S0-DOP-108

A HISTORY OF POLITICAL IDEAS

From Antiquity to the Middle Ages

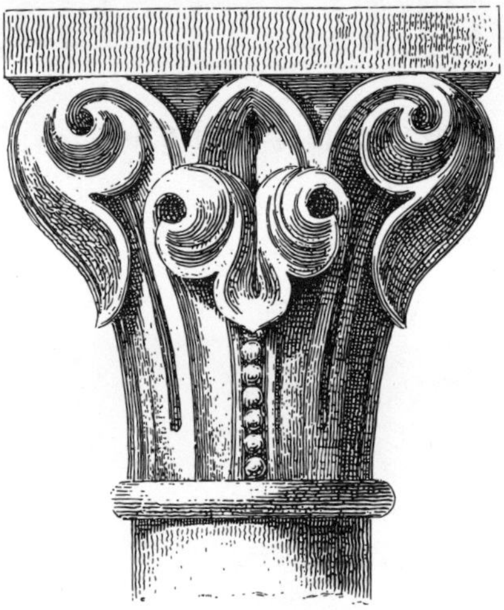

A HISTORY OF POLITICAL IDEAS

From Antiquity to the Middle Ages

PHILIPPE NEMO

translated by Kenneth Casler

DUQUESNE UNIVERSITY PRESS
Pittsburgh, Pennsylvania

First published in French as *Histoire des idées politiques dans l'Antiquité et au Moyen Age*, by Philippe Nemo, © Presses Universitaires de France, 2007

English translation copyright © 2013 Duquesne University Press
All rights reserved Published in the United States of America by
Duquesne University Press
600 Forbes Avenue
Pittsburgh, Pennsylvania 15282

No part of this book may be used or reproduced, in any manner or form whatsoever, without written permission from the publisher, except in the case of short quotations in critical articles or reviews.

Library of Congress Cataloging-in-Publication Data

Nemo, Philippe, 1949–
[Histoire des idées politiques dans l'Antiquité et au Moyen Age. English]
A history of political ideas from antiquity to the Middle Ages / Philippe Nemo ; translated by Kenneth Casler.
pages cm
Includes bibliographical references and index.
Summary: "Provides a context for understanding today's super states by tracing the origins of political thought from the earliest prestates through subsequent eras, including the philosophers and thinkers of the Greek city-state, Roman law, and the Christian Gospels; Nemo further examines the influence on political organization that extends from canon law and the influence of numerous Christian thinkers"—Provided by publisher.
ISBN 978-0-8207-0455-5 (pbk. : alk. paper)
1. Political science—History—To 1500. I. Title.

JC51.N44 2013
320.01—dc23

2013005016

∞ Printed on acid-free paper.

Contents

Part Two: Rome

Part Three: The Christian West

Preface

A History of Political Ideas from Antiquity to the End of the Middle Ages was first published in French by the Presses Universitaires de France in 1998. Its companion volume, *A History of Political Ideas in the Modern Era and Contemporary Times,* followed in 2002.

I would like to preface this English-language translation with a few comments on method along the lines of those I made in the first French edition.

Like the lecture series that was the starting point for this *History of Political Ideas,* the book is intended primarily for students and the educated reader with little prior knowledge of the topic. My intention is to present the material at face value—the lives and works of authors, the structure and argument of their doctrines—without scholarly commentary.

Though my primary intent is to provide an introduction to the topic, my approach is in no way superficial. The fact that the original publisher granted me so much space for the treatment of the material has permitted me to place appropriate emphasis on the principal doctrines, as well as to go into considerable detail on occasion and to present as often as necessary the moral and philosophical whys and wherefores of the arguments under study.

The history of political ideas entertains a special relationship with history in general. Both are tightly interwoven because political life provides theoreticians with the material for their thought at the same time that it urges them to take part in ideological debate. But the history of political ideas is by no means dependent on history. In general, doctrine builds on conceptual material from earlier doctrines according to a logic that is largely autonomous and theoretical. Because of this, one faces the problem of finding the proper balance between a presentation of the doctrines and the historical settings in which they appeared or, as the case may be, in which they played a role.

In an ideal world, and adhering to the proper academic division of labor, a work such as this *History of Political Ideas* should perhaps aim only to present the ideas, leaving it to the reader to place them in their proper historical context (with the help of specialist works when necessary).

However, my teaching experience informs me that contemporary students are woefully ignorant of history, whether classical, medieval, or modern. It, therefore, seems appropriate to provide at least some historical context throughout the work for a sound understanding of the relevant circumstances and key issues.

The historical treatment of political ideas over so many centuries demands a degree of expertise that outstrips the talents of an academic working alone. For this reason, general overviews in recent decades have tended to become projects for specialist teams, each member treating the authors and periods according to his or her particular expertise and specific knowledge. On occasion, and despite the project coordinator's best endeavors, this irreplaceable method has produced mixed results. It is why I believe that the traditional lecture, the work of a single author, can perhaps achieve in clarity and cohesion what it loses in wealth of detail. I hasten to add that science rarely advances by analysis alone. What would be the value of specialist expertise if it were not employed to produce an overview or to identify lines of convergence, extending into the present and giving it meaning? History most certainly does not move in a linear direction, as many historicist philosophers imagined. Neither is it an inscrutable, hydra-headed phenomenon. History sometimes appears chaotic, but there is an irreversible evolution of ideas that remains discernible despite the exhausting repetition of the same errors and illusions.

General Introduction

Anthropology and Politics:

Prestate Societies, Sacred Monarchies of the Ancient Near East, and the Greek City

It is customary to begin the history of political ideas with the works of the Greek thinkers. However, the relevance of this time-honored approach can be questioned. In recent decades, history, archaeology, and anthropology have progressed considerably, and our knowledge of societies before the Greek city is much improved. What was once thought to be a beginning may, in the light of new knowledge, be understood as a late moment, almost insignificant in the framework of a longer, more universal history. *A fortiori,* it is not possible to accept as a reason to begin the history of political ideas with the Greeks the fact—itself contingent—that the earliest surviving *texts* of political theory of any significant length are by Plato and Aristotle. Therefore, we need to go beyond tradition and ask if there is a more fundamental reason to begin the history of political science with the Greeks.

Two conditions seem necessary for a history of political ideas to begin: (1) that an *object* of political science exists—and for most writers[1] the *state* is that object; and (2) that the *instrument* of all science, *rational thought,* also exists. So the question is: are these two conditions satisfied by societies and thinkers before the Greek city?

1. The first condition is already fairly restrictive. The state did not always exist, and it did not exist everywhere. Anthropology teaches us that prestate societies continue to exist even today. History and archeology enable us to assert that societies without a state—called prestate

[1] Not all writers think like this. Georges Balandier, *Anthropologie politique* [Political anthropology] (Paris: Presses Universitaires de France, 1967; Quadrige collection, 1991), and others object to this reduction of *politics* to the *state.* Balandier claims that political realities exist in *all* societies, including "societies without a state."

societies—did indeed exist before societies with a state—called state-level societies. The first recorded "states" were those of the ancient Near East. We can date their appearance from the second half of the fourth millennium BC. So, it is only from this moment on, and in this region of the world, that we might expect to find *political* ideas, if we understand by this a system of ideas and principles that enable those responsible for ordering, administering, and modifying the institutions of state to give meaning to their actions.

2. The second condition is even more restrictive. By political "science" we understand not only a system of representations, but also a set of *theoretical* ideas based on *reason,* supported by *objective* arguments, having *universal* scope. But the political representations of the ancient Near Eastern states seem to reflect a prescientific mode of thought where *religion* and *myth* occupy the forefront as in earlier societies.

Let us try to characterize more exactly these two types of society—the prestate society and the ancient Near Eastern state—to see if by contrast we can capture the original features of the Greek city that make it the real starting point of a history of political ideas.

I. Prestate Societies

Prestate societies—also called *acephalous, archaic,* or *primitive* societies—are those where social order is maintained not by an institution towering over society, but by the solidarity of *lineages* sharing common ancestries, by a stratification according to *age groups* or *professional groups,* and by the entire community's spontaneous respect for more or less strict *customs* whose binding nature is sealed by strong *religious beliefs.*

A. A Typology of Prestate Societies

Anthropologists discern several types of prestate societies:[2]

1. *Groups* of hunter-gatherers, numbering between 20 and 100 members, with no permanent leaders, no strong social differentiations, other than "natural" ones associated with age and gender. Examples include pygmies and bushmen in Africa, Inuit in Greenland, and various tribes in the Pacific.

2. *Lineage* societies, like the Beti in southern Cameroon, and the *segmentary* societies, like the Tiv in Nigeria and the Nuer in Upper Sudan. Such societies are ancestral groups in which the elders have particular legitimacy, but there is no central power to speak of. Often each lineage has its own *council* of elders whose decisions must be more or less unanimous and taken in the name of the ancestors, who are considered the true leaders of the group.

The Beti ethnic group, with its 600,000 members, has some 20 lineages, each with this embryonic organization. But there is no common social order shared by the ethnic group as a whole, despite a strong sense of belonging. Within each lineage there are several sublineages or "houses"; each leader of a "house" has a degree of social authority depending on the size of his following, the number of wives he has, and his personal charisma.

Segmentary societies are a special instance of this social structure; lineages subdivide into opposing isomorphic "segments," but they stand together when they have to protect themselves against other lineages.

[2] Drawn from Philippe Laburthe-Tolra and Jean-Pierre Warnier, *Ethnologie, Anthropologie* [Ethnology, anthropology] (Paris: Presses Universitaires de France, 1993), chap. 6, "La vie politique" (Political life).

In the next two types, power tends to be concentrated, sporadically in the first case, more permanently in the second.

3. *Big men* societies, or societies with charismatic notables like in Melanesia and Papua or in Africa among the Efik and Igbo. The charismatic notable attains his high social position by means of his personal eloquence and a social network acquired by the exchange of gifts. His position, however, is insecure and often not transmissible to his descendants.

4. *Chiefdom* societies, like the Bamileke in southwest Cameroon, the Swat Pathans in Pakistan, and various societies in the Amazon. They have coordination structures, which are more or less independent of lineage membership and are led by men with distinct, hereditary responsibility for the *leadership* of the group.

The Bamileke, for example, are organized in some 100 chiefdoms of varying size (from several hundred to several tens of thousands). Individuals and subgroups move easily from one chiefdom to another, which means that each chiefdom is mixed, comprised of elements that do not necessarily include blood relations. On the other hand, the territorial base acquires greater importance. We are close here to the early forms of the state. The chief has many wives (in the past, up to 100); he marries off his daughters within the chiefdom to establish alliances; he exercises eminent religious functions (see below); he surrounds himself with a council and spokesmen of the chiefdom's various groups can come to him with their grievances.

Finally, to define the boundaries of prestate societies, we need to list the particular features that distinguish the *forms of a state*. A state exists when power is *concentrated* at the pinnacle of the social pyramid; when it is exercised freely within a well-defined *territory;* when the population grants it the *monopoly of legitimate violence* and, in particular, the mission to *administer justice;* when it employs personnel (governors, magistrates, public servants) chosen independently of *family ties*.

In terms of political order, there are different types of societies, from the most undifferentiated to the most structured, and the transition from one type to the other occurs imperceptibly. Furthermore, these types of societies are not steps in a necessary evolution toward a final ideal form of the state. Anthropological and historical findings show that societies can change from one form to another in virtually all directions.

State-level societies can become nonstate entities by dissolution of their central organization, division, or conquest. Examples abound in Africa, Asia, and the Americas, but they also exist in the West; for example, the dissolution of the Carolingian empire and the transition to feudalism that followed. This evolution corresponds to a return to a prestate society (see part 3, chapters 2 and 3).

What features do prestate societies share in common? "In most [of these societies], blood ties are stronger than any attachment or bond with a particular territory.... The number of conflicts appears to be limited by the *absence of social differences,* the impossibility of gaining the upper hand over others, and above all one's total *obedience to ancestral custom,* which functions as constitution, laws, and government.... The *penalty* for disobedience is either *moral* (social rejection) or *religious,* since a violation of 'taboos' implies automatic punishment."[3]

Let us examine these features more closely with the help of anthropological theory.

[3] Ibid., 110, 111.

B. René Girard: A Theory of the Sacred

René Girard posited that the rituals of archaic societies—societies permanently bound up in their myths and customs—are, without exception, directly or indirectly *sacrificial.*[4] Ritual sacrifices appear to serve the function of achieving a *katharsis* (purification or expunction) of violence within the group at regular intervals by channeling it toward a victim. Once violence is eliminated, the group itself is pacified, strengthened, united—in sum, ordered and prosperous. In this sense, rather than expressing a morbid inclination for violence and phantasmagoria among the members of archaic societies, ritual is more a *technique* for the resolution of a problem common to all societies: the avoidance of the spread of violence. Violence constantly threatens the break-up of the group through a process of "contagion," leading to revenge and retaliation in a self-sustaining dynamic, which soon becomes disruptive. According to Girard, sacral societies cope with the risk of contagion by turning to sacrifice as a *preventive* means. Sacrifice strengthens ties within the group, such that its members become "brothers" again, thereby reducing the risk that violence might reappear internally.

If, in spite of this, a crime is committed, these societies are at a loss. Numerous anthropologists (Bronislaw Malinovski, Robert H. Löwie, Sir Edward Evan Evans-Pritchard, and others) argue that since there is no *administration of justice* in such societies, it is not possible to tackle the problem and punish the guilty. The problem may be resolved, as among the Nuer, after long, drawn-out negotiations between two families, ending in the acceptance of a "blood price." But at any moment, an epidemic of vendettas can erupt and seriously threaten the prosperity, indeed, the existence of the group. For this reason, men in archaic societies literally dread the prospect of conflict. They ban all games, contacts with strangers, commercial exchange, all the while scrupulously performing rituals to avert the curse of evil.

Girard points out that modern societies, also confronted with the problem of regulating violence, come up with another solution: the *judiciary system.* Punishment is not carried out privately by the victim (or his family or clan), but by an organ representing the *community as a whole.* No one person is strong enough to oppose the combined strength of the group. Judicial punishment, therefore, puts an immediate end to the cycle of violence. It delivers a one-off vengeance, which cannot be "avenged." It is, so to speak, the "last word" in matters of violence.

This "curative" treatment is, in a sense, the equivalent of the "preventive" treatment of the ritual, since it solves the problem with the same efficiency (i.e., the containment of violence or, at any rate, its marginalization). But, Girard says, this solution is a vastly superior one. The social cost of sacrifice is high. For one thing, it supposes *unanimity,* and unanimity can only be achieved by maintaining society in the realm of *magico-religious thought* (see below). The judicial solution, however, does not need to prevent conflict because it has a means of stopping it after it erupts. Therefore, it can tolerate dissent, deviations, individual liberties, and consequently innovation and progress as well. Accordingly, archaic societies are "societies without history,"[5] while all *historical* societies are societies with a *judicial system,* that is to say, with a *state* (or *state-level societies*).

In a nutshell, this explains why neither a *state* nor *politics* can exist in primitive societies: it is not only that such societies have "not yet invented" a state; it is because the form of social order,

---

[4] See René Girard, *Violence and the Sacred*, trans. Patrick Gregory (Baltimore: Johns Hopkins University Press, 1979); René Girard, *The Scapegoat*, trans. Patrick Gregory (Baltimore: Johns Hopkins University Press, 1986).

[5] This does not mean that "nothing happens" in such societies, only that they do not invite change. When it does occur, it comes from outside. It is endured, unwanted, unaccompanied, and unstructured. Because change cannot be desired and imagined unanimously, it is only found in societies that accept individual differences and deviations from the norm.

represented by the state, supposes a thorough transformation of the modes of regulating violence and, consequently, of the underlying motives of human action.

If Girard's theory is correct, then the two systems—sacrifice and justice—are mutually exclusive; the first must disappear with the appearance of the second. There is no state where there is a "primitive religion," and there is no "primitive religion" (at least in a "pure" form) where there is a state that administers justice. This poses the problem of *transitional* forms, where archaic types of religion can be found together with an embryonic state. We will return to this problem below.

C. Magico-Religious Thinking

We must return briefly to a point made earlier: the mentality of people in societies rooted in ritual is necessarily *magico-religious*. Here is how to account for this.

We noted that ritual sacrifice is only effective if it is accepted unanimously, if every member believes unreservedly in the myth on which it is founded. This type of belief results only from *imitation*. Each person believes in the myth, not because the person personally and objectively accepts that what the myth says is true, but because he or she imitates the belief of his or her neighbor, who in turn imitates the belief of another neighbor, and so on, following a group sequence that runs "horizontally" from person to person rather than descending "vertically" from the spirit to the object. A myth is a collective illusion. But the person who dares to challenge the myth risks bringing down the wrath of the sacred gods on the entire group, and this lack of solidarity with the group is likely to provoke an accusation of sacrilege or sorcery. This explains not only why de facto rational thinking is absent from archaic societies, but also why it is the focus of active censorship that maintains the group in the realm of *mythical thought*. Girard notes,

> "Conservative" is too weak a word to describe the inflexibility of spirit and fear of change that characterize societies in which the sacred holds sway. The socio-religious order can appear as a boon and an unhoped-for act of grace, which the sacred can withdraw at any time. There is no question of making a *value judgment* of the existing order, of trying to *decide on, evaluate* or *manipulate* the "system" in some way. The primitive mind would regard such endeavors as both impious and insane, guaranteed to provoke the violent retribution of the gods. The proper attitude for men is vigilance and fixity. A single careless gesture can unleash a holocaust in which society can be utterly destroyed.[6]

Prestate societies are unable to *manage change* (which does not mean that they are immune from change; they are constantly in the throes of its destructiveness). Their *order* is intangible.

D. Mythical Order as Total Order—Both Cosmic and Social

Mythical order is both *cosmic* and *social*.

The same gods and heroes who set in motion the sun, the moon, the earth, the plants, and the animals at the beginning of time (during the primary events narrated in the myth) also decreed the social customs in use since that time. The transgression or challenging of such social customs would be as insane and senseless as calling into question the very laws of nature itself. "Primitive" man would have been as ill advised to do this as modern man to defy the laws of nature discovered by science.

---

[6] Girard, *Violence and the Sacred,* 298. The only change that is unavoidable by every society is the ebb and flow of new generations. For this reason, archaic societies take special precautions. Girard analyzes the "rites of passage" described by Van Gennep and finds that, in many societies, an adolescent does not become a full member of the community until he has completed the rituals, during which he can be excluded from community life, even for long periods of time.

The epistemologist Karl Popper makes this point in reference to the "magical attitude towards social custom": "Its main element is the lack of distinction between the customary or conventional regularities of social life and the regularities found in 'nature'; and this often goes together with the belief that both are enforced by a supernatural will."[7] It is just as unthinkable to alter the laws of nature as it is to modify social customs. A man from an archaic society rarely hesitates over *what is to be done* (even if he does not know or cannot or will not do what he must). Social obligation is never challenged.

If this is the case, then it appears that *free inquiry about society* and its rules implied by *political thought* is impossible in societies founded on myth and ritual. This is why we find no political theories in such societies, but only *myths of sovereignty* and certain practices and stratagems that some anthropologists regard as possible focal points of "political" analysis (but this is precisely the thinking of anthropologists). Men in archaic societies did not produce ideas that can be taken as a starting point for a history of political ideas. Girard's theory helps us understand that this absence of political ideas is not a contingent fact; it is implied in the very survival logic of these societies.

In a sense, however, it would be awkward to eliminate primitive societies from a study of political ideas completely. One way or another, they resolved the issue of human *coexistence* and *cooperation* with some degree of success, since humanity has lived the greater part of its history in such societies. Not only are their modes of social organization interesting from the point of view of the social sciences, it is difficult to imagine that nothing remains of archaic societies in our modern ones. In the course of our study we will have to consider the resurgence of "archaic" behaviors in the West—in particular *sacrificial* reflexes and *mythical* types of thought—both in post–Greco-Roman and medieval societies, as well as in contemporary societies.

II. Sacred Monarchies of the Ancient Near East

The sacred monarchies of the ancient Near East pose a slightly different problem. These societies show an unmistakable form of state organization that we know in some detail from the Sumerian, Egyptian, Akkadian, Babylonian, Assyrian, Hittite, Phoenician, Cretan, and Mycenaean states.[8] Thus, political science finds its *object:* the state. On the other hand, if we follow René Girard's theory, we can expect the mindset of these societies to differ from that of "primitive societies" since they have an *administration of justice:* ritual and myth no longer constitute the sole mortar of social order. For all that, can we make the case for the emergence of a political science? Let us first recall the principal historical developments of the age.

A. The Formation of States in the Ancient Near East

These are the first known *states.* Their emergence probably coincides with the development of *urban settlements,* datable to the second half of the fourth millennium BC, precisely in the Near

[7] Karl Popper, *The Open Society and Its Enemies* (Princeton, NJ: Princeton University Press, 1950), 168.

[8] See Jean-Claude Margueron, *Les Mésopotamiens* [The Mesopotamians], 2 vols. (Paris: Armand Colin, 1991); Samuel Noah Kramer, *History Begins at Sumer: Thirty-Nine Firsts in Recorded History* (Philadelphia: University of Pennsylvania Press, 1981); Jean Bottéro, *Mésopotamie* [Mesopotamia] (Paris: Gallimard, 1987), translated by Zainab Bahrani and Marc Van De Mieroop as *Mesopotamia: Writing, Reasoning, and the Gods* (Chicago: University of Chicago Press, 1995); François Daumas, *La civilisation de l'Egypte pharanoique* [The civilization of ancient Egypt] (Paris: Arthaud Éditions, 1987); Geneviève Husson and Dominique Valbelle, *L'etat et les institutions en Egypte des premiers pharaons aux empereurs romains* [The Egyptian state and institutions from the early pharoahs until the Roman emperors] (Paris: Armand Colin, 1992); Jean Gaudemet, *Les institutions de l'antiquité* [The institutions of antiquity], 3rd. ed. (Paris: Montchrestien, 1991).

East. These settlements are an unequivocal consequence of the *Neolithic revolution,* occurring some 10,000 years before Christ.

1. *The Neolithic Revolution*

The Neolithic revolution[9] is defined by the invention of *agriculture, animal husbandry,* and *the crafts;* in other words, by *sedentarization* and everything that derives from it: the establishment of *fixed dwelling sites* and the building of *permanent habitations.* Once this technological revolution occurred, new forms of social order became *necessary* and *possible.*

Agriculture and animal husbandry require specialized crafts. To build an irrigation system capable of controlling fluvial flood zones, the combined efforts of large numbers of people are needed. To protect crops and enjoy the harvest, a form of territorial organization is required, as well as a system of ownership and a system of defense against nomadic looters. Such problems can only be resolved within a social framework that enables division of labor and stability.

At the same time that these innovations become necessary, they are made possible by the existence of an *agricultural surplus* which, for the first time in the history of humanity, enables humans to specialize in technical activities that do not contribute directly to food production: artisanry, war, and administration (they were necessarily nonexistent in the hunter-gatherer subsistence economies of earlier Paleolithic societies). Collective organization and economic growth strengthen each other mutually by a process of "circular causality": the existence of food surpluses and security of supply foster the development of a division of labor, which in turn increases productivity. Consequently, the Neolithic revolution produced *unprecedented demographic growth.*[10]

2. *Urban Settlement*

This development seems to have accelerated markedly in southern Mesopotamia with the Ubaid and Uruk civilizations (early and mid-fourth millennium BC). It is at this time that the *urban settlement* appeared. It differed from earlier *villages* not only in terms of its size and number of inhabitants, but also in terms of the appearance of differences between small, medium, and large buildings for living, production, worship, defense, and authority. Understandably, these material differences reflect social differentiations (which did not exist in "primitive societies," or only weakly).

---

[9] In recent decades, spectacular advances in paleoanthropology and archeology make it possible to establish the following dates. The origins of the human species (*homo erectus*) are said to date back some four or three million years before our era in Africa (see Yves Coppens, *Le singe, l'Afrique et l'homme* [The ape, Africa, and man] [Paris: Hachette-Pluriel, 1985]). Depending on the author, *Homo sapiens* is said to have appeared between 200,000 and 100,000 year ago. The first burial places, a visible sign of symbolic thinking, date back some 70,000 years. Rock painting in Europe is 30,000 years old. From the origin of the human species until the dawn of the Neolithic revolution, humans lived like animals, producing nothing, subsisting from nature by *hunting* and *gathering.* The Neolithic revolution began about 14,000 years ago in the fertile crescent of the Near and Middle East. Around 5000 BC, irrigation appeared in the alluvial plains of southern Mesopotamia, enabling agricultural productivity to soar. See Margueron, *Les Mésopotamiens;* Jan Lichardus and Marion Lichardus-Itten, *La proto-histoire de l'Europe* [Proto-history of Europe] (Paris: Presses Universitaires de France, 1985) (the first chapters give a general overview of the Neolithic Age).

[10] The world population over the tens of thousands of years that the Paleolithic era lasted is estimated at some five million (between one million and ten million, with constant fluctuations between the extremes owing to climatic conditions, epidemics, the abundance or scarcity of prey, and so on; this demographic regime is the same as for animal species). World population increased dramatically with the Neolithic revolution, reaching 250 million by the time of Christ. See Jean-Marie Poursin, *La population mondiale* [World population] (Paris: Éditions du Seuil, 1976). This multiplication factor is such that it signals a genuine evolutionary "emergence," which can be compared only with what happened in the eighteenth century, when the market economy appeared and flourished. The market economy presided over a ten-fold increase in the world population, which grew from 750 million to 6 billion, in little more than two centuries, between 1750 and 2000. As we shall see, this revolution in the mode of economic production again went hand-in-hand with a total reconstruction of the sociopolitical structures of society.

Social differentiation seems to suggest, in turn, the appearance of some *central form of power* capable of regulating relations between various social categories. In fact, urban archeology has found traces of this power in the form of vast *palaces* around which the life of the country was organized. Numerous written documents confirm this archeological evidence.[11]

3. *Writing*

Hard on the heels of the city, shortly before 3000 BC, *writing* appeared.

Two writing systems arose more or less simultaneously: the *cuneiform* system in Sumer (southeastern Mesopotamia) and the *hieroglyphic* system in Egypt. For over 3,000 years, Egyptian civilization retained its writing system and the language it noted, constantly improving it along the way. As for the Sumerian cuneiform system, it was used (even after the disappearance of the Sumerians around 2000 BC) to note the language of other peoples of Mesopotamia and Asia Minor (the Akkadians, the Babylonians, the Assyrians, and the Hittites). It remained in use until the Phoenicians invented the *alphabet* writing system in the second half of the second millennium, from which the more recent writing systems of antiquity devolve, including Cretan, Mycenaean, Hebrew, Greek, Etruscan, and Latin writing systems.

The invention of writing played a crucial role in the evolution toward state-level types of social orders. As archeologists stress, since writing enables us to see for the first time what is happening directly, we are tempted to overestimate its role and to believe that it creates what it describes, whereas writing may only shed light on realities that existed long before it began.[12] Nevertheless, there is little doubt that possession of a system of writing had a direct, early influence on the organization and functioning of the state. Systems of writing enabled *messages to be transported over great distances, to produce a record of accounts,* and *to maintain archives,* all three helpful to the highest degree in administering a state. Many documents uncovered in archeological excavations in settlements throughout Mesopotamia (tens of thousands of cuneiform tablets) prove that the centralized administrative structures of the state, indeed, made use of writing. Many of these documents make explicit reference to the state and political power.

Our knowledge of such documents continues to progress thanks to the budding sciences of Egyptology and Assyriology. They are constantly uncovering and interpreting new tablets and inscriptions. In addition to administrative and accounting documents—the first to be inventoried—scientists have also uncovered genuine literature in the ancient Near East.[13] This literature is much older than either the Bible or Homeric poetry, long considered the first literary achievements of humanity.

4. *The Earliest Institutions of the State*

Early writing tells us that *state-level forms* of social life flourished from Mesopotamia to Egypt. We see the emergence of institutions with the characteristics of present-day state organizations: a *central government* under the leadership of a *monarch* assisted by *ministers* (for example, the Egyptian vizier); a *specialized army;* a *judiciary system* (while not independent of the king, it becomes a separate organ from him, with its courts and professional judges); a *central*

[11] It is not clear what the exact causal element was in this evolution. Did mentalities change, enabling a new organization of social life, which translated as the economic and technical progress mentioned above? Or was it this progress that resulted in a change of institutions and mentalities? It is impossible to confirm one hypothesis or the other in the current state of knowledge and theory.

[12] They also point to the examples of Africa and pre-Columbian America, stressing that major states may have existed in societies without writing.

[13] One of the crowning achievements of this literature is the Epic of Gilgamesh; the original core of this text is Sumerian, but it spread throughout the Middle East under the impetus of the Babylonians.

administration; a *local administration;* a fiscal system (with *population censuses* and *revenue control* mechanisms essential for tax collection purposes); administrative structures for large *building projects; foreign policy* organs (ambassadors, e.g.), attesting to the fact that the state now exercises exclusive jurisdiction over a clearly defined *territory.*

B. "Modern" Features of the State in the Near East

If by *political thought* we understand ideas concerned with the action of the state (either internal measures to order society or external ones to manage relations with neighboring peoples), it would be a singular paradox to deny the existence of political thought in the states of the ancient Near East.

In fact numerous written records provide irrefutable evidence of such political thought. Two striking examples illustrate this: the first bicameral congress, described by Samuel Noah Kramer,[14] and the Akkadian system of law brought to light in the famous "Code" of Hammurabi.[15]

1. *The "Congress" of Uruk*

There is historical evidence that a monarch consulted a *senate* ("an assembly of elders," to use Kramer's expression) and a *lower house* ("an assembly of arms-bearing male citizens"), that a discussion, deliberation, and joint decision took place, and that the decision even went against the will of the king. We have the "minutes" of this first "political" congress in the text of a poem on 11 tablets and numerous fragments (the critical edition of the 115 lines of this poem was first published in the *American Journal of Archeology* in 1949).[16]

The poem dates from approximately 2000 BC but tells of an event that occurred much earlier, around 3000 BC. At the time, "Sumer boasted may large cities centering about monumental and world-renowned public buildings."[17] A system of writing existed; there was already a literature.

The bicameral congress was convened to take a stand on a matter of war and peace. At the time, Sumer was comprised of a number of cities in competition for overlordship in the region. Kish was one of the largest; Uruk was also growing. For this reason, Agga, the king of Kish (in fact, the last king of the first dynasty of Kish) launched an ultimatum and commanded Uruk to accept him as lord and master or face war. The issue under debate in the two assemblies was to decide on the response to be given to Agga's emissary. The king of Uruk consulted the senate, which pronounced in favor of submission. Dissatisfied, the king turned to the lower house, which spoke in favor of war. The poem narrates the ensuing events. Agga's army laid siege to Uruk; an arrangement was found: the two kings became friends.

This is evidence of a genuine "political" problem, involving diplomatic thinking, a reasoned preference for peace, and a sort of right of reply by the opposition. Of course, we know nothing of the composition of the two assemblies, nor if there was anything resembling a vote or, for that matter, if an organized debate was actually held.

2. *The "Code" of Hammurabi*

In 1902, a magnificent stele was discovered in ancient Susa (present-day Khuzestan, Iran), now on display at the Louvre in Paris. The bottom portion of the stele is covered in Akkadian cuneiform script and was initially identified as a code of laws. At the time of its discovery, it was the oldest set of laws ever to be found; the stele itself attributes the work to the Akkadian king,

---

[14] See Kramer, *History Begins at Sumer,* chap. 5, "Government—The First Bicameral Congress."

[15] See Bottéro, "The 'Code' of Hammurabi," *Mesopotamia,* 156–84.

[16] Republished in Samuel Noah Kramer, *The Sumerians: Their History, Culture, and Character* (Chicago: University of Chicago Press, 1963), 186–90.

[17] Ibid., 31.

Hammurabi, who ruled Babylon from 1792 to 1750 BC. Since this discovery in the early twentieth century, ten more texts (some even older than the Hammurabi code) and some 40 incomplete versions of the same original have been found.

The original has about 3,500 decipherable lines, now identified as 282 "laws," all in the form "If…, then…" (e.g., "If a man bring accusation against another man, charging him with murder, but cannot prove it, then the accuser shall be put to death"; "If a man be in debt and sell his wife, son, or daughter, or bind them over to service, then they shall work for three years in the house of their purchaser or master; in the fourth year they shall be given their freedom"). Reading these "laws" one is reminded of civil and penal statutes; the impression is reinforced by the fact that the various articles of the laws are organized under "headings": 5 are devoted to *False witness;* 20 to *Theft;* 16 to *Royal fiefs;* 25 to *Farm labor;* approximately 10 to *Dwelling places;* at least 24 to *Commerce;* 15 to *Deposits and debts;* 67 to *Women and the family;* 20 to *Assault and battery;* 61 to *free,* then *servile professions;* and 5 to *Slaves.*[18]

On closer examination, however, it appears that the Hammurabi code is not a code of laws in the sense of the Roman codex of the Imperial period. In the first place, the Hammurabi code is not complete; many tablets dealing with administrative and judicial matters concern topics not covered in the Hammurabi code. Furthermore, the articles seem to be concerned with practical cases and thus refer to specific circumstances. There is also a certain non sequitur from article to article. Finally, the cases discussed in the administrative and judicial tablets of the period almost never make reference to the articles of the code, which they would do if the Hammurabi text were the law of the land, in the sense that we understand it.

More importantly still, Assyriologists tell us that the concept of "law" in the modern sense apparently did not exist for the Mesopotamians. They had no word—in Akkadian or Sumerian—to express the idea of "principle" or "law," whether in the domain of social rules or of nature. They seemed only to have reached an intermediary intellectual level between the special case and the law, the *exemplary case* or *paradigm,* that is, the "if…then" structure noted above.

Bottéro quotes other "scientific treatises" of Mesopotamian origin, dealing with medical and divinatory practices and, like the Hammurabi code, consisting of collections of paradigms. This way of thinking transcends empiricism in that it aims for universality and exhaustiveness. But it does not achieve the absolute and explicit generality of the law. In Mesopotamia, laws—as with most customs in traditional societies—remained *implicit,* that is to say, not only unwritten, but also *unformulated,* even verbally. All the same, they were known to all, though knowledge was intuitive.

> What took the place [of legislation in ancient Mesopotamia] was undoubtedly the "laws," but they were *unformulated,* just as the "laws" of science were unformulated. Mesopotamian law was predominately unwritten law. Unwritten does not mean nonexistent or unknown, but virtual: because it was constantly presented to the people in the form of positive or prohibitive customs, transmitted with education, or even in the form of traditional solutions to particular problems.… The principles of the laws were not deduced or formulated in explicit terms; it was as if they had been incorporated in a diffuse mass of traditions that generations automatically transmit to each other in any given cultural group, just as with language, or with a vision of the world, a feeling about things, different production processes and transformation processes, and so on.… the law is not a statement, a "letter," but a tendency, a "spirit."[19]

---

[18] Ibid., 159.

[19] Ibid., 181–82, with modifications to the translation.

Jean Bottéro concludes with the following interpretation of Hammurabi's code: rather than a compendium of *laws,* it is a collection of *judgments* that clarify the king's decisions in *cases presenting a problem for the first time* (either the occurrence of a set of circumstances for the first time or the existence of a "legal vacuum" that the king's decision is designed to fill). Thus, in Bottéro's opinion, the code concerns legal *amendments* or *innovations.* This explains why it is incomplete and unsystematic, and why the king took care to promote it very solemnly.

If Bottéro's theory is correct, we can deduce an important characteristic of the Babylonian state: the king, who pronounces judgments alone or through his representatives, is able to *interpret* the law; and, in this sense, Babylonian society can begin to *manage change.*

This characteristic is probably related to the invention of writing, which extends memory and fosters the accumulation of experience. Society no longer undergoes change; change can sometimes be managed by the state (more or less well, more or less after the fact, and with more or less difficulty). The following passage from the epilogue of the Hammurabi stele shows this: "Such are the just judgments delivered by Hammurabi, the wise king, in order to provide his land with firm discipline and upright conduct." There was disorder and unsolvable conflict, but the king arbitrated and restored stability, doing so with his innovative jurisprudence.

Thus, the situation of a Near Eastern society like Mesopotamia is very different from a society without history, where customs are set down absolutely and where change—when it does occur, despite the many obstacles raised by ritual and myth—is suffered, not managed. Gradually, people dared to interfere with customs and to think about them. This is undoubtedly an innovation, a "modern" feature of these societies, and reflects an early phase of "political" thought. It is indeed the transitional phase imagined by Girard.

C. "Archaic" Features: The Problem of Sacred Monarchy

Next to these modern features, another essential characteristic of state-level societies in the ancient Near East places them closer to archaic societies and distinguishes them as well from the later Greek city. Fundamentally, these societies still maintain a *magico-religious* mode of thought.

1. *The King-Priest in Anthropology*

The states in the ancient Near East were all *sacred monarchies.* The British anthropologist Sir James George Frazer showed that in numerous ancient societies the *sacred king* was an integral part of the magico-religious order. He was not only the object of rituals, he was himself a god, a sacred power, at any rate, whose words and actions played a direct and decisive role in maintaining the order of traditional societies, an order which was both cosmic and social.[20]

This feature already existed among chiefdoms. For example, among the Bamilekes, "the chief... makes offerings and libations to his deceased forbears in order to obtain their blessings for the people and the harvests. Priest of the earth and rainmaker, he organizes the annual festivities for the entire chiefdom at the end of the agricultural cycle. Then he fulfills the ritual against external acts of evil: tornados, locust plagues, swarms of bees that attack harvests, domestic animals and people. The chief has a body double who moves about the bush in the guise of a leopard. He presides over the detection and neutralization of sorcerers. He is often accredited the powers of a sorcerer, which are dangerous but domesticated."[21]

Precolonial African states showed the same traits: the pivotal role of religion, the participation of the king in ritual.

---

[20] See *The Magic Art and the Evolution of Kings (The Golden Bough),* 2 vols. (New York: Macmillan, 1911).

[21] Laburthe-Tolra and Warnier, *Ethnologie,* 123.

> In Cameroon, the king of the Bamum is the "father" of the kingdom, since the nation is an immense pseudo-lineage made up of his relatives and allies. Throughout the kingdom, the king is held to be "sacred"; he is set apart; even his body is not treated like an ordinary body.... He is held in a web of taboos and interdictions; he must not be seen eating; he cannot leave his land; he can only be addressed through an intercessor; he must use a special ancient language, like the emperor of Japan. He is a war chief and as such embodies the strength and health of the kingdom. He must prove his sexual prowess by impregnating women at his enthronement and demonstrate his physical stamina at annual tests like the Pharaohs of Egypt, who ran around the field at the Sed festival. The king is associated with the fertility of the realm: the emperor of China, Son of Heaven, plowed the first furrow; most of the African kings must know how to make rain and command the elements. Some societies (the Nyakusa) put their king to death as soon as he showed signs of physical weakness.[22]

This particular act of putting to death the king confirms Girard's idea that the "setting apart" of a godlike man is *a special case of the phenomenon of the emissary victim*. The fact that the king is set apart in an exceptional place—both inside and outside the group—enables him to accumulate all the social powers on his shoulders. This is why he can exercise superhuman power over the group or be a victim of its excessive ferocity. The omnipotence attributed to the king (his magical healing power) and, conversely, his particularly vulnerable nature (African kings can become ritual victims) lead us to believe that, in monarchy itself, there is a deeply archaic nature (because it is sacrificial).

These are precisely the features found in nearly all the sacred monarchies in the ancient Near East.

2. *The Pharaoh as Master of the Cosmos*

In Egypt, François Daumas writes,

> Ancient royal protocol...makes the king a *Horus,* who rules on earth like the god in heaven.... As heir to the universal creator and master, the Pharaoh assumes general cosmic power.... The king, through his own person, ensures the equilibrium of creation, threatened at all times with the backlash of chaos.
>
> The king *makes barley* and is *loved by Nepri,* the grain god. The Nile honors him by rising. His orders contain within them the power of their execution. He drove away the wild beasts and conquered the uncivilized peoples, pushing back the limits of chaos. His palace is provided with all the safeguards of divine life. He is the *universal Master*.... Royalty is knowledge and light for men, a giver of life like the sun and the *Nile. The king is life,* proclaims the author, the noble and princely Sehetepibre. He not only creates his civil servants, he is like Khnum, literally the creator god of humanity. He is Bastet and Sekhmet, the two daunting protector goddesses of the country....
>
> [The king,] by his sole presence and because he is the rightful heir of his father the creator god, upholds everything needed for life. The counterpart is found in literary works which describe the desolation of the country when royalty declines at the end of the Old Kingdom. The god Khnum no longer formed men and the birth rate declined. There is a metaphysical relationship between the king and the march of the world, which is not

[22] Ibid., 125–26.

> expressed in any personal royal miracle. In his essence, the king is a factor of order and continues the organizing work of creation.[23]

The analogy with the African chiefs and "rainmaker" kings described by modern ethnologists is striking.

3. *Cosmogonies and Myths of Sovereignty*

Above all, in sacred monarchies we find the same indissoluble bond between *cosmic order* and *social order,* which we said characterizes archaic societies. Throughout the Near East, in Egypt as well as in Mesopotamia, Creation myths are *cosmogonies* and *myths of sovereignty.* Social order is confounded with the order of the universe itself.

Jean-Pierre Vernant writes, for example,

> the Babylonian poem of the Creation, the *Enuma elish,* was sung every year in Babylon on the fourth day of the royal festival of the Creation of the New Year, in the month of Nisan. On that date, time was supposed to have completed its cycle and the world returned to its starting point—a critical moment at which the whole order was again threatened. During the festival the king mimed a ritual combat against a dragon. Thus each year he repeated the feat performed by Marduk against Tiamat at the beginning of the world. The ordeal and the royal victory had a double significance: even as they confirmed the power of the monarch's sovereignty, they symbolized a re-creation of the cosmic, seasonal, and social order. Thanks to the king's religious attributes, the structure of the universe, after a period of crisis, was renewed and upheld for a new temporal cycle. Babylonian ritual and myth reveal a particular conception of the relation between sovereignty and order. The king not only governed the social hierarchy, but also intervened in the workings of natural phenomena. The ordering of space, the creation of time, and the regulation of the seasonal cycle appear to have been part of the royal activity; they were aspects of the sovereign's function.
>
> *No distinction was made between nature and society;* in all its forms and spheres, order was made dependent on the monarch. In neither the human group nor the universe was it yet thought of abstractly or as existing in and of itself. To exist, it would have had to be established; to endure, it would have to be maintained; always it presupposed an ordering agent, a creative power capable of promoting it. Within the framework of this mythic thought one could not imagine an autonomous realm of nature or a principle of organization immanent in the universe.[24]

We shall see that this sacred mode of thought continues to exist, partly at any rate, in Homer and Hesiod. However, it is in relation to this thought that the early Greek "physicists" [*phusikoi,* or naturalist scientists] and political thinkers create a break.

Thus, the state in the ancient Near East did not yet have any autonomous existence. It was a mere constituent of the cosmic order, confounded with it, and obeying its laws. And just as cosmic order was created by divine agents—so say the dramatic events narrated in the Creation myth—and remained dependent at all times on the will of these agents, so the state too was created by extraordinary powers, with whom the king maintained privileged ties. Order can only be maintained as long as the people perform the proper rituals under the supervision and direct participation of the king.

---

23 Daumas, *La civilisation de l'Egypte pharaonique,* 111–15.

24 Jean-Pierre Vernant, *The Origins of Greek Thought* (New York: Cornell University Press, 1982), 111–12.

If this is correct, it is obvious that genuine political thought—that is, a debate on *the subject of order*—can only arise with difficulty in such societies; it is as unlikely as in sacred societies without a state. Because order is created by the gods, it is necessary, and it is inconceivable that it can be challenged. People will have their hands full simply meeting the requirements of such an order. They will not have time to make questions of the organization of the state an *intellectual concern* that can be debated and decided on with objective arguments. It is possible to debate, in the manner of the "early congress" described by Kramer, how matters should be dealt with in the framework of accepted rules (thus, issues of "executive power"). It is also possible to tackle new problems that come up in connection with the rules themselves, like in the case of the Hammurabi code.[25] But myth, law, and custom will never become *all together* focal points of explicit debate because they are matters of the sacred and the sacred alone.

Even the judicial system, although its very existence signals a big step forward in respect to archaic societies, is not entirely rational. It is rooted in "law," which is still essentially unwritten, outside the control of mortals. Judgments are delivered in the name of the gods. They are applied in terms that are predominately ritualistic.

It seems that not only the sacred monarchies of the ancient Near East, but nearly *all forms of state outside the Western tradition* (with the exception of states in the *Chinese sphere* of influence) adhere to this pattern: a state that rules society centrally but in accordance with a religious order that cannot be challenged and that holds society in the grip of a rigid structure. So, what happened in the West, and nowhere else, that led to forms of social order, moral attitudes, and thought without equivalence in other civilizations? Something absolutely unique: the emergence of the *city* in Greece.

III. The Greek City

The Greek city shows some *profoundly new features* compared with the states of the ancient Near East. We will examine them in depth in the chapters devoted to Greek political thought, but to set the scene for now, we can narrow the focus to five important ideas with Vernant:[26] *the crisis of sovereignty, the emergence of a public space, the promotion of reason and public speech, a demand for equality before the law, and the transformation of religion.* To this we will add a sixth: the emergence of a *critical* mind, resulting from a growing awareness of the *distinction between natural order and social order.*

A. The Crisis of Sovereignty

When the Greek city appeared at the end of the Dark Age (from twelfth to eighth centuries BC), what we note first is the *disappearance of monarchy,* both the Mycenaean *anax* (lord) and the Homeric *basileus* (sacred king). The king, who until then held the *monarchia* alone by virtue of his ritual powers, is replaced by several office holders.

The example of Athens, the only Greek city where the Mycenaean state disappeared gradually, is particularly instructive. Aristotle gave an account of its transformation in his Athenian

[25] It is even possible to play clever games with the gods, as with the curious practice of sacrificing a "royal substitute" for the king (cf. Bottéro, *Mesopotamia,* 150–53); this is attested in Sumer, among the Hittites, the Neo-Assyrians, and the Persians. When the astrologists predict an eclipse, a sign that the gods will cause the king to perish, the monarch repairs to a hidden place and designates an arbitrarily chosen victim to die in his place. The victim is disguised as the king, expecting to trick the gods. Such Machiavellianism is predicated on the assumption that reason is now slowly liberating itself from the stricture of magico-religious belief.

[26] See Vernant, *The Origins of Greek Thought.* We follow Vernant's analysis in the following discussion.

Constitution. A *polemarch* was put in charge of the armed forces; this means that responsibility for the military function was removed from the sovereign authority of the *basileus*. Then, *archons* were created, and *arche* (command) was also taken from the *basileus* (royalty). Initially elected for ten years, the archons were subsequently replaced every year. Thus, election to public office became a regular practice. This is a clear sign that the *arche* was "delegated every year by a human decision, through a choice that presupposed confrontation and discussion,"[27] whereas the *basileia* was relegated to a religious role and religion itself to a dependent role.

There was no longer a single sovereign, a quasi-divine character standing apart and above the various functional classes constituting society. The social body now appeared as an aggregate of heterogeneous elements, separate parts (*moirai* or *mere*) but united in the city itself. It is precisely the search for the proper balance between these parts that leads to the earliest *political speculation,* that is, the first *sophia,* the wisdom of the Seven Sages of Greece, at the dawn of the seventh century BC when the sages struggled to envison this "unity in plurality" and "plurality in unity" characteristic of the city. In this context, "*arche* could no longer be the exclusive property of any one person. The state itself was shorn of all private and personal character; having escaped the jurisdiction of the *genē,* it came to be everybody's business."[28]

B. The Emergence of a Public Space

It's everybody's business: the language is unequivocal. Political debate is moved *es to koinon* ("to the public commons"), *es to meson* ("toward the middle, or to the center").

The archeological record shows that the Mycenaean city had a closed royal residence ringed by fortifications; political matters were handled exclusively within this inaccessible, secret space. The next step was for "the city [to become] centered on the agora, the communal space... where problems of general interest were debated."[29]

This metamorphosis was not limited to political life in the narrow sense. It applied to all the sciences and the arts as well. Like the magistracies, the arts and sciences became "accountable" to a critical public. This evolution is already visible in Homeric poetry. At the origin it was court poetry, sung in the halls of the palace; then it left the inner circle and spread orally, by recitation from memory, then in writing to the public at large. By becoming public, this knowledge, these values, and the new intellectual methods became the focus of public *debate, interpretation,* and *argument*. This is an essential factor in the promotion of rationalism.

A key aspect in this process of making political and intellectual life a public concern is the *development of writing.*

The first script used to note the Greek language, Linear B, which the Mycenaeans had borrowed from the Minoans of Crete, disappeared entirely from the Greek mainland after the invasions of the twelfth and eleventh centuries. Around 750 BC, a new script was introduced, borrowed from the Phoenician alphabet. It spread quickly throughout Greece (there are almost no inscriptions prior to 730 BC; however, texts from the mid-seventh century are found in abundance). More easily accessible, the script was no longer reserved for a small, specialized caste of trained scribes. It became the public property of numerous citizens.

This is visible on two planes:

[27] Ibid., 42.

[28] Ibid., 47.

[29] Ibid., 47. In the city-states of the ancient Near East there was no agora, only a palace and temples (see Margueron, *Les Mésopotamiens,* 2:27: "If we trust available material, public spaces were not a normal feature of the oriental town, even if sometimes vast areas existed in front of a public building or around a *ziggurat*. But was there a place where the population could gather? Nothing proves the need for such a space.")

1. *The setting down of laws in writing.* "Setting them down not only ensured their permanence and stability; it also removed them from the private authority of the *basileis,* whose function was to 'speak' the law. Thus they became public property, general rules that could be applied equally to all." Incarnated in written/public law, justice descends from heaven to earth. In Hesiod's world justice, *dike,* remained on high; it was a sovereign divinity, remote and inaccessible, and therefore easily arbitrary when it spoke through the voice of kings, "devourers of gifts," takers of bribes, on earth. Now justice became "a rational standard . . . subject to discussion and modification by decree."[30]

2. *The first "publications"* (the first "books" like those by Anaximander, Pherecydes, and Heraclitus, and the monumental inscriptions in stone on which private citizens engraved various observations). The intention is not to communicate private thoughts to other private individuals. The authors speak to a "public"; they submit their ideas *es to meson* so that they become the "public property" of the city and, if possible, apply to everyone like the law. Like political debate, but unlike the religious mysteries, ideas now come under everyone's scrutiny and judgment.

C. The Promotion of Reason and Public Speech

In the public space of the city, decisions are only taken when there is a consensus. Therefore, the politician who speaks in public must *persuade* his audience, and he can do so only if he is *rational.*

Thus, *speech* in the Greek city takes on great importance, because it was the quintessential means of persuasion (*peitho*). Compared with its function in the archaic sacred society, speech in the Greek city changes its epistemological and metaphysical status completely. "Speech was no longer the ritual word, the precise formula [as it was in the pronouncements of the king when he rendered final *themis,* judgment], but *open debate, discussion, argument.* It presupposed a public to which it was addressed, as to a judge whose ruling could not be appealed, who decided with hands upraised between the two parties who came before him. It was this purely human choice that measured the persuasive force of the two addresses, ensuring the victory of one speaker over the other."[31]

Victory goes to the speaker who persuades his listeners with the most *rational* arguments, since reason is what all citizens share in common. As soon as it is no longer possible to impose one's opinion and that persuasion is required, *objective facts* visible to all must be set forth and the same *universal logic* meticulously applied by everyone. This urges public speakers to constantly search for greater objectivity and logical accuracy in their argumentation. "There was thus a close connection, a reciprocal tie, between politics and *logos.* The art of politics became predominately the management of language; and *logos* from the beginning took on an awareness of itself, of its rules and its effectiveness, through its political function."[32]

The Sophists formalized these rules in the second half of the fifth century BC. And, in the fourth century BC, Aristotle did the same for logic, and Isocrates for rhetoric.[33]

D. A Demand for Equality before the Law

The members of civic society, who have access to the public space, begin to see themselves as fellows, *homoioï,* and equals, *isoi.* "In the framework of the city, the tie that bound one man to another thus became a reciprocal relationship, replacing the hierarchical relations of submis-

[30] Vernant, *The Origins of Greek Thought,* 53.
[31] Ibid., 50; our italics.
[32] Ibid., 50.
[33] See Isocrates' magnificent praise of logos on pp. 169–72.

sion and dominance.... Despite everything that might set them at odds with one another in the day-to-day business of social life, on the political level the citizens conceived of themselves as interchangeable units within a system whose law was the balance of power and whose norm was equality."[34]

This demand for equality initially arises within the aristocracy and the *hippeis,* the mounted military nobility, who claim a right to share political power with the king because they take part in war. The same logic enters into play when the "*hoplite* revolution" (toward the middle of the seventh century) gives the middle-class citizen a military function similar to that of the aristocrats. Then he, too, stakes his claim to political equality in keeping with what he is psychologically and morally: a citizen-soldier. According to Homeric poetry, what counted for the *hippeis* was "the individual exploit, splendid performance in single combat." He threw himself into battle, driven by *menos* (the "ardor inspired by a god"). "But the *hoplite* no longer engaged in individual combat; if he felt the temptation to engage in a purely individual act of valor, he was obliged to resist it. He was the man of elbow-to-elbow warfare, or shoulder-to-shoulder struggle."[35] The worth of the warrior is no longer found in his *thymos* (his passion); it is in his *sophrosyne* (self-control, moderation) and his ability to submit to a common law. Thus,

> the phalanx made of the *hoplite,* as the city made of the citizen, an interchangeable unit, one element like all the others.... Even in war, *eris*—the desire to overcome an adversary, to affirm one's superiority over another—must give way to *philia,* the spirit of community.... Thus it condemned as excess, as hubris—in the same category as martial frenzy and the pursuit of purely personal glory in combat—the display of wealth, costly garments, magnificent funerals, excessive displays of grief in mourning, behavior that was too flamboyant in women or too confident and bold in aristocratic youths.
>
> All these practices were now rejected because, by accentuating social inequalities and the sense of distance between individuals, they aroused envy, produced discord within the group, threatened its equilibrium and cohesion, and divided the city against itself. What was now extolled was an austere ideal of reserve and restraint, a severe, almost ascetic way of life that obscured differences of manner and rank between citizens in order to bring them closer together, to unite them like the members of one big family.[36]

So the Greeks invent a new type of man, one who no longer accepts inequality, neither in regard to one person, a monarch or tyrant, nor in regard to a privileged few. The new man demands the equal participation of all citizens in the exercise of power, and expects all citizens to be subject to the same law. These ideas are expressed in two concepts—*isocratia* and *isonomia.* Later, Aristotle would say that politics is the art of finding a form of order, therefore differentiation, among a group of equals, a "squaring of the circle" that the Greek constitutions managed to achieve when they invented the rules of civic life: filling public offices by lot, elections, the orderly succession of magistrates, rotation, and for all citizens a position of command and obedience. For the Greeks at least, a hierarchical solution (royalty, tyranny, rigidly ordered societies) was ruled totally unacceptable, inhuman, and *barbarian.*

In Sparta, major reforms were carried out in the seventh century (ca. 650 BC), at the time of the Messenian wars. These reforms gave Sparta its final, very specific features. Approximately 10,000 equal portions of land were divided up among the citizen-soldiers. The new equals despised wealth and abhorred luxury. Private houses had to be built on the same model; *syssitia,*

[34] Vernant, *The Origins of Greek Thought,* 60–61.
[35] Ibid., 63.
[36] Ibid., 64–65.

communal meals, were instated (menus were austere and repetitive). Moreover, Sparta created a balance in the different components of its state (called a mixed regime): a dual royalty, a *Gerousia* (the council of elders) and an *Apella* (the assembly of the people, which elected the five ephors). Centuries later, as we will see, the commentators Polybius and Cicero expressed their admiration for this particular characteristic of the Spartan regime. However, since Sparta's reforms were a response to war and its military preoccupations, public speech had very little place in the new Spartan *polis*. The driving force was *phobos* (fear), not *peitho* (persuasion). The various magistracies continued to work in secret. It would be up to other Greek cities to assure the flourishing of rationality and critical thinking, the sciences and the law.

E. The Metamorphosis of Religion

The birth of the city went hand-in-hand with a complete metamorphosis of *religious life*. This metamorphosis had two symmetrical and complementary aspects: the *emergence of a public cult of the city,* and the appearance of *private forms of religious life*.

1. *The Emergence of a Public Cult*

Ancient priesthoods belonged to certain *genē;* this expressed the special relationship between a particular lineage and a particular divinity. But, by creating official cults, the city made the priesthood a public concern.

The sacred objects moved from the palace or the homes of the priests to the *temple,* an open and public place in the city; or they moved to diverse sanctuaries on the boundaries of the territory, dedicated to the *poliadic* divinities (i.e., the protectors of the city) and the city's founding heroes. Consequently, the old idols lost their magical, efficacious nature and became "simply 'images,' with no ritual function other than to be seen, no religious meaning other than their appearance.... The sacra, formerly charged with a dangerous power and withheld from public view, became a spectacle in full view of the city, a 'lesson on the gods,' just as the secret chronicles and occult formulas shed their mystery and their religious force to become the 'truths' debated by the sages in full view of the city."[37]

In other words, the *belief* in myths and the efficacy of the rituals went into decline. Only what *reason* revealed could be trusted. The public civic space was where the credit and discredit of reason appeared. Thus, the official public cult became dependent on the city and its political institutions. Religion *was subordinated to politics,* which was the exact opposite of the logic underpinning archaic societies and sacred monarchies.

Public rituals continued to exist in Greece until the extinction of paganism. They existed as sacrifices, oaths, divinatory practices (both before and after important decisions), declarations of war and conclusions of peace, the swearing in of magistrates, and so on. But they had become little more than a *formal framework for public life, which in effect no longer depended on them.*

2. *The Appearance of Private Forms of Religious Life*

The counterpart of this neutralization of religion was the flourishing of *private, noncivic varieties of religiousness.* In effect, the promotion of rationality found its limits before very long. Trust in reason was not total. Religious and philosophical associations (sects, brotherhoods, "mysteries") began to develop in response to human needs for salvation and an explanation of life and the world. But this religious sphere tended to lie outside the city and its official cults, precisely because they had lost their mysterious magical and salvific efficacy.

---

[37] Ibid., 55.

The sects promised a chosen few—based on a system of ranks and grades—spiritual fulfillment, including immortality (formerly reserved only for the king, as in Egypt). But this metamorphosis of the individual occurred independently of the social order and did not interfere with it. Religion and politics became autonomous spheres. However, the city could be governed without concern for the gods, whose oracles the magistrates now interpreted as they liked or completely ignored. On the other hand, an individual's salvation no longer depended on the performance of the rituals by the community. Politics broke free of religion, and religion, no longer the sole guardian of the social bond, could become the object of unfettered speculation. By inventing the city, whose social order obviated the usefulness of an order created by myth and ritual, the Greeks appear to have invented *religion* in the strict sense (i.e., as we, in the West, understand it).

F. The Physis/Nomos Distinction

The development of rationalism would have one further consequence for thought on social issues: the collapse of sacred order as the total order, an awareness of the distinction between *nature* and *culture, physis* and *nomos*—the final characteristic of the Greek contribution.

The systematic reflection of Greek thinkers (especially the Sophists of the second half of the fifth century BC) on their travel experiences, facilitated by Greek colonization, helped them to recognize that whereas people everywhere have the same universal physical *nature* (*physis*), with the same laws for all (eat, drink, reproduce), different people have different laws and customs (*nomoi*) compared with those of Greece. Therefore, a certain degree of difference in laws and customs, according to time and place, is compatible with life, and these laws and customs are largely a product of *human construction*. They are not founded in nature, nor are they imposed by the gods. They are a reality of another kind, accessible to human agency. Thus, the single order of earlier societies (primitive societies and the sacred monarchies of the ancient Near East) divides into two: *nature* and *culture*.

This principle of *physis/nomos*—a universal, unalterable *physis* and a multifarious *nomos,* changeable at will—opened the way for the development of *critical* thought: when something does not work properly in the social functioning, the necessary changes can be made. Therefore—and this is a very important corollary—individuals who propose changes are not necessarily enemies of society; critical debate is good and desirable; the community must structure such debate, take stock of opinions, and move to organize this debate, listen to opinions, then vote, because it is now accepted that total consensus is no longer feasible. Thus, the Greek city invented the procedures of *political pluralism: organized public debate,* and *voting* (including the secret ballot, unknown until then in Near Eastern states).

It is when the state is seen as artificial and mutable, and no longer as ordered by the gods, that "political science" becomes possible. With the emergence of the Greek city, it became feasible to develop a theoretical representation of what the state could and should be. A political science, which saw itself as objective, rational, and universal, was born in Greece.

We now have the answer to our question about the origins of political science. The Greek city gives us both the object and the intellectual tool of this science. Now we have a solid reason—because it is in the very nature of the thing—to begin the history of political ideas with the Greeks.

Nevertheless, one question remains. Was the Greek invention unique, and therefore can we argue that all societies today with an authentic "political" life and thought should be considered the direct or indirect cultural heirs of the Greek city?

The argument against this is the striking fact that at more or less the same time in other regions of the world other civilizational upheavals are observable: *Hebrew prophecy* in Judea, *Zoroastrianism* in Iran, *Buddhism* in India, *Confucianism* in China. All of these cultural mutations, occurring in the wake of the creation of the state, go beyond the model of the sacrificial society and the magico-religious thought with which it is associated.

It is, nevertheless, important to note, with Vernant, that the transformation originated *within religion itself,* whereas in the case of the "Greek miracle," it occurred "alongside and outside" religion and was characterized by *a profound mutation in the way of thinking,* which led to the birth of *science,* that is, to *rational knowledge of nature.* It is in this sense that political thought could only be Greek (and perhaps Chinese).

Similarly, for anyone wishing to retrace the history of political ideas, *Hebrew prophecy* also requires particular analysis. In comparison with the other religious reforms noted earlier, Hebrew prophecy engaged profoundly with the Western political tradition as early as the third century BC, and above all at the time of the Christianization of the Roman Empire, achieving over time a major inflection of this tradition.

This is why our study is organized around three themes:

1. We begin with the Greeks, the inventors of the city (part 1, "Ancient Greece").
2. Then we turn to the political and legal thought of Rome. Roman civilization inherited the Greek model of the city through the Etruscans and the Greeks of southern Italy. But it achieved an evolution of the model with its contribution of public and civil law (part 2, "Rome").
3. In its final centuries, Rome converted to Christianity. After a period of regression following the barbarian incursions, a true synthesis occurred in the Middle Ages between the Greco-Roman civic and legal contributions and the new moral and eschatological demands arising from the Bible (part 3, "The Christian West")

Part One

Ancient Greece

Chapter 1

Political Ideas in Greece before Plato

The first major works of political theory to come down to us are Plato's the *Republic* and Aristotle's *Politics*. It would be illogical, however, to begin the study of Greek political ideas with these two very late works. When Plato wrote the *Republic* around 375 BC, the Greek city-state was already in its final phase; Aristotle's *Politics* was written after Philip of Macedon's victory over the Greeks at Chaeronea (338), in other words, at a time when the independent Greek city, the theoretical object of his work, was on the point of disappearing in practice.

Therefore, the construction of the classical Greek city owes nothing to these works. If the Greek city was able to develop, the explanation must lie in the fact that from the outset bold thinkers and politicians performed the necessary intellectual and institutional work. In short, Plato and Aristotle found the spadework done already, such that their work was both a synthesis and a criticism of earlier work.

This process took place over some 350 years from the end of the Greek Middle Age until Socrates and the Sophists (750–400 BC). We discern three phases:

1. The formalization of notions on justice (*themis, dike*) and social order (*eunomia*), in contrast with "feudal" violence and excess; these ideas continue to be legitimized by reference to myths (see section I, "Homer and Hesiod: Justice and Social Order").
2. A realization that justice can only be ensured by a law (*nomos*), which is equal for all (*isonomia*), and that the law must be explicit and written, therefore, in the hands of men (see section II, "From Solon to Cleisthenes: The Emergence of the City and the Citizen").
3. Then it is realized that the law itself can be tyrannical and that, consequently, it can be criticized; to provide a basis for such criticism, a distinction is made between what is natural (*physei*) and what is conventional (*nomo*) (see section III, "The 'Great Generation of the Open Society'").

For each of these phases, we will present the historical context and the political ideas. However, none of the works by Greek political thinkers before Plato has survived; they exist only in fragments (excepting the poets Homer and Hesiod and the historians Herodotus and Thucydides).

Therefore, in order to present a reasonable interpretation of early political theories and representations, we are obligated to turn to history.[1]

I. Homer and Hesiod: Justice and Social Order

A. The Historical Context

The Greek city did not emerge gradually by way of an untroubled evolution from earlier forms of civilization. It appears to have been an *ex nihilo* creation that arose in mainland and Ionian Greece as a result of a largely *endogenous* process following from an interruption in the historical process. Some time around 1200 BC, Greece fell victim to a "disaster," which cut it off from the rest of the world; suddenly, all trace of civilization vanished, including the complete eclipse of writing. This is known as the Greek Middle Age, or the Dark Age. Out of this disaster, the Greek city emerged steadily. It was not a simple resurrection of what was destroyed, but a new, unprecedented reality. The term traditionally used to describe the new situation is the "Greek miracle." We might also borrow a term from evolutionary theory and speak of a genuine "emergence."

1. *The Mycenaean Civilization*

There is evidence of proto-Grecian populations in prehistoric times. The Greeks called them the Pelasgians.

Then, ca. 2000 BC, various peoples from Central Europe, speakers of Indo-European languages, migrated southward. Some—the Hittites—reached Anterior Asia; others—the Phrygians—crossed the Hellespont and settled in Asia Minor, relatively far from the Aegean Sea; others still moved into the Balkan peninsula. These latter populations were Greeks or *Hellenes*;[2] they trickled into the land over many centuries.

The first Greeks to arrive were the Achaeans, nomadic pastoral tribes, cattle and horse raisers. Compared with the indigenous inhabitants they encountered in Crete and the Cyclades islands, the Achaeans were barbarians. Gradually they became influenced by the local inhabitants, members of the Minoan civilization (the name comes from Minos, king of the Cretan city of Knossos). Reaching its zenith between 1900 and 1400 BC, this civilization was very similar to the civilizations of the Near East: large, centralized monarchies with power concentrated in the royal palace with its priests, scribes, and artists. Writing was known, its use widespread (a syllabic script, Linear A, was used for writing the language of the Cretans, which was neither Semitic nor Indo-European).

The Achaeans were influenced, dominated, and little by little transformed by the superior Minoan civilization. They invited Cretan artists to come and decorate their palaces. After, the

---

[1] The historical narrative of this and the following chapters provides only the minimum necessary to understand the evolution of the history of political ideas that follows. The full history of archaic and classical Greece can be found in many excellent studies and books.—*Translator's note:* Nemo quotes from the following works in this chapter: Claude Orrieux and Pauline Schmitt Pantel, *Histoire grecque* [Greek history] (Paris: Presses Universitaires de France, 1995); Matthieu de Durand, *Précis d'histoire grecque* [An overview of Greek history] (Paris: Éditions du Cerf, 1991); Marie-Françoise Baslez, *Histoire politique du monde grec antique* [A political history of the classical Greek world] (Paris: Nathan Université, 1994); Pierre Lévêque, *L'aventure grecque* [The Greek adventure] (1964; rev. ed., Paris: Le Livre de Poche-Références, 1997); Michel Humbert, *Institutions politiques et sociales de l'antiquité* [Social and political institutions in antiquity], 4th ed. (Paris: Précis Dalloz, 1991).

[2] "Greek" is the name of a tribe that had settled on the Greek coast on the Ionian Sea facing Italy. The Romans applied this name to all Hellenes.

pupils became more powerful than their master and some time around 1400 BC the Achaeans invaded and destroyed Knossos.

Mycenaean civilization reached its zenith between 1400 and 1200 BC. From the Cretans it borrowed its system of writing (which became Linear B and, for the first time, was used for writing a Greek language). Mycenaean civilization's influence spread throughout Greece and Asia Minor and even into Phoenicia, Palestine, and Egypt (Mycenae also borrowed maritime techniques from the Cretans and was able to conduct raids against Egypt).

Numerous Linear B tablets have survived. Its script was deciphered in 1954 and since then our knowledge of the Mycenaean civilization has grown. It was a replica of the Minoan civilization: centralized monarchic states administered by a bureaucracy centered around the palace, which ruled over political life, as well as over the economic and social life of the surrounding territory. The various states—Mycenae, Tiryns, Pylos in the Peloponnesus, and others—were independent of each other.

The only notable difference with Minoan states, due no doubt to the Indo-European origin of the Achaeans (because similar features are found among the Hittites), was the considerable importance attached to warfare. The Mycenaean palace was built on a strongly defended acropolis.

Sometime around 1200 the Mycenaean civilization went into decline and began to disappear. The reasons for this are complex and still debated by the experts. A series of wars seem to have some bearing on the situation.[3]

Archeological evidence exists of urban centers and palaces being destroyed by fire around 1200 BC. This destruction seems to have been caused by the "sea peoples." Other archeological and historical records tell us that these peoples traveled all the way to Egypt, ravaging Cyprus along the way and destroying everything in their path. Some seem to have settled in Palestine; they were perhaps the fearsome Philistines with whom the Hebrews tangled as they were federating their tribes at approximately the same time (see below, p. 388).

2. *The Dark Age*

The Dark Age takes its name from the complete disappearance of writing during this period (as we noted, writing only reappeared in Greece around 750 BC). There are no written records whatsoever from this period, neither from Greece nor from Eastern material referring to Greece. It is as if this wild and desolate land no longer interested anyone. The historian is literally "in the dark." Archeology is the only source of information.

The archeological record enables us to distinguish three phases of the "Dark Age":

1. *From 1200 to 1050 BC* approximately, civilization was broadly in stagnation. The population collapsed (three-quarters perished). The number and size of recorded archeological sites declined sharply, as if the country had become a desert. This stagnation impacted on material outputs as well; dwellings, technologies, and the arts and crafts all regressed. Stone construction disappeared entirely. Human and animal pictorial representation was abandoned. Gold, if it was found at all, came from tomb raiding or the chance discovery of a Mycenaean treasure.

2. *From 1050 to 900 BC,* abrupt changes occurred. Iron replaced bronze. Cremation replaced underground burial. These changes can no doubt be explained by the invasion of another wave of "Greeks," the Dorians, who migrated to the peninsula and conquered the Achaeans with their superior iron implements. The Dorians were true barbarians, impossible to assimilate. They left a path of destruction in their wake.

---

[3] Orrieux and Schmitt-Pantel, *Histoire grecque,* 35.

Fleeing the Dorian invasion, a tiny number of Achaeans took refuge in Asia Minor. There, the Achaeans came into contact with "oriental" peoples, or with peoples who had been in contact with oriental populations for a long time, like the Phrygians. On the one hand, these peoples were more developed than the Achaeans. On the other hand, the Achaeans entertained maritime contacts with Syria, because they needed metals found only in the Orient. In trade exchanges with the "orientals," the Achaeans offered their pottery. Cyprus was an important hub in this trade: copper was found on the island and iron was worked there. At one time or another Cyprus had been occupied by all the great oriental empires: Phoenicians, Assyrians, Egyptians, and finally Persians. Therefore, in Cyprus the Greeks encountered aspects of civilization that they could put to their advantage.

Thus, in the Archaic Age, Ionia and greater Greece (i.e., southern Italy), which the Ionians colonized and settled, saw the birth of the great cities of the new civilization and the appearance of the first great thinkers.

The Dorians moved farther south, into the Peloponnesian peninsula and across to Crete (later they invaded the southern coast of Asia Minor, facing the island of Rhodes.)

On the remains of the ancient Mycenaean states arose a "feudal" society, that is, a society of "chiefdoms," fragmented in many rival territories. The state as such disappeared (we will return to this feudal society, described at length in Homeric poetry).

3. *From 900 to 800 BC,* additional changes occurred, though their causes are difficult to explain (except for contacts with the Orient as noted earlier). The population grew again. Agriculture advanced. Pottery developed rapidly and changed significantly; paintings of human and animal figures reappeared. Metallurgy developed. Above all, the first characteristic features of the Greek city appeared. In urban centers, near the temples and aristocratic dwellings, a central public square—the *agora*—emerged; it was clearly intended for meetings of the *assembled people.* The countryside around towns also changed: plots were clearly separated and well cultivated. The territorial limits of the city were marked by a ring of *sanctuaries.* Sanctuaries inside and outside the city walls were devoted to *poliadic divinities* (protectors of the city) and *founding heroes*—mythical heroes dating back to Mycenaean times in mainland Greece, or historical heroes, founders of colonies, in the case of Greek settlements abroad. A new *public cult* began to flourish around these sanctuaries with the obvious purpose of safeguarding the identity of the city.

Between 800 and 700 BC, at the onset of the so-called Archaic period, the same trend continued, and the city emerged more distinctly. Throughout Greece, *aristocracies,* that is, collective and well-regulated power structures reserved for the nobility, began to replace the personal power of kings.

Our knowledge of the facts and ideas at the end of the Dark Age and the beginning of the Archaic Age comes from two collections of very important writings: the poems of Homer and Hesiod.

B. Political Ideas

1. *Homer*

a. Homeric Poetry

The *Iliad* and the *Odyssey* were composed in Ionia by one or two poets, the *Iliad* toward the middle of the eighth century, the *Odyssey* a little later toward the end of the same century.[4] The

[4] See Moses Finley, *Early Greece: The Bronze and Archaic Ages* (New York: Norton, 1970), 82–89. Since the Mycenaean period, bards had also existed; they sang the exploits of heroes. The authors of the *Iliad* and the *Odyssey* were probably two bards who collected traditional tales.

poems do not explicitly discuss Greek society of the age, primarily because the events they narrate occur supposedly in some distant past, dating back to the Mycenaean civilization. Nevertheless, they unintentionally reveal traces of the civilization in which they were composed, when the city emerged.

The Homeric poems narrate the epic of the Achaeans, who under the command of the Mycenaean king, Agamemnon, waged war against the city of Troy in Asia Minor, and the return to the homeland, Ithaca, of one of his generals, Ulysses, after years of wandering. The author or authors situate these events in a remote past, which they believe corresponds to their own origins. To maintain an impression of historical interval, they intentionally hide from view the realities of their own time, much as we moderns might do if we were writing a book or making a film about ancient times. But they are only able to hide the "modernity" of which they are fully aware. Their historical sense is weak. They unintentionally describe a society that is more recent than Mycenaean society, that is, Dark Age and Archaic Age (eighth century BC), although some descriptive elements date back to the Mycenaean period. For example, the Homeric heroes *cremated* their dead, but this practice did not arise before the eleventh century BC. "In sum, the Homeric poems retain a certain measure of Mycenaean 'things'—places, arms and weapons, chariots—but little of Mycenaean institutions or culture."[5]

Thus, an analysis of Homeric society is particularly complex: there are some features of a Mycenaean society; others are characteristic of the Dark Age, and still others of Homeric society, where urban centers arose; not to forget the purely imagined features typical of works of fiction. The work of historians nevertheless provides some insights.

b. Homeric Political Entities: Between Feudalism and Civicism

Homeric poetry touches on a number of political realities: in the *Iliad,* the city of Troy, the fabled seat of King Priam; the Achaean armies, each with an organization reflecting the Greek city it hails from: a general-king, noble companions, and citizen-soldiers. The *Odyssey* describes at length two states, the imaginary kingdom of Sheria[6] and Ithaca, Ulysses' homeland, where his wife Penelope and his son Telemachus await him. A few succinct references are made to Agamemnon's kingdom, Mycenae, and to Menelaus's kingdom, Sparta, as well as to the lands of the Myrmidons and the Lycians.

The descriptions of these various political entities show "archaic" elements (typical of society in the Dark Age), interspersed with "modern" ones (characteristic of the dawning world of the Greek city).[7]

i. *Archaic Elements*

• *Society in general showed a "feudal" character.* One finds a king (*anax, basileus*), nobles (*aristées, heroès*), and the people (*laos, laoi*). But the state as such, that is, the institutions of the Mycenaean age and the territory under its rule, have manifestly disappeared. "The world of Agamemnon and Achilles and Odysseus was one of petty kings and nobles, who possessed the best land and considerable flocks, and lived a seignorial existence, in which raids and local wars were frequent. The noble household (*oikos*) was the centre of activity and power. How much

[5] Ibid., 84.

[6] The island on which Ulysses landed and where he was greeted first by Princess Nausicaa, the daughter of the king, then by King Alcinoos himself. After honoring him with a banquet and listening to his adventures, Alcinoos lent him a ship and a crew of oarsmen to help him to return to Ithaca.

[7] See Claude Mossé, *La Grèce archaique d'Homère à Eschyle* [Archaic Greece from Homer to Aeschylus] (Paris: Éditions du Seuil, 1984), 38.

power depended on wealth, personal prowess, connexions by marriage and alliance, and retainers. There is no role assigned to tribes or other large kinship groups."[8]

Agamemnon possesses more than military power. He has a commander's baton, *skêptron* (scepters existed already in Sumer). He is the king-bearer of the scepter, *skêptroukos*. He has dominion over other kings—Nestor, Achilles, Ulysses—who are under obligation to answer his call in the event of war, and if they do not, they owe him compensation. He has bodyguards, young companions, and pages who eat at his table (as in Europe's Middle Ages). He governs with an assembly of *aristées*.

- *Hero morals*. Courtly values of a warrior aristocracy are dominant; the ideal attitude is bravery and fortitude in battle. "Strive always to be the best and to be superior to others" is the admonition. These are fundamentally individualistic values: the hero fights alone (with help from his page). The beauty of the physical body is glorified. The most magnificent outcome for the hero is to die young before experiencing the decrepitude of old age. Young companions surround the hero, learning the art of physical exercise and war at his side.[9]
- *The constant presence of the gods*. The Homeric world is full of gods. They constantly interfere with events, sometimes physically, taking sides for one party or another. For this reason, it is a world of marvels, escaping human reason. Moreover, kings are kings by the will of the gods and are more often than not also of divine origin. Pure heredity prevails only on rare occasion; objective merits almost never. On the whole, Homeric royalty is a "sacred" royalty, all the more that the role of the kings is still largely religious: he officiates at the sacrifices. To this we can add that Zeus himself is an absolute king; he takes decisions alone and does not share power with a council.
- *The non-fixedness of legal statutes*. The status of illegitimate children, slaves, and various categories of workers is, by and large, uncertain, as if there are no fixed rules in the matter. Homeric society has different social strata, but they do not yet have the class features of the later Greek city. There is a lower class made up of captives, called "slaves," who do not appear to be particularly ill treated. There is a small number of professions: blacksmiths, carpenters, medical physicians, seamen, and tradesmen (most trade and transport was in the hands of foreigners, the "Phoenicians"). There are also diviners and bards. Finally, there is an upper class of nobles and a king or chief who alone possesses power (the "people" do not yet have any political existence).

The devolution of political power is, on the whole, arbitrary. The uncertainty and vagueness of political structures in the Homeric world are plain to see when considering the kingdoms of Ulysses in Ithaca and Agamemnon in Mycenae.

During the 20 years that Ulysses is away from his island, the nobility maneuvers constantly to usurp his power, despite the existence of a "lawful" heir, Telemachus, Ulysses' son. But Telemachus cannot appeal to an uncontested constitution, a code of laws, or an unwavering administration, independent of the king's person, to ensure a smooth transition of power. In the Homeric world, power struggles are common.

Upon his return home, Agamemnon is assassinated by Aegisthus, the lover of his wife Clytemnestra. His son, Orestes, metes revenge for his cold-blooded murder. But had he not taken the initiative, no one would have sought revenge in his place. Thus, "there was no bureaucratic

[8] Finley, *Early Greece*, 84–85.

[9] On aristocratic paideia, see Henri-Irénée Marrou, *Histoire de l'éducation dans l'Antiquité* (Paris: Éditions du Seuil, 1948), translated as *A History of Education in Antiquity* (Madison: University of Wisconsin Press, 1982); and Werner Jaeger, *Paideia: The Ideals of Greek Culture* (New York: Oxford University Press, 1945).

apparatus, no formalized legal system or constitutional machinery. The power of equilibrium was delicately balanced."[10]

ii. *"Modern" Elements*

In the Homeric world, a "closed" archaic economy predominates, based on the exploitation of a single domain, the house (*oïkos*), where the master (even when he was a "king") supervises the work of his servants personally. There is, nevertheless, also evidence of *a mercantile economy* (no doubt the influence of the Phoenicians, who began to sail the Mediterranean after the eleventh century). While the customary exchange of gifts (particularly between hosts and guests) takes place as a gratis gesture (no one is "counting," so to speak), there are passages in Homeric poetry that suggest a concern for the fair value of things. Acts of piracy and raids are no longer the sole means of acquiring goods.

In addition to the great Homeric "figures" and warrior heroes, there are also *wise counselors* with fine intellectual and "political" skills: for example, the old Nestor, king of Pylos. Even Achilles and Agamemnon appear at times to distance themselves from hero morality concerned only with war and death. The *Odyssey* shows Ulysses challenging one of the suitors not to mortal combat but to an agricultural contest: the victor will be the one who can "plow the straightest furrow." In these nonheroic figures, and in the ambiguous features of the heroes themselves, we detect the emergence of a new morality, the morality of the citizen (this is even more marked in Hesiod).

The existence of a king-council-assembly structure is also a modern element. In Sheria, the king is assisted by a council of 12 scepter-bearing "kings" (*basileis*), sometimes expanded to include the "elders." Moreover, the *demos* is sometimes assembled in the *agora* (indicating that the public square existed already in Homeric times). But the people have no real power of decision; it is assembled only to hear and acclaim the opinion of the council. The same structures of king, council, and assembly are found in Ithaca as well: the council and the assembly are convened at irregular intervals to deal with the irksome problem of the devolution of royal powers after the disappearance of Ulysses. The same structure is found in the *Iliad* in the army of the Achaeans: Agamemnon governs with the advice of his council; in grave circumstances, he convenes a general assembly of warriors, though the assembly has no formal decision-making powers; it can only approve the decision of the "kings," which nevertheless suggests that the assembly served to channel expressions of protest and doubt: this was the first intentional political role of the *demos*.

Homer depicts the Cyclops as "wholly uncivilized" because they have no agriculture and, in particular, because they live alone. They have no public meeting place (*agora*) to debate issues or to take decisions collectively.

When Homer points out that the Trojans should have heeded the advice of the warrior Polydamas rather than the counsel of King Hector, he is subtly signaling his preference for an equal "right of expression" for all. When doubt is cast on the hereditary principle, when arguments are advanced in favor of an implicit right of the majority, these are signs of the new realities soon to flourish in the archaic and classical city.

Let us turn now to the topic of *justice*, which Homeric poetry addresses explicitly. We will find the same combination of archaic and "proto-civic" elements.

[10] Finley, *Early Greece*, 82.

c. Justice

As in the states of the ancient Near East, there is also in Homeric society an administration of justice, but it is probably closer to an unwritten "proto-law" without firm public laws and certainly not written. The belief is that justice (*dike, themis*) is spoken by the gods, and powerful figures claim to be their interpreters. A courtroom trial is still very much a ritual, if we are to judge by the incident of Achilles' shield in the *Iliad:*

> But the folk were gathered in the place of assembly; for there a strife had arisen, and two men were striving about the blood-price of a man slain; the one avowed that he had paid all, declaring his cause to the people, but the other refused to accept aught; and each was fain to win the issue on the word of a daysman. Moreover, the folk were cheering both, shewing favour to this side and to that. And heralds held back the folk, and the elders were sitting upon polished stones in the sacred circle, holding in their hands the staves of the loud-voiced heralds. Therewith then would they spring up and give judgment, each in turn. And in the midst lay two talents of gold, to be given to him whoso among them should utter the most righteous judgment.[11]

Dike is the pronouncement of a righteous or "straight" verdict, as opposed to excessive acts (*hubris*) or perverse acts. *Themis* is more solemn. It is the role of justice decreed by a god or a king capable of *themisteuein,* to ensure justice and make public laws and ordinances while holding the scepter (see *Iliad,* 1.278–79, Achilles addressing Agamemnon: "*Dikaspoloi, oi te themistas pros Dios eiruatai*" [Givers of *dike,* those who hand down justice and pronounce verdicts in the name of Zeus]).

Since justice supposedly comes from Zeus and is not rendered according to explicit public laws, will it not be arbitrary and generally unpredictable? Are not judges corruptible? Homer seems to have some concerns in the matter, since one of the merits that he attributes to Ulysses is precisely his sense of justice. Ulysses always made it a practice of allowing *dike* to triumph in Ithaca, while bad kings "twist the courses of justice aslant by false proclamations." Again in Hesiod, we will hear this accusation against the justice of kings, who claim divine powers but who, in reality, are corrupt.

2. *Hesiod*

Hesiod came from Ascra in Boeotia (the region of Thebes in northwest Attica). His works date from the middle of the eighth century BC and are, probably, contemporaneous with (or only slightly later than) the works of Homer. His major works are *The Works and Days* and *Theogony*.[12]

a. Two Types of Strife

The Works and Days is addressed to Hesiod's brother, Perses, who took him to court accusing him of stealing his inheritance. This poem expresses a genuine political philosophy: it claims the superiority of work, peace, and justice over aristocratic morals, the love of war, "excess," and the "right of might."

The poem begins with a bold "prophetic" assertion. There are two types of "strife" (*eris*). The one is fundamentally negative, destructive, and evil; it is pursued by the aristocrats. The other,

---

[11] *Iliad,* 18.496–510; *Translator's note:* quoted in A. T. Murray's translation of Homer, *The Iliad* (Cambridge, MA: Harvard University Press), 1985.

[12] *Translator's note:* We quote from Hesiod, *The Works and Days, Theogony,* and *The Shield of Herakles,* trans. Richard Lattimore (Ann Arbor: University of Michigan Press, 1959); hereafter cited in the text.

more benevolent, draws on the same vital force, but applies it differently, namely toward work. This second type of *eris* drives emulation and competition. It is fundamentally positive, productive, and benevolent: the bearer of peace and prosperity.

The good *eris* "pushes the shiftless man to work, for all his laziness. A man looks at his neighbor, who is rich: then he too wants work; for the rich man presses on with his plowing and planting and the ordering of his state. So the neighbor envies the neighbor who presses on toward wealth. Such strife is a good friend to mortals. Then a potter is potter's enemy, and craftsman is craftsman's rival; tramp is jealous of tramp, and singer of singer" (*Works and Days,* verses 20–26). Therefore, work is essential in order to be just. Work, production, and the competition that augments them both are the real solutions to civic quarrels and wars.

b. Work and Justice

Two myths illustrate the truth of these principles. The first, the *myth of Pandora,* shows that work, by the will of Zeus, is humanity's lot. The second, the *myth of race and blood,* recounts that, among the peoples who succeeded one another on earth, those who gave in to excess perished wretchedly, and those who chose justice were favored by the gods. The lesson here is twofold: humanity cannot escape the law of work; the human race cannot do without justice.

Hesiod sees an authentic *value* in work: "Famine is the unworking man's most constant companion. Gods and men alike resent that man who, without work himself, lives the life of the stingless drones,[13] who without working eat away the substance of the honeybees' hard working; your desire, then, should be to put your works in order so that your barns may be stocked with all livelihood in its season. It is from work that men grow rich and own flocks and herds; by work, too, they become much better friends of the immortals. Work is no disgrace; the disgrace is in not working" (*Works and Days,* verses 302–11).

Zeus, who commends men to work, also gives them justice by means of which every man can work in peace. Similarly, it is the will of Zeus that injustice be the lot of animals: "Here is the law, as Zeus established it for human beings; as for fish, and wild animals, and the flying birds, they feed on each other, since there is no idea of justice among them; but to men he gave justice, and she in the end is proved the best thing they have" (*Works and Days,* verses 275–79).

Now, in the society in which Hesiod lives, it is not the law of work and justice that predominates but the law of the predator, the law of the strongest. Judges, kings, and aristocrats "twist[ed] the courses of justice." Hesiod engages in genuine *social criticism* targeting the aristocracy and the ambivalent, arbitrary system of justice of his time, a system without established laws that Homer also denounced in his time.

> Their people must pay for the profligacy of their rulers, who for their own greedy purposes twist the courses of justice aslant by false proclamations.... The man who does evil to another does evil to himself, and the evil counsel is most evil for him who counsels it. The eye of Zeus sees everything. His mind understands all. He is watching us right now, if he wishes to, nor does he fail to see what kind of justice this community keeps inside it. Now, otherwise I would not myself be righteous among men nor have my son be so; for it is a hard thing for a man to be righteous, if the unrighteous man is to have the greater right. But I believe that Zeus of the counsels will not let it end thus. (*Works and Days,* verses 265–73)

[13] Plato also took up the metaphor of the lazy [stingless] drone; see section on Plato below.

c. Justice, the Gift of Zeus

It is true, Zeus strikes down the bad judges. The justice that Hesiod aspires to is primarily willed by Zeus. It is a gift of God; indeed, it is a goddess in its own right.

In his *Theogony,* Hesiod represents Zeus in union with *Themis;* the fruit of their union is Eunomia, Dike, and Eirene (Order, Justice, and Peace). "Next Zeus took to himself *Themis,* the shining, who bore him the Seasons, Lawfulness, and Justice, and prospering Peacetime (Eirene); these are concerned to oversee the actions of mortal people" (*Theogony,* verses 901–02).

Thus, Justice, the daughter of Zeus, is called to argue the cause of just men and convict the guilty at the court of Olympus: "Justice herself is a young maiden. She is Zeus's daughter, and seemly, and respected by all the gods of Olympos. When any man uses force on her by false impeachment she goes and sits at the feet of Zeus Kronion, her father, and cries out on the wicked purpose of men" (*Works and Days,* verses 256–60).

Good lawgivers are a gift from Zeus:

> All look in the direction [of the good king] as he judges their cases with straight decisions [good judgments], and, by an unfaltering declaration can put a quick and expert end even to a great quarrel: and that is why there are temperate barons [wise princes] because for their people who have gone astray in assembly these lightly turn back their actions to the right direction, talking them over with gentle arguments. As such a one walks through an assembly, the people adore him like a god, with gentle respect; he stands out among all assembled. Such is the holy gift the Muses give to humanity. So it is from the Muses, and from Apollo of the far cast, that there are men on earth who are poets, and players on the lyre. [But] the lords are from Zeus.[14] (*Theogony,* verses 85–95)

The lesson here: the reign of law must prevail over might. Internally and externally, society relies too heavily on violence and *hubris.* "Taking justice into one's own hands" is the negation of justice. When aristocrats demand that the people obey the laws, but are unrestrained in their own behavior, all is lost. In practice, those who are strong, and their allies, are able to impose injustice, but their rule cannot last, because the gods are watching.

Hesiod sees the dawn of a world that we know *a posteriori* is a new world: a world closer to the "rule of law," where each person respects the other; where kings, "devourers of gifts [i.e., bribes]," do not abuse their power with "twisted justice" and "crooked rulings"; where men enjoy modest, honest prosperity, the reward for their efforts. But the happiness of men—plentifully described in the rest of the poem: happiness at work, happiness in different seasons, happiness during the harvests—is still the gift of the gods. It is not yet fully the fruit of human will or reason.

II. From Solon to Cleisthenes: The Emergence of the City and the Citizen

A. The Historical Context

During the so-called Archaic Age[15] the city affirms itself in full, and the "Greek miracle" occurs.

---

[14] It should be noted in passing that justice and eloquence are already closely associated in the city of Hesiod.

[15] By convention, the term Greek Middle Age refers to the period when writing disappeared (1200–750 BC); the Archaic period refers to the years between the reappearance of writing and the ultimate founding of Athenian democracy under Cleisthenes (between 750 and 500 BC); the Classical period refers to the two seminal centuries of Greek civilization:

1. *Eighth and Seventh Century Transformations*

After ca. 750 BC, the societies emerging from the Greek Middle Age underwent several complex, accelerated transformations.[16]

a. Colonization

First of all, starting in the middle of the eighth century, the Greek world expanded remarkably. Over the next two centuries approximately, several hundred settlements were established around the shores of the Mediterranean, the Black Sea, and all the way to southern Italy, Gaul, and Spain. Most of these settlements were genuine cities, similar to those found in mainland and Ionian Greece.

Population movements to these settlements were well organized, nothing like the disorderly migrations of the Dark Age.

The Greeks called these transfers *apoïkia* (from *apo,* "away from," and *oïkos,* "home"). The word "colony" can be used, but nowadays it implies a relationship of dependence on a colonizing mother city, which was clearly not the case here. What we have is a permanent settlement beyond the seas. The people who embarked on the adventure, while hailing from a Greek city, did not always come from the same one. Thus, a colony did not necessarily have a single "metropolis."

i. *Motivation for Colonization*

The colonies seem to have been a response to a *political* problem: a resolution of the serious social crises in the cities of mainland Greece. If these cities mobilized for an enterprise as difficult and painful as colonization; if they succeeded in marshaling all imaginable material and human resources for the relocation of a portion of its population overseas, no doubt it was because they felt themselves to be under pressure to do so. It was, so to speak, a life and death issue.

Herodotus provides a firsthand account of this with his description of the circumstances surrounding the foundation of Cyrenae by the city of Thera (present-day Santorini, the southernmost island of the Cyclades). Departures were, by no means, voluntary. Lots were drawn to determine which members of each family would go. Those refusing to relocate faced the death penalty. Tarentum (present-day Taranto) was founded with people from Sparta, forced into exile.

The political motivation for colonization was not completely divorced from other reasons, such as economic and demographic pressures.

ii. *Phases of Colonization*

Two major waves of colonization (other than the earlier colonization of Asia Minor) are identifiable:

- In the direction of the western Mediterranean—southern Italy, Sicily, Gaul, and Spain. This wave of colonization took place roughly between 750 and 650 BC and continued sporadically until about 550 BC.
- In direction of the northeast, first toward Thrace, the neighboring islands, and the Troad (starting ca. 700 BC), and then toward the Hellespont, the coast of the Black Sea, the mouth of the Don, and Trebizond (between 600 and 500 BC).

---

the Age of Pericles is the Age of Philosophers until final submission to Philip of Macedon (between 500 and 338 BC); the Hellenistic period follows and lasts three centuries until the conquest of Egypt by Rome in 30 BC.

[16] For the presentation of these transformations we follow the order established by Mossé, *La Grèce archaïque.* This order does not imply linear causality. Colonization is not the cause of economic changes, which would be the cause of the Hoplite revolution, which in turn caused legislative reforms, and so on. The Greek "miracle" emerges from a multiplicity of causes, all mutually impacting on one another. Among these causes, political thought itself plays an important role.

All the lands toward which the Greeks emigrated were inhabited, so the resistance of wronged local inhabitants created a new problem. It was resolved in different ways. The Etruscans did rather well from their contacts with the Greeks. They assimilated aspects of Greek religion and political order, as well as the Greek alphabet (which they later transmitted to the Romans). In contrast, barbarian peoples, like the Thracians and the Scythians, were brutally expelled.

iii. *Colonization and Political Ideas*

Colonization played a decisive role in the development of political theories and representations. Each time a city was founded abroad, it was necessary to provide it with a constitution and a body of laws *before* settlement could take place. The leaders of the city, therefore, had to make explicit constitutional issues, which until then had only been implicit and a matter of custom. Likewise, *comparisons* became possible: this or that type of constitution had been successful here, failed there; such and such detail of organization produced good results here, created snags there. Politics became a matter of *expertise,* and we now know that cities *placed orders* for their constitutions with experts. Once the experts completed their investigations and experiments and proposed different solutions, the results became available for other cities needing constitutional changes at home to resolve political crises. Whether to establish new institutions or to modify old ones, theoretical political thought was now in motion.[17]

b. Economic Changes and the Stasis of Social Classes

Concurrently with colonization, archaic Greece was the theater of profound social and economic changes.

The archaeological record provides evidence of population growth and, more generally, of economic expansion, wealth progression, and technical advance at this time. It is conceivable that conditions were ripe for severe social instability, all the more so because the aristocracy, after the removal of the kings, withdrew inward and organized the economy for its own benefit. It controlled the best land and organized its apportionment to a small number of old families (it was at this time that emphasis was placed on genealogy: each noble family claimed ties with the city's mythical ancestors). But, in doing so, the aristocracy clashed with the other social classes of the city.

Several social categories thrived in the archaic city:

- Two traditional categories: the *aristocracy* and the *peasant farmers,* who cultivated the fields of the aristocracy in the country.

There were also two new categories (new in terms of size and mentality):

- The *rabble;* the underclass became increasingly poor as its numbers grew; it was deprived of land ownership and deeply indebted.
- A new *middle class* of wealthy farmers, merchants, shipowners, and artisans. The rise of this social category is evident in the lyric poetry around 650 BC. It subsequently acquired considerable political significance, playing a pivotal role in the most important military innovation in Greek history: the invention of the *hoplite phalanx* (see below).

Archaic Greece became the theater of serious political and social conflict. Politically, the various social classes sought a new distribution of roles in the government of the city; socially, they

[17] We will see below that Plato wrote the *Laws* as the Cretans were founding a colony.

expressed grievances about issues of ownership and indebtedness. The Greeks referred to these conflicts with the generic term *stasis,* meaning "secession," the breakdown of the traditional sociopolitical equilibrium. Five kinds of struggle are identifiable in archaic Greece:

1. *Internal struggles within the aristocracy.* These struggles were common in the Homeric world, but with the new political institutions, involving voting, coalitions, and so on, they changed shape. Some aristocratic fractions approved the idea of turning to the people for support against rival fractions: the Alcmaeonid family in Athens and the Bacchiad family in Corinth did this.
2. *The demands of a wealthier middle class.* The middle class had aspirations for a share in political power. Its claims were founded on its new military influence owing to the *hoplite* phalanx.
3. *Sporadic revolts of the poor.* Farmworkers lived in steadily worsening circumstances.
4. *Clashes due to food scarcity associated with population growth.* This was particularly acute around the small islands of the Aegean.
5. *Conflicts between cities.* This arose primarily from political factions of one city calling for assistance from the equivalent political factions of others (struggling aristocrats asked for help from aristocrats in power elsewhere, for example). Internal politics influenced external politics, and vice versa.

In his *Athenian Constitution,* Aristotle describes certain events in the life of Athens during the Archaic Age and tells us, "After this event there was contention between the upper classes and the populace.... The poorer classes, men, women, and children, were the serfs of the wealthy... [and] found themselves virtually without a share in anything."[18] Aristotle tells of widespread demands for land redistribution and debt forgiveness at the time of Solon (ca. 600 BC) and evokes the middle-class revolt against the aristocrats who monopolized all civic and religious offices, and the pressing demand of the middle class for the law to become public and fixed, while, until then, the aristocracy had claimed the formulation and possession of the unwritten law for itself.

c. The *Hoplite* Revolution

Legend accredits King Pheidon of Argos with the invention of the phalanx—the idea of organizing heavily armed foot soldiers in line formation. The archeological record shows that weapons disappeared from gravesites around this time, evidence that the possession of a weapon was no longer a privilege or a mark of nobility. But this does not imply that the ownership of weapons had become "democratic." With the disappearance of the charioteer as the primary weapon of combat, the nobility—the only class wealthy enough to maintain horses—lost its primacy of military functions. But to become a *hoplite,* it was necessary to be able to equip oneself with heavy iron weapons, and this excluded the masses.

The involvement of middle-class men in the military effort, at a time when conflicts between cities were frequent, necessarily had ramifications for the political life of the city. The same men, who agreed to defend the city with their lives, could not be expected to tolerate their exclusion from civic responsibility for very long.

d. The Age of the Lawgivers: The "Seven Sages of Greece"

In the metropolises, as in the colonies, there is evidence of the invention of *political concepts and institutions* intended primarily as solutions to the social and political problems created by stasis.

[18] Aristotle, *Athenian Constitution,* translated by Frederic G. Kenyon (London: G. Bell, 1914), part 2, lines 1–3.

Political thinkers began to appear, in particular those known traditionally as the Seven Sages: *Solon* of Athens; *Thales* of Miletus, statesman and founder of the Milesian school of "physicists"; *Pittacus,* tyrant of Mitylene; *Bias* of Priene; *Cleobulus* of Lindus; *Periander,* tyrant of Corinth; *Chilo* of Sparta; and others (the list of Seven Sages differs according to the source; some also include *Epimenides,* a philosopher-poet and seer). The Sages flourished toward the end of the seventh and during the sixth centuries. Their maxims were carefully preserved and taught during the Hellenistic Age. Along with others, *Zaleucus of Locri,*[19] *Charondas of Catania* (in Sicily),[20] they developed the key concepts of the state and politics: law, equality, various categories of penal law, and more.

Around 600 BC the same individuals (or perhaps others) invented new institutions: *tyranny,* and then other forms of regular participation of the *demos* in the government and administration of the city, which later became typical of *democracy,* such as the procedures of *election* and *appointment by lot* for access to public office, *councils, assemblies,* the *classification* of citizens, proper *territorial divisions.*

It is striking that virtually none of these political innovations owes a debt to religion: political thought in Greece was born "secular." Appeals to the Delphic oracle were, of course, made from time to time, but more often than not *after* an important decision had already been made. The men, whose ideas we will study below, defended their opinions and decisions with *rational* arguments (see above, p. 16).

Let us take a closer look at one of the most important of the new institutions: tyranny.

e. Tyranny

Tyranny made its appearance in numerous mainland Greek cities after the middle of the seventh century BC. It spread throughout the Aegean, to Asia Minor and the cities of greater Greece. There is a close (but not total) correlation between tyranny and the economic, political, and urban development of Greek cities. (Tyrannies did not exist in the more backward regions, such as Acarnania, Etolia, and Thessaly. It is as though tyranny became necessary only where stasis was strong, that is, where traditional hereditary aristocracies were destabilized and incapable of resolving the growing social conflicts and external wars indirectly instigated by them.)

In many places, tyranny successfully abolished the debilitating crush of stasis for a generation or two. Tyrants *protected the peasant farmer, encouraged trade,* and strengthened the sense of community with their policies of *public works* and spectacular *state-sponsored festivals.* They also maintained or reestablished *peace on their borders* through the agreement of alliances. But above all, tyrannies eliminated the outmoded habit of aristocratic government. Thus, paradoxically, they assisted the emergence of democracy.

However, the evolution of Greek cities under the yoke of *stasis* was not uniform. To understand this, we must leave the realm of generalities and discuss the two great cities that provided Greek political thinkers with two opposing political models: Sparta, the home of aristocracy; and Athens, the home of democracy.

---

[19] About 660 in Locri, Zaleucus decreed a law in favor of landowners to the detriment of aristocrats by birth; he caused the city to intervene directly in penal affairs, thus putting an end to personal revenge.

[20] About 600, Charondas of Catania introduced political reforms (increased role for the people's assembly) and penal reforms (procedures and sentences were established; the role of public action increased).

2. *The Evolution of Sparta*[21]

a. Origins of the Spartan City

Little is known about Sparta in the Archaic Age (and even the Sparta of more recent periods, for that matter, compared with the wealth of material for Athens).

After the decline of the Mycenaeans, the population of the Peloponnesus collapsed almost completely. Around 950 BC, Dorian tribes settled in the small plain of Laconia in the Eurotas valley on the eastern side of Mount Taygetus. Sparta was born of the political union of four villages and the subsequent annexation of a fifth.

Between 735 and 715 BC the Spartans crossed the Taygetus Mountains from east to west and conquered the rich *Messenian* plain. The pre-Dorian inhabitants were reduced to a condition worse than slavery elsewhere in the Greek world. *Helots* (literally, "captives") were slaves of the Spartan city-state itself. The *periekos* were subject peoples who remained semiautonomous in political terms.

b. The Great Rhetra

Initially, Sparta seems not to have differed much from other Greek cities.

The oldest text, providing insight into the political institutions of Sparta, is the "Great Rhetra" or the "Oracle," spoken when the fifth village, Amyclae, was annexed. The text is not easy to interpret. It is not clear who gives an injunction to whom: "Build a temple to Zeus Syllanius and Athena Syllania, divide the people into *phylai,* and divide them into *obai,* and establish a gerousia of thirty including the Archagetai, then from time to time convene the '*apella*' between Babyka [a bridge] and Knakion [a river], and there introduce and repeal measures; but the Demos must have the decision and the power."

In some respects this description calls to mind Homeric institutions. The *phylai* (clans) were the three Dorian tribes. The *obai* (localities) were the five founding villages. The *Archagetai* (founder-leaders) were the kings, a peculiarity of Sparta, which—until the third century BC—had two royal dynasties, the *Agiads* and the *Eurypontids,*[22] reigning jointly over the city; as "sacred kings," they presided over all rituals and, at the same time, held real political power (rare in ancient Greece). The *gerousia* ("senate") had 28 members and the two sovereigns *ex officio.* Senators had to be at least 60 years old and were elected for life (their election was by *acclamation;* the intensity of acclamation for each candidate was actually measured by election officials; this odd procedure greatly amused the Greeks). Finally, the *apella* was the assembly of ordinary citizens.

Judging solely by the Rhetra, Sparta was barely distinguishable from neighboring cities, politically speaking. We know that, in terms of its economy, it also engaged in trade and crafts production, like its neighbors, and that it was fairly open to the outside world. Similarly, it was known for its festivals, its music, and its poetry.

c. The Regime of Equals

Then, in the seventh century BC, the city changed profoundly. The Messenian wars were very brutal and continued until ca. 650 BC. It went through difficult times and suffered a calamitous defeat at Hysiai inflicted by Argos (669 BC). It appears that the wars were the impetus for a series of radical social and political reforms resulting in a form of government markedly different

[21] de Durand, *Précis d'histoire grecque,* 105–33; Orrieux and Schmitt-Pantel, *Histoire grecque,* 100–08.

[22] The origins of these dynasties are disputed. They may have been the kings of two Dorian tribes, the Hylles and the Dymanes (the third, the Pamphylii, never had a single head because of its composite character). Another theory is that the two families were descendants of the head chiefs of the two original villages with the joint reign beginning some time around 775–760 BC.

from other Greek governments: a *military aristocracy* dominating *helots* and *periekos*, *egalitarian within* but *closed to the outside world.*

The regime in Sparta can be characterized as follows:

- In political terms, the power of the dual kings was diminished by the invention of the *Ephors*—the five magistrates (literally, "overseers") elected annually by the assembly; the powers of the *gerousia* were bolstered to the detriment of the *apella*.
- In social and economic terms, there was a *land redistribution* in Laconia and a *division in equal lots* (*kleroi*) of the lands seized in the conquest of Messenia (some nine or ten thousand lots were created). As a result, the warrior class came to see itself as made up of "equals" (*homoïoï*).
- The citizens ceased participation in economic activity; *helots* worked the plots awarded to the heads of families, while *periekos* engaged in trade. The citizens of Sparta became a permanent army of citizen-soldiers.
- The citizen-soldiers were required to live communally: this included taking communal meals (*syssitia*) (the obligation extended to the kings as well).
- Children were reared by the state and given a military-style education, *agogè*.

The famous Spartan education applied to children and youths between the ages of 7 and perhaps 24. It involved physical education and military training, and nurtured a spirit of competition and rivalry. The final phase of the *agogè* required the near-adult to withdraw from the city for a year, hiding and sleeping by day, stealing food by night, primarily from the *helots,* it seems (this final test, *crypteia,* may have concerned only a minority).

- A number of other measures broke with the traditions of the other Greek cities; these measures were justified by the importance now attributed to the state, which had become a collective entity that all citizens were under blind obligation to follow. Among the measures were a strict application of *eugenics* (children deemed to be weak were "exposed," that is, killed) and a *semi-community of women* (particular worthy warriors were authorized to father a child outside their marriage).

These reforms introduced a gradual hardening, followed by a genuine sclerosis of life in the city. Laws remained unwritten, a "reactionary" characteristic, since after the diffusion of writing elsewhere in Greece ca. 650 BC, the law became codified in most urban centers (see below for the case of Athens).

Furthermore, Sparta refused to take steps toward a monetized economy, which the other Greek cities accomplished in the course of the sixth century. There is evidence only of barter with iron rods (common in western Europe in the Megalithic Age). The source of Spartan wealth was to be land, equally allotted.[23]

It seems that by the sixth century an elite with refined tastes and literary, artistic, and philosophical occupations had disappeared entirely from Spartan society. It became one big military camp.

Yet, a telling paradox remains. The Spartan *military* regime did not have a *conquering* spirit. It was far less oriented externally or concerned with expansion than Athens with its ostensibly more pacific principles. Sparta was content to secure its domination over Argos by strategic

[23] In truth, equality was more principle than fact. The list of winners of horse races at the Olympic games includes Spartan names, yet great wealth was required to participate in such races.

annexations. In the end, it controlled two-fifths of the Peloponnesus. The Peloponnesian League was an alliance of states organized around Sparta, but was not like the Athenians' Delian League, an empire with a hegemonic capital city.

Sparta did undertake a few military incursions outside the Peloponnesus. For example, it fought wars with Megara and Aegina, and, as we shall see, it intervened alongside Athens to expel the Pisistratidae. But these expeditions were exceptional. The city had no need of conquest; its political ideal was one of "reaction," the arrest of time, the maintenance of the city in the same permanent state (this would be Plato's ideal as well).

Did this military option at least enable Sparta to be a great power? This is debatable. Its army arrived late in Marathon in 490 BC because it had been involved in suppressing a *helot* revolt in Messenia. As a result, the full glory of victory accrued to Athens, the democratic city-state. Again, in 480 BC, it would require the strategic cunning of Themistocles, the Athenian soldier and statesman, to draw the Spartan admiral into the Battle of Salamis. However, Sparta did distinguish itself at the battles of Thermopylae and Plataea.

Sparta's constant military handicap, despite its ideology and determination, was its *demographic fragility* due to various causes: its strong resolve to shut itself off from the world, which denied it a demographic influx from immigration (Athens, in contrast, was something of an Aegean melting pot); the collective rearing of children; and finally, eugenic concerns that resulted in a form of Malthusianism. Sparta lacked men, and the problem only grew worse. Every military loss became an irreparable tragedy—in contrast, Athens was able to recover quite well. According to a census taken when Agis IV (244–241 BC) attempted his social reforms, the number of families had fallen from 10,000, the population size when the initial land allotments were made, to a mere 700.

It is true, Sparta triumphed over Athens in the devastating Peloponnesian War (430–404 BC), but it emerged thoroughly exhausted. In fact, in 371 BC, the army of Sparta collapsed before Thebes (the battle of Leuktra). This marked the end of its political history. The Theban chief, Epameinondas, restored Messenia and established a new political center in Arcadia: the city of *Megalopolis*.

The Greeks attributed Sparta's reforms to the legendary lawgiver Lycurgus of Sparta, a figure about whom virtually nothing is known (and who may never have existed). The extraordinary character of the Spartan regime fascinated Greek political thinkers throughout the ages. We will discuss the pro-Spartan attitudes of the Socratic circle below.

3. *The Evolution of Athens*

a. From Early Beginnings to Draco

Very little is known about Attica before the Greek Middle Age. The region had probably been in vassalage to Cretan kings in the distant past. According to tradition, a certain king Theseus unified the dozen or so independent countries of Attica and named Athens the capital city of the new entity. A citadel was built on the summit of the Acropolis and a *Mycenaean* form of state was adopted.

When Mycenaean civilization collapsed, Athens was one of the rare cases where the overthrow of the monarchic state was neither brutal nor total. The city's subsequent development, however, did fit the general pattern: a feudal regime during the "Dark Age," followed in the ninth and eighth centuries by the final disappearance of the kings and the emergence of aristocratic government. Power passed into the hands of annually appointed magistrates, the *archons,* and a council, the *Areopagus,* whose members were former archons. Access to the magistracies and judiciary functions was reserved exclusively for the *Eupatrids* or "well-born," that is, the nobles.

Although Athens managed to avoid, longer than most, the stasis of archaic Greece,[24] it nevertheless faced growing social conflict as early as the end of the seventh century BC. Such conflict involved the same social groups and produced the same outcomes as elsewhere: tyranny and the annihilation of the social and cultural substratum of the aristocratic regime. The first serious incident for which we have recorded evidence is Cylon's attempt to establish a tyranny around 630 BC.

The people apparently resisted en masse. Some of Cylon's partisans were slaughtered by members of a Eupatrid family, the Alcmaeonids, violating a safe conduct. The crime put an indelible curse on their descendants.

In approximately 620 BC the archon Draco was put in charge of terminating the vendetta from the Cylonian affair. He did so by enacting harsh "draconian" laws (Plutarch writes, "Draco's laws were written not with ink but blood").[25] And he also took a bold initiative: he *put his laws in writing* and obtained their indiscriminate application to all. This is the first record of an intention to establish *isonomia,* "equality before the law." Some of Draco's laws were still in use at the end of the fifth century BC.

b. Solon

But the dissatisfaction of the peasantry continued to grow. Civil war threatened. Then, in 594 BC, *Solon* became archon.

Solon (640–558 BC) was born into an impoverished noble family. He became wealthy through trade. With his knowledge of the seas and commerce, he played a significant role in the Athenian victory over the Megarans at Salamis (circa 612). Solon was a Eupatrid, but well disposed toward the people. In poems written before he became archon, he denounced the greed of the Eupatrids and the rich: "Unrighteous are the hearts of the rulers of the people, who will one day suffer many pains for their great pride (*hubris*); for they do not know how to restrain their excesses.... They grow rich through unrighteous deeds, and steal for themselves right and left, respecting neither sacred nor public property."[26]

During the civil disturbances, the *demos* approached Solon, aware of his stance, and asked him to impose a tyranny. He declined, though he did accept to become archon with strengthened powers so that he could undertake radical reforms and put an end to stasis.

i. *Social Measures*

Solon decided that a peasant in debt should no longer be enslaved. He made this law retroactive: anyone who was a slave because of debt or went into exile to avoid slavery was accepted back into Athenian society. His debts, however, were not forgiven, merely reduced by a third (a monetary expedient). Solon rejected the idea of land redistribution (as in Sparta), because he refused to commit an injustice against the nobles. His intention was to treat all social categories with fairness.

> For had I granted, now what pleased the one, then what their foes devised in counterpoise, of many a man this state had been bereft. Therefore I showed my might on every side, turning at bay like wolf among the hounds. I gave to the mass of the people such rank as befitted their need, I took not away their honour, and I granted naught to their greed; while

[24] This is why Athens did not need to found colonies like other cities; emigrants from Athens left for personal reasons.

[25] Plutarch, *Life of Solon XVII* (Cambridge, MA: Harvard University Press, 1914).

[26] Quoted in Finley, *Early Greece,* 123.

those who were rich in power, who in wealth were glorious and great, I bethought me that naught should befall them unworthy their splendour and state; so I stood with my shield outstretched, and both were sale in its sight, and I would not that either should triumph, when the triumph was not with right.[27]

ii. *Political Measures*

Following in Draco's footsteps, Solon undertook the first real *written codification of the law*. For ages the Athenians preserved the so-called "Boards," the four-sided structures of wood on which the laws were inscribed.

Solon established a new *law of persons*. This law took as its sole criteria of social distinction the criteria of wealth, shaking the traditional social order to the core. Henceforth, neither social origin nor inherited rank in the time-honored structure of kinship defined the rights or identity of an individual. An individual was no longer "how he was born," but "what he had." Yet wealth is mobile and a matter of personal freedom. Although it did not have an immediate practical impact, Solon's law was a philosophical revolution with wide-ranging implications.

Solon organized citizens in four classes according to wealth:

- The first class (*pentakosiomedimnoi*) had access to the office of archon, the Areopagus, and the high magistracies. Consequently, the wealthiest individuals gained access to the Areopagus. The Eupatrid privilege was broken.
- The next two classes, *hippeis* (horsemen or charioteers) and *zeugitae* (ox drivers), had access to the lower magistracies, as well as to Solon's new council, the *Boule of Four Hundred*.[28] This satisfied the middle classes, and in particular the *hoplites*.
- The last class (*thetes*) had access only to the assembly.

Finally, Solon established a new popular law court, the heliaia, and decreed that *the decisions of the courts could be appealed in the assembly*. In issuing his decree, Solon weakened the judiciary powers of the aristocracy, in keeping with the insistent demand of the other classes.

c. Pisistratids

In 561 BC a power struggle broke out between Lycurgus,[29] a member of the Eteoboutad *genos*, and Megacles, a member of the influential Alcmaeonid family. This struggle probably manifested the rivalry between two regional clans, since Attica had not yet been unified. Power finally fell into the hands of a third individual, Pisistratus, representing a third region, Diacria (a highland area in northeastern Attica). Instead of exercising power as an ordinary archon, he established a tyranny. Though a Eupatrid, Pisistratus turned to the disgruntled peasant masses for support, a classical example of the *demagogic tyrant*.

Pisistratus showed moderation. He left Solon's constitution in place and simply ensured that a member of his family was elected archon every year.[30]

---

[27] Aristotle, *Athenian Constitution*, part 12.

[28] This designation distinguishes it from the Boule established by Cleisthenes (see below), which had 500 members. For that matter, historians are not absolutely convinced that the Boule of Four Hundred ever existed; only Aristotle refers to it.

[29] Not to be confused with the mythical Spartan lawgiver.

[30] This behavior is common throughout history when ambitious individuals seize power in a republic and take steps to avoid shocking their fellow citizens with symbols of royal power: for example, Caesar Augustus in Rome, Cosimo de' Medici in Florence, Napoleon Bonaparte in France at the outset.

Pisistratus improved the lot of the farmers, extending *loans* and *facilitating repayment*. He also promoted *maritime trade* and developed *industry*. Small and medium-size property owners progressed economically and politically. The beautiful, much-sought-after painted pottery of Athens, which was found everywhere throughout Greece (including in greater Greece and Etruria), as the archeological record shows, is evidence that the age of Pisistratus experienced strong economic development. The minting of coinage is another sign of this development. The famous *tetradrachm* or *Athenian Owl* probably appeared first in the reign of Pisistratus's successor, Hippias.

Pisistratus undertook several *major building programs* in Athens—an aqueduct, a fountain, and temples—thereby providing work for the numerous poor among the urban masses. He built the large temple dedicated to Athena on the Acropolis (destroyed by the Persians in 480 BC and later replaced by the Parthenon) and another dedicated to Olympian Zeus.

The tyrant offered protection to *writers* and *artists*, and invited foreign poets and musicians to his "court." He gave more pomp to the Panathenian festival. He introduced recitals of Homer—undoubtedly the occasion to put Homeric poetry in writing or at least to ensure its publication. He organized competitions of tragic choruses every year on the occasion of the Dionysian festivals; theater came into being as an art and spectacle, distinct from the Dionysian rituals. These various collective projects and activities contributed to the emergence of a national sentiment.

Pisistratus "ruled" for over 30 years. He died in 527 BC and left power to his two eldest sons, Hippias and Hipparcus.

His sons behaved like princes; they had a court following and lived a life of luxury. After several years, the nobles revolted. Hipparcus was felled by the assassins Harmodius and Aristogiton, who were honored as "tyrannicides" and heroes of democracy (their descendants enjoyed certain privileges well into the fourth century BC). Following the assassination, Hippias tightened his grip on the tyranny. It lasted another four years during which time the nobles, including Cleisthenes the Alcmaeonid, went into exile. Cleisthenes attempted to seize power on several occasions, but without success. The *demos* remained passive.

Finally, in 510 BC, the Athenian nobles called upon Cleomenes, king of Sparta, who put an end to the tyranny of Hippias. On this occasion, in the eyes of all Greece, Sparta stood for the party of the aristocracy, just as somewhat later Athens epitomized democracy.

In conclusion, under Pisistratus and his sons, the Athenian aristocracy lost its power for good. If the 30 years of Solon's constitution and the 50 years of tyranny are put end to end, the result is a very long period during which Athenians lost the habit of an aristocratic social and political power. In the meantime, the ground beneath their feet shifted permanently, and the *demos* carved out a lasting place for itself on the political stage. Later, after democracy's victory, the Athenians presented Pisistratus's reign as a period of shameful regression squeezed between Solon and Cleisthenes. But this was historical hindsight. Without the neutralization of the old elite, achieved under the tyrant's rod, there would have been no democracy at all, as the example of Sparta shows.

d. Cleisthenes and the Flourishing of Athenian Democracy

Before long rivalry broke out between Cleisthenes and another aristocrat, Isagoras, a personal friend to the king of Sparta. Isagoras was elected archon in 508 BC. After two years of civil war, Cleisthenes finally won the power struggle and embarked on constitutional reforms, marking the true beginning of *Athenian democracy*.

His efforts at reform were no doubt bolstered by the "national" mood that the tyrants had cultivated throughout Attica. Athens inclined toward a city-state, and Cleisthenes consolidated the evolution with major civic and administrative reforms affecting the city's organization and public calendar.[31]

i. *New Tribes*

Cleisthenes began by replacing the four Ionian tribes with ten new "tribes"; the latter were no longer based on *ethnic origin* but exclusively on *geographic location.* In order to overcome the traditional political rivalry between the inhabitants of the city, the countryside, and the seaside, he created each new tribe with three *trittyes* ["thirds"], each *tritty* belonging to one of the three localities. In total, there were 30 *trittyes.*

Each *trittys* was comprised of three or four *demes.*[32] In the countryside, the *demes* were villages, sometimes combined when they were too small, sometimes broken up when too large. In the city, they were neighborhoods. The assembly of each *deme* elected a *demarchos* (like a mayor). The assembly administered the local finances and community properties; it oversaw the cults, held the civic and land registries, and provided the police. From that point on citizens identified with the *deme* in which they lived. All residents were recorded in the official population: citizens, former *metics* (resident aliens), and freed slaves, that is, a proto-melting pot. One's inscription on the registry was permanent, and population regroupings by political affinity became impossible. In addition to his first name, each person took the name of the *deme* as his last. According to Aristotle, no one was allowed to take his father's name. This was truly revolutionary.

Accordingly, the administrative identity of a citizen—his quality in the eyes of the law—was no longer bound up with one's birth or blood relations, but rather with one's place of residence. Citizens were no longer "sons of," but equal persons before the administration. The corollary of this was that men of foreign origin could also become citizens. Once naturalized, they would be the equals of the natives in the eyes of the law.

With these measures Cleisthenes undermined the social power of the old aristocracy and, in general, destroyed what was left of the lineage-based archaic society. He nurtured into existence an *abstract person,* the *citizen.*

ii. *Political Reforms*

As far as the mechanisms of government are concerned, Cleisthenes established the power of the *demos* once and for all with the Boule of Five Hundred. This council replaced the Areopagus, which was not entirely eliminated, since it retained its judiciary functions.

The assembly of each *deme* elected citizens with an aptitude for membership in the Boule (each of the 10 tribes provided a list of 50 Boule members; membership was determined by random lot). So the members of the principal democratic institution of the community were not chosen from the whole population but from a qualified list. Owing to its composition, the Boule was a city in miniature and genuinely representative. Since a citizen could only be a member of the Boule twice in his lifetime, each year 1 adult male in 60 could expect his name to be drawn from the urn. This arrangement meant that citizens became accustomed to a situation of obedience and authority alike, the very principle of democratic equality (*isotes*) (see below). Given its composition, the assembly could hardly avoid clashes with the Areopagus, which was composed of immovable professional politicians, nearly all born of noble families.

---

[31] Drawn from the presentation of these reforms in Humbert, *Institutions politiques et sociales,* 44–51.

[32] Each *deme* numbered between 300 and 1,000 citizens. There were roughly 100 *demes* in total, thus a population of between 25,000 and 50,000 citizens, and counting their families, between 80,000 and 100,000. In addition, there were 10,000 *metics* plus 30,000 to 40,000 slaves, making a total population in Attica of some 150,000 in 500 BC (ibid., 46).

Until then, real power was in the hands of the Areopagus and the archons[33] (they served at the discretion of the tyrants under the Pisistratids). The Areopagus controlled the archons, who convened the Assembly and directed its work. The Boule of Four Hundred (if it ever existed) had little impact on this situation. But the new Boule stripped the Areopagus of its power and responsibility.

The Boule became the fundamental organ of democracy. It prepared the meetings of the Assembly, which could not discuss texts unless the council had given its opinion. The Boule wrote decrees and functioned as the high court of justice after the reforms of Ephialtes.

The Boule was also the executive body. The year was divided into ten *prytaneis;* during each, the 50 Boule members of a tribe, the so-called *prytanis,*[34] took up residence near the council hall (*Bouleterion*), which Cleisthenes had erected in the agora. Each day lots were drawn to choose a president, the *epistates* of the *prytaneis;* he was the real head of state for 24 hours. In addition, the entire Boule met in regular plenary meetings.

From that point on, the tribes elected the archons.[35] But they were duplicated by a new college, the college of the *strategoi* (generals). The *strategoi* were also elected. Each commanded a part of the army and remained under the orders of the polemarch, for a time at any rate.

Because the *strategoi* were elected by the people (each tribe elected one), they played an increasingly important political role (like the ephors in Sparta and the tribunes in Rome). Little by little they encroached on the power of the archons; by the beginning of the fifth century, the archons were primarily restricted to judiciary and religious functions.

As for the *ecclesia,* it was no longer presided over by the eponymous archon and came under the responsibility of the daily *epistates* of the *prytaneis.* The venue for its meetings was also changed from the agora to the *pnyx,* the hill facing the Acropolis on which was built a vast amphitheater with a capacity of 25,000. Cleisthenes also established the principle of *isegoria*—an equal right of speech for all in the new *ecclesia.*

iii. *Change from a Religious Calendar to a Civic Calendar*

Another revolutionary measure with profound implications for the cultural traditions of the community was Cleisthenes' introduction of a new *calendar.* The 12 lunar months and traditional religious festivals would no longer regulate the rhythm of community life; this was replaced by 10 *prytaneis,* each longer than a month, during which the *prytanis* of each tribe governed the city. Because of the replacement of the religious calendar by the civic calendar, social life was punctuated by the city's main political events: solemn assemblies; elections; and the auditing and review of accounts. The celebration of religious festivals by a particular *genos* was not forbidden; they were merely relegated to secondary importance.[36]

iv. *Ostracism*

These revolutionary measures had to be protected from attack by nostalgic clients of the old aristocratic regime. Therefore, Cleisthenes enacted a law on *ostracism,* which made it possible to

[33] In Solon's time there were nine archons. Three existed since the disappearance of monarchy: eponymous archon (the chief magistrate), the archon basileus (responsible for religious arrangements), the polemarch (head of the armed forces). Solon added six *thesmothetus.* Cleisthenes added a secretary to the college, so that each of the ten new tribes would be represented. From Pierre Lévêque, *The Greek Adventure* (London: Weidenfeld and Nicolson, 1968), 178, 181–83.

[34] *Prytaneis* (pl.) means "the first" or "the leaders." They were the executives of the Boule.

[35] After Cleisthenes, another democratic reform replaced the election of the archons with appointment by lot.

[36] The inventors of the French revolutionary calendar (1793) copied this same artificial division of time.

send a prominent citizen, suspected of pursuing disproportionate personal influence, into exile. His measure targeted primarily the politicians of the aristocratic party.[37]

What models did Cleisthenes use for his reforms? One supposition is that he was influenced by Pythagorean speculations and the geometrism of the Milesian philosophers. One thing is certain, though: he thought through his reforms very carefully before implementing them. Cleisthenes is an early example of political constructivism, an approach that aims deliberately at ending conventions and forcing reality by the implementation of a rational action plan designed by abstract intelligence. Unquestionably, Cleisthenes ushered in the *age of politics* as we defined it in the introduction.

B. Political Ideas

Let us return now to each of the phases described above, examining them more closely in terms of the theories, ideas, and visions of society and humanity found in the all too few surviving texts.

The Greeks themselves attributed the first "secular" rational ideas on the organization of the city to the Seven Sages. Our knowledge of these Seven Sages is meager. In his dialogue *On Philosophy,* now lost, Aristotle writes, "They turned their attention to the organization of the *polis;* they invented laws and all the bonds that link the parts of a city together; and this invention they called Wisdom. Such was the wisdom . . . given to the Seven Sages, who invented the virtues suitable to a citizen."[38]

Because *stasis* was seen as *chaos,* the sages undertook to come up with new ideas on *social order (eunomia).* The "wisdom" of the Seven Sages and other thinkers of the sixth century BC consisted in defining a shared order—a general rule—that would make it possible to bridle the ambitions, arrogance, and excesses (*hubris*) of noble families, the violence of the masses, and the political demands of the middle class. This idea of order needed to be rational, based on objective observation, and no longer subject to myth.

In this respect, it is important to note that the sages were the contemporaries of the first Greek scientists, the "physicists" (one of the sages, Thales of Miletus, was in fact one of these early scientists). The same intellectual curiosity inspired the pursuit of the laws of the universe and the laws of society; these orders do not obey sacred anthropomorphic powers, but laws. In the *cosmos* and in the *polis, dike* rules. This principle is valid for all elements: they adhere spontaneously to a certain order, which is not decided at the sole discretion of any one element.

The astronomy of the Milesians, such as Thales, Anaximander, and Anaximenes, wrenched itself free from astral religion. Astronomy, geography, and physics were given a geometrical dimension. Anaximander is said to have drawn the first maps and built a physical model of the cosmos. He "placed a motionless earth at the center of the universe. He explained that if the earth stayed at rest in that place, with no need for support, it was because it was equidistant from all points on the celestial circumference, and so had no more reason to sink than to rise, or to move to one side rather than the other. Anaximander thus located the cosmos in a mathematical space composed of purely geometrical relationships."[39]

The earth no longer needed support—or roots—to hold it in place; nor did it depend upon a person (Atlas); there was no longer a high and a low in the world. Cosmic hierarchy disappeared as soon as the gods no longer set the world in motion. As Anaximander says, the world is no longer dominated by anyone or anything, *hypo medenos kratoumene* ("without submitting to

---

[37] It is not absolutely certain that Cleisthenes was the author of this law, since the first known date of its application was 488/87.

[38] Quoted in Vernant, *The Origins of Greek Thought,* 69.

[39] Ibid., 120–21.

the domination of anything whatever"), but submits to an impersonal principle of reason. No element or portion of the world could seize cosmic power to the detriment of the rest, no more than any one element of the city could exercise its *dynasteia* over all things. The *basileus* no longer held the city in his grasp; the role fell to the *nomos* (the rule of law). Similarly, the world held on its own, only by its laws.

This was the new spirit that expressed itself in the *administration of justice,* in ideas about the *law,* the virtue of *moderation* demanded of every citizen, and *equality* (see sections 1, 2, and 3 below).

1. *The Administration of Justice*

a. Criminal Legislation: Between Religion and Law

At the end of the seventh century BC, there emerged with the criminal laws (the laws of Draco and Solon in Athens, the laws of Zaleucus of Locri and Charondas of Catania, and the laws of other sages) what Rene Girard in his theory held to be the fundamental attribute of the state stripped of all sacredness: the *administration of rational justice,* which put an end to the cycle of violence by bringing down the full weight of the community on the guilty party, who by use of reason was found to be the perpetrator of a crime.

Initially, this evolution in the direction of rational justice continued to take into account the religious attitudes of society. The punishment of a crime by the judicial system was called for in order to *purify* a collective *stain;* one person's crime polluted all of society and everyone should feel threatened by it. This idea finds expression in the emergence of *Dionysianism* in the countryside and in the *Orphic cults.* Epimenides, one of the Seven Sages (in some lists), was a soothsayer—a sage in divine matters—called to Athens to drive out the *miasma,* the stain that had settled over the city after the slaughter of the Cylonians. He became Solon's political advisor and regulator of the rituals of mourning and the proper behavior of women. He also established sanctuaries and the rites of propitiation and purification.

Continuity across the boundaries of religion and civics was mediated by the "civic religion" of sixth century Greece as illustrated in the following examples.

Abaris was a sage in the Pythagorean tradition, a *shaman,* who "established new rituals of public worship (the *Proerosia* [a spring festival] at Athens). He opened sanctuaries for the community's protection (that of *Kore* the protectress at Sparta)."[40] *Onomacritus* was a political advisor, an envoy, and a constitutional expert for the Pisistratids; he was a soothsayer as well and an expert in secret oracles. Other examples include Lycurgus, Charondas, and Zaleucus, all of whom give their legislative codes a religious tonality; they believe criminals and opponents to be "possessed" individuals, who need to be restored to health by purifying rituals and chanted *katharsis.*

Jean-Pierre Vernant observes, however, that "this mystical ferment could continue only in the very narrowly circumscribed environment of the cults. It did not give rise to a widespread movement of religious renewal that ultimately embraced politics. What happened was the reverse."[41] Concern for social solidarity, which until then had been the business of religion and ritual (accordingly, it was spontaneous and without reflexive mediation), became an *intellectual* concern that could be explained and dealt with by rational means.

[40] Ibid., 120–21.

[41] Ibid., 80.

b. The Evolution of Legal Proceedings

This can be seen in the evolution of legal proceedings.[42] In the archaic trial, conducted under the authority of the *genē*, ritual expedients played an important role, such as in oaths, swearing, and the like. Such expedients retained their religious force and ensured automatic success, provided the ritual was followed properly. The judge was a priest of sorts, presiding over the ritual and providing a guarantee that it was correctly performed. He did not look into details. It was the gods who decided (the reader will have in mind our earlier examples of Homeric legal proceedings and the thoughts of Hesiod on this topic).

When the trial was held in the new context of the city, the judge began to personify the state: he was an impersonal being, sitting above the quarreling parties. He began to decide the suit himself with reference to the law (a law put in writing). He required only objective truth and instructed witnesses and the parties to the suit to give testimony and provide evidence. According to Vernant, "legal proceedings brought into operation a whole technique of proof, of reconstruction of the plausible and the probable, of deduction from clues or indications."[43] This was a complete change compared with the protolegal proceedings of the Archaic era.[44]

2. *The New Moral Ideal: Moderation* (Sophrosyne)

Another important development was the emergence of a new personal morality coupled with the new circumstances of community life. A *type of man*—the *citizen*—was born with the flourishing of the city. This did not happen on its own; it was the product of moral speculation by the sages and in the sects.

In contrast with the traditional, aristocratic *habrosyne* (beauty, grace), emphasizing refinement (as Homeric poetry eloquently illustrates), and the hubris of wealth (coveted by the nobles and the new wealthy classes), a novel ideal of *askesis* emerged, an ideal of restraint and self-control (*sophrosyne*), good sense, prudence, wisdom, moderation, and temperance. Such virtues formed the very foundations of human excellence (*arête*). "Pomp, ease, and pleasure were rejected; luxury in dress, in one's dwelling, in food and drink were forbidden. How furiously wealth was denounced!"[45]—because such behaviors could incite stasis and civic strife. Above all else, wealth was seen as the ultimate hubris: pure excess, without limit. This was a recurring theme of moral thought throughout the sixth century.

> *Solon:* "No end to wealth; *koros,* surfeit, begets *hybris.*"
> *Theognis:* "Those who today have the most want to have twice as much; wealth [*ta chremata*], turns a man to madness [*aphrosyne*]."[46]

Wealth was not the result of some anonymous economic mechanism. It came from a perverse will, a corrupted disposition, human wickedness, insatiable desire, boundless craving. In the wake of Hesiod's demands, the men of the new city praised the merits of *moderation.*

Spartan education (*agogè*), Vernant says, ensured that the young man maintained, in all circumstances, modesty and reserve. This was in striking contrast with the ludicrous vulgarity of the ordinary people and the haughty arrogance of the aristocrat. The Spartan educator attached the greatest importance to external behavior because he thought it expressed the proper

---

[42] See Louis Gernet, *Droit et institutions en Grèce antique* (Paris: Flammarion, 1982).

[43] Vernant, *The Origins of Greek Thought,* 81.

[44] A similar transformation would occur in Rome. We will see that, on the contrary, the High Middle Ages experienced a regression in this area.

[45] Vernant, *The Origins of Greek Thought,* 83.

[46] Quoted in ibid., 84.

moral attitudes for upholding the order of the city: the mastery of one's passions and emotions. The sages described these attitudes in their maxims: "nothing in excess," "moderation is best," "know thyself." The middle class, *oi mesoi,* embodied and corroborated these "bourgeois" values. It played a moderating role between the extremes, the minority of the rich who wanted to hold onto everything, the mass of people who had nothing and who wanted to take everything from the rich; both were agitators of constant civic strife.

a. Tyrtaeus

The poetry of Tyrtaeus (seventh century BC) drew its inspiration from the poet's Spartan experience in its new civic circumstances. Though a "warrior poet," Tyrtaeus vaunted the new moral ideal of moderation.

According to legend, a Delphic oracle instructed the Spartans to ask their Athenian adversaries to send them a moral adviser. The Athenians sent them Tyrtaeus, a lame, misshapen schoolmaster (in reality he may have been Lacedaemonian). Tyrtaeus composed the elegiacs known as *Eunomia* and *Ypothekia* (exhortations), collections of practical precepts. Most importantly, he wrote *Embateria,* war poems and songs, exhorting warriors to attack the enemy and celebrating Sparta's victory in the Messenian wars, which strengthened the unity of the city.

One fragment vaunts the soldier's virtue of courage, demeaning other values revered by the aristocracy: athleticism, beauty, noble birth, wealth, and eloquence. The moral lesson is this: a warrior should not aspire to individual exploits or the glory of the aristocrats; he should only serve the interests of the *polis.* Another fragment asks the Delphic oracle to endorse a Spartan constitution together with its provisions for a king, a council of elders, and citizens under strict obedience to the law.

3. *The Law*

In fact, there could be no *sophrosyne* without *nomos,* and no *nomos* without *sophrosyne.* The new man—the citizen—was the exact counterpart of the new form of community life—*isonomia*—where *by nature* no one commanded anyone else, where everybody paid strict obedience to the law.

Solon seems to have played an important role among the sages in bringing to light the logic of the law. He saw himself as a man of the center, a mediator, a conciliator. In order for the different parts of the city to reach agreement and achieve harmony, he said, there must be a *common law superior to all sides, a general rule,* a justice (*dike*) to ensure that it is well understood that it is in each and everyone's interest to respect it.

It is highly significant that Solon found an appropriate model for his ideal in the behavior of *merchants* (the reader remembers that Solon was by profession a merchant). Both sides in a transaction uphold the contract because they share a mutual interest that it not be violated. Why would citizens not agree on the law in the same way, simply because it is in their recognized interest?[47]

[47] Plutarch tells the following, slightly more than anecdotal, story about Solon. Anacharsis (a Scythian philosopher, the forerunner of the Cynics, who came to Athens and befriended Solon), seeing Solon in the act of compiling the laws, laughed at him for thinking that he could stop the injustice and rapacity of the citizens with written laws. "They are like spiders' webs; they will hold the weak and delicate who may be caught in their threads, but will be torn in pieces by the rich and powerful." To this Solon answered, "men keep their agreements with each other when neither party profits by the breaking of them; I am adapting the laws to the citizens in such a manner as to make it clear to all that the practice of justice is more advantageous than the transgression of the laws" (Plutarch, *Life of Solon,* 5).

Before long Solon put his idea into practice: "I wrote the same laws for the *kakos* [low born] and the *agathos* [high born], setting down impartial justice for each."[48] It was to preserve the rule of law, common to all and superior to each, that Solon declined the office of tyrant when offered it. Tyranny amounts to placing in the hands of one man what should remain in the hands of all. "What Solon accomplished, he did in the name of the community, by force of law [*kratei nomou*], joining together might with right [*bian kai diken*]. Kratos and Bia, the two ancient attendants of Zeus—who might not leave their places beside his throne for even an instant, since they embodied all that was absolute, irresistible, and irrational in the sovereign's power—had passed into the service of the law. Now they were servants of *nomos,* which reigned in place of the king at the center of the city."[49]

This is far from Hesiod's king: The good king, "whose religious virtue alone could resolve all quarrels and summon forth peace and all of earth's blessings.... [W]ith Solon, *Dike* and *Sophrosyne* came down from heaven to take up residence in the *agora*. That is to say, they would henceforth be accountable. The Greeks would most certainly continue to invoke them, but they would never again refrain from subjecting them to discussion."[50]

Here, at last, we encounter a key notion in the history of Western political thought: the *law* in clear differentiation from *power* (*kratos*),[51] the characteristic of earlier forms of the state. The law brought peace to the community *not by constraint, but because the majority was willing to submit to it*. Men who accepted the rule of law had more advantages, more security, and more prosperity. Obedience to the law was motivated by the use of reason, and not by fear of some magical force emanating from sacred power.

Like the judiciarization of the repression of murder, the endorsement of the law and the virtue of *sophrosyne* on which it depended remained shrouded in religious considerations for a long time.

In their way of life, the cults preached prudence and persuasion in the struggle against passion [*thymos*], a struggle that produced an education [*paideia*], which in turn enabled the rebellious spirit of the wicked to be vanquished. Certain Orphic gods personified abstract ideas like Arete (excellence), Sophrosyne (moderation), Pistis (trust), and Homonoia (peace).

But religion would never be able to dominate the system of ideas and behaviors that came to occupy an eminent place in the city.

4. *Equality*

The very idea of the law—whether natural law or civic law—implies that the elements under its rule are equal before it. And so, the idea of *equality before the law* gradually evolved from Solon to Cleisthenes.

a. Aristocratic Equality, I: Solon

"Equality breeds no war,"[52] Solon says: *isotes* [equality] is the precondition of *philia* [friendship]. Therefore, citizens must be equals, and equality—and its offshoots, reciprocity, role reversals—must be the mark of citizen relations.

Solon's understanding of equality was still hierarchical: geometrical rather than arithmetical, an equality of proportion. Equality does not mean that each citizen must be the equal of every other; rather, each person should receive a share (of power, wealth, honors) equal to his place in

[48] Vernant, *The Origins of Greek Thought,* 85.
[49] Ibid., 85–86.
[50] Ibid., 86–87.
[51] *Kratos:* power, stamina, strength; domination, might; royal power, sovereign might.
[52] Plutarch, *Life of Solon,* 14.2.

the city, that is, equal to his contribution to the common good. "To the *demos,*" Solon says, "I gave as much *kratos* [power] as it needs, without diminishing or adding to its *time* [honor, prestige]." As we saw, he refuses to redistribute the land that would "give the *kakoi* [the low born] and the *esthloi* [the high born] equal shares of the richest lands."[53] Solon also sees to it that there are two intermediary classes providing a smooth gradation between the two classes on the extremes.

The shares of each citizen, though *unequal in absolute terms,* were equal to *the merit of each.* It is an equality of proportion. It was no less a stable and impartial law, neutralizing the arbitrariness of magistrates.

The *demos* was wrong to claim an equality of condition (*isomoiria*), because it was only possible under tyranny, which transformed all citizens into slaves. Equality before the law (*isonomia*) was enough. And, when necessary, force could be used to obtain respect for the law. *Dike* and *bia* (violence) were necessary for social order.

In the end, since violence and personal pride no longer ordered social relations, harmony could prevail in the city. Plutarch says that Solon's constitutional reforms transformed the state by means of *reason* [or *speech*] and the law: "*hypo logou kai nomou metabole.*"[54]

The ideal of equality before the law also found expression in the coinage of *public money* (until then only wealthy private individuals were able to coin money). Henceforth, each city would use only one coinage, that is, a shared standard of value, facilitating transparency and equality in contractual and trade relations (a "public" currency also facilitated monetary adjustments and the redistribution of wealth without the usual violent despoliation). The state created—or improved—the market, which is coherent, since the market presupposes shared rules and regulations: rules about property rights and commercial transactions, as well as agreement on a common standard for the value assessment of goods and services bought and sold in the market. Only an entity above both parties—the state—could provide such a standard and guarantee its value.

b. Aristocratic Equality, II: Pythagoreanism

Pythagoreanism developed a very different stance in respect to equality before the law.

A native of the island of Samos, Pythagoras was thought to have left his homeland ca. 530 BC to escape the tyranny of Polycrates. He traveled to and settled in Croton on the Gulf of Taranto (southern Italy), where he apparently founded a sort of religious community. The 300-odd members shared their possessions and followed an ascetic life (with a special diet). They worked on mathematical problems and played music. Soon the inner circle became the ruling party of the town. It is not known whether they were allied with the local aristocratic families or with the new classes. Pythagoreanism spread to other towns and its devotees founded similar religious communities.

No works by Pythagoras have survived. Nor does he seem to have spoken very much, in keeping with the usual conventions of esotericism and secrecy. The scientific discoveries attributed to him are probably the work of the school he founded. His mathematical discoveries (multiplication tables, decimal system, the theorem of the square of the hypotenuse) were written down by Euclid in the third century BC. One of his disciples, Philolaus of Croton, a contemporary of Socrates, invented a theory of astronomy. Other disciples included Archytas of Taranto, who knew Plato (see below). The little we know about Pythagoras comes to us from Aristoxenus.[55]

[53] Quoted in Vernant, *The Origins of Greek Thought,* 92.

[54] Plutarch, *Life of Solon,* 14.2.

[55] Aristoxenus of Taranto was born about 350 BC. He was a disciple of Aristotle and is known for two works: *Elements of Harmony* and *On Rhythm,* the two oldest treatises on music to come from ancient Greece.

Pythagorean philosophy sees the principle of all things in *numbers* and in *harmony*—the laws of the universe. Pythagorean policy pursues harmony between the rulers and the ruled: "There is no greater evil than anarchy." An intellectual brotherhood, bound together by a shared philosophy and monastic life, can establish good government where each member of the community receives according to his or her merits and is educated to desire no more than his or her share. Archytas, the Pythagorean tyrant of Taranto, writes: "Once discovered, rational computation [*logismos*] puts an end to the condition of *stasis* and introduces *homonoia* [peace]; for there is truly no more *pleonexia* [greed, covetousness, or avarice], and *isotes* [equality] is achieved; and it is equality that permits business to be carried on in matters of contractual exchange. Thanks to all this, the poor receive from the mighty and the rich give to those in need, all groups having the *pistis* [trust] that by these means they will have *isotes* [equality]."[56]

Once again, what we have here is not strict equality between citizens, but an equal status of citizens in the eyes of the mathematical laws of the universe.

c. Democratic Equality: Cleisthenes

With the democratic current, we move from "geometrical" equality—a relationship of the type a/b = c/d—to a "mathematical" equality of the type a = b. Each citizen must enjoy equal participation in *arche,* which is to say in the processes of decision making and appointment to high office (voting, election by lot), and have equal access to magistracies and judicial appointments. This is the true sense of Cleisthenes' reforms.

We touched on these reforms earlier: the creation of ten new tribes instituting an abstract administrative order and replacing old ethnic and social divisions; the creation of the Boule, the *prytaneis,* guaranteeing the alternating participation of all citizens in the high magistracies; the guarantee of *isegoria* (equality in freedom of speech) in the *ecclesia* (assembly); the replacement of a religious calendar with a civic calendar; ostracism for the exclusion of citizens deemed too unequal. At the same time that these reforms reflected the new spirit of equality, different from that prevailing in Solon's age, they also contributed directly to producing such equality. Under Cleisthenes the city completed its transformation to a uniform society without hierarchical divisions, where all citizens took turns holding positions of authority and obedience, sharing a vision of themselves as equals, competent judges of a rational truth and of a law expressing neither the will nor the privilege of a class or a person, but incarnating an objective reality for all.

5. *The Response of the Aristocrats*

In the sixth century, however, certain thinkers refused to accept the new state of affairs; some rejected equality, the rule of law, liberty, others rejected the secularization of the city or the regime of constant innovation and the destabilization of traditional aristocratic society that the new civic values not only roused but actually called for. But a distinction is necessary between these various thinkers.

a. Theognis

Theognis of Megara lived in the second half of the sixth century BC. An aristocratic exile, banished by the democratic party, he expressed in his elegiac poetry pessimism, resentment, and contempt for the people.

---

[56] Cited in Vernant, *The Origins of Greek Thought,* 96. The Pythagorean ideal was not to the liking of all. In 509, fire destroyed the "house of the brotherhood" in Croton, and its followers were murdered. Was this the act of angry masses no longer willing to tolerate a government of eccentrics? Or was it the expression of classic factional infighting? Whatever the reason, additional attacks against the Pythagoreans took place in the following century as well.

There is, he argues, a close relationship between goodness, high-born birth, and fine education. Aristocrats are the best. The people are base and bad, *kakoi.*

Many of his fellow citizens married the daughters of rich parvenus. This mixture of good and base upset the poet more than access to political power by middle-class tradespeople. He recommended that the people and the aristocrats remain apart: "Avoid what is base, cultivate only what is high born." He presents such separation as a recipe for political stability. Only if justice is in the hands of the "good" can *stasis* be avoided. Theognis did more than formulate a spontaneous expression of aristocratic scorn at the misfortunes of his times. He actually showed signs of a reactionary *theory.*[57]

b. Heraclitus

Heraclitus is an altogether different case.[58] He does not express "visceral" contempt for the democrats like Theognis. While he accepts the idea of the law, he rejects the idea of equality that the demagogues of his age were spreading.

i. *Intelligence Is Threatened by Democracy*

Yes, "thought is common to all" (fragment 113). But some are more intelligent than others: "One is ten thousand to me, if he be the best" (fragment 49).

Intelligence is personal. I cannot evade responsibility by arguing that a demon is at work in my actions. "A person's character is his demon" (fragment 119). This is an expression of strong individualism, which, in a sense, is a philosophical argument in favor of aristocracy (or at least an aristocracy of the mind). For there is a serious risk that democracy and ostracism will expunge intelligence and excellence: "The Ephesians would do well to hang themselves, every grown person of them, and leave the city to beardless lads; for they have cast out Hermodorus, the best person among them, saying, "We will have none who is best among us; if there be any such, let him be so elsewhere and among others" (fragment 121).

ii. *Emulation Is a Form of Justice*

Of what use can exceptional individual qualities be in society? Heraclitus suggests that they are the very seeds of life, if they are free to express themselves, if emulation is allowed and required, if pluralism is the rule.

"War [*polemos*] is the father of all and the king of all; and some he has made gods and some humans, some bond and some free" (fragment 53).

"We must know that war is common to all [or universal] and strife is justice, and that all things come into being through strife" (fragment 80).

Thus, "strife" is *dike!* Heraclitus goes even further than Hesiod's approval of good *eris* (vigorous debate). Note that Heraclitus (unlike modern Nietzscheans who quote him) does not attach value to war as *violence,* but as *competition.*

---

[57] A century later, another poet, Pindar (518–438 BC) found inspiration in similar emotions. In his four *Epinician* (triumphal) odes, Pindar celebrates the victors of the games, who are mostly princes and large property owners. Like Theognis, he expresses his faith in heredity and scorn for the emergent equal society: "Unable to speak a compelling word among noble men.... Under every type of law the man who speaks straightforwardly prospers: in a tyranny, and where the raucous masses oversee the state, and where men of skill do. One must not fight against a god, who raises up some men's fortunes at one time, and at another gives great glory to others. But even this does not comfort the minds of the envious.... I hope that I may associate with noble men and please them" (Pindar, *Pythian II,* verses 81–95, trans. Diane Arnson Svarlien, Perseus Digital Library, available at www.perseus.tufts.edu).

[58] Heraclitus (ca. 576–ca. 480 BC) came from Ephesus in Ionia. He is the philosopher of the being as an eternal becoming, where opposites unite and oppose each other alike.

iii. *Strife Must Remain within the Bounds of Legality*

Heraclitus, too, expressed his attachment to the law: "For the Sun will not overstep his measures; if he does, the Erinyes,[59] the handmaids of Justice, will find him out" (fragment 94).

Stable and impartial laws govern both nature and the city. The law is to the *polis* what intelligence is to man: "Those who speak with understanding [intelligence] must hold fast to what is common to all as a city holds fast to its law, and even more strongly. For all human laws are fed by the one divine law. It prevails as much as it will, and suffices for all things with something to spare" (fragment 114).

The law can be made by one person, and government by one person is not necessarily illegal: "Submission to the will of even one person is also *nomos*" (fragment 33). The law, intelligence, and strife are universal principles, divine in origin, "the ultimate [cosmic] principles on which the order of the community rests";[60] they must not be left to democratic arbitrariness.

Here, a new concern emerges. Of course, government by law is preferable to the arbitrary rule of kings and aristocratic *genē*. But cannot the law also be arbitrary? Who should decree it? According to what criteria?

III. The "Great Generation of the Open Society"

These questions were raised pointedly in the last decades of the fifth century BC, at the time of Pericles and the Peloponnesian War. The experience of democracy under Cleisthenes, the violent confrontations with the barbarian world, and the frequent contacts between the Greeks themselves led thinkers of the time to examine the law more radically and to understand its *relative* character, the fact that it could and should be *examined critically* by those in pursuit of justice.

A. The Historical Context

The fifth century opened with the Persian wars, the two wars that the Greek coalition waged against the Persian Empire. These wars highlighted the strength and fecundity of the Athenian democracy instituted by the reforms of Cleisthenes.

1. *The Persian Wars*

Let us begin with the steps that led to the founding of the Persian empire.

Cyrus II of Persia, known as *Cyrus the Great,* unified the empire. Founder of the *Achaemenid* dynasty,[61] he was king from 550 to 530 BC. In 546 BC, he toppled the powerful Lydian king, Croesus, and brought under his control the Greek cities on the coast and the near islands: Chios, Lesbos, Rhodes. In 539 BC, he took Babylon and freed the Jews, allowing them to return to Jerusalem.

Cambyses II (530–522 BC) completed the work of Cyrus with his conquest of Egypt. But he was assassinated (or died an accidental death; the historical record is uncertain). A period of troubles ensued.

Darius I became king in 521. He embarked on a conquest of countries to the north of the Aegean Sea, Thrace and Macedonia. This led him to occupy the Hellespont region, which the Athenians considered to be of vital importance. When the Ionian cities, under the leadership

[59] The Erinyes were infernal Greek divinities. The Romans assimilated them with the Furies.

[60] T. A. Sinclair, *History of Greek Political Thought* (London: Routledge & Kegan Paul, 1952).

[61] His father was Persian, his mother Median.

of Miletus, revolted against the Great King, the Athenians decided to support the rebellion. They captured and torched Sardis, the Lydian capital on the banks of the Pactole, the seat of the Persian satrap (governor of the province). Darius went on the attack, taking Cyprus and Miletus (494), which he destroyed, enslaving the inhabitants. Then he resolved to take revenge on the Athenians.

a. The First Persian War

In the spring of 490 BC, a Persian fleet of 600 warships set sail from Cilicia, vanquished the Cycladic islands, then landed in Euboea. Eritrea was taken and the inhabitants deported to Persia. Miltiades,[62] the Athenian *strategos,* requested assistance from Sparta. But the Spartans failed to arrive in time, and in September 490 BC the Athenians won the Battle of Marathon, assisted only by a small force from Plataea, a small town in Boeotia.

b. The Second Persian War

Darius died in 485 BC and was succeeded by *Xerxes.* In 483/82 BC, *Themistocles* was appointed archon by lot. He was a new man, of foreign origin like Miltiades. It is thought that his father was one of the foreign-born to whom Cleisthenes granted Athenian citizenship.

About this time, the silver *mines at Laureum* in southeast Attica were discovered. They contributed 100 talents to the state coffers. Themistocles proposed to devote the windfall to the construction of a fleet of 100 trireme warships (one talent was given to each of Athens's 100 wealthiest men). This was truly inspired. It was the Athenian fleet that brought victory at the Battle of Salamis.

Faced with the threat from Xerxes, the Greek delegates held a congress in Corinth, where it was agreed to offer the command of the allied forces to Sparta. This was followed by the tragedy of Thermopylae where, owing to the defection of the Thessalians, the Spartans found themselves alone facing a Persian army of several tens of thousands. Under the command of Leonidas, 300 Spartan *hoplites* accepted to defend their positions to the death. A messenger was dispatched to Sparta to announce that they had died in obedience to the laws of the city. Their actions and words became forever famous for the Greeks.

Themistocles took charge of the situation. He ordered the evacuation of Athens and exposed the city to enemy plundering and destruction. He did so, however, in order to organize his counterattack. In September 480 BC Themistocles claimed victory at the decisive naval battle of Salamis.

There remained a Persian army in Thessaly under the command of Mardonius. It was defeated at *Plataea* in 479 BC, putting an end to the war.

2. *Persian Wars and Athenian Democracy*

The Persians wars had significant implications for the domestic and foreign policies of Athens.

In its foreign relations, Athens took the initiative to form the *Delian League* (478 BC), a military alliance designed to safeguard the region against a return of the Persians. It was agreed that cities, unable to engage in the fighting for lack of land or sea forces, should pay a tribute to be deposited in the treasury of the temple of Delos (an Aegean island near the Ionian coast).

---

[62] Son of Cimon Coalemos. He was the nephew of Miltiades the Elder, who had founded an Athenian colony in Thracian Chersonese. He succeeded his uncle, but he was driven out by Darius. He fled to Athens where he was elected *strategos.* Thus, at this time already, it was possible for a man of foreign origin to become *strategos* in Athens.

Military campaigns were led against two cities, which had rebelled against Athenian authority: Naxos, the largest of the Cycladic islands, was garrisoned by a permanent Athenian colony, known as a *klerouchía;*[63] the other was Thasos, the northernmost island in the Aegean Sea. Thus, virtually the entire coast of Asia Minor came under the direct control of Athens's fleet.

In terms of domestic policy, these troubles created the opportunity for more democratic development. Cleisthenes' democratic constitution had not prevented the aristocrats from playing most of the leading roles.[64] War, however, created a new situation. For one, it forced more frequent meetings of the *ecclesia*. The number of sessions for each *prytanis* increased from one to four (since there were ten *prytaneis,* this meant a meeting every nine or ten days). This led to a larger role for the *demos,* especially since Athens's military might now rested on its shoulders. When it came to the war effort, the *hoplites* no longer stood on their own. Because of the growing importance of naval combat, carpenters, shipbuilders, and *thetes* (oarsmen) shared in the responsibility. Themistocles chose Piraeus as the port of Athens. This brought about an expansion of the agglomeration. And the *demos* of Piraeus were not tied to the landed aristocracy like the populace of the countryside.

Since the *demos* elected officials to public office, new men appeared on the scene, men like *Ephialtes*. In 462/61 BC, in the absence of the pro-oligarchic *strategos* Cimon, who was away helping the Spartans suppress a helot revolt, Ephialtes passed a law dividing up the remaining powers of the Areopagus, transferring them to the Boule and the Heliaia, the popular legal court.

Upon his return, Cimon was ostracized by one of Ephialtes' young assistants, a certain *Pericles* (son of Xanthippus, grand-nephew of Cleisthenes). Following the assassination of Ephialtes, Pericles became the leading figure of Athenian democracy.

3. *The Age of Pericles*

a. Pericles

Pericles was an exceptional man, well known to us thanks to Thucydides in particular. His contemporaries called him the "Olympian" for his composure and capacity to handle difficult situations.

Though Alcmaeonid on his mother's side, and therefore belonging to the democratic tradition, Pericles was a nobleman, a man of culture and contemplation. In his youth he followed the lessons of Zeno of Elea[65] and Anaxagoras.[66] He welcomed into his home many foreigners, among them Herodotus and Protagoras. He was also a friend of many famous Athenians: Sophocles, the author of tragedies, Socrates the philosopher, Phidias the sculptor, and Alcibiades the politician (his nephew, in fact). All were members of his intellectual circle led by Aspasia, a Milesian woman of great renown.

---

[63] From *kleros,* plots of land allotted to soldier-citizens. Thus, a *klerouchía* is a colonial land settlement or military colony.

[64] This is because the *strategos* was an elected office. Election is an oligarchic principle, not a democratic one (our modern democracies have completely lost sight of this fact). Between 507 and 462 BC, all leaders with the exception of Themistocles belonged to prominent families; ostracism worked to their advantage in their struggle against their adversaries.

[65] Zeno of Elea, born ca. 490–85 BC, was a disciple of Parmenides. He was a representative of the *Eleatic school,* the other great school of Greek "physicists" alongside the Milesian school in the sixth to fifth centuries BC (the principal representatives of the school were Xenophanes, Parmenides, Zeno, Melissos; Elea was a Greek colony founded ca. 535 BC by the Phocaeans in ancient Lucania south of Naples).

[66] Anaxagoras, a philosopher born in Clazomenae ca. 500 BC and died ca. 428 BC in Lampsacus. He was a representative of the *Ionian school,* whose members included Thales of Miletus, Anaximander, Anaximenes, Heraclitus, and Archelaos of Miletus. They shared a materialist cosmogony, which sought to explain the universe through a first cause, usually one of the four elements.

Pericles took up the struggle again against the oligarchic party represented by Thucydides of Alopeke, the son-in-law of Cimon.[67] According to Plutarch, Thucydides formed the oligarchs into a genuine "party" for the first time, the *kaloi kagatoi,* the minority of "good and beautiful," who opposed the people. Pericles achieved the same result for the other side.

These were probably the first political parties in the modern sense: not just factions mobilizing the loyal followers or clients of an eminent person, but groups united on the basis of an ideology, a political project, deliberately assuming the status of a group of partisans with no claim to representing the whole population. The widening use of elections under the Cleisthenian constitution probably contributed to the emergence of this political phenomenon.

b. The Reforms of Pericles

In order to consolidate the power of the *demos,* Pericles strengthened and improved the rules of political process. He clarified procedures for the presentation of a bill in the *ecclesia* and the rules for scheduling its meetings. He spelled out the responsibilities of the Boule and, in particular, the rules by which it exercised control over magistrates entering and leaving public office (so-called rules of accountability).

Pericles also introduced the *misthos,* that is, pay for public service with money collected from taxes and tributes to the Delian League. He created a *misthos heliastikos* for jurors and judges in the law court (*heliaia*). This laid the foundation for an apparatus of state and the use of public office for electoral purposes. From this time forward, populist regimes made it a practice to increase the number of public servants. In contrast, oligarchs made it one of their propaganda themes to denounce such public expenditure and patronage. One of the first measures of the short-lived oligarchic government in 410 BC was to abolish *misthophory.* But when democracy was subsequently restored, a new payment was created, *misthos ekklesiastikos,* remunerating attendance in the Assembly, for the *demos* were not very assiduous.

According to Aristotle in his *Athenian Constitution,* the Athenian state under Pericles employed some 20,000 men from the public purse: permanent public servants, citizens whose duties warranted a *misthos,* settlers, *klerouchía,* military garrisons of allied cities, oarsmen, sailors, soldiers on board ships policing the Aegean, and a growing number of judges (the number constantly rose after Athens decreed that judicial matters must be sent to the metropolis for judgment). To pay all these salaries it became necessary to turn to the public purse or treasury, which had been transferred from Delos to Athens (treasury money was also used to build the Acropolis).

To a large degree, the democratic regime owed its survival to the social peace it secured, a peace largely paid for with the resources of the empire, which is why it was necessary to maintain the empire at all costs and without scruples.

Punitive expeditions were launched against Chalcis and Samos. Garrisons were created in large numbers. Inspectors (*episcopoi*) were sent on missions. Archons, virtual governors from Athens, were imposed on rebellious cities. Subject cities were required to adopt Athenian weights and measures, and its coinage. Aegina's surrender and the suppression of the Euboean rebellion enabled the elimination of two rival currencies and the triumph of the Athenian Owl, the most famous coin in the ancient Greek world.

c. The Apogee of Athens

It must be said in all fairness that Athens did provide security on the high seas, fostering the *expansion of maritime trade* and *economic development* for all.

[67] Not to be confused with Thucydides the historian.

The growth of *Piraeus* was a symbol of Athens's mercantile preeminence. The architect of the port city, Hippodamos of Miletus, built an emporium, docks, storehouses, and a corn exchange. A colorful population grew in Piraeus: sailors, port workers, merchants, Athenians, and resident aliens (*metics*), a development that worried the representatives of traditional society all the more that foreigners were often rich and powerful like Kefalos, the industrialist, whose workshop in Piraeus employed some 120 slaves.

At this time, Athens reached its cultural zenith. The Athenians, of course, were still a somewhat coarse people, inclined to bring accusations of immorality to the courts against the likes of Protagoras and Anaxagoras. But there were sophisticated classes too, and even the people attended performances of *Aeschylus* and *Sophocles*. As at the time of the Pisistratids, the Athenian festivals were magnificent and numerous, including the rustic religious festivals in honor of Demeter and Dionysus (the rural Dionysia) and, in Athens itself, three festivals for Dionysus: the Lenaia festival, the Anthesteria festival, and the Great Dionysia festival. Pericles built many splendid monuments, including those that adorn the Acropolis today. He also gave commissions to his friend Phidias, the sculptor, for work on the Acropolis.

4. *The Peloponnesian Wars*

The golden years of Athens did not last. Sparta and Athens had jealously observed each other for some time. They engaged in a first war in 460 BC, barely 20 years after their joint victory over the Persians at Plataea. A peace treaty was signed in 445 BC, but tensions between the two cities endured, for two reasons primarily: first, Athenian strength aroused envy; second, their ideological quarrels persisted. In fact, Athens and Sparta embodied the two opposing political models of the age.

A minor incident ignited the conflict again. A quarrel broke out between Corinth and two of its colonies, Corcyra and Potidea. The latter requested assistance from Athens, which accepted. But Corinth was a member of the Peloponnesian League, so Sparta intervened. Pericles could have retreated, but he opted for war instead. The war lasted from 431 to 404 BC, raging with the ferocity of a civil war, which in fact it was.

The Peloponnesian War can be divided into three phases:

- *The first ten-year war (431–421 BC)*. The Spartans invaded and devastated Attica. The inhabitants took refuge in Athens (the Long Walls between Athens and Piraeus enabled supplies to continue to be delivered). Then a plague struck, killing Pericles in 429 BC (the same plague had claimed his sons the previous year). Quarrels between individuals and political parties broke out. Both sides saw victories and defeats. Exhausted, peace was finally concluded. Each gave back to the other the territories it had seized.
- *The Sicilian expedition (415–413 BC)*. Then Alcibiades, a colorful Athenian figure, came onto the scene. A handsome man, the member of a prominent aristocratic family, nephew (or pupil) of Pericles, and a friend of Socrates, Alcibiades persuaded the Athenians to seize Sicily in order to gain control of the Mediterranean, as they had previously done in the Aegean. Once the expedition had departed, Alcibiades was called before the courts about a bizarre incident involving the smashing of the *hermai* in Athens. His enemies had succeeded in making accusations of his participation in the incident. Alcibiades immediately fled to Sparta. Without its leader and his inspiration, the Athenian expeditionary force suffered numerous setbacks. It finally collapsed during the siege of Syracuse and suffered humiliation at Latomia (a stone quarry near Syracuse where the Athenian army became cornered). Athens lost its elite military forces and a fleet of warships.
- *The second ten-year war (413–404 BC)*. Festering at the treatment inflicted on him by the Athenians, Alcibiades went over to the Spartans and convinced them to take up arms against

Athens again. Agis, the king of Sparta, fomented trouble among Athens's former allies in the Aegean. He placed a permanent garrison in Attica. Then Alcibiades defected to the great Persian king's satrap Tissaphernes.

This was followed by a violent coup, called the "first oligarchic revolution," which overthrew the regime in Athens.

The oligarchic party had never really ceased to exist in Athens. A minority movement, it found support in the *hetairai* (factions), particularly among the small landowners. In the armed forces, its representatives included wealthy trierarchs[68] and elected *strategoi*. Events provided the party with ample reason for revolt. Athens was ruined by the war, but the war itself was caused by a need to bolster the empire in order to pay the wages of the many public servants employed by the democratic regime.

With the Athenian fleet stationed in Samos, controlled by the democrats, the oligarchic party seized power in Athens. It called a meeting of the Assembly at Colonus, away from the *pnyx,* the habitual meeting place. It framed and imposed a new constitution. A new Boule of Four Hundred, chosen by cooptation, replaced the Boule of Five Hundred, appointed by lot. *Misthophory* was abolished. The conditions of access to the magistracies were modified. A decision was taken to draw up a list of 5,000 citizens who would enjoy full political rights. Antiphon the Sophist was said to be the theoretician behind the movement.

The new regime resorted to a reign of terror to intimidate the supporters of the *demos*. It lasted only a few months.

The armed forces in Samos revolted and eliminated the officers loyal to the oligarchy. They chose Alcibiades as their chief alongside the democrat leaders. He promised the support of Tissaphernes against the Spartans. As the newly elected *strategos,* Alcibiades returned to Athens in 407. Little by little the democratic regime regained control.

Athens suffered another defeat at the hands of the Spartan fleet at the naval battle of Notium, resulting in the final departure of Alcibiades. Then it won victory at the naval battle of Arginusae; this resulted in a controversial trial ending in the execution of Athens's six victorious *strategoi* on the grounds that they failed to recover the bodies of naval personnel lost in battle. It was, in fact, a political show trial. By inciting the crowd, the intention of the extremist democrats was to remove men known to be loyal to the oligarchy.

Finally, Lysander, the cunning Spartan general, delivered the coup de grace and defeated the Athenian fleet in the naval battle of Aegospotami in the Hellespont (404). Athens capitulated.

The oligarchic party made its return in Sparta's wake. For a time, democracy disappeared and Athens was ruled by a council of 30 citizens, the Thirty Tyrants. It engaged in a severe purge, exiling and executing opponents. Several hundred citizens and *metics* were affected and their personal property confiscated. The Thirty Tyrants became so abject that Sparta abandoned its support and allowed democracy to be restored (403 BC). An amnesty was declared, outlawing prosecution for past actions. On the whole, it was followed, with one terrible exception: the trial and execution of Socrates.

B. Political Ideas

Karl Popper refers to this entire period as the "Great Generation of the Open Society" for its political achievements and ideas.

---

[68] A *trierarchos* was the captain of a trireme, a Greek warship.

> This generation which marks a turning point in the history of mankind, I would like to call it the Great Generation.... There were great conservatives among them, like Sophocles, or Thucydides. There were men among them who represent the period of transition; who were wavering, like Euripides, or skeptical, like Aristophanes. But there also was the great leader of democracy, Pericles, who formulated the principle of equality before the law and of political individualism, and Herodotus who was welcomed and hailed in Pericles' city as the author of a work that glorified these principles. Protagoras, a native of Abdera who became influential in Athens, and his countryman Democritus, must also be counted among the Great Generation. They formulated the doctrine that human institutions of language, custom, and law are not taboos but man-made, not natural but conventional, insisting, at the same time, that we are responsible for them. Then there was the school of Gorgias—Alcidamas, Lycophron, and Antisthenes, who developed the fundamental tenets of antislavery, of a rational protectionism, and of antinationalism, i.e. of the creed of the universal empire of men. And there was, perhaps the greatest of all, Socrates, who taught the lesson that we must have faith in human reason, but at the same time beware of dogmatism; that we must keep away both from misology [anti-intellectualism], the distrust of theory and of reason, and from the magical attitude of those who make an idol of wisdom; who taught, in other words, that the spirit of science is criticism.[69]

We need now to look more closely at the principal representatives of this "Great Generation."

1. *Herodotus*

Herodotus of Halicarnassus (485–425 BC) was the first Greek historian and geographer of renown. His *Histories,* the record of his "inquiries," describes Greece and its neighbors by concentric circles in all cardinal directions. The countries of the "first circle" are ones that he personally visited, where he conducted first-hand inquiries and spoke to eyewitnesses of the events he narrates. Thus, from a rational and scientific viewpoint, his account of these countries is exemplary. For more distant countries, however, he contented himself to note the tales of traditions he heard, accepting them more or less uncritically.

Many passages in his *Histories* provide valuable information about the evolution of political ideas.

a. The Persian Discussion of Monarchy, Oligarchy, and Democracy

In his passages on the Persian Empire, we can read the oldest known discussions about "the best form of government."

The discussion took place ca. 522 BC. After the unexpected death of Cambyses, king of Persia and conqueror of Egypt in 525, a Magus claimed the throne for himself. The impostor styled himself Smerdis, after the son of Cyrus. But the Magian priest and his brother were murdered in a conspiracy fomented by seven important figures. Herodotus reports the discussion between these sages, shortly after the overthrow of the impostor. It concerns the best form of government to establish in Persia. What matters here is not whether the discussion actually took place, but how a Greek like Herodotus presented the issues sometime around 450 BC.

Otanes, one of the conspirators, wants to abolish monarchy, which in his opinion has been discredited by Cambyses:

[69] Popper, *The Open Society and Its Enemies,* 180.

"To me, he [Otanes] said, it seems advisable, that we should no longer have a single man to rule over us—the rule of one is neither good nor pleasant. Ye cannot have forgotten to what lengths Cambyses went in his haughty tyranny,[70] and the haughtiness of the Magi ye have yourselves experienced. How indeed is it possible that monarchy should be a well-adjusted thing, when it allows a man to do as he likes without being answerable? Such licence is enough to stir strange and unwonted thoughts in the heart of the worthiest of men. Give a person this power, and straightaway his manifold good things puff him up with pride, while envy is so natural to human kind that it cannot but arise in him. But pride and envy together include all wickedness—both of them leading on to deeds of savage violence. True it is that kings, possessing as they do all that heart can desire, ought to be void of envy; but the contrary is seen in their conduct towards the citizens. They are jealous of the most virtuous among their subjects, and wish their death; while they take delight in the meanest and basest, being ever ready to listen to the takes of slanderers. A king, besides, is beyond all other men inconsistent with himself. Pay him court in moderation, and he is angry because you do not show him more profound respect—show him profound respect, and he is offended again, because (as he says) you fawn on him. But the worst of all is, that he sets aside the laws of the land, puts men to death without trial, and subjects women to violence. The rule of the many, on the other hand, has, in the first place, the fairest of names, to wit, *isonomy;* and further it is free from all those outrages which a king is wont to commit. There, places are given by lot, the high official is answerable for what he does, and measures rest with the commonalty. I vote, therefore, that we do away with monarchy, and raise the people to power. For the people are all in all."

Such were the sentiments of Otanes. Megabyzus spoke next, and advised the setting up of an oligarchy: "In all that Otanes has said to persuade you to put down monarchy," he observed, "I fully concur; but his recommendation that we should call the people to power seems to me not the best advice. For there is nothing so void of understanding, nothing so full of wantonness, as the unwieldy rabble. It were folly not to be borne, for men, while seeking to escape the wantonness of a tyrant, to give themselves up to the wantonness of a rude unbridled mob. The tyrant, in all his doings, at least knows what is he about, but a mob is altogether devoid of knowledge; for how should there be any knowledge in a rabble, untaught, and with no natural sense of what is right and fit? It rushes wildly into state affairs with all the fury of a stream swollen in the winter, and confuses everything. Let the enemies of the Persians be ruled by democracies; but let us choose out from the citizens a certain number of the worthiest, and put the government into their hands. For thus both we ourselves shall be among the governors, and power being entrusted to the best men, it is likely that the best counsels will prevail in the state."

This was the advice which Megabyzus gave, and after him Darius came forward, and spoke as follows: "All that Megabyzus said against democracy was well said, I think; but about oligarchy he did not speak advisedly; for take these three forms of government—

[70] Before this, Herodotus narrates how Cambyses, afflicted by madness, murdered his subjects at random. He reports how Cambyses tried to kill Croesus, king of Lydia, drawing his bow and taking aim at him. Croesus fled into the next room and Cambyses ordered him captured and executed. The guards, knowing that Cambyses was raving mad and would regret his decision, secreted Croesus away and kept him alive. They reasoned that if Cambyses regretted his decision to have him killed, they could bring Croesus back; on the other hand, if he did not, there was plenty of time to carry out the execution order. After his folly had passed, Cambyses did have regrets and Croesus was brought to him alive. Cambyses expressed his delight, but ordered his guards put to death for disobedience. According to Herodotus, Cambyses committed many such outrages, including the desecration of Egyptian tombs and the statues therein. See Herodotus, *The Histories,* trans. George Rawlinson (New York: Alfred A. Knopf, 1997), 3.36–37.

> democracy, oligarchy, and monarchy—and let them each be at their best, I maintain that monarchy far surpasses the other two. What government can possibly be better than that of the very best man in the whole state? The counsels of such a man are like himself, and so he governs the mass of the people to their hearts' content; while at the same time his measures against evil-doers are kept more secret than in other states. Contrariwise, in oligarchies, where men vie with each other in the service of the commonwealth, fierce enmities are apt to arise between man and man, each wishing to be leader, and to carry his own measures; whence violent quarrels come, which lead to open strife, often ending in bloodshed. Then monarchy is sure to follow; and this too shows how far that rule surpasses all others. Again, in a democracy, it is impossible but that there will be malpractices: these malpractices, however, do not lead to enmities, but to close friendships, which are formed among those engaged in them, who must hold well together to carry on their villainies. And so things go on until a man stands forth as champion of the commonalty, and puts down the evil-doers. Straightway the author of so great a service is admired by all, and from being admired soon comes to be appointed king; so that here too it is plain that monarchy is the best government. Lastly, to sum up all in a word, whence, I ask, was it that we got the freedom which we enjoy?—did democracy give it us, or oligarchy, or a monarch? As a single man recovered our freedom for us, my sentence is that we keep to the rule of one. Even apart from this, we ought not to change the laws of our forefathers when they work fairly; for to do so is not well."
>
> Such were the three opinions brought forward at this meeting; the four other Persians voted in favour of the last.[71]

b. "Command and Obey Alternately"

Thus, the monarchy is restored in favor of Darius. But Otanes requests and obtains exemptions for himself and his family: "I have neither a mind to rule nor to be ruled" (*oute archein oute archestai*). His remarkable formulation is, after the principle of *equality,* the first solemn statement of the principle of *freedom.*

> Brother conspirators, it is plain that the king who is to be chosen will be one of ourselves, whether we make the choice by casting lots for the prize, or by letting the people decide which of us they will have to rule over them, or in any other way. Now, as I have neither a mind to rule nor to be ruled, I shall not enter the lists with you in this matter. I withdraw, however, on one condition—none of you shall claim to exercise rule over me or my seed for ever.
>
> The six agreed to these terms, and Otanes withdrew and stood aloof from the contest. And still to this day the family of Otanes continues to be the only free family in Persia; those who belong to it submit to the rule of the king only so far as they themselves choose; they are bound, however, to observe the laws of the land like the other Persians.[72]

This text can be compared with two others. In Sophocles' *Antigone* (more or less contemporaneous with the *Histories* by Herodotus), Creon identifies as a characteristic of the ordered state—one where anarchy does not rule—the fact that the citizen knows how to "command and obey alternately" (how to exercise authority over others and how to take orders). In Plato, we read: "A perfect citizen," the product of a good education, is one who understands "how both to

---

[71] Herodotus, *Histories,* 3.80–82.

[72] Ibid., 3.83

rule and be ruled righteously," or how to rule and how to obey.[73] These are clearly isonomic statements, but they express the exact opposite of Otanes' "liberal" position. He has a mind *neither* to rule *nor* to obey; he intends only to go about his own business. The regime Otanes desires is one that will give him the freedom to do so (and Herodotus, the friend of Pericles, put these words in the mouth of Otanes, no doubt to express his own preference). In other words, Herodotus understands perfectly the difference between political liberty—the freedom to exercise power—and civil liberty—the freedom to be independent of power. Democracy is surely preferable to tyranny, but it is not enough. Otanes-Herodotus does not seek power to oppress others, having experienced their oppression. He desires only freedom, regardless of who holds the reins of power. What is being sought here is the idea of "freedom under the law."

Other passages confirm that, indeed, this is what Herodotus, like many Greeks of this generation, is seeking. Throughout his work, he says that this penchant for *freedom,* which is inseparable from a penchant for equality before the law, is exactly what characterizes the Greeks—and what distinguishes them from the *barbarians.*

c. The Strength of a Society Where the Law Is the Only Master

Herodotus narrates a conversation between Xerxes and Demaratus, a former king of Sparta, who, banished from his homeland, joins the Persian expedition during the second Persian war. "Demaratus, it is my pleasure at this time to ask thee certain things which I wish to know. Thou art a Greek, and, as I hear from other Greeks with whom I converse, no less than from thine own lips, thou art a native of a city which is not the meanest or the weakest in their land. Tell me, therefore, what thinkest thou? Will the Greeks lift a hand against us?"

First, Demaratus asks Xerxes if he really wants to hear the truth. A useful precaution! The Great King is not accustomed to frank expression—more than one of his subjects has paid with his life for speaking too frankly. The Greeks, in contrast, Herodotus observes, have enjoyed *isegoria* (freedom of speech) for ages.

Since Xerxes insists on a reply, Demaratus resigns himself to stating his opinion: "they [the Lacedaemonians] will never accept thy terms, which would reduce Greece to *slavery.*"

> When Xerxes heard this answer of Demaratus, he laughed and answered. What wild words, Demaratus! A thousand men join battle with such an army as this! [If] you Greeks... are really men of this sort and size, how is the speech that thou uttered more than a mere empty boast? ... How could a thousand men, or ten thousand, or even fifty thousand, particularly if they were all alike free, and not under one lord,—how could such a force, I say, stand against an army like mine? ... If, indeed, like our troops, they had a single master, their fear of him might make them courageous beyond their natural bent; or they might be urged by lashes against an enemy which far outnumbered them. But left to their own free choice, assuredly they will act differently.

To this Demaratus answers, "Though they be freemen, they are not in all respects free; *Law is their tyrannical master;* and this master they fear more than thy subjects fear thee. Whatever he commands they do; and his commandment is always the same; it forbids them to flee in battle, whatever the number of foes"[74]

Xerxes laughs so heartily at this reply that he sends Demaratus away considerately. A few weeks later, the Greeks will celebrate their victories at Salamis and Plataea. Clearly, a city where

[73] Plato, *Laws,* 643e, trans. R. G. Bury, in *Plato in Twelve Volumes,* vol. 12 (1926; repr., Cambridge, MA: Harvard University Press, 2001).

[74] Herodotus, *Histories,* 7.102–04, with modifications to the translation (hereafter "with modifications").

the *law*, and not the *king*, rules is stronger—even militarily—than any other form of political organization.

d. Power Is Laid Down "in the Middle"

Herodotus also records that one day a certain Mæandrius, appointed by Polycrates the tyrant of Samos to succeed him, assembled the people upon receiving news of the tyrant's death and announced his decision to abolish the tyranny:

> Ye know, friends, that the scepter of Polycrates, and all his power, has passed into my hands, and if I choose I may rule over you. But what I condemn in another I will, if I may, avoid myself. I never approved the ambition of Polycrates to lord it over men as good as himself [*despozon andron homoion eauto*], nor looked with favour on any of those who have done the like. Now, therefore, since he has fulfilled his destiny, I lay down my office [*arche*] in the middle [*es meson*], and proclaim equal rights [*isonomia*].[75]

Thus, for Herodotus, the norms of the Greek world are the *public* character of power, *equality*, and the *freedom* of citizens, subject only to a faceless *law*. Tyranny is abnormal, a vestige of a bygone era, barbaric (meaning uncivilized).

e. *Physis* and *Nomos* in the Thought of Herodotus

But is the law itself an absolute? Herodotus's wide-ranging inquiry, conducted in different countries, proved to him that customs and laws (*nomoi*) are predominately relative and changeable; they are devoid of the fixity and intangibility of nature (*physis*). With Herodotus begins the debate on the distinction between *physis* and *nomos*, which reaches its climax in the second half of the fifth century BC with Protagoras and the other Sophists.

Herodotus tells the story of a significant event at the court of Darius:

> That people have this feeling about their laws may be seen by very many proofs: among others, by the following. Darius, after he had got the kingdom, called into his presence certain Greeks who were at hand, and asked—"What he should pay them to eat the bodies of their fathers when they died?" To which they answered, that there was no sum that would tempt them to do such a thing. He then sent for certain Indians, of the race called Callatians, men who eat their fathers, and asked them, while the Greeks stood by, and knew by the help of an interpreter all that was said—"What he should give them to burn the bodies of their fathers at their decease?" The Indians exclaimed aloud, and bade him forbear such language. Such is men's wont herein; and Pindar was right, in my judgment, when he said, "[Custom] is the king o'er all."[76]

Darius drew the following conclusion from the event: "if one were to offer men to choose out of all the customs in the world such as seemed to them the best, they would examine the whole number, and end by preferring their own."[77]

While some in the era of Herodotus celebrated *nomos* as a guarantee of essential freedoms against the arbitrariness of a tyrant, "a new generation sprang up and began to see that *Nomos* may itself be a tyranny—a series of customs and conventions imposed upon men who might not always wish to conform to them."[78] After a "good look around" (Sinclair) in all known countries,

---

[75] Ibid., 3.142.
[76] Ibid., 3.38.
[77] Ibid., 3.38.
[78] Sinclair, *History of Greek Political Thought*, 41.

one may adopt a preference for the customs of others and have doubts about the validity of one's own. A critical mind—perhaps even a revolutionary one—is awakened by this profound realization. The Sophists will further amplify it in due course.

2. *The Sophists: A Formulation of the Distinction between* Physis *and* Nomos

Archelaus the physicist[79] claimed that while he had discovered the objective foundations in nature of hot and cold, birth and decline, and so on, he could find no trace of *good* and *evil*, which clearly escape observation. He deduces that such notions can only come from convention: right and wrong are not "by nature but by custom" (*ti dikaion einai kai to aischron ou physei alla nomo*). Aristophanes, in his play "The Clouds" (ca. 421 BC), says through one of his characters, "Was not the lawgiver, who carried the law, [a man] like you and me?"

The Sophists take up the question and conduct a systematic analysis. Some go so far as to say that there is no moral model outside the various opinions of men, and that, therefore, right and wrong do not have an objective existence as such but derive only from circumstances or from power relations. Others, like Socrates, ask whether there exists an indisputable moral model for right and wrong to be found in "human nature" yet to be defined. But, however that may be, both schools agree that *nomos* must be freed from the yoke of convention and sacredness, that it can be changed by men, either by creating arbitrarily or by adapting it to bring it closer to an ideal norm.

What predisposed the Sophists to explore these ideas was the fact that they were *teachers*. In the new democracies, every citizen can, in principle, aspire to high office; but in practice political success depends on public speaking skills and on expertise, which, until then, was transmitted from generation to generation only in aristocratic families. The role of heredity will diminish only if advancement through *education* becomes possible. In fact, with the flourishing of democracy under Pericles, the *sophistai* poured into Athens from all over Greece, offering to educate young people in the art of political life.

But can these teachers educate youths who are not aristocrats, that is, who are not leaders "by nature"? Can education substitute for nature? Can virtue (i.e., excellence) be taught? Such are the questions that the Sophists and their pupils ask. Thus, they are the first to show concern for ideas about the relationship between nature and culture, *physis* and *nomos*.

a. Protagoras

Protagoras of Abdera[80] was born between 490 and 480 BC and died ca. 420 BC. Some time around 450–445 BC, he arrived in Athens where he became a close friend of Pericles. He traveled to Thurii in greater Greece and was in contact with Herodotus. Later, he returned to Athens where he frequented the company of Socrates and Euripides. He left Athens ca. 430 BC after publication of a decree against him for impiety at the instigation of Diopeithes. We know nothing about the constitution that Protagoras wrote for Thurii: it was probably a democracy on the Periclean model for Athens. In his lifetime Protagoras was famous for his speeches and writings. Among the latter was a *Republic* (*Peri politeias*), no doubt the first before the works of Plato and Aristotle. There was also a work titled "On the Original State of [Human] Things."

[79] Archelaus of Miletus was a fifth century philosopher of the Ionian school and a follower of Anaxagoras. Because of his preoccupation with morality, he is held to be a precursor of Socrates.

[80] A town in Thrace.

Only fragments of Protagoras's writings survive:[81] "About the gods, I am not able to know whether they exist or do not exist, nor what they are like in form; for the factors preventing knowledge are many: the obscurity of the subject, and the shortness of human life" (fragment 4, quoted in Freeman). "Of all things the measure is Man, of the things that are, that they are, and of the things that are not, that they are not" (fragment 1, quoted in Freeman).

According to Plato, Protagoras developed his thinking along the following lines: "Whatever seems right and honorable to a state is really right and honorable to it, so long as it decrees it to be so" (Plato, *Theaetetus,* 167c), which places full power in the hands of the orators. In truth, these opinions do not "possess *by nature* (*ouk esti physei*) an existence of [their] own," but simply what is held to be true by the group (*to koine doxan*) "remains true as long as it is held" (Plato, *Theaetetus,* 172b).

Thus, the state is the source of the law and morals. There are as many morals and laws as there are states. Morals and law are but a semblance, an illusion, for the greatest number. "To koine doxan" (what is held to be true by the group) is not an unchanging truth. Therefore, it can be criticized. Conversely, since what the greatest number believes can be law, even if it is not founded in nature, why not establish legislation and morality in a voluntary, artificial way? Here the seed of "legal positivism" now germinates.

b. Gorgias

Other Sophists held opinions similar to those of Protagoras. Among them, Prodicos of Ceos, Hippias of Elis, Hippodamus of Miletus, and Phaleas of Chalcedon. Gorgias of Leontini is one of the better known.

A student of Empedocles and a contemporary of Socrates, Gorgias (487–380 BC) was renowned and honored in his lifetime; his statue in solid gold was erected in Delphi. He was primarily a rhetor, one of the early inventors of the science of discourse. He gave considerable thought to the properties of language and to the fact that its effectiveness depended on the moment when things are said, on the "proper occasion." In his work *On Not-Being,* he explains that neither the being nor the not-being exists, or in any case there is nothing certain that we can say about them. Now, if being eludes speech, conversely speech eludes being and can permit itself to be autonomous. The science of discourse can free itself from the science of things. This is an assertion of a new morality, not of amoralism: discourse is creative, there are no lost causes, discourse can always produce a new point of view, changing the situation. Thus, Gorgias appears to sense the possibility of human progress, the forward march of humanity by way of culture. We can understand why his point of view was anathema to Plato, but also why it met with the positive approval of many of Socrates' and Aristophanes' contemporaries.

A beautiful illustration of this is found in the *Encomium of Helen,* one of the few works by Gorgias to have survived.[82] The aim of the *Encomium* is to prove the innocence of Helen, a woman whose reputation was tainted among the Greeks because she ran away to Troy with Paris while still the wife of Menelaus, king of Sparta (the cause of the Trojan War). Gorgias takes up her defense and produces a fictitious plea in her favor. She gave in to Paris, he argues, either because the Fates, the gods, or necessity decided it should be so; or she was taken by force, or persuaded by speech, or was a victim of desire. In all cases, except the last, she was compelled by an outside force, and it is this force that must be incriminated.

---

[81] See Milton C. Nahm, *Selections from Early Greek Philosophy* (New York: F. C. Crofts, 1947), and Kathleen Freeman, *Ancilla to Pre-Socratic Philosophers* (Cambridge, MA: Harvard University Press, 1948). Fragments from Freeman are indicated as such in the text.

[82] Dumont, *Les écoles présocratiques,* 710–14.

> [But] if it was speech which persuaded her and deceived her heart, not even to this is it difficult to make an answer and to banish blame as follows. Speech is a powerful lord, which by means of the finest and most invisible body effects the divinest works: it can stop fear and banish grief and create joy and nurture pity.... All who have [persuaded] and do persuade people of things do so by molding a false argument. For if all men on all subjects had both memory of things past and awareness of things present and foreknowledge of the future, speech would not have such power, but as things are now it is not easy for them to recall the past nor to consider the present nor to predict the future, and consequently it is easy for speech to convince of anything. So that on most subjects most men take opinion as counselor to their soul, but since opinion is slippery and insecure it casts those employing it into slippery and insecure successes. What cause then prevents the conclusion that Helen similarly, against her will, might have come under the influence of speech, just as if ravished by the force of the mighty? ... The effect of speech upon the condition of the soul is comparable to the power of drugs over the nature of bodies. For just as different drugs dispel different secretions from the body, and some bring an end to disease and others to life, so also in the case of speeches, some distress, others delight, some cause fear, others make the hearers bold, and some drug and bewitch the soul with a kind of evil persuasion. It has been explained that if she was persuaded by speech she did not do wrong but was unfortunate.[83]

So Helen is not guilty. But what about the last hypothesis claiming that Helen may have succumbed to desire? Again, she cannot be blamed, because the strength of an impression sometimes stops freedom of thought. A sense of duty is erased by particularly acute feelings and representations. "Some who have seen dreadful things have lost their presence of mind in the present time; thus fear extinguishes and drives out understanding."[84] This is true of other emotions as well, not just desire. And because human beings are not all-knowing, they are not all-powerful over their emotions either. In both instances, a human's responsibility is only relative.

These arguments resemble the reasoning of modern-day sociologists or criminologists who, through references to psychological and social determinisms put the criminal responsibility of the accused in perspective. We can understand why some see a humanist inspiration in the writings of Gorgias. From now on, because of the relativity of values, social thought can situate individual responsibility with greater accuracy and better judgment. Sophists develop a keen ability to overcome social prejudice and uncritical religious beliefs; they are no longer trapped in absurd and obscure tragic debates. We need only compare Gorgias's defense of Helen with the argument of Antigone in Sophocles' play of the same title.

3. *Socrates*

In the opinion of Karl Popper, Socrates (470–399 BC) was "the greatest of all" in the generation that lived and invented the "open society" in the second half of the fifth century BC. Although he left no writings of his own, we are familiar with his thought through his followers, primarily Plato and Xenophon. His intellectual contribution was twofold: his philosophy of knowledge is deliberately based on a *critical approach,* and he was a pioneer in making *morality a central focus of science.*

---

[83] English translation, Rosamond Kent Sprague, ed., *The Older Sophists: A Complete Translation by Several Hands of the Fragments in "Die Fragmente Der Vorsokratiker," Edited by Diels-Kranz with a New Edition of Antiphon and of Euthydemus* (Columbia: University of South Carolina Press, 1972), 50–54; with modifications.

[84] Ibid., 50–54.

With regard to philosophy of knowledge, Socrates complements and amends Protagoras's teachings. He does not claim that man is ignorant or that there is no truth; instead he argues that the discovery of truth depends on a critical mind and that the search for knowledge should never cease. He is, by no means, a skeptic. He is simply the first to realize that knowledge is open ended, constantly evolving, and that it is the recognition of this fact that allows for a fruitful scientific method.

As an illustration, here is a famous passage from Plato's *Apology*. Socrates is speaking:

> For if you kill me you will not easily find another like me, who, if I may use such a ludicrous figure of speech, am a sort of gadfly, given to the state by the god; and the state is like a great and noble steed who is tardy in his motions owing to his very size, and requires to be stirred into life. I am that gadfly which god has given the state and all day long and in all places am always fastening upon you, arousing and persuading and reproaching you. And as you will not easily find another like me, I would advise you to spare me. I dare say that . . . if you were to strike me dead, as Anytus [Socrates' accuser] advises, which you easily might, then you would sleep on for the remainder of your lives, unless god in his care of you gives you another gadfly.[85]

If knowledge is open ended, then the future itself is open ended. Socrates, like Gorgias, seems to have imagined the possibility of progress, of linear time rather than cyclical time. In this sense, there is a prophetic dimension to Socrates; he himself appears to have been perfectly aware of this. Humans are not prisoners of a "fixed" nature; there are intellectuals who, at the risk of passing for "monsters," introduce novelty in society by forcing nature: "Have you not known . . . that from the moment of my birth nature ha[s] condemned me to death?" (Xenophon, *Apology of Socrates,* sec. 27) (the argument has been made that this brings Socrates close to Jewish propheticism; see below, pp. 409–12).

Socrates does not personally apply this critical, scientific method to the natural sciences. He even shows a certain mistrust toward the sciences, which he accuses of being purely speculative. The study of science is worthwhile in youth, he argues, because it trains the mind, but later it is enough to retain only what is useful for practical life.[86]

The real topic worthy of inquiry is *morality*. Socrates was a pioneer in making morality a topic of critical debate and science; this involved wresting it from religion and unthinking convention. Morality is fundamentally useful, which is why moral behaviors can be assessed, criticized and, in the end, corrected.

Xenophon (*Memorabilia* 2.1.21–34) tells the story recorded by Socrates (according to Prodicos) of the meeting of Heracles with Virtue and Pleasure (a similar story is recounted by Dio Chrysostom, see below, pp. 358–64). Heracles, who has reached adulthood, is approached by both women to be his director of conscience. Pleasure promises ease without pain, riches at the expense of injustice. Virtue announces trials, demands restraint, but promises countless rewards during this life: honor, reputation, the loyalty of friends, security in the different phases of social and economic life, and finally immortal memory on earth after life ends. Socrates approves of this morality, which can be called positive and useful, and, broadly speaking, nearly "utilitarian."

---

[85] Plato, *Apology,* 30e–31a, trans. Harold North Fowler, in *Plato in Twelve Volumes,* vol. 1 (Cambridge, MA: Harvard University Press, 1914), 61–145; hereafter cited in the text.

[86] Xenophon, *Memorabilia,* 4.7.3–8, trans. E. C. Marchant (Cambridge, MA: Harvard University Press, 1923), 4:2–359; hereafter cited in the text by book, chapter, and section.

In reply to Hippias, who claims that the law is made and changed by men and that no one should take it seriously,[87] Socrates says that he is interested in unwritten moral laws, because they are universal and permanent. For this reason, those who do not heed such laws, even if they escape the punishment of human-made laws, will be punished in time because they behave against the nature of things established by the gods (Xenophon, *Memorabilia* 4.4.12–25). This is virtually a preliminary theory of natural law: true, the *nomos* is not intangible, but neither can it be amended at will. It must come near a transcendent norm, a natural law. Here Socrates distinguishes himself from other Sophists who criticize values either in the direction of nihilism (the Cynics) or in the direction of artificialism (any value can be created, if it can be enforced).

On this specific question of the respective contributions of nature and human artifice—the "innate" and the "acquired"—Socrates' stance appears well balanced. He sees clearly that, among individuals and within cities, *physis* and *nomos* are inextricably combined.

> When asked again whether Courage could be taught or came by nature, he replied: "I think that just as one man's body is naturally stronger than another's for labour, so one man's soul is naturally braver than another's in danger. For I notice that men brought up under the same laws and customs differ widely in daring. Nevertheless, I think that every man's nature acquires more courage by learning and practice. Of course Scythians and Thracians would not dare to take bronze shield and spear and fight the Lacedæmonians; and of course the Lacedæmonians would not be willing to face Thracians with leather shields and javelins, nor Scythians with bows for weapons. And similarly in all other points, I find that human beings naturally differ one from another and greatly improve by application. Hence it is clear that all men, whatever their natural gifts, the talented and the dullards alike, must learn and practise what they want to excel in. (*Memorabilia* 3.9.1–3)

And this other consideration:

> Excellent beings he [Socrates] recognised by their quickness to learn whatever subject they studied, ability to remember what they learned, and desire for every kind of knowledge on which depend good management of a household and estate and tactful dealing with men and the affairs of men. For education would make such beings not only happy in themselves, and successful in the management of their households, but capable of conferring happiness on their fellow-men and on states alike. His method of approach varied. To those who thought themselves possessed of natural endowments and despised learning, he explained that the greater the natural gifts, the greater is the need of education; pointing out that thoroughbreds by their spirit and mettle develop into serviceable and splendid creatures, if they are broken in as colts, but if unbroken, prove intractable and sorry jades; and high-bred puppies, keen workers and good tacklers of game make first-rate hounds and useful dogs, if well trained, but, if untrained, turn out stupid, crazy, disobedient brutes. It is the same with human beings. The most highly gifted, the youths of ardent soul, capable of doing whatever they attempt, if educated and taught their duty grow into excellent and useful men; for manifold and great are their good deeds. But untrained and untaught, these same become utterly evil and mischievous; for without knowledge to discern their duty, they often put their hand to vile deeds, and through the very grandeur and vehemence of their nature, they are uncontrollable and intractable: therefore manifold and great are their evil deeds. (*Memorabilia* 4.1.2–4)

[87] See Plato, *Protagoras*, 337c, trans. W. R. M. Lamb, in *Plato in Twelve Volumes*, vol. 2 (Cambridge, MA: Harvard University Press, 1924).

In short, a person never leaves the hands of nature as a fully completed being. The "final touch" is brought by culture, which in turn depends, in part (but only in part), on human artifice.

This stance distances Socrates from certain Sophists and from the idea of egalitarian democracy according to which anyone can achieve and become something as along as one receives an education. His stance earned him the enmity of the democratic party. But, at the same time, it created ample space for education and separated Socrates from an ignorant and arrogant oligarchy. Like other Sophists, Socrates believed in the renewal of the political class through education. He also went so far as to think that the sage would serve his country better if he educated good politicians at school, rather than participating in politics himself. "On yet another occasion Antiphon asked him [Socrates]: 'How can you suppose that you make politicians of others, when you yourself avoid politics even if you understand them?' 'How now, Antiphon?' he [Socrates] retorted, 'should I play a more important part in politics by engaging in them alone or by taking pains to turn out as many competent politicians as possible?'" (*Memorabilia* 1.6.15). This idea, which guided Plato his entire life, must be attributed to his teacher, Socrates.

All of this helps us to understand the politics of Socrates and his principal students. Socrates could not accept democratic egalitarianism: there are both good and not so good natures. Above all, he believed that only an elite could grasp and enforce the principle of "a government under the law." The masses were incapable of doing so, and the rich could not care less (*Memorabilia* 4.6.12). This novel political stance ultimately cost Socrates his life.

While chairing a meeting of the *ecclesia*,[88] Socrates brought down the wrath of the democratic party when, "in spite of popular rancour and the threats of many powerful persons" (*Memorabilia* 1.1.17–18), he refused to put to an illegal vote the sentencing to death of the supposed pro-oligarchic officers, who had won the Battle of Arginus. "When chairman in the Assemblies he would not permit the people to record an illegal vote, but, upholding the laws, resisted a popular impulse that might even have overborne any but himself" (*Memorabilia* 4.4.2).[89] In addition, he was critical of one of the founding principles of democracy, the *drawing of random lots,* when he proclaimed that it was folly to appoint public officials by lot; after all, no one would choose a pilot or builder or flautist by lot. The choice must be made based on the skills requisite "for work in which mistakes are far less disastrous than mistakes in statecraft" (*Memorabilia* 1.2.9).

The people did not like Socrates (but they were in no position to appreciate the quality of his arguments), and they suspected that he did not have unconditional sympathy for the *demos*. In fact, Socrates often expressed unkind opinions against ignorance, and the people erroneously interpreted his words as targeting the ignorant masses (*Memorabilia* 1.2.58–60). They were also aware that Socrates had had two students who were notorious opponents of the regime, Alcibiades and Critias (1.2.12).

Unfortunately for him, Socrates was on equally bad terms with the oligarchs, especially with the same Critias and his colleague Charides. When he found that Critias loved Euthydemus and sought to lead him astray, he said, "Critias seems to have the feelings of a pig: he can no more keep away from Euthydemus than pigs can help rubbing themselves against stones." Critias, one of the appointed members of the Thirty Tyrants, took revenge by obtaining a ban on Socrates' teaching (*Memorabilia* 1.2.29ff). Socrates worsened his case by refusing to make the accusations demanded by the tyrants.

---

[88] The year he was a member of the Boule, the month that the Boule members of his tribe were *prytaneis,* and the day that it was his turn to be *epistate* (chairman).

[89] See Xenophon, *Hellenica,* vol. 2 (books 5–7), trans. Carleton L. Brownson (Cambridge, MA: Harvard University Press, 1921), 1.7, 9–11.

4. *Democritus*

Democritus of Abdera, a compatriot of Protagoras, was the father of atomism and materialism in antiquity. He inspired both Epicures and Lucretius. While moral philosophy and political philosophy were not his principal fields of speculation, he did express views on the topics, all of which tend to corroborate regimes of *isonomia*.

Very little is known about the life of Democritus. He was born sometime between 500 and 457 BC and died between 404 and 359 BC, and some sources give him a life span of a century. In any case, he lived contemporaneously with Socrates and Protagoras. He produced a large body of writings, all now lost. Whereas Parmenides understands being as indivisible unity, for Democritus everything is composed of atoms and the empty space (or void) between them. Only atoms exist in reality; everything else—feelings, ideas, properties—exists only by convention or in our imagination. Atoms interact together; their trajectories overlap; they collide and bounce off one another. This activity of the atoms is what produces the forms of the universe. In turn, the universe can be represented in terms of figures, positions, movements, and oppositions, rather than in qualitative terms. Thus, atomism creates a new model of thought, more advanced than the theories of earlier Ionian *phusikoi*.

His rationalism encouraged him to approve regular civic institutions, which is evident in the few fragments where he discusses these issues. Discord and war have to be avoided at all costs (fragment 249). "A well administered city is the best safeguard; all else depends on it; its salvation is the salvation of all, its ruin the ruin of all" (fragment 252). The duty of the magistrate is to administer justice, and to do so he must be suitably protected (fragment 266). Democritus, like Socrates, appears to distrust the excesses of "direct democracy." Desires are to be held in check and *sophrosyne* to be exhorted: "You should consider the lives of the poor, reflecting on their intense sufferings, in order that your own possessions and condition may seem great and enviable, and you may, by ceasing to desire more, cease to suffer in your soul" (fragment 191). His concern for the poor is hitherto unparalled in Greek thought. "When the powerful prevail upon themselves to lend to the indigent, and help them, and benefit them, in this at last is pity, friendship, and mutual aid, harmony among the citizens, an end to isolation, and other blessings such as no man could enumerate" (fragment 255). Anticipating the cosmopolitanism of Alexander and the Stoics, Democritus writes: "The wise man belongs to all countries, for the home of a great soul (*agathè psyché*) is the whole world" (fragment 247).[90]

5. *Pericles: The "Open Society" of Athens versus the "Closed Society" of Sparta*

Most of the thought of the "Great Generation" can be found in Pericles. The great Athenian's ideas on democracy go far beyond a constitutional formula that secures the political ascendancy of the *demos*. They run deeper and hold the promise of a new kind of society where personal liberty is guaranteed, where reason is fostered through critical debate, and where foreigners are fully accepted, provided they comply with the law. We are familiar with his ideas on democracy from his famous funeral oration, delivered in honor of the first Athenian soldiers who died on the battlefield early in the Peloponnesian War, ca. 430 BC.[91]

Pericles opens by claiming, "if our more remote ancestors deserve praise, much more do our own fathers," which means that, for Pericles, the reforms of Cleisthenes embody *progress*. Then

---

[90] Nahm, *Selections from Early Greek Philosophy*.

[91] Thucydides, *History of the Peloponnesian War*, vol. 1, translated by C. F. Smith (Cambridge, MA: Harvard University Press, 1920), 2.35–47; hereafter cited in the text.

he praises the Athenian regime he has represented for over 30 years. He describes it as a balanced regime where election by lot gives everyone a chance, and where talent is recognized:

> Our political system does not compete with institutions which are elsewhere in force. We do not copy our neighbors, but try to be an example. Our administration favors the many instead of the few: this is why it is called a democracy. The laws afford equal justice to all alike in their private disputes, but we do not ignore the claims of excellence. When a citizen distinguishes himself, then he will be called to serve the state, in preference to others, not as a matter of privilege, but as a reward of merit;[92] and poverty is no bar.[93] ... We all participate in the government of the city through our vote.[94]

Athenian democracy was a regime of personal liberty and tolerance: "We govern ourselves in a spirit of liberty and the freedom we enjoy extends also to ordinary life; we are not suspicious of one another, and do not nag our neighbor if he chooses to go his way.... But this freedom does not make us lawless.... Further, we provide plenty of means for the mind to refresh itself from business.... [We] place the real disgrace of poverty not in owning to the fact but in declining the struggle against it." The city welcomed foreigners: "Our city is thrown open to the world; we never expel a foreigner" (2.39).

So, for the first time in history, if only in embryonic form, the formal recognition of citizenship extended beyond ethnic boundaries; a social system admitted to being rooted in something other than a community of origin, a real or mythical blood bond.

Moreover, personal liberty was conducive to the development of reason and genuine culture, the cultivation of the mind. "We [Athenians] do not look upon discussion as a stumbling-block in the way of political action, but as an indispensable preliminary to acting wisely.... We love beauty without indulging in fancies, and although we try to improve our intellect, this does not weaken our will."

This is the regime that Athenian soldiers were called on to defend against Sparta, an archaic regime described by Karl Popper in the following terms:

> (1) Protection of its arrested tribalism: shut out all foreign influences which might endanger the rigidity of tribal taboos. (2) Anti-humanitarianism: shut out, more especially, all equalitarian, democratic, and individualistic ideologies. (3) Self-sufficiency: be independent of trade. (4) Anti-universalism or particularism: uphold the differentiation between your tribe and all others; do not mix with inferiors. (5) Mastery: dominate and enslave your neighbors. (6) But do not become too large: "The city should grow only as long as it can do so without impairing its unity," and especially, without risking the introduction of universalistic tendencies.—If we compare these six principal tendencies with those of modern totalitarianism, then we see that they agree fundamentally, with the sole exception of the last.[95]

The Athens of Pericles was undoubtedly the culmination of the "Greek miracle." Many of the ideas and values of the modern liberal democratic state were already there in developed form.

---

[92] Allusion to the election of the *strategos* and the broadening of their political role, which is how Athenian democracy reintroduced a distinct oligarchic element in its constitution.

[93] Allusion to the misthophories.

[94] Thucydides, The Peloponnesian War, 2.35.

[95] Karl Popper, *The Open Society*, 177–78.

Chapter 2

Plato

Plato (429–348 BC) was born into an aristocratic Athenian family. He was perhaps a pupil of Cratylus, a philosopher of the school of Heraclitus. Subsequently he met his true mentor, Socrates, and remained his student for a dozen years. The death sentence handed down to Socrates in 399 BC outraged Plato.[1]

After this tragedy his first inclination was to travel. He left for Egypt some time around 390 BC, then traveled to southern Italy (greater Greece), probably intending to meet the Pythagorean scholar and politician Archytas of Tarentum (at the time, the city of Tarentum was ruled by the Pythagorean sect in the name of philosophy and science). From Italy Plato traveled to Sicily where Dionysius the Elder of Syracuse welcomed him. Some 15 years earlier, Dionysius had abolished democracy and now ruled Syracuse as a tyranny. The relationship between the two men quickly soured, either because Plato offered poor or unasked for advice, or because he developed a friendship with Dion, the brother of one of Dionysius's two wives (Dion was not on the best of terms with his brother-in-law). Dionysius embarked Plato on a vessel that, by coincidence or on orders from Dionysius, put into port on the island of Aegina, at war with Athens at the time. Sold into bondage, Plato was recognized and rescued in the nick of time by a rich Cyrenean. He returned to Athens in about 387 BC deeply humbled by his adventures.

Next Plato founded the Academy, inspired by ideas that we will discuss below. The name "Academy" comes from the legendary Athenian hero, Akademos; it referred to a sacred grove of trees outside the walls of Athens where Plato acquired a former gymnasium and park to set up his school. The Academy was a university of sorts, historically the first of its kind; it survived for centuries, until the complete Christianization of the Roman Empire. We know that students lived in residence. There were several teachers under the authority of a *scholarch* (Plato was succeeded by his nephew Speusippus, Xenocrates, Heraclides Ponticus, and others).

[1] Material in this section is from Léon Robin, *Platon* (1935; repr., Paris: Presses Universitaires de France, 1968), chap. 1.

The Academy met with resounding success as soon as it opened. Students flocked to it from all over Greece. It offered a structured curriculum and enjoyed a reputation as a breeding ground for future politicians and statesmen able to become what Protagoras was for Thurii, Parmenides for Elea, Heraclitus for Ephesus, and Pythagoras for Tarentum.

Several of the Academy's former students went on to establish new political regimes; among them Hermia in Atarnea on the northern Ionian coast (it is here that Aristotle opened his first school prior to the Lyceum), Coricos in Assos (north of Lesbos, where Aristotle also sojourned), and Erastus in Skepsis in the Troad.

Alongside his teaching, Plato wrote and published a large body of writings.[2] He appears to have completed his famous *Republic* ca. 375 BC.

Then, some time around 367 BC Dionysius the Elder died, leaving his son Dionysius the Younger (also called Dionysius II) to succeed him. His intellectual guide was none other than Plato's longtime friend, Dion.[3] Dion immediately invited Plato to come to Syracuse. Was this the unhoped-for opportunity to apply the ideas discussed in the *Republic*? Was perhaps the young and impressionable Dionysius II the ideal candidate for Plato's philosopher-king? Without a moment's hesitation, Plato left his school in Athens and set sail for Sicily.

At the outset, the relations between student and mentor were excellent; the pupil apparently delighted in the lessons of the master. However, things soured when Dionysius suspected Dion of coveting power for himself, fearing that Dion would overthrow him; before long he transferred his suspicions to Plato as well. Dion was sent into exile, while Plato was forced to remain in Syracuse. Finally Dionysius allowed Plato to leave, but extracted from him a promise to return at his bidding. Shortly after Plato's arrival in Athens, Dion (who had little hope of returning from exile unless Plato assumed an effective role at the court of Dionysius II) succeeded in persuading him to undertake a third journey to Sicily in 361 BC (at the age of nearly 70). But, again, relations between Plato and Dionysius II became embittered; Plato was virtually sequestered at court. He was only freed after a year, thanks to the energetic mediation of Archytas of Tarentum.

Realizing that nothing was to be gained from Dionysius, Plato and Dion developed a military plan to seize power in Syracuse. The young students of the Academy were to constitute the general staff and "cabinet" of the future tyrant. In 357 BC Dion set sail for Syracuse and succeeded in taking the city. However, he failed to neutralize the opposition of the partisans of Dionysius. After three years of indecisive rule, Dion was assassinated, putting an end to Plato's hopes of any workable application of his political ideas.

---

[2] Modern scholarship classifies Plato's dialogues in three chronological groups (within each group, however, the order is largely conjecture):

(1) *Early dialogues or Socratic dialogues: Ion, Hippias minor* (On lying), *Protagoras* (written perhaps during the lifetime of Socrates); next, the works intended to commemorate the life of Socrates after his death: *Apology* (of Socrates), *Crito, Euthyphro* (On religion); followed by the dialogues that illustrate Socrates' critical method: *Laches* (On courage), *Charmides* (On *Sophrosyne*), *Lysis* (On friendship), book 1 of the *Republic* (On justice), perhaps called *Thrasymachus* before inclusion in the larger work; and finally *Gorgias*.

(2) *Mature works: Menexenus* (a manifesto by the leader of the philosophical school who expresses an antirhetorical position), *Meno* (On virtue), *Euthydemus* (On the eristic method of argument), *Cratylus* (On language), *Phaedo* (On the immortality of the soul), *The Banquet* or *The Symposium* (On love), the *Republic* (On the ideal state and justice), *Phaedrus* (on love and on philosophical training in opposition to the training method of the Sophists), *Theaetetus* (On knowledge), *Parmenides* (On being).

(3) *Late works: Sophist* (On error and, again, On being), the *Statesman* (On the art of government), *Timaeus* (On cosmology), *Crito* (containing the myth of Atlantis), *Philebus* (On pleasure), *Epinomis* and the *Laws* (On the ideal state and its laws). There are also 13 *Letters*, several of which are considered authentic.

[3] According to Plutarch, *Life of Dion*, in *Lives*, vol. 6, trans. Bernadette Perrin (Cambridge, MA: Harvard University Press, 1918), owing to his tremendous wealth, Dion may have been an important financial backer of the Academy.

Throughout the last ten years of his life, Plato continued to teach and write. His death, in 348 or 347 BC, interrupted the completion of his final work, the *Laws,* again devoted to politics and the construction of a state, if not an ideal one, at least a better one. Plato's philosophy is frequently presented as a system where political thought occupies an important, though not central place alongside metaphysics, moral philosophy, philosophy of science (knowledge), and natural philosophy. However, in the autobiographical *Seventh Letter,* which today is widely accepted as authentic, Plato describes political interests as the primary concern of his life and his work. Philosophy was simply the journey that had to be undertaken before his return to politics, armed with the necessary intellectual skills.

To say that Plato was interested in the organization of the state would be an understatement. Combined, the *Republic,* the *Statesman,* and the *Laws* represent almost half of his entire output. In the *Laws* Plato examines the legal, administrative, and economic aspects of the state in exquisite detail; it is his longest and final work, undoubtedly his "testament."

Plato was by birth quite naturally destined to a career in politics (he was born into a grand aristocratic family whose members occupied the highest magistracies by vocation). However, the period in which he lived raised practical and moral obstacles to a political career.

The first 30 years of Plato's life were roughly the years of the Peloponnesian War. When he was more or less 20, he witnessed the political crisis accompanying the setbacks of the war: the replacement of the democratic regime, in 411 BC, by the oligarchy of the Four Hundred, followed by the oligarchy of the Five Thousand, the return of democracy, the Spartan occupation, and the Thirty Tyrants (404 BC). One of Plato's first cousins, Critias, and an uncle, Charmides, figured among the Tyrants.

It would have been easy for Plato to enter politics alongside his relatives at this time, but the barbarism of the regime, and especially the efforts of the Tyrants to coerce Socrates into denouncing its opponents, dissuaded him. "So when I beheld all these actions and others of a similar grave kind, I was indignant, and I withdrew myself from the evil practices then going on."[4] But democracy was restored before very long and Plato comments: "once again I was really, though less urgently, impelled with a desire to take part in public and political affairs" (*Seventh Letter* 325a), the more that the new regime presented a moderate face and honored the amnesty decreed at the departure of the Thirty. But before Plato could decide to enter politics, the new regime found Socrates guilty and sentenced him to death. After that Plato felt no more able to serve the new regime than to support the oligarchy.

At any rate, the fact that he had been the student of Socrates for some 12 years had made him critical and demanding. From oligarchy excesses are expected, from democracy only blindness. Socrates had awakened in him "the obligation of a total clarity of the Idea";[5] compared with this, the chaos of events and the corruption of political behaviors were for Plato immensely disappointing.

> When, therefore, I considered all this, and the type of men who were administering the affairs of State, with their laws too and their customs, the more I considered them and the more I advanced in years myself, the more difficult appeared to me the task of managing affairs of State rightly. For it was impossible to take action without friends and trusty companions; and these it was not easy to find ready to hand, since our State was no longer

[4] *Translator's note*: Quotes from Plato's *Seventh Letter* are from *Plato in Twelve Volumes,* vol. 7, translated by R. G. Bury (Cambridge, MA: Harvard University Press, 1966), 325a; hereafter cited in the text.

[5] See Auguste Diès, introduction to his edition (in French) of the *Republique* (Paris: Les Belles Lettres, 1932), vi (his text inspires this passage). *Translator's note:* Quotes from Plato's *Republic* are from *Plato in Twelve Volumes,* vols. 5 and 6, translated by Paul Shorey (Cambridge, MA: Harvard University Press, 1969).

> administered according to the principles and institutions of our forefathers; while to acquire other new friends with any facility was a thing impossible. Moreover, both the written laws and the customs were being corrupted, and that with surprising rapidity. Consequently, although at first I was filled with an ardent desire to engage in public affairs, when I considered all this and saw how things were shifting about anyhow in all directions, I finally became dizzy; and although I continued to consider by what means some betterment could be brought about not only in these matters but also in the government as a whole, yet as regards political action I kept constantly waiting for an opportune moment; until, finally, looking at all the States which now exist, I perceived that one and all they are badly governed; for the state of their laws is such as to be almost incurable without some marvelous overhauling and good-luck to boot. So in my praise of the right philosophy I was compelled to declare that by it one is enabled to discern all forms of justice both political and individual. Wherefore the classes of mankind (I said) will have no cessation from evils until either the class of those who are right and true philosophers attains political supremacy, or else the class of those who hold power in the States becomes, by some dispensation of Heaven, really philosophic. (*Seventh Letter* 325c–326b)

This, in a nutshell, is the program of the *Republic*. Knowledge determines action. It is only possible to establish order in the state if its true principles are understood. The truth commands the good in politics as in morality. Democrats are roused by opinion; oligarchs by the routine of conventions; neither the one nor the other have access to the truth. The practical failure of both the democrats and the oligarchs in rapid succession can be attributed to this fact.

Like other Athenian politicians, Plato founded his *hetairie*, his political faction or group of partisans. But his was not a group of conspirators; it was a *school*, a breeding ground for young people bent on entering politics, yet equally determined to postpone service until science was more advanced and the appropriate opportunity presented itself.

While awaiting their hour, these brilliant young minds engaged in intellectual debate and gradually succumbed to the beauty of their pursuit, delighting in knowledge *for its own sake*. For this reason Plato's philosophical work, the fruit of these years of waiting, sometimes leaves the impression that it is purely speculative and sufficient to itself. This impression, however, is misleading, because Plato—as the *Seventh Letter* tells us—constantly looks for the right moment to enter the fray and put his ideas into practice in the complicated events in Sicily. When after the third trip he understands that it will never happen, he returns to the topic of politics to which he dedicates his final work. Arguably, politics inspired Plato's entire philosophical enterprise, giving it its sense and direction.

In the following discussion of the *Republic*, the *Statesman*, and the *Laws*, we will see that Plato's political thought is essentially *a long argument against the very principle of democracy*.

I. The Republic

Plato's *Republic* is tightly constructed. Its ten books consist of five parts of varying lengths: a prelude (book 1), where the problem of justice is posed, if only cursorily; a conclusion (book 10), where the status of the poet in the city and the immortality of the soul are discussed through the myth of Er the Pamphylian. This leaves three main parts: (1) an inquiry into the essence of justice (books 2–4), which concludes that justice is the harmony of social categories in the state and the harmony of virtues in the individual soul; (2) a lengthy digression (books 5–7) on the philosophical training to provide to the elite of the state to ensure that they will be up to the task of government; (3) finally, a definition of the four types of injustice for the state and for the individual: timocracy, oligarchy, democracy, and tyranny (books 8–9).

A. Prelude: The Opinions of Common Men, Poets, and Sophists on Justice

Socrates went down to Piraeus for the festival of Bendis with Glaucon, son of Ariston. Setting out on the homeward journey to Athens, they run into Polemarchus and Adeimantus, Glaucon's brother. Polemarchus invites them to remain in Piraeus and spend the evening at his home. There they meet Lysias and Euthydemus, brothers of Polemarchus, together with Thrasymachus, Charmantides, and Cleitophon.

Cephalus, the elderly father of Polemarchus, strikes up a conversation with Socrates on the topic of old age and death. Old age, he says, is a time to think seriously about the afterlife and the rewards and punishments for good and bad living. He is pleased to have got his wealth honestly, freeing him from obligations to others, able to avoid lies and deceit. Thus, a good definition of justice might be "to speak the truth and pay your debts." Having said that, Cephalus leaves to attend the sacrifices, and the discussion continues around a proper definition of justice.

The initial discussion ends rather abruptly. Polemarchus recalls the words of the poet Simonides, who said that justice is the repayment to each what he is owed. But should we return a weapon to a madman, who lent it to us when he was sound of mind? Certainly not. The sense of Simonides is that one should do good for one's friends. But these claims, taken literally, snare Polemarchus innocently in a web of contradictions. He is unable to rival with Socrates' dialectical art. This angers another speaker, Thrasymachus, "who came at us," in the words of Socrates, "like a wild beast, seeking to devour us." Thrasymachus offers an entirely different definition of justice: "Justice is nothing else than *the interest of the stronger*.... And each form of government enacts the laws with a view to its own advantage, a democracy democratic laws and tyranny autocratic and the others likewise, and by so legislating they proclaim that the just for their subjects is that which is for their—the rulers'—advantage and the man who deviates from this law they chastise as a law-breaker and a wrongdoer" (*Republic* 338c–e).

Socrates argues that, like the physician who considers the interests of the patient rather than his own, the ruler defends the interests of the ruled. Thrasymachus grants him as much, but adds that the ruler does so like the shepherd who cares for the sheep in order to shear them. Life teaches that the naïve man is always wronged and the unjust man always has the advantage. The just man, who respects the terms of a contract scrupulously, loses. The same can be said about the honest man in public office: he makes no gain; if anything, he incurs the ill will of his friends by refusing to favor them. His private domestic affairs deteriorate from neglect, and he refuses to exploit his public position for personal gain. On balance, justice is truly negative.

In reply to Thrasymachus, Socrates argues that even thieves, who are by definition unjust with others, must be just together, otherwise their community would divide and they would be unable to act. Therefore, justice is useful. But the discussion ends with Socrates aware that he has strayed onto shaky ground. Before asking whether justice is useful and whether it increases happiness or unhappiness, it is better to ask: *what is* justice; that is, what is the *nature* of justice?

B. The Nature of Justice

1. *A Rhetorical Argument for Injustice*

Next, Glaucon sets out the theory stating that justice comes from *an agreement reached between men to escape the savagery of the state of nature.* Justice is a compromise between the greatest good—committing an injustice without punishment—and the greatest evil—suffering an injustice without any defense.

The story of the *Ring of Gyges* (verses 359d and following) provides an example of how committing an injustice without punishment can be a good. Gyges, a shepherd in the service of the king of Lydia, found a ring that made him invisible when he turned its collet toward the inside of the hand, and visible when he turned it back to the outside. He came to the palace with the ring, slept with the king's wife, killed the king, and seized the throne. Anyone with such power would behave like Gyges, which proves that "no one is just of his own will but only from constraint."

The problem can also be expressed as follows. Imagine an unjust man, who *seems* just, and a just man, who *seems* unjust. It is obvious that, "such being his disposition, the just man will have to endure the lash, the rack, chains, the branding-iron in his eyes, and finally, after every extremity of suffering, he will be crucified, and so will learn his lesson that not to be but to seem just is what we ought to desire." On the other hand, the unjust man, who seems just, will thrive, and the conclusion will be drawn that he is loved of the gods, and this will increase his wealth even more.

Before Socrates can give a reply to Glaucon, the latter's brother, Adeimantus, restates the argument by Thrasymachus. He puts himself in the skin of a quick-witted young man who, hearing all the arguments about justice and injustice, determines a course of action. Such a young man, he says, might reason as follows: "since it is the 'seeming,' as the wise men show me, that 'masters the reality' and is lord of happiness, to this I must devote myself without reserve. For a front and a show I must draw about myself a shadow-line of virtue."

He will have no trouble hiding from men and gods. He will organize societies and political clubs to hide from men, using "the arts of the popular assembly and the courtroom." And to protect himself from the gods, he will make "'sacrifice and soothing vows' and dedications," using the profits of his injustices (it goes without saying that if the gods do not exist—an open question—guarding against them is even easier). "In consequence, then, of all that has been said, what possibility is there, Socrates, that any man who has the power of any resources of mind, money, body, or family should consent to honor justice?" (*Republic* 365c–366b).

But if Glaucon and Adeimantus thus play the devil's advocate,[6] it is to hear Socrates' reply. In fact, they know (as everyone does) that Socrates believes *justice*—and not its "seeming"—is a good, and it is so independent of the advantages and disadvantages that it brings. By the time this dialogue takes place, Socrates "has already passed [his] entire life in the consideration of this very matter" (367e). What the others desire from Socrates is that he "prove in argument" the intuition they themselves hold against all arguments to the contrary, namely, that *justice is a good in itself, and desirable in and of itself.*

Their insistent and friendly petitions convince Socrates to rise to the task and answer the question fully. Now the dialogue can begin in earnest.

2. *Justice as Harmony between the Different Parts of the City*

It is a huge challenge. Socrates suggests a *methodological diversion* to get started. Just as it is easier, he says, to read large letters rather than small ones from a distance, it is easier to discuss justice in the state before going on to examine it in the individual person.

So, Socrates suggests starting with a simpler form of state (*polis*) as a suitable object of study, before turning—at the insistence of his interlocutors—to a more advanced one (369b and following).

---

[6] This same device of the rhetorical argument in favor of injustice is used again in Cicero's *Republic,* a deliberate imitation of Plato's *Republic.* Cf. below, pp. 291–92.

In passing, Plato presents a theory of *the founding of the state*. The state results from an association of men who accept the advantages of uniting together in order to satisfy their primary needs for food, lodging, and clothing, whereby they divide the work among themselves. Each will exercise his art—worker, builder, weaver, and shoemaker—for the common good of the community. For "our several natures are not all alike but different"; each man works better at one task, uninterrupted by other tasks. This is why it is important to intensify the division of labor: specialists will not make their own tools, other specialists will. So, there is a need for blacksmiths, but also cowherds, shepherds, and merchants for importing and exporting goods, sailors for transporting them, and salespeople in the settlement itself (people, Plato claims, incapable of any other kind of work), not to forget unskilled workers who sell their labor to anyone looking for someone who can do the strenuous tasks. In the case of an advanced state, one that covets the lands of its neighbors and the wealth of which attracts envy from people beyond its borders, an *army* specialized in warfare will be required. Finally, there will be a need for rulers specialized in the task of maintaining order and harmony among the various social and professional categories of the state.

In total, the well-ordered state will have three broad categories of citizens: "guardians" (rulers), "auxiliaries" (warriors), and "producers" (everyone else).

This model sets the scene to establish where justice fits in. Justice, together with prudence, courage, and temperance (or restraint), is one of the four "cardinal" virtues.[7] If the state described here is well ordered, it will possess all four virtues (*Republic* 427c). So, by identifying the seats of prudence, courage, and temperance, the place of justice will appear between the lines.

- Is our state really *prudent* (i.e., *wise*)? Yes, surely, if it is governed by guardians who possess the *sophia* or *phronesis* of government (428a–429a). If the guardians who rule the state are wise and prudent, then the state itself will be wise.
- Our state is also *courageous,* provided it is defended by auxiliaries who themselves are men of courage (429c) and able to impose on the other classes "the conservation of the conviction which the law has created by education about fearful things—what and what sort of things are to be feared" (430b; cf. 433c). Here again, the courage of the state derives from the courage of its auxiliaries.
- Finally, our state is temperate (i.e., moderate and restrained), because temperance is a kind of empire over the passions and pleasures. In a well-founded state, "the desires in the multitude and the rabble [are dominated] by the desires and the wisdom that dwell in the minority of the better" (431c). If there is agreement on this point between the rulers and the ruled, then the state will be temperate: temperance is "the concord of the naturally superior and inferior as to which ought to rule both in the state and the individual" (432a).
- All that remains is to situate *justice:*

> "Now then, Glaucon, is the time for us like huntsmen to surround the covert and keep close watch that justice may not slip through and get away from us and vanish from our sight. It plainly must be somewhere hereabouts. Keep your eyes open then and do your best to descry it. You may see it before I do and point it out to me." "Would that I could," he said; "but I think rather that if you find in me one who can follow you and discern what you point out to him you will be making a very fair use of me." "Pray for success then," said I, "and follow along with me." (432b–c)

[7] This four-part division of virtues, destined to a great future in moral philosophy, is attested since Socrates at least. Plato assumes it as common knowledge.

Of course, the prey is not hiding, it has been visible to all for a long time without their knowing; justice, Socrates says, is *the duty of each individual to do a single task, one for which he or she is by nature and aptitude best suited.* Only if each part of the state follows this rule will it be just and—possessing the four cardinal virtues—be perfect.

It is bad enough when a carpenter meddles in the work of a shoemaker (or vice versa) in a state where the division of labor is as described. But the confusion of responsibilities becomes acute if the three classes themselves are questioned. If, for example, a producer intrudes in the affairs of the state or enters the warrior class under the pretext that he is wealthy; or if a warrior, not being wise, takes it to mind to rule as a warrior. Then justice, indeed, will be jeopardized.

3. *Justice in the Individual*

Moving now from the "large letters" of the state to the "small letters" of the individual soul, it can be said that

> justice [in the individual] is indeed something of this kind, yet not in regard to the doing of one's own business externally, but with regard to that which is within and in the true sense concerns one's self, and the things of one's self—it means that a man must not suffer the [three] principles in his soul [craving, anger, reason] to do each the work of some other and interfere and meddle with one another.... [An individual] should dispose well of what in the true sense of the word is properly his own, and having first attained to self-mastery and beautiful order within himself, and having harmonized these three principles, the notes or intervals of three terms quite literally the lowest, the highest, and the mean, and all others there may be between them, and having linked and bound all three together and made of himself a unit, one man instead of many, self-controlled and in unison. (*Republic* 443d–444a)

In conclusion, both in the macrocosm of the state and in the microcosm of the soul, a certain organic division of labor must be maintained. Just as reason must govern courage, and reason and courage must rule desires, the individual turns vicious if the hierarchy is upset; and so it is in the state, each class must keep to its place (leader, intermediary, subordinate) and be satisfied with its lot. Evil is a liberal society, especially Athenian democracy, where elections and appointment by lot enable men of all social categories to enter the magistracies and where "capitalism" permits continuous social mobility, enabling, for example, non-Eupatrids, enriched by their mercantile activities in Piraeus, to exert the same social and political influence previously held by aristocratic families alone. Collectively, such a society is the equivalent of madness in the individual soul, the decomposition or cancer of a living organism.

So, the principle of justice is now established, and it is possible to look into various forms of injustice. But before Socrates can begin, his interlocutors plead with him to explain a curious idea he touched on when he was discussing the "guardians" of a well-founded state. Socrates said that goods, women, and children should be held in common as much as possible. Why?

C. The Communism of the Guardians

Because, Socrates replies, the task of the guardians is to uphold concord in the community. In order to fulfill their task, they must be as united as the parts of a body: "Is not, then, the community of pleasure and pain the tie that binds, when, so far as may be, all the citizens rejoice and grieve alike at the same births [successes] and deaths [misfortunes]?" (462b).

1. *Community of Goods*

In order to uphold concord, members must possess everything in common. So, "none must possess any private property save the indispensable. Secondly, none must have any habitation or treasure-house which is not open for all to enter at will."

This arrangement eliminates the usual quarrels over *mine* and *yours,* over money and other properties. There will be no loans, debts, or lawsuits among the guardians, and harmony will reign in the community.

Moreover, these "sheep dogs," with a duty to protect the flock, must not be tempted to harm the sheep in their care; in other words, they must not become wolves and use their power in the pursuit of personal interest, rather than in the general interest. They must, therefore, be sheltered from need and maintained by the state. They will remain extremely frugal.

> Their food, in such quantities as are needful for athletes of war sober and brave, they must receive as an agreed stipend from the other citizens as the wages of their guardianship, so measured that there shall be neither superfluity at the end of the year nor any lack. And resorting to a common mess[8] like soldiers on campaign they will live together. Gold and silver, we will tell them, they have of the divine quality[9] from the gods always in their souls, and they have no need of the metal of men nor does holiness suffer them to mingle and contaminate that heavenly possession with the acquisition of mortal gold, since many impious deeds have been done about the coin of the multitude, while that which dwells within them is unsullied. But for these only of all the dwellers in the city it is not lawful to handle gold and silver and to touch them nor yet to come under the same roof with them, nor to hang them as ornaments on their limbs nor to drink from silver and gold. So living they would save themselves and save their city. But whenever they shall acquire for themselves land of their own and houses and coin, they will be house-holders and farmers instead of guardians, and will be transformed from the helpers of their fellow citizens to their enemies and masters, and so in hating and being hated, plotting and being plotted against they will pass their days fearing far more and rather the townsmen within than the foemen without—and then even then laying the course of near shipwreck for themselves and the state. (*Republic* 416d–417b)

2. *Community of Women and Children*

For these same reasons, the guardians must also possess women and children in common: "these women shall all be common to all the men, and... none shall cohabit with any privately;... the children shall be common, and... no parent shall know its own offspring nor any child its parent" (457d).

Sexual unions will not be random; they will be closely guarded and decided by magistrates. This will permit eugenics and the constant improvement of the guardian race (here Plato is thinking about the eugenic practices of Sparta, but he "improves on" the Spartans by showing these practices to be dependent on a rigorous mathematical method).

---

[8] An allusion to the Spartan *syssitia* (common meals).

[9] Cf. below, p. 84.

Officials will only authorize unions of the best, concealing the reasons for their choices so as to avoid dissension among the guardians themselves; care will also be taken to keep the same number of guardians.

As for children, they will be raised in common by the state, except for the deformed, who will be eliminated (*Republic* 460c) (two Spartan practices).

Thanks to these measures, every member of the guardian class will "feel that he is meeting a brother, a sister, a father, a mother, a son, a daughter, or the offspring or forebears of these" (463c). Consequently, every guardian will belong to the guardian class like the members of a physical body: when the finger receives a blow, the entire body feels the pain; when one part heals the whole body rejoices. This is the true formula for unity.

Unafraid of scorn or ridicule, Plato goes against the thinking of his time in this depiction of community life and praises *the equality of the sexes.* Men and women should have the same tasks and receive the same education. Like their male counterparts, women will train in music, gymnastics, the art of war, and philosophy. Socrates refutes the argument that men and women are different by nature and should, therefore, have different social duties. The argument, he says, has no more weight than the objection that a bald man and a man with a full head of hair should not pursue the same profession. The only difference between a man and a woman is that the one fathers and the other gives birth. This does not affect their other abilities (454e). As a result, he affirms, "there is no pursuit connected with the administration of a state that is peculiar to woman" (455b). There are women who are well suited for medicine, music, and philosophy, why not for gymnastic, the art of war, or the administration of the state? Still Socrates admits that women are generally less talented than men in these various practices (456b): there are limits to his "feminism"!

D. A Theory of Government by the Elite

Pursuing his thinking on the guardians' particular way of life in a well-founded state, and the qualities they must have, Socrates develops a new idea: the guardians must constitute a moral and intellectual elite. This gives him the opportunity to present a *theory of government by the elite,* one of the most powerful refutations of democracy ever written.

For a just, happy, and harmonious state, Plato says, "either philosophers [must] become *kings* in our states or those whom we now call our kings and rulers (*basileis* and *dinastai*) [must] take to the pursuit of philosophy seriously and adequately, and *there* [must be] *a conjunction of these two things, political power and philosophic intelligence*" (473d).

1. *Philosophers, Contemplators of the Truth*

By "philosophy" Plato means science, that is, theoretical knowledge of the truth. Who are "the philosophers, who we dare to say ought to be our rulers" (474b)? The answer is those who are "able to *contemplate the truth*" (475e). Plato is referring to total knowledge, a sense and taste for exhaustiveness and synthesis: just as lovers love everything in the beloved, philosophers love the whole essence; they never intentionally overlook any of its parts (485b). Philosophers are inclined to apply justice throughout the state, not just in certain parts. Finally, philosophical knowledge (science) is a liberation from passions; philosopher-kings are preoccupied with "the spirit of truthfulness"; they are imbued with a "reluctance to admit falsehood in any form" (458c). They possess "the hatred of [falsehood] and the love of truth"; for the sole love of knowledge, they renounce the pleasures of the senses. It is because they see the ideal model "of the beautiful, the just and the good" that they will be able to make or keep good laws (484d) and, therefore, to hold the offices of the state.

2. *Demagogues, the Flatterers of that "Big Beast" the Multitude*

Plato prefers a government in the hands of philosophers because he believes that the current misfortunes of states stem from the fact that they are governed by *Sophists,* men with the opposite frame of mind. Such men are devoted servants of a degraded form of knowledge: *opinion*—the knowledge of appearances—also spontaneously the knowledge of the multitude, which is why Sophists dominate so easily in modern democratic states.

At this point Plato introduces a criticism of democracy as demagogy, an argument used by other thinkers in the fourth century BC. In the early days of the city, when freedom of speech in the agora and critical debate was open to all, democracy was literally the fountainhead of scientific rationality. But, left to the logic of the masses and the mob, it became a system in which rationality is *impossible.*

Plato uses an eloquent metaphor to describe the activity of the Sophists:

> Each of these private teachers who work for pay, whom the politicians call sophists and regard as their rivals, inculcates nothing else than these opinions of the multitude which they opine when they are assembled and calls this knowledge wisdom.
>
> It is as if a man were acquiring the knowledge of the humors and desires of a *great strong beast* which he had in his keeping, how it is to be approached and touched, and when and by what things it is made most savage or gentle, yes, and the several sounds it is wont to utter on the occasion of each, and again what sounds uttered by another make it tame or vicious, and after mastering this knowledge by living with the creature and by lapse of time should call it wisdom, and should construct thereof a system and art and turn to the teaching of it, knowing nothing in reality about which of these opinions and desires is honorable or base, good or evil, just or unjust, but should apply all these terms to the judgments of the great beast, calling the things that pleased it good, and the things that vexed it bad, having no other account to render of them, but should call what is necessary just and honorable, never having observed how great is the real difference between the necessary and the good, and being incapable of explaining it to another. Do you not think, by heaven, that such a one would be a strange educator?" "I do," he said. "Do you suppose that there is any difference between such a one and the man who thinks that it is wisdom to have learned to know the moods and the pleasures of the motley multitude in their assembly, whether about painting or music[10] or, for that matter, politics? For if a man associates with these and offers and exhibits to them his poetry or any other product of his craft or any political service, and grants the mob authority over himself more than is unavoidable, the proverbial necessity... will compel him to give the public what it likes, but that what it likes is really good and honorable, have you ever heard an attempted proof of this that is not simply ridiculous?" (*Republic* 493a–d)

In other words, the multitude cannot be philosophers, nor can it appreciate or elect them. Individuals who win the approval of the multitude do so, not because they speak the truth or act according to it, but because they pander to its sentiments and fantasies, which they grasp using a

[10] In Athens, the people's assemblies attributed the official prizes for poetry, tragedy, comedy, and so on. The internal contradictions of democratic logic did not put a strain solely on politics. Plato is particularly angered at the presumption of the crowd—stirred up and manipulated by the demagogues—because they think they can judge the beautiful. He returns to this topic time and again in the *Republic* and the *Laws.*

practical science. Though it is a doubtful science, it suffices to give them an advantage over those who speak the language of truth.

3. *The "Raison d'Être" of a Nondemocratic Form of Government*

An elemental political consequence of this situation is: if a government hopes to act for the good, then it must act *away from the public eye.* A just government is necessarily a nonpublic government (in the *Laws* we will see that it is a secret government, the Nocturnal Council). Moreover, it must be able to *lie* to the people in the interest of the state (*Republic* 389b).

Here Plato poses a direct challenge—no more, no less—to the underlying principle of the Greek city, a social order where power is essentially *public,* where questions of general interest are debated in the agora, where decisions cannot be taken unless they are first examined critically, a principle that supposes that all citizens are able to reason. In a sense, Plato's position amounts to a regression to a situation before the city. But does it mean a return to the magico-religious society? By no account: Plato intends to keep the gains of reason. But because he rejects the principles of public action and critical pluralism, which as we saw are structurally inalienable from the acquisition of rational thought, he raises here a serious point that we will return to at the end of this chapter.

At any rate, Plato's stance gives him the strongest argument ever raised against democracy: *the need for the state, for the sake of the common good, to be ruled not by the people, but by an intellectual elite.*

He reasons as follows: It is intrinsically impossible for the multitude to grasp the Truth. Demagogues stir up their passions and nourish their illusions; in this way they win the people's approval. In a democracy, the only person who comes to power is one who resorts to demagogy. Consequently, democratically taken decisions are necessarily flawed and detrimental to all, including for the multitude itself.

And yet, a true science exists, one that can inspire good decisions in the common interest. But those who possess such science can never *justify their ideas in the eyes of the multitude,* whatever efforts they may make in that direction. If good decisions are the aim, then a political system is required that enables an intellectual elite to impose its decisions *without consultation or approval by the rest of the community.* If the real aim is the good of the people, it is necessary to give up being understood by—or even communicating with—the people.

Since the misunderstanding between the elite and the people is unbridgeable, a separation between the two needs to be written into the constitution. What is needed is a form of government that protects the elite from the people, insulating it from the opinions, desires, and pressures of the people. This would include, for example, irremovable unelected magistrates, recruited by cooptation (or appointed by a perfectly wise king).

E. The Education of the Guardians

This brings us to a new question, one that is, in Plato's view, perhaps the most important for political science. How does the state find the wise rulers it needs to function, given that the choice cannot be left to chance or to the judgment of the multitude? The answer is that the state must pull out all the stops to identify individuals with the proper character and aptitudes, and then take responsibility for their *education* with appropriately adapted *educational principles.* Plato sets out his ideas on education in two lengthy passages of the *Republic* (2.374e–3.412b, 6.502d–7.540c).

Part of this education will be shared by the guardians in general, that is, both warriors and rulers; this will include music and gymnastic. Then the rulers, in the narrow sense of the term, will undergo further selection and receive a special training program in philosophy.

1. *Selection and Training of the Guardians in General*

a. Music

The "music" Plato refers to is more than the art of sound: it includes "three things, the words, the tune, and the rhythm" (*Republic* 398d). Here education will endeavor to strengthen the child's faculties of reasoning and protect him or her from everything in culture that falls in the category of imagination, symbols, and wanton or uncertain thinking. "Stories" will be banished, including those of Homer and, more generally, mythology. "Poets" will be chased from the city (Plato attaches great importance to this; he returns to it later in book 10).

On the other hand, the child will be exposed to rhythms and harmonies that foster a sense of measure and orderliness. The child will not be exposed to novelty or fashion, nor to complicated music with too many instruments, scales, or harmonies. Only classical, timeless songs and dances will be taught to the young, so that they will be able to fulfill their duties in public ceremonies appropriately.

b. Gymnastic

The same severity must be applied in the teaching of gymnastic. The term "gymnastic" means physical training as well as health, diet, and bodily habits. Again the goal is simplicity and orderliness. Excessive variety is to be excluded.

As far as diet is concerned, refined foods are forbidden; likewise, in matters of personal health, sophisticated medicines will not be allowed:

> excessive care for the body that goes beyond simple gymnastics is the greatest of all obstacles.... Asclepius knew this—... when bodies were diseased inwardly and throughout, he did not attempt by diet and by gradual evacuations and infusions to prolong a wretched existence for the man and have him beget in all likelihood similar wretched offspring. But if a man was incapable of living in the established round and order of life, he did not think it worth while to treat him, since such a fellow is of no use either to himself or to the state. (407cd)

Healing a complex illness is like trying to put an end in the courts to quarrels arising from complex social issues. It is vain to look for a solution after the quarrel has erupted; it is better to act in advance and prevent the problem from occurring in the first place.

Ideally, the best gymnastic will be "a simple and flexible gymnastic, and especially so in the training for war" (404b).

c. Nurturing the Soul of the Child with a Sense of the Good

The common thread of advice for the teaching of music and gymnastic is that a young person's soul should be instilled with a sense of the good long before he reaches the age of reason, at which time he will be able to judge rationally for himself what is good and what is bad (see 402a). This nurturing of the good in early education will develop an instinct for the good that will stand him in good stead throughout his entire life. The following passage argues the point remarkably:

> "It is not allowable for a soul to have been bred from youth up among evil souls and to have grown familiar with them, and itself to have run the gauntlet of every kind of wrong-doing and injustice so as quickly to infer from itself the misdeeds of others as it might diseases in the body, but it must have been inexperienced in evil natures and uncontaminated by them while young, if it is to be truly fair and good and judge soundly of justice. For which cause the better sort seem to be simple-minded in youth and are easily deceived by the wicked, since they do not have within themselves patterns answering to the affections of

> the bad." "That is indeed their experience," he said. "Therefore it is," said I, "that the good judge must not be a youth but an old man, a late learner of the nature of injustice, one who has not become aware of it as a property in his own soul, but one who has through the long years trained himself to understand it as an alien thing in alien souls, and to discern how great an evil it is by the instrument of mere knowledge and not by experience of his own." (409a–c)

It hardly needs saying that Plato—holding up the Spartan example as his rational ideal—believes that the education and training of the young is the responsibility of the state. The state alone possesses reason and is capable of teaching it. Childhood should be taken out of the hands of civil society and its negative influence.

2. *The Selection and Training of the Rulers: Special Training in Philosophy*

The foregoing concerns the guardians in general, but among them a tiny elite, called to govern, must be selected.

a. Souls of Gold, Silver, and Iron

First, there are certain special souls, destined to form the elite; they are superior to all others in morality and intellect. Plato calls them the "souls of gold."

Since Plato knows that the envious multitude do not accept the idea of superior individuals, he introduces his axiom that the state can lie for the right cause. The first rulers must persuade the citizens of the revitalized city that everyone comes from the same earth, that they are all brothers, but that the god who made them put *gold* in some, *silver* in others, and *iron* and *bronze* in yet others, establishing a difference in nature among men, such that the first are destined to rule, the second to be auxiliaries, and the third to be workers and craftsmen. Admittedly, these classes do not reproduce themselves identically from one generation to the next. A being of gold or silver can give birth to a being of iron and bronze, and vice versa. Which is why the role of selection and education is opposed to pure oligarchic heredity (this shows Plato to be the pupil of Socrates and the Sophists).

Officials monitor the talents of the young attentively in order to do justice to their nature (*Republic* 415c). They search for "souls of gold" like nuggets in the riverbed; they observe the young in their physical, intellectual, and moral exercises (412d–e). The members of the elite are recognizable by their life-long predisposition to put the interests of the state systematically above their own private interests. They are tested "much more carefully than men do gold in the fire, to see if the man remains immune to such witchcraft and preserves his composure throughout, a good guardian of himself and the culture which he has received, maintaining the true rhythm and harmony of his being in all those conditions" (413e).

The selection does not happen all at once. There are successive tests, each more demanding than the next. After the *ephebeia,* the state training institution for youths between the ages of 18 and 20, individuals are chosen who can benefit from the study of the sciences.[11] At age 30, it becomes clear which are best suited to dialectics, that is to say, those "who can view things in their

[11] The young guardians will be trained in arithmetic, geometry, stereometrics ("geometry in space"), astronomy, and harmony, successively. These various sciences share in common the fact that they require the mind to reach beyond physical perceptions to tackle purely theoretical problems, problems with no practical application and that cannot be resolved through the senses, but that require the intellect and the application of reasoning, especially unselfish reasoning. These various sciences are superior modes of knowledge compared with perceptual knowledge. They are ranked from the least to the most difficult, but they only lay the foundation for the one true science: dialectics.

connection" (537c) and "which of them is able to disregard the eyes and other senses and go on to being itself in company with truth." The study of dialectics lasts 5 years. Then, for the next 15 years, the chosen few return to a normal social existence in order to complete their training and their experience of life and of their fellow citizens, those they are called upon to rule. Then, and only then, at age 50, will they be hailed "leaders" and "guardians" (in the strongest sense) of the city. The others will be called "auxiliaries," the "implementers of decisions of their principals."

b. The Idea of the Good

Thus, the philosophical training of the guardians will involve the study of "the idea of the good," "by reference to which just things and all the rest become useful and beneficial" (*Republic* 505a).

It suffices for the ordinary citizen to pursue in practice what is just and honorable without speculating on what these virtues are. However, the guardians will need to go beyond appearances and grasp the essence of the good (cf. 506a). But on this, Socrates feels "blind," although he has spent his entire life contemplating the topic. He has already provided definitions of justice, temperance, and other virtues, but when it comes to defining the good, he is at a loss; at best, he is prepared to examine "the offspring of the good" and its nearest "likeness" (506e). By this he means the sun, "the offspring of the good which the good begot in its own likeness and which is in the visible world to vision and the objects of vision what in the intelligible region the good is to reason and the objects of reason" (508c, with modifications). In the daytime, when the sun illuminates everything, all objects are clearly visible to the eye, and the eye's sight is pure. Likewise,

> when [the soul] is firmly fixed on the domain where truth and reality shine resplendent, it apprehends and knows them and appears to possess reason; but when it inclines to that region which is mingled with darkness, the world of becoming and passing away, it opines only and its edge is blunted, and it shifts its opinions hither and thither, and again seems as if it lacked reason.... This reality... that gives their truth to the objects of knowledge and the power of knowing to the knower, you must say is the idea of good [*tèn tou agathou idean*]. (508d–e)

And, as the sun not only gives sensible objects visibility, but also generation, growth, and nurture, though it is not subordinated to generation itself, so the good gives knowable objects not only the faculty of being known, but in addition "their very existence and essence... though the good itself is not essence but still transcends essence in majesty and power" (509b, with modifications).

The famous *allegory of the cave* illustrates this ontological proposition[12] and, indirectly, the position of the rulers in relation to the multitude. The prisoners inside the cave understand the shadows on the wall to be reality, although they are mere images. The prisoners symbolize the multitude. The rulers are prisoners, who have been released; they have successfully climbed up the steep incline of the cave and reached the outside world. On the outside, they are dazzled by the light and suffer intensely. But, little by little, they see the reflections of objects in water, when previously only their shadows were visible. Then, they see the objects themselves, and next the night with the moon and the stars, and after that the day and the sun (this ascent of the soul compares with similar ones described by Plato in the *Banquet, Theaetetus*, or *Phaedo*). They realize that prior to this they lived in illusion. Now that they are awake to reality, they have no desire to go back down into the cave. In a word, by their education, they have been forced to "turn

[12] The myth leaves the reader dissatisfied with the climax, which is the superessential good, which according to Aristotle was the object of "esoteric" teachings at the Academy (reserved for students only); the *Republic* is an "exoteric" text, accessible by the public at large.

upwards the vision of their souls and fix their gaze on that [being] which sheds light on all." Plato continues:

> *when they have thus beheld the good itself they shall use it as a pattern for the right ordering of the state* and the citizens and themselves throughout the remainder of their lives, each in his turn, devoting the greater part of their time to the study of philosophy, but when the turn comes for each, toiling in the service of the state and holding office for the city's sake, regarding the task not as a fine thing but a necessity; and so, when each generation has educated others like themselves to take their place as guardians of the state, they shall depart to the Islands of the Blest and there dwell. (*Republic* 540b–c)

This is Plato's ultimate argument in defense of the rulers' right to govern the city. However, by no means does their right stem from the people's choice, or from its acceptance and acknowledgment of the ruler. A ruler's legitimacy comes from the connection his soul makes with the very structure of the universe on which the people must attune itself for its own good.

F. Injustice in the State and in the Individual

Socrates can now take up the argument again from before the interruption, that is, when, having provided a definition of justice, he was about to return to a discussion of the various types of injustice.

Applying his method of looking at the large letters first, Socrates begins his examination of injustice by focusing on the aberrations that the constitution of a state can result in. Then he deduces from them the types of wicked individuals that can exist. From this, it is possible to see how injustice, disharmony, and encroachment on the functions of others can lead to unhappiness in a community and in an individual.

The harmonious state has a name: *aristocracy*. The four "aberrations of the state" are: *timocracy, oligarchy, democracy,* and *tyranny* (544c). Thus, there are five forms of government, or constitutions. Other types are found among the Greeks or barbarians, but they are mere variants of these basic types. And since governments derive from "the characters of the citizens" and do not "spring from the proverbial oak or rock," "there must be as many types of character among men as there are forms of government." We have already been told that the man who corresponds to the aristocratic form of government is truly good and just. The other types of character are described with each corresponding constitution.

1. *Timocracy (Government Based on the Love of Honor)*[13]

An initial question must be posed: if aristocracy is a harmonious state, how can it be unstable? How can division exist in the city? The answer is simple enough: "everything that has come into being... shall surely be dissolved" (546a). For men to be as they should be, so that an aristocracy can perpetuate itself forever, the fathering of children, generation after generation, must be *determined mathematically at appropriate times* (Socrates uses extraordinarily complicated calculations to explain this, cf. 546b–c). This supposes perfect beings, which is, of course, impossible in a world of senses subject to becoming—and, therefore, some unions occur at the wrong time ("out of season"); the resulting offspring are of inferior birth. This, in turn, results in a mixing of strains in the population, followed by civil strife.

[13] "Oligarchy," "democracy," and "tyranny" are common words. In order to describe the "constitution based on the love of honor," Plato must create the words "timocracy" and "timarchy."

The iron and bronze races revolt and start wanting to accumulate more wealth. They alarm the higher races, who remain faithful to virtue and the established order of things. So, the guardians enslave "their former friends and supporters, of whose freedom they had been the guardians, subjecting [them] as *perioeci* [an allusion to Sparta] and serfs."

This is the form of government found in Lacedaemonia and Crete. It is dominated by a hard, uncultivated warrior class and is characterized by a "fear to admit clever men to office, since the men it has of this kind are no longer simple and strenuous but of mixed strain, and in its inclining rather to the more high-spirited and simple-minded type, who are better suited for war than for peace, and in honoring the stratagems and contrivances of war and occupying itself with war most of the time" (*Republic* 547d–548a).

This regime preserves some of the features of aristocratic government: a liking for hierarchies, military capabilities, disdain for commerce, and so on. But it has certain features of oligarchy as well; the former guardians, concerned about the rising social disorder, begin to cherish a lust for gold and silver; they store up wealth and begin living only for themselves (548ab). Under this form of government men behave deceptively and secretly, circumventing laws that have been imposed on them by force.

Timocratic *man,* one might say, is the opposite of an intellectual. He has lost his "best guardian," that is, "philosophy tempered with music." Timocratic man loves "gymnastics and hunting. He is brutal: "to slaves such a one would be harsh, instead of simply scorning them, as the really educated do" (549a, with modifications).

2. *Oligarchy*

Etymologically, oligarchy means the rule of the few; but the "few" are generally the *rich*. Thus, oligarchy is the type of government where power is held by a few wealthy citizens.

Oligarchy stems from the decline of timocracy. Self-interest is widespread; less and less importance is attached to virtue, more and more to wealth. This evolution becomes inscribed in the functioning of the institutions, when the criteria for access to the magistracies becomes one's level of wealth (Solon resorted extensively to this method, see above, pp. 39–40 and 48–49).

The new regime has many weaknesses, beginning with its basic principle: it is absurd to imagine that wealth qualifies an individual to rule. Is the pilot of a ship chosen because of the number of goods in his possession? Likewise, by opposing two broad categories of citizens, the regime instills discord in its midst. In situations of war, it will be weak; if oligarchs wage war in person, they will be too few in number to be effective; if they arm the people, the people may turn the weapons against them. An oligarchic regime destroys the qualitative social differences in a society and causes all identities to interpenetrate and interchange.

An oligarchic government tolerates "a man to sell all his possessions, which another is permitted to acquire, and, after selling them, to go on living in the city, but as no part of it, neither a money-maker, nor a craftsman, nor a knight, nor a foot-soldier, but classified only as a pauper and a dependent" (552a).

These men, Plato says rather curiously, are like "drones" in the social hive, lazy and unproductive. True, there are two types of drones, those with stings and those without. The drones "with stings" succeed in accumulating wealth illicitly; the others remain poor. But both are parasites, because they have no proper productive function in the organization of the hive.

Next, Plato describes oligarchic man, explaining how the oligarchic spirit is awakened in the individual by the education received from timocratic parents in childhood. A son sees how his father devoted himself to the honor of the state, but, "dashed, as a ship on a reef, against the state, and making complete wreckage of his possessions and himself, perhaps he has been a general, or has held some other important office... [he is] dragged into court by mischievous sycophants and put to death or banished or outlawed and has lost all his property" (553b), and all this because the state itself is disordered. So, the son ceases to revere timocratic values (e.g., honor and pride). He realizes that, in the circumstances, his interest is to build his fortune as quickly as possible. To this end he employs reason and courage but, in the process, upsets the order of values. He becomes thrifty, greedy, and even stingy. Magnificence and wealth are squandered. Culture is frittered away, because this new kind of citizen sets up "blind god Plutus... as the great king of his soul" (Plutus, the god of wealth, makes no distinction between good and bad). He holds education for little worth.

3. *Democracy*

Democracy follows on the heels of oligarchy as naturally as oligarchy from timocracy. The rulers have no respect for virtue; they refrain from chastening dissolute youth, thinking that youth will squander its wealth and that they can get rich at its expense. Thus, a mass of underclass citizens forms in the city. "There they sit, I fancy, within the city, furnished with stings, that is, arms, some burdened with debt, others disfranchised, others both, hating and conspiring against the acquirers of their estates and the rest of the citizens and eager for revolution" (555d).

Impoverished men and their children lose hope and lapse into idleness and gentleness, except when they find themselves lined up alongside the rulers in war. "Do you not suppose it often happens that when a lean, sinewy, sunburnt pauper is stationed in battle beside a rich man bred in the shade, and burdened with superfluous flesh, and sees him panting and helpless—do you not suppose he will think that such fellows keep their wealth by the cowardice of the poor, and that when the latter are together in private, one will pass the word to another 'our men are good for nothing?'" (*Republic* 556d–e).

When this happens, it takes no more than a spark for civil strife—the great struggle between oligarchs and democrats—to flare up. Each side then turns to foreign cities for help, the one to defenders of oligarchy, the other to supporters of democracy. This is exactly what happened in Greece.

When democracy becomes the form of government, opponents are either killed or banished, and public office and public wealth are divided up. All order vanishes.

The new regime is characterized by license. Every man "[leads] his own life in the way that pleases him" (557b). Which is actually rather appealing, especially to women and children; society resembles a harlequin's coat, "embroidered with all kinds of hues." Pluralism spreads: not only is there a constitution authorizing pluralism, there is an outright pluralism of constitutions, in Plato's words, "a bazaar of constitutions" (557d). No principle is fixed, none creates consensus; laws are not enforced; no one teaches the youth the proper maxims. Democracy is a dereliction of social and moral codes; it is "anarchic and motley, assigning a kind of equality indiscriminately to equals and unequals alike" (558c).

Plato can now define the democratic *individual;* he refers again to the family unit in which characters are formed.

The oligarch's son is at liberty to consort with the "drones," who procure all manner and kind of pleasures. "May we not say that just as the revolution in the city was brought about by the aid of an alliance from outside, coming to the support of the similar and corresponding party in the state, so the youth is revolutionized when a like and kindred group of appetites from outside comes to the aid of one of the parties in his soul?" (559e).

Thus, the "ruler of his soul" changes hands. The "citadel of the young man's soul" is seized by one of the factions, no longer defended by the "best watchmen" ("studies and honorable pursuits and true discourses"), which the oligarchic father failed to nurture in his son.

Now all is lost. When the virtues try to regain their rightful seat, they find the doors of the citadel closed. Reverence is called "folly," temperance "want of manhood," moderate expenditure "rusticity and illiberality." However, the vices of youth—"insolence and anarchy and prodigality and shamelessness, resplendent in a great attendant choir and crowned with garlands"—triumph. Again, names are turned around: "insolence will be called 'good breeding,' anarchy 'liberty,' prodigality 'magnificence,' and impudence 'manly spirit'" (560e).

The result is what we call today "nihilism." When a youth becomes an adult, he "establishes and maintains all his pleasures on a footing of equality"; he "lives turning over the guard-house of his soul to each as it happens along until it is sated, as if it had drawn the lot for that office." He does not choose between good and base desires; he "avers that they are all alike and to be equally esteemed." Thus, he

> live[s] out his life in this fashion, day by day indulging the appetite of the day, now wine-bibbing and abandoning himself to the lascivious pleasing of the flute and again drinking only water and dieting; and at one time exercising his body, and sometimes idling and neglecting all things, and at another time seeming to occupy himself with philosophy. And frequently he goes in for politics and bounces up and says and does whatever enters his head. And if military men excite his emulation, thither he rushes, and if moneyed men, to that he turns, and there is no order or compulsion in his existence, but he calls this life of his the life of pleasure and freedom and happiness and cleaves to it to the end. "That," Plato concludes, "is a perfect description of a devotee of equality." (*Republic* 561d–e)

4. *Tyranny*

"'And now,' said I, 'the fairest polity and the fairest man remain for us to describe, the tyranny and the tyrant'" (562a). Just as insatiable desire for what oligarchy holds to be the highest good (wealth), combined with disregard for all other values, opens the door to democracy, so democracy's insatiable desire for its highest goods—liberty and equality—leads to its downfall and spawns tyranny.

Everyone treats everyone else as an equal; the good ruler behaves as if he is the ruled and vice versa; a father is treated as an equal by his son, like the citizen by the foreigner, the teacher by the pupil, the elderly by the young (the same can be said of the elderly, who, "accommodating themselves to the young, are full of pleasantry and graciousness, imitating the young for fear they may be thought disagreeable and authoritative" (563b); but also the free by the slaves, men by women, and even humans by animals!

"Without experience of it no one would believe how much freer the very beasts subject to men are in such a city than elsewhere. The dogs literally verify the adage and 'like their mistresses become.' And likewise the horses and asses are wont to hold on their way with the utmost freedom and dignity, bumping into everyone who meets them and who does not step aside. And so all things everywhere are just bursting with the spirit of liberty" (563c–d). However, excessiveness always provokes a reaction: in nature as well as in society; "from the height of liberty [grows] the fiercest extreme of servitude," from democracy grows tyranny.

At this point we need to go into some detail. Plato says that the democratic state has three parts: (1) the "drones," that is to say, the breed of idle and spendthrift men, divided in two sorts, those with "stings" (troublemakers among the multitude) and those without, less harmful, happy to shut up their opponents; (2) the rich, in other words, those who in the context of general intemperance are the most orderly and thrifty natures; they are the producers of the "honey" so coveted by the drones; (3) and, finally, the "people." Herein lies the corruption of the system: in a democracy, the people are strong, because they have the numbers. But they do not know how to rule themselves; they are manipulated by the drones. The drones trick the people into believing that they will soon have the honey of the rich, but in reality they keep most of it for themselves. From then on, "those who are thus plundered are compelled to defend themselves."

They try to restore oligarchy. In reaction, the people hand over greater powers to a strong man of the democratic party. He, in turn, asks for a guard to protect himself from the intrigues of the oligarchs. His request is granted, and his adversaries run away. He becomes the ruler of the place (*Republic* 565b–566d).

In the beginning everything goes rather well (Plato is probably alluding to Pisistratus). The tyrant cancels all debts, redistributes plots of land to his supporters, and makes promises to everybody. Plato notes, however, a tyrant "is always stirring up some war so that the people may be in need of a leader... and that also, being impoverished by war-taxes, they may have to devote themselves to their daily business and be less likely to plot against him" (566d–567a).

This provokes criticism, especially among those who helped establish the tyrant in the first place and know where the source of his power lies. "Then the tyrant must do away with all such [i.e., 'those voicing their disapproval of the course of events'] if he is to maintain his rule, until he has left no one of any worth, friend or foe" (567b).

Surrounded by mediocre followers, who are not of much worth to him, the tyrant can only hold on to power—indeed, just stay alive—by hiring a mercenary guard: either a corps of foreigners to whom he pays high wages, or the slaves of his own citizens whom he sets free, so that their fates are bound to his—a new race of drones. Now that he holds total power, he can use all the resources of his people for himself and for his felonious gang of supporters. In exchange for total liberty, the people "has clothed itself in the garb of the most cruel and bitter servile servitude... *enslavement to slaves*" (569c).

Plato can now complete the family saga that serves as his illustrative principle. The democratic father allowed the "citadel of his soul" to be invested with passions. His son also became carried away by these same passions. But, just as the tyrant made himself the master of the people to protect it from the threats of the oligarchs, so the passions, as soon as they feel threatened by the father's appeals for restraint and moderation, find the means to place one passion at the top: "the monstrous winged drone" of love (573a)—the one with a terrible sting (a ferocious, insatiable beast slumbers in man—as dreams reveal when the defenses of reason are down—and it is awakened by democratic passions). This is how *tyrannical man* is formed; he is "continuously and in waking hours what he rarely became in sleep" (574e). He has no restraints, refuses no pleasure, holds back from no offense and no crime. When the state is well ruled, tyrannical men are usually only a few in number, reduced to fringe groups of delinquents that can be found in every society. But when the state weakens, these men come out of the shadows and occupy the high ground, until the most corrupt among them becomes the tyrant of the city.

The particular characteristic of tyrannical man is his inability to rule himself. Such a man can only be a slave; either he is slave to a tyrant, who will help him satisfy the appetites of his passions, or he is a tyrant himself and lives permanently in servile fear of a revolt. At any rate, he can never experience freedom or friendship (576a). He is not only the unhappiest of men; he is also the most unjust.

At the end of his argument, Plato is ready to give a decisive reply to the objections raised against justice by Socrates' initial interlocutors. In society happiness declines in proportion to the rise of injustice, across the spectrum from timocracy to tyranny. As for the individual, the just man is the happiest, because he is in harmony with others and with himself; and the supremely unjust man, tyrannical man, is the most miserable.

In book 10, Plato uses the myth of Er the Pamphylian, with its Orphic and Pythagorean influences, to illustrate that the happiness of the just and the misery of the unjust carry on into the afterlife. The immortal soul undergoes a series of reincarnations, and each unjust life is meted out horrible punishments in Hades. When the soul has meditated sufficiently on virtue, it is able to choose knowingly its next reincarnation and lead a just life on earth. Thereafter, the soul leads a series of earthly and heavenly lives in complete happiness.

G. A Theory of Revolution

Is the state that Plato sketches here in the *Republic* an "ideal state," a utopia as difficult to achieve as it is to draw a perfect circle with a piece of chalk? Or did Plato think he could establish an aristocratic state in Greece on the model of the *Republic*? Apparently he did believe that the model state could be founded in reality, but it would require a miracle or, at the very least, good fortune (he followed the events in Sicily for over 30 years on the lookout for both): that is, it would require a genuine philosopher-king able to impose change. An improbable circumstance, but not entirely impossible. Because, although most kings and tyrants are bad by nature, and even those who are good become corrupt, it is conceivable that *at least one king* can be a philosopher. Once this person in a million is found, it will be possible to make good laws in an already existing city, which then will gradually come closer to the model's ideal city.

But will the people accept this rule? If we are to believe Plato, this is highly unlikely, but again not completely impossible. The people may grow tired of the Sophists; and while they may not grasp the merits of the new rulers' actions in full, they will recognize in these rulers good men with good intentions in whom it is possible to have confidence (see 500e).

There is one remaining condition of success. The new rulers will have to create a race of guardians capable of guaranteeing the longevity of the regime. This will require the nationalization of education and the removal of children from the care of their parents.

"All inhabitants above the age of ten they will send out into the fields, and they will take over the children, remove them from the manners and habits of their parents, and bring them up in their own customs and laws which will be such as we have described" (541a).

Plato seems to have envisaged this revolutionary, and very violent step seriously, and he probably would have taken it in Syracuse, if the *putsch* had succeeded. We will come across this idea of society's total care of the youth again in our discussion of the *Laws* below, at which time we will discuss its moral and political implications.

II. The *Statesman*

In the *Statesman,* a dialogue written some 20 years after the *Republic* (ca. 357–354 BC), Plato reflects on the art of the statesman, which he calls the "political" or "royal" art. Ideally, the statesman will be to the citizens what a shepherd is to his flock; unlike the physician, the farmer, or the merchant, the shepherd does not have a specialized function in the community. His authority over his flock is total, like the cowherd over his herd, who oversees its couplings, feeding, health, and well-being (267e and following).[14] This ideal is difficult to attain nowadays, Plato says, because humanity is *corrupt.* He illustrates this with a myth.

A. The Myth of the Statesman

The state of the world has not always been as it is, Plato says. The present results from a reversal in the rotation of the heavens and the earth and consequently an inversion in the *flow of time.*

In the beginning, God ruled the universe personally. Men were earth-born, became younger, and never died; they were constantly born again in their parents in an endless reverse cycle. They had neither families nor cities, since they were ruled directly by God (demons governed the other animal species).

[14] *Translator's note:* Quotes from Plato's *Statesman* are based on Plato, *Plato in Twelve Volumes,* vol. 8, translated by Harold N. Fowler (Cambridge, MA: Harvard University Press, 1921).

Then God left the world and abandoned it to its destiny. The earth immediately reversed the direction of its rotation, like a spring that unwinds; time began to move in the direction as we know it. Instead of a creator-time, it became a corruptor-time. Men enjoyed a few technologies, such as fire and metallurgy—gifts from the compassionate deities—but they soon found themselves dispersed and without guidance. Then they built cities and began to govern themselves.

B. The Statesman Assumes the Function of God among Corrupt Men

Then men assigned the role of shepherd to one of their kind. But he is a fellow creature; to replace God, it would be better to appoint one of higher rank than the others (*Statesman* 303b). This allows Plato to formulate the key "political" question, namely: where is the human equivalent of divine authority to be found? The statesman, like God at the dawn of time, must be a "generalist," a true shepherd.

Actual political leaders, Plato says, have only a partial vision of things because the different cities known to us have partisan regimes; not one has a true statesman at its helm. Oligarchs are specialists of wealth, democrats are specialists of poverty, and others are specialists of religion or war. None of this knowledge is appropriate for the government of the city. The true science of command is found in only a few men: at best two (the philosopher and the head of state), maybe only one (the perfect monarch).

C. The Statesman Is Above the Law; in the Absence of a Philosopher-King, the Law Is Second Best

Possessed of true science, the statesman and the philosopher, or the philosopher-king, will not need laws. Plato says, laws are like "a stubborn and ignorant man, who allows no one to do anything contrary to his command, or even to ask a question, not even if something new occurs to some one, which is better than the rule he has himself ordained" (294a).

It is absurd, for example, for a professional athletic trainer to establish a general exercise regimen without adapting it to the best interest of each individual in the class. Similarly, we would think a physician out of his mind who treats all patients with the same remedy, without regard for changes in each one's health. And, finally, "the captain of a ship keeps watch for what is at any moment for the good of the vessel and the sailors, not by writing rules, but by making his science his law" (296e–297a).

Plato admits that if rulers are ignorant or insane, then written laws (or, for that matter, customs, which are the fruit of experience) would be a lesser evil. But a government truly possessed of political art and science will always be better than a government according to law. Two possibilities exist: either the law is decided rashly, in which case a wise man's decision is better; or it is made according to science, in which case science, the true objective standard, can undo what the law created.

Plato pays no heed to arguments formulated since the time of the Seven Sages, such as: the law forbids arbitrary decisions, or the law, the fruit of mutual agreement, is accepted willingly by all. This is not the problem. A government can easily dispense with the consent of the people. What is asked of a physician is to restore his patient to health, which he does if, and only if, he knows the art; and he cures the patient every time when he has the art. No patient will ever blame the physician for the cure, however harsh or painful, once he has been restored to health. It is no different in politics; only the truth is good, and it is always good, regardless of the method used to apply it.

D. A Typology of Constitutions

Today's cities, which have placed their destiny in laws and customs, Plato says, are illegitimate "bastard" forms of governments; and it goes without saying that cities that set aside the law, though they are not ruled by true philosophers, are even worse. This offers Plato the opportunity to paint a picture of the various types of political regimes.[15]

Three principal types of constitution are possible: constitutions where one man holds power alone; constitutions where power is in the hands of the few; and constitutions where power is held by everybody. This number can be doubled to account for forms of government that respect the law and forms that do not respect the law. This results in a total of six forms of government: monarchy and tyranny (monarchy is the best of the six, tyranny the worst; for the same reason, one man, imposing his will on all, can deliver the best results, provided his will is good; likewise, one man will produce the worst results if his will is corrupt); aristocracy and oligarchy (ranking two and five on the scale of six); and two forms of democracy, both with the same name—because, Plato says, democracy "is weak in all respects and able to do nothing great, either good or bad, when compared with the other forms of government, because in this the powers of government are distributed in small shares among many men" (*Statesman* 303a). Accordingly, democracy is both the worst of the best governments and the best of the worst (holding the third and fourth positions on the scale).

But the prize goes to the "seventh form of government," the one led by the true statesman. It "must be set apart from all the others, as God is set apart from men" (303b). In the other six forms, which are not under the rule of science (knowledge), the rulers are not statesmen, they are partisans and counterfeits, "the greatest of imitators and cheats"; and "the greatest of all [are] sophists."

E. Political Art and Inferior Arts

Just as it is not enough to wash the mud from gold nuggets to obtain pure gold, because gold has to be purified by fire to separate it from other metals amalgamated with it, similarly, to identify the true art of politics, it is not only necessary to distinguish this art from the competence required of the rulers of the six "partisan" forms of government, but also from certain other arts that resemble political art, though they are, in fact, different. "Herein are included the arts of the general and of the judge and that kind of oratory which partakes of the kingly art because it persuades men to justice and thereby helps to steer the ship of state" (303e–304a).

These three arts, which are not in themselves bad, would become bad if they were to become independent. It is one thing to know how to wage war and another to know whether one should or should not wage war; to know how to speak and to know what to say; to judge according to the law and to know whether the law is just and good. In all these areas of political life, a knowledge of what *should be* must have preeminence over the knowledge of what *is*. These arts, therefore, must serve the royal art.

F. The Royal Weaver

The "king" will not only rule the state, he will create it—and once again Plato's demiurgic yearning comes to expression—or more precisely, the king will "weave" the state with a "warp" of spirited characters and a "woof" of those inclined toward restraint (309b). In a beautiful passage (306b–308b), Plato shows that virtues, thought to be natural allies by superficial minds

[15] It is virtually the same picture we will find again in Aristotle.

(for the simple reason that they are virtues), are in reality irreconcilable enemies: social conflicts arise when citizens possess pure virtue but cannot recognize the utility of the others. Yet all are complementary and necessary for the success of the community. Royal art consists in weaving them together.

One way of doing this is for the magistrate to administer marriages authoritatively: for example, he will couple fiery tempers with restrained natures for the improvement of the "race"; fiery tempers have a natural tendency to intermarry, and this will produce a crop of insanely violent offspring within a few generations; likewise, temperate characters will couple and bear totally apathetic descendants. This can be remedied, of course, through eugenics dictated by the wisdom of the king (the same old Spartan concern found in the *Republic* and that we will come across again in the *Laws*). The truly useless human material will either be reduced to slavery or banished or destroyed.

Now we see how royal science works. On the one hand, it is characterized by access to eternal truths, on the other by the vision of the All. Thus, royal science can perceive *the dimension whereby the parts of the social body can achieve harmony,* a dimension ordinarily unknown to the parts themselves. Through the divine part of his soul, each citizen can commune with the others; the fiery-tempered citizen understands the need for restraint, while the more restrained citizen perceives the need for spiritedness. Once common ground is established, it is easy for the ruler to set down the necessary subordinate arrangements, laws, and measures that provide for good social organization. "[Royal art] binds the eternal part of their souls with a divine bond, to which that part is akin, and after the divine it binds the animal part of them with human bonds" (309c).

Despite everything he claims about the fundamental inferiority of the law in the *Statesman,* Plato summons again, in old age, his energy to produce a lengthy treatise on law. The passage of time seems to have influenced his thinking.

III. The Laws

The *Laws* reveal a different Plato from the one in the earlier dialogues. His commitment to his original aim—to bend politics to the intelligible world—remains as firm as ever. But, now older, his experience and knowledge of politics is much greater. He shows himself to be more alert to real concerns; he is more "practical," and—to some extent—he is more tolerant of human foibles. The depth of detail in the *Laws* is remarkable, as is the scope of its universal curiosity: it covers civil law, commercial law, criminal law, legal proceedings, and much more. Plato refuses to let anything slip through the grasp of his intellectual powers and structuring spirit. One is left with the impression that this time Plato is fully committed to reaching his goal and that after his long journey through speculative philosophy, perhaps little more than a diversion, the true passion of his youth—the topic of the *Seventh Letter*—finally triumphs: to establish the state on new foundations. It is as though the father of idealism now declares his love for the earth! He recalls that his lifelong aim and ambition has been to achieve this end (*Laws* 968b).

The intention of the *Republic* was to discover the nature of justice. Along the way, Plato produced a sketch of the ideal state. Here, in the *Laws,* his sole point is to provide a detailed constitution of the state. He imagines that because the Cretans are going to establish a colony, they will need all their laws at once. Greek political thinkers loved this kind of situation, because it enabled them to build entirely from scratch on a greenfield site.

The dialogue involves an Athenian stranger (his name is unknown, he is simply called the "Athenian" and is Plato's spokesperson, like Socrates in the *Republic*); a Lacedaemonian named

Megillus; and Clinias, a Cretan. Thus, we have a representative of the home of democracy and two representatives of oligarchic regimes. The three characters are all older, wise, and experienced; furthermore, they have time on their hands for contemplation and discussion.

Clinias poses the problem he faces in the following terms:

> The greater part of Crete is going to send out a colony, and they have entrusted the management of the affair to the Cnosians; and the Cnosian government to me and nine others. And they desire us to give them any laws which we please, whether taken from the Cretan model or from any other; and they do not mind about their being foreign if they are better. Grant me then this favour, which will also be a gain to yourselves:—Let us make a selection from what has been said, and then let us imagine a State of which we will suppose ourselves to be the original founders. Thus we shall proceed with our enquiry, and, at the same time, I may have the use of the framework which you are constructing, for the city which is in contemplation. (*Laws* 702c)[16]

A. A "Political Philosophy" Underlies Constitutional Law

1. *The "Second" Polity*

Clinias, Plato says (739a), has a choice between three models of government (or polities): (1) an ideal constitution (like the one in the *Republic* defined here as total communism, not just communism among the class of guardians); (2) an imperfect form of the ideal polity; and (3) other forms more distant still from the ideal model. The *Laws* set out to describe the "second" polity. It is far removed from the ideal, essentially because it accepts private property (though the state retains a sort of "preemptive" title on family land holdings); at the same time, the "second" polity resembles the ideal model in that it establishes a political order "very near to immortality" (739e).

Plato endorses a transition from the first to the second model, depending on the urgency: one must not squander an opportunity like the establishment of a colony; in situations like this one must play one's trump card. Future colonists, Plato well knows, will not want to give up private property, so he makes this concession to achieve success.

2. *The First Challenge: The Basis of Laws*

The first issue to be resolved is the basis of the laws. In whose name can the laws be justified? It can no longer be left to the gods, as "in the time of Cronos," that is, during the Golden Age (713c). In the *Laws*, as in the *Statesman*, Plato says that the tragedy of cities today is that they are not ruled by the gods, but by the laws of men, who lack the necessary wisdom and authority to govern (713e).

The solution is for humanity to be ruled by *something divine, immortal, and, at the same time, immanent in the human spirit: reason.* On the one hand, reason is something eternal; it is as external and transcendent in regard to humankind today as the race of Demons was in regard to humanity "in the time of Cronos." On the other hand, reason is immanent in humans, who can make something theirs if they have a clear intellection of it.

Thus, the laws will be a transcendent exteriority. But because they are rational, they will be thoroughly admissible to each individual. Each person can "immanentize" the laws, so to speak,

---

[16] Plato, *The Laws*, translated by Benjamin Jowett (1871); available at www.gutenberg.org. *Translator's note:* Quotes are from both Benjamin Jowett's translation and *Plato in Twelve Volumes,* vol. 12, trans. R. G. Bury (1926; repr., Cambridge, MA: Harvard University Press, 2001), which will be cited in the text as Bury.

in that he or she can grasp their necessity from within. The outward appearance of the laws will not take the form of submission, or humiliation of the intellect. The norm will be one that each person establishes for himself or herself, an *autonomy*—something close to what Rousseau and Kant formulate later.

Reason, as implied here, is not the reason of the demagogues, who manipulate the *nomos* arbitrarily with their sophistry. Rather, it is the reason that provides access to the nature of things. Accordingly, the real basis of *nomos* is Nature in the sense of the divine and eternal order of the universe.

Plato says, God, "holding in his hand the beginning, middle, and end of all that is, travels according to his nature in a straight line towards the accomplishment of his end" (*Laws* 716a; see also 733a, 733d, 734a). This straight line is opposed to "unreason" and "immoderation." Contrary to Protagoras, who said, "man is the measure of all things," Plato says that "God ought to be to us the measure of all things, and not [this or that] man" (716c, with modifications).[17]

3. *Civil Religion*

Because the city will be rooted in such transcendent norms, Plato also wants it to have a single shared and compulsory *religion*. Naturally, this religion will be attuned to reason; it will be the work of philosophy—Plato's philosophy.

Every citizen will take part in the cult of the gods through sacrifices, prayers, and offerings: these will be made first to the Gods, then to the Demons [Spirits], the Heroes, and finally to the ancestral Divinities. It will be a purified interior religion, emphasizing the intimate intentions of the heart. "From one who is polluted, neither good man nor God can without impropriety receive gifts. Wherefore, the unholy do only waste their much service upon the Gods, but when offered by any holy man, such service is most acceptable to them. This is the mark at which we ought to aim" (717a).[18]

Reason will pervade the entire cult, which must be worshiped according to mathematical laws, in keeping with the Pythagorean custom.

4. *The Preambles of Laws*

The purpose of the preamble or *preface* of a law is to make the connection between it and transcendent Nature intelligible to human reason.

In the *Laws,* we are dealing with citizens educated and trained in their motherlands. Accordingly, the revolutionary approach described in the *Republic* cannot be used when founding a new colony. Therefore, it will be necessary to persuade those who already have firm convictions. This will require a *preamble* or *preface* to explain the raison d'être of each new formulation of the law.

The *preamble* resembles a conversation between a physician and his patient before treatment begins. Because the treatment can be unpleasant, the patient needs to understand from the outset

[17] Plato reveals his fidelity to the teachings of Socrates here; like Socrates, and opposed to the other Sophists, Plato believes in the existence of a higher norm of *nomoï,* a "natural law." But the *Republic* shows us that Plato's version of the theory of divine or natural law is characterized by its hyperintellectualism. For Plato, Nature is the world of Ideas, accessible by mathematical and dialectical reasoning. For Aristotle and the Stoics, Nature is a reality that can be observed empirically with limited reason; consequently, it is not possible to identify the contours of a unique ideal State from Nature.

[18] We can almost hear the language of the prophets and the Psalms defying sacrificial religion (see below, p. 409). Is this the influence of "Jerusalem" on "Athens" (in view of the chronology, the hypothesis should not be rejected outright)? Is it the emergence of an independent "prophetic" force outside the tribal state? Or is it the inevitable, necessary consequence of what happens when a state is founded (regardless of where), nullifying and trivializing sacrifices and other public gestures of traditional religion?

what the purpose and probable effects of the treatment are, so that he can participate in his own recovery. (Only slaves are administered treatment automatically; see *Laws* 719e–720e.) It can be likened to the prelude of a piece of music that introduces the main composition. So, when making laws, it is necessary to "persuade as well as threaten" (721e), a threat being a mere half-measure used by the Lacedaemonians (again Plato takes a critical stance towards the Spartans; as we know, his preference is for timocracy, not democracy, but he weighs the threat of Sparta's deep-rooted anti-intellectualism).

Here is an example of a preamble for a law on marriage. In its simple laconic expression, the law reads: "A man shall marry between the ages of thirty and thirty-five, or, if he does not, he shall pay such and such a fine, or shall suffer the loss of such and such a privilege." The fully formulated law (with its preface) reads as follows:

> A man shall marry between the ages of thirty and thirty-five, considering that in a manner the human race naturally partakes of immortality, which every man is by nature inclined to desire to the utmost; for the desire of every man that he may become famous, and not lie in the grave without a name, is only the love of continuance. Now mankind are coeval with all time, and are ever following, and will ever follow, the course of time; and so they are immortal, because they leave children's children behind them, and partake of immortality in the unity of generation. And for a man voluntarily to deprive himself of this gift, as he deliberately does who will not have a wife or children, is impiety. He who obeys the law shall be free, and shall pay no fine; but he who is disobedient, and does not marry, when he has arrived at the age of thirty-five, shall pay a yearly fine of a certain amount, in order that he may not imagine his celibacy to bring ease and profit to him; and he shall not share in the honours which the young men in the state give to the aged. (721b–d)

Plato follows this program scrupulously throughout the *Laws*, placing a preamble before each law.

5. *The Need for a Tyrant to Found the State*

A further initial problem needs to be resolved. Most states were founded spontaneously in accordance with circumstances. In fact, "the same principle applies equally to all human things.... No man ever makes laws, but chances and accidents of all kinds, occurring in all sorts, make all our laws for us" (Bury, 708e–709a).

In sum, the source of social order is not just man, but the Gods, chance, and opportunity. Human faculty plays a role, but only in the last instance, doing what it can given the circumstances, like the pilot of a boat in rough seas.

Therefore, to form a state that is not too far from the ideal, one should pray to the gods for circumstances that enable the art of the lawmaker to produce its best results. In Plato's judgment, the optimal conditions for the application of the laws would be for the lawmaker to find a good tyrant (arguably Plato never recants the convictions he formed when writing his *Republic*). In fact, "the tyrant, if he wishes, can change the manners of a state: he has only to go in the direction of virtue or of vice, whichever he prefers, he himself indicating by his example the lines of conduct, praising and rewarding some actions and reproving others, and degrading those who disobey" (711b–c).

But the good tyrant will have to be young, temperate, quick at learning, and possess a good memory; he will also have to be courageous and of noble character: "When the supreme power in man coincides with the greatest wisdom and temperance, then the best laws and the best constitution come into being" (712a).

Plato would also settle for a small group of noble families (711d); monarchy is not, in his judgment, the only conceivable model; what matters is that power is as unified as possible, and that the men who possess it are, as much as possible, in possession of the most complete and balanced set of virtues. Plato recognizes that this is extremely rare: "The real impossibility or difficulty is... rarely surmounted in the course of ages; but when once it is surmounted, ten thousand or rather all blessings follow" (711d).

B. History as Decay and Corruption

To imagine appropriately the "next best" or "semi-ideal" form of government to be established, it is important to recognize the threat that the constitution must protect against: the danger of *corruption or decay,* arising from a lack of harmony among the parts of the city.

Here again is the core idea of the *Republic* and the *Statesman.* Plato sets out a theory of historical time as decay. From this he deduces a political program that is *reactionary* in a literal sense, since it involves founding a city in a homeland it can never leave. But instead of presenting his theory in the abstract, as in his earlier treatises, this time he discusses the *real* history of Greece. Though advanced in years, Plato does not shrink from writing practical history complete with names, facts, and dates.

1. *Historical Cycles*

Plato understands history as a past of undefined duration. The length of time that states have existed and people have lived together in politically ordered societies is "beyond imagination." "Have not thousands and thousands of cities come into being during this period and as many perished? And has not each of them had every form of government many times over, now growing larger, now smaller, and again improving or declining?" (*Laws* 676b–c).

The past must be understood as an endless succession of *cycles:* periods of civilization ending in destruction by a cataclysmic event (e.g., a flood), leaving nothing in its wake but a few shepherds, lost on the high mountain tops, survivors who painstakingly rebuild civilization "from this nothing," reinventing metallurgy, artisanry, and the art of politics (678).

With each new beginning, the survivors are so few in number that they share "a feeling of affection and good-will towards one another" (678e); thus, there is no occasion for wars or quarrels. These men are frugal, but happy: they have enough from their pastures, hunting, pottery, and weaving; they are simple and essential arts. They know neither wealth nor poverty. "The community which has neither poverty nor riches will always have the noblest principles; in it there is no insolence or injustice."

But the best quality of these primitive men is their "simplicity": "when they were told about good and evil, they in their simplicity believed what they heard to be very truth and practised it. No one had the wit to suspect another of a falsehood, as men do now; but what they heard about Gods and men they believed to be true, and lived accordingly" (679b–c).[19]

At the beginning of historical cycles humans have no laws; they cannot exist because there is no writing. Only customs exist. Their political organization is the first form described by Homer among the Cyclops: a sort of "state of nature" where families live dispersed without shared institutions, where the head of each family is the "ruler" (step 1). Then the families come together, their rulers acting as an aristocracy of sorts for the new group, which also chooses a few representatives to compare the customs of each original group and to agree upon some shared customs. Thus, the groups gradually unite into one (step 2). Then the communities settle in cities

[19] This praise of lost ignorance—coming from an intellectual like Plato—may puzzle. The worm that the Athens of the Sophists allowed into the apple of the Golden Age was *doubt,* which ate and spoiled everything. Doubt had to be banned from the city.

on the plain—long after the beginning of the cycle, because this dangerous decision assumes that the destruction of the flood has been lost from memory (step 3). Finally, they establish colonies abroad (step 4). Thus, decay and corruption begin as soon as "history" does.

Then Plato describes this deterioration at work in his own cycle of time. At this time the main actors are Greece and its neighbors, that is, the cities in the Peloponnesus (Argos, Messene, and Lacedaemon), Persia, and finally Athens.

2. *History of the Peloponnesus*

A sort of social contract is at the origin of the political regimes of the Dorian cities: an oath between six allies, the kings of three cities (i.e., three brothers, sons of Heracles) and three populations, each vowing to come to the assistance of the others in the event of a threat to the status quo (*Laws* 684a). What made this agreement possible was the social equality between the Dorian cities; it was not necessary to impose a land redistribution or to cancel debts before a just constitution could be established (problems that so many other Greek cities had to face).

In spite of such favorable circumstances, these regimes proved weak because their kings were excessive. They pursued their heart's desire and refused to be checked by wisdom. Soon dissension broke out among them, and the cities drifted toward what Plato (in the *Republic*) calls "timocracy": they organized for war, emphasizing only one virtue among the four principal ones. Sparta was less affected than the other two cities, owing to more favorable circumstances, and it was able to invent a more balanced form of government, the so-called mixed regime, a conflation of monarchy, oligarchy, and democracy.[20]

Sparta was indeed fortunate: it had not one but two kings, "twins," who held power in tandem.[21] This arrangement "restricted within due bounds the royal power" (691e).[22] Moreover, owing to their age and wisdom, the twenty-eight elders, making up Sparta's senate, were able to moderate the passions of the kings. Finally, the power of the senate itself was held in check by the power of the ephors. Thus, Sparta devised a system for keeping its various powers in balance. "We said...just now that there ought to be no great and unmixed powers; and this was under the idea that a state ought to be free and wise and harmonious, and that a legislator ought to legislate with a view to this end" (693b).[23]

The other two cities, Messene and Argos, went into decline, Plato says, because they failed to keep to this principle. Their behavior toward other states was bad. Messene waged war against Sparta just as Persia was invading Greece (this prevented Sparta from assisting Athens at Marathon); as for Argos, it simply sat on the sidelines, refusing to become involved in the fighting.

3. *The Decline of Persia and Athens*

The same lack of proportion is the cause of the decline of the other two forms of government discussed by the speakers in the *Laws:* Persia and Athens. Persia regarded itself as a pure monarchy; Athens saw itself as a pure democracy. The former emphasized wisdom, the latter

---

[20] These lines of the laws may have been the first formal analysis of the Spartan regime.

[21] Procles and Eurysthenes were brothers, sons of Aristodemus. Aristodemus, one of the three sons of Heracles, had inherited Sparta from his father.

[22] *Translator's note:* This quote is from Bury's translation of the *Laws*. Jowett's translation reads: "brought you more within the limits of moderation."

[23] This praise of the mixed regime of government is found again in 712b–713a: evidence that Sparta and Crete have "mixed regimes" exists in the fact that their forms of government cannot be given an exact name. They are neither democracies, nor oligarchies, nor aristocracies, nor monarchies, nor tyrannies, but a little of everything (Sparta tends more toward tyranny, Plato says, owing to the growing democratic power of the ephors).

liberty (693e). Both approaches can destroy harmony and, thus, weaken the bond of friendship and community.

a. The Persians

The cause of Persia's decline can be attributed to Cyrus's neglect for the *education of his children,* which he entrusted to women and eunuchs while he was away at war. Thus, his children became used to being waited on hand and foot, unopposed in any way. As a result, his son, Cambyses, lost his mind and murdered his brother; not long after he was stripped of power by the Medes. When Darius came to the throne, he managed to turn the situation around. Though he was not of royal birth, he had been "properly" educated (in the "school of hard knocks"). He reestablished equality and trust among the people. Unfortunately, Darius paid no more attention to the education of his son, Xerxes, than did Cyrus for his, and the same cause produced the same effect. The monarch lacked judgment and became a despot, and the basic minimum of freedom and equality that should exist in a monarchy disappeared again from Persia; with them vanished the bond of trust between citizens as well. Plato develops the same thought that Herodotus attributes to Demaratus the Spartan in a conversation with Xerxes. The cause of Persia's decline was

> that by robbing the commons [the people] unduly of their liberty and introducing despotism in excess, they destroyed in the State the bonds of friendliness and fellowship. And when these are destroyed, the policy of the rulers no longer consults for the good of the subjects and the commons, but solely for the maintenance of their own power; if they think it will profit them in the least degree, they are ready at any time to overturn States and to overturn and burn up friendly nations; and thus they both hate and are hated with a fierce and ruthless hatred. And when they come to need the commons, to fight in their support, they find in them no patriotism or readiness to endanger their lives in battle; so that, although they possess countless myriads of men, they are all useless for war, and they hire soldiers from abroad [mercenaries and strangers] as though they were short of men, and imagine that their safety will be secured by hirelings and aliens. (*Laws* 697c–698a)

And although the Persians numbered in the hundreds of thousands, they were vanquished by a handful of Athenians and Spartans. But even the Athenians were buffeted by the tempests of history.

b. The Athenians

Athens's vice was the exact opposite of the Persians': absence of authority and excessive freedom: "Entire freedom and the absence of all superior authority is not by any means so good as government by others when properly limited" (698a).

At the time of the Persian wars, Athenian citizens respected the laws and enjoyed "the bonds of friendliness and fellowship."s But the harmony that prevailed was not just the consequence of good political order and a profound respect for ancestral laws, Plato says; it stemmed from a fear of the Persian threat. After the Persian army massacred the entire population of Eretria, the Athenians dreaded the same fate. A community, especially one torn by factions, will come together temporarily against an external enemy. But when danger subsides, decay sets in again; this is precisely what happened in Athens.

Indiscipline appeared initially in music (a persistent theme in the *Republic*). There were certain well-defined, fixed types of music: hymns, lamentations, paeans, dithyrambs, and "citharoedic" nomoi (a kind of song)."The authority whose duty it was to know these regulations, and, when known, to apply them in judgments and to penalize the disobedient, was not a pipe nor, as now, the mob's unmusical shoutings, nor yet the clappings which mark applause: in place of this it was a rule made by those in control of education that they themselves should listen throughout in silence, while the children and their ushers [tutors] and the general crowd were kept in order by the discipline of the rod" (Bury, 700c).

But carried away by demagogy and a craving for pleasure, the Athenians soon combined lamentations with hymns, paeans with dithyrambs, "imitating the sounds of the flute on the lyre, and making one general confusion; ignorantly affirming that music has no truth, and, whether good or bad, can only be judged of rightly by the pleasure of the hearer" (*Laws* 700d–e).

Then a spirit of revolutionary lawlessness spread to every segment of society, and people felt no fear because they supposed they could judge for themselves. "For what is this shamelessness, which is so evil a thing, but the insolent refusal to regard the opinion of the better by reason of an over-daring sort of liberty?" (701a–b). This freedom was followed by disobedience to rulers, then to parents and elders, and finally to the laws themselves. Even oaths, pledges, and the gods were held in contempt.

The lessons learned from all this are clear. When even under servitude the Persians achieved a degree of freedom, as momentarily under Darius, they succeeded in their ventures. And when the Athenians, accustomed to freedom, but under the threat of circumstances, accepted the constraint of obedience to their leaders and the laws, they too succeeded. "When they [the two kinds of government] were carried to the extreme of either, slavery or licence, neither party were the gainers."

With the knowledge from history of what is to be avoided: inescapable decay owing to the loss of harmony, it becomes clear how to form the constitution of a new state: it must, in its very structure, *make any kind of change impossible.*

C. Plato's Preferred State: A Fixed, Immutable Society

1. *The Role of Mathematics*

In the first place, mathematics, whose truths are eternal, is destined to play a key role in the development of laws.

From the outset, Plato says, the number of families in the new state, and thus the number of plots of land to be allotted, should be 5,040 (737c). Why? Because "that number... contains the greatest and most regular and unbroken series of divisions." It is a number that can be divided by two, three, four, and so on up to ten. It is, therefore, the number "most likely to be useful to all cities," "for war and peace, and for all contracts and dealings, including taxes and divisions of the land" (738a).

Admittedly, mathematics can also be put to use for "illiberal" ("utilitarian" or "slavish") purposes—that is, for mercantile and greedy designs, as among the Phoenicians. But this is understandable because either these people had bad lawmakers or the climate corrupted their constitution (747b–e). Mathematics is not bad on its own.

Because mathematics is constant and fixed, any laws resulting from speculative mathematics are constant as well. All the same, safeguards against the threat of change, whether from internal or external causes, are necessary.

2. *Safeguards against Change from Internal Causes*

Plato's primary concern is to ensure the permanence of culture. In his opinion the best model of a changeless society is Egypt.

a. The Example of Egypt

Egypt was the model of a culture unchanged for so long that it seemed to exist outside the cycle of becoming.[24] *Music, painting,* and *sculpture* never changed there, because Egypt had the appropriate legislation.

> Long ago they appear to have recognized the very principle of which we are now speaking—that their young citizens must be habituated to forms and strains of virtue. These they fixed, and exhibited the patterns of them in their temples; and no painter or artist is allowed to innovate upon them, or to leave the traditional forms and invent new ones. To this day, no alteration is allowed either in these arts, or in music at all. And you will find that their works of art are painted or molded in the same forms which they had ten thousand years ago;—this is literally true and no exaggeration[25]—their ancient paintings and sculptures are not a whit better or worse than the work of to-day, but are made with just the same skill.—How extraordinary!—I should rather say, How statesmanlike, how worthy of a legislator! (*Laws* 656d–657a)

Things need to be set down in the new state in the same way.

b. Imposition of an Official Culture

Youth will always be obliged to sing the same music; the state should fix the program for the choruses, not caving in to fashion or conceding to the flying fancies of the public (653e–654a). "Nor shall any one dare to sing a song which has not been approved by the judgment of the guardians of the laws" (829de).

These arrangements will be completed by a state program of education. Most of the elements were already in the *Republic,* though Plato adds a few more tantalizing details in the *Laws.* The program should be implemented under the authority of a special magistrate, a "superintendent of education" of sorts, cloaked in honors and accorded the requisite discretionary powers.

c. A Fixed Number of Families, Equality of Lots, the Admissible Spread of Wealth

The other safeguard against internal change is the intangibility of the social and economic structures of the city. There will be 5,040 families, each with a dwelling and a plot of land. Since this is the "second-best" state, not the ideal one, a communist model will not predominate. Private property—or more exactly family property—will be the norm.

Here the notion of property is not the same as later in Roman law, a "right to use and abuse" in an "individualist" sense. The state retains eminent domain of the soil. It can reclaim the plots at will. Moreover, plots are inalienable: they cannot be transmitted, nor diminished or increased by means of bilateral exchanges, freely entered into by the beneficiaries.[26]

Neither can the land be shared among heirs. Each family will have a single heir. As for the other children, girls will be married off, and boys given to childless families.

If the overall population increases, the number of births will be reduced; if they cannot be reduced, the population surplus will be used to found new colonies. If the overall population

---

[24] Plato, it will be remembered, traveled to Egypt when he was about 40.

[25] Plato multiplies by four—in relation to his epoch—the antiquity of the Egyptian Empire.

[26] Consequently, a "property market" does not exist for the very reason that the whole purpose of the arrangement is to avoid the existence of the rich and the poor and the follow-on drift, of which Plato speaks in the *Republic,* namely a group of devil-may-care individuals, who become a sort of "lumpenproletariat," fostering discord and envy, until it becomes the army of the tyrant.

drops, a growth policy will be adopted.[27] The entire issue of population regulation will be placed in the hands of a high official, who will make use of the full range of solutions available to the state in such circumstances, including praise, reprimand, and coercion (*Laws* 740a–741a).

Not only will plots of land not significantly differ, money—another factor of inequality—will not be allowed either. Or rather, money will only be in circulation for trade; it will be forbidden to accumulate it (742a). Individuals authorized to travel abroad (see below) will be given the necessary money from the state. When they come back, they will return all remaining funds. Dowries will not exist. Interest-bearing loans will be forbidden under the threat of severe punishment.

This harsh assault against a liberal economy, against personal enrichment and every social change achieved in democratic Athens since the beginning of the fifth century BC, is, as far as Plato is concerned, justified by the aim he sets himself as a lawmaker. From the outset, his ambition for the state is the happiness of its citizens, not wealth and power. Happiness can only be achieved with virtue, and through social harmony or "fellowship"; both are undermined and destroyed by economic inequality.

Moreover, Plato speculates—without any hint of irony—that *virtuousness* is as impossible in a rich man as a poor man. The proof is as follows. It is possible to become rich justly and unjustly. A person, who resorts only to just means, will necessarily earn less than the one who combines the two means simultaneously. Furthermore, the virtuous individual will spend more because he will try to do what is good. For both reasons, his wealth will remain average. At the other end of the spectrum, the wasteful person will spend immoderately and impoverish himself. In the end, it is the absence of virtue that makes the rich person rich and the poor person poor; so, a virtuous man has only average wealth, and the government that maintains this middle position, averting excessive wealth and extreme poverty alike, will preserve virtue and achieve its goal (742d–743c).

Nevertheless, equality cannot be perfect: it will not be possible to prevent citizens—in the second-best state—from arriving in the new city with possessions and wealth acquired previously. Furthermore, distributive justice[28] implies that honors and offices cannot be distributed equally. There is a need for different classes ranked by a defined standard of wealth.

Plato recommends four classes. Individuals would move through the different classes as their wealth changes. The least rich will enjoy their plot of land and the income it produces (in any event, no less than this); the second will possess up to double this amount; the third class up to triple; and the fourth up to quadruple the amount. Any wealth in excess of this amount will go to the state, which will redistribute it. Penalties are foreseen for anyone attempting to keep the surplus for himself.

Plato is well aware that he will be accused of artificialism: he says, "all this is as if the legislator were telling his dreams, or making a city and citizens of wax" (746a). He also knows that the citizens are unlikely to accept any control of wealth and birth. Therefore, he accepts that there will be no perfect attainment of the goal; realism will prevail. The important thing is to come as close as possible to the goal.

---

[27] However, this policy will not extend to the risk of admitting immigrants into the community, even after a severe population collapse due to epidemics or wars; their education is simply too different from the local inhabitants (741a).

[28] Plato does not use this technical term. He speaks of "a law of inequality in proportion to his wealth" (or a "symmetrical inequality") and, elsewhere, of a "geometrical equality." See Plato, *Gorgias* 507e, trans. W. R. M. Lamb, in *Plato in Twelve Volumes,* vol. 3 (Cambridge, MA: Harvard University Press, 1925). But this is the basic idea of distributive justice (cf. below, pp. 564–65).

3. *Safeguards against Change from External Causes*

Similarly, the state will only remain itself over time if it is protected against change from external causes as well.

a. Distance from the Sea

It is calamitous for a city to be a harbor or to lie too close to the seaboard. Such a location virtually guarantees regular contact with foreign nations. Great danger—in the form of innovation, change, and pluralism—comes from such proximity. Here Plato is thinking about Athens and its port, Piraeus, whose location contrasted sharply with Sparta, situated geographically in the middle of its territories.

Without the necessary precautions a state faces the risk of "the sea filling the streets with merchants and shopkeepers, and begetting in the souls of men uncertain and unfaithful ways—making the state unfriendly and unfaithful both to her own citizens, and also to other nations" (*Laws* 705a). These threats increase with trade volume. They support the claim that a city should live as much as possible in economic self-sufficiency, even when it is close to the sea.

When a population lives near the sea, the risk is high that it will be harassed by a naval power and forced to pay a tribute (like the Athens of yore had to pay to Crete). The result is that the inhabitants imitate their tormentors and build their own ships; but then their best infantry soldiers—the *hoplites*—become sailors and, always quick to flee the fighting on their ships, invent any pretext to throw down their arms, which leads to the loss of the city. "Lions [trained to use triremes on the sea] might be trained in that way to fly from a herd of deer!" (707a).

Even if the city's navy succeeds in securing victory, the credit goes to the ship commanders and other sailing experts, in other words, to qualities of skillfulness, not to strength and courage. Furthermore, success is attributed to individuals, not to the group. For both these reasons, proximity to the sea is morally bad for the city. Lastly, Plato declares that, contrary to general belief, Salamis was not the decisive victory in the Persian wars; the true Greek victories were Marathon and Plataea, land victories, because "these battles by land made the Hellenes better." In estimating the goodness of a state, he says, we regard the moral value of its government, not its capacity to protect lives (707d). So, no harbor and no navy, or the very least possible, at any rate.

b. The Exclusion of Foreigners

The state in the *Laws,* deeply at odds with an open society, is encouraged to take all necessary precautions in its contacts with foreign nations and peoples.

"Now a state which makes money from the cultivation of the soil only, and has no foreign trade,[29] must consider what it will do about the emigration of its own people to other countries, and the reception of strangers from elsewhere" (949e).

The problem is, of course, that it is difficult to eliminate all contact, which would seem "ruthless and uncivilized." It is important that the city has a good reputation in the world (Plato attaches value to the moral judgment of foreigners, not because they are better than the native population, but because distance facilitates objective judgment) (949e–951a).

Here is what the law says: "In the first place, let no one be allowed to go anywhere at all into a foreign country who is less than forty years of age; and no one shall go in a private capacity" (950e).

As for travel abroad for reasons of state (not including military expeditions), it will be allowed only as embassies and delegations to the Panhellenic events, such as games and sacrifices in the sacred sanctuaries. Participation will promote the renown and glory of the city to the other

[29] This was the case of the Spartans, who left trade to the *periekos.*

Greeks. And when the delegates return home, they will teach the youth that the customs and laws of other states are inferior to their own.

There is one special form of foreign travel that the state should encourage: the study tour abroad. Some "inspired men," admittedly few in the world, have a deep grasp of the laws; it is worth seeking them out wherever they may be. Carefully selected citizens—Plato calls them "spectators"[30]—will be allowed to undertake foreign study tours. The applicants must be at least 50 years old, have an excellent "reputation, especially in war," and be "incorruptible." The "spectator" must return home before the age of 60—an age beyond which he may no longer have the strength to share what he has learned with the home community. His aim is to "establish more firmly institutions in his own state which are good already; and amend what is deficient; for without this examination and enquiry a city will never continue perfect any more than if the examination is ill-conducted."

Once again, contact with foreign lands is seen in terms of the preservation of the status quo, not innovation. Abroad, foreign sages may have discovered the root of corruption that causes even the closed state to decline, and this is what must be learned from them.

Upon his return home, the elders must determine if the spectator has become better or worse before he can meet with others in the community. If he has returned better, he will be praised and honored; if he has been "corrupted," he will be forbidden all contact with others. And if he does not accept this fate, he will be convicted in a court of law and sentenced to death "for interfering about education and the laws."

Finally, the welcome extended to visiting foreigners must be considered (*Laws* 952d–953e). There are "four kinds of strangers." The first kind, the merchants, come in summer, "like birds of passage [migratory birds], taking wing in pursuit of commerce" (buying and selling). They are welcome in marketplaces and harbors, but not within the city itself. They will be looked after by the appropriate trade officials, who will take care that they "shall not be allowed to make any innovation." The second kind are "tourists"; they visit the city out of curiosity. They will be welcomed very hospitably, but only by certain categories of citizens: the priests and ministers of the temples. The third kind of foreign visitor is one sent by his state on public business, either an ambassador or high official; he will be met by his counterpart with full public honors. Finally, Plato imagines that other states will also dispatch high-level "spectators" similar to those sent out by his ideal state on foreign study tours. They will be authorized to visit the high public officials of their choice for the purposes of their investigation.

But in none of these cases is the foreign visitor to be allowed direct contact with the population of the city. All contacts will be institutional. Individual liberty is completely banned from the system because it is a source of innovation, wrongdoing, and disorder.

4. *Totalitarian Supervision of Life*

To be effective, safeguards against internal and external changes must be coordinated by an all-embracing intelligence and implemented with a firm hand. This requires close supervision of every aspect of daily life. The state will keep close watch over the private morality of its citizens, a political affair that cannot be neglected. The state must "consider their pains and pleasures and desires, and the vehemence of all their passions; he should keep a watch over them, and blame and praise them rightly by the mouth of the laws themselves" (631).[31]

---

[30] *Translator's note:* Also translated as "overseas inspector" and "traveling inspector."

[31] In a curious passage (649b–650c), Plato says that the festivals can serve as "touchstones" to decide this. Officials will be dispatched to festivals to spy on the young and discover who drinks moderately and who excessively. Drunkenness momentarily removes fear and hesitation and enables a person's true character to shine forth. Some will show an aptitude for moderation, others will be boastful, lustful, and full of lies.

"The legislator has to be careful how the citizens make their money and in what way they spend it, and to have an eye to their mutual contracts and dissolutions of contracts" (*Laws* 632b).[32] This leads to a theory of the good use of *common meals* (the Spartan *syssitia*), *festivals, military exercises,* and *athletic games,* and the strict control of sexual unions. Thus, the state completes the efforts begun with public education on different registers.

It will ensure that there are at least 365 sacrifices per year, one a day. Thus, there is a "state religion," the product of collaboration between the guardians of the laws and the priests. The law will stipulate that there will be 12 celebrations in honor of the 12 gods, which give their names to each tribe (the city is divided into 12 tribes, each with 420 households; each tribe is dedicated to a god).[33] Each festival will perform the rites and sacrifices of the god it honors. It will include choruses as well as musical and gymnastic contests. Some of these will be reserved for women.

Each month at least one day will be set aside for military exercises, regardless of weather conditions. All citizens are concerned; for example, even women and children must train for the evacuation of the city. Not all cities follow this routine: many have gone soft in pursuit of wealth, which removes any "leisure" the citizen may have to reflect on the future (831c–832a). Such cities are not ruled by men with the true interests of its inhabitants at heart. They are ruled by factions pursuing the interests of one or only a few persons, or the mob; such factions depend on force and take care to avoid proper military training for the other portions of the population (832a–832d).

Each tribe will organize dances to enable young people of both sexes to meet, "seeing one another and being seen naked... [though] not transgressing the rules of modesty" (772a). The specifics of these entertainments will be ordered by those in charge and will be absolutely unchangeable (after an initial period of adjustment).

D. The Nocturnal Council

Such legislative measures can only be enacted by a superior authority, whose thought and action are inspired by the good. This is the role of the Nocturnal Council, the new incarnation of the government of the philosophers that Plato proposed in the *Republic* and the *Statesman.*

1. *Composition and Functions*

Plato is very clear as to the membership and functions of the Nocturnal Council, "the assembly of those who review the laws" (*Laws* 951d). It includes: (1) citizens "who have obtained the rewards of virtue"; (2) the ten oldest guardians of the law; (3) the "general superintendent" of education and his most recent predecessors.

Each of the senior members of the council sponsors a younger member, 30 to 40 years of age; his choice must be approved by the other council members (961b). If an unworthy junior

---

[32] In sum, it is absolute antiliberalism: the state is interested in every transaction, every contract, and, more generally, every interaction between citizens. Anything *social* is a *matter of state.* There is no distinction between private life and civic life. In the opinion of Plato, this is precisely the weakness of Spartan and Cretan institutions despite their reputations for authoritarianism: they are too liberal. They paid great attention to the conduct of their men on the battlefield, but they allowed them to live as they pleased in the city; in particular, they tolerated homosexuality and other sexual perversions (633 and following). They needed to be corrected on this score. Law and morality must coincide. There should be no distinction between a *civil order,* in which crimes and offenses are punished by the state authority, and a *moral order,* in which moral rewards and vices are sanctioned by praises and reprimands emanating from private individuals. The ideal city can choose to make praises and reprimands in certain instances, punishments in others. It alone has the prerogative, independently of the nature of the facts in question. The state has full responsibility for *all* social behavior.

[33] This is a return to the traditional organization, based on religion, which Cleisthenes sought to undo with the creation of his 10 tribes and his 10 *prytaneis* (his "secular" organization of the city). The 12 tribes occupy 12 districts organized in a star formation around the Acropolis. Each district includes an urban sector and a rural sector. Each of the 5,040 families is assigned to a tribe and receives an urban plot and a rural plot. The plots are equal in yield, though not in size.

member is chosen, the council will blame his sponsor. Note that the appointment of junior members is secret. Applications are impossible. A junior member learns that he has been considered for selection if and when the council confirms the appointment (*Laws* 961b).

The Nocturnal Council meets every morning between dawn and sunrise, "when everybody [is] most at leisure from all other business, whether public or private" (961c) (thus the word "nocturnal" used to designate the council throughout the text).

The items on the agenda of Nocturnal Council meetings include the making of laws and the type of government (thus, it is a "constitutional" council). In these discussions the council will use the information from abroad (the junior members of the council are required to absorb such information as is approved by the elders [952a–b]; this is one of the reasons for interrogating the spectators when they return from their travels).

The Nocturnal Council serves another no less important purpose. It supervises the House of Reformation: "There shall be three prisons in the state: the first of them is to be the common prison in the neighbourhood of the agora for the safe-keeping of the generality of offenders; another is to be in the neighbourhood of the nocturnal council, and is to be called the "House of Reformation"; another, to be situated in some wild and desolate region in the centre of the country, shall be called by some name expressive of retribution" (908a).

A certain category of impious men, unbelievers "with a righteous nature" (i.e., guilty only of not believing in the gods, but not of wrongdoing), will be imprisoned in the House of Reformation for no less than five years.

"And in the meantime let them have no intercourse with the other citizens, except with members of the nocturnal council, and with them let them converse with a view to the improvement of their soul's health. And when the time of their imprisonment has expired, if any of them be of sound mind let him be restored to sane company, but if not, and if he be condemned a second time, let him be punished with death" (909a).[34]

2. *Training Members for the Nocturnal Council*

Given these functions of the Nocturnal Council, it is not surprising that Plato attaches such great value to the philosophical training of its members, which he describes here again in the *Laws,* as earlier in the *Republic.* As one might expect, the members will be trained in mathematics and dialectics. But the *Laws* emphasizes that they must also know everything "respecting the gods," that is, "that they are, and... how great is their power." The council members will not be satisfied with the simple faith of a citizen, who believes because he must and by mere conformism. They must be fully convinced of the great truths of religion by reason and intellectual proofs, even at the risk of appearing impious in the eyes of vulgar citizens. Plato sums this up as follows:

> No man can be a true worshipper of the Gods who does not know these two principles—that *the soul is the eldest of all things which are born,* and *is immortal and rules over all bodies;* moreover, as I have now said several times,[35] he [the future ruler] who has not contemplated *the mind of nature* which is *said to exist in the stars,* and gone through the previous training, and seen the connection of music with these things, and harmonized them all with laws and institutions [moral conduct], is not able to give a reason of such things as have a reason. (967d)

[34] This form of "reeducation" or "brainwashing" will reappear in the Inquisition and in other totalitarian regimes. Like all regimes founded on an ideology rather than "values," the government needs to persuade its opponents. It eliminates them only as a last resort. A dissident who dies in defense of his convictions is more dangerous than one who is alive and can still be converted.

[35] Plato discussed this at length in book 10.

The guardians must not only *recognize* such essential truths, they must *formulate* them as well. As Plato puts it: "to *consider* only and to be unable to set forth what [one] think[s]...that would be the state of a slave."

Lastly, in addition to contemplating and formulating the good, proper rulers must be able to *perform* it, which is to say, they must be exemplary in their attitude and behavior themselves. But this is not sufficient in itself: virtuous but uneducated men are of no use to the state (966d). See 967a: "he who is unable to acquire this in addition to the ordinary virtues of a citizen, can hardly be a good ruler of a whole state; but he should be the subordinate of other rulers."

3. *The Nocturnal Council: The Guiding Intelligence of the City*

The Nocturnal Council is the anchor point of the city; it keeps it from drifting. It can do this because it is the city's "head," its brain, that is, *intelligence,* as well as its *eyes* and *ears;* also because it knows the ambition and aim the city has set itself (see *Laws* 960b–968b). Plato says, "In a ship, when the pilot and the sailors unite their perceptions with the piloting mind, do they not save both themselves and their craft?" (961e).

It is the same for an army (the general and the soldiers join forces) or a medical team (the physician and his assistants pull together). In all three cases—the ship, the army, and the medical team—the heads are worthy of their function and rank because they understand the *aim:* reaching the harbor for the captain, victory for the army, the patient's health for the physician. They ensure the constant pursuit of the aim. The statesman must also know the *aim of the state* (962b); otherwise, the government will behave erratically.

"There is nothing wonderful in states going astray—the reason is that their legislators have such different aims" (962e). For example, some laws fix that certain citizens should have political authority in the state, but they do not ensure that these individuals are virtuous or not. Other laws focus on ensuring prosperity, but lawmakers seem not to care about the "enslavements" that may result from this. Still other laws aim to achieve liberty for the citizens, often at the price of eliminating liberty for other peoples.

The absolutely coherent thinking of the Nocturnal Council will preserve the state from these contradictions. The Council must not allow its aims to "keep shifting...among a number of objects, but [must] concentrate its gaze always on one particular mark, and at that one mark to shoot, as it were, all its arrows continually" (Bury, 962d).

Plato theorizes that the aim of the state is "virtue [which is] of four kinds [courage, prudence, temperance, and justice]" (963a).

These virtues are both different and the same. This is evident in the fact that they have four different names (courage, prudence, temperance, and justice) and, at the same time, one single name: virtue.[36] It is important to recognize "which [principle] is the same in all the four—the same, as we affirm, in courage and in temperance, and in justice and in prudence, and which, being one, we call as we ought, by the single name of virtue" (965c–d).

What is the same in all four is that they all pursue a good. In a sense, they all share in a single idea of the good, that strange reality first encountered in the *Republic.* In the end, the government of the city should aim for the good, as the captain aims for the harbor.

Since these matters are the concern of only a tiny elite with special training and unique talents and aptitudes, we can easily understand why the council must be *nocturnal:* since the arguments supporting its legislative decisions will be intelligible only to the elite, this government by an elite must also be free from public control, which otherwise would put pressure on it to lower itself to

---

[36] Plato discussed the unity of virtues on different occasions: in *Protagoras* (329a and following), in *Menon* (throughout), in book 4 of the *Republic* (4.427d–434d), and in the *Statesman* (306a and following).

a level where the multitude can understand and approve. That said, there will be a *diurnal council* to appease the multitude; it will be public and accountable to public opinion for its decisions, but its authority will extend only to second-order decisions or insignificant matters.

Thus, Plato pursues the same *antidemocratic,* or indeed *anticivic* argument set out earlier in the *Republic.*

IV. Conclusion

Such, then, are the ideas that Plato bequeaths to the Western political tradition. Curiously, his political thought has had an unusual echo in French education in the modern period. While Lepeletier de Saint-Fargeau adopted the Spartan model of *agoge* and Plato's fantasy of removing children from the cultural influence of their parents as a central component of his "fascist" program for French youth—with the enthusiastic approval of the National Convention[37]—Lakanal's public statements (or more probably Dominique-Joseph Garat's), which paved the way for founding an *Ecole normale supérieure* in France, were similarly inspired by Plato, particularly his theory of "souls of gold" and government by the elite.[38] Thus, in France, Lakanal established the ideology of the *grandes écoles* and the government of a state in the hands of the "old boys" of these institutions.

Plato's arguments against *demagogy* remain true today. Modern politicians, who govern with opinion polls, correspond exactly to Plato's definition of the demagogue (one who studies the desires and changes of heart of "the beast," i.e., the *demos*). Likewise, Plato's initial intuition—that the state should be ruled by individuals who study the real issues and not their images or reflections in public opinion, who promote the long-term general interest rather than give in to the demands of pressure groups and an electorate unaware of its own interests—remains perfectly valid today as well. On the other hand, because he saw only the rule of illusion, confusion, and disorder in the institutions of democracy—that is, liberty of speech; critical pluralism; and social, political, and economic freedoms—Plato traveled down an antiscientific path and planted the seeds of totalitarian politics.

Perhaps the root of the problem lies in the fact that Plato adopted a model of scientism based exclusively on mathematics rather than on physics and the experimental sciences. Mathematics is apodictic—necessarily true and logically certain—it requires dogmatism, because it provides its own arguments. In contrast, the experimental sciences depend on a confrontation with an ontological exteriority. Plato imagined that political science was aprioric, like mathematics, whereas his pupil, Aristotle, and most of the great political thinkers after him, imagined political science to be experimental.

Still, Plato's ideal remains magnificent in its intention. If it is necessary to monitor every act and thought of the members of the community; if it is important to hunt down each and every deviation from the *nomos,* the reason is, as Christian Jambet observes, that

> the *nomos* expresses the providence of the gods, who in turn move the stars according to the laws of the universal Soul. Their providence finds expression in the tiniest of things, and these gods are models or generators of the virtues (wisdom, temperance, justice,

[37] Cf. Bronislaw Baczko, ed., *Une éducation pour la démocratie: Textes et projets de l'époque révolutionnaire* [An education for democracy: Texts and proposals from the revolutionary era] (Paris: Garnier, 1982), 345–87.

[38] Ibid., 471–82.

> fortitude). In keeping with this theodicy, nothing happens for just one person alone; rather it is this singular person that gives itself and owes itself to the universe. Each part is made for the whole rather than the whole being made for each part. This shows what is at stake in the struggle between virtue and vice: to be virtuous is to hold one's place in the order of the world that the King of the world providentially created to remove disorder and vice.... In this philosophical conception of the world, crime is never a crime against humanity; it is a crime against the divinity of the gods and against the deification of the human soul.[39]

The individual soul does not have its own existence; it is not a subject. The true subject is virtue, "a lone generator, like the Idea-Number. It cannot be said of a person that he is virtuous in the sense that he is predicated with a particular virtue, but he participates in the generator of virtue, he *proceeds* from it. He is the subject of the virtue, because the virtue is, as such, his true subject."[40]

For this reason the part must be subordinated to the whole, not so that it will be crushed or overwhelmed by it, but for its deification, its happiness, its life, so that it can be "transported along a holy path to a new and better place," so that it can return toward the One from which it proceeds.

It would be pointless to accuse Plato of some moral failing for the reason that his political vision clearly subverts our liberal ideas about society and the state (ideas that, one way or another, call for the political "whole" to serve the human "part"). Two additional revolutions (that we will study below) will have to occur before such ideas can emerge: the development of the individual human person in the protective framework of private Roman law, and the gift of biblical prophecy enabling man to reject and oppose any earthly injunction that might be contrary to ethics. Plato the thinker was necessarily ignorant of these innovations, and, moreover, he did not anticipate them, contrary to some of his contemporaries and his predecessors from the "Great Generation of the Open Society."

---

[39] Christian Jambet, "Le côté sombre de la loi, communication au Colloque Crimes et Vertus" [The dark side of the law, a conference communication at the Colloquium on Crimes and Virtues], *Corbières matin, Cahier philosophique*, Aug. 11, 1997; italics added.

[40] Ibid.

Chapter 3

Aristotle

Aristotle occupies a paramount place in the history of political ideas, not only for the range and robustness of his theories of society and state, formulated in his immense masterpiece *Politics,* but also for the relevance of his theories to thirteenth century thinkers in their efforts to restore the state on a natural basis against the tenets of "political Augustinism."

Life

Aristotle (384–322 BC) was born in Stageira, an ancient Ionian colony on the east coast of Chalcidice.[1] His father, Nicomachus (not to be confused with the addressee of the *Nicomachean Ethics,* Aristotle's son), was the personal physician to King Amyntas II of Macedon, father of Philip. Young Aristotle went to Athens in 366, at the age of 18, and entered the Academy as a pupil. He rubbed shoulders with the great orators of the age, among them Isocrates. Though Aristotle soon became Plato's favorite, it was Speusippus who followed the master as *scolarch* of the Academy upon his death in 348. Aristotle then left the Academy and Athens to teach at the court of the tyrant Hermias of Atarneus (also a former pupil of the Academy) in Assos, Asia Minor. There he pursued his studies in natural history and "sociology." Next he traveled to Mytilene on the island of Lesbos. In 343 he became tutor to the 13-year-old son of Philip of Macedon, the future Alexander the Great, a position he held for three years.

At the age of 50, Aristotle returned to Athens and established his own school, the *Lyceum,* named for its proximity to the temple of Lycian Apollo. The school grounds had colonnades through which Aristotle strolled as he lectured. This led to the name "the Peripatetics," used in later years to designate the pupils of the Lyceum. Before long the school rivaled the Academy, which continued to function under Speusippus, and then Xenocrates. Moreover, the Lyceum did not have permanent facilities like the Academy, and Aristotle resorted to subsidies from

[1] This section is drawn from Joseph Moreau, *Aristote et son école* [Aristotle and his school] (Paris: Presses Universitaires de France, 1962).

Alexander, who at the time ruled over Greece after the Macedonian victory at Cheronaea in 338 BC. But Alexander died in 323, and the national party raised its head again. Aristotle, a friend of the Macedons, took himself into exile in Euboea with his son, Nicomachus, to avoid the fate imposed on Socrates, adding, "I will not allow Athenians to wrong philosophy twice." Aristotle died in 322 at the age of 62.

Work

Aristotle left an enormous body of work, though only a fraction of his thinking and writing actually survive. His work can be divided into *exoteric* writings (intended for the general public) and *esoteric* or *acroamatic* writings (texts for a restricted audience). In the first century BC, his works were collected into a vast *Corpus Aristotelicum* by Andronicus of Rhodes, the tenth successor of Aristotle as the head of the Lyceum. Texts were collected from different places throughout the Mediterranean.

The corpus is structured into five categories:

1. *Organon,* his writings on logic.
2. Physics, his writings on the study of nature: *Physics* (a total of eight books), *On the Heavens, On Generation and Corruption, Meteorology* (on weather phenomena); *On the Soul* (introduction to the study of life), *Parva naturalia* (Little physical treatises), *History of Animals, Parts of Animals, Movement of Animals, Generation of Animals* (five books, a treatise on embryology).
3. Metaphysical writings (the term is not from Aristotle but from the expression *meta ta physica*, proposed by the authors of the corpus to refer to writings that came "after" the writings on physics): *Metaphysics.*
4. Ethics and politics: *Nicomachean Ethics, Eudemian Ethics, Magna Moralia* (Great ethics); *Politics,* the *Athenian Constitution* (a modern addition to the *Corpus Aristotelicum*).
5. Works of applied philosophy: rhetoric and poetics: *Rhetoric* (dialectics, the art of persuasion), *Poetics* (on education).

I. Aristotle's Conception of Nature

We will see that, for Aristotle, the city is not a human creation, but a "natural" organism. The meaning of this term is very precise in Aristotle's philosophy; it is, therefore, necessary to clarify his idea of nature before we turn to his *Politics.*

A. Criticism of Plato's Theory of Ideas

Aristotle was opposed to the idealism and pan-mathematicism of the Platonists. His own starting point is medicine, not mathematics. He is, first and foremost, a naturalist and a biologist. As far as he is concerned, the actual individual is no less real than ideas and numbers. In fact, he is *ousia,* substance itself.

Now this poses a problem. Plato had a reason for ascribing ontological value to intelligible matter: he thought that science was impossible if it focuses on things that "become." Aristotle admits the epistemological side of the argument: scientific demonstrations require necessary, universal concepts and cannot be made with singular sensible beings. But he rejects the ontological side of the argument: if science can have no other object than the universal, it is not necessary for the universal to be *separate.* Aristotle holds as absurd the notion that the world of ideas duplicates the world of phenomena. If the idea is separate, it cannot be cause. This leads to his famous "third man argument": if an idea were a substance, it would be an individual (a single being). Therefore, it would add to the individual sensible man, and the two together would participate in (i.e., have the form of) a *third* idea of man, and so on into infinity.

There are, indeed, intelligible realities, but they are immanent in sensible beings: they are their *form*.

B. Matter and Form

Form (*morphe* or *eidos*, i.e., "idea") is the organizing principle of matter. As far as form is concerned, a distinction must be made between beings created by art (*techne*) and by nature (*physis*). In the case of *techne*, the woodworker, for example, gives his wood the form of a "bed" or a "table": form is brought to the matter from outside. But for beings by nature, form is immanent in the matter and appears in and through the process of generation.

In both cases, the union of matter and form will be *substance* (*ousia*), that is, what possesses being to the highest degree; in other words, *substance* will be the actual individual, or the particular sensible being. This is where Aristotle parts company with Plato completely. (True, Aristotle hesitates in his work to some extent: in some places he says that *ousia* is a category, the species; but that does not make him a Platonist, because if the species differs from one of its individual models, it is not as such a separate form, an archetype; it exists only embodied in actual individuals.)

C. Becoming

The Aristotelian world divides into two: a *supralunar* world (meteors, planets, fixed stars in the heavens) and a *sublunar* world (everything on earth). The sublunar world is subject to generation and corruption, that is, to the phenomenon of becoming.

Beings, subject to becoming, are beings in which form does not exist permanently and to the same extent in matter. For a living being, becoming involves acquiring form (generation) and losing it (corruption). Becoming is not merely time; it is a continuous process of movement from the seed to the fully realized individual, from *dynamis* (potential) to *energeia* (actuality). A grain of corn is an ear of corn "in potential," which at harvest time becomes an ear "in actuality."

Note that, if potential precedes actuality, actuality also precedes potential. The form that achieves its perfection through becoming is not created by becoming. Before the child, who is a man in potential, there is the father, a man in actuality, who begets the child. God, however, is pure actuality.

Therefore, becoming is the tendency of all beings existing under the potency of generation and corruption to realize, unfold, and complete their form (in the sense of making the form perfect, *per-factum*, entirely made).

Now, in this endeavor, beings may succeed more or less well, because becoming is as *contingent* as it is *necessary:* the Aristotelian world, in contrast with the mechanistic sphere of the moderns, leaves ample room for contingency, that is, the unexpected.

A being is naturally under the obligation of its particular form: a child of a man cannot become a horse, and vice versa; an ostrich egg cannot become a duck, and so on. The form of a species never changes: the Aristotelian world is fixed; there is no place for Lamarckism or Darwinism, for adaptive changes or the evolution of the species (and none for historical progress or social "transformation" either). Becoming concerns only specific individuals, not species and their form.

However, it is not absolutely necessary that a given individual reaches perfection or achieves his or her particular form. A boy can experience normal growth and become a fully developed person, or he may fail to achieve the perfection of his form: he may be distorted, too small, too big, too fat, too skinny, and so on; he may even die before reaching adulthood because of contingent circumstances by accident. Both necessity and contingency contribute to the phenomenon of becoming.

Generally speaking, a natural being can fail to achieve the perfection of its form in two ways: either by *excess* (too much) or by *defect* (too little). Perfection is a *middle course* (here, "middle course" does not mean a compromise or a void between two positive extremes; to the contrary, it is positivity itself, because it is the perfection of the form).[2]

Whether a being attains perfection or not depends on contingent elements or *accidents:* a plant can germinate in fertile or arid soil; it may or may not receive water or light, be well or poorly attended, and so on. Now, Aristotle says, although there is a *science* of necessity (which consists of the knowledge of forms and substances), there cannot be a science of accidents. The Aristotelian world is not a mechanism: everything is not "written." This is why it makes sense, indeed why it is useful to develop *practical* sciences like ethics, rhetoric, and politics. Therefore, by the most exact knowledge possible of the essences, by studying the various attainments of these essences (for example, the myriads of particular individuals who ever lived,[3] examples of failures, of "monsters," of persons who failed to steer the "middle course" due to excess or defect), it is possible to guide human activity to the best possible degree amid the hazards of becoming and strive to genuinely improve one's fate and the fate of one's fellow citizens.

D. The Good and Happiness

For a natural being, everything that contributes to the perfection of its nature is *good*; everything to the contrary is *bad*. Moreover, in Aristotelian ethics and politics, the good is *defined* as the natural and the bad as the unnatural. There are no other criteria.

Nature has provided beings with *signals* that enable them to recognize which actuality is in keeping with their nature and which actuality guides them toward the perfection of their form: *pleasure* for animals, *happiness* for rational beings like humans (happiness and pleasure are not the same; our attainment of happiness can—indeed often does—imply forsaking pleasure when reason demands or requires it). Again, a definition of happiness results: for humans, happiness is what accompanies every act leading to a perfected nature as a human being.

So, Aristotelian ethics and politics are not in the least "ascetic." If toil is necessary to nurture virtues, to create beautiful, well-balanced, properly developed cities, the reason is to ensure a happy person and a happy city. The moralist and the politician must act like the horticulturist, who tends a beautiful plant with gentle, loving care: if the plant grows and flowers, if it is pleasing to the eye, the aim has been achieved. This can be seen in the splendor of the fully blossomed flower. Its splendor is the measure that signals the full attainment of its form. There is nothing more. The flower blossoms *for the sake* of blossoming and fructifying. Nature asks no more of it. The same is true of the moralist and the politician: the full "perfection" of the nature of human beings and the city is the end in itself. And happiness is the criterion of success (as we shall

[2] The "perfection" of a being of Aristotelian nature is not unique like the Platonic idea. A Platonic idea is an ideal; by definition, a sensible being is too different, too estranged, too fallen in regard to the ideal. There are myriads of sensible beings, but only one ideal. In contrast, Aristotle's perfect form is achieved only in and by individuals. There simply is no external model against which it can be said that one individual is more perfect than another. All that can be said is that a person is "right in the middle," that he or she is not a pathological reject, a failure, a monster. For every species there are several pathologies, as well as several paths to perfection, and several perfections. There are several kinds of beautiful women, several types of accomplished athletes. In this sense, Aristotle's theory is less inflexible than Plato's, more open to a plurality of becomings. This will have its importance when we discuss cities and political regimes. Aristotelian theory will become the model for moderate political theories, just as Plato's theory is the paradigm for radical theories.

[3] In addition to the *Athenian Constitution,* it is thought that Aristotle wrote or supervised the writing of some 160 studies of constitutions existing in Greece or in countries known to Greece.

see, the virtues of an individual and the virtues of the city are both conditions; there can be no individual happiness in a mean city, no thriving city with mean citizens). The ultimate goal for Aristotelian human beings is to be honored (to have a reputation for virtue) in an honorable city. This was the hope of every Greek in the classical age, and indeed of all Ancients until the onset of Christianity.

E. Virtue and Vice

Since our happiness is achieved in the perfection of our nature, and since there are accidents (and therefore contingencies) in the world of becoming that can impede this outcome, we must lead our lives in keeping with reason, which enables us to recognize the essence of human nature and to discern what does and does not agree with it. Aristotle is aware, on the one hand, of *the limits of human reason;* in this respect he does not share the faith of the Pythagoreans or the Platonists in the capacity of discursive intelligence to recognize the intimate nature of these essences; he is too much of a naturalist and too familiar with the rich complexity and diversity of reality for that. On the other hand, he is aware of the *power of passions,* which sometimes overwhelm reason.

Aristotle uses concepts known before his time, but to which he contributes his own robust ideas, which have come down to us over the centuries. Two in particular require our attention: the idea of *disposition* (*hexis, habitus*), and that of *vice* and *virtue.*

Habitus is a *disposition to behave in a particular way.* It is ingrained in us, such that in certain types of situations we behave in this or that way *without needing to engage discursive thought.* Its presence within us may exist because one day we desired it and we intentionally trained for it, or, conversely, because we failed to establish certain habits and others filled the gap more or less "on their own." At any rate, now that we have this disposition, it influences our action *spontaneously,* without our having to think about it. In fact, it can even cause us to act in a certain way although our conscience warns against it.

Thus, dispositions are an *intermediate* psychic link between the conscious and the subconscious, between our reason (which is free) and our passions (to which we are subservient). On the one hand, dispositions are accessible to reason; we can decide to acquire them or fight them. On the other hand, they escape reason because once our nature is ingrained it is no longer up to our reason alone to free us from something that causes us to act in certain ways against our will, particularly in critical circumstances where we have neither the time nor the strength to reason, which is why the ingrained pattern is so decisive.

By definition, *virtues* are dispositions that cause us to act in the *right* sense, that is, in the sense of the perfection of our nature. *Vices* are dispositions that induce us to act in the *wrong* sense.

It is the duty of each person to develop suitably robust virtues such that, whatever life's circumstances, including confrontations with the most complex and urgent problems, he acts spontaneously to preserve and perfect his human nature. A bad person is one who "lets himself go," who does not fight early inclinations to act wrongly. Locked into wrong choices, he turns increasingly away from his nature and stands helplessly by as happiness eludes him. Conversely, virtues are to be understood as a succor to achieve happiness (again there is nothing ascetic about the Aristotelian concept of "virtue").[4]

Human nature encompasses a range of virtues organized around four prime virtues, or "cardinal" virtues.[5] The list of these virtues has been fixed since Socrates and Plato: prudence (wisdom), justice, courage (fortitude), and temperance (restraint). Courage and temperance are permanent

---

[4] "Virtue" comes from the Latin *virtus,* which translates the Greek *arete,* for which the best translation is "excellence."

[5] *Cardo,* in Latin, means "hinge." The cardinal virtues are ones on which all others "hinge."

dispositions, which enable us to regulate, respectively, our *irascible* and *concupiscible* passions. Justice enables us to adjust the dispositions of those of our actions that affect others (it is the highest *social* virtue). Prudence is the virtue that enables us to regulate reason itself.

II. Politics

Aristotle wrote his *Politics* near the end of his life, after the *Nicomachean Ethics*. It consists of eight books, the order of which is disputed.[6]

A. Man, the "Political Animal"

Aristotle describes the city [*polis*] as the most perfect form of human community, one in which man can and must realize his nature. He also shows that the city is itself a natural phenomenon. Contrary to the Sophists' argument, the city is not an artificial or conventional creation. It is natural, spontaneous, and necessary. *It was not created or invented by man; on the contrary, man finds it complete when he comes to life*. Aristotle adds, "every City (polis) is a species of association (*koinônia*)... [but the polis is the most] inclusive association of all."

"The most inclusive" of all associations: the Greeks of the classical age could not imagine that cities might be gathered into a larger body, such as the Hellenic nation, or into something larger still, such as humankind.

1. *The Polis, a "Community of Communities"*

What are these communities that the city encompasses? They are of different levels. What they share in common, Aristotle says, is that they are made up of *different, complementary* elements, which in association produce the *common good* of the group. The primary association is "a union or pairing of those who cannot exist without one another, male and female."

The common good here is "reproduction" (1252a). Next comes "the union of the naturally ruling element with the element which is naturally ruled," meaning, the master and the slave. The common good is "the preservation of both." These "elementary associations" combine to form the *family* or household, where there is man and woman, parents and children, masters and servants. Then several households form a community at the next, higher level, the *village*. Again a distinction is made: the village is "governed by the eldest of kin," and all households are fixed in place "in virtue of the kinship between their members."[7]

This, Aristotle observes, was the model for monarchy, which is the form of government of a community whose ruling "father" is by nature different from the other members of the community. It is only the community, formed from a number of villages, that is the city in the real sense. It is like the parts of a Russian doll: all are of differing sizes, each with a distinctive body. Several implications for political theory result from this.

1. The Aristotelian city, unlike in modern political theory, is not a direct association of *individuals;* it is an association of *groups*. There are several intermediaries—several "natural

---

[6] *Translator's note: The Politics of Aristotle,* trans. Ernest Barker (Oxford: Clarendon Press, 1948); hereafter cited in the text. On occasion we quote from Benjamin Jowett's translation (Oxford: Oxford University Press, 1905), which will be noted in the text.

[7] Sometimes Aristotle inserts an additional level between the village and the city: the tribe, a pre-civil form of social organization.

communities"—between the individual and the state. It would be against the essential nature of the city to eliminate them. And it would result in the city reverting to an inferior form of human community, one less developed and more anomic.

2. The evolution from village to city is not a quantitative issue. Aggregating a few villages will not produce a city; or to say it differently, a city is not just a village bigger than others. The difference is *qualitative* in that the whole formed by the villages is of a radically different *nature* or *structure*. This new form or essence is defined notably by *autarkeia* (self-sufficiency), which means the existence of a sufficiently advanced and complex division of labor such that the city can satisfy its own needs and do without the outside world completely. This is because the city is self-sufficing; it presents all the necessary functions for independent living: agriculture and the mechanical arts, warfare capability, liberal arts, magistrates and judges, and so on. In contrast, a household or village is not autarkic.

3. Modern sociologists would refer to the various constituent communities of the city—and, for that matter, the city itself—as *systems* (it could be argued that Aristotle more or less invented the modern epistemological concept of "system"). Communities are made up of separate elements, which cannot exist independently of each other; accordingly, they must accept and cultivate their distinctiveness. For example, "the female and the slave are *naturally* distinguished" (from male and master). This is for *their* good. The common good is profitable to each part, whichever part participates. By completely assuming his or her function, even an inferior one, the individual works toward *his or her own happiness*.

All of this is the will of nature; if it were not, nature would not have taken pains to differentiate beings—*men* and *women*, men with *more capability* and men with *less capability*, *men* and *animals*, *animals* and *plants*, and so on. For Aristotle all of nature is *hierarchical*: each natural being has its place in these hierarchies. Moreover, its raison d'être is to serve other beings on the next level higher up, and so on, up to the person, the rational being, who occupies the top of the hierarchy. Because, as Aristotle puts it rather nicely, "Nature makes nothing in a spirit of stint [i.e., a small-minded way], as smiths do when they make the Delphic knife[8] to serve a number of purposes: she makes each separate thing for a separate end." But to repeat, by serving its superior, each being serves the organic whole, of which he and his superior are a part, and thereby he serves his own personal good.

2. *The Role of the "Polis" is to Fulfill Humankind's Nature*

The family enables men and women to live (*zen*), and its purpose is life and reproduction. The city does more: it enables men and women to live well (*eu zen*), to fulfill their proper purpose implied by their nature; in other words, the fulfillment of *human* nature.

People do not associate merely for material prosperity; if that were the case, a group of animals would be a state. Nor do they unite merely to form a defensive alliance against all forms of injustice, or simply for commercial purposes, because otherwise Tyrrhenians and Carthaginians and all merchant people would be citizens of a single state (see *Politics* 3.9). This is, of course, not the case: they may share contracts in common, but they do not share common magistracies for the enforcement of contracts. And no allied state is preoccupied with justice within the other states of the alliance. Thus, a state is manifestly more than an economic union. "[A] polis is not an association for residence on a common site, or for the sake of preventing mutual injustice and

[8] The Delphic knife was a multipurpose one like a Swiss army knife.

easing exchange.[9] These are indeed conditions which must be present before a polis can exist; but the presence of all these conditions is not enough, in itself, to constitute a polis" (*Politics* 3.12).[10]

For a city to be a city it must promote the good life for people, that is, it must help them to attain their own good, which is the fulfillment of their nature. "What constitutes a polis is an association of households and clans in a good life, for the sake of attaining a perfect and self-sufficing existence" (3.12). Several noneconomic factors are necessary for this:

> This consummation [fulfillment], however, will not be reached unless the members *inhabit one and the self-same place* and *practice intermarriage*. It was for this reason [i.e., to provide these necessary conditions] that the various institutions of a common social life—*marriage-connexions, kin-groups* [phratries],[11] *religious gatherings,*[12] *and social pastimes* generally—arose in cities. But these institutions are *the business of friendship*[13] [and not the purpose of the polis]. It is friendship [and not a polis] which consists in the pursuit of a common social life. The end and purpose of a polis is the good life, and the institutions of social life are means to that end. (*Politics* 3.12)

This brings us to Aristotle's famous formulation: "the state is a creation of nature, and man is by nature a political animal [*zoon politikon*].[14]

For a proper understanding of this definition, it should be remembered that, in Aristotle's judgment, science involves an exhaustive description of essences. Science must distinguish each species by its particular genus and particular differentia within the genus. The genus of "humans" is "animal" and the particular differentia or characteristic is "political" ("an animal intended to live in a polis"); it is what *characterizes* humans and is their true *nature*.

This definition means, in effect, that the fact that humans live in a city (or state) is not something that *adds* to their nature (an accident). It is a constituent attribute of their essence. A human being who is not also a citizen is inconceivable.

Proof to the contrary is that a person who lives outside the city (unless he or she has been exiled or has exiled himself or herself for some reason) is subhuman or superhuman. Separated from the city, such a person is like a member separated from the body. An arm cut off from the body is not an arm; it is a cadaver of an arm or, as Aristotle says, a "homonym" of an arm. Similarly, a human separated from the city would resemble a human, have the name of a human, but would not be a human.[15]

Aristotle adds that human beings are not mere *social* animals in the sense of social insects like bees.[16] Because "nature makes nothing in vain; and man alone of animals is furnished with the faculty of language (*logos*). The mere making of sounds serves to indicate pleasure and pain, and is thus a faculty that belongs to animals in general.... But language serves to declare what

---

[9] As some modern liberals think. Apparently, theories of this type existed already at the time of Aristotle.

[10] Aristotle might have said that it is not enough to create a European economic community for Europe to be a genuine state. What is precisely needed *in addition* will become clear in the following development.

[11] Associations of *genē*. A *genos* is an extended family, the association of all families with a common agnatic ancestor, i.e., a relative by the male line.

[12] One of the rare allusions to religion in Aristotle's *Politics*.

[13] Aristotle analyzes *philia* at length in his *Nicomachean Ethics*, trans. H. Rackham (Cambridge, MA: Harvard University Press, 1926); unless otherwise noted, this edition is hereafter cited in the text. The concept of *philia* undermines Plato's communism, as we will see below, pp. 124–26.

[14] *Zoon politikon* can also be translated as "civic animal." *Translator's note:* Translation by Jowett; Ernest Barker translates the same sentence as follows: "the polis belongs to the class of things that exist by nature, and... man is by nature *an animal intended to live in a polis.*"

[15] There is something almost therapeutic in Aristotle's observation. Had he personally observed, or had it been reported to him, that a person living alone becomes insane?

[16] The human being is a *zoon politikon*, a "political" animal, and not *koinonikon*, a "social" animal.

is advantageous and what is the reverse, and it therefore serves to declare what is just and what is unjust."

Now why is it that a sense of what is *just* and *unjust* is essential to fulfill a person's nature? And why is it that the question of justice is posed only in a civic context? These questions take us to the heart of Aristotle's argument.

3. *Citizen's Justice*

As we saw, human beings attain their fulfilled nature if their soul possesses all the necessary virtues (in the same way that their body achieves perfection if, and only if, every member and organ develops fully). Justice occupies the preeminent place among the virtues. It is the perfect virtue: *arete teleia* (*Nicomachean Ethics* 5). One can be courageous and temperate without being just, but it is impossible to be just without being courageous, temperate, and wise. For example, if intemperance leads a person to commit adultery, that person will behave not only intemperately but also unjustly. Likewise, a coward in combat will be unjust toward comrades in arms. Thus, it can be said of a truly just person that he or she possesses all the virtues, but the contrary is not true. In this sense, justice is the preeminent, all-embracing virtue. Only the just person will realize the essence of humankind.

But to be *just* one must live in a relationship with others. It is not possible to be just on one's own. Justice is a social virtue that regulates *those actions of ours that affect others* (as opposed to courage, temperance, and prudence, which contribute to our personal equilibrium). Moreover, to be *fully* just, one must live in a community where individuals are and remain *equal,* because justice is always a *form of equality,* whether "distributive" (consisting of a justice that provides each with the portion of common good equal to one's contribution) or "commutative" (which requires that, in an exchange, the things exchanged are of equal value).[17] The problem is that *equal individuals are found only in the city,* that is, a community where *isonomia*—equality before the law—exists. *Isonomia* does not exist in the household, the village, the tribe, or in monarchies. Thus, the city is *the only place where the development of one's humanity can be achieved fully.* It is in this sense that the essence of the human being is as a "political animal."[18]

From this it can be deduced, perhaps, that the barbarian, who lives only in monarchies and tribes, and who cannot be just in the full sense, is possibly less than human.[19]

---

[17] On the topic of distributive and commutative justice, cf. below, pp. 564–65.

[18] One question remains that is dealt with in book 7 of the *Politics*. There are two types of perfection: *scientific* (or "contemplative") life and *active* (or "political") life. Advocates of the former claim that it is the true "free" life, because it is a life liberated from action; an active life is not free because it is slavish. Advocates of the active life claim that it is impossible for one who *does* nothing to do *good*. Aristotle holds that each position recognizes only a part of the truth. Action is necessary because happiness is found only in activity; but freedom is also necessary because without freedom there is no "nobility." Therefore, one must seek out political power on the condition that, given the rivalries caused by politics, one does not practice "plunder and violence," which is not compatible with virtue (Aristotle, like Cicero after him, refutes (so to speak) Machiavelli before the fact: whatever good a politician does while in a position of power will not justify any reprehensible acts committed to gain power [see 1325b.5–6). Moreover, action and contemplation are not incompatible if it is noted that the statesman, like the architect, uses thought to direct the action of others. In this sense, political action remains noble and free. Otherwise, it will be necessary to admit that God, who clearly acts, but only by directing the action of others, occupies a position lower than human beings, which is patently absurd. In the end, the good city is one in which politicians enable peace and justice to prevail so that sages can contemplate the essences.

[19] Like the other Greeks of the classical age, Aristotle had a flattering view of his culture (we noted the first formal expression of this in the writings of Herodotus). We could almost call it "ethnocentrism" if the ideal that it expresses were not, by nature, *universalizable,* as shown by Stoic cosmopolitanism and the spread of Greek culture (*paideia*) throughout the Hellenistic and Roman world.

B. A Theory of Slavery

Let us return briefly to the household. We saw that there are three types of interdependence: husband/wife, parent/child, and master/slave. Aristotle takes a close interest in the last association. The Sophists of the fifth century BC opposed *physei* (what is by nature) and *nomo* (what is by law or convention). Accordingly, the question arises: is the slave a slave by nature or by convention? If by convention, suggesting that masters and slaves are equal by nature, then there is an injustice. Here is Aristotle's reasoning on the question.

1. *The Nature of Tools*

The goods used to ensure the livelihood of the family belong to the *oikia* (the household); as such, they *naturally* belong to the master of the house. We say "naturally" because they are needed to sustain the household, like craftspeople need to possess their own tools. The ultimate aim of the household is the survival of its members, which is the raison d'être or the good of this natural community. All means necessary for the attainment of this aim are good, like the goal itself.

There are two types of household instruments: animate and inanimate ones. For example, for the pilot of a ship the rudder is an inanimate instrument, while the lookout man is an animate one. Likewise, in the professions, one who helps (i.e., an assistant, an apprentice) is of "the *nature* of instruments" (Aristotle, *Politics* 1.4.1253b.30). So it can be said, "that the slave is an animate article of property," as if the shuttle of a loom should start weaving on its own, or the plectrum of a harp start playing. The slave is a part of the master, even though he or she is a *separate* part.

But can slaves exist *by nature*? Are there "persons for whom slavery is the *better* and *just* condition" (*Politics* 1.5.1254a)? The reply supposes that authority and hierarchy are necessary and useful things (already from the outset of life the soul rules the body, the intellect rules desire, humans rule animals, the male rules the female, and the major note rules the harmony; more often than not, it is the equality of these factors, or the reversal of their respective roles, that is damaging and cruel (the body of the wicked man rules his soul; the unbalanced household is ruled by the wife). "We may thus conclude that [for] all men who differ from others as much as the body differs from the soul, or an animal from a man" (*Politics* 1.5.1254b), there is *naturally* subordination.

2. *Slaves by Nature*

This case exists. There are people whose work consists solely of physical labor, and who can do nothing else. Such people are, Aristotle says, "slaves by nature," and it is better and just for them "to be ruled by a master."

Such beings are, of course, humans, and as such they are endowed with reason. However, their reason is of an inferior kind, narrowly linked to the senses and only able to distinguish types. Such beings are incapable of free speculation or independent knowledge [science]. Moreover, even the bodily form of such beings differ. The slave has muscles, but they are knotty and bulging; his silhouette is bent. The freeman is tall and straight. His athleticism is suitable for war, but useless for physical labor; he is quick and strong.

Since the master and slave share these differences, they complete each other: they form an organic community. Hence, even *friendship* can exist between them.

3. *Slaves by Nature, Slaves by Convention*

Having said this, Aristotle recognizes that there are slaves with the bodies of freemen and freemen with the souls of slaves. If this is so, it is because there *also* exist slaves *by convention,* made that way by positive law, particularly the law of war, which reduces some men to slavery who would otherwise be free by nature.

On this point there is controversy. Some say that force does not constitute right, others that force manifests a virtue, which as such creates right. However, even if it is just that some are reduced to slavery as a consequence of war, it is true that there are unjust wars, and the like. In sum, there are slaves by nature for whom slavery is just, and slaves by convention (some anyway) for whom slavery is unjust. Each needs to be looked at case by case.

Aristotle presents his theory of slavery in order to describe the household, the basic building block of the city. His description also serves to provide a definition of political power. The city, in fact, organizes relations between free and equal humans. *Thus, a regime like a tyranny, which reduces a naturally free citizen to slavery, is manifestly unnatural.*

The other two relationships within the household—parent/child and husband/wife—are qualitatively different from the master/slave relationship. The authority of parents over children is "royal"; the authority of a husband over a wife is "political" (because it preserves the equality between a men and a women).[20]

C. Political Economy

Aristotle argues that the city must be autarkic and that, therefore, it must be able to produce everything its citizens need. He then imagines an economic theory, one of the first ever recorded in the history of ideas (it comes just a few years after Xenophon's writings, which we will discuss below). Aristotle reflects first on the lawfulness of acquiring natural property.

1. *Good Chrematistics*

All beings in the animal world and in the human world have to eat and acquire the means of survival. All of nature is founded on this principle. "Plants exist to give subsistence to animals, and animals give it to men," to feed them, clothe them, or serve them. There is a universal teleology and hierarchy, and humans occupy the top: "as nature makes nothing purposeless or in vain, all animals must have been made by nature for the sake of men" (*Politics* 1.8.1256b).

Consequently, for human beings, the act of using what nature gives them is good and natural; it also determines the existence of the "natural arts of acquisition," such as fishing, hunting, farming, and so on. In a sense, even war can be a "natural art of acquisition," as in the case of people, who being destined by nature to obey, refuse to do so.

More generally, the art of wealth acquisition, which Aristotle calls *chrematistics,* is also natural to a degree because "it ensures a supply of objects, necessary for life and useful to the association of the polis or the household." In this sense the ownership of such wealth is lawful.

2. *Form as a Principle of Limitation*

But if what forms the basis of ownership is the acquisition of goods that are *naturally* necessary for life (like milk for the offspring of viviparous animals), then logically there is a limit to such ownership: *nature* itself. "There is a bound fixed [by nature itself], as is also the case in the means required by the other arts. All the instruments needed by all the arts are limited, both in number and size, by the requirements of the art they serve; and wealth may be defined as a number of instruments used in a household or state [and needed for their respective 'arts']" (*Politics* 1.8.1256b).

Let us recall here the theory of the fulfillment of nature and the "middle course." The handsomest man is not the tallest or the strongest, but the one who has greatness and strength of

[20] Thomas Aquinas later comments that the authority of a husband over a wife is restricted to what the law of marriage allows; just as the magistrate has only the authority given him by the statutes (*secundum statuta*), and not a universal authority (*quantum ad omnia*), it is in this sense that the authority the husband has over his wife is not "royal."

character, which contribute most to the realization of his essence as a human being. An *excess* of greatness or strength would cause him to miss or fall short of his form. Thus, his nature or essence fixes a limit on each of his features beyond which the beauty and balance of his form would be jeopardized. For this man, progress is coming as close as possible to his form, not expanding all of his potential infinitely.

If a man develops one of his faculties beyond measure, the consequence for his soul would be as if one of his arms or legs grew abnormally long for his body. Instead of being improved, he would be diminished, and he would be monstrous and incapacitated.

Form is a principle of limitation and finitude; unchecked, indefinite growth is hubris, an immoderation, a principle of illimitation. But being is form; quintessentially, *ousia* is the fully evolved form of the species in one of its members.

In contrast, what is limitless tends toward nonbeing. This is true in Greek metaphysics in general: unlike the later Christians and their ontotheology,[21] the classical Greeks do not believe that the being is infinite, and that whatever is limited is, therefore, by definition, ontologically imperfect. The Greek word for infinite is *apeiron*—literally that which has no limit and thus no form. For Plato, *apeiron* is quintessential nonbeing.

These general principles have very specific implications for the analysis of the economy in an Aristotelian world.

3. *Natural Economy and Artificial Economy*

For the head of the household and the head of the state, there is a *natural art of acquisition.* As long as this art is restricted to procuring what is necessary for the livelihood of the household and the city, *within the limits of their natural needs,* it is a good. It is good chrematistic.

But there is another kind of art of acquisition: the economy we would call "liberal" today (i.e., capitalism and business). Aristotle reckons it is *artificial* and *unbalanced.* It is bad chrematistic. In what respect is it not natural?

Every economic good has two possible values or uses, one that is proper to it, and another that is not. For example, a shoe can be worn—its proper use—or it can be used in exchange to obtain another good.

Exchange is natural, in a sense, when people have certain goods in excessive quantity and others in insufficient quantity; therefore, they have a certain interest in exchanging them to satisfy their needs (we saw earlier that this is what happens in the city, which has achieved economic self-sufficiency, *autarkeia;* or, better, a city is only a city if it is autonomous, and it can only be autonomous if it has achieved a sufficient level of division of labor; therefore, a city is only possible where there is exchange, which is enough to say that exchange itself is natural).

Aristotle approves of exchange up to the point of "retail trade." In a household, members "share all things in common"; therefore, there is no exchange in the literal sense. In an association of households, certain items are shared in common, others belong to a particular household; the two help each other through barter—the exchange of goods without any monetary intermediary (e.g., wine for grain).

In cities, *specie* becomes the medium of exchange. Precious metals were adopted at the outset, owing to their particular objective qualities: inalterability, divisibility, and transportability; at the same time its use value was not lost. Next, a stamp was made on the metal to indicate its weight. This, says Aristotle, is when coins began to be sought outright, without regard to their proper use as metal, and wealth began to be the simple possession of money.

---

[21] *Translator's note:* The ontology of God and/or the theology of Being.

This, he says, is "a sham" because (1) by convention it is possible to decide the value of currency; (2) money has zero use value, which is what the fable of King Midas illustrates: the king was granted his foolish wish that everything he touched would turn to gold, whereby he died of starvation.

True chrematistic is the art of acquiring wealth. Exchange is one normal means to achieve this goal, alongside other direct means such as farming, hunting, and so on. Bad chrematistic begins when trade, a simple exchange transaction, becomes an end in itself, when one pursues money for its own sake, when money is the be all and end all of the exchange. It is an unnatural and immoral way of behaving because "this form of the art of acquisition is unlimited"; that is, it is not limited by any object that it serves (*Politics* 1.9.1257b).

Aristotle's argument can be explained diagrammatically (Marx used the same diagram in his *Capital*). The healthy use of money (M) is one where it is merely a medium between two articles of merchandise or commodities (C, C'):

C ------------------------------ M ----------------------------- C'

In this case, the entire process remains within *natural* limits. At the beginning and the end of the process, a commodity is used for its natural use value. Since the consumers of C and C' are natural beings, whose needs are compatible with their respective nature, which is finite, they cannot nor will not consume an infinite quantity of C or C'. Consequently, the medium M remains limited.

Bad chrematistic corresponds to the following diagram:

M ----------------------------- C ------------------------------ M'

In this case, the commodity serves merely as an intermediary for someone bent on making money. It is a means, money is an end; and, as in every technique, the means is subordinated to the end. But money is a pure quantity; it has no use value. One never has too much money because it is not used for its proper and natural use value, which it does not have. The possession of money can never be limited by satiety or by achieving a balance. In this sense, money is a *principle of illimitation,* and, as such, a principle of *denaturation*. The desire for money can only create monstrosities—psychological monstrosities for people with money, and also social and political monstrosities because the unlimited growth of wealth disrupts the inner harmony and very form of the city.

All the more so, *lending at interest* is the most contemptible form of the art of acquisition because "it makes a profit from currency itself, instead of making it from the process [of exchange] which currency was meant to serve." Money "breeds" money, but it is an unnatural procreation because money itself is not a natural being.

Aristotle's theory of wealth acquisition is so robust and well structured that it has attracted followers throughout the long intellectual history of the West, up to and including the anticapitalist and reactionary social theoreticians of the late nineteenth century. All the same, it is a theory rooted in classical conceptions of *nature* and *time* and an arguably outdated *epistemology*.

Classical thought, and Aristotelian thought in particular, is "fixist": there is no idea of progress whatsoever. For Aristotle and Plato alike, the ideal is for the city to remain the same forever, or at best that a particular city of the species "cities" should succeed more, be healthier and more spirited than another—for example, Athens should be more beautiful than Sparta, or it should recover better after a period of decline. But while the individual is in a becoming mode, the species is permanent, as we noted. It is limited to and by its form. Therefore, a part that grows disproportionately cannot be perceived as the promise of a positive change or progress; it can only be seen as a mortal danger. For "capitalism" to emerge, an idea of history must arise that posits the possibility and desirability of change, the emergence of unprecedented social realities, and the surpassing of nature. As we will see, the Judeo-Christian tradition will play a critical role in the transformation of humanity's perception of time and, thus, contribute to the birth of a modern economy.

Added to that, Aristotle's economic ideas are related to his *epistemology*. Note that he condemns a liberal economy, "capitalism," the emergence of extravagant wealth in the city, and that he firmly backs the state control of wealth to preserve a certain equality of wealth, as we shall see. This proves that he believes in the "knowability" of the economic life of the city and thinks that its complexity does not exceed the ability of the magistrates to comprehend it.

In book 8 of his *Politics* Aristotle makes several important observations in this regard. The population of the city should be neither too large nor too small; otherwise it becomes *impossible to govern*. "Who can be the general of a [state] so excessively large? Who can give it orders, unless he has Stentor's voice?" (8.4.11). In his thinking, the government of a city is like the troops under a general's command. A general *knows the position of each of his soldiers* and, bearing in mind the common goal of the organization, *takes optimal decisions* in regard to their action. The magistrate also has to know every need and every resource of the city in order to coordinate them. A society that is too big to be controlled in this way escapes nature and is a monster. Other arguments reflect this same epistemological principle: "The function of the governors is to issue commands and give decisions.... In order to give decisions... and distribute the offices of government according to the merit of candidates, *the citizens of a state must know one another's characters*." From this Aristotle extrapolates a definition of the ideal size of the state: "the optimum standard of population... is, in a word, 'the greatest *surveyable* number required for achieving a life of self-sufficiency.'" It is easy to understand that when the great Hellenic monarchies and, even more so, the Roman Empire rose to predominance, Aristotle's economic categories were insufficient to contemplate the real economy.

D. A Criticism of Communism

In book 2 of his *Politics*, Aristotle examines different types of constitutions proposed by theoreticians, including Plato and Phaleas of Chalcedon (a proponent of land-sharing in the community). This poses again the question of communism. Aristotle is especially harsh on Plato's communism. Resorting to a number of theoretical and practical arguments, he makes a case against the community of goods (common ownership) among the guardians.

1. *Theoretical Arguments*

Plato's reason for promoting communism was his concern for unity among the guardians (see above). To this, Aristotle replies, "it is obvious that a polis that goes on and on, and becomes more and more of a unit, will eventually cease to be a polis at all. A polis by its nature is some sort of aggregation [i.e., it has the quality of including a large number of members]. If it becomes more of a unit, it will first become a household instead of a polis, and then an individual instead of a household" (*Politics* 2.2.1261a.2).

As we saw, a state in Aristotle's judgment is by no means a mere addition of identical parts (as is, for example, a *symmachy*;[22] or a barbarous nation, which is, as far as Aristotle is concerned, no more than an *ethnos*, a coalition of dispersed but identical villages, not an organized *polis* in the true sense). A state is an *organic* community made up of diverse but complementary elements.

[22] A military alliance among equal states for offensive or defensive purposes.

There are several kinds of occupations, and "a difference of capacities among [their] members," meaning a range of trades and activities. But even in an aristocracy, where some citizens are equal, and in a democracy, where all are equal, every one is ruler and ruled from time to time, and in this sense citizens are not identical. But if one insists on making them identical, though they play different roles and occupy different places in the hierarchy, the unity of the state will not be strengthened, and to the contrary one is likely to create an aggregation of disjointed elements, an accretion of juxtaposed households and individuals with no mutual ties. The city as city will be destroyed. Instead of pure unity, the result will be pure multiplicity. "It is as if you were to turn harmony into mere unison, or to reduce a theme to a single beat" (*Politics* 2.5.1263b.14).

2. *Practical Arguments*

(1) One takes less care of collective property: "Men pay most attention to what is their own; they care less for what is common; or, at any rate, they care for it only to the extent to which each is individually concerned. Even where there is no cause for inattention, men are more prone to neglect their duty when they think that another is attending to it; this is exactly what happens in domestic service, where many attendants are sometimes of less assistance than a few" (*Politics* 2.3.1262.4).

What is true of property is also true of people. If women are held in common, fathers will not love children equally, as Plato had hoped, but they will nurture equal indifference for all. There will no longer be direct parentage, nor parentage to the first, second, or *nth* degree, neither communities of phratries, nor tribes. Everything will be unclear, indistinct. Aristotle formulates this elegantly when he says, "it is better to be *own cousin* to a man than to be *his son* after the Platonic fashion." With communism, *philia* (friendship) ceases to exist because ties are no longer direct, which means paradoxically that social bonds—the very cement of society—become lax and weakened. Abstract love for the community is no substitute for the love that binds individuals together. Only the latter kind of love strengthens the social bond and creates the unity of the state. This powerful idea can be expressed with the following metaphor: the social fabric is held together by interpersonal friendships like clothing by its stitches. Accordingly, the threat of strife actually increases with Platonic friendship. And when strife breaks out, the moral means of suppressing it, inherent in filial devotion, is lacking. According to Aristotle, communist sociality dissolves in the group like a drop of wine in a large quantity of water. This is why, in order to maintain a united city, it is important to preserve the basic units: the family households and all the intermediate organic communities.

Anyway, Aristotle continues, Plato's plan is unrealistic because Herodotus reports a society in Libya where women are held in common to a degree; there the children are reclaimed by their original parents on the basis of imagined physical resemblances.

(2) On the issue of private property, Aristotle's conception is fairly moderate, neither "liberal" in the modern sense (attributing an absolute quality to private property) nor frankly "socialist." His view is that the lawmaker can act in an authoritarian manner according to the needs of the state, depending on its size, economic modes of production, relations with other states, and so on, by disposing of property, distributing land, making inheritance laws, levying taxes.

This is not to imply that Aristotle is a "socialist." Private property is a necessary condition for successful production. Only the *use* of the fruits of production should, if necessary, be common. Example: in Sparta, men use one another's slaves and, while traveling, they take from the fields of farms belonging to others (fields that were worked and cultivated by others).

(3) Finally, Aristotle develops a psychological argument against Plato's communism. It is human nature, he says, to love property, money, and self (self-love is a "natural human feeling"); therefore, possession cannot be bad. This same human nature gives us another instinct; the pleasure of doing a kindness and helping others (human nature rebukes self-love as well). But to

give, one must have. Therefore, communism is the negation of altruism. From these two viewpoints, communism is against human nature.

Similarly, temperance is a virtue that can be practiced in sexual matters as well, for example, by not coveting another's wife. But if women are held in common, this virtue will have no object. Therefore, the common ownership of women is not natural either.

Today this kind of reasoning can seem strange, but Aristotle takes nature as the standard against which all things can and must be measured. So, if individual human nature reflects these feelings and virtues, it is not "in vain." There must be a certain corresponding social order, and vice versa.

E. Different Kinds of Constitutions

Now Aristotle can pursue his analysis of the state in earnest. The state cannot be reduced to a *territory,* a *people,* or a *government* (because a state is bound by the obligations of an earlier government). Therefore, "it is obvious that the criterion to which we must chiefly look in determining the identity of the state is the criterion of the constitution" (*Politics* 3.3.1276b.9).

A constitution (*politeia*) is the order that frames and controls the various functions of authority and determines the highest authority, the *arche kyria panton* or sovereign authority—the ultimate authority on which all else depends, the final decision-making authority.

Consequently, constitutions can be distinguished by type of sovereign authority (a people's assembly, a select body or council, a single individual), and by the purpose of its action. A sovereign authority can act:

- in the interest of *all,* the only option corresponding to what a state should be naturally, that is, an organic community united to achieve the happiness of its constituent parts;
- in the interest of a *few,* in which case the constitution is wrong and unnatural.

"Those constitutions which consider the common interest are *right* constitutions, judged by the standard of absolute justice. Those constitutions, which consider only the personal interest of the rulers, are all *wrong* constitutions, or perversions of the right forms. Such perverted forms are despotic; whereas the polis is an *association of freemen*"[23] (*Politics* 3.6.1279a.11; my italics).

This gives us the following simple framework:

	One Person	A Few	All
Right forms of constitution	**Monarchy**	**Aristocracy**	[*Politeia*]
Perverted forms of constitution	**Tyranny**	**Oligarchy**	**Democracy**

Aristotle's classification completes the categories we found earlier in Herodotus (see above, pp. 58–60) and Plato (see above, p. 93); in time, they became the classical reference.

[23] *Arche despotike* is the authority of the master over the slave. The true *despotes,* the master, rules his slave in the *common interest of both,* as we saw, and not narrowly in his personal interest. In this sense, the tyrant is a doubly unnatural master: on the one hand, he rules free citizens as though they were slaves. In so doing, he perverts the state; on the other hand, he perverts the authority of the master.

Most doctrinal debate in Aristotle's *Politics* concerns two of these forms of government: oligarchy and democracy (monarchy is excluded de facto as barbarian). For the Greeks the real political debate oscillates between these two forms—as Aristotle says, "as winds, in ordinary speech, are simply described as north or south... [or] modes of music described as being Dorian or Phrygian" (*Politics* 4.3.1290a.7). However, Aristotle rejects both forms of government because they give only a partial view of the state.

Oligarchy, contrary to its etymology (the power of a few), is actually the power of the *rich.* But the claim of the rich to wield power *because* they are rich is absurd. The purpose of the state, as we saw, is not only to create wealth; it aims to fulfill human nature. But the rich know only how to accumulate wealth; they do not have the genuine competence to achieve the main goal.[24]

Likewise, *democrats* want to control all power, because they are *free.* But, as we saw, the aim of the state is not just the safeguarding of freedom.[25]

Moreover, both forms of government are *perversions.* The rulers defend the interests of a party and are, therefore, unjust. Because a democracy places all power in the hands of the people, they are able to seize the wealth of the rich, which is unjust. Oligarchy, in turn, is a deviation of aristocracy and results in giving power to those who are not the best, who do not care about the common interest. It favors the rich, who care only about their own personal interest (they are incapable of taking into account the full range of issues involved in the government of the city).

So the debate is narrowed down to aristocracy and a form of government that Aristotle does not really name, calling it simply a *politeia,* considered the best form of constitution, because it is the government of all acting in the interest of all.

What would this form of government look like? We will see that it must have certain features borrowed from the *government of the few* and others from the *government of the many.* In any case, it will steer a *middle course.* But before we can discuss this type of government, we must complete the description of the state.

F. Laws and Decrees: A Criticism of Assemblies

Aristotle identifies three elements or powers in the state, organized differently according to the type of constitution:

- the "deliberative element," which deals with "common affairs";
- a sort of "executive": the magistracies;
- the judiciary element.

"The deliberative element is sovereign (1) on the issues of war and peace, and making and breaking of alliances; (2) in the enacting of laws; (3) in cases where the penalty of death, exile, and confiscation is involved; and (4) in the appointment of magistrates and the calling of them to account on the expiration of their office" (*Politics* 4.14.1298a.3). Since the principal function of the "deliberative element" is law-making, its scope must be determined precisely.

The correct forms of constitution are, as we saw, ones where rulers rule in the common interest. Now the law is, quintessentially, common to all and in the interest of all. Therefore, the only lawful government is government by law. Aristotle says that the magistracies, whether they are one or a body (a council), should only be allowed to deliberate when the law is weak or blind, that is, in special cases. Even the king, if he is not a tyrant, must reckon with the law.

---

[24] This objection to the oligarchic principle was present in Plato as well.

[25] Another of Plato's arguments.

Aristotle emphasizes that opinions diverge on this point. The law cannot foresee everything; individual decisions play a critical role. The law is *reason without passion,* which is its advantage over the individual. But it can be *blind* reason, and owing to the wisdom of one person, the state can avoid situations that might arise by the creation of an inappropriate law (compare this with Plato, above, p. 92).

> Our inquiry will naturally start from the general problem, "Is it more expedient to be ruled by the one best man, or by the best laws?" Those who hold that kingship is expedient argue that law can only lay down general rules; it cannot issue commands to deal with various different conjunctures; and the rule of the letter of law is therefore a folly in any and every art [whether the art of politics, or that of medicine, or any other art]. In Egypt it is permissible for doctors to alter the rules of treatment after the first four days, though a doctor who alters them earlier does so at his own risk. If we follow this line, it is clear that a constitution based on the letter and rules of law is not the best constitution, in the same way and for the same reason [as medical treatment by strict rule is not the best treatment].
>
> But we have to remember that general principles must also be present in the ruler's mind. And that from which the element of passion is wholly absent is better than that in which such an element is innate. Law contains no element of passion; but such an element must always be present in the human mind. The rejoinder may, however, be made that the individual mind, if it loses in this way, gains something in return: it can deliberate better, and decide better, on particular issues.
>
> These considerations lead us to conclude that the one best man must be a law-giver, and there must be a body of laws [even in a state which is governed by such a man], but these laws must not be sovereign where they fail to hit the mark —though they must be so in all other cases. (*Politics* 3.15.4–6, with modifications).

Therefore, "executive" power must keep to the law at all times, yet be able to surpass it and complete it as well. The judge must also have this competence in order to judge equitably, as the following text from the *Nicomachean Ethics* shows:

> The same thing, then, is just and equitable, and while both are good the equitable is superior. What creates the problem is that the equitable is just, but not the legally just but a correction of legal justice. The reason is that all law is universal but about some things it is not possible to make a universal statement, which shall be correct. In those cases, then, in which it is necessary to speak universally, but not possible to do so correctly, the law takes the usual case, though it is not ignorant of the possibility of error. And it is none the less correct; for the error is [neither] in the law nor in the legislator but in the nature of the thing, since the matter of practical affairs is of this kind from the start. When the law speaks universally, then, and a case arises on it which is not covered by the universal statement, then it is right, where the legislator fails us and has erred by oversimplicity, to correct the omission—to say what the legislator himself would have said had he been present, and would have put into his law if he had known. Hence the equitable is just.[26]

Thus, the law must prevail in general and be corrected in certain cases. But, given these exceptions, "the question arises whether this authority [to decide what cannot be properly decided by rules of law] should be vested in the one best man or in the whole of the people. In the actual practice of our own day the people in their gatherings [assemblies] have both a judicial and a

[26] Aristotle, *Nicomachean Ethics,* 5.10, trans. W. D. Ross (Oxford: Oxford University Press, 1925).

deliberative capacity, and in both capacities they make decisions which are all concerned with particular matters [i.e., the matters that cannot be decided, or properly decided, by law]."[27]

Aristotle recognizes an extreme threat in this management of exceptional cases by a people's assembly. In a certain type of perverted democracy,

> the people, and not the law, is the final sovereign. This is what happens when popular decrees [*psephisma*] are sovereign instead of the law [*nomos*]; and that is a result which is brought about by leaders of the demagogue type. In democracies which obey the law there are no demagogues; it is the better class of citizens who preside over affairs. Demagogues arise in states where the laws are not sovereign. The people then becomes an autocrat—a single composite autocrat made up of many members, with the many playing the sovereign, not as individuals, but collectively.... A democracy of this order, being in the nature of an autocrat and not being governed by law, begins to attempt [resemble] an autocracy. It grows despotic; flatterers come to be held in honour; it becomes analogous to the tyrannical form of single-person government. Both show a similar temper; both behave like despots to the better class of citizens; the decrees of the one are like the edicts of the other. (Aristotle, *Politics* 4.4.1292a.7)

Nothing is worse than the democracy by assembly that Aristotle observes at work in Athens. Xenophon, Isocrates, and Demosthenes also held this form of government in contempt. When everything the *demos* votes is called "law," the *demos* is no longer held in check by the law. It is not content with making decisions on the exceptional cases where the law is silent, but makes decisions on whatever its passions inspire. When this happens, reason ceases to exist; true law disappears, the authority of the state is arbitrary, and the citizen becomes the slave of the mob. There is no liberty; there is no city. "Where the laws are not sovereign, there is no constitution.... This particular system, under which everything is managed merely by decrees, is not even a democracy, in any real sense of the word. Decrees can never be general rules" (4.4.1292a.7).[28]

G. The Powers of the State

Let us turn now to the question of how these powers come together in each type of constitution.

1. *Deliberative Power*

Several cases may arise. Decisions can be taken by all (democracy), by a few (oligarchy), and some by all and others by some (mixed regime).

---

[27] Ibid., 5.10. This occurs when *misthophory* (state pay for political service) is in practice, that is, "when there is a high rate of pay for those who attend the assembly. Men need not then mind their business; and therefore they hold frequent meetings and decide all issues themselves" (*Politics* 4.15.1299b.30).

[28] We see that Aristotle has already considered what the moderns (particularly the English theorists of the seventeenth and eighteenth centuries and the American constitutionalists) will attempt to clarify, namely what features the real law should have. It must be general, which means it must never be concerned with cases or individuals familiar to the authority who decrees the law. Otherwise, it is not a rule, merely an intentional act. But liberty is possible only if state coercion is applied following a rule, one that must be general, public, certain, and previously decreed. Otherwise, the action of the state is despotic. Of course, the government must have the leeway to take special measures, but such "regulations" must not contravene laws in application. This raises an intellectual problem: how to distinguish between the two types of norms and the special powers required to decree each of them. Popular regimes, of course, refrain from making these distinctions. Aristotle's thinking on this shows that the Greek constitutionalists gave careful thought to these issues and came up with answers: the power of the people to make and unmake law as the people see fit is no less despotic than the tyrant's power to do the same; it makes a government of *isonomia* and liberty, as imagined by the founders of the Greek polis (the Seven Sages) impossible.

a. Democracy

Again there are three possibilities: (1) Citizens decide by groups or by fractions in rotation (e.g., this is how the Boule in Athens functioned: the *prytaneis* followed one after the other); the people's assembly convenes only to vote laws and hear decrees read by the magistrates. (2) The people's assembly convenes to vote laws, elect magistrates, to decide war and peace; all other decisions are made by elected magistrates or magistrates appointed by lot. (3) The people's assembly convenes permanently and makes all decisions; magistrates simply prepare cases for decision. This is manifestly a deviant form of government, even though, Aristotle adds, it is "dominant in our time."

b. Oligarchies

Only citizens who pay the proper taxes are admitted to the assembly. If the tax is modest and the assembly does not have powers to change the constitution, the government is a "republican"-type oligarchy. If all tax-paying citizens do not participate in the assembly, but only those designated by the rulers, the government is a more marked form of oligarchy. If co-opted members or hereditary members make up the assembly, and if, furthermore, the assembly has powers to change the constitution, then it is a more extreme form of oligarchy. If the assembly deals with certain matters and magistrates with others, or if some magistrates are appointed by lot and others elected, they are *mixed* forms of government.[29]

The balance can shift between these powers, depending on whether certain parties have a right of proposal and others only a right of *veto*. The constitution will be held to be oligarchic if the assembly only has the right to vote measures prepared by special advisers (*probuli*) or guardians of the laws (*nomophylax*); this constitutional mechanism ensures that the assembly cannot make dramatic changes. In some constitutions, the assembly has a right of *veto,* but not the right to vote a measure without appeal. In others, the magistrates can reject a vote of the assembly, but cannot make a decision without appeal.

2. *Executive Power*

This is the power of the magistrates: "What is to be included under the term 'magistrate' (*archai*)?…The title should, on the whole, be reserved for those which are charged with the duty, in some given field, of deliberating, deciding, and giving instructions—and more especially with the duty of giving instructions, which is the special mark of the magistrate" (*Politics* 4.15.1299a.4).

Aristotle makes a distinction between the administration, with its officials (mere "subordinates"), and the government or true "magistrates," resembling our elected politicians or high civil servants.

Examples of low-level officials ("subordinates") include the market official in the *agora,* a choragus, a herald, an ambassador, an official in charge of grain distribution, even public slaves in low-level positions. Examples of magistrates include the office of the general (*strategos*), the superintendent in charge of surveillance of women (this was an aristocratic magistrate because the women of the people, who were obliged to leave the gynaceum to work, were not under surveillance), the superintendent of education for the youth, and so on. An interesting intermediary function was filled by advisors responsible for preparing decisions. Aristotle remarks that they were frequently rivals of the Boule members themselves.[30]

---

[29] Aristotle had collected a huge body of information about various constitutions in use in Greek cities and colonies: no doubt he had real examples in mind for each of these forms of government.

[30] Not unlike the rivalry between high public servants and elected politicians in modern states. Apparently, some Greek cities had an administrative elite, comprised of competent high public servants. Aristotle says that these "case

How are these different magistrates appointed? There are several questions here: Who makes the appointment? Who can be appointed? What is the method of appointment? The varied answers to each of these questions leads to the enumeration of the different types of constitution in use. The table below provides a simplified overview.

Voters	Eligible Candidates	Method Appointment
All	All	Elections
Some	Some	By lot
Some for certain positions, others for others	Some for certain positions, others for others	

Aristotle actually comes up with 12 combinations, not 18 ($3 \times 3 \times 2$). Three are democratic; that is to say, when everybody can choose and be chosen, either by election, by drawing of lots, or by both methods combined (appointment by lot for certain offices, appointment by election for others).

3. *Judiciary Power*

Aristotle clearly distinguishes this type of magistracy from the others. He identifies eight types of courts. At a glance, his list provides a hint of the level of administrative complexity—and sophistication—in Greek cities at the time:

1. a court for assessing the accountability of magistrates;
2. a court for offenses against any point of public interest;
3. a court for constitutional issues (where someone who attacks the constitution is judged);
4. a court for disputes between public officials and private individuals about the level of fines and taxes (fiscal concerns);
5. a court for major contract litigation between private individuals;
6. a court for cases of homicide (premeditated, involuntary, etc.) and decisions on whether a person exiled on charges of murder can return to his homeland;
7. a court for cases involving foreigners (foreigners in the proper sense of the term, i.e., with a legal status);
8. and, finally, a court for minor contract litigation between private persons (*Politics* 4.16).

The existence of an administrative court (4) to defend citizens from excessive taxation is telling.

H. Political Change

Book 5 of *Politics* is devoted to political changes and their causes.

1. *Causes of Political Change*

Civil strife, Aristotle says, has several causes.

advisors" reflect an *oligarchic* element within democracy. This is not unlike the situation in the French administration with its "*énarques*" (graduates of the École Nationale de l'Administration, which produces France's top civil service elite). The *democratic* element is the Boule member. When the two exist side by side, as in Corinth, Corcyra, and Eritrea, it is a mixed element, and an element of moderation. Sometimes the Boule members, or the Assembly, were ill at ease with this authority. The result was an extreme democratic government where the Assembly ruled without power sharing.

a. Disagreements about Justice

Differences of opinion arise when democrats deny that there is any disparity in merit or when oligarchs deny that citizens are equal in some degrees. "When one begins with an initial error, it is inevitable that one should end badly" (*Politics* 5.1.1301b.39).

When such disagreements on justice exist, conflicts arise; they can take various forms: either there is the will to change the constitution (i.e., to switch from a democracy to an oligarchy or an aristocracy, or vice versa), or there is the will to seize power without changing the form of government. Perhaps there is also a desire for more democracy or more oligarchy, or the will to create or eliminate certain magistracies.

b. The Loss of Equilibrium in the State

"The disproportionate increase of a part of the state is also an occasion which leads to constitutional changes. The analogy of the body is instructive. The body is composed of parts, and it must grow proportionately if symmetry is to be maintained.... The same is true of a state. It, too, is composed of parts; and one of the parts may often grow imperceptibly out of proportion" (*Politics* 5.3.1302b.33).

If in a democracy or a *politēia* the number of poor becomes disproportionate,[31] or if in an oligarchy the number of notables declines (as a result of war, for example), the impact can unbalance and, therefore, *distort* the state.[32]

The growing *reputation* of an institution or a segment of the population, acquired during wars or difficult periods, can also be the cause of constitutional changes. This is why it is best to be wary of "any person or body which adds new power to the state": they risk becoming seditious (to take advantage of their situation) or provoking seditions in others (by jealousy). Aristotle adds ironically that the cause of sedition is never the great moral superiority of a few men because there are never enough of them to constitute a political party.

c. The Great Effects of Petty Measures, Calculated or Not

Electoral intrigues can end in the vote of a decisive measure. Undetected demographic and economic changes can lead to fundamental shifts in the political balance—such as when the wealth of a city grows gradually and a greater number of citizens achieves access to office or wins voting rights, with the result that the very nature of the regime changes imperceptibly (cf. *Politics* 5.7.1306b).[33]

---

[31] This can be the result of deliberate policy; demagogues sometimes allowed illegitimate offspring and the sons of foreigners to be counted among the citizenry (cf. *Politics* 5.4.1319b.16).

[32] The thinking here is the same as in the case of bad chrematistic (cf. above, pp. 121–24). The value of the mean (*metriotes*) is illustrated with an example (*Politics* 5.9.1309b.7). A straight nose is ideal, but an aquiline nose or a snub nose can be pleasant. However, if the nose becomes too long or too bent, the face is disfigured: "What is true of the nose, and of other parts of the body, is true also of constitutions."

[33] "Even trifles may be the cause of revolutions—[this] is particularly true of aristocracies. They are especially apt to change imperceptibly, through being undermined little by little. Once they have abandoned one of the elements of the constitution, they find it easier afterwards to alter some other feature of a little greater importance; and they end eventually by altering the whole system of the state. This was what actually befell the constitution of Thurii. There was a law that the office of general should only be held a second time after an interval of five years. Some of the younger men showed soldierly qualities, and won a reputation with the rank and file of the guard. Despising the men who were in charge of affairs, and calculating on an easy triumph, these younger men set out to abrogate the law, wishing to make it possible for generals to serve continuously, and knowing that, in that case, the people would readily elect them for one term after another. The magistrates charged with the duty of considering such proposals—they were called the Board of Councillors—began by making an effort to resist the repeal of the law; but they were eventually led to agree, in the idea that when this change had been made the rest of the constitution would not be touched. They found themselves deceived; other changes were afterwards mooted; when they sought to oppose them, they failed to make any headway, and the whole scheme of the constitution was changed into an aristocratic *junto* composed of the revolutionaries" (*Politics* 5.7.1307b).

d. Immigration

Aristotle attributes an important role to immigration in political change. As a general rule, the population of a state must be fairly homogeneous (which is also why it takes time to form a state). If the city's homogeneity is disrupted, as when colonies are founded and large numbers of foreigners are admitted, the seeds of sedition are planted and can lead to grave dissension within the state. Again Aristotle illustrates this with several historical examples (*Politics* 5.7.1303a).

e. Geographical Factors

Such factors can also be the reason that the homogeneity of the population is insufficient. For example, the Athenians of Piraeus are different from those of the city: "more democratic than those who live in Athens" (*Politics* 5.7.1303b) Likewise, those cities with a portion of their territory on the continent and another on an island can face divisions.

f. External Causes

For example, political change can occur when a conqueror imposes his form of government on a vanquished state. As might be expected, Aristotle cites the example of the Peloponnesian War when Sparta imposed oligarchy on Athens.

2. *The Modalities of These Changes*

Political change takes place in different ways depending on the type of regime. In democracies, for example, demagogues influence the outcome. Sometimes they bring false accusations against wealthy individuals, finding an excuse to confiscate their property. Sometimes they attack them as a class by inciting the mob against them. In both instances, however, they frequently achieve the contrary of what they promise the people, namely, the ruin of democracy, since they create coalitions of the privileged in reaction (Aristotle comments, "a common danger unites even the bitterest enemies" [5.7.1304b]).

In oligarchies, the rich, when excluded from the ruling faction, will frequently seize the initiative and provoke unrest in order to obtain the offices they covet (the seditious can be individuals who have wasted their fortune in riotous living and hope to rebuild it by seizing power [5.7.1305b]). Sometimes the seditious become demagogues, flattering the mob and using force to overcome their rivals in the oligarchy. This is easier in oligarchies where the people are excluded from office but have voting rights. In contrast, when the ruling class is united and none of its members threatens to embark on seditious adventures, the power base of this class can be very sound, even when they are few in number. But oligarchies are weak in times of war: if the ruling class arms the people, the weapons risk being turned against it; if they hire mercenaries, the leader of these foreign soldiers may threaten to establish tyranny for his own benefit.

In the end, political changes are common and occur in all directions: from an oligarchy to a democracy, from a "republic" (moderate democracy) to a tyranny, and vice versa. In this regard, Greek history provides the observer with every conceivable example.

Other cases are frankly absurd: "Even petty seditions attain great dimensions when they involve the members of the government. There is an example in the history of Syracuse, where a constitutional revolution arose from a quarrel between two young men, who were both in office, about a love affair. In the absence of one of the two the other (in spite of being his colleague) seduced the affections of his friend; and the injured man, in his anger, retaliated by seducing his colleague's wife. Both of them, in the issue, drew the whole civic body into their quarrel and divided it into faction. The moral is that precautions ought to be taken at the very beginning of such feuds, and quarrels which involve men of leading and influence ought to be composed at once. The error is made at the start; and since, as the proverb goes, 'The start is half of the job,' a small mistake at the start is equal to all the mistakes made in the rest of the business" (5.4.1303b).

Incidentally, Aristotle disputes the legitimacy of Plato's law of becoming and decay outlined in his five forms of government in his *Republic*. Nothing in politics is ineluctable. True, nothing is permanent either. No regime is guaranteed to last forever, but it is possible to change from one to another, and each can survive for long periods if the proper means are used. In Aristotle's world, where contingency has its place, there is no *law of history*.

I. Politics of Moderation

What precautions can the different forms of government take to provide safeguards against these risks? What lessons should they learn from the experience? Through his commentary on the challenges facing each regime, we capture a glimpse of Aristotle's own political ideal, which might best be characterized with the notion of "moderation."

1. *Conditions of Political Stability*

a. Satisfy All Interests

The basic principle of stability is the *gradual and equitable satisfaction of everyone's interests,* even when these interests are not fully legitimate, and takes into account the balance of power and the threat of sedition. A balanced policy is the most likely sort to help a government—even an aristocratic regime—to achieve stability and sustain its longevity.

> We have to observe (and the observation is true of oligarchies as well as aristocracies) that some states owe their stability not so much to the solidity of their constitutional systems, as to the good relations in which their officers stand alike with the unenfranchised and the members of the civic body. In such states the unenfranchised are never treated unjustly; on the contrary, their leading members are promoted to share in constitutional rights; and while the ambitious among them are not wronged on points of honour, the rank and file are not maltreated in matters of money and profit. Similarly, in these states, the officers and the other members of the governing class behave towards one another in a democratic spirit of equality. Democrats seek to widen the principle of equality until it is made to include all the masses. What is certainly just—and expedient as well as just—is that the principle should extend to all who are really "peers." (*Politics* 5.7.1308a)

Generally speaking, Aristotle postulates, "stability—the aim of every 'polity'—is only to be found under a system of *proportionate equality, on the basis of merit,* by which each man *receives his corresponding due*" (5.7.1307a); in other words, on the basis of justice and, specifically, distributive justice.

Loyal to his policy of the middle course, Aristotle castigates excessive modern constitutions, where oligarchs seek the misfortune of the masses and the democrats the death of the rich, as social struggles are driven to exasperation. What is needed, on the contrary, is that the democrats, if they are clever, promise the rich that they will be treated with justice, and the oligarchs show concern for the interests of the people—like Solon.

b. The Struggle against Corruption

"The most important rule of all, in all types of constitution, is that provision should be made—not only by law, but also by the general system of economy—to prevent the magistrates from being able to use their office for their own gain" (*Politics* 5.7.1308b).

What annoys people is not so much that they are excluded from public office, but the thought that rulers are using their monopoly hold on power to enrich themselves. This explains Aristotle's recommendation for strict rules of transparency to prevent corruption; for example, public control of accounts. Thus reassured, the people will accept that competent individuals govern. Thus, vigilance against corruption is not just a "moral" concern; it is also a public order issue as well.

c. Maintain a Certain Equality of Wealth

Special attention will be paid to maintaining a certain equality of wealth and opportunity in society, as it is vital to sustain an "organic" balance that, if disrupted, leads straight to discord. The ways to achieve this are: nonconfiscatory taxation, equitable inheritance laws, access to well-paid offices for the poor, heavier penalties against the wealthy who commit crimes, compensation for citizens excluded from power by the constitution (the rich in a democracy, the poor in an oligarchy).

d. Assess the Quality of Magistrates and Public Servants

Aristotle holds that it is imperative to appoint magistrates of the highest caliber in order to maintain social harmony and peace.[34] It is important to select individuals with the appropriate qualities for office, taking into account the relative scarcity of such qualities: an honest treasurer is rare, as is an experienced general; it is less important that they are, respectively, moderately knowledgeable or moderately honest.

2. *Tyranny: An Immoderate Form of Government*

For Aristotle tyranny is the perfect example of an immoderate form of government, as can be seen from his somewhat ironic advice to a tyrant struggling to hold onto power:

> [Various measures for preserving a tyranny exist, such as] the "lopping off" of outstanding men, and the removal of men of spirit. [Another includes] the forbidding of common meals, clubs,[35] education, and anything of a like character—or, in other words, a defensive attitude against everything likely to produce the two qualities of mutual confidence and a high spirit. [Still another] is to prohibit societies for cultural purposes, and any gathering of a similar character: in a word, the adoption of every means for making every subject as much of a stranger as is possible to every other. (Mutual acquaintance always tends to create mutual confidence). Another line of policy is to require every resident in the city to be constantly visible to the tyrant and always hanging about the palace gates. (This is meant to give the ruler a peep-hole into the actions of his subjects, and to inure them to humility by a habit of daily slavery.) This line of policy also includes other measures of a similar character, common in Persia and among the barbarians, which have all the same general effect of fostering tyranny. Another line of policy is that of endeavouring to get regular information about every man's sayings and doings. This entails a secret police, like the female spies[36] employed at Syracuse,[37] or the eavesdroppers sent by the tyrant Hiero[38] to all social gatherings and public meetings. (Men are not so likely to speak their minds if they go in fear of a secret police; and if they do speak out, they are less likely to go undetected.) Still another line of policy is to sow mutual distrust and to foster discord between friend and friend; between people and notables; between one section of the rich and another. Finally, a

[34] To the long list of public offices mentioned above, Aristotle adds another very long and telling list (*Politics* 6.8.1322b–1323a), evidence that the Greek state in his time was highly developed with numerous functions found in large modern administrations (most of these functions had disappeared during the Middle Ages).

[35] In essence, any banquet or private reunion that might constitute a circle of resistance and unrest.

[36] Courtesans paid for out of the public purse.

[37] Under the tyranny of Dionysius.

[38] Another famous Sicilian tyrant. Xenophon devoted a study to him.

policy pursued by tyrants is that of impoverishing their subjects[39]—partly to prevent them from having the means for maintaining a civic guard; partly to keep them so busy in earning a daily pittance that they have no time for plotting. (*Politics* 5.11.1313a–1313b, with modifications)

Another measure Aristotle recommends is for the tyrant to artificially provoke wars "with the object of keeping their subjects constantly occupied and continually in need of a leader" (*Politics* 5.11.1313b). Tyrants will recruit foreigners to protect themselves against their own people.

Aristotle finds that *immorality* goes well with a tyrannical regime and vice versa (his argument is not exactly the same as Plato's in the *Republic*): "tyrants are always at odds with honorable good." They feel that "good men are doubly dangerous to their authority—dangerous, first, in thinking it shame to be governed as if they were slaves; dangerous, again, in their spirit of mutual and general loyalty, and in their refusal to betray one another or anybody else" (*Politics* 5.11.1314a). If citizens are capable of trust and loyalty to one another, they are capable of living independently, without a tyrant. Thus, the tyrant perceives the morality of citizens as a threat to his power.[40]

If a tyrant resorts to all these principles, he will, of course, hold onto power (Aristotle lists a sort of "hit parade" of long-surviving Greek tyrannies); conversely, a government that aspires to permanence without resorting to tyrannical measures will adopt moderate policies.

3. *Balance of Powers*

Aristotle starts from the premise that there are (and always will be, it seems) "two classes which compose the state—the wealthy class, and the poor" (*Politics* 6.3.1318a.4). As we saw, Aristotle rejects both oligarchy (power solely in the hands of the rich) and extreme democracy (power exclusively in the hands of the very poor, always the most numerous and therefore with the most to gain from democratic procedures), because "both of these answers involve inequality and injustice" (6.3.1318a.3). Greek cities adopted various intermediary solutions, such as giving more votes to the rich than to the poor, or allowing a council to exercise power where each member has a vote, but where half the members are elected by the poor class and the other half by the rich class.

Aristotle is in search of a general theoretical solution to this problem of weighting. It so happens that the two parties concerned agree at least on the principle of a majority vote. It will suffice, therefore, to adopt the principle that the law is made not by the majority of *individuals,* but by the major part of the *whole* made up of a combination of individuals *and* their wealth.

---

[39] By building monuments and major additions to them. Examples include the pyramids in Egypt and the erection of the temple to Olympian Zeus by the family of Pisistratus.

[40] Hannah Arendt, *The Origins of Totalitarianism* (1948; repr., New York: Schocken Books, 2004), and Friedrich August Hayek, *The Road to Serfdom* (1944; repr., Chicago: University of Chicago Press, 2007), reach similar conclusions in their analyses of twentieth century forms of tyranny. A society of trusting individuals, entertaining relations with one another based on stable moral rules and allowing for autonomy and "spontaneous order" in society, is incompatible with the arbitrary government of a totalitarian party that insists on "organizing" society instead of leaving it to "self-organize." The authoritarian organization of society from above involves the deferral of normal moral and legislative rules. People must do what higher authority commands them to do, not what they "should" do according to ordinary, so-called rules of proper conduct. Consequently, in totalitarian regimes, honest people are inevitably dismissed from important offices precisely because they will refuse to play the immoral role that authority commands them to play. They are replaced by depraved individuals who, because of their lack of morality, have no problem offering obedience to authority and carrying out unjust and criminal acts. This is how thugs and ruffians come to the highest offices of the regime (Arendt and Hayek target fascist and communist regimes indifferently).

An example will illustrate this idea. Suppose that the wealthy class is twice as rich as the poor; two votes could be given to each wealthy member of the council and one to each poor member. Suppose that there are 10 wealthy members and 20 poor members, and that a measure is adopted by 6 wealthy and 5 poor and rejected by 4 wealthy and 15 poor. If the vote were by college, there would be no solution, because the two colleges disagree. If the vote were by head count, the decision of the majority of the poor would win (19 to 11). With the proposed weighting, the result will be 17 votes [(6 x 2) + 5] to 23 [15 + (4 x 2)] (the same decision would be adopted in both cases, but just barely, and only 2 votes would need to shift to change the outcome). In the event of a deadlock, Aristotle recommends a decision by lot.

"The masses covet profits more than they covet honours," Aristotle remarks (*Politics* 6.3.1318b.6). This psychological principle enables oligarchies and tyrannies and most regimes (other than radical democracy) to function. In this respect, the ideal is a state where farmers are numerous: because they are occupied with farming, they give little thought to attending the assembly or getting involved in politics. It is enough that those who *want* to *can* and that they have the right to elect magistrates and control public accounts. Conversely, access to magistracies will be reserved for those who satisfy a property qualification or demonstrate certain capacities.

> A state which is governed in this way will be sure to be well governed (its offices will always be in the hands of the best of its members, with the people giving its consent and bearing no grudge against persons of quality); and the men of quality and the notables will be sure to be satisfied, under a system which at once preserves them from being governed by other and inferior persons and ensures (by giving others the right to call them to account) that they will themselves govern justly. To be kept in such dependence, and to be denied the power of doing just as he pleases, is an advantage to any man. (6.3.1318b.6)

This regime is obviously so much better that Aristotle approves the agrarian laws that aim to create a society of free small peasants, farmers, or herders. It is the other categories of people that pose a problem because they are "without exception of a much poorer stamp. They lead a poor sort of life: and none of the occupations followed by a populace which consists of mechanics, shop-keepers, and day labourers, leaves any room for excellence." But, paradoxically, such people always find time to attend the sessions of the popular assembly where their votes prevail over the farmers'! The best way around this is to adopt measures that bear on the structure of society itself—for example, some sort of agrarian law.

Demagogues in extreme democracies use property seizures indiscriminately, exasperating the notables. Laws are necessary, Aristotle argues, to ensure that the product of these seizures is paid to the temples and not to the public treasury. This will remove an important motivation from the assemblies and law courts. "Public prosecutions should be made as few as possible; and heavy fines should be used to deter prosecutors[41] from bringing them at random" (*Politics* 6.5.1320.4). Likewise, it is necessary to limit disbursements (*misthoi*) paid to Assembly members by restricting the number of meetings, because the funds for these disbursements are raised by taxation and property seizures, always to the detriment of the wealthy class. This is like trying to fill a leaky jar (6.5.1320a.29). (Besides, restricting the number of sessions will improve the work of the Assembly.) Moreover, the funds seized from the rich should not be distributed recklessly to the poor for their consumption, but should be used as capital grants to help them return to the land and work it productively.

[41] They are the *sycophants;* we will come across them again in the next chapter.

As for oligarchies, they should offer the multitudes a degree of participation in different powers. This requires the selection of those candidates from the general population who merit it. Oligarchies should also furnish grand celebrations, sacrifices, banquets, and games, and bestow gifts. Those oligarchies that refrain from such splendor are "limited democracies," in the sense that the rulers are as narrow and self-interested as those of democracies, who differ from them only in number (cf. *Politics* 6.5.1320a).[42]

III. Conclusion

This, then, is the essence of Aristotle's political thought. The state is a natural organism; it has no separate ideal norm; its highest and best models are provided by history itself in great variety. Aristotle deduces from this a political project that is neither radical nor tyrannical like Plato's, but moderate: various approaches are accepted, different balances among powers, and these balances are sought in the day-to-day practice of politics, not in the application of models derived from a priori reasoning.

Within the natural community of the state the division of labor thrives, so there are differences and inequalities, good by nature and necessary for the prosperity of all. Humans are capable of justice, and it is through justice, the hearth of virtues, that we fulfill our humanity. Inequalities, therefore, must be put in accord with the constitutive equality of justice. Aristotle lauds a policy of moderation: a limit must be set on the inequality of social conditions and roles, which supposes a constant process of *checks and balances*,[43] and two equally legitimate, but logically antagonistic demands must be reconciled: a demand for competence that excludes egalitarianism, and a demand for equality that excludes permanent privileges.

Informed by an immense body of empirical evidence on known constitutions, schooled by his own travels, Aristotle was alert to the wide range of institutional and administrative solutions invented by Greek states over the years to reconcile these demands. What struck his imagination were the details: this or that electoral expedient, fiscal measure, economic or demographic arrangement created a specific balance, warding off the risk of deviation. Thus, the permanence of the state depends on the capacity of its rulers to perform the painstaking work of development by turning their backs on easy solutions that require the use of violence; they must take into account existing reality and accept a boundless diversity of situations.

The Hellenes actually invented the solution: they "squared the circle" by creating organized structures, combining authority and hierarchy with free and equal citizens (who remained so). This implied the invention of the very art of "politics," that is, the art of bringing into agreement different wills, competing interests, even rival ambitions, without deliberately sacrificing one to

[42] The last two books of Aristotle's *Politics,* 7 and 8, deal with the ideal state. Experts believe that these two books were actually written before the others despite their place in the work, and that they were written by a young Aristotle when he settled in Assos, when the Academy's influence on him was still strong. Consequently, his model state resembles closely that of Plato's *Republic* and his *Laws*. We find the same pro-Spartan tendencies, the same emphasis on state-provided education, the same program of music and gymnastics, the same suspicion of innovations imported from abroad, and the same tight control over couples and child-bearing. And above all, the same starting point: the structure of the state must be in harmony with the structure of the individual soul (7.1.1323b.10–12). Virtue must prevail in the soul, and the state itself must be virtuous so that it can foster the perfection of virtues in each person. But these books are not original parts of the *Politics,* and for this reason we have made only one reference to them in the discussion.

[43] This is not a "liberal" policy: we discuss the difference between the concepts of "moderation" and "liberalism" when we discuss Montesquieu and modern liberalism in our *Histoire des idées politiques aux temps modernes et contemporains* (Paris: Presses Universitaires de France, 2002).

the benefit of others, without suffocating entire social classes (with the exception of slaves who were still not considered). This was the art of compromise, in a sense: not one that requires the forsaking of a praiseworthy, but out-of-reach ideal, but one where moderation itself is valued as an excellent ideal because it allows the largest number of citizens to thrive and flourish in the fertile soil of the city. Aristotle was by no means the first Greek to have thirsted for and experienced such "humanism," but he was certainly the first to have thought it through systematically. In fact, his theoretical conceptualizations of political problems remained decisive factors in political science well into the twentieth century.

Chapter 4

Xenophon, Isocrates, Demosthenes

Plato and Aristotle are not the only important fourth century writers for the history of political ideas. Their contemporaries, Xenophon, Isocrates, and Demosthenes, are also of great interest. Like Plato before them, and to a degree Aristotle as well, they address harsh criticism at the democratic form of government.

The quasi-unanimity of fourth century Greek intellectuals against democracy is thought provoking. Fifth century Athens offered the model of a "state under the rule of law"—providing equality before the law, freedom of thought and expression, pluralism, and commercial and cultural dynamism—which, though established by the democratic party after violent struggles with the aristocracy, gradually prevailed as it became apparent that it served the general interest and had enabled the flourishing of a brilliant civilization in Athens, so admired by the Greeks.

But fourth century democracy changed nature. Reestablished after the disaster of the Peloponnesian War and the tyranny of the Thirty, it became a "people's democracy" or, at any rate, a dictatorship of the people's party. Demagogues succeeded in distorting procedures of public debate and election. Justice became political. Systematic fiscal seizures served a policy of social relief (a kind of state socialism before that term existed). One consequence was the arousal of a suspicion of economic circles and chronic economic crisis. Democracy also demonstrated an inability to take the necessary foreign policy steps. In the opinion of some politicians, like Demosthenes, democracy was ill prepared to face the Macedonian threat. In short, democracy seemed to be leading to the ruin of the *state under the rule of law*. Plato's criticism and Aristotle's own lack of support can be understood in the context of Athens's political and cultural decline, resulting in its defeat in 338 BC (together with the other Greeks) at the battle of Chaeronea against the Macedonians.

I. Xenophon

Xenophon is the representative of "rightist" political ideas (we will see how below), though they are less extreme and of a different nature than Plato's.

A. Life

Xenophon of Athens (b. ca. 430 BC and d. ca. 355 BC) was a pupil of the Sophist Prodicos of Ceos. While very young he also studied under Socrates for five or six years. With Plato and Antisthenes (founder of the Cynics), he was one of the most celebrated Socratics. Perhaps disheartened by Athens's defeat at Chaeronea and the ensuing civil strife, Xenophon turned his back on an active political career in his native land. Like Plato, he looked abroad for his future.

In 401 BC, he joined other Greek mercenaries in backing Cyrus the Younger, who attempted to overthrow his brother Artaxerxes II, king of Persia. The attempt failed at the gates of Babylon, and the Ten Thousand, as the army of mercenaries was known, had to make their way back to Greece. Xenophon was one of five leaders elected by the soldiers to replace the generals killed by the satrap Tissaphernes. The army safely reached Greece after a long journey through Anatolia. Xenophon narrated this saga in his famous record of the expedition, *Anabasis*. Exiled by the Athenians, repelled by the circumstances surrounding Socrates' shameful death, he entered the service of Sparta and became a close ally of Agesilaus, king of Sparta; they fought together against Athens at Coronea (394 BC).

The Spartans granted him a property at Scillus, near Olympia in Ellis (Peloponnesus), and he settled there in 391 BC. He wrote most of his work there during the next 20 years of a peaceful retirement. After 371, the situation deteriorated in Sparta and he was forced to relocate to Corinth. (It may be that his exile was rescinded; in any case, he resettled in Attica ca. 364.) Our knowledge of the final 15 years of his life is poor.

B. Work

As a thinker Xenophon is very original and difficult to classify. His interests extend to military issues and matters related to war as attested by four of his works: *Anabasis, Art of Horsemanship, Cavalry Commander,* and *On Hunting*. He was a lifelong observer of political events and wrote a history of the end of the Peloponnesian War and of the events leading up to the Battle of Mantinea titled *Hellenica;* it was intended as a continuation of Thucydides' unfinished account. Xenophon fancied himself something of a political theoretician with his *Constitution of the Lacedaemonians* and the short treatise *Constitution of the Athenians* (perhaps apocryphal), and above all *Cyropaedia,* his reply to Plato's *Republic* (a historical—if not entirely fictitious—romance on the education of Cyrus the Elder, founder of the Achaemenid Persian monarchy). In this work he provides an exposition of the ideal monarch (again with long discursions on the military arts). His model in *Cyropaedia* is more Agesilaus, king of Sparta, than the Persian king, Cyrus. Later he devoted a second portrait to Agesilaus, titled *Agesilaus*. In his dialogue on government, *Hiero,* he describes tyranny as the opposite of true monarchy, to rival once again the last books of Plato's *Republic*. An admiring pupil of Socrates, he was revolted by his death and the slanders circulating against him in Athens. He wrote a series of works to do justice to his master: *Apology of Socrates, Memorabilia,* and *Symposium*. Finally, his interest in economics and agriculture inspired two additional works: *Oeconomicus,* which shines the spotlight once again on Socrates, and *Ways and Means*. Xenophon's work is vast but often neglected by philosophers, primarily because it is difficult to recognize an organized philosophical system. But it is rich in very original political viewpoints, the likes of which are found neither in Plato nor Aristotle. Importantly, his ideas are informed by the practical experience of power, absent in both Plato and Aristotle.

Xenophon's thought is marked by a "spirit of finesse" and, indeed, "spirit" on the whole. It expresses humor, benevolence, humanity; it displays great psychological insight (often reminiscent of the best seventeenth century French moralists); his powers of observation and eye for detail are acute. Nearly everything he writes is subtle and delightful. His style is lucid and graceful. He is understandably held up as one of the finest examples of the "Attic" spirit.

Xenophon's many talents explain, no doubt, why he left one of the finest psychological portraits of Socrates to come down to us, certainly more subtle and accurate than anything Plato wrote. For one, Xenophon does not intervene between the portrait and the model, nor does he create a wall of abstraction or some system like Plato. Furthermore, he was probably closer to Socrates in terms of his cast of mind, irony, and affinity for moral issues, but also in his concern for what is practical and useful. Xenophon's portraits of Socrates in his *Symposium, Memorabilia,* and the *Apology of Socrates* leave the reader thinking: surely, this is what Socrates the *man* must have been like.

Xenophon formulates a robust criticism of the declining morality of Athenian democracy. He also brings together the elements of a positive theory of the state and power.

1. *A Critique of Democracy*

Democracy in fourth century Athens ceased to be a form of government in the service of the public interest and became a regime serving a specific *clientele,* the people. Its chief characteristic was *irrationality.* It was a reign of demagogy, jealousy, and appearances.

a. Partisan Power

In Xenophon's time, democracy became the dictatorship of a faction. For his contemporaries, it was clearly the power of the "poor." Socrates addresses Euthydemus: "As the state you are preparing yourself to direct is governed by the people, no doubt you know what popular government is?—I think so, certainly—Then do you suppose it possible to know popular government without knowing the people?—Indeed I don't.—And do you know, then, what the people consists of?—The poorer classes."[1]

But the poor are *wicked:*[2] "And everywhere on earth the best element is opposed to democracy. For among the best people there is minimal wantonness and injustice but a maximum of scrupulous care for what is good, whereas among the people there is a maximum of ignorance, disorder, and wickedness; for poverty draws them rather to disgraceful actions, and because of a lack of money some men are uneducated and ignorant" (*Constitution of the Athenians* 1.5). "In no city is the superior element well disposed to the populace, but in each city it is the worst part which is well disposed to the populace" (3.10).[3]

Thus, the choice of democracy is problematic. It is understandable among the poor; they recognize their interest. But for those with a certain level of education, the choice of democracy is genuinely *evil:* "I pardon the people themselves for their democracy. One must forgive everyone for looking after his own interests. But whoever is not a man of the people and yet prefers to live in a democratic city rather than in an oligarchic one has readied himself to do wrong and has realized that it is easier for an evil man to escape notice in a democratic city than in an oligarchic" (*Constitution of the Athenians* 2.20).

---

[1] Xenophon, *Memorabilia,* 4.2.37, trans. E. C. Marchant (Cambridge, MA: Harvard University Press, 1923); hereafter cited in the text.

[2] Xenophon, *Constitution of the Athenians* 1.1, *Scripta Minora,* trans. E. C. Marchant and G. W. Bowersock (Cambridge, MA: Harvard University Press, 1925); all works by Xenophon are in this volume, hereafter cited in the text.

[3] In Rome as well, aristocrats were *boni* and *optimate,* "good" and the "best"; see below the chapter on Cicero.

While the upper classes may be morally and intellectually superior to the people, a pure, aristocratic form of government is not good; aristocrats display a class egoism that causes them to adopt unjust stances. Even a mean and stupid man of the people will defend the cause of his class. The Athenians are right to give everyone a voice.

> Their policy is also excellent in this very point of allowing even the worst people to speak. For if the good men were to speak and make policy, it would be splendid for the likes of themselves but not so for the men of the people. But, as things are, any wretch who wants to can stand up and obtain what is good for him and the likes of himself. Someone might say, "What good would such a man propose for himself and the people?" But they know that this man's ignorance, baseness, and favor are more profitable than the good man's virtue, wisdom, and ill will. (*Constitution of the Athenians* 1.6–7)

In the end, what is good is *pluralism,* not the people; it is democracy in the sense of *isonomia,* equality before the law, not class domination of the poorest (note that the *Constitution of the Athenians* may not be by Xenophon).[4]

b. Distortion of Justice

The meanness of the people, fanned by demagogy, leads to the failure of justice. "Do you not observe that the Athenian courts have often been carried away by an eloquent speech and have condemned innocent men to death, and often on the other hand the guilty have been acquitted either because their plea aroused compassion or because their speech was witty?" (*Apology of Socrates* 4). Witnesses are suborned and, worse, they allow it to happen (24). Justice is politicized: because the Athenians required their confederates[5] to come to Athens for their trials, they collected the court costs and systematically ensured the triumph of the democrats' causes—a combination of "racketeering" and political partisanship (*Constitution of the Athenians* 16).

c. Distortion of Reason

Similarly, Xenophon was critical of Athens's election procedures and its method of appointment by lot. In his opinion, both were irrational systems; what was required was *competence* (whereas people who owe their election to looks and intrigue often display crass ignorance [*Memorabilia* 3.1.3, and throughout]). These irrational systems were responsible for the lack of discipline and powerlessness of the Athenian armies: "This may be due to the incompetence of the officers. You must have noticed that no one attempts to exercise authority over our harpists, choristers and dancers, if he is incompetent, nor over wrestlers or wrestlers who also box? All who have authority over them can tell where they learned their business; but most of our generals are improvisers" (3.5.21).

Moreover, the system by election causes the best men to run away, because they are intimidated by the mob: As Socrates says to Charmides, "I mean to give you a lesson. The wisest do not make you bashful, and the strongest do not make you timid; yet you are ashamed to address an audience of mere dunces and weaklings. Who are they that make you ashamed? The fullers or the cobblers or the builders or the smiths or the farmers or the merchants, or the traffickers in the

[4] The same text goes even further in affirming a principle of universal *isonomia.* Xenophon believes that *isonomia* and equality of speech should benefit those who are useful to the city: for example, in addition to the *hoplites,* noblemen, and "honorable men," Xenophon includes the builders and operators of ships. They represent the lifeblood of the city; it is normal that they are able to speak, that they can enter the magistracies (*Constitution of the Athenians* 1.2). In Athens, freedom of conduct and speech is left to the metics, and, in certain cases, to slaves, insofar as they are useful to the state (*Constitution of the Athenians* 1.12).

[5] The reference is to the Second Athenian Confederacy.

market-place who think of nothing but buying cheap and selling dear? For these are the people who make up the Assembly" (*Memorabilia* 3.7.6).

Laws voted in these circumstances are not expressions of reason but of violence; this is what the young Alcibiades (not yet 20 years old) said with insolence to Pericles: "whatever the assembled majority, through using its power over the owners of property, enacts without persuasion is not law, but force" (*Memorabilia* 1.2.45).

d. Corruption

The worst evil of democracy is corruption. There are many in this form of government who "desire to win honour and to bear rule in their cities that they may have power to embezzle" (*Memorabilia* 2.6.24).

In Athens, tax fraud and property theft were rampant: "there are trierarchs who do not equip the ship for which they are responsible, and others who build on public property" (*Constitution of the Athenians* 3.4, with modifications).

In Xenophon's time, the political class was so corrupt that it was totally discredited. Honorable people avoided associating with it. Callias said as much to Socrates and his guests at the *Banquet:* "I think that my entertainment would present a great deal more brilliance if my dining-room were graced with the presence of men like you, whose hearts have undergone philosophy's purification, than it would with... office-seekers."[6]

Athens persecuted the rich, considering their money to be a state resource. Even if Critobuls—one of Socrates' interlocutors in *Oeconomicus*—had three times the wealth he did, it would not suffice to pay all the expenses his fellow citizens burdened him with. "Whenever you seem to fall short of what is expected of you," Socrates says, "the Athenians will certainly punish you as though they had caught you robbing them."[7]

The corruption of politicians is rivaled only by that of the "sycophants," the blackmailers who take the rich to the popular courts for their own personal gain. Criton, a wealthy man with ties to Socrates,[8] complains about this: "actions are pending against me not because I have done the plaintiffs an injury, but because they think that I would sooner pay than have trouble" (*Memorabilia* 2.9.1). In the *Symposium,* Charmides affirms that he is happier now that he is poor. Democracy leaves him alone now and no longer treats him like a slave: "when I was rich... I knuckled down to the blackmailers, knowing well enough that my abilities lay more in the direction of suffering injury than of inflicting it on them. Then, too, I was for ever being ordered by the government to undergo some expenditure or other.... Now, however, since I am stripped of my property... I am no longer subjected to threats but do the threatening now myself.... People now actually rise from their seats in deference to me, and rich men obsequiously give me the right of way on the street" (*Symposium* 4.30–31).

e. Complexity and Inertia of Democratic Institutions

Lastly, Xenophon finds that the democratic state cannot function properly because of the paralysis of its complex and unwieldy bureaucracy:

> I notice also that objections are raised against the Athenians because it is sometimes not possible for a person, though he sit about for a year, to negotiate with the council[9] or the

[6] Plato, *Symposium,* 1.4, trans. W. R. M. Lamb, in *Plato in Twelve Volumes,* vol. 3 (Cambridge, MA: Harvard University Press, 1925). Later, Isocrates and Demosthenes reaffirmed such contempt for politicians.

[7] Xenophon, *Oeconomicus,* 2.6, trans. E. C. Marchant (Cambridge, MA: Harvard University Press, 1923); cf. 7.3.

[8] The same Criton gave his name to the dialogue by Plato.

[9] The Boule of Four Hundred.

> assembly [the *ecclesia*]. This happens at Athens for no other reason than that owing to the quantity of business they are not able to deal with all persons before sending them away. For how could they do this? First of all they have to hold more festivals than any other Greek city (and when these are going on it is even less possible for any of the city's affairs to be transacted), next they have to preside over private and public trials and investigations into the conduct of magistrates to a degree beyond that of all other men, and the council has to consider many issues involving war, revenues, law-making, local problems as they occur, also many issues on behalf of the allies, receipt of tribute, the care of dockyards and shrines. Is there accordingly any cause for surprise if with so much business they are unable to negotiate with all persons? (*Constitution of the Athenians* 3.4)

In the perilous labyrinth of bureaucracy, it is virtually impossible to find a responsible interlocutor.

> For oligarchic cities it is necessary to keep to alliances and oaths. If they do not abide by agreements or if injustice is done, there are the names of the few who made the agreement. But whatever agreements the populace makes can be repudiated by referring the blame to the one who spoke or took the vote, while the others declare that they were absent or did not approve of the agreement made in the full assembly. If it seems advisable for their decisions not to be effective, they invent myriad excuses for not doing what they do not want to do. And if there are any bad results from the people's plans, they charge that a few persons, working against them, ruined their plans; but if there is a good result, they take the credit for themselves. (*Constitution of the Athenians* 3.4)

Xenophon draws the conclusion that democracy is leading Athens to certain decline. Consequently, like Plato, he recommends a reactionary Spartan-type political program. A return to the virtues of the ancestors is necessary; they can be learned from contemporary peoples, who have preserved them well because they have not been exposed to the erring ways of the Athenians.

f. The Example of Sparta

Admiration for Sparta was a common theme in Socratic circles, disappointed by Athenian democracy, as we know. The members of this circle hoped that if Athenians, like Lacedaemonians, showed more respect for their elders, if they refrained from mocking those who take physical exercise, if they lived in peace rather than constantly dragging each other before the courts,[10] then the city would flourish again. Of course, the most admirable thing about Sparta was its constitution, which enabled one of the least populous states of Greece to become one of the most powerful. Xenophon affirms this in his *Constitution of the Lacedaemonians,* written just a few years before the final collapse of Spartan authority at Leuctra in 371 BC.[11]

Unlike Plato, however, Xenophon is not an unconditional admirer of Sparta. On the one hand, although he hopes for a revitalization of Athenian morality through imitation of the Spartan model, he never calls for a revolution to establish suddenly an aristocratic form of government in Athens. He means for his antidemocratic reforms to be implemented step by step (see

[10] Xenophon, like Plato, fails to seize the significance of the rise in the number of lawsuits in Athens. Lawsuits exist only where pluralism (whether of business or ideas) thrives, regulated by the law. Lawsuits are the necessary price to be paid for handling such pluralism and for properly ordering society on the basis of personal liberty. It reflects a preference for the right of law over personal vendetta. Paradoxically, an increase in the number of lawsuits in society expresses moral progress. The resolution of disputes through the courts involves a decision not to use private force (here we follow Karl Popper analysis of Plato's disapproval of court trials in the *Republic*).

[11] Xenophon writes his work at the time Plato writes his *Republic*. Sparta was a shining example at this time.

Constitution of the Athenians 3.10). On the other hand, given his praise of individualism and its merits—which he backed with excellent arguments—and his support of family life, and given his formal denunciation of collectivism and egalitarianism, it is unlikely that he ever championed the Spartan model wholeheartedly. Agesilaus, the Spartan king whose portrait Xenophon sketched in a work with that title, was a very particular Spartiate. Anyway, in the end, Xenophon's intellectual curiosity turned him from the Lacedaemonian model.

The thrust of his investigations focused on the proper principles of organization, whether applied to a state, an army, a ship, an agricultural entity, or any other economic organization capable of making a collective body rich and powerful. Reflecting on his own experience in these fields, he formulates some very original ideas, and in so doing distances himself from a Spartan model of the "closed society."

2. *A Theory of Organizational Management*

Xenophon's thinking is often summarized by saying that he is a "royalist," but the formula is too simplistic. He believes in the role of strong personalities and leaders and, consequently under certain conditions, in the role of a king in the state. But for him, this is only the special case of a general principle, which applies to all organizations, and not just the state. The careful reader is soon persuaded that the true object of Xenophon's thinking is organization as such.

The defining characteristic of the leader or head of an organization is not that he gives orders; it is his capacity to plan, organize, enforce rules, and create systems and procedures within the organization that motivate others to work and perform to the highest degree of excellence. This includes being attentive to each person, ensuring that he feels—and is—treated justly. In sum, Xenophon formulates a genuine theory of "management."[12] He is a theoretician of monarchy only insofar as he is a positive, rational analyst of the skills, preoccupations, and methods of an *organizational leader*.

With Xenophon, Greek scientific thought moves forward another step: his analysis of autocracy as a political phenomenon drops all references to the sacred and emphasizes the universal mechanisms of human behavior. In a sense, Xenophon anticipates our most modern studies of "organizational sociology."

a. The Role of Individuals

Xenophon is a believer in the role of *individuals* in the life of communities and in history. Thinkers and actors are always individuals. When they think correctly, when they decide quickly and clearly, when they apply the law properly, and above all, when they motivate and inspire others, then things go well and fate can sometimes turn. Isomachus comments to Socrates,

> I grant you, Socrates, that in respect of aptitude for command, which is common to all forms of business alike—agriculture, politics, estate-management, warfare—in that respect the intelligence shown by different classes of men varies greatly. For example, on a man-of-war, when the ship is on the high seas and the rowers must toil all day to reach port, some boatswains can say and do the right thing to sharpen the men's spirits and make them work with a will, while others are so unintelligent that it takes them more than twice the time to finish the same voyage. Here they land bathed in sweat, with mutual congratulations, boatswain and seamen. There they arrive with a dry skin; they hate their master and he hates them. Generals, too, differ from one another in this respect. For some make their men

[12] Although anachronistic, we use this term because it is probably the best expression of the innovative concept that Xenophon constructs here.

unwilling to work and to take risks, disinclined and unwilling to obey, except under compulsion, and actually proud of defying their commander: aye, and they cause them to have no sense of dishonour when something disgraceful occurs. Contrast the genius, the brave and scientific leader: let him take over the command of these same troops, or of others if you like. What effect has he on them? They are ashamed to do a disgraceful act, think it better to obey, and take a pride in obedience, working cheerfully, every man and all together, when it is necessary to work. Just as a love of work may spring up in the mind of a private soldier here and there, so a whole army under the influence of a good leader is inspired with love of work and ambition to distinguish itself under the commander's eye. Let this be the feeling of the rank and file for their commander; and I tell you, he is the strong leader, he, and not the sturdiest soldier, not the best with bow and javelin, not the man who rides the best horse and is foremost in facing danger, not the ideal of knight or targeteer,[13] but he who can make his soldiers feel that they are bound to follow him through fire and in any adventure. Him you may justly call high-minded who has many followers of like mind; and with reason may he be said to march "with a strong arm" whose will many an arm is ready to serve; and truly great is he who can do great deeds by his will rather than his strength.

So too in private industries, the man in authority—bailiff or manager—who can make the workers keen, industrious and persevering—he is the man who gives a lift to the business and swells the surplus. But, Socrates, if the appearance of the master in the field, of the man who has the fullest power to punish the bad and reward the strenuous workmen, makes no striking impression on the men at work, I for one cannot envy him. But if at sight of him they bestir themselves, and a spirit of determination and rivalry and eagerness to excel falls on every workman, then I should say: this man has a touch of the kingly nature in him. And this, in my judgment, is the greatest thing in every operation that makes any demand on the labour of men, and therefore in agriculture. Mind you, I do not go so far as to say that this can be learnt at sight or at a single hearing. On the contrary, to acquire these powers a man needs education; he must be possessed of great natural gifts; above all, he must be a genius. For I reckon this gift is not altogether human, but divine—this power to win willing obedience: it is manifestly a gift of the gods to the true votaries of prudence.[14] (*Oeconomicus* 21)

b. Leadership Skills

Interestingly, Xenophon ranks *temperance,* not strength or intelligence, at the top of the list of *managerial* skills. The leaders he most admires—Cyrus and Agesilaus—are men of remarkable restraint. They eat, drink, and sleep very little. They are virtually indifferent to women (and boys), oblivious to comfort and luxury. They exercise daily; when they are not at war, they are hunting. "He [Cyrus] never dined without first having got himself into a sweat, nor would he have any food given to his horses without their having first been duly exercised."[15]

Magnanimity is another virtue of great leaders. "The rest of his preparations for war Cyrus now continued on a magnificent scale, for he was planning no mean enterprise" (*Cyropaedia* 6.2.4). The impact of great vision is admirable: only it leads to lasting works, the founding of empires and institutions. Cyrus is a political paragon because from his own genius he created the

[13] A light infantry soldier armed with a shield.

[14] Like Socrates, Xenophon attributes a role to both "nature" and "culture," to the innate and the acquired. This was the teaching of the Sophists. Xenophon's originality out of respect to the Sophists (but not out of respect to Socrates) is to add a pinch of religion.

[15] Xenophon, *Cyropaedia,* 8.1.38, 2 vols., trans. Walter Miller (Cambridge, MA: Harvard University Press, 1914); hereafter cited in the text.

Persian Empire, its territory, its dynasty and its institutions. Agesilaus is equally magnanimous. No doubt, Xenophon would have admired Alexander the Great.

c. Competence

Aristotle says that a magnanimous person is one who believes himself to be, and indeed is, capable of great things. *Competence* is the basic foundation of a *leader's* authority. "Under all conditions human beings are most willing to obey those whom they believe to be the best." In sickness, the patient obeys the doctor; on board ship, the traveler obeys the captain (*Memorabilia* 3.3.9). Moreover, where things continue to work properly in Athens is where power is in competent hands (*Memorabilia* 3.5.21). Socrates scolds Plato's brother, young Glaucon, for boasting of his intention to hold high political office, although he proves incapable of answering the most elementary questions on politics and the economy. In a concise cross-examination, Socrates demonstrates that Glaucon lacks a basic command of facts and figures and has not studied them in detail (*Memorabilia* 3.6). And yet, Glaucon, though manifestly incompetent, might well exercise power, proof, if need be, of the culpable negligence of democracy. The belief that competence breeds authority, all else being equal, is made with the following argument: "In spinning wool, he [Socrates] would point out, the women govern the men because they know how to do it and men do not" (*Memorabilia* 3.9.11).

Xenophon analyzes from within the mechanisms that cause people naturally to obey a leader with the requisite skills regardless of circumstance. It is not that men are cowardly or victims; they simply know that it is *in their interest* to obey. This is the conclusion drawn from a dialogue between Cyrus and his father, Cambyses, as the Persian army launched its war campaign (*Cyropaedia* 1.6). You might think that the strongest and most determined in battle are envied. Not at all! They are loved because the weaker soldiers know that the stronger ones play a leading role in victory; and, though it is not their primary intent, they provide assistance and protection in the midst of peril. Rather than envy, the weaker ones express admiration and gratitude. "[Cyrus] knew that common dangers make comrades kindly disposed toward one another, and that in the midst of such dangers there is no jealousy of those who wear decorations on their armour or of those who are striving for glory; on the contrary, soldiers praise and love their fellows even more, because they recognize in them co-workers for the common good" (*Cyropaedia* 3.3.10).[16]

It is because he attaches such importance to competence that Xenophon condemns the appointment of magistrates by democratic procedures, especially the drawing of lots and elections, which result in the choice of people without the proper qualities or qualifications for the job at hand. Still, an election offers more guarantees than appointment by lot. In Sparta it is used for all magisterial appointments. Even kings are chosen this way, if ever more than one candidate from the royal families is in contention (*Agesilaus* 1).

d. The Leader Serves the Interests of Those He Commands

Applying these general principles to the particular circumstances of political power, it becomes clear that the only person truly able to rule a state is one who can provide its citizens with services that warrant him occupying the position of ruler. There is an exchange of favors between the ruler and the citizens; neither party has any illusions about this, both cooperate with genuine *philia*. The enlightened despot is not entitled to behave with the city's resources as if they were private

[16] This calls to mind the *philia*, which Aristotle says exists among equals in "natural communities." Everyone understands that every task, even the highest, undertaken by another serves the common interest, and in this respect serves one's own as well. Consequently, what is superior, because and by means of its superiority, serves what is inferior. As far as the inferior understands this, there is *philia* of the inferior for the superior.

possessions for his personal enjoyment. But neither is he an altruist, content to achieve the happiness of his subjects while sacrificing his own. He enjoys the good he creates for himself indirectly, as a consequence of the good he creates for the citizens. The bad despot is one who competes with his subjects. The good despot is one who champions competition between the state he rules and other states; but with his own subjects he urges friendly collaboration and mutually profitable exchange (*Hiero* 11).

Such is the harmony achieved by Sparta's monarchy. The Spartans were never jealous of the prerogatives of their kings. The kings, in turn, never attempted to abuse their powers tyrannically (*Agesilaus* 1). This explains the exceptional stability of the regime: "no other government—democracy, oligarchy, despotism or kingdom—can lay claim to an unbroken existence, this kingdom [Sparta] alone stands fast continually" (*Agesilaus* 1.4).[17]

e. A "Cybernetic" Theory of Inequality and Emulation

From the principle that the power of the best is good for all, Xenophon draws several conclusions for the management of organizations, political or otherwise. Rules must be established whereby it is in one's vested interest to give the best of oneself, and against one's interest to contribute little or poorly. In this way, everyone will do his or her best and the general interest will be optimized. Conversely, egalitarianism is disastrous for the general interest, and especially for those at the lower end of the scale of talents and virtues.

Xenophon explains this rationally and objectively, leaving no hint of aristocratic contempt for the poor—in contrast with Theocritus and, at times, Plato. In fact, Xenophon affirms a scientific theory of inequality as a *transmitter of information* and a *factor of social dynamism,* prefiguring, in some respects, our modern "systemic" theories. Since he is well aware of the criticism that can be made against his theory in the name of principled egalitarianism and compassion, he has given thought to these objections but continues to think that the weakest are *advantaged by inequality, not disadvantaged.*

He insists on the universality of these principles, regardless of the type or size of organization, and whether public or private:

> [Socrates said,] Don't look down on business men, Nicomachides. For the management of private concerns differs only in point of number from that of public affairs. In other respects they are much alike, and particularly in this, that neither can be carried on without men, and the men employed in private and public transactions are the same. For those who take charge of public affairs employ just the same men when they attend to their own; and those who understand how to employ them are successful directors of public and private concerns, and those who do not, fail in both. (*Memorabilia* 3.4.12)[18]

What, then, are these principles? For an organization to perform efficiently, it is necessary to *reward effort and to punish laziness systematically.*

> The clothes that I must provide for my work-people and the shoes are not all alike. Some are better than others, some worse, in order that I may reward the better servant with the

[17] Xenophon, thus, proposes an explanation for the remarkable stability of the Spartan regime, so greatly admired by all Greek political thinkers. In his view it is its *mixed* character that ensured such stability (constitutionally, there were three powers: the people, the senate, and the kings; none of them abused their powers). Polybius took up this idea again later.

[18] Xenophon makes the claim that good "stewards" (today we would say good CEOs or managers) can make good generals because they know how to organize and lead (*Memorabilia* 3.4.7). Furthermore, "stewards" know how to wage economic battles. Xenophon's ideas are original for his time.

> superior articles, and give the inferior things to the less deserving. For I think it is very disheartening to good servants, Socrates, when they see that they do all the work, and others who are not willing to work hard and run risks when need be, get the same as they. For my part, then, I don't choose to put the deserving on a level with the worthless, and when I know that my bailiffs have distributed the best things to the most deserving, I commend them; and if I see that flattery or any other futile service wins special favour, I don't overlook it, but reprove the bailiff, and try to show him, Socrates, that such favouritism is not even in his own interest. (*Oeconomicus* 13.10–12)

This theory is fully comprehensible to the people. Cyrus proposes the principle that those who excel in war will be rewarded systematically, and those who waver will be punished or rejected. He even succeeds in obtaining democratic approval for this aristocratic principle. Of all the proponents of this principle, the most persuasive was an orator, and man of the people, by the name of Pheraulas, who sees that it offers him the only possible means to rise above his station and to equal or surpass the nobles (the so-called "peers") (*Cyropaedia* 2.3).

Next, Cyrus applies the principle in all of his campaigns, awarding honors and spoils after each battle, to each his merit according to the role he played (see, e.g., *Cyropaedia* 3.3). Importantly, his application of the principle is anything but random or arbitrary; it is very systematic: nobody escapes dishonor if he fails to perform, nobody is forgotten in the rewards if he excels through praiseworthy conduct. Between battles, Cyrus organizes exercises and games; there, too, he rewards generously those who show the most enthusiasm. Using various methods (some quite insane!), he takes pains to ensure that everyone understands how they have performed. He uses emulation as a *system* to signal and guarantee the rationality of collective action.

> So when invited guests came to dinner, he did not assign them their seats at random, but he seated on Cyrus's left the one for whom he had the highest regard, for the left side was more readily exposed to treacherous designs than the right; and the one who was second in esteem he seated on his right, the third again on the left, the fourth on the right, and so on, if there were more.
>
> For he thought it a good plan to show publicly how much regard he had for each one, because where people feel that the one who merits most will neither have his praise proclaimed nor receive a prize, there is no emulation among them; but where the most deserving is seen to receive the most preferment, there all are seen to contend most eagerly for the first place.
>
> Accordingly, Cyrus thus made public recognition of those who stood first in his esteem, beginning even with the places they took when sitting or standing in his company. He did not, however, assign the appointed place permanently, but he made it a rule that by noble deeds any one might advance to a more honoured seat, and that if any one should conduct himself ill he should go back to one less honoured. (*Cyropaedia* 8.4.3–5)

In Sparta, men with a reputation for shameful conduct in battle were held in disgrace and branded cowards. They were constantly singled out and forced to hide from public notice. Their presence in honorable houses was forbidden; they were refused entry to the *palestra,* and so on. Thus, finding the system praiseworthy, Xenophon says, it is preferable to die in battle than to live in Sparta in shame (*Constitution of the Lacedaemonians* 9).

Simonides, the poet, recommends to Hiero, the despot, that he should create a general spirit of emulation in his state, not just in the traditional fields of theater, the chorus, physical exercise, and military training, but in others as well, such as farming, commercial and industrial activities, and technical invention. In this way, such activities will be encouraged and develop. He also recommends that the tyrant himself should distribute rewards, which will increase his popularity, and that he should use low-ranking subordinates to administer punishments and reprimands, which make a leader unpopular (*Hiero* 9). He adds that this policy will not be costly to the despot: small rewards suffice because the real incentive is a spirit of emulation, which is, in fact, the true quality that distinguishes humans from animals: "For indeed it seems to me, Hiero, that in this man differs from other animals—I mean, in this craving for honour. In meat and drink and sleep and sex all creatures alike seem to take pleasure; but love of honour is rooted neither in the brute beasts nor in every human being. But they in whom is implanted a passion for honour and praise, these are they who differ most from the beasts of the field, these are accounted men and not mere human beings" (*Hiero* 7.3).

This is why a very small prize at the games suffices to unleash tremendous efforts. The competitors seek honor; the material prize is pure pretext.

f. The Importance of Friends

Cyrus understands that he owes his power to the people around him and especially to their personal devotion to him. He also recognizes that their devotion is proportionate to their well-being or wretchedness, and to the certainty or uncertainty of being able to count on their leader. Cyrus secures the loyalty of those on whom he depends by rewarding them generously for their service. His sense of justice, composure, and joviality contributes greatly to their loyalty. He wants to be, and is, richer in friends than Croesus in gold.

A delightful passage in *Cyropaedia* (8.2.16–23) illustrates this. Croesus, the rich king of Lydia, vanquished by Cyrus, said to Cyrus that had he kept the spoils of his campaigns for himself instead of distributing them to his soldiers, he would be immensely rich today. Cyrus asks Croesus to estimate the size of his wealth in this case. Croesus names "some large sum." Cyrus puts the sum in a letter to his officers and vassals, requesting their help for a "major project," and asking them to reply immediately in writing, quoting the sum they are prepared to send. After Cyrus's messenger makes the rounds and brings in all the promises, it is found that they total the sum named by Croesus many times over, proving that Cyrus's policy is the better advised.

The wealth Cyrus retains for himself is merely a reserve fund from which he can draw to support his comrades-in-arms when they are in need. This is essentially a policy of *clientelism:* the leader is less interested in amassing wealth for the sake of "private ownership," in the bourgeois sense, than in having enough to hand out to subordinates on whom he can count, whatever the circumstances (*Cyropaedia* 8.4.7, and following).

Nevertheless, if the friends of Cyrus become too close and strike an alliance together, they can be dangerous. For this reason Cyrus is careful to foster rivalries so that they are as incapable of taking action against him as political rivals "in a republic" (8.2.28). Cyrus also uses coercion when necessary: he "raises their children at court," a euphemism for holding them hostage. He urges his satraps to do the same with the children of notables in their provinces (8.6).

g. Theory of Reliable Confederates: The Example of Eunuchs

Cyrus is keen to ensure his personal safety within the palace. He concludes that the best guards are eunuchs because they are the only men whose attachment to others—women, children, and minions, except for their masters—cannot be exploited by their enemies.

Since eunuchs are held in contempt by the rest of society, the master who showers honors and privileges on them actually raises them in the eyes of his subjects and rivals, and he in turn becomes in their eyes the most important figure. On the other hand (Xenophon's love of nature and hunting is visible in the following example), just as gelded horses and castrated dogs, compared to normal animals, are deprived of their spirit but not of their physical strength, eunuchs can make excellent bodyguards (Xenophon notes, "on the field of battle steel makes the weak equal to the strong"). A further advantage of eunuchs is that, although they are deprived of sexual desire, they by no means lack in ambition, which distinguishes man from beast. Thus, Cyrus plays on the same psychological strings with eunuchs as with others (*Cyropaedia* 7.5.61–65).

h. Maintain the Vanquished in Subservience

Over and above his associates and faithful followers, Cyrus, like all leaders, has to attend to the large number of subject peoples that come into his possession after his victories in war. The conqueror must be careful to keep the art of war to himself and refrain from teaching it to his conquered peoples. Like a herd of animals, subject people will require only food and drink to remain content (*Cyropaedia* 7.5). Xenophon remarks—long before Hegel's master-slave dialectic—that Cyrus pushes wisdom and foresight so far as to say that it is necessary to avoid exhausting his subjects on demanding projects; to hold them in submission for any length of time, he must avoid giving them the training that might make them a threat in the future (*Cyropaedia* 8.1).

i. Controlling the Organization: The King, "the Law with Eyes"

A leader needs time to look after important matters and must, therefore, delegate responsibility, but in an orderly way. The hierarchical organization of the army will serve as a model for the financial and administrative functions of the state (*Cyropaedia* 8.1.14–15). In the provinces, for example, satraps will govern with the same methods as at court (8.6); but in these same provinces, garrison officers will be directly appointed by the king. Thus, both levels keep an eye on each other (Cyrus also established a postal service to stay in touch with all parts of his empire [8.6]).

While a good *manager* should not do everything himself, he should nevertheless supervise everything. There is no example, Xenophon says, of a negligent master with conscientious supervisors and servants. "I like the answer that is attributed to the Persian. The king, you know, had happened on a good horse, and wanted to fatten him as speedily as possible. So he asked one who was reputed clever with horses what is the quickest way of fattening a horse. 'The master's eye,' replied the man" (Xenophon, *Oeconomicus* 12.12).

Thus, Xenophon describes the king as the "law with eyes" or the "seeing law." The same idea appears later in Hellenic theories of monarchy. The king's friends and clients are there, among other things, to provide him with a valuable *network of indicators* ("the so-called 'king's eyes' and 'king's ears'" [*Cyropaedia*]). He never depends on a single source and constantly cross-checks all information:

> for by rewarding liberally those who reported to him whatever it was in his interest to hear, he prompted many men to make it their business to use their eyes and ears to spy out what they could report to the king to his advantage. As a natural result of this, many "eyes" and many "ears" were ascribed to the king. But if any one thinks that the king selected one man to be his "eye," he is wrong; for one only would see and one would hear but little; and it would have amounted to ordering all the rest to pay no attention, if one only had been appointed to see and hear. Besides, if people knew that a certain man was the "eye," they would know that they must beware of him. But such is not the case; for the king listens to anybody who may claim to have heard or seen anything worthy of attention. And thus the saying comes about, "The king has many ears and many eyes." ... [Thus] every one conducted himself at all times just as if those who were within hearing were so many eyes and ears of the king. (*Cyropaedia* 8.2.10–12)

When supervised in this way, an organization is sound. Cyrus likes his armies to be in a constant state of readiness and to engage in precision maneuvers, so he has them exercise continually to approach near perfection in this respect. Likewise, Ischomachus, the character in *Oeconomicus* who is probably Xenophon himself, patiently teaches his young wife the principles of strict domestic order; everything must be in its proper place at all times. For Xenophon, the perfect model of order is the Phoenician merchant vessel, which Ischomachus visits when it is anchored in the port of Piraeus:[19]

> Now I saw this man in his spare time inspecting all the stores that are wanted, as a matter of course, in the ship. I was surprised to see him looking over them, and asked what he was doing. "Sir," he answered, "I am looking to see how the ship's tackle is stored, in case of accident, or whether anything is missing or mixed up with other stuff. For when God sends a storm at sea, there's no time to search about for what you want or to serve it out if it's in a muddle. For God... saves you when you do your work well." (*Oeconomicus* 8.15)

Good principles of organization are revealed by the continuity they give to the community that they benefit. Xenophon never misses an opportunity to point out that the institutions established by Cyrus are still in place among the Persians and that they continue to function well. The founder of an empire, like a good *manager,* has a quasi-demiurgic quality about him.

All this is possible on condition that the organization has *a single leader* at its head. This is Xenophon's assumption in every example he gives. Even in forms of government that are not monarchies in the strict sense of the term, unity of command is necessary: "you will find that among states, even when the government is not a monarchy, that state which most readily obeys its officers is least likely to be compelled to submit to its enemies" (*Cyropaedia* 8.1.4).

j. The Leader as Moral Example

Thus, a good organization is one where the leader and the group function symbiotically. This has a final consequence for the leader. He is not free to do and be as he likes. He must at all times exemplify in his person the virtues and rules that he commands of others. The focus of attention of his subordinates, he is also their moral paragon. They imitate the good and bad in him. If he slackens, the bad immediately spreads throughout the organization: "whenever the officer in charge is better, the administration of the institution is purer; but when he is worse, the administration is more corrupt" (*Cyropaedia* 8.1).

> [Cyrus] made it plain how important he held it to be to wrong no one of his friends or allies, and if he always paid scrupulous regard to what was upright, others also, he thought, would be more likely to abstain from improper gains and to endeavor to make their way by upright methods. And he thought that he should be more likely to inspire in all respect for others, if he himself were seen to show such respect for all as not to say or do anything improper. And that this would be the result he concluded from the following observation: people have more respect for those who have such respect for others than they have for those who have not; they show it toward even those whom they do not fear—to say nothing of what they would show toward their kings; and women also whom they see showing respect for others they are more inclined to look upon in turn with respect. (*Cyropaedia* 8.1.26–28)[20]

k. "Civic" Autocracy

We can now apply these general principles of organization to the state. State structures must be open to the influence and authority of those with outstanding qualities. The constitution should

[19] Phoenicians were the best sailors of the time.

[20] This idea is found later in numerous other theories of monarchy. A political body rots from the head but also heals from the head.

grant such persons substantial powers of direct authority. Does this mean that Xenophon is a royalist? In a sense, it does, since Xenophon speaks favorably of the Persian and Spartan monarchies. But when we consider what he says about Cyrus and Agesilaus more closely, we understand that he does not reject the "republican" model of the Greek *polis*. In fact, he advocates a type of autocratic rule along the lines of the "principate" under the Roman High Empire (see below, pp. 307–55).

The king that Xenophon holds up as an example is not an oriental king, sacred and absolute. He is Agesilaus, a real person known to Xenophon personally, a "civilized" Greek king, deeply respectful of the law, with an authority strictly limited by the constitution; Xenophon insists on this again and again. As for Cyrus, he is indeed a Persian king, but Xenophon sees him as an "ideal" more than as an actual model.

Agesilaus prefers "to rule and to be ruled at home according to the constitution" rather than to be the "supreme power in" Asia (*Agesilaus* 2.16).[21] "Though the most powerful man in the state, [Agesilaus] was clearly a devoted servant of the laws. For who would be minded to disobey when he saw the king obeying?" (7.2). The obedience of the first magistrate of the land to the law contributes to social order. No one will want to revolt, seeing that the king himself does not abuse his dominant position.

Xenophon contrasts Greek *sophrosyne* and reason (or those of a hellenized Cyrus) with the splendor and magical spirit of the Medes and the Indians. At the grand reception of the Indian ambassadors, Cyaxares, king of the Medes, reprimands the young Cyrus for the plainness of his robes. He expects Cyrus to appear with as much magnificence as possible. Cyrus replies rather tersely that a disciplined, ordered, and efficient army is preferable to commanders in purple, adorned with bracelets and necklaces (*Cyropaedia* 2.4.5–6). The oriental king is invisible, concealed, difficult to meet, while the king of Sparta is accessible and transparent: an equal, a citizen (*Agesilaus* 9; this entire chapter compares the king of Persia and the king of Sparta; they are two public figures with very different statuses and roles). Agesilaus's own daughter uses public transportation in Sparta like everyone else! (*Agesilaus* 8.7).

Thus, an autocratic ruler does not replace the *law*. Xenophon understands that the law is not a command given by a ruler to his subjects; it is a stable public norm that enables every individual to know what is and is not allowed. On this basis, it is possible for everyone to comport themselves freely without fear of the ruler's arbitrary intervention. Repeating a formula found in Herodotus, Xenophon remarks that happiness is achieved neither through power nor through slavery, but "in a middle path . . . through liberty" (*Memorabilia* 2.1.11). True, Xenophon corrects this "liberal" interpretation of the law with another. It is important, he says, that the negative laws of Draco and Solon—which aim to punish individuals disrespectful of the law—be completed by "the Persian king's code," that is, by rules that reward merit positively (*Oeconomicus* 14.4–10).[22]

Another Hellenic feature of the ideal autocratic ruler, according to Xenophon, is his use of *reasoned speech*. In Xenophon's writings, political leaders constantly deliver speeches; they explain, persuade, listen to, and answer objections. Their style of leadership and command is anything but *laconic*. "In addition to his other duties a cavalry leader must take care to be a good

[21] Like the other Greeks of his age, Xenophon does not have a very high opinion of "barbarians" in the collective sense, even if he frequented certain exceptionally brilliant individuals from Persia. Xenophon scoffs at barbarians on various occasions—for example, when he claims that (1) Greeks are able to show respect for laws and customs, whereas barbarians break their bond and are deviously cunning; (2) Greeks are also capable of being more cunning than barbarians, these "children," when war is declared and cunning is officially allowed and just (*Agesilaus* 1).

[22] Later, Montesquieu would also remark that, in monarchies, the law is not enough: it is necessary to distribute honors and rewards to individuals who devote themselves to the service of the state and stand out through remarkable deeds.

speaker"—"Did you suppose that a commander of cavalry should be mum? Did you never reflect that all the best we learned according to custom—the learning, I mean, that teaches us how to live—we learned by means of words, and that every other good lesson to be learned is learned by means of words; that the best teachers rely most on the spoken word and those with the deepest knowledge of the greatest subjects are the best talkers?" (*Memorabilia* 3.3.11).[23]

1. The Status of Religion

Finally, Xenophon's typical autocrat is different from the oriental sacred monarch in that he is basically free from magic and ritual. Nevertheless, Xenophon's religious attitudes, like those of most of his contemporaries, are ambiguous. Personally, he is pious or, more exactly, superstitious; he makes sacrifices and prays to the gods (in *Anabasis,* for example, each time he faces a choice, at a fork in the road to take the left path or right path, or to engage or disengage from the enemy, he consults the gods). Politically, however, he is truly irreligious and he expects the religious cult to defer to civil imperatives, not the other way around. On campaign the Spartan king comports himself like a priest, a sacred personage; everyone believes, including the king himself, that he descends from the gods (*Constitution of the Lacedaemonians* 13.10). But this is a borderline case explained by the fact that, in life-threatening situations such as war, it is best to put all chances in one's favor by observing customary practices. Xenophon also points out that Lycurgus himself submitted his laws to the oracle in Delphi for approval (8.5). In spite of this, Agesilaus's religion is internalized and unencumbered by ritualism: "One of Agesilaus's favorite maxims was that the gods have pleasure in righteous deeds no less than in holy temples" (*Agesilaus* 11.2, with modifications).

Above all, we see Xenophon's emancipation from magico-religious thinking in his advice to make "cynical" use of the exterior signs of religion as a means of government. The "oriental" magnificence of Cyrus's court, for example, is a deliberate artifice to impress the people: "Next we shall describe how Cyrus for the first time drove forth in state from his palace; and that is in place here, for the magnificence of his appearance in state seems to us to have been one of the arts that he devised to make his government command respect" (*Cyropaedia* 8.3.1). Each time Cyrus leaves Babylon, he organizes, with the help of his communications advisors, a magnificent, stately procession to put his prestige on display to the population, accustomed to the sacredness of the monarchy. Xenophon assures his reader that Cyrus is not taken in by the "prostrations" the Greeks find so reviling. He imposes them on his subjects for reasons of politics (8.3.1).

> We think, furthermore, that we have observed in Cyrus that he held the opinion that a ruler ought to excel his subjects not only in point of being actually better than they, but that he ought also to cast a sort of spell upon them. At any rate, he chose to wear the Median dress himself and persuaded his associates also to adopt it;[24] for he thought that if any one had any personal defect, that dress would help to conceal it, and that it made the wearer look very tall and very handsome. For they have shoes of such a form that without being detected the wearer can easily put something into the soles so as to make him look taller than he is. He encouraged also the fashion of pencilling the eyes, that they might seem more lustrous than they are, and of using cosmetics to make the complexion look better

[23] Here Xenophon expresses himself like Thucydides: in his writings, politicians and generals speak, explain, and strive to provide justification for their decisions and opinions in front of an audience, listening with rational intelligence. We also recognize here the pupil of the Sophists and Socrates, the contemporary and compatriot of Isocrates (see below, pp. 159–74). One exception confirms the rule: the *prytaneis* have the right to remove laughable public speakers from the speaker's platform (*Memorabilia* 3.6.1).

[24] So Cyrus changed his mind (see the episode narrated above about the conduct of young Cyrus, p. 154).

> than nature made it. He trained his associates also not to spit or to wipe the nose in public, and not to turn round to look at anything, as being men who wondered at nothing. All this he thought contributed, in some measure, to their appearing to their subjects men who could not lightly be despised. (*Cyropaedia* 8.1.40–42)

Lastly, Cyrus understands religion as a safeguard of morality, which in a sense confirms the analysis: "Cyrus considered that the piety of his friends was a good thing for him, too; for he reasoned as they do who prefer, when embarking on a voyage, to set sail with pious companions rather than with those who are believed to have committed some impiety" (*Cyropaedia* 8.1.25).

In the end, Xenophon is more attached to traditional religion than rationalists like Thucydides. Perhaps this is attributable to his antidemocratic attitudes: all is not subject to discussion. On the whole, though, his political ideas are fully rational. He insists on providing proofs for his assertions and never resorts to convention or myth as such.

3. *Economics*

Prior to the relevant chapters in Aristotle's *Politics* (though in a slightly less theoretical tone), we find in Xenophon's writings a variety of ideas on the economy—some conventional, others quite original. They coincide closely with the political ideas just presented.

a. Farming

In a more traditional vein, Xenophon (like Hesiod before and Virgil after him) praises farming, an occupation he deems worthy of a free person because it encourages both justice and the defense of freedom.

"The earth willingly teaches righteousness," and the better she is served, the more gifts she gives in return. "The land also stimulates armed protection of the country on the part of the husbandmen [farmers], by nourishing her crops in the open for the strongest to take. What art produces better runners, throwers and jumpers than husbandry [farming]?" (*Oeconomicus* 5.4–12).

b. Division of Labor

Economic prosperity is linked to the division of labor. Xenophon provides one of the earliest analyses of this principle.

An elementary division of labor can be found in the family (here Xenophon presages Aristotle's study of "natural communities"). "For it seems to me, dear, that the gods with great discernment have coupled together male and female, as they are called, chiefly in order that they may form a perfect partnership in mutual service" (*Oeconomicus* 7.17). The body and spirit of a man are suited to outdoor work, demanding physical effort and fearlessness. A woman has less physical stamina, more affection for young children, and greater shyness; for these reasons, she stays at home. But both are equal in terms of prudence, memory, consideration, and temperance. "Because both have not the same aptitudes, they have the more need of each other, and each member of the pair is the more useful to the other, the one being competent where the other is deficient" (28).

On an entirely different scale, Xenophon also finds division of labor in the urban economy (on this point he is much clearer and more comprehensive than Plato in the *Republic*):

> it is, of course, impossible for a man of many trades to be proficient in all of them. In large cities…inasmuch as many people have demands to make upon each branch of industry, one trade alone, and very often even less than a whole trade, is enough to support a man: one man, for instance, makes shoes for men, and another for women; and there are places even where one man earns a living by only stitching shoes, another by cutting them out,

> another by sewing the uppers together, while there is another who performs none of these operations but only assembles the parts. It follows, therefore, as a matter of course, that he who devotes himself to a very highly specialized line of work is bound to do it in the best possible manner.
>
> Exactly the same thing holds true also in reference to the kitchen: in any establishment where one and the same man arranges the dining couches, lays the table, bakes the bread, prepares now one sort of dish and now another, he must necessarily have things go as they may; but where it is all one man can do to stew meats and another to roast them, for one man to boil fish and another to bake them, for another to make bread and not every sort at that, but where it suffices if he makes one kind that has a high reputation—everything that is prepared in such a kitchen will, I think, necessarily be worked out with superior excellence. (*Cyropaedia* 8.2.4–5)

c. *Ways and Means:* An Apology of the Open Economy

Xenophon's most original ideas on the economy are found in his *Ways and Means*—the last of his works, probably written in 455 BC, the year of his death.

Xenophon, the lover of war, became a pacifist. No doubt, he had grown old; at any rate, he had gained in intellectual maturity. For the previous two to three decades he had been a keen observer of endless and senseless civil wars among the Greeks. This experience was missing from his first works, written under the influence of his heroic and colorful memories of Asia. Xenophon wrote his *Ways and Means* under the watchful eye of Eubulus, the statesman presumably responsible for repealing the order of his exile. Eubulus pursued a deliberate policy of pacifism, distributing money to the people that would have been useful in the building of effective defenses against Philip of Macedon; in so doing he revealed his preference for what we would call today economic development.

With this example in mind, Xenophon developed what would become the ultimate liberal argument. Since poverty gives rise to needs and frustrations, and, thus, to pretexts for war, the one true remedy for war and international insecurity is not diplomacy, not defensive preparations, not even moral exhortations. It is economic development.

> For my part I have always held that the constitution of a state reflects the character of the leading politicians. But some of the leading men at Athens have stated that they recognize justice as clearly as other men; "but," they have said, "owing to the poverty of the masses, we are forced to be somewhat unjust in our treatment of the cities." This set me thinking whether by any means the citizens might obtain food entirely from their own soil, which would certainly be the fairest way. I felt that, were this so, they would be relieved of their poverty, and also of the suspicion with which they are regarded by the Greek world. (*Ways and Means* 1.1.1)

Xenophon then gives advice on the possible orientations of economic progress. He recommends, for example, working the mines of Laureum to the utmost: this will involve everyone—private citizens and the state—and everyone stands to earn handsome profits from this (*Ways and Means* 4). More generally, Xenophon praises the benefits of an economy based on trade and manufacturing activities.

Already in his *Memorabilia,* Xenophon expresses (through the voice of Socrates) his approval of market economic activity. It is not demeaning for individuals with a liberal education; on the contrary. With the wealth earned from such activity, one has the means to live. No less importantly, psychological relations are much improved and healthier, and virtues (and good health) are preserved.

Xenophon illustrated this very un-Platonist idea with a delightful anecdote. A noble family is struck by misfortune. Overcoming his initial revulsion for trade and manufacturing, the head of the household is persuaded to "start a business" on the advice of Socrates. He puts the women of the household—sisters, nieces, and cousins—to work in sewing activities. Soon business flourishes and hope is reborn. Pleasant banter and laughter fill the household anew: "There were happy instead of gloomy faces: suspicious glances were exchanged for pleasant smiles" (*Memorabilia* 2.7.12; see also chapters 8 and 9 in which Xenophon describes similar situations with the same solutions and the same outcomes).

One should not hesitate to borrow money to engage in economic activity. Though borrowing money for consumption is bad, borrowing to create value is fully justified (*Memorabilia* 2.7.11). Trade is good, provided it takes place between honest people.

In *Ways and Means,* Xenophon generalizes and formalizes this idea. Athens stands to grow more prosperous provided liberal rules are adopted, including "formal liberties" such as peace, public order, property and contract protection, quick and fair justice, and provided the state does not become an entrepreneur (excepting, of course, its ownership of the Laureum silver mines). If the state pursues such a policy, it will result in a *spontaneous proliferation of economic activity:* "[growth] need cost us nothing whatever beyond benevolent legislation and measures of control." The state needs only to provide *infrastructure development:* harbors, trade installations for merchants, and hotel accommodations (*Ways and Means* 3).

Moreover, to foster economic development, *the city must be open.* An invitation must be extended to "metics," who will come under the protection of "benevolent legislation." They must have civil rights. Local citizens must act as official protectors of foreigners and offer them assistance in case of need. Metics are industrious people; they have no need of public financial assistance. In fact, they pay more taxes than most (*Ways and Means* 2). The adoption of this policy will encourage Athenians to enter agreements with foreigners in ambitious economic projects. This will require maritime loans[25] [*daneismata nautika*] and investment capital.

> It would also be an excellent plan to reserve front seats in the theatre for merchants and shipowners, and to offer them hospitality occasionally, when the high quality of their ships and merchandise entitles them to be considered benefactors of the state. With the prospect of these honours before them they would look on us as friends and hasten to visit us to win the honour as well as the profit. The rise in the number of residents and visitors would of course lead to a corresponding expansion of our imports and exports, of sales, rents and customs. . . . I venture to hope that the citizens would contribute eagerly towards such objects. . . . I am also aware that large expenditure is frequently incurred to send warships abroad, though none can tell whether the venture will be for better or worse, and the only thing certain is that the subscribers will never see their money back nor even enjoy any part of what they contribute. But no investment can yield them so fine a return as the money advanced by them to form the capital fund. (*Ways and Means* 3)

Xenophon observes elsewhere that the presence of so many business partners in Athens is causing property values and service prices to rise to the benefit of Athenian merchants (1.17). Owing

[25] This is the earliest known form of business based on free contracts between persons, one side providing capital and the other labor. Thus, it is one of the earliest expressions of capitalism. It developed throughout the Hellenic and Greco-Roman world and spilled over into the Italian Middle Ages almost without pause; from there, with familiar improvements (joint-stock companies, banking techniques, and insurance), it spread to modern Europe. For a history of trade emphasizing the legacy of antiquity, see the short but excellent book by Yves Renouard, *Les hommes d'affaires italiens du Moyen Age* [Italian businessmen in the Middle Ages] (Paris: Armand Colin, 1972).

to the empire of the sea, Athenian citizens enjoy great material and intellectual wealth; compared with them, the other Greeks are mere peasants. Athens is a capital of world trade, the only place where every product made can be found. Its empire of the sea is both the cause and consequence of this phenomenon (*Constitution of the Athenians* 2).

Finally, Xenophon paints a striking picture of all the prosperities in the city in times of peace: business is good, products pour in, artists and intellectuals gather, and tourists flock to Athens as well. Prosperity, not war, is what gives the city its hegemony. War is costly and the returns can be less than the expense:

> For if the state is tranquil, what class of men will not need her? Shipowners and merchants will head the list. Then there will be those rich in corn and wine and oil and cattle; men possessed of brains and money to invest; craftsmen and professors and philosophers; poets and the people who make use of their works; those to whom anything sacred or secular appeals that is worth seeing or hearing. Besides, where will those who want to buy or sell many things quickly meet with better success in their efforts than at Athens? No one, I dare say, contests this; but there are some who wish the state to recover her ascendancy, and they may think that it is more likely to be won by war than by peace. Let such, in the first place, call to mind the Persian Wars. Was it by coercing the Greeks or by rendering services to them that we became leaders of the fleet and treasurers of the league funds? Further, after the state had been stripped of her empire through seeming to exercise her authority with excessive harshness, did not the islanders even then restore to us the presidency of the fleet by their own free will, when we refrained from acts of injustice?... Were you to show also that you are striving for peace in every land and on every sea, I do think that, next to the safety of their own country, all men would put the safety of Athens first in their prayers.
>
> If, on the other hand, any one supposes that financially war is more profitable to the state than peace, I really do not know how the truth of this can be tested better than by considering once more what has been the experience of our state in the past. He will find that in old days a very great amount of money was paid into the treasury in time of peace, and that the whole of it was spent in time of war; he will conclude on consideration that in our own time the effect of the late war on our revenues was that many of them ceased, while those that came in were exhausted by the multitude of expenses; whereas the cessation of war by sea has been followed by a rise in the revenues, and has allowed the citizens to devote them to any purpose they choose. (*Ways and Means* 5)

Thus, Athens is, in a sense, like America, and it is Xenophon's hope that it will grow in this respect. We can almost hear an echo of Pericles' eulogy of Athens in the funeral oration narrated by Thucydides. Rejecting Sparta's "closed" economy for good, Xenophon harbors ambitious projects for his homeland, where he is again allowed to sojourn. Unfortunately, Athens is no longer in a position to heed his advice, no more than that of any other intellectual or inspired politician. It has finally become the "blocked society" so harshly stigmatized by other fourth century thinkers.

II. Isocrates

Isocrates is an orator who thought that the raison d'être of his art was to express general ideas about politics; accordingly, we find in his work a detailed analysis of democracy and various proposals for its reform.

A. Life

Isocrates was born in 436 BC. His father was a successful flute manufacturer; he gave his son a first-class education. Like Xenophon, Isocrates was a pupil of the Sophist Prodicos of Ceos; he probably frequented Socrates as well, and may have been a pupil of Gorgias in Thessaly. With his background and training in oratory, he decided to make it his career, but his shyness and weakness of voice apparently ruled out the bar. Consequently, he became a logographer, a hired courtroom speechwriter. His enthusiasm waned with the mediocrity of the civil cases coming to court, and he turned his attention in two new directions. On the one hand, he *studied the theory of rhetoric* and *founded a school*. On the other, he *wrote political speeches* with the hope of influencing the politics of his times, though he did not speak from the tribune himself.[26] Isocrates never played an active political role except during the founding of the Second Athenian Confederacy between 376 and 374, when he worked with Timotheus.

Isocrates' school was founded in 393 and met with immediate success. It attracted and trained numerous pupils; many became renowned orators (Lycurgus, Hypereides), others historians (Theopompus, Ephorus), and still others politicians (Timotheus). Isocrates amassed considerable wealth from his teaching and was obliged to pay heavy taxes, such as the trierarchy (i.e., the financing of a warship).

The school of Isocrates was one of the earliest *schools of rhetoric,* perhaps the first to deserve the qualification of "school" in the proper sense, which is a collective teaching institution with a formal curriculum requiring a multiyear commitment from the pupils. Pupils had to complete a primary and secondary level of education before admission. Some studied for free. This can be compared with the one-on-one private tutoring paid for by anyone who could afford it, which had been the traditional approach of the Sophists until then. Isocrates actually established his school several years before Plato founded the Academy. According to H. I. Marrou,[27] Isocrates and Plato are the founders of the original educational establishment; each founded a branch, one applied and the other theoretical. Plato's Academy was the forerunner of the *university,* a teaching and research institution emphasizing the sciences. Isocrates' school was the precursor of the *professional school,* an institution emphasizing skills and know-how. The ambition of both institutions was to train politicians and statesmen.

Isocrates died in 338 BC at the age of 98. Legend has it that he let himself die of starvation after learning of Athens's calamitous defeat at Chaeronea.

B. Work

Academic tradition has succeeded in preserving a few of his *courtroom speeches,* the forms of which served as a rhetorical model for training purposes. Most of his surviving works are *political speeches (orations): Panegyricus, Plataicus, To Nicocles, Nicocles or the Cyprians, Evagoras, Archidamus, On the Peace, Areopagiticus, Panathenaicus.* Two speeches are particularly telling: *Against the Sophists,* in which Isocrates sets out his ideas about the art of rhetoric, and *Antidosis* (*On Exchange of Property*), his moral, philosophical, and political testament.[28]

---

[26] Such *epideictic speeches,* spoken off the tribune, were invented by Gorgias and Lysias. Both gave public exhibitions of their skills to the Greeks assembled in Olympia in 392 and 388 BC. Isocrates instituted the written form of the genre, the *Hellenic and political speech.* Before the invention of modern medias, such "speeches" were more or less the equivalent of pamphlet writing, satire, and opinion pieces in the press, that is, written forms of argument for the agora in the larger sense of public opinion.

[27] Marrou, *A History of Education in Antiquity.*

[28] Cf. *Isocrates with an English Translation,* 3 vols., trans. George Norlin (Cambridge, MA: Harvard University Press, 1980); all works by Isocrates are from this edition, hereafter cited in the text by title of work and section number.

Antidosis is an interesting instance of literary fiction. About 356 BC Isocrates lost an "exchange of property" case (a classical court action in fiscal matters: a citizen singled out to pay the trierarchy could sue another whom he thought to be wealthier in the expectation that that person would become responsible for the tax in his place). Two years later, in late 354 or early 353, he imagined himself the victim of a "public order offense," which charged him with corrupting the youth and illegally acquiring wealth by means of public speaking. He responded to this fictitious accusation with a real speech, *Antidosis,* which is a defense of his life, actions, and ideas.

Isocrates is an enthusiast of the civilization of the law and logos (*Antidosis* 1). This explains his foreign policy ideas: he argues for unity in the ranks of the civilized Greeks against the Persian barbarians, even should this mean appealing to Philip of Macedon for assistance (2); in terms of domestic policy, he formulates a sharp criticism of the failing Athenian democracy (3), and he advocates a mixed form of government (4).

1. *An Enthusiast of the Civilization of the Law and Logos*

Isocrates says that it is the virtues of the citizen—the practice of logos and *isonomia*—that made the Greeks stronger than the barbarians (since Herodotus, this idea had become a commonplace). The Athenians of old were the best examples of these virtues.

> [They kept] their word more faithfully than men now keep their oaths [*faith in* logos],...thinking it right to abide by their covenants as by the decrees of necessity [*their ability to abide by the law*]; they exulted less in the exercise of power than they gloried in living with self-control [acceptance of *sophrosyne*], thinking it their duty to feel toward the weaker as they expected the stronger to feel toward themselves [equality before the law, *isonomia*]; and...they considered Hellas to be their common fatherland [Panhellenism]. Because they were inspired by such sentiments, and educated the young in such habits of conduct [the role of education, *paideia*], they produced in the persons of those who fought against the Asiatic hordes [*during the Persian Wars*] men of so great valor that no one...has ever been able to speak in a manner worthy of their achievements. (*Panegyricus* 81–82)

These are not natural qualities. Isocrates, a student of the Sophists, posits that they are the fruit of reason and culture, which means of an education that transmits them. The corollary is that this much-vaunted civilization is not the exclusive property of the Greek tribe, and even less of the Greek race. It is universal and is beginning to spread throughout lands outside Greece. "So far has our city distanced the rest of mankind in thought and in speech that her pupils have become the teachers of the rest of the world; and she has brought it about that the name Hellenes suggests no longer a race but an intelligence, and that the title Hellenes is applied rather to those who share our culture than to those who share a common blood" (*Panegyricus* 50).

A contrario, the argument shows that the Greeks can become uncivilized as well: decadence is possible. Compared with Socrates, the originality of Isocrates' contribution to the *nature-culture* debate is to draw some important *geopolitical* conclusions: Hellenism is a *paedeia,* that is, a culture with a vocation to reach beyond the Greek tribe where it was born. In other words, the appeal of Isocrates for a defense of civilization against the threat of barbarism is by no means bound by a narrow or blind nationalism. He believes in the universality of reason and the law. In this sense he is a precursor of Stoic thinking, which would predominate in the Hellenistic Age.[29]

[29] For a presentation of his theory of logos, see "Isocrates' Theory of Logos," pp. 169–74.

2. *The Unity of the Greeks against the Barbarians*

In the field of foreign policy, Isocrates holds that the Persians must be fought for two reasons: (1) to defend civilization from barbarism: and (2) because this struggle will force the Greeks to put an end to their own internal quarrels. This Panhellenic objective implies that the classical model of the independent city-state must be transcended. However, to replace it, Isocrates imagines nothing better than political union under Athens's hegemony, as at the time of the Delian League.

a. The Enmity of the Barbarians and Greeks; the Need for Union among the Greeks

Given their culture, the barbarians will never escape being the enemies of civilization, and therefore of the Greeks. They can never be reliable allies.

> It is not possible for people who are reared and governed as are the Persians...to have a part in any...form of virtue....For how could either an able general or a good soldier be produced amid such ways of life as theirs? Most of their population is a mob without discipline or experience of dangers, which has lost all stamina for war and has been trained more effectively for servitude than are the slaves in our country. Those, on the other hand, who stand highest in repute among them have never governed their lives by dictates of equality or of common interest or of loyalty to the state; on the contrary, their whole existence consists of insolence toward some, and servility towards others—a manner of life than which nothing could be more demoralizing to human nature. Because they are rich, they pamper their bodies; but because they are subject to one man's power, they keep their souls in a state of abject and cringing fear, parading themselves at the door of the royal palace, prostrating themselves, and in every way schooling themselves to humility of spirit, falling on their knees before a mortal man,[30] addressing him as a divinity, and thinking more lightly of the gods than of men. So it is that those of the Persians who come down to the sea,[31] whom they term satraps, do not dishonor the training which they receive at home, but cling steadfastly to the same habits: they are faithless to their friends and cowardly to their foes; their lives are divided between servility on the one hand and arrogance on the other; they treat their allies with contempt and pay court to their enemies. For example, they maintained the army under Agesilaus[32] at their own expense for eight months, but they deprived the soldiers who were fighting in the Persian cause of their pay for double that length of time. (*Panegyricus* 150–52)[33]

However, the supposed superiority of the Greeks is compromised by a state of chronic disunity, which the Persians cleverly exploit to secure their own territorial expansion (133–34). It is, therefore, necessary—he argues—to unite the Greeks, which will have the added benefit of ending the civil wars in each state (173).

[30] The reference is to prostration (*proskynesis*), which was profoundly shocking to the Greeks.

[31] Asia Minor, where they were in contact with Greek populations.

[32] The king of Sparta, who was Xenophon's friend; he was constantly on military campaign in Asia Minor.

[33] In such circumstances, it was difficult to imagine great feats from the Persian army. In fact, the Persians were rarely victorious in their conflicts with the Greeks in the fourth and fifth centuries BC. Isocrates did not recognize distinctly (although he did sense) that the situation was fluid and changing. When the barbarians interact with the civilized world, they become civilized themselves. They are close to equaling and exceeding their betters, militarily in the first instance. At the time Isocrates was writing, the Greeks were being overrun by the Macedonians (who in turn were vanquished by the Romans not long after).

b. Athenian Merits Justifying the City's Hegemony

The unity of the Greeks will be achieved under the hegemony of Athens, the only power capable of accomplishing such an outcome. Isocrates' argument begins with a eulogy of Athens in which he provides an overview of the city's illustrious history and former glory. The Athenians, Isocrates says, "far surpass other men in the endowments of nature" (*Areopagiticus* 75). Athens is the mother of laws and the model for other states: "Those who in the beginning brought charges of homicide, and desired to settle their mutual differences by reason and not by violence, tried their cases under our laws" (*Panegyricus* 40–41).[34]

In the past, Athens was able to impose *isonomia* and democracy on subject states under its hegemony.

> We governed all the cities under the same laws, deliberating about them in the spirit of allies, not of masters;... supporting the people but making war on despotic powers, considering it an outrage that the many should be subject to the few, that those who were poorer in fortune but not inferior in other respects should be banished from the offices, that, furthermore, in a fatherland which belongs to all in common some should hold the place of masters, others of aliens, and that men who are citizens by birth should be robbed by law of their share in the government. (*Panegyricus* 105)[35]

Athens is open to foreigners and promotes trade. It was Athens that invented—or spread—the sciences and technologies. The Athenians were the first to pursue intellectual concerns and the art of oratory, doing so with the most success: "Our city so distanced the rest of mankind in thought and in speech that her pupils have become the teachers of the rest of the world" (*Panegyricus* 50). Furthermore, "all clever speakers are the disciples of Athens" (*Antidosis* 296–98). Eloquence and philosophy are among the principal "exports" that Athens has to offer, like the art of war is for Sparta and horsemanship for the Thessalians.[36]

c. The Indignity of Sparta

In any event, Sparta will never be allowed to extend its hegemony over Greece. Why? Because the Spartans are less "civilized." They and their allies do illegal, "anomic" things (*Panegyricus* 110–14; Isocrates often uses the term *anomos,* in the sense of "lacking any moral standard," i.e., lawless). With the Peace of Antalcidas (387 BC), Sparta did not hesitate to deliver Ionia to the Persians; after this some Greeks became slaves to the barbarians, a condition worse than slavery itself; now these same Greeks are forced to fight with the Persians against other Greeks, who are fighting for their liberty (122–28).

d. Union under Athenian Hegemony

Athens is the only state with sufficient authority to unite the Greeks. To every ally that accepts its hegemony Athens offers the benefit and guarantee of government by law, which, Isocrates says, is better than pure and simple independence. What is the worth of independence if one is powerless against a troublemaker? "Who would desire a condition of things where pirates command the seas and mercenaries[37] occupy our cities; where fellow-countrymen, instead of waging war

---

[34] Probably an allusion to the laws of Draco.

[35] This is achieved through census suffrage and limited access to magistracies in oligarchies.

[36] Isocrates adds that the Athenians would do better to heap praise on their intellectuals, rather than persecute them, because they contribute greatly to the reputation of Athens abroad.

[37] The Greek word is *peltasts,* a kind of light infantry. It was used as a figure of speech to refer to bands of mercenaries.

in defense of their territories against strangers, are fighting within their own walls against each other?" (*Panegyricus* 115).

However, an Athenian hegemony must not become an unjust tyranny (Isocrates, *On the Peace* 64 and following). This is the attitude that led Athens to its perdition in the past: strong during the Persian wars, exhausted ever since. Moreover, hegemony was just as disastrous for the Spartans (101–05). The same is true of the collective injustice of the empire as of the individual injustice of the tyrant (111–14): it is not only reprehensible, it is totally ineffective, and sooner or later it leads to decline and failure, like those led to ruin by courtesans (103) (earlier Thucydides had compared Athenian domination to tyranny).

e. The Macedonian Alliance

What Isocrates fears most is that, if the Persians are victorious, civilization will be destroyed. Therefore, he is prepared to turn to civilized non-Greeks to defend civilization. This explains his pro-Macedonian stance, which, unlike Demosthenes, he will continue to defend until a few years before Chaeronea.

Isocrates favors a sort of federal state in which member states "abandon a degree of sovereignty" in exchange for increased security. He is less convincing, however, in regard to the solution to be implemented. While he does not entirely abandon the idea of a hegemony, where one city provides the functions of the state and the others pay tribute, he does insist that the new confederacy be based on an equal treaty: "who does not know that a compact is something which is fair and impartial to both parties, while a command is something which puts one side at a disadvantage unjustly?" (*Panegyricus* 176). This will be the principle adopted for the Second Athenian Confederacy, founded in 377.

3. *Criticism of Athens's Failing Democracy*

Moreover, Isocrates says, Athens cannot possibly rule over a union of Greeks unless it cures itself of the chronic evils that weaken it. Isocrates has great international ambitions for his homeland, which is why he, at the same time as his contemporaries Xenophon and Plato, judges the Athenian democracy of his age.

a. A Reign of Corruption

Athenian orators, Isocrates says, are totally corrupt. They defend whoever pays the most (even taking money from foreign powers; see *Plataicus* 3, where the best payers are the Thebans), not who is in the right. The power of the "sycophants" has become brazen (*Antidosis* 312–19).

The politicians of the past were not corrupt. Pericles, for example,

> left an estate which was smaller than that which he received from his father, while he brought up into the Acropolis eight thousand talents, apart from the sacred treasures. But these demagogues have shown themselves so different from him that they have the effrontery to say that because of the care they give to the commonwealth they are not able to give attention to their private interests, although in fact these "neglected" interests have advanced to a degree of affluence which they would never have even dreamed of praying to the gods that they might attain, whereas our people, for whom they pretend to care, are in such straits that not one of our citizens is able to live with pleasure or at ease; on the contrary, Athens is rife with lamentations. (*On the Peace* 126–27)

Earlier politicians did not treat public goods like personal property. On the contrary, they used their personal wealth to rescue the public purse. Isocrates laments that the first thing politicians do when they take charge is to ask what is left to steal! (*Areopagiticus* 25).

In the past, the agora was a place where it was shameful to be seen: "so strictly did they [the Athenians] avoid the market-place that even when they were at times compelled to pass through it, they were seen to do this with great modesty and sobriety of manner" (*Areopagiticus* 48).[38] Today, "agora regulars" hold a choice position in society.

b. The Collusion of the Envious

Isocrates thinks that corrupt individuals are not the only guilty ones. He notes that an *intrinsically perverse system* is in place. The people vote for demagogues and sycophants, without calling them to account for their corrupt behavior, thereby excusing in advance their own immoral behavior.

> We pass a multitude of laws, but we care so little about them... that, although we have prescribed the penalty of death for anyone who is convicted of bribery, we elect men who are most flagrantly guilty of this crime as our generals and we pick out the man who has been able to deprave the greatest number of our citizens and place him in charge of the most important affairs.... We pretend that we are the wisest of the Hellenes, but we employ the kind of advisers[39] whom no one could fail to despise, and we place these very same men in control of all our public interests to whom no one would entrust a single one of his private affairs. (*On the Peace* 50–52)

The public purse is in the hands of such shady characters that one would dare not trust them with one's own money. The reason these characters are elected to public office is that the voters imagine they will refrain from poking their noses into the voters' business and that they will use every conceivable means to fight the political enemies of the *demos*. Of these two views, it is the very immorality of the politicians that causes the people to elect them, which is the same as saying that the people themselves are corrupt.

The cause of the people's corruption is envy:

> Some men... have been so brutalized by envy [*tou phtonou*] and want and are so hostile that they wage war, not on depravity, but on prosperity; they hate not only the best men but the noblest pursuits; and, in addition to their other faults, they take sides with wrong-doers and are in sympathy with them, while they destroy, whenever they have the power, those whom they have cause to envy. They do these things, not because they are ignorant of the issues on which they are to vote, but because they intend to inflict injury and do not expect to be found out; and so, by protecting those of their own kind, they think they are providing for their own safety. (*Antidosis* 142–43)

The social crisis in Athens presents many of the characteristics of René Girard's sacrificial *mimesis*.[40] Isocrates manages a glimpse of its underlying mechanism. The democratic mob is agitated by the demagogues and people encourage one another in the excitement of the agora. By persecuting the scapegoats designated by the sycophants, the mob does a favor to the sycophants, honoring and enriching them despite their corruptness and injustice, and a favor to itself inasmuch as this excuses in advance its own dishonesty. The man of the people, hiding in the crowd, lets loose his envy and hatred of the rich; at the same time he absolves himself of any personal

---

[38] Aristophanes often used the insult *agoraios*, "an agora regular" (see above; Xenophon made a similar observation: it is shameful to extend a formal dinner invitation to a candidate for elected office).

[39] The reference is to ordinary professional public speakers, that is, politicians.

[40] See general introduction to this volume, "Anthropology and Politics," pp. 1–20.

responsibility for the future of the state. Because the sycophants understand perfectly well how this mechanism—the source of which is the people's spinelessness and immorality—works, they repeatedly bring accusations against the rich in spite of their importance to the homeland (on this point the democrat Isocrates sides with the oligarchs Plato and Xenophon).

> When I was a boy, wealth was regarded as a thing so secure as well as admirable that almost every one affected to own more property than he actually possessed, because he wanted to enjoy the standing which it gave. Now, on the other hand, a man has to be ready to defend himself against being rich as if it were the worst of crimes, and to keep on the alert if he is to avoid disaster; for it has become far more dangerous to be suspected of being well off than to be detected in crime; for criminals are pardoned or let off with slight penalties, while the rich are ruined utterly, and it will be found that the number of men who have been spoiled of their property is greater than those who have been punished for their misdeeds. (*Antidosis* 159–60)

When sycophants, acting as protectors of the people against wealthy oligarchs, accumulate shameless wealth themselves, the people feign not to see the sleight of hand; one turns a blind eye while the other colludes (*On the Peace* 124).

c. Consequences of Corruption: Everything Is Blocked, Economically and Politically

Corruption and the activities of the sycophants upset justice. Obstructed by the demagogues, the Athenian courts decide against the law. This disrupts normal economic activity and, more generally, threatens public order. Isocrates thinks that this hurts the poor more than the rich. When well-to-do Athenians before the current corrupt period granted a loan,

> they had no fear that they might suffer one of two things—that they might lose their whole investment or recover, after much trouble, only a mere fraction of their venture; on the contrary, they felt as secure about the money which was lent out as about that which was stored in their own coffers. For they saw that in cases of contract[41] the judges were not in the habit of indulging their sense of equity[42] but were strictly faithful to the laws; and that they did not in trying others seek to make it safe for themselves to disobey the law, but were indeed more severe on defaulters than were the injured themselves, since they believed that those who break down confidence in contracts do a greater injury to the poor than to the rich; for if the rich were to stop lending, they would be deprived of only a slight revenue, whereas if the poor should lack the help of their supporters they would be reduced to desperate straits. And so because of this confidence no one tried to conceal his wealth nor hesitated to lend it out, but, on the contrary, the wealthy were better pleased to see men borrowing money than paying it back; for they thus experienced the double satisfaction—which should appeal to all right-minded men—of helping their fellow-citizens and at the same time making their own property productive for themselves. (*Areopagiticus* 33–35)

Since such a climate no longer exists and the wealthy are reluctant to lend, the number of poor has never been greater: "In that day no one of the citizens lacked the necessaries of life nor shamed

---

[41] We should not forget that the judges presiding over the Athenian courts, such as the popular court of Heliaea, came from the ordinary people. They were not professional judges. When they acquitted a debtor, they convinced themselves that it set a precedent for the forgiveness of their own debt.

[42] This is equivalent to what modern law calls a "judgment of fairness," which deviates from the letter of the law.

the city by begging from passers-by, whereas today those who are destitute of means outnumber those who possess them" (*Areopagiticus* 83).

Corrupt politicians knowingly hold the poor in the very vices that will force them to turn to the politicians again and again:

> I marvel that you cannot see at once that no class is so inimical to the people as our depraved orators and demagogues. For, as if your other misfortunes were not enough, their chief desire is that you should be in want of your daily necessities, observing that those who are able to manage their affairs from their private incomes are on the side of the commonwealth and of our best counsellors, whereas those who live off the law-courts and the assemblies and the doles derived from them are constrained by their need to be subservient to the sycophants and are deeply grateful for the impeachments and the indictments and the other sharp practices which are due to the sycophants. Wherefore these men would be most happy to see all of our citizens reduced to the condition of helplessness in which they themselves are powerful. (*On the Peace* 129–31)

A democratic vote never results in much-needed decisions of general interest; such a vote is marked by incoherence and irrationality: "We are versed beyond all others in discourse and in the conduct of affairs, but we are so devoid of reason that we do not hold the same views about the same question on the same day; on the contrary, the things which we condemn before we enter the assembly are the very things which we vote for when we are in session, and again a little later when we depart to our homes we disapprove of the things which we resolved upon here" (*On the Peace* 52).

d. "Single-Minded Thinking"

In order to make reforms, it should at least be possible to debate the problems posed by the institutions. Isocrates makes a devastating observation: when democracy is decadent and in the hands of the political market, it is virtually impossible to discuss real issues and speak openly. But no one dares to say the truth, nor can anyone bear to hear it. "Double speak" and "single-minded thinking" win the day. If and when the truth surfaces, it is usually in quick bursts, spoken by madmen and fools who are given the floor because no one imagines they will be taken seriously.

"You do not hear with equal favor the speakers who address you.... You have formed the habit of driving all the orators from the platform except those who support your desires.... But I know that it is hazardous to oppose your views and that, although this is a free government, there exists no 'freedom of speech' except that which is enjoyed in this Assembly by the most reckless orators, who care nothing for your welfare, and in the theater by the comic poets" (*On the Peace* 3, 14).

Pluralism and the equality of speech between parties are the necessary conditions for truth to emerge; otherwise, passions and false opinions triumph. Today, public speakers are not even allowed to pursue their arguments to the end. Democracy has become a reign of hurled insults (*Antidosis* 17, 173).

4. *The Reform of the State*

The breakdown of Athenian institutions is not only immoral and irrational; it will cause the ruin of the state:

> Yet we all know that success does not visit and abide with those who have built around themselves the finest and the strongest walls, nor with those who have collected the greatest population in one place, but rather with those who most nobly and wisely govern their state. *For the soul of a state is nothing else than its polity (psyche poleôs... politeia),* having as much power over it as does the mind over the body; for it is this which deliberates upon all

> questions, seeking to preserve what is good and to ward off what is disastrous; and it is this which of necessity assimilates to its own nature the laws, the public orators and the private citizens; and all the members of the state must fare well or ill according to the kind of polity under which they live. And yet we are quite indifferent to the fact that our polity has been corrupted, nor do we even consider how we may redeem it. (*Areopagiticus* 13–16)

Thus, for Isocrates, the only solution is wide ranging constitutional reform.

a. For an "Areopagitic" Democracy

Since evil is in the discretionary power of the Assembly, grossly manipulated by the demagogues, it is imperative that a balance of power be restored in favor of a new *Council of the Areopagus* with wise counselors who can put the true interests of the state first. Isocrates, of course, understands that this "areopagitic" democracy will resemble an oligarchy.[43] Still, he sticks to his position. The amputation of some of the people's powers, or at least the silencing of its direct voice in the Assembly, is the price to pay for a just and rational democracy: "in most of the discourses which I have written, you will find that I condemn oligarchies and special privileges, while I commend equal rights and democratic governments—not all of them, but those which are well-ordered, praising them not indiscriminately, but on just and reasonable grounds" (*Areopagiticus* 60).

The ideal democratic state should not be egalitarian: everyone should be rewarded according to his or her merits. The magistracies should go to "the most honest and the most capable"; they should not be drawn by lot (Isocrates says that making appointments by lot, in addition to its other faults, risks handing power over to the oligarchs).

So the elite must have more power. This poses no danger as long as the people are the sovereign authority over the magistrates. Besides, all this existed in the past; it is enough to revert to the earlier situation.

> So severely did they abstain from what belonged to the state that it was harder in those days to find men who were willing to hold office than it is now to find men who are not begging for the privilege; for they did not regard a charge over public affairs as a chance for private gain but as a service to the state; neither did they from their first day in office seek to discover whether their predecessors had overlooked any source of profit, but much rather whether they had neglected any business of the state which pressed for settlement.
>
> In a word, our forefathers had resolved that the people as the supreme master of the state should appoint the magistrates, call to account those who failed in their duty, and judge in cases of dispute; while those citizens who could afford the time and possessed sufficient means should devote themselves to the care of the commonwealth, as servants of the people, entitled to receive commendation if they proved faithful to their trust, and contenting themselves with this honor, but condemned, on the other hand, if they governed badly, to meet with no mercy, but to suffer the severest punishment. And how, pray, could one find a democracy more stable or more just than this, which appointed the most capable men to have charge of its affairs but gave to the people authority over their rulers (*auton touton ton demon kyrion poiouses*)? (*Areopagiticus* 25–27)[44]

---

[43] In fact, it is a mixed constitution establishing a compromise between the powers of the Assembly and those of experts, that is, the powers of the *demos* and the powers of the enlightened classes.

[44] Isocrates says this as if it were something quite natural. We will see in due course what efforts had to be made by the canonists, conciliarists, and thinkers of the sixteenth century, the likes of Bèze, Suarez, and so on to recover this idea of the "sovereign authority of the people."

Isocrates' proposals for constitutional reform prefigure those of Aristotle, and later, Polybius, Cicero, and other classical writers, rediscovered and reread in modern times: the best form of government, the most stable and the most reasonable in terms of law and justice, is a *mixed* form with democratic and aristocratic or oligarchic elements, a form where the people *control* but do not *govern*.

b. Education

Morals are more important than written laws. This is reflected in the overabundance of written laws, evidence of the deterioration of morals, from which comes, as a corollary, the fundamental importance of *education*.

"Those who are rightly governed, on the other hand, do not need to fill their porticoes with written statutes, but only to cherish justice in their souls; for it is not by legislation, but by morals, that states are well directed, since men who are badly reared will venture to transgress even laws which are drawn up with minute exactness, whereas those who are well brought up will be willing to respect even a simple code" (*Areopagiticus* 41).

Isocrates then sings the praises of the educator and his profession. The educator has more merit than the distinguished citizens who eat for free at the *prytanea;* they give only one good citizen to the state, while the educator supplies a great many (*Antidosis* 95). What, then, are Isocrates' ideas on education? We need to take a moment to examine his notion of logos, which conditions his pedagogy to a large extent.

5. *Isocrates' Theory of Logos*

Isocrates believes that it will not be possible to restore the state before the current generation of politicians, wallowing in corruption and mediocrity, is replaced by a new generation of politicians properly educated with sound principles. This is Plato's thought as well. The parallel is the more striking that both men, within a few years of each other, founded schools devoted to educating political leaders. As a complement to our discussion above, it is worth exploring the educational principles that Isocrates chose for his school, then comparing them with Plato's ideas on the subject. Two very different "visions of the world" arise in these two cases.

Isocrates proposes to teach political and judicial *eloquence*. He reflects on the nature and powers of the logos. In *Against the Sophists* and *Antidosis,* he forged a model of education and culture that dominated throughout the Greco-Roman world for seven or eight centuries. Much later, European humanism returned to his model, when it placed the emphasis of teaching and learning on "letters."[45]

a. The Nature of Speech: "True Opinion"

If rhetoric is so indispensable to good politics, it is not because of any superiority of seeming over being; otherwise, the criticisms of the Sophists, the demagogues, and the sycophants that we just read would be senseless. Rhetoric is indispensable, given the very *nature* of speech.

> In the other powers which we possess [i.e., other than speech], as I have already said on a former occasion, we are in no respect superior to other living creatures; nay, we are inferior to many in swiftness and in strength and in other resources; but, because there has been implanted in us the power to persuade each other and to make clear to each other whatever

[45] See Marrou, *A History of Education in Antiquity*.

> we desire, not only have we escaped the life of wild beasts, but we have come together and founded cities and made laws and invented arts; and, generally speaking, there is no institution devised by man which the power of speech has not helped us to establish. For this it is which has laid down laws concerning things just and unjust, and things honorable and base; and if it were not for these ordinances we should not be able to live with one another. It is by this also that we confute the bad and extol the good. Through this we educate the ignorant and appraise the wise; for the power to speak well is taken as the surest index of a sound understanding, and discourse which is true and lawful and just is the outward image of a good and faithful soul. With this faculty we both contend against others on matters which are open to dispute and seek light for ourselves on things which are unknown; for the same arguments which we use in persuading others when we speak in public, we employ also when we deliberate in our own thoughts; and, while we call eloquent those who are able to speak before a crowd, we regard as sage those who most skillfully debate their problems in their own minds. And, if there is need to speak in brief summary of this power, we shall find that none of the things which are done with intelligence take place without the help of speech, but that in all our actions as well as in all our thoughts speech is our guide, and is most employed by those who have the most wisdom. (*Antidosis* 253–57)

Speech serves not only to *express* oneself, but also to *think*. Or to put it differently, there is no need to distinguish sharply between thought and speech. Content and form are inseparable. In this sense, rhetoric is the essential tool for *training the mind*.

Isocrates explains why. The power of speech comes from the fact that it contains "true opinion." It is the only knowledge that matters and is useful in all human praxis, where uncertainty and, in modern parlance, complexity dominate. In concrete social practice, no situation resembles another exactly; this is why pure theories are inadequate. What is to be said and done in each circumstance always eludes theory: "No system of knowledge can possibly cover these occasions, since in all cases they elude our science" (*Antidosis* 184).

The reason certain philosophers are in error (Isocrates takes aim at the Platonists here) is that they are too attached to mathematics and the "exact sciences." To understand what is true in every situation, some knowledge of the sciences is necessary, but that knowledge needs to be combined with experience, acquired in contact with those who are experienced themselves. Then one will know how to use wisely the general ideas one has learned. The opinion formed may not be certain, but it will at least be probable. "For since it is not in the nature of man to attain a science by the possession of which we can know positively what we should do or what we should say, in the next resort I hold that man to be wise who is able by his powers of conjecture to arrive generally at the best course" (*Antidosis* 271).

Isocrates argues that "the power to speak well is taken as the surest index of a sound understanding" (*Antidosis* 255). The art of oratory creates an intimate bond, H. I. Marrou explains,

> between form and content. These... are inseparable; and this is so because the effort to find the right expression demands and develops a sensitivity of thought, a sense of different shades of meaning, which it is difficult to express in conceptual ideas, and even, sometimes impossible.... There are things that a poet feels and makes you feel at once, and which no amount of science can fathom. The result is that an "oratorical" kind of education, which in appearance is entirely a matter of aesthetics, whose one aim is to create "wizards with words," is in fact the most effective way of developing subtlety of thought.[46]

[46] Ibid., 90.

When comparing the art of writing with the art of discourse, philosophers, who believe in a mechanical connection between abstractions, rather than in the flexibility, flow, superposition, and contingency of words, make a mistake: the art of writing can give rise to an explicit learning method, presented in a written treatise; the art of oratory, however, rebels against it by nature. The authors of written treatises on discourse, the same who believe that oratory can be put in writing and communicated,

> do not attribute any of this power either to the practical experience or to the native ability of the student, but undertake to transmit the science of discourse as simply as they would teach the letters of the alphabet.... But I marvel when I observe these men setting themselves up as instructors of youth who cannot see that they are applying the analogy of an art with hard and fast rules to a creative process. For, excepting these teachers, who does not know that the art of using letters remains fixed and unchanged, so that we continually and invariably use the same letters for the same purposes, while exactly the reverse is true of the art of discourse? For what has been said by one speaker is not equally useful for the speaker who comes after him; on the contrary, he is accounted most skilled in this art who speaks in a manner worthy of his subject and yet is able to discover in it topics which are nowise the same as those used by others. But the greatest proof of the difference between these two arts is that oratory is good only if it has the qualities of fitness for the occasion, propriety of style, and originality of treatment, while in the case of letters there is no such need whatsoever.... [It is necessary] to choose from these elements those which should be employed for each subject, to join them together, to arrange them properly, and also, not to miss what the occasion demands but appropriately to adorn the whole speech with striking thoughts and to clothe it in flowing and melodious phrase. (*Against the Sophists* 10–16)

This can be glossed as follows: a man, whose speech is sufficiently rich and practiced, will find the proper range of ideas for each particular situation; each idea will be embodied in a word appropriate to the situation. The characteristics of the situation will not be concealed in abstractions, as in the case of a man whose command of language is poor. Rather, the situation will be characterized properly and finely through the intersection of the semantic fields of the various words used. It is in this sense that "true opinion," *doxa,* fostered by rhetoric, can be truer in all practical aspects than "science," *episteme* (in the Platonic sense), even if it is only probable and not certain.

This polemic between Isocrates and Plato[47] ran throughout history (even until fairly recently); it is, in fact, the debate between letters and science, between the "spirit of finesse" and the "spirit of geometry," between intuition and clear, distinct knowledge, found again from Pascal to Bergson (and which has become timely again with developments in the cognitive sciences).

b. The Political Efficacy of Speech: A Theory of Communication

A spirit of finesse enables efficacious action. Isocrates, like Xenophon, believes that intelligence in a good general is preferable to brute strength (*Antidosis* 116–17). This is even more true of the

---

[47] Above we discussed Plato's denunciation of opinion. Opinion is generally wrong and vague, he argues; it does not grasp true reality, that is, the reality of the Idea. And even when opinion is true, it is true by accident and cannot give its reasons. Thus, it is an illusion, a shadow in the cave, a nonbeing. There is strictly no difference between orators like Isocrates (the focus of attacks in *Phaedrus*) and the demagogues of the agora. Neither is able to grasp true justice, which supposes knowledge of the intelligibles, and cause it to triumph. But, to do justice to Isocrates' thinking on *doxa,* we have to admit that Plato, who in practice had a true spirit of finesse, somehow fails to seize an entire facet of the life of the mind.

politician: if he is to be able to persuade and inspire, he must have such a penetrating and skillful tongue as to pinpoint the concerns of every sort of citizen in every sort of circumstance.

These notions give rise to a genuine theory of "political communication," the antithesis of sophistry. The orator's art of persuasion can cause seeming (appearance) to pass for being, concealing, or dissimulating truth, purely and simply. However, a succinct Plato did not recognize that oratory can also involve the choice of a word that "hits the mark" in an infinite variety of social situations, something the philosopher does not do well: he often places his words at the wrong moment or in the wrong way, as he strings out his theories.

Is it really just an accident, Isocrates asks, that all the great Athenian politicians—Solon, Cleisthenes, Themistocles, Pericles (authors no doubt of great policies)—were also great orators? In contrast, Timotheus, an honorable politician, was only partially successful in learning Isocrates' lessons; he failed to grasp that the truth is welcome in a community only if it is properly presented and packaged. In his political action, Timotheus frequently failed to give "communication" its due:

> While he was no anti-democrat nor a misanthrope, nor arrogant, nor possessed of any such defect of character, yet because of his proud bearing—an advantage to the office of a general but out of place in dealing with men from day to day—everyone attributed to him the faults which I have named; for he was by nature as inept in courting the favor of men as he was gifted in handling affairs.[48] Indeed he has often been advised by me, among others, that while men who are in public life and desire to be in favor must adopt the principle of doing what is most serviceable and noble and of saying what is most true and just, yet they must at the same time not neglect to study and consider well how in everything they say and do they may convince the people of their graciousness and human sympathy; since those who are careless of these matters are thought by their fellow-citizens to be disagreeable and offensive. "You observe," I would say to him, "the nature of the multitude, how susceptible they are to flattery; that they like those who cultivate their favor better than those who seek their good; and that they prefer those who cheat them with beaming smiles and brotherly love to those who serve them with dignity and reserve. You have paid no attention to these things, but are of the opinion that if you attend honestly to your enterprises abroad, the people at home also will think well of you. But this is not the case, and the very contrary is wont to happen. For if you please the people in Athens, no matter what you do they will not judge your conduct by the facts but will construe it in a light favorable to you; and if you make mistakes, they will overlook them, while if you succeed, they will exalt your success to the high heaven. For good will has this effect upon all men.... Men cultivate the public orators and the speakers who are effective in private gatherings and who profess to be authorities on every subject, while you not only neglect to do this, but actually make an open breach between yourself and the orators who are from time to time the most influential. And yet... how many in the generations that are past have left no name, although they were far better and worthier men than those who are celebrated in song and on the tragic stage. (*Antidosis* 131–36)

Timotheus was emphatically a poor politician, because he was a poor orator.

[48] In Athens one is not in Sparta. Power is in the hands of civilians, not the military.

c. Teaching Oratory

But the art of oratory can be learned. Pericles had two teachers—Anaxagoras of Clazomenae and Damon—confirmation of the democratic idea that an aptitude for oratory can be taught, that it is not reserved exclusively for those with a natural inclination or for descendants of the great Eupatrid families (*Antidosis* 231–35; cf. 308).

How can oratory be learned? Isocrates dwells on the question at length. The teaching of oratory, as explained, must not be limited to abstractions. In his work, *Against the Sophists,* basically a school prospectus presenting his institution to prospective students, Isocrates criticizes the authors of *written* treatises of rhetoric. He argues that the knowledge and skill of oratory cannot be transmitted in writing. Teachers of rhetoric need to train their students with appropriate practical exercises and provide them with good models of speeches, together with examples of proper conduct for imitation (the speeches and virtuous personal lives of teachers will provide edifying examples [cf. *Antidosis* 277]). Learning depends on direct contact and a mimesis between the teacher's and the student's spirit of finesse. Furthermore, the teacher must also see to it that the student has direct personal experience of social and political matters.

These practical exercises are not mere "technical" exercises. They go hand-in-hand with the *broadest possible general education.*

We noted above that the mind must possess a sufficiently large vocabulary, each word expressing a general idea, to achieve a subtle characterization of situations in the subtlety of their uniqueness, to avoid being surprised by events as they arise, to "see things properly," to achieve a "true opinion" every time. This results in a strange paradox: that to prepare the mind for the mastery of unique situations and *practical life,* the mind must be trained in *generalities,* that is, possess broad knowledge in all domains, especially in fields of general interest with consequences for humankind.

This is why Isocrates wants future orators to practice on the "highest" topics. A speaker who trains only on narrow, material problems will never be more than a second-rate lawyer. Conversely, a speaker who aspires to success in politics and the handling of important matters will know how to make the link between the topic and general ideas. "When anyone elects to speak or write discourses which are worthy of praise and honor, it is not conceivable that he will support causes which are unjust or petty or devoted to private quarrels, and not rather those which are great and honorable, devoted to the welfare of man and our common good (*megalas kai kalas kai philanthropous*); for if he fails to find causes of this character, he will accomplish nothing to the purpose" (*Antidosis* 276).

Not surprisingly, Isocrates eliminates the pure sciences—greatly admired by the Platonists and the "physicists"—from his educational archetype. He relegates them, disparagingly, to secondary education, which—he suggests—is the proper place to "dabble" in them. The pure sciences, such as geometry and astronomy, are mere building blocks for useful sciences; they serve to exercise and sharpen the wit: a "gymnastic of the mind," they should be "banished utterly" by those "who want to do some good in the world" (*Antidosis* 265–69; Socrates held more or less the same opinion). The real reason for his disdain for pure science is that the true purpose of intellectual refinement is to be able to handle the affairs of the state. Pure speculation is childish. Teachers of rhetoric ought "to pursue the truth, to instruct their pupils in the practical affairs of our government and train to expertness therein, bearing in mind that likely conjecture about useful things is far preferable to exact knowledge of the useless, and that *to be a little superior in important things is of greater worth than to be pre-eminent in petty things* that are without value for living" (*Helen*, 5; cf. *Antidosis* 285).

The emphasis placed by Isocrates on a "broad general education" had a decisive impact on the curriculum of schools throughout the Greco-Roman world and even in schools in the West for a long time, following the rediscovery of classical literature.

d. The Political Ramifications of Teaching Rhetoric

One final point needs to be emphasized. On numerous occasions, Isocrates remarks that, to educate a good orator, several conditions are necessary, none of which may be neglected. It requires (1) a natural disposition; (2) a liberal education; (3) practice (*Antidosis* 189, 291–92). A natural disposition is more important than the rest. And this has important political ramifications.

If virtue and excellence are products of nature, social roles depend entirely on birth, which is the pro-aristocratic argument. But if everything depends on education, then anybody can be a good orator, provided he is properly educated, which is the pro-democratic (even revolutionary) argument.

But if excellence depends on a *mix* of nature, education, and effort through practical application, as Isocrates (like Socrates) believes, this pleads politically in favor of *a regime that is itself mixed.* We saw that Isocrates advocates just such a regime. It must be possible to have new men each generation, good natures educated by good teachers, but at the same time, it must be possible to stop the bad, uncultivated men, whatever their social class, from dominating the state. This is the goal of areopagitic democracy.

III. Demosthenes

Demosthenes is the famous orator and author of the *Philippics,* a masterpiece of oratory, imitated by Cicero centuries later. He is also a brilliant observer and analyst of Athenian domestic politics.

A. Life

Demosthenes was born in Athens in 384 BC, the son of a wealthy manufacturer.[49] His father died when Demosthenes was just seven years old. Demosthenes accused his tutors of misappropriating his inheritance after his father's death and took up the study of law and oratory in order to file a suit against them. He studied under the orator Isaeus and may have been influenced by Isocrates and Alcidamas, although he did not follow their lessons. He probably read Thucydides and Xenophon.

He was a successful logographer (professional speechwriter) until around 355 BC, when he turned to politics (he probably continued to write speeches for private civil suits occasionally). He pleaded political trials, then delivered harangues before the Assembly on the topic of the three Greek powers claiming political hegemony: Athens, Sparta, and Thebes. Subsequently, in the greatest political battle of his life, he warned against the Macedonian threat, which grew between the accession to the throne of Philip II of Macedonia in 359 BC and his victory over the Greeks at the battle of Chaeronea in 338 BC.

Demosthenes served as a member of the Athenian delegation that concluded the Peace of Philocrates in 346 BC. When the Macedonian king broke the peace, Demosthenes became the leading Athenian politician to oppose Philip's progress. His fellow Athenian citizens ultimately followed him in opposing the Macedonian, but it was too late. He personally fought at the battle of Chaeronea and, after Philip's assassination in 336 BC, he led the revolt against the Macedonians, a revolt quickly put down by the young Alexander.

[49] Demosthenes was born the same year as Aristotle; both died the same year (322 BC) as well. Quotations in this section are from *Demosthenes,* vols. 1–7, trans. J. H. Vince, A. T. Murray, N. W. and N. J. De Witt (Cambridge, MA: Harvard University Press, 1930); hereafter cited in the text by the work and section number.

After Chaeronea the Council awarded Demosthenes a golden crown for his political service to Athens. His long-standing rival, Aeschines, objected to the measure and sued him for its legal irregularity. In a ringing speech a few years later, Demosthenes defended his policies in *On the Crown* and was fully acquitted. But, in 324 BC, he was found guilty in another political show trial, apparently without a shred of evidence, and spent time in prison.

Upon the death of Alexander in 323 BC, the Greeks attempted a final revolt (the Lamian War), but it was stifled by the Macedonian Antipater. He commanded that all members of the anti-Macedonian opposition be turned over to him. Demosthenes escaped to a sanctuary on the island of Calaurea (today's Poros) and in the temple dedicated to Poseidon took poison to end his life (322 BC).

B. Works

Various civil courtroom speeches by Demosthenes have survived. The remainder of his work includes *political orations* (i.e., speeches delivered in the political process) and *harangues* (i.e., speeches delivered before the Council or the Assembly). Among his most famous political orations are *On the False Embassy* and *On the Crown;* among his harangues are *On the Navy-boards, For the People of Megalopolis, On the Liberty of the Rhodians, On Organization,* three *Olynthiacs,* four *Philippics, On the Peace, On the Chersonese,* and *On the Treaty with Alexander.*

1. *Background: The Macedonian Threat*

Demosthenes is persuaded that Athens and Macedonia stand for radically irreconcilable political principles. Athens represents democracy and civilization; Philip stands for despotism. One of the two must perish. Kings, as a matter of principle, are opposed to a system of freedom under the law: "'What is your object?' I said. 'Freedom? Then do you not see that Philip's very titles are utterly irreconcilable with that? For every king, every despot is the sworn foe of freedom and of law. Beware,' said I, 'lest, seeking to be rid of war, you find a master'" (*Second Philippic* 25).

As long as Athens stands, it represents a danger for Philip because all his other Greek possessions can turn to Athens, and all Greeks know that Athens does not want to be their despot (*On the Chersonese* 41–42). Demosthenes is certain that in case of victory Philip will embody a very different kind of power than that held by Athens, Sparta, and Thebes. Philip is not a Greek, "[nor is he] related to the Greeks" (*Third Philippic* 31). Thus, the loathing between the two rivals is irreconcilable, and Philip knows full well that of all his enemies only the Athenians see through his game. "He knows, then, these two facts—that he is intriguing against you and that you are aware of it. Assuming that you are intelligent, he thinks you are bound to hate him, and he is on the alert, expecting some blow to fall, if you can seize an opportunity and if he cannot get in his blow first" (*Second Philippic* 18).

Philip is a cynic, a fox, and a liar, who acts only in pursuit of his vested interests. In contrast, the Athenians have an ideal of justice. Philip promises mountains and miracles to the gullible in order to secure their backing or neutrality. As soon as he reaches his goal, he enslaves his allies and opponents. "He has hoodwinked everyone that has had any dealings with him; he has played upon the folly of each party in turn and exploited their ignorance of his own character. That is how he has gained his power" (*Second Olynthiac* 7).

The blindness and paralysis of Greek cities increase as Philip, gathering riches and military power, advances. Divided, the Greek cities become increasingly intimidated.

In the struggle against Philip, certain diplomatic alliances can be counted, likewise the virtual union of all the Greeks. Unlike Isocrates, who pleaded for an alliance with Philip against the Persians, Demosthenes sanctions an alliance with the Great King of Persia, Darius, against Philip. The Great King is in Susa, whereas Philip is in Euboea. Demosthenes' advice is to "drop the foolish prejudice that has so often brought about your discomfiture—'the barbarian' [i.e., the Great King of Persia], 'the common foe of us all'" (*Fourth Philippic* 31–34). As for the union of all the Greeks, Demosthenes suggests that the existence of a Panhellenic sentiment will make it easy. There is no reason to fear that some Greeks will side with Philip. "I do not think that any Greek would attack Greece. For where would he retire afterwards? Will he go to Phrygia and be a slave? For the objects at stake in a war against the barbarian are nothing less than our country, our life, our habits, our freedom (*peri choras kai biou kai ethon kai eleutherias*), and all such blessings. Who, then, is so desperate that he will sacrifice himself, his ancestors, his sepulchres, and his native land, all for the sake of a paltry profit? I cannot think that there is such a man" (*On the Navy-boards* 32).

2. *A Crisis of Democracy*

The weakness of the Greeks is their present disunity. Each city hopes misfortune will fall on its neighbor, not itself. Nobody takes the initiative to organize a common defense. Yet, in earlier times, union against the Persian threat was possible. So what has changed? The public spirit has been corrupted, and politicians are openly corruptible (*Third Philippic* 36–37). This helps Demosthenes realize the seriousness of the crisis gripping Athenian democracy. His political ideas on the topic are close to those of Plato, Xenophon, and Isocrates.

a. The Pomposity of Empty Words

In the *assembly form of government* or *direct democracy* that existed at this time in Athens, not only the law and key decisions were publicly debated and approved, but so was almost every day-to-day executive decision, especially in diplomatic and military affairs. But this led to a *regime of empty and pompous words* where words became mere incantations.

For example, the Athenians elected ten taxiarchs (division commanders) and ten *strategoi* (generals), two phylarchs and two hipparchs (officers). Of all these high-ranking officers, only one actually waged war. The others "marshal processions"; they are chosen "for the market-place, not for the field"; "[you] fight Philip... with decrees and dispatches," not with deeds (*First Philippic* 26, 30; cf. 45–46, and *Second Olynthiac* 11). The Athenians engage in shouting and arguing rather than listening to sensible orators.

Wrong decisions are always taken at the wrong time: "all other people deliberate before the event, but you after the event. And the result is that, as long as I can remember, the man who attacks any mistakes you have made gains your applause as an able speaker, but meanwhile the events and the real object of your deliberation wholly escape you" (*On the Peace* 2).

Time and again, the Athenians react too late, only to "incur additional ignominy." In comparison, because he knows "beforehand what he wants to do," Philip makes his decisions alone and puts himself in a strong position to seize every opportunity. While Philip takes up arms and marches into battle, "ready to risk all he has," the Athenians become embroiled in debate, some happy to have pleaded what is right, others to have listened to them, after which they all go home (*Fourth Philippic* 3). Thus, in this particular regard, democracy and autocracy fight with unequal weapons (*On the Chersonese* 11–12).

b. A Crazed Democracy

The result is that no one *governs* any more. "The real danger to democracy no one is bold enough to name; but I will name it. It is in danger when you, men of Athens are wrongly led, when in spite of your numbers you are helpless, unarmed, unorganized and at variance, when no general or anyone else pays any heed to your resolutions, when no one cares to tell you the truth or set you right, when no one makes an effort to remedy this state of things. And that is what always happens now" (*On Organization* 15).

Yet, democracy needs someone at the helm:

> But if all that a speaker passes over, to avoid giving offence, is passed over by the course of events also, then blandiloquence is justified; but if smooth words out of season prove a curse in practice, then it is our disgrace if we hoodwink ourselves, if we shelve whatever is irksome and so miss the time for action, if we fail to learn the lesson that to manage a war properly you must not follow the trend of events but must forestall them, and that just as an army looks to its general for guidance, so statesmen must guide circumstances, if they are to carry out their policy and not be forced to follow at the heels of chance. (*First Philippic* 39)

Without someone at the helm, the city adopts irrational, barbarian behaviors, a shame, to say the least, whereas Philip begins to rise above such a state in both military arts and diplomacy: "But you, Athenians, possessing unsurpassed resources—fleet, infantry, cavalry, revenues—have never to this very day employed them aright, and yet you carry on war with Philip exactly as a barbarian boxes. The barbarian, when struck, always clutches the place; hit him on the other side and there go his hands. He neither knows nor cares how to parry a blow or how to watch his adversary" (40).

If there were a government in Athens, there would be an intelligence. What imperils the Athenian political system—on this Demosthenes and Isocrates agree—is *the lack of any faculty to think and discover the truth;* truth was characteristic of democracy at the time of the "Great Generation," a process that involved critical debate, an exchange of views on the arguments, a consideration of the different sides of an issue. Valid objections removed illusions. The result was a shared, rational position. This is no longer the case. In the Council of Five Hundred, in the Assembly and in the courts, nobody listens to the arguments anymore ("let no one interrupt me till I have finished my story!" [*On Organization* 14]). Orators hijack public debate. The floor is no longer given to anyone who asks to speak. The public is no longer willing to listen to different points of view before judging. It ignorantly follows the first demagogue that strikes its fancy (cf. *Second Olynthiac* 31).

"I see how difficult it is to recommend the wisest course, because, when you share the delusions of your advisers, some wanting this and others that, anyone who attempts to suggest a middle course and finds you too impatient to be instructed, will please neither party and will be discredited with both" (*For the People of the Megalopolis* 2). "For he who would benefit the State, Athenians, must first purge your ears, for they have been poisoned; so many lies have you been accustomed to hear—anything, in fact, rather than the best advice" (*On Organization* 13).

The Assembly was warned, the worst predictions became true; but warnings went unheeded: "You are not remarkable for keeping in mind those who injure you" (*Second Philippic* 30; see Demosthenes, *On Halonnesus*, 18). The ambitious, who witnessed this, can count on the amnesia of the people, which amounts to an amnesty for the leaders.

It is claimed that Athens lives under a regime of free speech, that foreigners, servants, and even slaves have a voice: "but from your deliberations [at the speaker's platform] you have banished [freedom of speech] utterly" (*Third Philippic* 3).[50]

c. The Perverse Effects of the Democratic System

Demosthenes pursues the analysis further. The situation in Athens is not just a consequence of leniency, rectifiable by an increase in awareness. It reflects the intrinsic demands of the

[50] The parallel with Isocrates is striking. We noted earlier that for Isocrates truth was no longer heard from the lips of orators in the agora, only sporadically and ineffectually from the lips of fools and wits.

democratic *system,* given the present constitution. It is in the interest of politicians to say nothing and doing nothing; to prosper as politicians, all they have to do is "accuse and bribe and confiscate…[and obey] the promptings of greed or ambition" (*On the Chersonese* 71), in short, to be mere "sycophants" to varying degrees. Politicians who adopt this stance run no risk: they know this always thrills the Assembly. But a politician who argues in the public interest knows that he exposes himself to accusations, theft of personal belongings, and even death in some cases. Three examples illustrate this.

i. *The Egotistical Conduct of Generals*

Given that the Athenians do not provide their generals (*strategoi*) with the necessary human and material resources to fight the wars that the people have decreed; that the people are always slow to make the necessary military and diplomatic decisions; and finally, given the distressing habit of the Athenians to make accusations against their generals on the flimsiest of pretexts, the *strategoi* lose their nerve and sacrifice the general interest to their own self-serving needs.

> Why is it, think you, men of Athens, that all the generals you dispatch—if I am to tell you something of the truth about them—leave this war to itself and pursue little wars of their own? It is because in this war the prizes for which you contend are your own—(if, for instance, Amphipolis is captured, the immediate gain will be yours)—while the officers have all the dangers to themselves and no remuneration; but in the other case the risks are smaller and the prizes fall to the officers and the soldiers—Lampsacus, for example, and Sigeum, and the plunder of the merchant-ships. So they turn aside each to what pays him best. (*Second Olynthiac* 28)

ii. *The Boards*

The "boards" or "symmories" are officially constituted syndicates of taxpayers charged with contributing a specific sum of money; the members of the boards are expected to agree upon the fair amount to be paid by each member according to his means. Originally, the boards had no say in political decisions; they were simply under obligation to enact them. Then everything changed. Under the leadership of the demagogues, the Assembly gradually increased the tax burden on the various members of the boards, who were compelled to react. They organized into lobbies to weigh on decisions that threatened to ruin them. So they engaged in politics, but since they acted as members of the boards, their action was defensive and in the vested interest of their syndicate, not in the general interest. "The politicians, absorbed in their profession, neglect to devise the best policy for you and have joined the ranks of the office-seekers; and you conduct your party-politics as you used to conduct your tax-paying—by syndicates. There is an orator for chairman, with a general under him, and three hundred to do the shouting.…The rest of you are idle witnesses of their prosperity" (*On Organization* 20).

The board syndicates buy advisors and "shouters" (or media attention, so to speak) and sometimes negotiate with other boards; and it is on this basis that debates and votes are organized. In these circumstances, the final decision *never* reflects the common interest. The decision is what the best-organized syndicates are able to impose, in their own vested financial interest, to the detriment of the other categories of taxpayers and the community as a whole. In the meantime, the unorganized people suffer the consequences, although they vote.[51] Politics is no longer everyone's business.

---

[51] Demosthenes has a sharp eye for the familiar structural weakness known in modern sociology as "formless groups"; regardless of numbers, such groups are unable to weigh on decisions.

> Surely this system must be abandoned. You must be once more your own masters, and must give to all alike the same chance to speak, to counsel, to act. But if you authorize one class of men to issue orders like absolute monarchs, and force another class to equip the galleys and pay the war-tax and serve in the field, while yet a third class has no other public duty than to vote the condemnation of the latter, you will never get anything essential done at the right time. There will always be some class with a grievance, who will fail you, and then it will be your privilege to punish them instead of the enemy. (*Second Olynthiac* 28)

iii. *The Treasury of the Festivals and the Beginnings of "State Socialism"*

The Athenians were great lovers of festivals, as is well known. To stop them from fighting for seats, fixed dates for festivals were set and payment introduced. Then, to help the poor afford a seat on festival occasions, a special subsidy was introduced. This allocation became widespread and translated into a form of regular income (between 354 and 350 BC, Eubulus, a supporter and architect of social peace, administered the public purse and decided to use a special fund [called "theoric fund," *to theorikon*] from a budget surplus to pay for festival seats). Whereas, in the past, Demosthenes remarks, public money was used to pay soldiers, it became the custom to hand out money to the people without anything in return. Not only was this income support too meager to enable the poor to live decently, it also discouraged them from working. "These doles that you are now distributing neither suffice to ensure your safety nor allow you to renounce them and try something else" (*Third Olynthiac* 33).

Of course, once this happens, any suggestion that the state's defense budget needs to be increased—which, by definition, will reduce the budget surplus—is felt by the people as a threat to their income support. The result: democratic orators, assured of the people's backing, go on the attack against the proponents of such ideas or anyone who tries to put it on the agenda. Libanius, a later editor of Demosthenes, points out in his summary of the *First Olynthiac* that the Athenians even voted a law in favor of the death penalty for anyone who attempted to revive the original use of the fund, which was a war fund. The festival fund became an "entitlement" and a "taboo" (almost in the anthropological sense of the word). The topic could simply not be broached on pain of a lawsuit in witchcraft.

Demosthenes feels that it is vital to reverse this entitlement, or risk the recipients losing everything. As a precaution he defends his stance with denials: "'What!' someone cried, 'Do you actually move to use this money for military purposes?' Of course I do not. It is my opinion that we must provide soldiers and that there must be one uniform system of pay'" (*First Olynthiac* 19–20). So very cautiously, he recommends the election of *nomothetes*, special lawgivers authorized to review laws of constitutional importance; after this it will be possible to debate the issue freely (*Third Olynthiac* 10).

> Do not expect to find a statesman who will propose measures for your benefit, only to be ruined by you for his pains. You will never find one, especially as the only result would be that the proposer [who recommends reallocating the festival funds to another use] would get into trouble without improving the situation, and his fate would also make good advice more dangerous for the future.... Until you have set this right, Athenians, do not expect to find anyone so influential among you that he can break these laws with impunity, or so wanting in discretion as to run open-eyed into danger. (12–13)

To summarize, in the Athens of the time when (to use a modernism) the logic of the "political market"[52] dominated, *the vested interests of politicians, as individuals, were opposed to the interests*

[52] Demosthenes may not have used the term, but he certainly grasped the concept.

of the community they allegedly served. A solution in the public interest was an absolute threat for them, whereas a solution that would surely provoke a disaster was easy and far more profitable.

d. Professional Politics and Corruption

The fundamental problem for Demosthenes is the professionalization of politics. There are men who flatter voters for a living: "The orators profit by your disgrace" (*Third Olynthiac* 22). "None of the men whom you delight to honor speaks like that [i.e., speaks the truth], and I will tell you what their excuse is. Men who aim at office and at official rank go to and fro cringing to the favours of the electorate; each one's ambition is to join the sacred ranks of the generals, not to do a man's work.... The politicians, absorbed in their profession, neglect to devise the best policy for you and have joined the ranks of the office-seekers" (*On Organization* 18–20).

Demagogues grow rich by flattering the political market. The people, in turn, are duped and robbed. Demagogues build houses for themselves that are not only more beautiful than the houses of the people, but more beautiful even than public buildings, proof if need be of the decline of public-mindedness (*On Organization* 31). People grow fat on corruption. Yesterday's beggars suddenly become immensely rich (*On the Chersonese* 66). Selfish greed had no place among the earlier generations of Athenian politicians; "each thought it his duty to further the common weal" (*Third Olynthiac* 26).[53]

Demosthenes denies being in anyone's hire (*On the Peace* 12), which proves that he was suspected of corruption. Indeed, everyone who spoke at the *ecclesia* was under suspicion.

Corruption betrays the homeland to the enemy. Demosthenes points out that his opponents are in the pay of Philip (*Second Philippic* 32, 34). Such people are numerous and well organized in Athens: "what Philip would pray the gods to vouchsafe him, are some of us here trying to compass" (*On the Chersonese* 20). In this regard, Philip is a clever maneuverer. His manipulation of the *ecclesia* is part of his warfare. In fact, the reason Philip never openly declares war on Athens, according to Demosthenes, is to protect his "agents of influence," keeping them in place for as long as possible. They are more effective than many of his military campaigns.[54]

e. The Mediocrity and Envy of the People

Finally, Demosthenes, like Isocrates and Plato before him, casts doubt on the people. After all, demagogues merely follow in the footsteps of their cravings. "Your orators never make you either bad men or good, but you make them whichever you choose; for it is not you that aim at what they wish for, but they who aim at whatever they think you desire. You therefore must start with a noble ambition and all will be well" (*On Organization* 36).

i. *Sycophants Grow Rich on the Cravings of the People*

The real victims of pilfering are the rich, while the orchestrators are the sycophants, who cause them to vote by secret ballot and are assured of support from the envious "mob" (*Fourth Philippic* 35–45).

---

[53] Again we encounter the ideas and language of Isocrates.

[54] For example, mercenaries under the command of the general Diopeithes attacked Cardia in Thracian Chersonese, devastating the region under Macedonian rule. This was pernicious because Athens's claim on Cardia was questionable, and a state of war between Athens and Macedonia did not exist. But Athens's action was really a reply to Philip's own aggressions; he had recently conquered Thrace and was now poised to seize the straits, Athens's lifeline. Orators in Philip's hire demanded that the debate be confined to the doings of Diopeithes, demanding that he be recalled and punished (cf. *On the Chersonese* 4–8). It would be hard to imagine a more cynical service of foreign interests.

ii. *The Mob Is Self-interested*

Athenians are unable to "keep [their] hands off the public funds" and to decline public grants of money. Thus, they are not able to cover the costs of the city's defense (*On the Chersonese* 21–23).

iii. *The Mob Is Cowardly*

Because of its cowardice, orators hesitate to formulate concrete proposals for action: they know they can incur the hostility of the people (*Second Philippic* 3–4). Cowardice is the reason the military affairs of Athens are in such disarray. The Athenians refuse to fight themselves and prefer to hire mercenaries in their stead (*First Philippic* 16).[55]

iv. *The Mob Is Blind*

The people refuse to see the simple truth: Philip seeks the ruin of Athens. And while Athens sleeps, he advances inexorably toward his goal.

v. *The Mob Is Irresponsible and Places the Blame Systemically on Scapegoats*

> As to the reason for this—and in Heaven's name, when I am pleading for your best interests, allow me to speak freely—some of our politicians have been training you to be threatening and intractable in the meetings of the Assembly, but in preparing for war, careless and contemptible. If, then, the culprit named is someone on whom you know you can lay hands in Athens, you agree and assent; but if it is someone whom you cannot chastise unless you overcome him by force of arms, you find yourselves helpless, I suppose, and to be proved so causes you annoyance. (*On the Chersonese* 32)

Each individual passes off his personal obligations to a neighbor. Orators insult and accuse each other (*First Philippic* 7, 44). This leads nowhere. The transfer of blame is a shirking of responsibility.

> In the name of the gods, when we have abandoned all these places and almost helped Philip to gain them, shall we then ask who is to blame? For I am sure we shall never admit that it is ourselves. In the panic of battle the runaway never blames himself; it is always his general's fault, or his comrades', anyone's rather than his own. Yet surely to the runaways collectively the defeat is due; for he might have stood firm who now blames the others, and if every man had stood, the battle would have been won. (*Third Olynthiac* 17; *Second Philippic* 34)[56]

[55] Demosthenes proposes that for an army of 2,000 men at least 500 have to be Athenian citizens (*First Philippic* 21).

[56] The reflex of taking those to court who are responsible for diplomacy and defense is senseless for another reason as well, which Demosthenes shows clearly, demonstrating the maturity of legal and political ideas at the time. It is possible to take someone to court who violates laws *within* the state. But the politicians and military leaders that the demagogues indict are in action abroad for the most part. International relations are not subject to the law, but to the balance of power. In such matters, court sanctions are irrelevant (*On the Liberty of the Rhodians* 28–29).

> Men of Athens,... [you are being lied to when you are told]: "in the law-courts lies your salvation," and "it is the ballot-box that must save the State." I know that these courts are sovereign to uphold the rights of citizen against citizen, but it is by arms that you must conquer the enemy, and upon arms depends the safety of the State. For resolutions will not give your men victory in battle, but those who with the help of arms conquer the enemy shall win for you power and security to pass resolutions and to do what you will. For in the field you ought to be terrible, but in the courts sympathetic. (*On Organization* 16–17)

vi. *Finally, the Mob Is Fickle*

The Assembly invites "hirelings" to speak at the platform for the pleasure of hearing calumnies and to laugh. The citizen disappears under the disguise of a clown (*Third Philippic* 54). The cause of the loss and corruption of Greece is "envy of the man who has secured his gains; contempt for him who confesses"; pardon for those who are convicted; "hatred for him who censures such dealings; and every other vice that goes hand in hand with corruption" (*Third Philippic* 38–39).

Festivals and games are the only things that truly appeal to the Athenian mob and its demagogues, the only things they prepare with great seriousness. There is no risk that the Panathenian games or the Dionysian festivals will not be celebrated on the foreseen dates. What a contrast with the armies and navies that set out or arrive at the wrong moment, or not at all!

> The explanation is that at the festivals everything is ordered by statute; every man among you knows long beforehand who of his tribe is to provide the chorus or who to equip the gymnasium, what he is to receive, when and from whom he is to receive it, and what he is to do; nothing here is left to chance, nothing is undetermined: but in what pertains to war and its equipment, everything is ill-arranged, ill-managed, ill-defined. Consequently we wait till we have heard some piece of news, and then we appoint our ship-masters, and arrange suits for exchange of property, and go into committee of ways and means, and next we resolve that the fleet shall be manned by resident aliens and freedmen, then again by citizens, then by substitutes, then, while we thus delay, the object of our cruise is already lost. (*First Philippic* 36–37)

C. Conclusion: The Ideal of Demosthenes

On all these points the democrat Demosthenes is close to the oligarchs or aristocrats Xenophon and Plato. All three decry the tyranny of "popular democracy," which leads to Athens's moral decline, collapse, and ruin.

However, Demosthenes does not attribute the blame to the meanness and faults of the people as much as to the institutions.[57] It is they that must be reformed. Like Isocrates, he wants stronger "executive powers" and a change toward something like a "mixed regime." He also wants better-organized debates held in the general interest. Above all, he wants measures to be taken against corruption and says so in a remarkable passage: "It is impossible . . . to gain permanent power by injustice, perjury, and falsehood. . . . For a brief season such things endure . . . but at the last they are detected and fall to pieces. . . . In affairs of state the principles and the foundations must be truth and justice" (*Second Olynthiac* 9; he uses the same text again in *On the Treaty with Alexander*).

However, this ideal, it seems, can no longer be achieved in the context of the city.

[57] Like Thucydides, Demosthenes reasons like a sociologist, analyzing the "logic of situations"; he applies "methodological individualism." It will be a long time before anyone practices this scientific approach to the issues again. As early as the late Roman Empire and throughout the Middle Ages, and even for a long while during contemporary times, the most common practice is to "demonize" one's political opponents. Vast numbers of political leaders and intellectuals once again adopt the reasoning style of the mob.

Chapter 5

Political Ideas in the Hellenistic Age: Cynicism, Stoicism, Epicureanism

It seems that the fourth century Greeks did not foresee the historical evolution that finally condemned the political formula of the city-state. True, they considered uniting Hellenic countries against the kings of Macedonia and, later, against the Roman Empire, or at least to create political entities of a sufficient, critical size. But either they designed their federations on the model of symmachies without political integration, which were therefore extremely fragile, or whenever they tried to create large federal states, they failed. Obviously, the most effective political model appeared to be that of the Macedonian conqueror's, that is, monarchy.

And so, just as leading thinkers such as Plato and Aristotle were formulating comprehensive theories of the state and government for the first time, the *polis* itself was being overtaken by history (which does not mean that it disappeared: the institutions of the Greek *polis* and the Greek civic spirit endured for centuries). But another reality was emerging.

I. The Hellenistic World

The new model took shape after Alexander the Great's conquests (336–322 BC), which resulted in the creation of the great monarchic states.

Alexander's successors (called the "Epigones" or "Diadochi") founded three kingdoms: *Egypt*, governed by the Lagide dynasty, founded by one of Alexander's generals, Ptolemy, the son of a Macedonian nobleman by the name of Lagos (numerous Egyptian kings were named Ptolemy; the Ptolemaic dynasty lasted until Cleopatra and the reduction of Egypt into a Roman province in 30 BC with Alexandria as its capital); *Syria*, governed by the Seleucids, after another of

Alexander's generals, Seleucus (many Syrian kings bear the name Antiochos; its capital was Antioch); *Macedonia*, governed by the Antigonid dynasty, after Antigonus Gonatas; Pella was its capital. After 262 BC, a fourth Hellenistic kingdom was created in Asia Minor: the kingdom of Pergamon (governed by the Attalid dynasty; its kings took the name Eumenes or Attalus); Pergamon became a great cultural center, the rival of Alexandria.

No sooner were they created than these kingdoms engaged in endless wars that soon placed them in a position of inferiority against the rising power of Rome.

In theory, Greece came under the rule of the Antigonid kingdom of Macedonia, which created garrisons at strategic locations like Piraeus. Still, each city preserved its local government. Some managed to break free by inciting rivalries and wars throughout the kingdom, changing sides according to the dictates of interest. Moreover, they managed to create or maintain real federal states in Boeotia (11 "districts" around Thebes), Etolia (northwestern continental Greece), and the Peloponnesus (the "Achaean League" around Megalopolis). These political entities tried to re-create the "republican" institutions of the classical Greek *polis:* elected federal magistrates, councils with delegates pro rata to the population size of the federated cities, and even large people's assemblies. But these creations lacked internal harmony and continuity in diplomacy and war. In the end, they were unable to overturn the situation created by Alexander's conquests.

In many respects, the Hellenistic kingdoms remind us of the ancient sacred monarchies of the Near East (see the introduction to this volume). At the same time, they are something entirely new. They prolong the old monarchies because the king exercises absolute power without restraint and because his person is deified or quasi-deified. But they can no longer be "sacred monarchies" in the sense that ancient Egypt and the kingdom of Hammurabi were because they are basically multiethnic states (Macedonians, Greeks, Egyptians, Syrians, Persians, and the like), and their social bond is constituted essentially by Greek civic and scientific culture.

The creation of the Hellenistic kingdoms brought about an unprecedented mingling of peoples throughout the Mediterranean basin and the Middle East. Alexander himself pursued a policy of interethnic mingling (he initiated this with his own marriage to the Persian princess, Roxane; he imposed such mixed marriages on his officers as well). Thus, a new "Hellenistic" culture was forged that conquered ethnic groups could assimilate. We have already quoted Isocrates on this process of acculturation: "[Our city] has brought it about that the name Hellenes suggests no longer a race but an intelligence, and that the title Hellenes is applied *rather to those who share our culture than to those who share a common blood*" (*Panegyricus* 48).

Philosophy, in Greece and in the new cultural centers throughout the Hellenistic world, records this evolution and contributes to its strengthening.

II. The Cynics and Cynicism

We must look first to a school of philosophy—or philosophical tradition, at any rate—that appeared long before the conquests of Alexander: *Cynicism.*[1]

The distant founder of the Cynic tradition is a disciple of Socrates—thus, a contemporary of Plato and Xenophon (he appears at length in the latter's *Symposium*). His name is Antisthenes

[1] Material in this section is from R. Bracht Branham and Marie-Odile Goulet-Cazé, eds., *The Cynics: The Cynic Movement in Antiquity and Its Legacy* (Berkeley and Los Angeles: University of California Press, 1997).

(ca. 444–ca. 365). But the principal founder is Diogenes of Sinope[2] (ca. 413–ca. 327), described by Plato—who knew him—as "a Socrates gone mad." It was Diogenes who inaugurated the tradition of the philosopher in a worn cloak (*tribon*) with a walking staff in one hand and a beggar's bag in the other, living on handouts. Based on his example, Cynicism became a lifestyle based on begging in practice. His followers lived doglike in packs (*syn-kunizein*).[3]

After disappearing in the second and first centuries BC, Cynicism reappeared under the Roman Empire as a doctrine of resistance to the tyranny of the Julio-Claudian dynasty: its champions were *Demetrius* and *Demonax*. As earlier, the tradition recruited almost exclusively in the underprivileged classes, that is, among those that did not have the leisure to study (this explains the taunting of Julian the Apostate in the middle of the fourth century AD, who lumped Cynics and poor "uneducated Galileans" together).

The Cynics' ideas are known from many quotations and testimonies, but no complete work survives.

Cynicism reflects the profound *crisis of the polis*. As the etymology suggests, Cynics are "dogs" that bark and bite, which means that their intention is to upset and irritate, like Socrates, but they go much further, all the way to a kind of nihilism. They criticize *all* values. Diogenes had to flee Sinope after he (or his father, the master of the mint) got into trouble for counterfeiting the local currency. After this, he pretended to "counterfeit the currency" allegorically, that is, to systematically alter and confuse all values. Thus, the members of the school of Diogenes would truly be "cynics" in the modern sense, if they did not present a positive ideal of personal morality based on *asceticism,* as well as a genuinely intellectual ideal of *extreme lucidity,* an obsession with not being deceived by conventions, hypocrisy, and social prejudices that befuddle the masses. In this sense, the Cynics actually perpetuate the critical epistemology of the Sophists and Socrates.

The Cynics have precise theories on values and political institutions. Diogenes deliberately chooses *physis* over *nomos*. The universe forms a hierarchy; at the top are the gods and just below them are animals, not men, because animals are closer to nature. Cynics believe that by being more animal-like—by going about naked, sleeping outdoors in all seasons, performing sexual acts publicly, and behaving extravagantly[4]—man raises himself up.

---

[2] Sinope was a city on the shores of the Black Sea in the north of Asia Minor, a colony of Miletus. Like many Cynics, Diogenes came from the geographical periphery of the Greek world, and like most Cynics until the Roman times, his social origins were very modest.

[3] Among Diogenes's more or less well-known disciples were Monime, Onesicritus, Crates (whose own disciple was Zeno of Citium, the founder of Stoicism), Hipparchia, Metrocles, Menippus, Menedimus, and in the third century, Bion of Borysthenes and Cercidas (the latter, exceptionally for this school, played a direct political role, with the Stoic Aratus, in the reconstruction of Megalopolis and the introduction of a new constitution in 217 BC). Fragments of another teacher, Teles, also survive, giving evidence of Cynicism at this time.

[4] One example:

> Metrocles was the brother of Hipparchia; and though he had formerly been a pupil of Theophrastus, the Peripetician, he had profited so little by his instructions, that once, thinking that, while listening to a lecture on philosophy, he had disgraced himself by his inattention [breaking wind], he fell into despondency, and shut himself up in his house, intending to starve himself to death. Accordingly, when Crates, the Cynic, heard of it, he came to him, having been sent for; and eating a number of lupins, on purpose, he first persuaded him by numbers of arguments, that he had done no harm; for that it was not to be expected that a man should escape the laws of nature; and, then, he comforted him by breaking wind as well and showing him that he, in a similar case, would certainly have behaved in a similar manner. And subsequently, Metrocles became a pupil of Crates, and a man of great eminence as a philosopher.

From Diogenes Laertius, *The Lives and Opinions of Eminent Philosophers*, translated by C. D. Yonge (London: Henry G. Bohn, 1853), with modifications.

Here are some additional aspects of cynic "philosophy": In religion, Diogenes is an agnostic. He does not believe that the gods rule the world. He calls "illusions" such established practices as religious services, offerings, and sacrifices. Diogenes goes even farther and "falsifies" philosophy itself, which must not be a new illusory refuge. He refuses to examine certain problem issues that he considers unsolvable. All that is left is pure action. He advocates asceticism, which

The corollary of the Cynic bond with nature is *universalism*. The Cynics reject *nomos* because it is made up of customs, laws, and institutions, all of which are proper to a given country, whereas *physis* is universal. Therefore, Cynicism is fundamentally cosmopolitan (the idea that exile is not a misfortune is repeated frequently). But Diogenes does not understand cosmopolitanism in the Stoic sense of an organized world city (see below). His understanding is strictly negative: he is cosmopolitan only as far as he belongs to *no* city; he is *a-polis, a-oikos,* "houseless and citiless, a piteous exile / from his dear native land; a wandering beggar, / scraping a pittance poor from day to day" (Diogenes, after Diogenes Laertius, 6.38). "A citizen of the world" (*kosmopolitês*) (*Diogenes,* according to Diogenes Laertius, 6.63).

Crates takes up the idea and clarifies it after the conquests of Alexander: "'Tis not one town, nor one poor single house, / that is my country; but in every land / each city and each dwelling seems to me, / a place for my reception ready made" (Crates, after Diogenes Laertius, 6.38).

The laws of cities are all the same: worthless. It seems that Diogenes is the author of a *Republic* rejecting all laws, all fetters on freedom; he also apparently advocates outlandish behaviors like cannibalism, incest, common ownership of women and children, athletic games for women in the nude, and total sexual freedom. Political institutions and monetary currency are to be abolished. Nature is the only norm, the animal the only standard of reference. When the Cynics extol the animal, the free child of nature, they, in fact, laud a barbaric lack of culture.

Still, Cynicism is *not* cosmopolitanism because it is in no sense *civicism*. It cannot achieve universalism because it rejects the values of "civilization" (the law, reason, justice, and so on), which might enable different ethnic communities to coexist peacefully. The same comment applies to Epicureanism, to a lesser degree (see below).

III. Stoicism

The Stoic school,[5] also known as the Porch (owing to its location in Athens next to the *Stoa Poikile,* or Painted Porch), was founded—like Cynicism—by men who were not members of the privileged classes and who came from outlying, recently Hellenized regions:

- *Zeno of Citium* (ca. 335–264 BC), from Cyprus; his family may have originated in Phoenicia;
- *Cleanthes* (b. 331 BC; head of the school from 264 to 232 BC), from Assos in Troad;
- *Chrysippus* (b. ca. 281 BC; head of the school from 232 to 204 BC), from Cyprus or Cilicia (a southeastern region of Asia Minor).

prepares the body for action (the Cynic washes only with cold water, if he bothers to wash at all; he drinks only water and eats only after sweating heavily; he sleeps on a hard surface and wears his *tribon* in all seasons, doubled up or long; he possesses no garment other than his cloak). The Cynic must learn to forego the pleasures of civilization and to "go backward," that is, revert to simple animal life. Philosophy is not study, it is *parrhesia,* straight talk: the Cynic speaks the truth, regardless whether it generates scandal. Diogenes abandons any sense of modesty and human respect (he masturbates in public; Crates and Hipparchia make love in public). The Cynics claim that only individuals who can behave like this are true philosophers.

[5] This section is based on Emile Bréhier, *Les Stoïciens* [The Stoics] (Paris: Gallimard, 1962); Jean Brun, *Les Stoïciens: Textes choisis* [The Stoics: Selected texts] (Paris: Presses Universitaires de France, 1973); Emile Bréhier, *Chrysippe et l'ancien stoïcisme* [Chrysippus and ancient Stoicism] (Amsterdam: Gordon & Breach, 1971); Victor Goldschmidt, *Le système Stoïcien et l'idée de temps* [Stoicism and the concept of time] (Paris: Vrin, 1969).

A. Stoicism and the Cosmopolis

The Stoics teach that man is more than a citizen of a particular place; he belongs to a wider community extending to the limits of the world, the *cosmopolis*.

"The whole world is the City of the wise man."[6] He is no longer a citizen of a narrow, ethnically pure place; he lives in a "world-city" unified by Greek *paideia*. Plutarch writes:

> The much-admired *Republic* of Zeno [of Citium], the founder of the Stoic sect, may be summed up in this one main principle: that all the inhabitants of this world of ours should not live differentiated by their respective rules of justice into separate cities and communities, but that we should consider all men to be of one community and one polity, and that we should have a common life and an order common to us all, even as a *herd* that feeds together and shares the pasturage of a common field.[7] This Zeno wrote, giving shape to a dream or, as it were, shadowy picture of a well-ordered and philosophic commonwealth; but it was Alexander who gave effect to the idea.... He [Alexander] brought together into one body all men everywhere, uniting and mixing in one great loving-cup, as it were, men's lives, their characters, their marriages, their very habits of life. He bade them all consider as their fatherland the whole inhabited earth, as their stronghold and protection his camp, as akin to them all good men, and as foreigners only the wicked.[8]

B. Natural Law

How do the Stoics see the government of the *cosmopolis?* Chrysippus refers to what he calls *physei nomos,* "natural law." Thus, the Stoics do not dismiss *nomos,* like the Cynics, but they think that the *nomos* governing the fellowship of men and women must be different from the *nomos* governing cities, which is a particularist law; the former is closer to "natural law." Because nature is the same for everyone everywhere, human law based on natural law will tend to be a universal law.

For the Cynics, nature is the animal state, the uncultured barbarian: a stomach, genitals, muscles, and instincts. All morals, all institutions are dismissed as anti-nature. For the Stoics, nature is also the model, but within nature, globally speaking, there is a *particular human nature,* which is superior to animal nature (we will see why below); it has its own laws, different from the laws that animals obey. Civilization, *paideia,* expresses this superior nature of humanity: human beings are made to be "civilized." Thus, institutions and positive laws are by no means anti-nature.

1. *Nature according to the Stoics*

To understand what *natural law* is, we need to look at Stoic physics, which is different from the physics of Aristotle.[9]

Zeno asserts that a being is recognizable by its capacity to act, and that everything that acts is corporeal. Indeed, incorporeal phenomena exist as well, such as the void outside the world, place, "expressibles." But they are a "mere something" incapable of action or suffering. In this sense, Stoicism is a materialism.

[6] Chrysippus, frag. 2, in Bréhier, *Chrysippe.*

[7] Plutarch plays on the words *nômos* and *nomôs* here.

[8] Plutarch, *Moralia: On the Fortune or the Virtue of Alexander,* vol. 4 (Cambridge, MA: Harvard University Press, 1936), 6.

[9] Drawn from Pierre-Maxime Schuhl, preface to Bréhier, *Les Stoïciens,* xv–xxx.

Zeno does not dispute the eternal substance of the world. But, following Xenophanes, he observes that the earth deteriorates, that the seas rise and fall. He concludes that there are protracted cosmic periods during which the earth forms and dissolves. Hence the following cosmological pattern:

> A divine primordial fire gives birth to the element of air by condensation; then the element of water, the fount of the world, appears. Earth takes shape in the center, and the universe falls into place (*diacosmesis*), attaining perfection immediately. This recalls the cosmogony of the ancient Ionian "physicists." ... Then fire takes over again and progressively absorbs the other elements until the end of the "Great Year," which according to the calculations of Diogenes of Babylon[10] lasts 365 times 10,800 years. Then the fiery self-annihilation (*ekpirosis*) takes place and the universe, reduced to its fundamental principle, is purified, and the entire process begins all over again. This is the "eternal return," also familiar to the Pythagorians.[11]

Zeno (like Heraclitus) identifies the primordial fire with reason, logos. As it proliferates, logos produces "seminal reasons" (*spermatikoi logoi*) that guide the development of individual beings; these reasons are part of cosmic Reason. Nature is a "creative fire," "which, by virtue of its organizing strength, maintains the world and its parts, imbuing them with beauty. It is not a destructive, all-consuming fire, but a life-giving, wholesome warmth as well as the brightness of light."[12]

At different levels, this principle has various names. Among inorganic beings, it is a cohesive force called *hexis*. Among plants and animals, it is the soul, *psyche*, possessing *phantasia*, imaginative impression, along with *horme*, impulse. Among humans, *logos* comes—in addition to these capacities—after the seventh year. *Logos* causes humans to resemble the gods. "According to Zeno, the soul dwells in the heart; its substance is *pneuma*, i.e., the warm breath of life of the living animal (an idea borrowed from Greek medical writers). Chrysippus shows waves of *pneuma*, like the arms of an octopus, connecting the *hegemonikon* (the ruling or controlling principle of the soul) to the five senses and to the phonative and sexual organs."[13] The composition of the *psyche* is different from that of the *physis*. A cold, humid element is predominant in the *physis*; in the *psyche* it is a warm, burning breath formed of air and fire. This compound has fixed proportions, which cause illnesses when they are disrupted. The soul of animals is made up of corruptible elements of the universal soul, itself incorruptible.

This "creative fire," progressing methodically and penetrating the whole world and all humanity, exerts a true *providence*. "For Zeno, true piety is an awareness, respect, and adoration of this action, even if an obligation remains to revere the gods." Zeno believes that "beneath the official cult and the poetic myth there are nevertheless natural realities, or rather a deeper reality under different names."[14] Gods are just allegories.

For the Stoics, there is no void in nature; the void lies outside the world. The Stoics also believe that material bodies are not impenetrable. This is the contrary of the atomists, who theorize that atoms are indivisible and combine together within the void. "Thus, the unifying action of the spirit [breath] can penetrate any obstacle. The different parts exercise a mutual influence on one another. This explains the notions of *universal sympathy* and *total mixture*. ... Physics is the

[10] Also known as Diogenes the Stoic, a scholar of the Stoic school in the second century BC. We will come across him again.

[11] Schuhl, preface, xviii.

[12] Ibid., xix.

[13] Ibid., xx.

[14] Ibid., xx.

science of this order. It is not an abstract formula, but the link that connects the chain of events of our individual life to the general economy of the universe."[15]

2. *Political Consequences*

Since nature is like this, then so natural law must be as well. The closer the state and positive laws are to natural law, the more perfect they will be.

In practice, this can translate as contradictory aspects because Stoic natural law itself contains certain ambiguous features. As providence, fate, and universal solidarity, it makes less room for individual freedom and reason than Aristotle's natural law. Conversely, it substitutes a *cosmic* (thus distant) order for a (closer) *civic* order that strictly encloses the life of each citizen.

Stoic political philosophy plays on these ambiguities: at times it glorifies *absolute monarchy,* the embodiment of universal order; at other times it encourages the *dissidence of those who are wise,* those who are able to withdraw from involvement in the affairs of state because they are immediately part of universal nature and accountable to no one other than divine government.

When we come to Cicero and Dio Chrysostom, we will explore in more depth Stoic conceptions of *nature, human nature,* and *natural law.*

IV. Epicureanism

Almost simultaneously with Stoicism, another school of philosophy appeared: *Epicureanism.* It, too, reflects the transformation from the *polis* to the *cosmopolis* that occurred after the battle of Chaeronea. But while Stoicism develops a positive theory of the *cosmopolis,* it is fair to say that Epicureanism only embraces it between the lines. Epicurean wisdom thinking, rooted in private life and selfless scientific study, supposes that the citizen is allowed to live quietly, without active involvement in affairs of the state. The implication is that someone else—a Hellenistic king, a Roman senate—takes charge. The founder of this school was Epicurus.

A. Life and Work

Epicurus was born in 341 in Samos to a family of Athenian settlers.[16] At the age of 18 he went up to Athens. Alexander the Great had just died and the Athenian revolt had been crushed by the Macedonians. After a period of wandering, induced by the political instability of the times, he founded several schools of philosophy: in Mytilene, in Lampsacus (on the Sea of Marmara); then, in 306 BC, in Athens where he finally settled, he founded the Garden (shortly before Zeno of Citium founded the Porch). He died in 271 or 270 BC.

No complete work by Epicurus survives. The little we know about his thought comes from book 10 of Diogenes Laertius's *The Lives and Opinions of Eminent Philosophers* (written after 200 AD), which includes three letters by Epicurus to his followers (*Letter to Herodotus* on physics, *Letter to Menoecius* on ethics, and the *Letter to Pythocles,* though the authorship of this letter is disputed).[17] Fragments of his other writings do survive, including parts of his *On the Nature of Things* (discovered in Herculaneum). In addition to this work (37 volumes in length), it is said that Epicurus wrote as many as 300 works.

---

[15] Ibid., xxi.

[16] For material in this section, see Diogenes Laertius in *The Lives and Opinions of Eminent Philosophers,* 2 vols., trans. R. D Hicks (1925; repr., Cambridge, MA: Harvard University Press, 2006).

[17] Diogenes Laertius, *Lives and Opinions.*

B. The Philosophy of Epicurus

Epicurus subscribed to the materialist, atomic, and mechanical *physics* of Democritus. As an adolescent he had several teachers, notably Nausiphanes, a follower of Hecataeus of Abdera, himself a student of Democritus. The visible world consists of indivisible atoms and empty space or void. All reality, including psychological and intellectual reality, is made up of atoms. The world is ruled by chance and necessity, not by gods (the gods exist but they do not govern and do not care about human beings). Fate, in the Stoic sense, plays no role either because the existence of void creates a wide space for *chance* and *freedom* in the workings of the world and human affairs.

Sensation is the root of all knowledge; both feelings and reason depend on sensations. "Now, in *The Canon,* Epicurus affirms that our sensations and preconceptions and our feelings are the standards of truth. . . . Reason cannot refute them, for reason is wholly dependent on sensation."[18] Thus, Epicurus rejects all idealism, in particular Plato's: our knowledge is a reflection of material phenomena, knowable *because* they are perceptible, not *though* perceptible. He also rejects a bookish education, *paideia,* which he believes diverts us from our sensations and makes us approach truth circuitously. For deeper knowledge, Epicurus cultivates fine sensations (which is why he is the enemy of crude, degenerate pleasures).

Nevertheless, pleasure in the *ethics* of Epicurus is the greatest good. "As proof that pleasure is the end he [Epicurus] adduces the fact that living things, as soon as they are born, are well content with pleasure and are at enmity with pain, by the prompting of nature and apart from reason."[19] "The principle and the root of all good is the pleasure of the stomach" (*he tes gastros hedone*).[20] But however that may be, the soul has its own particular pleasures, the first of which is knowledge.[21] One should possess virtues not for their own sake, but for the pleasure that they procure (this argument is diametrically opposed to the Stoics for whom virtues and moral beauty are goods in themselves).

It is right to seek pleasure: it will be easier to bear suffering or deprivation if the aim is to attain stable, enduring pleasure; this is why the primary virtue of the wise is temperance. Diogenes Laertius presents Epicurus and his followers as prudent men, aspiring to a quiet life and cultivating friendship.

Epicurean communities avoid civic involvement and strenuous theoretical work. A wise man only earns money if necessary, only speaks in public if necessary, and founds schools, but does not recruit large numbers of pupils. He is moderate in everything.[22]

Lucretius praised Epicurus as the man who declared war on *superstition* and declared his faith in *rationalism.* But what political opinion can be deduced from such philosophical stances?

C. Epicurean Apoliticism

In the turmoil of the dying days of the Greek city, Epicurus no longer has any expectations from politics, nor from social life in general.

A wise person shuns participation in politics: "We must free ourselves from the prison of private and public affairs."[23] Again and again, a deliberate avoidance of civic responsibility is

---

[18] Ibid., 31–32.

[19] Ibid., 137.

[20] Quoted by Atheneaus; from Usener, *Epicurea,* frag. 409, available at www.Epicurus.com; hereafter cited in the text.

[21] From P. von der Mühl, *Epicuri epistolae tres et ratae sententiae* (Leipzig: Teubner, 1922), frag. 27; hereafter cited in the text.

[22] Ibid., 117–21.

[23] Epicurus, *Letters, Principal Doctrines, and Vatican Sayings,* trans. Russell Geer (New York: Pearson, 1964), frag. 58.

attributed to Epicurus and the Epicureans. We know from Diogenes Laertius that Epicurus is the author of a work "On Monarchy," like many writers of his time; however, none of his ideas on the topic have filtered down, other than these few sayings: "the wise man will pay court to a king, if need be"; "a free life cannot acquire many possessions, because this is not easy without servility to mobs and governments" (frag. 67, von der Mühl). "They [Epicureans] mention statesmen only to deride them and belittle their fame" (Plutarch, frag. 560, Usener).

Paul Nizan suggests the following interpretation of Epicurean apoliticism (closer to the Cynics than the Stoics):

> In the days of Plato, it was still possible to believe in the collective salvation of society. By the time of Epicurus, however, all that could be hoped for was individual salvation.... It is not easy for man to accept that his life is almost entirely negative, that it is characterized by misfortunes, shortcomings, and failings: fullness is man's most cherished law. By 300 BC thoughts of justice, duty, virtue, and progress were no longer entertained: these are not the values of a despairing world. The only hope was for "salvation." The great idea behind Epicurus is not that salvation offers an escape into the heavens, like Christianity later; it is that salvation can be a worldly pursuit. He does not promise heavenly riches or treasures in an afterlife. Salvation is not in heaven, in the spirit, or in death. Epicurus proposes a material wisdom that asks of the body and its qualities the secret of not dying in despair.[24]

Epicurus establishes a theoretical framework for his doctrine of apoliticism. "Among desires some are natural and necessary, some natural but not necessary, and others neither natural nor necessary, but due to baseless opinion" (*Principal Doctrine* 29). Thus, *seclusion from the life of the city* is a way to guard against ambition, vanity, constant struggle, and the errors of the crowd. "I have never wished to cater to the crowd; for what I know, they do not understand, and what they approve, I do not care" (frag. 187, Usener).

It is preferable for man to withdraw and live in isolation: Epicurus asks him to "live unknown" (quoted by Plutarch, frag. 551, Usener); "security in general [i.e., protection from others] depends upon peace of mind and social detachment" (*Principal Doctrine* 14). Once the person is in isolation, he will restore in himself a nature corrupted and removed by the group. He will find strength in natural and nonartificial things: his own body, senses, a knowledge of his needs, temperate pleasures.

Moreover, nature is not very demanding: Lucretius says in a well-known passage[25] "the nature of every man demands nothing more for itself, but that he, from whose body pain is removed and absent, may exercise his mind with a pleasurable feeling, exempt from care and fear." The needs of the body are few; it is enough to be without hunger, thirst, or pain. "Natural wealth is both limited and easily obtained, but vanity is insatiable" (*Principal Doctrine* 15). An anonymous Epicurean observes: "Anyone who fulfills the purpose of human life, even if his achievement goes unnoticed, is more or less an accomplished individual" (frag. 533, Usener).

However, a life in harmony with nature is not compatible with total seclusion. Life involves *friendship:* "Epicurus is right when, in one of his letters, he rebukes those who argue that the Sage is self-sufficient and for that reason does not stand in need of friendships" (quoted by Seneca, frag. 174, Usener). Accordingly, the Epicureans establish communities.[26] Such communities are

---

[24] Paul Nizan, *Les materialists de l'antiquité* [Ancient Greek materialism] (Paris: Gallimard, 1938), 14.

[25] Lucretius, *On the Nature of Things [De natura]*, trans. W. H. D. Rouse, rev. Martin Smith (1924; repr., Cambridge, MA: Harvard University Press, 1975), 2.1–61: *Suave mari magno.*

[26] A Marxist like Nizan saw in them the forerunner of socialist communities, but a closer reading of Epicurus leads us to conclude that he did not advocate a community of goods.

to be isolated from the overall community of the city and the human race. Epicurus addresses the following comment to one of his fellows: "I write this not for the many, but for you; each of us is enough of an audience for the other" (quoted by Seneca, frag. 208, Usener). This opinion stands in relief against that of the Stoics, who were also capable of seclusion and apoliticism but at the same time never lost sight of the *cosmopolis*.

In the words of Nizan, "naturalist optimism follows social pessimism" (20). In order for such optimism to be founded, humans—after finding safety from social terrors—need protection from the forces of nature, the gods, death, and time. Therefore, in retreat the Epicureans will busy themselves with *natural science,* the virtue of which is to banish these ghosts by discovering the neutral laws of nature. This is the fundamental difference from the Cynics (who are skeptical and lazy): Epicurean communities work, applying themselves to serious scientific study.

"I prefer, with my studies of nature, to discover what is useful to all men, whether or not I am understood, than to abide by vain opinion and win the praises of the people" (frag. 29, von der Mühl). "Philosophy [i.e., science] is an activity [that] secures the happy life by arguments and discussions" (quoted by Sextus Empiricus, frag. 217, Usener). "To win real freedom, you must be the slave of philosophy" (quoted by Seneca, frag. 199, Usener). "The love of true philosophy dissolves every anxious and painful longing" (Porphyry, frag. 457, Usener). This is also the theme of Lucretius's *Suave mari magno:* "it is sweet to contemplate the misfortunes of men from afar, i.e. from the serene heights of philosophy [the 'temple of learning']."[27] Science produces an overall vision of the world and enables us to put the misfortunes of our lives in proper perspective. "Remember that despite being mortal in nature, and despite being in receipt of a finite length of time, you have nevertheless ascended through your natural enquiries to infinity and eternity and have gazed down upon 'what is, will be, and was before' [Homer]" (frag. 10, von der Mühl).

D. Justice Is a Matter of Convention

Science tells us this about the creation of justice and laws by human societies:

"Natural justice is the advantage conferred by mutual agreements not to inflict nor allow harm" (Epicurus, *Principal Doctrine* 31).

"For all living creatures incapable of making agreements not to harm one another, nothing is ever just or unjust; and so it is likewise for all tribes of men which have been unable or unwilling to make such agreements" (*Principal Doctrine* 31).

"There is no natural justice, and crime should be avoided because one cannot escape the fear which results therefrom" (frag. 531, Usener).

In other words, the values and constitutive institutions of a political order have both a practical and artificial origin. Justice does not exist in a "state of nature," and a "nation" (tribe or people) can behave any way it likes with another nation with which it has not established a common code of justice. Here the ideas of Epicurus diverge radically from those of the Stoics (particularly the theory of natural justice that Cicero presents, see below, pp. 270–87).

Proof that justice is by nature contractual can be seen in its diversity: "Justice is the same for all peoples insofar as it benefits human interaction. But the details of how justice is applied in particular countries or circumstances may vary" (*Principal Doctrine* 36). These varied customs are also respectable. We find in Epicurus a slightly different variation of the idea of universalism emerging in Stoic cosmopolitanism at the same time: "As we respect our own customs, which we

---

[27] Lucretius, *On the Nature of Things,* 2.1–61: *Suave mari magno.*

consider praiseworthy of men, so must we respect those of others if they are set in their habits" (frag. 15, von der Mühl).

True, conventions are necessary for the creation of justice. To be happy one must be wise, and to be wise is to be just. Once a convention has been established, no one can avoid it under the pretext of returning to nature; a person may circumvent it a thousand times, but nothing guarantees that he or she will never be caught. When one is unjust, one lives in constant terror. Even the pursuit of pleasure requires just behavior. "The just life is without pain; in contrast, the unjust life is full of pain" (frag. 12, von der Mühl).

The definition of justice as an artificial creation, with a view to shared utility, has its corollary in the idea that laws can be judged in terms of their greater or lesser usefulness: "Where . . . things held to be just by law are revealed to be in conflict with the interests of the community, such laws do not suit the essence of justice" (*Principal Doctrine* 38). Moreover, according to this logic, a law may be just at a certain moment, and then cease to be just when circumstances change.

The intellectual movement established by Epicurus through the Garden lasted throughout antiquity. We will come across it again with Lucretius at the close of the Roman Republic. Though the movement continued to thrive, it remained marginal.

V. The King and the Law in the Hellenistic World

How should we characterize the transformation that occurred with the demise of the political model of the Greek city and the advocacy of incomparably larger political entities? This transformation has a "positive" and a "negative" aspect.

On the one hand, thanks to Alexander and his successors, Greek *paideia*, the fundamental principle of civicism, and the idea of "the rule of law" spread throughout the known world. In the Hellenistic *cosmopolis*, individuals enjoyed freedom to the same extent as in the smaller Greek city. In some respects people had greater freedom, because they enjoyed a more far-reaching public order and were farther from the power center.

Individuals were no longer under the close watch of the civic community in which every member knew and watched everyone else (the very wish of Aristotle, not to mention Plato's "totalitarianism"). They were no longer citizens in their city and foreigners everywhere else. They were at home everywhere, free to travel and develop broader cultural horizons. They could advocate more varied and bolder political and scientific opinions because if they were censured in one place, they could be accepted somewhere else (this was the age of great Greek science: Euclid (third century), Archimedes (287–212 BC), the astronomers Aristarchus of Samos (310–ca. 230 BC), Eratosthenes of Cyrene (ca. 276–ca. 195 BC), the Alexandrian grammarians, and so on). Individuals could also pursue more ambitious economic undertakings in regions of the Mediterranean where the same public order reigned. Likewise, they were free to withdraw from political life to explore the paths of an inner perfection, with no civic obligations whatsoever, in keeping with the wishes of the Epicureans and certain Stoics. In the final analysis, the citizen of the large state was noticeably freer, in practice and in theory, than the citizen of the small city.

However, the citizens of the new monarchies had to give up direct participation in the making, discussing, and amending of the law that presides over public order on such a grand scale. Greek efforts to establish federal bodies had failed because no assembly or council could properly claim to represent such vast territories; it became impossible to honor the venerable civic principle of open debate of public affairs in the agora or even the government of the state by a college of magistrates. In the new monarchies, government was administered and the law was made by one exceptional person—the *king*.

If in the eyes of the masses the king reigned, it was, first and foremost because he was an exceptional person, someone who clearly enjoyed the protection of the gods and "Fate." He was the one who, in troubled times, achieved victories when so many were swept to their deaths. The king personified the city when he ascended to his lofty position. It was asked and expected of him to unite in his person all the qualities that were once held by an entire community of citizens: justice, goodness, intelligence. He is an *internalized constitution*.

The Stoics say that the king is *nomos empsychos,* an "embodied law"—a living or animate law—because his soul contains, to a much higher degree than ordinary people, a fragment of the divine Logos that orders the universe. This alone explains why he rules an order that no longer satisfies the epistemological conditions postulated by Aristotle: that civic government assumed a tiny, surveyable territory and population, and human reason sufficed for its administration. The new monarchies required a higher, superhuman form of wisdom that Providence bestowed on a king.

Before long the exceptional character of the king warranted a *royal cult*. The Greeks, it is true, borrowed the idea from the lands they conquered in the Orient: the Lagide dynasty did little more than assimilate the indigenous cult of the pharaohs. At the same time, these ideas resonated with ancient Greek memories, notably with hero worship and death cults.

In the final analysis, the Hellenistic world constitutes, in political terms, a transformation, some aspects of which hold future promise, while others suggest worrying regression. The notion of *cosmopolis,* the emergence of a world where cultures intermingle, contributes to the development of the "rule of law" and personal liberty. In this respect, the Hellenistic world prolongs the Greek miracle and, at the same time, creates the conditions for an unprecedented cultural effervescence and economic progress. However, rationalism regresses and political power tends to resacralize itself.

The Roman world will inherit these ambiguities.

Part Two

Rome

Introduction

Roman Law and Western Humanism

The Greeks invented the city, a community under the rule of law—the same law for all, created by men, debated rationally in the agora, making possible personal liberty. While they created the form of the law, the Greeks did not progress very far in the development of its content. It fell to the Romans to take this decisive step and to activate the potentiality of personal liberty contained in the idea of the law. The law functions as a guide to enable one to know what and what not to do in order to eliminate violence and arbitrariness from social relations. The law performs this function best when exact limits are set on the scope of the legitimate action of each individual. This ring-fencing of *mine* and *yours,* the *proper domain* of each individual person, is what the Roman jurists achieved.

Roman jurists succeeded in this endeavor over the centuries—as military conquests transformed Rome into a colossal cosmopolitan state presiding over vast territories and diverse ethnic peoples—by inventing and perfecting legal concepts and increasingly abstract and universal legal tools, void of ethnic or religious particularisms. This includes notions of (1) *the law of persons:* minority, invalidity, trusteeship, legal guardianship, family, marriage, inheritance, adoption, legitimization, the notion of a legal (moral) person; (2) *the law of things:* ownership, possession, servitude, material and immaterial things, movable and immovable properties, prescription, bare ownership, usufructuary rights, co-ownership, joint possession, rent; and (3) *the law of obligations:* contract law, bailment, pledge, mortgage, guarantee, mandate, company, purchase, sale, synallagmatic pact, misrepresentation, fraud, testament, bequest, and trust, to name a few.

While the Greeks had a sense of *mine* and *yours* (Cicero reminds us that the definition of justice in Roman law—*ius suum cuique tribuere,* "give each man his due"—is Greek in origin) (see also Plato, *Republic* 331e), the Romans were the first to invent the legal apparatus for keeping close track of everything that is "mine" after I marry, have children, go into partnership, contract a debt, mortgage my belongings, after my children inherit from me, divorce, have children of their own (even illegitimate offspring, recognized or not), have their property seized, then restituted by court decision, and so on and so forth. It was Roman law that made possible the regularity and security of transactions and transformations that determine the future of each person's property.

These legal inventions have profound metaphysical implications despite their almost prosaic appearance. While the definition of the *proper domain* of each person is fixed and guaranteed over several generations, it is the *self* that acquires a dimension never before attained by all preceding civilizations. For the first time ever, the self is projected forward into the future: the self is no longer the being of a day, as short-lived as a blossom or a breath. It is part of something long term. This new time frame enables the self to make rational plans because it can anticipate the successive forms its properties will take; because the self alone knows what it will decide, as it exercises its own free will. In so doing, the self becomes totally *irreducible to any another* because, as its life unfolds through transactions and the successive forms of its property, which are also the forms of its personal experience, an absolutely singular path is plotted, which cannot be superimposed on the paths traced by other human lives and liberties. Individuals no longer melt into an anonymous throng, both in the sense of a complete fusion with the tribal group and in the sense of the tight solidarity that prevailed in the Greek city. For the first time in history, and thanks to the law, what we moderns know as *private life* becomes a possibility; a sphere of personal liberty, legally inviolate by others, becomes reality.

In this sense, it can be argued that the Romans *invented the idea of Man as we in the West understand it,* that is, a free, individual human person, having an inner life and an absolutely original destiny, which is irreducible to another; a person who can enforce his or her rights against others as well as against collective organization itself. All subsequent Western political forms, except in the high Middle Ages, will be conceived and developed on the basis of this Roman conception of Man. No political regime will be accepted on a permanent basis in the West that is not "humanist."

Judeo-Christianity will also play a fundamental role in the development of this Western humanism (we will spell this out below in part 3). But, originally, the invention of humanism is Roman; it is the work of Roman law, and within this law it is the work of everything that defines and protects private property.

We believe that it is because Rome's great authors of literary and philosophical works lived in a social world where, because of the law, the individual human person existed in a recognized social sphere where the self could flourish in relative safety, that their works possessed such a characteristic humanistic voice, differentiating them from the works of their Greek counterparts. Consider, for example, the difference between the social world of Plato's *Laws* and those expressed by the philosophy of a Lucretius, a Cicero, a Seneca, or the poetry of a Virgil or a Horace, the history of a Tacitus, to name only a few. It is a totally different civilization, one much closer to the civilization of modern Europeans.

These observations give us the plan for our discussion of Rome. We will present the concept of Roman law *before* undertaking a discussion of Roman political ideas, because these ideas will be easier to explain once the conditions of the emergence of Roman law are known.

There is a further justification for our methodological choice. The observation is frequently made that there are few great political thinkers in Rome—with the obvious exception of Cicero—in the Greek sense of theoreticians of systemic thought. The Romans had little inclination for abstract speculation. They were action-oriented, holding leisurely contemplation (the *schole* of the Greeks) in contempt. Their preference was not for *otium* (leisure), but for *negotium* (activity): military, administrative, and economic activity. Their interest in science came rather late and under Greek influence, and in fact they never really excelled in the sciences. Consequently, in Rome, political ideas rarely achieved expression in the form of general theories; more often than not, they were commentaries on Roman political life (though the commentaries of a Seneca or a Tacitus did have profound theoretical implications). But this is sufficient reason to devote considerable time and space to Roman institutions and Roman law. Because, in the last analysis, Roman laws and institutions have shaped the political realities of our Western world as much as if not more than Greek theories. It was Cicero himself who observed that legal practices and political institutions can *communicate a culture* and *shape a society* just as much as ideas themselves. Roman institutions are indeed the embodiments of ideas.

Chapter 1 begins our discussion with an overview of the principal phases of *Roman history*. Then, we turn to the question of Roman law. We approach this in two steps. First, we will discuss Roman *public law* and *Roman political institutions* (chapter 2); then, we will examine Roman *civil law* (chapter 3). Only then can we undertake a proper study of Roman political doctrines, beginning with those of the Roman Republic (chapter 4), then those of the High and Low Empires (chapter 5).

Chapter 1

The Historical Context

Traditionally, the history of Rome[1] begins in 753 BC and ends when Justinian I dies in Constantinople in 565 AD, not when the last emperor, Romulus Augustus, is deposed in 476 AD. Justinian momentarily restored the unity of the empire with his reconquest of Africa, Spain, and Italy, and in many respects his legal work represents a consolidation, and the crowning achievement, of all prior civilizational evolution. After this date the history of Byzantium begins in earnest and prolongs the history of Rome in the East for nearly a millennium (until the Turkish conquest of Constantinople in 1453). In some ways, however, the history of Byzantium is an altogether different story.

For Rome, strictly speaking, this represents almost 1,300 years of history, experienced by the Romans themselves as the exceptional, unbroken history of the same state—of the same Republic—and, in many respects, of the same people.

The history of Rome is traditionally divided into four well-defined eras, each corresponding to a political regime: *kingdom* (mid-eighth century BC to 509 BC); *Republic* (509 to 31 BC); *High Empire* (31 BC to 285 AD); and *Low Empire* or—the term often preferred today—*Late Antiquity* (285 to 565 AD).

[1] My presentation here draws on Marcel Le Glay, Jean-Louis Voisin, and Yann Le Bohec, *Histoire romaine* [Roman history] (Paris: Presses Universitaires de France, 1991).

I. The Founding of Rome and Monarchy (the mid-eighth to the end of the sixth century BC)

Little of certain is known about this period for which there are few written records. Toward the middle of the eighth century, Italy is occupied by pre-Indo-European and Indo-European peoples, whose civilizations are pre-civic and archaic. Two peoples stand out among these because they developed city-states: the Greeks, who settled in southern Italy and Sicily; and the Etruscans, who inhabited present-day Tuscany and the surrounding coastal areas.[2] Phoenicians were also to be found in Italy; some were itinerant merchants, some settled in local trading posts.

Recent historical and archeological evidence suggests that the founding of Rome as a city was the fruit of these more "advanced" civilizations, and in particular Etruscan colonization.

On the original site of ancient Rome, settlements grew up on the tops of each of the seven hills. In the middle of the eighth century, these settlements came together, forming a "Homeric" society, so to speak, with a king, a council of household heads, and a popular assembly. The king was a sacred figure: he alone was authorized to "take the *auspices,*" a necessary ritual before every public decision. When the king died, or was banished, the council (later the Senate) took charge of the auspices. Society was dominated by an aristocracy of families or *gentes,* whose chiefs chose the king. The *gentes* were divided into three tribes, each comprised of ten *curies;* together they made up the popular assembly or *comitia curiata* (curiate assembly). Justice and religion remained very much a concern of the *gentilicum.* This "sacred monarchy" lasted about a century and a half.

At the end of the seventh century, the Etruscans, who had already settled in Campania, moved into Latium. They were particularly interested in Rome with its "Tiberian island," making it easy to cross the river, ideal for trade and commerce.

Under the influence of these Etruscan invaders, a radical and, in some respects, revolutionary social transformation occurred: the emergence of a city in the Greek and Etruscan manner.

Archaeological findings show that a number of urban developments date from this time: marshes were dried out, a central square (*forum*) laid out; the city was paved and walls erected; civil and religious monuments were built of stone; a marketplace and a river port were created; a *pomerium* (the sacred boundary of the city to which the army was denied access) was laid out. The Roman annals (the earliest form of historical literature) date the rule of three Etruscan kings to these decades: Tarquin the Elder, Servius Tullius, and Tarquin the Proud.[3]

These Etruscan kings were responsible for establishing the social institutions of the city, in many respects analogous to the not-much-older Greek civic institutions (those of Solon and Pisistratus). A land reform was carried out. The population was divided into *territorial tribes,* replacing the ancient tribes and ethnic *curies* (there were now four "urban" tribes and ten "rural" tribes). Following a technological innovation (comparable to the Greek "*hoplite* revolution"), the fighting role of the aristocracy declined, and the army was reorganized so that each citizen could contribute to the cause of war according to his financial capability. Men were divided into

[2] The origins of the Etruscans remain a mystery to this day. Perhaps they came from the East or perhaps they are a local people who evolved under the influence of the Greeks (from Marseilles?) and Phoenicia.

[3] Before this date, the annals refer to Latin and Sabine kings and to various mythical origins (these myths were collected and organized by early Latin historians: Fabius Pictor, then Livy and Virgil in the first century BC). The annals mention Arcadian origins (Arcadia is a region of Greece); Trojan origins (Aeneas, the son of Anchises, is said to have arrived in Rome from Troy by way of Carthage, as told in Virgil's *Aeneid*); and, finally, the twins Romulus and Remus, suckled by a she-wolf.

classes according to their wealth. Each class had several *centuries*. On this basis, a second popular assembly was created, the *comitia centuriata* [*century assembly*]: personal wealth and military contribution now determined one's political role.

This new social order enabled the absorption of Rome's growing population, reaching some 100,000 by the end of the sixth century under Etruscan economic influence. Rome worked like a magnet, pulling in neighboring populations eager to share in its success. Since the new migrants did not belong to the original *gentes*, they were assimilated on the basis of a more abstract definition of citizenship. At work here was a process analogous to the reforms of Solon in Athens, which the Etruscans probably adopted from other communities in greater Greece. Direct Greek influence has also been supposed: legend has it that Servius Tullius came from Corinth. Rome, in other words, benefited from a tried-and-tested innovation, which spared it the lengthy development of homegrown solutions.

The revolutionary character of this transformation is marked by the decline of the aristocracy. The king in the age of the Etruscans was an ally of the new *populus* against the Senate, on the Greek pattern of tyranny. A land reform was put in place against the old families. The definition of citizenship, based on the new territorial tribes and the military role of the infantry (*pedites*), destroyed the old ethnic family-based social order and, therefore, undermined the power of the Senate, made up of the leaders of the *gentes*. The new masters also upset the Senate's recruitment system and canceled some of its privileges (e.g., the appointment of the *interrex*). With the growing importance of the marketplace, the Tiber river port, and economic ties with Etruria, tradespeople played a new role. Urban development projects provided craftspeople with work (these features recall the policies of Pisistratus).

The power of the Etruscan master was absolute. The Etruscans themselves contributed the notion of *imperium*, a civil and military command symbolized by the *lictors* holding the *fasces* (bundles of rods tied around an axe),[4] the symbol of Etruscan power. The king exercised his *imperium* over the entire population without the Senate's mediation. Accordingly, he could exercise power for the people and to the detriment of the aristocracy.

II. The Republic (509–31 BC)

We can understand that the aristocrats revolted: it was the origin of the Republic, traditionally dated to 509.

Roman legend presents this revolt as a triumph of liberty over tyranny. Since the last kings were foreign, their expulsion was seen as a national liberation. But from a social and political point of view, the founding of the Republic was really a power grab—or a retaking of power—on the part of the aristocracy, as well as a decline of the *populus*. Accordingly, this initiated a long war between the people and the patricians, which overshadowed the early history of the Republic. A balance was not struck until a century and a half later with the *Licinian Laws*.

[4] Other symbols of *imperium*, in addition to the lictor and the fasces, are found in the magistracies of the Republican period: the curule seat, the purple toga, the eagle-topped scepter, the gold-leaf crown.

A. The Apogee of the Republic (from the fifth century to the end of the second century BC)

1. *The Institution of an Oligarchy*

The new rulers were determined to protect themselves from a return of tyranny and from the power of the people. To achieve the first objective they replaced the *king* by *magistrates*—this was true of numerous other cities in the region as well—with temporary and limited powers; moreover, the number and functions of these magistrates changed over time. In the beginning a *praetor maximus* (borrowed from Etruscan institutions), then two *consuls,* then diverse other magistrates shared the powers possessed previously by the king alone.

For the second aim, the patricians closed themselves into a hereditary caste as time went by. Whereas the *fasti* (list of events occurring during the magistrates' year of office) show the consular offices and the Senate to be fairly open in the early days of the Republic,[5] a monopoly gradually asserted itself de facto and, before very long, de jure. Soon only the sons of high magistrates and senators could occupy the same functions as well, as if consular *imperium,* with its religious dimension, was supposed to be the source of enduring charisma.

2. *The "Popular Commune"*

But the common people revolted. There was a precise reason for that. Rome's incessant wars with the other city-states of Latium—a prelude to its extraordinary territorial expansion—threatened the economic prosperity that had prevailed since the time of the Etruscans. Farmers of rural tribes demanded debt relief and land reform. Perhaps the reforms of Cleisthenes, recently introduced in Athens, were an influence. However that may be, in 494 the common people retreated to the Sacred Mount, enacting a form of civil disobedience and refusing to make their contribution to the war effort. The patricians could not hold out against the threat: numerous foreigners joined the revolt, creating the additional risk of upsetting external alliances. The people only agreed to return to Rome in exchange for a patrician concession of two new institutions: the *plebeian tribune* and the *Council of the Plebs,* creating an alternative power to the power of the patricians in the Senate and the magistracies.

Tribunes were elected annually, at the outset by the Curiate Assembly (*comitia curiata*), and, once it came into existence, by the Council of the Plebs. There were two, then four, then (after 457 BC) ten tribunes. They had a right of *intercessio,* which enabled them to block the decisions and actions of other magistrates, including meetings of the Senate and the Assembly and the voting of laws, among others. The tribunes were sacrosanct. Any citizen could appeal to them for protection (the right of *auxilium*). It was only necessary to make an allegation that a person was a threat to the interests of the plebeians for him to be cursed and executed: this was a power of unlimited repression. Thus, the tribune was more or less a counterweight to the consular *imperium* (though the tribune's power was restricted to the *pomerium*—the sacred space within the boundaries of Rome—and to the immediate vicinity of the city; it did not affect the *imperium militiae* of the consuls in command of the army).

As for the Council of the Plebs, informal at first, it was formally organized in 371. From this time on, the people would be consulted through territorial tribes; within each tribe, every man had a vote (thus, there was no longer a privilege for wealth or age: this was a new "democratic" element). A majority was agreed in each tribe, then the tribes cast their votes (in 371 there were 25 tribes).

---

[5] In the Senate, *conscripti* (new junior members) were added to the *patres* (patriarchy).

The *concilia plebes* had an *electoral* function (the election of the tribunes, who were necessarily plebeians), and a *legislative* function (it voted *plebiscites,* i.e., the "decisions" of the plebeians, subsequently with the force of law).

Finally, the plebeians erected a temple for themselves outside the *pomerium,* at the foot of the Aventine Hill. It was served by Plebeian aediles, who, like Plebeian tribunes, were sacrosanct. The temple housed the archives and treasury of the plebeians. It was dedicated to the *Plebeian Triad* (Ceres, Liber, and Liberia), symmetrical to the *Capitoline Triad* (Jupiter, Juno, and Minerva).

3. *Consecutive Compromises: The Law of the Twelve Tables, the Laws of Valeriae Horatiae, the Licinian Laws*

This dualism of patrician and plebeian powers, which was fundamentally unstable and dangerous, was resorbed by successive compromises, resulting in what is called the *patrician-plebeian constitution,* that is, the classical republican form of government.

a. The Law of the Twelve Tables (451–450 BC)

For two consecutive years there were no consuls; they were replaced by a *decemvirate,* a special commission of ten men in charge of drawing up a new political and legal code. One particular grievance of the plebeians against the patricians was that they, as holders of the principal priesthoods, administered justice entirely alone on a spoken, secret, unstable, hence arbitrary basis. From that point on the law would be written, an obvious influence of Greek lawmaking (plebeian emissaries were probably sent to Greece to study the legislative system). The decemviral code formulated the basic principles of *private law, criminal law,* and *political order.*

- Private law: the code recognizes the family and private property as the building blocks of social order. The rights of the head of the family are exhaustively defined. Guardianship and inheritance laws are organized. Property and its methods of acquisition are defined. Civil procedures are established (see chapter 3 below for a more thorough discussion).
- Criminal law: the code grants the Century Assembly the right to declare capital punishment: thus, an important aspect of consular *imperium* disappears (though it survived outside Rome, notably in armies on campaign).
- Political order: the code institutes the principle of laws voted by the Century Assembly.

The Law of the Twelve Tables was very much a *compromise.* The plebeians did obtain guarantees but, in exchange, they recognized the patricians' monopoly of access to consular offices. They went so far as to admit the closed nature of the patrician caste, since the law prohibited marriage between patricians and plebeians.

b. The Laws of Valeriae Horatiæ (449)

The laws of Valeriae Horatiæ completed the Law of the Twelve Tables. One law validated the sacrosanctity of the tribunes (and, in practice, it legitimates their *intercessio*). Another admitted the official authority of plebiscites (but it was not until the *Lex Hortensia* of 287 that plebiscites were given the status of a law). A third law prohibited consuls from creating magistracies without consulting the people.

The new constitution, however, did not resolve the problem of the plebeians' access to the magistracies. The patricians invented loopholes by creating the "military tribune with consular power," a charge open to a plebeian, but which did not grant access to the Senate.

c. The Compromise of the Licinius and Sextius Plebiscite (367 BC)

Because Rome was constantly at war—in particular the war with the Samnites, which brought Rome in contact with Magna Græcia and Carthage, and above all the mortal danger it risked during the Gallic incursions in the first half of the fourth century—a new compromise had to be reached.

This was the work of two plebeian tribunes, Gaius Licinius and Lucius Sextius, both elected ten years running. A plebiscite was voted on debt cancellation, land reform (restricting ownership of *ager publicus*[6] to a certain number of tracts), and access to the consulship. From this point on, one of the two consuls could be a plebeian.

The patricians reacted again by creating new magistracies, which they reserved exclusively for themselves. But before long these new offices—*praetor, aedilis curulis*—were also opened up to plebeians, as were the older magistracies—*dictator, censor,* and *great pontiff.*

The result of this was not the mixing of social classes, but rather the creation of a new nobility (*nobilitas*) composed of old patricians and plebeians who had entered the magistracies. Quite naturally, the nobility tended to transmit its privilege to its descendants.

The new *patrician-plebeian constitution* inaugurated a period of relative institutional stability (fourth century to mid-second century BC), during which the Roman Republic reached its period of greatness. Also during this period Rome achieved most of its territorial expansion.

B. Roman Territorial Expansion

There would be no talk of Rome and Greece if the West had not been Romanized; without the Roman conquests, there would be no Europe. Roman conquest occurred primarily, but not exclusively, under the Republic. The following phases have been identified.

1. *The Conquest of Latium*

The conquest of Latium occurred in the fifth and fourth centuries BC. A Latin war pitted Rome against a league of cities from the Alban Hills ca. 496 BC (already under the regime of the Republic). This resulted in a Latin League, which defeated the Hernicii in 486, then vanquished other "neighbors": the Volsci, the Aequi, and southern Etruria (ca. 400 BC). A Gallic incursion in 390 BC was a serious alert, but Rome recovered. It suppressed a rebellion of its allies in 340–338 BC, putting an end to the Latin League.

Until then, the Latin cities had entered alliances on an equal footing (*foedus cassianum*): citizens of the various cities had reciprocal rights. For example, the Latins and Rome shared the right of marriage (*ius conubii*), the right of commerce (*ius commercii*), the right of inheritance, and the right to immigrate to Rome (*ius migrandi*); perhaps even the right to vote in Rome (*ius suffragii*). But they did not have the right to hold office in Rome (*ius honorum*); therefore, they were politically dominated, and it was against this state of affairs that these Latin cities revolted. After their defeat, their subjugation to Rome increased: now treaties were established on an unequal basis (*foedus iniquuum*); moreover, there were different treaties for different cities, and Rome was at liberty to change a treaty unilaterally. Its supremacy was thus ensured, even if the particular situation of the Latins was not all that bad.

---

[6] Land confiscated by the Roman state through conquest.

2. *The Conquest of Italy*

In 343 BC Rome went to war against the Samnites (losing an entire army at the battle of the Caudine Forks in 321), then against an alliance of Samnites, Umbrians, Etruscans, Gauls from Northern Italy, and Greeks from Taranto. It emerged victorious from this "Italian war" (312–290 BC), with its rule extended to the whole of central Italy.

Rome was now in direct contact with southern Italy, that is, greater Greece. At the outset Rome entertained peaceful trade relations with these cities, but rivalry with the largest of these, Taranto, was exacerbated as early as the Samnite wars. A long war ensued during which Taranto appealed for assistance to the Greek king of Epirus, Pyrrhus, but in vain: Taranto fell to Rome in 272. The rest of Italy—Tuscany and Northern Italy—was conquered in the course of the following century.

3. *The Conquest of the Mediterranean Basin*

a. The Punic Wars

With the capture of Taranto, Rome's expansion extended to the far reaches of the Italian "boot." A confrontation with Carthage, a more or less equal power at the time, was all but unavoidable.

- The *First Punic War* (264–241 BC) resulted in the conquest of Sicily, which became the first Roman "province." Immediately after, Rome annexed Corsica and Sardinia.
- The *Second Punic War* (218–201 BC) pitted Hannibal and Scipio Africanus against each another. With losses at the Battle of Lake Trasimene and the Battle of Cannae, Rome narrowly avoided disaster. Finally, Hannibal was defeated at the Battle of Zama (202 BC). Meanwhile, Hispania was conquered, providing Rome with strategic depth. The territory was organized into two provinces (197 BC).
- Finally, in a bid to crush the power of Carthage completely, Rome took the war to African soil. This was the *Third Punic War* (149–146 BC). Carthage was seized and razed to the ground by Scipio Aemilianus (who subsequently took Numantia and pacified Hispania). Africa became a Roman province (the war against Jugurtha, 113–05 BC, allowed Rome to extend its reach westward to Numidia—present-day Algeria—and Mauritania, and eastward to Tripolitania).

b. Macedonia and Greece

Rome's march toward the East began as early as the era of the Second Punic War. Three Macedonian wars were waged: in 210–205, 200–197, and 171–168 BC. L. Aemilius Paullus Macedonicus, father of Scipio Aemilianus Africanus, finally defeated and captured the last king of Macedonia, Perseus of Macedon, at the Battle of Pydna (168 BC). Initially under the supervision of a liberal protectorate, Greece revolted, but in 146 the Achaean League, the leader of the uprising, was crushed and Corinth was totally destroyed. Macedonia became a province in 147 (Greece did not become a province until 27 BC after its defeat at the Battle of Actium in 31 BC; but by then Greece was already de facto under Roman domination). Rome also occupied the Dalmatian coast (the province of Illyricum); though its conquests were still shaky, it had thus established full territorial continuity from northern Italy to Greece.

c. The Remainder of the Hellenistic East

Through a combination of wars and diplomatic efforts, Rome took possession of what remained of the Hellenistic East. It seized Asia Minor from the king of Syria, Antiochus III (192–189 BC), and in 133 it received the kingdom of Pergamon as a bequest from its king, Attalus III (this was at the time of the Gracchi crisis, see below). Thus, the province of Asia was created. In the first century, Rome received Cyrenaica, also by bequest (74 BC), and Bithynia (through the testament of Nicomedes II, also in 74). But the king of Pontus,[7] Mithridates, revolted against Rome, massacring tens of thousands of Italians and vowing to liberate Asia and Greece. This led to a long war (89–62 BC) in which Sulla, Lucullus, and Pompey distinguished themselves. It ended with the defeat of Mithridates and the creation of a new province, Pontus and Bithynia (65 BC). Crete came under Roman rule in 67, then Syria (conquered by Pompey) in 64, and Cyprus in 58. Egypt finally fell to Rome after the Battle of Actium despite efforts by Ptolomy and Cleopatra to maintain autonomy (Egypt became the personal property of Augustus and thereafter remained under the direct administration of the emperors).

4. *The Conquest of the West*

Italian merchants traveled extensively throughout western Europe long before any Roman military presence or conquest. They crossed the Alps through the high passes, traveled down the Rhine, and reached the North Sea. There are traces of Romanization in Gaul (farms) dating from before Caesar's conquest.

Southern Gaul (Provence) was conquered between 125 and 100 BC to establish territorial continuity between the Hispanic provinces and Italy (Aix-en-Provence and Narbonne were founded; the Via Domitia was built). Under Augustus ancient Provence was renamed Gallia Narbonensis. The rest of Gaul was conquered by Caesar between 58 and 51 BC. The resistance of the Gauls to the Roman conquest was initially murderous but after a few years disappeared (compare this, for example, with the reaction in Hispania). The Gauls almost seemed to welcome Roman civilization.

The left bank of the Rhine up to the North Sea (Belgium) came under Roman influence through alliances with Germanic tribes. Caesar, and later Agrippa (in 39–38 BC), crossed the Rhine. Caesar's two incursions into Britannia remained without consequence. Ireland was untouched. Likewise, northwestern Spain and the western Alps remained independent.

The Roman conquests will always retain an inexplicable, if not fascinating, quality. Why was Rome so successful? Why such continuity in its policy of expansion? Why such tenacity of execution? Rome, of course, enjoyed military and technical superiority, and above all organizational and rational superiority, against the brutal, disordered forces of the barbarians; even the Greeks could do very little (as Polybius and Aelius Astrides point out). Paradoxically, Rome's wars, seemingly conducted in a spirit of territorial expansion and conquest, were, in fact, defensive wars. Rome preempted the attacks of aggressive neighbors, responded to the calls of its allies under threat, then, having extended its frontiers far and wide, transformed its neighbors into client states, who then turned to Rome for protection. Thus, the Roman Empire spread like a stain over vast areas. The real reason for Rome's success—we will return to this in more detail—was, no doubt, the *superiority of its civilization*. It appears that the people under its authority came to the conclusion that they were better off being Romanized. This may explain the surprisingly enduring character of its conquests.

The conquests nevertheless gave rise to a number of new problems that the Romans would gradually resolve: the problem of *citizenship* and the problem of *provincial administration*. Above all, the conquests presented an unprecedented opportunity: the coexistence of diverse ethnic groups in a single, strong political body would lead to the development of a new abstract and, virtually, universal law.

---

[7] The Pontus was a province of the Persian Empire. After the defeat of the Persians by Alexander the Great and the dismantling of the Macedonian Empire following the death of Alexander, the Pontus became an independent kingdom under the former Satrap, Mithridates I, in 280 BC.

C. Crisis in the Republic (133–31 BC)

Whereas the Republic facilitated Rome's acquisition of a vast empire, it was a victim of its own success. After 130 BC it was shaken by a succession of crises, each more serious than the next.

1. *The Gracchi (133 and 121 BC)*

The growth of the state with these conquests resulted in various imbalances: *an excessive increase in wealth of the senatorial class,* which monopolized the *ager publicus;*[8] *the ruin of the middle class* due to competition from agricultural products produced in the conquered territories, and the constant use of citizen-soldiers in Roman military campaigns; the emergence of *a new equestrian class,* made up of public servants and financiers; this new class was needed to run a state grown excessively large, but it was frustrated that it had not yet acquired a social and political status corresponding to its real role.

It was the question of how to distribute the land tracts of the *ager publicus* that finally triggered the crisis. Two reformers, both members of a noble family in alliance with the Scipiones, appeared on the scene: Tiberius and Gaius Gracchus.

a. Tiberius Sempronius Gracchus

Tiberius Sempronius Gracchus was elected Plebeian tribune and sponsored a law, the *lex Sempronia.* Improperly acquired public land tracts were to be reconfiscated; lots would be redistributed and limited in size (500 *iugera,* roughly 300 acres, per person, an additional 250 *iugera* per child, up to a maximum of 1,000 *iugera*). A commission of triumvirs (*triumviri agris iudicandis adsignandis*) was put in charge of land redistribution, a measure that effectively sidelined the Senate. The confiscated land was redistributed to the poor on the basis of 30 *iugera* per person. Accused of revolutionary actions (the unseating of a tribune, who used his *intercessio* against the law; his own reelection as tribune two years running), Tiberius was murdered by a pro-senatorial faction.

Tiberius was perhaps inspired by Pericles, to whom he alludes. He even had a Stoic philosopher, Blossius, by his side. Was it his intention to establish a democracy in Rome? Plutarch in his *Lives* records the following speech allegedly by Tiberius Gracchus:

> "The savage beasts in Italy have their particular dens, they have their places of repose and refuge; but the men who bear arms, and expose their lives for the safety of their country, enjoy in the meantime nothing more in it but the air and light and, having no houses or settlements of their own, are constrained to wander from place to place with their wives and children." He told them that the commanders were guilty of a ridiculous error, when, at the head of their armies, they exhorted the common soldiers to fight for their sepulchers and altars; when not any amongst so many Romans is possessed of either altar or monument, neither have they any houses of their own, or hearths of their ancestors to defend. They fought indeed and were slain, but it was to maintain the luxury and the wealth of other men. They were styled the masters of the world, but in the meantime had not one foot of ground, which they could call their own.[9]

---

[8] *Ager publicus:* vast landholdings confiscated from subject peoples.

[9] Plutarch, *Lives,* trans. Bernadette Perrin (Cambridge, MA: Harvard University Press, 1921), "Tiberius Gracchus," 9.4.

b. Gaius Sempronius Gracchus

Gaius Gracchus attempted the same policy ten years later. He championed a new law, the *lex Sempronia frumentaria,* which organized grain distribution to the poor of Rome at low prices. He granted new rights to the equestrians to help them gain access to the courts on an equal footing with the senators. He also reorganized tribute payments from the province of Asia to their advantage. He wanted to send settlers to Taranto, Corinth, and Carthage, so that the empire would not be in the sole hands of the army and the Senate. The Senate opposed this and Gaius Gracchus made the fatal mistake of using force. The Senate enacted a *senatus consultum ultimum* (a "final decree" of the Senate) against him, and he was killed along with 3,000 of his followers (even the equestrians were allied with the Senate against him to prevent a drift toward democracy).

The failure of the Gracchi merely granted the aristocratic Republic a reprieve. Because the necessary reforms had not been carried out and social equilibrium had not been restored, the Republic was weakened. Increasingly, the generals arbitrated social conflicts with their coups d'etat that would undermine the Republic until the onset of the High Empire. The Gracchi themselves had shown the way by assuming extraordinary powers.

From the Gracchi rebellion onward, political life in Rome was dominated by two main political movements (not to say parties): the *populares* or "people's party," and the *optimates* (literally, the "best") or senatorial party. Both parties had their political leaders. Both went through phases of relative success and failure. The struggle between the two was political and electoral, but it frequently turned to bloody tactics: murders, militia, and mobs.

2. *The Slave Revolts*

The number of slaves in Roman society grew as a result of the conquests. In first century BC Italy, they represented from 30 to 50 percent of the total population, perhaps as much as 70 percent in some places. Their condition had worsened notably in the *latifundiae* (large agricultural estates), where they were employed in unprecedented numbers under the rod of particularly brutal overseers.

Hence, a string of more or less serious revolts, first in Latium (143–141 BC), then in Sicily (133–132), where the slaves managed to establish a state (under the leadership of a certain Eunous, who claimed divine status and had himself crowned Antiochus). This was followed by a revolt in Campania (103–101) where again the agitators (Salvius and Athenius) had themselves proclaimed kings. The leaders of these revolts were often from the east of the empire and acted with religious motivations. The consuls managed to put down the revolts and reestablish order, at the expense of long military campaigns.

The most serious revolt was in 73–71 BC, led by a Hellenized Thracian gladiator, *Spartacus,* and a Gaul, *Crixus.* This time the rebels had no intention of establishing a state. Their goal was to lead the slaves back to their countries of origin. This resulted in a series of erratic marches. Crassus and Pompey overcame the rebels and 6,000 were crucified along the Appian Way between Capua and Rome.

Compared with the Gracchi crisis, the slave revolts had no direct political implication, but they justified the award of extraordinary military commissions to generals, in itself a factor of instability.

3. *The Social War*

The Social war (91–88 BC)[10] pitted the Roman Republic against its Italian satellite states in revolt. At this time in Italy, people and territories were an intertwinement of different statuses. Romans, whether from Rome or the colonies, could invoke full citizenship rights. Inhabitants of *municipii* had only Latin rights, meaning (approximately) civil rights without political rights. The *socii,* that is, inhabitants of Rome's "allied" cities, had neither, though they had been loyal to Rome during the Third Punic War and continued to provide the Republic with auxiliary forces.

In 123 BC, Gaius Gracchus raised high hopes when he promised "Latins" Roman citizenship rights and the *socii* Latin rights. But the Senate vetoed both measures. In 91 BC, an aristocratic demagogue, Marcus Livius Drusus, proposed the measure again. It was his assassination that ignited the war. The Marsi in the north revolted first, followed by the Samnites in the south; soon all Italy rose up. It was a horrific civil war with unspeakable atrocities: Roman women were scalped; civilian populations were massacred. Both the Marsi and the Samnites established independent states with their own capitals and currencies. Marius and Sulla led campaigns against the rebels and peace was restored. Rome was magnanimous in victory and granted Roman citizenship to all Italy (with the exception of Cisalpine Gaul).

This had immense consequences: the number of Roman citizens doubled, surpassing 900,000.[11] Roman law spread. The political class began to renew itself. It was the dawn of big changes to come.

The rest of the history of the Republic is marked by the preeminence of men with ever-expanding powers obtained by increasingly illegal means.

4. *Marius*

A member of the equestrian class and an excellent soldier, Marius (157–86 BC) distinguished himself in Spain under Scipio Aemilianus. Although he was only a knight, the people's party elected him consul in 107 BC. He opened the army to the poor and the unemployed, making it stronger, but exposing it to manipulation by the ambitious. Reelected consul every year between 104 and 100 BC (an unprecedented occurrence), he defeated the Cimbri and the Teutoni (Germanic tribes that had migrated as far south as Provence in Gaul). But Marius was a poor politician; he clashed with his supporters in the people's party. He quarreled with his former deputy, Sulla, who disputed his leadership of the war against Mithridates. Several times they chased each other from Rome. Allied with Cinna, Marius engaged in notoriously bloody proscriptions; he died a few days after once again being reelected consul. He was the uncle of Caesar.

5. *Sulla*

Sulla (138–78 BC) was a relatively poor patrician. He led the debauched life of an aesthete under the influence of Hellenism. In 88 BC, he entered Rome at the head of his army (a sacrilege) and had the tribune Sulpicius Rufus executed (Sulpicius had revoked Sulla's command in the campaign against Jugurtha). He left for the East to wage war against Mithridates and captured Athens (86 BC) as well as other territories in Asia. In the Levant he discovered the oriental monarchies, a gripping encounter experienced by other Roman generals as well, one that may well

[10] "Social" does not have its modern meaning here; it comes from *socii*—allies—and refers to the Roman Republic's war with its client cities in Italy.

[11] The registration of the *novi cives* (new citizens) in the tribes had electoral implications; the result was protracted fighting between the *populares* and the *optimates.* According to census figures, there were 120,000 adult male citizens in 503 BC, 394,000 in 124 BC, and 910,000 in 86 BC. In 14 AD the number of citizens was 4,937,000, counting women and children (Le Glay et al., *Histoire romaine,* 111).

have nurtured the idea of empire. He returned to Italy with immense wealth from the spoils of war, and at the head of an army with some 40,000 men.

After a year and a half of civil wars, he took command of Rome, ordering massacres, banishments, and expropriations. The *lex Valeria* appointed him "perpetual dictator" with the title of "Felix," implying that the gods accorded him their special favor. He tried to establish a new regime, perhaps an imperial monarchy. He reformed the constitution in favor of the aristocracy by excluding the equestrians[12] from the courts and restricting the powers of the plebeian tribune. Then, suddenly, in July 79 BC, he voluntarily withdrew to his villa in Cumae, where he died the following year.

6. *Pompey, Caesar, Crassus: The First Triumvirate*

Caesar (101–44 BC), a relative of Marius, was a patrician who took up the cause of the *populares.* Praetor, then propraetor of Hispania, he formed the *First Triumvirate* (60 BC) with Crassus and Pompey, an informal, secret, power-sharing arrangement between the three men.

Caesar was elected consul in 59 BC. Then, as proconsul of Cisalpine Gaul and Gallis Narbonensis, he conquered Gaul (58–51 BC). After the death of Crassus in 53, Pompey had himself elected sole consul and put an end to the triumvirate. He ordered Caesar recalled and his army disbanded: this led to the *crossing of the Rubicon* (December of 50 BC). Caesar's arrival in Rome ignited a four-year civil war. Caesar pursued Pompey all the way to Greece and crushed his forces at Pharsalus (48 BC). Pompey was assassinated in Egypt on the orders of the young king, Ptolemy XIII; this act was punished by the award of the Egyptian kingdom to Cleopatra (wife and sister of Ptolemy XIII; she became Caesar's mistress and bore his son, Caesarion, Ptolemy XV). Caesar returned in triumph to Rome in 45 BC.

After these events, Caesar ruled as an absolute monarch. With the support of the *populares,* he had himself appointed dictator, at first for ten years, then for life. Many loyal followers of Pompey, including Cicero, went over to his side. He began a major campaign of reconstruction. He increased the number of senators disproportionately, causing a number of his party members to become senators (the Senate grew to over 1,000 members). He redistributed the *ager publicus* and created new colonies in Sicily, Greece, the Levant, Gaul, and Africa. He ended the extortionate practices of the publicans in the provinces.

Under suspicion of harboring thoughts of establishing a true monarchy, Caesar was assassinated on the Ides of March in 44 BC in a conspiracy led by Brutus and supported by Cicero.

7. *Antony, Lepidus, Octavian: The Second Triumvirate*

With the death of Caesar, Antony (83–30 BC), his second-in-command,[13] rose to power. Soon a second presumptive heir appeared, a young man of 18, Lucius Octavian, whom Caesar had adopted, which gave him strong legitimacy among the people and the army. Antony struck an alliance with Octavian and with a third man, Caesar Lepidus; together they formed the Second Triumvirate (43 BC), a formal, public alliance this time. The triumvirs eliminated the republican party with bloody proscriptions (Cicero was murdered). At the Battle of Philippi in 42 BC, they crushed Brutus and Cassius, the assassins of Caesar, and divided the Roman world between them: Antony received the East, Octavian the West, and Lepidus Africa.

[12] Originally, Gaius Gracchus had given them access to the courts (see above).

[13] See the excellent biography by François Chamoux, *Marc-Antoine* (Paris: Arthaud Éditions, 1986).

Antony married Octavian's sister, Octavia (such matrimonial alliances heralded a new form of stability in the absence of stable institutions). Antony left for the East to address problems and distribute offices. The Greeks looked on him as a Hellenic king, while Antony played along with this. In 41 he fell in love with Cleopatra at Tarsus in Cilicia and married her without repudiating Octavia: they had several children together. After long and careful thought, he announced in a solemn declaration that his children would be the future kings of the provinces of Cyrenaica, Syria, and Cilicia, in the orbit of the Kingdom of Egypt where he would share royal power with Cleopatra.

This was contrary to Roman tradition. Octavian spread the rumor of Antony's scandalous declaration throughout Italy, arousing envy and hate against Antony. All the same, several attempts at conciliation took place. One in particular (39 BC), the negotiation at Brindisium, celebrated by Virgil in his *Eclogues,* was followed by seven years of peace (40–33). But confrontation was unavoidable. It occurred at Actium (on the western coast of Greece, near Corfu) in 31. The two navies clashed. Antony was defeated and fled by sea to Alexandria, where he was trapped. The city was put to the siege in 30 BC and Antony committed suicide at the false news that Cleopatra had killed herself.

After these events Octavian ruled alone. He became the first Roman emperor, under the name of Augustus.

III. High Empire: Principate (31 BC to 285 AD)

Drawing lessons from Caesar's failure, Augustus created an absolute autocracy, sorely needed to consolidate a fragile state after decades of civil war. He worked this political miracle with respect for republican institutions, on the surface at any rate. This is not to say that Augustus did not dream of monarchy in his heart of hearts. Like all great Roman generals since Scipio Africanus, he was fascinated by the Hellenistic-oriental model of monarchy. In Alexandria, he visited the mausoleum of Alexander the Great and returned a glowing tribute to the great man. In Rome, on the north side of the Field of Mars, he erected an enormous mausoleum for himself, 87 meters in diameter, modeled on Alexander's. However, whether for reasons of prudence, psychological complexity, or pure political genius, Augustus constructed his kingship entirely from republican material.

The people of Rome swore an oath to him before Actium. Thereafter, Augustus assumed the consulship year after year. This, however, was illegal and could not last. In three steps, he managed to design a legal framework that fixed the problem and justified his exercise of absolute power.

On January 13, 27 BC, Augustus formerly surrendered all his powers to the Senate. The senators pleaded with him to stay and offered him a ten-year proconsular *imperium* over the 12 militarized provinces outside Rome's frontiers (the normal system of promagistracy awarded annually by the Senate remained unchanged for the other nonmilitary provinces).

In a second session, held three days later, the Senate bestowed on Octavian the title of "Augustus,"; that is, he was officially granted *auctoritas.* This notion had a certain religious tone about it: patrician senators with this style could take the auspices. It translates as a form of moral superiority, which gives the bearer a preeminence among equals. Augustus himself wrote in his "testament," *Res gestæ* (see below, pp. 322–23): "I exceeded all in influence [*auctoritas*], but I had no greater power [*potestas*] than the others who were colleagues with me in each magistracy."

This was literally the case: by virtue of his *auctoritas* alone, Augustus now surpassed all other magistrates cloaked in the proconsular *imperium*.

In 23 BC Augustus relinquished the consulship that he had held each year since 31 BC; in exchange he received the *tribunician power,* the civil power of Rome. Each year thereafter, he was entrusted with the tribunician power together with the provincial *imperium*. Augustus became inviolable. He could convene the Senate or the assemblies and have them vote laws. He did not need fear the *intercessio* of other tribunes, because he had *auctoritas.*

To these three pillars of absolute autocracy—proconsular *imperium, auctoritas,* and tribunician power—Augustus added the following necessary supplements:

- *sacerdotal* functions, the most important being the great pontificate;
- *censorial power,* which he used to re-form the Senate[14] and create a new equestrian order with men devoted to him;
- *consular power,* which he exercised to great effect without being consul (another useful fiction).

Augustus entrusted the provinces to handpicked men, who governed in his name, the so-called legates of Augustus.

In Rome, Augustus granted the equestrians the offices of *praetorian prefect* (military commander of the Praetorian Guard, the emperor's personal bodyguard), *prefect of the granary system* (*praefectus annonae*), and *prefect of the Vigiles* (commander of the "watchmen" [firefighters] and the police). When absent from Rome, he also appointed a *prefect of the city* (*præfectus urbanus*) from among former consuls to oversee Rome. He levied new taxes to supply a special treasury, the military *ærarium.* Finally, he surrounded himself with an advisory council, one of whose members was the celebrated thinker of the regime and patron of the arts, Maecenas, who rallied many influential writers (e.g., Virgil and Horace) to the service of the state.

And so, without a royal title, whose symbolism would have alarmed republican Rome, Augustus held the powers of an absolute monarch.

It is an irony of history that the "republican" titles held by Augustus subsequently became the very symbols of monarchy. He was *imperator* (a commander vested with *imperium*): the word "emperor" derives from this Latin word. The Russian czar and the German Kaiser took his name (Caesar). He was *princeps senatus* (the first member of the Senate by precedence), giving us the word "prince." Roman emperors surrounded themselves with *comites* and *duces:* they would become the counts and dukes of feudalism.

The High Empire is divided into periods corresponding to the "dynasties" of the emperors.

A. The Julio-Claudian Dynasty (31 BC–68 AD)

Augustus (31 BC–14 AD), *Tiberius* (14–37 AD), *Caligula* (37–41 AD), *Claudius* (41–54 AD), *Nero* (54–68 AD); then an interlude, the "Year of the Four Emperors" (69 AD): *Galba, Otho, Vitellius* (the fourth will be *Vespasian*).

During this dynasty no serious clashes with the people occurred: in Italy, the people supported the emperors (the lower classes regretted Nero). In the provinces, on the other hand, revolts were frequent. The type of regime was not the issue, it was Rome's presence. In fact, only the great senatorial families fomented opposition and instigated many ham-fisted plots. Emperors did not

[14] During the *lectio* in 28 BC, Augustus excluded 190 senators and upheld or appointed a further 600. He had himself officially appointed by the Senate *princeps senatus.*

shy from brutality or bloodshed in quashing these intrigues (antisenatorial repression was the topic of Tacitus's works).

The empire was no longer expanding (except for the conquest of Britain, see below). It was protected at its borders and pursued a policy of active diplomacy with client kingdoms.

B. The Flavian Dynasty (69–96 AD)

Vespasian (69–79 AD), *Titus* (79–81 AD), *Domitian* (81–96 AD).

The creation of the imperial regime was now complete. After the Roman patrician Julio-Claudian emperors, Italian emperors came to power. Henceforth, the ethnic diversity of the emperors increased.

In the aftermath of the crisis of 69 AD Vespasian restored peace and order. He launched a monumental building program (in Rome: the Capitol, the Coliseum), reconstructed and embellished provincial towns and cities, adopted a "social" policy and began to subsidize education; he also established a "cadastral system" for the entire territory, an authentic innovation for the time. He introduced an administrative reorganization of the provinces with the dual purpose of providing security and improving fiscal returns. He built the *limes,* a line of frontier forts that would protect the borders of the empire for centuries.

Domitian continued Vespasian's policies: monumental construction projects in Rome, reorganization of the territory using the cadastral system and land redistribution, the regularization of provincial government by placing governors under tight surveillance and establishing sound municipal institutions, reinforcement of the *limes* and reorganization of the army. A reign of peace and the efficient administration of the provinces brought about unprecedented economic development; provincial growth soon outstripped that of Italy.

C. The Antonine Dynasty (96–193 AD)

Nerva (96–98 AD), *Trajan* (98–117 AD), *Hadrian* (117–38 AD), *Antoninus Pius* (138–61 AD), *Marcus Aurelius* (161–80 AD), *Commodus* (180–92 AD), the *Pertinax* interlude (193 AD).

Empire was at its zenith in the second century AD, which was a century of peace and prosperity, traditionally called the *pax romana.* At this time it numbered 50 to 60 million inhabitants.

There were few "calamities" during the reign of the Antonine dynasty. By definition, the period of *pax romana* saw very few wars: only Trajan's conquest of Dacia (future Romania) and various security-enforcing border skirmishes (against the Arabs, the Parthians, and the Bretons); things did not take a turn for the worse until the reign of Marcus Aurelius (with the Germanic War on the Danube and the Parthian War to the east).

Domestically, the government and the administration functioned without major shocks. The law reached its zenith (see below). The emperors produced important legislative work: Hadrian caused the Praetor's Edict to be put in writing. Marcus Aurelius established a citizen's registry to stop the fraudulent acquisition of Roman citizenship. The *praetorian prefect* became the central figure of the regime, a sort of vice-emperor. The weight of the state grew: with his *alimenta* system Trajan introduced a "social" policy for the support of poor children.

Most importantly, perhaps, *the homogenization of the empire by the administration and the law* continued, and Italy underwent a *relative decline* compared with the provinces.

- *In economic terms,* Italy was no longer the sole trade hub. Interprovincial trade soared. Less costly provincial products were more competitive than Italian products. In the provinces, farmland acreage expanded apace; towns and cities underwent embellishments (baths, triumphal arches, amphitheaters, sewers and aqueducts, covered marketplaces); territorial infrastructure (roads, aqueducts) was developed.

• *In intellectual terms,* after a brilliant start to the century (e.g., Tacitus, Pliny the Younger, Juvenal, Suetonius, Aulus Gellius), second century Italian writers were simple old-fashioned scholars. Soon provincial writers (e.g., Florus, Frontinus, Apuleius, Plutarch, Arrian, Pausanias, Dio Chrysostom, Aelius Aristides) picked up the baton.

• *In political terms,* many provincial inhabitants gained full Roman citizenship rights, either individually or collectively (such as when their locality rose to the status of honorary colony; see below). The highest provincial political honor was when the emperor himself was a native of a province. The first three Antonines were "Spanish," descendants of Italians who had settled in Hispania. Another, Antoninus Pius, had ancestors from Nimes (Gaul).

Noteworthy in this context of provincial advancement is the progress of the eastern provinces. A new cultural identity arose: the Greek-speaking Roman (the Byzantines were called "Romans" throughout their long history).

D. The Dynasty of the Severi (194–235 AD)

Septimius Severus (194–211), *Caracalla* (211–17), *Macrinus* (217–18), *Elagabalus* (218–22), *Alexander Severus* (222–35).

The cosmopolitanism of the empire grew as the emperors came not only from the provinces, but from Africa and the Levant as well. Septimius Severus came from Leptis Magnus in Tripolitania; Elagabalus and Alexander Severus were of Syrian origin. In fact, the empire orientalized in various ways. The presence of oriental religions increased (Elagabalus was a priest of the god of Emesa, the sun god El Gebal); among these oriental religions was Christianity: its influence also grew, even at the imperial court. Power became increasingly monarchic, and monarchy itself more and more "oriental," religious, and absolute. The role of the praetorian prefect grew as well.

In social terms, the period saw the rise of the *equestrian order*. Politics became more social and popular: measures were taken to improve social mobility, and the tendency was to satisfy social demands.

Frontier wars intensified. Septimius Severus fought against the Parthians and the Bretons. Caracalla skirmished with the Alamans along the Rhine and the Danube and against the Parthians in the east.

In 212 AD the Edict of Caracalla (*Constitutio Antoniniana*) awarded all inhabitants of the empire the right of Roman citizenship. They were also allowed to keep their local rights and were not required to adopt private Roman law: many in the Orient embraced this position. As a result, mention of the citizen's tribe disappeared from the official registry and people adopted Roman names (frequently taking the emperor's gentilicum, Antoninus).

Under the Severi dynasty, intellectual movements—always centered on the province, especially the East—showed real vitality. There were historians (Dio Cassius, Herodian), scholars (Diogenes Laertus, Alexander of Aphrodisias), jurists (the greatest of the Roman legal tradition—Papinian, Ulpian, Paulus—lived at this time), doctors (Galen), Neoplatonist philosophers (Ammonius Saccus, Plotinus), and the first great Christian theologians or "church fathers" (Irenaeus of Lyon, Hippolytus of Rome, Clement of Alexandria, Origen, Tertullian). Most of these "Roman" intellectuals wrote in Greek.

E. Third Century Military Anarchy (235–84 AD)

Maximinus Thrax (235–38), *Gordian I and II, Pupienus Maximus, Balbinus, Gordian III, Philip the Arab* (244–49), *Decius, Trebonianus Gallus, Valerian* (253–60), *Gallienus* (259–68), *Claudius Gothicus, Aurelian* (270–75), *Tacitus, Probus, Carus, Numerian, and Carinus.*

It was a period of profound anarchy (15 emperors in 50 years), affecting power structures more than society itself, except for a growing threat on the imperial borders and the multiplication of increasingly uncertain wars against the Persians, the Moors, the Dacians, the Sarmatians, and all the Germanic tribes: the Franks and Alamans, the Carpi and the Goths, the Quadi, the Marcomanni, the Vandals, and so on.

F. Imperial Conquests

There were few new conquests under the High Empire, but many half-conquests became real with the attendant Romanization.

The rest of Hispania and the Alpine regions were conquered under Augustus. Augustus himself pacified the province of Illyricum: the lower Danubian provinces—*Rhetia, Noricum, Pannonia*—were organized. (These provinces roughly correspond, respectively, to modern Switzerland, Austria, and Hungary.) The greatest challenge was Germania. After several attempts at conquest, and the crushing defeat of the legions under Varus, achieved by Arminium in 9 AD, the Romans gave up their efforts and contented themselves with the occupation of the North Sea coast (Frisia) and the consolidation of the *limes* along the Rhine and the Danube; they did manage to annex the region between the two rivers, the *Agri Decumates* (present-day Swabia).

Britain was conquered under Claudius. Domitian expanded the conquest, but Rome never succeeded in occupying the entire island. Trajan conquered *Dacia,* the left bank of the *Danube* (future Romania). *Armenia,* which the Romans and Parthians had fought over since the time of Antony, was vassalized under Augustus and his successors. *Cappadocia* (in central-eastern Asia Minor), *Mauretania,* and *Thrace* were also acquired.

But the Roman legions suffered defeats. Expansionism ceased under Hadrian, after the army failed to hold the three most recently acquired provinces (Armenia, Mesopotamia, and Assyria).

IV. The Low Empire: Dominate (285–565 AD)

A. Principal Periods of the Low Empire

1. *Diocletian and the Tetrarchy*

Diocletian, Maximian, Galerius, Constantius Chlorus (284–305).

Diocletian, emperor in 284 AD, entrusted the west to Maximian, who assumed the imperial dignity of Augustus, the tribunician power, and the grand pontificate. Thus, there were two emperors, each ruling his half of the empire: one in Nicomedia (a town in Asia Minor near Byzantium), the other in Milan. Each appointed a junior co-emperor with the title Caesar: Galerius in Antioch, Constantius Chlorus in Trier. This system of rule was known as the "tetrarchy": its principal advantage was to allow for a more regular maintenance of order and control by virtue of the proximity of the rulers to the portion of the empire they governed, without compromising its overall unity, because a hierarchy existed between the tetrarchs who were, on the one hand, bound by a principle of collegiality, and on the other related to one another in some way (by blood or by adoption). In addition, a system of succession was introduced.

The tetrarchy put an end to domestic usurpation and kept foreign enemies at bay. Diocletian reorganized the army, the administration, and the finances of the empire. He attempted to control the economy (Edict on Maximum Prices in 301). He and Maximian carried out the worst Christian persecution (303–04 AD).

2. *Constantine and His Sons*

Constantine (306–37 AD) and his sons: *Constantine II, Constantius II,* and *Constans* (337–61 AD).

Constantine, the son of Constantius Chlorus, first divided the empire among various "Caesars" and "Augustuses" (Maximinus Daia, Severus, Maxentius, Licinius). But his accommodation with Christian monotheism after 312 AD (see below) prompted him to establish an absolute monarchy, which could not be shared. He completed the elimination of his rivals in 324.

Constantine pursued the domestic efforts of Diocletian: he strengthened absolute monarchy, hierarchized the administration (with an "official of the sacred chamber," questors, counts, *magistri,* and so on), reorganized the provincial administration by creating huge "praetorian prefectures," which grouped together the midlevel dioceses, which in turn were groupings of low-level provinces.

The three "praetorian prefectures" (Gaul, Ilyria-Italy-Africa, the East; subsequently Illyricum became a fourth), initially simple administrative divisions, became after Constantine's death separate entities over which his three sons ruled; thus, the collegiality of the tetrarchy again yielded to territorial division. This was reinforced by the new capital of the East, Constantinople, which Constantine created in 326 AD on the site of the ancient city of Byzantium. The separation of the East and the West was now a fact, except for occasional periods of unity with no real tomorrow.

Constantine's reign was especially important for its religious policy. As he had long been attracted to monotheism (he was a worshipper of the sun and, subsequently, of Apollo), his attraction to Christianity grew steadily. Although he was baptized only on his deathbed, already in 313 he established the "peace of the Church" with his famous Edict of Milan, which proclaimed religious tolerance and indulgence for Christians throughout the empire. In 325 he convened the Council of Nicaea, which condemned the Arian heresy.

Constantine's sons divided the empire among themselves. Constantine II took the East and passed for the first "Byzantine" emperor (his court was full of eunuchs, something unheard of in Italy; it remained a characteristic of Byzantium until the fifteenth century).

But wars erupted again on the borders: the new Persian empire of the Sassanids (under King Shapur II) struck several hard blows at the Romans, who were also under attack from the Germanic tribes—the Franks, Alamans, Quadi, Marcomanni, the Goths—the Huns, and the Scythians.

3. *Pagan Reaction: Julian the Apostate*

Julian the Apostate (361–63 AD), *Jovian* (363–64 AD).

In 360 AD at Lutetia Julian was proclaimed emperor by the army, even before the death of Constantius II. He was an intellectual in the Hellenic tradition (he left numerous literary and philosophical writings). Although raised a Christian, he became a follower of an "advanced paganism" (theurgy, Eleusinian mysteries, sun cult), thus he promoted the pagan cult again, banishing Christians from teaching positions and public office (which explains the epithet "Apostate"). He died in 363 in the war against Shapur II (as he lay dying, he is said to have whispered, "You have conquered, Galilean").

Jovian succeeded Julian; he was a moderate Christian and died in 364. After this date, a new crisis erupted and the destinies of the two halves of the empire diverged all but completely.

4. *The Collapse of the Western Empire*

Valentinian I (364–75 AD), *Gratian* (367–83 AD), *Valentinian II* (375–92 AD), *Honorius* (395–423 AD), *Valentinian III* (425–55 AD), *Romulus Augustus* (unseated in 476 AD).

Invasions occurred one after the other. The Western provinces were lost and became de facto barbarian kingdoms. The Vandals made their way through Gaul and Spain and settled in

Andalusia and Africa. Even Rome was captured by the Visigoths under Alaric in 410 AD, and then by the Vandals under Genseric in 455. The last emperor of the West was Romulus Augustus who, still a child, was deposed by Odoacer, a barbarian prince, appointed leader of the mercenaries.

5. *The East until the Time of Justinian*

Valens (364–78), *Theodosius I* (379–95), *Arcadius* (395–408), *Theodosius II* (408–50), *Justinian* (527–65)

Here again a series of wars and usurpations was the dominant theme of the age. But the reign of Theodosius I stands out for its success against the barbarians, and also because, under his rule, Christianity became the sole official religion of the empire (as early as 379, Gratian declined the pontifical priesthood; in 391, Theodosius banned all forms of pagan worship).

The East was also threatened by invasion, but it was farther away and resisted better. During the long rule of Theodosius II the *Codex Theodosianus,* the first great collection of Roman laws, was compiled.

Justinian was one of the greatest Roman emperors. He gave Roman law its final form (see part 2, chapter 3). Under his reign the empire was united for the last time, since he regained Africa, southern Spain, and Italy, thanks to the achievements of his general Belisarius (at the end of the sixth century, Italy succumbed to a new wave of barbarians, the Lombards, except for Ravenna, which remained a Byzantine "exarchate" for another two centuries). After Justinian the long history of the Byzantine Empire began, lasting until the fall of Constantinople to the Ottoman Turks in 1453.

B. The Main Features of the Low Empire

The Low Empire saw four major changes: the orientalization of monarchy ("Dominate") (actually in embryo since the Severan dynasty, as we saw); the growing burden of the state; Christianization; and the deepening divide between East and West.[15]

1. *The Orientalization of Monarchy*

A cult of living emperors grew up alongside that of the dead emperors. The epithets "sacred" and "divine" began to apply to everything touching the monarch. He is called *dominus,* lord, and no longer *princeps.* Astrological signs, once considered the mark of a deranged or tyrannical mind, were again accepted as symbols of a monarchy reflecting the cosmic order.

This tendency was initially nourished by late paganism and Neoplatonic philosophy, but it soon found additional sustenance in a certain Christian mythology, in particular Arian heresy, and in the theories of Eusebius of Caesaria (see below, pp. 369–78): "God is the model of Royal Power, for it is God who decides that one authority shall rule over men." "It is from the Lord of the Universe and through him that the emperor receives and puts on the image of his supreme royality."

An "oriental" ceremonial practice developed at court. The Persian ritual of *prostration* was introduced. The oriental "diadem" replaced the wreath of laurel leaves of the triumphant

[15] We mentioned earlier that the expression "Low Empire" no longer enjoys the favor of modern historians, who prefer the term "Late Antiquity." But, with this expression, the idea of empire disappears entirely. Furthermore, the expression is not as ideologically neutral as it sounds. What is at stake is an implied judgment contained in the expression "Low Empire." Those with a belief in a form of progress in history and the parallel risk of decline generally prefer the traditional expression, which has the added advantage of clearly signaling the collapse of the law, individual freedoms, and the Enlightenment, which occurred at the time of the Dominate.

republican general, still worn by the emperors of the High Empire. The emperor himself wore sumptuous robes embroidered with precious stones. His public appearances, and those of his court, grew rare, his gestures and attitudes became hieratic and fixed. His head was displayed surrounded by a halo of light.

The administration, mirroring the celestial hierarchy, became centralized and hierarchized. The dynastic principle was asserted (except when the army imposed its candidate, as it did with Julian; but Julian also had imperial blood).

2. *The Growing Burden of the State*

Because of this accentuation of absolute monarchy and, no doubt, under the pressure of barbarian encroachments, which accelerated militarization, the Low Empire is characterized by an unprecedented growth in the state apparatus in two respects: an increase in *bureaucracy,* and the emergence of unprecedented *interventionist practices.* Some scholars speak of a suffocating, fossilized "totalitarian" state. We will examine the institutions of the Low Empire in the following chapter. For now, we limit our discussion to the state control of the economy.[16]

Unable to halt economic decline or curb inflation, the state *regulated prices and trade.* The Edict on Maximum Prices in 301 set the maximum price of several hundred products. Wages were also fixed. Offenders risked death. Property rights were infringed: a person could settle on land with a simple promise to work it. Because taxes were levied on property and the village community was liable for collecting it, villagers were encouraged to work the holdings of negligent landowners.

The state also became an economic agent. It created *imperial manufactures:* arsenals, arms factories, weaving factories, paper mills, monetary workshops, and the like. These public enterprises enjoyed a monopoly.

Finally, the state established a corporatist organization of the *professions.* Corporations were state-owned structures. They, too, enjoyed a monopoly to exercise their respective professions. But in exchange, exacting rules and regulations were imposed. Cost-free services had to be available. To ensure that individuals remained attached to their station, heredity was imposed, and work mobility was banned entirely. This was a general tendency since even the military profession was made hereditary, as was the charge of the decurions. The condition of farmer was fixed as well: the system was known as the *colonate,* the precursor of medieval *serfdom.*

Attaching the farmer to arable land was an effective way of ensuring a regular income from taxes on individuals (*capitatio*). It also served the interests of landowners. The tenant farmer was a virtual slave. He was allowed to marry and own goods other than those that bound him to the landowner, but he was prevented from moving off the land and owed the landowner a substantial portion of his output and various *corvées.* The colonate system was generalized under Valentinian II and Theodosis I and led to a *regression of equality before the law:* after 396 AD the *colonus* could no longer subpoena his master in a court of law; on the contrary, the master exercised a right of correction and domestic jurisdiction. Poverty predestined individuals to sell themselves to a property owner and to accept the status of *colonus.* Other reasons to become *colonus* include: the decision by the state to settle barbarian peoples on the land; the legal loss of freedom for individuals who had been on the land for 30 years or more. But the most common reason for becoming a *colonus* was heredity.

Thus, all of society gradually became fossilized. As a consequence the economy collapsed and social forces emerged that were hostile to the power of the state, such as the development of

[16] The following section is from Humbert, *Institutions politiques et sociales,* 348–52.

potentes, a sort of landed aristocracy, which gradually became independent of central and provincial administration. This prefigured medieval *seigneuries* or manorialism.

3. *Christianization*

Since Constantine, Christianity was not only tolerated, it was actively encouraged. Christian symbols appeared on coinage. The clergy was exempted from taxes. Episcopal jurisdiction was officially recognized. Death sentences handed down to heretics by a church court were carried out by imperial power as early as the end of the fourth century AD. Perhaps even more surprisingly, in a sense, one of Constantine's laws stipulated, as early as 333, that episcopal courts would no longer be voluntary and arbitral; in time, they competed with and replaced civil courts (the measure was later revoked). Finally, church courts obtained a monopoly of authority over the clergy in civil affairs (though not in penal affairs): this was the origin of the "privilege of forum," which played an important role in canon law in the Middle Ages (see pp. 532–33, 586–88).

The more the Low Empire evolved and the secular structures of the empire weakened in the West, the more the sociopolitical role of the church increased, especially locally, where the bishop[17] upheld community life and became the de facto local leader, representing the Romans against the barbarians (e.g., Augustine during the Vandals' siege of Hippo, and Pope Leo the Great in Rome against the Huns and the Vandal Geiseric).

Because the bishops met in *synods* and *councils,* it was the church that maintained the idea of Roman civilization and unity over the divisions wrought by barbarian kingdoms. In a certain sense, when the bonds between the West and Byzantium finally dissolved completely, the church, organized around the papacy, took over from the empire; in so doing it transmitted the idea of empire to the Carolingian dynasty.

4. *A Deepening East/West Divide*

Institutionally, the deepening divide between East and West was accentuated by the system of *tetrarchy,* then by a *doubling of the administrative structures,* and finally *by a total dynastic separation.* Nevertheless, a semblance of institutional unity remained, and the laws established in one part of the empire were applied in the other. The founding of a second capital, however, moved the center of gravity of the empire toward the East. The Hellenization of the Orient was complete and Latin soon disappeared (except for the law, where Latin survived for a very long time). The East developed its own social, economic, and cultural traits, which laid the foundations of the Byzantine civilization, while the West plunged into anarchy and barbarism for several centuries.

Italy never really ceased to be "Roman." Byzantine presence survived in Italy for some time: in the "exarchate" in Ravenna, in Venice, and in large parts of southern Italy and Sicily. Even elsewhere the barbarian presence never fully eliminated urban civilization like it did in Gaul or in Hispania.

---

[17] There was roughly one bishop per town; in Gaul there were 118 dioceses for 112 towns and cities.

Chapter 2

Roman Political Institutions

Taking the categories of the classical nineteenth century study by Theodore Mommsen,[1] we can distinguish what, in Roman "constitutional" law and public law in the Republican period, comes under the magistracies, the people, and the senate. However, in the Imperial period the Roman state undergoes a change of nature and the institutions of this period, the Principate and the Dominate, must be considered as sui generis systems. Finally, we will devote separate presentations to the institutions of territorial administration and the social orders.[2]

I. Magistracies

At the apogee of the Republican period, there were no more than 30 high magistrates,[3] enough to run the state. It gives an idea of the remarkable efficiency of the system.

A. The Concept of *Imperium*

High magistrates in Rome (dictators, consuls, praetors, *interreges,* promagistrates in the provinces) were "vested with *imperium.*" *Imperium* was a legacy of Etruscan royalty. It was the civil and military power of command and was, at the outset at any rate, absolute (it encompassed the

---

[1] See Yann Thomas's preface to the republication of the French translation of Theodore Mommsen's *Droit public romain* [Roman public law] (Paris: De Boccard Édition Diffusion, 1984).

[2] In this chapter we draw on Gaudemet, *Les institutions de l'antiquité* [Institutions in Antiquity]; Humbert, *Institutions politiques et sociales de l'antiquité* [Political and social institutions in antiquity]; and Claude Nicolet et al., *Rome et la conquête du monde méditerranéen* [Rome and the conquest of the Mediterranean world], 2 vols. (Paris: Presses Universitaires de France, 1993–94).

[3] Not including junior officials.

right of life and death). Its symbol was the axe in the fasces[4] of the lictor (one or more lictors escorted the magistrate who was "vested with *imperium*"; the number depended on the rank of the official).

Imperium was, in essence, religious. It was not a power or mandate granted by the people, even if, under the *lex curiata de imperio* ("curiate law[5] on imperium"), the people ratified a magistrate's appointment. Strictly speaking, the people could not grant powers it did not have; it could only entrust certain citizens with the monopoly for taking the auspices, a de facto gift of power. The gods remain the true source of power.

Thus, Roman political power was neither as rationalized nor "secularized" as it was in Greece: the Romans, and the absolutist European tradition that followed after them, ceased to demand of power that it "use reason" in everything it did: power retained a sacred, awe-inspiring character.[6]

The transition from monarchy to republic did not fundamentally impact the essence of *imperium;* rather, it *divided it among several holders* and made it *nonpermanent* (*annual* appointments).

A distinction is made between *imperium domi* and *imperium militiae:*

- *Imperium domi.* This was the civil power inside the *pomerium;*[7] it was political, judicial, and coercive. As the political power it could convene the assemblies[8] or the Senate; it could pass laws (a right also held by the plebeian tribunes, although they did not "possess *imperium*"). Judicial power was exercised by the praetors. Coercive power included a right of life and death over citizens, which was soon withdrawn from magistrates inside the *pomerium* when a "right of appeal to the people" was granted (*provocatio ad populum;* the right of a citizen to be judged by the assemblies). For this reason the bronze axe disappears from the fasces of the lictors of urban magistrates after 300 BC.
- *Imperium militiae.* This was the authority to command the armed forces, to collect "tribute" (a tax to cover the costs of war paid by noncombatants), to raise an army, to share the spoils of war, to convene a *Century Assembly*[9] (promagistrates did not have this power), to engage armed forces in war outside Rome. Holders of this power also ran the civil and criminal courts in the provinces (for the governors). In due course, restrictions were placed on this power.

B. The General Principles of Roman Magistracies

The term "magistracy" was used by the Romans themselves: the *magister* is someone who is "greater than" his fellow citizens. He has *potestas,* a power or authority that allows him to enforce that part of the state's coercive force specified according to the magistracies, and to act in the name of the Republic.

[4] *Translator's note:* Bundles of rods tied around the sacred stave or axe of the lictor.

[5] For the meaning of this expression, see below, p. 226.

[6] It has to be added that Roman opinions about *imperium* are gleaned from a few late fragments of writing, dating from the crisis of the Republic. It is difficult to distinguish between reality and *a posteriori* reconstruction. It seems that the religious dimension weakened with time. A Greek like Polybius, who described the republican system in the middle of the second century BC, based on his observations and conversations with Roman politicians, hardly brings religious notions into play in his comments on the power of Roman officials. See the reservations of Nicolet, *Rome et la conquête,* 1:394 and following.

[7] The *pomerium,* it is recalled, was the city of Rome inside its sacred boundaries.

[8] They were political assemblies, of which several types existed in Rome; see below, pp. 226–28. We use the word "assembly" and only occasionally the term *curiata* throughout our discussion.

[9] This assembly, being of military origin, met outside the *pomerium* and, therefore, could not be convened by *imperium domi.*

A distinction must be made between *potestas* and *imperium*. All magistrates have *potestas*, but only certain higher magistrates are vested with *imperium* (and not all: for example, the censor was a high magistrate elected by the *Century* Assembly, but he did not have *imperium*).

We speak of *tribunician power, aedilitian power, censorial power*; it is said that two magistrates have *equal power* or that one has a power *superior* to the other. In addition, Roman magistrates share common features, such as the following.

1. *Election*

Magistrates are elected officials (except the dictator, his Master of the Horse,[10] and the office of the interrex: but they are exceptional magistracies). In the early days of the Republic, they were appointed by the presiding magistrate (*creatio*), until the assemblies obtained a say in the matter.

These elections, however, cannot be compared with modern democratic practices. The consul chose the candidates by arrangement with the Senate (see below); the people had a right of elimination, nothing more. However, the presiding magistrate of the assembly could require it to vote again, or he could simply halt the electoral process. A new magistrate assumed his office not by vote but by decree (*renuntiatio*), that is, by the announcement of his name after the vote. Finally, the assemblies had no right of dismissal. Nor can it be said that the magistrates were accountable to the assembly that elected them. In sum, the system was firmly under the control of the oligarchy in power.

2. *Annual Appointment*

Most magistrates were elected for one year. This was a basic principle of the Republic: it distinguishes it from monarchy and tyranny. But reappointment was accepted: it was possible to be elected consul, praetor, and the like several times, and the interval between two mandates tended to shorten.

3. *Collegiality*

All magistrates of a given sort held the totality of powers of the magistracy. There was no division of work between consuls, praetors, and so on, as in modern public ministries; each magistrate had full authority over everything and stood behind the decisions of his fellow magistrates. As a result, the magistrates could oppose each other either *a priori* (*prohibitio*) or *a posteriori* (*intercessio*), over the decision of one of their colleagues, which was the intended aim: the practice of collegiality was introduced to avert the risk of a return to personal power.

4. *Hierarchy*

A hierarchy existed among the magistracies; this was to be seen in a higher magistrate's right to oppose the decision of a lower magistrate (*intercessio*). The order of officials, however, was not set in stone, and some magistrates, like the tribune or the dictator, had trouble finding their place.

A law of 123 AD gives the following order: dictator, consul, praetor, Master of the Horse, censor, aedile, plebeian tribune of the Pleb, quaestor, *triumvir capitalis*,[11] agrarian triumvir, military

[10] The *magister equitum* served as the dictator's lieutenant, his second-in-command.
[11] The magistrate in charge of prisons and executions.

tribune in any of the first four legions, and so on. Only one order was truly fixed, the one by which magistracies were obtained: the *cursus honorum*.[12]

A distinction existed between higher magistrates (dictator, Master of the Horse, interrex, censor, consul, praetor), elected by the Century Assembly (*comitia centuriate*), and the lower magistrates (all others), elected by the Tribal Assembly (*comitia tributa*). The *curule* magistrates (quaestor and above) were so called because they had a right to the curule seat (*sella curulis*).

5. *Specialization*

Each magistracy had a set of well-defined powers and responsibilities, even if the scope of powers tended to be very broad for the higher magistrates.

Magistracies were held *without pay* (marking the oligarchic character of the Republic).[13]

6. *The Concept of Promagistracy*

One year was very short for many functions: this raised the risk of not fulfilling the duties of the function, which led to the notion of "promagistracy" and the idea of extending the term of office. The magistrate whose period of office was extended was no longer a magistrate as such. He could no longer convene an assembly or the Senate, for example. But he did retain *imperium*, either in the army or in the province (which often meant the same thing). Promagistracies (*propraetor*, *proconsul*) became the normal method of government in the provinces. A magistrate could be extended for a year, and sometimes longer (for example, Caesar in Gaul). Thus, the consulship became the prelude to a long and rewarding period in provincial government, the high point of a career.

C. Principal Magistracies

1. *Dictatorship*

If the Republic faced mortal danger, all powers could be concentrated in the hands of a dictator—a momentary resurrection of the monarchy. The function was very ancient, marked by religious taboos.

Twenty-four lictors escorted the dictator (the same number as the two consuls combined). The consuls nominated the dictator, the Curiate Assembly confirmed it; the dictator named his Master of the Horse. An appointment as dictator could not exceed six months. After 200 BC, the office fell out of use.

2. *Interrex*

When the seat of power was left vacant, the right of *auspicium* fell to the *patres*, that is, to the Senate, which co-opted an *interrex* (literally, a ruler "between kings"). He expedited current affairs for a period of five days, until such time as a consul was elected or a dictator appointed.[14]

---

12 The *cursus honorum* was the "sequence of offices" in the career of a Roman politician, meaning a career of magistracies. *Honos* is a magistracy.

13 Only wealthy individuals could afford to serve the state. In contrast, democratic Athens, as we saw, paid individuals for service in public office.

14 With the concepts of "dictatorship" and "interregnum" (as well as *senatus consultum ultimum*, which we will encounter again below), we have the appearance in constitutional law of special measures for exceptional circumstances, which exist in all modern constitutions (state of emergency, interim periods, and so on). The fact that these exceptional powers gave rise to precise, restrictive definitions is *a contrario* evidence that the rule of law was advancing. There are no formal "dictators" in truly dictatorial regimes.

3. *Censorship*

The censors were the highest moral authority of the Republic (a "censorship" was the highest rung of the *cursus honorum;* only men advanced in years with experience of high office rose to this level). The office was held every five years for a period of 18 months.

Two censors were responsible for taking the census and registering the population (this had implications for the composition of the Assemblies of Centuries and Tribes and for the registration of members in the equestrian class); establishing the list of senators (the censors held sovereign power to name new senators and to expel others); the censorship of public morality; financial responsibilities: maintenance of public buildings and roads, the administration of calls for tender, the adjudication of tax farms, the redistribution of the *ager publicus,* and so on.

4. *Consulship*

Consuls were chosen by the Senate, elected by the Century Assembly, and instated by the Curiate Assembly. Consuls possessed *imperium domi* and *militiae.* They had the right to "work with the Senate,"[15] convene assemblies, and pass laws. There were two consuls who ruled under a curious system of holding the fasces together (i.e., exercising power jointly): for the *imperium domi* each held power in alternate months, and for the *imperium militiae* on alternate days. This ensured that power remained unified.

5. *Praetorship*

Initially there was one praetor, then two (when the *praetor peregrinus,* the praetor for non-Roman citizens ("strangers" or "foreigners") was added to the *praetor urbanus* in 242 BC), then four (a doubling of the two functions), then six and more at the end of the Roman Republic (the objective being to create provincial government officials). The praetors had various functions connected with the *imperium* (powers similar to those of the consuls), but their main duty was the administration of justice: we will discuss this at length in the chapter on Roman private law below (chapter 3).

D. Lower Magistracies

Let us turn now to the lower magistracies, which did not have *imperium.*

1. *Office of Aedilis*

At the outset there were the *aediles plebis* (plebeian aediles), elected by the Plebeian Council (presided over by a tribune), and later the *aediles curules,* elected by the Tribal Assembly (presided over by a praetor or a consul). They have the same functions: the administration of justice (for less important cases than the ones handled by the praetors), public order maintenance, the supply of grain, the organization of public games (costs were borne by the aediles; the office of the aedilis involved significant personal expense for the office holder; upon completion of his mandate, the magistrate usually tried to recoup his costs when he took charge of a provincial government).

2. *Quaestorship*

Quaestors were elected by the Tribal Assembly. They led investigations into criminal cases and they had financial powers.

The *plebeian tribune* was one of the most important magistrates. But, because the tribunes were an emanation of the people, we will discuss it in the following section.

---

[15] They could convene the Senate, establish the agenda, preside over its meetings, obtain a vote.

II. The People

The people played a seminal role in the Roman Republic. They expressed themselves through *assemblies* and had their own *magistrates:* the *plebeian tribunes*. However, the term "people" was not the sum of all citizens. It was a closed, well-identified body whose members had *the right of Roman citizenship*.

A. Citizenship

The right of citizenship was obtained in various ways: by *birth* (certain restrictions existed in the case of mixed marriages and children born out of wedlock); by *emancipation* (with a few provisional restrictions: first-generation citizens could not embark on the *cursus honorum;* emancipated citizens were all registered in the same rural tribe in order to restrict their political impact as much as possible); by *assimilation after conquest* (this particular movement was slow at first, but accelerated under the empire until the publication of the Edict of Caracalla in 212 AD); and by *individual privilege* (for services rendered).

B. Plebeian Tribunate

Initially, this was a revolutionary institution, a counter power (see above) (Cicero wrote that the plebeian tribunate was "the child and the parent of endless seditions" (*De Legibus* 3.19). Starting in the third century BC, however, it became a normal part of institutional life in the Roman state, at the same time that it remained an element of instability or, at any rate, of reform. The tribunate was reserved exclusively for plebeians (certain politicians—for example, Clodius, the enemy of Cicero—made themselves plebeians to have access to the office). All ten tribunes were elected by the Plebeian Council. They did not have *imperium* powers, though they did possess special, awesome powers that even the curule magistrates did not have. Tribunician power was, in fact, so vast that in time it became one of the mainstays of the emperor's absolute power.

The person of the tribune was *sacrosanct,* that is, inviolable. An assailant of a tribune (even another magistrate) was declared *sacer,* a social outcast; anyone could take a *sacer's* life (another citizen or the tribune himself). The *sacer* was usually thrown from the Tarpeian Rock[16] and his goods confiscated; a judgment of the assemblies was not necessary, and there was no right of "appeal to the people." These risks held for anyone who made an attempt on a tribune's life or his authority, in other words, on the interests of the plebeians. In sum, a tribune had a virtual right of life and death over all citizens, including magistrates (in this respect, there is an asymmetry between magistrates and tribunes).

Because the tribune was inviolable, he could put the plebs under his protection: this was known as the power of *auxilium*. This was personal protection initiated by an individual who felt threatened ("*tribunos appello,*" "I appeal to the tribunes") or by a tribune himself; or it was collective protection called for by the plebs as such. In this case, the tribune could use his right of *intercessio* to suspend a magistrate's decision. The tribune's power could block anything; it could block the magistrate's power to convene the assembly or the Senate, to pass laws, to recruit soldiers (even in times of extreme danger): owing to their enormous powers, the tribunes were able to impose many concessions on the Senatorial class for the benefit of the plebs.

The tribunes' powers were, nevertheless, restricted to the city limits and one mile beyond; they had no power over the *imperium militiae*. Although one tribune could intercede against another

[16] A steep cliff at the southern top of the Capitoline Hill overlooking the Roman Forum.

(the principle of the collegiality of magistracies), and because there were ten tribunes, the senators always managed to elect a "traitor" and, thereby, to hamstring their opponents.

The tribunes played a positive role as well. They presided over the Plebeian Council and the Tribal Assembly. They could pass laws by *plebiscite* (in fact, the vast majority of laws originated with the tribunes). They could also "work with the Senate," in a manner of speaking. Many former tribunes became senators.

C. The Assemblies of the People

In principle, there were four assemblies: Curiate Assemby (*comitia curiata*), Century Assembly (*comitia centuriata*), Tribal Assembly (*comitia tributa*) and the Plebeian Council (*concilium plebes*); there is some debate as to whether the Tribal Assembly and the Plebeian Council (also called the People's Assembly) were, indeed, distinct. Their powers were electoral, legislative, and judicial. But however that may be, the complex Roman system was very different from the single assembly of Athenian democracy.

1. *Curiate Assembly*

a. Composition

The Curiate Assembly dates back to ancient times, when the population was divided into *curiae*. Gradually, this organization disappeared: in classical times, few citizens knew which *curia* they belonged to. Thus, the people were symbolically replaced by 30 lictors, each representing a *curia.*

b. Powers

Despite this ploy, the assembly retained an essential function: it approved the appointment of magistrates vested with *imperium* (*lex curiata de imperio*). Until this formality was finalized, the magistrate lacked the fullness of his powers. The Curiate Assembly validated certain procedures of civil law as well.

2. *Century Assembly*

a. Composition

The Century Assembly originated in a reform attributed to king Servius Tullius; its purpose was to obtain the contribution of various social classes to the war effort proportionate to their means (see above, pp. 200–01). The population was divided into five *classes,* on a scale from most to least wealthy (people with no wealth at all, the *proletarii,* were considered *infra classem* and could not be mobilized in the event of war). The classes were subdivided into *centuries.* Each class had the same number of *centuries* of *juniores* (under 45 years of age) and *seniores* (over 45). The outcome was that elders had more political importance than military importance.

Each "century" was supposed to represent an equivalent contribution of wealth. So, to form a century many more poor citizens were needed than rich. There were some 195 (or perhaps 193) centuries in total. Each century could cast one vote in the assembly; the century voted in its assembly beforehand. The first social class, with 18 centuries of equestrians (or "knights") and 80 centuries of infantrymen,[17] had a majority in the assembly. The other classes had 20 or 30

[17] In other words, 98 votes, at a time when the majority was either 98 or 97 (historians have not reached agreement on these numbers).

centuries, while the *proletarii* had only one (and in Cicero's time there were as many citizens in the class of *proletarii* as in the first class!). Thus, the system was extremely unequal; it was both oligarchic and "timocratic," since power was granted on the basis of wealth and military might.

b. *Powers*

The Century Assembly elected the higher magistrates: consuls, praetors, and censors: this was their primary function. It also passed laws (after ca. 200 BC the Plebeian Council took over this responsibility). Finally, they had judicial functions:

- They judged political and common-law crimes carrying the death penalty (a quaestor led the investigation in the consul's name).
- They also judged cases of *perduellio* (roughly equivalent to high treason), that is to say, infringements on the rights of the plebs, criminal misconduct of the magistrates, and crimes against the people (in all these cases the defendant risked the death penalty; a tribune led the investigation).
- It was before these assembly meetings that an "appeal for protection" was heard, raised by the plebeian tribune exercising his right of *auxilium* against a magistrate's ruling (after the enactment of the *Lex valeria* of 300 BC, an appeal could be brought by any citizen). In due course, the "right of appeal" to the people became a fundamental individual right in ancient Rome, which meant that consuls and praetors lost their discretionary power to mete out punishments, inside the city limits at any rate, which is why, as we saw, the bronze axe was removed from the fasces.

After 150 BC the criminal jurisdiction of the assembly was clipped by the creation of permanent criminal courts (*quaestiones perpetuae*), formed of judges acting as jurors and presided over by praetors.

3. *The Tribal Assemby and the Plebeian Council*

a. Composition

The Tribal Assembly and the Plebeian Council (or People's Assembly) differed in terms of the authority that convened them and in the purpose of their meeting, not in terms of their composition or method of election, since both came under the system of the territorial "tribes." Every Roman citizen belonged to a tribe, either the tribe associated with his place of residence or the tribe to which he was assigned by the censor when he became a Roman citizen (as we saw, emancipated slaves were assigned to a tribe at the discretion of the censor). There were 35 tribes in total.

In this case as well, there was a dual vote counting procedure: the majority vote of the tribe produced the tribe's vote for the assembly, and the majority vote of the assembly was based on the votes of all tribes. Within the tribe the social classes were mixed, which meant that the Tribal Assembly and the Plebeian Council were far more democratic than the other assemblies.

b. Powers

The Tribal Assembly elected the plebeian magistrates (tribunes and aediles) and the lower magistrates. It passed *laws* (when the assembly was convened by magistrates) and *plebiscites* (when convened by tribunes). Such texts primarily concerned "constitutional" or public law (we will see that, as far as civil law was concerned, the law and the plebiscite were actually secondary sources of law). Lastly, the Tribal Assembly also had judicial authority: they sat in judgment over public crimes liable to a fine.

4. *Procedure*

The striking feature is that these various assemblies were, to a large extent, subject to the magistrates; in this sense there was almost no "popular sovereignty" in the Roman Republic.

An assembly could not convene itself. It had no control over its agenda. Assembly meetings were rare (the religious calendar allowed only 195 "comitial days"[18] per year). Places of assembly were also subject to religious prohibitions: assemblies could only meet in Rome (unlike the Athenians, the Romans did not have *ecclesia* in the country); the Curiate Assembly met inside the *pomerium,* the Century Assembly met outside (in the Field of Mars). The meeting place had to be "inaugurated," that is to say, oriented in such a way that the magistrate could take the auspices ("read the omens"). A yes or no vote was cast (using the formulas *uti rogas,* "as you ask," or *antiquo iure utimur,* "use the old law"; *condemno,* "I condemn," or *libero, absolvo,* "I acquit/absolve," respectively).

No citizen was allowed to speak. Magistrates and tribunes were seated on the rostra; the people stood below. Voting was oral and public: each citizen stood before the "interrogator" (*rogare,* "ask for") and voiced his vote publicly. The popular party contested this practice, which made voters vulnerable to outside influences (patrons could coerce clients, the *nobilitas* could pressure the people to vote in its favor; vote buyers thrived). The procedure changed with the *Lex Gavinia Tabellaria,* which introduced secret votes or *tabellae* (enacted between 139 and 107 BC).

In the Century Assembly, the first classes voted first to show the *proper choice.* One century from among the first classes was chosen by lot; called the "prerogative," its vote was seen as an omen to influence the people. As for the Tribal Assembly, a meeting was held beforehand to enable prominent members to make their opinion known. This made it possible to manipulate the order in which the tribes voted or the order in which votes were counted. As soon as a majority emerged, the voting process was stopped: thus, this procedure rarely gave the lower classes an opportunity to even cast their votes. If the first votes pointed to an unsatisfactory vote, the magistrate commonly started the voting process again or interrupted it completely. He could also not announce the result or simply veto it.

Thus, in every respect, the people were under control. It was important, Cicero observed, "to place the suffrages, not in the hands of the multitude, but in the power of the men of property."[19]

In the first century BC, manipulations, cheating on a grand scale, assaults, and a combination of coercion and corruption perverted the electoral system entirely. However, judging by the efforts of the manipulators, the system was not simply a farce. The decisions of an assembly, however obtained, had full force.

III. The Senate

A. Composition

While all ancient cities had a council in one form or another, the Senate of Rome had particular importance. Foreign visitors to Rome in the Republican period would have noticed that real power was in the hands of the Senate.

The Senate had 300 members during the Roman Republic and 600 during the High Empire. The list of members was regularly updated with additions and removals; this was initially carried

[18] *Translator's note:* "Comitial" stems from *comitia,* or assembly, thus a day on which the assembly can be held.

[19] Cicero, *De Republica,* vol. 16, trans. Clinton Walker Keyes (Cambridge, MA: Harvard University Press, 1928), 2.39–40.

out by the king, then by the higher magistrates, and after 300 BC by censors, who undertook a "reading" of the Senate's list (*lectio senatus; legere* means "read" the album[20] as well as "choose").

Throughout the long crisis from the Gracchi to Augustus, which resulted in the collapse of the Republic, the Senate was a major prize in the struggle for power. Sulla and Caesar removed senators and packed the institution with their supporters.

The conditions of admission to the Senate were very restrictive socially, morally, and politically: membership in the Roman Senate did not depend on the drawing of lots, as did the Athenian Boule. The general rule was that entry into the Senate occurred after a period as a magistrate. Thus, the same conditions pertained as for admission into the *cursus honorum:* possess Roman citizenship, not be a freed slave or exercise one of several disqualifying professions, have the equestrian census,[21] have the *ius honorum* (the "right of honors," that is, be eligible to hold public office). And it was necessary to have been a magistrate (different levels depending on the era), but this was not always a sufficient condition: censors could reject a former magistrate considered unworthy. One entered the Senate immediately after serving as a quaestor; therefore, praetors, consuls, and promagistrates were chosen from among those who had a seat in the Senate. Note that, since magistrates were elected by the people, the Senate was as well, though only indirectly.

The assembly was *hierarchical.* Some senators were patricians: it was among their ranks that the *interrex* was chosen. Access to the speaker's platform was given to senators by rank order of the offices they had held: former dictators, former censors, former consuls (called the *consulars*), former praetors (the "praetorians"), and so on. Within these various categories, patricians spoke first; thereafter it was a question of seniority. The *princeps senatus,* the first senator to take the floor, was always the eldest of the patrician censors (emperors took this prestigious title for themselves). But the president of the session could also choose which among the former consuls could speak first. Finally, there were the second-tier senators, the *pedarii* (pedestrians), who had probably not yet held even a curule magistracy: these senators voted, but did not speak during the debates.

The rank of senator brought certain honors with it (special seats at the theater, special clothes,[22] the right to be a judge, judicial immunity). It also brought duties, such as exposure to certain counts of indictment, a ban on exercising selected professions and from taking part in public auctions: this particular restriction distinguished the class of senators devoted exclusively to state service from the class of equestrians devoted to economic and financial activities.

B. POWERS

The Senate could debate any issue of interest to the state. In this sense, its competence was universal; it nevertheless played a particular role in certain domains, such as those that follow.

1. *EXTERNAL RELATIONS*

The Senate received the credentials of foreign ambassadors and dispatched Roman ambassadors abroad. It confirmed the statutes of conquered countries and ratified the governors' laws (*leges datae*) given to the provinces.

[20] The *album senatorium* was the official list of senators presented on a white tablet.

[21] This means to have a certain level of wealth (possess a fortune of 400,000 sesterces).

[22] For example, the *laticlave,* a broad stripe of purple on the fore part of the tunic; see below, p. 241.

2. *WAR*

The Senate cooperated with the magistrates in raising armies and in setting the level of *tributum* for soldiers' wages. It allocated money to promagistrates for military affairs and to the provinces. It accepted (or rejected) the costs of triumphs for returning generals.

3. *CIVIL ADMINISTRATION AND JUDICIAL SERVICES FOR ITALY AND THE PROVINCES*

These responsibilities were an indirect result of the Senate's diplomatic role. Since the peoples of Italy were supposedly "allies" of Rome, all administrative matters and certain judicial questions were handled by the Senate, not by the assemblies or the magistrates, in these parts of the territory.

4. *FINANCES*

This was the proper sphere of competence of the Senate: the assemblies did not meddle here. The Senate administered Rome's monetary and property assets, and of course its revenues from the Roman people. It distributed the *ager publicus* and managed public contracts involving natural resources (mines, forests, and so on). It also dealt with tax disputes. When direct taxes disappeared almost entirely after ca. 150 BC, the Senate retained control of state revenues since it set the contributions of the provinces to the treasury. The Senate also controlled expenditure: magistrates with annual appointments could not engage in military operations (for example), unless the Senate voted the necessary credits. Even when magistrates managed funds available to them directly, they were still not the paymasters: payments were made in Rome by quaestors under the Senate's control.

In all of these areas, the Senate acted by advisory decree (*senatus consultum*), that is to say by majority vote on the matter at hand. The value of a decree resided in the Senate's *auctoritas*, which came primarily from the quasi-religious prestige of the native *patres*. *Auctoritas* did not have a precise legal definition: simply, it was almost impossible to go against it (*auctoritas* was a mainstay of the emperor's absolute power, as we saw). Accordingly, a magistrate intending to publish a decree required the opinion of the Senate, which could make amendments to his text. Only later, with the Gracchi, were attempts made to have the people vote without a preliminary consultation of the Senate.

The *senatconsults (senatus consulta)* acquired formal judicial value when comital legislation ceased to exist under the empire. The Senate had the authority to repeal a law already voted on a legal technicality. Although the Senate was, in some respects, the first permanent deliberative assembly in history, it was nevertheless anything but a "parliamentary assembly."

5. *SENATUS CONSULTUM ULTIMUM*

This was an emergency decree involving the suspension of normal constitutional arrangements; the Senate then exercised "full powers." It is an interesting example of ill-defined constitutional "emergency powers"; it lies in a gray zone between practice and law, but still makes an attempt at doctrinal justification.

The decree was first passed by the *Pontifex Maximus* Scipio Nasica in 133 BC, when the senatorial party opposed Tiberius Gracchus. Scipio declared the Republic in danger and had the tribune assassinated. Several years later, Gaius Gracchus attempted to have the practice declared illegal. But in 121 BC it was passed again, this time against him. After that the Senate formulated this theory: when a public enemy threatens the existence of the Republic, the Senate will have the right to take emergency steps: suspend laws, ignore tribunician power, execute the perpetrator who will not have a right of appeal to the people. In sum, the decree was a variant of dictatorship, but in favor of the Senate as a collective body. The decree was used in 121 BC (against Gaius Gracchus), in 100 (against a tribune), in 88 (in favor of Sulla), in 77 (in favor of Pompey), in 63 (in favor of the consul Cicero, who faced the Catilina conspiracy), and in 49 (against Caesar, who as a result crossed the Rubicon).

C. Procedure

The Senate assembled in the Curia, a building in the Forum, or in other "inaugurated" places (various Roman temples). The president set the agenda. When it was their turn to speak, however, the senators could ask the assembly to debate other matters. The *pedarii* did not speak unless given the *ius sententiae* ("the right to speak"). Voting was public; it involved senators moving physically to the side of the author of a legislative proposal they supported. A stenographer sometimes recorded Senate deliberations. As soon as it was adopted, a *senatus consultum* was put in writing by a commission. It was possible for a tribune of the plebs or magistrates, equal or higher in rank to the author of a proposal, to raise an *intercessio;* this suspended the validity of a senatorial text. *Senatconsults* were published and held in the archives.

IV. The Emperor and Imperial Government under the High Empire (Principate)

A. The Legal Foundations of Imperial Power

The legal foundations of imperial power were the same as those imagined by Augustus in the early days of the Principate: proconsular *imperium,* tribunician power, and *auctoritas.* We should note that, until Vespasian, it was the Tribal Assembly that voted the *lex de imperio,* vesting the emperor with his powers. Later, only the Senate chose and invested the emperor.

Auctoritas was very effective: it was *auctoritas* that ensured that a candidate for a magistracy nominated by the emperor always won the appointment. Likewise, a judgment returned by the emperor set legal precedent. Proconsular *imperium* and tribunician power together placed the highest civil and criminal judicial powers in the hands of the emperor: the emperor replaced the praetor in the administration of civil justice, and the law enforcement granted him by *imperium* was no longer limited by the *provocatio ad populum* (since there were no longer assemblies nor tribunes of the plebs). Furthermore, since the emperor now held tribunician power, he was sacrosanct. This gave him the authority to prosecute anyone he pleased for the crime of lese-majesty (against his own person, the members of his family, or close relatives and friends). Note that he also held various priestly offices, including most frequently the function of *Pontifex Maximus.*

B. The Imperial Cult

The Imperial cult probably originated in the East. During the lifetime of Augustus, various cities in the eastern provinces established cults to the "goddess of Rome" and the emperor with the appointment of priests, the erection of temples, and the organization of sacrifices; they were prolonging an ancient custom of the Hellenistic monarchies. Before very long the cult spread to the western provinces. Under the Julio-Claudians it adopted a less direct expression in Rome itself and elsewhere in Italy. Instead of the person of the emperor, the object of veneration was his "spirit," or the traditional divinities associated with his family (Venus and Mars were the tutelary gods of the *gens Julia*), or even the previous emperor, who was declared *divus;* brotherhoods were devoted to his cult: the *Augustales,* the *Flaviales,* and the *Antoniani,* to mention only a few).[23] Under the Flavians, the cult was organized in the provinces, as well as in cities.

It would be wrong to think that the Imperial cult was superficial because it was official. The people, it seems, participated enthusiastically. However, during the High Empire, with the exception of a few particular extravagances (Nero took himself for the sun-god; Domitian declared himself "*dominus et deus*" and demanded prostrations, for example), the Imperial cult did not really change the functioning of central power. The elite was not fooled and saw the prince as a citizen. Only later was the person of the emperor truly held to be sacred, and worship of his cult was imposed on everyone.

After Augustus died, the Senate took the decision to deify him (at the grand ceremony of deification, his body was cremated on the sacred Fields of Mars; an eagle was released, which supposedly transported the emperor's soul heavenward). The only other Julio-Claudian to be deified was Claudius. Alongside the public cult of the divinized emperor, a private cult existed within his family as well. The wives of the divinized emperor were also deified.

Emperors were careful to project their charisma, behaving as *providential men* whom the people could call upon for assistance at any time. They multiplied costly building projects (e.g., the Coliseum), gratis distributions, and support for orphans. The name of "Father of the Fatherland" was usually added (except for Tiberius and Hadrian) to their official titles. The emperor accepted the title of "patron" of towns and cities in the provinces and was often elected a magistrate of these places. He saw to it that they received his gifts. He devoted special attention to the army, showering it with gifts of money (*donativum*) upon his accession. Indeed, the army became the emperor's real pillar of support. In time the "praetorian cohorts" and provincial troops took over from the Senate (to a varying degrees of success) in the making and unmaking of emperors.

C. Imperial Government

1. *The Emperor*

As we said earlier, the emperor was a true autocrat. From Marcus Aurelius onward, however, a promising new practice developed: the collegiality of the emperors, probably an echo of the collegiality of the magistracies. Marcus Aurelius governed with Lucius Verus, sharing the same duties and obligations. With Diocletian the tetrarchy was established.

2. *The Imperial Council*

Augustus created a permanent council of the prince, which survived with changes until it became a formal institution under Hadrian. It was made up of confidants (*comitii*), relatives, close friends, military leaders, and senators, either handpicked or drawn by lot.

---

[23] In Rome, the soil for the Imperial cult was fertile. Romulus had been deified. At the end of the Republic, the generals were said to be the favored of the gods (*felix*) and superhuman. Caesar was immediately deified upon his death. His *gens*—Augustus, the Julio-Claudians, and the ensuing emperors, claimed a blood relation with Caesar whose name they bore—traced their ancestry from Venus. There were many Romanized barbarian populations in the west, notably in Spain, which had long practiced the deification of their tribal leaders; they too were well disposed to deifying the leader of the Romans. In fact, throughout all societies in antiquity, one comes across an anthropology of divine kingship behind the veneer of "civilization" (see introduction).

3. *The Senate*

The Senate continued to play a role, although it was under the total control of the emperor, who monitored membership using his censorial powers. It elected magistrates, passed *senatconsults,* and played a judicial role.

4. *Administration*

Augustus also created an efficient central administration, adapted to the length and breadth of the Roman world. It was well informed about the situation throughout out the territory and enabled instructions to be transmitted, statistics to be kept, and the state's fiscal resources to be managed. Under the rule of Claudius, departments entrusted to former slaves, now Roman citizens, developed into embryonic ministries independent of the Senate and the equestrian class, and devoted to well-defined matters. Over time this system became burdensome: gradually the central services of the state occupied the entire Palatinate (it is worth emphasizing again that, compared with modern states, the number of Roman public servants was quite small).

D. Succession

Roman emperors could not simply succeed one another from father to son, which would call to mind one of the most contemptible aspects of traditional monarchy. However, it was at his own peril that an emperor neglected the succession issue; ignoring it left the door wide open to anarchy. Normal forms of election had disappeared. Only imperfect solutions remained: the appointment of a supposed successor, joint power-sharing between the incumbent and his supposed successor (the ruling emperor usually delegated some of his duties to his supposed successor or shared them with him in imperial collegiality), dynastic marriages, adoption, and so on. The imperfection of these systems explains in great part the disorder and violence that went hand-in-hand with succession under the empire (except the Flavians and the Antonines).

V. The Emperor and Imperial Government during the Low Empire ("Dominate")

A. The *Dominus*

The first emperor to take the title "lord" and "god" (*dominus et deux*) was Domitian. He introduced oriental ceremonies such as prostrations and the kissing of feet. In time, the fiction of the Principate was forgotten. The empire became a monarchy and was accepted as such. The king was a lord because he was of a different fabric from his people. In some respects they were his "slaves." His power over them was total.

Even more than in the past, the emperor was the principal, indeed, supreme source of the law. He was the commander-in-chief of the army, the head of the executive and the administration, the highest judge in penal and civil affairs.

1. *The Imperial Cult*

The cult gained in strength. From Aurelian to Constantine, the emperors were identified with the sun, taking this farther than Nero and Domitian. They saw themselves as the visible face of the one, invisible god.

2. *The Court and Its Ceremonial*

The emperor lived in a palace (in Milan, Aquileia [near Trieste], Nicomedia [near Constantinople], Antioch, to name a few). Access to the emperor became increasingly difficult, and he became less visible. His public appearances, during which he was separated from the audience by a curtain, took on the aspect of an "epiphany." A ritual developed: prostrations were required; he was addressed as "lord." His progresses were codified and hieratic; his speeches were ceremonies.

3. *The Imperial Council*

It became known as the "sacred consistory"—"sacred" because everything concerning the emperor was holy, "consistory" because advisors were required to stand; no one was allowed to sit (and even to speak) in the presence of the emperor.

B. Roman Government and Administration

Under Diocletian, the praetorian prefect assumed the double role of chief minister and war minister, a grand vizier in the Egyptian style. When the praetorian prefectures became territorial under Constantine, the head of the administration took the title "quaestor of the palace." The dioceses were placed in the hands of vicars. The lord ruled through a network of spy-envoys, his *agentes in rebus*. A small number of other ministers headed up the administrative services, offices, and *scrinia* (archives). The officer of the sacred chamber was in charge of the imperial house. The *master of the office* was in charge of the police and the imperial guard. A *count of sacred bounties* and a *count of private estates* administered the imperial finances (these two counts, the quaestor of the palace and the master of the office, were members of the sacred consistory).

The Senate continued to exist but lost its political role. It gradually became a kind of municipal council.

VI. Territorial Administration

A study of Roman territorial administration is important in the context of our narrative. If Rome civilized the West, it did so first by Romanizing it through local, municipal institutions, established by Roman conquerors in barbarian countries. Here we need to distinguish between three periods: the Republic, the High Empire, and the Low Empire.

A. The Republic

In Italy, some territories were annexed, others were federated. Outside Italy, the conquered peoples and territories either became clients of Rome or were "relegated to the status of provinces."[24]

1. *In Italy*

The cities closest to Rome were granted full rights of citizenship "with suffrage," which included political rights. Others were given the status of *municipium* (literally, municipal township): their citizens retained their local rights, and the cities themselves retained their local institutions, though they lost their external sovereignty entirely. Some regions of Italy were without towns (northern Italy and the Adriatic coast), so it was not possible to establish *municipia* there. Still,

[24] See Humbert, *Institutions politiques et sociales*, 195–201.

Roman settlers occupied the territory, which could not be left without an administration. This is the origin of the appointment of Roman "prefects."

With cities more distant, or cities that had not been conquered under the same circumstances as the *municipia,* the Romans established equal and unequal alliances, or so-called alliances. "Federated" territories were allowed to retain their internal institutions and, to a degree, a semblance of external sovereignty: but they owed obedience, tribute, and military service to Rome (they recognized the preeminence—the majesty [*majestas*]—of the Roman people). This system was strongly amended after the Social War.

Twenty-five "Latin colonies" were founded between 334 and 184 BC. They were artificial creations: half the population was made up of Roman migrants, the remainder were Italian allies and local populations. Institutions modeled after those of Rome (magistracies, Senate, assemblies) were established. Plots of land were distributed to immigrants, but in order to preserve the Roman structure of oligarchic society the plots were unequal. The colonies played a vital military role: they maintained the peace and kept order.

2. *Outside Italy*

The statutes of the new province were drawn up by the Roman magistrate who conquered the territory. With assistance from a senatorial commission, he enacted a *lex provinciae,* which served as the constitution for the province (the *lex provinciae* was a *lex data,* i.e., an administrative decree; it was not passed by a vote of the assemblies like the *leges rogatae*). This law established the authority of the Roman governor over the local administration and management of economic resources in place of the prior authorities.

Rome seized some but not all local properties; it seized the personal holdings of conquered kings, which became *ager publicus,* the property of the Roman people. Public land was rented to private individuals for a rent called the *vectigal.* The remaining land was left in the hands of the native people, who were required to pay Rome a tithe on the harvest or a fixed property tax known as the *stipendium.* In addition, the province had to accept Rome's exploitation of its natural resources (such as mines), the payment of indirect taxes, requisitioning rights, and usurious interest rates that put provincials deeply in debt to their Roman bankers.

This system produced such profits for Rome that after 167 BC direct taxes were abolished. Magnificent buildings in Rome and public infrastructure developments (such as roads) throughout Italy were the fruit of this wealth taken from the provinces. Another social consequence, and a factor in the Gracchi crisis and in the imbalances that gradually brought about the downfall of the Republic, were the great landed estates (*latifundiae*), operated with armies of slave labor, which arose with the *ager publicus.* They supplied agricultural products at such low prices that the small traditional Latin landholdings were soon ruined.

Initially, governors were praetors, whose number was increased from two to six for this. Then the provinces were governed by promagistrates, propraetors, and proconsuls. On average they remained in office for two years. In their territories they possessed civil and military *imperium* (except for the immunities stipulated in the *lex provinciae*); in other words, they held absolute power. Their power was the greater that there was no one else to share their office—no college—and, therefore, no one to enforce a tribunician *intercessio.* The only right of opposition against them was the *provocatio ad populum* of a Roman citizen. The governor pronounced judgment on matters opposing Roman citizens in conflict with one another and between Roman citizens and peregrines (foreign subjects of Rome after the conquest of their country). To this end the governor enacted a provincial edict. He was the appellate judge in cases of local justice and could be assisted by legates (senators) and quaestors, and by an informal advisory council.

B. High Empire

1. *The Provinces*

Italy kept its own special status despite efforts to bring its status in line with that of the provinces. But this put an end to a "colonial" attitude. The compromise on which Augustus established his regime involved a distinction between senatorial provinces and imperial provinces, a distinction that lasted until the Severi emperors. The senatorial provinces were governed by proconsuls drawn by lot from a list of senators and appointed for one year with pay. They had only civil authority. In matters of criminal jurisdiction they were subject to appeal to the emperor. Their erstwhile financial powers soon passed into the hands of the *imperial procurators.* The far more numerous imperial provinces (30 of 40 provinces during the High Empire) were governed by "legates of Augustus," independently appointed by the emperor for periods of three to five years.

Emperors kept a close watch over the procurators and kept them in office for longer periods when they performed satisfactorily. Claudius saw to it that the inhabitants of the provinces were not overexploited or treated arbitrarily. *Provincial assemblies* existed to control the governors (e.g., the Concilium of the Three Gauls, a sort of governing body for the three new provinces known as Tres Galliae: Gallia Aquitania, Gallia Belgica, and Gallia Lugdunensis). Emperors established colonies and created *municipia* in the provinces. They granted citizenship rights to the Alpine nations, to provincial elites, and to auxiliaries at the end of their term in office. Beginning with Claudius, the Gauls were admitted into the Senate (they were granted the *ius honorum* [the right to hold civil or public office], required in addition to the census). A policy of infrastructure development (roads, aqueducts) was pursued.

2. *The Cities*

In stark contrast with the Roman Republic, the Roman Empire deliberately emphasized the urbanization of the provinces. The city was an important power relay. It was where the magistrates lived, where the laws of the Empire were published, where registry offices for civil and fiscal purposes functioned, where the Imperial cult was worshipped. It was also where the games and festivals were held. It contributed to the sedentarization of barbarian populations. Like the *limes,* the city established the frontiers of *Romanitas.*

Cities under the High Empire had different statuses:

- *Peregrine* cities preserved their institutions and their rights from before the conquest.
- *Municipia:* these provincial communities were granted "Latin rights," that is, the same rights as the *municipia* of Italy (with their municipal institutions and magistracies, as we shall see below). This right was granted all at once to the whole of Spain under Vespasian: all Spanish cities, big and small, became "Latin *municipia.*" This right was also widely granted in Gaul and in Africa. In the Latin *municipia,* officials with municipal responsibilities automatically acquired Roman citizenship rights. Thus, the provincial elite was quickly Romanized through its involvement in Roman municipal institutions.
- *Colonies.* They were the new towns populated with Roman settlers dispatched to the conquered territories. Examples in Gaul include Lyons, Arles, Nimes, Valence, Vienne, Frejus. Colonies were also established for the veterans of Augustus in Saragossa (*Caesaraugusta*), Aosta (*Augusta Praetoria*); and for the veterans of Claudius in Cologne (*Colonia Claudia Agrippinensium*). The inhabitants of colonies had Roman citizenship rights. There were also *honorary colonies,* such as already existing cities, which were granted Roman citizenship rights collectively *a posteriori.*

3. *Municipal Institutions*

In the peregrine cities, the traditional local institutions were preserved (the *archonte* in Athens, the *suffete* in Carthage, for example), while in the *municipia* and the colonies municipal institutions were set up that replicated the institutions of Rome on a smaller scale.

The *populus,* subdivided into *curiae,* met in *assemblies,* which in turn elected the *magistrates.* There was a three-rung municipal *cursus honorum* (two officials for each office): *quaestor* (financial affairs), *aedile* (supplies, markets, road network, buildings), and two *duumvirs* jointly sharing the office of the executive and the justice department (thus, at the local municipal level, they held the responsibilities of the praetor and the consuls, and even the censor, since they were in charge of taking the census every five years). Last but not least, there was a local senate, consisting of former magistrates and notables: a deliberative body in charge of all municipal affairs. To qualify for membership in the local senate, citizens had to belong to the *order of the decurions,* drawn from the *curiale class* (wealthy middle-class citizens). These decurions were responsible for tax collections; they also elected the priest in charge of the Imperial cult. Decurions were a breeding ground and talent pool for the emperor, who drew from them to renew the equestrian order.

In the eastern provinces and in certain regions of Italy, where there was no need to "municipalize" local life since cities already existed, the imperial administration paid more attention to ensuring that the autonomy of the cities did not lead to territorial disintegration. Accordingly, at times it suppressed autonomy momentarily by appointing "curators of the city" in charge of protecting citizens from disturbances and the abuses of local decurions and notables. This curatorship of urban centers led to greater uniformization of Roman administration.

From the time of Caesar, *Gallia Narbonensis,* which had been conquered between 120 and 117 BC, was quickly Romanized. The rest of Gaul, which proved remarkably peaceful (Rome withdrew its military presence and made no attempt to disarm the Gauls), was subdivided into three large provinces (Gallia Lugdunensis [Lyons], Gallia Aquitania [Aquitaine], and Gallia Belgica [Belgium]).

The Three Gauls had 60 subdivisions, not towns or cities but zones corresponding to ethnic groups or tribes (some 20 such zones were found in Gallia Narbonensis). Thus, urbanization and municipalization in Gaul were the work of Rome. The process began with each tribe being attributed a capital city, either a place of periodic assembly or a preexisting village where a *municipium* was artificially established.[25]

The Concilium of the Three Gauls, which met thrice annually in Lyons, was granted the right to praise and blame the governor, a privilege that strengthened the Gauls' sense that they were citizens (the council was a successor to an ancient Gallic "national" assembly; its primary purpose was to elect the priest in charge of the Imperial cult; however, it soon took on a political dimension: its discussions and grievances enabled the imperial administration to "keep its finger on the pulse" of the country).

---

[25] Sometimes it took several centuries for the *municipium* to establish its authority over the other villages (*pagi*) of the ethnic group. Thus, Lutetia asserted its authority over the Parisii, and Agedincum over the Senones. The city survived even after changing its Roman name back to its original ethnic name (Paris, Sens). Other examples in Gaul include the tribe of the Voconces and the city of Vaison, the Cavares (Cavaillon), the Rutenes (Rodez), the Biturges-Cubi (Bourges), the Limovices (Limoges), the Santones (Saintes), the Ausci (Auch), the Carnutes (Chartres), the Andecavi (Angers), the Namnetes (Nantes), the Veneti (Vannes), the Abrincati (Avranches), the Lexovii (Lisieux), the Aulerci Eburovices (Evreux), the Meldae (Meaux), the Tricassi (Troyes), the Atrebates (Arras), the Ambiani (Amiens), the Suessiones (Soissons), the Silvanecti (Senlis), the Remi (Reims), the Mediomatrici (Metz). Examples in Germania include the tribe of the Treveri and the city of Trier, the Vangoni and the city of Worms. See Jean-Pierre Martin, *Les provinces romaines d'Europe centrale et occidentale* [The Roman provinces of central and western Europe] (Paris: Éditions SEDES, 1990), 172–73.

This policy of assimilation had its ideology. The Senate mocked Claudius, who wanted to see "all the Greeks, Gauls, Spaniards, and Bretons in togas."[26] But how, Tacitus asks, could such men enter the Senate, whose ancestors "at the head of hostile tribes destroyed our armies with fire and sword, and actually besieged the divine Julius at Alesia"? Tacitus quoted the emperor as answering, in a speech preserved on the "Claudian Tables of Lyon":

> My ancestors, the most ancient of whom [Clausus, a Sabine] was made at once a citizen and a noble of Rome, encourage me to govern by the same policy of transferring to this city all conspicuous merit, wherever found.
>
> And indeed I know, as facts, that the Julii came from Alba, the Coruncanii from Camerium, the Porcii from Tusculum, and not to inquire too minutely into the past, that new members have been brought into the Senate from Etruria and Lucania and the whole of Italy, that Italy itself was at last extended to the Alps, to the end that not only single persons but entire countries and tribes might be united under our name. We had unshaken peace at home; we prospered in all our foreign relations, in the days when Italy beyond the Po was admitted to share our citizenship, and when, enrolling in our ranks the most vigorous of the provincials, under color of settling our legions throughout the world, we recruited our exhausted empire. Are we sorry that the Balbi came to us from Spain, and other men not less illustrious from Narbon Gaul? Their descendants are still among us, and do not yield to us in patriotism.
>
> What was the ruin of Sparta and Athens, but this, that mighty as they were in war, they spurned from them as aliens those whom they had conquered? Our founder Romulus, on the other hand, was so wise that he fought as enemies and then hailed as fellow-citizens several nations on the very same day. Strangers have reigned over us. That freedmen's sons should be entrusted with public offices is not, as many wrongly think, a sudden innovation, but was a common practice in the old commonwealth. But, it will be said, we have fought with the Senones. I suppose then that the Volsci and Aequi never stood in array against us. Our city was taken by the Gauls. Well, we also gave hostages to the Etruscans, and passed under the yoke of the Samnites. On the whole, if you review all our wars, never has one been finished in a shorter time than that with the Gauls. Thenceforth they have preserved an unbroken and loyal peace. United as they now are with us by manners, education, and intermarriage, let them bring us their gold and their wealth rather than enjoy it in isolation.
>
> Everything, Senators, which we now hold to be of the highest antiquity, was once new. Plebeian magistrates came after patrician; Latin magistrates after plebeian; magistrates of other Italian peoples after Latin. This practice too will establish itself, and what we are this day justifying by precedents, will be itself a precedent. (Tacitus, *Annals* 11.24)

This passage shows that Rome's policy of assimilation had not been passively experienced but, from a certain moment on, actively embraced and desired.

C. Low Empire

Italy continued to lose its special privileges: its administrative divisions were the same as elsewhere in the Empire. Without entering into detail about successive changes, let us focus on the state's organization at the time of Constantine.

[26] François Guizot, *A Popular History of France, from the Earliest Times*, vol. 1, trans. Robert Black (Boston: Dana Estes and Charles Lauriat, n.d.), chap. 3.

There were 85 *provinces* under governors (*præses*), who no longer held a military role, yet retained important judicial functions. These provinces were organized into fifteen *dioceses,* each led by a *vicaire,* and grouped under three, then four *praetorian prefectures* (two in the east, Illyricum and Orient, and two in the west, Italy-Africa and Gaul). This reflected an obvious effort to rationalize and harmonize the administration. At the same time, nonurbanized ("uncivilized") barbarian tribes were allowed to settle within the borders of the Empire: they retained their traditional tribal headmen and customs, though they remained under the governor's surveillance.

Under the administrative level of the province were the cities, the true building blocks of the Empire (under the cities were the *vici* and the *pagi;* small agglomerations were called *castella*).[27]

Rome and *Constantinople* were special cases. The people of Rome no longer held any political power, now in the hands of high public servants: city prefects, officers charged with the supervision of grain supplies (*praefectus annonae*), *vigiles* (the "watchmen," i.e., the police and firefighters of ancient Rome), and superintendents in charge of aqueducts and public works. Overseeing these officials was the prefect of the city (*praefectus urbi*), in turn supervised by the praetorian prefect. In Constantinople, there was a Senate based on the Roman model, albeit without the same prestige.

Sometimes, ordinary cities retained their names from when they were colonies and *municipia.* But their institutions were normalized. The three main organs of the High Empire—the *populus,* decurions, and magistrates—survived unchanged. The decurion council became known as the *curiale order:* membership in the order was based on a tax qualification and was hereditary. Since the *ordo* (the local council) was liable for the city's tax obligation from the pocket of its members, capital flight (toward the clergy and monastic life) increased steadily. Among the magistrates, the curator of the city was supreme (we mentioned the sporadic appearance of this institution under the High Empire above). The emperor also created a new function, the *guardian of the plebeians,* to protect citizens from unscrupulous local nobility.

VII. Social Orders

Social orders in Rome were not merely sociological or economic issues, as perhaps in other cities. They were clearly institutional and political because in the rigidly hierarchical Roman society social orders were established by law.

A. Under the Republic

At the beginning of the Republic, *patricians* and *plebeians* opposed each other. But, because the plebeians gained access to the magistracies rather quickly, additional social stratifications came into being. The ruling class gradually subdivided into two branches, which under the Empire became two legally defined classes: *senators* and *equites* or "knights" (the Roman equestrian class). The ruling fraction of the senatorial class was called the *nobilitas* (aristocracy).[28]

[27] The *vici* were villages, the *pagi* were districts. It is not clear whether the various parts of the administrative system—*vici, pagi, civitates*—were tightly structured in ancient Gaul. The *pagi* became the Carolingian "cantons."

[28] See Humbert, *Institutions politiques et sociales,* 201–07.

1. *Knights and Senators*

The origin of knights (*equites*) dates back to the founding of the censitary classes (based on an income and asset assessment), introduced by Servius Tullius.

The *knights* were the wealthiest citizens, those who could afford to keep horses in the service of the state. There were 1,800 knights. Censors updated the membership list every five years. The title of *eques* was for life, until it became hereditary after the second century BC. During the first half of the Republic, the entire wealthy class, including senators, belonged to the equestrian order. With the conquests, however, new wealth appeared throughout Italy and in the provinces. Senators also grew wealthier. The harmony and traditional moral ideals of the political class appeared to come under threat.

Then a plebeian tribune passed the *lex Claudia* (218 BC), which prohibited senators from participating in moneymaking ventures. They had to choose between wealth—and be only knights—or power—and be only senators. Thus, the two orders were separated (the separation became a legal reality in 129 BC: when taking their place in the Senate, senators had to surrender "the public horse" and formally ceased to be "knights"). No longer able to pursue a career of honors, the *equites* made up for this by undertaking careers in banking, trade, tax farms, public contracts (*publicans* were nonsenatorial knights, who entered into public contracts). Thus began a rivalry between the two orders, representing two opposing notions of power and social achievement. Soon the choice between the two became a family choice: in the second century BC, some three-quarters of the senators were sons or grandsons of senators.

2. *Nobilitas*

The *nobilitas* was comprised of all the patrician and plebeian families who could boast a former consul among its members. It totaled no more than a few dozen families. It was a closed caste: between 366 and 66 BC, only 15 consuls did not belong to the *nobilitas*. In the first century BC, 89 percent of consuls came from a consular family; 5 percent belonged to praetorian families (thus, the *nobilitas* represented only a small portion of the senatorial class; the two notions must not be confused).

Although it did not have the same sources of income as the *equites,* the *nobilitas* was, nevertheless, immensely wealthy. It owned vast tracts of land, having divided up the *ager publicus* among themselves. And because the proconsuls governed the provinces, again the *nobilitas* grew rich through spoliation.

Noteworthy is the failed attempt at democracy led by Appius Claudius. Censor in 312 BC, influenced by Greek ideas, Appius Claudius opened all the tribes to freed slaves (before this, emancipated slaves could belong only to the rural or "rustic tribe"). This was a harsh blow to the oligarchy of the senators and their clients. Appius Claudius went so far as to allow the sons of freed slaves to enter the Senate. However, in 304 BC, these measures were annulled and the *nobilitas* seized power again.

Rome's success can be attributed at least in part to the continuity of policies decided by this uniform group of aristocrats with shared interests and ideals. They accumulated vast political experience and transmitted it within their "caste" from generation to generation. Although Rome had no written constitution and boasted only a small number of political thinkers, political science nevertheless survived informally through this caste tradition. Caste members were genuinely devoted to the state. They held their rank (*dignitas*) and defended a sense of their duties (*officia*); they also had a claim on public honors (*honos*). They were widely respected and enjoyed immense influence and prestige (*auctoritas*).

The Roman Republic was an oligarchy: if everyone kept to their place prescribed by birth, all would be well. This was a far cry from the Athenian idea of democratic equality, based on the quick rotation of responsibility that enabled anyone to attain high public office through the drawing of lots. But Greece had been defeated; Rome was the victor. The *populares* would not achieve their aim. It seems that the *nobilitas* controlled all Roman institutions—the magistracies, the Senate, and the assemblies.

B. Under the High Empire

Augustus tried to define and control the structure of society through a series of legislative measures: some bearing on the family, others restricting the two forms of social mobility (the emancipation of slaves and the granting of citizenship to the peregrines); and others still establishing very strict conditions of membership in the upper classes.[29]

1. *The Senatorial Class and the Laticlave*

Since the time of Caesar, who had significantly increased the number of senators, many sons of senators and knights had taken to wearing the senator's *laticlave,* a distinctive mark of clothing with a broad purple band worn on the fore part of the tunic. In 18 BC Augustus restricted this privilege to the sons of senators; the sons of knights were only allowed to wear the *clavus angustus,* a new ornament of clothing with a narrow purple stripe running down the tunic. This was the first step in the creation of a hereditary senatorial class.

Between 18 and 13 BC, Augustus levied a *cens,* a tax assessment on senators. From this moment on, the qualification for a quaestorship, and therefore access to the Senate, would be one million *sestertii* (to become a knight, 400,000 *sestertii*). Even if one had such wealth, there was an additional requirement: the *ius honorum,* a special right of holding office, not granted to people of provincial origin. Finally, under Caligula, a true aristocratic senatorial class was established, since qualification for membership was the *laticlave* awarded by the emperor, and not the mere fact of being a senator. Thus, the senatorial class numbered many more members than there were senators in the Senate, no doubt between 2,000 and 3,000 members under Caligula.

2. *The Equestrian Class*

The emperor, as censor, personally granted the certificate of knighthood. A knight wore the *clavus angustus,* a golden ring, and enjoyed reserved seats at the games. The equestrian order organized an annual parade on July 15. The order was not hereditary (only sons of senators were born knights, as they waited to become senators); it was, therefore, an "open" order: the emperor awarded merits, thereby creating loyal followers, an elite of high-quality public servants who in time controlled all the major offices and functions of the state.

Throughout their reigns, emperors set aside a fixed number of positions and effectively established a *cursus honorum* that paralleled that of the senators. For senators the order of office was military tribunes, *vigintivirs,*[30] quaestors, plebeian tribunes, praetors, consuls. For knights it was prefects of the cohort, *clavus angustus* tribunes of the legion, prefects of the wing, procurators,[31] and, finally, prefects of the fleet, prefects of *vigiles,* prefects of provisions, prefects of Egypt,[32] praetorian prefects. There were some 10,000 to 15,000 knights (the total population at the beginning of the High Empire was approximately 4 million citizens).

---

[29] Cf. Marcel Le Glay, Jean-Louis Voisin, and Yann Le Bohec, *Histoire romaine* [Roman history] (Paris: Presses Universitaires de France, 1991), 197–203.

[30] Junior officials in charge of minting coins, judging certain legal cases, maintaining roads, and carrying out capital punishments.

[31] In the chancellery, in finance, in imperial provinces; different wages (60,000 *sestertii,* 100,000, 200,000, 300,000) corresponded to different grades.

[32] Senators were not allowed in this province, which was the special preserve of the emperor.

C. Under the Low Empire

Fourth century society was even more hierarchical. These hierarchies were fixed by the emperor's legislation. The law required certain professions to organize as *corporations;* it also imposed *hereditary* transmission. Before long it reached the point where there was no equality before the law because the state admitted a status difference between *honestiores* (senators, knights, decurions) and *humiliores* (all others), who were not given the same treatment in the courts.[33]

1. *The Elite*

At the top was the senatorial class. It, too, was ordered hierarchically. In the fifth century AD there were three categories of members for this class alone: *clarissimi, spectabiles,* and *illustri.* A nonhereditary title was created: "Patrice."

At this time, in addition to the great Italian and provincial families, bureaucratic officials from Ravenna as well as Germanic officers (Clovis held the title of Patrice) were allowed into the Senate of Rome. The less prestigious Senate of Constantinople was even more "democratic": it admitted bureaucrats, provincial figures, intellectuals (like the Neoplatonist Jamblic, in the middle of the fourth century), and even people from the popular social classes.

The equestrian class, which had now held the lion's share of high positions, was a victim of its own success: under Constantine, knights were finally incorporated into the senatorial class.

2. *The Curiales*

Landowners, provincial notables, the liberal professions (lawyers, physicians, academics) were admitted into the *curiale class,* the new name for the decurions. In each city the members of this class were in charge of the local municipal administration and the collection of local taxes. Since they were personally liable for meeting the tax collection targets of the entire city, they put their fellow citizens under enormous pressure and unsurprisingly were loathed. However, they could not resign their position, which was hereditary. Some tried to escape the profession by joining the clergy or becoming monks.

But the office remained honorary. Well-to-do youth prepared to take up their future office by joining and actively engaging in a municipal college or ephebia. Society in provincial cities was also hierarchical. Greetings were presented to the governor in a well-defined order: senators first, then the governor's cabinet members, the clergy (or, under Julian the Apostate, the former priests of the Imperial cult), the employees of the provincial administration, and finally the curiales.

At the bottom of the social order were the *humiliores:* workers, tradespeople, farmers, slaves (the Church did not abolish slavery: it asked only that slave masters treat their slaves more humanely), barbarians, which had settled on territory in the Empire but had not assimilated into local society. The majority of farmers, as we saw, were subject to the so-called *colonate,* which prefigured medieval serfdom.

Such, then, were the Roman public institutions. But it should be noted that public law itself served to frame civic, private, and economic life, for which the Romans developed a *private law* of unprecedented sophistication.

---

[33] Cf. Le Glay, Voisin, and Le Bohec, *Histoire romaine,* 492–501.

Chapter 3

Private Law

In the early days of Rome, it seems that there was a customary, spoken law, interpreted and enforced by the heads of family clans (*gentes*). It evolved with the emergence of federal monarchy: now the king was called upon when the security of the group was threatened, or in cases of parricide or betrayal (*perduellio*). When, under Etruscan autocrats, a city-state emerged, it took responsibility for handling the growing number of disputes and petty crimes. All the same, the law remained unwritten, interpreted by the pontiffs, all of whom belonged to the patrician class. This is why the plebeians protested, leading to the adoption of the Law of the Twelve Tables, where many of the rules of civil law were itemized and set down in writing.

From this time on, it is convenient to divide the history of Roman law into three periods, corresponding to three successive judicial *procedures*. The earliest period, ca. 450–150 BC, corresponds to the *legis actio* system of law (or the *actions of the law*). Next, from 150 BC until the end of the High Empire, we have the so-called *formulary procedure*. And finally, under the Low Empire, the *cognitio* or *extraordinary procedure*.[1]

[1] See Gaudemet, *Les institutions de l'antiquité* [The institutions of antiquity]; Humbert, *Institutions politiques et sociales* [Social and political institutions in antiquity]; Robert Villiers, *Rome et le droit privé* [Rome and private law] (Paris: Albin Michel, 1977); Gabriel Lepointe, *Droit romain et ancien droit français (Droit des biens)* [Roman law and ancient French law (property law)] (Paris: Précis Dalloz, 1958); P. G. Stein, "Roman Law," in *The Cambridge History of Medieval Political Thought*, ed. James Henderson Burns (Cambridge: Cambridge University Press, 1988).

I. The Period of *Legis Actio* (450–150 BC)

A. Judicial Organization

In Rome's early days, justice was a private affair, handled within the *gens*. For this reason, when disputes broke out between members of different *gentes*, the threat of *vendetta* was never far. It was largely to avoid this that the first federated allied monarchy was created. But the transition from "tribal" justice to "state" justice—that is, a justice under state control—did not occur all at once. The king undertook to channel private claims of revenge into fixed and controlled public practices under his authority, though he did not take complete charge of the process himself, nor did he administer his ruling personally. Traces of his hands-off approach survived in Rome for a very long time. The trial remained a private affair, at least partially, in the sense that the parties to a conflict continued to play a central role in every phase of the procedure. It was not until the Low Empire that justice became entirely an affair of the state, administered solely at the behest of the agents of the state and backed exclusively by the state's coercive powers.

This character is marked by the division of civil trials into *two stages*. First, the public magistrate "reads the law"; that is, he describes in legal terms the action to be opened, after which he appoints a judge. This is the *in jure* stage ("according to law"). Then comes the stage called *apud judicem* ("before the judge"). The state hardly intervened at all, since the *judge was a private person* and the parties to the conflict retained a central role in carrying out the ruling themselves.

In the early days, the magistrates in charge of *jurisdictio* (legal justice) possessed *imperium* (political power). Then, after 367 BC, a specialized magistrate with the title of *praetor* began to handle disputes. Later (from 242 onward, it seems), he doubled with a "praetor for non-Roman citizens" (*praetor peregrinus*) for trials between *peregrini* ("strangers," that is, foreigners) and, probably also, between *peregrini* and Roman citizens.

The magistrate administered justice in a given place—at the tribunal (*comitium*)—on given days, determined by a legal calendar of religious origin.

B. The Procedure

In this first period, the procedure was determined by the "actions of the law" (*legis actiones*), so-called because these actions were created or recognized by the law (the law stipulated that they should be used in specific cases; the magistrate's power was not arbitrary). The chief characteristic of the procedure was its rigid formalism: certain acts and exact words were required on pain of annulment: this restricted access to the procedures to individuals familiar with the proper forms, therefore to Roman citizens, to the exclusion of foreigners (which is why it was necessary to create a special praetor and a specific, adapted procedure for them). From Gaius we know of five procedures (see below). Some served to establish a right, others were "actions of execution." Some predated the Law of the Twelve Tables. One (the *condictio*) dates to the third or second century BC.

Actions in favor of recognizing a right:

- *sacramentum* (sworn wager)
- *judicis arbitrive postulatio* (request for a *judex*—trial judge—or arbiter)
- *condictio* (summons)

Actions in favor of executing the law:

- *manus iniectio* (seizure)
- *pignoris capio* (taking a pledge)

For a better understanding of how these actions worked in practice, we need to describe each phase of the proceedings step-by-step.

1. *The* In Jure *Phase*

The lawsuit begins with a summons (*in ius vocatio*). A person cites another against whom he has a claim. Neither the magistrate nor the state intervenes at this point in the proceedings. The plaintiff can use force to bring the defendant before the magistrate. Both the plaintiff and the defendant must appear in person: Roman law was not familiar with the concept of a legal representative, initially at any rate (it was gradually introduced in cases of tutelage or when one of the litigants was a prisoner of the enemy, or when he was in public service at some distance from the trial venue, or if he was too ill or too old to attend in person).

The *in jure* phase proper—before the magistrate—involved one of three possible actions.

The *sacramentum* (sworn wager) was the oldest and the most general procedure. It involved the following steps:

- *The rei vindicatio.* The plaintiff makes his claim on the "thing," which was present materially, either in whole or in part, if the "thing" was a movable item of property, or symbolically, if it was immovable (e.g., a piece of earth symbolized a piece of land). The plaintiff holds a wand [*vindicta*] in his hand, the symbol of his power. Placing it on the thing, he lays claim to it. At the same time, he speaks the ritual phrases.

Gaius, in his *Institutes* (see below), gives the example of a plaintiff's claim to a slave: "Hunc ego hominem ex jure Quiritium meum esse aio, secundum suam causam. Sicut dixi ecce tibi vindictam imposui" (I affirm that this slave is mine according to quiritary[2] right, based on the *causa* [uncertain meaning]. As I said, I lay claim to it by placing this *vindicta* on you). Whatever the exact meaning of these words, they clearly state the plaintiff's claim to his right of ownership of the thing. Then the defendant speaks exactly the same words and uses exactly the same gestures (*contra-vindicatio*). Thus, through such symmetry, the dispute becomes tangible (the suggestion has been made that this physical display of conflict in the procedure symbolizes the acting out of a fight).

- *The magistrate's intervention.* The magistrate immediately interrupts the dispute and says to both: "Release this man." This removes the threat of physical violence and makes way for the law.
- *The provocatio of the plaintiff by sworn wager.* The plaintiff now addresses his opponent, asking him by what right he claims ownership of the thing. The other simply reasserts his claim. The plaintiff then provokes his opponent in these terms: "Since you have made a wrongful claim of ownership, I challenge you in a wager (*sacramentum*) of 500 [or 50, depending on the thing's value] *as*."[3]

The other party replies in the same terms, making the same wager. Then the antagonists deposit the agreed sum with the pontiff, or promise to do so. The party found to be in the wrong loses his money (his money will be not handed over to the plaintiff; it will be deposited in the public treasury).

[2] Quirites: the ancient name of the Romans; it came from one of the original gods of the Roman pantheon, Quirinus (the name given to deified Romulus).

[3] The *as* was a Roman monetary unit. Writing in the second century AD, Gaius used a term contemporary to his time. However, in ancient times, when coins did not exist, the wager was cattle or sheep, depending on the sums at stake in the dispute. It is difficult to understand what the *sacramentum* actually was. It was not an oath in the true sense of the term (in which case, one would say *ius iurandum*); it was more likely a wager that the gods were called upon to witness, that is, a *sworn wager* (the words, at any rate, suggest a sacred act).

Thus, the focus of the trial is to determine which of the two has made a *sacramentum iniustum*, a false oath. This appears to be the magistrate's sole concern and the only decision he has to take. Of course, this decision will determine the outcome of the case. The entire procedure reveals traces of its ancient origins: the state is reluctant to involve itself in private quarrels; it concerns itself only with matters that might sully or pollute the community and, in so doing, bring down the wrath of the gods.

It is important to stress the *formalism* of the procedure. If the required words were not pronounced exactly as prescribed, the magistrate had a duty to void the legal action, regardless of his personal opinion on the merits of the suit.[4]

- *The appointment of a judge*. Next, the magistrate appoints a judge who must call a hearing within a prescribed time frame.

The final act in the *in jure* proceeding is the *litis contestatio,* that is, "confirmation of the trial by witnesses." The magistrate calls the audience to witness the legality of the formalities: "be witnesses," he proclaims. From then on the trial proceedings are "bound"; neither party can change its position. The suit must proceed along the exact lines and focus determined by the magistrate. The judge is not allowed to waver from this established framework.

Though complicated, the *sacramentum* remained the most widespread recourse to justice during this period, until the generalization of the formulary system of procedures. Two simpler, less ritualized procedures were also used: "a request for a judge or an arbiter" and a "summons," but they were only used for certain types of lawsuits.

2. *The* Apud Judicem *Phase*

In this phase, there is only one judge. As noted earlier, he is a private person, not a magistrate. Nevertheless, he is not just anybody: he is chosen from a list that contains only the names of notables. Initially, they were all patricians, but then the senators monopolized access to the judicial function. Finally, senators and knights rivaled each other for the privilege of judicial service (this lasted until the Low Empire, when the judge became a public servant).

The judge, like the magistrate, sits in the forum; the trial is public. A defendant, who fails to appear in court, automatically loses his case.

The court case itself is not formalistic. The judge hears both parties (or their lawyers), checks the facts, and gives his ruling—theoretically the same evening—which consists primarily in judging which of the two parties has spoken the truth and, therefore, sworn justly. His ruling must be utterly independent: the Law of the Twelve Tables, then the praetor, would punish a corrupt or partial judge.

The ruling was not an act of authority as such. It was an opinion; it showed the judge's way of thinking (*sententia*). The litigants had to draw their own conclusions, particularly who was the party in the right. And just as the plaintiff used personal means to force his adversary to appear in court, he had to personally execute the judge's ruling without automatic assistance from the coercive power of the public order.

The judgment, however, enabled the victor to carry out one of two legal actions (called actions of execution): the action of *manus iniectio* or the action of *pignoris capio*. It is worth

[4] For example, the Law of the Twelve Tables allowed for "legal action for the removal of a tree." Gaius explains that if a plaintiff, whose vines were damaged, makes a claim for "the removal of a vine," the case should be dismissed. The same happens if a plaintiff speaks of a *membrum ruptum* (broken limb), rather than of an *os fractum* (broken bone) as stipulated in the law.

looking at these actions somewhat more closely, as they reveal the very archaic nature of the entire system.

• *The manus iniectio (seizure).* This procedure applies to a defendant who refuses to appear before a judge (*manus iniectio vocati*) or who rejects the application of the judgment (*manus iniectio iudicati*). According to the Law of the Twelve Tables, the winner of a lawsuit obliges the loser to appear before the magistrate within 30 days of the judge's ruling. The winner places his hand on the loser and speaks the following ritual formula: "Because you were condemned to pay me 10,000 *sestertii* [for example], and you did not, I therefore engage against you *manus iniectio iudicati.*" If the loser still refuses to obey, and if he can find no one to put up a guarantee for him, the magistrate issues a conviction (*addictio*), following which the winner takes possession of the loser: he is entitled to seize the loser by force, to take him to his house and put him in chains where he can hold him for up to 60 days with the sole obligation to feed him and show him in public three times. If after 60 days either the loser or a close friend or relative still have not fulfilled the terms of the ruling, the winner obtains full rights over the debtor: he can kill him, sell him into slavery, or put him to work in his own household. In the event that several creditors hold claims on the debtor, the Law of the Twelve Tables stipulates that they can cut up the body among themselves.

Manus iniectio existed until the beginning of the Roman Empire, although it was relaxed somewhat (the right to kill or sell the loser into bondage fell into disuse).

• *The pignoris capio (seize as a pledge).* This is the seizure of an item of movable property from the debtor as a pledge. It was an ancient action that, by the classical age, was no longer in use except in very exceptional cases, all under public or religious law, not private law. A soldier could use the procedure to obtain his wages or the money he spent for his equipment; likewise a tax collector could resort to this action to coerce recalcitrant taxpayers, or a seller to obtain the agreed-upon price, if he sold an animal for the sacrifices. The application of the procedure does not require the intervention of a magistrate or a judge. Except for the observation of certain poorly understood forms and the utterance of solemn formulas, the procedure comes across as an act of pure violence.

This, then, is how justice was delivered in the early centuries of Rome. But, by what right were these procedures respected?

C. The Sources of Rights

At this time, there were fundamentally three sources of right: *custom, the law,* and *doctrine.*

• *Custom.* "Ancestral customs" (*mos maiorum*) had great authority, whether in the form of religious rules or civic practices (marriage, names, etc.).

• *The law.* The word *lex* (law or enactment) was widely used. It was applied to private contracts (*lex contractus*), corporate statutes (*lex collegii*), and in the proper sense of laws, *leges publicae.*

In Rome, public laws, that is, laws voted by the assemblies, were relatively rare, compared with the legislative activity of a modern state. Some 800 laws were passed in the period between the Republic and the Principate. Most concerned political matters (absorption and assimilation of the plebeians in the city) or economic issues (agrarian laws). Only 26 pertained to civil law (one of these was the Law of the Twelve Tables, which (as discussed above) contained numerous important dispositions of private law on matters of substance and procedure).

• *Doctrine.* To apply the law in real cases, it is necessary to be familiar with it, interpret it, and complete it. This responsibility falls to specialists, whose knowledge is called "doctrine." In ancient Rome, because the law still had a sacred character, these specialists were pontiffs, a council of priests familiar with the legal calendar (the auspicious and inauspicious days) and the customary ritual formulations to be used. Their intervention remained necessary even after the law was set down in writing with the Law of the Twelve Tables. All of these specialists were patricians, which explains why a "democratic" claim emerged in time for a disclosure of their science.[5]

D. The Period of the Formulary System (from the End of the Republic to the High Empire)

During this period more flexibility appeared in the procedure, which in time led to an entirely new civil law.

1. *Formulary Procedure*

The exact origins of the new system are not well known; it had been in use for some time when two laws made it official: *lex Aebutia* (end of the second century BC; it formally authorizes the formulary procedure) and *lex Julia* (17 BC, under Augustus; it totally abolished the old *legis actio*, except in a few residual cases).

One source may have been the constraints placed on the peregrine praetor in charge of deciding cases between foreigners. Because a foreigner's suit did not fit the familiar norms of the *legis actio*, the peregrine praetor had to give his instructions to the judge in concise *formulæ* (the origin of the name "procedure by formula" or "formulary procedure"). The body of formularies that the praetor intended for use in legal matters constituted his *edict* (see below).

The formulary procedure is flexible: for each new situation, that is, each new case, the praetor looks for and finds an appropriate formulary. The procedure is broad: the praetor is not restricted by the law; he can create many new rights. It is in the conciseness, exactness, abstractness, and versatility of the praetor's formularies that the full genius of Roman jurists, magistrates, and jurisconsults comes to expression.

The formulary system incorporates classical elements (such as the appointment of a judge) and secondary elements (such as "instructions"—conditions benefiting either the plaintiff or the defendant, or "exceptions"—the terms according to which the recognition of the plaintiff's rights are subordinated). But the core of the procedure is the "intention" (*intentio*)—a few words situating the category of offense that the praetor recognizes in the facts that he accepts for judgment, and the "condemnation" (*condemnatio*)—a statement as to the nature of the condemnation and the amount of compensation that the judge is authorized to award in the event that the facts invoked in the *intentio* are upheld. Actions are classified according to *intentio* and *condemnatio*. Over time, jurisconsults made distinctions between several classes of action. The following examples give a rough idea of this:

- *Civil* actions. They simply take over the old *legis actiones*,[6] adapting them to the style of the formularies.
- *Praetorian* actions. Civil law, for example, acknowledges an action of theft, but it is restricted to Roman citizens. In order to protect the peregrine against theft, the praetor resorts to a fiction. He instructs the judge to act "as if the plaintiff were a citizen." Such "fictive" action in praetorian law approaches the action of theft in civil law.

---

[5] The forms of action were divulged by Gnaeus Flavius, ca. 304 BC (thus, "Flavian law"). As soon as plebeians gained access to the great pontificate, the first titular office holder, Tiberius Coruncanius, made his consultations in public. Others followed his example and gradually a nonreligious science of the law developed. One of the earliest treatises on civil law was written by Sextus Aelius Paetus Catus, ca. 200 BC.

[6] In the *sacramentum*, for example, the plaintiff would say, "aio hunc hominem meum esse" ("I affirm that this man is mine"). The praetor's formula would say, "If it appears that this man is his, then, judge, you must give him satisfaction." The action is fundamentally the same.

• Actions *in factum* (as distinguished from action *in ius*). The praetor simply asks the judge to verify that certain facts of the case are true and to condemn or acquit, as the case may be. It is in such instances that the praetor has the greatest freedom and can deviate most from civil law. He can innovate, particularly in matters of contract law, and create useful concepts like *deposit, security, mortgage,* and so on.

• *Direct* actions and *actio utilis*. The latter is an extension of the former applied to new areas. For example, the action which punishes the occupant of an apartment for throwing something from a window and injuring someone below (*actio de effusis et deiectis*) is extended under the form of an *actio utilis* to something thrown from the bridge of a ship rather than from a building.

• *Real* actions and *personal* actions. These are used to assert, respectively, a right *erga omnes,* that is, in relation to everyone (such as the ownership of movable property of some kind), or a personal right, that is, a right of claim on a particular debtor.

• Actions of *strict law* and *bona fide* actions (*ex bona fide*). This second category includes the new actions created by the praetor to ensure that content prevails over form, and the spirit of the law over the letter.

• *Certain* and *uncertain* actions. The former concerns a particular object (specified movables or immovables, a specified amount of money); the latter refers to an object that has not yet been assigned a value.

Examples of Formularies[7]

• *For an action* in ius, *civil, direct, real, and certain*

"Titus, be judge. If it results (*si paret*) that this man belongs to Aulus Agerius, according to quiritary right, then as judge condemn Numerius Negidius to pay Aulus Agerius 10,000 *sestertii;* if it does not result so, then acquit him (*si non paret, absolve*)

(or) as judge, condemn NN to pay AA the value in money to be determined for this thing (if it belongs to AA); if it not be so, acquit him."[8]

• *For an action* in ius, *civil, direct, personal, strict, and certain, with transfer of persons*[9]

"Titus, be judge. If it results that NN should give Publius Naevus 10,000 *sestertii,* then as judge condemn NN to pay Lucius Titius 10,000 *sestertii;* if it not be so, acquit him."

• *For a praetorian action,* in ius, *direct, personal, bona fide, and certain, with a restitution clause*

"Titus, be judge. Given that AA has remitted a silver table in deposit to NN, and given that NN if he is in good faith must return [this deposit] to AA, then as judge condemn NN to do so to AA, unless he otherwise returns it; if it not be so, acquit him."

• *For a praetorian action,* in factum, *direct, personal, and certain, with the amount of the fine left to the appreciation of the judge*

"Titius, be judge. If it results that AA remitted a silver table to NN and that NN did not return it to him, thereby defrauding him (*dolus malus*), then as judge condemn NN to restore to AA the value in money that the thing has; if it not be so, acquit him."

[7] Quoted in Gaudemet, *Les institutions de l'antiquité,* 371–72.

[8] Aulus Agerius is a fictitious name identifying the plaintiff, the one who takes action (*agere*). Numerius Negidius is a fictitious name identifying the defender, the one who denies (*negare*).

[9] This is yet another procedure created by a praetorian formulary: the aim was to remedy the absence of a legal representation mechanism (which would be invented much later). If a son or a slave incurred a debt or a claim, and since he had no wealth of his own, either his father or master or guardian was named in the *condemnatio,* whereas the son or the slave were named in the *intentio.*

It is easy to see how such procedures could be instrumental in creating new rights and new legal concepts. With his *intentio,* the magistrate gives notice of the actions he promises to grant litigants. "With his promise of an action, the praetor creates a right, because he recognizes that a given circumstance merits legal protection . . . . Insofar as a citizen is able to obtain legal action before a judge, he can claim that he has rights."[10]

The concept of the *sales contract,* for example, comes into existence when the praetor decides one day to help the unpaid vendor by promising him an action: the *action of selling.* Because the praetor recognizes the vendor's right to make a claim if after selling an item he does not receive payment, and because the buyer is for all intents and purposes liable from a legal standpoint, the praetor's action introduces a specific legal relationship between the two parties: a *sales contract.*

The profound changes, which Roman society was undergoing at the time, offered the praetors countless situations for the creation of new formularies of action. It seems that the peregrine praetor played an active role in this. Foreigners were unfamiliar with the forms of quiritary right; neither did they observe Roman religious practices. Moreover, since the Empire was expanding, the parties to a lawsuit were not necessarily close neighbors with the opportunity of meeting face-to-face. In Rome itself, economic life was developing.

> It became necessary to consider various forms of nonformal commitment, which the law—basically the old, unchanged Law of the Twelve Tables—had not been able to conceive of up to this point. Goodwill was needed to establish and execute contracts that the archaic rituals, gestures, and solemn formulas were unfamiliar with. Legal practices had to keep pace with economic progress; a closed agrarian society could get by with cash sales and short-term loans among friends. But with the conquests, something more was required, such as credit (and the notions of trust and *fides*), transactions between absent parties, and above all obligations arising by mutual agreement. Since the law no longer kept pace with these changes, it was the praetor who, through his daily activity as an administrator of justice, could shake up the system.[11]

In recognition of their practical usefulness the urban praetor adopted many of the formularies initially developed for lawsuits involving foreigners.

It was during this period—from the middle of the second century BC to the end of the first century, when the formulary system was at the peak of its vitality—that family law, inheritance law, property law, and contract law—the most creative and most enduring of Roman contributions to universal law—made their appearance.

2. *The Magistrate's Edict (Praetorian Law)*

Rights created by the formulary procedure are crystallized in *the edict of the magistrate.* The edict is a text made public by the magistrate at the beginning (or sometime during the year) of his tenure; in it he notifies the rules he intends to be guided by in the performance of his duties during his mandate.

Since it was the praetors who made use of the formulary system (and the praetor was the signal point of reference for the other magistrates), the traditional term for the rights created by his edict was "praetorian law." Similarly, because praetors and other judicial magistrates were men vested with "honors," another expression for such rights is "honorary law." *Praetorian law* and *honorary law* are quite distinct (and separate doctrinally) from the old *civil law,* which was created or acknowledged by the law and that the two former laws sometimes complete and

---

[10] Gaudemet, *Les institutions de l'antiquité,* 327.

[11] Humbert, *Institutions politiques et sociales,* 318.

sometimes amend. Conversely, since civil law is by definition reserved to Roman citizens (*cives*), praetorian law is more universal and tends to be valid for all inhabitants of territories under Roman authority.

Ordinarily, the praetor's edict was applicable only during the year of his mandate. But it became the practice of each new praetor to reissue his predecessor's edict, adding a few decisions of his own (*pars nova*); this innovative license gave the legal system extraordinary flexibility and equipped it to assimilate whatever new situations were created by the evolutions of Roman society for over 250 years. At the same time, there was a sort of "natural selection" of the rules of law that produced a legacy of rules with permanent value.

Finally, under the Empire, because elected and independent praetors no longer existed, and accordingly no praetorian judicial creation existed either, the praetor's permanent legacy was set down in written form as a "perpetual edict" that not only collated all praetorian edicts, but also arranged them in order.

Edicts were organized under titles and sections (according to the phases of the lawsuit), and the formularies created by each successive edict were indicated. This made the edicts a useful guide for practitioners. The effort of "codifying the edicts" took place at the beginning of the second century and is thought to have been the work of the jurisconsult Julian by order of the Emperor Hadrian.

3. *Other Innovations in the Period of the Formulary System*

During this period there were innovations in the procedure, in the definition of the sources of the laws, and in jurisprudence. Concerning *procedure,* there were innovations at each phase of the legal process. Some appear minor, but they reveal general progress toward greater precision in justice.

For example, improvements were made to the *summons* procedure and to the use of *legal representatives.*[12] A solution was found to ensure the appearance of recalcitrant defendants before the magistrate and the judge. Thought was given to the *rules of evidence.* Even if an oath still played a role, written evidence had more importance than in the past. On the other hand, the judge was bound by the formula: in this sense, the trial remained very formalist. The judge could not hear new elements in the case if they were unknown to the magistrate. He could not correct material errors, which may have slipped into the formula. He could not condemn the party at fault to more or less than what was stipulated in the formula.

Another example is the principle of the binding force of the *res iudicata.* First, this was an indirect and imperfect consequence of the *litis contestatio,* then it became a general principle at the beginning of the Empire as legal experts put forward the idea of the public interest. A new trial could not be opened if it concerned the same suit, or if the claim was based on the same legal title, or if the litigants acted in the same quality (but if one of these three conditions was not met, a new procedure could go forward).

Forms of *appeal* were also invented, though the earliest forms were indirect and challenged the magistrate, the judge, or the ruling: in the early days of the Empire, the possibility of appeal to the prince or the Senate arose. Lastly, while the state remained firm in its refusal to carry out the judgment, the winner of a case was offered new solutions to coerce the loser (such as the public auction of his properties).

As for the *sources of the law, custom* continued to play a preeminent role, especially in the provinces; the *law,* relatively unimportant in civil affairs, was gradually superseded by the

[12] The notion of "proxy" appeared. We will see below (pp. 607–08) how this concept was used in corporate canon theory and, thus, in the development of democratic ideas during the Middle Ages.

senatconsults (all comital legislation disappeared by the end of the first century BC), and by *imperial constitutions* under the Empire: the term grouped together several categories of legal rules created by the emperor.

• *Edicta.* With several magistracies under his control, the emperor held the classical *ius edendi* of the magistrates. However, the emperor's edicts were very different from the praetor's. The emperor published edicts as often as he deemed necessary. Their validity was not limited to his lifetime or rule; they were permanent and applicable beyond the emperor's death. They were not mere promises of action, but abstract legal enactments with general effect for the entire territory of the Empire. They were genuine laws.[13]

• *Decreta.* These were judgments pronounced by the emperor and set jurisprudence throughout the Empire.

• *Rescripta.* These were imperial responses on a point of law, coming from either the emperor or his council (the best legal minds of the Empire), formulated in reply to petitions from subordinate officials, magistrates, or private individuals. Again, the quality of the person providing the response gave the ruling its force (in this sense, the emperor and his council competed with the other jurisconsults).

• *Mandata.* They were primarily administrative and fiscal instructions from the emperor to his governors and subordinate officials. In theory, they had validity only in the province to which they were sent and for the duration of the emperor's rule. But, again, the tendency was to accord them general applicability.

And finally, concerning *jurisprudence* or *doctrine,* its development during this period was extraordinary.

We saw earlier that the science of the law, once the exclusive privilege of the pontiffs, was secularized and divulged to the public. The names of the earliest jurisconsults appeared at the end of the third century BC. By the fall of the Republic, the origins of jurisconsults were increasingly diverse; they were no longer exclusively members of the senatorial class, nor were they all Romans from Rome. Ever-growing numbers came from the provinces and, by the end of the second century, from the East (Greek countries began to adopt Roman law at this time: and, in the end, Greek legal experts eclipsed their Roman masters). But the teaching of the law for the purpose of introducing common standards among experts was not organized at the "university" level, like philosophy and rhetoric, until the Low Empire. As early as the first century there were already two "schools" (in the sense of discussion circles or ideological circles) of jurists: the *Proculians,* supposedly more formalist, and the *Sabinians,* thought to be less formalist and more trusting of authority.

From a methodological standpoint, the jurisconsults were traditionalists. When faced with new situations, instead of creating new rules *ex nihilo,* they resorted to existing rules and conducted an extensive, analogical interpretation (we will discuss some examples below). Moreover, trained in schools of rhetoric, *they were thoroughly familiar with Greek moral philosophy, especially Stoic philosophy;* this guided them in their interpretations.

The writings of Roman jurisconsults also appeared as doctrinal works (commentaries on civil law, the praetor's edict, imperial constitutions, etc.) or as practical works and teaching manuals.

[13] In France, under the Old Regime, the term *édit* (edict) was the equivalent of *loi* (law); for example, the Édit de Nantes (Edict of Nantes).

None of these works have come down to us directly, excepting the *Institutes* (a teaching manual) by Gaius (fl. middle of the second century AD under Emperor Antoninus Pius). We know these works from passages cited in subsequent text compilations, notably the compilations of Paulus and Ulpian, abundantly quoted in the *Digest of Justinian*. These passages are sufficient to provide a fairly precise idea of the original texts.

These writers had recourse to reasoning to fill in the missing gaps in the law: silences, contradictions, and unclarified implications of the law. Their solutions were accepted and adopted because the first jurisconsults—pontiffs and members of the senatorial class—enjoyed immense religious and political authority. Later, when legal experts no longer belonged to this social category, their authority came from a new source of prestige, the Augustan institution of *ius respondendi* (the right of legal reply).

Augustus "certified" a number of legal experts with the authority to publish an official response on a point of law or to a question "in the prince's name." Under the High Empire this "right of legal reply" was granted to some 30 jurists. The replies of "certified" jurists did not have the status of an official, legally binding decision for judges as such. But they did have authority and created precedents. Because they were sometimes contradictory, one of Hadrian's *rescripts* stipulated that the opinions of these "certified" legal experts were legally binding on the judge only if they were all in agreement (the rule of unanimity).

E. The Period of the Low Empire: *Cognitio*, or Extraordinary Procedure

As we begin, let us note a curious paradox. It seems that the law itself fell into relative decline between the High and Low Empires: it was less creative, technically of a lower standard, and its application throughout the Empire was less uniform (despite the Edict of Caracalla of 212 granting Roman citizenship to all the inhabitants of the Empire). Curiously, it was at the very moment that the Dominate was being formed—under the Severi dynasty, the pivotal dynasty between the two phases—that the greatest Roman jurists were at their productive best: Papinianus, Paulus, Ulpian.

The explanation for this paradox is hard to find. Perhaps it was the corollary of a time lag: the jurists were heirs to a centuries-old legacy of legal work, which they began to compile at the very moment that the regime, fated to oversee the decline of the law, came into existence. Or, paradoxically, perhaps the despotic absolutism of the Severi dynasty itself played some positive role, facilitating the improvement and completion of the legal system and the science of the law, because for the first time a sufficiently strong and centralized state took charge of the law.

1. *Extraordinary Procedure or* Cognitio

The system of *legis actiones* and the formulary system were said to belong to the *ordo iudiciorum privatorum* ("order of private judgment"). In contrast, the procedure, which appeared at the beginning of the High Empire and became widespread under the Low Empire, was called "extraordinary" because it enabled the emperor and his officials to short-circuit the order of private judgment. The new system was also called *cognitio* (the emperor and his representatives "had knowledge" of the issues).

"Extraordinary" procedure first appeared in administrative usage during the Republican period. Then, it was extended to civil law, first in the provinces, as provincial governors were both administrative heads and magistrates of the courts, and especially in imperial provinces, where the governor was the emperor's direct representative with the same exceptional powers as the emperor (there was also the influence of monarchic traditions in the Hellenic provinces of the Empire).

From the provinces, where it was widespread by the end of the second century, the "extraordinary" procedure spread throughout all Italy. It soon became customary to consult the emperor for legal clarification. Even judges requested *rescripts*. Naturally, the emperor delegated his powers to his high officials, each in his particular area of competence.

An important characteristic of the new system was the enhanced role of the state, which *obligated both parties to appear before the state-appointed judge, tried the case on its merits,* took liberties with formal law, *enforced the execution of the ruling,* and ultimately left little leeway for conventional arrangements between the parties.

2. *Codification of the Law*

For this period three sources of the law can be found: (1) *custom,*[14] (2) *imperial constitutions* (now called, if the texts were general, "laws," "edicts," and "pragmatic sanctions"; and if they were particular exemplary decisions, they were called "decrees" and "*rescripts*"); and (3) *doctrine*. But the primary innovation was the *codification* of the law and its publication in *compilations*. This culminated in the work of Justinian, which was decisive for the spread of Roman law throughout the West in medieval and modern times.

a. Early Compilations of the Law: The *Codex Theodosianus*

We know of a collection of imperial constitutions in 20 books as early as the classical period (the work of Papirius Justus between 161 and 192 AD) and also a collection of decrees (the work of Paulus). In both cases, they were private initiatives, and the works were commentaries and analyses, but not the full text of the imperial constitutions. Then, at the end of the third century AD and the beginning of the fourth, the Gregorian code (*Codex Gregorianus*), probably written in 291–92, and the Hermogenian code (*Codex Hermogenianus*)[15] are mentioned. They were also private initiatives with no binding validity, but they included the original texts.

Finally, a century later, the *Codex Theodosianus* was compiled. It was a very original text and presaged Justinian's *corpus iuris civilis*. In 435 Theodosius II, emperor of the East, instructed a commission of 16 experts to compile every general constitution published since Constantine; they were also instructed to "freshen" them, that is, to remove obsolete passages and superfluous developments, to smooth over contradictions and gaps, and to organize everything by books and titles; each constitution was arranged under its relevant title in chronological order. The work was completed in 437 and published in 438. The Theodosian code is concerned principally with public law and, in book 16, with relations between the church and the state (private law receives much less attention because of the existence of the Gregorian and Hermogenian codes).

The main innovation of the *Codex Theodosianus* is that all of its laws have official authority; the codex itself was published as a law. *Henceforth, the laws were to be applied in the form in which they appeared in the codex* (nevertheless, the codex did not invalidate laws that it did not include). Furthermore, the codex applied to both parts of the Empire, east and west, regardless whether the source was oriental or occidental. Thus, the codex is the first example of a fully codified law by a state.

---

[14] A theory of custom was made. The premise was that a general consensus—tacit, but real—lay at the heart of the custom because custom is a product of the times, and oppositions to custom, if well founded, would have manifested themselves. If oppositions do not exist, it is because there is a consensus; therefore, it can be considered that custom has the same basis as the law: popular will. The theory is unproblematic, as long as custom is invoked only when the law is silent. But can custom be opposed to the law and, under the Empire, to the will of the prince? Roman jurists replied in the negative, thereby underscoring the voluntarist aspect of the law. We find this problem again in the Middle Ages.

[15] It completed the *Codex Gregorianus* by adding, in succeeding editions, the latest constitutions.

The *Codex Theodosianus* has additional relevance: it was the only form in which Roman law was known in the medieval West before the eleventh century rediscovery of the Justinian code. After the collapse of the Western empire, various barbarian kings published law codes for their Roman subjects. These codes used the *Codex Theodosianus* as their source.

b. Doctrine and Post-Classical Compilations of the Law

Jurisprudence under the Low Empire was different from what it was during the classical period. It was anonymous (jurists had become the emperor's public servants); it was more synthetical than analytical (it preferred classifications and was less expert in the analysis of cases); it tended to simplify problems rather than to search for creative solutions, because only the emperor made the law by this point. Authors simply adapted and completed classical legal texts. And, as the West sank into crisis, the imperial center of gravity shifted to the East.

There was one more development: the *teaching of the law* became *organized. Law schools* already existed in several cities, including in Rome. But the best schools were the school of Constantinople and, above all, in the fifth century AD, the school of Beirut. The existence of such schools in the East made possible the legal renaissance of the Justinian era.

Given the multiplicity of legal opinions and the difficulty of accessing the original texts, individual practitioners were inclined to petition authorities in support of their own preferences. Succeeding emperors took partial steps to establish a hierarchy among the authorities until Theodosius II, in 426 AD, enacted his *Lex citationum* (Law of Citations). It confirmed the prestige of five great jurisconsults: Gaius, Papinian, Paulus, Ulpian, and Modestinus, who henceforth could be cited in the courts (there were absurdities in this law: in the event of divergences of opinion between the authorities, the majority view carried the day; Papinian's vote was preponderant; it was only if he did not take a stand that the judge was free to give his own ruling). It should be noted that the Law of Citations subordinated the authority of the jurisconsults to a decision of the state: this consummated the state's total preemption of the law.

c. The Justinian Compilations

Justinian became emperor in Byzantium in 527 AD and ruled there until his death in 565. His dream was the restoration of the great Roman Empire. He fulfilled it by reconquering Africa and Italy. His reign produced "domestic" successes as well; he reformed the government, the central administration, and the provinces. But the jewel in the crown was his compilation of the texts of the law, which survive through his four great texts.

His aim was to address the shortcomings of the *Codex Theodosianus*. It was by no means complete. Many new texts had come into being since its compilation. Furthermore, knowledge of classical doctrine was in steep decline and ran the risk of being lost entirely.

Justinian appointed a talented jurist, Tribonian, to take on the immense task of compiling, correcting, and completing the numerous existing classical legal texts and commentaries. Tribonian assembled a team of eminent jurists (high officials, legal scholars, lawyers) to carry out the emperor's instructions. Their painstaking efforts resulted in the publication of four compilations: the *Codex Justinianus*, the *Digest*, the *Institutes*, and the *Novels*, which together comprise the *Corpus iuris civilis*.

- *The Codex Justinianus*. Two consecutive editions were published (in 529 and 534). It takes up the Gregorian, Hermogenian, and Theodosian codes, amending and completing them with every imperial constitution enacted since the reign of Theodosius II. The Justinian Code replaced its predecessors and became the only legal code in application. It is divided into 12 books, each subdivided into titles under which the laws are ordered chronologically, as in the *Codex Theodosianus*.

The Justinian code begins with ecclesiastical law (which was where the Theodosian code ended). Next, it deals with the *sources of the law, asylum law,* the functions of various *imperial agents, legal procedure, private law, criminal law, administrative and fiscal law.* Each imperial constitution is identified by the name of the emperor who enacted it, its date and place of enactment, and the name of the petitioner (in the case of *rescripts*).

• The *Digest* (or, by its Greek name, *Pandecta*) was a compilation of all known fragments by classical juristconsults. This massive project was initiated by Justinian in his pronouncement *Deo Auctore,* dated December 15, 530. Some 1,500 books, published over a span of several centuries, were to be surveyed, requiring the contribution of some 38 or 39 jurisconsults, many of whom held the *ius respondendi.* This immense task was completed in under three years and was solemnly published by the imperial constitution *Tanta,* dated December 16, 533.

The *Digest* comprises 50 books, following the same order as the material in the Justinian code. Each book is subdivided into titles under which the various quotations are organized, each with its exact references (author, work, place in the work). The most frequently quoted authors are the five eminent jurists of the *Lex citationum* (Paulus and Ulpian occupy the top spots). The quotations are not always accurate. Changes or interpolations were intentional, since the emperor's express instruction was for the jurists to amend and complete the texts (earlier amendments were made in the postclassical period).

At the time of its publication, the *Digest* was used as a reference manual and was not widely distributed. But when it was studied again during the Middle Ages in the West, it became a very important, normative reference.

• The *Institutes.* This was a short school manual, which included long passages from the *Institutes* of Gaius. It used the same plan as the earlier text. Being simpler and shorter than the *Digest,* its success was immense.

• The *Novels.* They were the constitutions enacted since the first publication of the Justinian code. Some were in Greek, others in Latin, and others still in both languages. They were released in a new compendium after Italy was reconquered from the barbarians and it became necessary to apply the law of the Empire again (Greek texts were translated into Latin).

II. Conclusion: Natural Law, "Law of Nations," Civil Law

If Roman law was so innovative, particularly during the era of formulary procedure, it was because the Roman Republic, followed by the Empire, was the first truly "multiethnic" state in the history of humankind. Legal expedients had to be invented to create a social bond between people originating in many different ethnic groups, and so that throughout the empire there could exist an equality before the law, which until then was found only in smaller monoethnic communities. Flexible political mechanisms facilitated the formulation of new legal rules, tested by trial and error, which gradually proved to be efficient, comprehensible, and applicable to people everywhere, with a reduced risk of social conflict and improved social cooperation.

Roman law, which was initially an expression of quiritary rights, evolved from a system of customs for a particular ethnic group (the Quirites) to a more universal law, natural law (*ius naturale*), or the "law of nations"[16] (*ius gentium*) (some texts combine the two notions, others make a distinction).[17]

These two universal laws, to which many philosophers under Stoic influence gave their attention, served as useful references and guides for the innovations of practitioners.

It made sense to search for a common legal category for, say, a Syrian and a Greek, if the belief was held that they shared the same "human nature": no doubt each had a neighboring sense of *mine* and *yours,* of lawful and unlawful, of notions of goodwill ("in good faith") and trust ("I give you my word"). Therefore, as the magistrate searched for legal concepts that litigants of diverse origins could understand and accept, he did not create an artificial situation; he simply tried to stick closely to the nature of things, and in doing so he invented efficient and permanent solutions. In this respect, the existence of Greek philosophy in Rome, precisely during the period of the formulary system's greatest vitality, undoubtedly played an important role (see the section on Cicero below).

The emerging praetorian law sought to clarify the common ground between natural law and the law of nations: it aimed to be simpler, less formalist, and less religious than civil law. It resulted in more "categories for all occasions" than the law of the Quirites, or, to be more precise, its categories were more *abstract* and *versatile,* with fewer references to institutions, places, gods, rulers, and events associated with a particular nation, thus with a vocation for universal recognition by all "nations" (*gentes*) of the Empire and beyond. The broad categories of civil law used to introduce this chapter reflect this remarkable character of abstraction: property, ownership, purchase, sales, contract, legal person, representative, and so on. This new law "developed above all in the field of contract law, because more often than not business relationships create situations where legal invention is necessary."[18] Here are a few examples of doctrinal definitions and the maxims by the jurisconsults.

---

[16] "Nation" here is a translation of the Latin word *gens,* which means "family," "clan," "ethnic group," "people." *Ius gentium* means, therefore, the "law of peoples" in the sense of the law shared by all nations. *Ius gentium* consists of the rules of behavior common to peoples everywhere; these rules underlie the diverse cultures of each ethnic group. This is so because all peoples belong to the human race and share the same human nature: this explains the connection between *ius gentium* and *ius naturale.*

[17] Some authors did make a distinction between the two. For example, according to the opinion of some jurisconsults preserved in the *Digest,* slavery was contrary to natural law because all humans are by nature equal (this was the opinion of the Stoics, who opposed Aristotle's hierarchism). Yet, slavery is found in all human communities, in every ethnic group, and therefore is legitimate according to *ius gentium.* It was invented because all people have been confronted with war. Slavery was seen as (1) a *product,* that is, a secondary outcome that was not in the original nature of man, and (2) a *universal* product, and in this sense no less legitimate than natural law, prevailing against the positive laws of each community.

Another interpretation of the distinction between natural law and the law of nations might be that natural law is common to all living beings, men and animals, whereas the law of nations is that part of natural law that concerns only humankind (it is not "historical," but natural and original). It is not easy to decide on the basis of the formulas presented in the *Digest* (see maxims in this chapter below). No doubt, the ancients could not take the argument further given the intellectual categories at their disposal, in particular their lack of a clear concept of *history* and *culture.*

[18] Gaudemet, *Les institutions de l'antiquité,* 340.

Natural Law, Law of Nations, Civil Law according to the Jurisconsults[19]

Gaius, *Institutes* 1.1: "The laws of every people governed by statutes and customs are partly peculiar to itself, partly common to all mankind. The rules established by a given state for its own members are peculiar to itself and are called *ius civile;* the rules constituted by natural reason for all are observed by all nations alike and are called *ius gentium*. So the laws of the people of Rome are partly peculiar to itself, partly common to all nations; and this distinction shall be explained in detail in each place as it occurs."

Justinian, *Institutes* 1.2: "The law of nature is that law which nature teaches to all animals. For this law does not belong exclusively to the human race, but belongs to all animals, whether of the earth, the air, or the water. Hence comes the union of the male and female, which we term matrimony; hence the procreation and bringing up of children. We see, indeed, that all the other animals besides men are considered as having knowledge of this law."

"*Civil law* is thus distinguished from the *law of nations*. Every community governed by laws and customs uses partly its own law, partly laws common to all mankind. The law which a people makes for its own government belongs exclusively to that state and is called the *civil law,* as being the law of the particular state. But the law which natural reason appoints for all mankind obtains equally *among all nations,* because all nations make use of it. The people of Rome, then, are governed partly by their own laws, and partly by the laws which are common to all mankind."

"*Civil law* takes its name from the state which it governs, as, for instance, from Athens; for it would be very proper to speak of the laws of Solon or Draco as the civil law of Athens. And thus the law which the Roman people make use of is called the civil law of the Romans, or that of the Quirites; for the Romans are called Quirites from Quirinum. But whenever we speak of civil law, without adding the name of any state, we mean our own law; just as the Greeks, when "the poet" is spoken of without any name being expressed, mean the great Homer, and we Romans mean Virgil."

"The law of the nations is common to all mankind, for nations have established certain laws, as occasion and the necessities of human life required. Wars arose, and in their train followed captivity and then slavery, which is contrary to the law of nature; for by that law all men are originally born free. Further, by the law of nations almost all contracts were at first introduced, as, for instance, buying and selling, letting and hiring, partnership, deposits, loans returnable in kind, and very many others."[20]

[19] English version of texts in *Gai Institutiones or Institutes of Roman Law by Gaius*, with a translation and commentary by Edward Poste, 4th ed., revised and enlarged by E. A. Whittuck, with a historical introduction by A. H. J. Greenidge (Oxford: Clarendon Press, 1904).

[20] The author of the *Institutes* is well aware that contract law is virtually universal.

The Maxims[21]

Under title 50 of the *Digest* concluding the work, certain assertions are made; this is because they are outside the context and therefore have a general character. They are known as the *maxims of Roman law*. For example,

- *Quod omnes tangit ab omnibus approbari debet* ("what touches all should be approved by all.")

The principle applies to the ward with several tutors, but, in the Middle Ages, it was extended from civil law to public law (in a "democratic" sense).

Other examples:

- "Justice is a constant, unfailing disposition to give every one his legal due" (*suum cuique tribuere*) (*Digest* 1.1.10; *Institutes* 1.1.pr.).
- "He who can consent can refuse."
- "In law one cannot claim immorality as a justification for one's acts"
- "Equal persons do not defer to one another."

Over 200 such maxims can be found in the *Digest*.

[21] Quoted in Stein, "Roman Law."

Chapter 4

Political Ideas under the Roman Republic

While Roman magistrates elaborated on principles of public law that were unprecedented in clarity and pragmatism from previously known states, and Roman jurists forged the basic vocabulary and analytical legal tools that would later form the common basis of all modern law, political ideas were also being framed in Rome, just as earlier in Greece.

The Romans, as we said, were by nature less contemplative than the Greeks, through whom they discovered only science. Moreover, the first author we will discuss in this chapter was actually a Greek, who settled in Rome: Polybius. But the Romans proved to be excellent learners, particularly in the field of politics. Their various forms of government, from the Republic to the Principate and the Dominate, yielded an experience of politics as abundant and rich as the Greeks. Moreover, they learned additional political lessons while administering a state with a global vocation. Their experience is reflected in works that rarely adopted the format of theoretical treatises (with the exception of Cicero), but nevertheless expressed a high degree of conceptual elaboration.

I. Polybius

A. Introduction: The Scipionic Circle

In the years following the Battle of Pydna (168 BC), Greece finally fell under Roman tutelage. We know that Greek civilization did not suffer from the loss of its political independence, but to the contrary, as Horace says, "Greece, the captive, made her savage *victor* captive"; Greece, in fact, hellenized Rome. While the Romans resisted Greek influence to some extent (e.g., Cato the Censor obtained in 161 BC an order of banishment of all philosophers from the Roman Senate), the first Romans to be won over by Greek culture were the great Roman generals. Polybius lived in the circle of one such general.

Scipio Africanus (235–183 BC) was proconsul of Hispania at the time of the Second Punic War. He undertook the conquest of Andalusia, then with his ally, the Numidian prince Massinissa, besieged Carthage in 204 BC. He went on to win the Battle of Zama in 202 BC. Next, he traveled to Asia to wage war against Antiochus III, king of Syria. However, he and his brother, *Scipio Asiaticus,* were indicted for embezzlement (the accusation came from the conservatives under their leader, Cato the Elder). He dedicated the last years of his life to Greek culture.

Scipio Aemilianus (also known as Scipio Africanus the Younger) (185–129 BC) was the younger son of Lucius Aemilius Paulus Macedonicus,[1] the conqueror of Macedonia, and the adopted son of the son of Scipio Africanus. Consul in 147 BC, he razed Carthage. Later, he pacified Hispania. As a defender of the interests of the senatorial class, he opposed the Gracchi reforms. Heir to the library of Perseus of Macedonia, bequeathed by his father, he cultivated a true interest in Hellenic culture.

The Scipionic Circle formed around the second Scipio; its members included *Gaius Laelius,* a politician and Scipio's dearest friend; *Gaius Lucilius,* the first Roman satiric poet; *Terence,* one of the first Latin comedy writers; *Panaetius,* a Stoic philosopher,[2] and *Polybius,* the historian. Panaetius and Polybius were Greeks.

B. Life and Work

Born ca. 210–208 BC, died ca.126 BC, Polybius was from Megalopolis, a city in Arcadia, in the north of the Peloponnesus.

Megalopolis was founded between 371 and 368 BC after the battle of Leuctra and the defeat of Sparta as a counterweight to the latter. Its founder was the Theban statesman and general, Epaminondas. From the outset, Megalopolis was constantly embroiled in wars with its Peloponnesian neighbors. In the third century, the city fell under the authority of the new Macedonian monarchy with the rest of Greece, but it struggled to maintain its independence, alone at first, then after 234 BC as a member of the Achaean League. When the Romans established a foothold in Greece and in the East, following the defeat of Philip V, King of Macedon (197), and the defeat of another Hellenistic sovereign, Antiochus III of Syria (190), the Achaean League found itself in a delicate position. Indeed, under Rome's long-armed protection it had succeeded in uniting and governing all of the Peloponnesus. (Lycortas, the father of Polybius, was one of the architects of this policy.) Nevertheless, the situation could hardly last. During the Battle of Pydna, the leaders of the Achaean League were accused of lukewarm support for Rome and were deported there (168 BC). Polybius, who was hipparch of the league (second only to the general), was among the exiles. He remained in Rome for 16 years.

---

[1] Not to be confused with the consul Lucius Aemilius Paullus, his father, who was killed in 216 BC at the Battle of Cannae in the war against the Carthaginians. Lucius Aemilius Paulus Macedonicus (227–160 BC) was his son; he captured Macedonia after his victory over the last king of Macedonia, Perseus, at the Battle of Pydna in 168 BC.

[2] Panaetius (185 or 180–110 BC) was one of the leading figures of Stoicism. With Posidonius he was also one of the two major representatives of what is called *Middle Stoa* (in contrast to *Early Stoa* with Zeno, Cleanthes, and Chrysippus, and *Late Stoa* with Seneca, Epictetus, and Marcus Aurelius). Born in Rhodes, Panaetius studied in Pergamon, then in Athens with the Stoics Diogenes of Babylon and Antipater of Tarsus. In 146 BC he joined Polybius in Rome and entered the Scipionic Circle. He was Scipio's constant companion on his travels and sojourns in the East between 146 and 129 BC. He had several pupils in Rome, including Lucius Aelius Stilo Praeconinus, the teacher of Varro the philosopher. When Scipio died Panaetius returned to Athens and succeeded Antipater as the head of the Stoic school. His thought is known through a few rare fragments and from Cicero's allusions to him. Panaetius's treatise *On Duties* (*Peri kathekontos*) inspired Cicero's *De officiis;* his treatise *On Providence* was also the inspiration for Cicero's *De natura deorum.* He also wrote a treatise *On Cheerfulness* (*Peri euthymias*), which inspired Seneca and Plutarch. Panaetius can be held as one of the great inspirations of Western humanism.

This was the beginning of an extraordinary intellectual adventure for Polybius. While his family and social circle were proponents of political independence, not to say the expansion of the Achaean League (a last attempt to preserve the classical Greek city against the rising power of Hellenistic monarchies and the emerging Roman Empire), Polybius himself was, intellectually speaking, completely won over to Rome.

In return the Romans welcomed him warmly. Already in Greece Polybius had frequented Roman public figures. Now, in Rome, he moved among senators and individuals who appreciated his personality and culture. He became the director of conscience and personal friend of the conqueror of Perseus, the young *Scipio Aemilianus* (who was 16 years old when Polybius reached Rome at the age of 40). With great enthusiasm Polybius studied Rome: its customs, its institutions, and its history, and he undertook to write a monumental history of Rome for his Greek compatriots so that they would be better acquainted with their conquerors. It was, in fact, a "universal" history, since Rome had conquered "the whole of the inhabited world," as Polybius wrote. The destiny of Rome now coincided with the destiny of the world. *The Histories* of Polybius narrate the events between 218 and 146 BC in 30 books (only 5 survive in full; fragments of others exist).[3] Years later he was granted permission to return to his home country, but preferred to return freely to Rome where he undertook official assignments for the Republic and accompanied Scipio on his military campaigns, traveling throughout Italy, Gaul, Hispania, and Africa.

Polybius is of interest to the history of political ideas for several reasons. First, in book 6, he pursues an *original constitutional thought* focused on the study of Roman political institutions (see section 1 and 2 below). Next, his entire work aims to substantiate the theory that Rome governs the known world lawfully: a sort of *philosophy of history* before the letter (see section 3).

1. *The Cycle of Constitutions*

Polybius outlines a theory of the *fundamental instability of political regimes,* or, at any rate, the regimes in power among most Greeks. These political regimes, he argues, are doomed to be replaced by another, which itself will be replaced, in a continuous "cycle of political revolution."

Polybius attributes his theory to Plato. But we will see that the order of succession of regimes is not the same for both thinkers. We should recall that Aristotle rejected the theory of a predetermined cycle of governments, arguing that any regime can be replaced by any other.

At the beginning of time, men, like animals, banded together in groups to face natural difficulties; they followed the strongest and bravest of their kind. This gave rise to *autocracy* (*Histories,* book 1), the rule of a leader by brute strength and bold courage (6.5).

In the next phase, ideas about goodness and justice were formed; people are different from animals because they possess faculties of intelligence and reason. With the ability to imagine the future and sympathize with the sufferings of others (which one can do by putting oneself in someone else's shoes), humans know which behaviors produce evil in the here and now and, conversely, which lay the foundations of good in the future. Polybius writes, "there arises in everyone a notion of the meaning and theory of duty, which is the beginning and end of justice." These virtues are transmitted by imitation. Therefore, the despot is forced to abandon government by "bodily strength and courage" and to respect justice and command respect for it. This gave rise to *monarchy* (*Histories,* book 2; book 6, sec. 6).

However, monarchy is not permanent either. While the first kings may be simple and good, their successors will not be their equal. They reach their position by inheritance and do not have the same personal qualities as their forebears. Furthermore, because general prosperity

[3] The texts fill six volumes in the Loeb Classical Library edition. Polybius, *The Histories,* translated by W. R. Paton (Cambridge, MA: Harvard University Press, 1922); hereafter cited in the text by book and section number.

has improved as a consequence of earlier reigns, the kings no longer know how to rule their appetites: they want better clothes and better food than their subjects; they are also inclined to lust and sexual indulgence.[4] This *tyranny* (*Histories,* book 3) stirs envy and contempt, and soon the tyrant is chased from power by a group of noble and high-minded men, with the approval of the people. This leads to *aristocracy* (book 4). It too lasts only a short while for the same reasons; the quality of rulers worsens, which leads to *oligarchy* (book 5), which in turn is overthrown by good individuals motivated by a desire to restore justice. Because the memory of the tyrant is still fresh in their memories, these people have no desire to bring back monarchy, so they turn to a third form of government, *democracy* (book 6). This form remains vibrant as long as it is led by those who experienced the abuses of earlier regimes, and while "civil equality and liberty of speech" (book 6) are upheld. But these memories are lost to the generation of their grandchildren—Polybius is precise—("when children inherited this position of authority from their fathers, having no experience of misfortune"). Then, a clique of ambitious individuals promises the people great riches to be taken from the wealthy. These factions draw on the corruptibility of the people and anarchy spreads until "a rule of force and violence" is established. Then the whole cycle starts over again: order is restored under the stick of a *autocrat,* followed by a *king,* and so on (6.8–10).

Polybius emphasizes that this cycle of political revolution cannot be avoided. It is a "law of nature" (*Histories* 6.10). It is so inevitable that reliable predictions can be made about the future of any form of government, if one knows the exact phase it has reached in the cycle. The tendency of each regime to decline, Polybius says, is not due to external or accidental causes. It is natural and inherent in each form of government, like rust to iron and woodworms and shipworms to timber.

2. *The Mixed Constitution*

There is one city, according to Polybius, that managed to escape the endless cycle of revolutions, thanks to the genius of its lawgiver. That city was Sparta and its lawgiver Lycurgus.[5] It was he who discovered the "law of nature" that orders the cycle of polities previously discussed. But he found that it applies only to *pure* forms of constitution or government. "Lycurgus, foreseeing this, did not make his constitution simple and uniform, but united in it all the good and distinctive features of the best governments, so that none of the principles should grow unduly and be perverted into its allied evil, but that, the force of each being neutralized by that of the others, neither of them should prevail and outbalance another, but that the constitution should remain for long in a state of equilibrium like a well-trimmed boat" (*Histories* 6.10).

Thus, Lycurgus created the Spartan constitution where the powers of the kings, on the one hand, and the *apella* (or assembly, where the people sat) and the *gerusia* (or senate, where the "best" convened), on the other, existed in a perfect state of balance. Polybius concludes that Lycurgus, by forming his constitution from these elements in this way, "left to the Spartans themselves a lasting heritage of freedom." In contrast, in Athens and in Crete, one power (democracy, as it happens) achieved hegemony over the others, and the cities collapsed.[6]

Polybius points out that Lycurgus worked out these things "by a process of reasoning"; consequently, he introduced a perfect constitution "all at once," such that the city achieved its

---

[4] Judging by the frequent references of classical writers to these excesses, the tyrants and oligarchs of the Greek cities must have been somewhat dissolute, clearly a major irritation to Greek public opinion.

[5] Lycurgus, it will be recalled, was probably not a historical person, but the Ancients unanimously attribute to him the creation of Spartan institutions after the Messenian wars.

[6] The idea of constitutional checks and balances, born of a mixed form of government, is not an invention of Polybius. It is also found in Thucydides (*The Peloponnesian War* 8.97), and in Plato (*Laws* 3.692–93, 4.712), as well as in Aristotle (*Politics* 6.1294a). Polybius, however, gives the idea new scope.

remarkable result "untaught by adversity." He notes, however, that Sparta did have other weaknesses: it was too frugal, did not engage in trade, and did not have a policy of territorial expansion.

But another city exists that succeeded in discovering the same system of government, which enjoys the same success, even if it did so by a process of trial and error—"by the discipline of many struggles and troubles," Polybius says—rather than as a result of abstract reasoning. That city is Rome. This is the crux of Polybius's argument, since throughout his *Histories* he endeavors to illustrate the dazzling superiority of the Roman Republic in the modern world.

Again one finds the three powers of a mixed constitution. The consuls control executive power alone. All other magistrates, with the exception of the plebeian tribunes, are subordinate to them. They organize the work of the Senate and the popular assemblies; they have near "absolute power" in matters of war: the recruiting of soldiers, the appointment of officers, the command over troops, allies, and operations, and the sovereign right of punishment. These are the prerogatives of a king.

For its part, the Senate also enjoys sweeping powers. It controls the treasury: nothing comes in or goes out without its knowledge. It is the highest judicial authority. It has control over Italy's "allied" cities, whose officials are directly subordinated to it. It decides foreign policy and dispatches and receives foreign embassies. All of these powers are the privilege of an elite body: the senatorial order, which is an aristocratic power.

Finally, the people, through its assemblies, also have a share of sovereign power. Only the people are allowed to try cases on capital offenses (life and death issues). In other cases, they hear appeals. Their assemblies grant high offices and vote on the passage of laws. "They deliberate on the question of war and peace" and, in this regard, they can override the Senate. The people are a democratic power. Polybius glosses:

> Having stated how political power is distributed among the different parts of the state, I will now explain how each of the three parts is enabled, if they wish, to counteract or co-operate with the others. The consul, when he leaves with his army invested with the powers I mentioned, appears indeed to have absolute authority in all matters necessary for carrying out his purpose; but in fact he requires the support of the people and the senate, and is not able to bring his operations to a conclusion without them. For it is obvious that the legions require constant supplies, and without the consent of the senate, neither corn, clothing, nor pay can be provided; so that the commander's plans come to nothing, if the senate chooses to be deliberately negligent and obstructive. It also depends on the senate whether or not a general can carry out completely his conceptions and designs, since it has the right of either superseding him when his year's term of office has expired or of retaining him in command. Again it is in its power to celebrate with pomp and to magnify the successes of a general or on the other hand to obscure and belittle them.[7] . . .
>
> As for the people it is most indispensable for the consuls to conciliate them, however far away from home they may be; for, as I said, it is the people which ratifies or annuls terms of peace and treaties, and what is most important, on laying down office the consuls are obliged to account for their actions to the people. So that in no respect is it safe for the consuls to neglect keeping in favour with both the senate and the people.
>
> The senate again, which possesses such great power, is obliged in the first place to pay attention to the commons in public affairs and respect the wishes of the people, and it

[7] The Senate grants or refuses "triumphs."

> cannot carry out inquiries into the most grave and important offences against the state, punishable with death, and their correction, unless the *senatus consultum* is confirmed by the people. The same is the case in matters which directly affect the senate itself. For if anyone introduces a law meant to deprive the senate of some of its traditional authority, or to abolish the precedence and other distinctions of the senators or even to curtail them of their private fortunes, it is the people alone which has the power of passing or rejecting any such measure. And what is most important is that if a single one of the tribunes interposes, the senate is unable to decide finally about any matter, and cannot even meet and hold sittings; and here it is to be observed that the tribunes are always obliged to act as the people decree and to pay every attention to their wishes. Therefore for all these reasons the senate is afraid of the masses and must pay due attention to the popular will.
>
> Similarly, the people must be submissive to the senate and offer respect to its members both in public and in private. Through the whole of Italy a vast number of contracts, which it would not be easy to enumerate, are given out by the censors for the construction and repair of public buildings, and besides this there are many things which are farmed, such as navigable rivers, harbours, gardens, mines, lands, in fact everything that forms part of the Roman dominion. Now all these matters are undertaken by the people, and one may almost say that everyone is interested in these contracts and the work they involved. For certain people are the actual purchasers from the censors of the contracts, others are the partners of these first, others stand surety for them, others pledge their own fortunes to the state for this purpose. Now in all these matters the senate is supreme. It can grant extension of time; it can relieve the contractor if any accident occurs; and if the work proves to be absolutely impossible to carry out it can liberate him from his contract. There are in fact many ways in which the senate can either benefit or indicate those who administer public property, as all these matters are referred to it. What is even most important is that the judges in most civil trials, whether public or private, are appointed from its members,[8] where the action involves large interests. So that all citizens being at the mercy of the senate, and looking forward with alarm to the uncertainty of litigation, are very shy of obstructing or resisting its decisions. Similarly everyone is reluctant to oppose the projects of the consuls as all are generally and individually under their authority when in the field.
>
> Such being the power that each part has of hampering the others or co-operating with them, their union is adequate to all emergencies, so that it is impossible to find a better political system than this... and consequently this peculiar form of constitution possesses an irresistible power of attaining every object upon which it is resolved. (*Histories* 6.15–18)

To what extent does Polybius's analysis of power in Rome reflect the historical reality at this particular moment in time? It seems that the consuls[9] had very little power compared to the Senate, and it seems that the power of the Senate was greater than Polybius suggests. By presenting the constitution as balanced, Polybius was reassuring the senatorial circles in which he moved and for whom he worked. Nevertheless, his analysis is invaluable for the details it provides about the checks and balances of powers in Rome.

[8] Shortly after Polybius's time, knights were granted access to judicial functions.

[9] Who, in addition, were two and, moreover, rivals: they gave only an imperfect image of monarchy.

3. *Rome, the Destiny of the World*

In his introduction to the *Histories,*[10] Denis Roussel says that "when one reads Cicero's *Republic,* it is clear that Polybius helped the Romans achieve true insight into the extraordinary originality of their institutions"—and especially their value as a universal model (much as Montesquieu would do in respect of England some 16 centuries later). Again according to Roussel, Polybius was the one thinker who led the Roman ruling classes to an awareness of Rome's *imperial* destiny. Polybius, an "oriental"—a Hellenistic Greek—may have even planted the seed of an idea of a Roman empire.

So what was the cause of the remarkable expansion of Rome? It cannot be attributed to the ambition of a single man, such as an Alexander the Great, or to a particular policy of the Senate at a given moment in time. Undeniably, Rome reaped immense material wealth from the spoils and tribute of the lands it conquered. As we said, after Perseus's defeat in 168 BC the Romans no longer paid direct taxes. Many leaders, though, felt only contempt for territorial expansionism and failed to see the positive benefits of empire. On this score, a man such as Cato the Elder had harsh words for Scipio the Elder. He recognized the danger for Rome in assuming the succession of the great Hellenistic monarchies. He cautioned it to pursue its external campaigns with the more limited aim of Italy's territorial security. Rome was not responsible for all humanity and would be well advised to let the Hellenic East rot in its vices. Because its victories were due to its collective discipline and republican form of government, it had every interest in preserving its national identity and in resisting cosmopolitanism.

Polybius could not share this last opinion. As a Greek, he was already committed to universalist thought. We noted earlier that, under the influence of Stoicism, many Greeks believed that humanity was one and that it was in its interest to live under a single political power. Polybius thought this one power should be monarchic. In his *Histories,* he ascribed ambitions of world dominance to Philip V of Macedon and Antiochus III of Syria. He was persuaded therefore that men such as Scipio Africanus, so manifestly exceptional and blessed by Fortune, could lead such a project. He was frankly astonished that one such as Scipio could refuse monarchy and prefer a mere Roman magistracy.

If individual Romans did not want to assume the burden of universal empire, Polybius thought, well then perhaps the *Roman people* would. He credited the Roman people with the same role and quasi-sacred status that philosophers had credited to Hellenistic sovereigns. In this respect, he was in step with a trend of his times. By the middle of the third century BC, the cult of the "goddess Rome" thrived in the cities of ancient Magna Græcia, and somewhat later in Athens, Delos, and elsewhere. It seems that Polybius was a believer in this goddess.

II. Cicero

Cicero (106–43 BC) is a colossal figure in the history of political ideas. He is seen quite rightly as one of the fathers of the doctrines of the *rule of law.*

Cicero's intellectual legacy includes

- a doctrine of society, man, and the dignity of humankind in general and of each man in particular, which is the key pagan source for Western *humanism;*

[10] Denis Roussel, introduction to Polybius, *Histoire* (Paris: Gallimard, 1970). We follow his argument in the following development.

- a doctrine of *law* as founded in human nature (Cicero is the primary classical reference for theories of *natural law*);
- a doctrine of the *state* as the organization dedicated to upholding the law;
- a doctrine of *private property* and *freedom of contract,* which is one of the fundamental sources of liberalism;
- a doctrine of a more political nature, that is, the doctrine of *mixed government.*[11]

Cicero is not always the most original in his various contributions; indeed, he draws on the Greeks, and especially the Stoics. But he towers above all of his sources and produces a commanding personal synthesis.

A. Life

Cicero was born in 106 BC in Arpinum, a *municipium* in the land of the Volsci, 120 kilometers southeast of Rome. His family belonged to the equestrian class. His grandfather had been a senatorial sympathizer and his father might have entered the *cursus honorum,* but he was too shy and did not make the attempt. Instead he ensured that his son received the necessary education to nurture such ambitions. In 91 BC Cicero, still an adolescent, was sent to Rome to study under Quintus Mucius Scaevola[12] and received his early legal training. He was then entrusted into the care of Marcus Pupius Piso, who became consul in 61 BC, two years after his pupil.[13]

In Piso's household there lived a peripatetic philosopher by the name of Staseas, who introduced Cicero to the philosophy of Aristotle. At this time, Cicero also began to study other Greek philosophers, notably the Epicurean Phedre, the Academician Philo of Larissa (a disciple of the Academician Carneades, a master and advocate of eloquence), and finally the Stoic Diodotus, who lived in Cicero's household for a number of years until his death in 60 BC. Another of his masters was the Stoic Aelius Stilo (Varro figured among his pupils). Cicero was close to the Greek rhetorician Apollonius Molon of Rhodes, who came to Rome as an emissary in 87 BC and again in 81 BC. He also frequented the Stoic philosopher Posidonius, another emissary from Rhodes and a student of the aged Panaetius (once a member of the Scipionic Circle), one of the two greatest masters (with Panaetius) of the Middle Stoa. Lastly, Cicero was acquainted with Archias the poet. With all of these people Cicero heard and spoke Greek, a language that the senators of Rome knew sufficiently well to authorize Molon to address a senatorial session in Greek without an interpreter (in 87 BC). Moreover, around this time Cicero was translating texts from the Greek by Xenophon, Plato, and Aratus the poet.

Joining the army, Cicero was assigned to the general staff of Pompey's father, where he and Pompey, both aged 17, were colleagues. After, Cicero served Sulla on campaign.

By 80 BC Cicero was sufficiently well trained in the law and in the art of oratory to take up a career as a lawyer. His early success enabled him to marry a young lady of excellent nobility, Terentia. But, because he was not yet 30 and could not aspire to the quaestorship, the first of the great magistracies, he left for Greece to complete his philosophical and rhetorical training. He set sail for the East in March 79. There he meditated in the places where Sophocles, Demosthenes,

[11] This is a reference to Cicero's major theoretical contributions. Obviously his work teems with references to other aspects of Roman political and social life, as well.

[12] Quintus Mucius Scaevola, consul in 95 BC, is credited with being one of the founders of Roman law. His father, Publius Mucius Scaevola, was one of the three founders of civil law alongside Manilius and Junius Brutus. Quintus was the author of a treatise on civil law in 18 volumes. Its plan was used again elsewhere for other treatises on *ius civile* and for this reason was called *ad Quintum Mucium* (Gaudemet, *Les institutions de l'antiquité,* 334).

[13] Material in this section is from the outstanding biography of Cicero by Pierre Grimal, *Cicéron* (Paris: Fayard, 1986).

Plato, and Epicurus had lived and worked. For six months he took lessons under Antiochus of Ascalon, the scholarch of the Academy. He was initiated into the Eleusinian mysteries. He visited Sparta, then traveled to Asia Minor, where he visited Miletus and Smyrna. Along the way he met famous orators in the different towns; finally he reached Rhodes, where he met Molon and Posidonius. He returned to Rome in the spring of 77 BC.

From this time forward Cicero pursued parallel careers as a lawyer and a politician. He served as quaestor in Lilybeus (Sicily) in 75 BC. This gave him the opportunity to defend the Sicilians in their case against Verres.[14] In 70 Cicero was elected Aedile for the year 69 (he gave the games three times); in 67 he was elected praetor for the year 66, and consul in 63. During his year in the highest office of the Republic, he thwarted the Catalina conspiracy. However, in 58 BC, under the First Triumvirate, he was exiled to Greece at the prompting of Clodius, a demagogic tribune. He returned to Rome in 57. In 52 BC he defended Milon, who had ordered the assassination of Clodius. In 51 he was appointed governor of Cilicia,[15] where he lived for a year. But in 49 BC Caesar crossed the Rubicon and established his dictatorship. After joining the senatorial party under the leadership of Pompey and fleeing Rome to join the resistance, Cicero and Caesar were finally reconciled after the latter's victory. Caesar was assassinated in 44 BC, leaving Cicero with renewed hope for the restoration of the Republic. This time he clashed with Mark Antony, who had plans for his own political hegemony. Mark Antony sent his soldiers to hunt down Cicero, and when they found him, they slit his throat.

B. Work

Cicero's writings include:

- *Orations,* which are pleas for civil and political trials (spoken or not) for both the defense and the prosecution: for example, *Against Verres,* parts 1 and 2 (70 BC), *Pro Cluentio* (66 BC), the *Catalinarian Orations,* also known as *In Catalinam* (63 BC), *Pro Murena* (63 BC), *Pro archia* (62 BC), *Pro Milone* (55 BC), *Pro Sestio* (54 BC), *Philippics*[16] (44 BC);
- numerous *Letters,* written between 68 BC and the eve of his death; they provide a wealth of information about Roman history and everyday life of the times (especially his *Letters to Atticus*);
- autobiographical writings, *On My Consulship* (in Greek), then *De consulatu suo* (60 BC), a poetic version of the same work, and *De domo sua* (57 BC);
- rhetorical treatises: long before the great Latin master Quintilian, Cicero excelled at the art of oratory; his writings include *De oratore* (55 BC), *Brutus* (46 BC), *Orator* (46 BC), *The Best Kind of Orator* (46 BC), *Divisions of Oratory* (46 BC), *Topics* (44 BC);
- political treatises: *On the Republic* (54–51 BC), *On the Laws* (52 BC);
- philosophical treatises: the *Paradoxes of the Stoics* (46 BC), *Hortentius* (45 BC, lost), *Academica,* parts 1 and 2 (45 BC), *On Ends* (45 BC), *Tusculan Disputations* (45 BC), *On the Nature of the Gods* (45 BC), *On Destiny* (44 BC), *Topics* (44 BC), *On Glory* (44 BC, lost), *On Old Age* (44 BC), *On Friendship* (44 BC), *On Divination* (44 BC) *On Duties (De officiis)* (44–43 BC).

---

[14] The former governor of Sicily and corrupt judge loathed for his greediness.

[15] A region in southeastern Asia Minor, close to Syria.

[16] The title was borrowed from Demosthenes' celebrated *Philippics,* a work attacking Philip of Macedon. The tyrant whom Cicero had in mind for his *Philippics* was Mark Antony.

Most of his works survive, due to the fact that Cicero was exceedingly famous during his lifetime; his works were constantly copied.

Cicero's most important political and philosophical texts were written in the years just before his death, when he no longer commanded political power and had withdrawn to his country villa, no doubt sensing a violent end to his life. Most of his political ideas can be found in *De republica, De legibus, De officiis,* his *Letters,* and in certain passages of *Pro sestia* (56 BC), *Pro cluentio,* and *De oratore.*

In the following pages, we provide a general overview of his political ideas based primarily on *De officiis, De republica,* and *De legibus.*[17]

The treatise *On Duties* (*De officiis*) is, perhaps, one of the most important works of all antiquity. Basing his exposition on a treatise by Panaetius, Cicero provides a complete moral philosophy with an analysis of the four cardinal virtues: prudence (wisdom), justice, fortitude (courage), and temperance (restraint). He examines the four virtues and positions them in a hierarchy; he discusses the conflict between the virtues and expediency; he considers their predominance over expediency for the attainment of *honestas,* that is, moral rectitude or goodness (moral beauty). Panaetius's moral philosophy, as presented and completed by Cicero, is rightly held to be one of the principal sources of Western *humanism,* because of the immense influence it exercised in antiquity and as late as the Renaissance.

Known and widely admired by classical authors, Cicero's *On the Republic* became lost, except for a few quotes and its last part, "the Dream of Scipio," and was not known to authors during the Middle Ages and the classical tradition. Miraculously, large portions were rediscovered in 1820 in a palimpsest. Cicero wrote the treatise between 54 and 51 BC in the form of a dialogue that allegedly took place in 129 BC[18] in the country villa of Aemilius Scipio, the friend of Polybius, Panaetius, and Terence. Scipio held conversations there with his close associates, among them many Roman officials and politicians.

On the Laws is the continuation of *On the Republic,* which together form a whole (like Plato's treatises that Cicero was deliberately imitating). This second work is devoted to the study of the law, or more exactly to the study of its higher principles, the *leges legum* (the law of the laws), to which legislation must conform if it is to have validity.

C. Human Nature: Ciceronian Humanism

Before undertaking a discussion of the law and the state, we need a definition of *human nature* that the law and the state protect as a sacred mission. In *The Laws* Cicero writes, "we must clarify the *nature* of justice, and *that has to be deduced from the nature of man* (*De Leg.* 1.5.17; see also 1.6.20: "we [should] look for the origin of justice in its source [i.e., *in nature*]; *once we have found that, we will have a reliable standard for testing our investigations*"; 1.10.28: "that what is just is based, not on opinion, but *on nature*").

In *On the Laws* and *On the Republic* Cicero sets out different theories on nature and natural law; but it is in *On Duties* that individual and collective human nature are given systematic examination.

---

[17] *Translator's note:* The Loeb Classical Library, Harvard University Press, has published Cicero's writings in 29 volumes. We quote the Loeb edition of *On Duties* (*De officiis*), vol. 21, trans. Walter Miller (Cambridge, MA: Harvard University Press, 1913), but prefer at times Niall Rudd's translation of the *Republic* and the *Laws* (Oxford: Oxford University Press, 1998). Cicero's *Republic* will be cited as *De Rep.* and his *Laws* will be cited as *De Leg.* in the text to distinguish them from Plato's works.

[18] In other words, between the tribunates of the first Gracchi, Tiberius (133 BC), and Gaius (123 BC).

1. *The Moral Ideal*

a. Human Nature

In *On Duties* (*De officiis* 1.4.13–15), Cicero lists the fundamental attributes of human nature, noting in particular:

1. the need for food, shelter, and the like;
2. the need to reproduce, and so on;
3. man is intelligent (he has a clear awareness of the past and the future and the chains of cause and effect);
4. man is sociable, he enjoys contact with others, and foremost with family members;
5. "the search after truth and its eager pursuit";
6. man's "greatness of soul and sense of superiority" such that he expresses "a hungering... for independence" and an unwillingness "to be subject to anybody";
7. "a feeling for order, for propriety, for moderation in word and deed" (no other being shares this feeling: *unum hoc animal sentit quid sit ordo*);
8. man's sense of individual and social property;
9. the need to exchange good offices with fellow men;
10. the endowment of men with *ratio and oratio,* reason and speech, the discriminating characteristics of human groups compared with animal groups.

These attributes of human nature can be narrowed down to four, corresponding to the four cardinal virtues identified by the moral tradition:

1. "the full perception and intelligent development of the true," regulated by the virtue of *prudence;*
2. the desire to preserve organized society through respect for property and contracts (*tribuendo suum cuique et rerum contractarum fide*), regulated by the virtue of *justice;*
3. the greatness (*magnitudo*) and strength (*robor*) of a noble and invincible spirit, regulated by the virtue of *nobility of spirit;*[19]
4. "the orderliness and moderation of everything that is said and done," regulated by the virtue of self-control (*modestia*) or temperance (*temperantia*).

This definition of human nature calls for a few comments.

It is social. There is not first an individual person, then a human society, conceived as a subproduct, an artificial and accidental construction. Man is *by nature a social being.* His nature flourishes only in association and in fellowship with other human beings. Aristotle expressed this idea forcefully against the individualism and artificialism of the Sophists.

It is spiritual. More forcefully than even Aristotle, Cicero insists on the importance of *reason, speech,* and *intellectual exchange* in the life of human society. A human society is not just a community of life (after all, animal groups live in communities as well); it is a "republic of mind and spirit." Humans are humans only insofar as they are citizens of this particular republic, that is, insofar as they can speak and dialogue with others. In modern terms, we would say that the characteristic feature of human society is *culture.*

[19] Philosophical tradition refers to this preferably as "courage" or "fortitude"; nobility of spirit (*macropsyches, magnanimitas, magnanimity*) is merely the most remarkable aspect assumed by this virtue alongside courage, long-suffering, and so on.

"The connection subsisting between all the members of the human race...is reason and speech, which by *the processes of teaching and learning,* of *communicating, discussing,* and *reasoning* associate men together and unite them in a sort of natural fraternity" (*On Duties* 1.16.50). If wants and comforts could be secured "by a magic wand" (*virgula divina*), man would not drop everything and devote himself exclusively to pure knowledge. "He would seek to escape from his loneliness and to find someone to share his studies; he would wish to teach, as well as to learn; to hear, as well as to speak" (*On Duties* 1.44.157–58; see also *De Rep.* 2.76).

It is divine. Humans are superior to animals because they possess "the divine fire of rational intelligence" (*De Rep.* 2.75). Faculties of speech and reason come from a divine source. This direct link with the gods suffices to ensure his dominion over all other earthly beings. Moreover, humans possess writing and the science of numbers, the latter being the only eternal and immutable beings. Because God created the universe, and because there is an essential bond between God and the human spirit, everything in nature is under the authority of God and humanity (*De Leg.* 1.8.25). The gods watch over the actions of human beings; divine providence exists (2.7.15).

In this sense human nature is *universal.* Cicero reaches beyond the ancient Greek categories, which created the opposition between Hellenes and barbarians. Cicero thinks in terms of Stoic cosmopolitanism. Any man, irrespective of race, nation, or tribe, can attain moral perfection, provided he engages in the culture of civilized men: "we are not concerned with nationality but with spiritual matters" (*non gentem, ingenia quærimus*) (*De Rep.* 1.37.58).

b. Honestum

Moral perfection is attained when one possesses the virtues in the developed state; this is the perfection of Form or human Nature. Cicero calls this perfection *honestas,* which can be translated as "moral rectitude" or "moral beauty."[20] "It is from these elements [those we enumerated above] that is forged and fashioned that moral beauty [*honestum*] which is the subject of this inquiry" (*On Duties* 1.4.14). Virtues give rise to *officia,* that is, duties, and the "beauty" (*honestas*) of life lies in honoring such duties (*On Duties* 1.2.4).[21]

Moral beauty (or moral goodness) is the supreme good. It is, therefore, "an end in itself," not a means to something else. Moral beauty is its own reward. Whoever possesses it possesses happiness. At best, moral beauty seeks glory and honor in the community. "Virtue clearly likes to be honoured, and it has no other reward" (*De Rep.* 3.40, with modifications).[22]

Cicero says that combining pleasure and moral rectitude is as absurd as confusing a man with a beast (*On Duties* 3.33.119). If a man does not accept this, then dialogue with him is simply impossible: "What sense is there to speak with a man who removes completely the human essence from man" (*quid cum eo disseras qui omnino hominem ex homine tollat*)? (*On Duties* 3.5.26, with modifications). Dialogue is possible with one's fellow man, not with a monster.

c. Morality and Expediency

Moral acts should be performed for their own sake, because they are right. But they can be useful or harmful for the person performing them, which brings us to the fundamental question in all

[20] *Honnête* has a restricted sense in modern French. But in the seventeenth century, the expression *honnête homme* referred to a "man of integrity" or, indeed, a "man of virtue."

[21] *Honestum* is a purity of mind, which is distinct from "physical" purity (*De Leg.* 2.10.24).

[22] Later we will see that the virtuous soul will be rewarded in the afterlife (see below, *The Dream of Scipio*).

moral philosophy: is it preferable to perform *right* acts, which are nonetheless *harmful*, or *base* acts, which are *useful?* Cicero's answer to the question is threefold.

1. In contrast with the Epicureans, who saw supreme good in pleasure and supreme evil in pain, and the Cynics, who made no distinction between what is right and what is base, Cicero establishes the absolute primacy of morals. It is necessary to do right (to do what is honorable and good) in *all* circumstances, whether the consequences are happy or unfortunate. The question of what to do simply does not arise, if one is certain of one's moral duty.

To imagine that one can hesitate in the performance of what is morally right is to imagine the existence of *better* goods than *honestas*, for example, health, wealth, honors, and pleasures. But this is wrong: the *sovereign good* lies in virtue alone (*De Leg.* 1.18.48–1.19.50). "Only the honourable [is] good and only the base [is] bad" (1.21.55).

Those who see the good in the expedient (*commodum*, i.e., the useful) are self-contradictory because they are not capable of "friendship, justice or generosity" (the reference here is to the theories of Pyrrho and the heterodox Stoics, Aristo of Chios, and Erillus) (*On Duties* 1.2.5).

The position of the Epicureans, who hold pleasure and pain to be the criteria of good and evil, is no less coherent. They cannot uphold temperance against expediency, whatever Epicurus claims. "For how can he [Epicurus] commend self-control [temperance] and yet posit pleasure as the supreme good? For self-control is the foe of the passions, and the passions are the handmaids of pleasure" (*On Duties* 3.33.118).

Thus, moral goodness admits only of "categorical imperatives." The mere fact of hesitation between the good [or honorable] and the expedient [or useful], weighing them on the same scales as if they are equal, is itself morally wrong (see *On Duties* 3.4.18 and 8.37).

One must act morally, even though one may "escape the eyes of gods and men." This is the true lesson to be taken from the Ring of Gyges. "For good men aim to secure not secrecy but the right" (*On Duties* 3.8.37–9.38; see also *On Duties* 3.19.78).

Again and again, the moral literature emphasizes the connection between rectitude and transparency.[23] Nothing is right that cannot be conducted openly and publicly; nothing is right that cannot be assumed with pride in the eyes of the city. Conversely, as soon as the need is felt to hide one's actions, there undoubtedly is some confusion or moral ambiguity.

2. This "idealism" does not prevent Cicero from being "utilitarian" and without contradiction. He thinks that *morality is by no means in fundamental contradiction with life*. The Stoic doctrine of "universal fellowship" teaches that something akin to preestablished harmony exists between man and nature because both have as their source the same "ordering *logos*," which ensures that *man, living "conformably to his nature," is generally neither at odds with human society nor with the universe*. Accordingly, neither human society nor the universe creates systematic hindrances that might prevent a person from living "honestly" (rightly); on the contrary, the more virtuous one is, the greater one's harmony with the events of nature and society. Thus, far from frustrating the course of life, moral rectitude (goodness) is in fact its fundamental condition: honest people are, in general, happier than dishonest ones. It is through some "slip" that moral rectitude (what is right) and expediency (what is useful) have become opposed. Socrates said that between the morally right and the useful expedient there is only a difference of reason, since both are inseparable by nature (*On Duties* 3.2.10).

[23] See Caesar, *De bello civili*, 1.67, *The Gallic War*, trans. H. J. Edwards (Cambridge, MA: Harvard University Press, 1917); Livy, *History of Rome*, trans. B. O. Foster (Cambridge, MA: Harvard University Press, 1919), 9.6, 3–7, 12; Tacitus, *Histories*, trans. Clifford H. Moore (Cambridge, MA: Harvard University Press, 1925), 4.72; John 3:19–21.

It is important to understand that "*nothing that is unjust is either advantageous or expedient;* a man who does not learn this lesson will never be able to be a "good man." "People overturn the fundamental principles established by Nature, when they divorce expediency from moral rectitude. For we all seek to obtain what is to us expedient; we are irresistibly drawn toward it, and we cannot possibly be otherwise. For who is there that would turn his back upon what is to him expedient? Or rather, who is there that does not exert himself to the utmost to secure it? But... we cannot discover it anywhere except in good report, propriety, and moral rectitude" (*On Duties* 3.28.101).

The only way to be happy is to be "honest" (i.e., honorable, good). Regulus[24] was happier remaining honest under torture than staying at home in safety and in shame: "And even as he was being killed, yet kept awake, his situation was better than if he had stayed home, aged prisoner of war, a man of consular rank foresworn" (*On Duties* 3.27.100, with modifications).

Cicero read in Polybius (*Histories* 6.58, 13) that when the news reached Hannibal that the Roman Senate refused to pay a ransom for the 8,000 soldiers left behind in order to teach them the lesson that they must either "conquer or die," Hannibal lost heart at such nobility of spirit. Morally right in appearance, nobility of spirit also proved supremely expedient (*On Duties* 3.32.114).[25] Cicero concludes: "For nothing can be expedient which is not at the same time morally right; neither can a thing be morally right just because it is expedient, but it is expedient because it is morally right" (3.30.110).[26]

In contrast, what is morally wrong and dishonorable is, generally, harmful and "calamitous" (*calamitosum*) for states and individuals. The immorality of Caesar, with his aspirations to be "the king of the Roman people," did not benefit him in the end (*On Duties* 3.21.82 and following).

Moreover, Cicero holds that immorality is a punishment in its own right, coming in addition to that of the law (Cicero regrets that, too often, shameful men escape the punishment of the law) (*On Duties* 3.8.36). Many make the calculation: the crime is small, but the reward large. To this Cicero replies, "Is there, then, any object of such value or any advantage so worth the winning that, to gain it, one should sacrifice the name of a 'good man' and the lustre of his reputation? What is there that your so-called expediency can bring to you that will compensate for what it can take away, if it steals from you the name of a 'good man' and causes you to lose your sense of honour and justice?" (*On Duties* 3.20.82; see also 81).

Let us return briefly to the example of Regulus. Some find his moral rectitude unwarranted and wrong. It cannot be argued that Jupiter's anger—which Regulus feared if he failed his oath—would have inflicted greater injury on him than Regulus brought on himself by keeping his word. To this Cicero replies, "Quite true, if there is no evil except pain" (*On Duties* 3.29.105). But he wanted to avoid the pain of dishonor. Which he did. In the end, his moral rectitude was more expedient than would have been his avoidance of torture and execution.

---

[24] Regulus, a Roman general, was taken prisoner by the Carthaginians in 255 BC. He was sent to Rome to negotiate an exchange of prisoners, promising to return even if he failed in his mission. On his arrival in Rome, he urged the Senate to reject Carthage's offer, arguing that the prisoners were young and gallant soldiers who would pose a threat to Rome if freed. Under no obligation other than his promise to his enemy, he returned to the Carthagean camp, where he was tortured and executed.

[25] Thus, there is a genuine mutual propriety between human nature and Nature, between humanity and the world. People can count on the fact that the world is not hostile to them, that as a rule it is possible for a person to succeed in the world. The reason for the urge to conduct oneself morally is not a transcendent call that detaches individuals from this world or pits them against it, confronting them with an impossible choice: either an immoral life or an unbearable morality. A person's obligation to behave morally arises under *the impulse of the same Nature that governs the universe.* Here we see the distance separating this conception from that of the Judeo-Christian world.

[26] In 1937 Pope Pius XI quoted these lines in an encyclical against Hitlerism.

3. Granted that expediency should never be given preference over moral goodness, it remains to determine what, for each opportunity in life, is *truly* morally right and good (that is, honorable) and morally base and wrong (that is, dishonorable) compared with what *only seems so*. In other words, to determine *where* duty lies in each circumstance.

For example, the killing of a tyrant,[27] who happens to be an intimate friend, is not something wrong that should be performed because it is expedient, although it is base to betray a friend; it is a tyrannicide and as such it is unreservedly right. Nevertheless, to put it in this particular light, the proper analysis must be undertaken.

So, Cicero sets himself the task of achieving in the field of morals what the praetor, with his "formulary system of procedure," achieved in the field of justice: the discovery of an inventive means of strictly applying general principles to every specific circumstance that arises (*On Duties* 3.4.19). Such casuistry is by no means an art of compromise; it is an application of prudence: through "experience" and "practice" we become "good calculators of duty" (*boni ratiocinatores officiorum*) (1.18.59).

It is, therefore, necessary to determine, in every circumstance of moral life, where duty lies; to do this, it is convenient to follow the order of the cardinal virtues.

2. *Moral Duties*

a. The Moral Duties of Prudence

As for discerning truth, there are two duties: avoid haste that leads to error, and avoid an unhealthy, purely speculative curiosity in things. For, indeed, "the whole glory (*laus*) of virtue is in activity" (*On Duties* 1.6.19). While speculation has its place in active life, it must not be the sole pursuit (this brings us to the debate on *otium* [a life of leisure] and *negotium* [an active life], see *De Rep.* 1.2 and *On Duties* 3).[28]

Political virtue consists largely of intelligence and prudence: a great politician is one who will never have to admit one day, "I never thought of that" (*On Duties* 1.23.81).

b. The Moral Duties of Justice

Justice is the virtue "by which society and what we may call its 'common bonds' are maintained" (*ea ratio qua societas hominum inter ipsos et vitae quasi communitas continetur*) (*On Duties* 1.7.20). There are two categories of justice: (1) strict justice, and (2) charity, kindness, generosity (*beneficiencia, benignitas, lieralitas*).

i. *Strict Justice*

The duty of strict justice is "to keep one man from doing harm to another, unless provoked by wrong," and to respect common and private property. It is founded on the principle *tribuere suum cuique*, "rendering to every man his due" (property), and *fides rerum contractarum*, the faithful discharge of obligations and honoring of contracts (*On Duties* 1.5.15).[29]

"The foundation of justice is good faith (*fides*)" (*On Duties* 1.7.23). Like the Stoics, who were fascinated by etymology, Cicero traces the origin of *fides* to *fiat quod dictum est,* "to make

---

[27] Cicero wrote this after Brutus assassinated Caesar on the Ides of March.

[28] See section titled "Active Life and Contemplative Life," below.

[29] Respect for *property* and *contracts* was the absolute basis of natural law until the modern period. Cicero understands that "the respect for contracts" is predicated on good faith. Thus, by definition, respect for a contract is good faith; others are expected to discharge their obligations; we count on their good faith. By introducing the assumption of good faith into the law, Roman jurisprudence and legislation also introduced an essential feature of natural law. The definition of justice as a fruit of *suum cuique tribuere* is solemnly recalled at the beginning of the Justinian *Digest* as an already immemorial formulation.

good what is promised." Justice depends on the proper respect for contracts and *good faith* in agreements.

There are two kinds of injustice: injustice by commission (inflicting wrong) and injustice by omission (not protecting from wrong). Its causes are fourfold: (1) the fear of an injustice being inflicted on one's self, (2) the desire for wealth and pleasures, (3) the ambition for power, and (4) the pursuit of a life of elegance and luxury. Injustice knows no bounds (*On Duties* 1.7.23).

Cicero allows wealth that is not based on injustice, that is, wealth that comes from fair transactions, "provided it hurt[s] nobody." He distinguishes between occasional injustice, committed under the impulse of passion, and deliberate injustice, committed wilfully, which is worse.

He condemns injustice by omission, which amounts to making action an obligation. Thus, once again he explicitly criticizes the *otium* of philosophers (*On Duties* 1.8.28),[30] which is a genuine injustice in the second sense (injustice by omission), though not in the first. Pure intellectuals are, literally, unjust individuals in that they do not accomplish the real essence of justice.

Likewise, the moral sense of action can change with the circumstances (*On Duties* 1.10.31). For example, it is right to return property to its owner, but if the item is a weapon and the owner is insane, it is wrong. Lower principles (e.g., returning property to its owner) have to be measured against higher ones (doing no harm to others, serving the common interest, *communis utilitas*). Another example: one should not keep a promise if doing so is hurtful to the person to whom it has been made, and if keeping it causes more harm than good. If you promise a friend to appear in court in his defense, and then your son falls ill, it is no breach of moral duty to temporarily abandon your obligation to your friend and attend to your son. Cicero notes that this order of priority is recognized by positive law, both by the praetor's edict as well as by the law (10.32). This is the origin of the adage, *summum ius, summa iniuria,*[31] "a now familiar saying," Cicero adds (10.33). The *intention* (or *spirit*) of the law counts for more than the letter.

ii. *Benevolence*

While strict justice consists of doing no harm and redressing wrong, benevolence involves something more, namely, it provides someone with help by means of a voluntary act that surpasses strict obligation. This benevolence is an integral part of human nature: we would not be perfect if we were happy only to be just.

In our discussion of biblical morality below (part 3), we will see that this new morality adds a further virtue to strict justice, namely *tsedaqa* or mercy, which involves giving to others more than their due. Biblical mercy or love is not the same as the benevolence of natural morality. Benevolence remains a natural virtue, regulated by equality and reciprocity, as we shall see, while love makes a break with nature (theologians speak of a "theological" virtue, which cannot be performed except for the gift of grace).

Although benevolence is different from *strict* justice, it is nonetheless a form of justice, in that the rule of equality applies to it as well. In the words of Cicero, "it shall be proportioned to the worthiness of the recipient" (*pro dignitate cuique tribuatur*). This, in fact, is the fundamental principle of justice (*On Duties* 1.14.45). "No one should be entirely neglected who shows any trace of virtue; but the more a man is endowed with these finer virtues—temperance, self-control, and that very justice about which so much has already been said" (1.15.46). Cicero adds that one should give more than he receives, like fruitful fields that return more than they receive (1.15.47). Thus, generosity is still measured by a rule of *nature*.

[30] Here Cicero takes aim at Plato as the leader, so to speak, of the pure "contemplatives."

[31] "The rigor of the law is the height of oppression," which can be paraphrased as "respect for the letter of the law, but hardly its spirit."

Conversely, "nothing is generous if it is not, at the same time, just" (*nihil est enim liberale quod non idem iustum*) (*On Duties* 1.14.43). One should abstain from being generous to someone at the expense of a third party. The supposed generosity of Sulla (a representative of the aristocratic party) or of Caesar (a representative of the "democratic" party) came at the expense of exiled citizens; it was not true generosity. At a private level, one should never give more than one has; by despoiling one's wealth one wrongs one's next of kin, and one is soon tempted to steal (1.14.44).

Lastly, we should do kindnesses to the meek rather than to the wealthy, from whom we anticipate rewards (*On Duties* 1.15.49).

iii. *The "Commonwealth of Mankind"*

Fundamentally, the functions of justice and benevolence are the *maintenance of human society,* which is an essential attribute of human nature. As we saw, humans are by nature social beings. Injustice, even abstaining from doing what is morally right and good, destroys a person's humanity.

Cicero describes in some detail the "commonwealth of mankind" and the duties that arise from it, as well as the relations between this commonwealth and the gods, and the relations with smaller communities, such as the city. The law, Cicero says, binds people with the immortal gods in a city; the universe forms *one immeasurable commonwealth, common alike to gods and mortals.*[32]

This "universal brotherhood" is thus not confined "within the walls of a city." It is cosmopolitan (*De Leg.* 1.23.61). Even the ordinary gods obey the laws set down by the supreme God, obeying "the celestial system, the divine mind, and the all-powerful god." Rejecting our duties as members of the universal brotherhood is an act of impiety because the gods themselves established this fellowship of all humankind (*On Duties* 3.6.28). The universal brotherhood follows from *natural equality,* and this equality ("one common nature") implies that one does not hold oneself in higher esteem than one's friends (*De Leg.* 1.12.34).

> Thus, however one defines man, the same definition applies to us all. This is sufficient proof that there is no essential difference within mankind. If there were, the same definition would not cover everyone. Reason in fact—the one thing in which we are superior to the beasts, which enable us to make valid deductions, to argue, refute our opponents, debate, solve problems, draw conclusions—that certainly is common to us all. While it may vary in what it teaches, it is constant in its ability to learn. For the same things are grasped by the senses of all, and those things that act on the senses act on the senses of all alike; and those rudimentary perceptions that are impressed on the mind...are impressed on *all* minds. Speech, which interprets the mind, uses different languages but expresses the same ideas. Nor is there any member of any nation who cannot attain moral excellence by using nature as his guide. The similarity between human beings is evident in their vices, bears some resemblance to what is naturally good; for it gives delight by its lightness and charm.... Death is shunned...life is sought.... What community does not love friendliness, generosity, and an appreciative mind which remembers acts of kindness? What community does

[32] *De Leg.* 1.7.23; the same idea is expressed in *De Rep.* 1.19, in *De natura deorum* 2.62, 154, and in *De finibus bonorum et malorum* 3, 19, 64. See Cicero, *De natura deorum* [On the nature of the gods], trans. H. Rackham (Cambridge, MA: Harvard University Press, 1933); and Cicero, *De finibus bonorum et malorum* [On the ends of good and bad things], trans. H. Rackham (Cambridge, MA: Harvard University Press, 1914).

> not reject the arrogant, the wicked, the cruel, and the ungrateful.... It is for these reasons that the whole human race is seen to be knit together. (*De Leg.* 1.10–11)[33]

Because all men share the same nature, they must also share the same "rule for right living" (*De Leg.* 1.10–11). In this sense, there is a fundamental equality among men. God requires, if not social equality, at least equal access for all to God's worship (2.10.25). It follows that we should be just and do good not only for our family and friends, but for the brotherhood of all humankind, which is a community of "reason and speech."

> [The] bond of connection [between all members of the human race] is reason and speech, which by the processes of teaching and learning, of communicating, discussing, and reasoning associate men together and unite them in a sort of natural fraternity (*conciliat inter se homines coniungitque naturali quadam societate*). In no other particular are we farther removed from the nature of beasts; for we admit that they may have courage (horses and lions, for example); but we do not admit that they have justice, equity, and goodness; for they are not endowed with reason or speech. (*On Duties* 1.16.50)

The preservation and triumph of human society is the very essence of a commitment to the common interest. It is more worthy to serve *the common interest* than one's own private interest. Paradoxically, I achieve more when serving the common interest than when pursuing my own personal interest. Hercules gives the example in this respect.

> Let us emulate the great Hercules, whom the judgment of men placed into the assembly of the heavenly gods in memory of his deeds. It is more in accord with Nature to undergo the greatest toil and trouble for the sake of aiding or saving the world, if possible, than to live in seclusion, not only free from all care, but revelling in pleasures and abounding in wealth, while excelling others also in beauty and strength. Thus Hercules denied himself and underwent toil and tribulation for the world, and, out of gratitude for his services, popular belief has given him a place in the council of the gods. The better and more noble, therefore, the character with which a man is endowed, the more does he prefer the life of service to the life of pleasure. (*On Duties* 3.5.25, with modifications)

Personal service in the public interest is a particular source of moral goodness and human excellence, which is why, *in the hierarchy of possible human lives, political careers rank at the top,*[34] above philosophy itself.

What is more, since man is not born for himself alone, but for the sake of all men, as Plato and the Stoics put it, it is necessary (Nature commands) that people should help one another: "we ought to...contribute to the general good by an interchange of acts of kindness, by giving and receiving, and thus by our skill, our industry, and our talents to cement human society more closely together, man to man" (see also *De Rep.* 3.8). The politician must work to establish (or restore) harmony among all, and particularly among fellow citizens. Cicero compares social harmony with the harmony of the different voices of the choir (*De Rep.* 2.69). This comparison was first made by Panaetius (see *On Duties* 1.40.145). Cicero's politics were based on the "harmony of orders"; he himself was something of a "centrist" and a "pacifist" (like Aristotle; see below his *cedant arma togae*, p. 283).

---

[33] This, then, is the lesson the Roman lawmakers learned from Greek philosophy, which stirred them to formulate proper rules of social behavior in all regions of the Empire. See above, pp. 256–57.

[34] This was the dominant belief in the Roman senatorial class.

It is because all human beings belong to the same natural order that laws and justice have legitimacy. The source of justice is the bond that "unites human beings and what natural fellowship exists between them" (*De Leg.* 1.5.16). "Our natural inclination to love and cherish our associates... is the true basis of justice" (*De Leg.* 1.15.43). Conversely, the principle of all legal punishment is that guilty persons banish themselves from society by doing wrong against it.[35]

iv. *Interlocking Human Societies*

Human society has several levels (*On Duties* 1.17.53–57): (1) infinite humanity (*societas infinita* [the *cosmopolis*]); (2) membership in the same people, tribe, and tongue (*eiusdem gentis, nationis, lingae*) (Is Cicero thinking of Italy here?); (3) the city-state (*civitas*), where fellow citizens have in common "forum, temples colonnades, streets, statutes, laws, courts, rights of suffrage, to say nothing of social and friendly circles and diverse business relations with many"; and (4) family and kindred, that is, husband, wife, and children living under the same roof.

Transcending these categories and hierarchies is the friendship of "good men of congenial character" (*viri boni moribus similes familiaritate coniuncti*), who recognize in others the moral goodness they possess in themselves. What hierarchy exists between these different societies? Which should receive our particular attachment? Cicero says, "when with a rational spirit [*ratione animoque*] you have surveyed the whole field, there is no social relation among them all more close, none more close, none more dear than that which links each one of us with our country [*res publica*].[36] Parents are dear; dear are children, relatives, friends; one native land embraces all our loves; and which honest man would hesitate to give his life for her, if by his death he could render her a service?" (*On Duties* 1.17.57, with modifications).

At any rate, to know how to place moral obligations towards members of various human groups in a hierarchy, "we shall have to consider what is most needful in each individual case and what each individual person can or cannot procure without our help. In this way we shall find that the claims of social relationship, in its various degrees, are not identical with the dictates of circumstances; for there are obligations that are due to one individual rather than to another" (*On Duties* 1.17.59). For example, I might help a neighbor in bringing in the harvest rather than helping my own brother in a lesser task, but in a court case, I would defend my kinsman instead of my neighbor. Only experience enables us to understand how this hierarchy works—just as experience and practice enable a physician or an orator to do their work—and thus to become a "good calculator of duty" (*On Duties* 1.18.59–60).

Despite such hierarchies, moral duties are universal. There is no distinction between brothers or father and fellow citizens, on the one hand, or between fellow citizens and the rest of humanity, on the other. "Others again who say that regard should be had for the rights of fellow-citizens, but not of foreigners, would destroy the universal brotherhood of mankind; and, when this is annihilated, kindness, generosity, goodness, and justice must utterly perish" (*On Duties* 3.6.28).

In fact, the very ideas of kindness, generosity, justice, and so on, suppose the universal. It is not possible to be just solely with one's own family and friends. It makes no sense.

v. *Property*

Just conduct is a show of consideration for public and private property. Cicero develops an intricate doctrine for both types: common property and private property.

---

[35] Killing a tyrant or stealing from him are not crimes because a tyrant is no longer a member of the *societas generis humani.* He is like a gangrenous limb that must be amputated from the healthy body (*On Duties* 3.6.32).

[36] The reference is to the Roman state. It is possible that the preceding list (*cosmopolis,* nation, city-state) was transcribed directly from Panetius.

The "brotherhood of mankind" implies that what is not considered by positive law to be private property is held in common, that is, it is *common property*.

> This, then, is the most comprehensive bond that unites together men as men and all to all; and under it the common right to all things that Nature has produced for the common use of man is to be maintained, with the understanding that, while everything assigned as private property by the statutes and by civil law shall be so held as prescribed by those same laws, everything else shall be regarded in the light indicated by the Greek proverb: "Amongst friends all things in common."[37] Furthermore, we find the common property of all men in things of the sort defined by Ennius;[38] and, though restricted by him to one instance, the principle may be applied very generally:
> "Who kindly sets a wand'rer on his way
> Does e'en as if he lit another's lamp by his:
> No less shines his, when he his friend's hath lit." (*On Duties* 1.16.51)

As members of the human race we must "let anyone who will take fire from our fire," give honest advice to one who is in doubt, and "deny no one the water that flows by." According to the test of Ennius,[39] however, the poorer classes should limit their generosity to what they can give without loss to themselves.

Private property is a natural right, although at the outset nothing is naturally private property. But "some of those things which by nature had been common property became the property of individuals" (either through original occupancy, through conquest, or "by due process of law, bargain, or purchase, or by allotment"). "Each one should retain possession of that which has fallen to his lot; and if anyone appropriates to himself anything beyond that, he will be violating the laws of human society" (*On Duties* 1.7.21).

> For a man to take something from his neighbour and to profit by his neighbour's loss is more contrary to Nature than is death or poverty or pain or anything else that can affect either our person or our property. For, in the first place, injustice is fatal to social life and fellowship between man and man. For, if we are so disposed that each, to gain some personal profit, will defraud or injure his neighbour, then those bonds of human society [*humanae generis societas*], which are most in accord with Nature's laws, must of necessity be broken. Suppose, by way of comparison, that each one of our bodily members should conceive this idea and imagine that it could be strong and well if it should draw off to itself the health and strength of its neighbouring member, the whole body would necessarily be enfeebled and die; so, if each one of us should seize upon the property of his neighbours and take from each whatever he could appropriate to his own use, the bonds of human society (*societas hominum et communitas*) must inevitably be annihilated. For, without any conflict with Nature's laws, it is granted that everybody may prefer to secure for himself rather than for his neighbour what is essential for the conduct of life; but Nature's laws do forbid us to increase our means, wealth, and resources by despoiling others. (*On Duties* 3.5.21–24)

Nature is not against "self-interest"; it is against theft and crime; it favors honoring and upholding the "private sphere" (*suum*) of all members of society.

---

37 See Aristotle, *Nichomachean Ethics,* trans. H. Rackham (Cambridge, MA: Harvard University Press, 1934), 7.9.1.

38 An early Latin poet.

39 We are far removed from Christian charity here: gifts are made only if they do not occasion loss; what is given does not form part of one's own flesh and blood; it is what is held in common *by nature*.

Cicero points out that this principle "of Nature, i.e. this 'law of nations'" (*natura, id est iure gentium*), is established in each human group or family (*gens*) by *laws*, the purpose of which is to safeguard the bonds of union between citizens. Positive law reinforces natural law. Cicero concludes, "the chief purpose in the establishment of constitutional states and municipal governments [is] that *individual property rights might be secured*" (*On Duties* 2.21.73).

Thus, logically Cicero condemns early attempts at socialism. The public official, he says, "must make it his first care that everyone shall have what belongs to him and that private citizens suffer no invasion of their property rights by act of the state." It is a "ruinous speech" (*capitalis oratio*) that favors "an equal distribution of property." The levying of a tax is sometimes necessary, when people "must bow to the inevitable, if they wish to be saved"; any other tax is unfair (Cicero argues against imposing a tax burden that takes from some for the benefit of others—although he does not state this explicitly, he argues for an equal or proportionate tax) (*On Duties* 2.21.73).

Moreover, the cause of recent wars,[40] Cicero says, has been Rome's plundering of its allies, or an obligation placed on allies to make gifts to Rome; in other words, a violation of private property rights (75). State confiscation of private fortunes serves not only demagogic purposes, but also the personal enrichment of politicians. Naturally, Cicero condemns this practice outright: "to exploit the state for selfish profit is not only immoral; it is criminal, infamous" (*On Duties* 2.21.77).

Cicero's praise of private property does not lead to him becoming personally involved in economic issues. There are "certain worthy gentlemen" at the Gates of Janus who are able to discuss "this whole subject of acquiring money, investing money," he says. They are more competent in these matters than any philosopher. Consequently he defers to them (*On Duties* 2.24.86).

vi. *Honoring Agreements*

Once Cicero perceives humankind as individual property owners—respectful of private property belonging to others and mindful of providing reciprocal services to one another—he naturally admits that such activities take place on the basis of contractual *agreement*. He points out that praetorian law requires agreements to be upheld *nec vi nec dolo malo* (neither through force nor criminal fraud) (*On Duties* 3.24.92–3.25.95).[41]

Of course, it is not the case that every agreement in every instance should be upheld. Once again, there are circumstances that can change the moral value of an act. If I promise a dying millionaire to dance publicly in the forum in order to become his heir, it will be morally better for me to break my promise and forego my inheritance than to lose my dignity; unless perhaps I dance and contribute the money to the public treasury to finance some public cause.

vii. *The Ethics of Trade*

But given all this, is one truly free to do whatever one wants with one's property? Cicero sets down a very interesting discussion between the Stoics Diogenes of Babylon and Antipater of Tarsus on a question of ethics in trade, namely, the right of the seller to remain silent, or indeed dissimulate,

---

[40] Probably the Social War (see above, p. 209).

[41] Here Cicero uses a text that is probably older than the equivalent one found in the *Digest* (2.14.7.7): "Ait praetor: Pacta conventa, quae neque dolo molo, neque adversus leges plebis scita senatusconsulta decreta edicta principum, neque quo fraus cui eorum fiat, facta erunt, servabo" (The Praetor declares: I will uphold contracts that have not been secured fraudulently nor against the law, resolution [*plebiscita*], decree or princely edict, and where none of these have been ignored).

concerning the quality of his goods. Cicero was directly familiar with these disputes, which the Stoic tradition had probably preserved for their exemplary value (*On Duties* 3.12.50–53).

Diogenes of Babylon was a Stoic philosopher and disciple of Chrysippus (b. in Seleucia ca. 240 BC). He was sent to Rome in 156 BC as a member of the famous Athenian delegation with Carneades the Academician and Critolaus the Peripatetic to appeal a fine. While the dialectic of Carneades created a scandal and provoked Cato's censorship, the more moderate arguments of Diogenes were highly esteemed and brought much credit to Stoicism in Rome. Antipater counted among Diogenes' students; he succeeded him later at the Porch. Panaetius was another; he also studied under Antipater and succeeded him.

Their discussion touches on two examples.[42] Is it right for a grain merchant in Rhodes to remain silent about the imminent arrival of a fleet from Alexandria with a cargo of grain so that he can sell his grain at a higher price? Is it right for the owner of a house to conceal its defects (the fact that it is infested with vermin, built with unsound timber, and on the verge of collapse) in order to sell it for more?

Diogenes, a native of Babylon, where commerce was a time-honored activity, answers yes to both questions. Antipater, his dialogue partner, answers no. Cicero takes the side of Antipater and adopts if not a hostile stance to commerce at least a hesitant one (all the while presenting Diogenes' arguments fairly). It is quite interesting to see what the Greeks had to say—in antiquity already—about a free economy from a philosophical standpoint. The refusal to allow a merchant to remain silent is a denial of a property owner's right to use his property as he pleases; yet the notions of selling and buying presuppose the legality of private property. Antipater's position is, therefore, contradictory. Conversely, one is under no outright obligation to say everything one knows. If this were the case, the philosopher would spend his whole life moralizing and sermonizing everyone! Diogenes provides a very "liberal" expression of the underlying ethics of a sales and purchase agreement: "he advertised for sale what he did not like; you bought what you did like." Nobody knows better than me my personal interest. By remaining silent, the grain dealer respects the personal liberty of the buyer, just as he expects his own liberty to be respected: both know the rules and there is nothing here that morality can condemn.

Roman civil law approves of this silence, except in just a few cases: defects in slaves and animals had to be declared, a wronged buyer could obtain the cancellation of a sales agreement; the same held for real estate transactions: silence was not permissible. The more recent civil law of Rome was stricter than the Law of the Twelve Tables (*On Duties* 3.16.65). Antifraud measures had become necessary primarily because of the influx of foreign merchants into Rome, a consequence of its imperial expansion (since foreign merchants were not domiciled in Rome, there were no guarantees).

Cicero finally takes the side of Antipater (*On Duties* 3.13.56), because, although it is licit to remain silent as long as nobody is hurt, *in the cases under discussion* silence is illicit. In both examples the sellers conceal facts from potential buyers who can benefit from the information, and the sellers do so in their own personal interest. This is not worthy of a "candid or sincere or straightforward or upright or honest man, but rather [of] one who is shifty, sly, artful, shrewd, underhanded, cunning, one grown old in fraud and subtlety" (3.13.57).[43]

---

[42] In *On Duties* 3.23.91–92, Cicero highlights other issues discussed by Diogenes and Antipater as well.

[43] This gives business and business people a bad reputation. Thomas Aquinas will argue that there is always a problem with business people, and the problem is not profit but untruth. If merchants have a reputation for immorality, it is not for what is opposed to *justice* in their conduct (while it is true there are dishonest merchants, there are many more honest ones); what is at fault is what in their conduct is opposed to *prudence*. The problem is with their relationship to truth. Sometimes their business practices are sharp and even the best among them are not above suspicion. Be that as it may,

The argument applies *a fortiori* to liars and cheats who "pretend one thing and practise another" (this was Gaius Canius's own definition; he was Cicero's fellow praetor—an excellent jurist, greatly admired by Cicero) (*On Duties* 3.14.58–60).

Moreover, Roman law always condemned the fraud of the dishonest seller, but it rarely condemned his silence. Likewise, the Law of the Twelve Tables condemned guardians who abused incapable persons. The *Lex Plaetoria* (193–192 BC) protected minors under the age of 25 from those who would abuse their inexperience. Near the end of the Republic, under the influence of new philosophical ideas and the influx of foreigners into Rome (a consequence of the expansion of the Empire), judges were asked more frequently to avoid literal interpretations of the law and instead to search for "whatever on that account he ought in good faith to pay or to do" (*quicquid paret dare facere oportere ex fide bona*). Around 90 BC, the judge Cato (the father of Cato of Utica, Cicero's contemporary) found in favor of a buyer who sued the seller of a building "in the name of good faith" for failing to declare its defects. Cicero extended this ruling to the above cases of the grain dealer and seller of the unsanitary, defective house (nevertheless, civil law condemned only certain silences; it was not a general rule).

Cicero was well aware that his moral condemnation of commercial and economic practices did not meet with general approval. Everyone respects the perfect good man, but he is seen as something of a misfit and, paradoxically perhaps, lacking in true wisdom. The "mischievous idea" is that the world distinguishes between the upright man and the wise man as if they were not the same (*On Duties* 3.15.62). The ideal of the good man, incapable of fraud or lying (even by omission), is virtually timeless.

Finally, some moral duties, concerning the final two cardinal virtues, also interest political thought.

c. The Moral Duties of the Nobility of the Spirit

Nobility of spirit (*magnanimitas*), also called courage (*fortitudo*), is the faculty to endure effort and pain. This virtue attracts the highest praise; to insult someone, we call them a coward; when statues of great men are made, they are represented in military garb (*On Duties* 1.18.61).

Courage is what differentiates men of leisure (scholars and philosophers) from men of political ambition (devoted "to statecraft and to conducting great enterprises"). Both types can be wise, morally upright, temperate, and in control of their passions. But philosophers are aloof from public affairs, rarely exposed to circumstances that enable them to build up their courage and endure the sudden and cruel reversals of fortune. Nobility of spirit can rarely manifest itself in such people, who consequently cannot achieve the fullness of moral goodness. On the other hand, politicians and statesmen do attain such heights because they are exposed to life's tests and develop a "hard shell" to face changes in fortune (*On Duties* 1.21.70–73). *Otium*—constant *otium* at any rate—must be condemned, except in cases of poor health, particular circumstances, or exceptional intellectual gifts. Philosophers may have clean hands, but in truth they have no hands; therefore, Cicero concludes, they are *not* clean. Without action, no complete virtue, therefore no man.

We should not be misled by Cicero's praise of courage: he is not referring to warriorlike expressions of this virtue. In a famous passage (*On Duties* 1.22.74–78), he praises *the supremacy of civil affairs above military endeavors*. The former are more lasting and provide the foundations for the latter. Solon's achievements were greater than those of Themistocles: "For arms are of little value in the field unless there is wise counsel at home."

---

business dealings are never really worthy of a freeman or a liberal profession. The corollary: a clerk who can work with his hands, pursue the liberal arts, be a statesman, and so on, should never be a merchant.

Praising his own consulship in 63 BC during which he crushed the Catilina conspiracy, Cicero wrote "*cedant arma togae, concedat laurea laudi*" (yield, ye arms, to the toga; to civic praises, ye laurels). In his triumph of 60 BC, Pompey proclaimed that his victory in war would have been in vain if there had been "no place in which to celebrate it," referring to the Republic Cicero had just saved.

d. The Moral Duties of Temperance

Temperance is the virtue that puts restraints on our appetites and ensures that all other virtues keep to a middle course and maintain an appearance of "propriety."

When the spirit is disordered by inappropriate passions, the whole body undergoes a change: expressions of rage, fear, or "extravagant joy" change a person's face (this explains why a respectable person modestly conceals his pleasure [*On Duties* 1.30.105]). This ugliness is a sign that the immodest person is dehumanized and inclines toward bestiality. This gives rise to various moral duties pertaining directly or indirectly to proper social life.

Modestia (*eutaxia,* i.e., orderly conduct) is "the science of doing the right thing at the right time" (*On Duties* 1.40.142): the importance of modeling one's conduct and speech according to the circumstances of time and place. For example, a praetor should not admire "a handsome person" while he is in office. Nor should one pursue long-winded reflections at a formal dinner, or "when upon a serious theme, introduce [jests or loose talk]" (1.40.144). Moreover, jesting must remain within bounds; some jests are elegant, others are vulgar (*ingenui et illiberalis ioci*). Similarly, certain forms of relaxation are proper (hunting), others are not (1.29.103–04).

A good person must be able to speak on the two registers of oratory and conversation. Rules exist for oratory; they have been laid down by rhetoricians. But there are none for conversation, and that is a pity. The voice should be clear and pleasing; one should avoid mumbling and affectation (*On Duties* 1.37.132–33). One who engages in conversation should not prevent others from participating. For the topic of the conversation, one should observe what is appropriate to the circumstance, avoiding anger, envy, apathy, maliciousness toward absent individuals, and swagger (see Plautus's *miles gloriosus,* the braggart). One must know how to end a conversation (*On Duties* 1.37.134).

Tiny infractions in these matters are almost more serious than grand extravagances. Like wrong notes in a musical harmony, they ruin everything. Indeed, false notes are the expression of serious hidden defects. The teacher must correct them. *Refinement* results from the systematic correction of moral shortcomings (*On Duties* 42.150–51).

One's use of goods in the public eye has moral significance as well. In choice of dress and home one must pay careful attention to rank and station and to the demands of time and place. For example, the dignity of a one's home enables a person to perform one's duties appropriately (*On Duties* 39.138–39).

From the foregoing discussion, it is possible to establish *a hierarchy of professions and social roles.* Trades and professions have varying degrees of respectability. For one reason or another, some are less respectable than others and are rightly held in less esteem.

The professions of tax-gatherers and usurers are "unbecoming of a freeman" (they are not "liberal professions"). Similarly, hired workers are considered base, as they are paid "for mere manual labour, not for artistic skill." Physical toil deforms the body. "Vulgar we must consider those also who buy from wholesale merchants to retail immediately; for they would get no profits without a great deal of downright lying." Vulgar, too, "are those trades which cater for sensual pleasures": fishmongers, butchers, cooks, perfumers, dancers, and gamblers living from "games of chance." On the other hand, professions that require "a higher degree of intelligence," such as medicine, architecture, and teaching, are proper and worthy, while trade on a large scale "is not to be greatly disparaged." "But of all the occupations by which gain is secured, none is better than agriculture, none more profitable, none more delightful, none more becoming to a freeman" (*On Duties* 42.150–51).[44]

e. Hierarchy of Moral Duties: The Primacy of Justice

Cicero concludes that it is possible to establish a hierarchy of virtues. The most important of the four is justice (*On Duties* 1.43.152). His argument is as follows:

1. *Justice* is better than *knowledge* because if a wise man did not live among men, he would cease to be a man. Without justice the wisdom of a wise man would be purposeless.

> The study and knowledge of the universe would somehow be lame and defective, were no practical results to follow. Such results, moreover, are best seen in the safeguarding of human interests. It is essential, then, to human society; and it should, therefore, be ranked above speculative knowledge. Upon this all the best men agree, as they prove by their conduct. For who is so absorbed in the investigation and study of creation, but that, even though he were working and pondering over tasks never so much worth mastering and even though he thought he could number the stars and measure the length and breadth of the universe, he would drop all those problems and cast them aside, if word were suddenly brought to him of some critical peril to his country, which he could relieve or repel? And he would do the same to further the interests of parent or friend or to save him from danger. From all this we conclude that the duties prescribed by justice must be given precedence over the pursuit of knowledge and the duties imposed by it; for the former concern the welfare of our fellow-men; and nothing ought to be more sacred in men's eyes than that. (*On Duties* 1.43.153–1.44.155)

Moreover (1.44.155), the best scholars are those who give their intellectual efforts meaning by training upright citizens; for example, Pythagorean Lysis taught Epaminondas of Thebes, Plato taught Dion of Syracuse, and Cicero's own teachers prepared him for public service to his country. This effort continues even after teachers pass away through their writings. "They seem to have devoted their retirement [contemplative leisure] to the benefit of us who are engaged in public business" (*otium suum ad nostrum negotium*) (1.44.156). "For that reason also much speaking (if only it contain wisdom) is better than speculation never so profound without speech; for mere speculation is self-centered (*cogitatio in se ipsa vertitur*), while speech extends its benefits to those with whom we are united by the bonds of society" (1.44.156).

Lastly, wisdom without justice becomes an imperfection. It is, in fact, worse than the coeval absence of wisdom and justice (nothing is more abhorent than an intelligent rogue or an intelligent tyrant).

2. Likewise, nobility of spirit, "if unrestrained by the uniting bonds of society, would be but a sort of brutality and savagery" (*On Duties* 1.44.157).

3. Again, the moral duty of *propriety* gives way to the duties owed to the *community*. Cicero adds that, fortunately, the state never demands repulsive or wicked acts of men (it never imposes excesses of food or wine or asks them to behave lustfully).

4. Finally, there is also a hierarchy among the duties owed to the community: "our first duty is to the *immortal gods*, our second, to *country;* our third, to *parents;* and so on, in a descending

[44] This moral hierarchy of trades and professions survived in the West for centuries.

scale, to the rest" (*On Duties* 1.44.160).[45] Cicero concludes that justice "is the sovereign mistress and queen of all virtues" (3.6.28).

f. The Art of Securing the Cooperation of Others

Cicero provides indirect proof of all this in part 2 of *On Duties* where he examines the kinds of support one can expect from others during one's lifetime.

Gods and animals can be of service to us in different circumstances. But of all the living beings, Cicero observes, the most helpful and the most harmful to humans are humans themselves. And yet, it is through the cooperation of others that we receive everything else, and without such cooperation we would have nothing and nothing would be available to us (*On Duties* 2.3.11–6.20). Even the influence of Fortune is lessened or increased by human beings (20). Cicero concludes, "I set it down as the peculiar function of virtue to win the hearts of men and attach them to one's own service" (17). He reasons as follows: men seek happiness, but it cannot be attained except through the cooperation of everyone together, and such cooperation is secured through moral goodness. Therefore, moral goodness is the highest expedient.

How can the cooperation of others be secured? By money, self-interest, and mutual service, but also through *fear* and *goodwill* [the love and affection of others] (*On Duties* 2.6.21–22).

Fear is the means used by rulers of barbarous or tyrannical states, but its use is discouraged in a "free state" (*libera civitas*) because it engenders hate. The assassination of Caesar shows the power of hate. "Those who wish to be feared must inevitably be afraid of those whom they intimidate" (*On Duties* 2.7.23–24).

Goodwill accompanies friendship. It must be equally present in the affairs of the public man with the people and in his private affairs. "The first and absolute essential [is] that we have the devotion of friends, affectionate and loving, who value our worth. For in just this one point there is but little difference between the greatest and the ordinary man" (*On Duties* 2.8.30).

The affection of others is obtained through kind services, generosity, justice, loyalty, "and all those virtues that belong to gentleness of character and affability of manner." While kind service is helpful in securing friendship, it is not the gift that leaves an impact, it is the moral goodness of the deed. An act of kindness that fails to produce a good result can have the same impact. It is the *intention* to perform an act of kindness that constitutes goodwill (*On Duties* 2.9.32). "And because that very quality which we term moral goodness and propriety [*honestum decorumque*] is pleasing to us by and of itself and touches all our hearts both by its inward essence and its outward aspect... we are, therefore, compelled by Nature herself to love those in whom we believe those virtues to reside" (2.9.32). We also show kindness toward people we admire and esteem (2.8.30). Admiration comes from the discovery of *unexpected* qualities of goodness in a person, for we all expect others to fear death and poverty and to be swayed by intense pleasures. But when exalted individuals show such expectations to be false, they shine with the splendour and beauty of virtue (2.10.36).

If we desire the affection and esteem of others, we must first of all be just. Justice is the one virtue "on the basis of which alone men are called 'good men.'" A just person is *a fortiori* one who inspires confidence, affection, and admiration. Conversely, an unjust person is vulnerable to injustice and to being without "friends with whom to enjoy social intercourse" (*On Duties* 2.9.33–34; 11.38). Justice is essential, especially in business.

> To buyers and sellers, to employers and employed, and to those who are engaged in commercial dealings generally, justice is indispensable for the conduct of business. Its importance

[45] Later Thomas Aquinas will give fuller development to this idea.

> is so great, that not even those who live by wickedness and crime can get on without some small element of justice. For if a robber takes anything by force or by fraud from another member of the gang, he loses his standing even in a band of robbers; and if the one called the "Pirate Captain" should not divide the spoils impartially, he would be either deserted or murdered by his comrades. Why, they say that robbers even have a code of laws to observe and obey. (*On Duties* 2.11.40)[46]

Cicero concludes that it is through confidence and affection, not through fear, that Rome rules its Empire, which is more a "protectorate of the world" (*patrocinium orbis terrae*) than a dominion (*imperium*).

3. *Cicero's Personalism*

In the foregoing discussion, our focus has been on human nature in general, that is, what it means to be human. But the Stoics and Cicero contribute a further important idea that appears nowhere else in Aristotelian moral philosophy (or, in any case, it does not receive special treatment): every person has their own *individual* nature or specific character, which deserves recognition, respect, and preservation by the brotherhood of men and by states. This may be Rome's special contribution: namely, the discovery of the potentialities of each individual human person, which is preserved by the sphere of individual autonomy produced by Roman law (see above, the introduction to part 2). "In the matter of physical endowment there are great differences: some, we see, excel in speed for the race, others in strength for wrestling; so in point of personal appearance, some have stateliness, others comeliness" (*On Duties* 1.3.107).[47]

We should follow the dictates of our own personal nature, just as we use our native tongue; if we lace our speech with foreign words, we are ridiculous; the same is true when we imitate others.[48]

Cicero illustrates this with his famous example from the *theater* (Panaetius probably provided the initial idea):

> Everyone, therefore, should make a proper estimate of his own natural ability and show himself a critical judge of his own merits and defects; in this respect we should not let actors display more practical wisdom than we have. They select, not the best plays, but the ones best suited to their talents. Those who rely most upon the quality of their voice take the Epigoni[49] and the Medus;[50] those who place more stress upon the action choose the Melanippa and the Clytaemnestra; Rupilius, whom I remember, always played in the Antiope, Aesopus rarely in the Ajax. Shall a player have regard to this in choosing his role upon the stage, and a wise man fail to do so in selecting his part in life? We shall, therefore, work to the best advantage in that role to which we are best adapted. (*On Duties* 1.31.114)

---

[46] This same idea appears in Plato's *Republic* 1.350c, 352b–c, as we recall.

[47] To prove this point, Cicero parades before the reader a "gallery of portraits" of famous Greek and Roman figures, one celebrated for his "wit," another for his "unusual seriousness," another for his "unbounded jollity," and another still for "his serious ideals . . . and austere life."

[48] Thus, at the very root of Western humanism, there is a refusal to mimic or imitate; imitation is the chief characteristic of tribal societies. The peculiar trait of an individual is what is not imitated and not able to be imitated. In this sense, the *crowd,* i.e., the *fusional group,* where everyone imitates everyone else, is inhuman. Here we have a *humanist* criteria for distinguishing the civilized human being, strictly speaking, from the barbarian.

[49] The sons of the seven heroes who took Thebes. Both Aeschylus and Euripides treated the subject.

[50] The son of Medea.

In the theater a character is called a *persona,* the Greek term for the mask and mouthpiece (*per-sona*) worn by actors. It seems that the word "person," and the "personalist" philosophy that Cicero develops in this passage, derives from the Stoic comparison of human nature with the roles and characters of the theater. Thus, Western humanism was a "personalism" long before Christianity transformed each individual human being into a unique creature blessed with God's love and promise of eternal salvation. Fortune can, of course, lead us astray from our Nature, but the struggle between Fortune and Nature is like the combat between a mortal and a god. Nature itself is unrelenting (*On Duties* 1.32.118). A young man must remember these things when he chooses what he will do with his life (1.32.117).

Cicero adds a final thought. Moral duties are contingent upon universal and individual nature, but also on age and circumstance. *Youth* has certain obligations: showing deference to elders, attaching one's self to wise counsel and influence. "The inexperience of youth requires the practical wisdom of age to strengthen and direct it." A young man must be protected from sensuality and beware of excesses. He must be "trained to toil and endurance of both mind and body." Likewise, *adulthood* has specific obligations: provide youth with good counsel and practical wisdom; serve the state; guard against idleness. The *magistrate, private citizen,* and *foreigner* (either resident alien or a visitor passing through) have specific obligations as well: "his duty [is] to attend strictly to his own concerns, not to pry into other people's business, and under no condition to meddle in the politics of a country not his own") (*On Duties* 1.33.122–26).

Having spoken so well of human nature and the moral duties it commands, Cicero proudly concludes, with Terence, that in human concerns nothing is foreign to him (*humani nihil a se alienum putat*) (*On Duties* 1.29; *De Leg.* 1.12.33).

D. The Law and the State

It is the purpose of the law to preserve the individual human nature described above. The law, in turn, is preserved by the state. These are the topics that Cicero develops in two works, the *Republic* and the *Laws,* to which we now turn. Taken together, these works form the first presentation of a *liberal* political doctrine in the history of philosophy.

1. *Natural Law and Positive Law*

In order to fulfill their respective functions and obligations, the law and the state must recognize that they do not create justice but receive it from nature: *iuris natura fons est* ("Nature is the source of right") (*On Duties* 3.17.72). There is a natural law, because nature did not create human beings without giving them bonds of law: "we have been made by nature to share justice amongst ourselves and to impart it to one another" (*De Leg.* 1.12.33).

This *natural* law is formally distinguished from *positive* law. "One must consider the science of the law to be derived, not from the *praetor's edict* (as most authorities hold today), nor from the *Twelve Tables* (as our forefathers believed), but from the deepest recesses of philosophy [as it is concerned with the study of nature]" (*De Leg.* 1.5.17, with modifications).

Citizens are justified in their judgment of the actions of jurists and political leaders, measuring them against this higher standard. This *right of judgment* is based on a distinction between *natural law* and *positive law,* or—what amounts to the same thing—between what is *legitimate* and what is only *legal.*

a. Universal Law and Eternal Law

> A true law exists: it is right reason in harmony with nature, [it] spreads through the whole human community, unchanging and eternal, calling people to their duty by its commands and deterring them from wrong-doing by its prohibitions. When it addresses a good man,

> its commands and prohibitions are never in vain; but those same commands and prohibitions have no effect on the wicked. This law cannot be countermanded, nor can it be in any way amended, nor can it be totally rescinded. We cannot be exempted from the law by any decree of the Senate or the people; nor do we need a Sextus Aelius[51] to expound or explain it. There will not be one such law in Rome and another in Athens, one now and another in the future, but all peoples at all times will be embraced by a single and eternal and unchangeable law; and there will be, as it were, one lord and master of us all—the god who is the author, proposer, and enacter of that law. Whoever refuses to obey it will be turning his back on himself. Because he has denied his nature as a human being he will face the gravest penalties for this alone, even if he succeeds in avoiding all the other things that are regarded as punishments. (*De Leg.* 3.33, with modifications)

Not only is it forbidden for a tyrant to overstep the bounds of natural law, it is also forbidden for the "Senate" and the "people" to do so as well. Natural law is not the product of human will, because *it is not founded on a consensus of wills;* natural law exists objectively, it is in the nature of things. No human, no group of humans, not even humankind as such command human nature. Nature is "transcendent."

> According to the opinion of the best authorities, law was not *thought up by the intelligence of human beings,* nor is it some kind of *resolution passed by communities,* but rather an eternal force which rules the world by the wisdom of its commands and prohibitions. In their judgement, that original and final law is *the intelligence* (*mens*) *of God,* who ordains or forbids everything by reason.... Since our childhood, Quintus, we have been taught to call "*If [plaintiff] summon [defendant] to court,*"[52] and other things of that kind, laws. But one must understand that this and other orders and prohibitions issued by communities do not have the power of encouraging people to right actions and deterring them from wrongdoing. That power is not only older than the existence of communities and states; it is coeval with that god who watches over and rules heaven and earth. (*De Leg.* 2.4.8–9)

Consequently, natural law, which the Senate cannot repeal, "does not come into force or lapse with the letters in which enactments are written down" (5.11). It is "the highest law." It comes into being "before all time" and is "eternal."

Thus, Cicero postulates the fundamental notion of "laws of laws" (*leges legum*) (7.18), that is, (natural) laws that (positive) laws must obey in order to have legitimacy, and that no lawmaker can ever transgress.[53]

Justice is natural, it is not based on a convention. It does not result from a contract, and neither does the state. Neither justice nor the other virtues nor the state itself can be based on a convention (*institutio*) (*De Rep.* 1.26.41; *De Leg.* 1.10.28).

Natural law, eternal and universal, is fundamentally stable. In contrast, positive law, when it fails to obey natural law, is doomed to instability. For if expediency, instead of the nature of things, forms the basis of the law, another expediency will subvert it (*De Leg.* 1.15.42).

---

[51] Author of the first civil law treatise, as we saw earlier.

[52] Cicero uses this formula to refer to the Law of the Twelve Tables and the praetor's edicts.

[53] This Ciceronian notion may be considered the source to which modern theorists of natural law, international law (the laws of nations), and constitutionalism, turn in their efforts to restrict the arbitrary powers of the absolutist state. Laws must obey higher principles, constitutional rules, and human rights: it is not possible to establish just any law, even if the "sovereign people" decide it. The sovereign—king, assembly, or people—is the highest power in the state, but the state is not higher than human nature.

b. Some Examples of Norms Drawn from Nature

Hierarchy is an example of natural law. The very idea of command and obedience is in nature; so, if natural law is followed, every city will have magistrates with authority (*De Leg.* 3.1.3). Similarly, people with fewer qualities readily accept the power of those with more; this establishes in natural law the principle of aristocracy (but a chosen or elected aristocracy, not a self-proclaimed one, even less an oligarchy where wealth rather than individual qualities constitutes the justification for power) (*De Rep.* 1.34.51). This explains why democratic equality, brought back to natural law, is an iniquity; it denies natural differences. "When the same respect is accorded to the highest and the lowest [*summis et infimis*] (who must be present in every nation), equity itself is most unequal" (*De Rep.* 1.34.53).

Other examples of norms from nature that are imposed on the lawgiver and ruler exist: the censors "shall not allow men to remain bachelors;[54] they shall regulate the behaviour of the citizens" (*De Leg.* 3.3.7); begging will be forbidden[55] (*De Leg.* 2.9.22).

Having established these principles, Cicero allows that many systems of positive law are in harmony with natural law. The Law of the Twelve Tables, for example, is "in accordance with nature, which is the criterion of law" (*De Leg.* 2.24.61). Since Cicero believes (*De Leg.* 2.23.59) that the Twelve Tables were "in the main imported from the laws of Solon," the latter in his opinion are an example of a *legitimate* law consistent with natural law.

c. Natural Law and Reason

Natural law is known through reason. This is not surprising since natural law is "*right reason* (*recta ratio*) in commanding and forbidding" (*De Leg.* 1.12.33). However, natural law cannot be fully penetrated by human reason and, furthermore, the doctrine of ancient natural law is not a "rationalism," if what is meant by this is an explicit, quasi-mathematical, logical-deductive knowledge of the law.

Cicero adds that this "right reason" is the law of Jupiter, which "came into being at the same time as the divine mind" (*orta est simul cum mente divina*) (*De Leg.* 2.4.10). Right reason is the divine Logos of the Stoics. Accordingly, there is a fundamental disproportion between this Logos and human reason. Far from human reason being able to claim that it serves as the measure of the universe, it must measure itself against the reason of the universe. "No one should be so stupid and so arrogant as to believe that reason and intelligence are present in him but not in the heavens and the world. Or that those things which are barely understood by the highest intellectual reasoning are kept in motion without any intelligence at all" (*De Leg.* 2.7.16).

Therefore, human intelligence, which is fundamentally limited, must find its marks in the objective intelligence that fills the entire universe and manifests itself in its order: "the procession of the stars, the alternation of day and night, the regular succession of the seasons, and the fruits which are produced for our enjoyment" (*De Leg.* 2.7.16). We must admit that there exists in the universe *an order that has not been created by us and that is infinitely greater than us.*

While the distance between human reason and natural law is irreducible, there is nevertheless a relation between the two. Human reason is a parcel of divine reason. The human soul is somehow "a sanctuary inhabited by God" (*De Leg.* 1.22.59, with modifications). Divine reason is firmly established *in* the human spirit (*De Leg.* 1.6.18). This is why human reason has at least some understanding, though only *roughly,* of divine law.

---

[54] Plato also forbids men from remaining bachelors, but for slightly different reasons; see above, p. 97.

[55] The explanation may be that begging contradicts the principle of mutual services that must exist between people in society. Begging is a one-way relationship.

Moral consciousness is one such form of understanding. Men, says Cicero, do not turn from wrongdoing for fear of punishment but because of their conscience. When guilty of wrongdoing, they are hounded "with the torment of their conscience and the agony of their guilt" (*De Leg.* 1.14.40; see *De Rep.* 5.4). This is proof that humans have an *inner* compass, which unfailingly points to right and wrong, which is precisely what natural law says. We have a sense of the just and the unjust.

Cicero adds that our ability to read our inner compass grows with the observation of nature and experience. This is true not only in the moral domain: human reason learns from nature by observation and imitation: "countless skills have been discovered thanks to nature's teaching" (*De Leg.* 1.8.26).[56] At any rate, for knowledge of our obligations it is advisable to consult others, in particular men of learning and practical wisdom, of whom "the majority usually drift with the current of nature." The best advisers are the high public servants of the state and elders (*On Duties* 1.41.147, with modifications).

d. Natural Law and Tradition

Hence the role of tradition. Cicero says that he does not intend to invent a new regime like Plato (*De Rep.* 1.8.13; see 2.11). In his opinion Rome's *traditional* regime is the best (*De Rep.* 1.46.70). Cicero does not intellectualize like Plato or develop an *a priori* system, which consists of neglecting the lessons of experience and rejecting as mere "opinion" the values handed down by forebears. He even suggests a novel hypothesis: that rights and institutions are the product of a long evolution involving scores of people over many generations, and their "trials and errors" eventually incorporate in institutions, which possess more knowledge than any one single individual. "Our own constitution . . . had been established not by one man's ability but by that of many, not in the course of one man's life but over several ages and generations" (*De Rep.* 2.1).

Cicero attributes this idea to Cato. The Roman constitution was not adopted wholesale from a foreign model. It is the fruit of an endogenous development (*De Rep.* 2.15). Therefore, time and the accumulation of experience play an intellectually creative role.[57]

e. Positive Laws Can Be Unjust

Since human intelligence has some knowledge of natural law—based on intuitive reason fed by experience—it is capable, when necessary, of *making critical judgments* about positive law. Here is an example. The second decemvirate added two new tables to the original Ten Tables of Law, forbidding marriage between patricians and plebeians. Cicero says that this law was a "most outrageous measure." The right to marry has always been allowed, even to foreigners. Why should it be forbidden to individuals of different social classes? The order was rescinded by the plebiscite (*De Rep.* 2.32).

Generally speaking, positive laws can be unjust. "Most foolish of all," Cicero exclaims, "is the belief that everything decreed by the institutions or laws of a particular country is just. What if the laws are the laws of tyrants?" (*De Leg.* 1.15.42). Positive laws, formulated to meet the

---

[56] The reference is to practical know-how and techniques.

[57] This particular hypothesis of the *epistemological* value of tradition, which incorporates knowledge that no *a priori* intellectual method can supersede, anticipates an idea that Anglo-Saxon representatives of the eighteenth century Enlightenment movement (Bernard de Mandeville, David Hume, Adam Ferguson, Adam Smith) developed in reaction to Cartesianism, playing a fundamental role in modern *liberal* theories. It is because human intelligence is incapable of an analytical understanding of social organization that the latter is best left to its own devices to find its point of balance; it must not depend on the commands and rigid plans of an authority. Freedom of thought and economic freedom must be allowed. In contrast, when socialism claims to rebuild society on a "blank slate" and organize its functioning, it postulates an *omniscience* of human intelligence that does not exist.

varied temporary needs of the community, enjoy the name of "law" only by consent. Among the "decrees" passing for laws, written and ratified by politicians, many are "harmful and pernicious" (*De Leg.* 2.5.11). Such false laws and arbitrary decrees should not have "the name of law," "even if the people have accepted [them]" (*De Leg.* 2.5.13). When the people behave like this, Cicero says, they are like a "gang of criminals"; Cicero had ample experience and evidence of such deviant behavior in Rome.[58]

Even with respect to customs, critical judgment should and must be exercised. Only the "best" customs should be preserved (*De Leg.* 2.16.40). This makes sense: the norm is not *the past* as such; it is *nature*. Customs can stray from the norm over time. Thus, there is a nonconservative, not to say hypercritical element in Cicero's thought. This is not unlike Plato's thought, and in the same way Cicero and Plato differ from Cato the Elder's conservatism.

Cicero's approval of critical judgment is illustrated in an idea that almost seems to be taken from Pericles: "anyone who blocks a harmful measure shall be deemed a public benefactor" (*De Leg.* 3.10; see 3.40; with this argument Cicero basically justifies parliamentary obstruction!).

Differences of *opinion* are admissible. It is possible to hold a different point of view in regard to what serves the common interest (Publius Africanus and Quintus Metellus, the conqueror of Macedonia, differed with "no trace of rancour" (*On Duties* 1.25.87).

In matters of politics and the law Cicero is a true "critical intellectual" in comparison with many Romans. He laments the fact that the Romans before him were pragmatists obsessed with petty interests. Even more, pragmatism leads to formalism and its abuses, whereas if one is able to judge from the bottom working up to the principles, the abuses of formalism can be corrected (*De Leg.* 1.4.14–5.15). Cicero is interested in everything; he is explicitly eclectic by choice: all philosophies, he observes, converge in the idea of natural law—except for Epicureanism, and perhaps the New Academy's Skepticism (1.13.38). Finally, Cicero explicitly expresses his debt to the "most perceptive Greek thinkers"—Theophrastus,[59] Diogenes the Stoic,[60] Plato, Aristotle, Heraclides of Pontus,[61] Dicaearchus,[62] Demetrius of Phalerum[63] (3.13). These were the sources of inspiration for his sense of critical judgment and taste for theory.

f. The Variability of Positive Law as a Function of Time and Place

Cicero recalls the famous embassy of Carneades, Diogenes of Babylon, and Critolaus to Rome in 156 BC. Speeches by the three men left a mark on certain Romans such as Scipio, Laelius, and Philus. But Cato had the three emissaries expelled after Carneades argued both sides of a case, speaking first in defense of justice, then arguing against it. Such dialectic juggling shocked the Romans.

In Cicero's *On the Republic* the interlocutors of the Scipionic Circle adopt the same dialectical method. In order to strengthen the arguments supporting natural law, they try first to weaken them, then they refute the refutation (*De Rep.* 3.6; cf. also Plato's *Republic* and the defense of injustice by his trio: Thrasymachus, Glaucon, and Adeimantus).

---

[58] It is difficult to express more clearly the doctrine of the necessary limitation of sovereignty, including the sovereignty of the people. In the modern period, royal absolutism abolished the bonds of natural law, as did Jacobin democracy, in its wake, with the doctrine of the people's unlimited sovereignty.

[59] Theophrastus was Aristotle's successor at the Lyceum (ca. 372–ca. 287 BC). A great botanist, a psychologist, and a moralist, he wrote *The Characters*, a work that inspired Jean de La Bruyère.

[60] Diogenes of Babylon, see above, p. 281.

[61] A student of Plato, astronomer, author of a semi-heliocentric theory, 388–312 BC.

[62] Historian, author of a history of Greek origins.

[63] Ca. 350–ca. 283 BC. An Athenian, he was a student of Theophrastus. Orator and politician. He instigated the creation of Ptolemy I Soter's library in Alexandria.

Thus, for one of Cicero's protagonists, Philus, the fact that customs differ from place to place and change over time is ample proof that natural justice does not exist; law is forged by society. "Justice is a *political* phenomenon, not an element in *nature.* If it were part of nature, like hot and cold or bitter and sweet, then just and unjust would be the same for everyone" (*De Rep*. 3.9). Furthermore, if natural justice existed, we could not harm animals (3.9). Interests are a zero-sum game: what some possess is what was taken from others (*De Rep*. 12). Neither nature nor good intentions created justice; human weakness did (*De Rep*. 13), and powerful men can permit themselves to be unjust: in truth, "government cannot be carried on without injustice" (*De Rep*. 3.43). Only the magnitude of the crime, Cicero says, makes Alexander any different from the ordinary criminal, alluding to Alexander's arrest of the pirate.[64] Moreover, the unjust person lives better than the just, and everyone agrees that the life of the former is preferable to the latter (Thrasymachus makes the same point in Plato's *Republic*). The true source of legislation is expediency. And, as Carneades said, given that expediency differs from nation to nation, it is hardly surprising to find a wide diversity and temporal variation of laws (*De Rep*. 3.12). Carneades added that if, in fact, a universal natural law existed, the Romans would have to relinquish their Empire, which of course they could not or would not do (*De Rep*. 3.12). (He concluded, according to Lactantius, that there is not only a *difference,* there is also an *incompatibility* between the "justice of the city" and "natural justice") (*De Rep*. 3.20).

Scipio (Cicero's spokesperson) replies: these arguments are all wrong; objective justice exists. Goodness and honesty are not matters of circumstance. The variability of laws proves nothing. When we make a judgment about a tree or a horse, we do so in reference to a model of what we think their nature should be. We make judgments about right and wrong in the same way. Beneath the diversity of opinions, we search for an objective right and wrong (*De Leg*. 1.17).

Of course, hot and cold, bitter and sweet, are not perceived in the same way by different individuals, but no one doubts that a thing is, objectively speaking, hot or cold, bitter or sweet, and it is possible to criticize the sense perceptions until some form of objective truth is reached. The same is possible in the search for justice and injustice, although it is more difficult given the variety of opinions involved (*De Leg*. 1.12.33; 17.47).

g. Natural Law, the Law of Nations, Positive Law

As we know, the brotherhood of men can be considered at different levels, human or state; there are also different levels of law. Cicero and the Roman jurists of his age tried to find their bearings within ideas of *natural law, the law of nations,* and *civil law,* the most elusive of the three being the idea of the law of nations, which lies midway between the other two.

The *rights of war* are a key component of the *law of nations.* War occurs between citizens of different states, who therefore do not share the same *ius civile*. And yet, one cannot fight without proper rules: for example, before war can be waged, a declaration of war is necessary. Tullus Hostilius "drew up a legal procedure for declaring war...he formulated the procedure himself in very fair terms, and then, by incorporating it in the fetials' ceremonies,[65] he enacted that every war which had not been declared and proclaimed should be deemed unjust and unholy" (*De Rep*. 2.17.31). The law was therefore enacted and was not "natural law"; however, it satisfied the deepest convictions of humankind; it was a law of nations (*ius gentium*).

[64] When Alexander captured a pirate and asked him by what criminal right he sailed the high seas on his tiny brigantine, the reply was: "By the same right which is your warrant for conquering the world."

[65] A "college of fetials" was made up of 20 priests from the patrician class, responsible for the rituals of declaring wars and concluding treaties.

It is by virtue of the law of war that an oath given to an enemy must be kept. Conversely, failure to keep an oath under the pretense that it was given to an enemy is to deny the law of nations (*On Duties* 3.29.107) (see the dilemma of Regulus above). When a defector from the army of Pyrrhus promised to kill the king, he was quite rightly handed over to his former camp (1.13.40). Likewise, cruelty in war is also forbidden (1.11.34–1.13.39). Pirates and brigands, however, are not held to such laws because they do not belong to the ranks of combatants; they are "a foe in all men's eyes" (they have removed themselves from society).

By and large, Rome respected the rights of war, which brought it further favor among the nations it conquered. Cicero borrows an idea from Polybius: Rome did not conquer unjustly, but "by defending its allies" (*De Rep.* 3.35). The vast reach of the Roman Empire cannot be explained by military might alone, but rather by the spread of the rule of law; like an unstoppable contagion, the empire garnered support for the "law of nations" from all peoples.[66]

> The early Romans anchored civil law in the law of nations when they granted *good faith* the force of law. "For how weighty are the words: *uti ne propter te fidemve tuam captus fraudatusve sim!* ("That I be not deceived and defrauded through you and my confidence in you")! How precious are these: *ut inter bonos bene agier oportet et sine fraudatione!* ("As between honest people there ought to be honest dealing, and no deception")! But who are "honest people," and what is "honest dealing"—these are serious questions. It was Quintus Scaevola, the pontifex maximus, who used to attach the greatest importance to all questions of arbitration to which the formula was appended *fide bona* ("as good faith requires"); and he held that the expression "good faith" had a very extensive application, for it was employed in trusteeships and partnerships, in trusts and commissions, in buying and selling, in hiring and letting—in a word, in all the transactions on which the social relations of daily life depend; in these he said, it required a judge of great ability to decide the extent of each individual's obligation to the other, especially when the counter-claims were admissible in most cases. Away, then, with sharp practice and trickery. (*On Duties* 3.17.70–71)

Thus, a body of praetorian law developed because the jurists, facing the challenge of regulating relations between people of different ethnic groups, "allowed their conscience to speak," and added its demands to positive law.

2. *The State*

But the law that is founded and developed in this way, Cicero says, can only be guaranteed in the framework of the state.

a. Definition

"A republic is the property of the public (*res populi*). But a public is not every kind of human gathering, congregating in any manner, but a numerous gathering brought together by legal consent and community of interest (*coetus multitudinis iuris consensu et utilitatis communione sociatus*). The primary reason for its coming together is not so much weakness as a sort of innate desire on the part of human beings to form communities (*naturalis quaedam hominum quasi congregatio*)"

[66] "A dominant state is just and in the interests of its vanquished populations, provided the state's dominion is lawful. When all faculty for wrongdoing is removed from the hands of the wicked, subjugated men fare better in general than before when they were their own masters" (St. Augustine, *Against Julian*, trans. Matthew A. Schumacher [New York: Fathers of the Church, 1957], 4, 12, citing a lost passage of Cicero's *Republic*). There are also obligations toward slaves, given that slaves also come under the law of nations (*On Duties* 1.13.41).

(*De Rep.* 1.25.39).[67] Corollary: tyranny is contrary to *humanitas*, because between the tyrant and the people there is no legal bond or civilized partnership (2.26).

Since the state is founded on the rule of law, it ends rule by force. This is the second part of Cicero's definition, drawn from a passage in his *Pro Sestio* oration. When humanity was young, people lived in a "bestial state," where murder, theft, and brutal force were the rule. Next, a few individuals of practical intelligence gathered all humanity into a single place.

> Then the institutions that bear on the common advantage, which we call "political" (*publicas*), were created along with human gatherings that were subsequently labelled "civil communities" (*civitates*), then the assemblages of dwellings that we call "cities" (*urbis*), which were marked off by walls when the principles of divine and human laws had been discovered. Nothing more clearly marks the difference between this way of life, refined by our distinctively human qualities, and that monstrous way of life [before the establishment of states] than the difference between *law* and *violence* [*ius* and *vis*]. *If we do not wish to use the first of these, we are obliged to use the other:* if we want violence to be eradicated, then law must prevail—which is to say the courts that embody the whole concept of law (*iudicia quibus omne ius continetur*); but if the courts fall out of favour or cease to exist,[68] then violence inevitably holds sway. (*Pro Sestio* 42.91–92, with modifications)[69]

A state in which there is not "one bond of justice," when "freedom itself [loses] all its rightful possessions," is not only a wicked state, it is *not even* a state, even if it is Syracuse with its wonderful buildings, citadel, and harbor. Syracuse was not a republic because "nothing belonged to the public" and "the public itself belonged to one man" (*De Rep.* 3.31).

The primary function of the state is to impose respect for the law and, in particular, to *safeguard property* (*On Duties* 2.11.40–2.12.41–42). When the state dies, it is as if "this whole world were to collapse and pass away" (*De Rep.* 3.23). Moreover, compared with a person for whom death is inevitable, the state should last forever.

b. Ciceronian Isonomia

Since the law is the "bond of justice" that makes the people, there can be no law unless each person is concerned in the same way. A just and equal law (*ius æquale*) must exist. There can be no stable civil society or partnership of citizens (*civilis societas, societas civium*) unless all citizens enjoy the same (*par*) conditions (*De Rep.* 1.32.49). "For what people have always sought is equality of rights under the law. For rights that were not open to all alike would be no rights" (*On Duties* 2.12.42) (thus, equality before the law forms an integral part of the law itself). "If it [liberty] isn't equal throughout, it isn't liberty at all" (*De Rep.* 1.31.47). This is the *isonomia* of Solon and Cleisthenes.

Cicero emphasizes that there should never be a law for one person in particular. "They [the presiding magistrates] shall not propose laws directed at private individuals" [*privilegia ne inroganto*] (*De Leg.* 3.4.11); "a law is something enjoined and binding on everyone" (3.19.44). This is true not only of a democracy. Even in a mixed form of government, it is necessary to maintain

[67] Augustine discusses this definition at length in his *City of God*. See part 3 below, pp. 455–56.

[68] Cicero sees perfectly well that the *courts* are a pivotal institution. There is no peace in the absence of law, no law without the administration of justice, and no law without a state to uphold the law (but the state does not *enact* the law).

[69] Cicero here recalls the conflicts of the Republican crisis, when armed factions triumphed over the rule of law and the courts, plunging society into an abyss.

a certain equality of rights (*quædam æqualitas*), which free people cannot do without (*De Rep.* 1.45.69).[70]

In this conception of the law all people are subject to it, including those who make and enact it (*De Rep.* 1.34.52). Executive power must command respect for the law, at the same time that it applies the law to itself. "As magistrates are subject to the laws, the people are subject to the magistrates. In fact it is true to say that *a magistrate is a speaking law, and a law a silent magistrate*" (*De Leg.* 3.1.2) (On the other hand, in the army, and especially in the field, "the decision of the commanding officer…shall be fixed and final" [3.6], which Cicero presents as an exception that proves the rule.)

Arbitrary power and subjective decision making must be excluded from the conduct of the state. This is the sense of judicial appeal. Cicero cites the Law of the Twelve Tables: "no sentence [that was not subject to appeal] could be passed on the life of a Roman citizen except in the Assembly of Centuries" (*De Rep.* 2.31). All things tainted with subjectivity will be mistrusted: "with any good judge, arguments have greater force than witnesses" (*apud bonum iudicem, argumenta plus quam testes valent*) (1.38.59).

Here Cicero formulates a doctrine of freedom under the law which is clearer and more radical than Aristotle's formulation. Personal liberty is based on a law that is equal, public, and precise. The function of the law is to safeguard liberty. A wicked state is one where "liberty ceases to be protected by the law" (*De Rep.* 3.32).

c. A Challenge to the "Reason of State"

Cicero's commitment to the rule of law is evinced in his formal disapproval of any doctrine of reason of state.[71]

This discussion is found in the casuistry of his *On Duties*. Earlier we saw that a person can never prefer the expedient to the good. But what about the expediency of the state? There is no difference, Cicero replies, because reason of state is cruel (e.g., when the Athenians amputated the fingers of the inhabitants of Aegine,[72] or when the Roman army razed Corinth).[73] He adds, "cruelty is most abhorrent to human nature, whose lead we ought to follow." In this sense, reason of state works against humanity and, in the end, against the state itself (*On Duties* 3.11.47).

States that put morality above public expediency do not suffer from their choice; on the contrary. Examples abound in both Greek and Roman history. Cicero mentions a fine illustration drawn from Greek history. Themistocles announces in the Athenian Assembly that he has a plan to weaken Sparta's military might. However, he cannot reveal it in public. The Athenians appoint Aristides to listen to the plan in secret. The plan is to set fire to the Spartan naval fleet. Reporting back to the Assembly, Aristides grants that the plan is indeed expedient, but not at all morally right. Without any detailed knowledge of the plan, the Athenians reject it for the sole reason that it is not morally right, and being thus wrong it would be inexpedient (*On Duties* 3.11.49).

While, in general, what is morally right should not be sacrificed for what is expedient, there are some who argue that an exception should be made in politics. Cicero cites the following lines by Euripides (from *Phoenissae* 524–25): "if we must do wrong, to do so for a kingdom

[70] Cicero appears to distinguish between political rights and civil rights: in an aristocracy or a mixed form of government, political rights are not equal, while civil rights are.

[71] This did not prevent him from resorting to exorbitant measures in practice—for example, in his quelling of the Catalina conspiracy. However, the logic was different in this case, given the state of emergency. In contrast, the use of unlawful measures for reasons of state is presented as a permanent necessity of government in the doctrines of Machiavelli and Richelieu.

[72] During the Peloponnesian War. Thucydides narrates the episode.

[73] In 146 BC. When Cicero visited the ruins of Corinth he was deeply affected by the depth of the destruction.

were the fairest cause, but in all else virtue [duty] should be our aim." Cicero firmly denies this exception. The proof: Caesar's fate (*On Duties* 3.21.82). The reason is always the same—means and ends must not be confused: "If supremacy is to be sought for the sake of glory, crime should be excluded, for there can be no glory in crime" (22.87).

d. Forms of Government

The function of the state is to uphold the law. The state can do this with several forms of government—monarchy, aristocracy, and democracy. Which form is preferable? Before concluding in favor of Polybius's mixed form, Cicero examines the arguments for each "pure" form of government. He recognizes that there are good ones for each and concludes that all their advantages should be *combined*.

i. *Monarchy*

Scipio says, it is a king, Jove, who rules the gods; we can gain inspiration from his example for society. Philosophers thought that the world was controlled by one mind [*mens*] (*De Rep.* 1.36.57); *a fortiori*, one mind can rule a state. Unity of power is essential: in the body politic, "if the thing is put in the hands of more than one person, clearly there will be no power in charge." This is evinced in the fact that, even after expulsing their unjust kings, in the face of war, the Romans placed all power in the hands of one person, a dictator, a "master of the people" (38.60). Indeed, "safety takes precedence over personal desires" (*valet enim salus plus quam libido*) (40.63).

But is not monarchy an *ancient*, even *barbarous* form of government? No, because even Rome had its kings, and it was neither ancient nor barbarous (Cicero thought Greece was already aging as Rome was born) (*De Rep.* 37.58).

Cicero also presents arguments against monarchy. The title of king suits only Jove, the best and the greatest of the gods. Where there are kings, the people are slaves (whether the king is good or bad does not change the problem) (*De Rep.* 33.50). So, monarchy is contrary to liberty (50.62).

ii. *Aristocracy*

The administration of the state exceeds the natural abilities of a single person; but it is also too complex for the people. Aristocracy (the power of the *optimates*) is, therefore, a "middle ground between the inadequate autocrat and the reckless mob" (*De Rep.* 1.34.52).

iii. *Democracy*

Again, there are arguments *for* and *against*. In support of democracy is the fact that it ensures the liberty of all, whereas in a monarchy, and even in an aristocracy, people are free in name only. In free cities, like Rhodes and Athens, anyone can be a magistrate (*De Rep.* 1.31.47). Frequently people under the rule of an aristocracy or a monarchy will aspire to life under a democracy, never the contrary. People do not willingly long for enslavement (32.48). "Since, then, law is the bond which holds together a community of citizens, and the justice embodied in the law is the same for everyone, by what right can a community of citizens be held together when their status is unequal? If the equalization of wealth is rejected, and the equalization of everybody's abilities is impossible, legal rights[74] at least must be equal among those who live as fellow-citizens in the same state" (32.49).

---

[74] Cicero makes a clear distinction between equality of rights and equality of conditions; in other words, between "formal" and "real" equalities.

On the contrary, democracy is an anarchy, a folly. The frenzy of the mob is more terrifying than a storm or a wildfire (*De Rep.* 1.42.65). More than any other excess, Cicero dreads the violence and irrationality of the masses.

iv. *The Cycle of Revolutions*

None of these three forms of government is workable as long it is in a *pure* form. Pure regimes are unstable and incline toward tyranny, oligarchy, or the excessive license of the masses (*De Rep.* 1.27.43). What is more, governments pass through "cycles and, so to speak, revolutions" in their transformation from one form to another (28.44–29.45).

For the most part, Cicero takes up the arguments of Plato and Polybius on the instability of governments when change appears. Thus, liberty leads regularly to tyranny. Power passes from one group to another, like the ball in a game (*De Rep.* 1.42.65–1.44.68). Scipio says the cycle begins to turn with the tyranny of Tarquinius Superbus: "You should become familiar from the start with its natural movement and circuit; for it is the crowning achievement of political wisdom...to divine the course of public affairs, with all its twists and turns." This results in the expulsion and exile of Tarquin by Brutus (2.25). Cicero paints a full-blown picture of Roman *stasis:* debt problems, the secession of the plebs, the creation of the tribunes, and so on.

And he concludes, "Accordingly, kings attract us by affection, aristocracy by good sense, and democracies by freedom (*caritate nos capiunt reges, consilio optimates, libertate populi*). So in comparing them it is hard to choose which one likes best" (1.35.54).

v. *A Mixed Form of Government*

Scipio finally states his preference for a *combination of all three forms* of government (*De Rep.* 35.54). "Unless a state maintains a fair balance of rights, duties, and functions (the magistrates having adequate power, the aristocratic council adequate influence, and the people adequate freedom) its constitutional organization cannot be preserved from change" (2.33).

Whatever the form of constitution, leaders must govern in the interest of the people and not in their own ("like the office of a trustee...conducted for the benefit of those entrusted to one's care"). This explains the absurdity of *factions,* both aristocratic and democratic, in Greece (with its *hetairies* or political clubs} and in Rome (*On Duties* 1.25.85–86).

e. *The Constitution of Rome*

As a matter of fact, like Sparta and Carthage before it, Rome enjoys a mixed form of government (*De Rep.* 2.23). The origins can be traced back to the censitary system, with the creation of the Assemblies of Centuries, usually attributed to Servius Tullius: every citizen has voting rights—if they didn't, it would have been humiliating—but the poor and the masses could not impose their will—which would have been dangerous for the community as a whole.

Cicero weighs the pros and cons of the plebeian tribunes. He favors their existence, a position consistent with his support for a mixed constitution. But his reason for this is very "political." Tribunes gave the people the *impression* they were equal, which in itself contributed to securing peace. Likewise, owing to tribunes, the people had leaders capable of reasoning; they were no longer a faceless, mindless mob. It was far better to have intermediaries.[75] A leader had to decide "not just what [was] best but also what [was] necessary.... It is the duty of a wise citizen, in dealing with an institution not evil in itself and so dear to the people that it could not be combated, not to leave its defense to a demagogue" (*De Leg.* 3.11.26, with modifications). Above and beyond

[75] This same reasoning was adopted in modern democracies by the ruling parties of the right to accept the existence of unions.

constitutional questions, this takes us to the heart of the political matter of *parties* competing for power.

f. Optimates and Populares

In the final century of the Roman Republic, two political parties were constantly opposed to each other. Their confrontation was not unlike that of parties in modern democracies vying for majority status (admittedly, the analogy is imperfect): a party of the "right," the *optimates* or "senatorial party"; and a party of the "left," the *populares* or "people's party." More often than not the two parties confronted each other normally (i.e., via elections), but at times their confrontation was violent, with one party inciting bloody street riots and the other hiring thugs to carry out political assassinations.

Cicero took a stand on this issue. His great idea was that *populares* and *optimates* were not just two rival political groups, but that the difference between the two was sociological and moral.

> All [honest] men belong to the best party [*optimates*], who are not guilty of any crime, nor wicked by nature, nor madmen, nor men embarrassed by domestic difficulties. [They are responsible for defending] religious observances, the auspices, the civil power of magistrates, the authority of the senate, the laws, the usages of one's ancestors, the courts of justice, the jurisdiction of the judges, good faith, the provinces, the allies, the glory of the empire, the whole affairs of the army, the treasury. [On the contrary, there are vast numbers of citizens who] are anxious for fresh changes and revolutions in the republic; or who, on account of some innate insanity of mind, feed upon the discords and seditions of the citizens; or else who, on account of the embarrassment of their estates and circumstances, had rather burn in one vast common conflagration, than in one which consumed only themselves. (*Pro Sestio* 45.97–46.99)[76]

So, the *optimates* are the conservatives, and the *populares* the revolutionaries. Cicero was by no means a *reactionary* in the modern sense (we saw earlier that tradition, in his judgment, can and must be criticized, especially when it diverges from natural law), but he was assuredly an antirevolutionary in his deepest philosophy, in the sense that he feared revolution could lead to an overthrow of the natural order with fatal consequences for justice and happiness. The *populares,* who campaigned for agrarian laws and debt relief, "undermine the foundations of the commonwealth: first of all they are destroying harmony, which cannot exist when money is taken away from one party and bestowed upon another; and second, they do away with equity, which is subverted, if the rights of property are not respected" (*De Off.* 2.22.78). And in the same vein, "there is nothing that upholds a government more powerfully than its credit [reputation]; and it can have no credit, unless the payment of debts is enforced by law" (*On Duties* 2.22.78).[77]

Cicero was, nevertheless, pessimistic about preserving a balance; like Plato, he believed in the inevitability of revolution. There is an asymmetry between the party of disorder and the party of order.

> The republic is attacked by greater forces and more numerous bodies than those by which it is defended because audacious and abandoned men (*audaces homines et perditi*) are impelled on by a nod, and are even of their own accord excited by nature to be enemies to

[76] Compare this with what Xenophon says above, pp. 142–43.

[77] Cicero made this very clear to all, when, under his consulship, he brutally suppressed the Catalina conspiracy, which included debt cancellation in its political program. The firmness of Cicero's response ensured peace and prosperity in the ensuing years: "for the hope of defrauding the creditor was cut off and payment was enforced by law" (*On Duties* 2.22.78).

> the republic. And somehow or other good men are slower in action, and overlooking the first beginnings of things, are at last aroused by necessity itself so that some times through their very delays and tardiness of movement while they wish to retain their ease even without dignity, they, of their own accord, lose both. (*Pro Sestio* 47.100)

Cicero had an excellent grasp of the mechanisms of *public opinion* and *rumor*. The *populares* endured only by manipulating these mechanisms; they were, essentially, demagogues, that is to say, not only immoral, but also intellectually dishonest; in sum, Sophists (Cicero agrees with the observations of many fourth century Greek intellectuals).

The masses often sway with the tide of rumor, but at times they are able to realize their error. When this happens, they vindicate those with honest expectations. Actually, Cicero says, there are two peoples. A formal distinction has to be made between the rabble of the assemblies and the *verus populus* (*Pro Sestio* 50.108), the *ipse populus Romanus* (57.140). "Do you not see, then, what a great difference there is between the Roman people and an assembly? Do you not see that the masters of the assemblies are the object of the hatred of the Roman people? and that those who are not permitted to appear without insult in the assemblies of these bandits, are honoured by every possible mark of respect by the Roman people?" (59.127, with modifications).

The *optimates* were often loved by the people and were "popular," in spite of efforts by the *populares* to tar them otherwise. On the other hand, the *populares* were just as frequently hated by the people. But then we are not referring to the same "people" in both cases.

E. Civil Religion: "The Dream of Scipio"

In the ideal state, a civil religion will be imposed on everyone (*De Leg.* 2.8.19–2.9.22). The real reason for this is that natural law, which is not the fruit of human will, must be anchored in transcendence, and the state must explicitly acknowledge this higher authority. Cicero rediscovers the inspiration of Plato's *Laws* here.

Cicero's religious laws favor a degree of religious eclecticism. He says, "we are framing laws, not just for the Roman people, but for all good and stable communities" (*De Leg.* 2.14.35). Religion, therefore, must be universal, which explains his acceptance of the Greek mysteries: "thanks to them we have become mild and cultivated, moving from a rough and savage life to a state of civilization; we have learned from so-called 'initiations' things which are in fact the first principles of life, and we have been taught a way of living happily and also of dying with brighter hopes" (2.14.36). On the contrary, Cicero is wary of the ecstatic, orgiastic religions of the Near East. When in 187 BC the consuls put some 3,000 (of 7,000) Bacchanalia participants to death, Cicero apparently approved their action.

Moreover, religion must be under the tight control of the state. Only state-approved faiths should be allowed, and the state should not authorize any new gods. Yet Cicero was sufficiently detached from popular religion to make use of it as a deliberate tool of government. For example, the augurs were used to cancel formal decisions (assembly meetings, legislative votes, election of a consul); such power was extremely useful in the hands of the politician (*De Leg.* 2.12.31–2.13.32). While the idea of the augurs is not ridiculous as such, if one accepts the existence of divine providence (2.13.32), it is best seen as a discretionary power held in reserve to enable the government to extricate itself from deadlocked situations, created by an overly strict legalism (2.13.33, 3.12.27, 3.19.43).

Cicero personally entertained genuine religious beliefs, though in a scholarly vein. This comes to the fore with brio in his famous "Dream of Scipio," which closes his *Republic,* much as Plato ends his *Republic* with the "Myth of Er" (Cicero obviously intends the parallel).

Scipio Aemilianius had a dream. He ascends to heaven, where he encounters his ancestor, Scipio Africanus. Aemilianius learns from Africanus that there is a place in heaven for those who "respect justice and do their duty"; that is, who put community interests before their own, and the rewards of heaven will make life's misfortunes seem insignificant. According to Stoic philosophy, the human soul is born of the eternal fires emanating from the stars and planets; the fetters of the body are like a prison. When the physical body dies and the soul is liberated, the soul returns naturally to the Milky Way. This is where the two Scipios meet and hold their conversation.

The spectacle of the heavens lying at their feet is magnificent. Seen from the Milky Way, the Roman Empire is but a tiny speck on Earth, itself the smallest of the stars. The two Scipios meditate on the relativity of human things: no one cares much about the fame of mortals in the cosmic immensity of time and space, especially since periodic conflagrations sweep through the universe and destroy everything. Still, one must be deserving of the rewards of the afterlife, and to earn them one must be just. Cicero's deepest conviction is that the only thing that counts are one's efforts on behalf of justice in the Republic. He formulates this in *Pro Sestio* (57.143):

> Let us then imitate our Bruti, our Camilli, and Ahalae our Decii, our Curius, and Fabricius, and Maximus, our Scipios, our Lentuli, our Aemilii, and countless others, who have given liberty to this republic; all of whom I consider deserving of being ranked among the company and number of the immortal gods. Let us love our country, let us obey the senate, let us consult the interests of the good; let us disregard present rewards, and fix our eyes on the glory which we shall receive from posterity. Let us think that the most desirable conduct is the most upright; let us hope for whatever we choose, but bear whatever befalls us. Let us consider, lastly, that the bodies of brave men and great citizens are mortal, but that the impulses of the mind and the glory of virtue are everlasting (*animi motus et virtutis gloriam*). And let us not, if we see that the opinion is consecrated by the most holy example of the great Hercules, whose body indeed has been burnt but whose life and virtue are said to have received instant immortality, think any the less that they who by their counsels and labours have either increased the greatness or defended the safety, or preserved the existence of this great republic have acquired everlasting glory.

F. Active Life and Contemplative Life

In his writing Cicero returns again and again to the question of *otium* and *negotium*, visibly a lifelong preoccupation. Looking at his personal life, one understands why. He was torn between the traditional Roman example of *negotium*, the active life lived out entirely in the *cursus honorum*, which his social origins made available to him, and the Greek example of *otium* and the *schole*, the life of "leisure," study, and contemplation, which his teachers provided and which he experienced in the prestigious schools of Athens and Rhodes, where he was an assiduous auditor. Since the collapse of the city-state and the rise of the great Hellenistic kingdoms—followed by the Roman Empire—the example of a private life of contemplative retirement, away from the agora, the forum, the court, devoted exclusively to speculation, competed in philosophical circles with Plato's exaltation of an active political life. As for Cicero, he wrote his philosophical treatises late in life after his involuntary sidelining from public affairs.

In the end, Cicero adopted a remarkably coherent philosophical stance in regard to this question.

1. He formulated and resolved the *otium/negotium* dilemma in the clearest of terms. On the side of *negotium*, the complete person obviously prevails over the incomplete person. What is the sense of prudent conduct if one is not also just, bold, and temperate? Justice triumphs over all other virtues. Our humanity lies in our service to the well-being of the community (see above, pp. 284–85, 119). Thus, the contemplative life can be but a brief moment in a free person's

existence. Cicero strongly disapproved of the Epicureans for advocating a total withdrawal from public life (*De Rep.* 1.2.2). Politics is a lifelong career; it does not tolerate amateurism or occasional participation (1.6.10).

Conversely, one cannot give proper service to the city if one is ignorant. The politician (and the jurist) must be cultivated and critical. "Only those who are skilled in the specifically human arts are worthy of the name [men]" (*De Rep.* 1.17.28). A senator must be competent and knowledgeable (*De Leg.* 3.18.41). A statesman must be knowledgeable in natural law and positive law, even if he is not an expert in these disciplines (*De Rep.* 5.3).

The ultimate solution to the dilemma is that a free person must not sacrifice *negotium* for *otium*, nor the contrary. Periods of *otium* belong to a largely active life devoted entirely to public affairs—like Scipio, who convened his "circle" between two sessions of the Senate, or Cicero, who withdrew to his country villa to study between two tenures as magistrate. The active life must embrace the contemplative life too. "What can be more impressive than the combination of experience in the management of great affairs with the study and mastery of those other arts?... Hence my opinion, that anyone who achieves both objectives, familiarizing himself with our native institutions and with theoretical knowledge [foreign learning derived from Socrates], has acquired everything necessary for distinction" (*De Rep.* 3.3.5). Cato formulated the same idea magnificently when he said "that he was never less idle than when he had nothing to do and never less lonely than when he was alone" (*De Leg.* 3.1.1) (because then he was in communion with the great minds of the past).

2. By giving precedence to public affairs in his life, which is essential for a life of distinction and moral excellence, the man of action does not shut himself off from a "life of contemplation." Cicero formulates a very bold and profound idea: the words and actions of a politician, the laws that he enacts, the institutions that he creates, sow intellectual seeds just as a work of pure abstract speculation does.

While it is true that some people nourish "natural potential by *verbal skills*, others do so through *laws* and *institutions*" (*De Rep.* 3.4.7) (Rome, in particular, was blessed with such people, who by implementing the ideas of the sages have taught wisdom to the world, albeit indirectly.) The creators of laws and institutions shape civilization as much as others with their speeches, as if there were a *sui generis* speech of laws and institutions, as if such law and institutions, in concert with words, were two equally valid and rich registers of logos and human reason. Aside from their verbal eloquence, the politician and the jurist work in their particular field to advance the "republic," that is, civilization, since the "institutions" and "disciplines" they impose on people forge a way of life and customs (5.4). As Ennius wrote, "on ancient customs and old-fashioned men the state of Rome stands firm," we might say that there is a "circular causality" between political-legal institutions and people. Institutions mold people, and people in turn sustain institutions. If institutions are designed with wisdom, they will form wise individuals; and wise individuals will know how to preserve or restore the ancient customs like the original colors of an old painting (5.1). The purpose of politics is to sustain a community of citizens living a happy and honorable life (4.3, 5.5, 5.6). Rulers provide an example for the whole community: their virtues spread throughout a society, just as their vices corrupt it utterly (*De Leg.* 3.13.30–3.14.32). Like Plato (only with less insistence), Cicero grasps that a good political system cannot function in the long run without an adequate *education* (3.13.30).

If Cicero asserts the limits of pure *otium*, the fault is neither his half-heartedness in regard to abstract speculation, nor a form of old-Roman traditionalism. Rather, his approach to culture is *global*. Culture must not be confused with ideas. The world of signs is not restricted to the world of words. Everything in human society can be a sign and have meaning. The human intellect is as

…ization as in speech, and magistrates and judges also contribute to the work of …through their right actions.

III. Lucretius

The poet philosopher Lucretius, author of a celebrated *De natura rerum* (On the nature of things), was not strictly speaking the creator of a political theory like Cicero, nor was he a political commentator like Sallust or Caesar. However, with his own brand of materialist, antireligious philosophy he was an important figure in the history of Roman social and political thought. His work proves that in Rome in the dying years of the Republic—before the Empire and its drift into sacred monarchy—there were genuine rational intellects who had fully assimilated the fruits of Greek science. Such minds raised the level of thought about the origins of society, culture, and institutions to heights that would not be attained again until the modern era.

A. Life and Work

Very little is known about the life of Titus Lucretius Carus (b. Rome ca. 94 or 98 BC, d. 55 BC). Born into a family of high officials, he might have pursued the *cursus honorum,* had he wished to do so. Instead he remained aloof from public life, perhaps because of the crisis in the Republic. He adhered to Epicurean doctrines,[78] which had many devotees in Rome (among them, Atticus, Cicero's friend). For Lucretius, Epicurean ideas were more than an inspiration, they were an illumination (on several occasions, he pronounced vibrant eulogies of Epicurus whom he held to be a god because he was the first to explain phenomena using rational laws, delivering humanity from the terrors of superstition). Hence, the long philosophical poem[79] "On the Nature of Things," in which Lucretius takes up the thinking of Epicurus, summarizes certain points, and develops others.[80] He left his work in manuscript form, not yet ready for publication. After his death, it seems that Cicero revised the final text and published it.[81]

1. *De natura rerum*

Lucretius's ideas about society and political institutions are found primarily in book 5 of *De natura rerum*. Before discussing this book, here is a brief overview of the others.

Book 1 is addressed to Memmius, a Roman aristocrat. The book begins with a presentation of the fundamental principles of Epicurean philosophy. Nothing can be produced from nothing, and nothing can be reduced to nothing. All things are shaped by primordial corpuscles, atoms too tiny to be visible, but reason proves they exist. Void also exists. Thus, everything in existence is a combination of atoms and void. There is no other reality. Furthermore, there is no center of the universe, which is why, as presented in book 2, atoms are constantly in motion (they have no reason to stop in one place rather than another). But their movements are not parallel, which

---

[78] See above, the paragraphs devoted to Democritus, the father of atomism (p. 69), and Epicurus, his intellectual heir, author of a moral system based on pleasure (pp. 190–93).

[79] It is a literary genre. Ennius, in his poem *Epicharmus,* did the same for the Pythagorean system of thought that Lucretius did for Epicurus 100 years before.

[80] In many respects, Lucretius added nothing to what Epicurus said. The writings of Epicurus survived only in a few incomplete fragments. In comparison, most of Lucretius's *De natura rerum* has survived. It is understandable that he is considered the author of the ideas found nowhere else but in his writings.

[81] *Translator's note:* We quote from the Rouse translation of Lucretius, *On the Nature of Things.*

explains why they enter into combinations and assume forms, which are always new: this is the origin of the diversity of things. These atoms not only produce our world, but an infinity of other worlds, as well. Like our own, these worlds are large "animals" that are born, grow, decline, and die. Book 3 discusses the human soul, which is also made up of atoms. It permeates the entire human body. Its constituent atoms are the most minute of any matter found in nature. Body and soul have no distinct, independent existence; they live and die together. As a result, death is not to be feared: death returns human beings to what they were before their birth and their constituent atoms continue to exist in other forms. In book 4, using these same principles of atomism, Lucretius attempts to explain the origin of the senses and ideas: they are very fine particles, emanating from external objects and entering our bodies with "semblances" of the things from which they come. Thus, the senses are the primary and infallible source of knowledge: when we experience optical illusions, for example, the mistake does not come from the senses as such, but from the interpretation produced too hastily by our minds. Lucretius also finds fault with finalism: the organs of our bodies were not designed for this or that usage; on the contrary, it is the fact that they were combined in this or that way that explains this or that usage. Atomism is a mechanism where there is only contingency and necessity. In book 6 Lucretius describes the stars and the astronomical phenomena.

2. *Book 5: The Origin of the World and Its Creations*

Lucretius attempts to give a rational explanation for the birth of the world, its plants, its animals, and human beings. Everything happens for exact, knowable reasons. Generally speaking, contingency and necessity preside over the entire evolutionary process, where all things came into being one after the other, each beckoned by what preceded it, and each opening up new pathways of creation after it. Even language and religion are not "original" or "transcendent" phenomena created by some god; rather, they are fruits of an evolution stretching across time, their origins traceable through their evolution. Today, we would call them the products of "culture." "The order of my design has brought me to this point, that I must show... in what manner the human race began to use variety of speech in their intercourse by means of the names of things; and in what ways that fear of gods crept into the heart, which in our earth keeps holy their shrines and pools and groves, their altars and images" (*De natura* 5.71–75).

First, it is erroneous to think that, because the gods are immortal and the earth is their abode, the earth itself is eternal. It, too, was born and one day will die. There is no reason to believe that the gods made the earth for mortals, that there is a Providence, and that it would be ungodly for mortals to attempt to understand the world and act upon it.[82] Even more radically, it is simply wrong that the gods created the world. Where would they have found the form of living beings? Form comes from random encounters of atoms. "The world was certainly not made for us by divine power; so great are the faults with which it stands endowed." Nature only produces what is useful to us, if we work on it. The world is not inexhaustible: even the sun and the stars will perish one day. Even rocks weaken and crumble.

The world took shape gradually, its constituent parts engaged in a mighty struggle. The earth came together around the core, then ether surrounded it. Next the sun and the moon were formed, and clods of earth sprang from the ocean heated by the sun. Since then everything is subject to the laws of necessity, which can be scrutinized—here Lucretius reveals an astoundingly critical mind, showing that the Chaldeans and the Greeks differed over possible causes, that various hypotheses can explain an eclipse of the sun or moon—but what is certain is that these laws

[82] This is directed at the Stoics and their hypotheses.

exist, since many phenomena (biological, as well as physical and astronomical) return at perfectly regular intervals.

After explaining the creation of the world, Lucretius turns to the creation of plant and animal life. First, plants and trees appeared, followed by animals and humans. Nature creates by trial and error, experimenting with many sorts of monsters. Gradually, like an old woman exhausted by age, the earth ceases to give birth to new species; the only life-forms to survive are those able to reproduce, finding in nature the necessary means to stay alive, and those domestic life-forms that find a protector in humankind (here Lucretius presages modern theories of "the survival of the fittest" and "ecological niches"). "But those to which nature gave no such qualities, so that they could neither live by themselves at their own will, nor give us some usefulness for which we might suffer them to feed under our protection and be safe, these certainly lay at the mercy of others for prey and profit, being all hampered by their own fateful chains, until nature brought that race to destruction" (*De natura* 5.871–77).

In passing, Lucretius condemns as childish illusions the belief in mythological animals—centaurs, Sylla, and chimera.

3. *THE EVOLUTION OF HUMANKIND*

Now Lucretius can focus his narrative on the story of humanity itself (beginning with verse 925).

The first race of humans, physically hardier and stronger than today, were hunter-gatherers; they had no knowledge of the crafts, no fixed abode. Their existence was precarious, but perhaps no less so than the lives of people today, because they did not die in large numbers in wars and on the seas (verse 1000). Then huts appeared and fire was discovered. Monogamy and families became the rule. Friendship and pity for the weak were born.

"Nevertheless, concord could not altogether be produced, but a good part, indeed the most, kept the covenant unblemished, or else the race of mankind would have been even then wholly destroyed, nor would birth and begetting have been able to prolong their posterity to the present day" (1024–27).

Then, in the same evolutionary and utilitarian way, language appeared, which Lucretius denies was an artificial and instantaneous invention. "Therefore to suppose that someone then distributed names amongst things, and that from him men learnt their first words, is folly. For why should he have been able to mark all things with titles and to utter the various sounds of the tongue, and at the same time others not be thought able to have done it?" (1043–45).

Even animals make different sounds to express the diversity of things; they have languages, too. Men had no need of gods or spirits for the collective invention of their tongues. And what about the first idea? Did it not require a transcendent revelation? It did not, because in these evolutionary processes the problem of the beginning is a nonissue. There is always a random phenomenon that produces the first idea of something; for example, the initial idea of making fire may have come to humans by two branches rubbing together under the effect of the wind. Via this process of evolution, something *more* always emerged from something *less*. Materialism has no need for hypotheses based on idealism or spiritualism.

Book 5 concludes with a discussion of various technical inventions: metal-working, weapons, agriculture, navigation, and the arts: sculpture, music, poetry. Each of these inventions is the product of the same evolutionary trial and error process; each is heralded by fortuitous events, resulting in a new, unprecedented pattern: forest fires melted mineral ore, revealing to humans the first molten-metal objects; "the zephyrs whistling through hollow reeds first taught the countrymen to blow into hollow hemlock-stalks" (1382–83). If different industries advance, it is because of changing tastes and fashion: humans desire foods more refined than acorns, softer beds than leaves and boughs, garments less coarse than wild animal skins.

"Ships and agriculture, fortifications and laws, arms, roads, clothing and all else of this kind, all life's prizes, its luxuries also from first to last, poetry and pictures, artfully wrought polished statues, all these as men progressed gradually step by step were taught by practice [experience] and the experiments of the active mind. So by degrees time brings up before us every single thing, and reason lifts it into the precincts of light. For they saw one thing after another grow clear in their minds, until they attained the highest pinnacle of the arts" (1448–57).

Abstract knowledge also progressed; the observation of the sun and moon taught humans "that the seasons of the year come round, and that all was done on a fixed plan and in fixed order" (1439). Lucretius is also aware that knowledge of the past is only possible if written records survive. Since the invention of writing was a late product of cultural evolution, there must have been a long prehistory unknown to us today. During this period, people similar to ourselves (though more primitive) obeyed the same utilitarian logic as people in the following periods. This is another reason for Lucretius to dismiss all mythological narratives of creation.

Having said this, as far as Lucretius is concerned, human progress is fundamentally ambivalent. History does not progress from *evil* to *good* like the messianic model that we will discuss below in our consideration of biblical ideas. Technical progress is not moral progress. We no longer fight each other for food the way animal-like primitive people did; but we do fight over silver and gold and wage wars, the horror of which primitive humans could not have fathomed. Such wars cause as many deaths as poverty itself before the invention of civilization. In fact, they reduce to nothing the achievements of civilization.

4. *Forms of Government*

As for the invention of forms of government, among the various other "cultural products," here is what Lucretius postulates. Beauty, strength, genius, and wealth caused some individuals to rise above others. This led to the birth of kings, towns, and citadels with the social structures associated with such institutions. Soon, however, even this hierarchy collapsed because the success of one gives rise to the envy of another.

"It is indeed much better to obey in peace than to desire to hold the world in fee and to rule kingdoms. Leave them then to be weary to no purpose, and to sweat blood in struggling along the narrow path of ambition.... All in vain, since in the struggle to climb to the summit of honour, they made their path full of danger; and even down from the summit... envy strikes them sometimes like a thunderbolt" (1131–34).

Anarchy took the place of proud kingships, collapsed in disarray. But such was the chaos of anarchy that magistracies and laws were soon invented.

> [An elite] taught them to create magistrates, and established law, that they might be willing to obey statutes. For mankind, tired of living in violence, was fainting from its feuds, and so they were readier of their own will to submit to statutes and strict rules of law. For because each man in his wrath would make ready to avenge himself more severely than is permitted now by just laws, for this reason men were utterly weary of living in violence. Hence comes fear of punishment that taints the prizes of life; for violence and injury enclose in their net all that do such things, and generally return upon him who began, nor is it easy to pass a quiet and peaceful life for him whose deeds violate the bonds of the common peace. For even if he hide it from gods and men, he must yet be uncertain that it will for ever remain hidden; seeing that often many men, speaking in dreams or raving in delirium, are said to have discovered [betrayed] themselves, and to have disclosed deeply hidden matters and their sins. (1143–60)

With these thoughts, Lucretius returns to Epicurus. In essence, the genesis of the state and the law follows a certain utilitarian logic. Law and state are products of humanity's reaction to the condition of all-out war, deemed unbearable beyond a certain point. Thus, law and state are not phenomena of nature, but of "culture." They are late inventions, subjective and revocable.

Religion, too, is a human invention, but more characteristic of primitive people, who had no understanding of the real causes of things. "It is not very difficult to explain in words, what cause has spread the divinity of the gods over great nations and filled the cities with altars, and has made customary rites to be undertaken, rites which now flourish in great states and places, from which even now remains implanted in mortal men the awe that raises new shrines to the gods all over the world, and drives them to throng together on festal days" (1161–67).

Here is the answer. Humanity stands in terror before the forces of nature. In ancient times, people could not explain such phenomena and looked for explanations in familiar causes. They imagined them to be the results of acts of intentional beings that they called "gods." And they imagined that the sentiments of the gods had a direct influence on their acts and words, whether good or bad. To explain thunder, for example, people imagined an angry god; when the sea raged, they thought the gods were picking a quarrel with them. So they prayed and felt remorse for their failings. But all this is stupid, Lucretius says, because these phenomena are totally dependent on the impersonal laws of nature, and nothing else. They are totally penetrable by human reason. Furthermore, experience shows that prayers are ineffectual.

He concludes that private and public worship is mere sham, in Rome and elsewhere. If we are to be wise, we must free ourselves from such delusions. Since all good and useful institutions throughout history were discovered by trial and error, and there is no reason to fear the fury of a sacred power if we forsake a traditional custom, a whole new horizon for political criticism and reforming activity is opened. But Lucretius himself never ventured into this arena; perhaps because he died too soon.

Lucretius's work had no tomorrow. It came at a time when the Greco-Roman world was entering a new era of religious syncretism and mysticism. The new era provided the loam in which the cult of the emperor could grow and thrive.

Chapter 5

Political Ideas under the Empire

When Augustus rose to power, Rome became a monarchy. This raises two important questions. Why had Republican solutions become obsolete after this time? And since a regression to a pre-civic form of "sacred monarchy" was impossible—among the elite at any rate—in a Greco-Roman world that was now deeply committed to a scientific and critical culture, what ideological justification could there have been for a monarchic constitution?

As for the first question, the most likely hypothesis is that the Republican solutions the Greek cities and early Rome experimented with—oligarchy, democracy, and "mixed" constitutions—were probably no longer suited to the immense political bodies created by Hellenistic and Roman conquests. The constitutions of the "cities" and "republics" supposed a unified *public opinion,* expressing itself either in a popular assembly or in a "senate" (or in a mixed form of both), the decisions of which reflected the mind of a public opinion that accepted them as legitimate in a more or less harmonious and reciprocal system of "resonance." The Hellenistic states and the Roman Empire, however, were largely multiethnic, nonhomogeneous polities. They were also geographic behemoths, and given the technical limitations of communication at the time, something like a *public opinion* would have had difficulty in shaping a response to the ebb and flow of social and political events at the time. Therefore, no assembly could be representative of so many dissimilar entities throughout the territory; any decisions taken by such an assembly would have inevitably faced the protestations and incomprehensions from other parts of the Empire (which is exactly what happened to the Roman Senate at the end of the Republic).[1]

[1] This would explain, *mutatis mutandis,* why the civic-republican ideal reappeared in the modern era. Because the modern era is the age of the printed document (which appeared in the sixteenth century) and the printing press (which appeared shortly thereafter in the seventeenth century), only then did it become possible for "public opinion" to reemerge once again in large states. (And with electronic media and communication, it may even be possible for continentwide public opinion to emerge in Europe.) This might also explain the failure of federalism, the one viable alternative to monarchy (federalism appeared in the form of leagues and alliances among Greek states, for example, the Aeolian League and the Achaean League in the third and second centuries BC). Federalism was unable to build on a shared public opinion

This, then, is the basic raison d'être of the monarchic form of government: in the absence of a coherent public opinion, it proposes another unitary principle—namely, a king and a system of government firmly under his command. The state is unified and coherent because it has one ruler, recognized by all, to whom anyone can appeal, and who guarantees the functional homogeneity—harmony (*synarmoga*)—of the different parts of the state in his person.

Of course, this transmutation comes at a price. The new form of government cannot have the same legitimacy as one based on open discussion in the *agora*, that is, in the Senate or in the Forum, which is a form of rationality more or less admitted and internalized by all citizens. By definition, a monarchic power is more distant, less comprehensible. To establish itself on a solid footing, it must either spread a holy terror to disarm the opposition; that is, it must fit the mold of the ancient sacred monarchies (certain hard facts support this attitude: military victories signaling the favors of Fortune, remnants of archaic mentalities among the uneducated masses); or it must have—in the eyes of the enlightened segments of the population—a philosophical foundation that presents the monarchy as the incarnation of a superior, objectively grounded rationality, inaccessible to average citizens. Roman monarchy would enjoy both types of legitimation.

Ideas on monarchy evolved significantly from the period of the Principate to the period of the Dominate.

Under the Principate, the king exercised his authority over the people through his religious *aura*, acquired either by the glory of arms or transmitted by his supposedly divine lineage as a descendant of the *gens* Julia. The *imperial cult* carefully preserved his *aura*. Furthermore, in keeping with a true state ideology, the monarchy encouraged efforts, such as Virgil's, to articulate this preeminence of the princely family with the ancient Roman legends in an original *epic* (see below). On the other hand, the jurists, the intellectual elite, and enlightened members of the political class—all guardians of the republican tradition and loyal to the spirit of Greek rationalism—described the prince as the "president of the Republic" who upheld the law. As the Republic faded into the past, these traditional civic values, instead of weakening, actually strengthened under Vespasian and during the dynasty of the Antonines (until Marcus Aurelius). Throughout this period the emperor ruled within the framework of constitutional constraints, which he respected on the whole.

Nevertheless, the evolution of certain reigns under the Principate (Nero, Domitian), which accelerated under the Severan dynasty, with the period of "military anarchy" (235–85 AD), and the advent of the Dominate (Diocletian), the sacred character of Roman monarchy became more marked in the popular sentiment and in the thinking of the intellectuals.

The person of the king itself became sacred, and a quasi-religious ceremonial appeared at court. The emperor no longer saw himself as a divine "hero" but imagined himself the equal of the other gods in the traditional polytheistic pantheon, and the earthly representative of a supreme sun god in a hierarchical polytheism, thereby paving the way for the Empire's conversion to Christian monotheism. At the same time, the intellectuals of the regime developed *political theologies*, inspired by Hellenistic Age ideas, and presented monarchic power as one of several elements of a single, intangible *cosmic order*. No one person's decision, or that of a collective assembly, could do anything to change this order. It is in the divine nature of things that the monarch's power remains exempt from constitutional control. The civic and liberal ideal of the foregoing centuries became jeopardized, and the drift toward Byzantinism was set in motion.

---

spanning the federated city-states; it necessarily came into conflict with the primary-level assemblies of each city-state, which did express local public opinion.

I. The Ideologies of the Principate

In the following pages we will discuss the religious and philosophical aspects of political ideas under the Principate.

The deification and heroization of Rome's autocratic ruler, a more or less spontaneous, collective phenomenon that by definition neither thought nor power controls entirely, gave rise to various official initiatives; the first of these was taken in the oriental half of the Empire (see section A below). Also, as early as the rule of Augustus, we come across a genuinely theological expression of this evolution in Virgil, which can be associated with Neopythagorism: the idea that the king inaugurates a new "golden age." Virgil also creates an imperial epic portraying the *gens* Julia, Caesar's family lineage, as predestined since the dawn of time to rule Rome (see section B below).

Simultaneously, arguments of another kind are formulated to provide the Principate with legitimacy. Theoreticians of the age begin to depict the Principate as an autocracy in which the state—with the emperor as its preeminent personality—remains a city under the rule of stable, public and equal laws for all, that is, a city under "the rule of law." Any power of the prince that exceeds the rule of law or that makes him the "lord and master" of the people is held by commentators to be an abuse of power, that is, a pathological and regressive power (a return to the ancient Roman monarchy or the oriental form of an absolute ruler). This is the opinion held by Augustus himself in his *Res gestae* (see section C), by Gaius and Ulpian (section D), by Seneca (section E), and, in slightly nuanced form, by Tacitus (section F), Pliny the Younger (section G), and the Greek rhetor Aelius Aristides (section H).

A. The Onset of Deification of Rome's Autocrat

From about the middle of the second century BC onward, Rome was in contact with the Hellenistic and oriental world.[2] Tacitus tells us in his *Histories*[3] that the Greeks of Asia said of Scipio Africanus, the conqueror of Greece, that he was a man of divine race who spent every day on the Capitol in conversation with his divine father; they compared him with Alexander the Great. Scipio, of course, was careful not to contradict such rumors. Other great Roman generals on campaign in the Eastern regions of the empire—from Sulla to Augustus by way of Caesar and Antony—came face-to-face with Hellenistic monarchy, underwent its influence, and experienced the adulation of the people; all this inspired dreams of transposing the system back to Rome. No doubt the Greeks of Asia Minor were a driving force in the deification of "Rome" and, ultimately, of its rulers.

As early as 195 BC, Smyrna devoted a cult to the "goddess Rome" (*Roma dea*); this was followed by Miletus and other cities of the region taking similar action. Chalcis (Euboea), ca. 190 BC, dedicated a religious shrine to "our Savior," Titus Flamininus (a rival general to Scipio), who was given equal standing with Hercules and Apollo.[4] Thereafter it was common to honor "Rome and Caesar," "Rome and Augustus." The Greeks of Asia had long seen their sovereigns as heroes (supermen) and gods. So it was quite natural for them to see "gods" in the generals of the armies that were besting their sovereigns in battle and, in some cases, unseating them. One further reason the Greeks held these men for exceptions, truly blessed with supernatural powers, was that

[2] This section is drawn from Ernst Barker, *From Alexander to Constantine: Passages and Documents Illustrating the History of Social and Political Ideas, 336 BC–AD 337* (Oxford: Clarendon Press, 1956), 204–14.

[3] Tacitus, *Histories*, 2 vols., trans. Clifford H. Moore and John Jackson (Cambridge, MA: Harvard University Press, 1925, 1931), 26.19. *Translator's note:* English quotations of works by Tacitus are from this edition.

[4] Plutarch, *Life of Flamininus*, in *Lives*, vol. 10, trans. Bernadette Perrin (Cambridge, MA: Harvard University Press, 1921), chapter 16.

they saw them extinguish chaos and establish peace where wars and confusion had reigned for ages. This too explains the titles given to the Roman generals: "savior" (*soter*), "benefactor" (*evergetus*), and "divine revelation" (*epiphanous*).

In 48 BC, the cities of the province of Asia dedicated an inscription to "Caius Iulius Caesar, the son of Caius, high-priest, *autocrator* (the equivalent of the Roman *imperator*) consul for the second time, descendant of Ares and Aphrodite (Mars and Venus), God Manifest (*Epiphanes*), and universal Saviour (*Soter*) of the life of mankind."[5] Likewise, the residents of the island of Lesbos decreed (sometime between 27 and 11 BC) that Augustus should be revered as a god. Around 9 BC, with the agreement of the Roman governor, the Greeks of Asia decreed that the birth date of Augustus, September 23, would be the first day of the civil calendar year. In this part of the world, since the early Hellenistic Age, the traditional first day of the year was September 21, the first day of the fall equinox. Nevertheless, the significance of the change is monumental: it is the equivalent of attributing a cosmological significance to the destiny of one man. The justification for this was expressed as follows: "the birthday of the most divine Caesar... is a day which we may justly count as equivalent to the beginning of everything—if not in itself and in its own nature, at any rate in the benefits it brings—inasmuch as it has restored the shape of everything that was failing and turning into misfortune, and has given a new look to the Universe.... Wherefore we may each of us count this [i.e., the birthday of Caesar] to have been the beginning of our own life."[6]

Even the fact that the new year originally began on September 21 is interpreted as providential, since it announced and made ready the coming of Augustus. Some time around 1 AD, the citizens of Helicarnassus expressed their belief that the birth of Caesar Augustus was another grace accorded by "the eternal and immortal nature of the Universe" because, thanks to him, "there is peace on land and sea." "Cities flourish in obedience to law and in concord (*homonoia*) and prosperity." The people of Assus in the Troad addressed Caligula in 37 AD as a god—"God Caesar Augustus"—associating him with Zeus the Savior and "our ancestral goddess the holy virgin [Athena Polias]." It became the tradition in the Roman Empire to consider each new emperor as the "Restorer of the World" (*restitutor orbis*), laying the foundations of a new golden age (*saeculum novum = diakosmesis;* see section below on Virgil).

Before very long, one of the principal grievances of imperial propaganda and public opinion against the Christians was that their rejection of the imperial cult upset the unity of popular beliefs in traditional religion; that it, therefore, inhibited the miraculous awakening of a new age of peace and prosperity (in short, they conducted a "witchhunt" against the Christians).

B. Virgil: The Fourth Eclogue, the *Aeneid*

Virgil rode this wave of popular sentiment when he formulated a political ideology in which he placed the accent on the divine and providential dimensions of the imperial figure.

1. *Life and Work*

Publius Vergilius Maro was born in 70 BC in Cisalpine Gaul in a village near Mantua. From early youth he was immersed in a rural setting and farming; both were strong influences on his poetry. He was educated in Cremona, Milan, and Rome, where he studied the Latin and Alexandrian schools of literature, as well as the philosophies of Epicurus and Plato. He acquired a vast culture

[5] Barker, *From Alexander to Constantine,* 209.
[6] Ibid., 211.

that extended to the sciences, including medicine and mathematics, two disciplines permeated by Pythagorism.

Virgil enjoyed the friendship of various writers of his age, in particular Gaius Asinius Pollio, who pursued a career in politics and was a lieutenant to Caesar and Antony. Imitating the *bucolics* or "eclogues"[7] of Theocritus, Virgil wrote a collection of *Eclogues* published in 37 BC. At this time Octavius was lord of the West. His "secretary of culture," Mecenus, noticed Virgil and asked him, it seems, to write a further collection of poems, the *Georgics* (published in 28 BC), in celebration of the life and work in the countryside that the Octavian peace had restored. A vibrant Italic nationalism came to expression in these poems. Virgil remained close to Mecenus, then established direct contact with Augustus himself. He next undertook to write his great epic poem, the *Aeneid,* in which his nationalism found even deeper expression under the benevolent patronage of a family and a dynasty. He worked on the poem for 11 years until he died in 19 BC, on the homeward leg of a journey to Greece (he had traveled there to see firsthand the places mentioned in his epic). The unfinished poem was published under the care of Mecenus and Augustus. Its success was immense. Before very long it was being used in schools for the study of Latin, much as Homer's *Iliad* and *Odyssey* were used to study Greek.[8]

2. *The Child Savior and the Return of the Golden Age*

The poem that Virgil wrote, aged 30, long before he knew Augustus, is important for the study of political ideology under the Principate. In his Fourth Eclogue, he refers to a *child restorer of the world* and *initiator of a new golden age.* Virgil could not have been announcing the founding of the Principate under Augustus at such an early date; but this is the meaning given to the poem by the partisans of Augustus retrospectively. This is by no means the sole interest of Virgil's poem. Christian propaganda and Emperor Constantine believed the poem to contain a messianic prophecy announcing the Christian destiny of the Empire.

Some modern scholars make the claim that Virgil received inspiration, via intermediaries, from biblical messianism (notably the books of Isaiah and Malachi). Others, among them Jerome Carcopino,[9] reject this claim and argue that the poem expresses pure pagan convictions, that is, Neopythagorist sentiments in vogue in Rome at the time of Virgil. This difference of opinion is not merely anecdotal. The question is: do the themes of the return of the Golden Age and what might be called a messianic monarchy allow for two interpretations of the poem, one pagan and another Judeo-Christian?

a. The Poem

We begin with the key passages of Virgil's Fourth Eclogue, which paint a very compelling picture of the coming Golden Age: a time of peace, prosperity, and happiness under the watchful eye of a providential king:

> Now is come the last age of Cumaean song; the great line of the centuries begins anew. Now the Virgin returns (*iam redit et Virgo*), the reign of Saturn returns; now a new generation descends from heaven on high (*iam nova progenies caelo dimittitur alto*). Only do you, pure Lucina [Diane], smile on the birth of the child, under whom the iron brood shall at last cease and a golden race spring up throughout the world! Your Apollo is king!

---

[7] They celebrate the charms of the countryside in verse.

[8] *Translator's note:* We use Virgil, *Eclogues, Georgics, Aeneid: Books 1–6,* trans. H. Rushton Fairclough, rev. G. P. Goold (Cambridge, MA: Harvard University Press, 1916); hereafter cited in the text.

[9] We follow Carcopino's widely respected interpretation throughout the present chapter: see Jerome Carcopino, *Virgile et le mystère de la IVe Eclogue* (Paris: L'Artisan du livre, 1930).

And in your consulship, Pollio, yes, yours, shall this glorious age begin, and the mighty months commence their march; under your sway any lingering traces of our guilt shall become void and release the earth from its continual dread. He shall have the gift of divine life (*ille deum vitam accipiet*), shall see heroes mingled with gods, and shall himself be seen by them, and shall rule the world to which his father's prowess brought peace (*pacatumque reget patriis virtutibus orbem*).

But for you, child, the earth, untilled, will pour forth its first pretty gifts, gadding ivy with foxglove everywhere, and the Egyptian bean blended with the laughing briar; unbidden it will pour forth for you a cradle of smiling flowers. Unbidden, the goats will bring home their udders swollen with milk, and the cattle will not fear huge lions. The serpent, too, will perish, and perish will the plant that hides its poison; Assyrian spice will spring up on every soil.

But as soon as you can read of the glories of heroes and your father's deeds, and can know what valour is, slowly will the plains yellow with the waving corn, on wild brambles the purple grape will hang, and the stubborn oak distil dewy honey. Yet will a few traces of old-time sin live on, to bid men tempt the sea in ships, girdle towns with walls, and cleave the earth with furrows. A second Tiphys will then arise, and a second Argo bear to carry chosen heroes; a second war will be fought, and great Achilles be sent again to Troy.

Next, when now the strength of years has made you a man, even the trader will quit the sea, nor will the ship of pine exchange wares; every land will bear all fruits.... The ram in the meadows will change his fleece, now to sweetly blushing purple, now to a saffron yellow....

"Ages so blessed, glide on!" cried the Fates to their spindles, voicing in unison the fixed will of Destiny. O enter your high honours—the hour will soon be here—dear offspring of the gods, mighty seed of a Jupiter to be (*cara deum suboles, magnum Iovis incrementum*)! See how the world bows with its massive dome—earth and expanse of sea and heaven's depth! See how all things rejoice in the age that is at hand! I pray that the twilight of a long life may then be vouchsafed me, and inspiration enough to hymn your deeds!

b. Jerome Carcopino's Interpretation

Carcopino's meticulous historical-critical analysis of Virgil's poem draws several important conclusions. The poem was written in early October 40 BC. The Treaty of Brindisi had just been agreed between Antony and Octavian. It was enthusiastically greeted by contemporaries exhausted by years of civil war ever since Caesar had crossed the Rubicon in 49 BC. The people lived in hope that life would return to normal again (mistakenly, as the civil war flared up again almost immediately), and they gave credit for peace to the Brindisi negotiators, notably Virgil's friend, Gaius Asinius Pollio, who was consul in that year. The child in the poem is identified by Carcopino as Saloninus, Pollio's son, born a few weeks or days after the treaty agreement.

The birth of Pollio's son provides Virgil with the opportunity to declare his Neopythagorean beliefs. Pythagoreanism was in vogue in Rome at the time, more so than previously; it had been revitalized by writers like Publius Nigidius Figulus and Lucius Cornelius Alexander Polyhistor. A Pythagorean "church" had even been established.

Pythagoreanism professed the dogma of the *Great Year,* a cosmic cycle that begins each time the heavens return to their initial position. This movement produces a total rejuvenation of the world: the return of the Golden Age.[10] The Pythagoreans postulated that the Great Year was

[10] According to Carcopino, ibid., 32–33,

> The unerring restoration of the world, which the Neopythagoreans inferred from the immortal divinity of the sidereal ether and, in their inner circles, called by the name *metakosmesis*, was one of the central truths

subdivided into a calculable duration of "months" or "centuries" (opinions diverged as to the exact number, somewhere between four and ten),[11] each with its own tutelary deity and specific characteristics. Thus, if with the help of certain indisputable signs it can be deduced that the last century is in progress, then it is possible to conclude that the Great Year is nearing an end and that a new era of renewal will soon begin. According to Carcopino, Virgil, like many of his contemporaries, interpreted the crisis of the Republic and the terrifying civil wars as the sign that the final century of the Great Year had indeed begun.[12]

When the peace of Brindisi was agreed, Virgil combined several elements into an overarching synthesis: first, contemporaries believed it would be a lasting peace; second, it had been concluded on October 5 or 6, 40 BC, when the zodiac constellation Virgo returned to the firmament; third, another Neopythagorean theory affirms that microcosm and macrocosm mirror each other. Carcopino postulates that Virgil interpreted the conjunction of these events—peace and astronomical conditions—as a harbinger of the end of the last century and the imminent return of the Great Year; further, in a vision, Virgil anticipated that the Golden Age to come would be reflected in the life of Pollio's son, one of the first children to be born after these omens.

Carcopino emphasizes that the Golden Age of Virgil's eclogue diverges profoundly from the paradise or messianic age of biblical tradition. In the Pythagorean golden age, as in paradise, everything is plentiful; honey flows from heaven, animals live in peace with one another and with all humankind. However, (1) this paradise does not *appear all at once:* Virgil insists that there will still be wars and economic turmoil; day does not break suddenly, the newborn babe is not instantly a man. And, (2) *the Golden Age is not, like the messianic age, an end-time;* because the movement of the universe is an "eternal return"; there was a Golden Age in the past, and there will be many golden ages in the future, which also means that there will be countless regressions to the Iron Age. Evil never disappears from the world entirely; it merely wanes or eclipses (in the astronomical sense of these two terms) from time to time. (3) Finally, the child in Virgil's poem does not appear to play an active role in the revival of things; he is incidental to it, a witness of sorts. The driving force of history is neither humanity, collectively speaking, nor a few exceptional men, nor is it a messiah. Rather, it is the movement of the stars and planets and the universe in general. They intrude on humanity from outside like the Fates (even if great men like Pollio and,

---

of Neopythagoreanism. They ascribed the discovery of this truth to the founder of their cult. Moreover, of the three teachings that Dicaearchus, a pupil of Aristotle, attributes to Pythagoras, and that Porphyrus recorded for posterity, one is that, at various verifiable moments in time, beings recommence their previous life. Accordingly, such rebirths occur again and again by virtue of the perpetual motion of the heavenly sphere, such that Nature, in each of its bodies and beings, reverts to its original form every time that the astronomical bodies return to their original positions on the orbital path. Thus, they claimed, it is possible to calculate the exact subdivisions of this cyclical motion by identifying specific conjunctions, imperceptible to the ignorant but obvious to the initiated of the "mathematics" of the Pythagorean school.

On the origin of the concept of the Great Year, Carcopino refers to Plato, notably *Timeaus* 39d, Cicero, *De Rep.* 6.22.24; *De natura deor.* 1.8.18; *De fin.* 2.5.15, and *Hortensius*, quoted by Livy, *De oratoribus* 16.7.

[11] See Carcopino, *Virgile*, 148. The Neopythagorean Publius Nigidius Figulus wrote in *De diis*: "Orpheus enumerates the rule of Saturn first, then Jupiter, followed by Neptune, and finally Pluto. Some, among them the magi, claimed that the rule of Apollo would be the last" (cited in ibid., 52). The Sibyl, however, speaks of ten *saecula*. Opinions vary likewise as to the length of these "centuries," which might be either 100 or 110 years. Cicero, also a believer in the Great Year, attributes to it a much longer duration, namely 15,000 years, of which only a few hundred have actually passed.

[12] It is classical that a generation of men, suffering under the affects of crises and wars, gain the impression that the "end of time" is near. The misfortunes they experience are so intense and unusual that they can not accredit them to the normal course of history that they expected to last forever. We will see that this psychological or moral disposition is characteristic of the prophets at the origin of messianism and the Jewish apocalyptic tradition (see part 3, introduction).

no doubt, his son, once he completes the *cursus honorum,* leave their mark, their deeds will not be sufficient to change the course of destiny).[13]

c. MESSIANIC INTERPRETATIONS

When Christianity emerged, Virgil's Fourth Eclogue was reinterpreted in a Christian sense in view of its messianic resonances and the role played by the child Savior. The author of *Oratio ad Sanctos* (326 AD), either Emperor Constantine or his advisor Eusebius of Caesarea (see below, p. 309), saw in Virgil's poem a prophecy announcing the birth and reign of Christ. What the pagan poet Virgil could only allude to, Constantine was able to say openly, and he did.[14] The return of the Golden Age is a figure for the reign of Christ. Verse 6, *iam redit et Virgo,* is, of course, a reference to Mary, mother of God. A child descending from heaven, born of a Virgin (*nova progenies caelo dimittitur alto* [verse 7]), with the gift of divine life (*ille deum vitam accipiet* [15]), the "dear offspring of the gods, mighty seed of a Jupiter to be!" (*cara deum suboles, magnum Iovis incrementum* [49]): this is Christ himself. When the poem says that the child shall "rule the world to which his father's prowess brought peace" (*pacatumque reget patriis virtutibus orbem*), the reference can only be to Christ the Son, who rules over the earth by the will of God the Father in heaven. The words used to describe the Golden Age, the peace between animals and humans (22), the superabundance of the fruits of the earth (18–30, 39–45), echo closely the descriptions of a messianic world by Isaiah and Malachi. The serpent that perishes (27) can only be Satan.[15]

Giving further credit to this messianic interpretation is Virgil's own reference to the oracles of the Cumaen Sibyl (verse 4: "Now is come the last age of Cumaean song"). According to some modern scholars, it is feasible that these oracles, when Virgil could know them, may have included passages from Jewish-Alexandrian texts as well.

The Sibyl was a pagan prophetess (comparable to the Pythia of Delphi). Since the fifth century BC, the Sibylline books were kept officially at the Capitol in Rome, and certain priests were assigned to their preservation and interpretation. Under the rule of Sulla a fire destroyed the oldest collections, leading to the compilation of a new collection of Sibylline oracles, including texts of Jewish-Alexandrian origin with elements of biblical messianism.[16] In one passage (book 3 of the surviving collection) the "Sibyl" prophesizes that "God [will send] a king who will make wars cease in all the earth." "Justice... will reign on earth, with Concord (*Homonoia*) at her side." Earth will yield the gift of an infinity of crops, and honey will drop from heaven like rain. Flocks and herds will abound. "There shall be deep peace all over the world,... wolves and lambs shall eat their meat together on the mountains,... the lion shall feed at the stall like the ox, and a little child shall lead him about in bonds."[17] More generally, Virgil may have been

---

[13] Tacitus shares this conviction; see below, pp. 332–35.

[14] In this he followed the Alexandrian scholars, who interpreted the coded passages and allegories of Homer and the Bible.

[15] This interpretation was common throughout the Middle Ages. Dante, author of the *Divine Comedy,* ca. 1310–20, believed in it firmly, and this is one reason why he chose Virgil to be his guide through hell: Virgil is virtually a Christian. The theme is found as late as Victor Hugo ("Virgil... God almost like an angel"), from *Les voix intérieures* [Inner voices] (Paris, 1837), 18.

[16] See Barker, *From Alexander to Constantine,* 217; Maurice Rat, introduction to *Virgile, L'Eneide* (Paris: Garnier-Flammarion, 1965), 340–41; Carcopino, *Virgile,* 65.

[17] Quoted in Barker, *From Alexander to Constantine,* 217–18. These same images are found in biblical writings. See, for example, Isaiah 11:6–9: "The wolf also shall dwell with the lamb, and the leopard shall lie down with the kid; and the calf and the young lion and the fatling together; and a little child shall lead them. And the cow and the bear shall feed;

influenced by various oriental religious movements, which had permeated Roman society for some time.[18]

d. Some Particular Aspects of the Poem

With these overall clarifications in mind, here is how certain details of the poem can be understood:

"At last, the final age of the Cumaean prophecy is come." The reference is to the last of the ten "centuries," comprising the Great Year.

"The great line of the centuries begins anew." The reference is to the Great Year, which begins anew from its starting point.

"Now the Virgin returns." According to Carcopino, the reference is to the *constellation* of Virgo, which escapes the brightness of the sun and becomes visible again in the zodiac exactly at the moment of the events that inspired Virgil (late September).

The poet Aratus and the Pythagoreans developed a symbolism associated with this constellation. The young woman it represents is Justice, because the Virgin and Justice are inviolate. In his *Georgics,* Virgil writes that long ago Justice inhabited the earth, but, pursued by humankind's villainy, she took refuge among simple country people—because their customs are most virtuous—before she was finally forced to flee to heaven. In Neopythagorean speculation, it was common to say that the fall of humankind after the Golden Age resulted from its use of the sword, ritual sacrifice, and the consumption of meat, all violent practices abhorred by Justice and which drove her to flee to heaven. Conversely, with the return of the Golden Age, Justice will redescend to earth.[19] Thus, clearly an age of peace and prosperity, and the rule of justice, are not exclusive to biblical messianism.[20]

"The reign of Saturn returns." The first "century" of the Great Year, the Golden Age, begins in the reign of Saturn.

---

their young ones shall lie down together: and the lion shall eat straw like the ox. And the sucking child shall play on the hole of the asp, and the weaned child shall put his hand on the cockatrice' den."

[18] See Carcopino, *Virgile,* 62–77. In addition to biblical and Jewish influences, Egyptian and Etruscan influences have also been proposed. During the rituals of the festivals of Aion and the sun in Alexandria, the *mystai* of Helios (the Sun) proclaimed, on December 25 after midnight, after they had confirmed the position of the night sky, "the Virgin has given birth, the light will grow." The myth of the child savior and lord of the world (*kosmoskrator*) allegedly stems from the book of revelations of the god Thoth. And the curious passage from Virgil's Fourth Eclogue (43–45)—"of himself the ram in the meadows will change his fleece, now to sweetly blushing purple, now to a saffron yellow"—is purportedly from the holy books of the Etruscans, and specifically from prophetic texts, which say: "If the fleece of a ewe or a ram put on a hew of purple or gold, it is a promise to the prince of a great happiness, the growth of his strength or the strength of his nation, which will be covered in glory and prosperity."

Carcopino, however, accepts only the direct influence of the Etruscans. He rejects all others, including the suggestion that Virgil may have read the Alexandrian texts of the Sibylline oracles. The themes of peace and the Golden Age are, he says, fundamentally pagan; they are already found among earlier poets who sang of the Golden Age—Hesiod, Aratus, Ovid, Empedocles. Perhaps Virgil had indirect knowledge of Egyptian and Jewish religions and of the prophecies attributed to the Greek Sibyls by the Alexandrian Jews through various books published in Rome in his lifetime; for example, the books of Marcus Terentius Varro and especially the writings of Neopythagoreans such as Lucius Cornelius Alexander Polyhistor. But it was primarily through the Neopythagoreans that these various oriental elements were transmitted, after being filtered by their own systems.

[19] Pythagoras banned blood sacrifices and prescribed a vegetarian diet. "Formerly, says Empedocles [490–435 BC], the altars did not flow with the blood of bulls; it was abominable to men to take the life of a living being and to delight in its inviolate substance.... All [animals], were gentle and obedient towards men, wild beasts and birds in the sky. Everywhere the flame of mutual love shone" (see Carcopino, *Virgile,* 102–03, who quotes similar passages from Aratus and Ovid). All of this recurs with the return of the Golden Age.

[20] Ibid., 133–42, 149–53.

"A new generation descends from the heavens." The followers of the Christian prophesy thought they recognized here the incarnation of Christ, according to the promise of the Jewish-Alexandrian Sibyl that a king would descend from heaven into the world and secure the rejuvenation of humanity through the salvation of the Savior. Carcopino recognizes in this verse the echo of *metempsychosis* modified by the Stoic Posidonius and adopted by Nigidius, Polyhistor, and Cicero (in the "Dream of Scipio," *Republic* 6; see above, pp. 299–300). According to this doctrine, souls are divine by nature. It is not possible for them to exist in this sublunar world, where all things are corrupt; they are emanations of the stars. If they are present in physical bodies on earth, it is because they *descended* from heaven, and they will *reascend* there one day.

"However, throughout the long succession of ages that fill the Great Year, only a small number of privileged souls descend from the ether to enliven earthly bodies. All the others, tethered to the chain of metempsychosis by Neopythagoreanism, must undergo—passively and more or less painfully—various humiliating transformations commanded by the cycle of life and death in a relentless repetition of necessity. Only after the series of *saecula* come to an end, and the Great Year begins again, will all souls—finally freed from the fetters of nature—be reincarnated in their primitive form. In keeping with the logic of Neopythagorean theodicy, the Golden Age is the moment when this miracle is accomplished, when the lives of creatures ignite from the sparks detached from the incorruptible ether…, [and] again all creation dips suddenly into the sidereal source of its divine substance."[21]

During this palingenesis[22] a new and rejuvenated life occurs, spreading throughout nature together with the divine; this is why the child is called *suboles,* "offspring" of God: at the blessed moment when the Great Year begins, it is as if God himself is increased by these new living beings.

"The iron brood shall at last cease and a golden race spring up." Then, the opposite of what happened at the beginning of the Great Year, in the first phase of the cycle, will occur. This explains why "Virgil, in more than one passage, put all verbs in the future tense, which Hesiod himself had conjugated in the past tense."[23] In his *Works and Days,* Hesiod describes the decline of humanity and the deterioration of the earth from an original state: the earth ceased to be fertile, and it became necessary to work, travel, and trade. The *metakosmesis* promised by the Neopythagoreans will restore, in inverse order, all the joys that time has eliminated, just as spring restores the leaves that fall in autumn.

"Your own Apollo now is king." As we saw, some say that the reign of Apollo is the last century of the Great Year. In contrast, the Sibylline oracles place the final century under the sign of the sun (perhaps in association with the ancient Stoic idea that the world is approaching the inferno, *ekpyrosis*). Virgil, or the Neopythagoreans that gave him his inspiration, replaces the sun with Apollo because Apollo is the metaphysical symbol of unity; in the periodic movement of the Great Year, the world approaches then recedes from the One and the Many. When "night" finally falls on the Great Year, "the monad, from which the multitude of beings and things grow and which [the Neopythagoreans] held Apollo to be the brightest symbol of all, that same monad recovers its original unity."[24]

"Te consule, te duce." This is a reference to the time when "Pollio is consul and foremost general" (it was expected that when his consulship would end, he would be appointed proconsul to

---

[21] Ibid., 84–85.

[22] "Return to life," from the Greek *palin,* "again," and *genesis,* "becoming, birth."

[23] Carcopino, *Virgile,* 59–60.

[24] Ibid., 52.

Illyricum, where he would command the army). This is a *simultaneity,* not a *cause.* Neither the child nor the father are heroes by the action that establishes the new age of justice; they are a father, who had the good fortune to sire a child, and a son, who had the good fortune to be born at the exact moment that the Golden Age returned. They are mere witnesses and reflections of this change in progress: the driving force of the change is the movement of the stars and planets, an incontrovertible force, independent of all human deeds.[25]

"Yet will a few traces of old-time sin live on." According to Carcopino, the persistence of evil for a while longer, although the new age is come, speaks in favor of the poem's Neopythagorean origin: it is because it is an astronomical cycle that the advent of the Golden Age is fundamentally progressive (similar to the dawn of day and the cycle of the seasons).[26] Virgil knows that Pollio has been appointed proconsul of Dalmatia, and does not deny that there will still be difficult wars to wage; but they will be the last; order is in view and soon within grasp.

"But for you, child, the earth untilled will pour forth its first pretty gifts. . . . But as soon as you can read of the glories of heroes and your father's deeds, and can know what valour is. . . . Next, when now the strength of years has made you a man." The different phases of the child's development, a young aristocrat destined to climb the ladder of offices of the *cursus honorum,* correspond exactly to the evolution of the century of Saturn (the Golden Age). The latter can be read in the former and vice versa, according to the law that Pythagoras himself taught, namely microcosm and macrocosm mirror one another: "It is said that Man is a microcosmos to the greater macrocosmos because all the powers of the cosmos are contained within him (*o anthrôpos micros kosmos legetaï hoti pasas echei tas tou kosmou dynameis*)" (the phrase is attributed to Pythagoras by a classical biographer).[27] The transformation of the cosmos when it enters the Golden Age is reflected and rejuvenated in the lesser model, namely, the life of the child celebrated in the eclogue.

In conclusion, we can say that, in his Fourth Eclogue, Virgil expresses a dearly held theme, shared by his contemporaries (among them some of the great luminaries of the age). It is possible that such mystical-religious representations played a role in the success of Augustus's political formula. Virgil, of course, was mistaken in his Fourth Eclogue: neither the peace of Brindisi nor the figure of Pollio had any lasting importance in Roman history. However, in other eclogues, Virgil alludes to young Octavian;[28] and in his *Georgics* (which he read to Octavian in 39 BC),

[25] Herein lies the true difference between pagan expectations of the Golden Age and Jewish and Christian messianic expectations. The latter postulates a *moral responsibility* of humankind: the advent of messianic time is inconceivable unless people build a world worthy of the Messiah, in which he can live. Humanity must wrestle with the circumstances to make this happen; they must remove injustice and wickedness in all their forms. The final victory over evil is possible, since the Torah and the Gospel command it. Time is no longer perceived as an "Eternal Return" of good and evil combined; it becomes linear and goal-directed. See below, part 3, introduction.

[26] A classical commentator, Servius, glosses Virgil's poem as follows: "In this passage, things seem to take place by *apocatastasis,* that is by restoration of the heavens to their original position" (Carcopino, *Virgile,* 44). Carcopino adds: "Like happy days that return little by little as the sad ones ebb away, and the sun nears the equinox by the same degree that it leaves it behind, the rebirth of the *aurea saecula* (golden centuries) comes about with a few ugly memories of former bad times in its wake, until it finally erases them completely. Already the Chaldeans used the term *apocatastasis* to describe the return of the stars and planets to their primordial positions in the heavens; Greek physicians employed it to describe a patient's return from illness to health" (ibid., 44). This method of restoration of happy times after times of sadness also distinguishes Pythagorean from Stoic doctrine. The Stoics also believed in a cyclical return of the Great Year, but for them the restoration came about after a cosmic cataclysm, a universal inferno (*ekpirosis*), destroys everything.

[27] This symmetry is the foundation of ancient astrology: every change in the stars and planets has its corresponding event in each individual person.

[28] In the First Eclogue (6–8), the character Tityrus, overjoyed that Octavian has restored peace, says, *O Meliboee, deus nobis haec otia fecit. / Namque erit ille mihi semper deux, illius aram / saepe tener nostris ab ovilibus imbuet agnus* ("O Meliboeus, it is a god [Octavian] who gave us this peace—for a god he shall ever be to me; often shall a tender lamb from our folds stain his altar").

he imbues the new hero and his family with the religious convictions exemplified in his Fourth Eclogue.[29] Finally, Virgil dedicates his monumental work, the *Aeneid*, to the glory of Octavian.

3. *The* Aeneid

a. The Imperial Destiny of the *Gens Julia* (*Aeneid* 6.752–885)

Rooted partly in myth or legend and partly in Virgil's "literary" imagination, the *Aeneid* is the story of thc founding of Rome by the descendants of Aeneas, the Trojan hero, as they traveled to the West after the calamity of the Trojan War. The *gens* Julia, the family of the Caesars, descends from Iulus, the son of Aeneas (or his grandson, also known as Ascanius), and also from Jupiter and Venus through Aeneas. The family was fated by the gods to rule the Roman Empire, which exists in turn by the will of the gods. It was also their will that Rome should unite the eastern and western Mediterranean worlds under the rule of Italy.

This grandiose divine project is revealed to the reader through a remarkable literary device. After Troy is conquered by the Achaeans, Aeneas flees to Carthage and becomes Queen Dido's lover; abandoning her, he arrives in Italy, where he pays a visit to the Cumaean Sibyl (the same Sibyl Virgil refers to in his Fourth Eclogue). She opens for him the gates of hell: on one side is Tartarus, where the wicked endure eternal punishments; on the other, Elysium, the Blessed Groves, where the virtuous reap their rewards and after a thousand years of purification are granted their reincarnation on earth (strong evidence for the Pythagorean doctrine of metempsychosis). Here Aeneas finds his father Anchises, who leads him to a long line of souls preparing for reincarnation. All will become famous in Roman legend and history. First, he sees the Alban kings, founders of the cities of Latium, then Romulus (the heavens have already decided that after his death he will be deified and revered as Quirinius). Immediately after, another soul captures his attention, that of Augustus, called to rule the entire world:

> Turn hither now your two-eyed gaze, and behold this nation, the Romans that are yours. Here is Caesar and all the seed of Iulus destined to pass under heaven's spacious sphere. And this in truth is he whom you so often hear promised you, Augustus Caesar, son of a god,[30] who will again establish a golden age[31] in Latium amid fields once ruled by Saturn; he will advance his empire beyond the Garamants[32] and Indians[33] to a land which lies beyond our stars, beyond the path of year and sun,[34] where sky-bearing Atlas wheels on his shoulders the blazing star-studded sphere. (*Aeneid* 6.788–97)

Only after Augustus does Anchises show Aeneas the other great Romans: the kings of Rome (Tullus Hostilius, Ancus Marcus, the Tarquins); the heroes of the Republic (Brutus, Decius, Torquatus, Aemilius Paulus [the conqueror of the Achaeans, and thus, in the eyes of Aeneas, the avenger of the Trojans], the Scipios, the Grachii, Cato, Fabius Maximus Cunctator). It is the will of the Fates that Rome will conquer and rule the world by the deeds of these men. This is the genius of Rome, even though the Greeks remain masters of the arts, the sciences, and eloquence: "Others [the Greeks], I doubt not, shall with softer mould beat out the breathing bronze, coax from the marble features to the life, plead cases with greater eloquence and with a pointer trace

[29] See the following three passages in the *Georgics*: (1) 1.32–34: the birth of Augustus on September 23, when the sun moves from Virgo to Libra, symbolizing his calling to restore the Golden Age; (2) 1.463–64: the eclipse of the sun at the moment of Caesar's assassination, attesting to his divinity; (3) 2.170: Octavian, "the greatest of all" Caesars.

[30] Augustus was the adopted son of Caesar, who himself had been deified.

[31] We find again the theme of the Fourth Eclogue.

[32] Inhabitants of the Libyan oasis, recently conquered by a Roman army.

[33] It was said that Augustus aspired to extend the Roman Empire to the banks of the Ganges.

[34] In other words, respectively, toward the great unknown of the north and the south.

heaven's motions and predict the risings of the stars: you, Roman,[35] be sure to rule the world (be these your arts), to crown peace with justice, to spare the vanquished and to crush the proud" (847–53).[36]

b. The Shield of Aeneas and the Battle of Actium (*Aeneid* 8.671–731)

Virgil finds another occasion to exalt Augustus in terms that foretell his deification. In preparation for the battle that her son, Aeneas, will wage against Turnus, the native king of Latium, Venus instructs her divine husband, Vulcan, to forge the weapons he will need. Among these weapons is a shield, richly embossed with the principal episodes of Rome's history.[37] In particular and by coincidence, the shield depicts in its center the battle of Actium.[38] It is telling that the kingdom instated under Augustus is presented as the kingdom of the West and conqueror of the barbarian East (Antony, of course, had Greece on his side, and the Greeks regarded the Romans, and all peoples in the West, as barbarians; the perspective here has been reversed).

> Among these scenes flowed wide the likeness of the swelling sea, all gold, but the blue water foamed with white billows, and round about dolphins, shining in silver, swept the seas with their tails in circles, and cleft the tide. In the centre could be seen bronze ships—the battle of Actium; you could see all Leucate[39] aglow with War's array, and the waves ablaze with gold.
>
> On the one side Augustus Caesar stands on the lofty stern, leading Italians to strife, with Senate and People, the Penates of the state, and all the mighty gods; his auspicious brows shoot forth a double flame, and on his head dawns his father's star [*sidus*]. Elsewhere, favored by winds and gods, high-towering Agrippa leads his column; his brows gleam with the beaks of the naval crown, proud token won in war.
>
> On the other side comes Antony with barbaric might and motley arms, victorious over the nations of the dawn and the ruddy sea,[40] bringing in his train Egypt and the strength of the East and farthest Bactra [Afghanistan]; and there follows him (oh the shame of it!) his Egyptian wife [Cleopatra].
>
> All rush on at once, and the whole sea foams, torn up by the sweeping oars and triple-pointed beaks. To the deep they race; you would think that the Cyclades, uprooted, were floating on the main, or that high mountains were clashing with mountains: in such huge

---

[35] This "division of labor" assigns science and oratory to the Greeks and politics to the Romans. Sallust formulates the same opinion: the Greeks were writers of great talent and eloquent speakers; as for the Romans, "the most able men were the most actively employed [men of action]"; from Sallust, *War with Catiline. War with Jugurtha. Selections from the Histories*, trans. J. C. Rolfe (Cambridge, MA: Harvard University Press, 1921), 8.

[36] Augustus excelled very certainly in this art particular to the Romans. The "clemency of Augustus" was famous. He restored peace through his intelligent policy of amnesty. He was proud of this policy, which he actively pursued in his dealings with the peoples conquered by Rome. The *Res gestae* of Augustus (see below, pp. 322–23) explains: "As for foreign nations, those which I was able to safely forgive, I preferred to preserve than to destroy" (quoted in Rat, *Virgile, L'Eneide*, 351n1654).

[37] Here Virgil imitates Homer, who described the shield of Achilles in his *Illiad*, 18.478, and Hesiod, who described the shield of Hercules in his *Theogony*, 139–321. Virgil was also imitated by later poets, among them Stacius.

[38] The Battle of Actium was the great naval battle in 31 BC, during which Octavian defeated Antony, finally putting an end to the civil wars (see above, p. 211). The battle took place on the western coast of Greece (across from Italy, slightly north of the Gulf of Patras). Cleopatra, queen of Egypt and wife of Antony (having previously been the wife of Caesar), was present at the battle. After the division of territories in 37 BC, Antony ruled over all the Roman provinces in the eastern Mediterranean, in addition to Egypt (including Greece). His dream was to establish a Hellenistic-type kingdom, subdivided into satrapies, to be handed over to his sons. At the Battle of Actium he engaged auxiliary troops originating from every region under his control. See François Chamoux, *Marc-Antoine* (Paris: Arthaud Éditions, 1986), 348 and following.

[39] The promontory on the island of Leucade in the Ionian Sea.

[40] An allusion, respectively, to the Parthians and the Armenians, recently vanquished by Antony, and to the countries bordering the Red Sea, the Persian Gulf, and the Sea of Oman.

ships the seamen attack the towered sterns. Flaming tow and shafts of winged steel are showered from their hands; Neptune's fields redden with strange slaughter.

In the midst, the queen calls upon her hosts with their native sistrum;[41] not yet does she cast back a glance at the twin snakes[42] behind. Monstrous gods of every form and barking Anubis[43] wield weapons against Neptune and Venus and against Minerva.[44] In the middle of the fray storms Mavors [Mars], embossed in steel, with the grim Furies from on high; and in rent robe Discord[45] strides exultant, while Bellona[46] follows her with bloody scourge. Actian Apollo saw the sight, and from above was bending his bow; in terror at this all Egypt and India, all Arabians, all Sabaeans, turned to flee. . . .

But Caesar, entering the walls of Rome in triple triumph,[47] was dedicating to Italy gods[48] his immortal votive gift—three hundred mighty shrines[49] throughout the city. The streets were ringing with gladness and games and shouting; in all the temples was a band of matrons, in all were altars, and before the altars slain steers covered the ground. He himself [Augustus], seated at the snowy threshold of shining Phoebus, reviews the gifts of nations and hangs them on the proud portals. The conquered peoples move in long array, as diverse in fashion of dress and arms as in tongues. Here Mulciber [Vulcan] had portrayed the nomad race and the ungirt Africans, here the Leleges and Carians and quivered Gelonians.[50] Euphrates moved now with humbler waves, and the Morini were there, furthest of mankind, and the Rhine of double horn,[51] the untamed Dahae,[52] and Araxes chafing at his bridge.[53]

Such sights he admires on the shield of Vulcan, his mother's gift, and though he knows not the events, he rejoices in their representation, raising up on his shoulder the fame and fortunes of his children's children. (8.671–731)

c. The Subordination of the Greek East to the Italian West (*Aeneid* 12.791–842)

Lastly, we must quote the very end of the poem. Here Virgil embellishes, somewhat artificially, the legend to justify the reconciliation of Greece and Rome under the aegis of the latter. If Aeneas faced so many challenges en route, and if in particular he had such difficulty reaching agreement with the native Italics, the reason, we are told, is because Juno was angry with him. Juno, the wife

---

41 The sistrum is an ancient musical instrument of the percussion family associated with ancient Egypt. It was an attribute of the priests of Isis. Virgil is being facetious here. Cleopatra's drums are ineffective against Roman trumpets.

42 To avoid falling into the hands of her conqueror, Cleopatra, back in Egypt, killed herself with an asp.

43 The Egyptian gods with animal heads strike the Romans as "monsters." The god Anubis had the head of a dog.

44 Facing the barbaric gods, the three Roman gods represented, respectively, naval might, beauty, and armed wisdom.

45 An Etruscan and Roman divinity (see the Greek Eris).

46 Goddess of war; the daughter, wife, or sister of Mars. Her name comes from *bellum*, war.

47 Octavian celebrated three "triumphs" in Rome for three different victories: over the Dalmatians, in Actium, and in Alexandria.

48 An expression of Virgil's nationalism for Italy and its religion.

49 Augustus restored many temples in Rome; Virgil had personally witnessed this work. Augustus ordered the erection of the Phoebus Apollo temple on the Palatine hill (we will return to this below); vowed in 36 BC, it was consecrated in 28 BC (Virgil knew it). It was made of white marble (the "snowy threshold") with ivory doors ("proud portal"). Great peacemakers aspire to be great builders and fulfill their promise because they create prosperity and optimism.

50 A people of Asia Minor and Asia.

51 The Rhine was symbolized in the form of a bull.

52 An Asian tribe of the region near the Caspian Sea.

53 The bridge built by Alexander over the Araxes River in Armenia was swept away by a flood. With these allusions to countries and peoples throughout the world, Virgil accredits the idea of Augustus as ruler and pacifier of the whole world, *restitutor orbis*.

of Jupiter, was jealous of Venus, the mother of Aeneas. Each goddess, like in Homer, gave systematic favors and supernatural gifts to her chosen camp, placing obstacles before its enemies. But Aeneas receives serious wounds in single combat with the Italic king Turnus. Virgil imagines the intervention of Jupiter, who until then had remained neutral in the quarrel. Jupiter commands Juno to leave off her taunting: she cannot alter the will of the Fates to allow the Trojans to settle permanently in Italy and Aeneas to be deified. Juno must comply, but she wrests from him one last compensation: the kingdom to be founded in Italy will be predominantly Italic, the name and language of the Trojans (and the Greeks in general) will disappear from Italy forever.

> "And now I yield [Juno says to Jupiter], yes, I yield, and quit the strife in loathing. This boon, banned by no law of fate, I beg of you for Latium's sake, for your own kin's greatness:[54] when anon with happy bridal rites[55]—so be it!—they plight peace, when anon they join in laws and treaties, do not command the native Latins to change their ancient name, nor to become Trojans and be called Teucrians,[56] nor to change their language[57] and alter their attire: let Latium be, let Alban kings endure through ages, let be a Roman stock, strong in Italian valour: Troy is fallen, and fallen let her be, together with her name!" Smiling on her, the creator of men and things replied: "You are Jove's true sister, and Saturn's other child: such waves of wrath surge deep within your breast! But come, allay the anger that was stirred in vain. I grant your wish and relent, willingly won over. Ausonia's[58] sons shall keep their fathers' speech and ways, and as it is now, so shall their name be: the Teucrians shall but sink down, merged in the mass. I will give them their sacred laws and rites and make them all Latins of one tongue. From them shall arise a race, blended with Ausonian blood, which you will see overpass men, overpass gods in loyalty, and no nation will celebrate you worship with equal zeal."[59] (12.818–40)

Thus, the story ends. Rome is founded; it dominates the world; the family of Augustus reigns. The different tribes of Italy form a single nation (Virgil, a Cisalpine Gaul, cherishes this extension of nationalism beyond the walls of the city of Rome; this was also the sentiment of another illustrious Roman citizen from the provinces a few years before: Cicero). This nation has Greek origins, which explains its noble spirit; but from the beginning, the gods desired that the Greek world should be subjugated to the Roman world. Opponents to the regime can now be presented as opponents to Rome itself and to its supernatural destiny; they are, in a sense, ungodly.

4. *Conclusion*

Through his writings, and particularly his *Aeneid,* Virgil nurtures a new type of political discourse: it might be called an "ideology of the state." This discourse is very different from the myths and legends spontaneously invented by a tribe (because the poet uses his imagination—or, better perhaps, the dictates of a shrewd political mind directed by Mecenus or even Augustus himself—to rearrange the mythological elements at his disposal). But it is no less different from the rational political philosophy of an Aristotle or a Cicero, or from the philosophy of history of a Polybius. Irrationality abounds to a large degree, contaminating Republican ideals and accrediting the idea, in the eyes of a yet uncultivated people impressionable by the supernatural, that

[54] Latinus, the king of the Latins, descended from Saturn, the father of Jupiter.

[55] The union of Aeneas and Lavinia, daughter of king Latinus.

[56] The Teucrians were descendants of Teucer, the first king of Troad; the Trojans are commonly referred to as the Teucrians in the *Aeneid.*

[57] They were a conquered people and by rights they should have taken the name of the conquerors.

[58] Ausonia first referred to Etruscan Italy, then to all of Italy.

[59] Junon had many temples in Latin lands.

the newly established autocracy is endowed with religious legitimacy. *Lineage* and *sacrality* are the two principles that emerge triumphant in this representation of Rome: the Republic and the anonymous rule of the law are a long way off. Furthermore, it is bewildering that Virgil presents Octavian's victory over Antony as a triumph of the West over the East: by accrediting the model of sacred monarchy in the West, Virgil's epic does more to orientalize the Roman Republic than to occidentalize Mediterranean civilization.

Be that as it may, Virgil's thought is still far from the ideas of the Dominate. The heroes of the royal *gens,* from Aeneas to Augustus, behave like human princes and are quite approachable. Although their origins are divine, they are fundamentally pious ("pious Aeneas"). The people do not prostrate themselves at their feet and retain a certain "civic" dignity. Virgil's own religion is very humanized and almost domesticated. The charm of *The Aeneid* resides perhaps in its combination of the sublime and restrained irony (found even in greater abundance in the other official poet of the regime, Horace).

C. Augustus: *Res Gestae*

Parallel to and in contrast with the religious and epic aspects we have been discussing, under the Principate there are also political ideas of a more traditional nature that emphasize the continuity between the Republic and the regime created by Augustus. These ideas are found in a text attributed to Augustus personally, the *Res gestae divi Augusti,* a quasi audit of his government's actions written in his seventy-sixth year a few months before his death; it was circulated throughout the Empire in Latin and in Greek. Several copies survive; the oldest and most complete copy was found in Ancyra (present-day Ankara, capital of Turkey) in the form of an inscription on the walls of a temple, explaining the name traditionally given to the document, "*monumentum Ancyranum.*"

The emperor recounts his life almost year by year, a life entwined with the history of the Roman people since the young 18-year-old Octavian's intervention in the civil wars. Some of his statements deserve particular mention; for example, when he claims that his sole purpose in establishing the Principate was to restore "the institutions of our ancestors," destroyed by the chaos in the aftermath of the collapse of the Republic. "[On three occasions], when the Senate and people of Rome agreed that I should be elected, without any colleague, to superintend laws and manners in the exercise of supreme authority, I refused to accept the award of any form of office which was not in accordance with the institutions of our ancestors; and it was by virtue of the tribunician power [and not as a dictator] that I executed the measures of policy which the Senate wished to see carried out by my means."[60]

Augustus personally requested and obtained additional tribunes to assist him in his functions. The only title he did accept was given by decree of the Senate.

> In my sixth and seventh consulships (28–27 BC), when I had extinguished the fires of civil war after receiving by common consent absolute control of affairs, I handed the commonwealth over from my own control to the free disposal of the Senate and the people of Rome. For this service done by me I received the title of Augustus by decree of the Senate, and the door-posts of my house were officially covered with laurels. . . . After that time I took precedence of others in dignity, but I enjoyed no greater power than those who were my colleagues in any magistracy.

[60] *Res gestae,* chap. 6, cited in Barker, *From Alexander to Constantine,* 226.

> While I was holding the consulship for the thirteenth time, the Senate, the order of knights, and the whole of the Roman people gave me the title of Father of my Country (*pater patriae*).[61]

Thus, Augustus emphasizes the fact that his powers were always expressly granted him by the Senate and the people, and that he did not proclaim them himself. Therefore, he is not king and does not claim to have legitimacy by dynastic inheritance or by providence. In fact, he claims that he is keeping the Republic alive as a "mixed form of government" with a democratic element (the people), an aristocratic element (the Senate), and a monarchic element (the consulship).

True, the monarchic element became more important compared to the other two, as it was augmented by the proconsular *imperium* granting Augustus military might without restrictions by virtue of his primacy over his fellow colleagues and his censorial power that enabled him to appoint members to the Senate and create the equestrian order, and finally, by virtue of his tribunician power that gave him civil powers and made him sacrosanct. In these circumstances it is easy to understand his low-risk decision not to hold the consulship continuously. The monarchic element was also stronger than the other two in the sense that it alone defined them and set their limits.

Even so, Augustus's explanations show that he felt bound by the "constitutional" law of the former Republic. He could manipulate it, but he could not, nor would not, eliminate it purely and simply. In this sense, the architecture of the "rule of law" remained intact. The result was a form of legal security for ordinary citizens.

D. The Principate: The View of the Jurists

Many other texts, written by jurists, survive from the period of the Principate and attest that the "ghost of the Republic [still] haunted the imperial palace."[62]

1. *Gaius*

In the second half of the second century AD, Gaius, author of one of the first training manuals of Roman law (*Institutes*), said this about the "constitutional" framework of the state: "The law of the Roman people consists of the following kinds of rules: statutes; plebiscites; *senatus consults*; constitutions of the emperors; the edicts of such magistrates as have authority to issue edicts; and the answers given by jurists to questions submitted to them." Gaius defines the first terms, then comes to the "imperial constitutions": "A *constitutio principis* is a rule laid down by the Emperor in the form of a decree, an edict, or a letter; and there has never been any doubt that such a rule has the force of law, since it is by virtue of a law [or statute] that the Emperor himself receives his authority (*imperium*)." Details follow on the last two "sources of law," the edicts of magistrates and the responses of jurists.[63]

Of course, the definitions Gaius gives for the first kinds of rules, laws, plebiscites, and *senatus consults* were already obsolete by the time he was writing. As we saw, by the end of the reign of Tiberius, laws and plebiscites were no longer passed by the assemblies, and by the end of the first century, there is no trace of a "law" in the strict sense (*lex rogata*). The *senatus consults* had become a mere formality: they were at the emperor's discretion. Only imperial constitutions and the jurists' responses to questions submitted to them created the law. But if Gaius presents things in these terms, it is no doubt because the Republican "hierarchy of norms" was not yet entirely forgotten. Most important is his way of defining imperial constitutions. If he says that they have

---

[61] *Res gestae,* chaps. 34–35, cited in ibid., 229.

[62] Barker, *From Alexander to Constantine.*

[63] Gaius, *Institutes,* 1.1.2–5, quoted in ibid., 257–58.

the "force of law," it is because he considers that they are not, in and of themselves, laws. They have this "force" only because beforehand the emperor received from the law, strictly speaking, the authority to issue these decrees.

2. *Vespasian's* Lex Regia *or* Lex de Imperio

Which law gave the emperor such authority? It was, of course, the ancient *lex de imperio* or *lex regia,* the same law that gave magistrates their authority upon taking office. We saw earlier that Augustus received his authority from this law on different occasions at the outset of his reign. It seems that a *lex regia,* in the form of a duly voted *lex rogata,* was established for the last time, explicitly at any rate, when Vespasian took office (it was, in fact, a *senatus consult,* approved by the people).[64]

It is interesting that the powers attributed to Vespasian by the law were restricted to certain duly listed categories. This can be explained by the historical context: the Senate demanded guarantees after the crimes of Nero and the horrors of civil war during the Year of Four Emperors (Galba, Othon, Vitellius, Vespasian). In the majority of articles, a formula was appended to say that power was given to Vespasian "as it was permitted to Augustus, Tiberius, and Claudius," indicating that these powers appeared at this time as already traditional and justified by precedents.

The emperor is "permitted" to make treaties, to summon and guide the Senate, to recommend candidates for office, to extend the bounds of the Empire. His action prior to being invested with authority by the law was nevertheless held to be lawful *a posteriori.* The law also stipulates that the emperor

- has the "right and power to do whatever he shall think to be for the advantage of the State, and for the greater dignity of affairs—both divine and human and whether they be public or private—as it was for *divus* Augustus, Tiberius, and Claudius";
- "that the Emperor Caesar Vespasian shall be exempt (*solutus*) from any laws previously passed by the people, and any enactments made by the *plebs,* which contained a provision that *divus* Augustus, Tiberius, and Claudius should not be bound thereby."[65]

The formula *solutus* is telling, in that it signals the exemption of the lawmaker from earlier laws. We will see that this is a characteristic of absolutism in the modern era; that is, that the king is *absolutus,* or absolved, released, or exempted from earlier laws, which means that not only can he make new laws, but he can also invalidate or ignore earlier laws. Vespasian, however, was exempt only from laws from which his predecessors were exempt, which seems to say that he was bound by all others (and that, accordingly, there was a large legacy of laws from the Republic that remained in force). In fact, while the emperor's hands were free to exercise executive powers, his praetors and his courts continued to administer traditional civil and criminal law.

3. *Ulpian*

By the end of the Principate there was no longer any mention of these restrictions. Nevertheless, the idea that the legitimacy of the prince's powers originated in a mandate from the people, and that therefore sovereignty existed originally with the people itself was reasserted, almost in the same terms as Gaius, by one of the great experts of Roman law, Ulpian, who worked at the end of the second century under the Severi emperors, the same dynasty that hastened the transition

[64] The text, inscribed on a bronze tablet, was discovered in the fourteenth century AD (see Barker, *From Alexander to Constantine,* 272).
[65] Cited in ibid., 272–73.

from the Principate to the Dominate (Ulpian's writings are preserved in the Justinian *Institutes* and the *Digest*).

> The pleasure of the *princeps* has the force of a *lex* (*quicquid principi placuit legis vigorem habet*),[66] inasmuch as by the *lex regia,* which gives the prince his sovereign power (*imperium*), the people confers on him and into his hand all its own sovereign power and authority. Whatsoever therefore the Emperor (*imperator*) has (1) determined by the issue and signature of a *letter,* or (2) decided by a *decree* given in the course of a judicial examination, or (3) settled out of court by a *provisional judgement,* or (4) enjoined by the terms of an *edict*—all such pronouncements form what we commonly call constitutions. Obviously some of these acts are personal, and do not constitute a precedent; for example, if the prince grants a favour to somebody for his services, or imposes some penalty, or gives some assistance to a man without creating a precedent, he does not go beyond the limits of his own private person.[67]

The restrictions observed in the law of accession for Vespasian have disappeared: now, whatever (*quicquid*) pleases the prince has the force of law.

However, Ulpian makes a distinction between acts that commit the emperor as a "political person" and have the force of law and acts that pertain to him personally and have no legal consequences. Fundamentally, Ulpian continues to see the emperor as a *magistrate,* a simple organ of the law, separate and distinct from the private person who is invested with the office.

Under the Low Empire this distinction tended to disappear: the monarchic "legal person" became indistinguishable from the private holder of the charge, and accordingly the *imperium* of the former became indistinguishable from the *dominium* of the latter. The state belonged to the king like his personal property or his family's patrimony. This confusion lasted throughout the High Middle Ages and the feudal period; the last centuries of the Middle Ages and the modern era had great difficulty ending it and reestablishing the classical Greco-Roman notions of an impersonal state and magistracy, a public mandate held momentarily and tenuously by a private person.

To be complete, we should point out that, throughout the period from Vespasian to the last Antonines, the emperors were, in fact, invested in office by an act of Senate. The Senate, of course, could not oppose the praetorians or the power of the legions. And when the emperor adopted the person he hoped would succeed him, as Nerva did with Trajan, the adoption meant a transfer of the emperor's *religious auctoritas* from his own shoulders to the shoulders of his adopted son. The act was all the more meaningful that it was solemnly performed by the pontiffs in the presence of the assembled people. Thus, the hands of the Senate were never free. Nevertheless, this formality was essential to lend legitimacy to the emperor's actions. The emperor is never emperor by his own making, nor by direct divine choice or patronymic legitimacy.

This spirit of relative loyalty to Republican civicism is reflected to varying degrees in the writings of Roman political authors in the first two centuries AD, notably in Seneca, Tacitus, and Pliny the Younger.

---

[66] We will come across this renowned formula again in the Middle Ages and the modern era.

[67] Quoted in Barker, *From Alexander to Constantine,* 262.

E. Seneca: *On Mercy* (*De Clementia*)

The Stoic Seneca, one of the greatest minds in antiquity, served as Nero's chief minister.

1. *Life*

Seneca (1–65 AD) was the son of a Roman equestrian from Cordoba.[68] Young Seneca studied philosophy in Rome (under masters of a rather eclectic Stoicism: Sotion, Attalus, and Papirius Fabianus). He began a career in administration, but rapidly abandoned it for health reasons. He sojourned in Alexandria for several years, moving in intellectual circles and completing his philosophical education. He returned to Rome in 31 AD and became a quaestor and an outstanding lawyer. Around 36 or 37 AD he held the office of aedile, but his career was derailed by a serious clash with the emperor Caligula, who both detested and envied him for his oratorical and literary talents. He was exiled to Corsica on a (no doubt false) charge of adultery with a rival of Agrippina. He spent eight years on the island (41–49 AD), where he devoted himself to the study of its history and customs and also took up the study of the natural sciences: astronomy, geography (he presented his findings in his *Naturales quaestiones*). Recalled to Rome by Agrippina, he was obliged to join her party, became praetor, and above all the tutor to Agrippina's son, Nero.

Three years into his service as Nero's tutor, Agrippina poisoned Claudius. Nero was proclaimed emperor. Seneca became the principal advisor or "chief minister" and mentor to the young 17-year-old prince. He wrote Nero's accession speech, delivered to the Senate, in which he announced a program of restoration of Republican liberties. When Nero ordered the assassination of his rival, Britannicus (the son of Claudius and his first wife, Messalina), Seneca did not protest and, in fact, inherited a large portion of the wealth of the deceased (land in Egypt). He committed other questionable acts, probably motivated by "reasons of state" and the price for maintaining a philosopher at the head of the Empire. First, Seneca banished his opponent, Sullius, to the Balearic islands, for reasons as arbitrary as those motivating his own exile to Corsica years before. Then, he was accomplice to Nero's murder of his own mother, Agrippina (March 59 AD), after which he governed alone for some three years. But, as early as 62 AD, he sought to retire from government. Nero, however, would not accept his request, fearful of the reaction of the Senate. Seneca was granted little more than semiretirement, enough for him to write his *Epistulae morales ad Lucilium*. His uncertain situation did not last. In 65, suspected by Nero of involvement in the Pisonian conspiracy (a plot to kill Nero), Seneca was ordered to kill himself. In total, he had governed the Roman state for some ten years.

2. *Work*

Seneca was the author of tragedies, poems, scientific works, and philosophical works. A large part of his writing is lost, in particular his books on geography (on Egypt) and natural history. Many of his works survive: (1) his dialogues (three *Consolations, On Providence, On the Shortness of Life, On the Happy Life, On the Firmness of the Wise Person, On Tranquility of Mind, On Leisure, On Anger;* (2) seven books *On Benefits;* (3) a satirical work: *Apocolocyntosis divi Claudii* (The Pumpkinification of the Divine Claudius); (4) two (or three) books *On Mercy;* (5) seven books on *Natural Questions;* (6) twenty books of *Letters to Lucilius.*[69]

---

[68] This section is drawn from Pierre Grimal, *Sénèque* (Paris: Presses Universitaires de France, 1966); *Sénèque ou la conscience de l'Empire* [Seneca or the conscience of the Empire] (Paris: Les Belles Lettres, 1979).

[69] Seneca, *Entretiens: Lettres à Lucilius,* ed. Paul Veyne (Paris: Robert Laffont, 1993). *Translator's note:* Seneca's works are available in ten volumes from the Loeb Classical Library (Cambridge, MA: Harvard University Press, 1928–72); we quote from this collection.

On Mercy

Seneca's *On Mercy* is a sort of solemn lesson addressed to Nero at the beginning of his reign (Seneca seems to have delivered the essence of the speech in Nero's presence).[70] Its principal purpose is to persuade Nero to show "mercy," but in Seneca's hands it becomes a genuine theory of power and of the *sociological* need for Nero to be autocratic.

a. The Monarch as the Soul of the State

Seneca takes for granted that Rome is now a monarchy. He is not fooled by the republican trappings of the Principate. Throughout his text, he frequently uses the name "king" to designate the prince. "King or prince," *rex* or *princeps,* the title is interchangeable (*On Mercy* 1.2.3). With one restriction, addressed below, Seneca subscribes to the new form of government. His reason? It alone can ensure peace.

Left to itself, he thinks, society will collapse. Its natural inclination is toward all-out war. "Man's spirit is by nature refractory" (*natura contumax est humanus animus*) (*On Mercy* 1.24.2). Political order can only be achieved if violence is done to human nature: peace must be *forced* on people. The iron fist of the autocrat can achieve this: only the emperor's yoke prevents the vast, unruly throng from destroying itself and others (1.1.1).

Seneca pursues this idea further. Because a community without a king will collapse and die, the king is the true *creator* of the political community. He is "the arbiter of life and death for the nations" (*On Mercy* 1.1.2). Because the body decomposes when the soul leaves it, and "if they lose their king, they all scatter" (*amisso rege totum dilabitur*) (1.19.2), it can be said that the king is the *soul* of the state: "you are the soul of the state, and the state your body" (1.5.1). The emperor is the head of the "body"; that is, the Empire, and the health or sickness of the head spreads to all its members (1.2.1). The emperor, in fact, identifies with the whole Republic; he personifies it (*in [eum] se res publica convertit*) (1.4.2).

A king has the power to "give and take life," to create;[71] is this not what defines the *gods*? He is, in fact, a "divine" being. Arguably, Seneca does not follow the popular form of imperial religion, but observes one of its more intellectualized forms. The crux of the argument is that the prince must be above the fray in order to arbitrate; he must *stand apart.* Accordingly, this requires a clean break with the Greek civic principle of *isonomia* and the old values of republican Rome.

Social life implies that it is possible to take unprecedented, and even *extraordinary* steps. But if the constitution is so designed that no one can take them, the state will race to its ruin and justice will reverse into injustice: *summum ius, summa iniuria* (the greater the right, the greater the wrong). The only solution is a power not bound by the laws, that is, an *absolute* power. The special privilege of the monarchic formula is that it enables one person to rise above justice to enable justice itself to triumph.

Seneca develops the idea that the one exceptional, "divine" quality of monarchy is that it must be construed in both a *positive and a negative way.*

---

[70] Seneca, "De Clemencia," *Moral Essays,* vol. 1, trans. John W. Basore (Cambridge, MA: Harvard University Press, 1928), 356–449.

[71] Having secured peace, the king is the reason that citizens have children again: "[The people] are eager to rear up sons, and the childlessness once imposed by public ills is now relaxed" (1.13). The king, then, is literally the cause of life of these new human beings.

b. The Privilege of Monarchy: The Positive Side

The king is, of course, the ruler of the people. He is the "father" (*On Mercy* 1.14.1) and the people are his "children." The father "is wont to reprove his children sometimes gently, sometimes with threats… at times admonishes them even by stripes" (1.14.1). He is like a "physician" who treats his "patients" (1.17.1–2).

Seneca resorts to even harsher comparisons. The king is like a dog trainer or a horse-breaker: if he is merciful, it is not for love; it is in the sense that the expert horse-breaker soothes the horse "with caressing hand" rather than "with the lash" (*On Mercy* 1.16.1–5). There is the same difference between the king and his subjects as between humans and insects: "[one] should recoil from… the tiny insects which defile the hand that crushes them." A king should not stoop to punish his subjects with his own hand (1.21.4).

The king's ontological superiority makes him a *model*. If the king is good and virtuous, the people will be good and virtuous. If he is cruel, the people will be cruel (*On Mercy* 1.25) (this topic is found again and again in monarchic theories).

Finally, Seneca admits—somewhat reluctantly—that Nero has quasi-divine qualities. He is a "star" (Nero believed that he had been born under the sign of the sun like an Egyptian pharaoh). These are old Hellenistic themes of the king and general who is protected and beloved of Fortune. Seneca does not shy from substantiating these qualities in his young pupil.

At times, Seneca—like Pliny, as we shall see—lapses into flattery. In order to exalt Nero more highly, he derides his predecessors. First, Claudius, after whose death Seneca wrote a bitter pamphlet, "The Pumpkinification of the Divine Claudius," not his "apotheosis" or "transformation into deity"). Seneca also lashes out at Augustus (*On Mercy* 1.9.1), observing that at the start of his reign he committed numerous crimes: his reputation for mildness in the later years of his rule was only a "weariness of cruelty" (*lassa crudelitas*) (1.12.2). Nero had committed no such crimes yet (but it is true, he was still only 17!).

c. The Privilege of Monarchy: The Negative Side

But there is an opposite side to the coin. Indeed, the king is a ruler, but he is a ruler *marked out to be seen.*

> Our movements [i.e., the movements of ordinary people] are noticed by few; we may come forth and retire and change our dress without the world being aware; you can no more hide yourself than the sun. A flood of light surrounds you; towards it every one turns his eyes. Think you to "come forth"? Nay, you rise [like the sun]. You cannot speak but that all the nations of the earth hear your voice; you cannot be angry without causing everything to tremble…; for when the doer is omnipotent, men consider not how much he has done, but how much he is likely to do. (*On Mercy* 1.8.4–5)

Thus, paradoxically, the king's visibility turns him into a prisoner and a slave. His privilege becomes an antiprivilege. Inversely, by way of symmetry, his subjects' inferiority changes into mastery, and the master has good reason to be jealous of his slaves, who enjoy freedoms that elude him:

> How many things there are which you may not do, which we, thanks to you, may do! It is possible for me to walk alone without fear in any part of the city I please, though no companion attends me, though I have no sword at my house, none at my side; you, amid the peace you create, must live armed. You cannot escape from your lot; it besets you, and, whenever you leave the heights, it pursues you with its magnificence. In this lies the servitude of supreme greatness—that it cannot become less great; but you share with the gods that inevitable condition. (1.8.2–4)

In the end, the promise held out to the prince is no less than death. Seneca carefully examines the mechanism at work here.[72] The purpose of the prince, we said, is to ensure the reign of justice—in other words, to prevent citizens from taking personal revenge for offenses committed against them. The prince monopolizes the use of force. But for this reason, he accumulates on his own head the hate of all the people who have somehow been wronged by the coercion of the state. When the state is an anonymous, deindividuated body, the risk of hate is low. But when the state is personified in an autocrat, he naturally becomes the focus of all hate. Such a man "is assailed by as many perils as there are many men to whom he is himself a peril" (*On Mercy* 1.25.3).

"Just as trees that have been trimmed throw out again countless branches, and as many kinds of plants are cut back to make them grow thicker, so the cruelty of a king by removing his enemies increases their number; for the parents and children of those who have been killed, their relatives too and their friends, step into the place of each single victim" (*On Mercy* 1.8.7). When Augustus understood this, he lost heart: "Why," Augustus asks himself, "do you live on if so many are concerned to have you die? What end will there be of punishments, and of bloodshed? I am the obvious victim for whom young men of noble birth should whet their swords. If so many must perish in order that I may not, my life is not worth the price" (1.9.5).

d. Mercy

It is in this context of a theory of the preeminent political role of royal exceptionalism that Seneca's discourse on mercy can be understood: "We have all sinned" (*Peccavimus omnes*), Seneca begins (*On Mercy* 1.6.3). If the state were completely impartial and just, would it not have to punish all the time? No less than the gods, Seneca replies, whose thunderbolts would never cease, if they resolved to punish systematically all the failings of men.[73] Yet the world is quiet. Therefore, the gods must be merciful. They have their reasons.

First, the merciful person expresses his excellence through his mercy. "Cruel and inexorable anger is not seemly for a king; for thus he does not rise much above the other man, toward whose own level he descends by being angry at him. But if he grants life, if he grants position to those who have imperiled and deserve to lose them, he does what none but a sovereign may.... To save life is the peculiar privilege of exalted station (*excellentia fortuna*)" (*On Mercy* 1.5.6–7).

Second, and above all, merciless punishment will lead to the opposite effect: *it will cause crime to spread rather than stop it.* For state-administered punishment to be effective, it must not be excessive. The guilty party must have something to gain from proper conduct, otherwise why bother behaving correctly. Severe strictness provokes despair and revolt (*On Mercy* 3.12.5). If punishment is excessive, crime becomes "trivialized," even incited. "Punishment showed [people] the way to the deed (*facinus poena monstravit*)" (1.22.1).

"A proposal was once made in the senate to distinguish slaves from free men by their dress; it then became apparent how great would be the impending danger if our slaves should begin to count our number. Be sure that we have a like danger to fear if no man's guilt is pardoned; it will soon become apparent how greatly the worse element of the state preponderates. Numerous executions are not less discreditable to a prince than are numerous funerals to a physician" (*On Mercy* 1.23.1). This points to the real reason to show mercy—both the mercy of the gods and the mercy of the emperors, which the first among them, Augustus, must exemplify: because

[72] He and his contemporaries had much leisure to contemplate these things, given the climate of conspiracy and crime surrounding the early Roman autocrats, from Marius and Sulla to Claudius, not to leave out Caesar, Pompey, Antony, and others.

[73] This recalls Psalm 130: "If thou, Lord, shouldst mark iniquities, O Lord, who shall stand?"

publicizing crime causes it to increase, only a "conspiracy of silence" can make it decline. The prince must seize the initiative by putting an end to violence so as to break the cycle of revenge. Only he can do this, because he is above the law. The fundamental legitimacy of absolutism lies in the fact that only the suspension of the ordinary course of justice secures social order, and only an absolute king can allow himself *not* to be just.

Seneca adds that the mercy he expects of a prince is different from *pardon*. Strictly speaking, mercy is the opposite of cruelty: "the hand must be held under control to keep it from cutting deeper than may be necessary" (*On Mercy* 1.5.2). Mercy is refraining from excessive or even minimal punishment; it is not pardon for the act to be punished (mercy is not forgiveness [2.7.1]). Seneca condemns pardon outright: "he who pardons admits that he has omitted to do something which he ought to have done" (2.6.2). He frowns on pity, which is not a virtue but a vice because it shows too much mercy: "pity is the sorrow of the mind brought about by the sight of distress of others" (2.5.4); it is akin to "wretchedness" (2.6.4). Nothing becomes a man more than a lofty spirit (*magnus animus*); but "sorrow blunts its [the mind's] powers, dissipates and hampers them" (2.6.5).[74]

The basic idea of Seneca's defense of mercy is that, at bottom, *the order of the state is based on crime*. The claim that crime cannot be stopped unless punishment for all and every crime is stopped is an admission that in every stable society a "residue of crime" subsists that *must* remain hidden, unpunished, unresolved.

Seneca's profound pessimism sets him apart from Cicero and the earlier Stoics. While Cicero inaugurated an optimistic tradition of liberal humanism, Seneca is the early representative of an absolutist, pessimist tradition, whose credo might be: people are *incapable of living justly,* and for this reason *they need an unjust authority*. A certain hubris of power is the response to the hubris of passions and social disorder.[75] At bottom, the Principate is the absolute power of the prince in the state; this is what enables the state to survive. Having said this, the exercise of absolute power by the prince must remain exceptional. The Principate is not the rule of a despot: the ordinary citizen (far from the centers of power, unsuspected of conspiracy) must be assured of the protection of the law.

Compared with the reign of Claudius, the young emperor restored the law, placing it beyond violation (*ius supra omnem iniuriam positum* [*On Mercy* 1.1.8]). Power must be adjusted to nature's law (*lex naturae* [3.19.1–2]). The Roman monarch must remain moderate in his conduct, amenable to legitimate claims, inflexible without cruelty to unjustified ones, affable, and easily accessible; the people should speak of him in public as they do in secret (1.13.5). Seneca concludes: the Principate represents "the fairest vision of a state which lacks no element of complete liberty except that it cannot be replaced" (1.1.9, with modifications).

Seneca lived under the reign of Nero, the last of the Julio-Claudian emperors. After his reign came the Flavians, then the Antonines. With the latter, a century of peace and prosperity began for the Roman Empire (second century AD). Rome ruled the entire known world and held it

---

[74] We see how different Seneca's *mercy* is from biblical *compassion*. There is no evangelical *agape* in his natural morality. The most secure haven against Fortune's tempests, says Seneca, is *mutuum auxilium*, the haven of mutual help (2.5.3). Seneca, like Cicero, adheres only to the rule of justice, which is symmetry. Mercy is opposed to pardon in that "mercy keeps freedom of decision" (*liberum arbitrium*). It is this freedom and this preservation of one's personal "reserve" that Judeo-Christian mercy sacrifices (although this self-effacement, this "enslaved will," an essential constituent of ethics, forms a higher ontological freedom, in the opinion of theologians). To Seneca's rejection of a pity that "blunts the mind" we can oppose Psalms 51:16 ("A broken and contrite heart, O God, thou wilt not despise") and the tears of Jesus when he learns of Lazarus's death (John 11:35).

[75] Curiously, this places Seneca close to certain later Christian political theories, for example, Augustine's: we are all sinners, which is why it is illusory, even impious, to think that power can be fully just. God gave us political power as a punishment for our sins, which is why tyrants are part of God's plan; it makes no sense to protest it.

under the *Pax Romana,* while its sole concern was to keep watch over its border regions. The Roman state extended its institutions everywhere and enforced its principles of administration and, in large portions of the Empire, its civil law.

How did contemporaries experience these developments? Several highly interesting expressions survive: two from the senatorial order (Tacitus and Pliny the Younger) about Trajan, one of the most remarkable Antonines and the true founder of the imperial system of rule; and one from a Greek (Aelius Aristides) about the empire under Antoninus Pius.

F. Tacitus

Tacitus was a historian, and not a political theoretician. Like Pliny the Younger, his friend, he witnessed the founding of the Principate with the reign of the Flavians and the ascension of the Antonines. Throughout his writings we find many original political ideas about the regime.

At times, his thought is ambiguous, but his fundamental political stance is never in doubt. He is loyal to the civic values of traditional Rome and condemns the tyrannies that the Romans suffered under most Julio-Claudians, and still more under the Flavian Domitian. All the same, he approves of the Principate on the basis of reason. On the one hand, like Seneca, he believes that the traditional Republic is incapable of upholding civil peace. On the other, while he admits that the early years of the imperial regime were indeed a failure, this cannot be attributed to the monarchic form of government itself. The true cause was the reprehensible behavior of the emperors, driven by a contrary destiny. With the rise of the Antonines to imperial office, the Principate actually flourished and fulfilled the promises made by Augustus years before.

1. *Life*

Tacitus (b. ca. 55 AD, d. 115 or 117) belonged to the provincial aristocracy (he was probably the son of a high-ranking public servant of the equestrian class, either from Gallia Narbonensis [perhaps Vaison-la-Romaine or Frejus] or from Gallia Belgica, near Germania; he frequently mentions this region in his writings).[76] He settled in Rome when quite young and studied rhetoric assiduously. He aspired to a career in politics. Vespasian bestowed the senatorial rank on him; he was the first in his family to achieve this distinction. Vespasian's intention was to strengthen the Senate, decimated by the Julio-Claudians; no doubt, the proven oratory talents of Tacitus had attracted the emperor's attention. In a sense, Tacitus is a *homo novus* and, in his senatorial ideology, he expresses all the enthusiasm of a neophyte, not to say a parvenu.

He held the office of military tribune in Gaul and in Germania, then the offices of quaestor and praetor. He became a member of the *quindecemvir,* the priest college in charge of various religious functions. Then, he probably held a high position in provincial government. In 93 AD the final years of Domitian's tyrannical Principate began. By this time Tacitus held a seat in the Senate and witnessed the collapse of public life, which recalled the worst years of the Julio-Claudians. In 97 he became consul. During his consulship he gave the funeral oration for Verginius Rufus, a general who rejected his army's appeal to make him emperor whereby he asserted the Senate's right to make the appointment. By publicly celebrating Verginius Rufus, Tacitus declared his attachment to institutional regularity, strongly reminiscent of the Republic. "Such speeches, and Pliny the Younger's *Panegyricus Traiani* on the occasion of his consulship in 100 AD, laid the foundations of an 'enlightened' Principate under the Antonines."[77] In this sense, it can be argued that Tacitus was both a spectator and, to a degree, an actor in the political events of his time.

---

[76] Our narrative here is drawn from Pierre Grimal, *Tacite* (Paris: Fayard, 1990).

[77] Grimal, *Tacite,* 91.

Tacitus may have exercised proconsular powers between 102 and 104 AD, after which he dedicated himself to the writing of his two major historical works, the *Histories* and the *Annals*. In 112 or 113 AD, he held the office of proconsul in the Roman province of Asia, the highest possible civilian governorship for a senator.

2. *WORK*

The Life of Agricola (ca. 98): an account of his father-in-law's life, Gnaeus Julius Agricola, who pacified Britannia between 78 and 84 AD.[78] Agricola is presented as an example: a man of the senatorial class who dedicated his entire life to the salvation and greatness of the state, holding himself aloof from political intrigue. *Germania* (98 or 99 AD): a geographic and ethnological description of the country and its inhabitants, probably written to familiarize Roman public opinion with a region that the Empire intended to occupy. *Dialogue on Oratory* (102 AD): a discussion supposedly held in 75 AD between three great orators to explore why oratory is no longer as scintillating as it was in the time of the Republic; in appearance the discussion is technical in nature, but it is actually of great political significance, as we shall see. *The Histories* (completed ca. 108–09 AD): a history of Rome between 69 and 96 AD; only the first five books of this work (up to the ascension of Vespasian) survive; Tacitus witnessed the period first-hand. *The Annals* (probably written between 112 and 117? AD): the history of Rome in the period 14–66 AD (with gaps); the reign of the Julio-Claudians from the death of Augustus to the death of Nero.

Tacitus is one of the greatest writers of antiquity. His sober, laconic, even mordant style employs succinct characterizations, struck at times like coins or caricatures. His penetrating psychological insights make him the equal—in another genre—of Thucydides.

3. *TACITUS'S PHILOSOPHY OF HISTORY*

Tacitus situates history on two planes: there are the cycles dominated by destinies, which we can do nothing to alter; and there are micro-events, which depend on the power of will and are largely contingent; such events cannot tip the scales of destiny, but they are instrumental in bringing it about. Thus, the history of Rome is fundamentally determined by destinies that desired the collapse of the Republic and the misfortunes of the early Principate, and now desire the renaissance that the contemporaries of Tacitus witness with the rise of the Antonines. But, the minutiae of this history, its particular hues and shapes, are the fruit of independent human actions and accidents. These two points require closer examination.

a. THE "CENTURIES" OF ROME

Tacitus was no atheist. (Machiavelli started the myth of his religious skepticism, but according to Pierre Grimal, the myth "does not hold up against the proof of his writing.")[79] Admittedly, Tacitus rejected superstition, an excessive form of religiosity running rampant among the credulous throngs of Romans, barbarians, and Jews. But he was a fervent believer that the gods watch over human affairs, directing fortune and misfortune according to the just rewards of human conduct.[80] The designs of the gods can be scrutinized by means of divinization, astrology, and the science of haruspication, "the oldest art of Italy" (*Annals* 11.15) (thus Tacitus does not share the skepticism of Polybius, who saw Roman religious practices as crass manipulation by the magistrates).

---

[78] *Translator's note:* English quotations of works by Tacitus are from the Loeb Classical Library in 6 volumes (Cambridge, MA: Harvard University Press, 1914–32. Nemo quotes from *Tacite: Oeuvres completes,* translation, presentation, and commentary by Pierre Grimal (Paris: Gallimard, 1990).

[79] Grimal, *Tacite,* 196.

[80] Tacitus wrote at the beginning of his *Histories:* "For never was it more fully proved by awful disasters of the Roman people or by indubitable signs that the gods care not for our safety, but for our punishment" (*Histories* 1.3.1).

Tacitus shows how virtually every emperor believed in the destinies and the signs that revealed them.[81] Tiberius, for example, practised the divinatory arts in secret and was versed in the "art of the Chaldeans" (i.e., astrology). He regularly consulted masters like Thrasyllus.[82] Thus, it is said that Tiberius foresaw and announced the Principate to Galba (*Annals* 6.20). A long commentary on the respective roles of fate and human freedom in history follows:

> For myself, when I listen to this and similar narratives, my judgment wavers. Is the revolution of human things governed by fate and changeless necessity, or by accident? You will find the wisest of the ancients, and the disciples attached to their tenets, at complete variance [Tacitus mentions briefly the opinions of the Epicureans and the Platonists, then goes on to discuss common beliefs]; in many of them [the Epicureans] a fixed belief that heaven concerns itself neither with our origins, nor with our ending, nor, in fine, with mankind, and that so adversity continually assails the good, while prosperity dwells among the evil. Others [the Stoics] hold, on the contrary, that, though there is certainly a fate in harmony with events, it does not emanate from wandering stars, but must be sought in the principles and processes of natural causation. Still, they leave us free to choose our life: that choice made, however, the order of the future is certain. Nor, they maintain, are evil and good what the crowd imagines: many who appear to be the sport of adverse circumstances are happy; numbers are wholly wretched though in the midst of great possessions—provided only that the former endure the strokes of fortunes with firmness, while the latter employ her favors with unwisdom. With most men, however, the faith is ineradicable that the future of an individual is ordained at the moment of his entry into life; but at times a prophecy is falsified by the event, through the dishonesty of the prophet who speaks he knows not what; and thus is debased the credit of an art, of which the most striking evidences have been furnished both in the ancient world and in our own. What is certain is the forecast of Nero's reign, made by the son of this very Thrasyllus. (*Annals* 6.20, with modifications)

Tacitus appears to accept this traditional opinion. If divinatory science appears to err at times, it is not because people are able to escape their destiny; it is because such science is extremely difficult, not to mention the fact that some experts give misleading information when it is in their interest to do so. And people's apparent liberty and the apparent contingency of events always contribute to the accomplishment of destinies.

Sometimes predictions can be "expiated"; in other words, divine signs can be recognized and understood and one's behavior can be amended so as to escape the intended punishment; but Tacitus also observes that Galba would not have been able to avoid the fixed decrees of fate, even if he had not held the portents in contempt (see *Histories* 1.18.2). More precisely, Tacitus is well versed in the vulgate of Roman syncretistic mysticism (Stoicism, Neopythagoreanism, for example) according to which there are great cycles in history, so-called Great Years with their "Great Months" or "Centuries." In 88 AD, Tacitus, as praetor, had been involved in Domitian's celebrations of the "Secular Games" (Claudius had celebrated such games in 47 AD).

---

[81] This belief was so widespread that divinatory practices, not immediately under the control of the ruling class, were systematically held to be acts of enmity and infidelity punishable by death: the consultation of divinities to know the end of a reign or to inquire who would ascend to the pinnacle of power was an expression of hostility against the actual emperor.

[82] With wry humor Tacitus tells the story of how Tiberius laid a clever trap for Thrasyllus. Tiberius had the habit of consulting an astrologer on a high cliff, then hurling him into the sea below after hearing his prediction in order to preserve the secret. Thrasyllus revealed to Tiberius that he would become emperor. Tiberius rejoiced, then asked Thrasyllus if he had thoroughly researched his own horoscope and ascertained the character of that particular year and day. Surveying the stars, making his calculations, Thrasyllus grew agitated and pale; he learned of Tiberius's intention to murder him. Tiberius, assured of Thrasyllus's competence as an astrologer, spared him (*Annals* 6.21).

He saw prefigurations of such cycles in the recent history of Rome. There was the civil war at the end of the Republic—the "iron century"—then the Principate of Augustus, when contemporaries thought they recognized the beginning of a Golden Age (see above, pp. 310–22). But before this century could flourish under the Principates of Nerva and Trajan, the gods, angry at the misconduct of the Romans and the collapse of their morals, brought about a regression. This intermediate cycle divided into two periods: the reign of the Julio-Claudians, between the deaths of Augustus (14 AD) and Nero (69 AD), then an ostensible improvement with the ascension of Vespasian and Titus, followed by a new collapse under the despotic rule of Domitian (70–96 AD). These two periods have a sort of cosmic unity, justifying the dedication of a body of work to each, respectively, the *Annals* and the *Histories*.

The transitions from one "century" to another are characterized by signs to which Tacitus grants great importance; he notes them carefully and attempts to untangle the authentic ones, certified by authorized specialists, from the uncertain ones, expressions of mere superstition. For example, the eruption of Mount Vesuvius during the reign of Titus on August 24, 79 AD, which destroyed the cities of Pompeii and Herculaneum; the destructive fires in Rome; the catastrophic high-water events of the Tiber; lightning strikes and strangely demented human behaviors at certain times ("Sacred rites were defiled; there were adulteries in high places. The sea was filled with exiles, its cliffs made foul with the bodies of the dead. In Rome there was more awful cruelty" [*Histories* 1.2.3–4]).

The unexplained destruction by fire of the Capitol, at the hands of the citizens, and of the temple of Jupiter during the fighting between the followers of Vitellius and Flavius (*Histories* 1.3.72), are particularly meaningful events. Jupiter was the god of the *imperium* vested in magistrates when they took office. His temple was very ancient and highly venerated; triumphant victors worshipped there to give thanks to the gods. Thus, its destruction by the furor of civil wars threatened the very survival of Rome.

b. Contingencies of History

While the general design of history is determined by the gods and obeys a fatal necessity, a certain place is left to contingencies and liberty. "For myself, the more I reflect on events recent or remote, the more I am haunted by the sense of mockery in human affairs" (Tacitus, *Annals* 3.18).

This explains in Tacitus's opinion the importance of personal motivation, psychology, and passions—the most common being the unrestricted appetite for power—that he presents in the *Annals* in carefully researched portraits: they remain famous to this day. Each of the historical figures, portrayed at length by Tacitus, moved events in a certain direction by his desires, personality, and choices (this, as we saw, is only apparently true; they only put their shoulders to the wheel of a grand cycle of events, already moving unstoppably in the predetermined direction).

Augustus, for example, was fundamentally a hypocrite: a two-faced character.[83] Sejanus, Tiberius's chief minister, was another scourge sent by the gods to blind the prince and facilitate the fulfillment of fate; nevertheless, his personal vices and ambition played a fundamental role in the sequence of events under Tiberius's Principate. Likewise, Messalina, the wife of Emperor Claudius, played a key role by way of her almost "insane" love for Caius Silius. Without Agrippina's all-consuming desire, Nero would never have ascended the throne (Tacitus wrote the famous line spoken by Agrippina, after her astrologer informed her that Nero would become emperor and murder his mother: "Let him slay so that he reign" (*Annals* 14.9). Nero's monstrous

[83] Among other vile acts, he chose Tiberius as his successor, knowing him to be mean and incompetent, in an attempt to improve his own reputation as an exemplary prince.

murder of his own mother is another example of an apparently independent human passion, but to the historian her murder is the accomplishment of destinies.

In his *Histories* and *Annals* Tacitus finds, at the heart of every human motivation in nearly every figure (large and small), two "faults especially common to the stronger" (*Histories* 1.51.7): greed and arrogance. His pessimism—which Machiavelli adored and which is similar to La Rochefoucauld's, whether there is a direct relation or not—explains in part his support for the Principate. The link between a "pessimistic" mindset and a political preference for a "strong state" is, as we saw when we discussed Seneca above, shared by the entire *absolutist* tradition. In the absence of an iron fist, stifling greediness and terrorizing crime, a society cannot for an instant be ordered. Throughout this tradition, we encounter the idea, in one expression or another, that human nature is fundamentally bad, or at any rate that it is violent and self-centered, and that, consequently, there can be no natural social order. Men cannot live in peace unless a "Leviathan" towers over them and instills fear, and even then such peace remains fragile. A certain level of crime and injustice is, therefore, a *sine qua non* condition that must be accepted for the state to survive. Moreover, this cruelty of the state is necessary in order to achieve the great ambitions of society. In a sense it is congenital to a state like Rome.

In sum, individual destinies, served by personal ambition and desire, preside over the transition from the Republic to the Empire. Is this perhaps a judgment on the two forms of government?

4. *The Republic and the Empire*

Tacitus, who was educated in the rhetorical tradition, has a tendency on every topic he approaches to weigh the pros and cons of each argument without drawing a final conclusion. He does the same when considering the respective merits of the republican and imperial governments.

a. The Mediocrity and Criminality of the First Principate

The historians of the Republic narrated accounts of great battles, the seizing of cities, and the terrible struggles between the patricians and plebeians. Tacitus, the historian of the Empire, tells us that he is not as fortunate. Because life under the Empire has become poorer, more narrow-minded, there are fewer ambitious projects, fewer monumental undertakings expressing the greatness of humanity. The regime is ugly, despicable, characterized by crime and pettiness. It merits closer examination, nevertheless, like one studies democracy or aristocracy (see *Annals* 4.32–33).

Freedom disappeared under the early princes. Augustus decreed the *lex maiestatis,* which was reinstated under Tiberius. This law invested the *imperator* with "majesty" (i.e., supremacy), traditionally the privilege of the Roman people. Accordingly, a criticism of the emperor became an insult of the Roman people, which was punishable by death. This law, which gave the emperor an arbitrary right of life and death over every citizen, became a devastating instrument of absolute power.

Freedom of speech was also suppressed. Power began to use "doublespeak." Altars were dedicated to Mercy and Friendship, while the prince himself was cruel and coerced even friends to bring accusations against one another (*Annals* 4.70). Under Sejanus, Tiberius's chief minister, unfair trials were conducted against writers. Tacitus, in his *Life of Agricola,* condemned the tyranny of Domitian during whose reign authors were eliminated and books burned.

> They imagined, no doubt, that in those flames disappeared the voice of the people, the liberty of the Senate, the conscience of mankind; especially as the teachers of Philosophy also were expelled,[84] and all decent behavior exiled, in order that nowhere might anything of good report present itself to men's eyes.

[84] A reference to the banishment of philosophers, including Epictetus and Dio Chrysostom (see below, pp. 358–59).

> Assuredly we have given a signal proof of our submissiveness; and even as former generations witnessed the utmost liberty, so have we the extremes of slavery. The investigations of the secret police have deprived us even of the give and take of conversation. We should have lost memory itself as well as voice, had forgetfulness been as easy as silence. (*Agricola* 2.2)

The Principate evolved into a reign of the *delatores*, that is, professional informers and informants who grew rich on the backs of their victims (*Annals* 11.5).

Finally, the princes destroyed the *aristocracy*. Nero, a true demagogue, slummed with riffraff and compelled aristocrats to do the same, forcing them to do in normal circumstances what they would never stoop to, all for the greater pleasure of the people, who rejoiced when they saw the despot drag down the high and mighty to the level of the common man.

b. Voluntary Servitude

The princes were not the only guilty ones. In keeping with his "pessimistic" vision of man, Tacitus says that tyranny can always count on the spinelessness of Roman society, whether the Senate, the equestrians, or the anonymous throng. This is how Tacitus describes the throng when it acclaims Otho as he set off on campaign against Vitellius: "The shouts and cries from the mob, according to their recognized fashion of flattering an emperor, were excessive and insincere. Men vied with one another in the expression of their enthusiasm and vows, as if they were applauding the Dictator Caesar or the Emperor Augustus. They did this, not from fear or affection, but *from their passionate love of servitude*" (*Histories* 1.90). Even the great and worthy were not exempt from this particular foible of human nature—a passionate desire to be enslaved (*libido servitii*): "At Rome," Tacitus wrote in his *Annals*, "consuls, senators, and knights were rushing into slavery" (1.7.1).

"The tradition runs that Tiberius, on leaving the curia [Senate-House], had a habit of ejaculating in Greek, 'These men!—how ready they are for slavery!' Even he, it was manifest, objecting though he did to public liberty, was growing weary of such groveling patience in his slaves" (*Annals* 3.65.3). Such groveling could still be heard decades later: "So the senators turned and twisted their proposals to mean this or that, many calling Vitellius an enemy and traitor; but the most foreseeing attacked him only with ordinary terms of abuse, although some made the truth the basis of their insults. Still they did this when there was an uproar and many speaking, or else they obscured their own meaning by a riot of words" (*Histories* 1.85.5).

Such cowardice actually justified, in Tacitus's opinion, the freedom-stifling initiatives of the prince. He stresses, however, that this cowardice was itself the consequence of the many murders the prince committed of the best senators, that is, those with a highly evolved civic sense. Given that power under the Principate was concentrated in the hands of one man, it was inevitable that political experts, now removed from the affairs of state, lapsed into intellectual and moral mediocrity, becoming easier to manipulate than under a regime of liberty (see *Histories* 1.1.2).

Thus, a vicious cycle set in: the arbitrariness and tyranny of the prince encouraged the spinelessness of the people and the aristocracy, which in turn excited the contempt and deceitfulness of the prince. This explains why Caligula cried out to be hailed *dominus* (*Annals* 6.45).

c. The Ideal of Equality before the Law Must Be Respected but Amended

So what is to be done? Should the Republic be restored, as these critics seemed implicitly to recommend? An answer to the question requires a reassessment of the republican ideal, which is intricately bound up in the ideal of equality before the law. Tacitus tackles the issue from a historical perspective. The ideal of *isonomia* shines at a particular moment in the history of societies.

> Primeval man, untouched as yet by criminal passion, lived his life without reproach or guilt, and, consequently, without penalty or coercion; rewards were needless when good was sought instinctively, and he who coveted nothing unsanctioned by custom had to be withheld from nothing by a threat.[85] But when equality began to be outworn, and ambition and violence gained ground in place of modesty and self-effacement, there came a crop of despotisms, which with many nations[86] has remained perennial. A few communities, either from the outset or after a surfeit of kings, decided for government by laws. The earliest specimens were the artless creations of simple minds, the most famous being those drawn up in Crete by Minos, in Sparta by Lycurgus, and in Athens by Solon—the last already more recondite and more numerous.[87] In our own case, after the absolute sway of Romulus, Numas imposed on his people the bonds of religion and a code dictated by Heaven. Other discoveries were due to Tullus and Ancus. But, foremost of all, Servius Tullius became an ordainer of laws, to which kings themselves were to owe obedience. Upon the expulsion of Tarquin, the commons, to check senatorial factions, framed a large number of regulations for the protection of their liberties or the establishment of concord; the Decemvirs came into being; and, by incorporating the best features of the foreign constitutions,[88] the Twelve Tables were assembled. (*Annals* 3.26–27)

In the rest of his account, however, Tacitus, by no means an idealist—his pessimism did not dispose him to see noble intentions in the actions of history's leading players—demonstrates that Roman laws were frequently little more than instruments of power in the hands of successive dominant players—magistrates, the Senate, the people, "strong men." And this was long before the triumph of the Principate. The lesson he learns from this is twofold: a pure "rule of law" can never exist, and today's discretional power of the princes corresponds to the nature of things. The Law of the Twelve Tables was

> the final instance of equitable legislation. For succeeding laws, though occasionally suggested by a crime and aimed at the criminal, were more often carried by brute force in consequence of class-dissension—to open the way to an unconceded office, to banish a patriot, or to consummate some other perverted end. Hence our demagogues: our Gracchi and Saturnini,[89] and on the other side, a Drusus[90] bidding as high in the senate's name; while the provincials were alternately bribed with hopes and cheated with tribunician vetoes.[91] Not even the Italian war, soon followed by the Civil war, could interrupt the flow of self-contradictory legislation; until Sulla, in dictatorship, by abolishing or inverting the older statues and adding more of his own, brought the process to a standstill. But not for long.

---

[85] It was something of a golden age, an uncorrupted state of nature.

[86] Tacitus believed that a barbarian world continued to exist and that it was still in a state of development before the levels achieved by Greece and Rome.

[87] Tacitus recognizes Greece as the forerunner in the development of political ideas and institutions.

[88] This is an allusion to the fact that, when the Law of the Twelve Tables was written, the constitutions of greater Greece and the Athenian laws of Cleisthenes were models.

[89] Saturnini resumed the policies of the Gracchi and was crushed by the Senate and Marius in 100 BC.

[90] Livius Drusus was a plebeian tribune in 91 BC. He attempted to drum up support from the people to regain certain lost privileges for the Senate, before he was assassinated. He used his personal wealth to buy votes for plebeians; this is why Tacitus calls him a "corruptor."

[91] An allusion to a promise made by Livius Drusus to grant Roman citizenship to "allies," that is, to residents of Italian cities other than Rome. Consul Philippus's intercession prevented the measure from being voted, which triggered the revolt of the "allies" and the Social War (see above, p. 209).

> The calm was immediately broken by the Rogations of Lepidus,[92] and shortly afterwards the tribunes were repossessed of their licence to disturb the nation as they pleased.[93] And now bills began to pass, not only of national but of purely individual application,[94] and when the state was most corrupt, laws were most abundant. (*Annals* 3.27)

Things worsened as the crisis of the Republic deepened under the two triumvirates: "Then came Pompey's third consulate. But this chosen reformer of society, operating with remedies more disastrous than the abuses, this maker and breaker of his own enactments, lost by the sword what he was holding by the sword.[95] There followed 20 crowded years of discord, during which law and custom ceased to exist; villainy was immune, decency not rarely a sentence of death" (*Annals* 3.28).

Thus, by inevitable necessity, Rome comes to the Principate system of government invented by Augustus. It is not, of course, a regime of equality before and under the law, but, seen against the broader historical backdrop described by Tacitus, it appears the *lesser evil.*

Tacitus draws the following conclusion from his historical analysis: a regime of equal laws for all is good, and preferable to the tyrannies that remain in existence among the barbarians. But such a regime was adapted to Rome only during the early centuries of its existence. In the last decades of the Republic the laws were controlled by certain interest groups—the rabble, the Senate, and certain factious generals—and used as instruments of tyranny until the situation became unbearable. In fact, the situation became so bad that when an absolute ruler used ostensibly illicit methods—secret police, informers, and the arbitrary right over life and death—he was no longer innovating; and if these measures enabled him to restore peace, order, and the semblance of rule of law, society won in the end. Tacitus believed that peace was an essential civic value (for the barbaric Germanic tribes it was war), because in troubled times the most despicable characters rule the streets and weaken all of society, attracting the wrath of the gods. Thus, whoever achieves peace, even at the price of crimes, is worthy of exaltation.[96]

d. The Principate, a Principle of Unity

The Principate is also required to achieve a principle of *unity* between the social orders (*Annals* 4.33). Alone one man can prevent the great body of the Empire from dismembering:

> When Lepidus [the triumvir] grew old and indolent, and Antony succumbed to his vices, the sole remedy for his distracted country was government by one man. Yet he organized the state, not by instituting a monarchy or a dictatorship, but by creating the title of First Citizen [prince]. The empire had been fenced by the ocean or distant rivers. The legions, the provinces, the fleets, the whole administration, had been centralized.[97] There had been law for the Roman citizen, respect for the allied communities; and the capital itself had

[92] The Roman statesman Aemilius Lepidus, not to be confused with Lepidus, the triumvir colleague of Antony and Octavian. He was consul in 78 BC, shortly after Sulla's dictatorship (82–79 BC). He, too, attempted to resume the policies of the Gracchi.

[93] In 70 BC Sulla's pro-Senate legislation was abolished and the powers of the tribunes and the plebeians restored.

[94] An example of such an *ad hominem* law was Clodius's law against Cicero (58 BC). When *isonomia* disappeared and *privilegium* took its place, the civic ideal was flouted.

[95] A reference to his defeat at Pharsalus before Caesar in 48 BC. For the members of the senatorial party, this date signaled the final loss of *libertas*.

[96] See Grimal, *Tacite*, 221, 227.

[97] Not only did the Principate establish a principle of unity on the domestic scene by putting an end to social and political squabbling in Rome; it established harmony and cohesion throughout the entire Empire as well, uniting armies, provinces, and virtually the entire world—everything on earth bounded by the ocean. Here Tacitus expresses a cosmic vision of Roman monarchy already; this aspect became more marked in the ideologies of the Dominate.

been embellished with remarkable splendour.[98] Very few situations had been treated by force, and then only in the interests of general tranquillity. (*Annals* 1.9.4–5)[99]

e. The Prince Chosen by the Gods

If the prince is to accomplish his mission as peacemaker and unifier, if Roman armies throughout the world are to fight under his banner, then he must have superhuman strength and be manifestly favored by the gods.

Such was the case for some members of the Julio-Claudian dynasty, descendants of divine Caesar and the *gens* Julia; as for others, the gods let their dissatisfaction be known through sinister or equivocal omens.

Nero, for example, bathed in the golden light of the rising sun at the summit of a tower, a divine "benediction" according to the Egyptians. This was the origin of his imperial sun cult. While this pleased the Stoic Seneca (he recalled the significance of the sun in the poem by Cleanthes, see *On Mercy*), Tacitus is wary: greater interest in the gods of the Orient poses a threat to the traditional alliance of the city and its native divinities.

Tacitus mocks Nero, the most Hellenistic of Roman emperors. Nero aspired to excellence in three areas of performance: as a citharede, an actor, and a driver of the quadriga. He displayed genuine love of beauty combined with *symmetria,* that is, harmony and just proportions. He claimed that it was the possession of these qualities, which justified his being emperor. Other precedents existed for Nero's attempt at "cultural revolution"; Tiberius and Germanicus, who participated in the Olympic games; Augustus, who reinstated the Actian games (following his victory at the Battle of Actium); and earlier still, Ptolemy Evergetes, Evander, and Achilles. And others followed: Hadrian, Marcus Aurelius. The *Neroniana* (the games created by Nero) made Greek-style clothing fashionable in Rome for a while. In the opinion of Tacitus, this preference for Greek clothing expressed the very opposite of the traditional values of Roman aristocracy, celebrated by Cicero in his *Dream of Scipio;* Tacitus himself gave an account of these values in his portrayal of his father-in-law's life, Gnaeus Julius Agricola. Thus, Nero was not chosen by the gods, in the eyes of Tacitus; he was a reprobate, and his subsequent destiny revealed this.

Neither Galba, Otho, nor Vitellius received any sign of divine election, which explains their instant failure.

In a certain sense, Vespasian and Titus did appear to have the favor of the gods. Vespasian showed signs of a divine calling from his earliest childhood. On his country estate, a towering cypress was felled; the next day it grew back higher and leafier. This, the haruspices agreed, was a portent of brilliant successes and great distinctions (*Histories* 2.78). At a most critical juncture of the Year of the Three Emperors (69 AD) Vespasian, in the East pondering his imperial ambitions, consulted an oracle on Mount Carmel. Basilides the priest said to him, "Whatever you are planning, Vespasian, whether to build a house, or to enlarge your holdings, or to increase the number of your slaves, the god grants you a mighty home, limitless bounds, and a multitude of men" (*Histories* 2.78). As he was leaving his villa in Caesarea, his troops hailed him, not with the name "legate," but *imperator;* and with inspiration from the gods they shouted, "Hail, Caesar," "Hail Augustus." Then, in Alexandria, he healed two invalids, who appealed to him in the name of Serapis.[100] Basilides, thought to be some 80 miles away, made a sudden appearance in the temple

98 Augustus contributed greatly to the embellishment of Rome.

99 Again, the idea that some crimes may be necessary to the detriment of a few, if that is the price of peace, order, and unity for the greater number and the state. Social order is rooted in a *sacrificial* logic.

100 Roman emperors, like the medieval kings of Europe and the wizard-kings of primitive societies, are "thaumaturges."

of Serapis. During the Battle of Bedriac, pitting Vespasian's supporters against those of Vitellius, a flock of birds darkened the skies above the gathering of Vespasian's enemies.

But only the regimes of Nerva and Trajan showed any real signs of a true "Golden Century" willed by destinies.

Tacitus intended to write a history of these regimes but died before he could fulfill his plan. Therefore, he did not leave a list of particular signs, which, in his view, express the divine aspects of the Antonine dynasty's rise to power. Still, there is little doubt that the new dynasty was *divine* in his opinion. (Pliny and Cassius Dio do list some signs: for example, Trajan is adopted by Nerva in the temple of Jupiter after a miracle, and Trajan is called "Optimus" [the best], the name of Capitoline Jupiter as well.)

f. The Ideal Principate according to Tacitus

With the rise of the Antonines, the promises of the Principate of Augustus—as expressed by Augustus in his *Res gestae*—seemed destined to be fulfilled (though Augustus himself neither could nor would fulfill them).

"Now at last heart is coming back to us" (*Agricola* 3.1). The rule inaugurated by Nerva and Trajan was the first to "[unite] things long incompatible, the Principate and liberty." The Antonines, as Galba said to Piso, will "rule over men who can endure neither complete slavery nor complete liberty" (*Histories* 1.16.9). Thus, the prince will be a *rector,* occupying a station above the republican institutions without abolishing them (see the passage quoted above from the *Annals* 3.28), as if Tacitus made a distinction between power in the state apparatus—this power must be autocratic—and the power of the state over society—which must respect civic values.

In the same speech attributed to Galba, when he formally adopted Piso—a speech that in the mind of Tacitus no doubt expressed the doctrine of Nerva when he adopted Trajan—Tacitus proclaims a central ideological plank of the new Principate: henceforth, succession is to be by adoption, and not hereditary in the *gens* (the cause of the downfall of the Julio-Claudians). "Adoption will select only the best [successor]; for to be begotten and born of princes is mere chance, and is reckoned higher, but the judgment displayed in adoption is unhampered; and, if one wishes to make a choice, common consent points out the individual"[101] (*Histories* 1.16).

The hesitation and uncertainty of Tacitus is clear: the emperors must be favored by the gods, but human reason and the consent of the Senate and the people are equally necessary—the sign of an intermediary period where the civic-mindedness and rationalism of ancient Rome has not yet disappeared entirely, while the mysticism of the coming Dominate advances.

5. *A Dialogue on Oratory*

A Dialogue on Oratory revealed many important arguments for and against the Republic and the Empire. Scholars today recognize the essay as the work of Tacitus, dating it to around the year 100 AD. Like the dialogues of Cicero, it is an invented dialogue between famous orators in 75 AD. Since this was the year Tacitus entered the *cursus honorum,* it is reasonable to assume that the question under discussion was one that Tacitus was contemplating at the time: to what purpose should one dedicate one's life? The matter is put in the form of two apparently unrelated questions: (1) what literary talent should one develop preferentially: oratory or poetry (i.e., primarily the writing of tragedies)? (2) Why are contemporary orators so inferior to the orators of the past?

---

[101] The Antonines respected the principle of adoption throughout their dynasty (with the exception of Marcus Aurelius, who chose his son, Commodus; and this was the end of the dynasty).

The first question concerns the old quandary of *otium* and *negotium.*[102] With the fervor of a neophyte, Tacitus—*homo novus*—inclines toward the old senatorial ideology: a Roman should dedicate his entire life to the city and be an orator and a magistrate. A solitary existence, devoted to the pointless practice of the arts and sciences, is a betrayal. Still, Tacitus is so impregnated with humanism and a desire for personal liberty, kindled by tyranny itself, that he is inspired to write this elegant defense of the poet's independence (it can also be read as an admonition to magistrates to remain independent in the performance of their duties):[103]

> As for your Crispus and Marcellus, whom you hold up to me as patterns for imitation, what is there about their boasted condition that we ought to covet? Is it the fear they feel, or the fear they inspire in others? Is it the fact that, besieged as they are from day to day by all sorts of petitions, they set the backs up of those whom they are unable to oblige? Or that, being constrained to curry favour in every direction, they can never show themselves either sufficiently servile to the powers that be, or sufficiently independent to us?... As for myself, may the "sweet Muses," as Virgil says, bear me away to their holy places where sacred streams do flow, beyond the reach of anxiety and care, and free from the obligations of performing each day some task that goes against the grain. May I no longer have anything to do with the mad racket and the hazards of the forum, or tremble as I try a fall with white-faced Fame. I do not want to be roused from sleep by the clatter of morning callers or by some breathless messenger from the palace; I do not care to have to write safeguards into my will in my anxiety as to what will happen; I wish for no larger estate than I can leave to the heir of my own free choice; for "some day or other the last hour will strike also for me." And my prayer is that my effigy may be set up beside my grave, not grim and scowling, but all smiles and garlands, and that no one shall seek to honour my memory either by a motion in the senate or by a petition to the Emperor. (*A Dialogue on Oratory* 13.4–6)

Yet Tacitus chose to enter the *cursus honorum*. Was that a contradiction? It was not, because he did not become an "orator" in the classical sense; he became a new type of statesman, one suited to the time of the Principate; on the contrary, as a historian he left intellectual accomplishments. In sum, he was engaged in the life of the city at the same time that he pursued an independent life of the spirit. This, in fact, is the deeper issue in the second question, almost anecdotal in appearance: why has contemporary oratory lost its eloquence?

Tacitus offers two preliminary explanations: the loss appears to stem from a laxity in education, to the benefit of empty formalism, and from the contemporary orators' weakening grasp of classical culture and philosophy, the source material for all orators. But such explanations are insufficient, and Tacitus dedicates the crux of his argument to a much more radical and innovative explanation. Eloquence is predicated on liberty; by abolishing liberty, the Empire made the development of eloquence impossible (in sum, the decline of oratory eloquence can be seen as a measure of the weakening of liberty under the Empire).

Tacitus sees clearly why this is so. Pluralism, the absence of a single decision center, obligated orators of the old Republic to develop the exercise of reason and the art of persuasion. Whereas contemporary trainee orators are reduced to abstract, academic exercises, the orators of

[102] See part 2, chapter 4, on Cicero, the section "Active Life and Contemplative Life."

[103] We quote this passage at length because it illustrates what was said earlier about the promotion of private life and the private person in a Roman civilization under the rule of law. The reader should note the strong demand for independence: to do what one pleases a person does not require the approval of some authority; one is a sufficient authority in one's own right.

the Republican period, attached to practicing orators with real power, made constant use of their intelligence and critical faculties:

> In this way they could command, firstly, a teacher, and him the best and choicest of his kind, one who could show forth the true features of eloquence, and not a weak initiation; secondly, opponents and antagonists, who fought with swords, not with wooden foils; and thirdly, an audience always numerous and always different, composed of friendly and unfriendly critics, who would not let any points escape them, whether good or bad. For the oratorical renown that is great and lasting is built up, as you know, quite as much among the opposition benches as on those of one's own side; indeed, its growth in that quarter is sturdier, and takes root more firmly.[104] (*A Dialogue on Oratory* 34.5)

In other words, there was under the Republic a public opinion in the sense of an anonymous agora. Though it was not comprised of people of good faith, but of envious and partisan types, truth could emerge in it at any time, simply because freedom of speech predominated, and this forced rulers to behave rationally, to adopt such conduct as they could justify on objective grounds and with universal value.

> Your public speaker can't get along without "hear, hear," and the clapping of hands. He must have what I may call his stage. This the orators of former times could command day after day, when the forum was packed by an audience at the same time numerous and distinguished, when persons who had to face the hazard of a public trial could depend on being supported by shoals of clients and fellow-tribesmen, and by deputations also from the country towns; half Italy, in fact, was there to back them. These were the days when the people of Rome felt that in quite a number of cases they had a personal stake in the verdict. (*A Dialogue on Oratory* 39.4)

Under the Republic the right existed to criticize anyone. No one was off-limits, there was genuine equality before the law. The final decision was in the hands of the assemblies, the Senate, or the *comitiae*. These groups, which could not be reined in by terror, voted one way or another only if one by one its members were convinced by the arguments. And only the speaker who argued most convincingly triumphed over all others. In the presence of such pluralism, the orator's skills flourished as a matter of course.

Here an aristocratic reflex causes Tacitus to step back from the brink, and he concludes his *Dialogue* with a bit of a theatrical coup in support of the Principate. If not even Publius Scipio, Sulla, and Gnaeus Pompeius were spared as they stood at the speaker's rostra, and if the jealousies of the lower classes could be excited against them, that is not liberty; it is license. No great state—meaning one that could be compared with Rome—could accept such a regime. Athens is the sole exception, but Tacitus shows calculated contempt for Athens—where "idiots" ruled—and, echoing criticism of fourth century Athenian democracy, he shows himself more faithful to Spartan values:

> The art which is the subject of our discourse is not a quiet and peaceable art, or one that finds satisfaction in moral worth and good behaviour: no, really, great and famous oratory is a foster-child of licence, which foolish men called liberty, an associate of sedition, a goad for the unbridled populace. It owes no allegiance to any. Devoid of discipline, it is insulting, off-hand, and over-bearing. It is a plant that does not grow under a well-regulated

[104] Remember these arguments. Not until Milton's *Areopagitica* and John Stuart Mill's *On Liberty* will we encounter such a defense of intellectual pluralism in the West again.

> constitution. Does history contain a single instance of any orator at Sparta, or in Crete, two states whose political system and legislation were more stringent than any other on record? It is equally true to say that in Macedonia and in Persia eloquence was unknown, as indeed it was in all states that were content to live under a settled government. Rhodes has had some orators, Athens a great many: in both communities all power was in the hands of the populace—that is to say, the untutored democracy, in fact the mob. (*A Dialogue on Oratory* 40)

Tacitus *appears* to have made his choice (we will see below why this restriction is necessary). In the timeless debate between a loquacious Athens and a laconic Sparta, Tacitus as an aristocrat and a man of order comes down on the side of Sparta. He claims to be even closer to the great monarchies of Persia and Macedonia. He would have preferred the latter as ancestors of the Roman Empire than "Athenian" democracy. It is time to draw a line under the past of "Athenian" Rome. If eloquence ever flourished on the banks of the Tiber, it was when the Republic was in the depths of its crisis. Even today, Tacitus says, eloquence subsists only where the state is imperfect and poorly ordered, where injustice, criminals, civic disorders, and foreign threats remain. In these instances, orators argue just causes and contribute to righting wrongs; but, he adds, "surely it were better to have no grievances than to need to seek redress." But now the Principate is heading in the direction of a more perfect order of the state, making abuse impossible. Orators will soon be condemned to a life of leisure.

> What is the use of long arguments in the senate, when good citizens agree so quickly? What is the use of one harangue after another on public platforms, when it is not the ignorant multitude that decides a political issue, but a monarch who is the incarnation of wisdom? What is the use of taking a prosecution on one's shoulders when misdeeds are so few and so trivial, or of making oneself unpopular by a defence of inordinate length, when the defendant can count on a gracious judge meeting him half-way?" (*A Dialogue on Oratory* 41)

Yet, the apparent frankness of this last tirade raises suspicion. Is Tacitus expressing himself at face value, or is he more Attic than he is willing to admit? Is he being ironic? It is difficult to say, especially given the ambiguity of his conclusion:

> Believe me, my friends, you who have all the eloquence that the times require: if you had lived in bygone days, or if the orators who rouse our admiration had lived today—if some deity, I say, had suddenly made you change places in your lives and epochs, you would have attained to their brilliant reputation for eloquence just as surely as they would show your restraint and self-control. As things are, since it is impossible for anybody to enjoy at one and the same time great renown and great repose, let everyone make the most of the blessings his own times afford without disparaging any other age. (*A Dialogue on Oratory* 41)

At any rate, Tacitus finds in this dialogue an answer to the question about his calling. He will be a magistrate, but he will be a "poet" magistrate, that is, he will retain his independence of judgment. In literary terms, he will be a historian; history-writing is a genre that reconciles the nobility of the orator's topic—that is, matters of state—with the supreme liberty of the poet, who is indifferent to his reputation with his contemporaries and whose eyes are riveted on the only glory that matters: the opinion of posterity. Tacitus makes himself worthy of such glory with his *Histories* and *Annals* by giving a narrative account of the cycles of misfortune traversed by the state, and emphasizing examples of virtue to be found there that opened the way, in the depths of decadence, to a renewal of eternal Rome. Thus, the *Annals* are a long *suasoria* (moral lesson) intended to provide the senators and optimates of Trajan's time with examples to follow and avoid so as to achieve the happiness of the Empire. The history of the Julio-Claudians will provide the material for this discourse. "[My conception of the first duty of history is] to ensure that merit shall not lack its record and to hold before the vicious word and deed the terrors of posterity and infamy" (*Annals* 3.65.1).

6. *The Civilizational Impact of Rome's World Domination*

Rome now controls a vast empire, also the object of Tacitus's thoughts. His *Agricola* and *Germania* are works devoted wholly to the barbarian world. The narrative accounts of the *Annals* and the *Histories* give Tacitus ample opportunity to discuss the military actions of Roman armies far from Italy, in Europe, and in the East. His opinion in this regard is important: does the Roman political class have an established doctrine on the question of conquest—at a time when many of its conquests, a wealthy source of experience and knowledge, lie in the distant past, and when new prospects of world domination are opening up?

His position on this is ambivalent as well, or more correctly critical and open. He supports Roman occupation and is convinced that it is a godsend for the barbarians, an opportunity for progress. At the same time, he uses these barbarian societies that he describes as primitive and cruel, and still close to "nature," as an indicator of the decline and corruption of civilized Roman society. With these ideas Tacitus initiates a long Western tradition of self-critical judgment through the eyes of the Other, that is, uncivilized tribes.

a. The "Noble Savage"

The barbarians, who had resisted Roman occupation stubbornly and pugnaciously, were admired not just for their military courage, but because their resistance expressed a sense of *libertas*, something the Romans had lost under the Principate. In a speech he attributes to Calgacus, a chieftain responsible for fomenting a revolt against the Roman army's occupation of Britain,[105] Tacitus describes the occupation in purely negative terms, as the result of greed and the passion to dominate:

> Robbers of the world, now that earth fails their all-devastating hands, they [the Romans] probe even the sea:[106] if their enemy have wealth, they have greed; if he be poor, they are ambitious; East nor West has glutted them; alone of mankind they covet with the same passion want as much as wealth. To plunder, butcher, steal, these things they misname empire: they make a desolation and they call it peace. Children and kin are by the law of nature each man's dearest possessions; they are swept away from us by conscription to the slaves in other lands; our wives and sisters, even when they escape a soldier's lust, are debauched by self-styled friends and guests; our goods and chattels go for tribute: our lands and harvests in requisitions of grain; life and limb themselves are worn out in making roads through marsh and forest to the accompaniment of gibes and blows. Slaves born to slavery are sold once for all and are fed by the masters free of cost; but Britain pays a daily price for her own enslavement, and feeds the slavers;[107] and as in the slave-gang the new-comer is a mockery even to his fellow-slaves, so in this world-wide, age-old slave-gang, we, the new hands, worth least, are marked out to be made away with: we have no lands or mines or harbours for the working of which we might be set aside. "Further, courage and high spirit in their subjects displease our masters; our very distance and seclusion, in proportion as they save

[105] Following his conquest of Gaul, Caesar continued north to the British Isles, where he landed twice but was unable to gain a permanent foothold. A century later, in 43 AD, Claudius finally achieved a partial conquest of the territory.

[106] In other words, having conquered continental Europe, the Romans are now exploring the coastlines and islands of the outer extremity of the world.

[107] With its payment of tribute and taxes.

> us, make us more suspected: therefore abandon all hope of pardon, and even at this late hour take courage. (Tacitus, *Agricola* 30, 31)

This praise for the *libertas* of the Britons is, no doubt, for Tacitus a way to criticize his Roman compatriots' cowardly acceptance of servitude.

Tacitus goes one step more in his *Germania,* since he offers an ancient version of the myth of the "noble savage." Humans closer to nature are better off in terms of basic moral virtues.

> None the less the marriage tie with them is strict: you will find nothing in their character to praise more highly. They are almost the only barbarians who are content with a wife apiece: the very few exceptions have nothing to do with passion, but consist of those with whom polygamous marriage is eagerly sought for the sake of high birth. As for dower, it is not the wife who brings it to the husband, but the husband to the wife. The parents and relations are present to approve these gifts—gifts not devised for ministering to female fads, nor for the adornment of the person of the bride, but oxen, a horse and a bridle, a shield and spear or sword; it is to share these things that the wife is taken by the husband, and she herself, in turn, brings some piece of armour to her husband. Here is the gist of the bond between them, here in their eyes its mysterious sacrament, the divinity which hedges it. That the wife may not imagine herself exempt from thoughts of heroism, released from the chance of war, she is thus warned by the very rites with which her marriage begins that she comes to share hard work and peril; that her fate will be the same as his in peace and in panic....
>
> So their life is one fenced-in chastity. There is no arena with its seductions, no dinner-tables with their provocations to corrupt them. Of the exchange of secret letters men and women alike are innocent;[108] adulteries are very few for the number of people. Punishment is prompt and is the husband's prerogative: her hair close-cropped, stripped of her clothes, her husband drives her from his house in presence of his relatives and pursues her with a lash through the length of the village. For prostituted chastity there is no pardon; beauty nor youth nor wealth will find her a husband. No one laughs at vice there; no one calls seduction, suffered or wrought, the spirit of the age. Better still are those tribes where only maids marry, and where a woman makes a pact, once for all, in the hopes and vows of a wife; so they take one husband only, just as one body and one life, in order that their desire may not be for the man, but for marriage, so to speak; to limit the number of their children, to make away with any of the later children is held abominable, and good habits have more force with them than good laws elsewhere. (*Germania* 18–19)

We could extend the list of quotes from *Germania* where the warriorlike qualities of the Germanic people are praised (modern German nationalism took great pride in these passages, seeing evidence of ancient Rome's recognition of the superiority of the German race). At the end of book 2 of his *Annals* (chapter 88), Tacitus offers a eulogy of Arminius, a German chieftain, who dared attack the Roman Empire at the height of its power.

Finally, we should note that Tacitus, in his descriptions of ancient Germanic religions, sees certain similarities with Greek and Roman mythologies; far from being a class of *Untermenschen,* these races are fundamentally similar. For all of these reasons, Tacitus seems to accept that barbarian revolts are justified, especially if Roman occupation is synonymous with corruption of

[108] This is not a reference to an exchange of love letters. Germanic women, on account of their lack of education, are preserved from literature and its examples of moral decadence. Literature had a bad reputation among the ancient Romans and among the Cynics.

wealth and estrangement from a "natural" life. In this sense, barbarians can serve Rome as guides, or at least as reminders of the threats facing the Roman people, once rustic and simple, but now conquerors of the world because of similar virtues, and who now let these virtues be corrupted by these conquests and by the luxuries they bring the victors.

b. The Superiority of Roman Civilization and *Pax Romana*

In the opinion of Tacitus, barbarians, of course, were not just endowed with qualities. In various passages of *Agricola* and *Germania,* he expresses a sense of superiority and disdain for the poor, technologically and socially backward barbarians; and he has scant regard for their morals: they are little more than animals (Germanic tribes dwell in dens and live virtually naked); they are cruel (they make human sacrifices and execute common criminals without due process); at the same time, they are unprincipled (they are addicted to drink and try to enrich themselves by commerce whenever possible). Above all, while Tacitus admires barbarians for their warriorlike courage, he chides them for prizing war as a supreme value.

Tacitus greatly admires barbarians in their natural habitat, but he cannot find words harsh enough to find fault with the savagery of the ragtag troops and hangers-on of Vitellius's army making their appearance in Rome.

As for the Romans, domination was not their sole motivation; they shared a genuine concern for order and peace; they knew these values to be precious for all; they even went to great lengths to deliver them to the barbarians themselves, often with generosity. The legate Petillius Cerialis made this point in a speech in Trier where he had put down the revolt of the Batavian Civilis. The Romans put their armies into the north of Gaul not because of cupidity, but in response to pleas from the ancestors of the inhabitants of Trier, exhausted by quarrels with their neighbor and by constant threats from Germanic tribes. "The Germans always have the same reasons for crossing into the Gallic provinces—lust, avarice, and their longing to change their homes, that they may leave behind their swamps and deserts, and become masters of this most fertile soil and of you yourselves: freedom, however, and specious names are their pretexts; but no man has ever been ambitious to enslave another or to win dominion for himself without using these very same words" (Tacitus, *Histories* 4.73).

Tacitus's realism is noteworthy. He claims not to take the speech literally and hints that political expediency requires a degree of cynicism or, at any rate, a distancing from ideology. And he continues: Rome's legitimacy resides in the fact that it is the policeman of the known world. "There were always kings and wars throughout Gaul until you submitted to our laws. Although often provoked by you, the only use we have made of our rights as victors has been to impose on you the necessary costs of maintaining peace; for you cannot secure tranquility among nations without armies, nor maintain armies without pay, nor provide pay without taxes."

This *Pax Romana,* guaranteed by an organized state, is a universal good that everyone can understand and enjoy thanks to Roman generosity and vision. "Everything else we have in common. You often command our legions; you rule these and other provinces; we have no privileges, you suffer no exclusion." The Gauls and Germans in the provinces under Roman rule are even happier than native Romans themselves: "You enjoy the advantage of the good emperors equally with us, although you dwell far from the capital: the cruel emperors assail those nearest them." Compared with these benefits, the passing excesses of bad princes and corrupt rulers, like the unpleasantness of taxes, were small; they bore them like bad weather. What really mattered was that the public order created by Rome endured. If revolts caused the Romans to leave, "what will follow except universal war among all peoples?"

Tacitus knows that this state of affairs—of which he is proud—is the fruit of a long history, of an unprecedented effort; and though initiated by Rome alone, it is now the common inheritance of all humankind: "The good fortune and order of eight hundred years[109] have built up this mighty fabric which cannot be destroyed without overwhelming its destroyers.... Therefore love and cherish peace and the city wherein we, conquerors and conquered alike, enjoy an equal right" (*Histories* 74).

7. *Conclusion*

The ambiguity of Tacitus's political thought remains intact; it is a mix of religion and reason. On the one hand, like Virgil, Tacitus believes in a new coming of a Golden Century for Rome, that the return of domestic order and peace, together with Rome's imperial expansion to the outer extremities of the world, marks a return of the favor of the gods. Empire is the fulfillment of Rome's eternal destiny; this alone justifies it. On the other hand, Tacitus, like Seneca, puts forward rational arguments in support of absolutism: human nature requires it—society cannot survive without an iron fist; *isonomia* is a temporary, unstable condition. Moreover, the people of the world are happier living under the yoke of Roman law than under the chaos of their own *libertas*.

All the same, the rational, critical aspect of this thought dominates distinctly. Tacitus is, more or less, the same sort of man as Seneca, Cicero, or Sallust. His work shows that, in his time, the Roman Empire had not yet entered into the mystical and totalitarian phase of the Dominate.

G. Pliny the Younger: Panegyricus to Trajan

Pliny the Younger is another important witness to the birth of the Principate and its time of greatness.

1. *Life*

Pliny the Younger (61–ca. 114 AD) was the nephew and adopted son of Pliny the Elder. Equestrian by birth, he achieved entry into the senatorial class by virtue of his election to a quaestorship while still in his late twenties. He led a dual career as a lawyer and a statesman. Close to Emperor Trajan he received a number of official appointments from him. He was consul in 100 AD, then imperial governor (*legatus Augusti*) of Bithynia and Pontus province (in present-day northern Turkey) in 111–12 AD.

2. *Work*

Pliny the Younger is the author of a large correspondence, including a set of exchanges of letters with Trajan while he was governor in Bithynia and Pontus. These are fascinating documents, showing the methods of administration at the time of the Empire. Earlier, prior to his elevation to the office of consul, Pliny delivered a long *Panegyricus* (praise) of the emperor to the Senate. It has come down to us.

Pliny's *Panegyricus to Trajan*[110] is not as such a general theory of monarchy. Everything he says relates to Trajan and can only be implicitly generalized to monarchy. The obsequious tone of Pliny's text is striking; it is, of course, tempered by rhetoric. Pliny avows that his praise is sincere, for he has nothing to fear if his words are unpleasing to the prince. This situation, he says, is very different from earlier regimes, notably the rule of Domitian. The newfound freedom of citizens to

[109] In reference to the traditional date of the founding of the city according to Roman annals, 753 BC.

[110] See Pliny the Younger, *Letters*, vol. 2, *Panegyricus*, trans. Bette Radice (Cambridge, MA: Harvard University Press, 1969); hereafter cited in the text by section and line number.

speak, without exalting the prince, is "a kindness... worthy of praise" (sec. 2). In the end, though, the impression that remains is that a certain terror continues to reign.

This does not stop Pliny from expressing the same convictions as Seneca and Tacitus. The Principate is fully justified as a system of government since it ensures order, peace, and stability. For this reason, the absolute ruler of Rome takes, in all legitimacy, several attributes of an oriental monarch. However, the strength and unity bestowed by the Principate on the Roman state make sense only if the state itself is a constitutional one, that is, a rule of law under which individual rights are recognized and protected. Pliny defends this other aspect of the Principate with greater fervor and conviction than even Tacitus.

3. *The Roman Prince Is Set Apart from Other Men*

The emperor is a divine being. His "purity and virtue make him [the equal of the gods]" (sec. 1). His personal qualities are proof that his predecessor, responsible for his selection as his successor, is worthy of the divine honors granted him (cult, shrine, flamines).[111] Trajan himself, Pliny says, will "deserve [his] seat in heaven" (deification) after his life is over (*Panegyricus* 35.4).

Pliny readily accredits the more antiquated and irrational portrayals of a sacred king: a rain-maker, father of the harvest, thaumaturge, and keeper of the order of the world. The emperor is a healer of maladies. He brings prosperity and ensures the fertility of the soil (*Panegyricus* 23.3). For Pliny, the emperor's teeming potency is, of course, as much the product of reason and effective administration as of magic. Because Trajan successfully organized the grain supply of Italy, it was possible to rescue Egypt in a time of famine (the opposite, in fact, of what ordinarily happened). This is the marvel of state power, which creates solidarity between its different regions.

> What a benefit it is for every province to have come under our rule and protection when we are blessed with a prince who could switch earth's bounty here and there, as occasion and necessity require, bringing aid and nourishment to a nation cut off by the sea as if its people were numbered among the humbler citizens of Rome!... [The emperor has it within his power] to banish hardships everywhere if not the condition of sterility, and introduce the benefits of fertility, if not fertility itself. He can so join East and West by convoys that those peoples who offer and those who need supplies can learn and appreciate in their turn, after experiencing licence and discord, how much they gain from having one master to serve. (Pliny, *Panegyricus* 32)

Thus, the emperor is a guarantor of prosperity and material protection. He is generous and fair (25). He funds educational programs for the young and pursues government policies for the family. He is "magnificent" and "evergetic." He builds circuses for the entertainment of the people, raises public buildings, and erects statues (51).

The emperor, Pliny continues, is graced with every virtue, and foremost with courage. He is a true huntsman (81). His virtues come from his person, not from his actions (56). His wife, too, is beyond reproach, modest, moderate, discreet, and virtuous. His sister also shares these qualities (83).

Set apart from others, visible to all, the prince is in every respect out of the ordinary; he is a model for imitation (45). To these recurring themes of monarchy Pliny adds a psychological dimension: individuals will only do good in the Empire if they *know* that the emperor *knows* what they are doing (70.3–8). Thus, the emperor is the *conscience* of the Empire, which he incarnates in his person (72.1). Last but not least, the emperor's justice is like a god's:

[111] *Translator's note:* The flamines were priests attached to the cult of an individual god.

> This is indeed the true care of a prince, or even that of a god, to settle rivalry between cities, to soothe the passions of angry peoples less by exercise of power than by reason: to intervene where there has been official injustice, to undo what should never have been done: finally, like a swift-moving star, to see all, hear all, and be present at once with aide wherever your help is sought. It is thus, I fancy, that the great Father of the universe rules all with a nod of the head, if he ever looks down on earth and deigns to consider mortal destinies among his divine affairs. Now he is rid of this part of his duties, free to devote himself to heaven's concerns, since he has given you to us to fill his role with regard to the entire human race. (80.3–4)[112]

4. *A Roman Prince Respects Right*

Nevertheless, with the accent placed on the monarch as an agent of impartial justice—because justice is divine, transcendent, detached, no respecter of persons, founded in an equal law for all—we see the sharp difference between Pliny's Roman prince and an Eastern monarch. Admittedly the Roman emperor is a despotic ruler, but the state he governs remains the Roman Republic (perhaps Pliny, like Seneca before him, is guilty of wishful thinking; but what matters here is the ideal he defends, that is, the body of principles he thinks it is normal to respect).

If one is obedient to the prince, it is because he *embodies the law:* "We are ruled by you and subject to you (*regimur quidem a te et subjecti tibi*), but *no more than we are to the laws,* for these too must regulate our desires and passions, always with us and among us. You shine out in splendour like Honour, like Sovereignty, for these are always above mortal men and yet inseparable from them" (*Panegyricus* 24).

Moreover, the emperor understands that *he, too, is subject to the laws:*

> In the Forum, too, you mounted the platform of your own accord and were equally scrupulous to submit yourself to the laws.[113] No one had intended these laws to apply to the Emperor, Caesar, but you were unwilling for your privileges to extend beyond our own.... There is a new turn of phrase which I hear and understand for the first time—not "the prince is above the law" but "the law is above the prince"; Caesar bows to the same restrictions as any other consul. He takes the oath of obedience to the law with the gods as witness. (*Panegyricus* 24)

Trajan forbids the widespread practice of denunciation, characteristic of earlier reigns, which presupposes a monarch with arbitrary powers. "No one was safe from them [the informers], no position secure." By forbidding denunciation, Trajan expresses his volition to enforce the law: "Your stern providence ensured that a state founded on laws (*fundata legibus civitas*) should not appear to perish through the laws' abuse" (Pliny, *Panegyricus* 34.1–2).

The same respect for the law exists in the administration of justice: "[Again] he gave proof of his scrupulous attitude towards equity and his deep reverence for the letter of the law.... No magistrate had his rights or authority diminished; indeed, he took pains to increase these, by delegating the majority of the cases to the praetors and addressing them as his colleagues, not with an idea of courting popularity among his audience, but because these were his genuine sentiments" (*Panegyricus* 77.3–4). Now, under the law, citizens are free. The Roman prince respects a citizen's liberty for the same reason that he respects the law (see 87.1).

---

[112] The recurrent theme of "king-minister," God's vicar on earth, is found repeatedly in Eusebius of Caesarea and in royal Christian theologies, as we will see.

[113] An equivalent formulation appeared later in the *Digest* (the *Digna vox* constitution, see below, p. 540) and gave rise to numerous medieval commentaries as a counterpoint to absolutistic expressions.

The emperor respects the law in financial matters as well. He is munificent, but he exercises restraint in his expenditures: "An emperor must learn to balance accounts with his empire, to go abroad and return with the knowledge that he must publish his expenses and account for his movements, so that he will not spend what he is ashamed to make known to all" (*Panegyricus* 20.5). He distinguishes carefully between his personal property and the public purse: "You do not dispossess existing owners in order to add to your vast domains every marsh and lake, and even pasture-land; rivers, mountains and seas are no long reserved for the eyes of one man alone. The Emperor no longer feels the need to own whatever he sees, and at long last the land subject to his sovereign rights extends farther than his personal property (*imperium principis quam patrimonium majus est*)" (50.1–2).

The law protects the property of private citizens. Trajan shows his respect for the law through the moderateness and regularity of his fiscal policy. He reduces the inheritance tax, demonstrating his respect for the rights of families and natural law. He puts an end to arbitrary despoliations (*Panegyricus* 36–37, 50). His tax officials could be summoned to court: "Anyone may call your procurator or his agent to justice, to appear in court—for an emperor's court is set up which differs from the rest only in the eminence of the person concerned in its workings. Lots drawn from the urn assign the exchequer [tax office] its magistrate, who can be rejected at any one's protest: 'Not him, he's weak and out of touch with the spirit of the age—that's the man, independent and loyal subject of Caesar!'" (36.3–4).

Did reality coincide with this ideal? It is difficult to say, but it is remarkable that such emphasis was placed on the independence of justice. The fact that the state accepts to subordinate itself to the judgment of a court is a formal sign that it acknowledges a law higher than the state itself. Thus, we see that, doctrinally, Pliny is aware of this fundamental aspect of the liberal "rule of law."

5. *The Roman Prince Is a Fellow Citizen*

The necessary corollary of an equal law for all is that all people are equal. In spite of so many appearances to the contrary, Pliny defends this crucial point that involves his whole conception of *humanitas.*

While earlier princes were carried about on the shoulders of slaves, thereby proving that they were the enemies of equality, Trajan used his own two feet and walked among men with whom he shared the same values of justice and respect for the law. This is what makes him worthy of his high station. "You are lifted to the heavens by the very ground we all tread, where your imperial footsteps are mingled with our own" (*Panegyricus* 24.5).

Because of his personality, his personal tastes, his psychology, Trajan accepts this civic equality with his subjects. It is the "engaging" side of his character. He is humble and humane. "You used to go on foot before, you still do now; you delighted in hard work, and still delight; though fortune has changed all around you, she changed nothing in yourself" (*Panegyricus* 24.2). The emperor is easily *accessible* to all:

> When the prince moves among his subjects they are free to stand still or approach him, to accompany him or pass ahead.... No forum, no temple is so free of access: not even the Capitol and the very site of your adoption are more public and open to all. There are no obstacles, no grades of entry to cause humiliation, not a thousand doors to be opened only to find still more obstacles barring the way. No, everything is peaceful before reaching you and on leaving you and above all, in your presence; such deep silence, such great reverence, that from the prince's house an example of calm and moderation returns to every humble hearth and modest home. (24.3, 47.5)

When one is in his presence, the prince is "normal"; he listens, he converses, he is *courteous* (*Panegyricus* 71.6). Perhaps his politeness is a form of vanity, nevertheless it comes across as an explicit and natural acknowledgment of the dignity of his less powerful interlocutors: it expresses a refined humanity, the combined result of republican tradition—Cincinnatus was humble and accessible as well—and Stoic universalism.

6. *The Principate Is Not a Despotism*

Pliny summarizes these arguments with the utmost clarity as follows: the *principatus* is not a *dominatio;* that is, the Principate is not a tyranny; the citizen's obedience to the Prince is not the same as the slave's submission to the master. "Tyranny and the principate are diametrically opposed (*sunt diversa natura dominatio et principatus*)" (Pliny, *Panegyricus* 45.3).

In spite of appearances to the contrary, the makings of the head of the Roman state are the same for a Brutus or a Camillus: Brutus drove out the Tarquins, Marcus Furius Camillus ousted the Celts from Latium: "they expelled the tyrant kings and conquering foe from the walls of Rome, while Caesar [Trajan] sweeps tyranny away, banishes all that captivity has bred, and makes sure that the imperial seat he holds shall never be a tyrant's throne" (*sedem obtinet principis ne sit domino locus*) (*Panegyricus* 55.7).

Respect for the law, which restricts the powers of the prince, increases his humanity. Good citizenship is the mold of humanism (and, conversely, despotic kings and enslaved subjects, found among the barbarians, are less than men): "A spirit which is above ambition, which can hold in check the temptations of power unbounded (*infinitae potestatis domitor ac frenator*), blossoms as the years go by" (*Panegyricus* 55.9).

This distinction between the prince and the master amounts to establishing the civic idea of the state—an abstract, permanent, and impersonal polity—as a common good distinct from the person of its leaders. We noted earlier that Pliny makes a distinction between public property and the emperor's personal property. His praise of *adoption* (5), like that of Tacitus, runs along the same lines. The normal mode of succession under the Antonines, adoption places common interest and public service above the special interests of the family.

This does not stop Pliny from emphasizing the difference between a situation *sub principe* and a situation *in libertate* (*Panegyricus* 44.6). Like Seneca and Tacitus, Pliny is aware that with the advent of the Principate a critical aspect of freedom, that is, *political* freedom, was severely compromised. But political freedom did not disappear entirely, since a right to criticize survived. Trajan tolerated criticism of former emperors; it amounted to giving future emperors (and the current one) a warning that the opinion of posterity matters (54.4–5, 65.4–5). Likewise, Pliny acknowledges Trajan's concern for a good reputation (*bona fama*) among "all" (*omnes*), a further sign of his regard for public opinion (62.9). This amounts to an admission that Rome is a community of free men, each with an independence of mind, a conscience, and rational judgment; Rome is not a faceless community where everyone's thinking is aligned. There is an agora in Rome like in Athens. Pliny hints that Trajan would have had no wish to retain power without the approval of the agora.

H. Aelius Aristides: The Oration "Regarding Rome"

The orator Aelius Aristides is interesting for his famous "Regarding Rome" oration in which he not only praises the emperor, Antoninus Pius, for conducting himself like a "President of the Republic" in the defense of justice, he also praises Rome itself as a properly administered state under the rule of law. The notions of "proper administration" and "rule of law" imply individual liberty; thus, the Romans ruled over "free men," and this is what set their Empire apart from all prior ones. The fact that the analysis and approval comes from non-Romans like Polybius or Plutarch is even more meaningful.

1. *Life and Work*

Publius Aelius Aristides was born into a family of rich landowners in 117 AD in Adriani, Mysia.[114] In 123, the family was granted Roman citizenship.[115] Publius received his education from the leading Sophists of the day in Smyrna, Pergamon, and Athens. He undertook a lengthy journey to Egypt. During this journey he began his career as an orator with the intention of pursuing it in Rome at the imperial court, but he fell gravely ill and was incapacitated for the next 13 years. During this time he became a devout follower of Asclepius, the god of medicine, and spent two years at his temple in Pergamon (he returned there frequently in later years). At the temple, the god came to him frequently in dreams and inspired remedies (Publius records some 130 such dreams in his *Sacred Tales*). He held regular conversations with a close circle of high society figures (writers, jurists, aristocrats, and officials), cultivated but neurasthenic temple goers. In time he began to write and speak again. He found himself frequently in the courts, pursued by his fellow citizens, who tried to impose upon him to accept honorific, but costly, distinctions ("liturgies"). Around 153–54 AD, his health fully restored, he again took up his profession as orator. This returned him to Rome. He also accepted students. After 165, his concerns for his health resurfaced, as did his religious obsessions. He died in 180 AD. A few dozen of his orations on wide-ranging topics survive to this day.

2. *"Regarding Rome" (Oration 26)*

Rome had everything; its markets contained produce and manufactured goods from the world over. The sun never set on its empire. In former times, a comparison with the majestic achievements of the ancients was made to belittle something. Now, the ancients were used to show the superiority of Rome.

The Persians once possessed a great empire, but to rule over it they weakened cities and countryside alike. They killed and destroyed. "The beauty of a child caused fear for the parents, that of a wife caused fear for the husband. The greatest criminal need not perish, but he with the most possessions. Survival was easier for an enemy than a subject. For in battle they [the Persians] were easily defeated, but in power they were immoderate in their crimes" ("Regarding Rome" 21–22).[116]

Aelius Aristides makes a similar observation about Alexander. He won wars, but he was not a true king. "What laws did he institute for each people? Or what lasting arrangements relative to finances, or to the army, or to the fleet did he make? Or with what kind of regular administration, one routinely proceeding in fixed cycles, did he direct affairs? ("Regarding Rome" 26).

The Romans dominated the world in an entirely different way. First, they dominated the whole world; they even conquered the islands of the sea. "Nothing escapes you, neither city, nor nation, nor harbor, nor land, unless you have condemned something as useless. The Red Sea, the cataracts of the Nile,[117] and Lake Maeotis,[118] which former men spoke of as at the ends of the earth, are for this city like 'the fence of a courtyard'" ("Regarding Rome" 28). Above all, "although your empire is so large and so great, it is much greater in its good order than in its circumference" (29). It is unaffected by endless, all-out war; peace reigns everywhere.

[114] A region in northwest Asia Minor, on the coast of Aegean Sea, between the Propontis in the north and Lydia in the south. The material in this section is from P. Aelius Aristides, *The Complete Works,* vols. 1–2, trans. Charles A. Behr (Leiden: E. J. Brill, 1981, 1986); quotations from his works are hereafter cited in the text.

[115] A full century before the Edict of Caracalla granted Roman citizenship to all free inhabitants of the Empire in 212 AD. In 110 AD Roman citizenship was still a privilege granted to the elite of conquered lands.

[116] Among Aelius Aristides' orations there is also one titled "Regarding the Emperor" (Oration 35). It appears to be apocryphal, dating from ca. 247 AD and addressed to the emperor Philip the Arab. It may even be a Byzantine text from the eleventh century. We will not discuss it in this study.

[117] Publius Aelius Aristides traveled to the first cataract on his visit to Egypt in 141.

[118] The present-day Sea of Azov.

> The whole inhabited world speaks in greater harmony than a chorus, praying that this empire last for all time. So fairly is it forged together by this chorus-leader prince. All everywhere are equally subjects.... No longer is there any difference between continent and island, but like one uninterrupted land and one tribe, all obey in silence. Everything is accomplished by edict and by a sign of assent more easily than one would strike the chord of a lyre. And if something must be done, it is enough to decree it and it is accomplished. The rulers who are sent to the cities and to the peoples are each the rulers of those under them, but in regard to their personal position and their relations to each other are equally subjects. And, indeed, one would say that in this respect they differ from their subjects, in that they first teach the duties of a subject. So much fear is instilled in all for the great ruler and president of the whole. ("Regarding Rome" 29–31)

The imperial administrators know that the emperor was informed of their efforts and actions. He communicated with them by letter without need for travel or personal meetings. His letters—the famous *rescripta* or "imperial responses"—arrived almost as soon as they were dispatched, as if carried by a winged messenger.

> You are the only ones ever to rule over free men. And Caria has not been given to Tissaphernes nor Phrygia to Pharnabazus, nor Egypt to another, nor are the people, like a household, spoken of as belonging to so-and-so, to whomever they were given to serve, although not even that man was free. But like those in individual cities, you govern throughout the whole inhabited world as if in a single city and you appoint governors as it were by election for the protection and care of their subjects, not to be their masters. Therefore governor is succeeded by governor [and none considers the land as his personal property]. (36)

Aelius Aristides raises a particularly important point about "government under the law": the right of citizens to appeal a governor's verdict and the real possibility that it may be overturned. The result is that judges have as much to fear from the verdict as the person under judgment, "so that one would say that people now are governed by those sent out to them in so far as it pleases them."

> How is this form of government not beyond every democracy?[119] There it is not possible after the verdict is given in the city to go elsewhere or to other judges, but one must be satisfied with the decision, unless it is some small city which needs outside judges.[120] But among you now a convicted defendant or even a prosecutor, who has not won his case, can take exception to the verdict and the undeserved loss. Another great judge remains, whom no aspect of justice ever escapes. And here there is a great and fair equality between weak and powerful, obscure and famous, poor and rich and noble. And Hesiod's words come to pass: "For easily he makes one strong and easily he crushes the strong,"[121] this great judge and governor, however justice guides him, like a breeze blowing on a ship, which does not, indeed, favor and escort the rich man more and the poor man less, but equally assists him to whomever it may come. ("Regarding Rome" 38–39)

After the Persians and the Macedonians, Aelius Aristides continues with the Athenians and the Lacedaemonians. Rome surpassed them as well. The Athenians and Lacedaemonians dreamed of

---

[119] A reference to the democracy of small traditional Greek cities.

[120] The use of outside judges was common in the Hellenistic world and responded to a lack of trust among inhabitants of the city proper.

[121] Hesiod, *The Works and Days,* verse 5: "Lightly he makes strong, and lightly brings strength to confusion, lightly diminishes the great man, uplifts the obscure one."

empire but succeeded only in achieving dominion over a few islands and a few small territories. Moreover, they only achieved hegemony alternatingly, never more than a generation at a time. Their subjects hated them and dreamed of destroying them. "Before you, the knowledge of how to govern did not yet exist" ("Regarding Rome" 51). The Athenians garrisoned cities under their control. They had a reputation for solving problems by force and violently. In addition, since they were not sufficiently numerous, and as they tried to rule the countries of others, they weakened themselves at home where division reigned. They could not decide between maintaining subject cities in a state of weakness, the better to control them, or strengthening them so that they might be useful in the struggle against their external enemies. "Thus then there was not yet an orderly procedure of government, nor did they consciously pursue this.... [They were] at the same time oppressive and weak" (57).

They were incapable of governing their cities "with generosity." The Romans succeeded because they had a science of government. When they created the greatest empire ever, their science served them. Likewise, the fact that they had an empire to govern enriched their science (58). The most admirable aspect of the Romans' conception of power was Rome's "magnanimity." Rome gave citizenship to all who were worthy, irrespective of whether they were from Europe or Asia. "[For the Romans] no one is a foreigner who deserves to hold office or to be trusted, but there has been established a common democracy of the world, under one man, the best ruler and director,[122] and all men assemble here as it were at a *common meeting place,* each to obtain his due. What a city is to its boundaries and its territories, so this city is to the whole inhabited world, as if it had been designated its common town" ("Regarding Rome" 60).

Now there is only one acropolis.[123] Rome receives people from every land, "just as the sea receives the rivers." And just as the sea does not change with the inflow of the rivers, Rome, because of its greatness, remains the same regardless of departures and arrivals. The word "Roman" is now "the name of a sort of common race." "You do not now divide the races into Greeks and barbarians," but into "Romans and non-Romans" ("Regarding Rome" 63).[124]

Aelius Aristides notes that the new Romans comprised only a portion of each conquered territory; they served the same function as garrison troops, but did not use force. "Under this government all of the masses have a sense of security against the powerful among them, provided by your wrath and vengeance which will immediately fall upon the powerful if they dare some lawless change" ("Regarding Rome" 65). This, according to Aelius Aristides, was why garrisons and cohorts were unnecessary and why Romans were able to maintain order throughout their vast empire. Taxes were happily paid, and this was normal. Cities had been resurrected like the souls of Plato's myth of Er; they had no recollection of having lived otherwise; the ravages of war had slipped from memory like a bad dream. Rome had recruited soldiers in every province of the Empire with the promise of citizenship and had made them "selected," "purified," and "set apart."

In political terms, Rome had a regime that combined the benefits of the three earlier forms of government: tyranny (oligarchy), kingship (aristocracy), and democracy. Aelius Aristides agrees with Polybius that a mix of all the constitutions is superior to its individual parts. Proof of this is in its stability (while the other regimes turned everything upside down). "[You] have discovered

---

[122] Antoninus Pius is cast virtually as a "president of the Republic."

[123] According to Plutarch, Alexander expressed the wish that his army might be the acropolis of all Greek cities (see above, p. 187).

[124] These are the same ideas and words used by Isocrates to signal the spread of Greek "culture" (*paedeia*) beyond the Greek tribe, except that now *Romanitas* has replaced Hellenism. Rome was far more successful at achieving the ideal of "cosmopolitanism" than Alexander (it is true that Alexander had only just begun to incarnate the ideal).

a form of government which no one had before, and have imposed unvarying law and order on all men" (91).

Romans had technical genius as well—and Aelius Aristides expresses his fascination for what we might call "Roman high-tech." The Romans knew how to build military fortifications. They invented the so-called *limes* (border defenses, the *nec plus ultra* of military art). The closed lines of their cohorts were impenetrable. Emulation reigned to the extent that the Romans were the only soldiers in the world who happily faced the enemy. Their tactical battlefield prowess made their enemies look like children. Strict, hierarchical lines of command ran from the emperor all the way down to the noncommissioned officer in charge of four or two soldiers. No subordinate envied his superior because everyone obeyed and commanded, and "the fruits of virtue [were] lost to no one" ("Regarding Rome" 89); everything worked to perfection.

Moreover, Rome filled its empire with cities and raised monuments instead of merely ruling over conquered places and leaving them in their original state. Greece now flourished again; Alexandria in Egypt was an ornament of the Empire. The Romans were as a "foster father" to the Greeks. They educated the barbarians "gently or harshly" as necessary. "The whole inhabited world... has laid aside its old dress, the carrying of weapons, and has turned... to adornments and all kinds of pleasures...: gymnasiums, fountains, gateways, temples, handicrafts, and schools." The world was "a pleasure garden." Rome's generosity was given to all. "[The Romans have] proved that well-known saying, that the earth is the mother of all and the universal country of all. Now it is possible for both Greek and barbarian, with his possessions or without them, to travel easily wherever he wishes, quite as if he were going from one country of his to another.... And what was said by Homer, 'The earth was common to all,' you have made a reality" ("Regarding Rome" 100–01).

Before the rise of the Romans there were many different peoples with barbarian customs; they were pleasant to behold, says Aelius Aristides, but not to live with. Everything was chaotic; there were factions; men ravaged the earth, weakening their fathers, as it were. "Before your empire everything was in confusion, topsy-turvy, and completely disorganized, but... when you took charge, the confusion and faction ceased and there entered in universal order and a glorious light in life and government and the laws came to the fore" ("Regarding Rome" 104).

The gods—"watching from above, in their benevolence"—made the Roman Empire successful and blessed Rome's possession of it. Each did so in the realization that the Empire magnified his glory. Moreover, Homer prophesized the rise of the Roman Empire. And it is because Hesiod did not have Homer's prophetic powers that he spoke of the golden race as something of the past. If only he had seen the Empire to come, he would have pitied those generations born before Rome!

II. Toward the Dominate and Byzantinism

A. Sun Cult, Pagan Monotheism, Ideologies of the Dominate

As early as Nero—and more with Domitian, then the Severi dynasty (the last dynasty of the High Empire), and finally with Aurelian, Diocletian, and Constantine, and after him all the emperors of the Low Empire—a new conception of Roman autocracy appeared. The cult of the emperor, as we know, existed as early as Augustus; it never weakened and was never contested under the High Empire. If the emperor was god, he was so in the framework of traditional polytheism, that is to say, at a rather modest cosmological level. Then a new development occurred.

Thinkers began to combine notions of philosophical monotheism (dating to the earliest Greek philosophers—the pre-Socratics—and continuing with Plato, Aristotle, the Stoics, and, finally, the Neoplatonists in the second half of the third century AD[125]) with the religious syncretism of an empire under the influence of oriental religions (notably Mithraism). Then they began to search for the philosophical and theological foundations of the idea of a sacred kingship where the emperor was no longer a god but the supreme earthly servant of a single heavenly God, that is, a "vicar of God" (*vicarius Dei*). This new philosophical and syncretistic monotheism, *which* clearly *predates Christianity,* buttressed absolute monarchy, which in turn imposed monotheism on the Empire; Constantine's conversion to Christianity brought this evolutionary development to its logical conclusion.

Let us try to clarify the principal phases of this evolution.[126]

1. Following the reign of Marcus Aurelius, the influence of the Orient grew, and before long a "solar theology" developed. Its origins were Greek (from the Seleucid monarchy in particular) and Iranian with the vogue in Rome at the time for Mithraism (Mithra was a god of light; Mithraism reached its zenith in the third century). The advent of an oriental imperial dynasty, that is, the dynasty of the Severi (the early Antonines were of old Italic and Hispanic stock), was the impetus for a development of this theology.

Septimius Severus (193–211 AD) was African (from Leptis Magna, present-day Tripoli, Libya; his family still spoke the Punic language). He married Julia Domna, the daughter of a hereditary priest king from Emesa (present-day Homs, Syria), a worshipper of the sun god Baal. Julia Domna exhorted the emperor to develop the imperial sun cult. The emperor and his wife were represented on coins as the sun and the moon. The inscriptions on their palace referred to it as the *domus divina.* After Septimius Severus's death, his son Carcalla became emperor (211–17) and after him, two Syrians, Elagabalus or Heliogabalus (218–22) and Alexander Severus (222–35) (Julia Domna's sister's daughters had married Syrians).

Understandably, these emperors of provincial origin were keen to eliminate any hint of difference between the Empire's older and more recent provinces; by nature the latter were more "cosmopolitan." Caracalla issued the famous edict of 212 AD, granting Roman citizenship to all inhabitants of the Empire. To implement a policy of imperial harmonization, the prince had to be reputed for his extraordinary powers and superhuman energy. The new solar theology was intended to justify his exceptional rank.

Earlier Nero had himself depicted on a coin with a radiate diadem, symbol of the rays of the sun. He called himself "the new Sun" (the new Apollo). Septimius Severus saw himself as a star illuminating the Empire like the sun lighting the world. He appears with a nimbus or halo of sun rays and a radiate diadem. Geta, his son, is shown on a coin as the offspring of the unconquered sun (*sol invictus*) and the sun-king. Elagabalus flaunted his rank as a hereditary descendant of the priest-king of the sun god Baal at extravagant processions and ceremonies in Rome; he brought to

[125] The first representative of Neoplatonism was Plotinus (205–70 AD), author of the *Enneads;* the other great Neoplatonists were Porphyry, Proclus, Jamblicus, Ammonius, and Simplicius. Neoplatonism is the extension of classical Platonism toward an expression of philosophical mysticism focused on the Platonic One, close to the one God of the Gnosis and the religious syncretisms of the Alexandrian world. The fundamental themes of Neoplatonism are: (1) a theory of *emanation* of all things from the godhead (the One or the Good); (2) a hierarchy of three *hypostases,* referred to as the objective reality of being, which includes the absolute One, the Intelligible, and the World Soul; (3) the World Soul's ascent and reunion with the One (*anagoge*).

[126] My account is based on Barker, *From Alexander to Constantine.*

Rome and put on display the black stone symbolizing the cult; he had himself styled "Elagabalus, priest of the unconquered sun-god."

2. The trend continued even after the Severi dynasty. Among the emperors of the period of military anarchy, lasting some 50 years until the accession of Diocletian (285 AD), two emperors stand out: Gallienus (259–68 AD), a protector of Plotinus and the Neoplatonists; and Aurelian (270–75 AD), the founder of the line of Danubian emperors, which continued with Diocletian and the other members of the tetrarchy, and was followed by Constantius, the father of Constantine. Many Danubians were of humble origin and owed their elevation to a military *pronunciamento* (the army of the Danube was the strongest and the nearest to Rome). These emperors had a pressing need for a more convincing and stable legitimacy.

Facing a mutiny of his army, Aurelian proclaimed: "the purple [the *paludamentum* or red mantle, symbol of imperial power] is the gift of God; God alone can limit that gift in time." Another story tells of an episode when Aurelian, on campaign in the East, attributed his victory at Homs to the sun-god of that city, the same solar Baal worshipped by Elagabalus. As a result, he exalted *sol invictus* as "lord of the Roman Empire" and raised a temple in his honor in Rome served by its own college of *pontifices dei Solis*. Aurelian gave *sol invictus* a syncretistic character, melding it with aspects of the Greek Apollo, features of the Iranian Mithras, and the Syrian Baal. Most importantly, he claimed to be *vicarius Dei*, servant to the Supreme God, rather than god himself; this was an innovation. Thus, monotheism and absolute monarchy join forces for the first time in history (the fate of this affiliation in the history of the West is well known). The new solar deity invigorated and united paganism and became the guarantor of loyalty to the emperor.

Thus, the idea of a king as the earthly representative of a heavenly God, ruling "by the grace of God" (*Dei gratia*), actually predates quite considerably Constantine, Christianity, and the theories of Eusebius of Caesarea that we will consider below. The idea was probably promoted in the age of Aurelian by Neopythagorean treatises on kingship, preserved by Stobaeus in his *Florilegium*, notably treaties by Diotogenes and by Pseudo-Ecphantus (see below, pp. 364–69).

Aurelian's doctrine is "one god, one empire, one emperor." He holds a scepter adorned with an eagle, reminiscent of Greco-Roman mythology (Jupiter or Homeric Zeus). He is depicted on coins as receiving a globe from the sun-god, a symbol of his dominion over the world. He wears a diadem of Persian origin: Macedonian kings wore this after Alexander's victory over Darius. Other coins from the period represent Aurelian with a radiate diadem, symbolizing the rays of the sun.

3. Though a polytheist, Diocletian adopts this same symbolism. His personal contribution is the creation of a new Byzantine court ceremonial intended to establish greater distance between the monarch and his subjects, now separated by numerous intermediaries at court. The *basileus* becomes distant, inaccessible, even hidden. Rules of *admissio*—or "presentation at court"—are established: it is no longer possible for just anyone to see the monarch, and those that can must obey strict rules. *Proskynesis* (prosternation) is imposed: in his presence one must kneel at the emperor's feet and kiss the hem of his robe; this expresses the very spirit of the Dominate: the king, his close associates, his subjects are men of a different essence, they are no longer the fellow citizens so dear to Pliny. The structure of society reflects the structure of the imperial court: one's social importance is on a par with one's worthiness to be admitted to the imperial court at a rank and place higher and closer to the emperor. Below we will return to the protests of Synesius of Cyrene against this (see p. 380). The new court ceremonial, based on ancient oriental patterns, is also supported by newer conjectures because the hierarchy of the royal court, which determines social hierarchy, is itself the reflection of the cosmic and celestial hierarchies.

4. Finally, Constantine, heir to the imperial ceremonial, returns to monotheism and sees himself as *vicarius Dei,* that is to say, both less and more than the old "gods" of the Principate.

The case of Constantine is complex. He appears to have undergone two conversions: the first, ca. 310 AD, when he turned from the Jovian-Herculian cult of Diocletian to the sun-worship of Aurelian's *Sol invictus* (his ancestors also paid devotion to this cult); the second, ca. 312–13, led him to Christianity, but only gradually and in some respects incompletely (see section D below, Eusebius of Caesarea). He was, in fact, a syncretist in search of a faith that could be embraced by all "nations." This was part political calculation, part personal quest, as well as a genuine acceptance of the Gospel's universal message.

Thus, Constantine's conversion was a continuation and a departure. For the rise of monotheism was organically entwined with the expansion of the Empire. The church itself absorbed the pagan history of Rome virtually unchanged into its political theology.[127] Let us turn now to some of the intellectual constructs that justified the new alliance between monarchy and monotheism (or a hierarchized polytheism).

B. Dio Chrysostom: Discourses on Kingship

With Dio Chrysostom we step back to Trajan's reign, the triumphant period of the Principate. But we shall see that Dio's ideas on kingship belong to a very different intellectual universe than that of his contemporaries, Tacitus and Pliny the Younger. Dio's ideas have their roots in an older Hellenistic Age, and at the same time they provide the substrate for a theology of monarchy to emerge in the following century. In fact, Dio's theory forms a bridge between Hellenistic thinking and the ideas of Byzantinism.[128]

1. *Life*

Dio Chrysostom (ca. 40–ca. 120 AD) was a native of Prusa (now Bursa) in the Roman province of Bythnia (present-day western Turkey), just south of Byzantium; he is also known as Dio of Prusa.[129] Born into a wealthy family, he received a classical education—focussed on rhetoric—in his native city. Dio arrived in Rome during the reign of Vespasian (emperor from 69 to 79 AD). At this time he switched from rhetoric to philosophy—two entirely different skills and attitudes. During Diocletian's reign, Dio was accused of associating with a local notable who had fallen into disgrace: he was found guilty and forced into exile, first from Rome, then Italy, and finally from Bythnia (probably in 82 AD). The sentence condemned him to a life of solitary wandering and poverty; he traveled from town to town, offering his services. This gave him the opportunity to test the Stoic maxim on the constancy of wise men and the Cynic maxim on the vanity of greatness. He traveled widely through the lands of the Danube and into southern Russia. Living among unfamiliar barbarians (e.g., the Getae), he was able to expand his knowledge of geography, politics, and morals. After the death of Diocletian in 96 AD, Dio's exile came to an end, and he was admitted back to Rome by the Emperors Nervas and Trajan. He struck a close personal bond of friendship with Trajan during the emperor's conquest of Dacia (present-day Romania);

---

[127] Perhaps Jewish and Christian representations of God, in spite of their shared biblical references, differ so greatly because of the influence of the imperial monarchic model in Christian theology. The God of the Christians is more Greco-Roman—more solar and imperial—than the God of the Jews.

[128] Moreover, we observe a decline of Roman thought and a renaissance of Hellenistic or Greek ideas in the first half of the second century: the leading intellectuals of the age are all Greek speakers: Epictetus, Plutarch, Marcus Aurelius, Aelius Aristides, Philostratus II (author of a *Life of Apollonius of Tyana*), and so on. In the following decades, the leading thought—i.e., that of the church fathers—continued to be dominated by Greek-speaking thinkers.

[129] See Dio Chrysostom, *Discourses,* 5 vols., trans. J. W. Cohoon and H. Lamar Crosby (1932; repr., Cambridge, MA: Harvard University Press, 2002). Dio's four discourses *On Kingship* are found in vol. 1 (cited by discourse and line number); the *Borysthenitic Discourse* is found in vol. 3 (cited by paragraph number).

it seems that Trajan held Dio's intellectual skills in great esteem. Dio used his contacts in high places to direct benefits to Prusa, his native city. On at least one occasion his contacts failed to protect him and he was again taken to court when Pliny the Younger was governor of Bythnia.

Dio is not what might be called an original thinker. He draws inspiration from the Stoics and from Plato and the Cynics. He is, however, a true philosopher. He does not believe that rhetoric, the science of speaking well irrespective of the topic, is a noble occupation for the mind (his opinion is all the more commendable given that, at the time, under Hadrian's reign, the Second Sophistic was triumphant in Rome).

2. *Work*

Many of Dio's works have survived. He wrote letters, numerous moral and political orations, and several treatises (now lost). Five discourses (or orations) are directly concerned with politics: (1) four "On Kingship" (*Peri basileias*), all four delivered before Trajan in Rome (the first spoken shortly after the emperor's ascension to office, the second and third probably in 101 AD, and the fourth in 103 AD); (2) the "Borysthenitic discourse," a conversation supposedly between Dio and the inhabitants of the Greek colony of Borysthenes, located on the northern shore of the Black Sea at the mouth of the Dnieper River, visited by Dio during his exile.

Dio Chrysostom opines that the art of politics is partly human (nurture), partly divine (nature); both registers are necessary. Thus, pure intellectuals, with no trace of the divine in their mind or soul, can be perfectly uncouth in politics. "Even if they stay with them night and day," Dio writes, they are as useless to politics as a eunuch to a woman; intellectuals "[grow] old in their ignorance, wandering about in their discussions far more helplessly than Homer says Odysseus ever did upon the deep" (*Kingship* 4.36–39).

An example of this divine wisdom is the idea that all rational beings form a single family. Such wisdom cannot be acquired through simple observation. Only poets, with their inspiration, grasp it "like a flash of fire from the invisible." But even they do not see it distinctly; they are more like attendants at the rites, standing just outside at the doors and catching only a few words of what is going on within (*Borysthenitic* 34).

The king, like the poet, "does not have to learn [the science of politics] but merely to recall" (*Kingship* 4.33) (by a sort of Platonic anamnesis). The science of politics exists within the monarch like an everlasting part of his soul or, Dio adds, like the unaltered teeth of a cremated body, "though the rest of the body has been consumed by the fire" (4.32).

3. *A City of Gods, a Cosmopolis, a City of Men*

There exists a city or a government of the gods, *theia polis* or *diacosmesis* (*Borysthenitic* 26), each god "pursuing an independent course," "dancing a dance of happiness coupled with wisdom and supreme intelligence" (22). Men are also part of this divine reality: they are to the gods what boys are to men (25). The city of men must be an approximation of the city of gods. The Stoics believe that all beings capable of reason (*pan to logikon*) belong to the same race, whether mortal or immortal. Together they form a community (*koinonia*) where justice (*dikaiosyne*) must reign. Dio also speaks of a "rational family" (*to logikos genos*) of gods and men who "share in reason (*logos*) and intellect (*phronesis*)" (38).

The consequence of this is that a city of mortals, like the city of gods, must be ruled by a government of reason, that is, a government of laws. A city is a community that obeys the law. Nineveh,[130] for example, is not a city (*Borysthenitic* 20). In the city of mortals, all men enjoy citizenship.

[130] Capital of the Assyrians, a people that the Greeks saw as especially cruel (e.g., Ashurbanipal) and disorderly (Sardanapallus).

Dio pointedly criticizes the Spartans because they excluded Helots from citizenship. This was wrong, he says, because Helots belonged to the *logikos genos* as well (38).

4. *Justification of a Monarchic Form of Government by Tradition and Natural Law*

All forms of government, with the exception of monarchy, are defective because they are the means by which any one part of the community can prevail over others. Only monarchy can preserve the *koinonia*, just as Zeus preserves the unity of the *cosmos* (*Borysthenitic* 31–32).

Dio, of course, is familiar with the three classical types of government—monarchy, aristocracy, democracy—and their lesser forms. But he expresses a clear preference for monarchy and turns to Homer for justification, as if the aristocratic and democratic Greek city was only a long and unattractive interlude between the Greek Dark Age and the time of Empire (*Kingship* 3:45–47).

Why are these collective forms of government of lesser value? Because only monarchy is founded on *natural law*. Animal herds and beehives have monarchs: proof that the weaker elements of society must be governed by the powerful. Likewise, the universe is ruled by a king, God (*Kingship* 3.50); the body by the soul (3.68); and woman by man (3.71–72).

5. *The King Does Not Rule by Force*

Various comparisons make it possible to approximate the concept of a good king.

A shepherd-king. First, Dio compares the good king to a shepherd (*Kingship* 1.1). The shepherd keeps watch over his flock; he does not slaughter his animals like the butcher (4.44). Kingship is described in terms of service (3.55). Great conquerors like Xerxes and Darius were butchers (4.45). They were no more kings than children who play at being kings and who are, in fact, the children of shoemakers and carpenters (when Alexander heard this, he was vexed and hurt)[131] (4.47–49).

A bull-king. A king leads a human herd. He is like a bull that leads the herd to pasture and protects it from wild beasts and other herds. The bull, of course, recognizes the superiority of humans. Likewise, the king rules over humans, but recognizes that he himself is subordinate to God's government. If the king shows himself weak before the enemy or brutal to defenseless citizens, God will unseat him (*Kingship* 2.67–78). Only the tyrant behaves like a lion with the herd.

A stingless bee. Diogenes claims to be the only man who taught Alexander the simple truth that he could not be a great king by brute strength alone. Just as the queen among bees has no sting, the king of men has no need to carry arms. This is the sign of his superiority over others (*Kingship* 4.60–64).

The king is the living law. The king must govern with the law, and not arbitrarily, yet he stands above it. Because he has no obligations whatsoever, not even to do what is good, he can do anything, including a higher good; and it is because he can be unjust that he can be truly just (*Kingship* 3.117).[132]

6. *Monarchy and Tyranny: Hercules' Correct Choice*

Dio uses a parable overheard on his wanderings in exile. Deep in the Peloponnesian countryside, a priestess of Cybele prophesied to him the end of Domitian's totalitarian reign and told him that

[131] *The Fourth Discourse on Kingship* is presented as a dialogue between Diogenes the Cynic and Alexander the Great.

[132] The king pays a high price for this power. Dio, like Seneca, emphasizes that the king, who is visible to all, is more vulnerable than anyone (*Kingship* 3.109). Dio quotes the Persian custom of the periodic sacrifice of a man standing as a substitute for the king. While the king himself is not actually put to death, the mere act of substitution suggests that the king is the target.

he would soon meet a good king (a reference to Trajan). She then instructed him to tell the following story in every detail when he met the king.[133]

The tale concerns Heracles, the mythic hero and king of all Greece. The son of Zeus and Alcmene, Heracles was half-god and half-man, making him capable of true political science. When Zeus heard that Heracles was to be entrusted with the kingship over all humankind, he decided to test him one last time. He sent his messenger (Hermes) to Heracles with instructions to lead him by paths unknown to mortals to an imaginary land (its traits are allegorical and transparent).

There are two mountains in this imaginary land that look like only one to anyone looking up from below. But, as one climbs higher, one sees that there are really two peaks: the Peak Royal and the Peak Tyrannous. Lady Royalty sits enthroned on Peak Royal surrounded by Justice (*Dike*), Civic Order (*Eunomia*), and Peace (*Eirene*). All three are supported by the Law (*Nomos*), also called Right Reason (*Logos Orthos*) (*Kingship* 1.26, 1.6–7), Counsellor (*Symboulos*), and Coadjutor (*Paredros*) (*Kingship* 1.73–75).

A series of crooked and perilous paths, drenched in blood and strewn with corpses, lead to the second peak. Tyranny is seated on a shaky throne. She tries to imitate Lady Royalty with her tiaras, diadems, and opulent raiment (perhaps an allusion to oriental monarchs?). But she is troubled, unable to sit with composure. Her eyes dart in every direction. One moment she smiles, the next she is in tears. She, too, is surrounded by her advisors: Cruelty (*Omotes*), Insolence (*Ybris*), Lawlessness (*Anomia*), and Faction (*Stasis*) (*Kingship* 1.76–82).

After his return home Heracles declares his preference for Lady Royalty over Tyranny. In this declaration Zeus recognizes the expression of Heracles' moral superiority, the reason he can be entrusted with the kingship over all humankind. Dio concludes that it is Heracles' moral superiority, not his famous "works," that makes him worthy of kingship (*Kingship* 1.84).

7. *The Qualities of a Good King*

For his description of a good king, Dio draws on examples from the Orient (Cyrus the Great, the Scythian kings, the pharaohs) (*Kingship* 2.77–78); at the same time, he attempts a general theory of kingship. The portrait he sketches of the good king matches Trajan perfectly, which Dio also admits (1.36).

What counts is the king's temperament (*Kingship* 1.3). He must possess all the virtues. He must be *temperate*. He must not be effeminate. The only music he should listen to is the *paean* (the warrior's charging song); the only dance he should dance is a quick step to dodge arrows in battle (2.57–62). Unfortunately, most kings are moved by a passionate spirit, either drunk on pleasures—either love of wealth or love of ambition—or on a combination of all three (*Kingship* 4.conclusion).

The king must be *prudent*. He must be a wise man in the strict intellectual sense of the term, that is, a man of truthfulness and *logos* (*Kingship* 1.26, 1.6–7). (A man without wisdom cannot be a competent ruler, neither of himself nor of anybody else [1.14].) The good king will pursue rhetoric and philosophy (1.18–24). Odysseus used wise speech to put an end to the quarrel between Agamemnon and Achilles (Dio casts both as rustic oafs, lacking common sense). Nevertheless, a king should not dedicate himself exclusively to speculation and study (1.25).

Added to this, kings are the sons of Zeus, inasmuch they share in his *omniscience* "and [Zeus] imparts it to whom he will" (*Kingship* 4.27). The good king has many friends; they are his eyes

133 The Sophist Prodicus of Ceos tells a similar tale recorded by Xenophon in his *Memorabilia* (2.1.21–34).

and ears in the kingdom and provide him with information about the goings-on (1.32). They enable him to be everywhere at the same time (3.104–08).[134]

He must have *fortitude*. His work is challenging; he has no relaxation or ease, unlike his subjects. He is like the pilot of a ship who remains fully alert so that his passengers can sleep peacefully while the ship sails over the reefs (*Kingship* 3.62–65). Just as the sun never tires of shining its light on humanity century after century, the king never dreams of abandoning his duties. The people live through him and suffer if he is bad (3.73–77)

Finally, the king is *just*. He is not to his subjects what a master (*despotes*) is to his slaves; he works for the good of all (*Kingship* 1.21); he prefers peace to war (1.27).

The consequence of all this is harmony between the people and the king. A king who is good and humane (*philanthropos*) enjoys the love—in the true sense of *erasthai*—of his subjects (*Kingship* 1.21–22). The love for a king is stronger than the love for a parent or someone close (3.111–15). Again, the city of men is a miniature reflection of the city of gods.

8. *The Government of Zeus Is the Model for Human Government*

Then Dio develops a Stoic theory of divine government. The king must respect and revere the "laws and ordinances of Zeus," just as the governors of the Roman provinces must obey the laws and statutes of the emperor.

> I might well speak next of the administration of the universe and tell how the world—the very embodiment of bliss and wisdom—ever sweeps along through infinite time in infinite cycles without cessation, guided by good fortune and a like power divine, and by foreknowledge and a governing purpose most righteous and perfect, and renders us like itself since, in consequence of the mutual kinship (*physis koine*) of ourselves and it, we are marshalled in order under one ordinance and law and partake of the same polity (*politeia*).
>
> He who honors and upholds this polity and does not oppose it in any way is law-abiding (*nominos*), devout (*theophilos*), and orderly (*kosimios*); he, however, who disturbs it, as far as that is possible to him, and violates it or does not know it, is lawless and disorderly, whether he be called a private citizen or a ruler, although the offence on the part of the ruler is far greater and more evident to all.
>
> Therefore, just as among generals and commanders of legions, cities or provinces, he who most closely imitates your ways [i.e., the ways of Trajan] and shows the greatest possible conformity with your habits would be by far your dearest comrade and friend, while he who showed antagonism or lacked conformity would justly incur censure and disgrace, and, being speedily removed from his office as well, would give way to better men better qualified to govern; so too among kings, since they, I ween, derive their powers and their stewardship from Zeus, the one who, keeping his eyes upon Zeus, orders and governs his people with justice and equity in accordance with the laws and ordinances of Zeus, enjoys a happy lot and a fortunate end. (*Kingship* 1.42–46).

The monarch in his kingdom is what God is in the world. He knows everything and takes care of everything. His logos provides for the cohesion and order of the community. His "ordering power" is expressed in the law. The law is the same throughout the kingdom, be it ever so vast as the cosmos itself.

---

[134] We saw earlier that Xenophon also develops this theme in his *Cyropedia*.

9. *The Myth of the Magi: The Monarch's Renewal of Society*

To explain the similarity of the monarch and God, Dio tells a myth that he says is learned in the secret rites of the Magi.

Dio's thought is syncretistic. If God is one, then all divine revelations to peoples the world over must coincide. Zoroaster, whose lessons the Magi teach, discovered the same truths revealed to Homer and Hesiod (*Borysthenitic* 39) He received these truths in a theophany not unlike the biblical "burning bush." He was on a mountain retreat when the mountain burst into flames; the Persians came to pray, and Zoroaster walked unharmed from the fire, explaining that the world is ordered and animated as follows.

The universe is propelled by a perpetual movement that keeps to the same cycles throughout all eternity (*Borysthenitic* 42). The movement comes from four divine chariots coursing the heavens in circles. The chariots correspond to the hierarchy of elements: fire, air, water, and earth. The outer chariot is pulled by a stead sacred to Zeus himself. It is "immeasurably superior in beauty, size and speed, since it has the outside track and runs the longest course" (43). It is a winged creature made of fire. The next horse, lesser than the first, bears the name of Hera; it is made of air. A third, lesser still to the second, is sacred to Poseidon; it is made of water. Finally, the last horse, the only one not to be winged, is made of earth; it is sacred to Hestia. It turns, yet it does not move, like the earth itself. These four horses are like a quadriga rounding the turn in the hippodrome: the inside horse hugs the marker while the other three race around him, the farther out the faster the pace.

This perpetual motion does not proceed without incident. It is affected by cyclical events, such as conflagrations and floods caused by the rebellion and excitement of the fire horse and water horse, respectively, which inflict disorder and panic on the other horses, and sometimes on the world itself. While these events are catastrophic for poor earthly creatures—as all myths attest—they really are little more than minor disturbances in the grand scheme of things, at least as far as the eternal movement of the quadriga is concerned. They do imply the total destruction of the world. The driver's action with the whip or goad quickly restores calm and order. Such incidents are even beneficial, since they allow the charioteer to rein in the steeds and resume a more regular pace.

There is, however, one particularly important event, rare though cyclical, when the quadriga is set ablaze and the horses "shift among themselves and interchange their forms." As Dio says, it is as if some magician had cast the horses in wax and the wax of the lesser horses melted under the effect of extreme heat, transferring their material to the ethereal horse.

This can be understood in the context of Stoic physics and its theory of *ekpyrosis,* the cosmic fire that will consume the world at the end of the Great Year). Everything comes down to fire. The Stoics did not consider divine fire destructive. They believed that fire ordered and impregnated everything. It was "creative." The Magi teach that the Great Year will end with a cosmic ejaculation, a burst of molten semen (as swift as thought, because it *is* thought) that will literally renew the world.

> It [the superior horse] became eager to generate [*dianemein*] and distribute everything and to make the orderly universe then existent once more far better and more resplendent because newer. And emitting a full flash of lightning, not a disorderly or foul one such as in stormy weather often darts forth, when the clouds drive more violently than usual, but rather pure and unmixed with any murk, it worked a transformation easily, with the speed of thought. But recalling Aphrodite and the process of generation, it tamed and relaxed itself and, quenching much of its light, it turned into fiery air of gentle warmth, and uniting with Hera and enjoying the most perfect wedlock, in sweet repose it emitted anew the full

> supply of seed for the universe. Such is the blessed marriage of Zeus and Hera of which the sons of sages sing in secret rites.[135]
>
> And having made fluid all his essence, one seed for the entire world, he himself moving about in it like a spirit that moulds and fashions in generation, then indeed most closely resembling the composition of the outer creatures, inasmuch as he might with reason be said to consist of soul and body, he now with ease moulds and fashions all the rest, pouring about him his essence smooth and soft and easily yielding in every part. And having performed his task and brought to completion, he revealed the existent universe as once more a thing of beauty and inconceivable loveliness, much more resplendent, indeed, than it appears today. For not only, I ween, are all other works of craftsmen better and brighter when fresh from the artistic hand of their maker, but also the younger specimens of plants are more vigorous than the old and altogether like young shoots. And indeed animals, too, are charming and attractive to behold right after their birth, not merely the most beautiful among them—colts and calves and puppies—but even the whelps of wild animals of most savage kind. (*Borysthenitic* 54–60)

This cosmic phenomenon has its equivalence in politics—and now we can understand why human government should model itself on divine government in ordinary and extraordinary circumstances.

Just as the divine charioteer uses the whip or the goad to rein in the panicky steeds, so the monarch must take firm hold of the reins and use routine acts of authority to keep a hold on the city of men. Like the material universe, the world of the city can weaken or tire and collapse into the disorders and dysfunctions that ordinary political action may not be able to rein in. Thus, the monarch, with Zeus as his example, will take all power into his hands and, guided only by the inspiration of his own thought and fully ignoring all earlier laws, he will be in a position to renew society entirely with radical measures of reorganization.

Dio's theory or theology of monarchy concurs with the popular, religious sentiment of the day whereby a new reign is actually the *re-creation of the world*. The monarch is a divinity: just as Zeus sees the need, at long cosmic intervals, to renew the living organism (*zoon*) of the universe, so too the monarch, as the earthly servant of Zeus, must from time to time establish new institutions and a new political order, especially when the city grows old and corrupt. Augustus succeeded in doing this in his age, just as Trajan did in the time of Dio. When everything seems corrupt and lost in the conventional institutions, the decisive action of one providential man is capable of renewing everything and bringing order to it again.

C. The Neopythagoreans: Diotogenes and Pseudo-Ecphantus

Let us turn now to the theories of kingship at the time of the Dominate.[136]

Two particularly interesting texts on kingship are found in the *Florilegium*, a compilation of texts by Stobaeus, dating probably from the second half of the fifth century AD. These texts are interesting because they provide detailed, innovative theories on what might be called the onto-

[135] A reference to the mystical, cosmic wedding—the "Sacred marriage," *Hieros Gamos*—celebrated in the mysteries. See the *Illiad* 14.294–96.

[136] *Translator's note:* Nemo quotes the French-language translations of Diotogenes and Pseudo-Ecphantus published by Louis Delatte, *Les traits de la Royauté d'Ecphante, Diotogene et Sthénidas*, Liege, Faculté de Philosophie et Lettres (Paris: Librairie E. Droz, 1942). Several years earlier, Erwin Goodenough produced an English-language translation of Stobaeus with the texts by Diotogenes and Pseudo-Ecphantus. See Erwin Goodenough, "The Political Philosophy of Hellenistic Kingship," in *Yale Classical Studies*, vol. 1, ed. Austin Harmon, 55–102 (New Haven: Yale University Press, 1928). We quote from this text.

logical foundations of monarchical power. Stobaeus attributed them to two unknown authors, Diotogenes and Ecphantus, calling them "Pythagoreans." Their texts can be dated to the third century AD, sometime during the reign of Aurelian. The authors no doubt sought the authority of older Pythagoreans in order to give their theories greater weight and antiquity (a Pythagorean by the name of Ecphantus lived in the fourth century BC, which is why we refer to Stobaeus's Ecphantus as "Pseudo-Ecphantus").[137]

1. *Diotogenes*

Diotogenes begins by posing an equation of sorts between kingship, the law, and justice: a king must never be a tyrant with arbitrary powers; he is the animate law of Hellenistic tradition. "The most just man would be king, and the most lawful would be most just. For without justice no one would be king, and without law [there would be no] justice. For justice is in the law, and the law is the source of justice. But the king is Animate Law, or is a legal ruler. So for this reason he is most just and most lawful."[138]

Next Dio enumerates the three principal duties of the king: military leadership, the dispensation of justice, and the cult of the gods (in short: war, justice, and religion).[139] The king's success in the performance of his three duties depends on his ability to pattern human government on the divine government of the *cosmos*. The king's leadership and command on earth, Diotogenes says, is the same as God's in heaven: the aim is to achieve *harmony:* "In judging and in distributing justice, whether as a whole in Public Law, or to individuals in Private Law, it is right for the king to act as does God in his leadership and command of the universe. On the one hand, in public matters the king is to bring the whole kingdom into harmony with his single rule and leadership, while private matters of detail must be brought into accord with this same harmony and leadership."

The parallel results in a genuine symmetry or equality of relations: "Now the king bears the same relation to the state as God to the world; and the state is in the same ratio to the world as the king is to God. For the state, made as it is by a harmonizing together of many different elements, is an imitation of the order and harmony of the world, while the king who has an absolute rulership, and is himself Animate Law, has been metamorphosed into a deity among men."

The metaphor of music, commonly used in Pythagorean thought, provides deeper insight into the duty of the king. Like the conductor of an orchestra, the king provides the pitch for the various elements of the state, who attune themselves to him and follow his beat. The king is

137 On Pythagoreanism, see above part 1, pp. 49–50, and part 2, pp. 312–13. Pythagoras lived in greater Greece in the fourth century BC. He left no writings and his direct followers very little. Consequently, a tradition of pseudoepigraphic Pythagorean writings flourished in Rome. Plato himself claimed inspiration from the Pythagoreans. Moreover, Platonism and Neoplatonism were constantly present in Rome; at times it was the dominant doctrine. Inventing "Pythagorean" texts is a way of being more Platonist than the Platonists themselves! As for political theories, we are faced with a special problem. We know that Pythagoras and his two successors, Alcmeon and Archytas, were not monarchists. They advocated a mixed form of government consistent with Pythagorean doctrine: in politics a harmony, defined by mathematical relations, is necessary between the various parts of society; the parallel in the human body is a balance between organs and tissue, in music a measured participation of the various notes of the scale. Now pure monarchy, in politics, would destroy harmony and order, just as unison destroys harmony in music. Thus, the presentation of monarchy in imperial Rome proposed by the third century authors Diotogenes and Pseudo-Ecphantus is a perversion of ancient Pythagoreanism, probably under the influence of late Platonism, and specifically Neoplatonism, which enjoyed the protection and encouragement of Gallienus.

138 All quotations in this section are from Stobaeus, *Florilegium* 4.7.61, 62, cited in Goodenough, "Political Philosophy," 65–73.

139 The re-inclusion of a religious duty in the public office of the king is noteworthy; the desire to have one man perform all three duties signals a regression in regard to the earlier division of sovereignty into several magistracies. We recall that Vernant, *The Origins of Greek Thought,* made this division a primary characteristic of the Greek city.

the giver of order and structure in the state and society; social order exists only through him. "The king should harmonize together [achieve *synarmoga* within] the well lawed city like a lyre. Knowing that the harmony of the multitude whose leadership God has given him ought to be attuned to himself, the king would begin by fixing in his own life the most just limitations and order of law."

Certain duties in regard to the social appearance of the *basileus* can be deduced from this. He must display his royal qualities outwardly: *majesty, might,* and *kindness.*

> [The] good king should present to the state proper attitudes in body and mind. He should impersonate the statesman and have an appearance of practicality so as not to seem to the mob as either harsh or despicable, but at once pleasant and yet watchful from every angle. And he will succeed in this if first he make an impression of majesty by his appearance and utterances, and by his looking the part of the ruler; if secondly, he be gracious both in conversation and in appearance, and in actual benefactions; and third, if he inspire fear in his subjects by his hatred of evil and by his punishments, by his speed of action and in general by his skill and industry in kingly duties. For majesty, a graciousness will make him popular and beloved; while the ability to inspire fear will make him terrible and unconquerable in his dealings with enemies, but magnanimous and trustworthy toward his friends.

Majesty is an attribute that allows the monarch to present himself as a god on earth, knowing that he is physically, ontologically, different from ordinary men. "Majesty must be one of his fixed attributes; he must do nothing base or worthy of the mob, but only things worthy of those who are admired, and to whom leadership and the power of the scepter belong; he must vie not with his inferiors or equals, but with his superiors."

When the *basileus* imitates God, it is so that men will imitate him. He is, in every respect, a model of life for them. "He must wrap himself about with such distinction and superiority in his appearance, in his thought life and reflections, and in the character of his soul, as well as in the actions, movements, and attitudes of his body. So he will succeed in putting into order those who look upon him, amazed at his majesty, at his self-control, and his fitness for distinction. For to look upon the good king ought to affect the souls of those who see him no less than a flute or harmony."

Whoever sees the king hears music and is morally transformed. This, no doubt, echoes Plato and the function he grants music in the *Republic* and the *Laws;* but this time the model to be imitated is not an Intelligible located in a separate world; it is incarnate in a man. Thus, Diotogenes spells out the contribution of *synamorga* (harmony) to society when everyone imitates the king. "Justice bears the same relation to communion [mutual relationship] as rhythm to motion and harmony to the voice; for justice is a good shared in common between the rulers and the ruled and is accordingly the harmonizing principle in the political community."

This system is, by the same token, quite subtle. The king, the centerpiece of the system, is not a blind, mechanical upholder of the law; he is especially attentive to the vulnerability of the least of his subjects; he is an orchestra conductor with a fine ear and gentle movements, fully aware of the danger of abruptness. "Equity and mercy share the throne of justice, the one softening the harshness of the injury, the other giving indulgence to those suffering from some delinquency. And the good king must be helpful to those who are in need, be grateful and not burdensome.... He must not be burdensome to any man, particularly not to the lowly and those in misfortune; for these, like men ill in body, are unable to bear a heavy load."

Are not the monarch's manifestations of majesty, strength, and indulgence in every respect "an imitation of divinity"? "For the gods, and especially Zeus, the ruler of all things, have such attributes."

2. *Pseudo-Ecphantus*

The author Stobaeus refers to as Ecphantus (our Pseudo-Ecphantus) develops ideas along similar lines to Diotogenes. He, too, establishes a close parallel between the purpose of God in the universe and that of the king on earth. But Pseudo-Ecphantus emphasizes the *distance* between the king and ordinary people.

a. The King Rules as He Contemplates Higher Worlds

According to Stoic doctrine, as Dio Chrysostom reminds us, the universe is a "living organism." It must have harmony, *synarmoga;* but in each of its *cosmic* regions there are different rulers. God assures harmony in the world of the stars and planets. A *daimon* does so in the region between the moon and earth. On earth, it is the king: "in our environment on the earth man has achieved the highest development, while it is the king who is most divine.... He is like the rest [of humankind] indeed in his earthly tabernacle, in as much as he is formed out of the same material; but he is fashioned by the supreme Artificer, who in making the king used himself as an Archetype."[140]

The king, because he is made of a higher essence than others, can communicate with higher worlds, and this is the power that enables him to organize society on earth. A blinding light radiates from the king, or rather from his royal function; only beings of royal heritage can contemplate such light, like the eagle—the king of birds—which alone can stare straight into the sun (an ancient topos).

> Royalty is explained in the fact that by its divine character and excessive brilliance it is hard to behold, except for those who have a legitimate claim. For bastard usurpers are confuted by complete bedazzlement, and by such vertigo as assails those who climb to a lofty height. But royalty is something with which people can live, if those who aspire to it are properly attuned to it, and are able to use it. Royalty is then a sure and incorruptible thing, very hard for a human being to achieve by reason of its exceeding divinity. And he who stands in it [i.e., the king] must be pure and radiant in nature, so that he may not tarnish its exceeding brightness by his own blemishes. (Stobaeus, *Florilegium*)

The king's superiority over ordinary people is such that royal power is irresponsible (the king is not obedient to law, he *is* the law). The wrongdoings of others are recognized and judged by their leaders, whereas the king's only judge is God. "In the case of ordinary men, if they sin, their most holy purification is to make themselves like the rulers, whether it be law or king who orders affairs where they are.... As for kings, if they had need of a higher principle, because the weakness of their nature led them to sinfulness; they can find comfort not in time or by wandering, but immediately by directing their gaze to the proper end."

The king, in search of an ideal, needs only observe how God rules the cosmos, since he has been given the capability to contemplate God. Thus, mystical contemplation becomes a normal mode of royal government (this idea will be found again in Eusebius of Caesarea). And what his contemplation of divine government reveals is that the stars and the planets are obedient to God and do not revolt. And this is what the king must obtain from his subjects. When the king succeeds, he resonates with God, and all the degrees of Being are, so to speak, in agreement.

> The greatness of cosmic order consists in the fact that nothing unruled can be found, and that it is in a sense the teacher of rulership. For its beauty is revealed straightway if the one

[140] The texts in this section and section b are from Stobaeus, *Florilegium* 4.7.64–66; quoted in Goodenough, "Political Philosophy," 75–89.

> [the king] who imitates [God] in his virtue is beloved at once by him whom he is imitating and by his subjects. For no one who is beloved by God would be hated by men, since neither the stars nor the whole cosmos are at enmity with God, but rather if they hated the leader they would not obediently follow him. But it is the very fact that God rules well which causes good rulership to apply to both the king and his subjects.

Thus, the condition for concord and harmony in the political community is a cosmic communication between the heavenly King and the earthly king. When the king establishes harmony among men, he does so because he himself is in harmony with God and the cosmos.

b. Economic Community and Political Community

Pseudo-Ecphantus adds the following idea. The political harmony a king establishes among his subjects, when he patterns his government on "love" and "communion" with the heavenly King, is of a higher nature than the mutual assistance earthly beings provide one another in the satisfaction of their material needs. Since the king and God are perfect beings, they have neither wants nor needs; their "love" is pure, not utilitarian; their only motive is harmony. When the king succeeds in communicating such harmony (in the pure sense) to his subjects, they surpass *economic* relations and establish a genuine *political* community:

> For apart from love and communion existence is impossible, as may be seen also in the case of bodies politic, leaving out of account what is ordinarily called communion. For such ordinary communion (mutual dependence) is beneath the nature of God and King, since they stand in no such need of each other as to be compelled to labor together to satisfy their wants and so render mutual assistance; for both God and King are perfect in virtue. But the love which shares in a common purpose in a city is a copy of the unanimity of the universe.

Aristotle observed that the purpose of politics is not to "live" but to "live well." Christian theologians commented that the shepherd-king not only takes his flock to pasture to ensure its earthly tranquility and prosperity; he also guides it to its supernatural destination. Pseudo-Ecphantus agrees with Diotogenes on this point: the king is responsible for the moral perfection of his subjects; the "love" or harmony that he establishes among them is directed toward a higher purpose.

To summarize, (1) a political bond is, strictly speaking, a "love [friendship] that shares in a common purpose"; (2) this bond is of a higher nature than mutual assistance and economic relations; (3) only the king can create this bond among men, the idea for which comes to him because of his special communion with God.

c. Spontaneous Social Order

For harmony to be perfect, it must be communicated through imitation, similar to musicians when they follow their orchestra conductor. Another innovative thesis arises from this: in normal circumstances, political power does not require *persuasion* or *coercion*. Political order is a peace-loving order, created by the king's imitation of God and the people's imitation of the king.

When everyone imitates the king—a paragon of harmony—social life is spontaneously harmonious, such that neither coercive institutions nor institutions of ideological control are needed to establish or maintain order. The miracle of harmony is that it conciliates the existence of a social bond and amiable cooperation among men and the maintenance of the total independence of each individual. The reason is that in pursuing the Good, each person obeys his own "virtue" and becomes an integral part of the objective harmonious order of the universe.

For the king's subjects, to imitate the Good is to be free:

> The resemblance which each man can achieve [through imitation of God or the king] consists in independence. For there is not one group of virtues which do what is pleasing to God, and another which imitate Him. Now the earthly king would be just as independent as the rest of us (by imitating God). For in making himself like God he would make himself like the Most Powerful, and everyone who tried to be like him.... Now when matters are put upon subjects by force and necessity their individual zeal for imitation is sometimes diminished, for without good will imitation is impossible, and nothing diminishes good will like fear.

Persuasion and coercion in government are expressions of a remnant of human weakness. "Oh, that it were possible to put from human nature all need for obedience! For the fact that as mortal animals we are not exempt from it is the basest trace of our earthiness, inasmuch as a deed of obedience is very close to being one of necessity; for what just escapes being brought about by the one is produced by the other. For whatever things can by their own nature use the Beautiful, have no occasion for obedience, as they have no fear of necessity."

God Himself rules the *cosmos* in this manner, that is, without persuasion or coercion:

> God, who has neither ministers nor servants, makes no use of anyone in giving His orders, nor does He crown or honor those who obey Him, or disgrace those who disobey; not such are the means he uses to extend his personal rule over a realm so vast. Rather, it seems to me, by offering Himself as one worthy of imitation God implants a desire to imitate Him in every man who has a nature like God's. God is Himself good, and to be so is His sole and easy function, while those who imitate Him do so as a consequence all things better than other people.

This, then, is the political program of monarchy: it should provide a higher model of behavior so completely in conformity with the Good that people imitate it spontaneously and live in perfect harmony withone another and with the entire universe.

D. Eusebius of Caesarea: Tricennial Orations

Although he was a Christian (and one of the most important of the church fathers), the ideas of Eusebius on monarchy must be presented in the continuation of pagan Greco-Roman political ideas. Moreover, his conception of monarchy is less specifically Christian than a prolongation of political thought on kingship since Dio Chrysostom. The monarchical structure of the state gains legitimacy in reference to the monarchical structure of the cosmos itself; since both structures are fundamentally hierarchical, it is inevitable that ideas of equality under the law and personal liberty tend to disappear. In fact, Eusebius casts the Roman Empire—now permanently focused on the Orient—in the ancient mold of native Hellenistic monarchies, which preserved many of the features of the pre-civic sacred monarchies of the East. He fully expresses the political philosophy of the Dominate. For centuries this philosophy survived in the "Christian" form of Caesaropapism in Byzantium.

1. *Life*

Eusebius was probably born in the early 260s.[141] He studied under the martyr Pamphilius of Caesarea, himself a student of Origen (Origen's magnificent library was continued by Pamphilius in Caesarea and was at the disposal of Eusebius). During the early decades of his life, before

[141] Material in this section is from H. A. Drake, *In Praise of Constantine: A Historical Study and New Translation of Eusebius' Tricennial Orations* (Berkeley and Los Angeles: University of California Press, 1976), and Eusebius, *Church*

Diocletian launched his anti-Christian persecutions, Christianity developed peacefully. At this time, Pamphilius and his school believed that the church and the Empire existed to fulfill God's plan. However, in 303 AD Diocletian launched his persecutions and Pamphilius was martyred. During the ten years the persecutions lasted, Eusebius, whose faith never wavered, wrote his *Church History* (also known as *Ecclesiastical History*), the first complete history of the Christian church since its origins, the single most important record of church history for this period even today. He finished the work by 313 AD. Eusebius, who became the bishop of Caesarea in 311, believed his life had been spared during the persecutions so that he could serve the renewal of Christianity. His apologetic writing intensified: he wrote a *Preparation for the Gospel* (*Praeparatio evangelica*) in 15 books (a refutation of pagan beliefs), and a *Proof of the Gospel* (*Demonstratio evangelica*) in 20 books (a refutation of Judaism).

Then the Arian controversies erupted. Eusebius subscribed to the Nicene statement, but some of the council's formulations gave him reservations. Gradually, he sided with the Oriental prelates, who were under attack from the intolerant anti-Arian, Athanasius of Alexandria. His support for the oriental prelates sowed seeds of doubt about his orthodoxy.[142]

However, Eusebius expressed such a strong desire to make theological concessions in order to preserve the unity of the church that he came to the attention of the emperor and won his sympathy. Apparently Constantine did not think Eusebius a very capable politician and opposed his transfer to the politically sensitive bishopric of Antioch and its unruly inhabitants. He did, however, consult him on biblical matters and, in 336 AD, entrusted him with an important *Oration*, which we will discuss at some length, as it expresses the official political ideology of the Empire in these years.

Eusebius dedicated himself to immensely important and wide-ranging intellectual undertakings. He died in 339 or 340 AD.

2. *Work*

In addition to the works cited above, Eusebius wrote a *Chronicon* (a universal history), apologetic works (*Against Hierocles, Against Porphyry* [two Neoplatonist authors]); *On Divine Manifestation* [*Peri theophaneias*]); polemical works (*Apology for Origen, Against Marcellus* [of Ancyra]); a *General Elementary Introduction* (to the Christian faith); a compilation of prophetic texts with commentaries, an essay *On the Celebration of Easter,* critical and exegetical works (critical editions of biblical texts, biblical dictionaries: biographies, place names, etc.), commentaries on Isaiah, the Psalms, the Gospel according to Luke, the First Letter to the Corinthians; *Orations* and *Letters*; and, to complete the list, various political writings.

3. *Political Writings*

Upon Constantine's death in 337, Eusebius wrote a *Life of Constantine,* a sort of hagiographic eulogy for the deceased emperor. Constantine is portrayed as a visionary enemy of paganism, the willful founder of a Christian empire forever bound to the church. Here Eusebius mentions Constantine's "conversion" and evokes the "Chi Rho," the miraculous Christian sign (a combination of the Greek letters *chi* and *rho* forming a cross). Under the banner of this sign, Constantine's army was victorious in battle against his rival Maximin Daia, the Augustus of the East. Appended to Eusebius's *Life of Constantine* is also an oration probably by Constantine himself. In it the

---

History; Life of Constantine the Great; Oration in Praise of Constantine, a revised translation with prolegomena by Ernest Cushing Richardson (1890; repr. Grand Rapids, MI: Eerdmans, 1986); hereafter cited in the text.

142 Eusebius belongs to a group of church fathers—among whom are Origen and Tertullian—whose thinking contributed greatly to the formulation of Christian doctrine, but whose imperfect orthodoxy excluded them from canonization.

emperor provides a Christian interpretation of Virgil's Fourth Eclogue. In publishing this work, Eusebius no doubt intended an ambitious philosophy of history: when Augustus established his pagan empire in Rome, he only laid the foundations for a Christian empire in Byzantium destined to save the world under Constantine. Together with Lactantius, another Christian intellectual in the emperor's circle, Eusebius set out to formulate the principal political directives of the new regime, just as earlier Horace and Virgil had formulated the ideology of the pagan Principate.

Eusebius may have put more words in Constantine's mouth than he actually spoke or thought. Constantine certainly converted to Christianity during his lifetime, but perhaps relatively late; he had pagan subjects he did not want to shock (the anti-pagan persecutions under the reign of Theodosius and Diocletian's parallel anti-Christian persecutions lay in the future). His principal concern was to maintain peace throughout the Empire and to win acceptance for the measures of appeasement in his Edict of Milan (313 AD). Thus, even after his final conversion (probably in 326, following the miraculous discovery of Golgotha and the Holy Sepulchre in Jerusalem), his goal continued to be the worship in his official presence of the "one God," the Supreme Sovereign of the universe, and his "servant" Logos (but not the Christ of the Gospels): these abstract theological notions were acceptable to the most enlightened pagans and to Christians alike.

Pagan philosophers, as we saw, had converted long ago to the idea of a single God, supreme sovereign of the universe. Moreover, the emperor's pagan entourage had little taste for the blood sacrifices of popular paganism, abhorred by Christians as well. Therefore, the subject of disagreement with Christians was neither monotheism nor the rejection of sacrifices. The real issue was dogma, like the dogma of Incarnation, the death of God on the cross, or the resurrection of the flesh. If the court of Constantine could be discreet on these issues, it might be possible to build a bridge between Christians and pagans.

The only thing that truly mattered to Constantine—and that could encourage educated and influential pagans at court and in high public office to accept his policy of appeasement with the Christians—was Christianity's *explicit acknowledgment and acceptance of the Roman Empire, including the totality of its political and social institutions;* and that, no matter who this one God and his Son, Logos, were, the emperor was their representative on earth, vested with earthly, spiritual, and temporal powers, ruling in their name with the benefit of their supernatural support. But while Celsius of Milan had clamored for these assurances, and Tertullian, Origen, and the other theologians of the early church refused, Eusebius of Caesarea accepted them and even theorized them (though this official ideology was probably not the actual thought of Eusebius).

Eusebius delivered his celebrated oration *De laudibus Constantine* ("In Praise of Constantine")[143] in the presence of the emperor and his court in 336 AD in Constantinople.

4. *Tricennial Orations*

In his oration Eusebius announces that he will deviate from the well-trodden path. Other orators lauded Constantine for his political virtues. Eusebius knows that the emperor bears responsibility for both spiritual and political concerns. Therefore, Eusebius will speak only to listeners who show an interest in the spiritual side of Imperial government and he will leave the others to "stand outside the sacred precincts."[144] "So let those who have penetrated the sanctuary of

[143] Modern scholarship has shown that under this one title tradition had erroneously compiled two orations by Eusebius; one delivered on July 25, 336, in Constantinople on the occasion of the jubilee or thirtieth anniversary of the emperor's reign (the emperor attended the event in person); the other had been delivered a year earlier in Jerusalem on the occasion of the inauguration of Constantine's monument at the Holy Sepulchre (an event that the emperor did not attend). We discuss the oration of 336 AD, the only one to concern the political theory of interest here.

[144] The reference is to the imperial palace, not the church. Moreover, his audience was composed of laity. As we know, imperial power itself went by the term "sacred" power.

the holy palace, that innermost, most inaccessible of places, having barred the gate to profane hearing, narrate the sovereign's ineffable mysteries to those alone who are initiated in these things.... Let the oracles of learned men... teach us in these ceremonies about sovereignty itself, about the Highest Sovereign and the holy escort around the Ruler of All" (Eusebius, *Tricennial Orations,* Prologue, secs. 4–5).[145]

a. The Supreme God and His Only Son, Logos

This will be a celebration of the Supreme Sovereign:[146] He whose "throne is the vault of the heavens, while the earth is footstool for His feet."[147] The Supreme Sovereign remains hidden by the stars and celestial armies; he is surrounded by hosts of angels, archangels, and holy spirits who draw sustenance from the "ever-flowing springs of light." He is master of the order of the world. Eusebius takes care to point out that this invisible God is higher than the visible sun to which Constantine had previously dedicated a cult. Now the earthly sovereign and his sons, the Caesars, laud the Supreme Sovereign; likewise, people of every race and creed, regardless of their divisions and separate opinions, recognize the one and only God. The entire universe, in fact—all the animals, plants, minerals, rivers, the deepest seas, the sun, the moon—recognizes that it is ruled by the law emanating from God, whose "will and word" order the All, the movements of the firmament, and the beauties of the earth (Eusebius, *Tricennial Orations* 1.1–4).

Coeternal with the sovereign lord is the Logos, God's only Son, who is second to him and mediator between God and the created world.[148] Because how could the Supreme Sovereign and his attributes be perceived and comprehended by humans, who possess only physical senses? "Who has looked on the face of Justice with his physical senses? So how did the concepts of legitimate authority occur to solid flesh and blood? Who made known to those on earth Ideas, which are invisible and formless, or Essence, incorporeal and shapeless? So there had to be a medium for these things, the one, all-pervading Logos of God, the Father of the rational and intellectual faculty in men, alone endowed with the Father's divinity, who channels the paternal emanations into His own progeny" (Eusebius, *Tricennial Orations* 4.1–2).

The Logos created the earth and all humankind. He created them in the image and likeness of the Father so that men have faculties similar to, yet very far from God's. Thus, humankind is able to perceive something of divine reality. "Hence [from the Logos] the natural and instinctive reasoning powers in all men, alike in Greek and barbarian; hence the concepts of Reason and Wisdom; hence the seeds of Prudence and Justice;[149] hence apprehension of skills; hence knowledge of Virtue and the sweet name of Wisdom, and noble passion for the training of philosophy; hence knowledge of all goodness and beauty; hence the ability to conceive of God Himself, and a life worthy of God's service; hence man's regal force and irresistible sway over everything on earth" (*Tricennial Orations* 4.2).

The Father and the Son preside over a court of heavenly hosts. "Heavenly armies encircle Him, an infinite number of supernatural troops, including God's attendant angels and those invisible

---

[145] In this prologue, Eusebius uses vocabulary to evoke the atmosphere of an initiation into the mysteries; the context is more pagan than Christian.

[146] In what follows, the expression "supreme sovereign" can apply either to God or to the emperor. It is a translation from the Greek *mega basileus,* "great king." Sovereignty translates *basileia* ("kingship").

[147] This is biblical imagery. See Isaiah 66:1; Acts 7:49.

[148] Eusebius introduces a Christian notion here with an Arian nuance: it echoes the Neoplatonist doctrine of "emanations," according to which a descending hierarchy of entities (Intelligence, Soul, and the World) emanates from the One; Eusebius's words are intended to avoid outraging pagan monotheists.

[149] The reader will recall that this is the explanation why, in the opinion of the Stoics, we as human beings are able to know natural law. See above, pp. 187–88, 289–90.

spirits within heaven who see to the order of the whole cosmos—over all of whom Logos takes precedence as a kind of prefect of the Supreme Sovereign" (*Tricennial Orations* 3.6).

The fact that the Logos is compared with the "prefect" (*hyparchos*), chief minister or vizier of the Roman emperor in the period of the Low Empire, shows the strict parallel in the mind of Eusebius between the two hierarchies of heavenly and earthly powers. God is assisted by his Son, who commands the universe and humankind in God's name. The emperor is assisted by his prefect, who oversees the administration of the Empire in the emperor's name. God on high is attended by angels and archangels, and by "holy spirits," who are to the Supreme Sovereign what the spear-bearer (*doryphorus*) or bodyguard is to the Byzantine emperor. The heavenly host are separated from the cosmos by a curtain, hiding them from view. The imperial court is also hidden from its subjects by a curtain.[150] It is also said that the sun and the moon and the stars in the celestial vault are to God in heaven what the emperor's torchbearers and bejeweled robes are to the imperial court on earth.[151]

The Logos has a manifestly *soteriological* vocation: he will lead his creation (humankind) to salvation, even descending to earth to assemble them together. Here Eusebius makes a subtle reference to Incarnation, not to the Cross. "He [the Logos] even came Himself—yes, the Father of His children did not shrink from coming into contact with mortals. Tending His own seeds and reviewing the commitments made from above. He preached to all to partake of the heavenly kingdom. He invites and exhorts all to be ready for the journey above, and to have prepared a proper garment for the call"[152] (*Tricennial Orations* 4).

b. Royal Power

The status and role of political power are thought through from the starting point of this cosmic theology and salvific economy. The analogy between the two reigns and two kings is very close and can be made on several registers:

> [1.] The Only-Begotten Logos [Son] of God endures with His Father as co-ruler from ages with no beginning to ages with no end. Similarly, His friend, supplied from above by royal streams and confirmed in the name of a divine calling, rules on earth for long periods of years.
> [2.] As the Universal Savior[153] renders the entire heaven and earth and highest kingdom fit for His Father, so His friend, leading his subjects on earth to the Only-Begotten and Savior Logos, makes them suitable for His kingdom.
> [3.] Again, our common Universal Savior, by invisible and divine power, keeps the rebellious powers—all those who used to fly through the earth's air and infect men's souls—at a distance, just as a good shepherd keeps wild beasts from his flock. And His friend, armed

[150] In Orthodox Catholicism a screen separates the "iconostasis," where the holy mysteries occur, from the body of the church, where the worshippers stand.

[151] Was the hierarchical structure of the Byzantine court perhaps inspired by the Christian theologians' descriptions of the heavenly kingdom, or did the influence perhaps run in the opposite direction? Religious structures and political frameworks mirror each other and entwine. This is not exclusive to the oriental Christian world. Certain elements of the Catholic ritual are undoubtedly borrowed from the Roman imperial cult: genuflection, incensing, sanctuary lamps, the practice of covering one's hands to perform a sacred act or to cover a sacred object (e.g., a paten), altar servers during the mass (e.g., candle bearers, incense bearers), and so on; all of these "rites of honor" are holdovers from the Roman monarchy, and the Roman Empire itself borrowed them in part from oriental court practices. Other elements of Catholic ritual are borrowed from the Orient through the direct channel of the Bible.

[152] This alludes to the white garment of the catechumenate, which Constantine himself donned on the eve of his death, casting off the purple robe, the attribute of his imperial power.

[153] That is, the Logos. As for the king, he will be a "savior" at a time and place to come. The Greek monarch traditionally held several titles: for example, savior (*soter*) and benefactor (*evergetes*).

against his enemies with standards[154] from Him above, subdues and chastises the visible opponents of truth by the law of combat.[155]

[4.] The Logos, being the Pre-Existent and Universal Savior, has transmitted to His followers rational and redeeming seeds (*logika kai soteriode spermata*),[156] and thereby makes them rational and at the same time capable of knowing His Father's kingdom. And His friend, like some interpreter of the Logos of God, summons the whole human race to knowledge of the Higher Power, calling in a great voice that all can hear and proclaiming for everyone on earth the laws of genuine piety.[157]

[5.] The Universal Savior throws wide the heavenly gates of His Father's kingdom to those who depart hence for there; the other, in imitation of the Higher Power, has cleansed all the filth of godless error from the kingdom on earth, and invites bands of holy and pious men into the royal chambers, taking care to preserve intact each and every one of all those entrusted to his care. (*Tricennial Orations* 2.1–5)

Thus, humankind must live in a monarchy. The same autocracy that reigns in heaven must also reign on earth. Like the one God in heaven above, the one king reigns on earth below, where he decrees his one law. The earthly king models his conduct on the example of the one and only heavenly God.

> Thus outfitted in the likeness of the kingdom of heaven, he pilots affairs below with an upward gaze, to steer by the archetypal form.[158] He grows strong in his model of monarchic rule, which the Ruler of All [*panbasileus*] has given to the race of man alone of those on earth. For this is the law of royal authority, the law which decrees one rule over everybody.[159] Monarchy excels all other kinds of constitution and government. For rather do anarchy and civil war result from the alternative, a polyarchy based on equality. For which reason there is One God, not two or three or even more.[160] For strictly speaking, belief in many gods is godless. There is one Sovereign, and His *Logos* and royal law (*nomos basilikos*) is one, not expressed in words or syllables nor eroded by time in books or tables, but the living and actual God the *Logos*, who directs His Father's kingdom for all those under and beneath Him. (*Tricennial Orations* 3.5–6)

On earth as well, there can be only one king and one law; though less perfect than the Supreme Sovereign, they aspire to the same unity and harmony; otherwise, anarchy will prevail.[161] Later,

---

[154] Probably a reference to Constantine's sign, the Chi Rho Cross.

[155] The political *opponent* becomes the adversary of God, and opposition to God is a sin; consequently, the dissident is designated as a victim to the sacrificial mob.

[156] We recognize the Stoic idea of *logoi spermatikoi*. In addition to the seeds of reason, Eusebius's God also plants seeds of salvation in each creature.

[157] Thus, the emperor is the pastor, preacher, prophet, and priest of humanity. He holds indistinctly spiritual power and temporal power (the Bible separates them, as we shall see).

[158] Drake notes: "In the courtyard of Rome's Palazzo dei Conservatori on the Capitoline Hill stand the remains of a statue of Constantine the Great." The enormous head, entirely preserved, measures almost two meters, depicting a solemn, meditative Constantine: "[his eyes] are fixed upward, away from the cares of this world, in an eternal gaze on the heavens" (*In Praise of Constantine* 3).

[159] Monotheism is the foundation of monarchy. The same reasons justify the one and the other. This explains the predicament for some created by the Nicene statement on the Trinity; in one sense, it is too "democratic," with its strict equality between the divine persons. Eusebius is more comfortable with a semi-Arian interpretation, which maintains a strict hierarchy with one supreme God, the Father.

[160] This may be a criticism of tetrarchy, the system of government established by Diocletian. Constantine did everything he could to eliminate it.

[161] This is the traditional idea of the *logos empsychos* king (the living or animate law). In their intention (spirit) and form (letter), all explicit laws, oral and written, betray the spirit of the king by their resolve and externality. Only the king can cause the spirit to prevail over the letter.

Eusebius observes that polytheism leads to civil war; but by embracing monotheism, the emperor establishes peace among men. In the mind of Eusebius, it appears that the earthly monarchy of the Roman *basileus* is quasi universal; he is called to rule over the whole world and all humanity, even beyond the actual borders of the Empire.

c. The Qualities of the King, True Copy of the Logos; the Vices of the Tyrant, False Copy

The king is able to perform his function as sovereign because the Logos has blessed him with superior abilities. Eusebius explains this with traditional arguments: "God's friend... [has] been furnished by God with natural virtues and received in his soul the emanations from that place. His ability to reason has come from the Universal Logos, his wisdom from communion with Wisdom, goodness from contact with the Good, and justness from his association with Justice. He is prudent in the ideal of Prudence, and from sharing in the Highest Power has he courage" (*Tricennial Orations* 5.1).[162]

He who aspires to rule must pattern his virtues on the divine archetype. He who strays from these virtues and follows the wrong model, or creates a false copy, has "in place of reason and wisdom, the ugliest of all things, irrationality." He is not fit to govern and will be a source of anarchy, war, and bloodshed. He may be able to control his empire with despotic power, but he can never be called sovereign in the proper sense.

Like Plato in the *Republic,* Eusebius describes the tyrant as someone whose soul is exposed to chaotic passions and "malignant masters." The true *Autokrator* is "above care for money, stronger than the passion for women, victor of physical pleasures and demands" (*Tricennial Orations* 5.4). He is a "philosopher-king" (5.4). Though he rules on earth, he aspires to ascend to the spiritual kingdom of God and prays to the heavenly Father night and day. He knows that his earthly rule is "a small and fleeting authority over a mortal and temporary life... not much greater than the rule exercised by goatherds or shepherds or cowherds" (5.4). Only, as emperor, his job is harder and the creatures difficult to satisfy.

The king is more devoted to heaven than to the herd; this is why he can lead the latter. He is not troubled by his entourage of minions and heavily armed men. He is not vainglorious.

> The cheers of the crowds and the voices of flatterers he holds more a nuisance than a pleasure, because of his stern character and the upright rearing of his soul.[163]... He laughs at his raiment, interwoven with gold, finished with intricate blossoms, his royal robe with the diadem itself, when he sees the people astounded and marvelling at the sight, like children at a hobgoblin. He himself has no experience, no such sensation, but through acquaintance with the divine he clothes his soul in raiment embroidered with temperance and justice, piety and the remaining virtues, truly the fitting attire for a sovereign. (5.6)

d. Eternity and Numbers; the Sign of Salvation

Such is the model of the ideal sovereign, a man endowed with the highest virtues, chosen and protected by God. It remains to be seen how Constantine measures up to it.

Eusebius shows that Constantine clearly enjoys divine favor, since God has granted him and his sons long years of rule. God also gave Constantine the opportunity to associate one of his sons in the service of the Empire for each ten-year period. Now the fourth decade of his rule has

[162] We recognize the list of cardinal virtues from pagan natural morality, but missing are the theological virtues, i.e., the specific virtues of the Gospel.

[163] Constantine was, on the contrary, sensitive to flattery. Eusebius uses a common rhetorical device here—the inversion of an attribute—to rebuke Constantine politely for his weakness.

begun, and all four of his sons have been "Caesars."[164] Constantine has sent each of them out to the four corners of the world to rule, like the rays of the sun shining on the farthest reaches of the earth. They are like four colts pulling the royal chariot, which Constantine leads "with the reins of holy harmony and concord" (3.1–4).

Eusebius interprets such earthly joy as a sign of the everlasting felicity promised to Constantine, a reward for his lengthy and commendable service as sovereign. To make his case, he uses Neopythagorean arguments in the knowledge that his listeners will recognize the references.

Eternity is formless and beyond man, but not beyond God, who defines it with all kinds of numbers. God guides eternity with his creative wisdom of numbers like a horseman commands his mount with harness and reins: "He [God] rides it [eternity] from above... bridled as if to reins by bonds of an indescribable wisdom. By punctuating it with complete harmony of months and dates, seasons and years, and the reciprocating intervals of nights and days, he circumscribes it with manifold boundaries and measurements.... He has delimited it with all kinds of numbers, rendering the diversity in it many-formed instead of formless" (*Tricennial Orations* 6.4).

The first numbers are the unit, the dual, the triad, and the "double dualed" (four). These numbers order the world, because matter is one; the dual is all-encompassing substance and form; the triad is space in its dimensions of breadth, length, and depth; and four is the number of elements—earth, water, air, and fire. The quarternion (1 + 2 + 3 + 4 = 10) produces the decade. Everything else derives from this; three decades make up the month, four times three months make the four seasons and one year, and so on.

The *triad* is particularly remarkable: "The triad is akin to this [the unit], similarly indivisible and inseparable, since it is the first to be composed of even and odd numbers. For the first even number, combining with the unit, produces the first naturally uneven number, the triad. And the triad first revealed Justice, pointing out the way of equality, inasmuch as it partakes equally of a beginning, a middle, and an end. It is an image of the mysterious, all-holy, and royal triad [the Trinity]" (*Tricennial Orations* 6.13). Equally remarkable is the *decade,* since it can be used to compose all the other numbers, in keeping with the principles of the decimal system.

Our reasoning, says Eusebius, has reached its end. Today is the thirtieth anniversary celebration of Constantine's rule: the number 30 is made up of these perfect numbers. Through these numbers we can fathom the eternity promised to Constantine. He deserves the reward of eternity, Eusebius notes emphatically; his work has been truly great. He put an end to the anti-Christian persecutions and established the peace of the church. He fought against idolatry, ridiculed the ancient gods, and destroyed their statues.[165] He razed an Aphrodite temple on Mount Lebanon.[166] Through the denial of the plurality of the gods, wars have vanished from the Empire; now that the "madness" of polytheism has ceased, the blood of men is no longer shed. Only an exceptional man could have achieved such an exceptional change of history.

Moreover, he could not have produced these achievements without the help of Providence. This help is palpable in the Chi Rho Cross—a sign of salvation and symbol of eternal life—revealed to Constantine in miraculous circumstances. Here is how Eusebius tells the episode in his *Life of Constantine.*

---

[164] Eusebius takes some liberties with dates, and he conveniently passes over the fact that Constantine had his eldest son, Crispus, executed in 326 AD.

[165] In order to recover precious metals for a better use.

[166] In Aphaca (modern-day Efqa). For specifics on this episode, see Pierre Chuvin, *A Chronicle of the Last Pagans* (Cambridge, MA: Harvard University Press, 1990). Chuvin's book provides accounts of even graver pagan persecutions perpetrated by Constantine's successors.

In 310 AD, upon hearing that his armies had defeated the enemy in his name, though he was personally absent from the battlefield, Constantine had a vision of Apollo with his own features. He concluded that he was the blood relation and protégé of the sun god. Then, about noon, he saw a cross of light in the heavens, above the sun, bearing the inscription: *in hoc signo vinces,* "In this sign, you shall conquer." When night fell, the Christ of God appeared to him in his sleep and commanded him to mark the shields of his soldiers with this same sign. Constantine obeyed and defeated Maxentius at the Battle of the Milvian Bridge on October 28, 312. In a subsequent battle Licinius defeated the persecutor Maximin Daia under the same banner. Thus, Constantine had proof, so to speak, that the one true God was neither a pagan deity nor the sun, but Christ. Immediately after these events, the Edict of Milan was decreed.

There is no certain agreement as to what the sign actually was. Apparently it combined the Greek letters X (chi) and P (rho), corresponding to the first two letters of the word "Christ" and graphically presentable in the form of a cross. However, the graphic presentation could also portray a solar symbol: the sun rising over the mountains (it could also be a Germanic or Celtic symbol known to Constantine and his armies, who had spent long years with him in Gaul and Brittany). No doubt this ambiguity served Constantine's "ecumenical" purpose: Christians saw the cross in the sign; pagans recognized the emperor and his house, both concluded that the emperor must be God's protégé.[167]

Eusebius, who of course prefers the Christian interpretation of these events, notes that Constantine comported himself as the true *spiritual* leader of his people.

> Thus indeed did the sovereign himself—incredible as it sounds—become the teacher of rules of worship to his army, and he transmitted pious prayers in accordance with divine ordinances—to raise their outstretched hands above toward heaven while fixing the eyes of the mind on the highest point, the Heavenly Sovereign, and then to invoke Him in their prayers as Giver of Victory, Savior, Guardian, and Rescuer. In fact, he even ordained one especial day of prayer, the one which is truly supreme and first, belonging to the Lord and to salvation, the day, indeed, both of light and of life, named for immortality and every good.[168] He himself practises what he preaches, and celebrates his Savior in his royal chambers. (*Tricennial Orations* 9.10–11)

Constantine built many beautiful churches to the glory of God throughout the Empire, especially in Palestine and Constantinople. In Antiochus, he built the Golden Octagon. In Jerusalem, at the site of the Holy Sepulchre itself, he built an enormous house of prayer dedicated to the sign of salvation; the ornaments of this house, says Eusebius, are beyond description. He also built other monuments in Palestine, all of which were sacred to the "Saving Sign":

> the Sign that, in turn, gives him compensation for his piety, augments his entire house and line, and strengthens the throne of his kingdom for long cycles of years, dispensing the fruits of virtue to his good sons, his family, and their descendants. And surely this is the greatest proof of the power of the One he honors, that He has handled the scales of justice so impartially and has awarded to each party its due. On the heels of those who beleaguered the houses of prayer followed the wages of their sin, and straightaway they

[167] A vast literature exists about Constantine's Chi Rho Cross. Questions remain about the sign itself, its religious meaning and Constantine's use of it. Some have suggested that the Chi Rho is the distant ancestor of the fleur-de-lis, the symbol of the French monarchy (see below, part 3, pp. 509–10).

[168] Sunday, which for the first time was set aside in a law by Constantine as sacred and as a day of rest; the law was enforced throughout the Empire.

> became rootless and homeless, lost to hearth and lost to sight. But he who honors his Master with every expression of piety—at one time erecting imperial palaces for Him, at another making Him known to his subjects by votive offerings everywhere on earth—has found in Him the Savior and Guardian of his house, his kingdom, and his line. Thus have the deeds of God become clear through the divine efficacy of the Saving Sign. (*Tricennial Orations* 9.18–19)

Finally, Eusebius praises Constantine for his omniscience. The acts of abomination carried out at the temple of Aphrodite had remained unknown because of its location in a remote mountain place. But the *basileus* saw them because nothing escapes his eagle eye (like an eagle he can look straight into the sun).

These are proofs of Constantine's special "friendship" with God and legitimatize his hold on a universal empire. "God Himself, the Supreme Sovereign, stretches out His right-hand to him from above and confirms him victor over every pretender and aggressor" (*Tricennial Orations* 10.7). Eusebius calls him the "friend" of God.

In conclusion, Eusebius's political theology is not particularly Christian (if, indeed, it is Christian in any sense at all). If anything, it suggests Hellenistic kingship. Eusebius says the same thing about the king as the pagan Sthenidas: he must be a "copy and an imitator of the first God" (*mimatas ara kai hyperetas*).[169] Eusebius may have also found inspiration in a text preserved in the *Corpus hermeticum* with numerous references to a Supreme Sovereign God of the universe—immortal, eternal, and all-powerful—and to sovereigns who reign in his image on earth. As for Constantine's omniscience, it reminds us of Xenophon's all-knowing wisdom of Cyrus and Dio Chrysostom's omniscience of Trajan; at least these two authors knew that such omniscience was the product of a skillful policy: the regime's formation of an effective secret police.

E. THEMISTIUS

Two other Greek pagan deliberations on kingship warrant our attention. The first is that of Themistius.

1. *LIFE AND WORK*

Themistius (317–ca. 388 AD), a philosopher and orator, is known in the history of ideas as one of the principal commentators of Aristotle in antiquity. A friend of Julian "the Apostate" (emperor from 361 to 363), he was also one of the dignitaries of the Empire; he served as a senator and a proconsul, and was also director of the "university" of Constantinople. He was personally entrusted with the education of the eldest son of Theodosius I. He left two works: *Paraphrases* and *Orations.*

2. *THEMISTIUS'S SPEECH ON KINGSHIP AND TOLERATION: AN ADDRESS TO THE EMPEROR JOVIAN (364)*

Julian "the Apostate" went back on the policies of Constantine and his sons, reestablished paganism, and took harsh measures against Christians.[170] His successor to the imperial office, Jovian (363–64), reversed these measures. Then it was the turn of the pagans to live in fear of persecu-

[169] Quoted by Stobaeus, *Florilegium* 48, 63.

[170] Drawn from Barker, *From Alexander to Constantine* 377–80.

tion. Themistius rose to their defense. The intellectual novelty of his stand is not his defense of paganism per se, but his appeal for *toleration.*[171]

> You, and you only, as it appears, are aware that a king is not able to apply compulsion to his subjects in all things. There are some things which have escaped the yoke of necessity—things which are stronger than threats or commands; and among them are all the virtues, and especially the virtue of reverence for the Divine. You have recognized in your wisdom that a man in whom the movement of the mind is to be really and truly unforced, self-governing, and voluntary must be a leader in these good things. If it is not possible even for you, Sire, to bring it about that a man should be kind by rule and prescription without choosing internally to be so, how much more is it impossible to make a man reverent and dear to heaven by inspiring him with fear of transitory necessities and poor weak bugbears, which time has often brought in its course and as often carried away? We stand most foolishly convicted if we do honour to the purple instead of to God, and change our worship as easily and as often as the tide veers in the Euboean channel. . . .
>
> Not such are you, most godlike of kings. You, "autocrat" and self-governor in all things, as you are and will be to the end, assign by law to all men their share in the rights of worship; and in this, too, you emulate God, who has made it a common attribute of the nature of men that they should be duly disposed to piety, but has made the mode of their worship depend on the will of each. To apply the compulsion of necessity is to deprive man of a power which has been granted to him by God. This is the reason why the laws of Cheops and Cambyses hardly lasted as long as their makers, but the law of God and *your* law remains unchanged for ever—that the mind of each and every man should be free to follow the way of worship which it thinks [to be best]. This is a law against which no confiscation, no crucifixion, no death at the stake has ever yet availed; you may hale and kill the body, if so be that this comes to pass; but the mind will escape you, taking with it freedom of thought and the right of the law as it goes, even if it is subjected to force in the language used by the tongue.[172]

Toleration not only requires the efforts of a wise statesperson, its strongest rampart is a genuine ontological pluralism willed by God:

> Nor is your army, Sire, all ordered on one and the same scheme. Some are infantry and some cavalry; some bear arms, and some carry slings; some have their station by your person, some near it, others far away from it; some are content if they are known to the bodyguard, and some cannot get so far. But all depend, none the less, on you and on your judgement; and this is true not only of the men in the army but also of all other men—all who serve you otherwise than in war—farmers, orators, administrators, philosophers, and all the rest. Bethink you, Sire, that the Author of the universe rejoices in this diversity. It is His will that Syria should have one sort of polity, Greece another, and Egypt another; nay, Syria itself is not all alike, but divided into small parts. No man conceives things in exactly the same way as his neighbour; one has this opinion, and another that. Why, then, attempt to force men to the impossible?[173]

---

171 Perhaps because he was an Aristotelian scholar and an advocate of Aristotle's policy of "moderation."

172 Themistius, *Speech to Jovian, On Tolerance* 67b–d, 68a, qtd. in Barker, *From Alexander to Constantine* 377–78.

173 Ibid., 69c–70a, qtd. in Barker, *From Alexander to Constantine* 379–80.

F. Synesius

The last great political voice illustrating the Dominate and its ideas—at a time when the ideas of the church fathers were flourishing and announcing new political realities—was Synesius of Cyrene.

1. *Life and Work*

Synesius (373–414 AD) was a native of Cyrene (present-day Libya). He was a *defensor civitatis.*[174] At the end of his life he also served as bishop. He studied Neoplatonist philosophy at Alexandria, and his ideas combined Christian and Platonist themes. His writings included *On Dreams, On the Gift of a Planisphere, Letters,* and *Hymns.*

2. *An Address to the Emperor Arcadius (circa 400 AD)*

Synesius developed ideas that were quite conventional: the king is a copy of God.[175] He should bear one or the other of the titles of the great King in heaven. He must be king of himself, have many friends, unite the army behind him, enlist in his army Romans, not "Persians" or other barbarians whose numbers grow constantly.

But Synesius's most original idea was that the king should *appear in public.* In a final outpouring of classical civic-mindedness, Synesius protested against the sacralization of the *basileus* and Byzantine power, which was increasingly secluded and hidden from the public view (the agora). Secrecy and seclusion undermined politics and replaced it with ritual and magic, which Synesius clearly held in contempt. He shouts in anger: the Byzantine *basileus* is a "barbarian."

> I contend that nothing in the past has had a worse influence on Roman affairs than the pomp and ceremony surrounding the person of the King, a ceremony conducted for you in a secrecy of seclusion by your attendants, as if they were celebrating a ritual, *with all the "barbarian" apparatus used in your court.* Appearance and reality do not usually go together. Do not be angry with me for saying this; it is not your fault; it is the fault of those who started this mischief and transmitted to the present an evil which is accentuated by the passage of time. The result is that this majesty—this fear of your being brought down to the level of ordinary men by becoming a common sight—makes you a recluse; you are besieged, as it were, by your own self; you see very little, and hear very little, of the experiences that produce a stock of practical wisdom; your only delight is in the pleasures of the body, and in the most material of those pleasures, such as come from touch and taste; you live, in a word, the life of an anemone in the sea.[176]

In literary imagery, capturing the spirit of Aristophanes, Synesius declares that the emperor is "kept in [his] chamber like a lizard that hardly ever puts out its head into sunlight"; instead he should be living a plain and simple life out of doors, with the armies under his command.

Greece invented the model of a secular state, the idea of individual liberty resulting from an equal law for all, democracy, and the concept of rational political science. As the heir to these accomplishments, Rome went a step further in the development of political ideas, inventing an abstract, virtually universal law enabling individuals from different ethnic groups of the Empire to cooperate, and developing a state apparatus where aristocratic, democratic, and monarchic elements were coherently associated. All of these political institutions and doctrines were suf-

---

[174] *Translator's note:* "defender of the state," an office often held by a bishop.
[175] Material in this section is from Barker, *From Alexander to Constantine* 380–86.
[176] Synesius, qtd. in ibid., 383.

ficiently robust to enable a grand "Greco-Roman" civilization to thrive for five or six centuries, leaving its indelible mark on all the civilizations of the Mediterranean basin and Europe. But before this legacy could be transmitted to modern Western civilization, it would undergo a complete transformation by an extraneous addition from the biblical world. At first, the two very different mindsets coexisted side by side, more or less in conflict. In the Middle Ages, however, a genuine synthesis was achieved, giving birth to modern political institutions and theories. It is toward these developments that we now turn our attention.

Part Three

The Christian West

Introduction to Part Three

Together with Hellenism and *Romanitas*, Judeo-Christianity is the third pillar of the Western political tradition. It ushers in an entirely new political and legal inspiration, one foreign to the spiritual universe of the Greco-Roman world: a new moral sense—a rejection of the normality of evil—implying a radical transformation of the perception of time, the idea of history as directed toward improvement, and the idea that spiritual power outweighs temporal power and that the state, a "sinful Babylon," must be harnessed to avoid constituting the ultimate horizon of human existence.

The "West" was born in the Middle Ages, more precisely between the eleventh and thirteenth centuries, such that, after centuries of contact, an innovative synthesis occurred between the new moral element from "Jerusalem" and the great civic legacy of ancient Athens and Rome. This synthesis made possible the rise of European modernity, rooted in social and scientific progress, and structuring itself on the model of liberal democracies where the state has conditional and limited powers.

For an in-depth understanding of this history, we must step far back in time to the Bible itself. At its deepest origin, biblical thought is free of Greek influence. In terms of its reference model of social organization, the biblical world offers an alternative route out of the magico-religious universe of the ancient Near Eastern sacred monarchies, a route very different from the Greek city-state. Furthermore, the intellectual product of the Bible, in terms of profundity and insight, holds its own against Greek philosophy. We will discuss how this original thought developed and will examine its specific contributions.

Our discussion begins with the "political"[1] ideas in the ancient biblical world and in the New Testament. We will attempt to identify the most original concepts of this thought: the relegation of temporal power to a secondary role relative to spiritual power, the eschatological orientation of time in history (see the introductory chapter to part 3, "The 'Political' Ideas of the Bible").

Then we will discuss the political ideas and attitudes of the first Christians under the Roman Empire, and in particular the work of Augustine, the most important political thinker during the early centuries of Christendom (chapter 1, "Christianity and Politics at the Time of the Roman Empire").

---

[1] For a discussion of why the word "political" is in quotes, see below, pp. 386, 406.

Next we will turn to the first period of the Middle Ages, that is, the Early Middle Ages. At this time the civic model collapsed; the regions of what was formerly Roman Europe, now dominated by barbarian Germanic kingdoms, again resembled pre-civic societies. Despite a brief resurrection of the Empire (under the Carolingian and Ottonian dynasties), the state regressed until it disappeared altogether (at any rate in certain times and places). The church, as keeper of the classical world and conveyor of new values, struggled against this decline and imposed its spiritual and moral authority over the young states of Europe in the context of "political Augustinism" (chapter 2, "The Early Middle Ages: Fifth to Eleventh Centuries").

Feudalism emerged from the ruins of the Roman state. Since this social model was never the focus of theoretical speculation (or, at best, *a posteriori*), our emphasis will be less on the history of political ideas and more on a history of social representations and attitudes. We will also discuss the topic of sacred kingship (chapter 3, "Feudalism and Sacred Kingship").

The classical Middle Ages opens with the great reform of the church, the Papal Revolution (eleventh to thirteenth centuries). The papacy, establishing itself at the very heart of Western Christianity, believed it had been entrusted with a mission to lay the foundations of a universal Christian society. To achieve this aim, it drew on all classical culture and sought to conciliate Christian and Greco-Roman contributions. It encouraged the study of *Roman law* and developed *canon law* (chapter 4, "High Middle Ages [Eleventh to Thirteenth Centuries]: The Papal Revolution").

We will consider the writings of Thomas Aquinas, who saw his views as an explicit doctrinal synthesis of Aristotle's political and moral philosophy and Christianity. In matters of social justice, commerce, finance (interest-bearing loans), and forms of government, Aquinas invented concepts that would reemerge in the Catholicism of modern and contemporary times (chapter 5, "Saint Thomas Aquinas").

Toward the end of the Middle Ages, the separation of spiritual and temporal powers, the shoots of which were already visible during the Papal Revolution, finally flowered. States began to assert their independence, and the European nation-states resolutely staked their claims to the detriment of feudal lords. The modern "machinery of state" emerged. The widespread study of Roman law, Greek philosophy, and Latin humanism provided the framework for thinkers and politicians to lay the intellectual foundations of the modern concept of the state (chapter 6, "The End of the Middle Ages [Fourteenth to Fifteenth Centuries]: Toward the Modern Concept of the State").

With the flourishing of urban life in the twelfth and thirteenth centuries came the outbreak of revolutionary movements under the cloak of religious "millenarianism," a feverish hope for the destructions of the end-times and the thousand years of earthly bliss, prophesied in the book of Revelation. These eschatological perspectives took a pacifist turn in the writings of Joachim of Flora and the Franciscan "Spirituals." Others were more violent, for example, the Brotherhood of the Free Spirit, the Taborites, Thomas Müntzer, and the Anabaptists. These movements were the first to attune the West to the idea of revolution. We will discuss the idea of whether revolution crowns or opposes the idea of progress inherent in the theological and juridical innovations of the medieval church (chapter 7, "Medieval Millenarianism").

Preliminary Chapter

The "Political" Ideas of the Bible

Any mention of "political" ideas in the Old Testament has to be put in quotation marks, according to our definitions (see the general introduction above, "Anthropology and Politics"). The state—in the sense of an object of political thought—did not exist in the earliest periods of Hebrew history; then, for nearly four centuries after its creation, the Hebrew state was associated with the sacred monarchies of the Near East (we will stress some important nuances below); after this, the Jews had no state of their own, except for one short period, and the state became something foreign, ruled by the Assyrians, Chaldeans, Persians, Greeks, or Romans. As for scientific thought, the precondition for political thought, it came into existence only much later in the biblical world, and then in broad brushstrokes under the influence of Hellenism; it disappeared, in fact, from rabbinic Judaism with Hellenism itself. So, for all these reasons, there is nothing in the Bible, strictly speaking, that can be compared with the political thought of Greco-Roman philosophers and orators. This, of course, did not prevent the biblical people from inventing original social models, different from the Greek city-state and from the magico-religious inventions of the Near Eastern sacred monarchies.

We will begin our discussion with an overview of the history of the ancient Hebrew-Jewish people. Then we will explore the principal "political" ideas of the Bible, beginning with the Old Testament, followed by the New Testament.

I. A HISTORY OF THE HEBREW PEOPLE

A. THE SEDENTARIZATION OF THE "HEBREWS" (THIRTEENTH CENTURY BC)

The earliest record of people in Palestine claiming descent from the patriarchs Abraham and Isaac dates to the thirteenth and eleventh century BC.[2] At this time Palestine was a protectorate of Egypt. Town-states thrived under the rule of kinglets often at war with one another. The term "hebrew," a common noun before becoming a proper noun, referred to nomadic peoples in the process of sedentarization. These groups—or large families and clans which had "crossed over" into the region—were fairly uncontrolled. Like mercenaries, they offered their services to the highest bidder, especially to cities involved in military conflicts with other cities; they were also itinerant laborers employed on large construction projects. The word "hebrew" at the time was more a social marker than an ethnic identifier.

Each clan had its own history and founding myth. Some of these clans were related to Abraham, Issac, Jacob, and Israel. At the outset, however, they seem to have been independent. Only after they united politically in one state did their respective founding myths converge retrospectively into a single, coherent history as told in Genesis.

Evidence suggests that one clan, associated with Abraham, sedentarized in the region of Hebron (30 kilometers south of Jerusalem). Its main sanctuary was located in the plain "by the oaks of Mamre" where Abraham pitched his tents.[3] Another clan, claiming ties with Isaac, apparently settled in the Negev near the sanctuary and springs of Beer-sheba (southwest of the previous group). It may have been in contact with the city-state of Gerar. Another community, claiming descent from Jacob, left upper Mesopotamia in the early thirteenth century, crossed the Jordan River and its tributary, the Jabbok River, and settled some 50 kilometers north of Jerusalem, in the proximity of the Canaanite city of Shechem (present-day Nablus); its relations with the city and its inhabitants were conflictual. Lastly, there is evidence of a clan of *Bene Israel* (Sons of Israel) in the region of Mount Ephraim; its sanctuary was at Silo (some 30 kilometers north of Jerusalem). The Bene Israel were probably the same clan that had sojourned earlier in Egypt and founded the cult of "Yahweh."

We said that some Hebrew groups went to work on large construction projects for various city-states in the region. The tribe of Israel, claiming Joseph as its founder, may have worked on building projects in the Egyptian store-cities of Pitom and Ramses to the east of the Nile river delta. They left Egypt under the leadership of Moses during the reign of the pharaoh Ramses II, sometime between 1270 and 1250 BC. They roamed the desert between the Negev and the Sinai, where Moses wrung from them obedience to the cult of Yahweh, the one nonrepresentational god. Under Joshua's leadership, the group moved north, bypassing the land of the Moabites and

[2] Our sources for this section are André Lemaire's remarkable overview, *Histoire du people hébreu* [History of the Hebrew people] (Paris: Presses Universitaires de France, 1981). For the Hasmonean period, we consulted André Caquot and Marc Philonenko, *La Bible, Ecrits intertestamentaires* [Intertestamental writings] (Paris: Éditions Gallimard, 1987). See also Hans Küng, *Judaism between Yesterday and Tomorrow* (New York: Crossroad, 1992), with a very rich bibliography on the history of the Hebrew people at 57–216; Pierre Grelot, *L'espérance juive à l'heure de Jésus* [Jewish messianic expectations at the time of Jesus] (Paris: Desclée de Brouwer, 1994); André Neher, *L'essence du prophétisme* [Quality of prophecy] (1955), republished as *Prophétes et prophéties* (Paris: Payot, 1995); A. Cohen, *Everyman's Talmud* (New York: E. P. Dutton, 1975); Berl Gross, *Before Democracy: A Study in the History of Error and Justification* (Melbourne: Globe Press, 1992); and Graham Maddox, *Religion and the Rise of Democracy* (London: Routledge, 1996).

[3] Later, King David located his kingdom in Hebron for a period of seven years. This probably explains why Abraham was identified as the eldest of the patriarchs after the founding myths were combined into a single narrative.

crossing the Jordan River near Jericho. Then, after various battles or alliances with local rulers, the group settled on Mount Ephraim.

These different groups gradually came together to form a loose "Israelite confederation."

B. The Israelite Confederation

At first, two neighboring clans, the Bene Israel and the Bene Jacob, concluded the "Shechem alliance" (Josh. 24).[4] The Bene Israel clan imposed religious unity, that is, the Yahweh cult, rejecting the deity (or deities) of the Bene Jacob. At the same time, Joshua imposed on both clans an early form of the Decalogue. Thus, a degree of social unity existed in the confederation, but each tribal group maintained its autonomy in its territory, uniting under a single leader only in war.

Other "Hebrew" groups—the Zebulun and Neftali—attacked the Canaanite city of Hazor. Then, in order to counter the threat from the "Sea peoples,"[5] they too joined the Israelite confederation. With a complicated history, rich in alliances, betrayals, mobilization against shared threats, and withdrawal after threats declined, the various Hebrew tribes—those in the north and in Galilee, those in central Cisjordan, those in Transjordan, and finally those in the south—joined the Israelite confederation.

The southern tribes, worshippers of Yahweh, probably broke off at some point from the group moving out of Egypt in a northerly direction. These tribes had close contacts with the land of Judah, home to the tribe of Abraham, which had remained outside the Israelite confederation, separated as it was by the non-Hebrew city-state of Jerusalem. It was they who introduced the Yahweh cult to the tribe of Abraham, thereby facilitating the later rapprochement of Judah and Israel (see below).

Thus, in the twelfth and eleventh centuries BC, a loose grouping of "peoples"—extended families, clans—lived in close contact under the predominant influence of the tribe of Israel and its Yahweh cult. Except in wartime, these people had no central political unity. Their names appear in the biblical books of Joshua and Judges: Ephraim, Benjamin, Simeon, Zabulun, Neftali, Issachar, Reuben, Gad, Dan, Asher, Manessah, and so on. Their numbers were soon fixed at 12 and were codified as the "Twelve Tribes of Israel."[6] At this time the people and the land of Judah continued to remain outside the confederation.

C. Unified Monarchy (ca. 1030–931 BC)

The land of Canaan was dotted with numerous city-states ruled by kings. This pattern gradually imposed itself on the entire Israelite confederation, perhaps by an internal evolution related to sedentarization and the development of an urban and rural economy, but no doubt in the first instance owing to the growing external threat posed by Philistine expansionism.

Transition to monarchy and the development of a state probably occurred in two phases: the creation of a "chiefdom" under the reigns of Saul and his son (ca.1030–ca.1003 BC); the creation of a monarchy, strictly speaking, under the kingships of David (1003–970 BC) and Solomon (970–931 BC).

---

[4] We quote from the Revised Standard Version (New York: Thomas Nelson and Sons, 1959) and use the usual conventions for modern biblical references.

[5] The "Sea peoples" is a term found in Egyptian inscriptions to describe certain groups of invaders. They reached the region of Palestine around 1200 BC. They may be the same invaders who destroyed the Mycenaean civilization (see above, pp. 24–25). The Egyptians, under Ramses III, succeeded in driving them back, after which they settled in the surrounding regions of the eastern Mediterranean. One of these groups, the "Philistines," settled on the central coast of Palestine, giving the land the name of "Philistia" (which became "Palestine" in time).

[6] Various passages of the Bible provide different lists of the 12 tribes. Some list as many as 14.

1. *Saul*

After Ebenezer's defeat by the Philistines (1 Sam. 4:1–2) and the seizure and removal of the Ark of the Covenant from Shiloh, the prophet Samuel acquired religious authority among the Israelites of Mount Ephraim (predominantly the tribes of Ephraim, Benjamin, Israel, and Gad). He was able to achieve the proclamation of Saul, the great military commander of these tribes, as king (Samuel's action immediately met with political opposition; see below). With the help of his son Jonathan, Saul liberated Mount Ephraim from Philistine occupation. However, the Philistines reacted to these military maneuvers and overwhelmed the Israelites at the Battle of Mount Gilboa, during which Saul and three of his sons were killed. At the urging of Abner, the head of the Israelite army, another of Saul's sons, Ishbaal, was proclaimed king. Within two years Ishbaal also lay dead, assassinated by his political opponents. The royal title fell to David, a Judean of simple origins. David had initially befriended Jonathan, but then he revolted, switched his allegiance to the Philistines, and succeeded in being proclaimed king of Judah. Ishbaal's death made him "king of Judah and Israel."

In speaking of the monarchy of Saul and his son, we used the term "chiefdom," not state, because at this moment in Israelite history there was no *territorial unity* or central bureaucracy. David and Solomon managed to achieve both.

2. *David*

After his proclamation as king, David continued to build on his military successes and used war and diplomacy to expand his kingdom to the maximum extent.[7] He defeated the Philistines in battle and captured the fortress town of Jebus, where he built his capital, Jerusalem, because it enabled him to establish territorial unity between the southern parts of the kingdom (Judah and Benjamin) and the Ephramite tribes in the north. For centuries thereafter Jerusalem was known as "the city of David." He fought the Amalakites, the Moabites, the Ammonites, and their Aramean allies. His kingdom extended north as far as Damascus and southeast as far as present-day Amman. However, he made no attempt to conquer Philistine territories to the southwest or Phoenician territories to the northwest.

Domestically, David eliminated Saul's descendants from political contention. He had to confront chronic dissensions in the south and in the north, the armed revolt of his son, Absalom, and difficulties with his own succession: finally, with backing from the priest Zadok, the prophet Nathan, and Benayahu, the head of David's personal guard, one of his youngest sons, Solomon, was crowned king during his father's lifetime.

David instituted several of the specific attributes of a state during his reign: a standing army; a judiciary system directly appointed by and under the authority of the king (the traditional system of the tribes could appeal to this higher system); and a tax system based on an accurate population census (most of the state's income came from the spoils of war, as under the rule of Saul, and from the income of David's own personal estates). David installed the Ark of the Covenant in Jerusalem. Imitating the other sacred monarchies of the region, he made plans to build a great temple, but his project ran into stiff opposition from his enemies (the significance of this will be discussed below).

3. *Solomon*

Likewise, Solomon brutally eliminated his domestic opponents. In his foreign relations he established an alliance with the pharaoh, who gave him his daughter in marriage (an exceptional feat

[7] David remains the reference for modern-day Israeli ultra-nationalists.

and a testimony to the influence achieved by the kingdom of Israel in only a few short years). Solomon continued the work of his predecessor, David, in pursuing the creation and consolidation of the machinery of state. These efforts won him a reputation for extraordinary "wisdom" in the Jewish historiography.

Solomon surrounded himself with advisors and public officials, whose positions were apparently hereditary, including priests, secretaries, heralds, army chiefs, palace chamberlains, and the heads of "prefectures." The family of the prophet Nathan was rewarded for its role in making Solomon David's successor. The House of Judah was favored with numerous appointments, rousing the jealousy of the other tribes.[8] This body of state-appointed officials went by the name of "Levites."[9] The territory of the kingdom (including the annexed Canaanite cities) was divided up into 12 districts; each had a prefect at its head. Each prefecture attended the king and the royal court for one month every year. Since the spoils of war were no longer available to finance the state, tribute money from vassal states and taxes levied on international trade (including maritime trade, trade with Phoenicia, and the desert caravans) had to be collected. David's professional army remained intact and was even equipped with chariots.

Last but not least, Solomon was renowned for his grand building projects: military fortifications and, in Jerusalem itself (1 Kings 9:15–24), the temple, the royal palace, the citadel of Millo (a rampart or stepped-stone structure connecting the temple and the palace), and the city walls. These projects took years to complete and required technical assistance from the Phoenicians (Solomon granted them territory in return). Above all, it required forced labor, which Solomon obtained from the conquered Canaanites but also from the Israelites themselves. His use of forced labor led to revolts, notably in the House of Joseph (it had suffered under slavery in Egypt for years until Yahweh delivered it, which is why Solomon's decision roused religious opposition).

The social transformations, stemming from the establishment of monarchy, left their mark in the archaeological record; fortified cities emerged along with sharp social distinctions, e.g. larger houses for notables, an obvious sign of wealth and esteem. It is estimated that between the start of Saul's reign and the end of Solomon's (less than a century), the population doubled, a phenomenal rate of growth.

While David had succeeded in unifying the Israelites in the Yahweh cult, Solomon's state and cities indulged in *syncretism*. His numerous foreign wives led to the presence of foreign cults and foreign temples in Jerusalem (the temple of Chemosh, god of the Moabites; the temple of Milcom, god of the Ammonites; the temple of Ashtoreth, goddess of the Zidonians; see 1 Kings 11:1–8). Canaanite cities were allowed to retain their cults as well.

D. The Two Kingdoms: Israel and Judah (931–722 and 587 BC)

When Solomon died, his son and successor, Rehoboam, was unable to hold the northern territories, which revolted against his regime over the issue of forced labor; they chose another king, Jeroboam. This ushered in a period of division in the kingdom: in the south, the tribes of Judah and Benjamin formed the "kingdom of Judah" with Jerusalem as its capital; in the north,

---

[8] These favors granted to family and friends of the royal family are evidence that the state was still organized on the archaic model (the Greek and Roman models featured equality before the law, which usually—if not always—implied the disappearance of lineal primacy in public appointments).

[9] In Jewish mythology, Levi was one of the 12 sons of Jacob. He was older than Judah, but Jacob punished him for his wrongful conduct toward the inhabitants of Shechem (Gen. 34:25–31, 49:5–7). This punishment meant that the descendants of the Levi were not entitled to receive tribal lands and were scattered throughout the territory of Judah. When Solomon, a member of the tribe of Judah, ascended to the throne and took control of the entire confederation, he gave favors to the Levites, who were close to him. Because they had no land, he ensured their specialization in sacerdotal functions. We will discuss the sociopolitical consequences of the sacerdotal specialization of the Levites below.

the "kingdom of Israel" united the remaining ten tribes and chose Shechem, then Samaria as its capital with new cult centers in Dan, Bethel, and later on Mount Gerizim to counter the temple in Jerusalem.

The two monarchies differed from a political standpoint. In the northern kingdom, a "charismatic" principle prevailed: each king was expected to establish his leadership by virtue of his military prowess. In addition to provoking the political opposition of the prophets (as we will see), this led to bloody clashes with each succession and great dynastic weakness (nevertheless, there were two fairly robust dynasties: the Omri dynasty [ca. 881–841 BC] and the Jehu dynasty [841–749]). As for the southern kingdom, it respected the dynastic principle on the whole: all the kings of Judah came from the "house of David."

On the other hand, the process of "Canaanization" was much stronger in the northern kingdom, which entered into an alliance with the Phoenicians (Ahab [ca. 874–853 BC], the king of Israel, married Jezebel, the daughter of Ittobaal, king of Tyre). The cult of Baal continued to spread throughout the region, scandalizing traditional Israelite circles, which chose the prophet Elijah as their spokesperson.[10]

But when the new Assyrian threat materialized, the kingdom of Israel knew to form an alliance with the kingdom of Judah (Ahab's daughter, Athaliah, was given in marriage to Joram, son of Jehosaphat, the king of Judah, 2 Kings 8:18–26).

Israel and Judah also had to support conflicts with various neighboring kingdoms—Moab, Aram, Edom, Philistia—which were often obligated to pay tribute. Sometimes the reverse occurred, when, for example, the kingdom of Israel under King Jehu was forced to pay tribute as a vassal to the Arameans of Damascus.

Jehu's coup d'état and the policies of his successors, Jehoahaz and Jehoash, brought an end to the process of "Canaanization" in Israel. Their policies were backed by traditionalist circles led by the prophets Elisha and Yonadab. The reaction was the same in Judah, where the foreign-born Queen Athaliah was executed in 835 BC on the orders of the priest Yehoyada, who caused the young Joash to be proclaimed king (2 Kings 11:4–16).

In the north the long reign of Jeroboam II (ca. 790–750 BC) is noteworthy; it has been compared to David's. Under Jeroboam II the economy expanded greatly, as evidenced by the archeological record; in response, numerous social problems associated with the accumulation of wealth in the upper class came to the fore; they were fanned by the inflammatory admonitions of the prophet Amos. Writing developed for administrative purposes, as attested by an increase in the number of inscriptions. The first prophetic books (*Amos* and *Hosea*) were put into writing at this time. Finally, Israel vassalized Judah (Jerusalem was captured ca. 800 BC), and its domination lasted almost until the end of Jeroboam's reign.

1. *The End of the Kingdom of Israel (722 BC)*

After the death of Jeroboam II, the northern kingdom entered a period of unrest, which ended in the final destruction of the kingdom by the Assyrians. Beginning with the reign of Tiglath-Phalazar III (744–727 BC), the Assyrians embarked on a systematic conquest of Syria-Palestine.

[10] The Israelites were attracted to the cult of Baal primarily for two reasons: (1) in the eyes of poor nomadic peoples, the cult of a dominant civilization offers great prestige; (2) a predominantly agrarian cult based on fertility has obvious "utilitarian" advantages for former nomads now become sedentarized farmers (sacrifices to Baal are intended to bring rain and abundant harvests; in most archaic religions, such sacrifices are, generally speaking, deemed effective). Therefore, it is not for "sentimental" reasons: the recently sedentarized Hebrew farmers adopted the cult of Baal, like their long-settled Canaanite neighbors, to satisfy existential needs. One can appreciate the difficulties that the proponents of the strict Yahweh cult had to face to impose a god of the desert and nomadic life on the newly sedentarized population. See Neher, *Prophétes et prophéties,* 176–81.

The Israelite kingdoms were unable to present a united front against the Assyrian threat. In less than 30 years, the regime changed four times. The prophet Hosea bitterly lamented such instability. Several anti-Assyrian coalitions were formed. The last united Pekah, king of Israel, with Rezin, king of Damascus, in an alliance supported by Philistia and Edom; the coalition attacked Jerusalem in an effort to force the tribe of Judah to join the alliance. Against the warnings of the prophet Isaiah,[11] the young king of Judah, Ahaz, appealed to Tiglath-Phalazar III, who was only too eager too intervene in the conflict. The war, in fact, enabled Tiglath-Phalazar to become ruler of the entire region. A few years later, in 722, after Israel refused to pay tribute and revolted again with the help of Egypt, the new king of Assyria, Salmanazar V, laid Samaria to waste and forced 30,000 Israelites into exile; he dispersed them throughout his empire so that they would never return (Judaism later knew them as the "ten lost tribes"). Furthermore, Salmanazar repopulated the land of Israel with many foreign settlers and effectively transformed the territory into an Assyrian province. The Yahweh cult was virtually eradicated from the region.

2. *The End of the Kingdom of Judah (587 BC)*

The kingdom of Judah underwent the same fate as the kingdom of Israel some 135 years later. For the first 100 years of Assyrian domination, the kings of Judah chose to pay tribute in order to avoid the destruction of their kingdom. This implied a degree of tolerance toward foreign cults: Ahaz went so far as to offer one of his sons as a human sacrifice in the classical Canaanite fire ritual (2 Kings 16:3). But the prophets Micah and Isaiah railed against this syncretism. Their efforts bore fruit, since two major religious reforms—the reforms of Hezekiah and Josiah—gradually restored the Yahweh cult. At the same time, they disrupted the status quo and led to the final crisis.

King *Hezekiah* (719–699 BC) sought the religious reunification of Judah and what remained of the Israelites of the north. He ordered the destruction of Canaanite places of worship and attempted to reestablish the Yahweh cult around the one temple in Jerusalem.

His project included an essential component, *the fusion of the northern and southern religious traditions into a single text.* Two accounts of the origins of the Hebrew people had long existed (the creation of the world, patriarchal narratives, sojourn in Egypt and deliverance, Moses and the gift of the Law on Mount Sinai, arrival in the Promised Land): one in the north (the Elohist[12] narrative), and another similar (but not identical) account in the south (the Yahwist[13] narrative). There would now be a single Yahwist-Elohist account. After revisions and additions it became the basis for the Pentateuch, the first five books of the Bible.

Another critical aspect of the project was *the bringing of tithes to the Temple.* The great Temple in Jerusalem became the center of economic activity, and the surplus it accumulated was available to the king for his commercial and military ventures. The number of Levite officials grew steadily.

Under pressure from the Assyrians, Manasseh (ca. 699–645 BC), Hezekiah's successor, put religious reform on hold and returned to syncretism. However, Assyrian power went into decline

[11] The reference is to First Isaiah. The book of Isaiah contains the prophecies of several individuals: the first Isaiah, who actually bore the name, and one or two anonymous authors, who made their prophecies in the name of Isaiah (a common practice known as *pseudoepigraphy*). We will also discuss Second Isaiah (also known as Deutero-Isaiah) from the postexilic period and author of chapters 40–55 of the book of Isaiah (see below). Chapters 56–66 may have been the work of Trito-Isaiah (Third Isaiah) from the Second Temple period. Such pseudoepigraphy is characteristic of a number of other books in the Bible, in both the Old and New Testaments; it can also be found in the so-called *intertestamental* writings, in the books of Zechariah, Daniel, Enoch, Ezra, John, and others.

[12] Given this name because God is called "Elohim" in the northern account.

[13] God is called "Yahweh" in the southern account.

when a new power from the east began to rise: the *neo-Babylonians* or *Chaldeans*, who seized the Assyrian capital of Nineveh in 612.

With the death of the last great king of Assyria, Assurbanipal, in 630 BC, the young king Josiah resumed the reform of Hezekiah. He strengthened the Yahwist Law by requiring all Israelites to make the pilgrimage to Jerusalem for the Passover celebrations. He also promulgated a new text of religious law, Deuteronomy.

Josiah claimed that the scrolls were found buried in the Temple walls. Is this plausible? Or did Josiah have the scrolls written, then stage the announcement of their discovery? However that may be, the scrolls are clearly the work of priestly circles.

Deuteronomy, presented as a "new covenant," strenghtened Yahwism and justified the *centralization of the cult in the Temple of Jerusalem*, where Yahweh was said to abide. All the Yahwist priests in the kingdom were ordered to Jerusalem and told to enter Temple service. And Josiah added an *obligatory value* to Deuteronomy: it became the first "book of the Law," before even the Torah itself.

Deuteronomical thought shifted the hope of Judah from the classical model of temporal kingship to that of an "everlasting kingship" (see the amended verse by the Deuteronomist in 2 Samuel 7:16: "your throne shall be established for ever"). This idealization of the royal archetype gave rise in due course—when a Jewish king and Hebrew state no longer existed—to a *messianic* ideology: the "Messiah" as the ideal Davidic king. However, Josiah died unexpectedly in a military campaign against the Egyptians, who arrived to save the Assyrians.

Josiah's son, *Yehoyakin,* tried to resist the emerging geopolitical power in the region, the Chaldeans, led by King Nebuchadnezzar II (604–562). Nebuchadnezzar had extended his power throughout Syria-Palestine and had even attempted to enter Egypt itself. Yehoyakin's resistance, however, was in vain: Nebuchadnezzar seized Jerusalem in 597 and deported as many as 10,000 people from among the social elite; he then enthroned a new king, *Sedecias* (another of Josiah's sons), subordinated to his authority.

Despite the prophet *Jeremiah's* warnings, Sedecias led a revolt backed by other chieftains in the region. The repression of the Chaldeans was terrible. Nebuchadnezzar retook Jerusalem in 587 BC and burned its principal buildings to the ground (the temple,[14] the royal palace) and pulled down the city walls. Then he butchered the king's sons and blinded the king, before forcing him, his retinue, and what remained of the local population[15] into exile in Babylon. Jeremiah fled into Egypt with a few survivors. This was the beginning of the Exile.

Why did Judah last longer than Israel in the struggle with the great powers of Mesopotamia? Probably due to the bond that the people of Judah maintained with the Davidic dynasty, which had created an effective bureaucracy, a well-designed defense system, a hereditary caste of high officials in the service of the Temple (whose high priest was allied to the royal family), and a "people's assembly" comprised of traditional tribal heads. Facing this southern state, which inherited David and Solomon's political legacy, the kingdom of the north—which grew out of resistance to the state—never attained the same degree of solidity. The king, as we said, was really a "charismatic" warlord, like Saul, discredited as soon as he lost a battle; the whole system was looser, more feudal. The weakness of power enabled feudal chiefs to abuse the mass of people quite easily. Contacts with Phoenicia enriched the merchant class, provoking incomprehension and jealousy. Last but not least, the land was more exposed to Aramean and Assyrian threats than Judah. The

[14] The ancient Ark of the Covenant, which David had brought to the Temple, disappeared in the catastrophe. The only sacred ornament in the Second Temple's Holy of Holies—the most remote and most secret room of the sanctuary—was a menorah, a seven-branch candelabra.

[15] This catastrophe is described at length in the book of Lamentations, traditionally (but, according to modern text criticism, erroneously) attributed to Jeremiah.

weakness of central government was both a cause and consequence of the critical stance of the prophets—Elijah, Elisha, Amos, and Hosea—who protested against the "Canaanization" of the land.

E. Exile (587–538 BC)

Because the state no longer existed in the north and in the south, the Jewish people faced the threat of pure and simple extinction. This threat grew in intensity when the greater part of Judah came under the occupation of the Edomites (a people of the southeast) and there was no longer a single people living on a piece of well-defined territory. Aware of the situation, those in exile took innovative initiatives to perpetuate the identity of the people. Since a state and a territory could no longer safeguard the people's identity, it became the role of religious and cultural institutions to do so.

In Babylon, the Judean exiles were not dispersed and absorbed in the local population, as had been the fate of the Samarian exiles. This union of exiles enabled community life to be organized around the people's various leaders, an assembly of the "Elders of Israel," priests, and prophets like Ezekiel and, between 597 and 587 BC, Jeremiah (Jeremiah was not in Babylon, but corresponded with the exiles by letter). The prophets encouraged the exiles to turn to Yahweh, mysteriously present among them in spite of the distance from Mount Zion. They convinced the exiles that their sojourn in Babylon would be long, and that it was therefore necessary to play an active role in Babylonian society, while at the same time ensuring the survival of the Israelite community through endogamous marriages. Since the exiles represented the administrative, economic, and industrial elite of Israel, they were able to occupy a place in Babylonian society with relative ease.

The elite also kept alive the hope of a return to the homeland at some time in the future (their hope was sustained by Ezekiel's vision of the resurrection of the bones, Ezekiel 37, and by a rising *messianic* fervor during this period, as we will see). For this reason the Israelites were careful to preserve their identity and to avoid their dissolution in Babylonian society. The only sure way to achieve this was to keep the *history* and *laws* of the Jewish people alive in their memories, to teach them to their young people, to worship the *cult of God's word* rather than the *cult of sacrifice,* which in the context of exile was impossible anyway, and to honor the *ancient customs* (*endogamous marriage, dietary taboos, circumcision, religious festivals,* etc.), none of which required the possession of a territory. This formed the embryo of an institution called the "synagogue" and the functions of the "scribe" or the "doctor of the law."

The requirement for this was the preservation of texts, both the narrative accounts (*haggada*) and the laws (*halakhah*). As a consequence, the Jewish traditions were revised, sorted, and compiled in collections, laying the foundations for what would become the "Bible."

We said earlier that this process began during the monarchic period with the compilation of the Yahwist texts from the south and the Elohist documents in the north, then the Yahwist-Elohist texts from the south again, and finally by the addition of the Deuteronomic code during the reign of Josiah in 621 BC. Thereafter, the process gained pace.

The exiled Jewish priests in Babylon prepared a guide or catechism of their traditions based on their sacred narratives and their moral laws. German scholars refer to this document as the *Priesterkodex.* At the same time in Palestine the writing of the Deuteronomy continued (this included the book of *Deuteronomy,* and the books of Joshua, Judges, 1 and 2 Samuel, and 1 and 2 Kings).

Another important point needs to be made here. The prophets foretold the collapse of the two states, unless the people converted in their hearts and returned to strict monotheistic belief. As a manifestation of this threat, the Exile accredited the truth of the prophets' words retrospectively.

This is why the ideas of the Yahwist religion—universalism, radical monotheism, internalization of ethical norms, the election of the Jewish people—became the *organizing and unifying principles* for the compilation, codification, reinterpretation, and revision of the texts.

After the fall of Jerusalem, the people of Judea took refuge in the surrounding countries, primarily in Egypt, but also in Ammon, Moab, Edom, Phoenicia, and Philistia. Thus, the period of Exile marks the onset of the *Diaspora* (Greek for dispersal or "scattering") of the Jewish people. Before very long the religious reforms imagined by the exiles were adopted throughout the Diaspora.

Then Babylon itself was vanquished by another empire, the empire of the *Achaemenid Persians.* Cyrus, the founder of this empire, captured Babylon in 539 BC. What would be his attitude toward the Jewish exiles?

F. The Hebrew People and the Persian Empire (538–332 BC)

Either through cold calculation or genuine religious tolerance (associated with his Zoroastrianism), Cyrus[16] signed the Edict of Cyrus authorizing the Jewish exiles to return to Jerusalem and to rebuild their Temple. His successors, Cambyses (530–522 BC) and Darius (521–486 BC),[17] adhered to the same policy of tolerance and hands-off administration of the Jews. Nevertheless, the territories of Judah and Israel were made part of the Persian satrapy of "Transeuphratene," although initially the Persians appointed princes of the Davidic line as governors of the district of Jerusalem: Sheshbasar, then Zorobabel (the first rebuilder of the Temple), then Hannanah and Elnathan. Likewise, the high priests, also appointed by the Persians, were descendants of the legitimate line of the sons of Zadok,[18] including Zorobabel's ally, *Joshua.* The prophet Zechariah drew attention to this fact and its messianic significance. The new Temple was inaugurated in 515.

The Persians did not go so far as to allow the full restoration of the Davidic kingdom. Gradually, governors were selected from other families. Furthermore, the reconstruction of the walls of Jerusalem was halted. From this moment on, the Hebrew nation rallied around the high priest, his clergy, and the Temple rather than around the king. This change of emphasis marks the transition from a Davidic monarchy to a theocracy.

Theocracy is the organization of society around God's Law—the Torah—and the sacrificial cult of the Temple entrusted to the priestly class. The state occupies a secondary role, either because its control is conceded to foreigners (Persians, then Greeks) or, when in the hands of the Jews, with the approval of the occupier, it is under the control of the priestly class. The foreign power (initially the Persian satrapy in Palestine, and thereafter the Hellenistic monarchies) gave legal force—not just moral force—to the Jewish Law. Lawbreakers were vulnerable to the full arsenal of punishments, including the death penalty. A judgment about whether the law had been

[16] Cyrus was the king idealized by Xenophon in his *Cyropaedia* (see above, p. 141).

[17] The same Darius who launched into the first Persian war and whom the Greeks stopped at Marathon.

[18] Zadok was a priest at the time of David and Solomon. Along with Nathan, he spoke in favor of Solomon during the succession debates (1 Kings 1:32–34). In return, Solomon rewarded his family. Thereafter, the descendants of Zadok were considered the only legitimate high priests. Ezra was a Zadokite descendant.

The book of Chronicles describes Zadok as a descendant of Aaron, the brother of Moses. Aaron was the leader of the tribe of Levi, and since Moses had entrusted him with priestly functions, the Levites (who, it will be recalled, had no tribal land contrary to the other Hebrew tribes) became the primary Israelite priestly caste. Nevertheless, a distinction is necessary—or was made at some point—between *priests* and *Levites:* the former were Levites, but they were, above all, descendants of the line of Aaron and/or Zadok; only they could fulfill the function of sacrificial priest and high priest. The latter were persons of lower rank, priestly assistants, usually public servants, temple administrators, court clerks, judges, and teachers. Thus, the expression "priests and Levites" does not oppose two separate categories; rather, it pits one (privileged) party against the whole.

broken was made by the priestly caste; its supreme body was the *Sanhedrin*. The Law included a number of *cultic requirements* (the cult, strictly speaking, and the organization on which it rests: the sanctity of the Temple, clerical privileges, etc.), as well as *fiscal* and *civic* obligations (the day of rest on the Sabbath, the Sabbatical Year, and the Jubilee Year), not to forget certain requirements associated with *social norms* (sexual, hygienic, and dietary measures, to name only a few).

The features of this theocracy were accentuated by two new initiatives taken by the Persians, anxious to maintain peace and order in the province: the missions of *Nehemiah* and *Ezra*.

1. *Nehemiah*

The son of King Artaxerxes's cupbearer, Nehemiah was a typical representative of the exiled Jewish families, who managed to gain access to the Persian court. He was appointed governor of Jerusalem. In 445 BC, he rebuilt the city walls, repopulated the city, forgave debts to restore civil peace, imposed respect for Deuteronomic law, reformed the collection of the tithe, commanded observance of the Sabbath, and carried out an exacting "ethnic cleansing" policy by forbidding marriages between Israelites and foreigners. (He excepted from this policy the High Priest himself, who was keen to extend his influence to the surrounding districts and continued to arrange marriages with non-Israelites for members of his own family.)

2. *Ezra*

Nehemiah's restoration work was continued by Ezra, another Jewish governor dispatched by the Persians to Jerusalem. The exact date of his mission is not known: perhaps it was contemporaneous with Nehemiah's, but in all likelihood it was sometime after 398 BC.

Ezra was a priest trained in exile by circles close to the Persian court. The Persians apparently charged him with the mission of gathering, unifying, and codifying the various traditions comprising the Jewish cult and legislation in view of producing an official text that would facilitate relations between Persian authorities and Jews dispersed throughout the empire: the Jews of Judah and Samaria, as well as those of Egypt, Babylon, and Asia Minor. The "law of God in heaven," which Ezra was responsible for enacting, obtained full government recognition for civil application. By taking this political and administrative decision, the Persians unwittingly made a decisive contribution to the creation of *Judaism*.

Ezra's "law" was probably the Pentateuch as we know it today, that is to say, the Jewish Torah, the final synthesis of the above elements in a single coherent text: a Yahwist-Elohist document (about the origins of Israel and the alliance in Sinai, Deuteronomy, and the *Priesterkodex*, encompassing every ritual and civic requirement in detail). The entire text was rewritten and harmonized, all events included in a rigorous and accurate calendar, all heroes of Israel's history properly identified in association with their lineage, and connecting them to the twelve tribes of Israel. The text was no doubt put together in Babylon by Jewish priests and Ezra's immediate associates. Ezra then enacted the laws in Jerusalem in a series of solemn ceremonies. This proved highly successful since the texts became the religious and legislative standard in Samaria and Judah. Henceforth, obedience to the same Law became the principal criteria of collective Jewish identity.

Under Ezra's governorship, ethnic cleansing was resumed: "foreign women" were systematically expelled, clan by clan, by authority of the traditional leaders (Ezra 9–10); the revised text of the Law and the new genealogies provided the basis for these exclusions. Once this messianic fervor abated, a golden age of theocracy began in earnest.

The long period of Persian domination—two centuries—was globally a period of peace, prosperity, and demographic growth for Palestine. Exiles returned to the homeland in successive waves. Aramaic became the most commonly used language under Persian domination; the

Persians themselves adopted Aramaic as the official language of administration in their territories of Babylon and Syria-Palestine. And because Assyrian and Babylonian exiles used Aramaic, they brought it with them when they returned to Judah. Henceforth, Hebrew was used only in the country. Beginning with Ezra's efforts, biblical Hebrew was written with the Aramaic alphabet; until then it had used a more archaic Phoenician alphabet.

Given the new authority of the Law, the question of a *scriptural canon* came to the fore. If the Law forms the basis of government, what is the "Law" exactly? What particular texts speak for the Law? It is not hard to see why the Jewish scriptural canon became permanently established during the theocratic era.

At the time of Nehemiah and Ezra, the Hebrew Bible (*Tanakh*) contained three sets of books in descending order from the divine, so to speak: the first books were written directly by God, the second by the prophets, and the third, for the most part, by the hand of man:

- the *Pentateuch* or *Torah:* these books were completed either under Nehemiah or Ezra, as we saw;
- the *Prophets* or *Nabi'im:* the books of the scriptural prophets; the three "great prophets" (Isaiah, Jeremiah, Ezekiel), and the twelve "minor prophets" (from Hosea to Malachi), to which the doctors of the Law add the Deuteronomic writings: Joshua, Judges, the books of Samuel, and the books of Kings;
- the *writings or Ketuvim:* these are works of prayer, wisdom, and poetry: Psalms, Proverbs, Job, the Song of Songs, the book of Ruth, Lamentations, Ecclesiastes, and the book of Esther.

Before very long the other historical books were added to this last group: 1 and 2 Chronicles and the books of Ezra and Nehemiah. These books were written at the request of the new leaders by a writer known as the "Chronicler."[19] These new texts contain a clearly biased theology and political philosophy. They glorify *Jerusalem,* the *Temple,* and *Davidic kingship,* something never done before in such terms, not in the north at any rate. For this reason, the Samaritans rejected the texts, accepting only the Pentateuch as the Law, and refusing the political/religious glorification of Jerusalem, its Temple, and kingship. The Samaritan schism became final in the fourth century. By then the biblical religion had merged with the religion of Judah, justifying the subsequent name of "Judaism."

G. The Hebrew People and the Hellenistic Monarchies (332–142 BC)

When Alexander the Great, the conqueror of Persia, arrived in the region in 332 BC at the head of his Macedonian and Greek armies, Judah and Samaria succumbed to his rule. Thereafter, the two regions became a part of the mainstream Hellenistic kingdoms, first under the *Lagides* of Egypt (until 200 BC), then under the *Seleucids* of Syria (200 to 167 BC).

1. *Judah-Israel under the Lagides*

The first of these two periods was relatively peaceful and prosperous. The provinces were not under the rule of a single governor, but were administered by officials with special purviews, reporting to a central authority. Communities were founded or refounded on the Greek model of

[19] Much later, under the influence of the Pharisees, the last prophetic book, the book of Daniel, was added to the Hebrew Bible. The final text version of the Hebrew Bible dates from the first century AD. We will return to the circumstances of its compilation below.

the *polis* and a certain hellenization occurred. In fact, Greek became the administrative language, though Hebrew continued to be used locally; Aramaic declined. Nevertheless, hellenization was more or less limited to Jerusalem, where the lineage of the Zadokite high priests, with figures such as Onias I, Simon I, Manasseh, Onias II, Simon II, and Onias III, embodied the Jewish tradition and remained influential throughout the period. In Samaria, a high priest of the Zadokite family named Manasseh obtained an authorization to build a temple on Mount Gerizim (near Shechem). This contributed to maintaining the tradition of the Law in Samaria.

In the aftermath of Alexander's conquests, social changes such as equal civic and political rights led to an intensification of the Jewish Diaspora throughout the Hellenistic world, in particular with the founding of new cities like Antioch, Ephesus (in Asia Minor), Kition (Cyprus), and above all Alexandria in Egypt (along with towns in Cyrenaica and the Delta). The attitude of the Ptolemies to the Jews was positive.

In all likelihood, *the translation of the Hebrew Bible into Greek* (the "Septuagint"),[20] in about 270 BC in Alexandria, was an initiative of the Ptolemies, and recalls Persia's instructions to Nehemiah and Ezra to produce an official version of the Torah. The translation improved working relations between the administrative authorities and the Jews. It also promoted a dialogue between the intellectual circles of the library and the museum, the foremost center of learning in Alexandria, and it stimulated Jewish religious life itself. Greek became the everyday language of the Diaspora: teaching in the synagogues and proselytizing among the Jewish Diaspora also took place in Greek.

It was during this period that *Jewish wisdom writing* emerged. God and the history of redemption were no longer the central focus. The emphasis turned to man and the organization of daily life in a stable world now held to be permanent. Fixed rules became necessary in a stable, permanent social world. Great dreams and radical eschatological hope had to be set aside (we will say more about this below). Jewish literature *began to resemble the literature of its neighbors in this regard.* The Wisdom of Solomon was borrowed from Egypt; at the time of the Babylonian exile, banished members of the Jewish community were exposed to an "international intellectual culture"; when the Greeks arrived, the Jews discovered Greek *sophia*; some read Plato and the Stoics.

In this regard, it can be argued that international contacts, and particularly the quasi-immersion of Judaism in the Hellenistic world, represented an extraordinary challenge for the Jews, an opportunity for unprecedented developments and a mortal threat for Jewish identity. Some Greek Jews were tempted by the hellenization of Judaism (among them the historiographer Jason of Cyrene, the philosopher Aristobul, and above all Philo of Alexandria (15/10 BC to 40/50 AD), who lived contemporaneously with Christ and authored an immense body of biblical interpretation inspired by the allegorical exegesis used in Hellenic intellectual circles on Greek literary texts).

The world, now enlarged by Hellenistic expansion, experienced unprecedented demographic, economic, technical, and urban growth and progress. The intellectual and social elite of the cities of Palestine, including Jerusalem, were hellenized. Increasingly, even the names of the high priests were Greek. It is also true that certain populist circles cut themselves off from Hellenic influence in the name of devotion to the Law. The hellenization movement might have even been irreversible, if the new occupiers, the Seleucids, had not prompted unprecedented persecutions of the Jews.

---

[20] Called by this name because 72 elders, placed in 72 separate chambers, miraculously produced the same text in Greek.

2. *Judah-Israel under the Seleucids*

A series of wars between Hellenistic Egypt and Syria led to the Seleucids' occupation of Coele-Syria, including Judea and Samaria. The new overlord proved to be much harsher than the previous one. Nevertheless, culturally speaking, the age was one of the most creative.

At first, change was imperceptible. Antiochus III, whose rule began in 200 BC, issued a decree confirming the enactment of the Law for Jews and the political authority of the Senate and the Council of Elders (*gerousia*). Severely damaged during the wars, the Temple was brilliantly reconstructed under the watchful eye of the high priest Simon II (Jesus ben Sira, the author of the book of Ecclesiastes, also known as the book of Sirach, provides a lively account of this age, during which the priestly circles became rich and were hellenized). Exempting the Jews from certain taxes, Antiochus III encouraged the Diaspora. Through his efforts, many Jews resettled throughout Asia Minor.

The Romans also intensified their involvement in the region. In 188 BC the army of Antiochus was defeated at Magnesia (in the region of Smyrna in Asia Minor) by Scipio Africanus,[21] who imposed a heavy tribute. Antiochus's successor, Seleucus IV, attempted to seize the Temple treasury in Jerusalem in order to meet his additional expenses. However, the high priest Onias III resisted and took a hand in his assassination in 175 BC.

It was in these troubled times that a *policy of forced hellenization in Judea* began. The new king, Antiochus IV Epiphanes (176–164/163 BC), rewarded Jason, a brother of the high priest Onias III, with the high priesthood. A usurper, he was only able to hold on to his priestly position through a policy of collaboration with the occupier. Under Jason, Jerusalem was renamed Antioch and transformed into a Hellenistic city. A new gymnasium was built and delegations were sent to the new quadrennial games at Tyre. Then, following these events—and various court conspiracies and assassinations involving Jason's rival, the high priest Menelas—Antiochus IV Epiphanes forcefully seized the Temple treasury and the sacred vases. He tore down the city walls, massacred a part of the population, sent the rest into exile, and decreed the total hellenization of the religion and the social customs of Judea and Samaria.

The temples of Jerusalem and Mount Gerizim were rededicated to Zeus; pig sacrifices were made before the altar; this is the "abomination of desolation" referred to in the book of Daniel. The books of the Law were torn up and burned. The observance of Jewish customs (Sabbath, circumcision, and so on) were punishable by death. In Samaria, where Hellenistic cities had developed to a considerable degree, hellenization was more or less accepted; but in Judea only the hellenized elites were favorable. The level of violence was so great that it triggered the revolt of the Maccabees, which spelled a lasting division of Jewish society into parties and sects, which became bitter rivals.

3. *The Revolt of the Maccabees (167–142 BC)*

The book of Daniel—critically important for the "political" ideas of the Old Testament—is contemporaneous with the revolt of the Maccabees. The revolt began in 167 BC, when Mattathias the Hasmonean, a non-Zadokite priest,[22] hurled thousands of Hasideans (*hassidim* or "pious" Jews) into battle against the Greco-Syrian occupier. The revolt continued through 165 BC under the leadership of two of Mattathias's sons, Simon and Judah. At the head of a growing number of rebels, they successfully carried out numerous daring military campaigns, including the liberation of the Temple, which was purified and rededicated in 164 BC (this episode is commemorated

---

[21] For more on Scipio Africanus, see above, pp. 260–61.

[22] This fact is important. Many Jews considered the Hasmonean dynasty to be illegitimate because it descended neither from David nor from Zadok. Such Jews held the Hasmoneans to be usurpers of the kingship and the priesthood.

in Judaism as Hanukkah, the Festival of Lights or Festival of Dedication). The revolt ignited an all-out war with the Greco-Syrians. Both sides used every weapon in their arsenals: the Jews enlisted Roman diplomacy and exploited the internal divisions of the Seleucid kingdom; on their side, the Greco-Syrians took advantage of the fractures in Judean society and leaned on the hellenized elite in Jerusalem for support. The new king Antiochus V was forced to allow the Jews to live by their own Law.

After many successes, Judah was finally killed with 800 of his men in a desperate battle in 160 BC. The Seleucids resettled in the land with the help of the high priest Alcimus. But another of Mattathias's sons, Jonathan, soon took up the struggle in the wake of Judah's defeat. Jonathan escaped into the desert and gradually regained control of all Judea until he finally wrested the title of high priest from one of the Seleucid parties. Such were his successes that he did battle at Antioch at the head of the Greek armies. Jonathan expanded his territories (even at the expense of Samaria), then he, too, fell into a trap and was killed. His older brother, Simon, took over and became the high priest (*archiereus*), general (*strategos*), and leader (*hegoumenos*) of the Jews. In so doing, he took all temporal and spiritual powers into his own hands.

So, at a cost of 25 years of war, the Maccabean brothers[23] returned its political independence to Judea.

H. The Rebirth of Monarchy, Quarrels with Rome, and the Final Crisis (142 BC–70 AD)

The last period during which the Jewish people existed as a political body occurred under Roman rule. Rome had become the overlord of the entire Near East. Initially the Hasmonean monarchy—the name given to the dynasty founded by the Maccabean brothers—was allied with Rome (142 to 63 BC); then it came under Roman domination (63 to 37 BC). Roman rule continued indirectly with the collaboration of a new dynasty, the Herodians (37 BC to 66 AD), and after by direct administration. Roman authority, however, was so unstable that a war of independence, the Jewish War (66–70 AD) ensued, whereupon the Romans destroyed the Temple, chased the Jews from Jerusalem, and ended the existence of an independent Israel.

We must briefly recount these four phases, then examine an important phenomenon, noteworthy for its ideological impact: the division of Jewish society into parties and sects, each with a profoundly different worldview.

1. *The Hasmonean Dynasty in Alliance with Rome (142–63 BC)*

The dynasty was accorded recognition under Simon, and his title was granted by an assembly gathered for this purpose in 140 BC. Simon ruled until 135 and was succeeded by *John Hyrcanus* (134–104 BC), who assumed the title of king. Then followed *Aristobulus* (104–103 BC), *Alexander Jannaeus* (103–76 BC), *Alexandra* (76–67 BC)—since a woman was not allowed to assume the function of high priest, she entrusted it to her son Hyrcanus—and *Aristobulus II* (67–63 BC).

John Hyrcanus conducted wars that led to an expansion of the territory. He also destroyed Samaria and the Samaritan temple on Mount Gerizim (the cause of an inextinguishable hate between the Samaritans and the Judeans). Alexander Jannaeus pursued his predecessor's policy of territorial expansion; it was under his rule that the Jewish kingdom achieved its maximum geographical reach (Judea, Idumea, Galilee, Samaria, Philistia, the Plain of Sharon, the Golan Heights, Gaulanitis, and Moabitis).

---

[23] "Maccabeus" (which means "hammer" or, perhaps, "chosen by Yahweh") was the surname given first to Judah. Thereafter, by convention, it was extended to all five brothers.

2. *The Hasmonean Dynasty under Roman Domination (63–37 BC)*

After Pompey took Jerusalem in 63 BC, two rulers followed in succession: *Hyrcanus II* (63–40 BC) (the Romans refused to grant him the title of king), and *Antigonus* (40–37 BC). This was a period of great turmoil because of the Roman civil war and Parthian attacks. There was constant conflict between the various parties.

3. *The Herodian Dynasty under Roman Rule (37 BC–66 AD)*

Herod was a non-Jew and son of the governor of Idumea.[24] He was clever enough to conclude an alliance with the Roman occupier. For his efforts the Roman Senate appointed him king. Several years later Augustus confirmed his appointment and his title. With assistance from the Roman army, Herod conquered the rest of the country still in the hands of Hasmonean partisans. He ruled from 37 BC until 4 AD under the name of "Herod the Great."

Herod pursued a policy of grand public works, relying heavily on Roman technologies. He restored and embellished the Temple, the royal palace, the city walls, and siege towers. He was a great admirer of Greco-Roman culture (he sent his two sons to Rome for an education) and surrounded himself with hellenizing scholars (Nicholas of Damascus). He did not personally hold the office of High Priest. He ended lifelong appointments to the high priesthood and appointed both Pharisees and Sadducees to the office (see below). Finally, he obtained from Rome the right of the Jews in Judea and throughout the Diaspora to live according to their Law and to sacrifice at the Temple.

When Herod the Great died, the kingdom was divided into three "tetrarchies" under the overall authority of the legate of the Roman province of Syria. Each was held by one of his sons: Herod Philip, Herod Archelaus, and Herod Antipas. Other members of the family (Herod Agrippa I, Herod Agrippa II) administered the country on behalf of the Romans, so that it is possible to speak of a Herodian "dynasty."

4. *Palestine under Direct Roman Administration*

Between 6 AD and 41 AD, the Romans had no other choice but to administer Judea, Samaria, and Idumea directly (Pontius Pilate, who held office between 26 and 36, was one of these direct administrators, or Roman prefects, as they were known). Rome did not abolish the Sanhedrin, which continued to legislate and pass judgment under the presiding high priest. The latter position now belonged to four great families, who alternated in the function.

Beginning in 44 AD, all of Palestine came under the rule of Roman "procurators," who from time to time traveled to Jerusalem from their residence in Caesarea[25] (e.g., Felix and Festus, who sat in judgment of Paul; cf. Acts 25).

This policy proved unsuccessful for the occupier. The procurators, ignorant of local customs and motivated only by gain, repeatedly made mistakes. The threat of revolt simmered, then flared into the open in a series of crises. Finally it broke into an all-out *war of independence* that involved the entire population, including the learned and moderate elite, who until then had collaborated with the Greeks and the Romans.

The war swept throughout Palestine and enveloped Alexandria. Rome dispatched one legion, then three more, under the command of the future emperor Vespasian and his son Titus.

---

[24] Idumea is a Greek name formed from "Edom." After the Exile, the Edomites spread west and north, such that, at the time of the Maccabees and the Roman occupation, Idumea referred to a vast territory located south of Judea between the Dead Sea, Hebron, Gaza, and Bersabe (Beersheba).

[25] Caesarea was a new city located on the Mediterranean coast midway between Jaffa and Mount Carmel. It was founded by Herod the Great between 12 and 9 BC.

In 70 AD, Titus laid siege to Jerusalem, captured the city, razed it to the ground, massacred the population, and carried off the survivors as slaves. He made Judea into a Roman province with a permanently garrisoned legion. Above all he destroyed the second Temple completely and dissolved the Sanhedrin. Henceforth, the traditional cult could no longer be practiced. The future survival of the Jewish religion depended on its *radical transformation*.

Outside Jerusalem, the war lasted until 74 AD. The remaining 870 inhabitants of Massada, a fortress on the Dead Sea under Roman siege, preferred collective suicide to surrender.[26] According to Flavius Josephus and Tacitus, some 600,000 Jews lost their lives during the war, roughly one-quarter of the total Jewish population of Palestine.[27]

Then, in 132–35 AD, a final revolt erupted. Its leader, Simon ben Kosiba (called "Bar Kokhba," "son of a star"), was thought by some Jews to be the Messiah (among them some of the most important scholars of the age, including Rabbi Aqiba, also put to death by the Romans). The revolt was crushed by the emperor Hadrian. Fifty fortresses and a thousand fortified places were taken; an additional 850,000 victims lost their lives. This time, the Jews were forbidden entrance to Jerusalem on pain of death. For nearly two millennia they were denied a homeland and the Diaspora became the "normal" way of life.

5. *The Divisions of Jewish Society: Sadducees, Essenes, Pharisees; Zealots, Baptists, Nazoreans*

The often violent and cruel struggles, in the final decades of the Hebrew state, cast a long shadow over the Jewish observance of the Law. Some factions of the population refused to admit religious collapse. Moreover, the Hasmoneans bore the titles of king and high priest, as we said, although they descended neither from David nor Zadok: consequently, they met with fierce resistance. These conflicts resulted in *deep divisions* in Jewish society.

Some "Hasideans" (*hassidim*), the early followers of the Maccabees, broke away when the Hasmoneans sought to be kings and high priests. This led to the following divisions.[28]

a. Sadducees

Some Hasideans argued that the high priest had to be a Zadokite descendant: they were the Sadducees. In general, they belonged to the traditionalist and wealthier segments of society and were members of the priestly caste, the notables, and the senior ranks of the army. They adhered to the written Law (as opposed to the unwritten or oral Law preferred by the Pharisees, as we shall see). The Sadducees believed that the only qualified interpreters of the Law were the priests. Moreover, they rejected the more recent doctrine of the resurrection of the righteous.[29] From a political standpoint, they progressed. They finally came to support the Hasmonean dynasty, which it found to be legitimate as a consequence of the times. They accepted Roman rule until the great Jewish War, at which time they joined the army of resistance *in extremis,* to their detriment.

---

[26] The fortress on the Dead Sea was identified in 1838 and thoroughly studied by archeologists in the twentieth century. It is a national monument of the State of Israel today.

[27] It was a common Roman practice to estimate the loss of human life at one-quarter of the population. Similar estimates were made for losses in Gaul a few decades earlier, roughly 1.5 million people (either by the sword or by famine).

[28] Scholars continue to debate the various groups and sects in ancient Jewish society. The following descriptions should be considered as tentative.

[29] For the same reason, the Sadducees were particularly hostile to Christ and his followers, more so than the Pharisees, who tolerated the new doctrine of the resurrection of the just. Indications here and there in the New Testament show that the Sadducees were responsible for Christ's death and the ensuing anti-Christian repression.

b. Pharisees

Other Hasideans attributed more importance to the written and unwritten Law than to the legitimacy of the priesthood. They were the Pharisees (*perushim,* from the Hebrew root "to be separate" or "set apart"). Their origins were more populist. They did not belong to the priestly circles and were versed in the "secular" study of the Law and the tradition of jurisprudence it inspired (*halakah*). They formed virtually a new intellectual elite, the more that they established training centers and schools. They enjoyed great prestige among the people for their wisdom and uncomplicated life in compliance with the Law. They represented religious purity against the corruption and miscegenation of a hellenized and Romanized elite.

c. Essenes

When the Sadducees finally put their support behind the Hasmonean dynasty, the hardliners in favor of a dual Davidic and Zadokite legitimacy distanced themselves and entered permanent opposition against them. This led to the founding of several well-organized, independent communities outside urban settlements. The first such community was probably founded by the last scion of the Zadokite line known by his sect as the Master of Justice. These Essenian communities were monasteries before the letter. They nurtured the hope of an imminent coming of a messianic king and priest. They also entertained innovative ideas about the impending triumph of Good and the extermination of Evil in the world. The Essenes were also responsible for *a messianic, apocalyptic vibrancy in the Jewish literature of the time.* Ultimately, they laid the foundations for the coming of Christianity.[30]

The Hasmonean kings leaned on one or the other of these factions in turn (they held changing political positions). The Pharisees, who enjoyed the backing of populist circles, often opposed the king, who repressed their actions harshly. In 88 BC, Alexander Janneaus, the perpetrator of various massacres, ordered the crucifixion of 800 Pharisees; prior to this he slaughtered their wives and children before their eyes. Alexandra, in contrast, ushered many scribes and doctors of the Pharisees into the Sanhedrin (thus Pharisaic law acquired the force of law). In reality, under the Hasmonean and Herodian monarchies, the Pharisees and Sadducees took turns holding power. Around the time of Christ, more sects sprang up after troubles in Galilee and Peraea[31] under the rule of Herod Antipas.

d. Zealots

The followers of Judas of Galilee were given the name "Zealots" for their "zeal" (Judas of Galilee was the leader of a violent revolt against a census ordered by Quirinus, legate of Syria, in 6 AD). The Zealots played an important role in the Jewish independence movement under the Roman prefects and procurators, leading up to the destruction of the Temple (perhaps even up to the last revolt in 132–35 AD). After 60 AD, the Zealots were called "Sicarii" (wielders of small concealed daggers) because they were organized in small terrorist units to commit political assassinations and kidnappings.

e. Baptists

About 27 AD in Peraea, a certain John the Baptist attracted followers by practicing full immersion baptism, a symbol of spiritual conversion (it was a sort of liberation from the Jewish Law and

[30] The famous Dead Sea Scrolls from Qumran, discovered in 1947, were the remains of an ancient library in an Essenian community, which had survived for decades in this isolated place. The scrolls have proved to be highly important for our understanding of the so-called intertestamental Jewish literature.

[31] An area east of the Jordan River, between the Sea of Galilee and the Dead Sea.

the official cult practices). John was executed by order of Herod Antipas. Some of his followers rallied to the cause of Jesus of Nazareth.

f. Nazoreans

Shortly after the death of John the Baptist, another preacher from Galilee by the name of Jesus of Nazareth developed a following among the people; he was admired for his speech and miraculous deeds. He was proclaimed the Messiah. He, too, was put to death, this time by order of the high priests of the Sanhedrin. However, his followers, who believed in his resurrection, formed the sect of the "Nazoreans." They were renamed "Christians" (in Greek) ca. 39–40 AD. Their influence spread to Damascus and Antioch, and pagans were also admitted to their numbers. "James the brother of Jesus," the leader of the Nazoreans in Jerusalem, was executed in 62 AD by order of the high priest Annas, a Sadducee. Annas also obtained the conviction of Paul by the Roman authorities (Acts 23–26).[32]

I. Jewish Revival under the Pharisees after the Destruction of the Second Temple

After the disaster of 70–74 AD, a Jewish king ceased to be. The Temple was gone and all hope had vanished from Jerusalem, at least for the foreseeable future. The Zealot, Essenian, and Sadducean uprisings were pitilessly crushed.

Still, the Romans were keen to find a *modus vivendi* with the Jewish people, whose religious identity was so strongly asserted. This explains why they agreed to work with the Pharisees, who had not played a leading role in the struggle. The Pharisees were less concerned with the renewal of the state than with obtaining their religious freedom.

The Pharisees obtained permission from the Romans to open a school for rabbis and the provision of services for the synagogue in Jamnia, a coastal town near Jaffa. The new school gradually assumed some of the judicial functions of the Sanhedrin as well. It was under its auspices that in 90 AD the canon[33] of the Hebrew Bible and the liturgy of Jewish services[34] were decided for good. After the revolt of Simon Bar-Kosiba, the school was transferred to Tiberias in Galilee. Moderate Pharisees continued to preside over the school, primarily under the leadership of the patriarchs of the Hillel family.

Another historical consideration plays a significant role in the transformation of Judaism: namely, its *growth in non-Roman circles in the Orient.* During the events of the year 70 AD, many rabbis fled to Babylon, where an active and prosperous Diaspora community existed. Strengthened by the arrival of the new exiles, this community was led by an "exilarch," who traced his descent from the royal Davidic line (the community thrived under the tolerance of the Parthians and, subsequently, the Sassanid Persians).[35] Higher rabbinic schools were also established in Babylon, and as early as the third century AD Babylonian Judaism began to outweigh Palestinian Judaism in importance.[36] During this period the Talmud appeared. A new written

---

[32] Other groups, fewer in number, were involved in anti-Roman agitation at this time.

[33] The process was actually negative in that the rabbis decided to accept only the Hebrew "TaNaKh" (a symbolic acronym made up of the Hebrew words *T*orah, *N*abi'im, *K*etuvim) and to exclude the more recent books, though considered holy in many respects, but only available in Greek or quoted, a little too insistently, by Christian apologetics for their messianic and apocalyptic content. Among them are the books of Baruch, Sirach, Tobias, Judith, Maccabees I and II, and the Wisdom of Solomon, as well as the pseudoepigraphic Enoch, the Testaments of the Twelve Patriarchs, and the Sibylline Oracles.

[34] In particular, the daily personal prayers and the collective prayers recited in the synagogue.

[35] The Sassanids were a new dynasty that restored the Persian Empire and ruled until the Muslim conquests.

[36] The preeminence of Babylonian Judaism was confirmed after the arrival of the Muslims in the seventh century.

tradition, it provided Judaism with its foundations throughout the entire Christian era down to the present day.

Three concepts characterize the new form of Judaism after its renewal by the Pharisees: the *rabbinate*, the *synagogue*, and the *Talmud*.

1. *The Rabbinate*

Specialists of Jewish law and the commentaries, the *Pharisaic rabbis* dominated the school at Jamnia and its subsidiaries in Palestine, Babylon, and elsewhere in the Diaspora. They took the place of the temple *priests* and formed a new class at the top of the social hierarchy; their legitimacy came from their learning and not their lineage. Their knowledge and moral purity, as well as their scrupulous observance of the religious laws, upheld their elite status (yet they never cut themselves off from the rest of society as did, for example, the monastic Christians).

2. *The Synagogue*

The synagogue (Greek for "assembly") emerged as the replacement of the Temple. It became a place of collective prayer, where the Torah was read, teachings were given, and nonliturgical meetings of the community were held. Although the synagogue emerged as an institution during the Babylonian exile, the earliest archeological remains of stand-alone buildings of worship date only from the first century AD. The synagogue was a revolutionary innovation in the history of religions; it provided a model for Christian *churches* and for Muslim *mosques*. The synagogue was the focal point around which all other institutions of the community were organized, notably schools.

3. *The Talmud*

The canon of Scriptures, decided at a meeting in Jamnia in approximately 90 AD (as we saw), is read only in the context of rabbinic exegesis. The rabbis themselves referred to this as the "oral Torah," handed down by successive rabbinic experts giving an opinion on this or that passage from Scripture. The discussion topics are theological (*haggada*) and especially moral and legal (*halakhah*). In the early days, the commentaries were memorized and handed down orally, then little by little they were put into writing. Two phases in this process can be identified, reflecting the growth in rabbinic commentary and its complexification: the Mishna and the Talmud.

The *Mishna* is a written collection of oral traditions assembled in Palestine during the first three centuries of the common era. The patriarch, Rabbi Judah, produced the first version, probably with a team of experts, around 200 AD. The collection was no doubt intended for rabbinic training purposes and used a very helpful codification system by topic. Other versions came into existence near the end of the third century. It is probable that the Mishna was the work of five or six generations of doctors of the law, perhaps as many as 260 experts.

During the following three centuries, the Mishna itself became the focus of commentaries in Palestine and—most importantly—in Babylon. These new commentaries are called *Gemara* (Aramaic for "learning by tradition"). It is the final compilation of these combined commentaries (the *Mishna* and the *Gemara*) that make up what is called *the Talmud* (Hebrew for "study, teaching"). The Jerusalem Talmud was probably completed in the middle of the fifth century in Tiberias (the Romans abolished the patriarchate there ca. 425 AD). It comments on 39 tractates of the Mishna. The Babylonian Talmud, completed in the seventh and eighth centuries, is longer (some 6,000 pages) and better organized. This became the standard text for all rabbinic Judaism.

What does the Talmud contain? A trove of knowledge of two principal kinds: the *halakhah* and the *haggada*. It should be noted that the purpose of all this was not to establish a single doctrine or "orthodoxy" (the equivalent of a Christian dogmatism never existed in Judaism). Instead, it was to specify the acts to perform in order to live according to the Torah. The rules for a righteous life in the real world (an "orthopraxis") are revealed in the Torah, Mishna, and Talmud by God, either directly or indirectly. All 613 prescriptions (248 commandments and 365 prohibitions) must be observed. Thus, in terms of knowledge there is no rigidity, but in terms of practical living there is great strictness. Jews are under obligation to study the Torah, constantly and intensely, their whole life long. It is in this sense that Judaism is by definition the "religion of the Book." This explains why the tradition of study in Judaism is so strong. Moreover, because no state or other institution existed outside the synagogue for the organization of the community, at least until the Jews became integrated in modern states, the study of the Torah was identical with study and learning in the broad sense. For traditional communities, Judaism was a culture in its own right and permeated the personal and social spheres of all its members.

This brand of rabbinic Judaism, rooted in the synagogue, abandoned attempts at establishing an independent Jewish state by force. It did, however, keep alive an eschatological vision in a different form. Rabbinic thought holds that the fruit of strict observance of the Torah will be the advent of a messianic kingdom.

The problem is that the Jewish way of life, based on the strict observance of particularist practices vis-à-vis surrounding societies (notably, a strict ban on mixed marriages and endogamy, resulting in talk of a Jewish "race"), produced incomprehension and, little by little, the hostility of Christian and Muslim host societies. Thus, the history of rabbinic Judaism gradually merged with the history of *anti-Semitism*.

II. "Political" Thought in the Old Testament

The Israelite confederation was formed of poor nomads in the process of sedentarization, living a precarious existence. They aspired to building a state to ensure their military security and to advance their social and economic well-being: they wanted to "be like all the nations" (1 Sam. 8:20). But the neighboring states were typical Near Eastern sacred monarchies of the kind we know: centralized, bureaucratic, and militarized kingships with a sacrificial religion rooted in myth and ritual. Would the Hebrew people be able to fit the same pattern? As we shall see, the answer is no, because at the very outset they missed their rendezvous with the classical model of the sacred state. The Hebrew people were driven to invent an entirely new social model, contrasting significantly with the traditional monarchies in the Near East and with the contemporaneous model of the Greek city. Israelite *social* thought was genuinely original, but it was not *political* thought in the Greco-Roman scientific sense, which is why we refer to it as "political" in inverted commas.

A. Antimonarchic Ideology

In Judges, the book that narrates the events of the time of the Israelite Federation, the Bible bears witness to an unprecedented *antimonarchic rebelliousness*.[37]

[37] Material in this section is drawn from Maddox, *Religion and the Rise of Democracy*, 27–45.

1. *JUDGES*

In his *Kingship of God,* Martin Buber discusses the "seven anti-monarchic" stories narrated in the book of Judges.[38]

• The first story mocks the fall of Adoni-bezek, brought down by the tribes of Judah and Simeon: Adoni-bezek had cut off the thumbs and big toes of threescore and ten kings to no avail; then he suffered the same fate as well. Once-mighty kings fall; their power is fundamentally frail (Judg. 1:1–7).

• The next story praises the accomplishment of the first judge, Othniel, who delivered Israel from the yoke of King Cushan-rishathaim ("man from Cush, he of the twofold crime"), a king of Mesopotamia (Aram of the two rivers) (Judg. 3:7–11).

• The third story ridicules the taste for luxury and extravagance displayed by Eglon, king of Moab. He was "a very fat man." When Ehud plunged his sword into his belly, "the fat closed over the blade" (Judg. 3:12–25).

• Barak and two women, Deborah and Jael, *exterminated* King Jabin of the Canaanites (Judg. 4–5).

• *The story of Gideon.* Also named Jerubbaal, Gideon assumed military leadership over the tribes following a face-to-face meeting with God who appeared in the form of an angel. Gideon won a great victory over the Midianites and was offered the kingly crown, which he refused. "Then the men of Israel said to Gideon, 'Rule over us, you and your son and your grandson also; for you have delivered us out of the hand of Mid'ian.' Gideon said to them, 'I will not rule over you, and my son will not rule over you; the LORD will rule over you'" (Judg. 8:22–23).[39]

• *The fable of the trees.* After killing all his brothers except for Jotham, Abimelech, one of Gideon's many sons, had himself proclaimed king of Shechem. Jotham, however, thwarted Abimelech's grab for royal power when he addressed this allegory to a gathering of citizens from Shechem:

> The trees once went forth to anoint a king over them; and they said to the olive tree, "Reign over us." But the olive tree said to them, "Shall I leave my fatness, by which gods and men are honored, and go to sway over the trees?" And the trees said to the fig tree, "Come you, and reign over us." But the fig tree said to them, "Shall I leave my sweetness and my good fruit, and go to sway over the trees?" And the trees said to the vine, "Come you, and reign over us." But the vine said to them, "Shall I leave my wine which cheers gods and men, and go to sway over the trees?" Then all the trees said to the bramble, "Come you, and reign over us." And the bramble said to the trees, "If in good faith you are anointing me king over you, then come and take refuge in my shade; but if not, let fire come out of the bramble and devour the cedars of Lebanon." (Judg. 9:8–16)[40]

• *The story of Jephthah.* Jephthah, the illegitimate son of a harlot, lived the life of a freebooter until he was invited by the elders of Gilead to be their leader and rid them of the threat of an Ammonite invasion. Jephthah stipulated that, if successful in the struggle with the Ammonites, he was to continue as their leader and be king of Gilead. He won the victory over the Ammonites but at the expense of the following vow to Yahweh: he would make a burnt offering to Yahweh of whatsoever would come from his door to greet him upon his return from war. The battle is

[38] Quoted in ibid., 28.

[39] In Israel, God alone is king: we will return to this theme shortly.

[40] Not a good start for the reputation of temporal power in Israel!

fought, Jephthah is victorious, and the first to greet him upon returning home is his daughter and only child. The sacrifice is made, depriving Jephthah of a royal dynasty (Judg. 11).

Buber concludes: "The kingship . . . is not a productive calling. It is vain, but also bewildering and seditious, that men rule over men. Every one is to pursue his own proper business, and the manifold fruitfulness will constitute a community over which, in order that it endure, no one needs to rule—no one except God alone."[41] From the very outset of their history, the Israelites appear to hold the institution of monarchy as indissolubly bound up with pagan polytheism.

2. *Samuel and Nathan*

After the time of the Judges came the Saulic and the Davidic-Solomonic lines of royalty. Almost immediately they became the target of prophetic admonitions. Monarchy was not at all an endogenous product of Hebrew culture, as it was in the neighboring sacred monarchies; to the contrary, it was an artificial borrowing from these foreign kingships. For the people the king cannot be a magico-religious figure endowed with supernatural powers. The people had their own customs, and probably had an earlier version of the Mosaic law. It was in reference to these customs and to this covenant that the prophets explicitly denounced the *principle* and *practice* of monarchy.[42]

Antimonarchic ideology finds expression in several verses in the first book of Samuel, which tell of the prophet Samuel's rejection of the people's demand for a king.[43]

> Then all the elders of Israel gathered together and came to Samuel at Ramah, and said to him, "Behold, you are old and your sons do not walk in your ways; now appoint for us a king to govern us like all the nations." But the thing displeased Samuel when they said, "Give us a king to govern us." And Samuel prayed to the Lord. And the Lord said to Samuel, "Hearken to the voice of the people in all that they say to you; for they have not rejected you, but they have rejected me from being king over them. According to all the deeds which they have done to me, from the day I brought them up out of Egypt even to this day, forsaking me and serving other gods, so they are also doing to you. Now then, hearken to their voice; only, you shall solemnly warn them, and show them the ways of the king who shall reign over them." (1 Sam. 8:4–9)

The will to be ruled by a king is the will to no longer be ruled by God. The state is not complementary, but antithetical to theocracy. "[By asking for a king] you have this day rejected your God" (1 Sam. 10:19). Because God "brought up Israel out of Egypt and delivered [the children of Israel] from the hand of the Egyptians, and from the hand of all kingdoms, and from them that were oppressing [them)" (1 Sam. 10:18).

> He said, "These will be the ways of the king who will reign over you: he will take your sons and appoint them to his chariots and to be his horsemen, and to run before his chariots; and he will appoint for himself commanders of thousands and commanders of fifties, and some to plow his ground and to reap his harvest, and to make his implements of war and the equipment of his chariots. He will take your daughters to be perfumers and cooks and bakers. He will take the best of your fields and vineyards and olive orchards and give them to his servants. He will take the tenth of your grain and of your vineyards and give it to his officers and to his servants. He will take your menservants and maidservants, and the

---

41 Quoted in Maddox, *Religion and the Rise of Democracy,* 28–29.

42 As such, prophets did not form a "political" opposition; by no means did they see themselves as an alternative to the ruling power (they did not wish to oust the king). Their opposition is *sui generis* religious and moral.

43 It is possible that these verses are from a later date, perhaps even post-Exile. Be that as it may, they express fairly accurately the position of the classical prophets.

> best of your cattle and your asses, and put them to his work. He will take the tenth of your flocks, and you shall be his slaves. And in that day you will cry out because of your king, whom you have chosen for yourselves; but the Lord will not answer you in that day.
>
> But the people refused to listen to the voice of Samuel; and they said, "No! but we will have a king over us, that we also may be like all the nations, and that our king may govern us and go out before us and fight our battles." And when Samuel had heard all the words of the people, he repeated them in the ears of the Lord. And the Lord said to Samuel, "Hearken to their voice, and make them a king." (1 Sam. 8:10–22)

In the end Samuel gave the Hebrew people a monarchy, albeit a *limited* one, under obligation to uphold the customs of the Israelite federation and follow God's commands as interpreted by the prophets (what later became known as "spiritual power"). Furthermore, at the first opportunity, Samuel revoked Saul's royal commission (1 Sam. 15.10–31). And when David dreamed of building a temple in Jerusalem as a concession to the influence of Baal's religion, he was stopped by the prophet Nathan's *veto* (2 Sam. 7): David did not build a house for Yahweh, it was Yahweh who made a house—that is, a dynasty—for David, which is the proper order of things.

In whose name did the prophets criticize kingship? In the name of *justice* and, more exactly, in the name of *social justice.*

B. Justice and Social Justice among the Classical Prophets, the New Messengers of Yahweh

1. *Justice*

Canaanite religious practices were not merely rejected as foreign—they were held to be idolatries. Conversely, the worship of Yahweh began to be understood as a different form of thought entirely, a form of morality, an interiority and a truth, opposed to vain cultural practices rooted in magic. In other words, the prophets introduced a new interpretation of religion: true religion is a matter of conscience, not ritual.[44] "I hate, I despise your feasts, and I take no delight in your solemn assemblies. Even though you offer me your burnt offerings and cereal offerings, I will not accept them, and the peace offerings of your fatted beasts I will not look upon. Take away from me the noise of your songs; to the melody of your harps I will not listen. But *let justice roll down like waters, and righteousness like an ever-flowing stream*" (Amos 5:21–24). The contrast is harsh: "I despise your offerings," then, without transition, "I want justice." One century later, Jeremiah argues the same cause: "To what purpose does frankincense come to me from Sheba, or sweet cane from a distant land? Your burnt offerings are not acceptable, nor your sacrifices pleasing to me" (Jer. 6:20).

"Will you steal, murder, commit adultery, swear falsely, burn incense to Ba'al, and go after other gods that you have not known, and then come and stand before me in this house, which is called by my name, and say, 'We are delivered!'—only to go on doing all these abominations? Has this house, which is called by my name, become a den of robbers in your eyes? Behold, I myself have seen it, says the Lord" (Jer. 7:9–11). Jeremiah made these claims in public before the gate of the Temple. He, in fact, held the Temple itself to be idolatrous: "sacred" but not "holy":

[44] We observe here a development among the Israelites that was contemporaneous among the Greeks: a realization that rituals are ineffective and myths are an illusion. But in the case of the Hebrew people, magico-religious practices are not discredited in the name of pure human *reason* but in the name of a *moral consciousness* that God's law teaches humankind.

> Do not trust in these deceptive words: This is the temple of the Lord, the temple of the Lord, the temple of the Lord. For if you truly amend your ways and your doings, if you truly execute justice one with another, if you do not oppress the alien, the fatherless or the widow, or shed innocent blood in this place, and if you do not go after other gods to your own hurt, then I will let you dwell in this place, in the land that I gave of old to your fathers for ever. (Jer. 7:4–7)

Jeremiah's attack on the Temple is an attack on the entire *establishment,* including an assault on royal power itself. The prophets frequently singled out the king in person for moral censorship. The prophet Nathan held King David to account for killing his servant Uriah and taking his wife (2 Sam. 11, 12). When King Ahab allowed his wife Queen Jezebel (a foreigner) to murder Naboth and seize a vineyard he coveted, the prophet Elijah took him to task:

> Then the word of the Lord came to Eli'jah the Tishbite, saying, "Arise, go down to meet Ahab king of Israel, who is in Sama'ria; behold, he is in the vineyard of Naboth, where he has gone to take possession. And you shall say to him, 'Thus says the Lord, "Have you killed, and also taken possession?"' And you shall say to him, 'Thus says the Lord: "In the place where dogs licked up the blood of Naboth shall dogs lick your own blood."' Ahab said to Eli'jah, "Have you found me, O my enemy?" He answered, "I have found you, because you have sold yourself to do what is evil in the sight of the Lord. Behold, I will bring evil upon you; I will utterly sweep you away [eliminate your posterity]." (1 Kings 21:17–21)

Again, as so often in the northern kingdom, spiritual power caused temporal power to fall.

2. *Social Justice*

The prophets were stern critics, and their criticism contained an undisputed *social* element. The ruling class, that is, the royal and priestly *establishment,* were idolaters. Those closest to Yahweh were the "poor," the mass of weak and propertyless individuals. Hosea spoke to the tradition of the slaves out of Egypt; first Isaiah, who belonged to the citified world of Jerusalem, spoke to the urban poor. And both spoke over the head of the *establishment* directly to the masses.

Jeremiah, who lived under five different kings (of Judah), created an opposition party against the successor to Josiah, whose name was Zedekiah, accusing him of failing to provide protection for the helpless: "And to the house of the king of Judah, say, Hear the word of the Lord: O house of David! Thus says the Lord: 'Execute justice in the morning, and deliver from the hand of the oppressor him who has been robbed, lest my wrath go forth like fire, and burn with none to quench it, because of your evil doings'" (Jer. 21:11–12).

In the prophecies directed against Jehoiakim, another son of King Josiah, the criticism is more economic, "anti-rich":

> Woe to him who builds his house by unrighteousness, and his upper rooms by injustice; who makes his neighbor serve him for nothing, and does not give him his wages; who says, "I will build myself a great house with spacious upper rooms," and cuts out windows for it, paneling it with cedar, and painting it with vermilion. Do you think you are a king because you compete in cedar? Did not your father eat and drink and do justice and righteousness? Then it was well with him. He judged the cause of the poor and needy; then it was well. Is not this to know me? says the Lord. But you have eyes and heart only for your dishonest gain, for shedding innocent blood, and for practicing oppression and violence. (Jer. 22:13–17)

Amos chided the new urban and state economic system that exploited the poor: "Hear this, you who trample upon the needy, and bring the poor of the land to an end, saying, 'When will the new moon be over, that we may sell grain? And the sabbath, that we may offer wheat for sale, that we may make the ephah small and the shekel great, and deal deceitfully with false balances, that we may buy the poor for silver and the needy for a pair of sandals?'" (Amos 8:4–6).[45]

Isaiah echoes him: "The Lord enters into judgment with the elders and princes of his people: 'It is you who have devoured the vineyard, the spoil of the poor is in your houses. What do you mean by crushing my people, by grinding the face of the poor?'" (Isa. 3:14–15).

And Micah: "Can I forget the treasures of wickedness in the house of the wicked, and the scant measure that is accursed? Shall I acquit the man with wicked scales and with a bag of deceitful weights?" (Mic. 6:10–11).

The rich tilt the scales in their favor and behave shamelessly with the laws of society—this accusation is even harsher than the previous one. The rulers manipulate institutions and abuse justice and the law; they are no more than a gang of "thieves": "Your princes are rebels and companions of thieves. Every one loves a bribe and runs after gifts. They do not defend the fatherless, and the widow's cause does not come to them" (Isa. 1:23). "Their hands are upon what is evil, to do it diligently; the prince and the judge ask for a bribe, and the great man utters the evil desire of his soul" (Mic. 7:3).

The high and mighty change the law to suit their purpose: "Woe to those who decree iniquitous decrees, and the writers who keep writing oppression, to turn aside the needy from justice and to rob the poor of my people of their right, that widows may be their spoil, and that they may make the fatherless their prey!" (Isa. 10:1–2).

It is only to be expected that God takes issue with a nation whose positive laws run counter to God's own: "Hear the word of the Lord, O people of Israel; for the Lord has a controversy with the inhabitants of the land. There is no faithfulness or kindness, and no knowledge of God in the land; there is swearing, lying, killing, stealing, and committing adultery; they break all bounds and murder follows murder" (Hos. 4:1–2; see Jer. 2:8–9; Isa. 3:13–15).

This propaganda was comparatively effective. Perhaps the prophecies of Isaiah and Micah played a part in the religious reforms of King Hezekiah at the end of the eighth century. As for the book of Deuteronomy, made public under King Josiah in the second half of the seventh century and probably written in the northern kingdom during the age of the classical prophets, it obviously includes some of the demands of the prophets discussed above. It insists more than ever on the covenant between Yahweh and his people, particularly on the demand for social justice, which heretofore had not been translated into the laws. In Deuteronomy, Moses is quoted as saying: "If there is among you a poor man, one of your brethren, in any of your towns within your land which the Lord your God gives you, you shall not harden your heart or shut your hand against your poor brother, but you shall open your hand to him, and lend him sufficient for his need, whatever it may be. . . . For the poor will never cease out of the land; therefore I command you, You shall open wide your hand to your brother, to the needy and to the poor, in the land" (Deut. 15:7–11). The author of Deuteronomy also discusses the issue of wage justice and fair

---

[45] This alludes to indentured service, a form of debt obligation. Maddox observes:

> Around the monarchy had grown what Max Weber called an urban patriciate. . . . Not only did this parasitic class live off the travail of the poor; they won their easy power by dispossessing the weak, wrenching away their means of subsistence. Much of the property of the rich had been taken over from smallholders who had secured loans on their land and had surrendered it on default of payment. They continued to pay ruinous rents to their landlords and there is a strong presumption that, deprived of the security of their land, they raised further loans on the security of their persons, on default becoming bondservants or even permanent slaves of the wealthy. . . . So Amos accuses the wealthy of a complex system of exploitation. (*Religion and the Rise of Democracy*, 38–39).

dealing over debt (Deut. 24:18). Every seventh year all debts are to be cancelled, and slaves are to be offered their freedom (Deut. 15:1–6, 12–17).[46]

3. *Beyond Natural Justice:* Mishpat *and* Tsedaqa

One point deserves special attention: the significant difference in tone and intention between the prophetic appeal for justice and the criticism of injustice that we find in the Greek world, for example in Hesiod. The prophets do not simply fault the *hubris* of kings and the wealthy to the exclusion of all else; that is, excess and immoderation were not the sole explanations for injustice. They also accused them of being *indifferent* to the poor. In the opinion of Maddox, there is a stronger sense of justice in the concepts of *mishpat* and *tsedaqa. Mishpat* is more or less simple justice, that is, the judgment of an honest judge giving each party his due; it approximates Greek *nomos. Tsedaqa,* in contrast, extends beyond mere obligation: it is a deep desire to repair justice where it is disturbed, and to usher it in, by instituting love and charity where it is absent. The words *mishpat* and *tsedaqa* can be translated as "justice" and "a burning compassion for the oppressed," respectively. Jeremiah advocated a circumcision of the heart: "Circumcise yourselves to the LORD, remove the foreskin of your hearts" (Jer. 4:4).[47]

A call for justice (*tsedaqa*) in public discourse has profound political implications: it means *the impossibility of leaving matters as they are;* the illnesses of society have to be faced and fully cured. This is the responsibility of the leaders of the people; and for that matter, it is the only one that makes them legitimate leaders. Leadership of the community is more than mere "government"; it includes *an obligation of social transformation.*

Compared with the Greco-Roman world, Hebrew prophets introduced something totally different in the art of government. Henceforth, politics becomes inseparable from *eschatology* and *messianism.*

C. Messianism and Eschatology in the Classical Prophets

Let us begin with a definition of these terms:[48]

- Etymologically speaking, *eschatology* is concerned with the end of history or the end of the world (the Greek *eschaton* means "last" or "ultimate"); more generally, it concerns the end-time, also called the End of Days. The claim of *tsedaqa* (i.e. the conviction that God demands a higher form of justice) leads to the idea that the end-time will be *different* from the present. There is still room for progress; God's Creation can yet be perfected. Time no longer moves in a *cyclical* direction; it is now *linear.* In other words, *tsedaqa*—anticipating the Gospel's command of *agape* or "love"—introduces the idea of history into human thought.

---

[46] The author of Deuteronomy also demanded that the king accord legal rights not only to the poor but to *aliens, orphans,* and *widows* as well. These last three categories are *scapegoat* categories, according to Girard's theory (*The Violence and the Sacred*). Messianic Scripture says that the saints defend their cause in particular. Thus, prophetic thought offers a new "escape route" from the sacrificial logic of primitive societies. Prophetic morality sees a *victim* in the person who is accused, despised, and rejected by the multitude; such a person is held by the masses to be diabolical and guilt-laden. Like the Greek city, which promotes equality before the law, the Bible offers *another avenue of escape from the sacrificial logic of archaic societies.*

[47] See Joel (end of the seventh century BC): "Return to me with all your heart. . . . Rend your hearts, and not your garments" (Joel 2:12–13).

[48] See Neher, *Prophètes et prophéties;* Benjamin Gross, *Messianisme et eschatologie* [Messianism and eschatology], in *Encyclopédie de la mystique juive* [Encyclopedia of Jewish mysticism], ed. Armand Abécassis and Georges Nataf (Paris: Editions Berg International, 1977); republished in one volume as *Messianisme et histoire juive, Encyclopédie juive* (Paris: Editions Berg International, 1994); Grelot, *L'espérance juive.*

• *Messianism* is the conviction that the advent of the end-time will require divine intervention through a prominent human or anthropomorphic figure, such as a king ("messiah" means the "anointed" one), a priest, perhaps an entire nation—the people of Israel—or an angel.

These ideas can be found in the writings of the early prophets, and they develop over time. Three partially overlapping phases can be identified in their development:

1. *Messianism as hope in the restoration of classical Davidic monarchy.* In the earliest days, the prophets claimed that the misfortunes of the land were a consequence of the people turning away from Yahweh's Law; as soon as they return to the strict observance of the Law, Yahweh's anger will cease and things will become normal again. The improvement to come is represented as the *restoration of the classical Davidic monarchy throughout the land of Israel.* Thus, the messianic era is essentially a restoration, a "return" (*techouva*).

2. *Messianism as hope in a perfect Israelite society, from which injustice and misery will disappear entirely.* At the same time that the Mesopotamian threat made the restoration of a classical monarchy in Israel less and less probable, the messiah figure became less realistic, more idealistic and miraculous. The new Israel will be radically different from the old one. Either the king of Israel will be a "holy one," who will bring about perfect social justice and put an end to war, or there will be neither king nor state because God will rule over the people directly in a New Covenant. This situation will last forever. At this stage there is no escaping time and history: only the real Israel, its land and people, and the generations that follow will experience the messianic era.

3. *Messianism as hope in the end of history: the "apocalyptic" Scriptures.* Toward the end of the period of Exile, then again much later, after a dwindling of messianic hope (reflecting the apogee of priestly "theocracy" during the Maccabean crisis) until the destruction of the Second Temple, there were moments when messianic and eschatological ideas reached a tipping point. The "world to come" became the "end of time." In a sense, this reflected an exit from history (which does not mean an end to the life of the flesh as such). Alongside this development, the idea of the *resurrection of the dead* appeared: a coming time of justice and messianic joy would be experienced not only by those who are alive at the moment of the epic eschatological struggle, but also by the righteous of an earlier time, miraculously resurrected. These events will concern all nations, not just Israel alone. God himself will sit in judgment over all humankind in a "Last Judgment."

Let us first examine the primary messianic and eschatological themes found in the writings of the classical prophets. Then, we will turn to the apocalyptic literature.

1. *The Figure of the Messiah*

a. The Messiah Is a King in the Davidic Line

For the classical prophets, the messiah is a Hebrew king[49] in the line of David: "And there shall come forth a shoot from the stump of Jesse,[50] and a Branch shall grow out of his roots" (Isa. 11:1).

"Behold, the days are coming, says the LORD, when I will fulfil the promise I made to the house of Israel and the house of Judah. In those days and at that time I will cause a righteous Branch to spring forth for David (Jer. 33:14–16; see also 23:5). This primacy of the "house of David" reflects the collapse of the northern kingdom.

[49] In some instances, he may not be a Hebrew. Second Isaiah (also known as Deutero-Isaiah), the author of chapters 40–55 of the book of Isaiah, calls Cyrus, the king of Persia, the "messiah." Cyrus was the rising star in politics; his successes portended the imminent downfall of the Chaldeans and the liberation of Israel (see Isa. 40:13, 41:1–5, 41:25–29, 45:1–13, 46:8–13, 48:12–16).

[50] Jesse is the father of David, see 1 Sam. 16:1.

b. THE MESSIAH IS A RIGHTEOUS PERSON, A SAINT, INFUSED WITH THE SPIRIT OF GOD

The king, who may be a child, is chosen by God, who gives him his Spirit (*ruah*). This gift makes the chosen one a powerful king, a righteous person, and a saint: "For to us a child is born, to us a son is given; and the government will be upon his shoulder, and his name will be called 'Wonderful Counselor, Mighty God, everlasting Father, Prince of Peace.' Of the increase of his government and of peace there will be no end, upon the throne of David, and over his kingdom, to establish it, and to uphold it with justice and with righteousness from this time forth and for evermore. The zeal of the LORD of hosts will do this" (Isa. 9:6–7). "And the Spirit of the LORD shall rest upon him, the spirit of wisdom and understanding, the spirit of counsel and might, the spirit of knowledge and the fear of the LORD" (Isa. 11:2). The legitimate offspring of the house of David "shall execute justice and righteousness in the land. In those days Judah will be saved and Jerusalem will dwell securely. And this is the name by which it will be called: 'The LORD is our righteousness'" (Jer. 33:15–16). This righteous king will preside over the destiny of a reunited Hebrew kingdom (combining Judah and Israel), and all its institutions, including the Temple and the priestly class that serves it.[51]

c. THE "KENOTIC" FIGURES OF THE MESSIAH

Over time, the Jewish Messiah was so idealized and so completely identified with a figure of pure justice that the prophets projected an image of him in which the temporal king became absorbed almost entirely in the figure of a saint. Far from being a glorious and triumphant king, he became a humble person capable of suffering for others.

First Isaiah says: "Behold my servant, whom I uphold, my chosen, in whom my soul delights; I have put my Spirit upon him, he will bring forth justice to the nations. He will not cry or lift up his voice, or make it heard in the street; . . . the coastlands wait for his law" (Isa. 42.1–4).

Then Deutero-Isaiah transformed the Messiah into a "suffering servant": "He was despised and rejected by men; a man of sorrows, and acquainted with grief; and as one from whom men hide their faces he was despised, and we esteemed him not. Surely he has borne our griefs and carried our sorrows; yet we esteemed him stricken, smitten by God, and afflicted. But he was wounded for our transgressions, he was bruised for our iniquities; upon him was the chastisement that made us whole, and with his stripes we are healed" (Isa. 53:3–5).

The messianic figure is predestined to triumph. But like certain prophets—for example, Jeremiah[52]—the messianic figure will triumph in excruciating pain, resulting in physical humiliation and complete social annihilation. His voluntary sacrifice will redeem the "sins of the many."

The same theme, perhaps with less emphasis but essentially the same meaning, is found in Deutero-Zechariah.[53] God will act through a mediator in the form of several figures: a *messianic king* (Zech. 9:9–10), successor to the Davidic-Solomonic line and the prophets (because he is

---

[51] This is why, in the prophecies of Haggai and Zechariah dating from the early days after the Exile, it is not only a question of restoring the Davidic monarchy, but also the Zadokite priesthood. The accession of a new high priest is described in terms as wonderful as for a new king. In later intertestamental literature, notably in the Qumran writings, there are many references to a "Messiah of Aaron" (i.e., a messianic priest) alongside the "Messiah of David." Together they form a pair, so to speak, and rule together over the restored nation.

[52] See Neher, *Prophètes et prophéties,* 276–301, for a description of the trials and tribulations of the prophets, which make them all, in a sense, "suffering servants."

[53] The prophecies attributed to Deutero-Zechariah, especially the messianic passages (chapters 9–11), may date from 330 BC, the beginning of the Greek era. If this date is accepted, the text expresses the ideological fermentation taking place at the time of Alexander's conquests and the associated political upheaval. Deutero-Zechariah's messianic ideal (see 9:1–8, 9–10, 11–17; 10:3–11) is close to Isaiah's ideal of apocalyptic revelation (Isa. 24–27).

both righteous and poor); a *good shepherd* (Zech. 11:4–17, 13:7–9)—therefore he is close to the Lord who is himself a shepherd of men (see Ezek. 34:11–22, 31); and finally a "pierced" man:

> And on that day I will seek to destroy all the nations that come against Jerusalem. And I will pour out on the house of David and the inhabitants of Jerusalem a spirit of compassion and supplication, so that, when they look on him whom they have pierced, they shall mourn for him, as one mourns for an only child, and weep bitterly over him, as one weeps over a first-born. . . . On that day there shall be a fountain opened for the house of David and the inhabitants of Jerusalem to cleanse them from sin and uncleanness. (Zech. 12:9–13:1)

Is this perhaps an allusion to the assassination of Onias III or of Simon Maccabeus?[54] In any case, the Covenant is reinstated by a humble, rejected, and persecuted figure (Zech. 13:7–9), recalling Isaiah's figure of the suffering servant. The Messiah's sufferings, like those of the servant, are a source of transformation of hearts (Zech. 12:10) and purification (Zech. 13:1). Though there is a constant link with David, the person is not "royal" in the human sense of the term: he is a source of salvation, not through glory, but through destitution and frustration. It is hardly surprising that the New Testament often refers to Deutero-Zechariah in association with the coming of Jesus Christ. When Jesus rode into Jerusalem, his act is a virtual restaging of the prophet's vision: "Rejoice greatly, O daughter of Zion! Shout aloud, O daughter of Jerusalem! Lo, your king comes to you; triumphant and victorious is he, *humble and riding on an ass,* on a colt the foal of an ass. I will cut off the chariot from Ephraim and the war horse from Jerusalem; and the battle bow shall be cut off, and he shall command peace to the nations; his dominion shall be from sea to sea, and from the River to the ends of the earth" (Zech. 9:9–10). These passages show that biblical prophecy laid the basic foundations for the New Testament theme of a God who "humbled" or "emptied" himself (*kenos* in Greek) and accepted the Cross.

At a time when temporal kings were harshly criticized, the transformation of a messianic king into an essentially humble person left a lasting mark on the attitudes of the Jews and the Christians in regard to temporal power and social majesty in general. In due course, it becomes a point of dogma in every Judeo-Christian faith that earthly hierarchies do not reflect actual spiritual hierarchies, and that pure spirit, stripped of all external trappings, produces deeper, more lasting social transformations than visible power.

d. The "Holy Remnant"

In addition to the theme of the Messiah as a "branch" from which the tree will grow again, there is also the notion of the select few, a remnant of pure individuals destined to assume the sufferings of the servant who brings salvation. This theme is already present in Amos: "'Behold, the eyes of the Lord God are upon the sinful kingdom, and I will destroy it from the surface of the ground; except that I will not utterly destroy the house of Jacob,' says the Lord. 'For lo, I will command, and shake the house of Israel among all the nations as one shakes with a sieve, but no pebble shall fall upon the earth'" (Amos 9:8–10; see 3:12, 5:15).

Thus, God makes a "selection," sometimes using a moral standard, sometimes a purely arbitrary, "gratuitous" one. Some of the remnant may be "saints," some mere "cast offs" (see Mic. 4:7; Songs 2:7–9, 3:12–13; Jer. 3:14, 5:18). In Ezekiel, the select few are those who reject pagan "abominations" and are set aside by a mark upon their forehead to escape the punishment of

[54] In any event, the compilation is more recent than suggested above. Onias III was the high priest, who opposed the confiscations of Heliodorus, the minister of Seleucus IV Philopator. The usurper high priest, Menelas, reinstated the confiscations, then treacherously ordered the assassination of Onias III in 170 BC (2 Macc. 4:32–38; see Dan. 9:26). Simon Maccabee was assassinated in 134 BC (1 Macc. 16:11–17).

extermination that Yahweh placed on the people of Israel (Ezek. 9:4–7; see 6:8, 11:13, 12:16, 14:22–23). Gradually the characteristics of the holy remnant and the Messiah overlap and entwine. When this happens, the Messiah becomes a collective figure, combining all the faithful of Israel, that is, those who resisted the temptation of idolatry. Moreover, in subsequent Jewish thought, the figure of the Messiah increasingly identifies with the entire Jewish people[55] because the nation of Israel is held to be the "holy remnant" among all nations, and through it will come the salvation of all humanity.

The theme of a select minority, authorized to take revolutionary action by virtue of its moral and religious purity, will grow in importance in the political history of Christian societies. It can be found among millenarian groups, in heresies, and even in the activist minorities of modern revolutionary parties.

2. *Messianic Time*

Messianic time is always attributed the same broad features:

a. A Time of Justice

The Messiah-king will mete out justice, in particular social justice: "He shall not judge by what his eyes see, or decide by what his ears hear; but with righteousness he shall judge the poor, and decide with equity for the meek of the earth; and he shall smite the earth with the rod of his mouth, and with the breath of his lips he shall slay the wicked. Righteousness shall be the girdle of his waist, and faithfulness the girdle of his loins" (Isa. 11:3–5). "Give the king thy justice, O God, and thy righteousness to the royal son! May he judge thy people with righteousness, and thy poor with justice! . . . For he delivers the needy when he calls, the poor and him who has no helper. He has pity on the weak and the needy, and saves the lives of the needy . . . . From oppression and violence he redeems their life; and precious is their blood in his sight" (Ps. 72:1–3, 12–14).

When God is come, justice will reign everlasting: "Lift up your eyes to the heavens, and look at the earth beneath; for the heavens will vanish like smoke, the earth will wear out like a garment, and they who dwell in it will die like gnats; but my salvation will be for ever, and my deliverance will never be ended" (Isa. 51:6).

b. A Time of Peace

Another essential characteristic of the messianic era is *peace*. According to Scripture, peace will reign among men and throughout all Creation. This is what the following celebrated texts say: "He shall judge between the nations, and shall decide for many peoples; and they shall beat their swords into plowshares, and their spears into pruning hooks; nation shall not lift up sword against nation, neither shall they learn war any more" (Isa. 2:4).

"The wolf shall dwell with the lamb, and the leopard shall lie down with the kid, and the calf and the lion and the fatling together, and a little child shall lead them. The cow and the bear shall feed; their young shall lie down together; and the lion shall eat straw like the ox. The sucking child shall play over the hole of the asp, and the weaned child shall put his hand on the adder's den"[56]

---

[55] "Israel was holy to the Lord" (Jer. 2:3); "The Lord called me from the womb, from the body of my mother he named my name. . . . And he said to me, "You are my servant, Israel, in whom I will be glorified" (Isa. 49:1–3). In the Middle Ages, the Jewish philosopher Judah Hallevi identified the "suffering servant" of Isaiah 53 with the people of Israel (Neher, *Prophètes et prophéties*, 311).

[56] The reader will recall that the essence of this passage, if not the very same words, was transposed to the "Sibylline oracles" written by the Jewish community of Alexandria. It then entered the new compilation of oracles in Rome after the destruction of the official ancient oracles. It may have inspired Virgil's *Fourth Eclogue*, as we saw earlier (see p. 314).

(Isa. 11:6–8). "The wolf and the lamb shall feed together, the lion shall eat straw like the ox; and dust shall be the serpent's food. They shall not hurt or destroy in all my holy mountain, says the Lord" (Isa. 65:25).

c. Jerusalem and "Mount Zion": The Center of the Kingdom

The restored kingdom will be a united kingdom, and its center will be Jerusalem and "Mount Zion" (this is consistent with the fact that the Messiah will come from the Davidic line: Jerusalem is the quintessential "city of David").

> It shall come to pass in the latter days that the mountain of the house of the Lord shall be established as the highest of the mountains, and shall be raised above the hills; and all the nations shall flow to it, and many peoples shall come, and say: "Come, let us go up to the mountain of the Lord, to the house of the God of Jacob; that he may teach us his ways and that we may walk in his paths." For out of Zion shall go forth the law, and the word of the Lord from Jerusalem. (Isa. 2:2–3; see Mic. 4:1–3)

Many *Psalms* are hymns to Zion (e.g., Ps. 137).

d. The Gathering of the Dispersed Jews in Jerusalem

In this messianic Zion will be gathered the exiles, the deportees, and the captives desiring to return home, as well as all the Jews of the Diaspora settled in faraway countries, even Jews who are now non-Jews, because they are unable to create communities for the preservation of their Jewish identity (a reference to the "ten lost tribes" cast far from the kingdom of Samaria by the Assyrians). All these peoples will settle on Mount Zion. This gathering of the Jewish people will be a sign of the end-time.

"I will bring your offspring from the east, and from the west I will gather you; I will say to the north, Give up, and to the south, Do not withhold; bring my sons from afar and my daughters from the end of the earth, every one who is called by my name, whom I created for my glory, whom I formed and made" (Isa. 43:5–7). "For I will take you from the nations, and gather you from all the countries, and bring you into your own land" (Ezek. 36:24). "I will bring them home from the land of Egypt, and gather them from Assyria; and I will bring them to the land of Gilead and to Lebanon, till there is no room for them" (Zech. 10:10). *A fortiori,* Judah and Israel will be united as one kingdom (Ezek. 37:15–28).

These themes played a leading role throughout Judeo-Christian history and continue to drive Zionist ideology today. The primate of Jerusalem ordered the Crusades. In medieval cosmology, Jerusalem was the center of the world. Dante organized his *Divine Comedy* (1320) around Jerusalem, the center of all land mass. When at the time of the great discoveries Europeans attempted to reach the East by circumnavigating Africa or crossing the Atlantic, the idea was to thwart the Muslims and to open the road again to Jerusalem for all converts. The convergence of Christians the world over on Jerusalem is the unmistakable sign of the end-time.[57]

e. Messianic Exaltation

Already for the early prophets, who nurtured a dream of a restored "classical" kingship, contingent on the people and their leaders mending their ways and heeding the Law, it was obvious that happiness would return and life would begin anew:

[57] See Jean Delumeau, *Mille ans de bonheur* [A thousand years of bliss] (Paris: Fayard, 1995). The early explorers of the New World recognized the natives of the Americas as the remnants of the ten lost tribes. Their conversion was considered a direct prelude to the end-time.

> In that day I will raise up the booth of David that is fallen. . . . "Behold, the days are coming," says the Lord, "when . . . the mountains shall drip sweet wine, and all the hills shall flow with it. I will restore the fortunes of my people Israel, and they shall rebuild the ruined cities and inhabit them; they shall plant vineyards and drink their wine, and they shall make gardens and eat their fruit. I will plant them upon their land, and they shall never again be plucked up out of the land which I have given them." (Amos 9:11–15)

"Return, O Israel, to the Lord your God, for you have stumbled because of your iniquity . . . . I will be as the dew to Israel; he shall blossom as the lily . . . . They shall return and dwell beneath my shadow, they shall flourish as a garden" (Hosea 14:1, 5, 7).

This happiness has something miraculous about it. Subsequent prophets would lift their language to poetic heights to describe it. For example, these words by "Trito-Isaiah":[58]

> be glad and rejoice for ever in that which I create . . . ; no more shall be heard in [Jerusalem] the sound of weeping and the cry of distress. No more shall there be in it an infant that lives but a few days, or an old man who does not fill out his days, for the child shall die a hundred years old, and the sinner a hundred years old shall be accursed. They shall build houses and inhabit them; they shall plant vineyards and eat their fruit.[59] They shall not build and another inhabit; they shall not plant and another eat; for like the days of a tree shall the days of my people be, and my chosen shall long enjoy the work of their hands. They shall not labor in vain, or bear children for calamity; for they shall be the offspring of the blessed of the Lord, and their children with them. Before they call I will answer, while they are yet speaking I will hear. (Isa. 65:17–24)

Deutero-Zechariah writes: "On that day the Lord their God will save them for they are the flock of his people; for like the jewels of a crown they shall shine on his land. Yea, how good and how fair it shall be! Grain shall make the young men flourish, and new wine the maidens" (Zech. 9:16–17).

There is also Isaiah's celebrated description of an "eschatological banquet": "On this mountain the Lord of hosts will make for all peoples a feast of fat things, a feast of wine on the lees, of fat things full of marrow, of wine on the lees well refined" (Isa. 25:6).

Ezekiel, who foretells the liberation of the Israelites from the Babylonian exile, announces the New Jerusalem, which they will build upon their return to Zion. In nine long chapters (Ezek. 40–48), the prophet provides minute details about the architecture of the Temple and the city (which combine as a citadel). He also describes the royal and priestly organization of the country, its borders, its religion and its festivals. The glory of God will fill the Temple. The name of the New Jerusalem will be "YHWH-Shamma," which is to say, "The Lord is there" (Ezek. 48:35). The city will be perched on a "very high mountain." Earlier the prophet criticized the construction of pagan temples in high places. Henceforth such heights will be purified; like a flock, the people will be led by Yahweh to the best pastures in the mountains of Israel. And the New Jerusalem will be raised on the highest of these mountains, with the Temple on the summit.

Trito-Isaiah offers a description of the new city, which is magnificent and almost unreal: "O afflicted one, storm-tossed, and not comforted, behold, I will set your stones in antimony, and lay your foundations with sapphires. I will make your pinnacles of agate, your gates of arbuncles, and all your wall of precious stones. All your sons shall be taught by the Lord, and great shall

[58] Trito-Isaiah ("Third" Isaiah) is thought to have authored the last part of the book of Isaiah, from chapter 56 to the end. He probably prophesied after the return from the Babylonian exile.

[59] This was an obsession of these people constantly subject to invasion and plundering.

be the prosperity of your sons" (Isa. 54:11–13). Later these same images would inspire Christian literature on "Paradise."[60]

3. *The New Covenant: A Society without Institutions*

We need to emphasize another new idea, which many centuries later would inspire utopian and revolutionary currents of Western political thought: the idea that the perfect society of the messianic era might be a society without institutions, or at best with weak, barely visible ones, resulting at any rate in the elimination of the use of coercion.

As we saw, the classical prophets introduced the idea that what God requires is not active participation in the performance of rituals but an inner conversion of the spirit. If all people convert, then peace will prevail among all people as between "the lion and the lamb." Thus, peace and happiness in the community no longer depend on the coercion of the state but on the moral perfection of the individual, who heeds the voice of Yahweh: then the community will become spontaneously peaceful and prosperous. In this sense, the strictly institutional prospect of a restoration of the state and the priesthood fades into the background.

No doubt this is the sense of Jeremiah's somewhat odd political behavior. In the context of modern ideas about the nation and the state, his ideas may seem opportunistic, almost traitorous, because against the party of the king and the aristocrats, who aim to resist the invader Nebuchadnezzar militarily, Jeremiah advocates pure and simple surrender. He walks the streets of Jerusalem with a yoke around his neck, a symbol of bondage, which he holds to be inevitable and invites the people to embrace it.

Behaving in this way, Jeremiah places his hopes of salvation on a nonpolitical plane. Resistance—the preservation of the state at any cost—will expose Judea to total destruction by the armies of Nebuchadnezzar or to the success of a political regime that Jeremiah thinks will be religiously questionable (as we saw, the ruling class scorns all values, and the king is the worst offender). Under these conditions, dealing with the enemy is right, not wrong. Of course, the people will have to pay tribute to the Babylonians, but the cost will be relatively low compared to the looming massacre and loss of religious freedom. For Jeremiah, safeguarding Israel's religion is vital. Compared with the possibility of following the Law of Moses, the question of temporal power comes in second.

God does not want a strong and independent state; God wants a faithful people, who defend the law and peace in their midst. What is needed is a reorganized community, which no longer attempts to impose itself among nations by force, but a community that pursues peace and general prosperity, including among the non-Jews. This is what Jeremiah says in his letter to the captives in Babylon:

> Thus says the Lord of hosts, the God of Israel, to all the exiles whom I have sent into exile from Jerusalem to Babylon: Build houses and live in them; plant gardens and eat their produce. Take wives and have sons and daughters; take wives for your sons, and give your daughters in marriage, that they may bear sons and daughters; multiply there, and do not decrease. But seek the welfare of the city where I have sent you into exile, and pray to the Lord on its behalf, for in its welfare you will find your welfare. (Jer. 29:4–7)

This community will be so holy and pure that no intermediary will be necessary between it and God. A new covenant will be established in which political and priestly institutions will be almost unnecessary, because each member will have interiorized the same morals.

[60] They would also inspire the description of the "Celestial Jerusalem" in the Revelation of John.

> Behold, the days are coming, says the Lord, when I will make a new covenant with the house of Israel and the house of Judah, not like the covenant which I made with their fathers when I took them by the hand to bring them out of the land of Egypt, my covenant which they broke, though I was their husband, says the Lord. But this is the covenant which I will make with the house of Israel after those days, says the Lord: *I will put my law within them, and I will write it upon their hearts;* and I will be their God, and they shall be my people. And no longer shall each man teach his neighbor and each his brother, saying, "Know the Lord," for they shall all know me, from the least of them to the greatest, says the Lord; for I will forgive their iniquity, and I will remember their sin no more." (Jer. 31:31–34)

Ezekiel also expresses the same idea:

> For I will take you from the nations, and gather you from all the countries, and bring you into your own land. I will sprinkle clean water upon you, and you shall be clean from all your uncleannesses, and from all your idols I will cleanse you. *A new heart I will give you, and a new spirit I will put within you; and I will take out of your flesh the heart of stone and give you a heart of flesh. And I will put my spirit within you, and cause you to walk in my statutes and be careful to observe my ordinances* [the Torah]. You shall dwell in the land which I gave to your fathers; and you shall be my people, and I will be your God." (Ezek. 36:24–28)

Thus, the holiness of the people, converted inwardly, will ensure respect for the law and create social harmony. Ezekiel offers a fierce criticism of temporal power, which claims to safeguard order by external means and coercion. This ruling class does not govern in the general interest, but in its own:

> Ho, shepherds of Israel who have been feeding yourselves! Should not shepherds feed the sheep? You eat the fat, you clothe yourselves with the wool, you slaughter the fatlings; but you do not feed the sheep. The weak you have not strengthened, the sick you have not healed, the crippled you have not bound up, the strayed you have not brought back, the lost you have not sought, and with force and harshness you have ruled them. So they were scattered, because there was no shepherd; and they became food for all the wild beasts. . . . Therefore, you shepherds, hear the word of the Lord; . . . *Behold, I am against the shepherds; and I will require my sheep at their hand* . . . for I will rescue my sheep from their mouths, that they may not be food for them. (Ezek. 34:2–10)

Ezekiel is certain that in messianic times there will be a shepherd, "my servant David," but he will simply be "a prince among them," whereas "I, the Lord, will be their God" (Ezek. 34:24). It can be said that this prince will only exercise *ministerial* functions: he will not be the master of the flock by his own authority; rather, he will be God's humble servant in the task of keeping God's sheep. The true ruler will be God in person: "For thus says the Lord God: Behold, I, I myself will search for my sheep, and will seek them out. As a shepherd seeks out his flock when some of his sheep have been scattered abroad, so will I seek out my sheep" (Ezek. 34:11–12).

Thus, the Bible *lessens the importance of the state* either because it restricts temporal power to a subordinate role or imagines that a community can function without political institutions. The state is a relative reality; it is temporary and can be dispensed with; at any rate, it would be immoral to make it an absolute. *True justice and true social harmony are rooted in the dispositions of the heart, which are not created by the state but by God (and his prophets).*

Augustine recalled these passages after the catastrophic seizure of Rome by Alaric in 410 AD. He knew that it was senseless to combine the destiny of Christianity with that of the Roman Empire. The Empire might well perish under the onslaught of the barbarians, but that would not sound the end of Christian society, even one consisting of converted barbarians. Fundamentally, the two cities—the heavenly city and the earthly city—are separate. This is the theme of his *City of God* (see below, chapter 1).

The even more radical idea that society can do without political institutions altogether appears in all millenarian movements and in secular millenarianisms, that is, modern revolutionary ideologies. We will see later that Lenin, too, imagined a society outside history, one thriving peacefully and prosperously without institutions, in which the interiorization of the law in the people's hearts would replace the external coercion of the state.[61]

D. Messianism: The End of History and Apocalyptic Literature

At two particularly tragic moments in the history of Israel—during the Babylonian Exile and in the long period from the persecutions of Antiochus IV Epiphanes (175 BC) to the destruction of the second Temple (70 AD)—eschatology took a radical turn. In addition to the restoration of the state and the founding of a holy and joyful community on Mount Zion, it became possible to imagine *the "end of History" or an "exit" from the cycle of time.*

The corresponding texts and ideas belong to the *apocalyptic genre*. Strictly speaking, the literature of this genre flourished for over 300 years, roughly between 200 BC and 150 AD. However, apocalyptic themes also appeared in the oracles of the exilic prophets, or slightly thereafter. The persecutions of Antiochus IV Epiphanes disrupted 300 years of stability—the fruit of theocracy—and awakened a more anxious tone of eschatological thought among the prophets. This disquiet dawned in Hasidim circles on the periphery of theocracy.

In Greek, the word "apocalypse" means a "lifting of the veil" or "revelation." The new prophetic literature aspired to unveil or reveal the secrets of God's plans for humanity. The inspiration for this came from above through the agency and ministry of the angels, or in the form of visions and dreams rich in imagery.

The authors of apocalyptic literature often gave voice to their messages through historical figures. This enabled such a figure to announce what was already known to have occurred (a process known as foreshadowing or back-dating; sometimes it involves misattributed authorship called pseudoepigraphy). Such figureheads include Daniel, Enoch, Moses, Ezra, the patriarchs, Baruch, and even Adam.

The books belonging to apocalyptic literature include Daniel, the deuterocanonical second book of Maccabees, and texts that are not part of the Old Testament, the so-called intertestamental literature, including the Jewish (Essenian and Pharisaic) Scriptures from the second and first centuries BC and the first century AD (e.g., the Hebrew Revelation of Enoch, the Testaments of the Twelve Patriarchs, the Psalms of Solomon, and the Fourth Book of Ezra).

1. *Eschatological Struggle and the Last Judgment*

A new idea emerged with the exilic prophets and those immediately after them—Ezekiel, Deutero-Isaiah, Trito-Isaiah (the author of the Revelation of Isaiah), Deutero-Zechariah, and Daniel (awaiting the Revelation of St. John the Divine): in order to hasten the end of history, a final, ferocious battle must occur; it will be more fierce and extreme than any other in the history of humankind. It will be followed by the *Last* Judgment, which brings final retribution for all merits and mistakes.

[61] We noted the existence of this theme in the texts of the Neopythagoreans of the third century AD above (see part 2, pp. 368–69).

a. Eschatological Struggle

Toward the end of the seventh century BC,[62] the prophet Joel spoke at some length about the Day of the Lord, a day of disaster when innumerable armies would advance on Israel and destroy all life, casting the entire population into the depths of despair and folly—the only ones to be spared would be the handful who underwent an inner conversion and whom God would recognize as "innocent" and "cleared of the guilt" (Joel 3:19, 21). He would remove their enemies (Joel 2:20) and open up an idyllic existence characterized by abundance, fertility, and joy.

The theme of an eschatological struggle appears again in the writings of Ezekiel and Deutero-Zechariah. All the forces of evil gather under the command of the diabolical figure Gog. Facing them are the forces of good, the army of the saints under the leadership of the Lord's commander-in-chief (an angel, perhaps God himself).

Here is Ezekiel's version. "In the latter days," God will "put hooks into [the] jaws" of Gog, the chief prince of Meshech, and bring him forth in war against Israel, which believes it dwells safely in the mountains. "Persia, Cush, and Put," "a great company," "all of them with buckler and shield," "wielding swords," will join the armies of Gog and come up against the people of Israel (Ezek. 38:16). Then God, in his fury, will bring about a great earthquake in the land of Israel; it will throw down the mountains and hasten the victory of all creatures faithful to God, who will conquer the coalesced armies of evil.

Sometime around 330–300 BC, Deutero-Zechariah had a similar vision:

> For I will gather all the nations against Jerusalem to battle, and the city shall be taken and the houses plundered and the women ravished; half of the city shall go into exile, but the rest of the people shall not be cut off from the city. Then the Lord will go forth and fight against those nations as when he fights on a day of battle. On that day his feet shall stand on the Mount of Olives which lies before Jerusalem on the east; and the Mount of Olives shall be split in two from east to west by a very wide valley; so that one half of the Mount shall withdraw northward, and the other half southward. . . . And the Lord your God will come, and all the holy ones with him. (Zech. 14:2–5; see 9:1–8)

b. *The Last Judgment*

What will be the aftermath of this final battle? God's intervention will take the form of a judgment, which occurring at the end of time will be the "Last Judgment." Let us recall that in early messianic thought the royal Messiah, the "righteous man," brings about universal judgment: "He shall judge among the nations, and shall rebuke many people" (Isa. 2:4). This will happen on the Day of the Lord. The enemies of Israel will be judged and found guilty, and Israel will be innocent. And the enemies of Israel will be exterminated. The words of the Bible are especially strong here: "With pestilence and bloodshed I will enter into judgment with him; and I will rain upon him and his hordes and the many peoples that are with him, torrential rains and hailstones, fire and brimstone. So I will show my greatness and my holiness and make myself known in the eyes of many nations. Then they will know that I am the Lord" (Ezek. 38:22–23).

God will throw fire into the land of the enemy. He will destroy its armies. Seven months will be necessary to bury the dead, such will be their number. The birds and the animals will rejoice before so much blood and flesh to be devoured. "And this shall be the plague with which the Lord will smite all the peoples that wage war against Jerusalem: their flesh shall rot while they are still on their feet, their eyes shall rot in their sockets, and their tongues shall rot in their mouths" (Zech. 14:12; see Isa. 13; Mic. 7:13; Zeph. 3:19). Israel will rule over all nations (see Ezek. 39:21–25).

[62] The most probable date.

Every year the surviving nations will be required to go up to Jerusalem for the feast of the tabernacles and "worship the King, the Lord of hosts" (Zech. 14:16–21), and the Lord will smite the heathen "that do not go up to keep the feast."

"Then every one that survives of all the nations that have come against Jerusalem shall go up year after year to worship the King, the Lord of hosts, and to keep the feast of booths" (Zech. 14:16). "May his foes bow down before him, and his enemies lick the dust! May the kings of Tarshish and of the isles render him tribute, may the kings of Sheba and Seba bring gifts! May all kings fall down before him, all nations serve him" (Ps. 72:9–11).[63]

Perhaps the vanquished nations will convert, in which case they will also enjoy messianic happiness. Such joy will be of a new kind. In Trito-Isaiah (probably around 530/510 AD) a new, radical theme appears in complete break with the past: "For, behold, I create *new heavens* and a *new earth:*[64] and the former shall not be remembered, nor come into mind" (Isa. 65:17–24). Happiness will be *everlasting*. Deutero-Zechariah refers to a true exit from the cycle of time, a "day" when the succession of days and nights will cease:

> [After the last battle], the Lord shall come, and all the holy ones with him. And that day there shall be neither cold nor frost. And there shall be continuous day (it is known to the Lord), not day and not night, for at evening time there shall be light. On that day living waters shall flow out from Jerusalem, half of them to the eastern sea and half of them to the western sea; it shall continue in summer as in winter.[65] And the Lord will become king over all the earth; on that day the Lord will be one and his name one. (Zech. 14:5–9; see 9:1–8)

c. *The Resurrection of the Dead*

Will all the "saints" of Israel see this "one day"? Now an astonishing idea appears: the righteous will enjoy everlasting happiness, either because they will be alive on the Day of the Lord, or because they will be "resurrected," though they are already dead.[66]

During the Exile, the prophet Ezekiel referred to the restoration of Israel as a resurrection of the dead. The spirit (*ruah*) of God—the breath of life—would return them to the living. Here is the entire passage in Ezekiel on the valley of the bones:

---

[63] See Isaiah 49:22–23: Thus says the Lord God: "Behold, I will lift up my hand to the nations, and raise my signal to the peoples; and they shall bring your sons in their bosom, and your daughters shall be carried on their shoulders. Kings shall be your foster fathers, and their queens your nursing mothers. With their faces to the ground they shall bow down to you, and lick the dust of your feet."

[64] This theme is also found in the Revelation of St. John the Divine, see below.

[65] This is the theme of the return of an earthly paradise. The theme of living waters gushing forth from Jerusalem (a symbol for the Temple) and nourishing the land, is also found in the books of Joel (4:18), Ezekiel (47:1–12), and Psalms (46:5). The writings of the Gospel of John will proclaim that it is the fulfillment of Ezekiel's prophecy when the waters gush from the pierced side of the crucified Christ—the new Temple—"a spring of water welling up to eternal life" (John 4:14, 7:37–39; 19:34). Saint John the Divine refers to "a river of the water of life" "flowing from the throne of God and of the Lamb" (Rev. 22:1–2).

[66] The emergence of this theme of the resurrection of the dead is the continuance of a tradition of biblical thought on retribution and reward. At the outset, the traditional Torah taught that God rewarded the righteous—the observers of the Law—and punished the wrongdoer. Then, skepticism arose—perhaps because Israel gradually became part of a multiethnic, "international knowledge culture" with Egypt, Babylon, and the Hellenistic world with their relativistic leanings. The skeptics objected that the wrongdoers prospered while the righteous suffered. This was Qohelet's (Ecclesiastes') position. Then came a third period: the righteous will indeed be rewarded, but their reward will be in heaven. God's justice is fundamentally different from the justice of men; it transcends all understanding. This theme, already found in the book of Job, intensifies in the apocalyptic writings, until it finally crystallizes in the Gospels and the letters of Paul.

> The hand of the Lord was upon me, and he brought me out by the Spirit of the Lord, and set me down in the midst of the valley; it was full of bones. And he led me round among them; and behold, there were very many upon the valley; and lo, they were very dry. And he said to me, "Son of man, can these bones live?" And I answered, "O Lord God, thou knowest." Again he said to me, "Prophesy to these bones, and say to them, O dry bones, hear the word of the Lord. Thus says the Lord God to these bones: Behold, I will cause breath to enter you, and you shall live. And I will lay sinews upon you, and will cause flesh to come upon you, and cover you with skin, and put breath in you, and you shall live; and you shall know that I am the Lord." So I prophesied as I was commanded; and as I prophesied, there was a noise, and behold, a rattling; and the bones came together, bone to its bone. And as I looked, there were sinews on them, and flesh had come upon them, and skin had covered them; but there was no breath in them. Then he said to me, "Prophesy to the breath, prophesy, son of man, and say to the breath, Thus says the Lord God: Come from the four winds, O breath, and breathe upon these slain, that they may live." So I prophesied as he commanded me, and the breath came into them, and they lived, and stood upon their feet, an exceedingly great host.
>
> Then he said to me, "Son of man, these bones are the whole house of Israel. Behold, they say, 'Our bones are dried up, and our hope is lost; we are clean cut off.' Therefore prophesy, and say to them, Thus says the Lord God: Behold, I will open your graves, and raise you from your graves, O my people; and I will bring you home into the land of Israel. And you shall know that I am the Lord, when I open your graves, and raise you from your graves, O my people. And I will put my Spirit within you, and you shall live, and I will place you in your own land; then you shall know that I, the Lord, have spoken, and I have done it, says the Lord.'" (Ezek. 37:1–14)

Thus, Israel's return to the promised land from Babylon will be the greatest miracle of all: the omnipotence of the God of Israel will vanquish the most unexpected obstacle. A little later perhaps, and in equally beautiful words, the Revelation of Isaiah insists on the power of God to return the dead to the living and to transform every ordeal of suffering into consolation: "And he will destroy on this mountain the covering that is cast over all peoples, the veil that is spread over all nations. He will swallow up death for ever, and the Lord God will wipe away tears from all faces,[67] and the reproach of his people he will take away from all the earth; for the Lord has spoken" (Isa. 25:7–8).

After the second century BC, all Jewish writing takes up this theme of belief in the resurrection of the dead and develops it.[68] Similarly, this belief figures, in one form or another, in the intertestamental literature coming from Essenian and Pharisaic circles.

The political consequences of this theme are, of course, overwhelming. The deep-seated certainty of the resurrection contains the seed of an irrevocably negative judgment on temporal power, dedicated solely to worldly concerns: it establishes the possibility of *an absolute resistance to political power.*

Two Old Testament books, inspired by apocalyptic thinking, are of particular interest, not only because the themes of eschatological struggle and the resurrection of the dead are developed further, but because the political significance of the two themes becomes absolutely clear

[67] The idea and image is repeated textually in the Revelation of St. John the Divine (see below).

[68] Only the Sadducees remained immune to this literature. They kept strictly to the written Torah. As representatives of the priesthood, they never raised the books of the prophets to a level of authority comparable to the Torah, meaning that they did not adopt the eschatology of the prophets.

against the backdrop of Seleucid persecutions. They are the *book of Daniel* and the *second book of Maccabees.*

2. *The Book of Daniel and the Theology of History*[69]

The book of Daniel can certainly be attributed to an author writing during the persecutions of Antiochus IV Epiphanes and hiding behind the authority of a figure from the time of the Babylonian exile.

The author imagines that King Nebuchadnezzar raised several young Jews in his court; among them Daniel. Like Joseph in the service of the pharaoh, Daniel interprets King Nebuchadnezzar's dreams on various occasions. Daniel is much more proficient at this than his idolatrous rivals at court—"the magicians, the astrologers, the Chaldeans, and the soothsayers"—because he is guided by the spirit of the one true God. The king and his servants are grateful to Daniel and shower him with honors. He is given many important duties at court.

a. The Theology of History

Daniel is either commanded or takes it upon himself to explain various visions and mysteries.

Nebuchadnezzar's dream of the statue (Dan. 2): in his dream the king sees the image of a great statue with a head of fine gold, a breast and arms of silver, the belly and thighs of brass, legs of iron, the feet part iron and part clay; but a single stone, uncut by human hand, smites the image and breaks it into pieces.

Daniel's vision of the four beasts and the Son of Man (Dan. 7): the four winds of the heaven bring up four great beasts from the sea: a lion with eagle's wings, a bear, a leopard with four wings on its back and four heads, and a fourth dreadful beast with iron teeth; it has ten horns, then an eleventh with eyes like the eyes of a man and a mouth speaking great things; then "the Ancient of days" appears, and "one like the Son of man came with the clouds of heaven."

Then come the *dream of the tree* (Dan. 4), the *vision of the writing on the wall* (Dan. 5), Daniel's *vision of the ram and the goat* (Dan. 8), and the *mystery of the 70 weeks* (Dan. 9).

Daniel manages to resolve all of these mysteries using one simple key: *an all-embracing sense of history, its phases, and its meaning.* Each dream or vision, taken on its own, remains a mystery; but placed against the backdrop of an all-embracing History, it acquires its own stark significance. God, the sole master of time and history, reveals this plan to the prophet: "He changes times and seasons; he removes kings and sets up kings" (Dan. 2:21).

As the master of history, God has written the *script,* so to speak, for a history destined to accomplish God's mysterious designs.

This "history"—as far as the memory of the prophet and his contemporaries can grasp it—involves the *passing of four great empires:* the Babylonians, the Medes, the Persians, and the Greeks (the four materials of the great statue in reverse order of their baseness: iron and clay represent the Lagids and the Seleucids (Dan. 2); the four beasts (Dan. 7). The Seleucid kingdom went through a succession of kings (the ten horns of the fourth beast). Antiochus IV Epiphanes (the eleventh horn) ascended to the throne by betraying his three rivals.

Although all these empires arose from the realm of evil, the quintessential empire of evil was the empire of Antiochus. Not only did Antiochus not worship Yahweh, he intended to forbid the worship of the God of the Israelites and to be venerated himself as the "manifest god" (this being the meaning of his self-proclaimed name: "Epiphanes"). Thus, history is conceived of as a *dramatic process,* a mystery of injustice, *which constantly aggravates the triumphs of evil.* Moreover,

[69] See the introduction to the book of Daniel in *Traduction oecuménique de la Bible (TOB)* (Paris: Éditions du Cerf-Les Bergers et les Mages, 1976), 1671–78.

the people of Israel, at the heart of the process, must face countless trials and tribulations for their sins (Dan. 3:28–32, 9:4–19; see also 2 Macc. 7:32–33).

However, a righteous elite continues to resist the powers of evil incarnated in the pagan empires and accepts martyrdom; but the outcome of their struggle depends solely on God: it is God, or God's angels, not the hand of "man," that intercedes (cf. the stone, "uncut by human hand," that smashes the statue with the head of gold). And God, the inspired scriptwriter, *chooses to intervene exactly at the moment when the figure of absolute evil seems on the point of victory.*

All the details of the mysteries presented to Daniel can be explained with reference to this general plan; the well-known events of Near Eastern history since the Exile fall into place, including the most recent episodes of the Maccabean struggle.

b. The Son of Man and the Coming of God's Kingdom

While he takes up the exilic prophets' message of hope (at times explicitly, as in Daniel, chapter 9, where he quotes Jeremiah 25:11–12), Daniel deliberately transposes it to a higher level than world history. He announces a *kingdom of God* that will last forever.

The empires of evil are not destroyed by a "classical" messiah; in this regard, the book of Daniel achieves a genuine transformation of traditional messianism. At the time of the Babylonian Exile and the prophesy of Isaiah, redemption was expected to come from a king of the Davidic line. Now it is expected from an already-existing "Son of Man" ("a son of mankind," "a son of man"), standing at the right hand of God, sent directly by him for the salvation of the world. "I saw in the night visions, and, behold, with the clouds of heaven there came one like a son of man, and came to the Ancient of Days [God] and was presented before him" (Dan. 7:13).

The expression "Son of Man" is to be understood in opposition to the conquering kings of pagan empires, who are like the "beasts" from the Great Sea, the realm of evil. The supreme judge of the world and savior of the Jewish people will arrive "on" or "with" the clouds of heaven, attesting to *his heavenly origin*. He has a human shape (like an angel).[70]

The kingdom of this Son of Man is everlasting: "And in the days of these kings [the last Greeks] shall the God of heaven set up a kingdom, which shall never be destroyed: and the kingdom shall not be left to other people, but it shall break in pieces and consume all these kingdoms, and it shall stand forever" (Dan. 2:44). Then a transfigured world will come to pass: "And to him [the Son of Man] was given dominion and glory and kingdom, that all peoples, nations, and languages should serve him; his dominion is *an everlasting dominion,* which shall not pass away, and *his kingdom that shall not be destroyed*" (Dan. 7:13–14).

c. Confirmation and Development of the Theme of the Resurrection of the Dead

Who will inhabit this transfigured world? Those whose names are written in the "Book" (in heaven, there is a list of individuals worthy of citizenship in the new Jerusalem) (Isa. 4:2–3). That is to say the righteous, those tested by trials. They include the doctors and the prophets charged with instructing the people (Dan. 11:35).

What will become of those who, before the day of redemption, are exposed to martyrdom? The prophet's creative imagination introduces two additional hypotheses.

---

[70] In the new Jewish revelation, angels occupy an important place (perhaps a Persian influence?). In the book of Daniel, an angel of the Lord intervenes to save the three young people in the fiery furnace and to rescue Daniel in the lion's den. Again an angel provides the keys for an interpretation of dreams and visions. God accomplishes his plan for the world through the agency of angels. In fact, the Son of Man himself is an angelic creature.

1. First, God will *prevent their death*. This is the meaning of the two episodes when three young people are saved from the fiery furnace and Daniel is rescued from the lion's den.

Nebuchadnezzar makes a statue of gold, then orders the entire population of his kingdom to fall down before it and worship it at the signal. Those who refuse will be cast into a fiery furnace. Of course, Daniel's three young Jewish companions, Shadrach, Meshach, and Abednego, refuse to worship the golden image. Nebuchadnezzar commands the furnace to be heated, and the young Jews are cast into the inferno. While the fiery flames of the furnace kill the king's servants who throw them in, the three men walk about, untouched by the flames, serenely praying to God (Dan. 3).

The presidents of the kingdom and the king's governors and counselors, jealous of Daniel, advise their ruler to establish a royal statute and make a decree that whoever seeks a petition of God or man, other than Darius, will be cast into the den of lions. But Daniel, in obedience to the Jewish law, kneels down three times a day and prays before the God of Israel. Daniel is brought to the king, who commands that he be cast into the den of lions. The next day, the king finds him untouched: an angel of the Lord "hath shut the lions' mouths, that they have not hurt me" (Dan. 6).

2. The prophet goes further. He knows that many martyrs have died. Does that mean that God has abandoned them? No, because God plans to resurrect them. Once again the theme of the resurrection of the dead is presented, now for the first time with clarity.

> At that time shall arise Michael, the great prince who has charge of your children. And there shall be a time of trouble, such as never was since there was a nation till that time; but at that time your people shall be delivered, every one that shall be found written in the book. *And many of them that sleep in the dust of the earth shall awake, some to everlasting life, and some to shame and everlasting contempt.* And those who are wise shall shine as the brightness of the firmament; and those who turn many to righteousness, like the stars for ever and ever. (Dan. 12:1–4)

The book of Daniel was included in the Hebrew Bible on the insistence of the Pharisees. For centuries, like the Revelation of St. John the Divine, it was one of the principal references for millenarians and those who speculate about God's intention in history. As late as the sixteenth and seventeenth centuries, Daniel's description of the successive empires provided a basis for speculation on the political future of Europe.[71]

3. *Contempt for Temporal Power in the Second Book of Maccabees*

The idea that God promises the faithful and martyrs a new, everlasting life actually bolstered the courage of the Maccabean rebels. We have striking evidence of this in the second book of Maccabees, which is rich in political implications.

Written in Greek around 124 BC, the work seems to be a summary of a longer work in five parts authored by a hellenized Jew, Jason of Cyrene, sometime around 160 BC, shortly after the events of the narrative (i.e., the persecutions of Antiochus IV Epiphanes) occurred.

The most powerful moment of the narrative is the story of the pagan king's persecution of an entire family (seven brothers and their mother). It remains one of the most memorable biblical examples of martyrdom (a phenomenon already illustrated by earlier prophetic figures).[72]

---

[71] See Delumeau, *Mille ans de bonheur*. On the topic of millenarianism, see below, part 3, chapter 7.

[72] Neher, *Prophètes et prophèties*, 299, evokes prophets who suffered martyrdom for their faith: Moses, perhaps; Hur, who with Aaron was left in charge of the people, when Moses ascended Mount Sanai; contemporaries of Elijah, who

No doubt the story has historical roots, but it is embellished and presented with a deliberately apologetic intent. Even before Jason's narrative, it had passed into legend.[73]

We quote the entire text because the thoughts and affirmations are of great doctrinal interest.

> It happened also that seven brothers and their mother were arrested and were being compelled by the king, under torture with whips and cords, to partake of unlawful swine's flesh. One of them, acting as their spokesman, said, "What do you intend to ask and learn from us? For we are ready to die rather than transgress the laws of our fathers." The king fell into a rage, and gave orders that pans and caldrons be heated. These were heated immediately, and he commanded that the tongue of their spokesman be cut out and that they scalp him and cut off his hands and feet, while the rest of the brothers and the mother looked on. When he was utterly helpless, the king ordered them to take him to the fire, still breathing, and to fry him in a pan. The smoke from the pan spread widely, but the brothers and their mother encouraged one another to die nobly, saying, "The Lord God is watching over us and in truth has compassion on us, as Moses declared in his song which bore witness against the people to their faces, when he said, '*And he will have compassion on his servants.*' "
>
> After the first brother had died in this way, they brought forward the second for their sport. They tore off the skin of his head with the hair, and asked him, "Will you eat rather than have your body punished limb by limb?" He replied in the language of his fathers, and said to them, "No." Therefore he in turn underwent tortures as the first brother had done. And when he was at his last breath, he said, "You accursed wretch, you dismiss us from this present life, but the King of the universe[74] will raise us up to an everlasting renewal of life,[75] because we have died for his laws."
>
> After him, the third was the victim of their sport. When it was demanded, he quickly put out his tongue and courageously stretched forth his hands, and said nobly, "I got these from Heaven, and because of his laws I disdain them, and from him I hope to get them back again." As a result the king himself and those with him were astonished at the young man's spirit, for he regarded his sufferings as nothing.
>
> When he too had died, they maltreated and tortured the fourth in the same way. And when he was near death, he said, "One cannot but choose to die at the hands of men and to cherish the hope that God gives of being raised again by him. But for you there will be no resurrection to life!"
>
> Next they brought forward the fifth and maltreated him. But he looked at the king, and said, "Because you have authority among men, mortal though you are, you do what you please. But do not think that God has forsaken our people. Keep on, and see how his mighty power will torture you and your descendants!" After him they brought forward the sixth. And when he was about to die, he said, "Do not deceive yourself in vain. For we are suffering these things on our own account, because of our sins against our own God. Therefore astounding things have happened.

---

were killed by Queen Jezebel; Isaiah, according to one Jewish tradition; Michaiah. Jeremiah was threatened with death on several occasions.

[73] The story of the seven martyred brothers, known as the "Maccabean martyrs"—also called the "martyrs of Antioch" because Antiochus IV Epiphanes resided in the city during the persecutions—was the topic of frequent commentaries by the church fathers, who considered the martyrs to be Christians before the letter. A cult was established in favor of the "Saint Maccabeans" in the early Christian centuries.

[74] Yahweh is the only king: Antiochus IV Epiphanes is a usurper.

[75] Clearly, the belief in the resurrection of the dead is already well established in the theology of the times.

"But do not think that you will go unpunished for having tried to fight against God!" The mother was especially admirable and worthy of honorable memory. Though she saw her seven sons perish within a single day, she bore it with good courage because of her hope in the Lord. She encouraged each of them in the language of their fathers. Filled with a noble spirit, she fired her woman's reasoning with a man's courage, and said to them, "I do not know how you came into being in my womb. It was not I who gave you life and breath, nor I who set in order the elements within each of you. Therefore the Creator of the world, who shaped the beginning of man and devised the origin of all things, will in his mercy give life and breath back to you again, since you now forget yourselves for the sake of his laws."

Antiochus felt that he was being treated with contempt, and he was suspicious of her reproachful tone. The youngest brother being still alive, Antiochus not only appealed to him in words, but promised with oaths that he would make him rich and enviable if he would turn from the ways of his fathers, and that he would take him for his friend and entrust him with public affairs. Since the young man would not listen to him at all, the king called the mother to him and urged her to advise the youth to save himself. After much urging on his part, she undertook to persuade her son. But, leaning close to him, she spoke in their native tongue as follows, deriding the cruel tyrant: "My son, have pity on me. I carried you nine months in my womb, and nursed you for three years, and have reared you and brought you up to this point in your life, and have taken care of you. I beseech you, my child, to look at the heaven and the earth and see everything that is in them, and recognize that God did not make them out of things that existed.[76] Thus also mankind comes into being. Do not fear this butcher, but prove worthy of your brothers. Accept death, so that in God's mercy I may get you back again with your brothers."[77]

While she was still speaking, the young man said, "What are you waiting for? I will not obey the king's command, but I obey the command of the law that was given to our fathers through Moses.[78] But you, who have contrived all sorts of evil against the Hebrews, will certainly not escape the hands of God. For we are suffering because of our own sins. And if our living Lord is angry for a little while, to rebuke and discipline us, he will again be reconciled with his own servants. But you, unholy wretch, you most defiled of all men, do not be elated in vain and puffed up by uncertain hopes, when you raise your hand against the children of heaven. You have not yet escaped the judgment of the almighty, all-seeing God.[79] For our brothers after enduring a brief suffering have drunk of everflowing life under God's covenant; but you, by the judgment of God, will receive just punishment for your arrogance. I, like my brothers, give up body and life for the laws of our fathers, appealing to God to show mercy soon to our nation and by afflictions and plagues to make you confess that he alone is God, and through me and my brothers to bring to an end the wrath of the Almighty which has justly fallen on our whole nation."

[76] This is the first time that the idea of creation "out of nothing" (*ex nihilo*) is expressed in the Bible. It contrasts with the Greek idea of creation from "first matter" (*prote hyle*), and even the idea in the book of Genesis of creation from "chaos." God created chaos from nothing. If the author, Jason of Cyrene, provides this detail, it may be because of his Hellenistic education and his desire to underscore the greater radicality of Jewish thought compared with Greek thought in this regard. Subsequently, Christian theologians, and notably Augustine, would pursue the implications of a more radical metaphysical feature of creation.

[77] In paradise, where the elect will gather.

[78] Earthly royal law has no value, or only insofar as it is a faithful reflection of divine Law.

[79] Antiochus will have to face the Last Judgment.

> The king fell into a rage, and handled him worse than the others, being exasperated at his scorn. So he died in his integrity, putting his whole trust in the Lord. Last of all, the mother died, after her sons. (2 Macc. 7)

This text can be seen as a particularly eloquent example of the biblical stance toward temporal power.

The struggle of the seven brothers and their mother against the Greek king revolves around respect for the Law. The Jewish family refuses to eat pork and worship the king, Epiphanes, the so-called "Manifestation of God." The king cannot tolerate such resistance, nor understand why torture and death are preferable to the (in his eyes) insignificant act of eating pork, or living in respect of the laws of the state. In other words, he fully realizes that the defiance of the Maccabean martyrs is not an act of personal courage but the expression of a cultural reality that he cannot grasp. By intensifying the cruelty of his tortures, he is not behaving sadistically. He is attempting to overcome their resistance and the threat it poses to his power (which is why he offers the youngest son and his mother a way out). Religion in the Greek city-state was never truly independent. It was always organized and controlled by the state; or if it was independent, it never raised any political claims. Furthermore, in the context of the Hellenistic kingships, which had more or less merged with the model of Near Eastern sacred monarchies, where the state and the king (the "incarnate law") were one, the mere existence of a sovereign will, independent of the state, was scandalous.

The text dwells on the reasons the king is nothing and the principle defended by the martyrs everything. The sole "king of the universe" is the God of Israel. He created everything: the world and flesh-and-blood human beings. In an instant, the same God can re-create everything that the king destroys; he can even destroy the king and all his descendants. The world and the king are of no significance. Everything important in human life takes place in the alliance between God and man. What is at stake in this alliance is whether the person is a saint or sinner. *The entire functioning of the world depends on this single issue of conscience.* The happy and unhappy phases of history are bound up in the sins of humanity and God's grace ("we suffer because of our sins"; it is "for our punishment and edification" that God expresses "his anger"), and not in the initiatives of earthly kings, who command neither individual salvation nor the general course of history. Temporal power is nothing. Nothing in the Greek mental universe compares with this outlook.[80]

E. Conclusion

Today, most Jewish scholars believe that apocalyptic literature, with its prospect for an end of history and an everlasting life in paradise, represents a deviation from Judaism. Benjamin Gross,[81] for example, examines the three responses of the Sadducees, the Essenes, and the Pharisees to the Greco-Roman persecutions of the Jews and concludes that only the response of the Pharisees is metaphysically and morally correct.

1. The Sadducees keep to the Temple and the state, that is, to human history; they aim for a "restoration" and forget the "transfiguration," which is part of the Torah. In the end, they fall in the very arena where they elected to make their stand.
2. The Essenes aspire to a "transfiguration" and flee into the desert. In other words, they look for succor outside history. They cast off the burden of historical transformation, the Torah's gift to Israel. Christianity, with its spiritual roots in Essenism, will undergo the same fate.

---

[80] Even if the prospect of the survival of the soul (see the myth of Er in Plato's *Republic* and "Scipio's Dream" in Cicero's *Republic*) can strengthen the courage of the wise in the struggle against a tyrannical power.

[81] See Gross, *Messianisme et histoire juive*, 35–47.

3. Only the Pharisees satisfy both requirements. They propose to live in history at the same time that they sustain a transcendent tension with its fulfillment. This explains their political "moderation," which preserves the future, and their patient desire to reconstruct after the disaster.

For Gross, the apocalyptic hypothesis of an imminent end of history brought about by God without human intervention—an idea found primarily in Assidean circles which gradually evolved into the Essenian faction—was a sign of renunciation of Israel's calling.

III. "Political" Thought in the New Testament

And yet it was from the bosom of Israel that a new prophet emerged who began his public life ca. 30 AD and changed the very nature of the problem. He called himself Messiah, "christos" (the "anointed" one in Greek). But instead of accepting the part of a royal messiah, according to Jewish expectations of the time, Jesus proclaimed: "my kingdom is not of this world" (John 18:36).

A. The Moral Revolution of the Sermon on the Mount

The new kingdom is indeed messianic in the sense that it is a reign of justice, but Jesus says that it will be a reign of a *new kind of justice*, a higher justice than the old one. "For I tell you, unless your righteousness exceeds that of the scribes and Pharisees, you will never enter the kingdom of heaven" (Matt. 5:20).

The Sermon on the Mount, with which the Gospel of Matthew begins, summarizes the principles of this new justice. It is again the theme of a distinction between *mishpat* and *tsedaka* that we came across earlier in our discussion of the prophets; a distinction between simple justice, which is content to reverse injustices and return to the *status quo ante* so that the world can continue its existence as before (in this sense, it is close to the natural justice of the Greco-Roman world)—and another justice that acts positively on the world, transforming it entirely, *making it just*, removing all unrighteousness from it permanently. In a sense, Jesus only repeats the original distinction made by the prophets; but at the same time, he gives it a more explicit, more radical expression.

> You have heard that it was said to the men of old, "*You shall not kill* [Exod. 20:13; Deut. 5:17]; whoever kills shall be liable to judgment." But I say to you that every one who is angry with his brother shall be liable to judgment. . . . You have heard that it was said, "*You shall not commit adultery.*" [Exod. 20:14; Deut. 5:18]: But I say to you that every one who looks at a woman lustfully has already committed adultery with her in his heart. . . . It was also said, "Whoever divorces his wife, let him give her a certificate of divorce" [Deut. 24:1]. But I say to you that *every one who divorces his wife*, except on the ground of unchastity, *makes her an adulteress* and whoever marries a divorced woman commits adultery.
>
> Again you have heard that it was said to the men of old, "*You shall not swear falsely, but shall perform to the Lord what you have sworn*" [Exod. 20:7; Num. 30:3; Deut. 23:22]: But I say to you, Do not swear at all. . . . Let what you say be simply "Yes" or "No." . . .
>
> You have heard that it was said, "*An eye for an eye and a tooth for a tooth.*"[82] But I say to you, Do not resist one who is evil. But if any one strikes you on the right cheek, turn to him

[82] The law of retaliation, *Lex talionis;* see Exod. 21:23–25.

the other also; and if any one would sue you and take your coat, let him have your cloak as well; and if any one forces you to go one mile, go with him two miles. Give to him who begs from you, and do not refuse him who would borrow from you.

You have heard that it was said, "*You shall love your neighbor* [Lev. 18:19], and hate your enemy." But I say to you, Love your enemies and pray for those who persecute you. . . . For if you love those who love you, what reward have you? Do not even the tax collectors do the same? And if you salute only your brethren, what more are you doing than others? Do not even the Gentiles do the same? . . .

Beware of practicing your piety before men in order to be seen by them. . . . Thus, when you give alms, sound no trumpet before you, as the hypocrites do in the synagogues and in the streets, that they may be praised by men. Truly, I say to you, they have received their reward. But when you give alms, do not let your left hand know what your right hand is doing, so that your alms may be in secret; and your Father who sees in secret will reward you.

And when you pray, you must not be like the hypocrites; for they love to stand and pray in the synagogues and at the street corners, that they may be seen by men. Truly, I say to you, they have received their reward. But when you pray, go into your room and shut the door and pray to your Father who is in secret; and your Father who sees in secret will reward you. . . .

Do not lay up for yourselves treasures on earth, where moth and rust consume and where thieves break in and steal, but lay up for yourselves treasures in heaven, where neither moth nor rust consumes and where thieves do not break in and steal. For where your treasure is, there will your heart be also. . . .

So whatever you wish that men would do to you, do so to them; for this is the law and the prophets. (Matt. 5:20–7.12; see Luke 6:20–38)

1. *Asymmetry in the Ethical Relationship: Mercy*

The new justice, as outlined in the Sermon on the Mount, presents many remarkable features. In every instance Jesus describes, the new justice differs from the old like *asymmetry* from *symmetry*.

Natural or traditional justice is symmetry: it involves giving to each his or her due according to a principle of equality. It is the same notion of justice that Greek philosophy and Roman law defended. Ancient Jewish law—as presented by Jesus in the Sermon on the Mount—involves the same symmetry with its notion of *lex talionis:* "an eye for an eye, a tooth for a tooth."[83]

But Jesus says it is necessary to go beyond the rule of symmetry; we must give *more* than is required. And even if we give the same that we receive from another, we are still not quit with him. Not only is it forbidden to kill another person, we must not be angry with that person either; not only the same formalism applies to marriage and divorce, but marriage is now deemed permanently binding; not only are promises under oath to be honored, now we must keep our word in every circumstance. Not only are we under obligation to love those who love us, we must also

[83] Later in the Bible, Paul will also emphasize the similarity between the natural justice of philosophers and the ancient Jewish law: "For when the Gentiles [pagans], which have not the law, do by nature the things contained in the law, these, having not the law, are a law unto themselves: which shew *the work of the law written in their hearts, their conscience also bearing witness,* and their thoughts the mean while accusing or else excusing one another" (Rom. 2:14–16). It seems that Paul is familiar with Stoic theories on natural law and knows of its inscription in the minds and conscience of all men (see Cicero's views on natural law and reason, p. 289–90).

love those who hate us; not only should we refrain from lifting our hand against another person, but if we are struck we must not strike back but "turn the other cheek." Not only must we admit that we have as many faults as our neighbor, but we must also recognize that, if there is a "speck" in our neighbor's eye, there is a "log" in our own (Matt. 7:1–5). In a word, Jesus commands *an end to the mirror-symmetry in human behaviors* on which traditional justice is defined.

Thus, Jesus describes the features of an ethical relationship among human beings as radically different from justice. The Gospel calls this ethics by various names: *mercy, compassion, charity, love (agape).* While the old justice, as defined by the Ancients from Aristotle to Cicero, is of the type $a = b$ (i.e., an equality on finite terms),[84] it can be said that *mercy* is an inequality and an injustice because it requires infinite gifts in exchange for finite goods. Indeed, it is not, in any sense of the word, an *exchange:* it is fundamentally an *asymmetrical* relationship. It involves feeling concern for another person whatever befalls that person, and regardless of whether one is at fault or not. It implies answering another's call, precisely because that person has made a call, and not because we have any particular obligation toward the person making the call. In a word, it involves *accepting a debt, which one has not contracted as one's own.*

The philosopher Emmanuel Levinas analyzed this ethics in detail (his emphasis was on the prophetic morality of the Old Testament and not on the New Testament; however, it can be argued that the same formal features apply in both instances, that is, that the same ethics runs throughout the Bible). Levinas insists on the *asymmetry* of this ethics and argues convincingly that the true content of the mysterious concept of "original sin" was its asymmetry.

Original sin does not mean some form of collective guilt affecting individuals from outside by virtue of their membership in the human family, though they may have done nothing wrong personally. Rather, it means that we are truly individual sinners, inasmuch as we do not repay infinitely the debt we owe since the commandments of the Torah (or of the Gospel) have been revealed to us. Such sin is "original," in that it is related to our human condition: our moral conscience creates for each of us an ancient, unconditional debt in regard to others (i.e., it is a debt even before we contract a commitment, even before we formulate a thought or conjecture). As long as suffering exists in the world, although we may not be the cause, we have an obligation to feel *responsibility* for it. Likewise, although we have fulfilled our commitments, we have no moral right to turn our back on another human being. Our moral response, Levinas says, must be the same as Abraham's instant, unconditional, uncalculated response to God's call: "Here I am, Lord" (like Kant's categorical imperative). That a person is a "sinner" means that the person's moral debt is never payable.

Levinas argues eloquently that our acceptance of an uncontracted debt is what constitutes our *humanity.* For Levinas, humanity—in a radically different sense from the Latin humanist notion—introduces a "responsibility for the other." Without his or her humanity, a person is pure *conatus essendi,* like a rock or a star, in "pursuit of his existence" in complete disregard for others. Such a person may well abstain from wrongdoing; and when that person causes someone hurt, he or she makes amends and pays his or her debts "on the nail." But once these obligations have been fulfilled, the person abandons and loses interest. In the opinion of Levinas, this morality leads to Auschwitz. Only the prophetic ethics of the Bible can liberate humanity from this ontological status. Biblical "man" is an "otherwise than being"; he does not identify his being with a "being" as such. He aspires to perfect creation, to transform it. He *is* only inasmuch as he

[84] Such is the case, it will be recalled, for commutative justice (the items for exchange must be of equal value) and distributive justice (each individual receives a proportion of the common good equal to his or her contribution).

is involved in the messianic becoming of history. Biblical man is not an *ousia* in the Greek sense, and this is the real reason why he cannot be satisfied with simple Aristotelian or Stoic "justice."[85]

2. *The New Justice and the Kingdom of Heaven*

Now, if the new ethics is unequal and inequitable, how can Jesus claim that it is "justice"? The answer is found in the text of the Beatitudes, which comes immediately before the Sermon on the Mount:

> Blessed are the poor in spirit: for theirs is the kingdom of heaven (*basileia ton ouranon*). Blessed are those who mourn, for they shall be comforted. Blessed are the *meek*, for they shall *inherit the earth* (Ps. 37:11; Gen. 13:15). Blessed are those who hunger and thirst for righteousness, for they may be satisfied. Blessed are the merciful (*eleemones*), for they shall obtain mercy. Blessed are the pure in heart, for they shall see God. Blessed are the peace-makers; for they shall be called the sons of God. Blessed are those who are persecuted for righteousness' sake, for theirs is the kingdom of heaven. . . . Rejoice and be glad, for your reward is great in heaven. (Matt. 5:3–12)

It is true that the merciful, those who extend the moral requirement of what is owed beyond an exact arithmetical accounting of natural justice, are condemned to pay much more than they will ever receive in exchange on this earth. In this sense, they incur a loss. But, Jesus promises them the kingdom of heaven, access to the promised land, consolation, mercy, and the beatific vision of God. These, in all their mystery, are disproportionate realities as difficult to calculate as the debt of love. The merciful give more than they owe, but in return they receive *much more than their due*. Thus, we see that mercy, which eliminates all calculations, such as those found in statutes and laws, nevertheless contains a novel and mysterious measure of equitable exchange, and therefore of justice. Simply, this new justice is *an equality between two infinites,* the infinite love of humanity and the infinite love of God.

If it is true that there is no common measure between what is owed to others according to the law and what is owed according to mercy, then there can be no common measure between the good expected from justice, which is a finite quantity, and the infinite delight that God promises to the merciful. If we cease to calculate our mercy, God will cease to count his reward. Inversely, if we admit that God places no restraints on his reward, then it makes sense for us not to limit our mercy. This is the new covenant that Jesus proposes. It is not a covenant sealed on Mount Sinai with a written Law, establishing mutual obligations on both parties. It is a covenant of love.

Jesus of Nazareth is a continuation of the Old Testament prophecy after the period of the Exile (Jeremiah, Ezekiel, Deutero-Isaiah, etc.), which also promoted a new covenant with the same intention. But Jesus radicalizes and systematizes its expression.

B. The Paradoxical Eschatology of the Gospel

The new justice singularly transforms humanity's relationship with life on earth, and thus with social and political life. Jesus says that his "Kingdom," promised to the merciful, "is not of this world." Since it is no longer possible to ascertain and put limits on what one "owes" to others in this life, the only alternative is death and escape from this world. If one's aspiration in life is to be merciful; if one is dissatisfied with ordinary justice; if one desires to frustrate the plans and

[85] Emmanuel Levinas's most important works are: *Totality and Infinity,* trans. Alphonso Lingis (Dordrecht: Kluwer Academic, 1961); *Otherwise than Being, or Beyond Essence,* trans. Alphonso Lingis (Dordrecht: Kluwer Academic, 1981); *Difficult Freedom: Essays on Judaism,* trans. Seán Hand (Baltimore: John Hopkins University Press, 1990).

calculations that define social order, then one must empty oneself of one's rights and being, and provoke the incomprehension, bitterness, and hate of others. Such a person is doomed to an ill-adapted life, a life of failure, suffering, danger, persecution, and death. While natural justice makes life possible, mercy leads to the Cross.

By radicalizing the ethical message of the prophets, Jesus brings full circle the evolution of the Messiah figure from earlier centuries. The Messiah was initially a triumphant royal figure, then evolved toward an increasingly "kenotic" figure (the suffering servant of Deteuro-Isaiah, the "Pierced One" of Deutero-Zechariah), as we saw.

But death itself leads to the kingdom of God. The Gospel provides new and fairly numerous details[86] about paradise and hell. The heavenly world is already available to those who die (the crucified Christ says to the good thief, "Truly, I say to you, today you will be with me in paradise" [Luke 23:43]). For the living, the heavenly world is the standard for their every act. It gives meaning to the pledges and sacrifices of human life ("your Father who sees in secret"). The life of the Christian changes direction compared with the life of the Assidean at the time of the book of Daniel. Assideans lived in the hope that the Messiah would come *one day* (even if they believed that his coming was *imminent*); nevertheless, the timeline of the Assidean's hope remained "horizontal." Suddenly, the tension becomes "vertical." The eschatological end-time is here and *already* now; it is "above" us. History does not bring about the end-time for the faithful; it is each individual's behavior that creates a place (or not) in the kingdom of God, which has no specifiable time or place; his kingdom is "present" without being visible.

The Gospels attest to this transformation of traditional biblical eschatology into a paradoxical "eschatology of the present." Jesus confirms that he is, indeed, the long-awaited Jewish Messiah: therefore, the Jews need not await his coming any longer. Just as he, the Messiah, exists in God even before his Incarnation,[87] he continues to exist in heaven where he is now returned. After Christ's assumption, Christians no longer await his coming, but await his "return," or more exactly, his Second Coming, his "Parousia." The kingdom is forever pending and imminent: "Know that he [the Son of Man] is near, at the very gates. . . . But of that day or that hour no one knows, not even the angels in heaven, nor the Son, but only the Father" (Mark 13:29–32). "Being asked by the Pharisees when the kingdom of God was coming, he answered them, 'The kingdom of God is not coming with signs to be observed; nor will they say, "Lo, here it is!" or "There!" for, behold, the kingdom of God is in the midst of you'" (Luke 17:20–21). But the Kingdom is only present for those who hear the Word of God and are "ready": "Therefore you must also be ready; for the Son of man is coming" (Matt. 24:44).

The parable of the "ten virgins" (Matt. 25:1–13) tells the story of ten maidens who took their lamps and went to meet the bridegroom. Five of them were wise and took extra oil with their lamps; five were foolish and did not. The bridegroom arrived while the foolish virgins were away looking for oil. Conclusion: "Therefore, you must also be ready; for the Son of man is coming at an hour you do not expect."

Eschatological hope, therefore, changes its meaning. Christ demands a conversion of the heart, giving rise to immediate personal action. He places no direct hope in an outer, social, or

---

86 These details were inspired by earlier Essenian intertestamental writings.

87 This was the case of the Messiah in the prophetic texts as well. The Messiah exists from the beginning of time and is coeternal with God. Daniel's "Son of Man" came "with the clouds of heaven"; he is a son of heaven. The New Testament inherits the idea (John 1:1–2), and Christian theology develops it until Jesus becomes the Son of God, "begotten, not made," one of the three figures of the Trinity.

political transformation of the world. This will occur as a consequence of the transformation of hearts.[88]

C. Christ's Doctrine, "Render unto Caesar"

This results in a clear principle on the status of temporal power. When the Jews make clear their intention to proclaim Christ as their king, he flees alone into the mountain (John 6:14–15);[89] and again when he is presented before Pilate, Christ rejects the temporal kingship.

> Pilate . . . called Jesus and said to him, "Are you the King of the Jews?" Jesus answered, "Do you say this of your own accord, or did others say it to you about me?" Pilate answered, "Am I a Jew? Your own nation and the chief priests have handed you over to me; what have you done?" Jesus answered, "My kingship is not of this world; if my kingship were of this world, my servants would fight, that I might not be handed over to the Jews; but my kingship is not from the world." Pilate said to him, "So you are a king?" Jesus answered, "You say that I am a king. For this I was born, and for this I have come into the world, to bear witness to the truth. Every one who is of the truth hears my voice." Pilate said to him, "What is truth?" (John 18:33–38)[90]

Thus, the kingship of Jesus and his messianic calling are an agency of truth rather than an exercise of political power. It is not possible to express more clearly the difference between spiritual power and temporal power, the power of the spirit and the power of might. Jesus wants to transform the world, but he will do so with the agency of "truth."

Beginning with the kings, and Solomon in particular, the Bible emphasizes the quality of wisdom (the Greeks also insisted on this quality in their theories of monarchy, as we saw). For the prophets, the royal Messiah was a man filled with the *ruah* of God (spirit) and its "gifts": wisdom, intelligence, counsel. Here the two levels, spirit and power, are completely separate.

Does Jesus actually condemn temporal power? The episode of Caesar's tribute provides clarification of this point.

> Then the Pharisees went and took counsel how to entangle him [Jesus] in his talk. And they sent their disciples to him, along with the Herodians, saying, "Teacher, we know that you are true, and teach the way of God truthfully, and care for no man; for you do not regard the position of men. Tell us, then, what you think. Is it lawful to pay taxes to Caesar, or not?" But Jesus, aware of their malice, said, "Why put me to the test, you hypocrites? Show me the money for the tax." And they brought him a coin. And Jesus said to them, "Whose likeness

---

[88] In the Gospel one finds texts with a more classical eschatological tone: Mark 13 is a prodigious eschatological discourse, which alludes to the pains of childbirth, the tribulation of Jerusalem, and the glorious manifestation of the Son of Man.

[89] He was no doubt aware of the misfortunes that befell Jewish agitators of his time, who made literal interpretations of messianic and apocalyptic prophecies; for example, Judas son of Ezekias, Athronges, Judas of Galilee (founder of the Zealots), Barabbas (an insurrectionist freed in exchange for Jesus), Theudas, and others after Christ's ministry and death. According to the narratives of the Jewish historian Flavius Josephus, a contemporary of these events, all of the prophets see themselves as, or accept being seen as, the "king" of the Jews. They promised God's help, proclaimed indifference to death, and drew a following, who shared their aspirations (notably, for freedom from the yoke of Roman taxes). They carried out insurrectionary acts and were pursued, captured, and executed by the occupying forces. See Grelot, *L'espérance juive,* 168–79.

[90] The synoptic Gospels tell the same story (Matt. 27:1–2, 11–14; Mark 15:1–5; Luke 23:1–5) without explicitly quoting Jesus' reply, "My kingdom is not of this world." In these other versions, the refusal of Jesus to answer Pilate's question, "Are you the King of the Jews?" is almost more eloquent. Jesus claims neither the throne of David nor the priesthood.

> and inscription is this?" They said, "Caesar's." Then he said to them, "Render therefore to Caesar the things that are Caesar's, and to God the things that are God's." When they heard it, they marveled; and they left him and went away. (Matt. 22:15–22; see Mark 12:13–17; Luke 20:20–26)

Jesus, who works through the agency of truth to bring about the kingdom of God, does not deny the rights of temporal power. He appears to believe that both powers have their own rights in their respective spheres. He is firmly anchored in the traditional prophetic vision, according to which temporal power must accept the moral standards and eschatological horizon revealed by God. However, his tone is almost the reverse of the Maccabean martyrs. He does not call for the hatred, contempt, or destruction of the state: in the scenes of the Passion, he expresses no hostility toward Pilate, not even a defiant tone. Moreover, he no longer seems to pursue the ideal of a "community without institutions." He even appears to offer support for the Empire, as if he believes that for spiritual power to devote itself to truth, it is necessary for temporal power to preserve public order. He envisions a separation of roles: "Caesar" commands the temporal sphere, while God and his representatives on earth—the saints and prophets, that is, those "on the side of truth"—look after the message of redemption.

Christ's position may be due to the fact that he is not speaking at the same time as Jeremiah or Ezekiel. For him, "Caesar" is not "Babylon." He lives in a civic, secular state, one that is no longer sacred but is ruled by human law. Furthermore, the model of the state is provided both by the Hellenistic communities on the borders of Judea and by Rome in Herod's Judea itself. This is where Jesus was born and raised, or at least he rubbed shoulders with the state sufficiently to understand its fundamental principles.

In religious matters, the Roman state is more or less tolerant or indifferent. The Empire's pluriethnicity and vastness actually intensify its religious tolerance (cf. Pilate's skeptical, disillusioned response to Jesus: "What is truth?"). We are left with the impression that Jesus is counting on the relative neutrality of the state, which creates the conditions for the prophets to do their work of "truth," provided that the prophets leave the responsibility for maintaining order to the state. This enables us to understand the symmetrical form that Jesus gives in his response: "Render therefore unto Caesar the things which are Caesar's; and unto God the things that are God's." God must recognize the legitimacy of Caesar if Caesar himself is to recognize the religious and moral freedom of the followers of the new justice.

Arguably, Jesus could not recommend this doctrine of religious and moral freedom until history had produced the model of the city-state. His statement is inconceivable in the Pharaoh's Egypt. Jesus and his early disciples, Paul in particular, are the first people of the Bible to think in *political* terms (without quotation marks).

Historically, Christianity and—in part—rabbinic Judaism (though not Islam) developed in the context of civic and quasi-secular states. Arguably, they could not have developed the theme of an independent spiritual life otherwise.

In summary, the Bible expresses a religious and moral principle, which discredits temporal power in regard to spiritual power. The gap between the two powers grew in the final centuries of ancient Judaism because temporal power was in the hands of foreign powers. Then, rabbinic Judaism and Christianity built "churches," or "pure" spiritual powers, because they evolved in Hellenic and Roman societies, where the model of a secular state existed already. It is, in a sense, the "miraculous" encounter of these two totally independent cultural developments that made possible over time the establishment of modern Western states characterized by the radical separation of the two powers. This relative rehabilitation of temporal power is found in the writings of the apostle Paul.

D. The Political Theology of the Apostle Paul

1. *Life*

Paul (ca. 5–10 AD to 67 AD) was a Pharisaic Jew born in Tarsus in Cilicia (southeast Asia Minor). He was a Roman citizen by birth. Following a period of anti-Christian persecution, Paul converted (ca. 34 or 36—the famous vision "on the road to Damascus" [Acts 9:3–6]). From his base in Antioch, the center of Hellenistic Christianity, he became the organizer of several churches in the pagan world. Owing to his rabbinic education, he was probably the preeminent theologian of the new Christianity. Arrested in 58 AD on orders of the Sadducees, he was sent to prison in Rome where he was freed, then subsequently martyred during Nero's anti-Christian persecutions in 67 AD.

2. *Work*

Paul is the author of 13 epistles: the epistle to the Romans, 1 and 2 Corinthians, Galatians, Ephesians, Philippians, Colossians, 1 and 2 Thessalonians, 1 and 2 Timothy, Titus, and Philemon. Modern scholarship no longer attributes the Epistle to the Hebrews to Paul, although it shows his influence (Hebrews establishes the doctrinal relationship between Judaism and Christianity). The writings of Paul represent fully one-quarter of the New Testament and provide the very foundations of Christian theology. His theology is essentially a "Christology"—that is, a doctrine of Christ, his nature, his death, and his Resurrection.

3. *A Legitimization of Temporal Power: "There is no power but of God"*

First of all, Paul endorsed the Christian doctrine we have been analyzing: since the kingdom of God is not of this world, Christians are not to conquer or create a state and exercise temporal power therein. Like the Pharisees, Christians abandoned the war of independence against Rome (moreover, in the event of social and political agitation, the nascent Christian church would have been exposed to Roman repression and the risk of extinction, just as much as the Jewish national movements). The sole purpose of the Church is to preach the Gospel as commanded by Jesus; for this, it needs time and must live in peace with the authorities.

Therefore, in his Epistle to the Romans, Paul advocates a "conservative" policy:

> Let every person be subject to the governing authorities. For there is no authority except from God,[91] and those that exist have been instituted by God. Therefore he who resists the authorities resists what God has appointed, and those who resist will incur judgment. For rulers are not a terror to good conduct, but to bad. Would you have no fear of him who is in authority? Then do what is good, and you will receive his approval, for he is God's servant for your good. But if you do wrong, be afraid, for he does not bear the sword in vain; he is the servant of God to execute his wrath on the wrongdoer. Therefore one must be subject, not only to avoid God's wrath but also for the sake of conscience. For the same reason you also pay taxes, for the authorities are ministers of God, attending to this very thing. Pay all of them their dues, taxes to whom taxes are due, revenue to whom revenue is due, respect to whom respect is due, honor to whom honor is due. (Rom. 13:1–7)

---

[91] In Latin: *nulla potestas nisi a Deo*. This formulation is noteworthy, as it will reappear again later.

This is also the position of Jesus of Nazareth: render unto Caesar that which is Caesar's. The Epistles are full of other political and social calls for calm: "Slaves, obey in everything those who are your earthly masters, not with eyeservice, as men-pleasers, but in singleness of heart, fearing the Lord. Whatever your task, work heartily, as serving the Lord and not men, knowing that from the Lord you will receive the inheritance as your reward; you are serving the Lord Christ. For the wrongdoer will be paid back for the wrong he has done, and there is no partiality. Masters, treat your slaves justly and fairly, knowing that you also have a Master in heaven" (Col. 3:22–4:1).

Paul repeats these same exhortations: it is necessary to remain obedient to principalities and magistrates (Titus 3:1), and one should even pray for the civic authorities, the height of indignity for many Jews (Jeremiah, it will be recalled, also demanded this of the Jewish captives in Babylon): "First of all, then, I urge that supplications, prayers, intercessions, and thanksgivings be made for all men, for kings and all who are in high positions, that we may lead a quiet and peaceable life, godly and respectful in every way" (1 Tim. 2:1–2). Thus, the sociopolitical order of this world receives a divine guarantee, be it ever so precarious.

It is striking that Paul's conservative political stance, summarized in scarcely nuanced words here, was to have major consequences for the Christian political tradition. An entire school of Christian conservatism, not to say Christian absolutism, was founded on apostolic authority.

4. *The Universalism of Christianity*

Up until the apocalyptic age, Jewish messianism never lost its nationalist color: the aim of the prophets had always been to restore the kingdom of Judah-Israel in Jerusalem, and the moral burden to complete the great work of the Creation was on the shoulders of the "remnants of Israel." While prophetic morality was charged with an obligation to protect the poor, widows, and orphans from injustice, the Old Testament never advocated social equality as such. But now, Paul proclaims, "Here there cannot be Greek and Jew, circumcised and uncircumcised, barbarian, Scyth'ian, slave, free man, but Christ is all, and in all" (Col. 3:11).

In this text Paul affirms a twofold *universalism:* Christianity rejects divisions of humanity rooted in ethnicity ("neither Greek nor Jew") and divisions based on social class (neither "bond nor free"). No doubt, his Hellenic culture and Jewish origins influenced his stance. He traveled the length and breadth of the Roman *cosmopolis* in which, as a Roman citizen, he felt more or less assimilated. Above all, he expresses the essence of Jesus' ideas on the morality of compassion and provides a profound, "abstract" formulation of universal validity: all men are called ("elected") to apply the new justice, not just the Jews. A Samaritan, who understands that every man is his fellow man, is able to instruct "priests" and "Levites" in this morality (Luke 10:29–37); and a sinful woman is able to teach a Pharisee (Luke 7:36–50).

In the name of such universalism, Christianity (like Judaism before the Maccabean crisis and Islam later) becomes a proselytizing religion with the aim of converting the whole world.[92]

5. *The Church Is a Necessity*

However, the conversion of hearts depends on one condition: the presence of the *church* in the world. The Apostle Paul shows this with a strong argument (strong at any rate for those who accept his theological premises).

Man alone does not have the strength to bring a response to the disproportionate demands of the Sermon on the Mount. A sinner cannot be just, because he cannot love unto death. But

[92] Moreover, Christ sent his disciples out into the world explicitly: "Go therefore and make disciples of all nations" (Matt. 28:19).

Christ's sacrifice on the cross, followed by his Resurrection, results in the elimination of the power of death, not only for Christ but for all humankind. "Therefore as sin came into the world through one man [Adam] and death through sin . . . , so by one man's [Jesus Christ's] act of obedience many will be made righteous" (Rom. 5:12–19).

Christ, the new Adam, enables all humankind to participate in his victory over death. This participation in the death and Resurrection of Christ takes place through *baptism:*

> Do you not know that all of us who have been baptized into Christ Jesus were baptized into his death? We were buried therefore with him by baptism into death, so that as Christ was raised from the dead by the glory of the Father, we too might walk in newness of life. For if we have been united with him in a death like his, we shall certainly be united with him in a resurrection like his. We know that our old self was crucified with him so that the sinful body might be destroyed, and we might no longer be enslaved to sin. (Rom. 6:3–6)

Through baptism we become members of the church, the "mystical body" of Christ.[93] We are "incorporated in him." This "incorporation" creates a new person, defined as a man or woman of the "spirit" (*pneuma*) and no longer of the "flesh" (*sarx*). "Those who belong to Christ Jesus have crucified the flesh with its passions and desires" (Gal. 5:24). The baptized become again what humankind was before the Fall. In this capacity they can practice the new justice.

This explains why there are individuals on earth who are, so to speak, sufficiently "inflamed" to desire to surpass the old justice. Without the grace of baptism, such people would be unable to triumph over themselves and exceed their nature, and therefore the world would continue as before. Of course, it is necessary to believe in the sanctity of Christ and in his Resurrection: only the believer in Christ can be "justified" in the new sense of the word.[94]

Let us conclude the argument. If only the baptized person can be justified, and if the church, the mystical body of Christ, is the only authority that can baptize, then the sacramental action of the church is the essential condition for true justice to reign in the world, and also for the world to begin the march toward its eschatological end. We understand why Paul was more interested in this new "spiritual power"—the only power capable of bringing about a total transformation of humanity—than in "temporal power," which only rules over the old Adamic self.

E. The Community of Goods in the Early Church according to the Acts of the Apostles

One passage in the Acts of the Apostles was much quoted during the Middle Ages by the proponents of the new egalitarian millennium, and again in modern times by Christians under the sway of socialism. It refers to the community of goods, which apparently existed in the early church. Since, by definition, the early church is the model to be followed, Christianity must therefore be either socialist or communist in its essence. "Now the company of those who believed were of one heart and soul, and no one said that any of the things which he possessed was his own, but they had everything in common. . . . There was not a needy person among them, for as many as were possessors of lands or houses sold them, and brought the proceeds of what was sold and laid it at the apostles' feet; and distribution was made to each as any had need" (Acts 4:32–35).

---

93 "[God] has put all things under his [Christ's] feet and has made him the head over all things for the church, which is his body" (Eph. 1:22–23). "He [Christ] is the head of the body, the church; he is the beginning, the first-born from the dead, that in everything he might be pre-eminent" (Col. 1:18).

94 This notion of *justification by faith,* which is developed in several of Paul's epistles (e.g., Rom. 3:21–26, 3:28; Eph. 2:8; Phil. 3:9; Titus 3:4–5), also fascinated Protestant theologians in due course.

The same passage adds some terrifying threats for anyone disinclined to share everything he owns:

> But a man named Ananias with his wife Sapphira sold a piece of property, and with his wife's knowledge he kept back some of the proceeds, and brought only a part and laid it at the apostles' feet. But Peter said, "Ananias, why has Satan filled your heart to lie to the Holy Spirit and to keep back part of the proceeds of the land? While it remained unsold, did it not remain your own? And after it was sold, was it not at your disposal? How is it that you have contrived this deed in your heart? You have not lied to men but to God." When Ananias heard these words, he fell down and died. And great fear came upon all who heard of it. (Acts 5:1–5)

The same fate befell Ananias's wife not long after, and "a great fear came upon the whole church."

Of course, Peter's accusation concerns the lie told by Ananias and his wife, not their refusal to share their possessions (they were free not to give). This is why the passage underwent a more restrictive interpretation during the Middle Ages; the councils proclaimed that the community of goods should not be the ideal for all, but only for those with a special calling, namely monks. All the same, it became a valuable scriptural reference for the opponents of private property ownership.

But it remains an isolated text. In the Gospel there are many *logia* [sayings] by Christ where he not only sanctions private property but moves the moral requirement to another level (e.g., the parable of the talents, the parable of the Good Samaritan; see also the Epistles of Paul).

F. The Revelation of St. John the Divine and the Millennium

The New Testament closes with a book—the Revelation of St. John the Divine—that appears to go back to the classical figures of eschatology (it contrasts sharply with what has been called the paradoxical eschatology of the Gospel). Revelation portrays an extraordinary picture of the end-time, in the tradition of the book of Daniel and the Jewish apocalypse. It also appends an original idea: prior to the end-time proper, there will be a happy period of 1,000 years—a "paradise" on earth.

The text of the book of Revelation dates either from the period of Nero's persecutions and the Jewish War (65–70 AD) or, more likely, from the end of the reign of Domitian (91–96 AD).

It is presented in the form of an inspired vision. The speaker is the prophet John.[95] While on the island of Patmos, John fell into a state of ecstasy. The "Son of Man," described in the same terms as in the book of Daniel but clearly identifiable with Jesus Christ, appeared to him in a vision. This celestial being spoke to him and said, "Write the things which thou hast seen, and the things which are, and the things which shall be hereafter" (Rev. 1:19). Then he had a series of visions and auditory sensations: he heard messages of conversions to be transmitted to the seven Christian churches located in Asia Minor. Next he received the vision of the final phases of history: the prelude to the end-times, the coming tribulation, the great eschatological struggle, and finally the fulfillment and final manifestation. In these last phases, the main role is played by the "Lamb," that is, Jesus Christ, in whose hands God has placed the destiny of the world.

We begin by quoting several passages from the final chapters of Revelation, then we will discuss the two interpretations these texts have prompted.

---

[95] It is possible that the John of the Revelation is the same as the John of the Gospel, but most theologians now think they are two different people.

1. *The Text about the Millennium*

Then I saw an angel coming down from heaven, holding in his hand the key of the bottomless pit and a great chain.

And he seized the dragon, that ancient serpent, who is the Devil and Satan, and bound him for a thousand years, and threw him into the pit, and shut it and sealed it over him, that he should deceive the nations no more, till the thousand years were ended. After that he must be loosed for a little while.

Then I saw thrones, and seated on them were those to whom judgment was committed. Also I saw the souls of those who had been beheaded for their testimony to Jesus and for the word of God, and who had not worshiped the beast or its image,[96] and had not received its mark on their foreheads or their hands. They came to life[97] and reigned with Christ a thousand years.

The rest of the dead did not come to life until the thousand years were ended. This is the first resurrection.[98]

Blessed and holy is he who shares in the first resurrection! Over such the second death[99] has no power, but they shall be priests of God and of Christ, and they shall reign with him a thousand years.

And when the thousand years are ended, Satan will be loosed from his prison. and will come out to deceive the nations which are at the four corners of the earth, that is, Gog and Magog,[100] to gather them for battle; their number is like the sand of the sea.

And they marched up over the broad earth and surrounded the camp of the saints and the beloved city; but fire came down from heaven and consumed them[101] and the devil who had deceived them was thrown into the lake of fire and sulphur where the beast and the false prophet[102] were, and they will be tormented day and night for ever and ever.

Then I saw a great white throne and him who sat upon it; from his presence earth and sky fled away, and no place was found for them.[103]

---

[96] A reference to those who rejected the cult of the Roman emperor.

[97] A confirmation of the doctrine of the resurrection of the righteous formulated in the book of Daniel.

[98] Only the righteous are raised during this "first resurrection."

[99] Hell.

[100] These two names are found in the Old Testament as well, but with various meanings. Gog is a descendant of Ruben, according to 1 Chronicles 5:4. Magog is the son of Japheth, according to Genesis 10:2. Ezekiel 38–39, we recall, refers to Magog in his struggle against a restored Israel. Finally, Jewish tradition refers to Gog and Magog as two peoples who will attack Israel either before, during, or immediately after the messianic era.

[101] This is a repetition of the classical narrative of eschatological struggle.

[102] Thus, at the end of time, a "false prophet" will appear, one who will pretend to be a saint or a priest, but he is the devil himself in disguise. Later millenarian prophecies will pick up and amplify this same theme. It is on the basis of these traditions that medieval millenarians and, later, Protestants represented the pope as a diabolical figure, an Antichrist. Note that the expression "Antichrist" does not appear in the book of Revelation, although Christian millenarians designated as such the leader of the armies of evil in the final eschatological struggle preceding the advent of the millennium. The word "antichrist" figures in the epistles of John (1 John 2:18–22, 4:3–4; 2 John 7). Revelation does refer to the "Beast" (chapter 13); other passages of the New Testament also refer to the "impious man," the "lost," the "Adversary." In the Old Testament this figure corresponds to "Satan" (1 Chron. 21:1; Job 1:6; Zech. 3:1–2) or the "devil" (Song 2:24; Gen. 3).

[103] The old world—historical "earth" and "heaven"—disappear entirely.

> And I saw the dead, great and small, standing before the throne,[104] and books were opened. Also another book was opened, which is the book of life.[105] And the dead were judged by what was written in the books, by what they had done.
>
> And the sea gave up the dead in it, Death and Hades gave up the dead in them, and all were judged by what they had done.
>
> Then Death and Hades were thrown into the lake of fire. This is the second death, the lake of fire; and if any one's name was not found written in the book of life, he was thrown into the lake of fire. (Rev. 20:1–15)

Then follows the vision of the "New Jerusalem," the ultimate aim of all human and cosmic existence. To describe this, the text uses the term "new" many times, a sign that the perception of time had changed. Ecclesiastes said, "There is *nothing new* under the sun" (Eccles. 1:9). To the contrary, an eschatological perspective supposes a time of creation.

> Then I saw a new heaven and a new earth; for the first heaven and the first earth had passed away; and the sea was no more.
>
> And I saw the holy city, *new* Jerusalem, coming down out of heaven from God, prepared as a bride adorned for her husband;[106] and I heard a great voice from the throne saying, "Behold, the dwelling of God is with men. He will dwell with them, and they shall be his people, and *God himself will be with them;*[107] he will wipe away every tear from their eyes, death shall be no more,[108] neither shall there be mourning nor crying nor pain any more, for the former things have passed away."
>
> And he who sat upon the throne said, "Behold, I make *all things new*. . . . I am the Alpha and the Omega." (Rev. 21:1–6)

Two types of interpretation have been given to this text in the Christian tradition.

2. *Millenarian Interpretation*

Taken literally, what is being announced is an age of peace and happiness *on earth,* as part of history, before the end-time. The righteous will rise from the dead; Christ will come again and reign for 1,000 years. Then the eschatological struggle and the Last Judgment will occur. This interpretation is that of *millenarianism.* It circulated in the early centuries of Christianity when the Christian community, suffering under Roman persecution, anxiously awaited the end of the world.

---

[104] This is the Last Judgment. This time, all people are raised from the dead, sinners and the righteous alike, and appear before the Judge.

[105] These are the books in which all human deeds are recorded, see Daniel 7:10 and Revelation 3:5. See also the text *Dies irae: liber scriptus proferetur . . . quicquid latet apparebit* ("Day of wrath: the written record will be brought forward . . . all that which is hidden will be revealed").

[106] This marriage symbolism—Yahweh as groom and Israel as bride—is very common in the Old Testament in the writings of the prophets and in the Song of Songs. This symbolism is taken up again by the Christians (and, first, by Jesus himself: the reader will recall the parable of the ten virgins).

[107] Here the Greek transcribes the Hebrew "Emmanuel" ("God with us").

[108] The references in these two verses are similar to formulations in the Revelation of Isaiah (Isa. 25:6–8). This text, and the verses about the "eschatological feast," were often quoted, commented on, and amplified in the first century, even in Pharisaic circles, for example, in the "targums" (the Aramaic translations/interpretations of the Bible). See Grelot, *L'espérance juive,* 261–63.

3. *Symbolic Interpretation*

Starting with Origen and especially Augustine, as Christianity was about to triumph in the Empire on a permanent basis, the passage was given a symbolic interpretation. The figure 1,000 was understood to refer to an indefinite period of time, one that began with the Incarnation. As soon as Jesus was born, Satan was "bound" (Matt. 12:25–29: "If it is by the Spirit of God that I [Jesus] cast out demons, then the kingdom of God has come upon you"). In this sense, the *millennium* is not a future time to come, even less one provoked into being; it is the present time, the age of the church, a time energized by the moral entreaties of the Gospel and the paradoxical eschatology of the hoped-for Second Coming (*Parousia*). During this time, Christ already rules, the kingdom of God is already open to the righteous—even though this kingdom is not of this world.

This dual interpretation has great consequences for the history of political and social ideas: depending on whether one considers it an earthly or a heavenly kingdom, one's degree of patience concerning injustice and the other evils of this world may not be the same, and one has a different conception of the ideal goals that a political power can set itself in a Christian society. On the one hand, the millenarian approach is revolutionary, attaining extraordinary heights of intolerance and fanaticism, or it is reformist, nurturing an idea of social, economic, and scientific progress. On the other hand, the symbolic interpretation, developed as early as Augustine's *City of God,* accepts as unavoidable and providential that *evil will exist in the world until the end of time:* thus, it nurtures a *conservative pessimism.* While the church condemns millenarianism officially, it oscillates between these two poles, as we will see.

Given the extreme importance of numbers and dates for millenarian movements—in antiquity, in the Middle Ages, and in the modern era—it may be helpful to provide some information about their meaning in the Revelation of St. John.[109]

There is nothing comparable to this 1,000 years in the Old Testament, which prefers multiples of seven, such as the "Jubilee," a week of weeks of years (i.e., 49 years). The significance of the number 1,000 probably has a Babylonian or Persian origin. Already in Psalm 90 we find this verse: "a thousand years in thy sight are but as yesterday when it is past." The book of Jubilees (prior to 100 BC) speculates on the age at which Adam died. God said to Adam, "The day you eat of it you will die." Genesis indicates that Adam lived to be 930 years old. By "day," God understands 1,000 years.

If 1,000 years are like a "day" for God, then the Hexameron, that is, the six days of Creation, can be understood as follows (this is the interpretation given by Pseudo-Barnabas in a text dating from the beginning of the second century AD). The six days of Creation last, in fact, 6,000 years. At the end of the six days, the Savior will arrive and inaugurate the seventh day, the day of rest, the *millennium.* Then, at the end of these 1,000 years, and after the resurrection of the dead, an "eighth" day will begin, which is the other world or the kingdom of God. Thus, in total, the world will be led to its proper end in 7,000 years.

Other numbers in the book of Revelation are crucially important for millenarians: for example, the 144,000 (12 times 12,000) Israelites sealed as servants of God on their foreheads (Rev. 7:4); "the number of the beast" 666 (Rev. 13:18), an evil number because it is three times removed from the perfect number 7. (As the year 1666 approached, many European millenarians believed that the time of eschatological wars and the time of the Antichrist was come.) According to Daniel, as the reader recalls, the trials and tribulations experienced under Antiochus IV Epiphanes lasted three and a half years ("a time, times, and a half"), in other words, the time to erect the altar of Zeus in the Temple, then the time for the "purification" of the Temple by Judas Maccabeus. The

[109] See Delumeau, *Mille ans de bonheur,* 20–21.

book also mentions "1,290 days" and "1,335 days" (Dan. 12:11–12); likewise, Revelation mentions 1,260 days in which two witnesses prophesy clothed in sackcloth (Rev. 12:3) and a woman flees into the wilderness (Rev. 12:6).

Other examples in Revelation include the opening of the seven "seals" by the angel (chapter 6), the sounding of the seven "trumpets" (chapter 8–11), the pouring out of the seven "vials" of the wrath of God (chapter 15–16): once again, these numbers inspired the speculation of many commentators, who attempted to interpret the episodes and tragedies of history as so many signposts heralded in the book of Revelation and marking the imminent coming of the end-time.

Finally, it must be pointed out that the symbolism of millenarianism is exclusively bound up with the *length* of Christ's earthly reign, not with its exact moment in *time:* the "terrors of the year 1,000" are completely divorced from millenarian speculations and never really had the importance that is attributed to it.

G. Conclusion

It seems that the Bible's contribution to the Western tradition of political ideas, however rich, can be organized around two points: the eschatological "energizing" of historical time, and the discrediting of temporal power. These two ideas, or two existential attitudes, unknown to the Greco-Roman world, shaped the social and political ideas of the medieval and modern West, through a series of transformations.

1. *An Eschatological Energizing of Historical Time*

Animated by messianic and eschatological hope, the time of the Bible moves in a *linear* direction; it is not *cyclical time.* This difference in the idea of time between Athens or Rome and Jerusalem is well known and has often been discussed, but it is usually presented as a raw, more or less inexplicable anthropological fact. In my opinion, however, this transformation of time is clearly a consequence of the moral revolution initiated by the prophets and radicalized by the Sermon on the Mount.

Biblical morality is fundamentally a morality of compassion; it leads to a sharper perception of human suffering than ever before; it is an invitation to view the evils, until then held to be part of the eternal order of things, as *abnormal* and *unacceptable.* The new morality is *a principle of revolt against nature and its fixed forms.*

This development is fundamentally different from the natural morality of the Greco-Roman world formalized by Aristotle and the Stoic tradition until Cicero or Seneca. In the Greco-Roman tradition, a person was fundamentally an essence. A person's destiny was to become the actual Form one received in potentiality at birth. Now the Form of a person is finite. Just as the body has four limbs, and not one more, the soul possesses four cardinal virtues, and not one more. Its only prospect is to develop the exact form of these virtues, no more and no less. Justice, in particular, is essentially measure and limit. As the *Digest* says, it is "to give to each his own"; this gives rise to precise calculations to determine one's duty. To exceed one's duty is a vice. For the Greeks, the infinite, *apeiron,* is a negative; it is seen as excess, *hubris.* Generally speaking, the world is considered to be fixed. When the suspicion arises that nature or society can present certain developments, the idea is spurned and the observed changes are seen as mere phases in a cosmic cycle, thought to repeat themselves throughout eternity.

On the contrary, for messianic humankind, which is called by God to perfect the work of creation, historical existence cannot be an "eternal return." In the words of Augustine, ours is a "restless heart" (*irrequietum cor*). Historical time is "energized" by an eschatological perspective: it becomes a time of urgency, the "time that remains," to struggle as much as possible against evil in order to lessen the sufferings of humanity by all available human means. History becomes a *project to improve the world.* Man can and must act in the world (with God's help) in order to contribute to the coming—or at least the new manifestation (the nuances between Judaism and Christianity are irrelevant here)—of the Messiah and the advent of God's kingdom.

We saw that archaic societies accepted the sacral order—regardless of whether it was cosmic or social—as an external, absolutely intangible fact set down in the founding myth and sealed by ritual. Whoever deviated from this order risked the wrath of the sacred powers. Such societies stood entirely outside historical time.

In contrast, the Greek world—rational, critical, and desacralizing—was capable of desiring and accepting change. However, critical of the *nomos,* it then also sacralized the *physis,* starting with human nature. In our earlier discussion of the natural law, we saw that the Greek world regarded *physis* as the absolute, transcendent norm. It was comprehensible only if one studied the most perfect creatures of each species, thus taking past realities as a reference. Consequently, the Greek world never developed the concept of History as a progressive process; nor did it ever have a political and social "program."

The religion of the Bible is an unprecedented special case, where it is sacred power itself that, through the agency of the prophets, demands a profound transformation of man and the world and creates the prospect of a totally new future. Thus, *in the knowledge that God sustains him, and that he is his co-worker, man can and must transform history into a program.* He can begin by *thinking* history, by developing the concept itself.

Historical progress does not so much involve providing solutions to problems as *recognizing problems* and *anomalies* where previously nothing of the sort was visible, where the normal and eternal nature of things was all that was possible. In this sense, the greatest merit goes not to the *problem solvers* but to the problem *creators,* irrespective of their impact on the conventions of the age. This is precisely what the biblical prophets did. In the words of André Neher, the biblical prophets—that is, wounded and "altered" men—identified and created problems and made unprecedented moral demands, even at the expense of their own personal ruin.

Jesus did exactly so: there had been no problem with divorce; then he created one; there had been no problem condemning publicans and prostitutes or throwing the first stone at someone the community found guilty, of fighting with one's enemies, and so on. Now, all these attitudes are *problematic.* Therefore, new solutions may loom behind each of these new problems—for example, the creation of an institution, and historical progress. The injury of mercy or compassion (love) has a *creative* virtue.

The new morality, wherever it prevails, will carry a disruption of perspectives on time; Judeo-Christian societies see themselves as transformative societies. In fact, no civilization other than Judeo-Christian civilization has intentionally pursued progress. If the West devotes itself to social, economic, scientific, and technological progress, it owes it to its Judeo-Christian heritage.

2. *The Discrediting of Temporal Power*

The second conviction of the people of the Bible—a conviction that also passes into the political tradition of the West—is that temporal power as such plays no more than a secondary role in human life, because it plays no part in the economy of salvation, which depends entirely on the inner conversion of a person. Exposed to every temptation, covering social injustices with its authority, political power is fundamentally suspect. It must be kept under the constant supervision of inspired individuals—prophets, saints, and priests, guided by their conscience inhabited by the spirit of God—who collectively constitute what became known as "spiritual power" in due course.

We noted this fundamental discordance of the two powers ever since the criticism of kingship by the prophets, then the transformation of the messianic king and priest, who became less and less identified with real institutions and increasingly "spiritualized," then, under theocracy, the disinterest manifested by priests for the institutions of state relinquished to foreign powers (albeit reluctantly), and finally in the Seleucid and Roman eras when the Jewish sects openly led wars against the occupying powers and their Hasmonean and Herodian representatives. Finally, the separation of spiritual and temporal power became total with rabbinic Judaism and early Christianity.

In this regard the contrast between the biblical world and the Greek world is striking. In Nathan's harsh moral judgment of David, in the contempt and defiance of the "Maccabean martyrs" toward Antiochus IV Epiphanes, and in the irenic attitude of Christ to Pontius Pilate, there is more than mere distance; there is an absolute certainty of *superiority*.

This is a long way from Socrates' *irony* toward the Athenian authorities, or the *insolence* of Diogenes the Cynic towards Alexander; or the *indifference* of the Epicurean communities, who withdrew and shunned all semblance of power. The Stoic sage could, of course, detach himself from power, but in the same sense that he could detach himself from all things associated with temporal existence: Seneca removed himself from public life and from the affairs of state when circumstances went against him. But, except for such circumstances, it was self-evident for the Stoic that benevolence for the human race required his total and unreserved participation in the affairs of state.

In the attitude of the biblical prophets and saints, we encounter a genuine feeling of superiority in regard to the state, as well as the will to direct it from a distance by the exertion of moral pressure on the people and their leaders. There is a profound conviction that the state can do absolutely nothing for or against the redemption of the righteous, which is in the hands of God alone and the righteous themselves. Every state is necessarily and always a "Babylon," one of the beasts from the sea. The righteous can never completely trust it and cooperate with it.

This biblical contempt for temporal power—the conviction of the "saints" that they exist in a history that lies outside the realm of action and beyond the sight of the powerful of this world—plays a fundamental role in the political history of Christianized societies, including those of Western Europe, which continue to hold in high esteem the civic traditions of antiquity. *But the Greco-Roman trust in the state would never be fully restored.*

I believe that the biblical idea of a fundamental indignity of temporal powers will contribute—as much as the Greek idea of a government by law, but in a completely different way—to the development of *freedom* as the highest political value in the West. If the state is a Babylon, a perdition; if true salvation comes only from God and God's messengers; it is essential to preserve human conscience from the abusive intrusion of temporal power. Its right of involvement must be restricted to an external sphere of action alone. The protection of a private sphere of conscience and thought, which assumes a legal basis during the Middle Ages, is the consequence of the biblical tradition's distrust of temporal power.

Graham Maddox[110] believes that the very idea of *democracy* is the fruit of a biblical tradition of state mistrust. In fact, modern democracies are regimes that have established a set of

[110] Graham Maddox, *Religion and the Rise of Democracy* (London: Routledge, 1996). Maddox's argument is consistent with the Anglo-American tradition, which sees religion playing a positive role in the efflorescence of modern democratic regimes (see such writers as John Locke, J. S. Mill, and Lord Acton for the English tradition; see also the American preachers of the U.S. colonial period, the founding fathers, and the heralds of the "Great Awakening" of the early nineteenth century: for all of these Puritans, it goes without saying that Jerusalem is the primary inspiration of democracy). This argument is surprising from the Catholic European point of view, which sees the modern, secular, and liberal state, on the contrary, as the product of a radical revolt *against* Judeo-Christianity and the church. We will see that Maddox's argument is well supported by the history of ideas.

institutions for the systematic control of the state: a free press, public schools, elected representatives, an independent judiciary, and so on. The idea that the state needs constant control could only come to those who, in principle, were suspicious of its villainy and perversions. The secularization of the state—that is, the reduction of the state to a simple technical tool serving objectives that it has no authority to define for itself—is the brainchild of *Calvinist* countries (The Netherlands, England, the United States) whose political thinkers and leaders were deeply immersed in and influenced by the biblical tradition (especially the Old Testament). Conversely, it was under the influence of atheistic or neo-pagan ideologies—Marxism and Nazism—that the state became totalitarian in the twentieth century. It was the Judeo-Christian tradition that preserved the West from the temptation of looking at the state as an *absolute* entity.[111]

[111] It is true that certain Christian states sometimes suppressed the distinction between temporal and spiritual power: for example, Byzantine "Caesaropapism," the Spain of the Inquisition. But this is a deviation from biblical inspiration.

Chapter 1

Christianity and Politics at the Time of the Roman Empire

Christianity's fundamental theological stances in regard to history and temporal power, outlined in the introductory chapter to part 3, would translate into a number of specific political choices. Progressively the church fathers[1] established a true political doctrine. It evolved between the time that the church was a persecuted, almost clandestine minority, and the period after the Edict of Milan (313 AD), when it became an official institution of the Empire.

I. The Political Attitude of Christians under the Roman Empire

A. Christianity and the Imperial Cult

Christians, of course, could not accept the imperial cult; their refusal to venerate the emperor as a god put them at odds with the rest of Roman society.[2] Theophilus of Antioch (d. ca. 182 or 183 AD),

[1] The expression "church fathers" refers to the ecclesiastical writers of the first centuries of the Common Era responsible for establishing Christian doctrine. The timeframe for the Western "fathers" stretched from the early beginnings of Christianity until Gregory the Great (ca. 600 AD); in the East it extended until the ninth century. The church fathers wrote primarily in Greek and in Latin. They are not to be confused with the "doctors of the church," fewer in number, who received their title by formal decision of the Magisterium. The doctors can belong to any period.

[2] Material in this section is from H.-X. Arquillière, *L'augustinisme politique: Essai sur la formation des théories politiques du Moyen Age* [Political Augustinism: Essay on the development of political theories in the Middle Ages] (1933; repr., Paris: Vrin, 1972); Jean Sirinelli, "Rome et les débuts du christianisme" [Rome and the beginnings of Christianity],

a converted pagan and bishop of Antioch in 169 AD, categorically outlawed Caesar worship by Christians:

> Wherefore I will rather honor the king [than your gods], not, indeed, worshipping him, but praying for him. But God, the living and true God, I worship, knowing that the king is made by Him. You will say, then, to me, Why do you not worship the king? Because he is not made to be worshipped, but to be reverenced with lawful honor, for he is not a god, but a man appointed by God, not to be worshipped, but to judge justly. For in a kind of way his government is committed to him by God: as He will not have those called kings whom He has appointed under Himself; for king is his title, and it is not lawful for another to use it; so neither is it lawful for any to be worshipped but God only. . . . Accordingly, honor the king, but love him, obey him, and pray for him with loyal mind.[3]

The punishment for refusing to worship the emperor could go as far as martyrdom (see Saint Polycarpus, bishop of Smyrna, ca. 155 or 177 AD).

The situation changed as members of the Roman elite converted to Christianity. For them it became necessary to clarify the relationship between loyalty to the church and participation in public life.

B. Celsus: Opposition to the Christians

Celsus was a second century, anti-Christian polemicist. He is known to us through Origen's treatise *Contra Celsus* (248 AD), which quotes lengthy passages from his *A True Discourse.*

Celsus criticized Christians who sought to enjoy the benefits of a *Pax Romana,* like other citizens, but refused to abide by the associated civil and military obligations. Christian abstention or withdrawal might have been defensible when it was only a tiny sect; but given the increasing number of Christians, and the growing threat from the barbarians, such an attitude was no longer admissible.

Once again, the conflict sharpened around the Christians' refusal to worship the cult of the emperor. In so doing, they isolated themselves from the other citizens and placed everyone at risk of incurring the wrath of the sacred powers. In the opinion of Celsus, their stance threatened the entire Roman community. Christians claimed religious truths known only to them, and foreign to those of the Empire. According to Celsus, the Christian's loyalty was to these truths, not to the Empire. And this, in his opinion, was treachery.

Later Eusebius of Caesarea would claim that a prosecuting magistrate was mistaken when he interrogated and accused a Christian as though he were a spy of some foreign power. In fact, Christian communities increasingly resembled states within a state. Throughout the Roman Empire, Christians were regarded as "barbarians of the interior."

C. Tertullian

Tertullian (Carthage, 155?–220? AD), another apologist known for his antagonistic style and the severity of his opinions, claimed the very same status for Christians that Celsus called a crime. He rejected the idea that barbarians were enemies (this, it is recalled, was the position of the Cynics as well) and asserted, "*my republic is the world,*" adding, *secessi de populo,* "I have withdrawn from society [i.e., public life]." As for Caesar, he is only God's tool, seated on the throne to hold the world in check in expectation of the Parousia. In and of himself, Caesar has no value. "They

in *Histoire des idées politiques* [History of political ideas], vol. 1, ed. Jean Touchard (Paris: Presses Universitaires de France, 1959). For the historical context of this period, see above, part 2, chapter 1.

[3] Theophilus of Antioch, *To Autolycus,* chap. 11, quoted in Arquillière, *L'augustinisme politique,* 96.

[the emperors] know who gave them empire, they know...that He is the only God [the living God], in whose power alone they are."[4]

Still, he argues, Christians pray for emperors and kings in order to enjoy the peace and benefits they are able to provide for one and all. "A Christian is enemy to none, least of all to the Emperor of Rome, whom he knows to be appointed by his God, and so cannot but love and honour; and whose well-being moreover, he must needs desire, with that of the empire over which he reigns so long as the world shall stand."[5]

Tertullian emphasizes that an unjust law is null and void, adding that the church, which now defines what is just, often has objections to imperial legislation. At the time of Tertullian, however, such criticism had to remain muted.

D. Origen

Origen (185–255? AD), one of the most important of the church fathers, was educated in Alexandria (he and Plotinus, the founder of Neoplatonism, were contemporaries, perhaps even classmates). Origen authored a large body of theological writings, including exegetical commentaries on most of the books in the Bible.

In contrast to Tertullian, Origen attached great importance to Greek philosophy; he believed that pagans had achieved glimpses of the truth. He was a Platonist and a dualist. Thus, he thought the Scriptures allowed for two interpretations, one "corporeal" (or "physical" in the sense of "according to the flesh"), and the other "spiritual";[6] he developed the idea of "two cities" before Augustine. However, he did not see an antagonism between the City of God and the City of Man; rather, he imagined a hierarchy from one to the other. They are parallel, each moving toward its goal. Therefore, Caesar could rule uninhibited in his realm. Deep down, Origen, who was a Greek, had no quarrel with the Empire; in fact, in his opinion, the Empire greatly facilitated the spread of the Gospel message.

E. Constantine Places the Church under Imperial Tutelage

Everything changed when Constantine (ca. 280–337 AD), with his Edict of Milan (313 AD), put an end to Diocletian's persecutions.[7] The two cities would have to become involved together, and it was in that involvement that they discovered the depth of their antagonism.

Constantine convened the Council of Nicaea (325AD) with the intention of reestablishing the unity of the church, under threat from the Arian heresy. At this synod, Arius[8] was condemned

[4] Q. Septimi Florentis Tertulliani [Tertullian], *Apologeticus: The Text of Oehler,* annotated, with an introduction by J. E. B. Taylor, trans. A. Souter (Cambridge: Cambridge University Press, 1917), 30.

[5] Tertullian, *The Address of Q. Sept. Tertullian to Scapula Tertullus, Proconsul of Africa,* trans. Sir David Dalrymple (Edinburgh: Murray & Cochrane, 1790).

[6] We saw above that Origen rejected a literal interpretation of the book of Revelation and preferred a symbolic one.

[7] For a discussion of the religious and political views of Constantine, see the chapter devoted to Eusebius of Caesarea above pp. 369–78.

[8] Arius (280–336 AD), a priest, denied the consubstantiality (*homoousia*) of the Father and the Son; rather, the Son is the first creature of the Father. Despite the decisions of Nicaea, the Arian controversy agitated the Eastern Empire for a very long time, and Arian and Orthodox bishops competed for episcopal seats. Arianism seemed to triumph after the Councils of Sirmium (357–59 AD) and Rimini (359 AD); it was defended by the emperors Constantius II, Valens, and Valentinian II, but opposed by the Cappadocian fathers; Basil the Great, bishop of Caesarea; Gregory of Nyssa, his brother; and Gregory Nazianzus. With the ascension of Theodosius I, who reunited the eastern and western portions of the Empire, the Council of Constantinople (381 AD) renewed its condemnation of Arianism. Meanwhile, it spread outside the Empire among the barbarian peoples under the impetus of Ulfilas's mission (Ulfilas or Wulfila [311–83 AD], a translator of the Bible, was a Goth of Cappadocian origin). As the Arian heresy spread, it contributed to a strengthening of the differences between the civilizations of Rome and the barbarians. In Gaul, as late as the sixth century, bishops like Caeserius of Arles continued the struggle against the Arian heresy, which disappeared from Spain only around 589 AD with the conversion of the Visigoth king Reccared I.

and a "symbol of faith" adopted, which would become the basis of the Christian creed: the only Son of God [*Logos*] is said to be "begotten, not made" and "*one in Being* (*homoousios*) with the Father."

It is because the Roman emperors convened the ecumenical synods that the church, with state backing, became the powerful organization that we know today, professing the one doctrine. Before that, Christian communities were somewhat divergent and autonomous, lacking unity on important dogma.

The period between the Edict of Milan and the death of Pope Leo I (Leo the Great) in 461 AD was the golden age of *patristics*[9] with its great controversies on christology and the Trinity. Worship became public, great church buildings were erected, and liturgical ceremonies were conducted with hitherto unknown pomp.

F. The First Church Protests against Imperial Tutelage

Soon the church began to complain about this all-invading solicitude of temporal power that threatened its freedom.

Already a letter from Ossius, a bishop of Cordoba, warned the emperor against personal involvement in ecclesiastical and dogmatic affairs in Nicaea. Athanasius, bishop of Alexandria, patriarch and doctor of the church (295–373 AD) refers to the letter in his *History of the Arians*. He does not hesitate to criticize the emperor for his lukewarm anti-Arian stance. Likewise, Lucifer, bishop of Calaris (Cagliari on the south coast of Sardinia), criticized Emperor Constantius II for coming to terms with the Arians. Disregarding the synodical canons, Constantius proclaimed, "my will is also a canon of the church" (in this respect, he may be considered one of the founders of Caesaropapism in the Eastern Empire). Lucifer retorted, "You may claim to have divine authority and be superior to the bishops, but if you do not obey them, God has already condemned you to death! How can you, a lay ruler, assume such authority over the family and priests of God?"

The church asserted its authority more forcefully with Ambrose, bishop of Milan (333–97 AD). Several controversies led him to define the frontiers between church and state.

1. *The Altar of Victory*

Augustus had erected the Altar of Victory in the Curia (the Roman senate house). Constantius II had it removed, then Julian the Apostate reinstated it; then it was removed again. Now the senators were demanding its restoration once more, and the new emperor, Valentinian II, hesitated. Ambrose wrote to him, strongly opposing restoration: "it is a religious cause, and I the bishop make a claim [to be heard]." Then he uttered a threat: if the emperor comes to the church, he will find it empty ("either no priest there, or one who will resist you").

2. *The Portian Basilica*

The Arians, supported by Justina, Emperor Valentinian's mother, demanded the Portian Basilica in the suburbs of Milan for their place of worship. Ambrose rejected the request adamantly, arguing that the emperor cannot dispose of what belongs to God. In 386 AD, the Arians renewed their claim, and again Ambrose refused. The ministers of the church have dominion over all Christians, he wrote, including the emperor: "Because the king's sins are great, he must not be spared the harsh criticism of the priests, so that he may be corrected.... The emperor is in the church, not above the church."[10]

[9] The thinking of the church fathers.

[10] *Commentary on Psalms XXXVII*, in Arquillière, *L'augustinisme politique*, 110.

3. *The Callinicum Synagogue*

Some Christians in the Syrian city of Callinicum were responsible for destroying a synagogue. Theodosius issued an order for its reconstruction at the expense of the local bishop. Challenging the emperor from church premises, Ambrose flatly rejected the imperial order, arguing that Christian assets were not to be allocated to the building of a synagogue. Arquillière observes, "This is a stark illustration of natural justice (compensation for damages) being absorbed by bishopric sacerdotal justice, which in the end would be imposed on a Christian emperor. It was a rare example for the times but marked the onset of a trend with a promising future."

4. *The Thessalonican Massacre and Theodosius's "Excommunication"*

The emperor Theodosius was held responsible for the massacre of 7,000 people at Thessalonica. The bishops were sitting in synod when the news of the massacre reached Milan and immediately asked Ambrose to excommunicate Theodosius. When the emperor returned, Ambrose withdrew from the city, sending him a letter, in which he instructed him to follow David's example in repentance and to utter the words "I have sinned greatly." In another letter, Ambrose described the following scene: the emperor "stripped himself of all royal symbols; he wept publicly in the church, begging his pardon with groans and tears. His innermost circle was mortified at his humiliation, but the emperor himself showed no shame at doing public penitence."[11]

To what doctrine did Ambrose have recourse for his actions? A former imperial official in the Roman west, he was well versed in Roman law. He was also knowledgeable in pagan philosophy and in the doctrine of the "cardinal virtues."[12] Thus, he was familiar with the conflict between the pagan and Christian systems of justice. He deliberately chose the latter: "But that very thing is excluded with us which philosophers think to be the office of justice. For they say that the first expression of justice is, to hurt no one, except when driven to it by wrongs received. The authority of the Gospel did away with this. For the Scripture wills that the Spirit of the Son of Man should be in us, Who came to give grace, not to bring harm."[13]

Thus, Ambrose recognizes that divine justice necessarily interferes with state justice, and in some instances contradicts it. He claims the authority of the church in spiritual matters and in combined spiritual and temporal matters (e.g., the synagogue in Callinicum), including over the emperor himself in matters of sin, *ratione peccati.* Since the emperor had committed a sin in the affair of the Thessalonican massacre, the church was entitled to intervene.

G. John Chrysostom

John Chrysostom (b. 344, bishop of Constantinople in 397, d. 407 in exile) was a contemporary of Ambrose, but he belonged to Eastern Christianity. Here is how he saw the conflictual relationship between the church and the state: "The king is entrusted with bodies, the priest with souls; the king remits the balance of debts, the priest the balance of sins; the former obliges, the latter exhorts; the former by pressure, the latter by free will; the former has material weapons, the latter spiritual weapons; the former wages war on savages, the latter on demons. The latter office is

[11] Quoted in Arquillière, *L'augustinisme politique,* 110.

[12] He wrote a *De officiis* with the aspiration of producing a Christian version of Cicero's great work.

[13] Ambrose, *De officiis ministorum* [On the duties of the clergy], trans. H. de Romestin, E. de Romestin, and H. T. F. Duckworth. In *Nicene and Post-Nicene Fathers,* 2nd ser., vol. 10, edited by Philip Schaff and Henry Wace (Buffalo: Christian Literature Publishing, 1896), 1.28.131.

higher; hence the king submits his head to the priest's hands, and at all points in the Old dispensation priests anointed kings."[14]

In the East, however, practice did not follow theory. Indeed, in political matters the gap widened between Christian attitudes in the east and the west of the Empire. In both cases, Christianity's espousal of radical monotheism led to celestial monotheism becoming a justification for a quasi-totalitarian imperial autocracy. And in both cases, *monachism*[15] developed in reaction to a growing osmosis between church and Empire: it became necessary for one class of men to renounce society altogether, something the Christian community could no longer do, as it was now fully a part of both society and the state.

Progressively, however, the East moved in the direction of "Caesaropapism," that is, toward an entwining of spiritual and temporal powers. This was well suited to this part of the Empire where the memory of sacred monarchies and their Hellenistic extensions remained robust. In the West, which was suffering from an early collapse of the Empire under the barbarian incursions, the church survived as a powerful and respected institution. But none of the new states had sufficient authority to maintain the church under its tutelage, at least not until Charlemagne reestablished the Empire. Meanwhile, in the West, Augustine's astonishing theology provided new arguments for the supremacy—or independence, at any rate—of the church.

II. Augustine's Political Doctrine

A. Life and Work

Augustine (354–430 AD) was born in the Numidian city of Thagaste in North Africa (present-day Souk Ahras, Algeria); he was the son of a pagan father, Patricius, and a Christian mother, Monica. He received a classical education and became a professor of rhetoric in Carthage, then in Rome. At first, he followed Manichaeism, then Neoplatonism, before converting to Christianity at the age of 30. Soon after he became an ordained priest, and, in 396, the bishop of Hippo (the most important city in North Africa after Carthage). He held this episcopal office until his death, all the while producing an immense body of doctrinal writings. Augustine authored philosophical treatises, polemical (anti-Manichean, anti-Donatist) tracts, Old Testament and New Testament commentaries (*De genesi ad litteram* [Homilies on the Gospel according to John], etc.), a spiritual autobiography (his *Confessions*), and last but not least, his *City of God (De civitate Dei)*. His work runs to many volumes.[16]

Augustine was not particularly attracted to political questions. The first half of his work is devoted exclusively to philosophical and theological concerns. But, in 410, Rome was sacked by the Visigoths of Alaric. Pagans—still numerous at the time; the cause of Christianity had by no means triumphed—argued that the disaster came about because Rome had abandoned its ancient gods. Augustine's *City of God*, written between 413 and 427, was his response to these allegations.

---

[14] Saint John Chrysostom, *Homily IV on Isaiah*, in *Old Testament Homilies: Homilies on Isaiah and Jeremiah*, vol. 2, trans. Robert Charles Hill (Brookline, MA: Holy Cross Orthodox Press, 2003), 89–90.

[15] *Translator's note:* The religious practice of renouncing all worldly pursuits in order to fully devote one's life to spiritual work.

[16] *Translator's note:* For quotes from the *City of God*, we use the Loeb Classical Library translations: *The City of God against the Pagans*, 7 vols., trans. William M. Greene (Cambridge, MA: Harvard University Press, 1963). The author uses Saint Augustine, *La Cité de Dieu*, 5 vols., general introduction and notes by G. Bardy, trans. G. Combès (Paris: Desclée de Brouwer, 1959–60).

Augustine's work is monumental. It is more a reflection on history than on the state—political matters are discussed in book 19 (of a total of 22) and in a few other passages. The remainder of his work is concerned with philosophical and theological issues: the errors of paganism, the creation of the world, the creation of man, original sin, the history of salvation, the Last Judgment, and hell and paradise.

B. The Two Cities

Humankind is divided into two cities: "The two cities... were created by two kinds of love: the earthly city by a love of self carried even to the point of contempt for God; the heavenly by the love of God, even to the contempt of self" (*City of God* 14.28). There is no succession. Like Origen, Augustine rejects the notion of millenarianism. Both cities have existed side-by-side since the beginning of time. One descends from Abel, the other from Cain. They are both radically at odds and inextricably enmeshed (importantly, their opposition is not exactly the same as that of the church and the state). On earth, the heavenly city is on pilgrimage, in exile, like the Jews in Babylon. God alone knows which city each person belongs to; there is no question of a "community of the pure," whose members recognize each other mutually (like in the doctrine of the Manicheans or, in the Middle Ages, that of the Cathars).

C. Only Christian Justice Can Form the Basis of the State

What, then, in these circumstances happens to the state and in particular to Rome, whose sacking by the Visigoths revealed its vulnerability and whose collapse seemed possible and even imminent?

In his *De Republica,*[17] Cicero defined the republic (i.e., the state) as a "common sense of right" (see above, p. 293). But such a sense among Christians is only possible if the Gospel forms the basis of the new justice, the only justice capable of bringing about a reign of peace. "The peace of the heavenly city is a perfectly ordered and fully concordant fellowship in the enjoyment of God and in mutual enjoyment by union with God" (*City of God* 19.13).

Roman pagans never practiced such true justice: "Justice is that virtue which assigns to every man his due. What sort of justice is it that removes a man from the true God and subjects him to unclean demons? Is that assigning to every man his due? If we are to pronounce unjust the man who keeps back a piece of land from its purchaser and hands it over to another who has no lawful claim on it, are we also to pronounce just the man who takes himself from the Lord and God who made him and serves evil spirits?" (*City of God* 19.21).

Conclusion: if the republic is a consensus on the law and the Romans never experienced the true law, then "*there never was a Roman state*" (*City of God* 19.21). Rome never enjoyed more than de facto rule, the rule of a "nondescript mob unworthy of the name of people." Knowledge and worship of the true God is necessary to establish a true people and a true republic; therefore, the pagan Empire is null and void. Thus, *Alaric could not destroy what did not exist;* his carnage was simply one further contribution to Rome's thousand-year history of plundering and murdering. The sacking of Rome, regrettable in its own right, has no deep significance in history. The real historical development would be the conversion of the Romans—and the barbarians—to Christianity under the guidance of the church, the dispenser of baptism and mediator of the grace of Jesus Christ. Thus, with individuals who believe in the true God, whose grace enables them to love, it will be possible to practice true justice and lay the foundations of a genuine republic. The only true state is a Christian state; a state cannot exist without the church.

[17] Augustine had Cicero's complete text of *De Republica* in his possession.

These arguments form the basis of what H. X. Arquillière calls "political Augustinism," the political ideology dominant in the West from the end of antiquity until the eleventh and twelfth centuries. We will discuss this ideology in chapter 2 below.

D. Political Authority as a "Ministering" Authority

Augustine rounds out his vision with a new idea, one that proved fatal for the "natural" law of the state. In the individual, reason can command passions only if God commands reason. Likewise, in the city, *men cannot command other men lawfully unless they themselves are commanded by God, which is to say by the law of God's love* (see *City of God* 19.21.2).

Thus, before God, *natural hierarchies fail.* Men who differ from one another in nature are equal before God by reason of their ontological nothingness. Accordingly, the natural subordination of one person to another has no merit. This is a deeply subversive principle, one that poses a threat to all human powers in the pagan city.

Some individuals will have powers over others, but these powers must be exercised as a *service,*[18] not as power. "In the home of the just man who lives by faith and who is still a pilgrim in exile from the celestial city, even those who give commands serve those whom they seem to command. For they command not through lust for rule but through dutiful concern for others, not with pride in exercising princely rule but with mercy in providing for others" (*City of God* 19.14).

But does the secular state, or the insufficiently Christian state, have any legitimacy at all? Or, to ask the same question differently, should civil authority have no independence with regard to ecclesiastic authority? Augustine does not go so far. He adopts a more nuanced position for practical and theoretical reasons.

The practical reason is that, in Augustine's lifetime, the Roman state was still functioning; its strength was impressive and majestic, the product of 1,000 years of history, almost all of it pagan. In contrast, the church itself was yet young, and comparatively small and weak. It could hardly claim to overthrow the Roman state or to rebuild society and the state on an entirely new, purely Christian basis, especially since, for the Christians at the time of Augustine, the end of the world was thought to be near. It is for this event—the end of the world—that the church must prepare the faithful, and not the establishment of a society on earth destined to be permanent.

In this period of transition, however, it is necessary to find a theological status for a secular state and civil government that have to be lived with for a while, and it is necessary to explain why God allows such a state with its injustices to exist. Augustine solves these problems by establishing, on the one hand, *a doctrine of political authority as punishment for sinners,* and, on the other, *a doctrine of the action of Providence in history.*

E. Political Power as Punishment for Original Sin

In a famous text that we have already quoted, the apostle Paul says, "there is no authority except from God" (*nulla potestas nisi a Deo*) (Rom. 13:1–7; see above, p. 438). Augustine understands this to mean that by right of nature no person has authority over another; therefore, all authority has a supernatural origin. Before the Fall (before nature was wounded), love was sufficient to bind together human society. Then people sinned and the race of Cain was forever condemned to rend itself to pieces. Therefore, to live together and restrain their hatred and murderous impulses, people need some kind of authority. In his goodness, God filled this need by establishing political powers. Political power, therefore, is the consequence of original sin.

Augustine formulates this in a key passage from book 19:

[18] This idea exists in Ezekiel already; see above, p. 420.

> This is the prescription of the order of nature, and thus has God created man. For, he says: "Let him have dominion over the fish of the sea, and over the birds that fly in heaven, and over every creeping thing that creeps upon the earth" [Gen. 1:26]. For he did not wish a rational creature, made in his own image, to have dominion save over irrational creatures: not man over man, but man over the beasts. So it was that the first just men were established as shepherds of flocks, rather than as kings of men, so that even so God might indirectly point out what is required by the principle of gradation among his creatures, and what the guilt of sinners demands (*quid postulet ordo creatuarum, quid exigat meritum peccatorum*); for of course it is understood that the condition of slavery is justly imposed on the sinner. Wherefore we do not read of a slave anywhere in the Scriptures until the just man Noah branded his son's sin with this word; so he earned this name by his fault, not by nature.... But by nature, in which God first created man, no man is the slave either of another man or of sin. Yet slavery as a punishment (*paenalis servitus*) is also ordained by that law which bids us to preserve the natural order and forbids us to disturb it; for if nothing had been done contrary to that law, there would have been nothing requiring the check of punishment by slavery. For this reason too the Apostle [Paul] admonishes slaves to be subject to their masters, and to serve them heartily and with good will, so that if they cannot be freed by their masters they may themselves make their very slavery in some sense free, by serving not in crafty fear but in faithful affection, until all wickedness pass away[19] and all lordship and human authority be done away with (*donec transeat iniquitas et evacuetur omnis principatus et potestas humana*) and God be all in all. (*City of God* 19.15)

Thus, the secular state or the natural state, or civil authority—even if it is Babylon—has a certain legitimacy (*City of God* 19.24). A Christian can live within the state; it is even in his interest that the state exists, regardless if it is imperfect. But his support for the state will not be unconditional, because he knows that the world and with it the social and political order, are only temporary:

> so long as the two cities are intermingled we also profit by the peace of Babylon;[20] and the people of God is by faith so freed from it as meanwhile to be but strangers passing through. For this reason the Apostle too admonished the church to pray for its kings and other high persons, adding these words: "That we may live a quiet and tranquil life with all piety and love." And the prophet Jeremiah,[21] in predicting the captivity that was to befall the ancient people of God, and in bidding them by divine inspiration to go obediently to Babylon and by their very patience to do God service, added his own admonition that they should pray for Babylon, saying: "Because in her peace is your peace"; that is, of course, the temporal peace of the present that is common to the good and the evil alike. (19.26)

What, then, will this coexistence of people with and without God, in the same political order, look like?

---

[19] That is, until the advent of the kingdom of God.

[20] Here it is important to recall that in biblical symbolism, "Babylon" is the figure of absolute evil, that is, the quintessential society where sin has triumphed. Christians in Rome, and in all subsequent states following the demise of Rome, whatever the form until the end of time, are like the Hebrews in Babylon: that is, in exile, in a temporary camp. As a Christian, one should never align one's destiny with that of an earthly homeland—and its temporal authority—whatever it may be.

[21] See above, pp. 419–20.

> "But a household of human beings whose life is not governed by faith pursues an earthly peace by means of the good things and the conveniences of this temporal life, while a household of those who live by faith looks to the everlasting blessings that are promised for the future, using like one in a strange land any earthly and temporal things, not letting them entrap him or divert him from the path that leads to God, but making them a means to brace his efforts to ease the burden and by no means to aggravate the load imposed by the corruptible body, which weighs down the soul. Therefore both kinds of human groups and of households use alike the things that are necessary for this mortal life; but each has its own very different end in using them. So, too, the earthly city, that lives not by faith, seeks an earthly peace, and its end in aiming at agreement concerning command and obedience on the part of citizens is limited to a sort of merging of human wills in regard to the things that are useful for this mortal life. Whereas the heavenly city, or rather the part of it that goes its pilgrim way in this mortal life and lives by faith, needs must make use of this peace too, though only until this mortal lot which has need of it shall pass away. Therefore, so long as it leads its life in captivity, as it were, being a stranger in the earthly city, although it has already received the promise of redemption, and the gift of the spirit as a pledge of it, it does not hesitate to obey the laws of the earthly city whereby matters that minister to the support of mortal life are administered to the end that since this mortal life is common to both, a harmony may be preserved between both cities with regard to the things that belong to it. (*City of God* 19.17)

It remains to be explained why God allows non-Christian political power, and indeed blatantly anti-Christian power, to exist in the world, and why God tolerates historical disasters, which eliminate some states and lead to the creation of others in an apparently erratic and unjustified fashion. This brings Augustine to the concept of *Providence,* the thread of his argument.

F. The Role of Providence in History

Augustine writes in book 5 of his *City of God:* "Neither heaven nor earth, neither angel nor man, not even the inner organs of a tiny and despised animal, not the pin-feather of a bird nor the tiny flower in the meadow nor the leaf on the tree did God leave unprovided with a suitable harmony of parts, a peace, so to speak, between its members. *It is impossible to suppose that he would have excluded from the laws of his providence the kingdoms of men and their dominations and servitudes*" (5.11).

The order of things and time are incomprehensible to mortals, but they are perfectly known by God (*City of God* 4.33). God gives earthly realms to both the good and the wicked (4.33). "And yet the power to dominate is granted even to such men only by the providence of the supreme God, when he deems mankind worthy of such masters. The voice of God states the matter clearly in the following passage (the speaker is the wisdom of God): '*By me kings reign, and by me tyrants hold the earth*' [Prov. 8:15]. . . . Another passage plainly says of God: '*That he causes a hypocrite to rule because of the perversity of the people*' [Job 34:30]" (*City of God* 5.19). Augustine concludes: "Sometimes the unrighteous arrive at worldly honours: when they have arrived at them, and have been made either judges or kings; for *God doth this for the discipline of His folk,* for the discipline of His people; *the honour due to their power must needs be shown them* (*ut exhibeatur illis honor debitue potestati*)" (*Exposition on Psalms CCXXIV,* 7).

Although such men are knaves and rogues, Christians must obey them. Julian was an infidel emperor, a pagan and an apostate, yet his soldiers remained obedient; they refused only to offer incense before idols. "Christian soldiers served an infidel Emperor; when they came to the cause of Christ, they acknowledged Him only who was in heaven. If he [Julian] called upon them at any time to worship idols, to offer incense; they preferred God to him: but whenever he commanded them to deploy into line, to march against this or that nation, they at once obeyed. *They distinguished their everlasting from their temporal master;*[22] and yet they were, for the sake of their everlasting Master, submissive to their temporal master" (*Exposition on Psalms CCXXIV*, 7). This is, indeed, a doctrine of submission, although a very relative one. The state touches the limits of the Christian *conscience*.

With these doctrines on authority and Providence, Augustine's *City of God* effectively answers the questions raised by the pagan protests after the sacking of Rome, and more broadly it provides a solution to the political problem that Christians faced at the time. It is not right for Christianity to demonstrate too much support for a transitory form of politics or history. Rome will disappear, but so what? The destiny of a Christian is not identical with the destiny of Rome, or with any other earthly homeland, for that matter.

III. The Birth of Canon Law

The existence of a law pertaining specifically to the church has been debated since the beginning.[23] Is there not a contradiction between grace and law (or rule), between the spirit and the letter? Did not Augustine say, "Love and do what you will"? Experience shows that rules were needed to simplify social life and limit the chances of conflict. At any rate, the law elaborated by the church, or under its direct influence, will have absolute characteristics; it will not be reducible—in form or content—to any of the secular laws of the West.

A. First to the Fourth Centuries

The Old Testament contains many rules for social life. The New Testament did not abolish them all; canon law would draw on such rules. For example, in the Epistles of Paul, and in other Epistles, there are many provisions for a Christian marriage (1 Cor. 7; Eph. 5:21–33; Heb. 13:4; 1 Phil. 3:1–6). Since these rules are in the Bible, the authors of canon law consider them "divine law."

Immediately after, we come across other rules in ecclesiastical writings; this time they are human in origin. The first letter of Clement of Rome is considered to be the first legal text of the church. In it Clement discusses the organization of the Christian community. There are references to the Bible, but they are made in a spirit of Roman legalism, with "examples of the ancients" (*mos majorum*). Other letters (the Letter of Ignatius of Antioch, the Epistle of Barnabas) also offer rules for ending quarrels in the early Christian communities.

1. *Canonical-Liturgical Writings*

Between the first and early fourth centuries some writings were produced on the liturgy, the organization of the church, and married life. The *Didache* (end of the first century) gives the rules for baptism and the election of bishops and deacons. The *Apostolic Tradition* by Hippolytus of Rome (ca. 200) expressed a desire to "keep the tradition" or face the threat of heresy. It established the

[22] In this compact formulation we have an early condemnation of "Caesaropapism," i.e., the intertwining of spiritual and temporal powers; or, to put it differently, this is a *desacralization* of political power.

[23] Drawn from Jean Gaudemet, *Eglise et cité: Histoire du droit canonique* [Church and state: A history of canon law] (Paris: Éditions du Cerf, Montchrestien, 1994), 35–55.

Eucharistic rites, ordination, and the hierarchic organization of the church (with bishops, priests, and deacons). Around 230 the *Didascaloi of the Apostles* treated similar topics and the charitable functions of the church (visiting the sick, and so on). Around the year 300, the *Ecclesiastic Constitution of the Apostles,* written in the East (either Syria or Egypt), provided rules that it attributed directly to the apostles; thus, the hierarchy as such did not appear to be authorized to establish rules. The *Canons of Hippolytus,* dating from ca. 336–40 in Egypt, also appeared.

At the end of the fourth century, an important work, the eight books of the *Apostolic Constitutions,* was produced. It deals with the status of people (the laity, clergy, widows, orphans), with the cult, Christian initiation, and the like. The apostolic canons are found in book 8, a collection of 85 decrees, which appear in canonical compilations until the twelfth century.

Originating in Syria or Palestine, this text deals with questions of community life, states of life, the cult, church governance and hierarchy, baptism, repentance, family life, marriage, relations between husbands and wives, parents and children, masters and slaves, and relations with authorities. The intention is literally to organize community life—a Christian society—in all its important aspects. It is genuinely "law" since each rule or prohibition carries with it a punishment (removal of clergy from office, excommunication, and so on).

Church law for this period, from the first to the fourth century AD, may be said to have had two characteristics: it originated principally in the *East,* and it invoked the *authority of tradition,* reaching back to the apostles themselves, because the church did not yet have a fixed hierarchy that could lay claim to a law-making function in its own right.

B. Fourth and Fifth Centuries

After the Roman Empire became Christian, the organization of the church changed and other sources of church law were added to the tradition: the *canons of the synods* and, in due course, *pontifical decrees,* as well as other parallel sources such as the *patristic tradition* and the *lay legislation* of the Roman Empire. The first *collections of canon law* date from this time.

1. *The Synods*

Synods or councils (*concilia*) were held in the East and in the West as early as the second century AD. They defined dogma, fought heresies, and decreed disciplinary measures: for example, the invalidity of baptisms performed by heretics, and setting the date for Easter. Official records were not regularly produced at this time, but some conciliar decrees exist from later recensions. Until the fifth century the acts of some 50 synods were preserved. They recorded decisions, for example, about regular and lay clergy; laity; the government and hierarchy of the church; the administration of the sacraments; liturgy; family and social life; church jurisdiction and punishments; the attitude to adopt with regard to pagans, Jews, heretics, and so on.

Often the emperor or local patriarchs convened these synods, rather than the pope. Decrees applied only to those in attendance, as the concept of representation was not yet clearly established. Gradually, the idea prevailed that decrees were binding for the entire church, depending on the hierarchy of synods, which ran the gamut from general council to local synod. Pope Gelasius distinguished between good and bad councils: good councils followed Scripture, the doctrine of the church fathers, and ecclesiastical rulings approved by the entire church and especially Rome. Imperial confirmation put the full weight of secular law behind conciliar decrees (Theodosius confirmed the decisions of the Council of Constantinople, as Marcian did for the Council of Chalcedon). At the same time, imperial confirmation was not considered a source of canon law in its own right.

2. *The Decretals*

The decretals, or "decretal letters"[24] were papal replies to questions raised by churches; such replies were intended to provide instructions for an overarching solution to the issue at hand (that is to say, the answer applied beyond the particular case submitted to the Holy See for direction): as a procedure, it was closest to the imperial "rescripta."

We have decretals from the fourth century (they are known from subsequent recensions, but it is believed that they were recorded and archived from the outset). The decretals of Innocent I (401–07), Leo I (440–61), and Gelasius (492–96) (known as *Liber regularum*) were intended as law when they first circulated. The justification for such authority was the idea that the pontiff was the successor to Peter: this doctrine of Roman primacy was asserted as early as the fourth century; we will come across it again below. However, the papacy at this time made no claim to innovation: it based its instructions on Scripture, tradition, and earlier papal decrees. *Non nova instituentes, sed vetera renovantes* (Leo I). Only "divine law" was invoked. Gradually, church law was added to by other sources.

3. *Patristic Doctrine*

The church fathers wrote not only about theological and moral issues, but about the law as well. When their opinions were included in canonical collections, they began to acquire normative value in their own right.

4. *Roman Lay Legislation*

Christians obeyed secular civil law in their private lives; the church used Roman legal techniques for the formulation of its own law, first adopting its terminology (*auctoritas, potestas, ordo,*[25] *decreta, edicta,* etc.), then accepting its procedures (for holding a synod or a court session, for the law of evidence), and also its basic institutional concepts (e.g., associations), and even its theology: God is *dominus,* the sinner/Redeemer relationship is described as a debtor/creditor one (all of these laws were found in Tertullian and at the time of the persecutions).

More directly still, when the Empire officially became Christian, there was *secular legislation in church matters,* for example in the codices of Theodosius and Justinian: the granting of donations to the church, matters of fiscal immunity, the protection of church patrimony, laws pertaining to foundations,[26] clerical privileges (jurisdictional and fiscal), recognition of episcopal jurisdiction, measures pertaining to Jews and heretics, and so on. A large number of these prescriptions came to be included unchanged in the medieval canon collections.

5. *Early Canon Law Collections*

Nothing in antiquity and the Early Middle Ages compares with the great Roman legal codes by Theodosius and Justinian. The church did not yet have its own legal experts for this. The first collections of church canons were the fruit of private and local initiatives.

Here are a few examples of the kinds of canon law collections and their sources. The Antioch collection dates from the middle of the fourth century. In Rome, a *Vetus romana* contains the

---

[24] The decretals go by several names: *decretalis epistula, decretum, constitutio, decreta,* etc.

[25] In Roman law, the word *ordo* refers to social classes (senators, knights, e.g.); in canon law *ordo* refers to different kinds of clergy (for example, "enter the order of…") or the major categories of Christian life (monks, clerics, laity), or more narrow statuses (widows, virgins, etc.).

[26] See Jean Imbert, *Les hôpitaux en droit canonique* [Hospitals in canon law] (Paris: Vrin, 1947).

canons from the Council of Nicaea. Another contains canons from various synods and includes the Antioch collection. These collections were added to in the fifth and sixth centuries. In Africa, where a legal outlook existed, and where the turbulent history of the church created serious disciplinary problems, we have the "Acts of the Synod of Hippo" from 393 (called the "breviary of Hippo"), the Decision about Apiarius, and passages from the church register of Carthage. In Gaul, the acts of a "Second Council of Arles" (in fact, a collection of acts from several synods) have been preserved, as well as some 40 manuscripts of "Statutes of the Ancient Church," pertaining to the ordination of bishops and clerics of various degrees of Holy Orders, and likewise concerning the status of virgins and widows.

Before very long, *collections of decretals* began to appear. At the time of Pope Gelasius, the papal chancery (*chartarium*) kept a registry of papal decisions and collected various legislative texts (decretals and synodical canons). The Dionysiana collection (named after the Scythian monk, Dionysius Exiguus, who was responsible for its compilation), with some 50 "apostolic canons," became an important contribution to Western canon law.

Thus, as the "barbarian age" dawned, the church was well supplied with texts, concepts, and legal practices; these would enable it to be the strongest institution of the Early Middle Ages, as the state went into decline.

Chapter 2

The Early Middle Ages (Fifth to Eleventh Centuries)

There is something of a paradox in devoting a chapter to the Early Middle Ages in a book on the history of political ideas. After all, the same arguments that led us to begin our narrative with classical Greece and not before—because in earlier periods and in other geocultural areas either the object of "political science" (the state) or its subject (scientific thought) was absent[1]—should logically lead us to interrupt it in the West between the fifth and eleventh centuries.

During this long period of precipitous civilizational decline, the state withered away except in a small number of countries at certain times. In its place came another social organization, *feudalism*, similar, it would seem, to the "chiefdoms" of prestate societies. And while the scientific spirit of the age did not disappear entirely, it was confined to an extremely small circle. The mentality of the rest of the population—including most of the secular leaders—could best be described as "magico-religious." So, if we stick to our definitions, true political thought is hard to find during the Early Middle Ages.

Yet, it would be even more perplexing to simply break off our narrative for this period. The civilization of the Early Middle Ages remains a "written" civilization; unlike that of the Greek Middle Age, the past cannot be forgotten. The highly educated men of the church were familiar with the political and legal theories of antiquity (to a degree anyway: Aristotle's *Politics* was lost; Justinian's *Corpus iuris civilis* was inaccessible), and they drew on them to frame the problems they encountered in the feudal context concerning government, the administration of justice, and the relations between the church and the secular authorities. Even if, in the absence of the institutions described in the Greek, Latin, biblical, and patristic writings, they could not criticize these classical texts nor add their own innovative contributions, they nevertheless managed to

[1] See our general introduction, "Anthropology and Politics."

ensure a certain continuity in intellectual life. It was on the basis of their contributions, however modest, that it was possible for political thinking to reawaken sometime around the eleventh to thirteenth centuries. Therefore, the history of political ideas in the Early Middle Ages must direct attention to this period of transition just as to other periods.

We will begin with an overview of the main political developments of the Early Middle Ages (section I). Then, we will examine the arguments for what has been called "political Augustinism," that is, a doctrine of the subordination of the state to the church (section II). Alongside this sort of apogee of church power—awaiting the decline of church power that would occur at the time of the Holy Roman Empire of the German Nation and during the greatest period of feudalism—is a revival of *canon law* (section III).

In the next chapter we will discuss the two main "political institutions" of the Early Middle Ages: feudalism and sacred kingship. We will also explore the representations or ideologies that are associated with them.

I. The Historical Context

The history of the Early Middle Ages can be divided into five periods.[2]

A. The Establishment of the First Barbarian Kingdoms

Since the sack of Rome, in 410, the barbarians had mounted growing pressure on the Empire's borders; by the dawn of the fifth century, they had established their first kingdoms with "federated" status within the Empire itself: the new realms included the *Visigoth* kingdom in Aquitaine (418 AD), the *Vandal* kingdom in North Africa (435 AD), the kingdom of the *Suevi* in northwestern Spain (after 406 AD). The *Angles, Jutes,* and *Saxons*[3] invaded Great Britain and, in the fifth and sixth centuries, they pushed native Britons to the north and west as far as Armorica. Meanwhile, following additional disturbances in the aftermath of the Hun invasion,[4] the *Ostrogoths* of Theodoric the Great conquered Italy, not before threatening Byzantium and being expulsed by Zeno, the Roman emperor of the East. The *Alamans,* the *Burgundians,* the *Quadi,* the *Marcomans,* and the *Bavarians* moved into the territories of present-day southern Germany, Switzerland, northern Italy, and Burgundy. And the Frankish kingdom also began its expansion around this time.[5]

There followed a brief resurrection of the Roman entity in the sixth century. The armies of Justinian, the Roman emperor of the East (525–68), recaptured North Africa, Italy, and a part of

---

[2] Material in this section is from Michel Balard, Jean-Philippe Genet, and Michel Rouche, *Le Moyen Age en Occident* [The Middles Ages in the West] (Paris: Hachette, 1990).

[3] The Angles and Jutes originated in Denmark and the region of contemporary Germany near Denmark. The Saxons came from present-day Saxony.

[4] The Huns were finally defeated at the battle of the Catalaunian Plains in 451.

[5] The Franks originated in the valley and delta of the Rhine (present-day Rhineland and the Netherlands). In comparison with other Germanic peoples, the Franks were fortunate to have united quickly under the leadership of strong kings—Merovius, Childeric I, Clovis (481–511)—and to have converted to Catholicism (Clovis was baptized by Saint Remi, bishop of Reims, in 496 [or in 498 or 499: the precise date is still disputed by historians]), whereas the other Christianized peoples of Germania converted to Arianism (unlike the Franks, they were not able to reach agreement with the Roman Church and the peoples of the lands they conquered). Clovis defeated the last Roman general Syagrius in Gaul in 486; then he vanquished the Visigoths, confining them to their Spanish territories. Thus, he came to control large parts of what constitutes modern-day France. After these victories, his Frankish kingdom continued to expand. Burgundy was conquered in 536, then Provence was seized from the Ostrogoths. Given the weakness of the other Germanic peoples, the descendants of Clovis were able to capture all of western and southern Germany between 530 and 555.

Spain after 533. However, once again another barbarian Germanic people, the *Lombards*, invaded Italy (all of the north and part of the south) between 568 and 572.

Toward 600 AD, the following kingdoms existed on the territory or immediate frontiers of the old Western Roman Empire: the Frankish kingdom in Gaul and in western and southern Germany (depending on the reign, the kingdom was divided between different heirs into two parts: Austrasia in the East and Neustria in the West);[6] the Visigoth kingdom, extending the length and breadth of Spain; the kingdoms of the Anglo-Saxons (Kent, Northumbria, Mercia, and others) in the eastern half of Great Britain; the kingdom of the Lombards in the north of Italy and in part of the center and the south (Byzantium still had possessions in Italy, but they were increasingly scant and scattered).

B. The Destabilization of Barbarian Kingdoms (550–750 AD)

These realms proved extremely fragile, primarily because the principle of neutrality and impersonality of the *res publica* was replaced by a principle of patrimonial kingdoms as Roman political and administrative practices declined. At the death of each king, the kingdom was divided among his sons, who then went at one another's throats; this led to devastating civil wars that exhausted the country.

Weakened by these struggles, the Franks came under external threat from the Alamans, the Thuringians, and the Bavarians, all of whom revolted; other unconquered peoples posed a similar threat: the Frisians, the Bretons, and the Vascons (Basques). Groups of Asiatic invaders, the Avars and the Slavs, also arrived from the East, settling in Bohemia and on the right bank of the Elbe.

Around 700 AD, the creation of *territorial principalities* (Austrasia, Neustria, Aquitaine, Burgundy, Frankish Provence, Septimania, Visigothic Tarraconesis, and so on) resulted in a fragmentation of the Germanic kingdoms. Royal influence was reduced to almost nothing despite efforts by the Visigothic church to strengthen the sovereign's prestige by "anointing" him in the tradition of the kings of ancient Israel—this custom was to have a bright future—and despite the rising power of the "mayors of the Palace,"[7] who federated the aristocracy. As for the Anglo-Saxon kingdoms, though they faced a common enemy—the Britons (i.e., ancient Celts, the original inhabitants of the Isles)—they remained divided as well.

Reacting to the constant insecurity caused by the exhaustion of these kingdoms and the gradual disappearance of any state administration in the Roman sense of the term, the aristocracy employed practices common to Celtic, Germanic, and Roman societies and seized all public powers. If the resulting small entities had any legitimacy at all, it came from their ability to effectively enforce small-scale public order. Thus began a process of fragmentation that intensified and lasted without interruption (except for the Carolingian empire) until the end of the Early Middle Ages.

C. The Creation and Apogee of the Carolingian Empire

1. *The Rise of the Pepinids*

In the Frankish kingdom, the Pepinids,[8] an Austrasian family (Pepin I, Pepin of Herstal, Charles Martel, Pepin the Short), rose to the office of mayor of the palace, the true "power behind the

[6] Austrasia was the ancient realm of the Ripuarian Franks (Metz was its capital); Neustria was the kingdom of the Salian Franks (its capital was Paris). The rivalry between Austrasia and Neustria raged throughout the Merovingian era.

[7] Superintendents of the king's household.

[8] The possessions of the Pepinids in Austrasia were concentrated around the Meuse River valley.

royal throne." Thereafter—early eighth century—the Pepinids continued their rise to power through their successes over internal and external threats to the kingdom.

In 751, repaying the support provided him during his struggles with the Lombards, Pope Zachary granted Pepin the Short the right to unseat the last Merovingian king, Childeric III, and to take the title of king for himself. Then, in 752, he was "anointed" or "consecrated" by archbishop Boniface. In 754, Pope Stephen II personally traveled to Gaul to "consecrate" Pepin and his sons anew; in so doing, he inaugurated a new dynasty, the Carolingians.

The Franks intervened victoriously against the Lombards in 754 and 756, and whether or not Pepin was shown the famous Donation of Constantine (see below), he accepted the legitimacy of the pontiff's possession of central Italy. It was the beginning of the pontifical state that existed roughly within the same borders until 1860.

2. *Renovatio Imperii*

These events brought about the re-emergence of the idea of empire. Pepin had conquered the south of Gaul and Aquitaine; Charlemagne (768–814 AD), his son and sole heir to the throne after the death of his brother Carloman, returned to Italy and vanquished the Lombards, after which he assumed the title of king of the Lombards (774). He then led a series of conquests that expanded his kingdom toward the north, east, and south: he subjugated the Saxons and various Germanic tribes in the north (as far as Denmark) and in the south (the Bavarians). He made the Lombards of southern Italy his tributaries, he drove back the Avars into the Danube region of Europe. Finally, in Spain, in what is today Catalonia, he established a Frankish "March" to keep the Muslims at arm's length.

In the wake of these events, numerous scholars and eminent ecclesiastics (the Anglo-Saxon Ealwhine, bishop of York, the Lombard monk Paul the Deacon (Paulus Diaconus), and the Visigoth Theodulf, bishop of Orleans) were attracted to Charlemagne's court, impressed by the extent of his conquests and by the fact that the pope had been safely reinstated in Rome. They went so far as to establish a parallel between Charles, whom Pope Hadrian I called "magnus," and Emperor Constantine, the patron of early Christianity. As early as 778, Alcuin spoke of restoring the Roman Empire, which was achieved on Christmas Day in the year 800 in Rome.

The restored Empire consisted primarily of the Germanic and Latin realms, excluding the Hispano-Visigothic kingdom of Asturias and the Anglo-Saxon kingdoms, and in Western Christendom, but far from its economic and intellectual mainstream, the Celtic realms (Wales, Cornwall, Scotland, Ireland). "Europe" was born (the name had existed since antiquity, but scholars and ecclesiastics now loaded the word with civilizational implications, not just geographic meaning): it was the part of Christendom where Greek was not spoken, its center of gravity was in the West, and it had its own political institutions and its own church. Thus, even before the official schism of 1054, the creation of Charlemagne's empire deepened the split between Byzantine and occidental Christendom.

Charlemagne undertook to shore up his empire with the necessary military and administrative machinery. He organized his own palace, established his capital in Aix-la-Chapelle, and held his provinces tightly in his grip. He appointed *earls,* assisted by professional judges, and organized earldoms into "duchies" and, on the imperial borders, into "Marches." He placed local officials under the control of his royal commissioners, the *missi dominici.*

In religious affairs, in imitation of Byzantium, he created a sort of "Caesaropapism," weaving the hierarchy of the church into that of the Empire. He saw himself as an ecclesiastic and intervened in dogma (he dared to add a few very important words to the Christian Creed: the *filioque* clause), and imposed the Roman liturgy throughout the Empire [until then, the Roman liturgy was one of many]; in this sense, Charlemagne was arguably one of the principal founders of the "Roman Catholic Church").

3. *Louis the Pious and the Onset of Imperial Decline*

A number of coincidental deaths led to Louis the Pious (814–40) being sole heir to the throne, like his father, Charlemagne. The idea of a European empire grew, at least at the onset of his reign. Various intellectuals—Benedict of Aniane, Agobard, archbishop of Lyon, abbot Adalhard of Corbie and his brother Wala—worked tirelessly to this end. Louis the Pious convened synods whose rulings and proclamations were applied throughout the Empire. He also imposed the authority of ecclesiastical chapters on all bishoprics and the rule of Saint Benedict on all monasteries. The church, however, gradually slipped from the grasp of secular power.

Louis the Pious recognized the pontifical state. He renounced his titles of king of the Franks and king of the Lombards in exchange for the sole title of emperor, granted him by the pope a second time in 816 (as though the coronation by his father in 813 had not sufficed). Louis did not yet dare dispossess his sons in favor of an indivisible imperial power; but, instead of dividing their inheritance into equal shares in the Germanic tradition, he provided that the imperial title should go to his eldest son, Lothair, and that his other sons and nephews should receive kingdoms (Italy, Bavaria, Aquitaine) as integral parts of the Empire. These provisions were de facto the renunciation of a Germanic conception of royal power in favor of a Roman "hierocratic" conception. The latter was further strengthened when Lothair, crowned by his father in 817, was recrowned by the pope (in 823 in Rome), influenced by bishops in the royal entourage. It became increasingly clear that the devolution of the Empire was now a clerical and Roman prerogative.

D. The Dislocation of the Carolingian Empire, the "Government of the Bishops," the Rise of Feudalism

The Carolingians, however, were unable to maintain order and unity in such a vast territory with its deep linguistic and ethnic divides. Succession wars between the sons of Louis the Pious, together with a new wave of raids and incursions from external forces, led to the dislocation of the Empire.

1. *The Succession Problem of Louis the Pious*

The supposed heirs of the royal realms, threatened by dispossession if Roman conceptions of empire prevailed, rejected Louis's conciliatory measures. Already in his lifetime three conflicts had erupted between the ecclesiastic and Germanic camps; in 833 a council of bishops divested the emperor; then in 835, after a reversal of alliances, another council solemnly reinstated him. At his death, the Empire was divided into two, the East granted to Lothair, the West to Charles the Bald. But Aquitaine, Bavaria, and Italy more or less seized their own independence.

Such turmoil had grave consequences: with each crisis territorial vassals saw a change of king, and they had to swear new oaths of loyalty, only to retract them with the next change; gradually this broke the bonds of fealty. Thereafter, barons became preoccupied with consolidating their authority in their own territories.

With the treaty of Verdun (843 AD), written in Old French and Old High German, the empire was divided into three:

- Louis the German received all the territories to the east of the Rhine (East Francia);
- Charles the Bald was granted all territories to the west of the rivers Scheldt, Meuse, Soane, and the Rhone (West Francia);
- Lothair received the very long central portion, from Frisia in the north to Provence in the south, including Italy, and the two capitals Aix-la-Chapelle and Rome; he also received the imperial title (in theory, the empire embraced the two Francias); this region was called Lotharingia (the origin of the word "Lorraine," designating an eastern French province). It was the most fragile part of the Empire, without linguistic or geographic unity.

This situation could hardly last. Further divisions occurred (primarily to the detriment of Lotharingia). The imperial title, transmitted either to a king of East Francia or West Francia, began to lose its significance. In the end, it was no longer bestowed (the last Carolingian emperor died in 924, but anarchy was already widespread by this time).[9]

2. *The Last Invasions*

The kings were unable to reach agreement or gain the upper hand over their adversaries because Europe was under severe threat from the last invasions of the Muslims, Hungarians, and Scandinavians, and each parcel of its territory was dangerously insecure and preoccupied with its own survival. The crisis began on the continent around 840.[10]

The *Scandinavians* ("Vikings," "Normands") left their lands for unknown reasons (the simplest explanation seems to be that they were attracted by the wealth of the southern countries, the same reason the Germanic tribes invaded the Roman Empire). They plundered the coasts and the inland regions of Great Britain, Germania, France (as far as Aquitaine), and Spain. Then they crossed the straits of Gibraltar and sailed as far as Sicily and southern Italy. They penetrated so far inland (Paris was taken several times, Troyes was devastated; they even sailed up the Rhone from the Mediterranean) that insecurity reigned throughout the Frankish realms (except in Germany far from the coasts). The sentiment of insecurity increased after 850 as the invaders began to build permanent settlements at the mouths of major river systems (the Scheldt, the Seine, and the Loire in France), from which they were able to organize attacks at will. They held the terrorized populations to ransom and exacted a heavy tribute, the so-called *Danegeld*.

Their repeated attacks resulted in the conquest of great swaths of territory in Great Britain and France. In Great Britain, the whole of the east (a territory known as the *Danelaw*) was annexed by the end of the ninth century; Alfred, the Anglo-Saxon king of Wessex (871–899), succeeded in stopping the Danes at the very last moment. For one 20-year period, the whole of the Isles belonged to Cnut the Great, a Viking (995–1035), who succeeded in uniting Denmark, Norway, and England under his authority. In addition, after 870 the Scandinavians occupied the Shetland Islands, the Feroes, and Iceland, and even established several small coastal kingdoms in Ireland.

In France, with the Treaty of Saint-Cler-sur-Epte (911), Charles the Simple, King of Francia, authorized Rollo, the chieftain of the Vikings, to settle vast territories around Rouen and Evreux. Rollo pressed Charles militarily and extended his hold to the west, to the Cotentin peninsula, and to the south (Sées and the region of Maine, which were reached in the early eleventh century). This produced a powerful, well-administered duchy. As early as 1016 cadets of this duchy left for southern Italy and Sicily to serve the Lombardian dukes there; but they soon turned against them and established their own Norman Kingdom of Sicily. (Roger I, brother of Robert Guiscard, seized the island from Arab Muslims between 1061 and 1091.) In 1066, the duke of Normandy, William, conquered England.

In the period before the Viking settlements, local inhabitants shut themselves away in strongholds behind castle walls; not surprisingly, the economy collapsed. Such events merely strengthened a tendency toward feudal autarky.

---

[9] The title of Emperor was held by Louis II (king of Germania and emperor from 855 to 875), Charles the Bald (king of West Francia and emperor from 875 to 877), Charles the Fat (Charles III, king of Italy and Germania, regent of France, and emperor from 881 to 888), Guy III of Spoleto (king of Italy, emperor from 891 to 894), Arnulf of Carinthia (king of Germania and emperor from 896 to 899), Louis the Blind (Louis III, king of Provence and Italy until 928, emperor from 901 to 905), and Berenger I of Friuli.

[10] For a detailed narrative of this crisis, see Marc Bloch, *Feudal Society,* trans. L. A. Manyan (Chicago: University of Chicago Press, 1961), 3–87; originally published as *La société féodale*.

Between 827 and 902 *Muslims* conquered Byzantine Sicily, before the Normans chased them out. They also established bases in Italy (Garigliano) and in southern France (at Fraxinet, present-day La Garde-Freinet); from their French base they plundered towns and monasteries throughout Provence. Their incursions reached north as far as Paris (where the earl Odo, an ancestor of Hugh Capet, stopped them; he also defended Paris against the Normans). Resistance was impossible until the devastating intervention of William I, the count of Provence, who destroyed the military base at Fraxinet in 972–73.

The *Hungarians* added their own brand of terror to the existing ones. These nomads of Turco-Mongolian stock drove out the Avars and settled in the plains that became Hungary. Swift horsemen, accustomed to autonomy and mobility because they were nomads, these peoples embarked on expeditions throughout western Europe, terrorizing and plundering everything in their path, except fortified towns. Their reign of terror lasted from 862 to 955; Otto the Great finally defeated them at the Battle of Lechfeld, after which they settled permanently in Hungary and, following the example of their king, Saint Stephen I (baptized in 995), converted to Christianity.

3. *Feudal Collapse*

The lack of reaction to these threats was due to divisions among the Frankish kingdoms. The aristocracy had already achieved quasi-independence from royal authority and the latter was incapable of coordinating an effective defense or mobilizing the necessary money and men. Such weakness fed on itself: since the kings were unable to defend the population, they increasingly abandoned power to the earls, placing them in charge of huge commands for defensive purposes (duchies, marches); later, these leaders, in possession of huge territories, proved disloyal to their kings.

The church sought to react to the anarchy. Its first move was to consolidate royal power by distinguishing a king (from among the many small and great lords), using a rite borrowed from the Bible: royal *unction*. The first anointed kings were the Spanish Visigoths, followed by the Carolingians. Hincmar, archbishop of Reims, revived and embellished the theory and symbolism of consecration; he went so far as to establish a legend: *the miracle of the Holy Ampulla* (see below, p. 504). Increasingly, the councils of bishops intervened in the transfer of royal and imperial titles to put an end to succession quarrels. This was known as the "government of the bishops."

4. *Feudal Collapse in West Francia: Principalities and Castellanies*

However, these efforts did not fully curb the breakdown of the state. Following the Empire's collapse in favor of kingdoms, power "trickled down" to regional entities, the "principalities," then it seeped even further to the microlevel, the so-called "castellanies," which were purely local entities. This feudal fragmentation reached its apogee in the tenth and eleventh centuries between the Rhine and the Rhone.

Principalities were established by the grandees of the realm who disallowed a direct intervention of the king in their affairs. Princes were more often than not former Carolingian officials, who had seized royal prerogatives. They swore oaths of fealty to the king, but did not obey him. Drawing on local, ethnic, and linguistic characteristics, they were able to establish more uniform entities than the kingdom they controlled through their vassals on whom they bestowed fiefdoms. Aquitaine, Gascony, Brittany, Normandy, and Flanders were established in this way.

In Lotharingia, the earl Boson proclaimed himself king of Burgundy and Provence. These realms were placed under the tutelage of the kings of Germania. Then, in 890 in the north of the kingdom of Burgundy, the Earl of Autun, Macon, and Chalon created a duchy of Burgundy under the tutelage of the kingdom of West Francia.

The kings acknowledged these various usurpations, which in their view were more or less normal, since they too were descendants of families of earls, for example, Odo and Robert I, two members of the Robertian dynasty before Hugh Capet (election by the barons had become the normal method of appointing kings). The principality was a formal division, functioning under a remnant of "public law."

However, given the circumstances in which power was exercised at the time, principalities were still too large and unwieldy. Inevitably, at the end of the tenth century, the princes who had stripped the king of his authority were in turn divested of theirs by earls and lords. Thus, the *castellany* or *lordship* triumphed: a community of peasants and a handful of knights banded together around the feudal lord of a fortified stronghold capable of guaranteeing the safety of the group; this lord became the sole upholder of law and justice in his territory.

Feudalism reached its apogee, and the state its nadir, in the territory of West Francia between 950 and 1100. One number alone gives an idea of the fragmentation of the kingdom of West Francia at the end of the tenth century: it seems that some 300 quasi-independent feudal entities (of various sizes) existed at this time.

5. *Feudalism in Other Parts of the Regnum Francorum: Italy and Germania*

A similar territorial collapse occurred in Lombardy with the emergence of secular and episcopal principalities: Modena, Parma, Piacenza, Cremona, Bergamo, the Marquessate of Friuli (on the eastern March), the Marquessate of Ivrea (in the Piedmont where its sovereign ruled over the earldoms of Turin and Asti), Tuscany, Spoleto, and so on.

In Germania the *Stämme* (the old German tribes) reappeared on well-defined territories. Chieftains resurrected ducal titles in Bavaria, Franconia,[11] Swabia,[12] and Saxony; Lorraine, which was claimed and contested by West Francia, became a fifth *Stem* duchy. However, the king refused to formalize these secessions, as in West Francia, and ducal titles were never hereditary. The Marches—Frisia, Thuringia, Bohemia, Carinthia—also fell into the hands of strongmen.

In conclusion, the break-up of the Carolingian empire resulted in the disappearance of the Roman idea of the state for centuries. But a reaction set in before long.

E. Attempts by Otto I to Restore the Empire, the Rise of the Capetian Dynasty

1. *The Holy Roman Empire of the German Nation*

The idea of empire was resurrected in a new land created by the Carolingians—Saxony. Carolingian kings had ruled over Germania until Louis IV the Child (d. 911). Then, Henry I the Fowler, duke of Saxony, was elected king of Germania in 918. His family reigned until the death of Henry II the Holy (also called Henry II the Saint) in 1024. The next dynasty to succeed him was the Salian dynasty founded by Conrad II, Duke of Franconia.

Henry I won victories over the Slavs and the Hungarians, thereby enhancing his prestige. His son, Otto I, succeeded him in 936 and defeated the rebel German dukes, replacing them with members of his own household. As a key element of his policy, he relied on the royal investiture of *ducal bishops,* temporal feudal lords and direct representatives of the king, whose titles and charges reverted to the crown after their deaths. In this way, Otto succeeded in halting the process of fragmentation of the kingdom.

---

[11] On both sides of the Main River, between Mainz and Bamberg.

[12] On the upper Danube, between Würtemberg and Bavaria.

Externally, he also defeated the Slavs, coerced the Duke of Bohemia into becoming his vassal, and expanded the kingdom to the northeast (he founded the town of Magdeburg). He permanently removed the Hungarian threat in 955 with his victory at the battle of Lechfeld (as we saw). He seized the Lorraine from the king of West Francia, turning to his advantage the virtual absence of the state in this part of the Frankish kingdom. He placed the kingdom of Burgundy under his tutelage and finally took Italy when he married the heir to its throne, Adelaide of Italy, in 951.

All that was needed for him to become emperor was a consecration ceremony in Rome. He obtained his wish in 962 when the pope called him to free him from the hands of the Roman princes. Shortly after his consecration, Otto proclaimed an edict stating that henceforth he would appoint the pope: this imperial prerogative lasted until 1059. The Empire was effectively restored, though it was not the same as Charlemagne's Empire, since it did not include the Latin countries that later formed France: it was truly a "Germanic" Roman empire.

Otto II (973–82) did not have time to build on the conquests of his father. Otto III (983–1002), son of the Byzantine princess Theophano, came under the influence of Greek and Roman ideas of empire. His ambition was to resurrect Constantine's eternal Rome; moreover, he gave his own appointee to the papacy, Gerbert d'Aurillac (a former Episcopal schoolmaster in Reims), the name of Sylvester II, a reminder of the earlier pair Sylvester-Constantine.

2. *The Rise of the Capetian Dynasty*

About the same time in West Francia, a Robertian[13] prince, Hugh Capet, was elected king. He was the duke of the Franks and held the titles of Duke of Aquitaine and Duke of Burgundy. He was more powerful than the earlier Carolingian kings, Lothair and Louis V, and more powerful than the legitimate heir of the latter, Charles of Lorraine, his uncle. He was elected because he was less inclined to extend his domains toward the Lorraine, and therefore posed less of a threat to the supporters of Otto II, who were led by Gerbert d'Aurillac. Thus, West Francia came under imperial tutelage at this time. But here, as in Germany (and in England because of William's conquest), a spectacular revival of the royal state lay just ahead.

So, what then were the doctrines, or thoughts at any rate, occupying the minds of the key political actors during these difficult times?

II. "Political Augustinism" in the Early Middle Ages

H.-X. Arquillière[14] coined the expression "political Augustinism" in reference to the theocratic (or hierocratic or sacerdotalist) political doctrines dominant in the West from the end of the Roman Empire until the restoration of the secular state between the twelfth and fourteenth centuries.

[13] The Robertians (also called Robertines) were an aristocratic family, apparently descendants of Witukind, a Saxon official of the Carolingian Empire. The most important members of the dynasty, before Hugh Capet, were Robert the Strong (d. 866), who received the titles and charges of earl of Touraine, Anjou, and Blesois from Charles the Bald; his sons, Odo, count of Paris (ca. 860–98) and Robert I (ca. 865–923) (these last two were both kings of France, elected by the barons, Odo from 888 to 897 and Robert from 922 to 923); the son of Robert I, Hugh the Great (d. 956), Count of Paris and Duke of France, the true "power behind the throne," since he arranged the election of the Carolingian princes to the throne; he was the father of Hugh Capet. The rise to power of the Capetians mirrored that of the Carolingians, the preceding dynasty: by the time they became kings they had long been a powerful family.

[14] Material in this section is based on H.-X. Arquillière, *L'augustinisme politique: Essai sur la formation des théories politiques du Moyen Age* [Political Augustinism: Essay on the development of political theories in the Middle Ages] (1933; repr., Paris: Vrin, 1972).

These doctrines, which tended to absorb the state into the church, deserve only partially the label of "Augustinism." It is true that Augustine dominated the ideas of the Early Middle Ages; this is all the more true that two of the main doctors, who influenced the medieval West, Gregory the Great and Isidore of Seville, were steeped in his thinking. Thus, the bishop of Hippo exercised his influence both directly and indirectly. But political Augustinism is quite different from Augustine's actual thought, which, as we saw in chapter 1, was quite nuanced. It asserted the principle of the absolute primacy of supernatural justice over natural justice; it also showed the futility of Stoic and Ciceronian definitions of natural law and the state for a humankind facing the alternative between damnation and redemption. But, during Augustine's lifetime, the Empire was still powerful and retained its traditional pagan foundations; vast regions of the Empire remained unchristianized or were Arian. As for the church, it was still a young and relatively weak institution. Therefore, the doctors of the church, from Paul to Augustine, were inclined to argue that the Empire had a "natural right" to exist, or at the very least Providence tolerated its existence and the sins of its leaders; earlier in chapter 1 we touched on Augustine's doctrinal justifications for this argument.

A few centuries later, after the disappearance of the Roman Empire, when medium-sized powers of questionable legitimacy were the sole vestiges of temporal authority, it was again possible to return to Augustine's basic intuitions.

A. From Gelasius (492–96) to Gregory the Great (590–604)

In a letter to Anastasius, the Byzantine emperor of the East, Pope Gelasius posited the following principle:[15] "There are two powers . . . by which this world is chiefly ruled, namely, the sacred authority of the priests and royal power. Of these, that of the priests is the heavier, since they have *to render an account for all men, even the kings of men* on the Day of Judgment."[16]

Gelasius emphasizes that since the coming of Christ clear limits have been placed on the spheres of authority (e.g., "Render unto Caesar the things that are Caesar's"), such that the emperor can no longer proclaim himself *pontifex maximus,* and in turn a pontiff can no longer lay claim to royal power. Each authority is autonomous in its realm, but is subordinate to the other in the other's realm. Likewise, divine order has need of both powers, but they are unequal: the *auctoritas* of pontiffs dwarfs the *potestas* of kings.

Gregory the Great (590–604 AD) was a Roman official who founded a monastery on the Coelian Hill; he was called to the papal function in response to threats to Rome posed by the Lombards. Gregory was an expert in questions of law and administration. In the Roman tradition he held the Empire of Byzantium in great respect (he had seen the lavishness of the Byzantine court firsthand). But, against the young barbarian kingdoms, he asserted the authority of the church.

Pope Gregory's political doctrine was, by and large, Augustinian. He believed that political power had existed since the creation of the world, but that before the Fall such power was paternal and that human beings only exercised coercive authority over animals. By nature, all men were equal. But, after the Fall, only force kept them in order. Thus, the inequality among people and the existence of powers are a consequence of original sin.

Gregory believed, therefore, that Providence created kings, even bad ones. He even took the argument a step further than Augustine when he said that subjects have the rulers they deserve and can even make good kings bad. On the other hand, he also emphasized the "ministering" facet of political power.

---

[15] Ibid., 27.

[16] Translated in J. H. Robinson, *Readings in European History* (Boston: Ginn, 1905), 72–73.

> This rhinoceros [the emperor] which was before proud and stubborn is now bound and fastened by the bands of faith.... The Lord asserts that he has confidence in the strength of the rhinoceros; because He inclined the powers, which He had conferred for a temporal mission on an earthly prince, to minister to His reverence, in order that by the power he had received, through which he had heretofore been puffed up against God, he might now bestow on God religious obedience.... For the Lord left His labours to the rhinoceros, because He entrusted to an earthly prince, on his conversion, that Church which He purchased by His own death, because, namely, he committed to his hand the great anxiety of preserving the peace of the faith.[17]

Gregory, however, did not formulate a clear doctrine of the limits of the two powers. He would have liked a perfect union of the two, based on shared intentions. But he took strong exception each time the emperor raised a question of dogma, challenged canon law, or placed the universal primacy of the Roman Church in doubt. Gregory, however, did not go as far as taking disciplinary measures against him for insubordination. He "consents to what he cannot prevent," but clarified his own responsibility, according to the principle, *in quantum sine peccato nostro, portamus.*

Then, in 593, the Byzantine emperor Maurice and his eldest son Theodosius banned public officials from assuming church offices and taking up monastic life. Gregory accepted the first principle, but rejected the second, arguing that it would "close the way to heaven to many." His argument was based on the idea that a king's only mission is to help his subjects attain salvation. "But what am I, in speaking thus to my lords, but dust and a worm? Yet still, feeling that this ordinance makes against God, who is the Author of all, I cannot keep silence to my lords. For power over all men has been given from heaven to the piety of my lords to this end, that they who aspire to what is good may be helped, and that the way to heaven may be more widely open, so that an earthly kingdom may wait upon the heavenly kingdom."[18]

Nevertheless, Gregory accepted the application of imperial law in the western bishoprics because at this time the Empire of Byzantium was still held in great esteem in the West. However, when it succumbed to internal and external difficulties, the papacy immediately raised the level of its claims.

So, in the West at any rate, Gregory already had full church powers. Kings continued to interfere in the nomination of bishops, convene synods and councils, and grant canons the full force of law. But in truly difficult cases, appeals were made to the pope as the head of the church. The pope also intervened in his own right in matters of faith and discipline. He punished the abuses of the Frankish church, such as lay people acceding to the episcopate, simony,[19] the undisciplined morality of the clergy, and pagan survivals in the countryside. As a result, Gregory was led to oppose kings, the sponsors and accomplices of such abuses, and asserted that his "primacy of jurisdiction over the church is greater than that of barbarian kings." Accordingly, he wrote to two Merovingian kings, Theoderic and Theodebert, "It is the chief good in kings to cultivate justice, to preserve the rights of every man, and not to suffer subjects to have done to them what there is power to do, but what is equitable."[20]

---

[17] Saint Gregory the Great, *Morals on the Book of Job,* 31.8, trans. John Henry Parker and F. and J. Rivington, vol. 3, pt. 2 (Oxford: Oxford University Press, 1844), 428, 431.

[18] Epistle LXV to the emperor Maurice, trans. J. Barmby, *Selected Epistles of Gregory the Great,* in *Library of Nicene and Post Nicene Fathers,* 2nd ser., vol. 12 (Buffalo: Christian Literature Publishing, 1895), 140–41.

[19] The practice of taking payment to obtain holy offices or a position in the hierarchy of the church (see below, p. 512).

[20] Epistle CVI to Theoderic and Theodebert, kings of the Franks, in Barmby, *Selected Epistles,* 32.

To Childebert, Gregory writes, "There is nothing exceptional about being a king, for there are many kings. What matters is to be a catholic king."[21] And to Queen Brunehaut, "For in submitting the neck of your mind to the fear of the Almighty Lord you confirm your dominion also over subject nations, and by subjecting yourself to the service of the Creator you bind your subjects the more devotedly to yourself.... If therefore you know of any that are violent, if of any that are adulterers, if of any that are thieves, or bent on other wicked deeds, make haste to appease God by their correction."[22]

Gregory goes so far as to imagine the excommunication and removal of kings who rebel against the commands of the church. When a papal charter given to the abbey of Sainte-Marie d'Autun requires a surety, he writes, "If any person among the kings, bishops, judges, and lay people, recognizing the seal of our authority on this constitution, violates it nonetheless, let him be stripped of all power, honor,[23] and dignity, for he shall be held responsible for his iniquity before Divine judgment. Furthermore, if he fails to return sequestered property and do worthy penance, let him be separated from the body and blood of our Redeemer and tested by a harsh retribution."[24] This is an explicit threat of excommunication. The formal right to depose a king—a claim later made by Gregory VII—is not yet fully asserted. But the intention is clear.

Thus, while the Byzantine emperor "made religion an office of his administration," Gregory "makes politics a subdivision of morality."[25]

B. A New Institution: The Consecration of Kings

The clearest sign of political Augustinism's progress is the institution of *royal consecration*.[26] It is a direct imitation of the Old Testament consecration of the Israelite kings by the prophets, recorded in several passages of the Bible. The revival of this idea and its application to the heads of barbarian kingdoms was inspired by church clerics and intellectuals. Gradually, it crystallized into a permanent institution.

Before the consecration of Pepin the Short in 752 and 754, a precedent was set by the consecration of the Visigoth kings of Spain, certainly before 672 (the consecration of King Wamba) and perhaps as early as the first Catholic Visigoth king, Reccared I (586–601).

After the Carolingians organized the consecration rites, the practice spread throughout the monarchies of the medieval Christian West: in the Holy Roman Empire of the German Nation (where it was a natural continuance of Carolingian consecration and anointment), in England (beginning with King Egbert in 787), and in other western countries such as Spain (where it was revived after a period of absence), Portugal, and even in smaller realms such as Burgundy, Provence, or Navarra.

Pepin, the son of Charles Martel, was a usurper. His dynastic line, the Pepinids, had held the office of "mayor of the palace" for several generations, but legitimate Merovingian kings, descendants of Frankish royal families invested with sacred powers, continued to occupy the throne. By bestowing the title of king on Pepin, the church replaced a royal pagan-Germanic rite with its

---

21 Arquillière, *L'augustinisme politique,* 160.

22 Epistle XI to Brunehaut, queen of the Franks, in Barmby, *Selected Epistles,* 8.

23 In other words, he should be stripped of his public authority.

24 Arquillière, *L'augustinisme politique,* 160.

25 Ibid., 137.

26 See Marc Bloch, *The Royal Touch: Sacred Monarchy and Scrofula in England and France* (London: Routledge & Kegan Paul, 1973); originally published as *Les rois thaumaturges,* 1924. On the early beginnings of the Carolingian dynasty, see Louis Halphen, *Charlemagne et l'Empire Carolingien* [Charlemagne and the Carolingian Empire] (1947; repr. Paris: Albin Michel, 1968); Stéphane Lebecq, *Les origines franques, V–IX siècles* [Frankish origins, fifth to ninth centuries] (Paris: Éditions du Seuil, 1990). We will discuss the ceremony and symbolism of consecration below (p. 507).

own Christian rite. This was a new assertion of power. What makes political power legitimate is not an automatic right of succession; it is the good of the people, and the church claims to be its legitimate exponent. When the successor of a royal household is manifestly incapable of protecting his people, he can be replaced, and the church assumes this responsibility.

Inevitably the institution of royal consecration finally regressed with the decline of political Augustinism. We will see that, in the fourteenth and fifteenth centuries, certain theoreticians in France would argue that the king holds his power by right of royal blood and divine privilege, not as a consequence of any church investiture.

In the meantime, political Augustinism made further advances at the time of the "government of the bishops" under Louis the Pious and his successors.

C. Jonas of Orleans

1. *Life and Work*

Jonas of Orleans was born ca. 760 in Aquitaine.[27] He was a member of Charlemagne's court and, later, the court of Louis the Pious, who was king of Aquitaine before becoming emperor. Likewise, Jonas sat at the court of Pepin, a son of Louis the Pious (Pepin was crowned king of Aquitaine in 817). In 818, Jonas became the bishop of Orleans, one of the most important bishoprics in Neustria. He was a close associate of Louis the Pious, who entrusted him with several challenging missions (e.g., he dispatched him to Rome during the iconoclastic controversy). Jonas sat at many synods. He also lived harmoniously with Charles the Bald and died in 841.

Jonas wrote a *Life of Saint Hubert* (*Vita S. Huberti*); a *Rules of Christian Life for Laymen* (*De institutione laicali*), dedicated to Count Matfrid of Orleans (a moral treatise with large portions devoted to marriage); a work titled *On the Veneration of Images* (*Du cultu imaginum*), a criticism of the iconoclastic views of Claudius, bishop of Turin; *On the Necessity to Not Seize Church Possessions* (*De rebus ecclesiasticis non invadendis*), addressed to Pepin of Aquitaine.

Jonas also addressed a *Rules of Christian Life for Princes*[28] (*De institutione regia*) to the same Pepin, probably in 831, written against the backdrop of intense struggles between the emperor and his sons. The document is a compilation of various texts written by Jonas in his capacity as "notary" at numerous synods and council meetings (the "notary" drew up the official acts). He drew on material from the Councils of Paris (825 and 829) and Worms (829); he used some of the same material again for the Council of Aix-la-Chapelle (836). Thus, his text is historically important because it not only gives the personal opinion of the bishop of Orleans, but also the view of the Carolingian episcopate itself, for whom Jonas was the official spokesperson.

2. *Royalty Bows to the Priesthood*

The *Institutio regia* is nevertheless an extremely weak text, representative of the extent of decay of ideas and culture in this intermediary period.

Jonas begins by recalling the theological argument of the secondary or empty nature of earthly life in relation to heavenly life, thereby establishing a hierarchy between temporal and spiritual powers: earthly life is transient; we are mere pilgrims on earth (*Le métier de roi,* 157).

[27] Material in this section is from Jonas d'Orléans, *Le métier de roi* [On the institution of kingship], ed. Alain Dubreucq (Paris: Editions du Cerf, 1995); hereafter cited by page number in the text.

[28] Also known as *On the Institution of Kingship.*

The church, which is the mystical body of Christ, has two preeminent figures at its head: "All the faithful must know that the universal church is the body of Christ, that the same Christ is its head and that there are in it mainly two exalted persons, the priestly and the kingly. The former is all the more important that he is accountable to God for the king himself" (*Le métier de roi,* 177).

The basis of priestly authority is the "power of the keys." Jonas quotes three Gospel references to support this power: Matthew 16:19 and 18:18, and John 20:20–23. The priesthood holds the "keys" to heaven for all Christians. Therefore, it has the authority to judge kings, but eludes human judgment itself. To support his argument, Jonas quotes the words of Constantine to the bishops, which he borrows from the books added by Rufinus to his translation of Eusebius's *Church History:*

> God has appointed you priests and given you power to judge even concerning us, and therefore we are rightly judged by you, while you cannot be judged by men. For this reason, wait for God alone to judge among you, and whatever your quarrels may be, let them be saved for that divine scrutiny. For you have been given to us by God as gods, and it is not fitting that a man should judge gods, but only he of whom it is written: God has stood in the assembly of the gods, in the midst he has judged between gods. (Ps. 81:1; Rufinus 10:2)[29]

Thus, the priesthood is quasi-deified, and temporal power accepts that it is vastly inferior to it. "Hatred for the priests of Christ amounts to hatred for Christ himself" (Ps. 81:1; Rufinus 10:2). There is, in fact, only one true power, the power of the priesthood. The *regnum* and *imperium* are only offices or ministries; their exercise is conditioned. Referring to a "study of word origins" by Isidore of Seville (*Reges a regendo, id est a recte agendo*), Jonas writes, "A king who rules piously and justly and mercifully is rightly called king; but if he lacks such virtues, he fails the name of king" (*Le métier de roi,* 185; see also 195).

Only the clergy is capable of judging the king's righteousness because it alone is competent in divine matters. The fact that royal power is justified only to the extent that it implements divine justice is supported by numerous passages in the Bible (for example, Deut. 17:14–15, 17:17–20; Prov. 29:14, 20:28; Eccles. 32:1). Jonas also quotes a dense passage attributed to Saint Cyprian:[30]

> The justice of a King is this: not to use his power to oppress any one; to judge between a man and his neighbor without respect of persons [see 1 Pet. 1:17]; to be the defender of pilgrims and orphans and widows [see Deut. 24:20, 26:12; Jer. 7:6]; to prevent thefts: to punish adultery; not to exalt the wicked to power; not to nourish unchaste persons and actors; to destroy the wicked from the face of the earth; not to permit parricides and perjurers to live; to defend churches; to sustain the poor by alms; to place righteous men in charge of the affairs of the realm; to have old men and wise men and sober men for his counselors; not to give ear to the superstitions of magicians, soothsayers [see 2 Kings 23:24] and pythonesses; to put away anger; to defend the land bravely and righteously against foes; to trust to God in all things; to hold the Catholic faith in God; not to permit his sons to act wickedly; to attend to prayers at regular hours; not to take food before the appointed hours. "Woe to thee, O land, when thy king is a child, and thy princes eat in the morning! [Eccles. 10:16]. (*Le métier de roi,* 189–91)

Many of these duties that the king commits himself to fulfill are explicitly listed in the "oaths" sworn at the consecration ceremony, inspired by the Carolingian bishops (see below,

---

[29] *The Church History of Rufinus of Aquileia, Books 10 and 11,* trans. Philip R. Amidon, S.J. (New York: Oxford University Press, 1997), 10.

[30] Circa 200–258, church father, bishop of Carthage.

pp. 502–03). If the king does not fulfill them, various misfortunes ensue: foreign and civil wars, failed harvests, plagues, natural disasters, doomed dynasties: the kingdom will be removed from the bad king and placed in the hands of others, as God did in the Old Testament (and as Childeric III was dethroned and replaced by Pepin). Jonas quotes Fulgence:[31] "Now it is clear to see how the justice of the king invigorates the age: it is a gift of peace, the bulwark of the nation, the protection of the people, the fortification of the homeland (*munimentum gentis*), the cure for illness, the happiness of men, the clemency of the air, the serenity of the sea, the fertility of the earth, the consolation of the poor, succession for his sons,[32] and for himself, the hope of happiness to come" (*Le métier de roi,* 193).

According to the Bible, God alone is king. Earthly kings are merely his "ministers." All Jonas could do was copy at length a passage from the *Wisdom of Solomon* (6:2–8):

> Give ear, ye that rule the people, and glory in the multitude of nations. For power is given you of the Lord, and sovereignty from the Highest, who shall try your works, and search out your counsels. Because, being ministers of his kingdom, ye have not judged aright, nor kept the law, nor walked after the counsel of God; Horribly and speedily shall he come upon you: for a sharp judgment shall be to them that be in high places. For mercy will soon pardon the meanest: but mighty men shall be mightily tormented. For he which is Lord over all shall fear no man's person, neither shall he stand in awe of any man's greatness: for he hath made the small and great, and careth for all alike. But a sore trial shall come upon the mighty. (*Le métier de roi*, 201)

Before God, the king is nothing.[33] He must be humble in his station, not puffed up with pride, especially since all people, though different in merit, are equal in nature (see *Le métier de roi,* 211). It is neither heredity, nor strength, nor anything that comes from man that makes a king; it is God, either by his gift or by his leave (in the case of a sinful king) (see 217). The duty and royal ministry (*regale ministerium*) of the king is to "govern the people of God and to rule with equity and justice, to strive that they may enjoy peace and harmony" (199).

Jonas, like Augustine, believes that all ancient pagan monarchies were tyrannies, because they did not uphold true justice. Fulgence also says that the first duty of the king is to defend the patrimony and tranquility of the church. He will do so by the force of arms, a more important duty for the future of the "Christian Empire" than the acquisition of new territories. "The king's duty is to defend the churches and the servants of God. His office is to safeguard the priests and their ministry and defend God's Church with the force of arms" (*Le métier de roi,* 193).

The king must achieve by force what the church cannot obtain by preaching, that no one shall commit crimes and injustices. The king must be watchful over his officials in particular. It is also the duty of the king to safeguard those under the protection of the church: widows, orphans, foreigners, and the poor. He must "present the cause of the poor" (*Le métier de roi,* 199) at his audience; this is, we recall, what the prophets demanded of the Old Testament kings, as well. And it is only if he fulfills his duty of religious ministry that his subjects owe him obedience.

These, then, are the ideas of political Augustinism that the bishops invoked when they divested Louis the Pious in 833 in Compiègne—even if Jonas himself was not among the bishops who backed Louis's sons and in fact denounced these bishops in a council in 835. Though the

[31] A Latin Christian writer (467–533), monk, bishop of Ruspe in the province of Byzacene (modern-day Tunisia), and founder of the monastery in Cagliari, Sardinia.

[32] Again, the emphasis is on the precariousness of dynastic succession, which is never guaranteed; succession must be earned at each turn (the church decides if the dynastic heir merits his station or not).

[33] The Augustinian theology of the Carolingian bishops is far removed from the Greek world of Eusebius of Caesarea. In the latter, the king is said to be a "friend" of Logos, ontologically and cosmically above all others.

church was politically divided in this business, it does not follow that there was any disagreement about political Augustinism. Once again the church participated in the divestiture of a king, the clearest possible expression of the subordination of the right of the state to the judicial ethics of the church.

D. Agobard of Lyon

We can see the limitations of political Augustinism in the controversies involving a contemporary of Jonas, Saint Agobard, bishop of Lyon (a more distinguished thinker than Jonas).[34]

1. *Life and Work*

Agobard was born in 769 in Spain, which he left at the age of 13 for the province of Narbonne. At the age of 23 he arrived in Lyon and became an assistant to Leydrade, bishop of Lyon, responsible for the reconstruction of the settlement on the Rhone after its total destruction by the Muslims in 732 (Lyon became a center of high culture during the so-called Carolingian renaissance). Agobard was named bishop sometime around 804 and held the position until his death in 840. A supporter of Lothair, who rebelled against his father, Louis the Pious, Agobard participated in the synod in Compiègne that divested the emperor in 833. When Louis was returned to the throne in 835, Agobard was unseated as bishop and went into exile. He was reinstated in 838, two years before his death.

Agobard was the author of pastoral, liturgical, and theological works, a treatise against popular superstitions (notably the ordeals of fire and water), a treatise against the law code of the Burgundians (*Loi Gombette*)[35] and for the unity of the Law in the Empire and the extension of testimonial evidence,[36] various political treatises (*On Injustices; On the Division of the Frankish Empire among the Sons of Louis the Pious; Apology of the Sons of Emperor Louis against Their Father; On the Comparison of Ecclesiastical and Political Regimes* (in this treatise Agobard clarifies the instances when the dignity of the church is to be placed above the majesty of the Empire).

Finally, Agobard authored a number of vitriolic opuscules against the Jews: *On the Insolence of the Jews; On Jewish Superstitions; On the Baptism of Slaves Belonging to Jews; Against an Impious Law Decreed by the Palace on the Subject of the Baptism of Slaves Belonging to Jews; On the Dangers of Consorting with Jews.* Agobard's controversy with the Jews is worth discussing at length, as it offers a concrete example of the position of legal and political thought during the Carolingian era.

2. *The Question of the Personality of Laws*

The rule of the *personality of laws* predominated in the barbarian kingdoms and in the Carolingian Empire. The personality of laws means that a single code of laws does not apply in a given territory, that the applicable law is the code of the community to which the individual belongs. For example, in Lyon (the former capital of the kingdom of Burgundia) in the lifetime of Agobard, it was possible to find Burgundians, Ripuarian Franks, Salian Franks, Alamans, Bavarians, and Visigoths, each ruled by a code of laws for his or her particular nation. There were also

[34] Material in this section is from Monseignor Bressolles, *Saint Agobard, évêque de Lyon, 769–840* [Saint Agobard, bishop of Lyon], vol. 1 (Paris: Vrin, 1949); Capucine Nemo, *Louis le Pieux et les Juifs: Etude de trois diplômes de protection* [Louis the Pious and the Jews: A study of three diplomas of protection] (graduate thesis, University of Paris X-Nanterre, 1997).

[35] The *Lex Burgundionum* was proclaimed by Gondebaud (ca. 480–516), king of the Burgundians. It was a classical code of barbarian laws written after the conquests at the initiative of the Germanic kings, who were keen to set down in writing—following the example of Roman law—the heretofore exclusively oral customs of their tribe. Other examples include Salic Law and Ripuarian Law, the laws of Frankish tribes. The *Lex Burgundionum* was written in Latin.

[36] Agobard was especially critical of trials by combat and purgatory oaths, admitted by the barbarian *Loi Gombette*.

Gallo-Romans ruled by the Roman code of law, which was different from the *lex romana Burgundionum* or the "Breviary of Alaric" (which was the law that applied to Romans living in the Visigothic kingdom). Also, among the peoples ruled by Roman law were Jews, who had been granted the right—by Roman law—to live under their own Jewish law.[37] To say the least, the situation was complex.

Thus, justice could almost never prevail. For example, if someone committed a crime, and if the witnesses were from Burgundia, whereas he himself belonged to another nation, no one could testify against him; so all that was required to clear his name was a "purgatory oath," even a false one. Conversely, if five friends from five different "nations" and laws lived together under the same roof, if one was unjustly accused, none of the others could testify in his favor. And so it became necessary to resort to so-called Germanic methods, deeply rooted in superstition and known for their cruelty: ordeals by fire or water, purgatory oaths, trials by combat (the latter enabled strongmen to wrong the elderly and the poor in health, and to challenge them to a combat to the death; this, they claimed, was sanctioned by God). The church had little choice but to pay lip service to such methods. But Agobard rejected them outright, declaring, "God does not defend the powerful and the greedy."[38]

Proper justice becomes possible only if there is *unity of law*. But for Agobard, who was a good political Augustinian, a return to pure Roman law—a mystery of inequity, a source of injustice and disorder—was simply out of the question. The only possible source of unity, in his opinion, was a law inspired by the Christian faith. Agobard paraphrased the words of the Apostle Paul: "There is now neither Gentile nor Jew, Scythian nor Aquitanian, nor Lombard, nor Burgundian, nor Alaman, nor bond, nor free. All are one in Christ."[39] What is required is a unity of law and of faith in a single Christian empire: "Would that it might please God the Almighty that everyone were ruled under one most pious king by one law.... It would indeed accomplish much on behalf of the concord of the City of God, and the equity of the people."[40] If any one should be excluded from providing evidence, let it be a non-Christian or a sinner, one who has not done appropriate penance. If there is to be a division, let it be between the kingdom of God and the realm of the devil.

3. *The Jewish Question*

But then the Jewish question was acutely posed. The large Jewish community in Lyon lived under the protection of Louis the Pious. Some had "diplomas of protection," which entitled them to the king's special protection (*maimbour* in medieval French, derived from *mundium, mundeburdum,* or again *mitium,* the protection extended by the powerful man to his weaker neighbor). The Jews were granted this favor primarily because of their economic role; as merchants they

---

[37] See Capucine Nemo, *Rome et ses citoyens juifs* [Rome and its Jewish citizens] (Paris: Editions Honoré Champion, 2010).

[38] As for ordeals by fire and water, it must be said that nothing remotely similar is found in the Roman judicial system of the Low Empire. Confronted with this Germanic custom, which most barbarian societies appeared to believe in, the church decided against condemning it entirely. Instead, it christianized the practice by including it in a ceremonial involving the exorcism of individuals, the blessing of instruments, and so on. One of Charlemagne's capitularies did approve such ordeals. Agobard was one of the first to offer a theoretical condemnation of this pagan practice, and he worked hard to eliminate it in practice as well. It was only in the twelfth century, under the influence of canon law, that ordeals finally disappeared from the legal procedure (but Roman tortures were reintroduced at this time).

[39] Quoted in Bressolles, *Saint Agobard,* 92. *Translator's note:* English translation of Agobard's epistle by R. H. C. Davis, *A History of Medieval Europe: From Constantine to Saint Louis,* 3rd ed. (New York: Pearson, 2005), 165.

[40] Ibid., 92. *Translator's note:* English translation of Agobard's epistle by Courtney M. Booker, *Past Convictions: The Penance of Louis the Pious and the Decline of the Carolingians* (Philadelphia: University of Pennsylvania Press, 2009), 229.

were suppliers to the royal court where they had powerful friends, notably in the entourage of the Empress Judith.[41]

In light of this royal protection, the emperor went so far as to forbid the Christians of Lyon and their bishop from converting slaves belonging to the Jews. Roman law actually denied Jews the right to own Christian slaves. If Christians were to baptize slaves owned by Jews, the effect would be their emancipation, which would constitute theft of Jewish property (compensation was provided for, but it was far less than the market value of the slaves). Therefore, the Jews took their grievance to the royal court.

There were other issues under dispute as well. The slaves took their daily meals with their masters and participated in prayers that cursed Christians and the Lord Jesus Christ. The market day was changed from Saturday to Sunday to enable the Jews to honor their Sabbath, and so on. Since the emperor's diplomas of protection apparently did not suffice, Louis resorted to the absolute weapon: he issued *missi dominici* in order to frighten the bishop and the count (Agobard writes of the intervention of these *missi* Gerric and Frederick as veritable persecutions). What arguments did the emperor use to justify such a harsh decision fraught with danger for his soul?

Although the attitude of Louis the Pious to the Roman conception of a unitary state was more favorable than his sons', he was, nevertheless, a Frank, and the principle of the unity of laws was not a foregone conclusion for him. As a member of the Frankish "tribe," he no doubt did not wish Roman law or any other foreign law to be applied to the Franks, or Frankish customs to be extended to other peoples. Perhaps he even used the diversity of laws as a method of government, since diversity made it possible to maintain antagonism between the different communities. Finally, whenever his personal interests and sympathies were involved, his intention was probably to uphold the laws of the state—and the might of his warriors—against the claims of a subject, be he a bishop. Moreover, in the case at hand, the bishop was attacking the right of the Jews to worship according to the religion of their fathers, which was a right accorded them as subjects of the Roman Empire—paradoxically perhaps, but such was the case. Therefore, as king of the Franks and as the Roman emperor, Louis the Pious felt wholly justified in resisting Agobard's religious intolerance.

4. *Agobard's Protestations*

No dogma in the Christian faith is more central than the universality of redemption through Christ, inaugurated with the institution of baptism. Therefore, Agobard had recourse to an arsenal of theological arguments at his disposal. Because a Jewish merchant could purchase a slave for a mere pittance, could he also acquire the right to the slave's soul (which belonged only to Christ)? Could the right of ownership be a hindrance to salvation? How could the emperor deny a bishop the right to baptize pagans who sought it? Agobard went so far as to deny the very material existence of such an impious decree. Either the decree was a fake, or it was wrung from the prince by bad counselors. "It is not possible that a most Christian and most pious Emperor has taken a decision so contrary to the laws of the Church and Apostolic practice."[42]

Agobard set great store by his knowledge of the Jewish religion and talmudic tradition. He fought the basic beliefs of Judaism as being superstitions. He argued that to allow the Jews to practice their religion and expose those in their proximity to their influence and propaganda posed a fundamental threat to Christianity, which had not yet won all people to its cause. He

[41] The relations between the palace and the Jews of Lyon may not have been exclusively economic: on the one hand, Jewish culture was greatly appreciated at court, and on the other Jews were on intimate terms with the aristocracy throughout the Empire. See Bressolles, *Saint Agobard*, 109.

[42] Ibid., 107.

added that some people claimed that rabbis spoke more eloquently than their priests. In the end, Agobard failed to win both arguments: against the Jewish question and against the personality of the laws. The Carolingian emperor was still sufficiently powerful at the time to impose his will on both issues. The triumph of political Augustinism was only partial.

The regime of the personality of laws met its end in the next century, but Agobard's arguments were not the reason. It was, rather, a consequence of a complex, historical process. First, the nations of the Empire were increasingly intertwined, so that it became increasingly difficult for the administrative services and judges to identify with certainty the nationality of individuals, given the absence of a public registry. Second, in time, national laws exercised influence over one another, while at the same time they came under the influence of laws originating in church chapters and synods. Finally, as early as the end of the ninth century, the impact of laws and justice (whatever the origin) weakened as the feudal system began to develop. At the heart of feudalism, there was neither unity of law nor, indeed, the centrality of the law. Once again, the system was complex, but not because of individuals, rather due to the diversity of territories. Each feudal body had its lord who dispensed justice in accordance with local customs. More often than not, such customs were oral, and the old written codes of law fell into neglect (except for Roman law in the south of France). Unity of law and respect for the law reappeared much later, in the twelfth and thirteenth centuries, under the influence of the papacy (see below, chapter 4).

E. Hincmar, Archbishop of Reims

Hincmar (born ca. 806) received his education at the Abbey of Saint-Denis under the direction of the Abbot Hilduin.[43] He became a first-rate theologian. When Hilduin was appointed chaplain to the court of Louis the Pious, he brought with him the young Hincmar, who became an advisor to Louis the Pious. Later, Hincmar also served Charles the Bald (in 869 he consecrated Charles king of Lotharingia). In 845 Hincmar was raised to the Archepiscopal See in Reims as successor to Ebbo; he held the seat until his death in 882. Thereafter, he was the intellectual power behind the episcopate of Gaul for a quarter century.

Hincmar authored a number of works on relations between the church and the Christian monarchy, culminating in *De ordine palatii* (On the governance of the palace) (882). He gave political Augustinism its deepest meaning: as spiritual power on earth, the church must be *prophetic*. In its dealings with the kings of the Christian empire, it needed to regain the posture of the Old Testament prophets toward the kings of Israel: an attitude of harsh scrutiny and moral censorship. Furthermore, etymologically speaking, *Episcopi* (bishops) means "overseers."

The overseen (the king) could not be allowed to appoint and control the overseer (the clergy). For this reason, Hincmar addressed a protest to Louis the Pious, finding him guilty of intending to appoint bishops: "If it is true, as I have heard, that when you grant an election requested of you, bishops, priests, and people must appoint the one you crave and command (which is not an election by Divine law but an extortion by human authority), if it is so—and I repeat, as I have heard—then it is the same evil spirit, in the form of the serpent which betrayed our forefathers and chased them from the Garden, who through flattery whispered it into your ear."[44]

Hincmar strengthened the hold of sacerdotal power on royal power when he prepared the royal consecration ordinals and royal oaths. He also introduced the legend of the Holy Ampulla (see below, p. 504). In 869, he inserted into the royal consecration ordinals a promise by

[43] Material in this section is from Halphen, *Charlemagne et l'Empire Carolingien*, 317 and following.

[44] Quoted by Louis Bodin, in Jean Touchard, *Histoire des idées politiques*, vol. 1 (Paris: Presses Universitaires de France, 1959), 138. In 868 Hincmar wrote to Charles the Bald, "It is to your anointing, an episcopal and spiritual act, and to the blessing that flows from it, much more than to your temporal power, that you owe your royal dignity" (quoted in Bloch, *The Royal Touch*).

the king to the church to the effect that if the king failed to keep his promise, he would be guilty of perjury and liable to excommunication, and his subjects could forsake him. This amounted to placing the king under the formal tutelage of the church. Hincmar declared the following to Louis III, the successor to Charles the Bald: "Remember the *professio* (promise) signed by your own hand and made to God at the altar in the presence of all the bishops."[45]

Hincmar refers to the *bishops,* not the *pope.* Thus, the king is indeed subordinated to a sort of "government of bishops." Such had been the case since the first quarrels of Louis the Pious with his sons. Hincmar justified the demands placed on Louis the German at the synod of Metz in 859 by the fact that he had provoked a division of the Christian faith, whereas the bishops, as we know, must assure the unity of all Christians. Moreover, the general assemblies of the various Frankish realms were now held in the presence of, and under the leadership of the archbishops, bishops, and abbots of each kingdom. With responsibility for nearly all the ecclesiastical provinces of ancient Gaul, they intended to establish the "unity of the church" against the fragmentation of royal power. It was probably Hincmar who wrote the following sentence in article 2 of the statutes of the synod of Savonnières (near Toul) in June 859: "The bishops, in accordance with their ministry and the sacred authority invested in them, shall unite to direct and correct the kings and the multitude of realms and the people entrusted to them, lending them the encouragement of their counsel."[46]

The kings were invited to attend the synods of the bishops and participate regularly in the sacraments of the altar. They were truly placed under surveillance. The kings themselves (Louis, Charles, Lothair II) took note of this at the reconciliation meeting in Coblenz in June 860. In due course, the emperors also became "creatures" of the pope. At any rate, their real powers only declined until the extinction of the title altogether in 924.

III. The Development of Canon Law: The Pseudo-Isidorian Decretals and the Donation of Constantine

Charlemagne's attempts at "Caesaropapism," the strengthening of the bishops under Louis the Pious, and more generally the osmosis of church and state in European kingdoms encouraged the development of *canon law.*[47] The texts of canon law in this period belong to the following categories.

- *Decretals.* The correspondence of Gregory the Great, which contains declarations of normative value, was collected in two volumes under Pope Hadrian II (772–95); the basis for this work was the registry of correspondence maintained by the papal chancery.
- *Conciliar canons.* Numerous synods were held under the Visigoth kings of Spain and throughout Charlemagne's empire. Conciliar canons regulated church life, as well as conjugal morality and the fight against crime.
- *Episcopal statutes.* They were important in the ninth century (Hincmar, bishop of Reims).

[45] Quoted by Bodin in Touchard, *Histoire des idées politiques,* 138.
[46] Quoted by Halphen, *Charlemagne et l'Empire Carolingien,* 321.
[47] Material in this section is from Gaudemet, *Eglise et cité.*

- *Monastic rules.* This is a special kind of law. The Rule of Saint Benedict was written between 534 and 547 and the Rule of Saint Colomban between 590 and 595. Benedict of Aniane revised the Rule of Saint Benedict; officialized by Louis the Pious in 817 (his "monastic capitulary" was valid for the entire Empire).

Political Augustinism demanded that secular power lead the fight against evil; but by "evil" those of the time understood crime and sin indifferently: the two concepts overlapped. Thus, there was also an overlapping of conciliar canons and secular legislation. King Clothair II, in his Edict of 614, confirmed the provisions of a synod held in Paris, but introduced some changes of his own. As early as 769, and for a century, Carolingian capitularies fixed the recruitment and training of priests, defined the election and responsibilities of bishops, assured the administration of church patrimony, and oversaw the observance of the Sabbath and payment of tithes.

A. The Principal Canon Collections

The legislation of the Carolingian capitularies was compiled by Ansegisus, abbot of Saint-Wandrille (near Rouen). His four books contain 29 "ecclesiastical capitularies," which for the most part are known only through this compilation (a mere selection).

Until the eleventh century, the Spanish church used a collection of Visigoth-period canons, the *Collectio Hispana,* possibly the work of Saint Isidore of Seville. It includes several conciliar canons dating back to the fourth century; successive editions were augmented with canons from the synods of Toledo until the Arab invasion (711). The entire compilation contains no fewer than ten books, that is, 1,633 canons organized under 227 titles. Sometime around 700 AD another compilation was published in Ireland under the title *Hibernensis;* in addition to canons, it contains 600 fragments by the church fathers.

Charlemagne, who as we know aspired to unify and Romanize the Frankish church, sent a request to Rome for a code of canon laws. In 774, Pope Hadrian I (772–95) sent him a modified and enlarged version of the ancient *Collectio Dionysiana,* known as the *Collectio Dionysio-Hadriana.* It circulated throughout the Empire; Hincmar used it. But its chronological classification made it unwieldy. It was, therefore, replaced by other collections: the *Dacheriana* (ca. 800), the *Concordia canonum* by Cresconius, the *Vetus Gallica,* a collection of canons from Angers dating from the seventh and eight centuries (24 titles, 400 canons). Other collections, based either on the *Vetus Gallica* or the *Dionysio-Hadriana,* were compiled in the Carolingian Empire until the ninth century.

B. The Pseudo-Isidorian Decretals

The Pseudo-Isidorian collection also deserves attention. This collection contains several elements favorable to the clergy. Subsequently it was shown that many of these elements were deliberate fabrications from the eighth and ninth centuries, probably by clergy members who felt threatened by lay influences. One of the four parts, the "False Decretals" (known as the *Pseudo-Isidorian Decretals*), is a composition attributed to "Isidore Mercator," a legendary figure. It is an *Hispana* augmented by apocryphal papal letters—some are forgeries, others authentic—and 172 patristic texts. In total, some 10,000 fragments are presented together in three sections: (1) false decretals based on forged texts of Roman law and attributed to the early Popes Clement I (88–97 AD) and Miltiades (311–14 AD) (false attributions were a means of lending texts greater authority); (2) canons, many falsified, from 54 synods spanning the period from the Council of Nicaea to the last Spanish synods; and (3) papal decretals from Sylvester (314–35 AD) to Gregory II (715–31 AD), for the most part authentic.

The Pseudo-Isidorian decretals were probably written between 847 and 857, possibly in Saint-Denis (near Paris). Responding to an obvious need, they circulated quickly and widely (more than 100 manuscript copies survive). Whether pure inventions or calculated choices, they testify to a constant preoccupation: to ensure the primacy of the Roman See (probably with a view to protecting church property under threat of spoliation from the rising tide of feudalism). Subsequent collections borrowed heavily from the false decretals. They were used in France as early as 850–70 and in Rome in the following century.

C. The Donation of Constantine

Among the Pseudo-Isidorian decretals, one fabrication, more famous than the others, stands out. It dates from the same period and was perhaps produced in the same workshop: it is known as the Donation of Constantine. It declares that Constantine, after his conversion to Christianity, entrusted the pope with temporal power over the western Empire.

The forgery was not mere invention. A similar myth circulated in Rome as early as the sixth century. Miraculously cured of leprosy, Constantine is said to have entrusted Pope Sylvester with western imperial powers, while he, Constantine, retreated to the east and established a new capital, Constantinople. He gave the pontiff the Lateran palace and transferred to him all imperial symbols. He also recognized the primacy of the Roman See.

Although it promoted pro-papal interests in spectacular fashion, the false Donation of Constantine was not without certain risks for Rome. Some argued that since the pope held his states as a concession from the emperor, nothing prevented a future emperor from revoking the concession. The pope did not hold the Empire as the "vicar of Christ."

Not long after, doubts surfaced about the authenticity of the text, which was not included in the Decree of Gratian in 1140 (see below). Accursius declared it void. Nicholas de Cusa expressed his doubts in 1432. Finally, in 1440, the scholar and humanist Lorenzo Valla proved that the text was a forgery. All the same, others defended its authenticity well into the sixteenth century.

D. The Penitential Canons

Also significant are the collections of canon law of a rather special kind, the *penitential canons,* the model for which arrived from the East. They are lists of rules about the penances to be done for various crimes and sins, both religious (e.g., magic, idolatry, desecration of tombs) and profane (rape, adultery, bigamy, incest, and subsequently murder, theft, perjury, abortion, and infanticide). Exact guidelines are given for the penances (the length of the fast, particular mortifications, charitable works to be performed). Penances correspond mechanically to each wrongful act; there is no examination of circumstances or of the subjective guilt of the accused. Sexual misconduct, in particular, was given obsessive attention.

Chapter 3

Feudalism and Sacred Kingship

Two major political phenomena mark the end of the Early Middle Ages: the development of the *feudal system* and *sacred kingship*. Technically speaking, these phenomena do not belong to a book on the history of political ideas because only retrospectively were these phenomena presented in theoretical texts as a coherent system, indeed as a political ideal in its own right. In fact, they evolved from customary practice rather than through theoretical thought. They are no less the missing link between the political institutions inherited from antiquity and the new model of the state that ultimately emerged in the period of the eleventh to the thirteenth centuries. It was *against* the feudal institutions of lordship, vassalage, and sacred kingship that the canonists, "legists," and philosophers (i.e., the founders of the "modern" state) took a stand. We cannot fully appreciate the thinking of the latter unless we develop a sufficiently clear picture of the ideas of the former.[1]

I. Feudalism

In the nineteenth century, the word "feudalism" acquired a very broad sense: almost every feature of pre-revolution French society in Europe was labeled "feudal." The word, in fact, refers to a very specific institutional and anthropological reality: a system of *feudal-vassalic relations*. This type

[1] This chapter draws from Bloch, *Feudal Society;* F.-L. Ganshof, *Feudalism* (New York: Harper & Row, 1964); originally published in French as *Qu'est-ce que la féodalité?,* 1944. See also on specific topics: Halphen, *Charlemagne et l'Empire Carolingien* 174–80; François Olivier-Martin, *Histoire du droit français des origins à la Révolution* [A history of French law from the origins until the revolution] (Paris: Éditions du CNRS, 1988), 80–93; R. van Caenegem, "Government, Law and Society," in *The Cambridge History of Medieval Political Thought,* ed. James Henderson Burns (Cambridge: Cambridge University Press, 1988), 174–210; Harold J. Berman, *Law and Revolution: The Formation of the Western Legal Tradition* (Cambridge: Cambridge University Press, 1983), 295–315.

of social bond replaced the classical model of the state after its collapse; it, in turn, declined as the state gradually revived. The feudal-vassalic system culminated between the ninth and twelfth centuries when the state had virtually disappeared (notably in France). It remained vibrant until the early fourteenth century, at which time feudalism disappeared, almost without a trace.

A. The Origins of Feudalism

1. *Celtic, Germanic, and Roman Origins of Vassalage and "Commendation"*

The institution of vassalage had forerunners in the Low Empire and among Celtic and Germanic tribes. In the Low Empire, large landowning *potentes,* whose estates were far from the city, assembled private militias made up of comrades in arms called *buccellarii* ("biscuit eaters"); basically, they were the master's henchmen. As for the ancient Germanic tribes, Tacitus, in his treatise on Germania, mentions an institution of companions (*comitatus*): a group of warriors organized around a chief.

These two institutions came together at the time of the Merovingian dynasty. The Merovingian king employed members of a bodyguard known as *antrustions*, free men of Frankish descent who swore an oath while their hands were held in the king's (an ancient Germanic custom found elsewhere in Europe: the *thanes* among the Anglo-Saxon, *gardingos* among the Visigoths, *gasindi* among the Lombards). As a consequence of widespread turmoil in the seventh and early part of the eighth centuries, the practice of swearing oaths grew between local petty chieftains and impoverished warriors for their common defense. It was more or less a personal bond, in a sense an enlargement of the family household.

2. *Vassalage at the Time of the Carolingians: A Deliberate Political Project*

The institution developed rapidly in the Carolingian era. This time royal authority provided the impetus; soon vassalage took a political turn. The Pepinids resorted to it while still mayors of the palace; then, the Carolingians actively encouraged the system. They were convinced that it would provide the new fighting machine—the heavily armed horseman—required by the wars of the time.

Around the time of the Arab invasions, the use of the horse became permanent in combat. The kings and dukes could no longer be satisfied with mustering simple foot soldiers, the mass of free men in the ranks of a *host* (*hostis,* an armed expedition). The need now was for well-trained, readily available professional horsemen who could be counted upon to supply their own costly equipment (with their own horses and weapons). By entrusting territories to vassals,[2] who made further distributions to sub- or rear-vassals, it was possible to patch together a network of properties capable of supporting and equipping a man for combat (the minimum requirement was roughly 15 farms with their peasants). This system provided the kings with the professional fighting contingents they so badly needed. These fighters came in addition to the normal recruits (*hosts*) provided by the counts and to the additional troops contributed by the immunists.[3]

Although Charlemagne required all free men over the age of 12 to swear an oath, there was no intermediary institution between the king and the populace. With the vassal system, the king

[2] It was at this time, under the Carolingians, that the Celtic word "vassal" (*vassus* or *vassalus,* "young lad") came into use.

[3] "Immunists" were clergy members whose lands, by royal privilege, evaded the ordinary administration of local counts.

could depend on direct vassals, who in turn controlled their own vassals all the way down to the individual fighter. Thus, a vassal network was a pyramid system with the king at the top. The task of the king was made easier, and the large contingents of vassals were more dependable, since they were held in bond by personal acts of homage and oaths of fealty.

From the moment that the grandees of the realm accepted vassalage, together with the gift of large parcels of land, the status of the vassal, and especially the "royal vassal," became supremely honorable (before it was a position of social dependence): this gave rise to a new *nobility*.

However, the vassal system could not survive over the long term. On the one hand, in order to avoid a fatal conflict with the church it became necessary to stop the policy of the Pepinids, who *enfiefed* their vassals on lands at the expense of church properties. Thus, vassals had to be given land from the royal domains, rather than from church holdings; royal properties shrank quickly. As early as Charles the Bald, royal domains did not suffice to secure the attachment of new vassals. Since the kings gave their vassals lands as private hereditary property and entrusted them to exercise public offices over each of these lands, the state itself was virtually dismembered.

3. *Feudal Fragmentation*

This is indeed what happened under Louis the Pious and his successors. Given the irremediable disunity between the second emperor's successors and the general insecurity arising from the invasions of the Vikings, Muslims, and Hungarians, the concern for survival forced communities to rally around a local chief for protection. Since the local chief could no longer rely on a strong central authority, and fearful of the appetites of his neighbors and rivals, he became increasingly independent and entered alliances or fought wars with others as his own personal interests dictated.

At this time, the principle of the *heredity of fiefs* became widespread: neither the king nor the feudal lord could take back a gift of land or office, which had been granted in earlier feudal times basically under a precarious status. Custom required that the feudal lord also placed his trust in the son of the man who had served him faithfully.

Means and ends soon became reversed: at the outset, the possession of a fief was intended to support a horseman; the obligation of an increasingly light service, satisfied increasingly by an equivalent monetary—or sometimes purely symbolic—reward, became the means to preserve for one's self and one's heirs a parcel of land in perpetuity.

Gradually, the inheritance of a fief and the emerging practices of feudal heredity became important features of seigneurial policies. Matrimonial alliances and vassal ties were cleverly used to guarantee security and satisfy personal ambitions; at the same time, they progressively undermined the original idea of a feudal pyramid culminating in the king.

Thus, by "seizing the fief," lineages became the building blocks of the social bond, like in pre-civic times. This, in turn, led to the disappearance of the very notion of "magistracy" (in its sense in antiquity), and with it, too, the disappearance of the state, to the benefit of a regime of "chieftains."

4. *Regional Variations*

In the eleventh and twelfth centuries, feudalism was throughout Europe a widespread phenomenon, though there were significant differences from one country to another, especially as regards the ties between vassalage and fiefs or the degree of royal control.

a. France

It was in France, particularly in the north, that feudalism advanced the most. In the south, *alleux* (that is, allods)—freehold land owned outright by free men and not granted by a lord—were numerous; for this reason, feudalism developed late and only partially. Despite these differences, the disintegration of the state in France by the late twelfth century was so advanced that the only system that enabled the king to assert his authority outside the royal domains was feudal law.[4]

b. Germany

In Germany, three phases of development can be identified: (1) During the first phase (the ninth to the twelfth centuries), the feudal system began to develop, but the Saxon and Franconian emperors were able to preserve the fabric of the Carolingian state, using the means of the imperial church to strengthen it: they appointed bishops as counts (and because they were not presumed to have children, the counties could not become hereditary). (2) In the second phase (the second half of the twelfth to the thirteenth centuries), the investiture controversy (see below, pp. 518–20) weakened the authority of the German emperors. Frederick Barbarossa attempted to strengthen the feudal pyramid of the state, creating an order of imperial princes (*Reichsfürsten*), composed of his direct vassals; to be a member it was necessary to be a lord of at least two counties, and thus to hold the title of duke or marquess (or the equivalent ecclesiastical title). Beneath them was a strict hierarchy, extending from the princes to the "serf knights" (*ministeriales*); no one could hold a fief from a lord, who did not belong to a higher rank in the hierarchy. (3) However, before the system could prove its worth, that is, by the second half of the thirteenth century (after the papacy had defeated the Hohenstaufen), the German Empire lost every ounce of its political clout over the princes. Accordingly, Germany collapsed into a heap of independent states.

c. England

In pre-Norman England, there was *thanage,* a system of Germanic origin, consisting of the personal dependence of a "thane" on a superior. But the resemblance of thanage to the debris of the Carolingian state was quite distant. Mere humble servants (though free) could be thanes together with noble warriors and powerful feudal lords. There were no fiefs.

The feudal vassal system in its mature form made its way into England with the Norman Conquest of 1066. From the outset it acquired a more systematic aspect than in the duchy of Normandy. The shape of the feudal pyramid was virtually perfect. By right of conquest, William was able to grant vast tracts of land seized from the Saxons to his own military leaders in exchange for an agreed contingent of fighting men. His military leaders or "tenants-in-chief" (later barons) had to raise the contingents themselves by granting smaller fiefs to their inferiors; this was the very blueprint of the Carolingian idea of a feudal pyramid. Moreover, feudalism in England was total in that it extended throughout the entire territory; not a single parcel of land was left in free hands (allods). Every master of a parcel held it from a lord or directly from the king. In addition, this highly central and well-administered system fit on top of another relatively effective form of administration, an earlier development of the Anglo-Saxon kings: a network of local royal officers, so-called *sheriffs* or counts of each *shire;* it continued to function intact alongside the new feudal system.

d. Italy

Around 1060, in central Italy, the great abbeys and the pontifical states imported a fully formed feudal system with a view to building dependable armies for their protection. The pontifical monarchy gave this feudalism the character of a public law institution, something it lacked elsewhere. Moreover, feudal law also evolved into written law in Italy. In the south, feudalism was associated with the Norman kingdom in place there. In the north, the imperial heartland, feudalism

[4] Ganshof, *Feudalism,* 249.

sputtered slowly to life, then rapidly evolved into a regime of hereditary fiefs. But it collapsed almost as quickly, when the independent urban republics began to rise in the eleventh century.

e. Spain

Feudalism was firmly in the grip of the Spanish kings owing to the constant Muslim threat to their lands and peoples; vassalage and fiefs were never systematically linked, and fiefs never became hereditary; close to a rich Muslim Spain, Spanish kings paid for their armies with money, not fiefs.

It should be noted that, in the Holy Land and the eastern Mediterranean (Greece, Asia Minor), feudalism was an import from the West, forming the basis of the crusader states for the two centuries that they existed.

Finally, a feudal system never developed in large swaths of northern Europe (Frisia, Scandinavia, Ireland), primarily because the primitive fabric of a lineage society continued to survive there.

B. The Structure of Feudalism

Let us turn now to a fuller description of feudal institutions and the "political" intentions that underpin them.[5]

1. *Bonds of Vassalage*

a. Vassalage contract

The "vassalage contract" was not an institution under public law, but in principle under the competence of private law: it tied one private person to another private person. However, the particular character of this relationship between two private persons was indirectly altered when the parties became public figures—a king, church dignitaries, or grand officers of the realm. In this instance, a distinction was made between *vassalage* and *royal vassalage,* which truly was a political institution.

Initially, the vassalage contract was written, but as writing regressed, the formalities were reduced to a ceremony in the presence of witnesses: it became an oath of *homage.* Then, around the turn of the twelfth and thirteenth centuries, it became a written contract again.

Vassalage was the act by which a vassal (*vassus, vassalus*) entered into an obligation with another person: he "commended himself" to the other person (*se commendat*) and owed obedience (*servitium, obsequium*) in exchange for assured protection. This other person was called "master" (*dominus*) or "lord" (*senior*) ("suzerain" is a later expression primarily reserved for kings and great princes).

We quote below a passage from a vassalage contract, dating probably from the middle of the eighth century (the text is perhaps a model used for many contracts). In it the vassal explains why he has decided to "commend himself to the power of another man."

> Inasmuch as it is known to all and sundry that I lack the wherewithal to feed and clothe myself, I have asked of your pity, and your goodwill has granted me, permission to deliver and commend myself into your *mundoburdus* (= place myself under your personal protection).[6] This I have therefore done, in such fashion that, (1) you have undertaken to

[5] This section is drawn from ibid., part 3.

[6] The Old French word *maimbour* and the Latin word *mundeburdium* (or *mundium*) that it denotes come from the German *Mund,* which refers to the protection of a lineage over its members (the head of the lineage guarantees protection). Kings could grant their *maimbour* to vassals, churches, monasteries; this act placed these individuals and institutions (and their properties) under the protection of the king, who considered them as members of his household. (From this it must be concluded that the king's other subjects did not enjoy such protection.) See above, pp. 479–80.

> aid and sustain me in food and clothing, while I have undertaken to serve you and deserve well of you so far as lies in my power; (2) and for as long as I shall live, I am bound to serve you and respect you as a free man ought, and during my lifetime I shall not have the right to withdraw myself from your authority and *mundoburdus;* (3) furthermore I must be for the remainder of my days under your power and protection. And in virtue of this action, if one of us tries to alter the terms of the agreement, he will have to pay *solidi* (a fine) to his peer [the other], but the agreement itself shall remain in force. Whence it has seemed good to us that (4) the two parties concerned should draw up and confirm two documents of the same tenor, and this they have done.[7]

It is interesting that the vassal claims to be the "peer" of his lord in terms of his social rank. This claim actually strengthens the equality of station of the two parties: the contract between the two is, in fact, synallagmatic (each party is bound to provide something to the other by contractual agreement); there are equal penalties for each party, and the contract exists in two copies. Moreover, the future vassal understands that he will not be required to perform any demeaning duties (e.g., the manual work of a serf); this would not be appropriate given his status as a "free man." The vassalage contract is for life; it is irrevocable as long as the parties to the contract are alive (unless one of the parties breaks his commitment);[8] and it is void as soon as one of the parties dies.

It is a contract between two free men. Naturally, the vassal alienates his freedom, as soon as he becomes the man of his lord, but he accepts obedience to his lord by choice. This is the distinction between vassal dependence and the dependence of a serf: one is born a serf, but one is vassal by choice. However, excluding demeaning obligations, as noted, the dependence of a vassal is total: a person is no longer his own master and must follow the lord wherever he is needed, even to a foreign land.

Because the contract binds two free persons and is for life, it must be renewed explicitly in the event that it is to be transferred from a lord, or a vassal, to a son or another relative.

b. Homage

A vassal contract is sealed with a ceremony, which before long replaces the written act entirely; it is called homage (*hominium, hommagium, Mannschaft*). It involves specific gestures: the vassal places his bare hands (i.e., without weapons) between the hands of the lord, a sign of submission to him; the lord receives the hands as a sign of protection (*immixto manuum*). A further aspect of the ceremony is a short declaration of intention spoken by the vassal: "I become your man from this day forth," or "I am willing to become your man"; sometimes the lord also declares his willingness to accept him. Through the act of physical homage, feudalism displays its very primitive nature by attaching less importance to words than to gestures.

In all primitive rights a symbolic, material act is required (for example, in ancient Roman law, when a field was sold, a lump of earth was given). Thus, in the eyes of the masses, to become a vassal is to "come into the hands" of someone. Before long another gesture was added: a kiss (on the mouth, rarely on the feet). The expression used to describe vassal homage is "a homage of hands and mouth."

The bond of a man to his lord, sealed by an act of homage, became a universal model. In courtly poetry, the lover (admirer of his lady) proclaimed that he was the "vassal" or "man" of his lady. Today, when a man presents his respects ("homages") to a lady, in fact he is declaring

---

[7] Quoted in Halphen, *Charlemagne et l'Empire Carolingien,* 175.

[8] If the lord makes death threats against his protégé or makes attempts on the virtue of his wife or daughter, or makes other insults of similar gravity, the contract is void.

himself her vassal. This worldly use of the expression comes directly from the old vassal institution by way of "courtly" culture.

Marc Bloch points to another striking imprinting of feudalism on the human psyche: our modern Western gesture of prayer, two clasped hands (in antiquity one prayed with open, outspread palms), is apparently the same gesture as the *immixtio manuum,* which the vassal performed as a sign of submission to his lord, inviting him to take his hands in his.[9] God is addressed in prayer as a feudal lord.

c. Oath of fealty

Toward the middle of the eighth century, an *oath of fealty* was added to the vassal commitment. The kings required their vassals to swear this oath in addition to the one owed by every free subject of the realm. "Fealty" follows immediately upon homage. The difference is that the oath has religious value. It is sworn at the altar or by holding a holy relic or placing one's hands on a liturgical missal, and so on. Failure to keep one's oath is perjury. It is in reference to the vassal's oath of "fealty" that we speak of the vassal's "fidelity." At the outset, the members of the aristocracy entering a commitment of vassalage probably swore the oath to distinguish their vassal bond from other less honorable bonds of submission. In fact, only a free man can swear an oath. Thus, the vassal bond becomes a bond "of fealty and homage," according to a widespread formula.

Oaths of fealty dating from the classical High Middle Ages include formulas such as: "From this hour forth, I, X, shall be true to you, Y, in good faith and spirit, as a man should be to his lord, without deception.... I vow here never to hold you captive, neither to take your life nor limb, neither I nor a man nor woman on my advice or at my command.[10]... I shall be a friend of your friends, an enemy of your enemies."[11]

d. Obligations of the vassal contract

Whether written or oral, the vassal contract supposed obligations on both sides.

i. *Obligations of the Vassal*

The vassal was under obligation to perform certain duties and services.

- *Military duties.* The original purpose of vassalage was to provide the lord with armed service on military campaigns. If the vassal lived nearby, he owed his master constant readiness. If he was *enfiefed* with an estate, he owed a number of days of service each year. A vassal traveled on military campaigns with his own supplies and at his own expense. A lord could ask his vassal to extend the duration of campaign duty, but in that case the lord had to cover any additional expenses.

The obligations of military service varied: the vassal might be called to duty alone or accompanied by a number of men. He might come fully armed or partially equipped (as in the case of *vavasours,* vassals of vassals, who were less well off). A distinction was made between an *expeditio,* a campaign with a "military host" (armed expedition), and an *equitatio,* a simple ride or policing expedition. Occasionally, a monetary tax called "scutage" (Old English) or *ecuage*

[9] The Catholic liturgy revived this practice, in part, in the years after Vatican II.

[10] Although it goes without saying, it goes even better said. The naïveté of the expression is astonishing, as is the suggestion of violence and tenuousness of the social bond that is implied.

[11] This last formula reveals better still the total ruin of the civic relationship and moral bond in society. One is no longer another's friend or enemy on the basis of his virtues or vices, as was natural at the time of Aristotle or Cicero; now the reason is because both belong (or not) to the same group. This is fundamentally a "tribal" principle, and in a world where Celtic and Germanic tribes had long since disappeared, together with their myths and rites that bound them together, this restrictive principle loses its innocence and becomes a "mafia" principle.

(Old French) was levied in place of actual military service. This solution soon found favor among the great lords of the realm, making it possible for them to assemble the first fully reliable armies on call.

There was also nonmilitary vassal service; for example, a vassal might be called to carry on his shoulders into the cathedral a newly consecrated bishop; or to hold the stirrup for his lord as he mounted his horse; or to deliver messages.

- *Aid.* A vassal owed his lord special monetary obligations under certain conditions. Soon these obligations were itemized in the feudal custom, then spelled out in detail in the written feudal law. They included payment of a ransom for the release of the lord if he was captured; a contribution to the cost of knighting the lord's eldest son; a contribution to the wedding costs of the lord's eldest daughter; a contribution to costs when the lord left for the Crusades.
- *Advice and counsel.* The vassal was obligated to attend to his lord at court and provide him with wise counsel. He could be summoned to court at least once a year and on special occasions. At these council meetings, the business of the realm was discussed and justice delivered (the vassal was seated with the lord and his co-vassals in the feudal *curia*).

ii. *Obligations of the Feudal Lord*

The feudal lord owed his vassal protection: he looked on his vassal as a member of his own household; whoever attacked a vassal was guilty of a personal attack on the lord; the attacker was then exposed to retaliation by the lord's sworn supporters.

The lord also had an obligation of generosity toward his vassal. He owed him gifts, originally called a "benefice" (*beneficium*), implying something free and exceptional. Because the lord expected assistance from his vassal in times of war, he had to provide him with the necessary means to wage war. This is why the benefice soon became a payment, that is, a "fief."

iii. *Other Aspects of the Vassal Contract*

In principle, the contract was binding between two men only. Even if the vassal called up his vassals to serve in his lord's army, these vassals were only obligated to obey their own immediate lord; they owed no obedience to the higher lord. "The vassal of my vassal is not my vassal."

It was possible to break off one's commitments, but only by mutual consent. This required a special ceremony during which feudal homage was renounced and "fealty" withdrawn (*diffidatio, diffidentia*). The implication was that the fief must be returned. Usually, a rupture of the bond arose because one party held that the other had not honored his commitments. When the *diffidatio* did not result in the restitution of the fief, the consequence could be war (the sense of the English words "defy" and "defiance" is traceable to the notion of *diffidatio*).

When either vassal or lord took it upon himself to break the bond unilaterally, it was termed a "felony." If the vassal was at fault, the punishment decided by the feudal court was usually the confiscation and permanent loss of his fief (*commissio*). The punishment for the lord was called the "disavowal," which involved a solemn ceremony (in this event, the vassal retained his fief, which he now held from the lord of his former lord). These "feudal penal rights" were only formulated and introduced in the later stages of feudalism.

e. Multiple commitments, the system of "ligeancy," the illogicalities of vassal hierarchy

The thirst for benefices led vassals to swear an oath to more than one lord as early as the late ninth century. Count Siboto of Falkenstein, for example, was vassal to 20 lords. This created many difficulties and undermined the very notion of vassal service. When several lords required the service of the same vassal, which lord was the vassal to serve? And when several of these lords waged war against one another, to which did the vassal owe fealty? The custom was for the vassal to serve the lord from whom he held his most important fief, or to explicitly preserve the rights of the first lord in the provision of a new homage.

In the eleventh and twelfth centuries, another solution was tried—"liege homage," which involved naming the lord to be served on a priority basis in the actual vassal contract. It became increasingly common to be the vassal of one lord for one property and to be the lord of that same lord for another property. This created an "interlocking hierarchy" of sorts, which contradicted the initial concept of fidelity and subordination altogether.

Thus, a king of France became the vassal of his own vassals in order to obtain a strategically important fief: in 1124 Louis VI became the vassal of the abbey of Saint-Denis in order to receive the county of Vexin—at least Suger prevented the king from swearing an oath of fealty to the abbot; in 1185 Philip II Augustus received the county of Amiens as a fief from the bishop of Amiens.[12]

The original intention of the Carolingians was to strengthen the state by doubling its structures through the addition of the feudal pyramid. But these departures from classical feudal hierarchy resulted in a grave failure.

2. *The Benefice or Fief*

The original system of vassalage guaranteed the warrior, who swore an oath to his lord, a house over his head and food on the table; the lord also undertook to clothe and equip him. In order to enable their vassals to perform their military service the Carolingians took to the habit of granting benefices (*beneficia*), later called "fiefs" (*feoda*).

a. Landed fiefs

Benefices came in various forms, but more often than not the vassal was granted a parcel of land, enabling him to support himself.

The principle reason for a gift of land was no doubt that the economy of the early Middle Ages was largely nonmonetary: neither a lord nor a king had sufficient money to provide a regular income to those who served him; furthermore, in the absence of a developed economy, even with money his servants would not have had the wherewithal to live and equip themselves. The only alternative was to remunerate the vassals with land so that they could, in turn, exploit it with the help of the local dependent population.

Some lords actually granted their lay vassals church properties to help them derive additional income. This produced a number of "lay abbots."

The *fiefs de reprise,* or allods, were lands transferred by freehold owners to a lord in exchange for protection; these free men swore an oath to the lord, who immediately returned the land to them as their fief.

b. Other Types of Fiefs: Noble Fiefs, Honors, Money Fiefs

A fief could also include the gift of a public office, either a lay office or a church office; such offices conveyed benefices in their own right. When a vassal held full public authority over a parcel of territory, his fief was known as a "noble fief" or *fief de dignité,* also called an "honor" in the Carolingian age and in twelfth century Germany. An abbey could grant an "avowry" (from the Latin *advocatus,* Old French *avoué*)[13] to a military man, who held the property in fief and acted as an

[12] See van Caenegem, "Government, Law and Society," 193.

[13] An *avoué* was a layperson who exercised public authority over an ecclesiastical fief (since the clergy could not bear arms).

agent for the abbey; as an *avoué* he could be granted certain rights: he could collect taxes and tolls, coin money, as well as administer the mayoralty of a village or the lordship of a domain. The fief could also provide a monetary income ("money fief," Old French: *fief de bourse* and later *rente,* "annuity"). This particular type of fief enabled a lord to extend his reach beyond the boundaries of his own domains. For example, in the twelfth and thirteenth centuries, the English crown extended its vassal network to many lords on the continent, primarily in Flanders and Lotharingia; these vassals received annuities in exchange for their allegiance.

c. Investiture

The vassal received the fief in an investiture ceremony, the counterpart of the ceremonies of homage and fealty, which it traditionally followed. As with any legal commitment at this time, the investiture involved the remittance of symbolic objects to the beneficiary; for example, a lump of earth representing the gift of land or, if the fief was an honor, a scepter, a rod, a gold ring, a knife, a glove, a military standard or banner, or a cross for the investiture of bishoprics as in Germany and Italy before the Concordat of Worms (see below, pp. 514–15). As soon as the investiture ceremony was celebrated, the vassal was enfiefed (i.e., he became the lawful possessor of the fief), and he was entitled to full legal rights with respect to third parties. Since the concept of holding a fief was similar to the notion of possession in Roman law, the two concepts were thought of as akin when the study of Roman law was revived later. In certain instances, investiture, fealty, and homage resulted in the production of written instruments.

A vassal could voluntarily abandon his fief (a bond of fealty, as we saw, could be dissolved if both parties agreed); this required a symbolic act equivalent to the solemn investiture ceremony, an act known as *werpitio.*

d. Rights over the Fief

In theory, a feudal lord retained full rights of ownership over the property of the fief (*dominium supremum* or *directum,* which later became *eminent domain*) and granted usufructuary rights, or useful possession, to his vassal (*dominium utile, ius utendi et fruendi*). However, by the twelfth or thirteenth century, the vassal's hold on the fief moved in the direction of quasi-ownership, with rights of "use and abuse," a consequence as much of the de facto situation as of the influence of Roman law. The first step in this direction was the hereditary transmission of fiefs.

e. Inheritance of Fiefs

Because the gift of a fief and an oath of fealty were directly linked, it goes without saying that, in the early phase of feudalism, the gift lasted only as long as the vassal bond was kept. Thus, possession of the fief was fundamentally precarious; at best it was restricted to the holder's lifetime. The perpetuation of the feudal bond and the possession of a benefice beyond the lives of the two initial parties of an agreement also became a focus of attention; in short, the question of the hereditary transmission of a vassalage and fief was raised.

As we saw, it was accepted as early as the late ninth century that a fief could be inherited. The practice spread rapidly and soon the king admitted it: Charles the Bald confirmed it at the council of Quierzy-sur-Oise in 877 (he even recommended to bishops and abbots that they should allow their "men" to enjoy the favor).

While the development of the practice was slower in Germany, Conrad II imposed it on his vassals by edict to win the favors of his rear vassals. Lifelong fiefs remained common in Germany until the thirteenth century. The inheritance of fiefs was also widespread throughout England, but much later than in France.

Of course, the transfer of the fief to the vassal's direct or indirect heir meant that the legatee had to become the vassal of the lord master of the fief. Hence, the repetition of the ceremonies of homage and fealty, followed by the ceremony of investiture, occurred with each inheritance: the inheritance of a fief was never automatic, like the inheritance of an allod. But a lord could not refuse the act of homage of a vassal.

In the early phase of classical feudalism, when inheritance had not yet become a full right, a lord could exact a payment for his consent to reinvest the heir. The amounts involved for the purchase of the domain of a large principality enfiefed to a person who was not a direct heir (e.g., a son-in-law) could be quite considerable. For example, Ferrand of Portugal had to pay 50,000 pounds in 1212 in order to marry the heiress of Flanders and thus become the count of the land.[14]

f. The Inheritance System of Fiefs

Given that the original function of the fief was to enable the vassal to fulfill his obligations (primarily military), a special system of inheritance began to emerge as soon as fiefs became hereditary. It was out of the question, at least in the early days, to divide up the fief or to transmit it to an underage direct heir or to a woman, for the simple reason that the service portion of the obligation could not be properly met in such cases.

To counter the risk of property division, it was common to bequeath the fief to the firstborn son (a practice known as "primogeniture"). Less common was the concession of a domain to the younger son (known as the right of "juveigneur"); rare was the system of *parage* or *frérage*, which involved sharing the domain between all the sons, including the obligation of every son to assist the eldest in performing his vassal duties. Finally, in Germany, the devolution of undivided lands to all brothers existed as well. Irrespective of these different methods of succession, a system of shared inheritance gradually emerged throughout Europe.

If the heir was underage, the lord could claim the fruits of the fief, on the condition that he covered the child heir's living and education costs; he could also bring the child to his court as a page or a squire. The lord could accept the temporary homage and oath of fealty of a relative who had agreed to perform the vassal service. Finally, a procurator could provide the required vassal service as a representative of the child heir.

As for female heirs, they too were admitted into the line of succession under certain conditions. A woman could present a representative to the lord, and the representative would swear an oath of fealty and homage under certain circumstances. More often than not, the representative was the woman's husband, which meant that the lord had an interest in her choice of husband. It soon became the custom for the lord to intervene in the marriage affairs of his vassals' daughters. In the twelfth century (and later still in Germany), women became accepted as normal heiresses.

Also in the context of a fief reverting to the patrimony of the vassal, the option of subinfeudation existed. This involved the vassal granting parcels of his fief to subvassals at his pleasure. In the early days of the practice, the lord's authorization was required, but the requirement was dropped before very long.

Over time the vassal was allowed to dispose of his fief freely, as though it were a piece of property in the Roman legal sense. In particular, he could sell it to any buyer for money, and the lord could not object. Though this process came to an end in the thirteenth century in England, restrictive forms continued for some time. First, the seller had to transfer the fief to the lord, who could invest the buyer with the fief; in this case the buyer swore homage and an oath of fealty. If the buyer was an ecclesiastical institution, which of course could not swear an oath, the lord had to convert the property into a freehold and sell it himself, in which case the process involved a

[14] A lord had a right of veto in regard to the marriage of an heiress to a fief (see below).

series of transactions. The lord did have a sort of right of preemption, if his vassal put the fief up for sale.

The survival of the one word "feudalism" to designate all feudal-vassal institutions can be explained by the fact that, over time, vassalage became conflated with feudalism, and vassal duties ceased to be viewed as the consequence of a contract between two parties but rather as the offshoot of the possession of a fief. This or that service was required for the possession of this or that fief. Thus, the idea of "pure" vassalage gradually disappeared altogether.

C. Chivalry and Nobility

A ruling class is not necessarily a nobility.[15] An entire process of institutional and ideological history was necessary before the ruling class of feudalism could see itself first as a "chivalry," then in the twelfth and thirteenth centuries as a "nobility," and before this separation of the ruling class from the other classes (peasants, clergy, tradespeople, urban craftspeople, and so on) passed from custom to law.

Socially, the defining characteristic of nobility was its possession of land, which it worked with its dependents. Nobility itself was fully devoted to war and its offshoots, hunting and tournaments. Another characteristic of this social group was *court* and "courtly life." The knight lived in his castle with his soldiers, his squires, and his vassals. Justice was delivered at court, which explained the existence of a certain legal culture in noble circles. Similarly, because one spoke at court where ladies were present, a man of arms no longer stood out or outshone his rivals solely with his fighting skills and gruff language. Beginning in France in the eleventh century, then spreading by imitation throughout Europe, there was a development in civil society of various courtly practices—civility, gallantry, and *courtoisie* or *prudhommie* (the moral courage of a man of valor)—and certain literary talents.

Toward the middle of the twelfth century, nobility began to see itself as a separate group. In the opinion of the nobles, they belonged to the better families and described themselves as *gentilhommes*—men of good *gent* (race) or lineage—in order to emphasize their qualities of birth. But the group was ill defined and had no legal recognition. An initiation rite, *dubbing* or *knighting*, contributed to drawing a boundary between this group and the other social classes.

1. *Formalization of Membership—Dubbing*

The dubbing ritual appeared in the second half of the eleventh century. Performed by an older knight, the ceremony formally made a young man a "knight." It consisted of three acts: (1) the ceremonial girding of a sword; (2) the application of a heavy blow with the flat of the hand on the young man's neck or cheek (dubbing comes from the Old English word "dubbian," derived from an Old Germanic word meaning to strike; the blow was intended to make an impression on the mind of the young man so that he remembered his promise for the rest of his life; the intention may also have been to transfuse a magical influx); (3) an athletic display: the young knight sped on his horse and transfixed with his lance a suit of armor attached to a post; this was known as the "quintaine." Sometimes the young knight's hair was cut.

Early forms of this initiation ceremony, comparable with rites of passage in primitive societies, existed among the ancient Germanic tribes. While in primitive societies the initiation rite concerned every young free man—warriors all—in feudal times it was restricted to the small

---

[15] See Bloch, *Feudal Society*, 359–440; Martin Aurell, *La noblesse en Occident (Ve–XVe siècles)* [Nobility in the West] (Paris: Armand Colin, 1996); Jean Chelini, *Histoire religieuse de l'Occident médiéval* [A religious history of the medieval West] (Paris: Armand Colin, 1997), 372–76.

caste of professional warriors (various corporations adapted the practice to their specific rites of passage).

The dubbing ritual became widespread in the twelfth century. Before very long a knight was not merely "made"; he was "ordained." The whole body of dubbed knights became an *ordo* ("order"), and as a class it was set apart, since increasingly only the sons of knights were dubbed and very rarely newcomers.

2. *The Code of Chivalry*

The intervention of the church encouraged a transformation of the ceremony into an institution. First, the church blessed the sword given to the future knight. Then, little by little, priests performed the act of dubbing itself at the ceremony; they did so as feudal lords, but of course added considerable religious pomp. As early as the twelfth century, a liturgy of dubbing began to be established. The blessing of arms expanded from the knight's sword to his spurs, his banner, and his lance; sometimes a prayer vigil or purifying bath was added (or, more prosaically, an evening of festivities). A *pontificale,*[16] written by William Durandus, bishop of Mende at the end of the thirteenth century, and another Roman *pontificale* from the fourteenth century, ordered the official rites for all Christendom. Lay people, however, did their best to resist efforts by the clergy to control the entire ceremony.

When the church began its involvement in the knighting ceremonies, it made efforts to transform, little by little, knighthood itself. The "peace movements,"[17] organized by the church, reviled the knights, who profited from the declining power of the state to abuse the church with their misdeeds and insults. The church attempted to convert the knights into a "militia of Christ" acting for the best causes: the armed defense of the church, the maintenance of public order and peace, the repression of heresies, and the fight against infidels.

To this end the church imagined certain high moral precepts comprising a "code of chivalry," which every knight accepted explicitly or implicitly when he was dubbed. These precepts were first introduced into the oath and prayers that accompanied the dubbing ceremony, then they became a commonplace of the literature—examples are found in Chrétien de Troyes's *Perceval,* in the prose romance of *Lancelot,* in the German *Minnesang* (a fragment of the "Meissner"), in the *Ordene de Chevalerie,* an Old French didactic poem, much copied in other European countries, and last but not least in Saint Bernard's *De militia christiana.*

In a sense, this theme merely made explicit the values spontaneously created since feudalism: for example, an attachment to fidelity, the values of fortitude and courage. But the church purified them and infused them with spirituality, adding explicit religious concerns.

The true knight goes to mass daily or at least regularly. He makes his sword available to good causes, in particular those listed above. War ceases to be a value in its own right (as it was in Germanic mythology); it is now a means subordinated to higher ends. Fighting skills and arms are subject to rules as well: a knight is expected to behave properly in battle; he may not slay a defenseless enemy. Acts of treason and false accusations are forbidden; a knight does not participate in parodies of justice; he does not give bad counsel to a lady; he assists a fellow being in distress. These precepts, still a little thin in the writings of Chrétien de Troyes in the twelfth century, became more substantial in the entourage of Saint Louis in the next century.

Here is a passage from the *Pontificale* by William Durandus: "Most Holy Lord, Almighty Father...thou who hast permitted on earth the use of the sword to repress the malice of the wicked and defend justice; who for the protection of thy people hast thought fit to institute the

---

[16] A liturgical commentary.

[17] See below, p. 516.

order of chivalry... cause thy servant here before thee, by disposing his heart to goodness, never to use this sword or another to injure anyone unjustly; but let him use it always to defend the Just and the Right."[18] The impact of the ideal of chivalry on the history of the West is well known. It went well beyond the strict military sphere. Such a noble mission gave the order of chivalry pride of place in society (after the church, of course). The knight dominated and directed the laity like he sat on a horse; as per the saying, "who sits above it controls it."

Thus, from the middle of the eleventh to the thirteenth century, "professional" men of war were transformed by this largely ecclesiastical work of the institution of chivalry (the attitude of the church in this regard can be explained by the great reforms of the church itself; see chapter 4 below). The fighting men, who throughout the Carolingian era and the early feudal age had remained semibarbarian and semipagan, devoted to feuding and plundering, were transformed. The church gave them a social status, created them into an *ordo* that was fully integrated into Christian society, alongside the clergy,[19] and placed them at the pinnacle of laity. Knights had their own quasi-sacramental rites of initiation, which set them apart from the people; they had their missions: inside the realm, they served the cause of public order and peace; outside, they were encouraged to use their bountiful energy and fighting skills against the infidels in Palestine and Spain, the pagans on the doorsteps of Europe, and heresiarchs wherever they could be found. Thus were laid the foundations of a legal institution of *nobility.*

3. *The Transformation of a De Facto Nobility into a Legal Nobility*

Toward the middle of the thirteenth century, it became inscribed in law that what constituted chivalry and nobility was neither one's military profession nor the act of dubbing; it was *birth.*

Among soldier-monks like the Templars, Christian humility did not prevent the existence of two well-distinguished categories of fighting men: the higher category of knights and the lower category of ordinary "serjeants." Even the color of their mantles differentiated them: knights wore white and serjeants brown. But to be a knight, it was not only necessary to be dubbed before entering the order; it was a requirement to be a knight's son or descendant of knights on one's father's side.

Similarly, in peace ordinances issued in 1152 and in 1187, Frederick Barbarossa (like other kings after him) said no to peasants bearing the knight's sword and lance; he also forbade rewarding an act of gallantry on the battlefield with an accolade of knighthood. Thus, gradually the class of knights narrowed and closed.

For a long time, petty lords, abbots, and bishops continued to claim the right to dub knights, as in the past. Soon, the right to dub became an exclusive royal prerogative: only the king, in this domain as in others, had the authority to go against custom. The king, of course, had high hopes of profiting from his privilege. Be that as it may, the first "letters of nobility" appeared in France under the signatures of Philip the Bold and Philip the Fair.

Suddenly the ritual ceremony of dubbing regressed or disappeared. Now, according to Beaumanoir, the defining feature of a nobleman (*gentilhomme*) was membership in a "lineage of knights." And when, by exception, an aspirant was made a new knight by a letter of nobility, his descendants were also entitled to "the privileges, rights and franchises which the nobles are accustomed to enjoy by virtue of the two lines of descent" (the chancery of the king of France at the end of the thirteenth century). Thus, nobility acquired a strict legal status.

In former times, one was noble because one had sworn an oath to a lord and received in exchange the gift of a fief, which provided the means to maintain the arms and equipment of a

---

[18] Quoted in Bloch, *Feudal Society,* 319.

[19] This also became a single *ordo;* until then, regular and secular had been carefully distinguished.

knight. Now, on the contrary, one had to be noble to have the right to possess a military fief,[20] unless the king gave (or sold) his derogation to the requirement. Even religious orders (other than the Templars noted above), which until then rejected only postulants of servile origin, decided to write in their rules the distinction between noble and non-noble descent. Dueling (i.e., the practice of exacting private vengeance) became a prerogative of nobility. Nobility had coats of arms. They enjoyed generous fiscal exemptions (by virtue of the fact that they paid with their blood).

It was only when nobility, until then a social class, became a "legal class" that a strict aristocratic hierarchy began to form, from base to summit, with dukes, marques, counts, barons, and vavasours.

The inaccessibility of the nobility was partly a defensive reaction against the rise of a new, increasingly wealthy and dominant social class, the bourgeoisie (which counterreacted, in turn, using communal charters to ban nobility from entering commerce). The bourgeois actively bought rural domains and their dependents (most were seigneury; see below). And since access to the social class of nobility was denied to it, the bourgeoisie could not acquire a seigneurial right of *bannum* (*droit de ban*).

D. Seigneurialism

What we have been discussing pertains exclusively to the ruling class.[21] But feudalism trickled down through society to the bottom. Each knight oversaw a group of dependents (peasants, craftspeople, servants), which formed a seigneury (manor). While the seigneurial system (manorialism) is closely tied to the feudal system, the two should not be confused. There is a dependence between the lord and those who live under his authority, but the logic and customs of this dependence are fundamentally different from the vassal bond.

The seigneury was a landed estate of variable size; it frequently consisted of land parcels separated by considerable distance (parcels were transmitted from one seigneury to another by the twists and turns of inheritance and alienation). Usually each domain was divided into a reserve for the master (exploited for him directly by his representatives) and tenures. Land tenures were granted against an annual tax (the *cens,* a *perpetual and imprescriptible* monetary payment, which eroded over time) or against a *field-rent* (*champart,* a portion of the harvest). The lord had the right to levy other taxes as well.

1. *The Right of Bannum*

When feudalism was at its apogee, the possession of a fief implied—in practice if not always in law—that *in his territories the lord exercised public authority, indeed performed the full spectrum of public duties:* law courts for high and low justice, administrative authority, the right to open markets and to levy taxes, and so on.

In the early period of feudalism, particularly in Germany, a distinction was made between the gift of a territorial fief and a gift of "honors," that is, the delegation of some part of public authority. But, as time went by, the distinction was gradually forgotten.

The discretionary power exercised by lords over the people in their domains is known as "the right of bannum." A lord can also claim the right of bannum over a territory outside the limits of his own estate (the territories of weaker lords or of freehold landowners [allods] in search

[20] Remember that as late as the eighteenth century in France the rank of officer was restricted to aristocrats with 16 quarters of nobility.

[21] See Robert Boutruche, *Seigneurie et féodalité* [Seigneurialism and feudalism] (Paris: Aubier, Éditions Montaigne, 1968); "Seigneurs et seigneuries au Moyen Age" [Seigneurs and seigneurialism in the Middle Ages], proceedings of the 117th National Congress of Scholarly Societies (Paris: Éditions du CTHS, 1995), with introductory reports by Robert Fossier and Philippe Contamine.

of protection). This practice was at its greatest in western Francia after the dismantling of the Carolingian state; it was less developed in Germania, where the power of the state remained intact for longer, and in England, where the state was more or less preserved by the Anglo-Saxon kings and even strengthened by the Norman kings and the Plantagenets.

The right of bannum applied first to the administration of *justice*. The lords held courts of "high" and "low" justice. The distinction between *high* and *low* law courts dates to Carolingian times when the customary judicial assemblies in Germania, called "*mallus,*" were still in use in the villages or groups of villages. The *mallus* dealt with minor and civil cases. Only the high courts under the authority of the count could hear criminal cases involving the death penalty, corporal punishment, or banishment; the low court heard cases for misdemeanors and most civil cases. As feudalism developed, jurisdiction over life and death criminal cases was moved from the level of the state representative (i.e., the count) to the lower district level. Nevertheless, the distinction continued to exist between the two levels of jurisdiction, each with clear and separate competencies. Even small lords could dispense high and low justice, while even smaller lords could only hear cases in the low court.

It should be pointed out that although justice in France was very fragmented, it was far less so than land ownership; this was especially true of high justice. In Plantagenet England (in the twelfth century), the king's justice gradually reduced the importance of *feudal courts*.

In both cases, when feudalism was at its apogee (and aldermen and professional magistrates had virtually disappeared), the lord of a territory heard a case surrounded by a seigneurial court of illiterate participants. The procedure was summary and at times involved trial by ordeal or trial by combat (judicial duel). The lord collected all fines personally.

Seigneurial protection involved other counterparts, primarily the right to levy taxes and collect payments: market taxes on goods, fees for protecting a castle, transaction rights, personal taxes, other exceptional appeals for funds, the quartering of troops and accommodating of officials, requisitions, economic monopolies, and banalities.[22] These fees and dues were called exactions (banal exactions) or new customs duties; they yielded more income than the fees charged on the land itself. They were collected by a vast army of administrators, "mayors," serjeants, and, in Germany, *ministeriales*.

Accordingly, the dependents of an estate were tempted to flee either to the city or to the new colonies (e.g., the lands reconquered from the Muslims in Spain). This put pressure on the lords to grant relief and manumission; "charters" were drafted against payment, stipulating and restricting the nature and amount of the exactions. Sometimes peasant communities were permitted to form "communes" or "consulates" with the right to dispense justice.

Medieval jurists, trained in both canon and Roman law, challenged the seizure of public offices by local lords and claimed back the exclusive right of the kings and their officers to exercise public functions.

2. *Serfdom*

Serfdom is a very complex issue and divides the experts. It is certain that serfdom replaced slavery sometime during the Carolingian era, and that it, too, disappeared toward the thirteenth century. The complexity of the issue can be explained as follows. A serf is "unfree." The word "free" can have several meanings: it can refer to a person who is not *legally* dependent on another, but also a person who is *exempt from obligations*. Thus, a peasant can be "unfree" without being a "slave."

---

22 *Banalities:* the dependents of an estate were under obligation to use the mills, ovens, wine presses, and so on, which belonged to the lord, or to sell their wine after the lord had sold his.

Such a peasant is called a *manant* or a *villein,* which are marks of servitude. Because a serf's obligations vary, the notion of "serfdom" itself is somewhat uncertain.

Serfs were not allowed to belong to religious orders (they could not have two masters). They could not bring a suit in a court of law, nor freely dispose of their property. Serfs usually did not participate in the defense of the village; they had no freedom of movement (the lord had the right to pursue them into neighboring estates); they paid a head tax on dependents and were banned from marrying someone not a dependent of the same manor. A serf's properties were subject to a regular succession tax (*mainmorte*);[23] therefore, their children had to pay the lord a fee to repossess the property. In the case of mixed marriages, the quality of serf (the "servile stain") was transmitted through the male line. To this must be added various direct and arbitrary taxes, the unpaid labor service owed by a tenanted serf, and the humiliations to which the *villein* class was at times exposed.

Of course, individual and group manumissions existed. A master on his deathbed could manumit one or more of his men. Kings, monasteries, and cities also granted or sold collective manumissions to their subjects; this required the drafting of a charter of manumission.

The occurrence of this increased with the development of a monetary economy: Louis IX and Philippe the Fair needed money for their wars and crusades; monasteries needed money for their building projects. But manumitted serfs often went into considerable debt in order to pay the sums for their manumission; this created a new form of dependence.[24] All in all, there was a clear social distinction in rural society between the well-to-do peasants, who purchased their freedom at a high price, and the "poor villagers."

Feudalism offers us a key to understanding the development of political ideas between antiquity and the classical Middle Ages. It produced a very novel kind of social bond, as different from what came before it as what came after. It was not the social bond of the city in antiquity, and it was not yet the bond of the modern state. And although it may seem to have been a regression compared with Roman civicism, it was not a retreat to tribalism.

The particularity of feudal institutions lay in the fact that *all social relations tended to become private, person-to-person relations;* private relations, in the ruling class at least, were the only threads of the social fabric. The person was no longer submerged in a group as in archaic societies; nor was an individual bound to others by virtue of a law formulated and guaranteed by the state, as in classical or modern civic models. In feudal times trust existed only between those with a personal bond. There was no longer a public collectivity. This truly represented a regression because, in the absence of being able to entertain relations of trust in a large, anonymous, civic society, nothing could be attempted which supposed a strong division of labor or knowledge. For this reason, the ninth, tenth, and two-thirds of the eleventh centuries were periods of unprecedented cultural and economic barrenness in western Europe.

We will see below that the work of the church, and the work of kings, would concern the patient reconstruction and repair of a social bond mediated by the public space. Classical texts from antiquity provided them with a model for their work.

---

[23] *Mainmorte* refers to the legal impossibility of transmitting the serf's property, movable and immovable alike, to his heirs or of alienating them; the hand (*main*) holding the title of ownership of a tenament is said to be dead (*morte*), the only "living" hand being the hand of the lord.

[24] Serfdom did not exist in Picardy, Normandy, Forez (the eastern Massif Central in France), Saxony, or in Lombardy. In Germania, a class of free men, under the sole authority of the baron courts, managed to survive, but in the twelfth century "territorial" serfdom (as opposed to "personal" serfdom) appeared, where the lord granted a servile tenure attaching the tenant to the land; then in the thirteenth century, a new form of personal serfdom emerged, combining arbitrary and unlimited servitude. In the end, there were more serfs in Germania than in France. Likewise, in England, the lower strata of the peasantry wound up as serfs with an hereditary attachment to the soil (for example, *sokemen*, bordars, etc.).

II. Sacred Kingship

Feudal society had another clearly archaic institution: *sacred kingship*. We noted earlier that after the Visigoth kings of Spain the kings of the Franks, then the kings of France, and most of the kings of Europe, were anointed by bishops or the pope in imitation of the Old Testament tradition of anointing the ruler. The Christian sacred replaced the pagan sacred of the ancient Germanic realms. Thus, in certain respects, *medieval European societies prolonged the pre-civic model of sacred kingships,* taking their legitimacy from representations of a mythical order, accrediting the idea of a divine election of the king and an intervention of sacred powers in the affairs of the realm, and finally reverting to magical practices (e.g., the miraculous healing powers of the French and English kings).

However, the religion of medieval monarchy was not that of Egypt or Mesopotamia; nor was it the religion of syncretic Roman paganism, which triumphed under the Low Empire. The religion of medieval monarchy was Christianity. Thus, the king and his faithful followers embodied the moral and political values of Judeo-Christian eschatology.

Therefore, medieval monarchy is profoundly ambiguous. It seems that it never managed to achieve a synthesis between the two strands of logic it was connected with. These strands merely coexisted side by side: the feelings and enthusiasm of the people never really coincided with the thinking of the church. Moreover, the magico-religious perception of kingship persisted among the masses for centuries, long after clerics, jurists, and university philosophers began to discover the authentic political ideas contained in the ancient texts which ultimately discredited the archaic model of kingship.

This is why the study of medieval monarchy, like feudalism, cannot be easily located on the historical timeline. The principle of royal consecration, the legends of the miracle of the Holy Ampulla, and the affirmation of the quasi-sacerdotal character of the king can be traced back to Carolingian times. As for the dynastic epics and the edifying speeches about the monarchical symbols (e.g., the fleur-de-lis, oriflamme), they date from no earlier than the twelfth century, when monarchies began to reappear after the long night of feudal fragmentation. Even the belief that scrofula could be healed by the sacred power of the "king's touch" dates to this period. As for the consecration ceremony proper, it was only elaborated by intellectuals at the court of Charles V in the fourteenth century.

A. Royal Consecration

Consecration rites are familiar to us through the documents known as the *ordines ad consecrandum regem*.[25] They were added to over time; likewise, the spoken words and physical gestures changed meaning from one age to the next. All the same, there was a certain consistency in the structure of the ceremony; it had three parts: *an oath, the anointment,* and *the coronation*.[26] The ritual begins with a prayer vigil. Alone in the cathedral, the king prays for a portion of the night.

---

[25] This section is based on the following works: *Le sacre des rois* [The consecration of the kings] (collective work) (Paris: Les Belles Lettres, 1985); Stéphane Rials, ed., *Le miracle capétien* [The Capetian miracle] (Paris: Librairie académique Perrin, 1987); Bloch, *The Royal Touch,* 262–74; Emmanuel Le Roy Ladurie, ed., *Les monarchies* [Monarchies] (Paris: Presses Universitaires de France, 1989); Charles Petit-Dutaillis, *La monarchie féodale en France et en Angleterre* [Feudal monarchy in France and England] (1933; repr., Paris: Albin Michel, 1971).

[26] In France, the ritual reached its maturity in the fourteenth century: the *ordo,* written for the consecration of Charles V in 1364, established the pattern for all future consecrations. The *Treatise on Consecration* (*Traité du sacre*) by Jean Golein, an intimate of the king, also dates from this period and established the meaning for the different elements of the consecration. The consecration of French kings took place, unless otherwise prevented, in Reims. The archbishop of Reims officiated at the ceremony. The tradition dated back to Saint Remi, bishop of Reims, who in 496 baptized the first

1. *Oaths*

On the morning of the first day of the ceremonies, the king *swears an oath.* The principle of an oath dates back to 869 and the consecration of Charles the Bald with the title of King of Lotharingia. Bishop Hincmar of Reims provides us with an idea of some of the words spoken by the participants on the occasion. The bishop said to all in attendance, "If this be your opinion, that after you have heard Charles, here present, speak the words, we shall show by a certain sign (*unction*) that he has been chosen and given to us by God." To this the king replied,

> Since the honorable bishops, speaking as one voice through one of theirs, have shown by their unanimity that God has chosen me to defend you and govern over you, know therefore that I will uphold the honor of God, his worship, and respect for his holy church, and I will cherish and honor each one of you according to his rank with all my knowledge and all my power, and I will keep the ecclesiastical and civil laws to which each of you holds; this being the condition for each of you to grant me respect and obedience, which I am due as your king.[27]

Before very long, the oath was divided into two promises, one to the church, the other to the realm.

- *The oath to the church:* "I promise and grant to each of you, and to the churches committed to your charge, that I will preserve the canonical privilege, law and justice due, and, God willing, I will defend you to the utmost of my powers, as a king is bound by the law of his kingdom to defend bishops and churches committed to his charge."[28]
- *The oath to the realm was then taken:* "In the name of Jesus Christ, I promise to the Christian people of my realm these things. First, that by our will all Christian people will find true peace in the Church of our Lord God. Item, that I will defend against all rapine and iniquity whatever the measure. Item, that I will be merciful and equitable in my judgments, so that our Lord God may grant me and you His mercy. I confirm all of the aforesaid things by oath."[29] The king's hands were then placed on the Bible.

2. *Anointment*

The act of anointing the body with holy oil (olive oil), an act called unction, was also part of the consecration ceremony. The Hebrews borrowed it from their Canaanite neighbors, though it is attested throughout the ancient Middle East and Egypt (and probably in other ancient societies as well).

---

king of France, Clovis. But, the rule stipulating that the king of France should be consecrated in Reims was established much later; it is attested only from the tenth century.

[27] Hincmar of Reims, quoted in Arquillière, *L'augustinisme politique,* 145.

[28] Passage quoted by Abbé Jean Goy, *À Reims: Le sacre des rois* (Roissy: N.p., 1980), 64. The Latin text is quoted by Jean de Viguerie: "Promitto vobis et perdono, quod unicuique de vobis et Ecclesiis vobis commissis Canonicum privilegium, et debitam legem atque iustitiam servabo, et defensionem (quantum potero, adiuvante Domino) exhibebo, sicut Rex in regno suo, unicuique Episcopo, et Ecclesiae sibi commissae, per rectum exhibere debet."

[29] "Haec populo Christiano, et mihi subdito, in Christi promitto nomine, in primis, ut ecclesiae Dei omnis populus christianus veram pacem nostro arbitrio in omni tempore servet.

"Item ut omnes rapacitates, et omnes iniquitates, omnibus gradibus interdicam.

"Item ut in omnibus iudiciis aequitatem, et misericordiam praecipiam ut mihi, et vobis indulgeat suam misericordiam clemens et misericors Deus" (ibid., 65).

An additional clause was added in 1215, whereby the king swore "to exterminate, in all lands subjected to my rule, the heretics declared to be so by the church" (this clause is important for the psychological insight it provides into Louis XIV's decision to revoke the Edict of Nantes). An additional clause, added for the consecration of Louis XV in 1722, called for the king to enforce the edicts relative to duels. Lastly, there was a clause in the *ordo* of Charles V exacting a promise from the king to preserve the crown estates in tact, but apparently it was never pronounced.

The last Hebrew king to be anointed was the king of Judah in 586 BC. After the Exile, unction acquired a spiritual significance more or less synonymous with divine election: for Ezekiel, all the "elect" [the holy remnant] were "anointed." As we saw, messianism ("messiah" means the "anointed" one, as we recall) is the doctrine of the election of one or a few and of the salvation for all people.

a. THE HOLY AMPULLA

The oil used at the consecration ceremony for the kings of France was not the pure olive oil used in Palestine; it was a scented oil perfumed with balsam, called *chrism;* it also contained a residue of the holy oil from the "Holy Ampulla."

Sometime in the ninth century, a legend originating with Hincmar was established. It asserted that on the day of the baptism of Clovis a dove descended from heaven with a vial of ointment, which it delivered to Saint Remi for the anointment of the king. The legend of a *chrism* provided by heaven gave the French monarchy extraordinary prestige everywhere in Christendom. The Holy Ampulla was preserved in Reims, in a tabernacle that sits in the Abbey of Saint Remi, built for the purpose (the abbey was bigger than the cathedral at the time). When the reliquary was taken to the cathedral for the royal consecration, the elders were locked in the abbey church of Saint Remi and became the "hostages of the Holy Ampulla."

b. THE ANOINTMENT RITUAL

After the swearing of oaths and the *Te Deum laudumus,* the king was literally disrobed and left standing at the altar in his long white shirt with special slitted openings. Everyone knelt and chanted long litanies:

> Lord, have mercy on us. Christ, have mercy on us. Lord, have mercy on us. Christ, hear us. Holy Mary, pray for us. Saint Michael, saint Gabriel, saint Raphael, All ye holy Angels... All ye holy Apostles... All ye holy Martyrs... All ye holy Bishops and Confessors... All ye holy Virgins... All ye holy Saints of God, make intercessions for us.[30] ... That you would give us peace, that keep us merciful and pious, that you would deign with clemency to instill in our hearts the grace of the Holy Spirit, that you would deign to direct and defend your Church, that you would deign to keep the Apostolic See and all the prelates in your holy service,... that you would deign lead your servant to the royal dignity.[31]

Then, the archbishop spoke three more prayers. Here is an example:

> Almighty God, who counsels thy people with virtue and governs them with love, grant thy servant wisdom with the rule of discipline. Grant that he, devoted to you with all his heart, may be a suitable ruler of the kingdom and, by your grace, protect the church.... Grant that in the days of his rule may be born fairness and justice for all, help for friends, obstacles for enemies, consolations for the afflicted, correction for the arrogant, learning for the rich, pity for the poor, pacification for the pilgrim, and peace and protection for the subjects of the realm.[32]

After these prayers the archbishop consecrated and anointed the king in six places: on the head, the breast, on both shoulders, front and back, on the arms at the joints and on the back

---

[30] These same litanies—systematic invocations of all the saints of Christendom by name or by category (in any case, several hundred invocations)—are still pronounced today at baptisms and at the ordination of priests.

[31] Goy, *À Rheims,* 70–72.

[32] Ibid., 74.

(sometimes on the hands as well). At each place he spoke these words: "I anoint you with this holy oil in the name of the Father, the Son, and the Holy Spirit," and those in attendance replied, "Amen." Meanwhile, an anthem was sung.[33]

Then the archbishop spoke again: "Lord God, anoint this king as ruler of this realm, as you anointed the priests, kings, prophets, and martyrs, who conquered realms, established justice, and gained promises. May your most sacred unction pour upon his head and, entering into him, penetrate the depths of his heart. And, by your grace, may he be made worthy of the promises gained by the most victorious kings, so that he may reign happily in this century and join their company in the heavenly kingdom."[34]

c. The Outpouring of the Holy Spirit on the King

In the Bible we read that a king, after receiving the anointment of his peers or a prophet, is "seized upon" by the "spirit of Yahweh" (*ruah*). There is no hiding the connection between this outpouring of the Holy Spirit and the "trance" of more archaic religions, as can be seen in the book of Samuel: "Then Samuel took a vial of oil, and poured *it* upon his [Saul's] head, and kissed him, and said, *Is it* not the Lord who hath anointed thee *to be* captain over his inheritance? *You are the man who is to govern Yahweh's people and save them from the power of the enemies surrounding them. The sign for you that Yahweh has anointed you as prince of his heritage is this:*[35] Thou shalt come to the hill of God... and meet a company of prophets coming down from the high place with a psaltery [lyre], and a tabret [tambourine], and a pipe, and a harp, before them; and they shall prophesy.[36] And the Spirit of the Lord will come upon thee, and thou shalt prophesy with them, and *shalt be turned into another man....* [From this day forward] God [will be] with thee" (1 Sam. 10:1, 5–7).

In the context of royal and messianic biblical theology, the anointed one knows that he has been changed and that everyone now looks on him as another person with new powers and gifts. As we saw, the outpouring of the spirit (*ruah*) of God upon the Messiah, the Anointed one, constitutes the reception of the "gifts of the spirit": wisdom, judgment, justice, concern for the meek, equity, and the desire for peace.

The Visigoth, Frankish, and other medieval kings inherited this mythology, as did the kings of France through the legend of the Holy Ampulla. They, too, were said to receive the "gifts of the Holy Spirit" through the action of anointment. They were transformed into saints of a sort and suffused with Christian virtues: faith, mercy, heroism, and the spirit of peace.

The consecration rites predestine the king to become a new Christ, to imitate Christ. He is convinced that this is the fundamental condition for receiving the immense powers of a king. His duty is to defend the church, to promote peace and justice, and to ensure the triumph of equity and mercy (see the text of his oath to the people).

There is no other sanction than divine sanction, which is imagined as potentially awesome. The king cannot escape his responsibility as monarch, which is a great honor, but which also represents a risky and perilous commitment: the everlasting fate of his soul. There is no doubt that the kings of France consecrated in Reims were for the most part deeply religious and performed the sacrament in the proper mental attitude with the utmost sincerity, aware that they had been destined to it since youth. At a time when virtually everybody believed that even the most ordinary sacrament was efficacious *ex opere operato,* a sacrament as exceptional as consecration, bathing

[33] The queen was also anointed. In certain periods, the queen's ceremony was performed separately in the basilica at Saint-Denis (near Paris).

[34] Goy, *À Rheims,* 76–77.

[35] *Translator's note:* The verse in italics is not found in the Revised Standard Version of the Bible; it figures in the Catholic version. We quote here from the Jerusalem Bible.

[36] They will be in a state of ecstasy.

in amazing pomp and ceremony and the transports of enthusiasm of the people, necessarily left the deepest impression on its beneficiary. Each consecrated king virtually became a Saint Louis.

d. The Internal Transformation of the King

The transformation of the consecrated king is emphasized by certain particulars of the rite itself. During the prayer vigil on the eve of the consecration ceremony, the king spoke a prayer asking to be stripped of his old self. The next morning, the bishops of Beauvais and Laon arrived at the Palace of Tau[37] to "wake the king from sleep," as if the elect in being awakened would take on a new self. And the disrobing of the king in the cathedral made clear that he had left behind his former self as a mere layperson: "he abandons the worldly condition . . . to take up that of the royal religion."[38]

A new king of France was almost always a young man, and sometimes a child or an adolescent. In the consecration ceremonies there is an echo of the *extraordinary return of the Golden Age,* announced by Virgil's Fourth Eclogue. There are also elements of Dio Chrysostom's *Discourses on Kingship.* But it is above all a response to the "magical" expectations of the uneducated masses of traditional societies.

3. *Other Aspects of the Rites*

a. Royal robes and regalia

Without acknowledging the growing reservations of the church, the rite retained signs that the king not only changed personality after his anointment, but also acquired a *sacerdotal function:* he was robed (immediately after being anointed) with the tunic of a subdeacon, the dalmatic of a deacon, and the chasuble of a priest.

The "emblems of royalty" or *regalia,* blessed at various moments during the ceremony, also had great symbolic significance: spurs, sword, scepter, the *main de justice* (topped with a carved hand of benediction, shorter than the scepter), crown, and royal ring.

The *royal ring,* for example, is the symbol of the mystical union of the king and the realm (it seems to allude to biblical marriage symbolism). The *sceptre* is the sign of divine power descended from heaven. The *main de justice* symbolizes the *justice* that the king must dispense. When the archbishop hands the king the *sword,* he speaks these words: "Take this sword with the blessing of God and use it by the virtue of the Holy Spirit to resist and repel the enemies of the holy Church. Defend the realm committed to your charge, and keep the army of God with the help of our Lord Jesus Christ, invincible conqueror, who reigns with the Father, etc."

b. Coronation

After 816 a *coronation ritual* was associated with the act of anointment. The 12 peers of France (that is to say, the most important vassals of the land) held the crown above the head of the king as a prayer was spoken. Then the archbishop placed the crown on the king's head.

c. Enthronement

Finally, the king was led to the throne and seated on it: this was the act of enthronement, as such. After removing his miter, the archbishop gave the king a kiss and declared, "May the king live forever." Then the peers, laypeople, and church leaders stepped up to the throne and each in turn lifted the crown from the king's head and spoke the same words.

---

[37] *Translator's note:* The residence of the kings of France in Reims before their consecration.

[38] Jean Golein, quoted in Bloch, *The Royal Touch,* 275.

Lastly, the mass for the day was celebrated. After the celebration of the mass, the shirt worn by the king for the ceremony of anointment was burned. The king left the cathedral for the palace, preceded by a great lord of the realm bearing the naked royal sword. The Holy Ampulla was returned to its sanctuary.

4. *The Effects of Consecration*

The effects of the consecration are many and lasting.

a. Sealing the Choice of a King

First, consecration *seals the official choice* of a king over the possible rivals and claimants. Although Pepin the Short did not belong to royalty, consecration alone made him a king. After Pepin, and for as long as the heredity principle was not fully accepted under the Frankish dynasty,[39] consecration continued to be the important event that "made the king." This was the case even more so when election was the usual method for designating the king (885–987).

It took a long time for the idea to disappear. Even after heredity made its way into the customs of the French kingdom, Joan of Arc held that it was an insufficient condition. In her opinion, what transformed the "gentle Dauphin" (Charles VII) into a true king was his consecration in 1429. Just two years later, in 1431, the king of England, Henry VI, was consecrated king of France at Notre Dame de Paris; the ceremony was performed with greater solemnity than Charles VII's consecration in Reims two years before. Yet Henry's consecration in Paris failed to establish his authority.

The closer we come to modern times, the more the heredity principle becomes the norm.[40] In the sixteenth century, Jean Bodin admitted in his theory of sovereignty that he had slight regard for consecration: "The king does not cease to be king in the absence of coronation or consecration."

b. The Consecrated Nature of the King's Person

For those who believed in the significance and values of royal consecration, the institution retained its extraordinary ideological importance throughout the Enlightenment Age and well into the nineteenth century. It confirmed that the king and the dynasty were established by God, and not by man.

Augustine wrote, "For we can rightly call christs all those who are anointed with His chrism" (*City of God* 17.4). The king is the image of God on earth, a "God on earth" (Terremerveille, early fifteenth century), a "king-priest" (Chancellor Aguesseau, seventeenth century), a "bishop outside the church" (judgment of the King's Council, 1766). In the end, consecration placed royal authority beyond human challenge.

Furthermore, consecration protected the king's person. After the kings of Israel were anointed, they were considered "sacred": it was a sacrilege to raise one's hand against them.[41] When David held Saul at his mercy in the cave in the wilderness of Engedi, his heart pounded at the mere thought that he had cut off Saul's skirt: "He said to his men, 'The Lord forbid that I should do this thing to my lord, the Lord's anointed, to put forth my hand against him, seeing he is the Lord's anointed.'" So David persuaded his men with these words, and did not permit them to attack Saul (1 Sam. 24:6–7; see also 2 Sam. 1:14).

---

[39] For the Franks, the key principle of choice was the lineage—or line of descent—rather than the particular individual. The dynastic line was invested with the magical powers required to exercise royal power; the particular holder of the royal office was chosen for his personal qualities, and notably his warring skills.

[40] For the evolution of the succession laws, see below, pp. 579–80.

[41] This was truly an archaic, magical mark. The plebeian tribune in pagan Rome was similarly sacrosanct.

The king of France was also sacrosanct, which is why horrible punishments were inflicted on regicides (e.g., Ravaillac), and why the members of the Convention, responsible for deciding the execution of Louis XVI, had such diabolical reputations well into the nineteenth century.

c. Royal Consecration and Church Sacraments

But is the royal consecration a sacrament? It was at the time of Pepin and Charlemagne, but with the Papal Revolution (see chapter 4 below) and the increasingly strict separation of the priesthood and laity, the church sought to limit the sacramental nature of the royal consecration: this was its way of safeguarding its own authority against claims by kings for a Byzantine style of Caesaropapism.

When in the thirteenth century the sacraments were officially codified and a list of seven official sacraments was drawn up, royal consecration was not among them. Therefore, it was not a sacrament in the proper sense, but rather a "sacramental," that is, a simple yet subtle sign bestowed by the church with certain spiritual consequences. Moreover, anointment with the holy chrism was extended to the ordination of bishops and to baptism. In the eyes of the church, the king was at best a subdeacon; in some chapters (e.g., Saint Martin of Tours), the king held the low rank of canon. He had access to the chancel and to the altar, and he could take communion under both species, but he could not touch the host. He was, in sum, of little significance in the eyes of the church. But, in the eyes of the people, the matter was very different.

d. The Miraculous Healing Powers of the King: Healing Scrofula

Among the corollaries of consecration there is one especially important to the population; it is one of the most archaic features of the institution itself: the king's sacred power to heal certain diseases, scrofula in particular. This power was claimed rather late by the kings of France (in the eleventh century), and later still by the kings of England. It is a miraculous power acquired the day after consecration.

If we look more closely into medieval anthropology, we discover that this power was not the exclusive right of kings, though it took spectacular forms at the French and English courts. The Middle Ages, and especially the Early Middle Ages, were awash in magic. Relics had special healing powers; they were fought over and seized for the income they brought to the places—churches, monasteries—where they were kept. It was said of Saint Louis that he performed more miracles after his death by his relics than during his lifetime with his "official" healing powers. In fact, virtually all the great figures of society had sacred and miraculous healing powers; they were all "wizards." However, the problem for the church was that many of the figures it branded as heretics, such as the sect of the Flagellants, the Taborites, the Brothers of the Free Spirit, had immense healing powers in the mind of the people. The king could hardly accept to have less.

B. The Emblems of the French Monarchy

Sacred monarchy, which does not claim to be a scientific political doctrine, spontaneously uses many other emblems, in addition to those of consecration, with a powerful effect on the hearts and minds of the people of the age.[42] We know that many of these emblems date back to times prior to the Christian age. In other words, ancient pagan symbols became Christianized through a series of transformations.

[42] In this section we follow Hervé Pinoteau, "Armes de France et symboles capétiens" [Arms of France and Capetian emblems], in Rials, *Le miracle capétien* [The Capetian miracle]; Anne Lombard-Jourdan, *Fleurs de lis et oriflamme: Signes célestes du royaume de France* [Fleur-de-lis and Oriflamme: Heavenly signs of the kingdom of France] (Paris: Presses du CNRS, 1991).

Anne Lombard-Jourdan points out that political power and sacerdotal power are helpless in creating effective symbols. Owing to their great antiquity, symbols are rooted in deep emotions, providing powerful cohesion to the people of a community. Successive authorities can only adopt these symbols, which have already acquired great religious strength. Conversely, contemporaries can contribute to changing their interpretation.

Thus, the Christian kings of France could do very little to eliminate Celtic or Germanic symbols, nor could they impose biblical or Christian symbols in their place, if such symbols had not already triggered deep emotions in the psyche of the people. But, from the moment that the Christian monarchy began to assert itself against feudalism and to demonstrate a need to rally the people in its favor, the kings were able to change the meaning and material appearance of certain highly venerated symbols: a *solar sign* becomes the *fleur-de-lis;* a "talisman" became the *oriflamme of Saint Denis.*

a. The Fleur-de-lis

We find on ancient Merovingian coins an emblem that symbolizes the rising sun and the growth of life and fertility, specifically that of the royal family. The unshorn hair of the Merovingian kings, parted in two, apparently also suggests these symbols and their esoteric meaning.

Perhaps the emblem also replicates the Celtic sign that was the probable source of Constantine's famous Chi Rho Cross: the miraculous sign that handed him victory at the Battle of the Milvian Bridge in 312, resulting in his conversion to Christianity. Constantine, of course, had spent time in Gaul and Brittany before these events, as we know (see p. <X-REF>).

In the twelfth century, during the reign of Louis VI and Louis VII, when Suger was abbot of Saint-Denis, a new royal emblem appeared: the *fleur-de-lis.* Its shape appeared to have evolved from an ancient Gallic symbol. Set on a blue background, the golden fleur-de-lis was affixed to crests and military banners as well as to royal vestments. The writings of the time invented new meanings for the emblem: for Saint Bernard, the cerulean blue—the color of the material heaven—and the fleur-de-lis—strewn like stars across the heavens—symbolize the heavenly abode and the saints who live there. The white of the *lis* is the symbol of purity. The three lobes of the lily are a Trinitarian symbol (this hermeneutic was reinforced deliberately at the end of the fourteenth century when the fleur-de-lis started to be grouped in clusters of three).

The new floral symbolism of the French kings broke radically with the older symbolism of the emperors, kings of England, and other lords of the time, who in an expression of their physical strength and military might used figures of wild beasts (lions, bears, eagles) or representations of weapons (swords, axes) on their coat of arms. The king of France, a messianic prince, was a peacemaker, which was expressed in his floral symbolism.[43]

b. The oriflamme of Saint Denis

Another emblem was the red *oriflamme of Saint Denis* called the "Montjoie." It was taken on military campaigns and unfurled as a sign of "war without mercy" along with the battle cry, "Montjoie Saint Denis"! Thus, it was a "talisman."[44] Usage of the oriflamme is attested only rather late, as is its Christian interpretation: red is the blood of Christian martyrs.

Again, according to Anne Lombard-Jourdan, the roots of the symbol can be traced back to the ancient Celtic and Germanic past of Gaul. First, she says, the magico-religious value of Saint

[43] Capetian princes other than the kings of France—French noblemen, foreign sovereigns like the kings of Naples and Spain—preserved the fleurs-de-lis on their coats of arms because of the prestige of the symbol.

[44] It was brandished at the battle of Agincourt in 1415 for the last time, then permanently stored at the Abbey of Saint-Denis.

Denis is attributable to the fact that the holy martyr's tomb was erected on the site of a pan-Celtic sanctuary (the "plain of Saint-Denis" just north of Paris).[45] This was the famous "omphalos of the Gauls"—a consecrated burial place—about which Caesar wrote in his *Gallic Wars* (*De bello gallico* 6.13.10). The tumulus of Teutates, the ancestor of the Gauls, was located there. The Romans associated the god-father Teutates with Jupiter.

Then, Lombard-Jourdan continues, the word "Montjoie" in the battle cry apparently has no connection whatsoever with either a hillock (*mont*) or joy (*joie*); its origin was Germanic and came from the word *mundgawi,* protector of the land;[46] when Germanic tribes arrived in the land, they attributed this name to Teutates. Finally, as for the oriflamme, a cloth banner tied to the end of a lance, Lombard-Jourdan traces its origins to the ancient Gallic *labarum,* a weapon with amazing powers, which the druids kept in the same holy place on the plain of Saint-Denis. They passed on a replica to Constantine, who used it to win a victory for himself and his armies of Gaulish warriors. An equivalent of this talisman was found in other Celtic regions (e.g., Ireland). The cloth fabric attached to the end of the lance was painted so as to symbolize a dragon, the purpose of which was to terrorize the enemy.

Later, the same weapon reappeared in Germany in the arsenal of kings and emperors: it is the same German imperial lance described by Liutprand of Cremona in the tenth century. In France the first mention of the oriflamme being used as a magical weapon (lance or "Holy Nail") dates from the Song of Roland in the eleventh century. There is no use recorded before 1124, though it was said to be in use at the time of Charlemagne. According to Suger, Louis VI had the weapon brought from Saint-Denis and unfurled at the head of his army, which was assembled to resist the invasion of Emperor Henry V. The word "oriflamme" means "golden flame";[47] the fluttering part of the fabric is cut in tongues or "flames." There are later references to the Holy Lance in France, in the German Empire, and in Burgundy, Poland, and Hungary.[48]

These royal emblems, even more than the consecration rites, take us back to the magico-religious time of prestate societies. However, while the royal entourage finalized the rituals and activated (half-sincerely, half-manipulatively) the different emblems of power, other thinkers were exploring the more rational ideas of antiquity to find arguments on which to base the authority of the king and the state more solidly.

---

[45] Very little is known about Saint Denis. He was probably the first bishop of Paris, martyred in 250. At the beginning of the ninth century, thanks to Hilduin, abbot of Saint-Denis, his identity was cleverly combined with that of Dionysius the Areopagite, a figure referred to in the Acts of the Apostles (Acts 17:34) as the only Athenian who believed Paul after his sermon on the Areopagus hill. Dionysius the Areopagite was held in high esteem during the Middle Ages; he was thought to have authored many important theological and mystical works (*On the Divine Names, On the Celestial Hierarchy, On the Ecclesiastical Hierarchy*); today these works are attributed to a Syriac monk of the sixth or seventh century.

[46] We recognize the word *mund,* the root of *mundium* and *mainbour* (protection), discussed earlier in the context of Germanic customs and the vassalage contract.

[47] In French, *or* means gold.

[48] On all of this, see the riveting essay by Lombard-Jourdan, *Fleurs de lis et oriflamme,* 131.

Chapter 4

The High Middle Ages (Eleventh to Thirteenth Centuries): The Papal Revolution

By the second third of the eleventh century, feudalism had triumphed everywhere, albeit to varying degrees and with significant regional differences. Loyalty to the feudal lord outweighed loyalty to the kingdom and the importance of the law. In addition, spiritual and temporal powers had become deeply entwined. But, in a matter of decades, various developments would transform the situation.

The church was revitalized and grew stronger under the leadership of inspired popes, who changed it into an institution outside civil society, capable of pursuing independent projects. Since the church included among its number the only learned men of the age, it was the church that led a reflourishing of classical culture—Greek philosophy, public and private Roman law, the Bible, and patristics. This powerful church, led with a firm hand from Rome, with its new institutions—ecumenical councils, mendicant orders, universities—became a virtual counter-power to feudalism.

Moreover, new secular powers—local communities and national kingdoms, partially under the influence of the church—also rose up against feudalism. The joint and antagonistic efforts of these two players—church authority and secular power—resulted in a true synthesis of biblical elements and Greco-Roman culture.

During the Early Middle Ages, Christians continued to live in a pagan world without any true synthesis between the Christian and classical worlds. They aspired to make their way to heaven without changing the world. Held to be deeply sinful and doomed to an early destruction, the world was abandoned to paganism. This is why the most highly prized lifestyle was that of the monk, who avoided engaging with the world by living apart in a monastery, preparing for everlasting salvation through prayer and contemplation. On the hierarchy of "orders" (*ordines*), in which society in the Early Middle Ages was divided, monks occupied the top place.

Now popes and kings were committed to *building a Christian world.* They turned to the legal techniques inherited from Greco-Roman antiquity as a tool to transform this world prophetically and to bring it closer to its eschatological goal, to make it less sinful, more just, and more peaceful. This is why the rediscovery of Roman law and Greek philosophy did not lead to a simple "renaissance" of ancient civicism but resulted in the emergence of a new civilization: the civilization of the West.

We begin our discussion with a historical overview of these developments: first the reform of the church, then the growth of secular powers, and finally their struggle together (section I, "Historical Overview").

Next we turn our attention to the ideological aspects of the "Papal Revolution": the doctrine of papal "plenitude of power," the formation of a new canon law after intense doctrinal debate combining Christian elements and legal techniques from Justinian's Roman law. We will see how these efforts led to a Christianization of the law and a juridicization of Christian morals (section II, "Ideological Aspects of the Papal Revolution"). Then we will discuss the doctrinal terms in which the antagonism between spiritual and temporal powers came to be formulated (section III, "The Doctrine of the Two Swords"). Finally, we will discuss the "constitutional" law that emerged from the semihostile, partially cordial confrontation between these two powers, keen to establish the limits of their own respective spheres. We will see that they did agree on one point: that a sovereign power, standing above all feudal powers, is entitled to enact the law (section IV, "The Right to Make Laws").

I. Historical Overview

A. Reform and Culmination of the Church

1. *The Crisis of the Church in the Eleventh Century*

By the end of the Early Middle Ages, the church and religious life in general were in deep crisis.[1] The growth of feudalism occurred at the expense of the church's independence. In Germania, the emperor controlled the bishops and the popes. In western France, the lay clergy and the monasteries gradually came into secular hands; the heads of principalities and castellanies took control of church matters. The result was a regression of Christianity.

In a Europe that had undergone an authoritarian, even violent conversion, at any rate beyond the Roman *limes,* the church was weak. When the state declined and feudalism spread, it was almost inevitable that religious disorder would break out.

As soon as Charlemagne's empire collapsed, prestate customs (such as blood feuds, private wars, witchcraft, polygamy) roared back to life. Even the former Roman and Christian territories were affected. The church purchased its survival only at the cost of compromising and coexisting with this very archaic society.

The crisis had three main aspects: (1) a *secular hold on ecclesiastical investitures* at all levels, from village parish to the papacy itself; (2) *simony,* the taking of payment to obtain holy office or a position in the church hierarchy, became progressively widespread; and (3) *nicolaism,* which means priestly marriage (clerogamy) and, more generally, licentious living, and living in concubinage.

[1] This section is based on Chelini, *Histoire religieuse de l'Occident médiéval,* and Gaudemet, *Eglise et cité.*

2. *The Reform of Cluny*

Individual bishops had tried to react to these problems, but their efforts were in vain. The only significant attempt before the Gregorian reform was the reform of Cluny.

The Benedictine abbey at Cluny, in Burgundy, was founded in 909 by William the Pious, Duke of Aquitaine. In 932, Pope John XI granted the abbey a privilege of exemption, that is, a release from diocesan and lay authority (in other words, from the authority of kings, bishops, counts, and even relatives of Duke William). Cluny came under the direct authority of Rome. This gave it immense prestige and enabled it to establish a widespread network of monasteries with similar aspirations of independence. The order developed quickly and powerfully under the rule of only six abbots over two centuries (909–1109).[2] Cluny reformed many great monasteries (such as Fleury, Charlieu, Ganagobie, Vezelay) and created new ones for which huge donations were received. Hugh of Semur, successor to the abbot Hugh, erected the great abbatial cathedral, which was the largest church in Christendom until its destruction in the early nineteenth century.

By 1200, the order held authority over some 1,450 establishments: 850 in France, the others principally in Germany, England, Italy, and Spain. At the time of Hugh, the mother abbey alone numbered some 400 monks. Former Clunisian monks became bishops, legates, and pontifical dignitaries; two became pope (Urban II, Paschal II). The abbots of Cluny traveled widely and played a prominent role throughout Christendom.

Finally, Cluny played a leading role in achieving the Peace of God (*Treuga Dei*), by which the church hoped to end the incessant private wars destablizing the world (see below). All of these characteristics made Cluny a model for what could be a clergy truly autonomous from the secular authorities.

3. *Papal Reform before Gregory VII*

What is conventionally called the "Gregorian reform" began in the middle of the eleventh century, in other words, before the pontificate of Gregory VII (1073–85), who gave it his name. The reform continued until the 1120s. It was led by fervent men—popes, legates—with the help of learned doctors whose writings explained and justified in theological terms the decisions of the church leaders.

Four major figures standout during the reform: Frederick of Lorrain, chancellor of the Holy See, abbot of Monte Cassino, and pope (in 1057) under the name of Stephen IX; Humbert of Moyenmoutier, the cardinal-bishop of Silva Candida from 1057, the central figure in Pope Nicholas II's entourage; Saint Peter Damian, cardinal-bishop of Ostia from 1058; and finally Hildebrand, the future Pope Gregory VII.

The reformers pursued the implementation of the following principles:

- the free election of bishops by the clergy and the people;
- the ecclesiastical appointment of minor clerics to office by the elimination of secular *dominium* over local churches;
- the election of the pope by a college of cardinals;
- the restitution of estates and tithes to churches;
- the initiation of a moral and administrative reform of the church;
- the firm and irrevocable imposition of celibacy on monks and priests from the subdiaconate on up;
- the establishment of an autonomous government of the church, a blend of monarchy and collegiality.

[2] Bernon, Odon, Aymard, Maiolus, Odilon (abbot from 994 to 1049), and Hugh (abbot from 1049 to 1109).

The rallying cry of the reform was *libertas Ecclesiæ*—the full independence of the church from temporal power, under the exclusive leadership of the Roman See.

Three facts, illustrative of this frame of mind, can be identified before Gregory VII's personal involvement in the reform:

1. The papacy encouraged a popular revolt against the clergy in Milan and Lombardy, said to be corrupted by wealth and living in concubinage. If we consider that this movement, known as the *Pataria*, presaged a revolt of the poor, who rose up and threatened the clergy and the papacy (see below, chapter 7), and the fact that the papacy and especially Hildebrand, the pontiff's legate in Milan, encouraged the movement, we recognize the extent to which the church was animated by a genuine "revolutionary" spirit. Ultimately, one of the leaders of the *Pataria* became pope (Alexander II) and led the fight against attempts by Emperor Henry IV to put down the reform movement.

2. The papacy engineered its own independence with the papal decree of 1059 instituting the election of the pope by the "cardinals" (i.e., the principal Roman leaders of the church, from Rome and the surrounding region); the clergy and the people of Rome approved this decision by acclamation. Henceforth, the emperor's only role was the confirmation of the pope's election. The final formal procedure of papal election was adopted at the Third Lateran Council (1179), which decreed that the pope had to be elected by at least two-thirds of the cardinals.

3. The papacy multiplied *synods* or *councils* which enacted the various points of the above program in succession; they also imposed severe punishments if they were not adhered to strictly; for example, married priests and priests living in concubinage were forbidden from attending Mass.

4. *The Action of Gregory VII*

In 1074, following his accession to the papacy, Hildebrand decreed the deposition of simoniacs and Nicholaites through a synod in Rome. Papal legates, dispatched throughout Christendom to supervise the application of the papal decree, were not well received. In France, a synod decreed that the law on celibacy was contrary to reason and natural law. In northern Italy the episcopate simply ignored the decree. In Germany, the measures provoked a "struggle for power between the Papacy and the Holy Roman Empire" (see below). Everywhere temporal power defended *simoniacal* and *Nicolaite* clergy.

Gregory concluded that he would not be successful in his internal reform of the church until he first resolved the issue of the church's independence, in other words, until the elimination of lay investitures. Consequently, in 1075, he adopted two new measures: (1) In a famous text of major doctrinal importance, the *Dictatus papæ* (to be discussed below), he asserted the primacy of spiritual power and the primacy of the Roman See. (2) He obtained, from a Roman synod held in 1075, an absolute and general ban on *lay investitures*. "No cleric shall receive a church from the hands of a layperson, either gratis or against payment, on pain of excommunication for the giver and the taker of such a benefit."

This time his decrees began to produce results. They were adopted without resistance in the Spain of the *Reconquista*. In the Normandy and England of William the Conqueror, the prince appointed bishops and abbots of great worth, which the papacy greeted with approval (the rivalry between spiritual and temporal powers in England only erupted much later). In France the papacy faced a serious challenge with the Capetian kings, notably Philip I; a large portion of his income came from simony. But an energetic papal legate, Hugh of Die, succeeded in imposing the reform and purged the episcopate, using as his weapon the threat of popular revolt against corrupt clergy: the terrifying example of violence during the *Pataria* bore its fruit. In all these countries, doctrinal solutions to the various problems posed by the papal Reform, such as the investiture controversy, simony, and Nicholaism, were found and implemented.

The primary cause of the investiture controversy resided in the fact that, in the feudal system, the bishop was a temporal lord at the same time that he was invested with spiritual duties. For his temporal lordship he was dependent on a temporal superior, who gave him his "investiture" (see above, p. 494). The doctrinal solution was not found in a single stroke. Guido of Ferrara distinguished between the "lay" and "spiritual" aspects of the episcopal function; basing his argument on forgeries regrettably dating from the early eleventh century, he continued to accept that a secular lord could appoint a bishop. In France, Saint Ivo of Chartres and Hugh of Fleury[3] drew a sharp distinction between the archbishop's granting of ecclesiastical *jurisdictio* (with the symbols of the crosier and ring) and the "investiture of temporal things" by the secular seigneur. In England, Lanfranc and Saint Anselm[4] adopted similar positions: there was to be no investiture by laypersons with the symbols of the crosier and the ring, but the bishop must swear an oath of fealty for his fiefs. In time, these solutions were widely accepted.

Simony was treated as a heresy (Cardinal Humbert wrote a treatise with the title *Adversus simoniacos*), which made it possible to nullify investitures tainted with simony. As for Nicolaism, doctrinally, priests were forbidden to enter into marriage and common law arrangements (Peter Damian, *De celibatu sacerdotum*). Virginity was proclaimed to be spiritually superior to the state of marriage, as was also the necessity, in the name of the "freedom of the church," to protect church properties from the inheritance claims of women and children.

Thereafter, for centuries (until the Lutheran Reform, later still for Catholic nations) the clergy *lived sociologically apart from civil society,* by virtue of its ecclesiastical celibacy. This revealed dramatically (and, in practice, strengthened) the idea of a separate "spiritual power" with a special historical, social, intellectual, and moral purpose. It also pointed to the opposite side of the coin, namely that temporal power had no equivalent spiritual mission; *for the first time since the Roman Empire, political power was stripped of its sacred powers, and was, in essence, desacralized.*[5]

For a long time, the church reform, set in motion by the papacy in the eleventh century, continued to create resistance from secular, seigneurial, and royal powers across Europe; in particular, there was a lively controversy with the Holy Roman Empire of the German Nation. Generally speaking, however, the reform was a success. This can be seen at several levels: the monastic movement was revived; the universal mendicant orders (Franciscans and Dominicans) were created under Rome's direct oversight; the struggle against heresies was pursued. Ecumenical councils, convened by the popes, pursued the work of organizing Christendom; universities were founded; "Roman canon" law was created; and western Europe was strengthened geopolitically by the Spanish *Reconquista,* the Crusades in the Orient, and the *Drang nach Osten* of the Germans (i.e., population migrations toward northeast Europe). Within Europe itself, feudal brigandage was neutralized with the ideal of chivalry. Finally, owing to the papal monarch's example, the modern idea of a state with law-making and administrative powers dawned.[6]

---

3 Chartres was the seat of an important episcopal school; Fleury was an abbey near Orleans under the special protection of the Capetian dynasty (see below, p. 597).

4 Both were former abbots of the Abbey of Bec in Normandy, and both subsequently were appointed archbishop of Canterbury by William the Conqueror.

5 At the time, this idea was held only by intellectuals; for a long time, the people continued to believe in the sacred power of kings created and manifested by anointment (see the previous chapter). Increasingly, the popes denied royalty a sacred function, thereby making a contribution—perhaps more than intended—to the process of state secularization.

6 On these various points, see Chelini, *Histoire religieuse;* J.-M. Mayeur, Ch. and L. Pietri, A. Vauchez, M. Venard, eds., *Histoire du christianisme* [A history of Christianity], vol 5, *Apogée de la papauté et expansion de la chrétienté* [Apogee of the papacy and the spread of Christianity] (1054–1274) (Paris: Desclée Fayard, 1990). On the revival of monasticism

B. Communes and States Claw Back Gains from Feudalism

While the church prepared to carry out this work, another type of institution, namely, *communes* and *kingdoms*, began to whittle away at feudalism and gradually contributed to its decline.

1. *Communal Movement*

The communal movement took place in towns, which experienced exceptional growth between the eleventh and thirteenth centuries, due in large part to the very considerable expansion of trade throughout the period. As a purely political phenomenon, it originated in the peace movements.

a. The Peace Movements

Feudal society at the end of the Early Middle Ages was a world of permanent insecurity for people and property.[7] Pillaging warlords, which no state power could restrain, looted shamelessly and made life impossible for their neighbors. *Blood feuds—vendettas*—had become widespread again. Under the influence of the church, communities began to react to put an end to this violence, swearing truces for agreed-upon periods of time—a few days a week—and specified places.

Synods of bishops in the southwest of France, one of the regions most harshly affected by these disorders, were apparently the origin of these "peace movements" (the council of Charroux in 990, the council of St. Paulien in 990–94). The solution spread widely and rapidly, with the Order of Cluny playing a pivotal role.

b. The Oath Establishing the "Commune"

In towns, adhering to the logic of the peace movements, the diocesan peace associations, or groups of neighborhoods and professions (societies, charities, guilds), accustomed their members to the idea of mutual aid. The "communal movement" arose from this effort to obtain from all the inhabitants of the town (not just a few associations) the formal swearing of an oath of mutual peace and protection.

Thus, a "bourgeois" elite was the true instigator of these peace movements. It cleverly exploited the political vacuum prevailing in towns at the end of the feudal age: neither the squires, living in their castles far from the centers of urban life, nor the bishops, discredited by their participation in the feudal system, could achieve order and justice in the towns and communes.

c. Charters

Once a commune was formed, it needed a charter of population and franchise from the local lord, whether he was secular or ecclesiastical; the charter enabled the commune to preserve its customs, to appoint magistrates, to administer justice, and to create an armed militia for purposes of internal and external order.

---

and the founding of the mendicant orders, see, among others, Marcel Pacaut, *Les ordres monastiques et religieux au Moyen Age* [Monastic and religious orders in the Middle Ages] (Paris: Nathan Université, 1993); on universities, see Jacques Le Goff, *Les intellectuels au Moyen Age* (London: Wiley-Blackwell, 1993); translated as *Intellectuals in the Middle Ages* (Paris: Éditions du Seuil, 1985]; Marie-Dominique Chenu, *Introduction à l'étude de saint Thomas d'Aquin* [An introduction to the study of St. Thomas Aquinas] (Paris: Vrin, 1974); Léo Moulin, *La vie des étudiants au Moyen Age* [Student life in the Middle Ages] (Paris: Albin Michel, 1991).

[7] On the peace movements, see Dominique Barthélémy, *Nouvelle histoire de la France médiévale* [A new history of medieval France], vol. 3, *L'ordre seigneurial, XI–XII siècles* (Paris: Éditions du Seuil, 1990), 57 and following. This book represents the most recent scholarship on the topic and challenges many received ideas on feudalism. Simultaneously, it reveals that our knowledge and understanding of the period remain still patchy.

Feudal lords and kings often granted such franchises, realizing that they could wring more financial resources and military backing from a well-organized, peaceful community, where trade thrived and taxes could be collected. Many joined the pact and gave their warrant; others resisted. Local differences were numerous.

By the end of the thirteenth century, these communes began to regress, and kings soon took charge, exploiting the financial difficulties of the communes. Furthermore, the institution of a strong state responded to the need for peace better than a purely local arrangement by an association. As for economic privileges, they now profited an oligarchy, against whom it was easy to incite the poor and common people. In moments of serious urban crisis, when these classes were openly in conflict with one another, the king was called upon to mediate; in Italy, the call was made to a *podestà,* then captains, who in time became absolutist princes (see, for example, the Visconti and the Sforza in Milan).

2. *Monarchic Renaissance*

Thus, in the twelfth and thirteenth centuries, the monarchic state began to assert itself. It had never entirely disappeared, partly because of the consecration accorded to kings by the church[8] and the memory of states in antiquity preserved by clerics and the royal entourage. But now, the reform of the papacy and the model it gave of a centralized monarchy, on the one hand, and a deliberate policy of the kings on the other, enabled monarchies to assert themselves.

In the Empire, the policy of the Hohenstaufen failed as a consequence of their conflict with the papacy (see below), and the country collapsed into a myriad of principalities and autonomous towns. Yet the overall picture was not so bad: the emperors proclaimed a "peace of the Empire" with real results.

In Italy, a strong monarchic power was not possible because the country was divided between two powers, the papacy and the Empire; for various reasons neither could gain the upper hand in the territory, nor could it enable a local royal power to emerge.

It was particularly in England and in France that a monarchic state was able to re-emerge. As a consequence of the Norman Conquest in 1066, the kings of England were in a strong position compared with principalities. They had inherited centralized power from the former Anglo-Saxon kings and had created a highly structured form of feudalism with, in principle, all power in the king's hands. Henry II (1154–89) asserted his royal prerogative strongly. However, his successors, either absent (Richard the Lionheart) or weak (John "Lackland"), faced a revolt of the barons, resulting in the Magna Carta (1215), followed by the Provisions of Oxford (1258). These measures put severe restrictions on royal prerogative.

In France, the Capetian kings cleverly used the feudal system against the feudals themselves (by returning to the original idea of the Carolingians). They set themselves up as supreme sovereigns and created a "feudal monarchy"; their methods included thorough investigations into the performance of their vassals; the generalization of liege homage to their rear-vassals; intervention in the transmission of large fiefs to heirs; extension of the appellate procedure to the royal judiciary; enactment of general ordinances with the consent of barons; and, lastly, the assertion of the principle that the "king is emperor in his realm"; that is, he is vassal to no one (see below, pp. 590–91). Saint Louis succeeded in prohibiting private wars and the possession of weapons. The Capetians took full custody of the realm.

With the revival of Roman law taught in universities, a new conception of political authority came to the fore. Scholars presented authority as inalienable and indivisible, abstract and

[8] The religious prestige of the monarch was likewise augmented by the canonization of certain kings (Stephen, Wenceslaus, Louis IX, and others).

independent of the holder, and legitimate by its general utility. It was in the name of this general utility, and not in his own name, that the king made laws or repealed them.

Kings, of course, had to be sufficiently powerful and rich for this new idea of the state to triumph. For this reason, they created a number of instruments, specific to monarchic power; they achieved their full maturity only in the fourteenth and fifteenth centuries, though their origins went back to the eleventh through thirteenth centuries. They included

- *currency:* kings owned a monopoly over currency;
- *tax system:* various feudal taxes were systematized and taxes were levied on every "hearth"; other sources of income associated with the exercise of state sovereignty, currency manipulation, import-export duties, and so on, were also created;
- *central administration:* the king's council (*curia Regis*) was transformed into a government with specialized functions, including legislative, fiscal, judicial, and other functions; secular specialists trained in the Roman law—previously the domain of churchmen—held these offices;
- *local administration:* in France, the creation of provosts, bailiffs, and seneschals.

C. The Conflict between the Church and the State

The two powers, church and state, grew in strength more or less in parallel. Under the circumstances, rivalry and conflict could only be expected as they benefited mutually from the erosion of feudalism.

1. *The Beginnings of Rivalry between Papacy and Empire*

The toughest and most threatening reaction to church reform came from the Empire, which had dominated the church in Rome and in Germania up until the immediate predecessors of Gregory VII.

When Gregory VII sent his legates to Germany for the purpose of instituting his reform, the German bishops, who benefited from the status quo and had no intention of relinquishing their political role, initially put their weight behind the emperor. A synod went so far as to decree the deposition of the pope. Gregory reacted vehemently; he excommunicated and deposed the emperor and absolved all his subjects from their oaths of loyalty. Henry IV had to do penance before the pope at Canossa (at the northern end of the Appennine mountains) before the excommunication was lifted (1077). Then, in 1080, Gregory excommunicated Henry a second time and recognized Rudolf of Swabia's claim to the crown. Henry's response was to appoint an antipope, Clement III. Gregory VII was forced to flee Rome and died in exile in 1085.

His successor, Urban II, renewed papal condemnations of lay investiture, simony, and clerogamy at the synods of Melfi (1089) and Clermont (1095). The papal clash with Henry IV continued when the emperor refused to join the pope's first crusade (1095). Then, the new emperor, Henry V, insisted on appointing bishops and was himself excommunicated in 1118.

Finally, an agreement was reached, known as *the Concordat of Worms* (1122); it incorporated the distinctions proposed by Ivo of Chartres: the emperor was to give up his right of investiture with the ring and the crosier and accept the independence of papal elections; in turn, the pope was to accept that such elections should take place "in the presence of the emperor," and that the emperor would bestow the *regalia* (including the *scepter,* the symbol of temporal power) on the elected bishop.

The agreement was ratified a few months later at the First Lateran Council (1123). This was the first ecumenical council to be held since the Fourth Council of Constantinople in 869. Most importantly, it was called by the pope (Callistus II), and not by the emperor as in antiquity and in Byzantium. The Concordat of Worms effectively ended Caesaropapism in the West.

2. *The Struggle between the Priesthood and the Empire in the Twelfth and Thirteenth Centuries*

But the quarrel between the popes and the emperors did not cease. It continued in different forms through a succession of dramatic episodes into the fourteenth century.

In the footsteps of the pope, Frederick Barbarossa (1152–90) encouraged the revival of the study of Roman law in Bologna. According to Roman law, the emperor was *dominus mundi;* he interpreted this as a right of direct government for himself over all Christendom. The emperor waged war throughout Italy, including Rome, to establish this principle. However, he was defeated by an alliance of cities in northern Italy and the papacy.

The son of Barbarossa, Henry VI (1190–97), was even more ambitious than his father: he wanted to reign not just over all of Italy (he had also inherited the Norman kingdom of Sicily and therefore held the papacy between pincers); he also planned to reunite the empire of the Orient with his western Empire. But, he died before achieving his goal. He left behind a young heir: a two-year old infant, the future Frederick II.

The pope thought he was acting wisely when he made this child his ward and ensured his election as emperor against two pretenders, Philip of Swabia and Otto of Brunswick. He went so far as to have Otto deposed by the Fourth Lateran Council in 1215 in application of his doctrine, declaring that the pope disposes of the empire at his pleasure (the same council deposed Raymond VI, Count of Toulouse, under the pretext that he had not fought the Albigensian heresy in his territories hard enough; this was a strict application of the principle of papal *plenitudo potestatis* ("plenitude of power," or papal authority).

But, Frederick II championed the projects of his Hohenstaufen predecessors and, in turn, became a staunch adversary of the papacy. In Sicily, he developed a centralized state with an absolutist government, which, it has been said, anticipated in many ways the modern state long before England and France. He started an all-out war against Popes Gregory IX and Innocent IV and also tried to invade Italy like his predecessors. But, again the cities united against the German emperor. He was deposed in 1245 at the council of Lyon (Innocent IV reinstated the principle agreed in 1215) and suffered military defeat in 1248. These events finally brought to an end the rule of the Hohenstaufen dynasty. The Holy German Empire never recovered its power again. The papacy had triumphed.[9]

In the following century, the contest between the papacy and the Empire went through some final twists and turns (we will return to the endgame in chapter 6 below).

3. *The Two Powers in England and France*

In England and France, after some initial clashes, the relations between the church and the state stabilized. The main reason was that, on account of its constant rivalry with the Empire, the papacy needed the support (or at least the neutrality) of the French monarchy and, to a lesser degree, the English monarchy. The reality of the situation in both countries, except in periods of crises, was the independence of temporal power and the existence of a royal control (including the right of taxation) over the clergy.

[9] Frederick II was an exceptional figure, one of the most remarkable during the Middle Ages. See the famous biography by Ernst Kantorowicz, *Frederick the Second* (New York: Ungar, 1957).

Nevertheless, the relationship between temporal power and spiritual power went through two major crises in England; the first opposed King Henry II Plantagenet (b. 1133; ruled 1154–189), and Thomas Becket; the second pitted King John of England "Lackland" (b. 1167; ruled 1199–1216) against Pope Innocent III.

Thomas Becket was the friend and confidant of Henry II, who appointed him chancellor of the kingdom of England. When Henry became embroiled in a dispute with the church, he thought it a good idea to appoint Thomas archbishop of Canterbury (1162). But, to his surprise, the new prelate adopted all the tenets of the Papal Revolution and declared his opposition to the Constitutions of Clarendon (1164), intended to impose restrictions on ecclesiastical privileges and bring church courts to heel. Finally, Henry sent four knights to assassinate Thomas in the cathedral of Canterbury (1170). Such was the scandal that the king was forced to do public penance and retract, formally at least, the Constitutions of Clarendon in 1172.

Nevertheless, Henry II was able to secure that even though all members of the church enjoyed the "benefit of clergy" (which allowed them to be tried by church courts), the entire procedure would remain under royal control. Thus, the monarchy secured a decisive advantage.

King John of England "Lackland" found himself opposed to Pope Innocent III over the nomination of Stephen Cardinal Langton as archbishop of Canterbury. John was excommunicated in 1208 and remained so for four years. Furthermore, the pope placed all of England under an interdict (which meant that religious acts by local clerics were invalid). Finally, the pope deposed King John and authorized Philip Augustus, the king of France, to seize England. In extremis, John reconciled with the pope and agreed to become his vassal (1213); he also accepted a charter on the free election of church dignitaries.[10]

Thus, a sort of balance of power was finally achieved. The notion of the primacy of papal power was thwarted in favor of a reasonable compromise, even though a "hot war" continued to rage on the boundaries between the two authorities; but neither had any desire to push to the extreme.

In France, as in England, what was at stake was the division of powers between church courts and secular courts. After a succession of clashes—the most serious being the one between Philip the Fair and Pope Boniface VIII—a compromise, slightly in the king's favor, was reached in France (a similar compromise was reached in England as well).

The origin of the quarrel was the papal interdiction on the king (in 1296) to levy taxes on the clergy (an attempt by the pope to resurrect a decree approved by the Fourth Lateran Council in 1215). The pope knew that the king needed this money to wage his European wars. In the opinion of the pope, it was more urgent for Christian princes to worry about the Holy Land, where Acre had just fallen to the Mamluks (1291). Philip replied with a total ban on the exit of gold and silver from the territory; in sum, the king made it impossible for Rome to collect its religious taxes. This was followed by a lull during which Saint Louis was canonized (1297). The clash flared up again in 1301 during the trial of Bernard Saisset, Occitan bishop of Pamiers, accused of treason. The opening of such a trial was a blatant aggression against the pope, because in canon law a bishop could not be tried by a secular court. The clash provided fresh opportunity for doctrinal debate (see below, pp. 538–39).

The historical context now set, we can attempt to pinpoint the ideological innovations of the age. They were particularly important and numerous, and it can be argued that in the course of these two or three centuries the basic pattern of "Western" states and law was established.

---

[10] This, by no means, put an end to John's troubles. Shortly after, he faced a serious revolt from his barons, which led to the signing of the Magna Carta (1215); we will return to this in detail below.

II. Ideological Aspects of the Papal Revolution

A. *Dictatus Papæ, Plenitudo Potestatis,* and Pontifical Monarchy

Pope Gregory VII's reform program was strengthened by a doctrinal manifesto, the so-called *Dictatus papæ,* a set of 27 declarations or short theses, dated March 3 and 4, 1075, written by the pope himself, expressing his thoughts on central issues of church reform.[11]

1. *Primacy of the Roman See*

The first principle is the primacy of the Roman See—its primacy in relation to local churches, but especially its primacy over the Byzantine Patriarchate. "The Roman church was founded by God alone" (not exclusively by the Apostle Peter).[12] Already in 1062, Saint Peter Damian wrote, "All churches... were founded by an emperor, a king or a man whatsoever his condition. But the church of Rome was founded by He who entrusted the Blessed [Peter] with the keys to everlasting life and the right of government on earth and in the heavens."[13] Several precedents exist for this declaration of primacy of the Roman church: the Decree of Gelasius, the letter of Nicholas I to Emperor Michael in 865, and the false (Pseudo-Isidorian) decretals quoting Gelasius and Pseudo-Anaclet.

Thus, the pope has universal spiritual power, and the Roman church is "catholic" in the sense that its decisions on matters of faith and discipline are valid for all Christians. It is also infallible: "the Roman church has never erred; nor will it err to all eternity, the Scripture bearing witness" (*DP* 22).

2. *The Privileges of the Pope*

Consequently, the bishop of Rome—the pope—has certain essential prerogatives. "That he alone [the pope] may use the imperial symbols" (*DP* 8). These symbols include the miter, the imperial purple, the scarlet cloak, purple sandals, a white horse, and so on. Gregory VII does not refer explicitly to the Donation of Constantine (part of the false decretals, see above pp. 483–84) because it would have been an admission that the pope holds his powers by imperial concession. He nevertheless laid claim to these privileges for the church of Rome, which was the same as denying them to the Patriarch of Constantinople.

"That of the pope alone all princes shall kiss the feet" (*DP* 9). This is the *adoratio,* an imperial ceremonial gesture borrowed from royal oriental rituals and dating from the Low Empire. The popes adopted it in the sixth century.

"That his [the pope's] name alone shall be spoken in the churches" (*DP* 10), excepting perhaps only the name of the bishop, certainly excluding laypeople; this was so that the practice would be resumed in the Orient where it had fallen into disuse. The pope is said to be "a saint" "by the merits of St. Peter" (23).

3. *The Legislative Authority of the Pope*

The pope's *legislative* power is asserted in two theses of the *Dictatus:* "That for him alone is it lawful, according to the needs of the time, to make new laws" (*DP* 7), and "That no chapter and

---

[11] This section is drawn from Gaudemet, *Eglise et cite.*

[12] *Dictatus papæ,* 1, in Ernest F. Henderson, *Select Historical Documents of the Middle Ages* (London: George Bell and Sons, 1910), 366–67; hereafter cited in the text as *DP.*

[13] Quoted in Gaudemet, *Eglise et cite,* 303.

no legal book shall be considered canonical without his [the pope's] authority" (*DP* 17). In other words, the pope must approve the law implicitly or explicitly.

This does not mean that the pope claims to make the laws of the church himself, but rather that he wants to be the arbiter on all legislation (as one commentator observes: "Peter acts as a touchstone for testing whether gold is true or false").

4. *The Pope Is the Head of the Church Hierarchy*

The pope holds the highest office in the Roman Catholic Church hierarchy. Gregory revived earlier provisions, but changed the emphasis to the advantage of the papacy. The pope had the authority to ordain a cleric, regardless of his original diocese (*DP* 14); he could assemble new congregations, creating, dividing or uniting bishoprics (7); he was authorized to transfer bishops from one diocese to another "if need be" (13). The exclusive right to depose and reinstate bishops was removed from the synods and granted to the pope ("That he alone can depose or reinstate bishops" [3]); "That he may depose and reinstate bishops without assembling a synod" [25]). The pope was sovereign over the synods: "That no synod shall be called a general one without his order" (16); in short, only the pope had the authority to convene a universal synod.

This doctrine had been affirmed in the past, but in practice synods were convened without the pope's authorization and their decisions were binding without his approval. With the false decretals and the *Dictatus papæ,* the pope's supremacy over the synods was confirmed, as was his exclusive right to convene universal synods.

In jurisdictional matters, three principles were affirmed (again Gregory VII approved measures taken by earlier popes, notably Innocent I and Nicholas I):

1. The pope had his own sphere of competence. "That to the latter [the pope] should be referred the more important cases of every church" (*DP* 21)—in other words, not just appeals. Court trials of bishops belonged to these "important cases."
2. The pope heard appeals. "That no one shall dare to condemn one who appeals to the apostolic chair" (*DP* 20). Thus, an appeal was a right. This measure resulted in a judicial centralization of the church. Adopting a suggestion from Saint Peter Damian, Gregory VII introduced a further provision, which strengthened the papacy: the right of "recourse to the pope," that is, the right to bring an accusation against a church superior, in matters of faith and church property at any rate, before the pope (24).
3. The pope "may be judged by no one" (*DP* 19), a principle already formulated in the false decretals.

In their commentary, some canonists, such as Cardinal Deusdedit, added the restriction, "unless he is a heretic." This restriction took on major importance during the conflict between Philip the Fair and Boniface VIII, and again during the Great Schism of the West and the Conciliar movement (we will return to this below.

5. *The Pope's Primacy over Secular Princes*

The *Dictatus papæ* are even more revolutionary with respect to the relations between the church and temporal powers. "That it may be permitted to him [the pope] to depose emperors" (*DP* 12). In 1080, Gregory VII justified his right to excommunicate and depose Henry IV by referring to the power to "bind and unbind" granted to the Apostles: "If you [Peter and Paul] can bind and unbind in heaven, you can much more, on earth, take from all men empires, kingdoms, principalities, duchies, marquisates, counties and possessions of whatsoever nature they may be." The pope did not exercise temporal power himself; therefore, he was not the temporal ruler of lords, but he could "bind and unbind" each individual "in terms of his sin," *sub ratione peccati.*

In particular, the pope could *absolve subjects from their fealty* (*DP* 27). In a sense, this right is a logical consequence of the papal right to excommunicate a prince (contact with an excommunicated person is forbidden).

6. *Plenitudo Potestatis*

The doctrine of *Dictatus papæ* can be summarized in the famous declaration of *plenitudo potestatis* ("plenitude of power"). It says that the pope, as the "general vicar of Christ," has full authority over the church hierarchy as well as over all humankind in every domain, spiritual and temporal. Therefore, he also has authority over emperors and kings.

The formula *plenitudo potestatis* was old; it is already found in a letter by Saint Leo I (the Great), pope from 440 to 461. It is used again in the false decretals, but in these texts it does not yet have the absolutist sense it achieves in the *Dictatus papæ.* Cardinal Humbert of Silva Candida (Humbert of Moyenmoutiers) uses it in this new sense just before Gregory VII. Cardinal Humbert acknowledges the Apostolic See's "divine and human authority," adding that "the church justly holds the reins in heaven and on earth, *specialius in Petro*"; the pope's authority is placed directly below Christ's. The canonist Tancredo says of the pope: "he governs in place of God" (*Dei vicem*).

At the outset, the theory of the *plenitudo potestatis* raised eyebrows among the canonists, but it gradually won acceptance by the majority, even among the early Romanists. The canonist Hostiensis went so far as to apply a formula of Roman law to the pope reserved for the emperor: owing to his plenitude of power, the pope is *legibus solutus,* he is not "bound by the laws"; that is, his power is "absolute."

On this basis, Gregory VII and his successors built an *absolute pontifical monarchy,* which because it believed that its prophetical mission was to Christianize the world—we will return to this in detail below—used *the instrument of legislation and the law without reservation.*

B. The Birth of Roman Canon Law

In this regard, the pontifical monarchy rediscovered the many virtues of *scholarly Roman law,* which had fallen into total neglect in the Early Middle Ages. It used this law as a model for the formulation of a new *canon law.*

1. *The Revival of Studies in Roman Law*

Sometime around 1070, in the city of Bologna under the control of the Countess Mathilda of Tuscany (an ally of the pope), scholars took up once again—for the first time in the Middle Ages—the study of Justinian's *Corpus iuris civilis.* The University of Bologna was the first medieval university; it served as a model for all others. The initiator of this first study of Roman law was *Irnerius* (d. 1130).

We can distinguish two schools of Roman law subsequently: the "glossators," who applied Roman legal texts in their literal sense; and "postglossators" or "commentators," who tolerated a broader liberty of interpretation. In table 1, we list some of the important names in Roman law that we will cite in our discussion below.

Though the study of Roman law began at the instigation of the papacy, it soon provided jurists in the employment of the emperor and kings *arguments against the papacy,* because it was (1) an imperial law, favorable to the absolute and universal authority of the emperor (at least in terms

Table 1
Luminaries of Roman Law

Irnerius (d. 1130), chief contributor to the revival of Roman law, professor at the University of Bologna.

1. The school of glossators (early twelfth-thirteenth centuries)

Placentinus (d. 1192), taught Roman law at the University of Bologna and at Mantua and Piacenza, before migrating to Montpellier; wrote *Summa Codicis*.

Azo (b. ca. 1150, fl. 1198–1230), taught Roman law at Bologna, author of a *Summa Codicis* (1208/1210) and a *Summa Institutionum*.

Accursius (ca. 1191–1263), taught Roman law at Bologna, author of a *Glossa ordinaria* (Ordinary gloss on the *Corpus Iuris Civilis*, ca. 1230); it became a classic for the study of Roman law and was still in print in the seventeenth century.

2. The school of commentators (post-glossators):

This new generation of legal doctors distanced itself from the letter of the text and applied the dialectical method and Aristotelian logic to the study of the law in accordance with the Scholastic method, which had reached maturity. In the legal opinions or *consilia* that they delivered, the doctors of the law attempted to adapt Roman law to contemporary society (in the *Libri feudarum*, they sought to translate feudal rules in terms of Roman law).

Jacobus de Ravannis (Jacques de Révigny), d. 1296 and **Petrus de Bellapertica** (Pierre de Belleperche), d. 1308 (both taught in the law schools of Orleans and Toulouse; both influenced Cynus de Pistoia, thus the school of Bartolus and Baldus).

Guilelmus de Cuneo (Guillaume de Cunh) (d. 1335; a teacher in the law school at Toulouse).

Cynus de Pistoia (Cino) (1270–1336/1337). He studied at Bologna and in France. Under the influence of Petrus de Bellapertica he adopted the Scholastic method of the commentators and introduced it to Italy; taught at Perugia and Bologna.

Bartolus of Sassoferrato (Bartolo da Sassoferrato) (b. 1313/1314, d. 1357), a student of Cynus at Perugia and at Bologna. He was a magistrate and professor of law at Pisa; taught at Perugia from 1343 until his death. Author of commentaries on Roman law and constitutional legal theories, *De Tyranno, De regimine civitatis*, and a work on the Guelfs and the Ghibellines.

Baldus de Ubaldis (Baldo degli Ubaldi) (b. ca. 1327, d. 1400), a student of Bartolus in Roman law (he also studied canon law and wrote a commentary on the *Decretals*).

Other important fifteenth and sixteenth century commentators include **Alexander Tartagnus, Jason de Maino, Philip Decius**.

Significant is the contribution of the influential school of *Neapolitan jurists*, which was independent at the outset then merged with the school of the "commentators." It contributed theories on absolute monarchy for the kings of Sicily. Members included **Marinus da Caramanico** (d. 1288), **Andreas de Isernia** (d. 1316), **Lucas de Penna** (d. ca. 1390)

Source: James Henderson Burns, ed., *Cambridge History of Medieval Political Thought* (Cambridge: Cambridge University Press, 1988).

of its "public law" aspects), and (2) it was a "secular" law.[14] Furthermore, with the rediscovery of Aristotelian philosophy, which took place at the same time, the study of Roman law provided *arguments against Christianity itself.* This is why it aroused many objections and much opposition among theologians and canonists. Several synods in the twelfth century actually condemned its study. It was forbidden to teach Roman law in Paris under the pretext that it was an imperial law that justified the subordination of the king of France to the Empire.

However, its language, concepts, and techniques were essential to the formation of the new canon law, which the reformed church intended to use to gradually transform civil society.

2. *The Constitution of the Corpus Iuris Canonici*

a. Sources of Canon Law

Up to this point, the main source of canon law was the "canons" of the synods. Then everything changed when the decretals became the main source.[15] We must distinguish between broad texts (general decretals, *decretalis generalis, constitutio*) and specific texts (rescripts).

A rescript does not derogate from an earlier law (that is to say, it must comply with it), whether a general law or a conciliar canon. Conversely, a general decretal can change preexisting general rules (according to the principle, *lex posterior derogat priori*). The chief canonists—Huguccio, Hostiensis (discussed further below)—accepted that a decretal could go against the canons of synods (though this remained a topic of debate).

Decretals covered all aspects of canon law, including "civil" law, marriage law, and so on. Decretal output was abundant: some 1,000 decretals were produced during the twelfth century, which was not an exceptionally productive one.

Conciliar legislation, no longer the main source of law, continued to exist. *General synods,* also known as *ecumenical synods,* were now western and pontifical, whereas in the fourth and fifth centuries they had been oriental and imperial. Nine such synods took place between the First Lateran Council (1123) and the Council of Basle-Ferrara-Florence-Rome (1431–45). Other special and local synods (so-called national and provincial councils) and diocesan synods established the *synodical statutes.*

Following the example of the Roman jurisconsults, the canonists also formulated a theory of *custom* (*consuetudo*) as a source of true law, distinct from simple *usus* and "tradition," a word used to refer to the transmission of belief.

b. The Codification of Canon Law

The new canon law, the combined fruit of all these sources, was soon codified, initially at the private initiative of certain legal luminaries, then at the initiative of the papacy itself, which desired to encourage the use and study of the law. It was first codified in the Decree of Gratian, then in the huge collection of the *Corpus iuris canonici.*

The Decree of Gratian was the culmination of earlier efforts of codification undertaken in the early days of the Church reform. Of note are the decrees of Burchard, bishop of Worms, dating from the early eleventh century. They include the Carolingian collections but adopt a systematic plan. Next came the collections of Gregorian reforms (works by Peter Damian, Humbert, the *Liber canonum* by Deusdedit). Also important are the collections of Yvo of Chartres (b. 1040, bishop from 1090 to 1115) in the following century, used by Gratian directly. At the end of the

---

[14] Roman law, of course, did not take into account the Scriptures (except in certain post-Theodosian circles), and it was founded (1) on nature and (2) on the legislation and tradition of praetorian jurisprudence.

[15] This section is drawn from Gaudemet, *Eglise et cite.*

eleventh and the beginning of the twelfth centuries, other collections were compiled with borrowings from Roman law (an osmosis or hybridization of Roman law and Christian rules of conduct was achieved by including Roman legal texts in the canon collections). Another collection, the *Liber de misericordia et justitia* by Alger of Liege (ca. 1106), merits a mention for its method: for the first time, the author did not simply quote the canon, but he added his personal view on each question supported by quotes from texts of the canon. Gratian adopted this method in his work.

Very little is known about Gratian (he may have been a native of Bologna); even the date of his decree (the *Decretum Gratiani*), 1140, is uncertain. The *Decretum Gratiani* combines some 4,000 canons organized in three parts: (1) 101 "distinctions"; (2) 36 "causes" divided into "questions"; (3) *De consecratione* (added subsequently); it deals with the sacraments, the consecration of churches, sacred objects, mass, festivals, fasts, and so on.

The first part follows a strict plan: sources of the law, basic concepts (natural law, divine law, positive law, etc.). This first part imitates the classical structure of the Roman legal texts. The next part concerns issues pertaining to priests (ordination, duties, etc.). The overall plan of the second part is not clear, although coherent sections within this part do stand out; they include sections on simony, monks, and marriage, for example. Each *quæstio* begins with a real or "textbook" case; then the appropriate authorities are quoted for a solution of the case.

The original text went through modifications and additions before it was finally stabilized in 1150. Among the additions were numerous texts from Roman law.

In schools of law everywhere, the traditional title for Gratian's work was the *Decree.* Gratian himself had called it *Concordantia discordantium canonum,* "Concord of Discordant Canons." Gratian applied the new dialectical method perfected by Abelard and developed in universities; he brought contradictory canon texts together, then drew distinctions to reveal why such texts were contradictory in appearance only (Thomas Aquinas also applied this method, as we will see). In this sense, Gratian's work is much more than a collection of texts: it is an original effort, an interpretation that organizes and clarifies questions without eliminating the problems.

Before long his work met with success on a grand scale. The doctors of the law accepted the *Decree* even before Rome gave its official approval. During the Middle Ages, the faculties of canon law at universities were called "Faculties of the Decree," that is, schools where Gratian's "textbook" was studied.

Between 1140 and 1234, the popes continued to produce decretals, and the synods produced their canons. Therefore, it became necessary to make additions to the *Decree* of Gratian. Several doctors, including Bernard of Pavia and the great canonist Johannes Teutonicus, undertook private initiatives in this respect. Then a papal initiative, replicating Justinian's gesture in the sixth century, resulted in the compilation of several new collections. Together with Gratian's *Decretum,* they became the so-called *Corpus iuris canonici.*

- The *Decretals* of Gregory IX, dating from 1234, were given this name since they were produced at Gregory IX's initiative. It adopted a strict plan of presentation in five books and 2,000 chapters; 87 percent of its texts were published after the *Decree* of Gratian.
- The "sixth book" of the *Decretals* (*Liber sextus*), dating from 1296, was the work of Boniface VIII (called the "sixth" book because it came after the five of Gregory's *Decretals*); two thirds of the book contains decretals by Boniface VIII and canons from the Second Council of Lyons in 1274).
- The *Clementinæ* were the decretals of Clement V, the first pope at Avignon, produced in 1314 at his request and published by John XXII in 1317. All decretals issued up to this date were not systematically included in this collection. Therefore, private publications completed the work; two are important:

• The *Extravagantes* by John XXII ("extravagantes" means "that which circulates outside"), 20 constitutions by Pope John XXII published between 1325 and 1327, for example the decretal *Cum inter nonnullos* (1323).[16]

• The *Extravagantes communes,* 70 decretals issued between 1295 and 1483. They include *Unam sanctam*[17] and several other important texts.[18]

In total, in the various editions of the *Corpus iuris canonici* published since 1500, we find: *Gratian's Decretum, the Decretals of Gregory IX, Sextus, Clementinæ, the Extravagantes of John XXII, and the Extravagantes communes.*

The resulting compilation remained the official legal code of the church for an exceptionally long time, from the Middle Ages until the twentieth century. A new canon code was published only in 1917.

3. *Types, Schools, Great Canonists*

Canonist doctrine flourished between 1150 and the end of the fifteenth century. Many scholars at the Faculties of the Decree contributed to the doctrine. The *genres* of doctrine evolved:

1. First were the *summæ,* systematic commentaries of Gratian's *Decretum;* and later the decretals of Gregory IX, both in the manner of commentaries like those of Bible exegetes.
2. Next were *apparatuses,* selections of the most important glosses on a range of topics.
3. Questions (*quæstiones*), unlike the *summæ* and apparatuses, did not comment on the Decree or the decretals in the order of the texts; instead, they focused on a particular question, usually a real case or a textbook case, and developed their thinking with comments and quotes according to the intellectual demands of their argumentation. Some material of the *Digest* was already written in this manner; Gratian himself wrote a large number of *quæstiones* (in the second part of his *Decree*).[19]
4. Independence in regard to the *Corpus iuris canonici* was further accentuated by *treatises.* They dealt with issues of marriage, legal procedures, penitence, and questions of benefices (an echo of similar developments in civil and Roman law).

Bologna, where the *science* of Roman and canon law was born around 1070, remained a great center of legal learning throughout the Middle Ages. Students poured into Bologna from around Europe to study with the great legal luminaries of the Western world. Other centers developed in France (Paris, by the end of the twelfth century [before it was closed], Montpellier in 1221), in England (Oxford), in Spain (Salamanca), and during the fourteenth and fifteenth centuries in Bohemia and Poland (Krakow).

The law professors at these centers were as international as their students. A distinction was made between the *decretists*—commentators of Gratian's *Decree*—and *decretalists*—later canonists who attached greater importance to the decretals enacted after Gratian's *Decretum.* In addition to the canonists Deusdedit and Anselm at the time of Gregory VII, there are many other great names (see table 2).

[16] This text condemns the extremist Franciscans, who advocated total poverty, and who claimed that neither Jesus nor the Apostles had any personal possessions.

[17] The bull on the pope's superiority issued by Boniface VIII on November 18, 1302, during his dispute with Philip the Fair, King of France.

[18] For example, *Quorumdam exigit* (1317), which also condemns the Franciscan spirituals.

[19] Similarly, theology at this time evolved from biblical exegesis toward *quæstiones,* and thereby toward a more systematic and demonstrative science.

Table 2
Great Canonists

Gratian of Bologna, his life remains obscure, his chief work was the *Decretum* (completed ca. 1140).

Huguccio (Uguccione) (date of birth unknown, *fl.* 1180–1210), taught canon law at Bologna and was later Bishop of Ferrara from 1191 until his death in 1210); wrote a *Summa decretorum* [i.e. a systematic commentary of Gratian's *Decree*] (1180–1191) and a *Liber derivationum.*

Johannes Teutonicus (unknown date of birth and death, *fl.* 1210–1245), taught canon law at Bologna and, later, in Halberstadt; wrote an *Ordinary Gloss* to Gratian's *Decretum,* various *apparatuses, quæstiones,* and *consilia* (legal opinions).

Bernard of Parma (d. 1266), studied and taught at Bologna. His major work was an Ordinary Gloss on the *Liber extra* (i.e., the decretals of Gregory IX).

Hostiensis (Henricus de Segusio, cardinal-bishop of Ostia) (d. 1271), elected bishop of Sisteron, 1244, archbishop of Embrun, 1250, and cardinal-bishop of Ostia, 1263. Taught canon law at Paris and perhaps at Bologna. His chief works were *Summa aurea; In primum-quintum decretalium librum commentaria; Apparatus in Novellam Innocentii quarti.*

Other significant canonists include **Laurentius Hispanus**, **Stephen of Tournai**, **Tancred**, **Ricardus Anglicus**, **Raymond of Penyafort**, **William Durandus** (the **Older** and the **Younger**), and several great canonist popes such as **Innocent III**[20] and **Innocent IV**,[21] and, in the fourteenth and fifteenth centuries, **Johannes Andreæ**, **Franciscus Zabarella**[22] and **Panormitanus** (Nicholas de Tudeschis).

Note that in Italy (up until the end of the fifteenth century, at any rate) these doctors were considered "noble" like *milites* or knights.

Source: James Henderson Burns, ed., *Cambridge History of Medieval Political Thought* (Cambridge: Cambridge University Press, 1988).

Increasingly canonist doctrine was differentiated from adjacent disciplines: theology, Roman law, and Aristotelian philosophy. It is worth repeating that its relations with Roman law were ambiguous: it borrowed many texts, basic concepts, and methods, and at the same time accused it of not pursuing the same purpose.

The canonists held tradition in great respect and often cited the "authorities" (Roman jurisconsults, physicians, theologians, philosophers, and so on), as well as what they called the "common opinion of the doctors" (all the while debating whether the doctors should reach a unanimous or a majority opinion, or whether only a small number of well-respected doctors sufficed). The canonists were active in the life of their century and helped to govern, which is why their work influenced the creation of innovative political doctrines.

If Pope Gregory VII and his successors labored so passionately to build this astounding institutional edifice—the doctrine of *plenitudo potestatis,* absolute and sovereign pontifical monarchy

[20] Born ca. 1160, studied theology at Paris and law at Bologna; elected pope in 1198; d. 1216.

[21] Born ca. 1200, taught canon law at Bologna; lawyer at the papal curia from 1226; pope 1243–54; wrote a celebrated *Apparatus in V libros decretalium,* completed shortly after 1245; as a private doctor, wrote commentaries on his own papal decretals, as well as on the text deposing Frederick II (1245).

[22] We will discuss his role in the development of conciliar theories below (see chapter 6).

(the model for all secular European monarchies), and a full and universal system of canon law—the inspiration was *a profound conviction that it provided the necessary means for the church to pursue and accomplish its prophetic mission: the Christianization of the world.*

C. The Christianization of the Law and the "Juridicization" of Christian Morals

For the American legal historian, Harold J. Berman, what happened in Europe between the eleventh and thirteenth centuries was nothing less than a "Papal Revolution," by which he means a "total change," the opening of a new era in which everything—ideas, values, institutions, morals—were reframed. In other words, in terms of its scope and civilizational impact, it was comparable with the Greek and Roman "miracles."[23]

Berman highlights the fact that paradoxically it is the institution of an absolute, universal spiritual power, distinct and separate from the different temporal powers, which led to a secularization of the power of the state in the West. From the moment that the church claimed exclusive jurisdiction over souls, the calling of temporal power could only extend to secular matters. This represented a complete break with the Caesaropapism of the Early Middle Ages, which nevertheless continued to survive in Byzantium and throughout the oriental Christian world.

The confrontation between spiritual power and temporal power that followed, Berman argues, resulted in two mutually fertile developments: on the one hand, the *Christianization of ancient pagan law,* and on the other the *juridicization—that is, the provision of viable rules—of an unlivable Christian morality.*

Thus, for the first time, the strands of a Greek, Roman, and Judeo-Christian civilization came together and were tightly entwined. It made possible a totally new civilization: the "West." Berman argues that the "West" exists only where the Papal Revolution, with all its moral and legal corollaries, had a significant impact.[24]

1. *Penance and Incarnation: The Works of Man Lead to Salvation*

This civilizational synthesis begins in the theology of the eleventh and twelfth centuries, particularly in the new doctrines of *penance* and *Incarnation.* This theology involves certain innovative choices, which enable life to be imagined and directed in more positive and rational ways.

In the old doctrine, penance was the ability of the church (as possessor of the "power of the keys" given to Peter) to deliver the sinner from eternal damnation. Since man's sin is infinite, penitence is "all or nothing." The church can give or withhold its absolution.

In the new doctrine of atonement proposed by Saint Anselm of Canterbury (1033–1109), and other theologians living contemporaneously with the Papal Revolution, the path was opened for a calculated assessment of *sins and punishments.*[25]

Saint Anselm posits that Christ's sacrifice on the cross redeems once and for all humankind's collective original sin. Accordingly, it remains only for each individual to atone personally for the sins he has committed during his lifetime to achieve the salvation of his soul. These sins are not infinite; they are knowable and measurable, and as such they are not inaccessible to atonement through human merits (whereas original sin was). The church can deliver a person from hell and eternal damnation in exchange for the finite fruits of a penance. Thus, for atonement, it becomes possible to record a person's sins and fix a "tariff" proportionate to their gravity. The notion of

---

[23] See Berman, *Law and Revolution.*

[24] Berman, ibid., recognizes a major turning point in European history in this event, more important than the traditional rupture between the Middle Ages and the modern era.

[25] See Brian Davies and G. R. Evans, eds., *On the Incarnation of the Word in "Anselm of Canterbury: The Major Works"* (Oxford: Oxford University Press, 1998).

purgatory appears in the next century (twelfth) and makes sense in this new logic: purgatory is an additional period of time to pay off the debts of sin.

Saint Anselm also asks: *cur Deus homo,* why did God become man? Again, his answer has social consequences of the utmost magnitude. If Christ wanted to atone for the sins of man with his death on the cross, it is to involve all men more intimately in the redemption that follows the cross. When the Word became flesh it became imitable by man, enabling him to pursue salvation through *imitatio Christi.* Thus, salvation could be something other than an external grace falling on an irresponsible humanity; it became a process whereby individuals worked together to build step-by-step a less sinful world with human means: with reason and moral conscience. Thus, heaven came closer to earth, and transcendence combined with immanence. From this perspective as well, the dialectic of *zero* and *infinite* was replaced by an arithmetic of *plus* and *minus.*[26]

With this return to reason and measure it was possible to glimpse a solution to the problem—until then a real conundrum—by combining *justice* and *mercy* in a viable morality (see above, pp. 412, 431–32). The ground was prepared for a Christian society to reclaim classical culture based on the rational calculation of what was just in order to safeguard vital individual rights and the conditions of a properly ordered community life.

Now we can understand the true reason behind the papal initiative to revive the study of Roman law and to use it as a model for the formulation of a new law of Christian society. In the High Middle Ages, Roman law could not be of much interest: salvation did not depend on a little more or a little less commutative or distributive justice. But now, every good and every bad work, however small, contributed to determining one's salvation. It became important to be able to appraise human works and to calculate what each person was due in terms of justice in the context of life's complexity and social exchanges. Roman law makes this possible, which is why it recovered its eminent moral legitimacy. At the same time, it was to be transformed by the charitable inspiration of its new Christian sponsors.

What we observe is a sort of mutual transposition: the law incorporates more Christian values, while evangelical love is "juridified" and humanized, becoming more "humanist" in the Greco-Latin sense of the term; thus, it becomes less tyrannical, more compatible with a society called upon to endure and prosper.

These transformations were the fruit of canon law, which at this time, as we saw, was undergoing on the one hand a new phase of development under the influence of decretals issued by the papal legislative authority, and on the other was beginning to be codified and organized in large compilations. Now, this living law had the vocation to concern virtually every aspect of social life in both the public and private sphere.

A simple list of the powers of the church courts shows the universal calling of canon law.

Church courts have authority over six categories of *individuals:* (1) the clergy and clerical employees; (2) students; (3) crusaders; (4) *personæ miserabiles,* that is, the poor, widows, and orphans; (5) Jews, in claims against Christians; and (6) travelers, including merchants and sailors, whenever their security is at risk.

The *issues* that come under the jurisdiction of a church court are spiritual causes or issues associated with spiritual problems (even when laypersons are concerned). This makes for a very wide spectrum: (1) the administration of the sacraments in all circumstances (therefore marriage and matrimonial matters); (2) last wills and testaments (owing to the sacred character of a person's

---

[26] It is telling that the accent in Eastern Christianity is not placed on Incarnation to the same degree (Eastern icons reveal a Christ in divine glory rather than a Christ suffering in the flesh). The realism of Man-God's suffering, the pains and weaknesses of the flesh—his passions and agonies—is characteristic of Western Christianity after the eleventh and twelfth centuries.

last will, affecting the salvation of the soul of the deceased); (3) benefices, that is, the administration of church properties, foundations, bequests, and gifts made to the church; (4) oaths, because they are made before God (thus all aspects of civil law—property law and contracts—where an individual might be accused of "false swearing"); (5) sins punishable by ecclesiastical censure (an area of criminal law which includes heresy, sacrilege, witchcraft, usury, slandering, fornication, homosexuality, adultery, attacks on religious places, aggressions against a member of the clergy, and so on).

Furthermore, the intellectual superiority of the church court, and the fact that many of the jurists of secular courts and administrations were highly educated churchmen, meant that the legal formulations of the canonists worked their way progressively into the full framework of the law, for example, in matrimonial law, inheritance law, property law, contract law, penal proceedings, and finally public and "constitutional" law. The canonists combined Roman and Christian concepts in innovative associations in their new formulations of the law.

2. *"Will," "Conscience," "Person"*

For example, the "will" of the testator was a precise legal concept in Roman civil law. But, in Rome, it took seven qualified witnesses and strict procedures for a testator to change the customary rule of succession, which in principle favored the preservation of the *gens*. But from a Christian standpoint, the testator's will was sacred, since the everlasting salvation of his soul depended on it. Accordingly, canon law greatly simplified the formalities for a testament. A single verbal statement of will sufficed; it could be authenticated by a witness—with an interest—such as a priest, who heard the dying person's "last wishes."[27]

The canonists postulated as well that, in contracts, promises were binding because they were a matter for the "conscience." It was always better if such promises were "solemnized" (i.e., put through a formal procedure involving writing, signature, gestures, presence of a witness, oaths, etc.), though it was not absolutely necessary: in God's eyes, one's "conscience" is bound by the fact that one has given a sincere promise. According to Berman, this new flexibility paved the way for a modern law of contract inexistent in the Justinian corpus.[28]

3. *The "Peace of God": The Roman-Canonistic Doctrine of Violence and War*

A new doctrine of violence and war appeared. The canonists were confronted with a new challenge: the reconciliation of the natural right of defense (the right of an individual to defend his or her life or property; the right of a society to defend its order) with the commandments of the Old and New Testament: "you shall not kill" and "turn the other cheek." The solution was the systematic promotion of legal remedies to the detriment of physical assault. For example, in the case of a defrauded bishop who attempts to recover his property by force, the principle states that property transfer by violent means is never lawful, even if the aim is to reestablish one's ownership rights. A victim may not mete out his own justice. His rights can only be recovered by a legal remedy. Failing that, the *statu quo ante* must prevail. In other words, violence itself is unlawful. This principle is generalized by Gratian's *Decretum* (the *reintegranda* and *actio spolii* canons).

Another example is the "Peace of God" advocated by the church as early as the tenth century (see above, p. 513 and pp. 516–17). Reading the texts, it becomes clear that the canonists placed war outside the law. It was restricted to a small category of "professionals" (knights) and forbidden to the peasantry (the great mass of people). Of course, it was also forbidden to the

27 Berman, *Law and Revolution*, 232–33.
28 Ibid., 247.

clergy (the learned and enlightened segment of society). Likewise, war was restricted to certain days of the week and certain times of the year. Peace was guaranteed by a collective oath; as we saw, this oath played a key role in forming the guilds and communes in towns and urban centers; it also played a role in the declarations, by dukes, kings, and emperors, of the peaces of the land (*pax terræ, Landfriede*).[29] Berman adds,

> The European jurists of the twelfth and thirteenth centuries converted the Roman law rule [*vim vi repellere licet,* "force may be used to repel force"] into a general principle, which they juxtaposed with the so-called pacifistic utterances of Jesus ("turn the other cheek"), and from the opposing maxims they developed a general concept of justification for the limited use of force applicable to a whole series of interrelated categories systematically set forth: *force necessary to execute the law, to defend oneself, to defend another, to protect one's own property, to protect another's property.* These principles were applied not only to civil and criminal law but also to political and theological questions about a "just war."[30]

Gratian's *causa* 23 on "just war," and the commentaries it inspired, provided Grotius with many of his ideas on the law of war and peace and, by extension, on the natural law guaranteeing future "human rights."[31]

4. *The Decriminalization of Sin: Internal Forum, External Forum*

Another major innovation of canonists and theologians such as Peter Abelard and Peter Lombard was the *separation of morals and law* by means of a clear theological distinction between the concepts of "sin" and "crime."

In the Middle Ages, law and morals were still largely intertwined (as in all traditional sacred societies and in most Muslim societies today). Now a distinction was made between the "internal forum" and "external forum."[32] Some deeds and thoughts are reprehensible, but they come under an "internal jurisdiction": God sees and hears them and judges them, the priest has the authority to discuss them with the sinner in the confessional, but the secular court, or even the church court, cannot know them or punish them, because they do not disturb the public order, which is the sole concern of such courts; these deeds and thoughts are intimately linked to the conscience of the sinner and are known, therefore, only to God.[33]

---

[29] Ibid., 90.

[30] Ibid., 148; my italics.

[31] See Peter Haggenmacher, *Grotius et la doctrine de la guerre juste* [Grotius and the doctrine of the just war] (Paris: Presses Universitaires de France, 1983).

[32] The word "forum" refers to a place where tribunals were held in Rome and, therefore, by extension, to a judicial court.

[33] See Peter Abelard, *Ethical Writings, Ethics*, trans. Paul Vincent Spade (Cambridge, MA: Hackett, 1995): "human beings do not judge about what is hidden but what is plain. They don't think so much of the guilt belonging to the fault as of the performance of the deed. Rather God alone, who pays attention not so much to the deeds as to the mind with which they are done, is truly thinking about the guilt in our attention and tries the fault in a true court. Thus he is called the tester of the heart and reins [Jer. 20:12], and is said to see in the darkness [after Ezek. 8:12]. For where no one sees, there he sees most of all, because in punishing sin he doesn't pay attention to the deed but to the mind, just as conversely we don't pay attention to the mind that we don't see but to the deed we know" (18, sec. 5).

The two registers of sin and crime (morality and law) are completely separate. A judge will find a woman guilty of unintentionally smothering her child: and yet she is not guilty in her intention; if he does not punish her, it will encourage recklessness among other mothers. The maintenance of public order, for which the judge is responsible, requires that the woman be punished for her deed, but God will surely pardon her. Likewise, a judge must find a man guilty, despite suspicions of false testimony, if he cannot prove the testimony to be false; otherwise judicial credibility itself would be compromised. The contrary of this is implied: even people, who are sinners in the eyes of the Lord, should not be found guilty if they do not upset the public order.

External justice encounters what could be called an epistemological limit. An external jurisdiction, whether secular or ecclesiastical, can only apply public coercion to deeds that trouble the public order and that are sufficiently external so as to be objectively recognizable and certain, so as to persuade the reason and conscience of the judge (now valued by the new Roman-canonist procedures). All deeds and thoughts that do not meet these standards, regardless of how reprehensible they may be, are a matter for God's judgment alone, or for the sacramental authority of the priest, who is entitled to administer the sacrament of penance with his *ordinatio* (which is neither an *imperium* nor a *jurisdictio*); such deeds and thoughts lie totally outside the scope of politics.

One imagines that the implications of this innovation must have been enormous, since in due course it would produce the freedom of ideas and morals that characterize Western civilization.

Henceforth, the state would be concerned only with crimes and misdemeanors. It would have no legitimacy in matters of conscience and, in general, in the private lives of individuals.[34] This is not to say that immorality would go unpunished, only that it would not be subject to *penal* punishment. Punishment came from words, invectives, and discredit, not from the "secular branch."[35] Thus, *an inner sphere for ideas and for a certain scope of private action was established.*

It was probably as a consequence of this innovation that universities were able to develop as places of independent research (Abelard was one of the early theoreticians and practitioners of this new freedom), and that profane science could emerge some time later.

5. *Law and Politics as Instruments of Social Transformation: The Status of Natural Law Changes*

The real motivation for the formulation and widespread diffusion of a new law by the post-Gregorian church was the idea that the law and legislative action would have a vocation to serve as instruments of deliberate social *transformation;* in other words, they could be the object of a *political program* and, for the very first time, substantiate the prospects of a Christian eschatology.

This is what can be seen in the reform work of the church throughout the eleventh to thirteenth centuries and in the action of temporal leaders like Saint Louis and other temporal leaders, for example, in towns and corporations. All of them aspired to use the law and politics as instruments to improve society and make it more Christian and more ordered.

The status change of the concept of "natural law" played an important role in this development. Traditionally, since antiquity, the standard for positive law was natural law; but natural law in the eyes of the Greeks and Romans, as we saw, expressed a fixed-structure universe, unchanging and cyclical; therefore, natural law represented a principle of social and cosmic *preservation.* In contrast, in the eyes of the canonists, no sooner had God created nature than it was damaged

---

See also section 7: "we punish house-burnings with a greater penalty than we do for carrying out fornication, when before God the latter is regarded as much more serious than the former. These things are done not so much out of duty to justice as out of the proper balance for its administration, so that, as we said, in preventing public injuries we have regard for general expediency.... In such cases we pay more attention to administering—that is, to the standpoint of foresight we noted—than to pure fairness" (19).

[34] In the particular case of *heresy,* the crime/sin distinction does not hold. Throughout the Middle Ages, the "sin" of heresy was held to be a "crime," and the ecclesiastical courts delivered the "sinner" to the secular branch for trial.

[35] Thus, the state must let people do and say many immoral things freely, which Thomas Aquinas in his own sound logic concluded it would. In his *Summa Theologica,* Aquinas went further, arguing that some sins, such as *usury,* even have *social utility:* "Human laws leave certain things unpunished, on account of the condition of those who are imperfect, and who would be deprived of many advantages, if all sins were strictly forbidden and punishments appointed for them. Wherefore human law has permitted usury, not that it looks upon usury as harmonizing with justice, but lest the advantage of many should be hindered" (*Summa Theologica* IIa IIæ, q. 78, art. 1, reply to the third objection; see below, p. 554).

in the Fall; then it was restored by grace; therefore, natural good is not *behind* us but *before* us; it is not a state of being, it is a must-be. In order to know what is consistent with "natural and divine law," we must never base ourselves on empirical reality, that is, positive law, or custom, which has never been consistent with natural law; we must examine the reason and conscience of a Christian.

Pontifical absolutism became the instrument of this transformation called for by Christian eschatology: if the prince was to be *legibus solutus* (not "bound by the laws"), it was so that he could ensure that politics triumphed over custom, will over fate, and so that he could innovate and legislate to bring about a transformation.

Such Christian "progressivism" is accentuated in the following statement by Thomas Beckett: "Christ said, not 'I am the custom,' but 'I am the truth.'"[36] Reform was possible and necessary. Gregory VII said as much in his reply to Henry IV when he was pressed to justify his openly "revolutionary" initiatives (Gregory made no effort to deny their "revolutionary" character). Gratian, too, asserted that the Christian legislator was justified in abolishing unreasonable customs (especially unjust feudal customs such as "exactions," abuses of power, arbitrary taxes). On his deathbed, Saint Louis said to his son: "Preserve the good customs of the realm and abolish the bad."[37]

Such, then, were the principal ideological aspects of the Papal Revolution. By virtue of the doctrine of the Two Swords, the point of view of the reformed church prevailed over the renascent secular powers.

III. The Doctrine of the Two Swords

For the canonists, the relationship between spiritual power and temporal power and the implications of the doctrine of *plenitudo potestatis* are inextricably tied to an image from the Gospel: the "two swords."[38]

A. The Image of the Two Swords

Jesus of Nazareth is with his apostles at the Last Supper. He knows that he will soon be arrested and says, "'What is written about me has its fulfilment.' And they said, 'Look, Lord, here are two swords.' And he said to them, 'It is enough'" (Luke 22:37–38).

Later on the Mount of Olives, when Judas arrives with the guards, his apostles inquire: "'Lord, shall we strike with the sword?' And one of them struck the slave of the high priest and cut off his right ear. But Jesus said, 'No more of this!' And he touched his ear and healed him" (Luke 22:49–51; see Matt. 26:51; Mark 14:47). Traditionally, this passage is interpreted allegorically. The two swords are said to represent the two powers, spiritual and temporal.

Temporal power is a "sword": that goes without saying, it is the power of coercion. Several passages in the Bible make explicit reference to the "temporal" or "material" sword as an allegory for political power. According to Paul, political authority "is God's servant for your good. But if you do wrong, be afraid, for *he does not bear the sword in vain;* he is the servant of God to execute his wrath on the wrongdoer" (Rom. 13:4).

---

[36] Quoted in James Henderson Burns, ed., *Cambridge History of Medieval Political Thought* (Cambridge: Cambridge University Press, 1988), 258.

[37] "Bad customs" were feudal customs established by the seigneurial class. Jean de Joinville, *Memoirs of Saint Louis,* trans. Ethel Wedgwood (New York: E. P. Dutton, 1906), §745.

[38] This section is drawn from J. A. Watt, "Spiritual and Temporal Powers," in Burns, *Cambridge History,* 367–424.

But spiritual power is also a sword. Elsewhere in the Scriptures, the Word of God[39] is compared with a "two-edged sword" (Heb. 4:12),[40] the "sword of the Spirit" (Eph. 6:17). A sword is used to separate and strike; this is what the clergy must do in its mission of evangelization. Various texts refer to the "sword" of excommunication, anathema, just canonical sanction, and papal anger (Gregory VII spoke of "the anger of God and the sword of Saint Peter").

The canonist Deusdedit (1040–1100) summarizes the situation as follows: "the priest fights, as the Apostle says, with the sword of the word . . . the king fights with the material sword, since he is the Lord's minister, avenger in wrath on those who act with evil."[41]

The image is open to numerous interpretations. Are the two swords equal or unequal, independent or interdependent? The question was debated in schools for a century and a half.

During his quarrel with Gregory VII, the emperor Henry IV published a broadside against the madness of Gregory, called the *Hildebrandica insania.* Quoting Luke 22:38, he argued that there is a *duality* of power. There are two swords because there are two distinct authorities. They must, of course, cooperate, but neither is subordinated to the other. Frederick Barbarossa, Frederick II, Philip the Fair, Dante, and William of Ockham held this "dualist" position as well.

To the contrary, the theory underlying "political Augustinism" is that temporal power is subordinate to spiritual power: we saw this expressed variously by Saint Ambrose, Gelasius, Gregory the Great, and Jonas of Orleans. Likewise, Hugh of St. Victor[42] (1098–1142) expressed this idea in a text that found its way into Gratian's *Decretum,* whereby it gained widespread diffusion. There is only one society, one body or one "congregation" of Christians; it indeed has two orders: one secular, the other clerical, but the secular order has no autonomy. It is subordinated to the clerical, just as temporal realities are inferior to spiritual realities and ordered beneath them. Spiritual power institutes temporal power and rules over it. In reference to the image of the two swords, therefore, it must be said that *the pope holds both swords.*

Saint Bernard formulated (1091–1153) this as follows: "Both swords are Peter's: one is unsheathed at his sign, the other by his own hand." In his *De consideratione,* Saint Bernard writes the following to Pope Eugene III: "Both swords, spiritual and material, then, belong to the church; the one exercised on behalf of the church, the other by the church: the one by the hand of the priest, the other by the hand of the soldier, but clearly at the bidding of the priest (*ad nutum sacerdotis*)[43] and the order of the emperor."[44] This is known as the "hierocratic" conception of power, opposing the "dualist" conception advocated by the imperial party.

B. The Two Swords in Canon Law

Gratian included the doctrine of the Two Swords in his *Decree.* He personally maintained a cautious dualist position: priests are forbidden to wield the material sword, and the prince "does not bear the sword in vain." Gratian, in fact, compiled evidence in favor of both positions. Thus, the debate was carried on in the schools.

One of the most important *quæstiones* on the Two Swords is attributed to Richardus Anglicus. It was written sometime around 1200. Richard weighed all the available arguments. Supporting

---

[39] It is the mission of the church to preach this message.

[40] "For the word of God is living and active, sharper than any two-edged sword, piercing to the division of soul and spirit, of joints and marrow, and discerning the thoughts and intentions of the heart. And before him no creature is hidden, but all are open and laid bare to the eyes of him with whom we have to do" (Heb. 4:12–13).

[41] Quoted in Watt, "Spiritual and Temporal Powers," 371.

[42] The Abbey of Saint Victor in Paris was the seat of a famous school founded by William of Champeaux in the Middle Ages before universities began to develop. The school taught the liberal arts, exegesis, and theology. Its principal teachers were Richard, Andrew, Hugh, and Godefroy, all of whom were given the patronym "of St. Victor."

[43] *Nutus* is a reference to a "nod of command."

[44] All quotes from Watt, "Spiritual and Temporal Powers," 372–73.

the pope's possession of the two swords, he found the "authority to bind and unbind," given to the Apostles by Jesus. It should be remembered that in the past the pope unseated kings (e.g., Childeric III, the last Merovingian king): hard evidence that kings received their authority from him. Likewise, Paul said. "Do you not know that the saints will judge the world?" (1 Cor. 6:2): therefore, it must be possible to appeal from the lay court to the church court. But Gratian's *Decree* also included "dualist" texts, emanating from popes who insisted on the boundaries between the two powers. Alexander III posited that, in temporal matters, it was not possible to appeal from the civil judge to the pope. The logical conclusion was that the emperor did not receive his authority from the pope; otherwise, such an appeal would be possible. Richardus noted that there were kings in history before there were priests: therefore, their power came from God, not from the clergy. Finally, Richardus weighed the arguments, emphasized the nuances, and drew his own "dualist" conclusion: the emperor held his authority directly from God.

Johannes Teutonicus continued to argue the dualist position in his *Ordinary Gloss* on Gratian's *Decree* (ca. 1216). Then, Bernard of Parma, in his ordinary gloss on the *Liber extra* of the decretals (1241–63), returned to the idea that the pope held both swords. Thomas Aquinas also accepted this argument in his *Commentary on the Sentences,* against the opinion of Peter Lombard, the author of this famous theological treatise. This was, in fact, the dominant argument at the time, since Innocent III had reestablished it on a solid footing during his quarrel with the Emperor Henry VI. He claimed that the pope had transferred the Greek Empire to the Germans at the time of Charlemagne when he realized that the Greeks could no longer protect the church of Rome (the primary mission of the temporal sword). It is true that since this time, the Germans had chosen their emperor by election, but it was the pope's responsibility to confirm the election or, if the candidate was incompetent, to veto it. Furthermore, the authority of the elected emperor only came into force with his anointment, a ritual during which the pope placed the temporal sword in the hands of the emperor.

The "hierocratic" interpretation finally won the day in the texts of the decretalists[45] in the early thirteenth century. "For there is one body of the Church and therefore it ought to have only one head. Also, the Lord himself used both swords... but it was Peter alone that he made his vicar on earth, therefore he left him both swords. Further, Moses had both swords and his successor is the pope. Moreover, the pope is the emperor's judge because he confirms him, consecrates and crowns him and can depose him."[46] Therefore, the state cannot be considered an independent reality. A body with two heads would be a monstrosity. This was full circle back to Hugh of St. Victor's idea.

Preluding the full-scale offensive on the hierocratic interpretation that occurred in the fourteenth century, new forms of resistance appeared as early as the twelfth and thirteenth centuries. In 1157, Frederick Barbarossa seized the opportunity to reassert dualism against Adrian IV in Besançon. The imperial crown comes from God through the election of the princes, and not through the church. Claims that the Empire is a fief or a *beneficium* from the pope are contrary to Luke 22.

On his side, Frederick II accepted that the pope, as the "holder of the keys," had the authority to impose spiritual penances, but he rejected the argument that the pope had any authority, in either divine or human law, to "transfer empires at will or punish kings temporally by depriving

---

[45] They were no longer commentators of Gratian's *Decretum* alone; but they also commented on the new pontifical legislation by decretals.

[46] *Ordinary Gloss,* quoted in Watt, "Spiritual and Temporal Powers," 381.

them of their kingdoms, or judge temporal rulers at all."[47] Of course, priests anointed kings and princes, but no one could claim that this gave them the right to unseat them.

The hierocratic interpretation was taught at the University of Oxford. In a controversy over the legitimation of children born before marriage—a principle that was admitted by canon law but not common law—Bishop Robert Grosseteste (ca. 1168–1261) claimed that common law should be made to correspond with canon law because the relationship between temporal law and ecclesiastical law is the same as the relationship between the two swords: "the laws of princes which contradict the decrees of Roman pontiffs are of no validity." The English jurist, Henry of Bracton,[48] replied that the English earls and barons "did not wish to change the laws of England which had hitherto been used and approved." Therefore, there must be a primacy of English custom.

In thirteenth century France there was a moderate interpretation of hierocracy: the clergy held the temporal sword, but it could not wield it directly; it could only command temporal power (*nutum*) to use it. It was at the instigation of spiritual power that temporal power embarked on crusades and battled heresy (the Cathars, Flagellants, Lollards, etc.). In this sense, the clergy held the temporal sword to defend its autonomy, as illustrated in a celebrated anecdote from the *Life of Saint Louis* narrated by Joinville:

> Bishop Guy of Auxerre addressed him [the king] for them all [the prelates of the kingdom of France]: "Sir" said he "these archbishops and bishops here present, have charged me to tell you that Christendom is falling to pieces and melting away in your hands, and will fall away still further, unless you study to remedy it; inasmuch as no one, nowadays, has any dread of excommunication. Wherefore we desire you, Sir, to order your serjeants and bailiffs to use compulsion on such as have been excommunicated a year and a day, that they may give satisfaction to the Church." And the King, without taking counsel at all, made answer, that he would willingly order his bailiffs and serjeants to use compulsion on those that were excommunicated as they demanded; but that he must be allowed to have cognisance whether the sentence were legal or no. They consulted together and replied to the King; that they would not give him cognisance of what pertained to religion; and the King in his turn replied; that he would never give them cognisance of what pertained to him; nor would he ever order his serjeants to force those who were excommunicated to procure absolution whether right or wrong. "For if I did so, I should be flying in the face of God and of justice; and I will give you this as an instance: The bishops of Brittany kept the Count of Brittany no less than seven years under sentence of excommunication, and in the end the Court of Rome absolved him. Now, if I had put compulsion on him after the first year, I should have done so wrongly."[49]

Like Bracton in England, Beaumanoir opposed "the custom of France" to claims of hierocracy; in other words, he advocated dualism under royal control. The temporal sword, he argued, is not to be applied at the "*commandement*" of spiritual power; it is called into action only at its "*supplicacion.*" The king responds to the demands of the church only "*par grace.*"

---

[47] Ibid., 386.

[48] Bracton (d. 1268) was a royal judge in the court of Henry III and famous for his writings on law. He is the presumptive author of *De legibus et consuetudinibus Angliae* (On the laws and customs of England).

[49] In Joinville, *The Memoirs of the Lord of Joinville*, 348–49.

C. The Confrontation between Philip the Fair and Boniface VIII

The confrontation between Philip the Fair and Boniface VIII gave the pope an opportunity to reaffirm the fundamental principles of hierocracy in an extreme—but already obsolete—form in the bull *Unam sanctam* (1303); in turn, the quarrel gave the king and the learned men in his service (including several independent university professors) an equal chance to set out their positions. In doing so, they outlined for the first time some of the "secular" features of the modern state, a state not only free of the church, but a state claiming spiritual influence over its subjects.

The papacy put forward an extreme case in defense of hierocracy. Boniface VIII reminded the king's ambassadors that the papacy had deposed French kings in the past (Childeric III, Louis the Pious) and that it might indeed unseat Philip as well. The pope used the bull *Ausculta fili* to call the French clergy to Rome and sit in judgment over the king's exercise of government. Various legal scholars backed the pope's interpretation.

Gilles of Rome reworked St. Bernard's Two Sword doctrine in the *De potestate papæ*, arguing that the pope possessed a plenitude of power *sine pondere, numero et mensura* (i.e., unrestricted).

James of Viterbo wrote another treatise, *On Christian Government:* "the vicar of Christ has fullness of power, because the whole of that power to rule which Christ has given to the church, priestly and royal, spiritual and temporal, is held by the pope, vicar of Christ." The state cannot be autonomous because society is identified with the church.

Cardinal *Matthew of Aquasparta*, who was close to the pope but not part of university circles, emphasized the same time-tested logic: "the pope has cognisance and judgement of all temporal causes by reason of sin (*ratione peccati*)."[50]

But the clinching argument in the hierocratic debate was the bull *Unam sanctam*, which defended the idea of a universal papal monarchy. As the vicar of Christ, the pope had the right to judge, depose, and establish temporal powers, while no one could sit in judgment of the pope. Thus, the autonomy of the temporal realm is denied.

The papal bull provoked strong reactions from the secular experts and led to a number of important texts: The *Disputation between a Knight and a Clerk* (anonymous author) presented the case as follows: "Curb your tongue, sir clerk, and acknowledge that the king, in right of his royal power, is supreme over the laws, customs and liberties granted to you clergy and that he may add to them or take away from them or amend them according as equity and reason or the advice of his magnates counsels."[51] Others upheld the "custom of France" and assailed Boniface's text, which was said to include "bad and outrageous novelties."

The king's close councillors advised him to convene a general synod which would have the authority to put Boniface VIII on trial (such advice presaged the arguments of the Conciliarists, which came to expression in the next century). The arguments put forward were as follows. The canonists had always admitted that a pope could be judged in certain exceptional circumstances, particularly if a pope is guilty of heresy. While the canonists never devised a procedure for bringing an accusation against the pope, they retained the idea in doctrine and included it in the *Decretum* and in the *glossa ordinaria*, where it was applied to cases other than heresy (e.g., scandal, notorious crime, incorrigibility). The breach only needed to be widened.

William of Nogaret, an advisor and keeper of the seal to Philip IV of France, plotted a strategy. At a meeting of the king's council in the Louvre palace on March 12, 1303, he opened for

---

[50] All texts quoted in Watt, "Spiritual and Temporal Powers," 400–01.

[51] Ibid., 403.

the prosecution. He accused Boniface of being a "manifest heretic, usurper of the chair of Peter, simoniac, blasphemer, destroyer of churches, incorrigible public sinner." He branded him "the very personification of that abomination of desolation of the Temple" (i.e., the Antichrist) which Daniel speaks of, and demanded that he be arraigned. He called on Philip to act with the sword to save the church. It was for the king to take the initiative, he argued, because he was king, and because it was a duty, especially incumbent on the kings of France—and the Capetian monarchy—to uphold and spread the faith. Philip accepted Nogaret's petition, as did another group of senior clergy and members of the University of Paris (this became the rule: if the king was to stand up to spiritual power, he needed his own domestic "spiritual power" capable of arguing the wisdom of God and Reason as eloquently as the pope [and perhaps even against the pope]).

There followed the "affair at Anagni" (September 7, 1303), when William of Nogaret allowed soldiers to occupy the hall in the pontifical palace where the pope awaited them, leading indirectly to the death of the pope.

Next, two new scholarly treatises were published: the *Quaestio in utramque partem* (unknown authorship) and the *On Royal and Papal Power* written by John of Paris.[52]

The novelty of the *Quaestio* was that it quoted Aristotle and Cicero and recalled the idea, with reference to Greco-Roman philosophers, that the existence of the state was intrinsically natural: that it existed before and independently of ecclesiastical sanction. Rather than bring weak facts and feeble dialectical subtleties against political Augustinism, the author advocated an entirely different intellectual principle, raising the issue to a new philosophical plane.

Likewise, the text emphasized that Christ had forbidden Peter to use the material sword, that he had refused to be made king, and that he had commanded "to render to Caesar" what was his. Spiritual power was only spiritual. But the argument did not lead to the unfettered liberation of the state because the *Quaestio* accepted that the pope, though he had no direct power to depose kings, could absolve vassals and subjects of a temporal lord from their oaths of allegiance.

John of Paris anticipated the arguments of the Conciliarists (see chapter 6 below). He granted that the pope had the authority to absolve subjects from allegiance to a disreputable king. However, the opposite was also true: the pope could be summoned to judgment. The papacy was an institution that came only from God; it could not be challenged by men. But the decision as to who should be pope was human, and not divine. The college of cardinals, representing the whole church and responsible for electing the pope, could also depose him: "the body whose consent in the place of the whole church makes a pope might, conversely, unmake him."[53]

This deposition mechanism had to be available in the event that the pope's conduct became scandalous for the church, or if he contributed to the disunity of the Lord's flock. Likewise, it was required if he was illegally elected or advocated theological novelties without counsulting a general council (this argument took sharp aim at *Unam sanctam*). Thus, there was genuine symmetry between the Two Swords; each controlled the orthodoxy of the other.

---

[52] The Dominican John of Paris (real name Jean Quidort) was born ca. 1240 and died 1306. He studied and taught at the University of Paris. A supporter of the ideas of Thomas Aquinas, he wrote several works of philosophy and theology, including *Commentary on the Sentences* (ca. 1285).

[53] Texts quoted in Watt, "Spiritual and Temporal Powers," 407–08.

IV. The Right to Make Laws

The birth of "constitutional" law in the last centuries of the Middle Ages was no doubt the fruit of the rivalry between the Two Swords.[54] The representatives of the two powers did everything they could to limit encroachments on their authority. They had to define, exactly and narrowly, their respective responsibilities and their relationship to each other; at the same time, they gave thought to the limits that respect for certain transcendent norms imposed on one another. This led to an intense debate on the right that the monarch—the pope or the king—had *to make laws.*

A. The Authority to Legislate

This was a new idea. Until then, life in traditional medieval society transpired under the powerful influence of custom, and custom was backed by intangible, sacred powers; no one would dare to change it deliberately. The powers that be could act only within the scope of its authority; their intervention was strictly limited to punishing transgressions.

As we saw, the papacy was the first authority to wriggle free from this restriction, arguing its own eschatological perspective. The idea proved contagious; soon the secular authorities seized on it as well, especially since they believed that they were simply reviving powers held earlier by the Roman emperor. Thereafter, rivalry between the Two Swords only escalated.

In time the result was the modern idea that men, through the intermediary of an absolute monarch, or as a "sovereign people," were able to change the law by choice. It was possible, in other words, to *use reason and will to build a society artificially,* liberated from higher norms, whether natural law, custom, or historical law.

Civilists and canonists debated the various facets of the issue. The challenge was to conciliate what was found in Roman law, theology, and the vestiges of Germanic custom surviving in the feudal institutions (in the spirit of the latter, a ruler was forbidden to encroach on custom because his own authority came from a contract with the people embedded in these customs). The awkwardness of the situation was further aggravated by the existence of two incompatible principles in the Justinian code: on the one hand, the principle contained in Ulpian's celebrated formulations: *Quicquid placuit principi legis vigorem habet* ("what pleases the prince has the force of law") and *Princeps legibus solutus est* ("the prince is not bound by the law") (see above, p. 325); on the other hand, the principle contained in the text of *Digna vox* (Codex 1.14.4; 6.23.3; the constitution enacted by Theodosius II in 429 AD), stating that while the prince is the source of all law, he must direct his actions according to the law.

Another maxim of Roman law was also invoked in support of the monarch's legislative authority: *par in parem imperium non habet* ("an equal has no power over an equal"). Thus, the prince was not bound by existing laws (i.e., laws made before his rise to power), since these laws were made by his equals.

Roman law was not clear about the *source* of legislative authority. A debate intensified on the question of whether legislative authority had been transferred from the people by the *lex regia* to the prince on a permanent or a revocable basis. Azo postulated the latter: "the people did not completely abdicate their power, for what is once transferred may be taken back." He also dared to say to the Emperor Henry VI that the prince did not possess *merum imperium* (pure imperium) alone; he shared it with the other high magistrates.

---

[54] This section is based on K. Pennington, "Law, Legislative Authority, and Theories of Government, 1150–1300," and J. P. Canning, "Law, Sovereignty, and Corporation Theory, 1300–1450," in Burns, *Cambridge History,* 424–519.

There was even greater hesitation to grant the prince the right to change custom at his will. Irnerius said, "Today all power of law-making has been transferred to the emperor"; thus, a custom could not prevail against the edict of a prince. And, Johannes Bassianus, a civilist at the end of the twelfth century, declared, "Nature creates many new things daily; God on High established the emperor on earth in order to adapt *leges* to the *varietas naturæ.*" But it should be recalled that Roman law granted custom the authority to make, interpret, and abrogate law. Thus, most civilists held that the prince could not change the law without just and necessary reasons, since in a sense custom represented the will of the people toward the prince.

B. The Influence of the Canonists

Given these scruples of the secular jurists, canonists close to Rome, under the "prophetic" influence that inspired the *Dictatus papæ,* tipped the balance in favor of a monarch's "revolutionary" and "demiurgic" right to make laws. The pope must have the authority to act against the customs and traditions of a sinful humanity.

There is a difference between the authority of the pope and the authority of the Roman emperor: according to Roman law, the authority to legislate is transferred from the people to the prince by the *lex regia;* therefore, the origin of such authority is the people (whence the role—even indirect—of custom in the legislative framework); whereas the authority of the pope comes directly from God—he is *vicarius Christi*—possibly against the will of the sinful people.

Around the year 1200, the pope—the celebrated canonist Innocent III—argued in his decretal *Quanto personam* that papal authority is "not human but divine."

What was at stake was to prove that the pope had the authority to transfer bishops. "God, not man, separates a bishop from his church because the Roman pontiff dissolves the bond between them *by divine rather than human authority,* carefully considering the need for and usefulness of each translation. The pope has this authority because he does not exercise the office of man, but that of the true God on earth."[55]

Laurentius Hispanus (first half of thirteenth century) commented this text in the following terms: "Hence [the pope] is said to have a divine will. O, how great is the power of the prince! He changes the nature of things by applying the essences of one thing to another... he can make iniquity from justice by correcting any canon or law; for in these things his will is held to be reason.[56]... He is held, nevertheless, to shape this power to the public good."[57]

The important words here are "change the nature of things" and "make iniquity from justice." The pope is like a demiurge who can change creation itself. Johannes Teutonicus says, "He can make something out of nothing" (*de nihilo facit aliquid*). It suffices that the pope *wills* and he is *right.* He is under no obligation to provide reasons for his decisions.

By emphasizing the exceptional powers of the pope, the *source* of the law was sharply differentiated from its *contents:* even an unreasonable law could be valid if it came from a person as "exceptional" as the pope.

Thus, Laurentius Hispanus unknowingly opened the door to *legal positivism,* that is, the doctrine that says that the law is the work of human will and posits that a law is valid or invalid not by virtue of its "standards of justice" or "precepts of reason," but on the grounds that it emanates or not from a person with the authority to make the law; in more modern terms, the doctrine

---

[55] Quoted by Pennington, "Law, Legislative Authority," 429.

[56] This is an allusion to Juvenal's formula *pro ratione voluntas* (*The Satires,* 6.223); we will return to the meaning of this below.

[57] Quoted by Pennington, "Law, Legislative Authority," 427–28.

equates *legitimacy* and *legality*.[58] The commentaries of Laurentius Hispanus were echoed over the next four centuries, and his quotation of Juvenal, *pro ratione voluntas,* became a classical designation of absolutism.

Hostiensis (see table 2 above) pushed these formulations in new directions with his distinction between the pope's *potestas absoluta* and *potestas ordinata* (or *ordinaria*). In normal times, the pope can only exercise "ordinary" authority—that is, he must adhere to existing positive law; but in extraordinary circumstances, he can use the extraordinary power invested in him as the vicar of Christ. For example, he can do such "extraordinary" things as undo marriages and exempt clergy from the religious vow of chastity. In this sense, he is "above the law."

The canonists revived various older expressions from Hellenistic theories of monarchy: the pope is the "living law" (*lex animata*); he "has all laws within his breast" (*omne ius habet in pectore suo*). And from the phrase *princeps legibus solutus* he derived the expression *potestas absoluta* ("absolute authority"), which enjoyed a long and illustrious career.

C. Resistance to Absolutism in the Name of Fundamental Norms, Customs, Natural Law, and Divine Law

Civilists like the royal English judge Bracton (middle of the thirteenth century) rejected these doctrinal developments: "The king himself ought not to be subject to any man, but he ought to be subject to God and the law, since the law makes the king (*lex facit regem*). Therefore let the king render to the law what the law has rendered to the king, viz., dominion and power, for there is no king where will rules and not the law (*non est enim rex ubi dominatur voluntas et non lex*)."[59]

Laws are made by customs, tradition, and time; the king has legitimacy because he serves a justice established before him and independently of him, and to which the people are unfailingly attached. If the king claims to be the source of the law by his will, he upsets the established order of things, and he betrays the very mandate he holds to maintain public order.

In the seventeenth and eighteenth centuries, English jurists like Edward Coke remembered Bracton's protestations against absolutism and the emphasis he placed on the intrinsic wisdom of *common law,* which was held to be higher than any person, even the king. Similarly, the eminent theologian Thomas Aquinas rejected the idea that the content of the law could be wholly divorced from its source. For a law to be genuine and have force, it must be absolutely "rational" (see below, pp. 549–50).

Even for the canonists there were certain bounds that the pope could not overstep. Such limits were determined by the *status Ecclesiæ,* that is, the "statute" of the church. For example, the pope could not change the structure of the church, its dogmas, or the basic rules established in

---

[58] Pennington, ibid., recognizes this as a major development: "His [Laurentius] was an important step in the development of political thought. . . . This was a necessary step before a theory of sovereignty could evolve that was untrammeled by morality, reason, and age-old customs. . . . If a sovereign's will was the source of law, and not restricted by the strictures of reason and morality, and if, under certain circumstances, a monarch could promulgate and act contrary to standards of justice and the precepts of reason—even though in the Middle Ages these acts were always justified because of the common good or because of great necessity—all the necessary elements were in place for what later would be called 'reason of state'" (Burns, *Cambridge History,* 428, 430, 436). Pennington's presentation can be objected to on several grounds. If the canonists believed that it was possible to make and unmake the law, it was because the law was subordinate to the eschatological purpose of the church, which was to foster good and hasten the advent of the messianic end-time; it was most certainly not because they did not want to be "restricted by the strictures of reason and morality." If the freedom to make laws is to be extended to a freedom of immorality—the point of view of extreme "legal positivists" such as Machiavelli and Hobbes and Marxist and Nazi legal theorists—then Pennington's idea of modernity has aged badly under the totalitarian experience of the twentieth century.

[59] Quoted by Pennington, "Law, Legislative Authority," 487.

apostolic times. He could unseat a bishop but not eliminate the office of bishoprics, because it had been instituted by Christ himself.

If the pope took such a step, he faced the problem of *resistance to the unlawful authority of the pope*. Hostiensis claimed that a bishop could refuse to obey a papal order if it was against his conscience.

Concerning the authority of the emperor, Accursius in his *Ordinary Gloss* to the Roman law posited that his power was limited by his obligation to respect the property rights of imperial subjects by virtue of natural law and *ius gentium*. This position was not so clear-cut for theology because some of the church fathers were against private property—but most civilists came around to the idea in due course.

In the end the High Middle Ages did not clearly settle the debate. During the eleventh through thirteenth centuries, kings were still in the early phase of their struggle against feudalism, and largely under the moral authority of the church. Consequently, they were far from being able in practice to change the laws of their kingdoms at will. The progress of absolutism in the next period (the fourteenth and fifteenth centuries) went hand-in-hand with the growth of a state apparatus and the development of a national consciousness; then, other ideological innovations occurred, which provided theoretical justification for this progress.

Chapter 5

Saint Thomas Aquinas

Thomas Aquinas was born ca. 1224/25 at the castle of Roccasecca near Aquino in southern Italy (the Holy Roman Emperor Frederick II ruled the region at the time). He died in 1277.

Count Landulf of Aquino, Aquinas's father, was a feudal lord. Aquinas was his youngest son. Landulf offered his son as an oblate to the Benedictine Abbey of Monte Cassino in 1230. In 1239 Aquinas left Monte Cassino for schooling at the Faculty of Arts in Naples. This was the start of a university career that absorbed him until his death. At the age of 20 (1244) and against his family's wishes, he joined the Dominican Order. He was sent to Paris where he lived in the convent of St. James (at this time the College of St. James was one of the leading centers of learning of the Dominican Order). He studied under Albertus Magnus (Albert the Great), professor in the faculty of theology.[1] In 1248, Aquinas followed Albert the Great to Cologne. In 1252, he returned to Paris and remained there until 1259.

In Paris, Aquinas wrote his commentaries on the Bible and on the *Four Books of Sentences* by Peter Lombard.[2] (This was the normal first and second step in the career of a young academic: one became *baccalaureus biblicus* [bachelor of the Bible] and *baccalaureus sententiarum* [bachelor of the *sentences*].)[3] Aquinas quickly rose to fame at the same time that he became a nuisance: it took the intervention of Pope Alexander VI for him to obtain his *licentia docendi*. He became a professor at the university and took part in the fight between the seculars and the regulars.

Aquinas returned to Italy between 1259 and 1268, living in Anagni, Orvieto, Rome, and Viterbo (he taught at the Roman Curia). Aristotelianism spread throughout universities, reaching Paris, where it triggered a moral and intellectual crisis. For the third time, Aquinas returned to Paris,

---

[1] Albert was the first great translator and commentator of Aristotle's texts, rediscovered through contacts with the Arabs in Spain and the Crusades to the Holy Land.

[2] During the Middle Ages, Lombard's *Sentences*—written toward the middle of the twelfth century—was the principal textbook in use in the faculties of theology before Aquinas's own *Summa theologica* replaced it.

[3] See en.wikipedia.org/wiki/Thomas_Aquinas.

living in the capital of the Capetians between 1268 and 1272.[4] For him these were extraordinarily productive years during which he produced the greater part of his *Summa Theologica*. Finally, in 1272, he was called to Naples to lead the faculty of theology. He died at the Cistercian Fossanova Abbey on March 7, 1277, after falling ill en route to the Second Ecumenical Council of Lyon. His life is quite simple: with the exception of his travels, it was a life of inquiry and teaching.

Aquinas was a prolific writer. His work includes the following.

1. *Commentaries on Aristotle,* from translations by Robert Grosseteste and the Dominican friar William of Moerbeke: the commentaries covered the *Posterior Analytics,* Aristotle's *Physics, On the Heavens, De anima, Metaphysics, Nicomachean Ethics, Politica* (up to 3.10), and so on. These commentaries remain authoritative today.
2. *Commentaries on Pseudo-Dionysius the Areopagite:* commentary of *the Divine Names, Mystical Theology, On the Celestial Hierarchy,* and *On the Ecclesiastical Hierarchy.*
3. *Commentaries on the Bible:* in the course of his academic career, Aquinas wrote commentaries on the entire Bible. The commentaries by his students remain as well: commentaries on Isaiah, Jeremiah, Lamentations, Psalms, Job, the Gospel according to Matthew, the Gospel according to John, and the Letters of Paul.
4. *Commentary on the Sentences,* by Peter Lombard: this was Aquinas's first major work, written at the age of 30.
5. *Quaestiones disputatae.*[5] Some 510 disputations survive, organized in seven categories : *De veritate, De potentia, De malo, De spiritualibus creaturis, De anima, De virtutibus, De unione Verbi incarnati.* In addition there are 12 "quodlibetal" (miscellaneous) questions, organized by the disputation leader without a predefined topic.
6. *Summa contra Gentiles.* This was Aquinas's first major *summa.* The Gentiles were pagans, usually Arabs, thus Averroes (Ibn Rushd) and his reading of Aristotle.
7. *Summa theologica.* Several thousand pages in length, the work is organized in three parts: *Prima pars:* the focus is on the one God (subparts include God, the Creation, the world, man); *Seconda pars:* God is the ultimate End (the focus is on morality and politics); *Tertia pars:* the Christian conditions of a return are explored, the Man-God mediator, Christ, and his church (i.e., christology, ecclesiology, the sacraments); there is also a *Supplement to the Third Part,* which Aquinas did not have time to write personally (it was completed by his students); this part concerns the last things, paradise, purgatory, and hell.

---

[4] In total, Thomas Aquinas spent some 15 years in Paris.

[5] In the Scholastic system of education, *disputations* were a formalized method of debate designed to discover and establish truths in theology and the sciences. They were led by a professor of the university following fixed rules. The professor announced a topic formulated as a question (*An Deus sit* ["Does God exist?"], *Utrum aliquis possit pro pecunia mutuata aliquam aliam commoditatem expetere* ["Whether it is right to ask for any other kind of consideration for money lent"], etc.). On the appointed day, the parties presented each side of the argument, *pro* and *contra*; generally, their arguments were derived from the traditional written "authorities": the Bible, the church fathers, philosophers, jurisconsults, and so on. *Aristoteles dicit…, sed contra, Tullius…,* and so on. The presiding professor decided the outcome of the disputation either on the day or at another session; then he presented his conclusion in a detailed argument beginning *Respondeo dicendum…* (I answer that it must be said…). Against the backdrop of his general answer, he provided a reply to each individual objection. The entire process was usually recorded in a written argument. Aquinas held two disputations a week between 1256 and 1259; all were recorded.

I. Nature and Grace in the Thought of Thomas Aquinas

Aquinas's thought was directed by an aim in complete harmony with the spirit of the Papal Revolution: the reconciliation of Christian faith and reason.

A. A Reversal of Perspective

Latin theology of the Early Middles Ages, dominated by the thought of Augustine, opposed the "two cities"—the rule of grace and the rule of nature—against each other. Augustine rejected—or at least denied the legitimacy of—the philosophical and legal thought of antiquity; this he did in favor of the new Christian eschatology that claimed that this world is nothing, or at best a mere transition toward a heavenly kingdom. Aquinas, who with his epoch discovered the culture of antiquity and the work of Aristotle in particular, was intellectually captivated by the positive knowledge contained in such texts as the *Nicomachean Ethics* and *Politics,* completely unknown to the thinkers of the Early Middle Ages. Aquinas believed that the science of antiquity, a description of the world below, was intrinsically good—despite its pagan character—because it was a product of reason; he believed that it was important to make a place for this science within Christianity, as the Papal Revolution inspired Christians to intensify their involvement with the world and make efforts to transform it rather than flee it. Accordingly, Aquinas's intellectual approach was to *combine the scientific culture of antiquity and Christian theology* and show evidence of their fundamental complementarity.

Aquinas's entire oeuvre is directed toward this aim. In order to understand the future impact of his thinking on political and legal ideas, we need here at the outset to emphasize a particular aspect of his synthesis: the new relationship that he establishes between *nature* and *grace.*

Fundamentally, Aquinas modified the theological status of nature. For Augustine, nature was totally corrupted by the Fall. Aquinas, in contrast, posits that nature was indeed damaged by the Fall, but not corrupted: nature was only "wounded," and the wound can be healed.

If left to itself, nature can no longer produce a good life or a good society, nor can it lead one to perfection; its dynamic has been broken. In this sense, it is true that the ideals of antiquity are illusory. Only God's grace can give meaning to human life anew. For Aquinas, however, the action of grace is not extrinsic: it will not divert human beings from their nature in order to save themselves; on the contrary, grace heals nature, and it is the immanent dynamism of nature, now restored, that brings about salvation. The normal action of grace is to restore in humanity the powers of nature paralyzed by the Fall, that is, in the first place, reason and free will, which recover their capacity to discern and desire the true good.

Consequently, *nature can once again become the central focus and aim of science, including divine science, that is, theology.* Everything that the Ancients—beginning with Aristotle but including Cicero, the Roman jurisconsults, and the many others—said about a moral and political life in harmony with nature, regains its full value.

However, the train of natural or "cardinal" virtues must be pulled by the engine of theological virtues, which are the fruits of grace. The metaphor is brought to mind by the second part of the second part (*Secunda pars secundæ partis*) of the *Summa* where the emphasis, certainly not accidental, is on the three theological virtues, *faith, hope,* and *charity,* then the four cardinal virtues *prudence, justice, fortitude,* and *temperance.*

In practice, however, the natural virtues, even when they are directed toward a supernatural goal, preserve their structure and properties in full—beginning with justice, which commands

Aquinas's entire thought in social and political matters. In many respects, the thousands of pages devoted by Aquinas to moral and political ideas are a mix of pure Aristotelian gloss and Christian theology, where the one does not modify, nor is modified by, the other. Aquinas merely grafts, so to speak, the nonbiblical philosophy of nature of Aristotle and the Ancients to the body of biblical theology, between the doctrine of Creation and the doctrine of the end-time.

This reversal of perspective on nature and grace occurs at different places in the *Summa,* notably in the treatise on sin (Ia–IIæ, q. 71–89) and the treatise on grace (Ia–IIæ, q.109–14). Let us present this briefly.[6]

B. Original Sin

All humanity descends from Adam (q. 81, art. 1); Adam sinned; therefore, all human beings are sinners because the members of a body are accountable for the sins of the head. Therefore, in each person, sin affects his or her nature, which is transmitted by Adam to each. As such, original sin is a "sin of nature" (*peccatum naturæ*).

Sin is a *habitus*—an inclination to act in this or that way—which disturbs human nature; it is like a sickness (q. 82, art. 1). Since bodily sickness is both a privation of health and a positive production of malignant humors, original sin is both a privation of "original justice" (Aquinas takes this idea from Augustine) and a permanent disposition to act wrongly. Aquinas writes: "a certain inclination to an inordinate act does follow from Original Sin, not directly [such as other *habits* that incline a power to act, e.g., force, which inclines to an act of courage], but indirectly by the removal of the obstacle that original justice once opposed to the inordinate movements [of the soul and the body]: just as an inclination to inordinate bodily movements results indirectly from bodily sickness" (q. 82, art. 1, sol. 3).[7]

Original sin consists in the lust after (*concupisciencia*) or attachment to perishable goods in a material world, rather than in ignorance (ignorance exists in the sinner, but it is the result of an obscuration of reason by lust). Sin is "formally" an absence of original justice and "materially" a concupiscence (q. 82, art. 3).

All of question 85 is devoted to the "corruption of the good of nature" by original sin. Sin "diminish[es] the good of nature" (*diminuit bonum naturæ*). Because of sin, humanity is "stripped of the gifts of grace and [only] wounded in his natural gifts" (*expoliatur gratuitis et vulneratur in naturalibus,* as Venerable Bede formulates it) (q. 85, art. 1, *Sed contra*). For Aquinas, these formulas reflect a precise diagnosis. First, the "diminution" in question does not affect "the principles of which nature is constituted, and the properties that flow from them, such as the powers of the soul, and so forth" (q. 85, art. 1, *Sed contra,* concl.).[8] What it does, on the one hand, is to remove entirely the "gift of original justice," which was previously a part of human nature; and on

[6] *The Summa Theologica of St. Thomas Aquinas,* 2nd and rev. ed. (1920), literally translated by Fathers of the English Dominican Province (The translator used the online edition, copyright © 2008 by Kevin Knight with corrections, www.newadvent.org/summa); hereafter cited in the text. For a complete edition in Latin, see *Summa theologica Curia fratrum eiusdem Ordinis,* 5 vols. (Salamanca: Bibliotecca de autores cristianos, 1964).

[7] Sin wounded nature so completely that humans were rendered mortal. In this respect, Aquinas diverged from Aristotle, for whom death, of course, belongs to the natural order: all sublunary beings are subject to "generation" and "corruption." Aquinas is pressed into subtle arguments to reconcile the Aristotelian concept of nature with the biblical idea that "God did not make death" (Wisd. 1:13) and that death—like physical defects and sickness—is the punishment for sin; in the words of Paul, "sin came into the world through one man and death through sin" (Rom. 5:12). Aquinas explains that, in the state of nature, the soul being the form of the body, the immortality of the human soul itself makes the body immortal, the law of generation and corruption being valid solely for other natural beings (see q. 85, art. 5, concl.; q. 85, art. 6, obj. 2 and concl.; see Ia, q. 97, art. 1).

[8] A few lines further, the text adds to this list: "being, living and understanding." None of this is affected by sin.

the other hand, it "diminishes" (in the strict quantitative sense of the term) the "natural inclination to virtue." This "diminution" of inclination to virtue does not mean that the inclination is affected at the source, only that an obstacle prevents it from reaching its goal; and that obstacle is sin. Diminution is not "by subtraction" but "by raising obstacles" (reply to obj. 1). It is true that the more man sins the more the obstacle grows until the salvation of humanity becomes virtually impossible. However, as long as the root is not pulled up, there will always be an authentic inclination to good in humanity—it is in this sense that nature is *wounded*, not *corrupted* by the Fall.[9]

Although Aquinas admits that sin "diminishes mode, species and order" in humanity, he nevertheless maintains that "there is a good belonging to the very substance of nature, which good has its mode, species [beauty] and order, and is neither destroyed nor diminished by sin" (q. 85, art. 4, concl.). For example, contrary to Augustine's opinion, "in order to know the truth in all things, [humanity] does not need in all cases a [divine] light in addition to his natural light" (q. 109, art. 1, concl.). Likewise, Aquinas accepts that, corrupted by sin, we cannot desire the good completely, but "because human nature is not altogether corrupted by sin, so as to be shorn of every natural good, even in the state of corrupted nature [we] can, by virtue of its natural endowments, work some particular good, as to build dwellings, plant vineyards, and the like" (q. 109, art. 2, concl.). He is like "a sick man [who] can of himself make some movements, yet he cannot be perfectly moved with the movements of one in health, unless by the help of medicine he be cured." Without the help of *grace* he cannot reach his supernatural good; however, "he can perform works conducing to some good proportionate to his nature" (q. 109, art. 5, concl.).

C. Grace Restores Nature

Thus, Aquinas redirects attention to nature and its immanent laws and to the classical authors who discussed this in antiquity.

The Aristotelian idea of justice regains its interest again. Aquinas recognizes, of course, that Aristotelian justice cannot fully apply to Christians because it is based on an equality, and between human beings and God there is absolute inequality.[10] Whatever the sinner does or does not do, his or her acts contain neither merit nor demerit in the eyes of God; the works of human justice are simply void. It is only by grace that a person does something good. Aquinas says that it is indeed God's grace that restores human nature with a free will: he conciliates the omnipotence of God and human liberty by making the latter the consequence of the former. From this moment on, human justice becomes meaningful again. *God surely rewards our works of righteousness,* not because they make God our debtor (which God cannot be because he is the giver of all things, including our personal gifts), but because God owes it to himself to respect the good nature that he places in us: "as our action has the character of merit only by virtue of divine ordination, it does not follow that merit makes God our debtor; it makes God His own debtor, inasmuch as it is necessary that the ordination [that He imprinted in creatures] should be carried out" (q. 114, art. 1, rep. to obj. 3).[11]

---

[9] Aquinas adds that even among the damned this inclination to good exists, because it is requisite for a *remorse of conscience* (reps. to obj. 3).

[10] We know that pure justice applied to humans leads to their loss. Aquinas writes, "For the sinner deserves not life, but death, according to Romans [6:23]: 'The wages of sin is death.'"

[11] God must reward our just works according to our supererogatory merits, that is, those that build up our "credit" in the great ledger of life's works. These works can be deducted from another's debts (q. 114, art. 6, concl.: "it is congruous and in harmony with friendship that God should fulfil man's desire for the salvation of another").

For these reasons, and in keeping with the spirit of the Papal Revolution, Aquinas the theologian offers a systematic discussion of the principal categories of rational political and legal science in his *Summa theologica:* the *law, justice,* and the *state.*

III. The Law

The "treatise on laws" in the *Summa theologica*[12] was particularly important in an age when the papacy and the secular monarchies were rediscovering the instrument of legislation. With customary clarity, Aquinas places his treatise on laws in the context of his moral philosophy: "We have now to consider the extrinsic principles of acts. Now the extrinsic principle inclining to evil is the devil, of whose temptations we have spoken in the First Part [of the *Summa theologica*], [q. 114]. But the extrinsic principle moving to good is God, Who both instructs us by means of his Law, and assists us by his Grace: wherefore in the first place we must speak of law [q. 90–108]; in the second place, of grace [q.109–14]."

Let us begin with a discussion of the very concept of law, then turn to the different kinds of law: *eternal* law, *natural* law, *human* [i.e., positive] law, *divine* [i.e., revealed] law, itself subdivided into the *Old* Law (the Torah, the Old Testament law) and the *New* Law (the law of the Gospel).

A. The Concept of the Law

The law is defined as follows: "an ordinance of reason for the common good, made by him who has care of the community" (*quæam rationis ordinatio ad bonum commune, ab eo qui curam communitatis habet, promulgata*) (q. 90, art. 4, concl.). Each part of this definition is important.

The law (art. 1) is dependent on "reason" (it is *aliquid rationis*); that is, it is an order by which human acts are authorized or forbidden. It is a "rule and measure of human acts." It is so, inasmuch as it relates acts to an end (this is the very purpose of reason: to link means and ends with a view to illustrating the meaning of things). The end in question is *the common good of the community* (art. 2).

While recognizing the legitimacy of life and private property (see below), Aquinas nevertheless establishes a hierarchy, in Aristotelian fashion, between the individual and the community. The law of the community (the law of all) predominates over a law framed for a single person or a community of inferior rank (a private law), because the good of the community is superior to the private good of the part, even for the part itself.

This relationship between the law and the common good defines another fundamental attribute of the law. It must be *framed for and by the community as a whole or by the representative of the community* (art. 3). "Now to order anything to the common good, belongs either to the whole people (*alicujus gerentis vicem totius multitudinis*), or to someone who is the viceregent of the whole people. And therefore the making of a law belongs either to the whole people or to a public personage who has care of the whole people (*personam publicam quæ totius multitudinis curam habet*)" (art. 3, concl.).

An individual cannot frame the law because he or she does not have sufficient coercive powers but can only provide advice. From this, two conditions arise (q. 97, art. 3, rep. to obj. 3): either the people are "free" (*libera multitudo*)—that is, they form a republic, and they make their own

[12] The Old Law, Ia–IIæ, q. 98–105; the New Law, Ia–IIæ, q. 106–08.

laws (Aquinas is thinking of examples from antiquity and of the republics existing in Italy in his age); or sovereign authority is in the hands of a monarchy, and in this case the king does not act as a private person but as a representative of all the people. What is important to know is how and when such a representative mandate is given, and whether it is provisional or permanent, conditional or unconditional; Aquinas does not address these questions here. What is certain, though, is that the people are the law-making authority. Aquinas undoubtedly continues the ancient Greco-Roman tradition and disagrees with the Pauline and Augustinian idea of a direct God-given authority to certain individuals because of sin.[13]

Finally, the law must be publicly *promulgated* (art. 4). Its public character is part of its essence. The law is addressed to human intelligence; it can only work if one has knowledge of it. Now, the source and purpose of the law is the same; everyone must know the law and know that everyone knows it: it must be public knowledge, which it can be only if it is promulgated. Therefore, an unpromulgated law is not a law. Setting down the law in writing is the way of continuing its promulgation indefinitely.

Thus, Aquinas denounces every form of government based on secrecy (Platonic government, for example, and later still, Machiavellian and absolutist government), and as a corollary he condemns the retroactivity of the law.

He gives an interesting reply to the objection that *natural law* remains valid, though it is not promulgated: natural law is promulgated and public to the extent that God inscribed it in every person's heart, that is, in everyone's *conscience* (Cicero, we recall, made the same claim). Consequently, no one can say that he or she does not know the law. Let us examine the different kinds of laws.

B. Eternal Law

In the continuum of ancient philosophy—Stoic philosophy in particular—Aquinas says that "the whole community of the universe is governed by Divine Reason" (q. 91, art. 1, concl.), and since God is eternal, there is also an "eternal law," eternally promulgated because it is one with the divine Word. By anticipation it contains all the forms of creation in the divine intellect, just as a craftsman has in mind the form of the object he will produce before he creates it.

Augustine said, "the eternal law is the divine order or will of God, which requires the preservation of natural order, and forbids the breach of it" (*Contra faustum,* 22.27; see Cicero, *De legibus,* 2.4, no doubt Augustine's source of inspiration). Aquinas says, "the eternal law is nothing else than the type of Divine Wisdom, as directing all actions and movements" (q. 93, art. 1, concl.). Aquinas, like Augustine, identifies this Wisdom with the Word, the second person of the Trinity, so that eternal law, without being strictly speaking the Son, is "appropriated to the Son, on account of the kinship between reason and word" (*appropriatur filio propter convenentiam quam habet ratio ad verbum*) (q. 93, art. 1, rep. to obj. 2).

Furthermore, the idea of Providence is related to the idea of eternal law, but it differs from it in that Providence is the execution of the eternal law in each creature. Finally, because God creates each creature and directs it toward its end, eternal law cannot be considered static; it is a dynamic reality through which "God governs the movements of all beings in order to attract them to him and enable them to achieve their end."[14] All laws derive in one way or another from eternal law.

---

[13] Aquinas's position had enormous repercussions for the subsequent history of political ideas. In particular, it provided a defense against absolutism when later, in modern times, the principle of the ultimate sovereignty of the people was set out by theorists with Thomist training, such as Francisco Suarez.

[14] See introduction to *Somme théologique*, vol. 3, *Prima pars*, ed. Jean-Marie Aubert (Paris: Edition du Cerf, 1993).

C. Natural Law

Natural law is the active and organizing presence of eternal law in all creatures, and particularly in human beings. "Since all things subject to Divine providence are ruled and measured by the eternal law...; it is evident that all things partake somewhat of the eternal law (*aliqualiter participant legem æternam*) in so far as, namely, from its being imprinted on them, they derive their respective inclinations to their proper acts and ends" (*ST* q. 91, art. 2, concl.).

The creatures subject to divine providence fall into two broad categories: rational creatures and irrational creatures. Irrational creatures partake in the eternal law by their subjection: inert things are subject to determinism, animals are subject to their instincts, and so on. As far as the rational creature is concerned, it is "subject to Divine providence in the most excellent way, in so far as it partakes of a share of providence, by being provident both for itself and for others" (q. 91, art. 2, concl.).

The rational creature possesses reason, which is the ability to think about the relationship between means and ends. In this sense, a man is, so to speak, called to be "his own providence, a providence over himself received as a delegation of Divine providence" (Jean-Maris Aubert). People do not receive imprints of eternal law passively; they receive the capacity to make laws and to conduct themselves in respect of these laws.

In the irrational creature, eternal reason expresses itself as an invincible inclination to perform this or that act and to pursue this or that end. In the rational creature, it expresses itself as an inclination to discern what is good and what is evil. Aquinas describes a theory of "conscience" in almost the same terms as Cicero (see above, pp. 289–90):

> Hence the Psalmist after saying (Psalm 4.6): "Offer up the sacrifice of justice," as though someone asked what the works of justice are, adds: "Many say, Who showeth us good things?" in answer to which question he says: "The light of Thy countenance, O Lord, is signed upon us": thus implying that the light of natural reason, whereby we discern what is good and what is evil, which is the function of the natural law, is nothing else than an imprint on us of the Divine light. It is therefore evident that the natural law is nothing else than the rational creature's participation of the eternal law. (q. 91, art. 2, concl.)

But before they are governed by reason, the chief characteristic of their species, humans are substance and animals. Therefore, natural law translates as particular attributes for each of these levels:

> in man there is first of all an inclination to good in accordance with the nature which he has in common with all substances: inasmuch as every substance seeks the preservation of its own being, according to its nature.... Secondly, there is in man an inclination to things that pertain to him more specially, according to that nature which he has in common with other animals: and in virtue of this inclination, those things are said to belong to the natural law, "which nature has taught to all animals" [*Pandect. Just.* I, tit. i], such as sexual intercourse, education of offspring and so forth. Thirdly, there is in man an inclination to good, according to the nature of his reason, which nature is proper to him: thus man has a natural inclination to know the truth about God, and to live in society: and in this respect, whatever pertains to this inclination belongs to the natural law; for instance, to shun ignorance, to avoid offending those among whom one has to live, and other such things regarding the above inclination. (q. 94, art. 2, concl.)

This brief list of attributes of human nature corresponds by and large with the attributes identified by the Ancients.

Natural law has two additional attributes: it is *universal* (q. 94, art. 4), and it is *unalterable* (q. 94, art. 5). It is universal like the primary axioms of science, although there is a difference between speculative reason and practical reason. In both cases, the first principles are common to all, and are therefore universal. But, whereas the particular logical conclusions of the general principles of knowledge remain universal truths, the particular applications of the principles of practical reason can differ according to circumstances, and in particular when knowledge of natural law is "perverted by passion, or evil habit, or an evil disposition of nature; thus formerly, plundering, although it is expressly contrary to the natural law, was not considered wrong among the Germans, as Julius Caesar relates (*De Bello Gall.* vi 23)" (*ST* Ia, q. 94, art. 4, concl.; translation with modification).

The observation is very important. First, it happens that nature creates monsters. Then, "passions" or "custom" can obscure natural law. Consequently, a reference to natural law will not always play a conservative role. Aquinas holds that the Germanics did not live "according to nature" as Tacitus thought, and manifestly Aquinas believes that the civilization of Caesar is closer to natural law than barbarian custom is. Consequently, for the barbarians Romanization was neither a denaturing nor a replacement of an arbitrary custom by another equally arbitrary one; rather, it was progress toward a life closer to nature as created and desired by God. This confirms what we said earlier about the status change of natural law during the Papal Revolution (see above, pp. 533–34).[15]

When the law of nature was momentarily erased from a person's soul (art. 6)—"either by evil persuasions, just as in speculative matters errors occur in respect of necessary conclusions; or by vicious customs and corrupt habits"—it became necessary to restore it.

Even revealed law does not change natural law: Aquinas, who could not, of course, call into question prophecy, states that the revelation does not change natural law, it simply adds to it, just as clothes do not change the human body. Beneath the clothes, the naked being remains with all its natural properties.

D. Human Law

One might believe that humans are sufficiently guided by natural law. However, this is not the case: first, because nature only provides an aptitude to virtue, not fully perfected virtues, human law plays an important role in the development of virtue (1); second, because natural law is general, certain additional determinations are necessary to direct human life *hic et nunc* (2).

1. It is for virtue as for other human aptitudes for which nature provides the pattern but which must then be cultivated and developed. Nature, for example, provides a man with "reason and his hands," which he will use to develop technical skills, but he will only be able to use such skills when, through effort and experience, he has thoroughly internalized them. Here, Aquinas comes very close to the modern notions of "nature" and "nurture" (culture), in the sense that he demonstrates that culture is a *sui generis* product added to nature, yet distinct from it; such skills are not to "reason and the hands" what the mature animal is to the embryo, that is, an actualization of what exists in the egg in its virtual state. Similarly, the perfection of virtue results from a process involving the intervention of society:

[15] Another example: homosexuality, the supreme "unnatural crime," was not considered a vice by the Greeks (see q. 94, art. 6, concl.); this does not mean that the natural law is different for Greeks and Christians, but that passions prevented the Greeks from recognizing and admitting natural law.

> A man needs to receive this training (*disciplina*) from another, whereby to arrive at the perfection of virtue. And as to those young people who are inclined to acts of virtue, by their good natural disposition, or by custom (*consuetude*), or rather by the gift of God, paternal training suffices, which is by admonitions. But since some are found to be depraved, and prone to vice, and not easily amenable to words, it was necessary for such to be restrained from evil by force and fear, in order that, at least, they might desist from evil-doing, and leave others in peace, and that they themselves, by being habituated in this way, might be brought to do willingly what hitherto they did from fear, and thus become virtuous. *Now this kind of training, which compels through fear of punishment, is the discipline of laws.* Therefore, in order that man might have peace and virtue, it was necessary for laws to be framed. (q. 95, art. 1, concl.)

2. Just as science does not fully exist when we only posit the first principles, similarly the law is not full and "operative" when the first principles of natural law are only inscribed in our conscience; other determinations are required. They can be obtained in two distinct ways: either by *derivation of particular principles from generalities,* or by *adaptation of these principles to the diversity of circumstances.* Aquinas defines the first mode in these terms: "Just as, in the speculative reason, from naturally known indemonstrable principles, we draw the conclusions of the various sciences, the knowledge of which is not imparted to us by nature, but acquired by the efforts of reason, so too it is from the precepts of the natural law, as from general and indemonstrable principles, that the human reason needs to proceed to the more particular determination of certain matters" (q. 91, art. 3, concl.). For example, the commandment "you shall not kill" derives, as a conclusion from principles, from the more general precept, "you shall do harm to no one."

The second mode is "likened to that whereby, in the arts, general forms are particularized as to details: thus the craftsperson needs to determine the general form of a house to some particular shape." Thus, the terms of criminal punishment derive, as a determination, from the principle that a given wrongdoing must be punished (q. 95, art. 2, concl.).

It is the proper task of human or positive law to reach these conclusions and to make these determinations. From this we see that human law is legitimate only if it derives from natural law in some way; it is not autonomous; whatever is just in human law comes from the natural law immanent in it.

Aquinas posits that "the law of nations" derives from natural law according to the first mode, and "civil law" according to the second (q. 95, art. 4, concl.).

But these derivations from natural law could come about bit by bit. Why, then, do they appear in the form of this general rule, which is the law? Because, although the law cannot anticipate all particular cases, and it is necessary in this sense to leave the judge a certain role—only the judge, the living law, can decide questions of fact—it is preferable all the same to resolve as many issues as possible through the law.

> Firstly, it is easier to find a few wise men competent to frame right laws, than to find the many who would be necessary to judge aright of each single case. Secondly, because those who make laws consider long beforehand what laws to make; whereas judgment on each single case has to be pronounced as soon as it arises: and it is easier for man to see what is right, by taking many instances into consideration, than by considering one solitary fact. Thirdly, because lawgivers judge in the abstract and of future events; whereas those who sit in judgment of things present, towards which they are affected by love, hatred, or some kind of cupidity; wherefore their judgment is perverted. Since then the animated justice of the judge is not found in every man, and since it can be deflected, therefore it was necessary, whenever possible, for the law to determine how to judge, and for very few matters to be left to the decision of men. (q. 95, art. 1, rep. to obj. 2)

But human law, in order to be legitimate, must possess certain attributes, which can be deduced from the above definitions of its origin and purpose. It is both a rule and measure of human acts; the rule itself is governed by two hierarchically superior norms: divine law and natural law; its purpose is the common good. Therefore, human law must be *in harmony with religion,* attuned to the *natural aptitudes* of those for whom it is intended (for example, the law does not place the same demands on children as on mature adults), *clear,* framed for the *common good,* and last but not least, *general* in its source and in its purpose. In its source: we saw above that the law is framed by the community or its representative. In its purpose: since the very idea of the "law" implies this: "For if there were as many rules or measures as there are things measured or ruled, they would cease to be of use, since their use consists in being applicable to many things. Hence law would be of no use, if it did not extend further than to one single act. Because the decrees of prudent men are made for the purpose of directing individual actions" (q. 96, art. 1, concl.).

What is the scope of human action covered by the law? Again Aquinas continues and officializes in Catholic theology the distinction between *crime* and *sin* made by Abelard and the canonists (a distinction important for the idea of freedom in the West; see above, pp. 532–33). *The law punishes crime, not sin.* The reasoning is as follows: the law must be adapted to the nature of those it governs; it accepts of a child things that are forbidden to an adult. Similarly, because of the law,

> many things are permissible to men not perfect in virtue, which would be intolerable in a virtuous man. Now human law is framed for a number of human beings, the majority of whom are not perfect in virtue. Wherefore human laws do not forbid all vices, from which the virtuous abstain, but only the more grievous vices, from which it is possible for the majority to abstain; and chiefly those that are to the hurt of others, without the prohibition of which human society could not be maintained: thus human law prohibits murder, theft and such like. (q. 96, art. 2, concl.)

Furthermore, since the law is a teaching, it must be progressive: if the commandments given to imperfect people are too severe, it is like putting new wine in old bottles: the bottles break and the wine is lost. Severe laws will not be obeyed, and consequently less demanding laws will also be ignored.

Elsewhere, Aquinas mentions a rather curious idea hinted at above: certain sins—for example, usury—cannot not be forbidden by law for reasons already stated, nor should they be, because they are *useful,* and to forbid them would harm public interest. Aquinas has an intuitive understanding of the social usefulness of trade, free enterprise, and banks, but he only wants to tolerate them in the name of this particular paradox. We will have to wait for Calvinism, Bernard de Mandeville and Adam Smith for "private vices," and producers of "public goods" to be analyzed as new expressions taken by virtue itself in a transformed social context.

Are people obligated in their consciences to obey human law? Can they not resist it? Cannot the "court of conscience" (*forum conscientiæ*) find against it (art. 4)? This is a delicate question, but Aquinas manages to formulate a seemingly balanced response; his merit is to posit clear distinctions. Concerning laws that are just in their purpose and their modes, we are bound in conscience to obey them. As for unjust laws, in one way or another, there is no obligation in conscience to obey them, "except perhaps in order to avoid scandal or disturbance" (*scandalum vel turbationem*). In this case, "a man should even yield his right" charitably (Aquinas quotes the Sermon on the Mount: "If a man . . . take away thy coat, let go thy cloak also unto him; and whosoever will force thee one mile, go with him other two"). The only argument for resisting power, even at the risk of scandal and disturbance, is when the laws are wholly opposed to divine law, for example, a law obliging idolatry.

Is everyone subject to human law? Are there not some enlightened people, directly led by the law of the Holy Spirit, who are exempt from human laws? Is not the prince, according to the *Digest, legibus solutus* (art. 5), one of these? As for "spiritual men," "the very fact that [they] are subject to law, is due to the leading of the Holy Ghost, according to 1 Peter 2.13: 'Be ye subject... to every human creature for God's sake'" (q. 36, art. 5, rep. to obj. 2).[16] As for the obligation of the statesman to obey the law, a distinction must be made between directive force (*vis directiva*) and coercive force (*vis coactive*).

> The sovereign is said to be "exempt from the law," as to its coercive power (*vis coactivam*); since, properly speaking, no man is coerced by himself, and law has no coercive power save from the authority of the sovereign. Thus then is the sovereign said to be exempt from the law, because none is competent to pass sentence on him, if he acts against the law. Wherefore on Psalms 50.6: "To Thee only have I sinned," a gloss says that "there is no man who can judge the deeds of a king." But as to the directive force of law, the sovereign is subject to the law by his own will, according to the statement [in the decretals of Gregory IX] that "whatever law a man makes for another, he should keep himself."[17] And a wise authority [Dionysius Cato or Ausonius] says: "Obey the law that thou makest thyself." Moreover the Lord reproaches those who "say and do not"; and who "bind heavy burdens and lay them on men's shoulders, but with a finger of their own they will not move them" (Matthew 23.3–4). Hence, in the judgment of God, the sovereign is not exempt from the law, as to its directive force; but he should fulfill it to his own free-will and not of constraint. Again the sovereign is above the law, in so far as, when it is expedient, he can change the law, and dispense in it according to time and place.[18] (q. 96, art. 5, rep. to obj. 3)

Next, Aquinas reflects on the *interpretation* to be given to human law. Should we keep to the letter of the law or to its "spirit," when the letter leads to a manifestly absurd decision in a particular case? The law must be interpreted according to the lawgiver's intention. The lawgiver pursues the common good and frames the law as a means to this end, not as an end in itself; if he had known that the means would go against the end in a given case, of course he would have chosen another means, and this is why we can interpret his text. Even an individual can interpret the law in cases of necessity, when there is not enough time to turn to a higher authority or the legislator himself.

That said, the best interpreter of the law is *custom*. Here Aquinas shows (q. 97) that he has a certain understanding of cultural evolutionism and of these phenomena of selection and rule-fixing by circular causation that theories of "spontaneous order" endeavor to explain much later. First of all, human law, though it derives from eternal law and natural law, which are unchangeable, can change for two reasons: first, because reason makes progress in its way to determine and adapt divine laws; second, because, human things being changeable, a fixed rule would provide different results under new circumstances, and therefore in order to "stick" to natural law as closely as possible, positive law must amend itself constantly (art. 1). Nevertheless, change is intrinsically dangerous because it disrupts habituation to the law, which is a necessary condition for collective obedience to the law ("laws derive very great force from custom" [Aristotle, *Politics* 2.1269a.24]). Thus, we should only accept change when the expected rewards compensate the inconveniences arising from the fact of changing (Aquinas quotes the *Digest:* "in establishing

16 Again we come across the doctrine of Romans 13 as developed by Augustine (see above, pp. 456–58). In the name of humility and the penance due for original sin, a Christian must accept an unjust and incomprehensible power.

17 A formal transcription in canon law of the maxim *Digna vox*.

18 This reservation defends the idea of absolutism, although in a spirit of equilibrium with canon law.

new laws, there should be evidence of the benefit to be derived, before departing from a law which has long been considered just").

Yet, serious objections can be raised against the force of custom (*consuetudo*) (q. 97, art. 3, obj. 1–3). If human law is just because it derives from natural law and divine law, custom, in turn, possesses nothing that can add or subtract from the justice of the law. Moreover, "many evils cannot make one good. But he who first acted against the law, did evil. Therefore by multiplying such acts, nothing good is the result," and a custom, produced by numerous acts against the law, can never legitimately force out the law. Custom "grows by the acts of private individuals," whereas the law must be framed either by the people or by its official representatives.

In response, Aquinas sets out to prove that there is a *rationality* of custom, despite appearances to the contrary. Though it is true that human reason expresses itself in written and spoken words, it is also true that it expresses itself through acts, "since seemingly a man chooses as good that which he carries into execution" (q. 97, art. 3, concl.). Therefore, just as one can explain the law with words and change it, the same is possible through acts as well, especially when acts are repeated a number of times by large numbers of people, because it proves that such acts are not accidental but are performed for a particular reason.

Moreover, we said above that the law can and must change because, when circumstances change, the same law changes meaning, and while it was useful in the past to the community, it can become harmful. When people act against the law, they only implement the change they feel is necessary. Finally, since the source of the law is the community, it is not surprising that a practice involving the whole community (custom) influences the law. Accordingly, "custom has the force of a law, abolishes law, and is the interpreter of law" (*consuetudo et habet vim legis, et legem abolet, et est legum interpretatrix*).[19] The fact remains that custom, like human law, cannot go against natural and divine laws.

E. Divine Law: Generalities

Almost all of the above is drawn from doctrines dating from antiquity: what is said about eternal law comes from the doctrines of Stoicism; what is said about natural law and its relation to positive law is inspired by Aristotle, Cicero, and the *Digest*. Aquinas breaks free from these traditions when he posits the idea that added to eternal, natural, and human law there is "Divine law," or *revealed* law (that is to say, the two successively revealed laws of the Old and New Testament). Here we have the other aspect of the spirit of the Papal Revolution, which places moral and political life in the perspective of an "economy of salvation." We can see that Aquinas tries to adopt balanced positions on the millenarian controversies of his time.

Here we need to clarify a point of vocabulary. The expression "Divine law" applied to revealed law does not suggest that the other laws under discussion are not also "divine": eternal law and natural law also come from God, of course; the "divineness" of the revealed laws is an attribute not of their origin but of their mode of promulgation.

Four reasons justify that divine laws, known to humanity by supernatural ways, are needed to lead them toward their proper aim, eternal happiness. The first and strongest—or, at any rate, the one that shows best the difference with the tradition of natural law—is:

> if man were ordained to no other end than that which is proportionate to his natural faculty, there would be no need for man to have any further direction of the part of his reason, besides the natural law and human law which is derived from it. But since man is ordained

[19] This same formula is found in canon law as early as Gratian's *Decretum*.

> to an end of eternal happiness which is inproportionate to man's natural faculty, as stated above (Question 5, Article 5), therefore it was necessary that, besides the natural and the human law, man should be directed to his end by a law given by God. (q. 91, art. 4, concl.)

Just as in the *Divine Comedy* Virgil cannot be Dante's guide beyond purgatory and Beatrice must descend from heaven to reveal the path known only to celestial beings, likewise, when people have a calling to perfect their essence in heaven as beings "capable of God"[20] rather than on earth as natural beings, to do so they must be initiated in paths that lead them by grace not by nature, that is, by the holy Scripture rather than by natural reason.

There are other reasons. If we were only to count on natural reason, we would never have any certainty; the Revelation that we accept through faith gives us certainty. Furthermore, "human law [which knows only exterior acts and not intentions] could not sufficiently curb and direct interior acts"; the divine law fills this gap.[21]

As soon as Aquinas introduces a transcendent, nonphilosophical element, he makes a dramatic departure from Aristotelianism in a fundamental way: divine law is not a timeless science, defining and revealing fixed essences; divine law is part of a temporality, a history that is also an economy of salvation and a pedagogy. Divine law is successively the *Old Law* and the *New Law*. This is normal, or at least it is not shocking: it is not for us to find an order of exposition in things which by definition are beyond us. "The Apostle [Paul] [Gal. 3:24–25] compares the state of man under the Old Law to that of a child "under a pedagogue"; but the state under the New Law, to that of a full grown man 'no longer under a pedagogue'" (q. 91, art. 5, concl.).

This does not mean that there is not a deeper logic in this revelation, perceptible at least *a posteriori*. Human beings naturally believe that they are called to natural, earthly futures: the Old Testament announces the kingdom of heaven in a still concealed mode—the promised land (which is earthly); but, in this way, it teaches them the very existence of God and his concern for them. This prepares the way for the New Testament, which reveals in a second moment that this kingdom, to which humanity is destined, is not earthly but heavenly. Likewise, from the Old Law to the New, there is greater interiority. The Old Law placed norms on external acts, the New Law will direct intentions: "the Old law restrains the hand, but the New law controls the mind." Lastly, the two laws do not use the same means: according to Augustine, "there is little difference between the Law and the Gospel—fear and love" (*brevis differentia est Legis et Evangelii, timor et amor*).

The progressive character of this divine pedagogy can be summed up as follows:

> As the father of a family issues different commands to the children and to the adults, so also the one King, God, in his one kingdom, gave one law to men, while they were yet imperfect, and another more perfect law, when, by the preceding law, they had been led to a greater capacity for Divine things (*ad majorem capacitatem divinorum*). The salvation of man could not be achieved otherwise than through Christ, according to Acts 4.12: "There is no other name given to men, whereby we must be saved." Consequently the law that brings all to salvation could not be given until after the coming of Christ. But before his coming it was necessary to give to the people, of whom Christ was to be born, a law containing certain rudiments of righteousness unto salvation, in order to prepare them to receive him. The natural law directs man by way of certain general precepts, common to both the perfect and

---

[20] Aquinas posits that humanity, by grace, is *capax Dei*, "capable of God." The word "capable" is to be understood in the sense of capacity, as in the capacity of a container (a one-liter-capacity bottle). The human soul is in a privileged sense a creature with an infinite capacity able to receive the infinity of God. We will come across this idea again a little later.

[21] There may be an incoherence here: it seems that natural law has already enlightened a person's inner conscience.

> the imperfect: wherefore it is one and the same for all. But the Divine law directs man also in certain particular matters, to which the perfect and imperfect do not stand in the same relation. Hence the necessity for the Divine law to be twofold, as already explained. (q. 91, art. 5, reps. to obj. 1–3)

F. Divine Law: The Old Law

Therefore, it is necessary to study the Old and New Testaments one after the other. Aquinas sees the Old Testament in terms of the moral and legal norms that it establishes. His aim is to show that these norms added a first supplement to natural law—and, in this sense, they were "good"—but that they should be abolished for the most part, when the time came to move to the second stage of the revelation—and, in this sense, these norms were "bad." In fact, the Old Law was good in that it was directed to a good end, eternal life; and bad in the sense that it did not yet include everything necessary to reach this end. Thus, the Old Law was ambiguous and could constitute no more than a transition.

The Old Law does two things: it "showed forth the precepts of the natural law, and added certain precepts of its own" (q. 98, art. 5, concl.). In this respect, its work is comparable to that of human law in that it guides external acts and preserves the order of the community; but the Old Law does not wholly amend our inner intentions, which becomes possible only through the grace of Christ (q. 98, art. 1, concl.).

Paul's Letter to the Romans (7:11) says that the Old Law taught us what sin is,[22] but it did not bring the grace to vanquish it. It is in this sense that Paul says that the Law "kills."[23] Moreover, it is because the law was imperfect that God did not give it in person, as he did the New Law; He gave the Old Law through intermediaries ("messengers") (q. 98, art. 3). The Old Law was nevertheless good as a preparation, and it came authentically from God: Aquinas insists on this (q. 98, art. 2) against heresies such as Marcionism, which "demonized" Judaism. The Old Law was good in two ways: it contained precepts that are still valid, and it prefigured the coming of Christ (this is what is identified by the "typological" reading suggested here of the Old Testament texts). The Old Law was given exclusively to the Jews and not to all humankind because Christ was to be born among the Jewish people according to God's promise to Abraham (q. 98, art. 4; see art. 5, concl.: "the Old Law was given to the Jewish people, that it might receive a prerogative of holiness, in reverence for Christ Who was to be born of that people"). There is no "respecter of person" in relation to the rest of humankind because Aquinas, building on the stringent argumentation of Augustine, says that sinful humanity is wholly condemned; that some will be saved is the result of "gratuitous election," to which other people are not entitled as a due.[24] The Old Law was given exactly at the appropriate time, that is, "between the law of nature and the law of grace" (art. 6, concl.). At the time of Abraham, people sinned by ignorance and turned to idolatry;[25] it was necessary to teach

---

[22] The Old Law demanded *tsedaqa* and *mishpat* (see above, p. 412). However, we cannot meet this requirement; by the law we are made sinners.

[23] "The written code kills, but the Spirit gives life" (2 Cor. 3:6); by "written code" Paul refers to the Old Law. Moreover, "God sometimes permits certain ones to fall into sin, that they may thereby be humbled. So also did He wish to give such a law as men by their own forces could not fulfill, so that, while presuming on their own powers, they might find themselves to be sinners, and being humbled might have recourse to the help of grace" (q. 98, art. 2, sol. 3).

[24] "All whom God teaches, He teaches out of pity; but whom He teaches not, out of justice He teaches not." Though Aquinas attributes this text to Augustine, it cannot be found literally in Augustine's writings, but many of his texts do say roughly the same thing. The text cited by Aquinas became traditional in the Middle Ages.

[25] Aquinas holds that at this time humankind had become more sinful and idolatrous than it had been immediately after the original sin; the habit of sin aggravated sin. It was this aggravation that motivated the gift of revelation at this time rather than another.

them monotheism. Then, enlightened by the good, they discovered that they lacked the force to attain it; this opened the way to grace. Aquinas says that divine pedagogy delivered natural humans from both their ignorance and weakness.

Finally, the Old Law (q. 99, art. 6) was based on fear of God's commandments and not yet on the love of their observance. It "induced men to the observance of its precepts, by means of temporal promises and threats." It did not do so because the people to whom the Law was given were wrongdoers in particular. It did so because Old Testament law, though more advanced than pagan law, was "as yet imperfect in comparison to the perfection which was to result from Christ's coming."

The Old Law subdivides into *moral, ceremonial, and sociopolitical (or "judicial")*[26] precepts. These three categories express the demands of natural law. The first category contains general precepts. The next two contain the "specifications": the ceremonial precepts explain in detail how to worship God, the judicial precepts set out how justice is to be practiced among men and women.

The moral precepts retain some of their value under the New Law. The precepts of the other two categories are entirely abolished, their purpose being to announce and prepare Christ's coming; after his coming, they become obsolete.[27]

1. *Moral Precepts*

The Old Law contains moral precepts because it aims to establish friendship between God and humanity, but this is possible only if people maintain good relations among themselves, which is the purpose of natural morals. But, this morality is forgotten and disfigured in sinful humans. The Old Law—and particularly the Ten Commandments—reminds him of this. Here we see firsthand how grace restores the nature of humanity wounded by sin: it does so by reformulating natural moral law. Thus, the Old Law presupposes and confirms this law: "just as grace presupposes nature, so must the Divine law presuppose the natural law" (q. 99, art. 2, reps. to obj. 1–2).

Aquinas's study of the Decalogue (Ten Commandments) continues a long Christian tradition. Although most of the provisions of the Jewish law are declared obsolete by the Letter to the Hebrews, and by the church fathers, the Decalogue is still considered valid (Irenaeus, Theophilus of Antioch, and Augustine recommended its study and observance). In the ninth century, it was recommended for the catechism of children and the simple-minded; thereafter, until the *Summa* that immediately preceded the work of Aquinas, the Decalogue was the focus of constant commentary; it was even put to verse and rhyme in order to make it easier to learn. In articles 4 to 7 of question 100, Aquinas accepts the already traditional division of the Decalogue into two tables (*tabulae*), three rules ordering humanity in their relations to God and seven relating to human justice.

2. *Ceremonial Precepts*

The "ceremonial precepts" are rules about worship; they are particularly numerous in the Old Testament (in Leviticus, Numbers, and so on); they pertain to worship in the strict sense: ceremonies, sacred objects, circumcision, dietary laws, and the like.

---

[26] This classification is commonly attributed to Alexander of Hales, who wrote a *Summa theologica* before Aquinas. Alexander was a Franciscan friar.

[27] The ceremonial precepts "were annulled so far as to be not only 'dead,' but also deadly to those who observe them since the coming of Christ, especially since the promulgation of the Gospel. On the other hand, the judicial precepts are dead indeed because they have no binding force: but they are not deadly. For if a sovereign were to order these judicial precepts to be observed in his kingdom, he would not sin" (q. 104, art. 3, concl.).

What, Aquinas asks, is the purpose of these rules? Can they be explained? Argued with reason? Or, because the New Testament abolished most of them, are they to be seen as the remnants of pagan rites? In his reply, Aquinas begins with the observation that, since the transition from paganism to monotheism, the status of religion has changed entirely. Among the pagans the purpose of religion was to underpin social order; worship was organized around this one criteria. Biblical religion, in contrast, aims to ensure the salvation of all and, therefore, organizes society in the best possible way to achieve this: religious functions are no longer subordinated to social ones; social functions are subordinated to the religious. Thus, worship loses its preeminence as social activity, at the same time that it assumes a new role ordained by divine teaching. The principle of worship is that "man is [now] directed to God not only by the interior acts of the mind, which are faith, hope, and love, but also by certain external works, whereby man makes profession of his subjection to God" (q. 99, art. 3, concl.).

The ceremonial precepts of the Old Law have two functions: to ensure the adoration of God and to prefigure the coming of Christ. In several long passages in questions 101 to 104, Aquinas develops how these two functions are fulfilled.

3. *Social and Political ("Judicial") Precepts*

The *præcepta judicialia* are not "judicial" precepts in the strict sense, which is why the expression must be translated as "social and political precepts": they are precepts that enable people to live together in a given society.

There are four categories of precepts, which correspond to the four levels of organization of the people: "one, of the people's sovereign to his subjects; a second of the subjects among themselves; a third, of the citizens to foreigners; a fourth, of members of the same household, such as the order of the father to his son; of the wife to her husband; of the master to his servant" (q. 104, art. 4, concl.).

Aquinas's discussion of the first category gives him an opportunity to state his preference for the "mixed regime" of government praised by the Ancients: this was, he argues, the type of government of the Israelite people, who had great leaders (Moses) and kings (monarchic element), assemblies of the elite (aristocratic element), and others chosen from among the people (democratic element) (q. 105, art. 1) (see below, p. 573).

The second category concerns private law, questions related to property ownership, trade, interest-bearing loans (usury), penal law (q. 105, art. 2). Aquinas judges the provisions of the Old Testament on these subjects favorably: they appear to him to correspond more or less with Aristotle's opinions, which says everything. The Old Testament recognizes private property, which is excellent for the administration of private goods, but it imposes restrictions. The rich must share at least some of their wealth; the fruit of the earth must also be shared, in part at any rate. The nonurban real estate of a family cannot be permanently alienated; indentured slaves must be freed after a period of time ("jubilee"); interest-bearing loans are forbidden and debts must be canceled every seven years. All of these measures are designed to ensure that the imbalances in wealth are not too great. The punishments noted in the Old Testament seem fair to Aquinas: they are not only proportionate to the harm inflicted, they are also adapted to the circumstances and the risk of recurrence, and so on. The penal process also has its virtues in his eyes.

The third category concerns precepts for foreigners. Aquinas approves of the legislation of the old Jewish state, which imposed limitations on immigration (see q. 105, art. 3).

He also approves of the Jewish-Hebrew law concerning legal relations within the family, parent-child, husband-wife, master-slave (q. 105, art. 4). Slavery is permitted, but strongly attenuated; poor treatment of slaves is limited. Divorce is formalized.

How are we to understand Aquinas's positive opinions on ancient Jewish society? They appear to be intended as replies to critics, who traditionally pointed a finger at the cruelty, archaism, and contradictions of this society. This may be a new sign of Aquinas's own traditionalism. To him, the Western society of his age, which was still feudal in character, seemed not to progress; if anything, it appeared a regression compared with ancient societies.

G. Divine Law: The New Law

The New Law is the New Testament law of the Gospel: another divine law, but one that could only be revealed after the law of the Old Testament, and that could only be heard after the teachings of the Old Testament had been received.

The New Law differs from the Old not only in content but more fundamentally, by the fact that it is not exactly a law; it is a grace—an outpouring of the Holy Spirit into the innermost part of humanity ("instilled in the heart").

Like the Old Law, the New contains "provisions" guiding human actions, but such provisions are of "secondary importance": "The New Law contains certain things [in addition to an outpouring of grace] that *dispose* us to receive the grace of the Holy Ghost, and pertaining to the *use* of that grace: such things are of secondary importance, so to speak, in the New Law; and the faithful need to be instructed concerning them, both by word and writing, both as to what they should believe and as to what they should do" (q. 106, art. 1, concl.).

The Gospel contains "the teachings of faith" and "those commandments which regulate human affections and human actions"; in this sense, the New Law, like the Old Law, "kills." "Augustine explains this by saying that the letter denotes any writing external to man, even that of the moral precepts such as are contained in the Gospel. Wherefore the letter, even of the Gospel would kill, unless there were the inward presence of the healing grace of faith" (q. 106, art. 2, concl.).

As for grace, the primary and principal element of the New Law, "the grace of the Holy Ghost bestowed inwardly," it "quickens" and "justifies" (q. 106, art. 2, concl.). It gives a desire to do good, which paradoxically also begets a passiveness toward the outpouring of grace. The law of the Gospel is a law of love that not only *says,* "love your neighbor as yourself"; it also provides the *propensity* to love (which, as we know, the Old Law does not do).

1. *The Contents of the Law*

"Whatsoever is set down in the New Testament explicitly and openly as a point of faith, is contained in the Old Testament as a matter of belief, but implicitly, under a figure" (q. 107, art. 3, rep. to obj. 1). Hence, the New Law is "contained" in the Old like the fruit in the seed; it adds nothing of substance to the Old Law. The New Law, as we saw, eliminates the ceremonial precepts, whose reason to exist disappears because the figure they proclaim has become reality. It also eliminates the need for most of the "judicial" precepts and, henceforth, Christian people can act according to their will in social and political matters as long as they do so with charity. Lastly, Aquinas posits—and argues closely—that all the moral precepts are fully preserved in the New Law, which adds nothing new or, more exactly, provides clarifications. The Sermon on the Mount does not bring a new morality; it brings a perfected version of biblical morality, which can be opposed to the flawed interpretations of the Pharisees (q. 198, art. 3).

> Now Christ fulfilled the precepts of the Old Law both in His works and in His doctrine. In His works, because He was willing to be circumcised and to fulfil the other legal observances, which were binding for the time being; according to Galatians 4.4: "Made under the Law." In His doctrine He fulfilled the precepts of the Law in three ways. First, by explaining the true sense of the Law. This is clear in the case of murder and adultery, the prohibition of which the Scribes and Pharisees thought to refer only to the exterior act: wherefore Our Lord fulfilled the Law by showing that the prohibition extended also to the interior acts of

> sins. Secondly, Our Lord fulfilled the precepts of the Law by prescribing the safest way of complying with the statutes of the Old Law. Thus the Old Law forbade perjury: and this is more safely avoided, by abstaining altogether from swearing, save in cases of urgency. Thirdly, Our Lord fulfilled the precepts of the Law, by adding some counsels of perfection: this is clearly seen in Matthew 19.21, where Our Lord said to the man who affirmed that he had kept all the precepts of the Old Law: "One thing is wanting to thee: If thou wilt be perfect, go, sell whatsoever thou hast," etc. (q. 107, art. 2, concl.)

On the one hand, the New Law is less difficult to observe than the Old, in that it does not include all of the rites, ceremonies, and obligations to which the Jews were subjected; on the other hand, the New Law is more burdensome in that it imposes an inner perfection on which the Old Law did not insist (q. 107, art. 7).

Finally, the New Law contains "commandments" and "counsels." Commandments are sufficient to bring eternal happiness because they compel us to pursue spiritual goods as the supreme end rather than the goods of this world. But we "will attain more speedily thereto [eternal happiness] by giving up the goods of this world entirely: wherefore the evangelical counsels are given for this purpose" (q. 108, art. 4, concl.). The reference is to the renunciation of all three worldly goods: riches, pleasures, and honors; all forms of religious life are based on this threefold renunciation. However, salvation does not depend on the choice of a religious life; it is not a precept. The strict evangelical commands are only a not-absolutely-necessary addition, for example: do good to one's enemies, forgive an offense even when one is entitled to compensation. Perpetual poverty or perpetual chastity is only necessary if one desires to attain perfection (this is how Aquinas interprets the story of the wealthy young man in Matthew 19:21).[28]

2. *The Joachimist Controversy*

Now that the law of the Gospel is revealed, it is final; there will be no other until the end of time (q. 106, art. 4). Here Aquinas's position is diametrically opposed to Joachimism, the doctrine of Joachim of Flora (1135–1202), which stated that after the age of the Father (the Old Testament) and the age of the Son (the New Testament) would come the age of the Holy Spirit.

We will examine Joachimism and the millenarian movements it inspired in greater detail below (see chapter 7), but we need to take a moment here to explore Aquinas's view, which is of the utmost importance if we are to understand his idea of history and, therefore, the true nature and role of politics.

Aquinas admits that there are three states of humankind. However, he notes that the list to retain is that of Pseudo-Dionysius (the Areopagite) rather than that of Joachim of Flora: after the Old Law, then the New Law, the third state is "not of this world," it is in heaven. "The first state is figurative and imperfect in comparison with the state of the Gospel; so is the present state figurative and imperfect in comparison with the heavenly state, with the advent of which the present state will be done away as expressed in that very passage [1 Cor. 13:12]: 'We see now through a glass in a dark manner; but then face to face'" (q. 106, art. 6, rep. to obj. 1).[29]

There is therefore no reason to expect an age of the Holy Spirit different from the age of Christ. The Holy Spirit came at Pentecost when Jesus was glorified, and he taught the Apostles "all truth

[28] Thus, love is not an obligation, that is, the love that leads to the Cross. Aquinas shares the same desire as others at the time of the Papal Revolution to make Christian morality livable. He advocates a morality directed toward heaven but applicable on earth.

[29] The theme of the three states—one where there are figures without the realities, another where there are figures and realities, and the last where there are no figures and only realities—is recurrent in Aquinas's writings.

in respect of matters necessary for salvation," even if he did not "teach them about all future events" (q. 106, art. 6, rep. to obj. 2).

Does this mean that, in the hope of these things, there will be nothing new on earth? Not exactly.

> The state of the world may change in two ways. In one way, according to a change of law: and thus no other state will succeed this state of the New Law. Because the state of the New Law succeeded the state of the Old Law, as a more perfect law a less perfect one. Now no state of the present life can be more perfect than the state of the New Law: since nothing can approach nearer to the last end than that which is the immediate cause of our being brought to the last end. But the New Law does this: wherefore the Apostle says [Heb. 10:19–22]: "Having therefore, brethren, a confidence in the entering into the Holies by the blood of Christ, a new way which He hath dedicated for us let us draw near." Therefore no state of the present life can be more perfect than that of the New Law, since the nearer a thing is to the last end the more perfect it is.
>
> In another way the state of mankind may change according as man stands in relation to one and the same law more or less perfectly. And thus the state of the Old Law underwent frequent changes, since at times the laws were very well kept, and at other times were altogether unheeded. Thus, too, the state of the New Law is subject to change with regard to various places, times, and persons, according as the grace of the Holy Spirit dwells in man more or less perfectly. Nevertheless we are not to look forward to a state wherein man is to possess the grace of the Holy Spirit more perfectly than he has possessed it hitherto, especially the apostles who "received the first fruits of the Spirit, i.e. sooner and more abundantly than others." (q. 106, art. 4, concl.)

Therefore, historical change is possible, although it can be for better and for worse. History has no direction. Paradoxically, this leaves us in an existential situation similar to that of the eternal return of paganism. Evil, whether it meets success or undergoes decline, remains. Safeguards against evil do not change, either: "The Church began from the time of Abel and will last to the end of the world" (*Commentary on the Symbol of the Apostles*); "the faith of the Church will endure to the end of the world; this is said against those who claim it should last only a certain time (Aquinas, *Commentary on Matthew 24:34*); "Adam introduced one state, namely of guilt; Christ [the state] of true glory and life. Hence, since after that state no other one followed in that life, therefore he is called the last" (*Commentary on 1 Corinthians 15:45*). So it can be said that grace seems to concern *individuals* (whether it saves or damns them) and does not impact on *history*.

In a "quodlibetal question," Aquinas observes that the church changes: once the object of persecutions, when "the nations of the earth trembled," in his time it was no longer persecuted and even had the strength to command the secular arm of the state. This reflects true progress. However, "between yesterday and today, the state of the church has changed, but the church itself has not changed." Here Aquinas's thought is close to what Aristotle says about the age of perfection: "with regard to man's state we find that the perfection of manhood comes in youth, and that a man's state is all the more perfect, whether before or after, the nearer it is to the time of his youth" (IIa–Iiæ, q. 1, art. 7, rep. to obj. 4). Time is decidedly not a creator. As for the great figures who left their mark on the history of salvation—Abraham, Moses, and Jesus—Aquinas notes that "the most excellent revelation was that which was given first." Likewise, the Apostles made better use of the New Law than those who came after.[30]

[30] See Thomas Aquinas, *La loi nouvelle,* Ia–IIae, q. 106–08, trans. J. Tonneau (Paris: Éditions du Cerf, 1981).

In conclusion, like Origen and Augustine before him, Aquinas refuses to take the revelation in a literal sense; he "depoliticizes" eschatology. In doing so, he will stand as a reference for conservative Catholicism in the Counter-Reformation and much more so in the European Counter-Revolution.

III. Justice

That said, even if salvation is personal, political leaders, like good shepherds, have an obligation to ensure the salvation of their flock, in particular by the way they make and apply laws. Lawmakers, judges, and rulers must be *just*. For this reason, Aquinas reflects at length on the question of justice and explains with exemplary clarity the legal philosophy underlying the sanction of Roman canon law by the church of the Papal Revolution (*ST* IIae, q. 57–80).

A. The Virtue of Justice

The proper object of justice (*iustitia*), Aquinas says, is what is just (*iustum*), that is, what is required by the law (*ius*). The law subdivides into natural law and positive law. Whatever the nature of the law under consideration, it should be argued with the jurists that justice is "the perpetual will to apportion to each his right" (*ius suum unicuique tribuere* or *reddere,* which can also be rendered as, "to each according to his due").[31]

True, Augustine attributes the role of "succoring the unfortunate" to justice. But, in this case, Aquinas replies, we do not give them what is theirs but what is ours. Mercy is *another virtue* than justice, which consists in giving to each *his or her own*. The proper matter of justice is an act adapted and proportionate to the objective demands of another; another can demand his or her due, but not my mercy.

Thus, Aquinas implicitly rejects Augustine's argumentation, which asserts that a non-Christian state cannot exist, because a state supposes "an agreement on justice" (according to Cicero's definition) and the only true justice is the justice of the Gospel. Aquinas says no; natural justice exists, and though it is insufficient for salvation, it is fully legitimate in its order. Any community that recognizes this constitutes a legitimate political community, a legitimate state. The Christian order, based on the church, emerges as an indispensable principle of salvation; but it does not replace the political order. Political order is not absorbed in the theological order.

Justice involves giving to each his or her due *according to a rule of equality*. However, equality is understood differently according to whether justice is distributive or commutative.

Commutative justice is the form of justice that apportions exchanges between individuals. Such exchanges must be equal in the sense that what one gives must be of equal value to what the other gives according to an "arithmetical" equality:

$$a = b$$

Distributive justice is the form of justice that apportions the just distribution of common goods (or evils) among the members of a group, whether these goods are material or immaterial. Justice is attained when each individual receives a share of the common good corresponding to

[31] Here Aquinas provides, for the most part, a gloss on Aristotle, but his gloss has the advantage of being clearer and more explicit than Aristotle's original.

his place in the group. In this case, the equality is "geometrical"; it is an equality of relations, a proportion:

$$\frac{a}{b} = \frac{c}{d}$$

For example, the king should receive a greater share of the wealth of the state than his subjects, the general a greater share of the victory honors than the common soldier (or he should be more severely punished than the soldier in the event of defeat). But if all the reapers worked an equal amount, they would receive an equal share of the harvest. So it is clear that shares can be unequal from one individual to another (for example, the range of salaries of different employees in the same company can be quite large), there is nevertheless in this second form of justice a principle of *equality,* since each individual receives as much as he gives.

B. Property (IIa–IIæ, q. 68)

Question 66 of IIa–IIæ of the *Summa theologica,* devoted to "theft and robbery," is a true *treatise on property.* Aquinas concludes, while flagging some very important reservations, that private property is lawful. From this point of view, he distances himself—as does the entire official church of his time—from a certain communistic and apocalyptic Christianity and from the radical position of the Franciscan Spirituals (see below, p. 629).

Question 66 has eight articles, but the main argument can be summed up in three questions: (1) whether it is natural for a person to possess external things? (art. 1); (2) whether it is lawful for a person to possess a thing as his or her own? (art. 2); whether it is lawful to steal through stress of need? (art. 7) (another way of saying: is private property an absolute?).

Article 1: *"Whether It Is Natural for Man to Possess External Things?"*

It would seem not (*videtur quod non…*)[32] because the world belongs to God. Furthermore, we cannot change the nature of things external to us. Therefore, it is not natural to possess external things. However (*sed contra*), the Psalmist says that God gave "natural dominion of man over other creatures" and Genesis 1:26 says, "Let us make man in our image, after our likeness; and let them have dominion over the fish of the sea, and over the birds of the air, and over the cattle, and over all the earth, and over every creeping thing… upon the earth."

Aquinas replies: external things are to be considered in two ways: in terms of their *nature* and in terms of their *use.* Considered in terms of their nature, external things are subject only to the power of God and belong to God. But human beings have natural dominion over such things and can use them for their own profit, for the imperfect beings exist for purpose of the perfect beings.

Aquinas adds that humans, being made in the image of God, are undoubtedly the most perfect of creatures of the material world, and everything in the world is directed to their use.[33] Thus, their possession of all material goods—mineral, vegetable, or animal—is wholly lawful, as long as they do not presume to change the nature of such goods.[34]

---

32 We will develop the argument following the various steps of the Scholastic technique of *disputatio* (see above, note 5 to this chapter).

33 This is a very humanist but "antiecological" argument.

34 This argument forms the basis for the church's mistrust of the "demiurgic" power of science (e.g., genetic manipulations, eugenics, etc.).

So far, the argument has only proven the overall legitimacy of humankind 's stewardship of the earth. What about ownership of *private property?*

Article 2: "*Whether It Is Lawful for a Man to Possess a Thing as His Own?*"

It would seem not. The church fathers, and among them Basil,[35] argued that the rich amassed their wealth by seizing common goods, that is, the goods intended for all.

Basil uses a metaphor borrowed from Cicero (who in turn took it from Chrysippus[36]): the rich person is like someone who arrives at the theater first to prevent others from seeing the play, although it is intended for everyone; this is what the rich do when they seize the common goods of nature.[37]

However, Augustine affirms the contrary and criticizes the monks who refuse any contact with those who marry and possess their own external goods. He calls them "heretics" and says they are full of "arrogance," the more so that they falsely call themselves "apostolic."[38]

Aquinas's conclusion: it is necessary to distinguish between the power to administer external goods (*potestas procurandi*) and their *use* (*usus*). In regard to the first point, Aquinas observes,

> it is lawful for man to possess property. Moreover this is necessary to human life for three reasons.[39] First because every man is more careful to procure what is for himself alone than that which is common to many or to all: since each one would shirk the labor and leave to another that which concerns the community, as happens where there is a great number of servants. Secondly, because human affairs are conducted in more orderly fashion if each man is charged with taking care of some particular thing himself, whereas there would be confusion if everyone had to look after any one thing indeterminately. Thirdly, because a more peaceful state is ensured to man if each one is contented with his own. Hence it is to be observed that quarrels arise more frequently where there is no division of the things possessed. (q. 66, art. 2, concl.)

---

[35] Basil the Great (330–79), the bishop of Caesarea, was a fourth century Cappadocian father.

[36] One of the founders of Stoicism; see above, pp. 186–87).

[37] Aquinas was familiar with other material by the church fathers condemning ownership of private property, which they held to be theft and the fruit of original sin. For example, Saint Ambrose: "The world was created for all men, and you, the rich minority, try to claim it for yourselves. Nature knows no rich men, she made us all poor. For *we* are *born without* clothes and are brought forth without *silver* or *gold.* It is not yours, that you give to the poor, it is his." Saint Basil wrote: "The earth was made for all, it is a common inheritance which the brothers received from the common Father. They enjoy air, sun, and rain, why should they not enjoy the soil that nourishes them?" Saint John Chrysostom: "You possess the result of theft though you are not a thief yourself.... *Mine* and *yours,* those chilly words, which introduce innumerable wars into the world, should be eliminated! The community of goods is more appropriate and better suited to nature." Saint Jerome: "At the origin of all wealth is always an injustice. A rich man is either a thief or the son of a thief. Not to give to the poor what belongs to the poor is a sacrilege." Saint Clement of Rome said: "In strict justice, everything should belong to all. Iniquity alone has created private property." Text material is quoted in C. Spicq, ed., *Summa theologica: La justice,* IIa, IIae, q. 63–79 (Paris: Desclée et Cie, 1947), 1:304–08. See below, chapter 7 on millenarianism).

[38] These so-called "communists" of the third and fourth centuries claimed that their argument was based on the testimony of the Acts of the Apostles, which said that the Apostles shared their goods in common (see above, pp. 440–41). In quoting this text, Aquinas may be taking indirect aim at the false apostles of his time, specifically the sect of the Apostolics started by Gerard Segarelli in Parma in 1260. The Council of Lyon in 1274 and the popes Honorius IV in 1286 and Nicholas IV in 1290 condemned these communist tendencies. It was a serious matter for the church and was revived by the "quarrel of poverty" concerning the Franciscans. John Hus, who was also opposed to private property, was condemned at the Council of Constance in 1415. Pius IX condemned communism in 1846 and again in 1864, as did Leo XIII in *Rerum novarum* in 1891 and Pius XI in *Quadragesimo anno* in 1931. Note that the church has been equally harsh in its condemnation of liberalism.

[39] Aquinas quotes almost verbatim the corresponding chapter from Aristotle criticizing the communism of Phaleas of Chalcedon and Plato (see above, pp. 124–26).

On the other hand, with respect to external things, "man ought to possess external things, not as his own, but as common, so that, to wit, *he is ready to communicate them to others in their need.*" This too comes from Aristotle.[40] But Aquinas also cites Paul: "As for the rich in this world, charge them not to be haughty, nor to set their hopes on uncertain riches but on God who richly furnishes us with everything to enjoy" (1 Tim. 6:17–18). In other words, private property is not an *absolute;* this is confirmed by the last step of the argument in spectacular fashion.

Article 3: *"Whether It Is Lawful to Steal through Stress of Need?"*

It would seem not, because for Aristotle the mere word "theft" instantly suggests wickedness. Now that which is wicked in and of itself cannot become good merely because it is directed to a good end.

However, Roman law says, "in cases of need all things are common property" (*in necessitate sunt omnia communia*).

Aquinas concludes:

> Things which are of human right [i.e., positive law] cannot derogate from natural right or Divine right. Now according to the natural order established by Divine Providence, inferior things are ordained for the purpose of succoring man's needs by their means. Wherefore the division and appropriation of things which are based on human law, do not preclude the fact that man's needs have to be remedied by means of these very things. Hence whatever certain people have in superabundance is due, by natural law, to the purpose of succoring the poor.... Since, however, there are many who are in need, while it is impossible for all to be succored by the property of one man, it depends on the free will (arbitrium) of each of us to give his own things, so that out of them he may come to the aid of those who are in need. Nevertheless, if the need be so manifest and urgent, that it is evident that the present need must be remedied by whatever means be at hand (for instance when a person is in some imminent danger, and there is no other possible remedy), then it is lawful for a man to succor his own need by means of another's property, by taking it either openly or secretly: nor is this properly speaking theft or robbery.

Likewise and for the same reason, "a man may also take secretly another's property in order to succor his neighbor in need" (q. 66, art. 7, concl.).

What happens when a rich person has an abundance of food and the poor person is hungry? Inferior creatures (victuals) are redirected from their natural ends, which is to serve the fulfillment of the natural ends of higher creatures (human beings). The reason is that positive law forms an obstacle. But, positive law cannot derogate from natural law. Therefore, the private ownership of food is illegitimate in such a case, which is why *the poor do not commit theft* when they seize food. This is not to excuse or acquit the poor with the argument that hunger leads to the loss of self-control—*they are merely seizing their due, what is theirs, their natural good.*

Aquinas emphasizes, however, that it should be the personal initiative of the owner to redistribute surplus goods: he rejects the notion of millenarian communitarianism. Likewise, state socialism is simply beyond his ken. The only collective assistance that the poor are entitled to receive is the property of the church (Aquinas must have been familiar with the canon doctrine

---

[40] "Notables who are men of feeling and good sense may also undertake the duty of helping the poor to find occupations—each taking charge of a group, and each giving a grant to enable the members of his group to make a start. The example of the citizens of Tarentum may also be commended for imitation: the well-to-do share with the poor the use of their property, and thereby conciliate the goodwill of the masses" (Aristotle, *Politics* 6.1320b).

which says that the church is "the steward to the property of the power"). As for the rest, Aquinas gives legitimacy—subject to an obligation of mutual assistance—to a form of society based on private property, private administration of goods, and therefore trade.

C. Trade and the Question of the Just Price (IIa–IIæ, q. 77)

The church condemned trade in even harsher terms than private property. Restoring Aristotelian natural law in this area as well, Aquinas repeats Aristotle's principled condemnation of speculative trading. But because he does so on the basis of natural law, as well as on the grounds of evangelical precepts, he opens the way for the development of a positive theory of trade and modern economic activity.[41]

1. *The Morality of Trade*

All human affairs are ordered by "the rule of reason." Trade must also adhere to this principle. It must demonstrate that it pursues proper ends and that its methods are beyond reproach. This is the price for its acceptance as a healthy activity with a proper place in Christian society.

But it cannot be denied that the Scriptures and the Christian tradition are full of hostile comments on trade. The merchant is suspected of greed, and greed is immeasurable. Isaiah said: "Woe to those who join house to house, who add field to field" (5:8). Ecclesiastes 5:9: "He who loves money will not be satisfied with money." Greed also leads to unfairness; it stifles the love of one's neighbor as well as the love of God ("No one can serve two masters;...You cannot serve God and mammon" [Matt. 6:24]). Jesus chased the merchants from the Temple (hardly flattering for the profession!). The church fathers and the church tradition pursued this line of thought as well. Tertullian (second century): "When the motive for acquiring ceases, there will be no necessity for trading."[42]

Another idea: trade is blamed for showing too much concern for the affairs of this world and for turning the mind away from God. Aquinas interprets the etymology of *negotium* thus. It is the negation of *otium*—the *scholè* of the Greeks—the active leisure, which alone enables study and contemplation. A merchant is the *quintessential* noncontemplative. This is why commerce is strictly forbidden to clerics.

Aquinas found in Aristotle's writings the same condemnation of commerce and speculative capitalism, argued this time from the philosophy of nature. Nature is finite, whereas speculation is infinite; therefore, "capitalism" is antinatural (see above, pp. 121–24).

Later we will see that Aquinas's personal opinion is more nuanced.

2. *A Just Price*

Things must be sold at their "just" price. Like Augustine, Aquinas believes that an objective value can be ascribed to things corresponding to their use value; selling for more than this value is a breach of the equality that defines commutative justice. All the same, Aquinas provides two very important correctives to this rule.

---

[41] On the development of trade in the twelfth and thirteenth centuries in Europe, see Renouard, *Les hommes d'affaire italiens;* Régine Pernoud, *Histoire de la bourgeoisie en France* [A history of the bourgeoisie in France], vol. 1, *Des origines aux temps modernes* [From its origins until modern times] (Paris: Éditions du Seuil, 1960); Philippe Dollinger, *La Hanse, XII*^{e}*–XVII*^{e} *siècles* [The Hanseatic League from the twelfth to the seventeenth centuries] (Paris: Aubier, 1988).

[42] See Spicq, *Summa theologica: La justice,* 411 and following.

1. There is a "work" component that contributes to the creation of value. While it is true that "trading, considered in itself, has a certain debasement attaching thereto, in so far as, by its very nature, it does not imply a virtuous or necessary end,"[43] gain, which is the aim of commerce,

> though not implying, by its nature, anything virtuous or necessary, does not, in itself, connote anything sinful or contrary to virtue: wherefore nothing prevents gain from being directed to some necessary or even virtuous end, and thus trading becomes lawful. Thus, for instance, a man may intend the moderate gain which he seeks to acquire by trading for the upkeep of his household, or for the assistance of the needy: or again, a man may take to trade for some public advantage, for instance, lest his country lack the necessaries of life, and seek gain, not as an end, but as payment for his labor (*quasi stipendium laboris*). (q. 77, art. 4, concl.)

2. There is also a "subjective" component to the creation of value.

> We may speak of buying and selling, considered as accidentally tending to the advantage of one party, and to the disadvantage of the other: for instance, when a man has great need of a certain thing, while an other man will suffer if he be without it. On such a case the just price will depend not only on the thing sold, but on the loss which the sale brings on the seller. And thus it will be lawful to sell a thing for more than it is worth in itself (*plus quam valeat secundum se*), though the price paid be not more than it is worth to the owner (*quamvis non vendatur plus quam valeat habenti*). (q. 77, art. 1, concl.)

Thus, Aquinas takes the first step toward a "subjective" theory of value. The scarcity of goods, or the intensity of demand, forms part of the value, and this is lawful.

Aquinas supports his analysis with a passage from the *Nicomachean Ethics* about "useful friendship." Exchanges between friends are equal not if they exchange things of *equal value* but if they both derive *equal utility* from the exchange (art. 1, rep. to obj. 3). In other words, equality is not to be considered from a material or objective point of view but as an "equality of usefulness." Only the parties to the exchange can determine this because each exchange involves an original calculation, which no one—not even a civil authority—can make for them.

D. Interest-Bearing Lending (Usury) (IIa–IIæ, q. 78)

Usury is, incontestably, a "sin" in Aquinas's opinion. He is familiar with Aristotle's reasoning and with his remarks on the usury practices of his time (see Aristotle, *On Politics* 1.10.4, 5; *Eudemian Ethics* 1.3; and *Rhetoric* 1.5, 16).

In trade, even "speculative" (i.e., unregulated) trade, a product enters into play between the sums of money exchanged. In contrast, "the lender, who lends with interest, exchanges two unequal sums of money directly; and in usury, money becomes principle, means, and end. Money begets itself and produces 'little ones' (*tokos, fœnus*)."[44] But, according to the scholastic formula *nummus nummum non parit,* money does not beget money. Therefore, the interest-bearing loan is even more antinatural than speculative trade. It is a monstrosity.

[43] Because trading involves the handling of money and goods; but from the outside it is difficult to ascertain *a priori* whether money is handled with a view to the acquisition of goods by the user (which is good) or if goods are handled with a view to increasing the trader's profit (which is wicked); in other words, it is not clear whether the final cause which directs trading activities—and gives it meaning—is money or goods.

[44] Spicq, *Summa theologica: La justice.*

Aquinas also knows the biblical facts. Usury is condemned in the Old Testament, at least within the Hebrew community (see, e.g., Exod. 22:25; Lev. 25:33–37; Sir. 29:1–7; Deut. 15:6–8, 23:19–20, 28:12).

One has a duty of mercy toward one's neighbor to lend without counterpart and to decline to make unwarranted gains by taking advantage of the poverty of those whose wages or goods or person have been withheld (see note 37 to this chapter). Usury is tolerated only toward foreigners (it was a common practice in the ancient Near East).

The New Testament intensifies this condemnation (see Matt. 5:42; Luke 6:34–36). Mercy, the ideal of holiness, must take precedence over simple justice and its economic utility. The Christian not only lends without interest, he sometimes neglects to ask for the repayment of the principal.[45]

Last but not least, Aquinas was also familiar with church tradition, itself hardly favorable to usury. The church fathers saw themselves as the defenders of the meek. The barbarian incursions impoverished the Low Empire. Consumer loans became widespread again. Lenders profited handsomely from the situation, seizing the goods and even the persons of the borrowers (many were driven to suicide). Seneca had asserted earlier that a usurer was a murderer. Basil the Great, Ambrose, and Augustine echoed him: the usurer strangled the poor; there was no distinction between an interest-bearing loan (*fenus*) and a funeral (*funus*).[46] For all of these writers, the evil in usury (whether the transaction was in money or anything else) resided in the fact that it was offensive to charity and to mercy toward others. For Saint Ambrose, the fact that the Deuteronomist tolerated interest-bearing loans to foreigners was evidence that usury was an act of war and the antithesis of the Christian law of brotherhood.

As for canon law, it placed a formal ban on clerical usury (the Councils of Elvira in 305, Arles in 314, Laodicea and Nicaea in 325; the ban was periodically renewed in later times). But in the eighth and the eleventh centuries, the ban was extended to laypersons by different councils and in several of Charlemagne's capitularies, and they were threatened with excommunication (again this corresponded to the prevailing economic circumstances—an economic crisis precipitated by the Norman invasions; interest rates were exorbitantly high during this age: as high as 100, 200, and 300 percent). Various decretals confirmed this position.

In the twelfth and thirteenth centuries, the nobility, cities, kings, and even bishops were deeply indebted to wealthy bourgeois and Italian bankers. Moneylending became a profession in its own right. For this reason, the Lateran Council of 1179 pronounced an absolute and universal ban on the practice. The church also stepped up its pressure on civil authorities to force them to take coercive measures in support of the church's spiritual punishments against moneylenders (the church refused to endorse the last will and testament of impenitent usurers). The Council of Lyon in 1274 placed usurers under the jurisdiction of church courts, regarding them as heretics. Only Jews were allowed to lend money, provided they did not commit excesses. Finally, in 1311, at the Council of Vienne, Pope Clement V nullified all civil legislation in regard to usury and declared, "If someone falls into the error of presuming to affirm perniciously that the practice of usury is not sinful, we decree that he is to be punished as a heretic; and we strictly enjoin on local ordinaries and inquisitors of heresy to proceed against those they find suspect of such error as they would

[45] Nevertheless, we should point out that in biblical societies, as in ancient Greece, loans were made for consumption purposes; the Ancients would have viewed things differently if they had witnessed situations in which the borrower used borrowed money to make productive investments, yielding huge profits; it would seem more "natural" in this case that the lender should be remunerated. This is precisely the new logic of reciprocal economic service that Aquinas saw emerge in the thirteenth century. He sensed that it required a new formulation of the moral problem.

[46] See Spicq, *Summa theologica: La justice*, 453.

against those suspected of heresy."[47] To conclude, the Christian spirit rejected unambiguously and banned outright all interest-bearing loans.

Yet theology provided no *specific rational arguments* against usury, especially since the church fathers and canonists had expressed different positions at different times. Even the Scriptures are not very clear on the matter. When the economic development of the thirteenth century brought usury back to the fore, it became necessary to clarify the issue again. Never daunted by major theoretical challenges, and full of confidence in the power of reason, Aquinas took up the task in his *Summa theologica*. Here, then, is his personal opinion:

> To take usury for money lent is unjust in itself, because this is to sell what does not exist, and this evidently leads to inequality which is contrary to justice. In order to make this evident, we must observe that there are certain things the use of which consists in their consumption: thus we consume wine when we use it for drink and we consume wheat when we use it for food. Wherefore in such like things the use of the thing must not be reckoned apart from the thing itself, and whoever is granted the use of the thing, is granted the thing itself and for this reason, to lend things of this kind is to transfer the ownership (*cuicumque conceditur usus, ex hoc ipso conceditur res*). Accordingly if a man wanted to sell wine separately from the use of the wine, he would be selling the same thing twice, or he would be selling what does not exist, wherefore he would evidently commit a sin of injustice. On like manner he commits an injustice who lends wine or wheat, and asks for double payment, viz. one, the return of the thing in equal measure, the other, the price of the use, which is called usury.
>
> On the other hand, there are things the use of which does not consist in their consumption: thus to use a house is to dwell in it, not to destroy it. Wherefore in such things both may be granted: for instance, one man may hand over to another the ownership of his house while reserving to himself the use of it for a time, or vice versa, he may grant the use of the house, while retaining the ownership (*dominium*). For this reason a man may lawfully make a charge for the use of his house, and, besides this, revendicate the house from the person to whom he has granted its use, as happens in renting and letting a house.
>
> Now money, according to the Philosopher [Aristotle] was invented chiefly for the purpose of exchange: and consequently the proper and principal use of money is its consumption or alienation whereby it is sunk in exchange. Hence it is by its very nature unlawful to take payment for the use of money lent, which payment is known as usury. (q. 78, art. 1, concl.)

The distinction between *consumable* things—things destroyed by use—and *non fungible* things—things that use does not destroy—comes from Roman law. Aquinas applies it to moneylending. He does not take into account the factor of time, which in his opinion changes nothing in terms of the equality of the exchange (in contrast, modern economists define interest as the "value of time"). Likewise, he accepts Aristotle's argument, which says that money does not beget "little ones"; it is essentially sterile, merely the intermediary of trade; only one's work creates wealth. Therefore, "if the borrower uses the money from the lender and makes it productive through his work, the lender has no claim to the added value from it."[48]

But, after reformulating the fundamental reasons for forbidding interest-bearing loans, Aquinas provides a few correctives.

[47] Ibid., 461.
[48] Ibid., 466.

1. He admits the idea of compensation for a lender who suffers a loss through lending (*damnum emergens*):

"A lender may without sin enter an agreement with the borrower for compensation for the loss he incurs of something he ought to have, for this is not to sell the use of money but to avoid a loss. It may also happen that the borrower avoids a greater loss than the lender incurs, wherefore the borrower may repay the lender with what he has gained. But the lender cannot enter an agreement for compensation, through the fact that he makes no profit out of his money: because he must not sell that which he has not yet and may be prevented in many ways from having" (q. 78, art. 2, rep. to obj. 1).

A compensation may be admitted only if the money lent is not returned according to the terms of the loan (q. 62, art. 4). However, it is not possible to include such compensation in the *initial* contract. Compensation can only be lawfully expected in the initial loan contract if the lender suffers a loss other than a mere cessation of gain (*lucrum cessans*).

But, Aquinas does not accept what the fourteenth century jurisconsult Paul de Castro allows: the justification of interest as remuneration for taking a risk on the money lent, *periculum sortis* ("risk of chance"). In the end, his position nevertheless opened a breach with the canon's absolute prohibition of usury.

2. However, in order to better condemn usury in a sense, Aquinas does approve of capitalism, strictly speaking; that is, the form of economic activity associating *capital* and *work*.

> He who lends money transfers the ownership of the money to the borrower. Hence the borrower holds the money at his own risk and is bound to pay it all back: wherefore the lender must not exact more. On the other hand he that entrusts his money to a merchant or craftsman so as to form a kind of society, does not transfer the ownership of his money to them, for it remains his, so that at his risk the merchant speculates with it, or the craftsman uses it for his craft, and consequently he may lawfully demand as something belonging to him, part of the profits derived from his money. (q. 78, art. 2, rep. to obj. 5)

The "big-venture loan" and joint stock companies (not yet with limited liability) were invented and developed at this time in Italy.[49] Aquinas was familiar with these new economic forms and approved of them.

All of these rules of justice should be included in proper human laws, which should be promulgated and enforced by the state. Once again Aquinas attempts to show how the ancient doctrines of a state, thought of as "a being of nature," can be wholly integrated into a Christian theology.

V. The State

In the years 1265–67, Aquinas worked on a short pamphlet titled *De regno* (*On Kingship*, also known under the title *De regimine principum*), a sort of instruction manual for the 14-year-old king of Cyprus, Hugh II (Cyprus was one of several principalities established by the Crusaders in the Levant). But the young king died while Aquinas was working on the material, and Aquinas abandoned the project (Ptolemy of Lucca, one of his followers, later completed it). Greatly influenced by Aristotle's ideas, the pamphlet contains a number of original ideas.[50]

---

[49] See Renouard, *Les hommes d'affaire italiens.*

[50] *Translator's note:* Several editions of Aquinas's pamphlet are available in English. We used the online edition by Gerald B. Phelan, revised by I. Th. Eschmann, O.P. (Toronto: The Pontifical Institute of Mediaeval Studies, 1949);

A. A Definition of the State

First, Aquinas embraces Aristotle's fundamental ideas on the nature of the city. Humans are social and political animals by nature. Animals form into groups naturally. But people could not survive if they did not form a society, because their only resource is reason, and one person's reason embraces very little in reality: a division of knowledge is imperative, as is a sharing of the fruits of knowledge, so that all can enjoy the basic minimum for survival. The mere existence of language, for example, proves that "man communicates with his kind more completely than any other animal known to be gregarious" (*On Kingship* 1.7). Such cooperation must be established at a level that allows for self-sufficiency and the mutual satisfaction of needs: thus, not at the level of the domestic household, the small town, or the village, but at the level of the city.

However, such a multitude requires a "directive principle" ("a governing power") (*On Kingship* 1.1) to avoid breaking up and dispersing, like a body requires a central organ—the heart or the head—to govern its members, or like reason rules the other parts of the soul, or the celestial body that rules the other bodies. "Now it is manifest that what is itself one can more efficaciously bring about unity than several... [and] it is evident that several persons could by no means preserve the stability of the community if they totally disagreed" (3.17, 18). Nature shows us the way: the body has one heart, bees have one queen, and the universe one God. Experience also proves that where one person rules, unity is stronger.

B. A Mixed Form of Government

For reasons of principle, therefore, monarchy is the best form of government. But if it becomes a tyranny, it is the worst. So where the power of government is vested in one, there is more risk. Is there not a more balanced solution? Aquinas comes to a conclusion a little later when in his *Summa theologica* he formulates a praise of "mixed government":

> Accordingly, the best form of government is in a state or kingdom, where one is given the power to preside over all for the sake of his virtue (secundum virtutum);[51] while under him are others having governing powers, they too chosen for the sake of their virtues; and yet a government of this kind is shared by all, both because all are eligible to govern, and because the rules are chosen by all. For this is the best form of polity: a good mix between kingship; aristocracy, in so far as a number of persons are set in authority; and democracy, i.e., government by the people, in so far as the rulers can be chosen from the people, and the people have the right to choose their rulers. (Ia–IIæ, q. 105, art. 1)[52]

Aquinas notes in his *De regno* that the mixed form of government was the true strength of the Roman Republic; soldiers knew that they fought in their own mutual interest, not in the interest of the prince. Unfortunately, republics do not last because of internal quarrels and must make room for tyrannies: thus, the Roman Republic was replaced by the Empire, where most emperors behaved like tyrants. In sum, a truly ideal form of government does not exist, and the mixed government is the lesser evil.

---

available at dhspriory.org/thomas/DeRegno.htm. Aquinas's ideas on the state can also be found in his commentary on Aristotle's *Politics*.

[51] As a proper representative of the church, Aquinas does not seem to hold heredity in high esteem. His monarchy, like that of Nicolas Oresme in the following century, is elective, or at any rate, the person of the head of the state must be able to be changed if his virtue falters.

[52] We recall that Aquinas believed that this mixed form of government was what characterized the political regime of Ancient Israel.

But, whatever the form of government, it is important that it is not tyrannical. A good government can be established if proper rulers are chosen at the outset (like Samuel chose Saul and David), if their power is moderated, if a procedure is set up to remove rulers who become tyrants despite precautions.

C. A Doctrine of Tyrannicide

In fact, Aquinas provides a justification for revolt against an unjust political power; he even goes so far as to justify violence and the assassination of the tyrant.

He does place a condition on revolt motivated by the injustice of the rulers: the remedy must not be worse than the evil it replaces. He illustrates this with the following story:

> In Syracuse, at a time when everyone desired the death of Dionysius, a certain old woman kept constantly praying that he might be unharmed and that he might survive her. When the tyrant learned this he asked why she did it. Then she said: "When I was a girl we had a harsh tyrant and I wished for his death; when he was killed, there succeeded him one who was a little harsher. I was very eager to see the end of his dominion also, and we began to have a third ruler still more harsh—that was you. So if you should be taken away, a worse would succeed in your place. (*On Kingship* 7.44)

The Scriptures provide somewhat contradictory evidence on this score. The Old Testament (Judges) seems to authorize tyrannicide, whereas the New Testament forbids it (all power comes from God; Christians did not kill their persecutors, the Roman emperors). Aquinas reaches the conclusion that it is wrong for a person to remove a tyrant *on his own private initiative*. Because, in the eyes of the wicked, even good monarchs can be tyrants. "This is because the wicked usually expose themselves to dangers of this kind more than the good, for the rule of a king, no less than that of a tyrant, is burdensome to them since, according to the words of Solomon [Prov. 20:26]: "A wise king scatters the wicked." Consequently, by presumption of this kind, danger to the people from the loss of a good king would be more probable than relief through the removal of a tyrant" (*On Kingship* 7.47).

Therefore, a revolt must result from a *public* initiative. And the people can lawfully remove a king, *because they put him in power in the first place*. "If to provide itself with a king belongs to the right of a given multitude, it is not unjust that the king be deposed or have his power restricted by that same multitude if, becoming a tyrant, he abuses the royal power" (*On Kingship* 7.49).

This is a firm affirmation of the *democratic* principle: political power, even the power of a king, derives from a *mandate* of the people. As soon as the king betrays this mandate, he becomes an unlawful ruler. "It must not be thought that such a multitude is acting unfaithfully in deposing the tyrant, even though it had previously subjected itself to him in perpetuity, because he himself has deserved that the covenant with his subjects should not be kept, since, in ruling the multitude, he did not act faithfully as the office of a king demands" (*On Kingship* 7.49).

How should the people go about the removal of a tyrant? By means of a *senatus consultum* or a popular vote (e.g., the unseating of Tarquin the Proud [Lucius Tarquinius Superbus] and Domitian). Also, the act of a higher authority, such as that of a king if he exists, would be appropriate (e.g., Tiberius unseated Herod; Aquinas certainly has in mind the papal depositions of princes and feudal lords).

And, of course, the people can also pray to God, who can remove a tyrant: many examples exist. But for God to act, the people must be worthy, which means it must repent of its sins. Aquinas quotes Hosea 13:11: "I will give you a king in my wrath," and Job 34:30: "[God] makes a man that is a hypocrite to reign for the sins of the people." And he concludes, "Sin must therefore be done away with in order that the scourge of tyrants may cease" (*On Kingship* 7.52).

D. The Motives of Rulers

Tyrannicide would not be an issue if the exercise of power remained moderate. But power cannot be exercised moderately as long as rulers are motivated by pleasures and riches because these things can only be attained at the expense of their subjects; the pursuit of such things inclines rulers inexorably to tyranny. It would be better for them to seek honor and glory because they are compatible with the good of their subjects. But even this is not without risk of immoderation. Aquinas posits that rulers are only moderate in government if the ultimate aim of their action is eternal happiness (*beatitudo*).

All rewards come from a higher authority. All political power comes from God (the Apostle Paul); kings are his servants (Wisdom of Solomon); therefore, the rewards of kings also come from God. Such rewards are not earthly success because God grants this to wicked kings as well (like Nebuchadnezzar); they are rewards of happiness, which is a form of glory, but much higher, because it is "a never-fading crown of glory." First of all, happiness is promised to kings as men.[53] Nothing earthly can quell their desire. The king as a man is *capax Dei,* "capable of God" (see above, note 20 to this chapter). Only God can satisfy human desire. And because humans are by nature rational beings, their nature can only attain perfection through an intellectual vision of God, a vision of the essence of all things through a vision of the creator of all essences. The king shares with all people this prospect of salvation.

But the happiness of the king will be even greater. For if happiness is the reward for virtue, a higher degree of happiness is owed to a greater virtue:

> It is said also in Sirach (31.8, 10): "Blessed is [the man]...who could have transgressed with impunity and did not transgress, who could do evil and did not do it." Wherefore, having been tried in the work of virtue, he is found faithful and so, according to the proverb of Bias:[54] "Authority shows the man." For many who seemed virtuous while they were in lowly state fall from virtue when they reach the pinnacle of power.[55] *The very difficulty, then, of acting well, which besets kings, makes them more worthy of greater reward;* and if through weakness they sometimes do amiss, they are rendered more excusable before men and more easily obtain forgiveness from God provided. (*On Kingship* 10.73)

Conversely, tyrants will be punished more harshly than ordinary sinners. Especially since the tyrant has no possibility of repentance; he is accountable for his own sins and for those he incited his followers to commit by example.[56]

E. The Essence of Government

Fear of punishment and hope of reward are insufficient for a ruler to be just and moderate. The ruler must also meditate on the art of government and understand what it entails. "To govern is to lead the thing governed in a suitable way towards its proper end. Thus a ship is said to be governed when, through the skill of the pilot, it is brought unharmed and by a direct route to

[53] Aquinas studies happiness—the ultimate aim of human life being a vision of God—in a famous treatise in his *Summa theologica,* Ia–IIæ, q. 1.

[54] Bias was one of the Seven Sages of Greece.

[55] We saw this idea in our discussion of Cicero (see above, pp. 482–83).

[56] Dante remembered this idea in his *Inferno* when he placed tyrants in the deepest circles. See *Inferno,* canto 12, verses 103–12: in this seventh circle of hell, the circle of the "violent" sinners, Alexander the Great, Dionysius of Syracuse, and Dante's contemporaries (Ezzolino di Romano, Lord of Padua, Obizzo of Este, Marquis of Ferrara and of the Marca d' Ancona) atone for their wrongdoing (see also *Purgatory,* canto 6, verse 125: "Italian cities all o'erthrong'd with tyrants").

harbour" (*On Kingship* 15.103). "It is the governor's duty, not only to preserve the thing unharmed, but further to guide it towards this end" (15.103).

We saw that the end of man is external to him: it is the fruition of God. Rulers can choose to ignore this and limit their concern to the preservation of the state. But if they do, the same thing will happen to the ship of state as to the ship on the sea; the ship's carpenter will repair damage and other specialists will look after the onboard functions; the ship will survive, but no one will direct the ship to its port of destination. Likewise, if the rulers of a country imagine that the end of man is in man himself, that is in his prosperity or his health, in science or in good behavior, they will be mere economists, physicians, doctors, and educators (*institutores morum*). This is what happened in pagan nations where the spiritual plane was directed to the temporal. But under the New Law, the state is directed to Christ, the true King, and therefore to a transcendent end. "Consequently the Christian man... needs another and spiritual care to direct him to the harbour of eternal salvation, and this care is provided for the faithful by the ministers of the church of Christ" (*On Kingship* 15.105).

Thus, Aquinas comes full circle to the fundamentals of political Augustinism. The rulers of a state can only perform their role as servants of the church, a church under the legitimate authority and direction of Peter's successor, the pope, "to him all the kings of the Christian People are to be subject as to our Lord Jesus Christ Himself" (*On Kingship* 15.110). Nevertheless, the rulers have one specific function: to institute and preserve a good life for the multitude in society under their authority, leading it "to a higher perfection." It is unfortunate that Aquinas broke off his *Summa theologica* before developing this last formulation.

Chapter 6

The End of the Middle Ages (Fourteenth to Fifteenth Centuries): Toward the Modern Concept of the State

The fourteenth and fifteenth centuries may be looked at from two points of view. On the one hand, from an economic and demographic viewpoint, it was a period of crisis and decline, due in particular to the Black Death and the Hundred Years' War. In terms of culture as well, these two centuries seem less bright than the classical Middle Ages of the twelfth and thirteenth centuries. On the other hand, the period was rich in political developments. Throughout Europe the state as an institution experienced spectacular growth. The state apparatus grew decisively (a tax system, a judiciary, central and local bureaucracies, a standing army, etc.), nations asserted themselves. In doctrinal terms, the important attributes making up the modern idea of the state were developed in theoretical texts, which became numerous again since the link with ideas from antiquity was reestablished. If during the fourteenth and fifteenth centuries the state was, in some respects, in transition between a feudal monarchy and an absolute monarchy, it nevertheless showed original features: it was at this time, against the backdrop of the crisis of the church and the rise of Conciliarism, that "democratic" ideas appeared. Absolute monarchy triumphed in practice, but the intellectual seeds of new political ideas planted at this time began to grow again in the sixteenth century.

In the following pages we will discuss the different characteristics of the state as they came into sharper focus during the fourteenth and fifteenth centuries. This will include its *abstraction* (section I), its *secularity* (section II), its *sovereignty* (section III), *the notion of the nation-state* (section IV), *absolutist expressions of government* (section V), and *representative or democratic expressions of the state* (section VI). We will also describe the historical context.

I. The "State" as an Abstraction

A. From the King to Crown and State

In the Middle Ages a word for a "state" still did not exist.[1] It was not until the end of the fifteenth century that "status" was used in this sense. Before this time, one spoke of *res publica, regnum; civitas* was derived from Latin translations of Aristotle. There were also several transitional concepts. In the twelfth century, John of Salisbury spoke of a "body politic," and his definition circulated widely.

His metaphor implied that all parts of the "body" were mutually dependent; this made it possible to condemn tyranny and rebellion both. Around the year 1400, Jean de Terre Rouge (also called Jean de Terremerveille) wrote that the supporters of the duke of Burgundy were but "putrefying members of the French body politic, and that they ought therefore to be amputated for the health of the whole."[2] Bishop Stratford used the same metaphor in 1327 to ratify the deposition of Edward II, labeling him the sick head of the body politic and calling for a new head. This image of the "body politic" is related to the rediscovered and much discussed Aristotelian idea of the "natural community." According to Aristotle, the defining characteristic of this community is its self-sufficiency. This raises the question of the desired boundaries of the body politic: it must be sufficiently vast to live independently.

The words "crown" and "royal crown" (*corona regni*) also came into use around this time. By the mid-twelfth century, the symbolic material object of the crown came to be an abstract concept, especially in England.[3] Soon thereafter in France, Abbot Suger used the word "crown" in the same abstract sense. We find it used again in this way in 1158 in Bohemia and in 1197 in Hungary. Philip Augustus distinguishes his "person" from the "crown" in a letter to the chapter of Reims in 1197: he appealed for military aid against the Flemish "for the defence of my person and of the crown of the kingdom."[4] But, it was only in the fourteenth century that the idea became widespread throughout the West.

Obviously, restrictions had to be placed on alienations of crown properties. Jean de Terre Rouge makes the point that kings had only usufructuary rights over the properties of the crown. Charles VI did not have the right to dispose of crown properties at the Treaty of Troyes:[5] he did so to the detriment of the heir to the French crown. This was the beginning of the idea of the realm's "fundamental laws" (a sixteenth century formulation).

In addition, before long—that is, during the conflict between the king of England, Henry III, and his barons (1258–65)—it appears that, the kingdom being a community, a *communitas regni,* every subject of the king had a legitimate interest in the crown. In a way, the crown itself was public property, and legislative and fiscal decisions were no longer to be made by the king alone. Vassals owed allegiance to the crown, and not to the king; therefore, they could, if necessary, oppose the person of the king. The return of an abstract idea of the state facilitated the return of civic notions from antiquity.

---

[1] This section is drawn from Jean Dunbabin, "Government," in Burns, *Cambridge History,* 477–519. See Bernard Guenée, *L'Occident aux XIVe et XVe siècles: Les etats* [The West in the fourteenth and fifteenth centuries: The state] (Paris: Presses Universitaires France, 1993).

[2] Quoted by Dunbabin, "Government," 482.

[3] See Dunbabin, "Government," 499–502.

[4] Quoted ibid., 501.

[5] Shortly after France's defeat at the Battle of Agincourt in 1420, Charles VI made Henry V, king of England, heir to the French crown.

B. The Evolution of Succession Laws in France

This process of abstraction and depersonalization of the concept of the state is illustrated strikingly by the evolution of succession laws in France.[6] At the outset, the kingdom was almost completely combined with the person of the king. The greats of the realm were his loyal subjects, personally and according to the logic of a private contract of vassalage; by the time the evolution was complete, the kingdom was virtually detached from the person of the king, and it was to the state that subjects were loyal.

Succession laws, framed by jurists such as Jean de Terre Rouge, were firmly established by the fifteenth century after several rules were adopted: hereditary primogenital succession (twelfth century), masculine and lateral succession (fourteenth century), accession to and continuity of the crown (fifteenth century).

Throughout the ninth century, Frankish kings were *elected* (among privileged families). Then, gradually, the hereditary principle prevailed; Philip Augustus was the last king to be elected and anointed during the lifetime of his father (1179).

The right of *primogeniture* (the firstborn's right of inheritance) was soon added to the hereditary principle. It became permanent with the House of Capet.[7] The first two dynasties customarily shared the kingdom among sons, like private property according to Germanic custom (as the Treaty of Verdun did in 843). The principle that the entire kingdom became the birthright of the eldest son reflects a partial return to the Roman idea of the state: a permanent public person, manifestly distinct from the private person holding the office.

For over three centuries the House of Capet enjoyed a long, direct line of male heirs, from Hugh Capet to Louis X the Stubborn. Since Louis X only left a posthumous son, John I, who died after a few days, Louis's brother, Philip, who became regent, pressed his own claims to the crown and had a royal council proclaim him king under the name Philip V. In so doing, he usurped the normal feudal rights of Princess Joan, Louis X's surviving daughter: by a new advance of the Roman concept of public law, royal law stood apart from feudal law. Once more the new rule was applied for Philip V's succession because he left only daughters. His immediate successor in 1322 was the brother of the deceased king, a third son of Philip IV, Charles IV the Fair.

The problem was that, when Charles IV of France died, the closest male heir was the king of England, Edward III, the grandson of Philip the Fair by his mother Isabella. But was she able to transmit to her son the right of accession to the throne, being unable to accede herself? Could she be both "bridge and pillar" for two kings? A new council of dignitaries gave a negative reply: one cannot transmit a right that one does not possess oneself. And so, a distant cousin, Philip VI (the nephew of Philip the Fair), became the rightful king of France and the first in the line of the House of Valois.

It is clear that in both cases (the designation of Philip V and Philip VI), "Salic law"—the code of the Salian Franks—played a lesser role than political considerations: the kingdom, a most precious public property, could not be entrusted to a child too weak to protect it or to a foreign sovereign too strong to respect its integrity. From this time on, the French law of succession was settled: "In the absence of a direct successor of the deceased monarch, the crown descended infinitely to the first-born son of the eldest lateral branch."[8]

---

[6] This section is drawn from Stéphane Rials, "La devolution de la couronne" [The devolution of the crown], in Rials, *Le miracle capétien.*

[7] In regard to the inheritance of fiefs, the reader recalls that various principles were in play at different times and places: paternal choice of the successor, choice of the younger son over the eldest, etc. See above, pp. 495–96.

[8] Rials, "La devolution de la couronne." Hereditary law prevailed primarily by custom. But it could also be supported by theoretical justifications: according to intuitive biological theory, sons were said to reproduce and prolong the nature and virtues of their fathers; thus, a royal nature existed. It was perhaps also the almost priestly quality conferred on kings

Then a new rule was posed, which was further progress of the principle that royal right was public right: the right of succession to the crown of France could not be transmitted at will; in other words, the bearer of the crown could not transmit it to whomever he pleased. The king, unlike a private property owner, lacked the testamentary freedom to dispose of his properties.

The question arose with the Treaty of Troyes (1420), when Charles VI the Mad dispossessed his son Charles (Joan of Arc's "beloved dauphin" and future Charles VII), removing him from the royal line of succession in favor of Henry V, king of England. (Charles the Mad "adopted" Henry like the Roman emperors adopted their successors.) Jurists rejected his act of disinheritance, declaring royal succession to be a "statutory" right, not a "patrimonial" right. The king was not at liberty to choose his successor. The rules guiding the designation of future kings were those outlined above, independently of any human will.

In keeping with the same principle, the rightful royal heir was not at liberty to refuse his inheritance (in private law an heir does have such a right of refusal): a king of France cannot abdicate the crown. (For this reason, the abdication of Charles X in 1830 was contested.)

One final principle will be discussed: the immediacy of royal succession and the unbroken continuity of the crown. As soon as the king died, his successor began his reign without interruption. (This is the meaning of "The king is dead. Long live the king!," "the dead holds the living in its grasp," and "the king never dies in France.") This principle was established sometime between the end of the thirteenth century and the beginning of the fifteenth. It amounted to diminishing the importance of ceremonial anointment and, accordingly, reduced the church's role in the legitimation of royal authority.

These last two measures moved the concepts of kingdom and crown decisively away from the concepts of patrimony and *dominium* and closer to the idea of a "republic" in the Roman sense, that is, toward the idea of a state.

In fact, the idea moved so close that hereditary succession, that is, the essential bond of the state with a lineage, was understood as an anomaly, an arbitrary survival of archaic practices. If the state was truly a public body, that is, an abstract reality—permanent and independent of its successive physical officeholders—neither a private person nor a private family could have a hold on it, just as it was not possible for magistrates in the ancient *polis* to control their offices. The evolution of monarchic public law, inspired by Roman law and moving away from the biblical idea of a God-elected messianic figure over the flock, could only lead to a republican form of government, and this is what finally happened in France.

Thus, at the very moment that succession laws were being "definitively" framed—and in a sense because this was so—they immediately became null and void, since they canceled out their object, the monarchy. The physical body of the king became unnecessary and superfluous with his abstract body, the state.

II. Secularity

However, this state could not flourish as long as a church existed within it with claims of autonomy and superiority. A body politic cannot have two heads; it cannot be ruled by two parallel

---

by sacred anointing that excluded women from the royal succession (since women cannot be priests). Finally, jurists were quick to confirm the law of succession because they understood that automatic succession stifled the possibility of claims and quarrels. This point was made vigorously by the French royalists in the nineteenth and twentieth centuries, scandalized by the extraordinary, even unnatural (in their eyes) instability of the political regimes of France since the interruption of the direct line of hereditary rule in 1792.

organizations; otherwise, it ceases to be one body. The embryonic "nation-state" instinctively rejected the biblical notion of a permanent distinction and an irreparable competition between a spiritual power and a temporal power. In particular, the idea that the church had its own legal jurisdiction and that certain citizens could escape secular justice by "privilege of forum" offended the legal experts reared in Roman public law. In the fourteenth century, first-rate minds began to establish the rational foundations of what might be called, in modern terms, the "secularity" of the state. The dying days of the controversy between pope and emperor in Italy offer insight into the moment and manner of the eruption of this new ideological struggle.

A. The Germanic Emperors and Italy in the Fourteenth and Fifteenth Centuries

The Italians themselves were among the first to contest clerical and papal tutelage. They suspected that the pope, who had fervently supported Italian cities in their wars against the Germanic emperors, was using these struggles to build excessive power.

The papal ideology of *plenitudo potestatis,* engineered by the great legal popes Alexander III, Innocent III, Innocent IV, and Boniface VIII (cf. his bull *Unam Sanctam* of 1302), had become utterly suffocating. Italian cities started to react: Padua refused to pay taxes to the church in 1266; in Orvieto a revolt against the presence of the *curia* (the papal court) took place. At the beginning of the fourteenth century, fulminations against church courts and clerical privileges were widespread. Revolts erupted in territories newly united with the pontifical states. In the struggle between popes and emperors, two new incidents at the end of the fourteenth century exacerbated antagonisms and encouraged defenders of the imperial cause.

Henry VII of Luxembourg invaded the Italian peninsula in 1310. The first Avignon pope, Clement V, had encouraged him to conquer Italy to foil the power of the Angevin king, Robert of Naples. Henry had himself crowned emperor by the pope's representative in 1312. But, following in the footsteps of his predecessors, he laid claims to all of Italy and expressed the intention to depose the king of Naples. The pope and Robert reconciled their differences, and the kingdom of Naples was declared "outside the Empire"; the pope declared it a fief of the church again. A war would have been fatal for the papal camp, but Henry VII died suddenly in 1313.

In 1314 two rival clans in Germany elected two different emperors: Frederick I of Habsburg (Frederick the Fair) and Louis IV of Bavaria (Louis the Bavarian). The second Avignon pope, John XXII, announced he would recognize neither, then declared himself imperial vicar for Italy (thus, the highest temporal sovereign). Louis defeated Frederick on the battlefield in 1322, but the pope refused to recognize Louis as emperor; in 1324 he excommunicated him. In 1327, Louis invaded Italy, the fourth German emperor to risk the Italian adventure, but again he failed to seize the whole country; he did, however, capture Rome, where he had himself crowned emperor by the excommunicated bishop of Venice; he then deposed the pope after declaring him a heretic (1318).[9]

It was in this historical context that the imperial argument received a full-scale intellectual defense; this had not been the case in the twelfth and thirteenth centuries, when the proponents of "dualism" were few in number and not very talented. Henry of Luxembourg received the

[9] This is how the story ends: in 1338, at the Diet of Rhens, it was decreed that the emperor's election by the German princes was sufficiently legitimate without additional need for papal approval. In 1356, the Golden Bull of Emperor Charles IV confirmed this decision and declared the sovereignty of the prince-electors. Henceforth, the pope conferred only the imperial title; the capacity to reign as emperor was established by election (which also conferred the title of "king of the Romans"). Thereafter, several German emperors reigned without the imperial title (Wenceslas, Rupert, Albert II). Thus, the division between the papacy and the Empire reflected the fact that the Empire ceased to be a universal reality and became the form of state particular to the German nation.

intellectual backing of leading intellectuals such as the Florentine historian Dino Campagni and, above all, the great poet *Dante*. Louis the Bavarian was supported by—and the Avignon popes lambasted by—*Marsilius of Padua* and *William of Ockham*. These writers made constant, almost obsessional doctrinal reference to Aristotle's authority, which had in the meantime become the new vulgate of the universities.

B. Dante (1265–1321)

Dante Alighieri is the great Italian poet and author of the *Divine Comedy,* which tells of a visionary journey into hell, purgatory, and paradise with two guides: the Roman poet Virgil and Beatrice.[10] In literature, Dante's creation is the poetic equivalent of cathedral architecture and, in theology and philosophy, the *Summa theologica*. With the *Divine Comedy* and these other achievements, the Christian Middle Ages reached its period of greatness.

Dante, a Florentine exile chased from his native city by the outbreak of political turmoil after the death of Frederick II, also wrote a work of political theory titled *De monarchia* (On monarchy). In this work he comes out in favor of the Holy Roman Emperor's universal domination and argues for restricting papal power to the spiritual domain. *De monarchia*—short, tight, and coherent in its development, but more philosophical than political in scope—is representative of a nascent Italian humanism that revolts against what is in appearance an increasingly irrational and outdated attitude of church authorities.

Dante Alighieri was born in 1265 in Florence. At the time, on a papal commission, Charles of Anjou had conquered the Hohenstaufen kingdom of Naples and Sicily. In Florence, the Guelphs retook power from the Ghibellines. In 1300, already famous as a poet, Dante held various public offices (ambassador, adviser) and was briefly "chancellor of Florence," the most important office in the bureaucracy of the Florentine Republic. But the Florentine Guelphs were split between a "bourgeois" party (the White Guelphs) and a "people's" party (the Black Guelphs), around which the aristocracy rallied in support. The two parties clashed; to separate them Pope Boniface VIII sent a mediator, Charles of Valois, the brother of Philip the Fair. Upon his triumphal entry into Florence, Charles handed over power to the Black Guelphs. Absent from Florence at this time, Dante was sentenced to exile and to death at the stake, if ever he fell into the hands of the Commune (the government of Florence). These were good reasons for Dante to give his native city a wide birth for the rest of his life (he lived in exile for 20 years, successively in Verona, Ravenna, Mantua, and Piacenza; during this time he wrote his *Divine Comedy*). It also explains his political stance against the pope and in support of the emperor (Dante did not like the Black Guelphs, but he despised the White Guelphs as well, and distanced himself from them). He placed his hopes in Henry VII of Luxembourg, elected king of the Romans in 1308 and crowned emperor in 1312 in Saint John Lateran Church. Dante was the most fervent of the Ghibellines (supporters of the emperor). Henry died suddenly in 1313 near Sienna, and all that was left for Dante was to complete his literary oeuvre. He died in 1321.

The *Divine Comedy* is by far Dante's most significant work. He completed the third part, *Paradise,* shortly before his death. His first verses for Beatrice, interspersed with prose commentaries, the so-called *Vita nuova* collection, were written between 1292 and 1295. The *Banquet* (*Convivio*) is an unfinished second collection of didactic poems written in 1305 and 1306. *De monarchia* is written in Latin; its date of composition is unknown.

---

[10] See Dante Alighieri, *The Divine Comedy: Inferno, Purgatorio, Paradiso,* trans. Robin Kirkpatrick (London: Penguin Classics, 2012). See also Dante Alighieri, *Monarchy,* ed. Prue Shaw (Cambridge: Cambridge University Press, 1996).

Dante's *De monarchia* is very robustly constructed and uses the explicitly logical method of the Scholastics, almost to the extent of puerility at times. The work is divided into three parts, each with a clear thesis: (1) monarchy or universal empire is necessary for the well-being of the world; (2) the Romans are the God-given holders of the imperial office; (3) the papacy has no right of interference in the temporal power of the emperor.

1. *Monarchy or Universal Empire Is Necessary for the Well-Being of the World*

Dante argues for the need of a centralized state to preserve civil peace; universal peace, he posits, is the condition for the well-being of the world. "There must therefore be one person who rules and governs mankind, and he is properly called 'Monarch' or 'Emperor'" (*De monarchia* 1.5.9). Because

> wherever there can be conflict there must be judgment to resolve it, otherwise there would be an imperfection without its proper corrective; and this is impossible, since God and nature never fail in their provision of what is necessary. There is always the possibility of conflict between two rulers where one is not subject to the other's control; such conflict may come about either through their own fault or the fault of their subjects (the point is self-evident); therefore there must be judgment between them.... [Thus], the world requires the existence of a monarchy. (*De monarchia* 1.10.1–2, 1.11.20)

Quoting Aristotle, he says, "Things do not wish to be badly ordered; a plurality of reigns is bad; therefore let there be one ruler" (*Metaphysics* 12.3.16).

Dante insists on this principle of unity. "What can be done by a single person is better done by a single person than by several." It is "unnecessary and pointless" for more than one person to do something, if one suffices. "Mankind can be ruled by one supreme ruler, who is the monarch." Not that he should take every decision in the affairs of his people; he should leave these to lesser officials because "nations, kingdoms and cities have characteristics of their own, which need to be governed by different laws" (the northern Scythians cannot be ruled like the Garamantes, living below the equator). Nevertheless, the supreme monarch can provide a universal principal to all, just as the speculative intellect provides its law for practical intellects; it is even essential for this shared law "to come from one person, to avoid any confusion about universal principles" (*De monarchia* 1.14).

The superiority of unity is, for Dante, metaphysical; it depends on the very structure of the being, in which the being conditions the one that conditions the good. So, the more we are, the more we are one, and the better we are: "unity seems to be the root of what it is to be good, and plurality the root of what it is to be evil" (*De monarchia* 1.15.3).

The experimental evidence of this: there never was "peace throughout the world except under the divine monarch Augustus, when a perfect monarchy existed. That mankind was then happy in the calm of universal peace is attested by all historians and by famous poets" (*De monarchia* 1.16.1–2). The New Testament itself attests to this.

"What the state of the world has been since that seamless garment was first rent by the talon of cupidity[11] we can read about—would that we might not witness it. O human race, how many storms and misfortunes and shipwrecks must toss you about while, transformed into a many-headed beast, you strive after conflicting things" (*De monarchia* 1.16.3–4).

[11] That is, when the Empire of Augustus began to collapse. The "seamless garment," *tunica inconsultilis*, is Christ's robe for which the Roman soldiers cast lots without tearing it (John 19:23–24). For Dante the garment became the symbol of an indivisible monarchy.

2. *The Romans Are the God-Given Holders of the Imperial Office*

If the Empire is so necessary to the higher good of humankind, there must be a head to exercise the highest office. Dante's aim is to demonstrate that the Roman Empire is the rightful universal monarchy.

It is clear that, for him, the Holy Roman Empire is the continuation of the Augustan Empire. However, this is only implicit. Nowhere is there praise for the Germans; the entire demonstration is to the glory of Rome, or more exactly of Italy. The philosophical argument in support of a universal monarchy is expressed with marked Italian nationalism.

Dante believes that Rome's domination of the world is God-given; this is proven by the countless wonders by which it was founded. Surely such wonders were willed by God; accordingly, Rome's domination is wholly lawful.

Dante endorses Virgil's epic narrative. Aeneas founded Rome. He had three wives: the first was Asian (Creusa, daughter of Priam), the second African (Dido), and the third European (Lavinia, daughter of Latinus). Thus, he was promised the whole world (*De monarchia* 2.3). The history of Rome is a succession of miracles, which Dante proudly tallies, citing Virgil and Livy abundantly, from the geese of the capitol to Hannibal's failure to exploit his victory at the Battle of Cannes.

But Rome's victories were made possible by the superior virtues of the Roman people (Dante refers to Cicero here) (*De monarchia* 2.5.5). When the Roman people conquered the world and subordinated it to their rule, they introduced the rule of law everywhere; it was therefore just that they assumed the dignity of Empire (2.5.18). If one finds these qualities among the Romans surprising, Dante refers to Aristotle, who said that there are masters and slaves by nature; the same idea applies to peoples. "Certain peoples are born fitted to rule, and certain others to be ruled and to serve.... Such people should be ruled, even if force has to be used to bring this about" (2.6.7–8).

Dante cites Virgil when he compares the respective merits of the Greeks and the Romans (see above, pp. 319–21), and he concludes that the Romans are called to rule the world. Once again, this is God's choice because "the resolving of a universal dispute is of greater concern to God than the resolving of a limited dispute" (*De monarchia* 2.8.1). By handing the Romans military victory, God announces his choice. All other empires—Persian, Macedonian—were incomplete and disappeared; only the Roman Empire is universal and survives (Dante does not make any allusion to Byzantium).

Lastly, the highest proof: the New Testament confirms the primacy and God-given mission of the Roman people. For Christ's sacrifice to purchase the sin of humankind, it was necessary that it was not accidental, it had to bear witness to humankind's rejection of Christ's messianity. By choosing to die by the authority of Pontius Pilate, Christ gave Roman authority its universal legitimacy: "If Christ had not suffered under an authorized judge, that penalty [the Cross] would not have been a punishment [but a simple injustice]. And no judge could be authorized [in Jerusalem] unless he had jurisdiction over the whole of mankind" (*De monarchia* 2.11.5).

3. *The Papacy Has No Right to Encroach on the Temporal Power of the Emperor*

Last question: did the Roman Empire, which Providence had called to rule the world, receive its mission directly from God or through the intermediary of a "vicar" or "officer" of God, for example, the papacy?[12]

[12] Again we are faced with the question of the Two Swords. Here Dante defends a particularly radical version of the dualist argument.

Dante's answer: since the Roman Empire is necessary for the well-being of the world, whatever interferes with its mission is contrary to divine plan, whether it is the pope or the decretalists, those who think that the pope can legislate in all domains, even against the law of the Empire or against the Scriptures. Because "the traditions of the Church come after the Church" and "tradition must come after the law." Therefore, "it must be the case that the Church does not derive its authority from the traditions, but that the traditions derive their authority from the Church"[13] (*De monarchia* 3.3.16).

Dante refutes a series of arguments traditionally used by theologians, committed to the cause of Rome, to establish the primacy of the church over the Empire; some we encountered in the writings of the advocates of hierocracy.

a. The two great lights

These theologians favored a symbolic interpretation of the two great lights in Genesis, the one that rules the day and the other the night (the sun and the moon, Genesis 1:16). The sun represents spiritual power, the moon symbolizes temporal power. Since the moon merely reflects light received from the sun, temporal power must receive its authority from spiritual power. This, Dante says, is farcical, because both the sun and the moon were created on the fourth day, that is, before the creation of humankind, which occurred on the sixth day; therefore, the symbols cannot refer to human powers. Moreover, if the moon receives the light of the sun, it does not owe its existence to the sun. Accordingly, even if the symbols apply to human institutions, that does not prove that the Empire owes its existence to the papacy (*De monarchia* 3.4).

b. Levi and Judah

The Bible says that Judah is the father of temporal power, and Levi is the father of the priesthood. Now Levi preceded Judah in birth; therefore, spiritual power has primacy over temporal power. But the fact that one is older does not imply higher authority in the least. Otherwise, a young bishop would have less authority than an older archdeacon.

c. Samuel placed King Saul on the throne, then removed him

Although this is true, in both cases he was commanded to do so by a messenger from God. This does not mean that God's vicar on earth, the pope, can dispose of kings at will. God's legatee does not have all of God's powers (*De monarchia* 3.6).

d. The power to bind and unbind

Peter received the power to bind and unbind from Christ, but such power applies only to the things that the keys of the heavenly kingdom in Peter's possession can open or close. It does not mean that, on earth, the pope can bind or unbind subjects from the laws of the Empire.

e. The Two Swords

It is wrong to see a symbol in the Two Swords. The passage must be understood literally, which is made clear by the context. Christ merely said: two swords suffice, if money is not available for 12 (one for each apostle).

---

[13] A return to a time before the Papal Revolution, back before its decretals and synods, to the *Sola scriptura* and the early church. Dante feels that it is necessary to remove from Christianity the thick layer of "traditions" compiled at the beginnings of the Roman Church: this particular idea, which we will come across again in the thought of Marsilius of Padua and William of Ockham, announces the Reformation.

f. The Donation of Constantine

This gift, it is said, made the pope the true head of the Roman Empire in the West. By appointing, crowning, and deposing the Holy Roman Emperors, the pope simply looks after his interests. Dante does not say or does not know that the Donation is a forgery. He argues from the legal point of view: Constantine could not legally alienate a part of the Empire because the Empire was not private patrimony; it was a function or office: "his task is to hold mankind in obedience to a single will . . . as can easily be seen from the first book of this treatise" (*De monarchia* 3.10.5). Had Constantine given away half of the Empire, he would have failed his mission and destroyed his legitimacy. Furthermore, the church could not accept the gift because Jesus denied it the exercise of temporal powers once and for all when he said to his disciples, "Take no gold, nor silver, nor copper in your belts, no bag for your journey" (Matt. 10:9–10) (*De monarchia* 3.10).

g. Charlemagne owed his imperial office to the church

He did not inherit it legally since there was still an emperor (Michael) in Constantinople. Dante turns the argument around: inasmuch as, on several occasions, the emperors put the popes on the seat of Rome—or back on it—all popes should consider that they are indebted to the Empire.

A fundamental argument in support of the autonomy of the Empire and its primacy in temporal matters is that the Empire existed before the church *De monarchia* 3.13.3). Both Christ and Paul recognized this when they accepted the judgment of Caesar, and Christ added, "My kingship is not of this world" (John 18:36) (3.15.5).

These ideas were radicalized by Marsilius of Padua and William of Ockham.

C. Marsilius of Padua (1275–1343)

The son of a notary[14] at the University of Padua, Marsilius was born between 1275 and 1280.[15] He studied law and medicine. Later he was the rector of the University of Paris (1312–13). He traveled to the papal court in Avignon and to Padua before returning to Paris, where he taught Aristotelian logic and metaphysics in the faculty of arts. In 1326 he sojourned in Germany at the court of Louis IV of Bavaria, the rival of Frederick I of Habsburg and enemy of the Avignon pope, John XXII (see above). He was the imperial vicar when Louis was in Rome in 1328. Louis appointed him Archbishop of Milan. Later, he probably returned to Louis's Bavarian court. He died toward the end of 1342 or in 1343. His main work was his *Defensor pacis* (1324) (Defender of the peace). He wrote three other works: *De translatione Imperii Romani, Defensor minor,* and *De jurisdictione Imperatoris in causa matrimoniali.*

In the first part (Discourse I) of his *Defensor pacis,* Marsilius says that it is totally wrong to believe that the church has any legal authority or coercive power at all, or that it can claim exemption from ordinary taxes or have separate courts. Because Christ said, "render unto Caesar," all power is Caesar's. Then Marsilius writes, "does not Paul say in his *Letter to the Romans* (chapter 13) that every person is subject to the governing authorities, for there is no authority except from God? And does not 'he who resists the authorities resist what God has appointed'?" Marsilius proposes a return to the early church and a vision before the development of political Augustinism.

---

[14] Notaries belonged to an influential corporation, one of the "major Arts" of Padua: they were something of a gentry class and belonged to the *popolo grosso*.

[15] See Jeannine Quillet, *Marsile de Padoue, Le défenseur de la paix* [Marsilius of Padua, defender of peace] (Paris: Vrin, 1968); *translator's note:* Alain Gewirth, *Marsilius of Padua: Defensor Pacis* (New York: Columbia University Press, 2001).

Next, he posits, referring to Aristotle and the *lex regia,* with the examples of the Holy Roman Empire of the German Nation and the Italian republics, that the people are the highest authority in society. Since there is only one people, there can be only one authority: "The supreme government in a city or a kingdom must be only one in number" (*Defensor pacis* 3.2.11; see 1.17). Thus, Marsilius rejects the divine character of the papal office and attacks the very core of hierocratic logic. Papal authority, he says, is not "given immediately by God but rather by the decision and will of men, just like any other office in society" (1.19.6). The function of the pope is human in origin; it was created because the congregation of believers in Christ needed a leader, and it was administratively convenient to have a centralized organization. But the function could have fallen to anyone; it did not have to be the bishop of Rome. "Gradually and secretly," the primacy of the first bishop of Rome, established on the basis of reverence for the martyred Peter and Paul originally, became stronger and, once it became official under Constantine, evolved into a tyranny and a source of corruption. Papal *plenitudo potestatis* was the chief cause of clerical corruption and of the misery of Italy and the Empire.

What, then, is the role of the church? Christ rejected for himself and his disciples (and their successors) all forms of rule in this world and all coercive jurisdiction on earth. Therefore, the church founded by Christ is in no sense a legal authority or jurisdictional body. It is a "congregation of faithful" (*congregatio fidelium*). The mission of the priest is "to teach and exhort people in the present life, censure and rebuke the sinner and frighten him by a judgment or prediction of future glory or eternal damnation [beyond the grave]"; but he cannot "coerce" in this life (*Defensor pacis* 2.10.2).

Furthermore, bishops and priests must accept secular authority and its jurisdiction in their community. "The ruler by authority of the legislator [for Marsilius, the whole body of citizens] has jurisdiction over all bishops, priests and clergy, lest political society be destroyed by the existence of an unordered multiplicity of governments" (2.8.9; 3.2.15).

This is what Christ did, according to the Scripture. He "sought to remove himself from any type of earthly rulership, wishing always to subject himself to the coercive jurisdiction of temporal authority" (2.4.13). Temporal power, even within the church, must be the jurisdictional authority in all conflicts of power, crimes, and so on, and (the consequence is more ambiguous) in questions of doctrine. Sovereign power belongs to the whole of Christian society (*universitas civium,* the "corporation of citizens"; *universitas fidelium,* the "corporation of faithful"). This idea produced Conciliarism and its theories (see below, pp. 610–14).

Now Marsilius can direct a broadside against *plenitudo potestatis* in the second part (Discourse II) of his *Defensor pacis.* He rejects the pope's claims to be the only authority capable of a proper interpretation of the Scripture; to make points of doctrine without interference; to convene general synods; to excommunicate or place a prince, state, or country under an interdict; to make appointments to ecclesiastical offices anywhere in the world.

To this he opposes the argument that the church itself should be subordinate to secular authority. Since the church has no coercive authority of its own, it should turn to the "believing human legislator" whenever Christian life requires measures of authority. The human legislator should be the only one to make ecclesiastical appointments, convene synods, and so on. Thus, secular authority must be delivered of all clerical tutelage. Marsilius says that papal attempts to seize northern Italy—"by this bishop [the pope] and his accomplices"—are acts of usurpation and despotism.

Thus, Marsilius goes much further than Dante. Dante rejected hierocratic rule in the name of dualism; Marsilius disputes dualism and defends the exact opposite of hierocratic rule: imperialism. Like a good Aristotelian, Marsilius has an "organicist" view of the body politic. As we saw, a body cannot have two heads and two organizations. The *critical* role of spiritual power is denied. In this sense, Marsilius anticipates the absolutism of the modern state as formulated by Hobbes, in very Marsilian style: "Temporal and spiritual government are but two words brought into the world to make men see double and mistake their lawful sovereign."[16]

D. William of Ockham (1295–1350)

William of Ockham lived contemporaneously with Marsilius of Padua and, like him, was an ardent defender of the emperor Louis IV of Bavaria. William also led an attack against the papacy in a string of astoundingly radical political writings that challenged the pope's claims to exercise control over temporal power and to have sole jurisdiction in spiritual matters.

William was born in the village of Ockham, Surrey, England, in 1295. He entered the Order of Saint Francis and studied at the University of Oxford (from 1309 to 1321), where he also taught (from 1321 to 1324). His teaching displeased the papacy, and he was called to the papal court in Avignon, where he spent four years. After 1328 he took up the cause of Louis IV of Bavaria. In Louis's defense he formulated the celebrated line: *Tu me defendas gladio; ego te defendam calamo* ("Defend me with the sword and I will defend you with the pen"). Like Marsilius, he took refuge at the emperor's court in Munich, where he remained until his death, pursuing his theological and polemical writing. He continued to lambaste the Avignon popes and successors of John XXII, Benedict XII, and Clement VI, criticizing them for their conflict with the Empire as well as for their attempts to strengthen papal absolutism and their interventions on the subject of Franciscan "poverty." Thus, William's quarrel with papal authority was profound; his criticism contributed to destabilizing the papacy and to what became the "Great Schism." Alongside John Wyclif in England and Jan Hus in Bohemia, William of Ockham is rightly seen as announcing and paving the way for the Reformation.

William's philosophical and theological writings belong to the first period of his life in England before 1324: *Summa totius logicae, Commentary to the Sentences, Quodlibetal Questions.* The ensuing periods were dominated by his political writings. Noteworthy among these are *Breviloquium de potestate tyrannica* (A Short Discourse on Tyrannical Government) (1339–40), which we discuss below; *Dialogus inter magistratum et discipulum de imperatorum et pontificum potestate* (Dialogue between a Master and a Theology Student about the Powers of Popes and Emperors), which contains, in its third part, his *De potestate et juribus romani imperii* from 1338 and *De potestate papæ et cleri;* also noteworthy are *Tractatus de potestate imperiali* (1338–40), his *Octo quæstionum decisiones super potestatem Sumi Pontificis* (1339–41), and various pamphlets and works against John XXII.

In book 1 of his *Breviloquium de potestate tyrannica,*[17] William develops at length the idea that freedom must exist to discuss the pope's powers, and that this is in the very interest of the pope himself. Neither the pope nor the emperor can be judge and party in their own cause. They must be separated by a recourse to the Holy Scriptures, which are superior to the canons of Rome and the laws of the Empire. Theologians will debate the powers granted to the pope by the Scriptures; jurists will deliberate on the limits of the various temporal powers established by the legal tradition.

William's arguments have a very modern ring to them; they anticipate the Protestant theory of *Sola Scriptura,* and they reflect by and large an Enlightenment-like spirit: human concerns are best considered freely, rationally, and consciously, with all sides of the argument out in the open ("truth emerges when it is thoroughly probed by arguments for and against" [*Breviloquium* 1.5]),

---

[16] *Leviathan,* quoted in J. A. Watt, "Spiritual and Temporal Powers," in Burns, *Cambridge History.*

[17] See William of Ockham, *A Short Discourse on Tyrannical Government,* ed. Arthur Stephen McGrade, trans. John Kilcullen (Cambridge: Cambridge University Press, 1992); all of William of Ockham's works hereafter quoted in the text are from this edition.

and popes, emperors, and kings need to understand the basis of their powers with the same critical insight as scholars so as not to exercise them in the dark. Christians must have the right to judge the constitutional limits of the pope's power as well as his conduct of affairs, for he might be a heretic or a criminal.

In book 2 of *Breviloquium,* William takes aim at the notion of *plenitudo potestatis.* The pope does not have "plenitude of power" in either spiritual or temporal concerns. This doctrine, said to be founded on Matthew 16:18–19 ("You are Peter, and on this rock I will build my church, and the powers of death shall not prevail against it. I will give you the keys of the kingdom of heaven"), is wrong and heretical because it contradicts the freedom of the Gospel. If the pope had "plenitude of power," then all Christians, including the emperors and kings, would be his slaves. Even if he is the sole vicar of Christ on earth, he can not have more power than Christ, who never sought to be a temporal ruler. On the other hand, the powers of kings and emperors are lawful in and of themselves; and, furthermore, they existed before the coming of Christ; the same can be said of the natural and divine rights of men.

Book 3 argues that it is a mistake to think that the emperor receives his power from the pope. This appears nowhere in the Scriptures. Temporal power results from natural law, which is given to all. Even infidels have legitimate temporal attributes and can rightfully appoint rulers and judges: these attributes and magistrates are not given to them by the pope. The claims of Pope John XXII to the contrary are arrogant and heretical.

In fact, the Empire comes from God and the people, not from the pope (book 4). It comes from God as all pagan kingdoms do, no more, no less (when Jesus said "render to Caesar the things that are Caesar's," he did not mean "I appoint Caesar as emperor," but rather, "Give to Caesar what is due to him by human law").[18] In certain exceptional cases, the people can take back their power from the emperor without offending God. At any rate, the Roman Empire was the lawful temporal power at the time of Christ and his apostles.

Following the same logic, the theory of the Two Swords is also wrong: it is based on a misinterpretation of the Scriptures.[19] The speech on the Two Swords can be interpreted very differently from the way most canonists suggest. Saint Ambrose, for example, saw in the Two Swords an allusion to the Old and New Testaments because in the Scriptures the word of God is often compared to a sword of the Spirit (*Breviloquium* 5.5).

Equally absurd is the idea that the sun and the moon in Genesis denote the papacy and the Empire (imperial power being only a reflection of papal power): there is nothing in the Scriptures which supports this interpretation (*Breviloquium,* chap. 6).

William also rejects the argument derived from the anointing of the kings of Israel (chap. 7) and castigates it for being "empty and frivolous" and "manifest heresy." First, it is wrong that the church resorts to the Old Testament for its political, legal, and cult practices; it can only claim the moral law.[20] Next, "it cannot be inferred from [the practice of] anointing that the emperor or other king is inferior, especially in temporal matters, to him who anoints him." Consider the son of a king, when he is baptized or confirmed by a priest or a bishop, or a pope who is elected although he is not yet a priest and is anointed by the same person who ordains him a priest. In both cases, it is not possible to argue "that the son of the king is inferior in temporal matters to him who baptizes or confirms him, or that the pope is inferior to him who ordains him" (5.7). As for the Donation of Constantine, it is dubious; but if it is true, the church did not approve it.

[18] William of Ockham concedes that in certain cases the Scriptures says that God did set up some kingdoms directly, for example, the kingdom of Nebuchadnezzar and the kingdom of Cyrus. However, this is not said of the Roman Empire.

[19] The following arguments parallel those of Dante.

[20] Thomas Aquinas says more or less the same thing (see above, pp. 561–62).

The three thinkers under discussion advanced considerably the idea of the secular nature of the state. But, in order to free themselves from the authority of the pope, they had to accept the authority of the emperor, and in so doing they had to renounce the idea of independence for the Italian states (as well as the notion, for these states, of a republican form of government, because the Guelphs—the enemies of the Empire—advocated a republic). So, we can say that they established the idea of *laicity* to the detriment of the idea of *sovereignty*. Advocacy of the idea of sovereignty would be the work of other thinkers both inside and outside Italy (but within Guelph and republican circles).

III. Sovereignty

The construction of the idea of "sovereignty" was necessary to justify the claims of the new political entities—kingdoms and cities—that were emerging in the fourteenth and fifteenth century in Europe and seeking the right to decide, judge, and legislate independently of the Empire.

A. The King of France and the Emperor

It was initially in France that the need was felt to justify the political independence of the nation-state toward the universal empire. Political theory crystallized this in a paradoxical formula: "a king is emperor in his kingdom."[21]

Initially, nothing was very clearly articulated to justify the coexistence of the Empire and several kingdoms in the Frankish realm. Time and again, the Empire was simply handed down to the most important Frankish kings: for example, Lothair, followed by Charles the Bald, then Charles the Fat, and later Odo. When the Capetians came to the throne, in their opinion as successors to the Carolingians, they did not hesitate to establish their claim to the imperial title as well: had not God left the charge of *renovatio imperii*—the restoration of the Roman Empire of the West—to the Franks in general, which is to say neither specifically to the eastern nor the western Franks? Thus, until the end of the eleventh century, meetings between the king of France and the emperor occurred on the basis of strict equality.

Everything changed after the Hohenstaufen dynasty came to power in 1137. The Hohenstaufen had no ties with either the Carolingians or the Capetians. In addition, certain national myths began to be forged separately in the two countries. The unification of France with the German empire became increasingly improbable. But it remained necessary to develop judicial arguments supporting France's independence vis-à-vis the Empire.

It was at this time that the Justinian code, and with it the full panoply of Roman law, became the focus of renewed study. According to this law, the Roman emperor was *dominus mundi*, lord of the world, and nobody contested that the Holy Roman Emperor of German Nations was his legitimate successor. Naturally the first jurists—the *glossators*, interpreters of Roman law in literal terms—supported the claims of the Hohenstaufen to *dominium mundi*.

Thus, Frederick Barbarossa (1122–90; reigned 1152–90) received the ideological backing of the Bolognese doctors at the Diet of Roncaglia (1158). In the following year already, Frederick began to behave like a new Constantine, convening a synod, using the title *Dei gratia imperator*

[21] For this section, see Marguerite Boulet-Dautel, "Le roi et l'empereur" [The king and the emperor], in Rials, *Le miracle capétien;* also J. P. Canning, "Introduction: Politics, Institutions and Ideas," and "Law, Legislative Authority and Theories of Government," in Burns, *Cambridge History*, 341–65, 424–76.

et semper Augustus, and so on. Thereafter, he and his successors saw the kings of Europe as their subordinates; they attempted to obtain the homage of Richard the Lionheart, king of England, and Philip Augustus, king of France.

The position of the House of Capet would have been untenable if the pope, embroiled in conflict with the Empire at the time, had not supported French claims and tolerated their statements "a king is emperor in his kingdom" and "the king of France recognizes no superior in temporal affairs."

The idea that the king was *imperator in regno suo* appeared in canonist writings in the last decade of the twelfth century, and again in a "question" discussed by Azo at the beginning of the thirteenth. The formula was apparently common at the time of Louis IX, king of France (later, Saint Louis). It means that, within the French realm, the king had no superior and held all sovereignty: accordingly, he would be attributed the totality of powers that Roman law attributed to the emperor.

The other formula, "the king of France recognizes no superior in temporal affairs," comes from a decretal by Innocent III, *Per venerabilem* (1202). The pope wrote, probably using the terms of an earlier letter addressed to the king of France, Philip Augustus: "Since the king [of France] himself recognizes no superior in temporal affairs" (*cum rex ipse superiorem in temporalibus minime recognoscit*). Jurists adopted the view that the pope, who only quoted Philip Augustus's words, had in fact adopted them as his own and formally asserted that the king of France had no temporal superior.

This second formula went much further than *rex in regno suo est imperator in regni sui,* which could be construed to mean that the king exercised the powers of a prince in his realm as long as the emperor allowed; in other words, by implicit but revocable delegation. In the end, the two formulas were conflated into one. In addition, in 1219, Philip Augustus obtained a papal ban on the teaching, in Paris, of Roman law, which was considered favorable to the emperor.[22]

The cause, however, was difficult. The French position prevailed only because the unbridled ambition of Frederick II led to the destruction—by the papacy—of his dynasty, his power, and to the elimination of the Empire itself as the dominant political authority in Europe. Thereafter, the Holy Roman Empire of the German Nation never acquired the necessary political authority to recapture its advantage over France or England. Moreover, by making a gift of Frederick's inheritance to the brother of Saint Louis, Charles of Anjou, the pope augmented the power of the House of Capet and exacerbated the need for civilists and canonists to find sound theoretical reasons for kingdoms to remove themselves from the authority of the Empire.

B. The Work of the Neapolitan Jurists

Thus, Neapolitan jurists, in the service of the Angevin kings of Naples, attempted to deny the emperor's universal sovereignty and to prove that there should be a plurality of independent kingdoms. Marinus da Caramanico (d. 1288) wrote: "long before the empire and the Roman race from of old, that is from the *ius gentium* which emerged with the human race itself, kingdoms were recognized and founded." Thus, the Empire, created by the force of arms, was merely a de facto power; neither natural law nor the law of nations made it a necessity.

[22] This law was to be taught in Orleans. The legal luminaries of the School of Orleans included Pierre de Belleperche (Petrus de Bellapertica) and Jacques de Révigny (Jacobus de Ravannis), who remained skeptical at the idea that the king of France was not a mere subject of the emperor: "Some say that France is exempted from the Empire. This is impossible *de jure*. You have it in C.I.27.2.2 [reference to the Justinian code] that France is subject to the empire.... If the king of France does not recognize this I do not care" (Jacques de Révigny, quoted in Canning, "Politics, Institutions and Ideas," 467).

Oldradus da Ponte also denied the emperor's *de jure* claim to be lord of the world (*dominus mundi*). The emperor invoked the *lex regia,* but the Roman people could not transfer more rights than it had, and it did not have the right to legislate for other peoples, which was contrary to the law of nations (*ius gentium*). Therefore, the emperor could not have such rights either. Marinus allowed that imperial Roman law could be applied in Sicily, but added that its application resulted from the Sicilian people's customary acceptance of the constitution given by its monarchs and was not the corollary of Sicily being part of an empire with a universal calling.

Finally, Andreas de Isernia (d. 1316) wrote: "With cause another king will be able to do in his kingdom what the emperor can in the land of the empire, which is small these days. In Italy he possesses only Lombardy, and not all of that, and part of Tuscany; the rest belongs to the church of Rome, like the kingdom of Sicily also. The first lords were kings as Sallust says.... The provinces therefore (which have a king) have returned to the pristine form of having kings, which is easily done. Free kings have as much in their kingdoms as the emperor in the empire."[23]

Little by little the idea of sovereignty gained ground in the fourteenth century. Pope Clement V (the first Avignon pope) confirmed it with his bull *Pastoralis cura* (1313), which sought to protect the king of France and Robert of Naples from the imperial claims of Henry VII. Thus, the bull and the Neapolitan jurists concurred (Oldradus was a legal adviser at the *curia* in Avignon). Now, the Empire was considered to be a territorially defined body; the papacy officially gave up the idea of the Roman Empire's universality (this, no doubt, provided it some consolation for its loss of *plenitudo potestatis* over the Empire). For a long while, the canonists remained divided on this issue. Boniface VIII continued to press for the universality of the Empire.

C. The Sovereignty of the Republics of Northern Italy in Relation to the Empire

In the fourteenth century, the legitimacy of sovereignty in legal theory was defended by the civilists (the so-called Commentators, among them *Bartolus* and *Baldus*), to the benefit, this time, of the Italian city-republics.[24]

In their struggle with the Empire, the city-republics had proclaimed their "liberties," that is, their right to a republican government and to "sovereignty" with respect to all external powers. But what legal argument did they have to back their claim? Bartolus made the principal contribution. First, he innovated methodologically. When the law and the facts were in contradiction, he said, the law must accommodate itself to the facts. In substance, he conceded that the emperor was the *de jure* lord of the world. But, de facto, many people no longer obeyed him. Therefore, Bartolus concluded, "in the case of present-day Italy, and especially those of Tuscany where no superior is recognised, I judge that they [the cities] constitute in themselves a free people, and hence possess *merum Imperium* in themselves, having as much power over their own population as the Emperor possesses generally." And this was true, Bartolus added, whether or not the cities obtained explicit concessions from the emperor.

Bartolus put this in a famous formula. The independent city was *sibi princeps*—its "own prince"—which, in English, became "self-government." This is similar to the notion that the king is "emperor in his kingdom," but Bartolus went one step further, as it was audacious to think that the people, like a corporation, could be everything that a *princeps* was (the transposition from emperor to king was, after all, more natural).

[23] Texts cited in Canning, "Politics, Institutions and Ideas," 465–66.

[24] This section is drawn from Quentin Skinner, *The Foundations of Modern Political Thought,* vol. 1, *The Renaissance* (Cambridge: Cambridge University Press, 1978), chap. 1.

His argument begins with customary law. Jurists shared the view that custom was lawful because it was the expression of tacit popular consent, which did not require the authorization of a superior. But laws were equal, not superior, to custom. Therefore, they did not require the authorization of a superior either.[25]

Bartolus also provided a legal basis for the *republican* idea in a commentary on a passage in the *Digest* on the right of appeal. In the feudal hierarchy, appeals were referred to the emperor. But in a republic, who will judge appeals? Bartolus replied unflinchingly, "in such a case the people themselves must act as judge of appeals, or else a specific class of citizens appointed by their government." The reason was that "the people themselves constitute the only superior to be found, and so constitute *sibi princeps*, an emperor unto themselves." Thus, not only was the state sovereign, but also the true sovereign entity within the state was the people.

Baldus (ca. 1327–1400) applied the same arguments to monarchies that Bartolus applied to the sovereignty of independent republics. By virtue of custom, certain kings were no longer the emperor's subjects, although the emperor remained their *de jure* sovereign. Accordingly, there was a hierarchy of sovereignties—a contradiction in terms—which corresponded to the situation in northern Italy where everyone accepted the titular sovereignty of the emperor, and no one recognized his authority in reality. Baldus went so far as to allow, in the name of *ius gentium*, that free peoples could elect their kings.

The intellectual efforts of the civilists were wide-ranging and influential. Ever since the ruin of Greek cities at the end of the fourth century BC, and under the successive influence of Stoicism and Christianity, the idea predominated that the civilized world—the Hellenistic *cosmopolis*, the Roman Empire, Christendom—should be united in a single political body. Of course, feudal fragmentation blatantly opposed this ideal, but it was not supposed to weaken Christian unity. Moreover, the period in which the Empire and secular kingdoms collapsed into countless principalities and chatellanies was the same in which the papacy succeeded in creating unprecedented cultural unity. With the advent of peace, prosperity, and the development of trade and cities, the need for renewed political unity was felt again; but since the Hohenstaufen squandered the opportunity to recreate a universal Empire, another more realistic solution rose on the horizon, that of the nation-state.

IV. The Nation-State

Throughout the feudal age, new political entities arose through the fortunes of marriage, inheritance, or the sudden extinction of a dynastic line; to a large extent, the feudal map of Europe was a kaleidoscope of unstable and artificial entities.[26]

With his marriage to the daughter of Louis de Male in 1369, Philip the Bold was able to add Flanders to his own Duchy of Burgundy. Thus began an adventure the first phase of which ended in 1477 with the death of Charles the Bold. Another phase began in 1469, when Maximilian I of Habsburg married Mary of Burgundy: this marriage gave the contours to the extraordinary future empire of Charles V. It was because Louis the Great, king of Hungary, inherited the kingdom of Poland from his uncle, Casimir III the Great, that a personal union between the two countries was achieved; before long, the Duchy of Lithuania was added to his realm for similar reasons. Examples abound.

[25] See Canning, "Politics, Institutions and Ideas," 470.

[26] This section is drawn from Guenée, *L'Occident*, 113 and following.

Yet, at the beginning of the fourteenth century, exceptions to this rule existed, which in modern times would become the norm. In 1328, Edward III of England could not succeed Charles IV, king of France, although his titles and claims—important in the feudal logic of the devolution of estates—were far better than those of the Valois. The single very powerful reason that stopped him from mounting the French throne was that the local population could see him only as a *foreigner*. Such national sentiment continued to deepen, becoming more commanding, until it finally triumphed in the events surrounding Joan of Arc.

For an understanding of why national sentiment emerged, we need to go far back in time. The phenomenon was particularly strong in England and France, but it applied throughout Europe.

A. The Building Blocks of a Nation

1. *Race*

Cicero gave a definition of the "nation" adopted by Isidore of Seville: a nation, as its etymology suggests (*nascor, natus*), is a body of people born of the same stock; it is, therefore, first and foremost a question of blood or race. This is why the people of the Middles Ages took it to a much lower level than the French and German "nations" and spoke of the "nation of Paris" and the "nation of London" in reference to the natives of these cities and others.

As for the overlap of these groups of men and women, related by blood, with political organizations, that happens when they begin to reach across territories. Augustinian theologians held that no relation existed, in principle, between *natio,* a racial community, and *populus,* a political community. But their view met with resistance in the thirteenth and fourteenth centuries with the spread of Aristotelianism, which held that, since a city was a natural community, it must have a certain homogeneity, regardless of the criteria retained.

2. *Natural Territory*

The Aristotelian idea of "natural community" implies the notion of *autarkeia,* self-sufficiency: a healthy, enduring "political body" is a community able to live independently on a sufficiently large territory and to ensure its own self-defense. Giles of Rome wrote in his treatise *De regimine principum* that the kingdom constitutes the true state and the best political body because it is better able to defend itself than a simple town. In contrast to Dante, who believed—anachronistically—that the whole of Christendom should be organized in a universal empire, thinkers such as John of Paris,[27] opposed to the subordination of France to the Empire, and later Nicholas Oresme,[28] eager to establish France's independence vis-à-vis the Empire and England, argued that (1) the kingdom offered the most effective coercive jurisdiction, and (2) that differences in climate, geography, race, and national temperament justified separate political organizations in different countries.

3. *Name*

The identity of a human group also depends on a *name*. In this respect, the situation in medieval Europe was very shaky.

The Romans called the region to the west of the Rhine *Gallia* and to the east *Germania,* though these names were quickly forgotten and familiar only to the learned. It took the Germans centuries to forge an identity under a single name. They saw themselves first as "teutonic" and

---

[27] On John of Paris, see above, p. 539.

[28] On Nicole (or Nicholas) Oresme, see below, pp. 604–05.

"teutons"; the terms referred first to the language, then to the people who spoke it, and only lastly to the country where the people lived, *Teutonia*. Then, during the Renaissance, the old term *Germania* reappeared, accompanied by a new name, *Alemania*. But the absence of political unity prevented the one or the other from being adopted. The cases of *Polonia* and *Catalonia* are clearer because they appeared after the founding of their respective kingdoms. We can also cite Guenée's particularly eloquent counterexample, the case of Burgundy: "the fact that neither the states nor the subjects of the Duke of Burgundy had a common name was more threatening for Charles the Bold than the policy of Louis XI."[29]

4. *Language*

A common language is another essential parameter. Latin, of course, was shared throughout Europe, but it was the language of a small group of clerics. The masses spoke many different languages, belonging to one of three large linguistic families—Germanic, Romance, and Slavic. From the earliest times, the speakers of these languages distrusted and despised one another, which led to their respective communities being regrouped politically.

The separation of the German nation and the French nation was due in large part to the radical difference of their languages. An *a contrario* confirmation of this can be seen in the chronic instability of the borders of plurilingual Lotharingia, which was never able to form a nation.

Toward the end of the thirteenth century, rulers began to build on the nation as a linguistic community: the celebrated *Grand Chronicles of France* (see below) were translated from Latin into French. Not long after, the king of Portugal made Portuguese the official language of his kingdom. France is exemplary in that, fairly early on, a state and a language coincided with a territory (admittedly, real linguistic unity did not exist throughout the population until modern times, but there was unity among the cultural and administrative elite, and the unity of language was, for all, an early ideal).

5. *National Saints*

National unity is also *religious*. There is a paradox here that it is important to clarify. By all expectations, Christianity should work against the splintering of territories into nation-states; moreover, the papacy struggled hard to avoid such territorial breakup that only the Great Schism—and even more the Reformation—made inevitable. But religion can be understood at different levels, and although the nations of Europe professed the same Christian faith, they each had their own *national saints* as embodiments of unity.

For France there was Saint Martin, Saint Remy, and Saint Denis. The last named, the evangelist of Paris, capital of the Capetians, became the most important saint after the Capetian dynasty triumphed. The banner carried into battle by the king of France was that of Saint Denis (see above, p. 509). And Louis VI recognized Saint Denis as the official protector of the realm.

Other saints, associated by the faithful with a particular nation, include the patron saints Ambrose (Milan), Mark (Venice), Stephen (king of Hungary), Olaf (king of Norway), and the saint, martyr, and duke of Bohemia, Wenceslas. In Poland, after Saint Wojciech, the bishop of Cracow, Stanislaus, canonized in 1253, became the official patron of the nation.

On this point, England diverges somewhat from the rest of Europe: it was only much later (under the reign of Edward III, 1327–77) that Saint George, not a hero of national history but a legendary figure of the early church, became the patron saint of England.[30]

---

[29] We will discuss the case of France and the origin of its name below.

[30] The concurrence of the religious community and the political community presented the Jews with a dilemma: because they could not belong to the former, they had difficulty joining the latter.

6. *Myth of Origin and National History*

European nations formed around their respective *origin myths* and *national histories*. An extraordinary rumor of unknown source surfaced in the seventh century with the Chronicle of Fredegar: it claimed that the German, French, and English nations descended from the Trojans, making them cousins to Rome (Virgil, in his *Aeneid*, narrates Trojan lineage through Aeneas). Fanciful etymologies supported the myth. Thus, the Trojan Brutus was said to be the ancestor of the Britons, another Trojan, Francion, the father of the Franks, while Paris, Helen's lover, gave his name allegedly to the capital of Gaul; and the Germans received their name from their Roman relatives who called them "brothers," and so on.

The rumor intensified as the Middle Ages progressed (see the twelfth century *Historia regum Britanniæ* by Geoffrey of Monmouth, and the *Grand Chronicle of the Kings of France*). Only the revival of classical knowledge from antiquity in the Renaissance was able to quell the rumor, much to the chagrin of the populations concerned (it took time for them to accept the naked truth; meanwhile they shifted the focus to other narratives to boost their national sentiments, for example, Tacitus's *Germania* for the Germans, Caesar's *Gallic Wars* for the French).

These origin myths, based on pure invention, must be distinguished from national history which, even when distorted or embellished, has its roots in objective fact.

Medieval Romans proudly believed that they were the direct successors of ancient Rome. Florence and the Florentines made similar claims, but took care to emphasize the Roman Republic and its virtues as the model for their republic, not the Rome of kings and emperors, the countermodel followed only by the tyrants of Milan (see below, section VI). Switzerland reveled in the story of William Tell, who terrorized the tyrannical reeve of the Habsburgs. The Welsh established their national narrative on the Celtic King Arthur. And the French and Germans both staked claim to the emperor Charlemagne, whom Frederick Barbarossa had canonized.

We will focus on the case of France at some length, because it clearly illustrates the role of another important element, *political will*, in this case the patient, stubborn, political will of the Capetian dynasty.

B. The French National Epic

As we saw, the House of Capet was fortunate to enjoy exceptional longevity and unbroken continuity, as measured by the usual standards of the feudal age: 14 direct male heirs from Hugh Capet to Charles IV, followed by an equally robust lineage of the Valois, the cadet branch of the Capetian dynasty, which succeeded the Capetians (however, during the Hundred Years' War, the French monarchy encountered grave threats, which it outlasted, emerging strengthened in the end).[31] Such longevity enabled the French kings to pursue coherent policies: domestically, they strengthened centralization, established the most impressive state apparatus anywhere in Europe at the time, and developed a certain linguistic unity; geopolitically, in a manner of speaking, they expanded their national territory to its "natural" borders. In addition, the unbroken continuity of the dynasty enabled the Capetians to add to their territorial expansion an ideological contribution.

When the Capetians ascended the throne, they began work on a national "epic,"[32] in which the Holy Ampulla (the glass vial of anointing oil) and the deliberate intervention of God at Reims

[31] This section is drawn from Colette Beaune, "Les Capétiens et la naissance d'une histoire nationale" [The Capets and the birth of a national history], in Rials, *Le miracle capétien*.

[32] Or a "myth." But this word is best reserved for the foundation stories of ancient societies for which there is no identifiable author or person who created it. We will see that the French national epic emerged from a simultaneous process of deliberate political will and spontaneous tradition; the two factors reinforced each other in a sort of "circular causality." Thus, the appropriate word is "epic," such as the epics composed by Virgil and Livy at the behest of Augustus (or the

in support of the Franks occupied the leading place. The anointing of the king, as far as the church was concerned, was intended to prove the biblical subordination of temporal power to spiritual power, as well as the quasi-messianic calling of the king and, indirectly, of the kingdom and people under his charge. In the Bible, however, there is only one chosen people, the people of Israel. As soon as several kings from several nations are anointed, and there is no emperor over the whole of Christendom, there are, in fact, multiple messiahs and shepherds of "chosen peoples." This led to a competition among European nations to become the true "new Israel" chosen by God to lead Christianity. The popes declared (more in the spirit of accommodating the universality of Christianity and flattering the naïve arrogance of the Frankish barbarians) that France was the new Israel's "tribe of Judah," now representing Christianity.[33] Carolingian and Capetian kings were particularly adept at fostering national pride and galvanizing their troops in battle, and they were able to rally the servants of the king to a feudal society under threat from countless centrifugal forces.

The earliest written "French" history, *Historia Francorum,* the work of Gregory of Tours, dates from the end of the sixth century.[34] At the time of the Merovingians, there was also the Chronicle of Fredegar and the *Liber Historiæ Francorum,* which suggested a Trojan origin for the Frankish people in order to put the Franks on a par with the Romans. The Carolingians did not commission a "national" history of western Francia, perhaps because the universal Roman Empire was said to live on in their lineage. Only with the Capetian dynasty did the "national" concern finally crystallize on western Francia in dialectical opposition to the Germanic world.

When the Capetians ascended to the throne, the cultural centers that could have produced a "national" history—Reims, Sens, Laon—actually defended the deposed royal lineage; consequently, they were not particularly disposed to glorify the usurpers or offer proofs of their legitimacy as successors to the Frankish kings.

1. *Fleury*

Therefore, it cannot be a coincidence that the first efforts to write a *national* history took place in an abbey, which had figured among the possessions of the Capetian family for generations. The Abbey of Fleury,[35] as it was known, possessed Saint Benedict's relics and was an important

biblical narratives about the patriarchs written at the request of a priesthood anxious to emphasize national continuity; in this sense, the sacred history of the Hebrew people is also a national epic).

33 See Pinoteau, "Armes de France," 319. Pepin the Short's new promulgation of the *lex Salica* included a proclamation that the Franks were the beloved people of God. Charlemagne's victories were presented in the *Royal Frankish Annals* as victories of "the Franks with the help of God." The reason for the "election" of the Frankish people was so that it could protect Peter's church under threat from the Lombards. The church in Rome appealed to the Frankish aristocracy (and not just the Pepinid family) as "its adopted sons." / Pope Paul I—the successor of Popes Zachary and Stephen, who anointed Pepin and his sons—said that the Franks are "Peter's chosen people," just as the Israelites are Yahweh's chosen people. The pope called them "a holy people, a royal priesthood." From on high, God and Peter (the pope imagined himself to be their spokesperson on earth) recognized the physical strength of the Franks and the "energy" of the Pepinids, in contrast with the slackness of the last Merovingians. Thus, the new power was apt to provide for the defense of the church (see Janet Nelson, "Kingship and Empire," in Burns, *Cambridge History,* 211 and following).

34 Although the name "France" is older than the names of other European countries, it is less old than one might think. The name "Frank," *Francus,* appeared as early as the fourth century, and *Francia* soon after. But, at the time, it designated neither a kingdom nor the country of France (for a long time both were called *Regnum Francorum,* referring to eastern regions of the Merovingian and Carolingian territories, as well as to the regions comprising present-day France). Until the twelfth century, only scholars used the term "Francia" to designate the kingdom of Charlemagne and Charles the Bald. For the population at large this term represented an ill-defined region in the north corresponding more or less to what, today, is called the Ile de France. When the reference is to the whole kingdom, the expression used is *tota Francia* or *regnum.* "Francia" only began to designate the whole kingdom at the end of the twelfth century. In June 1204, King Philip Augustus officially called himself *Franciæ rex,* "king of France." There are written documents from the following year that use the expression *Regnum Franciæ.*

35 Located about 30 kilometers from Orleans. The Robertians were the counts of Fleury.

pilgrimage center. It had developed a large library and become a respected intellectual center, one of the seats of the Cluniac reform. In about the year 1000, the abbot of Fleury was the half brother of the second Capetian king, Robert the Pious. It was at this time that the *Gesta Francorum,* a history of the Franks up to Pepin and Charlemagne, was compiled and written by a team of monks under the direction of Aimon.

The monks of Fleury borrowed from Hincmar the legend of the Holy Ampulla, which became the official narrative. The story of the vase of Soissons, told by Gregory of Tours as an example of Frankish indiscipline, was invoked this time as evidence that Clovis was recognized as the rightful authority throughout the nation.

Another monk from Fleury, by the name of Helgaud, wrote the first French royal biography. His *Life of Robert the Pious* dates from ca. 1033, two years after the king's death. In it Robert is portrayed as a holy man. Not a word is said about the change of dynasty: Robert is said to be of royal lineage[36] and high birth, without further detail.

At the beginning of the twelfth century, Hugh of Fleury wrote a *Universal History* in six books, which covered the period from Genesis until the end of the reign of Louis the Pious in 840. Writing between 1110 and 1114, Hugh brought the narrative forward from 840 to 1108 in his *Book containing the acts of the modern kings of France.* He developed a positive theory for the succession of the three dynasties; all changes were brought about by God who "elevates and humbles whomever he will" and does so wisely: the last Merovingian king, Childeric, was incompetent and a consensus emerged between Pope Zachary and the greats of the realm to replace him with the dynasty of the Pepinids.

Over the years, these different texts were copied and augmented at the Abbey of Fleury. The overall picture is one of a remarkable nation, the Franks, who enjoyed God's favor, whose kings were anointed ones and true saints. The divine origin of anointing kings was evidenced by the miracle of the Holy Ampulla and by the thaumaturgical powers of anointed kings. Conversely, dynastic justification was weak: God put the Capetians on the throne, but why would God not remove them with equal suddenness? The center of learning at Fleury, influenced by political Augustinism, believed that God alone, not heredity, made kings; it was for this reason that no attempt was made to show a continuity of lineage between the three Frankish dynasties. This task fell to later royal chroniclers.

2. *Saint Denis*

In time the Abbey of Saint Denis, north of Paris, replaced Fleury as the dynastic church. Clearly, the Capetians felt sufficiently well established in their royal office that they could abandon their former fief in Orleans.

Pepin the Short was raised and educated at the Abbey of Saint Denis. Charles Martel, Pepin, and Charles the Bald are interred there; after Louis VI, Saint Denis became the royal tomb of all Capetians. In 1127 the great Abbot Suger introduced a reform of the abbey, after which it replaced Fleury. The king, Louis VI, carried into battle the abbey's banner, said to be Charlemagne's oriflamme. The abbey became the guardian of the French crown and its royal insignia.

Suger wrote a *Life of Louis VI,* an unfinished *Life of Louis VII,* and a *Historia Francorum* (now lost). He also oversaw the compilation of earlier histories, in particular the histories produced by Fleury. Thus, an authentic tradition of national history and epic was inaugurated at the Abbey of Saint Denis. It soon received official backing: Philip Augustus appointed a monk from Saint

[36] This is a fact: two members of the Robertian family before Hugh Capet, Eudes and Robert I, had been elected kings of France.

Denis, Rigord, to be the king's chronographer (he wrote a history of his royal patron's reign); thereafter, every king had his official chronicler.

The clerics were now able to tackle the formidable challenge of dynastic discontinuity, left only partially resolved at Fleury. They recalled the prophecy of the two saints—Saint Valéry and Saint Riquier—who allegedly promised Hugh Capet the throne for seven generations in reward for his piety. This meant that God had explicitly forsaken the Carolingian dynasty in favor of the Capetians. But then, the seventh Capetian, Philip Augustus, married Princess Elisabeth of Hainaut, said to be a descendant of the last Carolingian pretender, Charles of Lorrain. Thus, their son, Louis VIII, and his descendants, became the direct heirs of all three dynasties combined;[37] this was, at any rate, the official written version throughout the thirteenth century. The royal tombs in the Abbey of Saint Denis were rearranged in accordance with this version: left and right, the Merovingian and Carolingian tombs, respectively, and in the middle the tombs of their common successors, the Capetians.

The chronicles were also rewritten. Sometime around 1250, one manuscript combined all earlier texts, chronologically ordered, in a single compilation, which in 1274 was translated into French and dedicated to King Philip III by the monk Primat. This *Roman des rois,* a vernacular history of the kings of France, embraced all of the wonders associated with the royal dynasties of France: the Holy Ampulla, the fleur-de-lis,[38] the unbroken line of kings from Meroveus, the grandfather of Clovis, until Philip III, the minor adjustments to the dynasty willed by God. All of this combined to paint a picture of the providential triumph of a very Christian race of kings.

Chronicles continued to be written about the reigns of French kings until the end of the Middle Ages. Every king had his biographer at the Abbey of Saint Denis; his task was to narrate the sovereign's every word and deed. The condensed versions of these narratives constitute the *Grand Chronicles of France.* It was copied repeatedly, frequently embellished with rich illuminations, and widely distributed. With the invention of the printing press, the work became even more widespread.

Thus, this national narrative, "thought of as the Bible of that other sacred history which was the history of France" (Colette Beaune), resulted from a process lasting some five centuries. In retrospect it was riddled with distortions, omissions, and outright lies, yet it inspired a heartfelt consensus among the population at large, as well as among the learned elite. The history of France forged a strong identity, bravely expressed at the battle of Bouvines[39] and again in efforts to pit the papacy and the empire against each other. It crystallized during the Hundred Years' War, when Joan of Arc became its first martyr.

The new nation-states had to be ruled, but this was not possible with the means inherited from the feudal age. It became necessary to invent a new apparatus of state, different from anything ever seen: a paid army, central and local administrative structures, a tax system, a national currency, a customs system, and so on. This state apparatus posed a threat to many interests, since it depended on a state with exorbitant powers; no king had held so much power since the end of antiquity.

For this reason, the state—and its theoreticians—hesitated between two solutions: either magnify the king's person to the point of justifying his "absolute" power over his subjects; or present state power as more or less an emanation of the collective will, of which the king was just a component.

[37] The Carolingians laid claim to descent from the Merovingians through Princess Biltilde, although she probably never existed.

[38] According to legend the fleur-de-lis was a miraculous, God-given gift to France; perhaps a deformation of an ancient pagan sun symbol, it appeared under the abbotship of Suger and, thereafter, spread rapidly. See above, p. 509.

[39] *Translator's note:* The Battle of Bouvines between the king of France, Philip Augustus, and a German, Flemish, and English coalition led by Emperor Otto IV, confirmed the French crown's sovereignty over the regions of Brittany and Normandy, and was, therefore, important to the early development of the French state.

V. Absolutism

A. The Radicalization of Absolutism by the Jurists

In the fourteenth and fifteenth centuries, political theoreticians held back nothing to free the princes of the new, national, independent, and sovereign states from the constraints of "fundamental norms" which, in earlier periods it was agreed, should place limits on the powers of rulers: customs, natural law, church-formulated divine law.[40]

To understand the motivation of these theoreticians, we must remember that at this particular juncture in history, monarchy as a power was still weak. Consequently, very few authors thought in terms of imposing doctrinal restrictions. On the contrary, they were keen to justify the monarchy's acquisition of new powers, convinced that only a strong royal power could protect the vulnerable, ensure peace, legislate for the good, and put an end to "bad" feudal customs.

For Baldus, the power of the king was decidedly unbound from positive law; it obeyed reason alone. He transferred *potestas absoluta* to secular rulers, which had been, until then, the sole privilege of the pope. He adopted Hostiensis's distinction between "ordinary" and "absolute" power (see above, p. 541). In ordinary cases, the king obeyed the law (according to the maxim *Digna vox*); in extraordinary cases, he could unmake it.

Can the ruler derogate from fundamental norms? This depends on a distinction between the particular and the general case. The prince can derogate from natural law or customary law *ex causa,* that is, in a particular case. However, he will not be thought of as freed from it in all other cases (this was clearly stated as an imitation of papal absolutism). In any case, the ruler is the sole judge of the validity of the *causa.*

Jurists focused their attention on *the role of will* in the creation of positive law. Many of their texts emphasized the sovereignty of the ruler's *voluntas.* The bridge between the law that is good, if and only if it is rational, and the law that is valid, if and only if it comes from the prince, was established by Juvenal's well-known formula, *pro ratione volutes,* "let my will replace reasoned judgment" (Accursius glossed this statement as follows: *magna et justa causa est ejus voluntas,* "his own will is accounted a great and just cause").

Baldus: "Plenitude of power is a plenitude of will (*arbitrii plenitudo*) subject to no necessity and limited by no rules of public law"; "Nothing can resist the ruler's plenitude of power, for it is superior to positive [human] law, and the ruler's will is sufficient to replace reason."[41]

Baldus and Jacobus Butrigarius (ca. 1274–1348, a teacher of Barolus) further strengthened absolutism by weakening *property rights.* Such rights, Jacobus argued, do not fall within the *ius gentium.* Therefore, the prince can remove his subject's property rights *sine causa.* Baldus agrees: to deprive a subject of his private property "any reason which so moves the emperor is cause enough." Guillaume de Plaisians (d. 1313, advisor to Philip the Fair) says that the king owns the whole kingdom as a public good or for its defense.

The absolutist trend is particularly well illustrated in the case of France. It was there that the very "uncatholic" idea of divine right of kings flourished particularly vigorously. According to this theory, (1) kings received their crown directly from God, not from the church; (2) the power of kings could not be limited either by the moral authority of the church or by any social contract with the people.

Theories of absolute monarchy were formulated at times of great distress in the French realm: after Poitiers (1352) and at the time of the partition with Burgundy. Moreover, the theoreticians succeeded in persuading public opinion of its necessity. And when the monarchy in France

[40] This section is drawn from Canning, "Law, Sovereignty," 454–76.

[41] Ibid., 457.

emerged from the dangers of the Hundred Years' War under Charles VII, it became quasi-absolute without any transition.

Under the reign of Charles VII the king was genuinely *resacralized* and put on a pedestal as a reincarnation of the *divine* Roman emperor. This implied the near total submission of his subjects. The leading French intellectuals of the age—Buridan (ca. 1295–d. after 1348), Gerson, Christine de Pisan, Jean de Terre Rouge, Jean Juvénal des Ursins (1388–1473)—accepted this outcome. Disobedience to the king would be a crime of *lèse majesté.*

B. "The Mirror for Princes"

In truth, if a monarch must be absolute, the only guarantee his subjects have is in his wisdom.[42] Understandably, theoreticians—keen to free the royal monarch from restrictions placed upon him by feudal custom and excessive respect for "fundamental norms"—insisted on the need for the ruler to be "wise." It is of the utmost importance to properly educate the future monarch in his youth and to advise him well in his exercise of power. This explains the development of a new kind of political writing that emphasizes the rules of proper personal conduct of a good king: the so-called "Mirror for princes."

Works of this kind multiplied dramatically at the end of the Middles Ages and throughout the sixteenth century. Quoting from a list by Jean Barbey, the following are representative of the age: Hugh of Fleury, *De regia potestate;* Honorius of Autun, *Summa gloria;* John of Salisbury, *Policraticus* (1159); Helinand of Froidmont, *De regimine principum* (On the governance of princes, 1200, dedicated to Philip Augustus); Guibert of Tournai, *Eruditio regum et principum;* Vincent of Beauvais, *De eruditione filiorum regalium* (On the education of princes, thirteenth century); Giles of Rome, *De regimine principum* (written for Philip the Fair); Jean Gerson, *Vivat rex;* Christine de Pisan, *Livre de paix* (Book of peace); J. Legrand, *Livre des bonnes mœurs* (Book of good manners).

In addition to these works, there were the thoughts of the royal biographers such as Suger (Louis VI and Louis VII),[43] Joinville (Saint Louis), Christine de Pisan (Charles V),[44] Commynes (Louis XI),[45] and Philippe de Mézières's work, *The Dream of the Old Pilgrim.*[46]

This literature reflects the ideas of the time for a good king and good government. One observes a certain evolution between the thirteenth and sixteenth centuries. At the time of Saint Louis, the Christian virtues of the prince were extolled; they were markedly different from the virtues of the ancient kings lauded by Dio Chrysostom, Virgil, and Tacitus; to prudence (wisdom), temperance, and courage were added, in the Christian prince, humility, "justice" (i.e., fairness and mercy), and the pursuit of peace. But as natural philosophy was restored and grew in strength to the detriment of biblical revelation; as Aristotle, Roman law, and Latin authors were studied again, the ideal of the king became "renaturalized" as well. Gradually, these ideas moved in the direction of the humanist ideal, burnished in the sixteenth century by thinkers such as Rabelais, Guillaumé Budé, and Morisot. The king is expected to practice asceticism, not to mortify himself but so as to

---

[42] This section is drawn from Jean Barbey, "Le modèle du roi" [The example of the king], in Rials, *Le miracle capétien.*

[43] Suger, Abbot of Saint Denis, *Life of King Louis VI the Fat,* trans. Jean Dunbabin; available at www.fordham.edu/halsall/basis/suger-louisthefat.html; *The Deeds of Louis the Fat,* trans. with introduction and notes by Richard Cusimano and John Moorhead (Washington, DC: Catholic University of America Press, 1992); and a history of Louis VII (*Historia gloriosi regis Ludovici*).

[44] Christine de Pizan, *Le livre des faits et bonnes mœurs du roi Charles V* [The book of the deeds and good manners of the wise King Charles V], trans. and presented from Latin by Eric Hicks and Therese Moreau (Paris: Stock, 1997).

[45] Philippe de Commynes, *The Reign of Louis XI,* trans. with an introduction by Michael Jones (New York: Penguin, 1972).

[46] Philippe de Mézières belonged to the inner circle of Charles VI and was the tutor to the future Charles VI.

dominate his passions. The wisdom he is meant to possess becomes "science." A king should study works of political and economic science; he cannot be content with being an uneducated soldier.

The authors of the "Mirrors for Princes" revived the ancient virtue of *prudence:* the prince must use his knowledge and reason with discernment and moderation; he must look for inspiration in the experiences of the past and be surrounded by advisors. The king becomes a specialist in "the art of politics," which wins its autonomy from theology and morality, which also means that advisors begin to accept more or less immoral conduct in the king—lies, dissimulation, cunning, as well as realism, pragmatism, and the art of exploiting circumstances with little or no scruple—provided they are for the good of the state.

Just as the king increasingly becomes a dual person, as we saw earlier in our discussion of inheritance laws, with a private and public person (the latter associated with the abstraction of the state), similarly the head of state has two models of conduct: one a Christian or traditional humanist morality for his private person, and the other called "reason of state" (the term is from Guichardini, a student of Machiavelli) for his public person. Of course, the king-person cannot uncouple the good from the moral; but the king–head of state can and must resort to immoral means. He is licensed to practice individual evil in order to defend the common good.[47]

What is true for the kings is even more so for his advisors; if they have virtues, all is well and good; but it is more important that they also have competence. Before very long, the king's advisors were being recruited from outside the narrow circle of the clergy. The "legists" in the service of Philip the Fair were university professors trained in Roman law. Beginning in the thirteenth century, throughout Europe, as a rule the servants of the state began to be recruited from universities where they were expected to acquire knowledge and develop skills of an increasingly secular nature. With the birth of humanism, an additional need for eloquence developed.

VI. Representative Institutions

If, as we just saw, absolutist tendencies were strong among many thinkers of the fourteenth and fifteenth centuries, such tendencies were by no means dominant.[48] Other theoreticians opposed the idea of "community" to the idea of absolutism. Somehow or other, government must be shared.

What form would the sharing of government responsibility take? Feudalism had already initiated a dialogue of sorts between the king, his vassals, and the people; this was manifest in the

[47] This principle is the essence of absolutist thinking. The idea that an independent state unsubordinated to moral principles should exist over the heads of every individual in society—an idea later formulated theoretically by the likes of Machiavelli, Thomas Hobbes, and G. W. F. Hegel, and that Friedrich Nietzsche summarized as "the coldest of all cold monsters"—is thoroughly new. It is found nowhere in antiquity. Conversely, in Antiquity there were sacred powers, which also transcended humankind by their force and were, morally speaking, fundamentally ambivalent; such sacred powers were held responsible for the residual evil in society. But what happens here, at the turning point between the Middle Ages and modern times, is a sort of *transfer of this amoral character of archaic sacred powers to the abstract notion of the state,* call it a *divinization* or, more exactly, a *sacralization of the state;* it grew in strength as society was declericalized. This sacralization of the state appears later in the contemporary political theories of the most secularized states, for example, the French republic, as well as twentieth century Nazism and communist totalitarianism. The new God that the state becomes is an archaic, nonbiblical God: one who loves good and evil alike; the state incarnates a transcendent destiny, indifferent to individuals. However, this sacralization of the state does not exist in countries where modernization was inspired by religious motives, for example, the Calvinist states of northern Europe and America: the Netherlands, England, and the United States. As we saw, the Bible, far from deifying kings and temporal power, has nothing but suspicion for them.

[48] This section is drawn from Dunbabin, "Government," and Guenée, *L'Occident.*

coronation oath and the vassal contract. Subsequently, in some countries at least, the sovereign was obliged to swear increasingly demanding, increasingly solemn oaths; some of these prefigured treaties that come close to modern "constitutions."

In 1283, under threat of deposition, the king of Aragon swore an oath to uphold the *privilegio general,* a body of rules establishing the relationship between the king and his vassals, the cities and his people. Likewise, in 1308, the king of England, Edward II, swore to uphold the laws and customs that the "community of the realm" might establish; but because he did not do so, he was unseated in 1327. This resulted in a number of exceedingly long texts and oaths, solemnly enacted by the sovereign at the beginning of his reign (e.g., the "Joyous Entry" in the duchy of Brabant in 1356 and the Treaty of Tübingen in the duchy of Württemberg, to name only two).

The people's participation in government primarily took the form of *representative assemblies,* which grew out of feudal "advisory councils" and were influenced by the model of ecclesiastical assemblies (chapters of convents and dioceses, synods, general chapters of monastic orders, etc.); they developed as early as the twelfth and thirteenth centuries, moving in new directions in the fourteenth and fifteenth centuries. In many respects they prefigured our modern governments and parliaments.

A. Councils, Parliaments, States

1. *The Notions of Council, Parliament, and State*

Monastic origins can be found for the idea of the "council": Saint Benedict's Rule requires the superior to have a small group of advisors. But the royal council is primarily feudal in origin. Very early, in England and in France, the king was surrounded by a "court" (*curia regis*), a high court of justice, and a political advisory council. The monarch selected his advisors himself. Then, when the functions of the state became more complex, the council was divided into various committees with specialized functions, for example, finance, justice, and policy.

The word "parliament" initially comes from the old French word "parlement," a translation of the Latin *colloquium,* meaning "speaking," "conversation," "conference." Curiously, the French word gave rise to a Latin word *parlamentum* or *parliamentum,* which spread throughout Europe. Initially, it referred to a session of the court (a "conference"), then came to refer to the deliberating institution itself. But its meaning was different from country to country. In France, the custom was to speak of "parlement" in reference to that part of the court which assembled as a court of justice, that is, the royal tribunal (later extended to the provinces). Conversely, in England, "Parlamentum" referred to the entire court, extended to the delegates of counties as well. The reason for this was that the membership of the *curia regis* had changed. In feudal councils, the only participants were vassals and clerics, each representing his own personal interests. But the prince soon brought the people in urban areas into his *curia.*

Initially, council members were appointed at the discretion of the prince, who sought wise council; these members had a consultative voice only. Then, around the end of the twelfth century, in the south of France, a significant change occurred; the appearance of the "proxy" enabled members of the bourgeois class to be chosen by their peers to advise the king; this was soon followed by elected representatives of the clergy, who sat with the prelates.

In 1189, an assembly with elected bourgeois from each town met for the first time in the kingdom of Leon: soon after, the same occurred in the pontifical states, in Castille, and again in England, when the *knights of the shire* were summoned to the king's council for the first time in 1213; bourgeois representatives were added in 1265 and representatives of the clergy in 1297. The phenomenon spread to France and several other states of the Empire in the fourteenth and fifteenth centuries.

In all of these cases, assemblies continued to exist with unelected members, barons, and prelates; each continued to speak in his own name and for himself. Gradually, and without fanfare, elected representatives took their seats alongside these unelected individuals; their numbers slowly grew, and the presence of all social orders became the rule. When the French assembly met in 1484, it was truly a "national" assembly.

Another development: at the outset, the members of all social orders sat and deliberated together; then, in some countries, the members of a given order or "estate"—nobility, clergy, bourgeois—began to want to deliberate separately, without the others. This led to the expression, assemblies of the "three estates" or simply "estates," divided into general and provincial estates (these French expressions soon spread throughout Europe). In Germany, there was a "Diet" (local or imperial). Gradually, it became the habit to vote by social order rather than by individual voice.

In England, owing perhaps to the weakening of the monarchy under the reigns of Richard the Lionheart and King John, the sequence of events accelerated and went farther. A provision of the Magna Carta (1215) stipulated (article 14) that certain taxes could not be levied without the consent of a council comprised of archbishops, bishops, abbots, dukes, and the principal barons of the realm. The king's direct vassals were to be convened by name 40 days in advance by the sheriff. Conversely, unlike the king of France, the king of England did not have a local public service appointed and paid for by the royal monarch (e.g., bailiffs, seneschals, etc.). Power was exercised locally by the *gentry,* the so-called *knights of the shire.* Without their cooperation the king had no local authority; consequently, he was forced to accept their delegates in his Parliament, which is why, very early on and perhaps from the outset, the English Parliament—as the recipient of petitions from small towns and villages—had a political function, in contrast to the French "parlement." The English Parliament even sought to participate in the making of laws and defend custom from the aggressive legislative initiatives of the king. But what theoretical arguments could be put forward to justify such practices?

2. *French Contributions: Godfrey of Fontaines, Nicholas Oresme, Philippe de Mézières, John Gerson*

Godefroid de Fontaines (ca. 1250–ca. 1306–09) elaborated a doctrine on consent: "When therefore any man rules over other freemen, not slaves, and only enjoys the right to rule by virtue of the whole community either electing or instituting or accepting him and consenting in his rule, his dominion can only be for the common good and the common utility. And therefore he has no right to impose anything burdensome or binding on them unless it meets with their consent. For as free men they ought to obey willingly, not under compulsion."[49]

In the writings of Nicholas Oresme (1320–82),[50] especially his commentary on Aristotle's *Politics* and *Nichomachean Ethics,* we come across ideas on the functions of the council. Since Oresme was an advisor to Charles V the Wise, we can assume that his writing and ideas reflect those of the king's counselors toward the middle of the fourteenth century.

Oresme thinks that the king can profit from listening to the people. "Though the common people do not know how to govern or make laws, it can see mistakes and recognize truths so as to advise law-makers and prevent them from erring; for this reason they should be listened to."[51]

Oresme's preferred form of government is *la policie royale* (royal government or monarchy). After discussing the advantages and disadvantages of hereditary and elective monarchy, he voices

[49] Dunbabin, "Government," 514.
[50] Nicole or Nicholas Oresme, bishop of Lisieux, tutor of the future king of France, Charles V the Wise.
[51] Oresme, quoted in Guenée, *L'Occident,* 153.

a preference for the latter. In any case, power in a monarchy has to be shared with a representative group of people. "That which is done and approved by all is stronger and more stable, more acceptable and more agreeable to the community, and provides less opportunity for murmur or rebellion than there might be otherwise." Oresme had also read in Aristotle that a "multitude" "knows best how to consider and order everything that is good for the public realm."[52]

As a matter of fact, the members of the king's council are the representatives of the reasonable multitude (public opinion). In this sense, their power is greater than the king's: royal power, Oresme writes, "must be less than that of the whole multitude, or its weightier part."[53] Oresme also asks how often the council should be assembled and by whom; he concludes that the "chief princes" should have the power to convene the participants even without the king's consent. In Oresme's opinion the royal council represents the entire kingdom; he admits the idea of *sanior pars* ("the sounder part," see below) rather than the majority. The idea is that wisdom guarantees *representativeness* better than numbers.[54]

In Sparta, the "sovereignty of the polity" was not in the hands of the democratic masses; it was held by the "multitude and universal congregation of all the princes and magistrates and principal citizens."[55] Oresme notes that at the University of Paris, decisions about the community are taken by the "general assembly of the Masters of the University," not by all members.

What are the competences of the council? Oresme's answer shows that he sees it as a mechanism of *government.*

> In counselling, the first necessity is to establish the end that is required, such as the peace of the city or the country in time of war. Then one must think, search and discover the shortest means to that end, which might mean negotiating with the enemy, or fighting them, or so to order and rule one's country as to prevent the enemy from doing any harm. Then one must choose by good judgement one of these means, such as fighting them. Then one must counsel how this should be done, and when, and by whom, and in what numbers. Then they must be chosen, and armed, trained, and so on to the point where the decision has to be put into practice, such as finding money or making arms or any other demands consequent upon the deliberations, and proceeding further in procuring and pursuing the known end by the means agreed upon.[56]

Another of Charles V's advisors, Philippe de Mézières (1327–1405),[57] insists that advisors should defend the public interest even in the face of challenges to their personal interests. The good advisor must be able to oppose prelates and clerks as well as the influential members of the council.

For Jean Gerson (1363–1429), the council is a useful auxiliary to the intellectual limits of the king. "How much sense has one single man? Wherefore the wise man says: do everything by counsel and you will never repent."[58] In Gerson's opinion, an advisor must be sincere, work in the public interest, and keep secret the council's deliberations. Writing at a time when nobility claimed ever more exclusive privileges, Gerson thought that advisors should be recruited from all "orders." His concern is not so much democratic as opportune: he felt that advice to the king

---

52 Ibid., 153.

53 Oresme, quoted by Jeannine Quillet, "Community, Counsel, and Representation," in Burns, *Cambridge History,* 566.

54 Quillet, "Community, Counsel, and Representation," 567.

55 Ibid., 565.

56 Oresme, quoted in ibid., 550.

57 Tutor to the heir apparent and future Charles VI.

58 Gerson, quoted by Quillet, "Community, Counsel, and Representation," 578.

had to be the most fully informed possible; the "head on a body" should have "eyes, ears, [and] nose."[59]

These various theoretical contributions notwithstanding, it is clear that in fifteenth century France under the monarchy the status of the council was never very clear in either juristic or doctrinal terms.

3. *English Contributions: Song of Lewes, Sir John Fortescue*

We saw earlier that representative institutions in England were more advanced than in other European countries. English theoreticians were convinced that the whole *communitas regni* had a right of participation in government. They contested the legislative and executive "prerogatives" of the king. When the Magna Carta of 1215 was adopted, the idea was introduced (article 61) that if the king departed from the law (even the human law), the community of the realm could compel him to obey it.

In the thirteenth century, the anonymous author of the English text the *Song of Lewes* (1264) calls attention to the fact that God alone has the prerogative of unlimited monarchy. The author thinks that the king should not be allowed to choose his own advisors. Henry III should have a council of barons, and he justifies his opinion as follows: "Since the governance of the realm is the safety or ruin of all, it matters whose is the guardianship of the realm, just as it is on the sea, all things are confounded if fools are in command."[60]

The kingdom must be governed in the public interest: "Whoever is truly king is truly free, if he rules himself and his kingdom rightly; let him know that all things are lawful for him which are fitted for ruling the kingdom, but not for destroying it."[61]

John Fortescue wrote, "The statutes of England . . . are made, not only by the prince's will, but also by the assent of the whole realm, so they cannot be injurious to the people nor fail to secure their advantage."[62] Fortescue was very aware of the uniqueness and advance—compared to France—of England's constitutional situation. While France was a *dominium regale,* a royal dominion, England was a *dominium politicum et regale,* which might be translated as "a *polis* or *res publica* ruled by a king."

The king does not decide the ends of common life; on the contrary, the people have established him to "protect the law, the subjects and their bodies and goods, and *he has power to this end issuing from the people,* so that it is not permissible for him to rule his people with any other power."[63]

B. Canonist Corporate Theory

One of the principal sources for these "democratic" ideas was *corporate theory,* developed by canonists to resolve legal problems within the church. This theory reached maturity toward the middle of the thirteenth century.[64]

---

59 Ibid., 578.

60 Dunbabin, "Government," 502.

61 Ibid., 506.

62 Ibid., 507. Fortescue was an English lawyer (ca. 1385–ca. 1476). He was elected a member of Parliament (1421) and appointed chief justice of the king's bench under Henry VI in 1442. He was appointed chancellor of England in 1461. He wrote *De laudibus legum Angliæ* ("In praise of English law"), which sets out a theory of constitutional monarchy.

63 Ibid., 516.

64 This section is drawn from Burns, *Cambridge History,* and Guenée, *L'Occident.*

In late antiquity and during the Middle Ages, the church was a "democratic" element—compared to Roman aristocratism or, later, feudalism—if only because ecclesiastical orders had always been open, in principle, to individuals of every social category.

Canonists were confronted—virtually on a daily basis—with problems between a bishop and his chapter of canons, or between an abbot and his monks. Who could represent the church or the monastery externally, for example, at important synods and councils? How were decisions to be taken in the chapter? How were votes to be counted? Could an ecclesiastic bring a suit against his chapter or against a bishop? Could a bishop oppose the will of a chapter?

It is important to distinguish between theories of *representation* and *election*.

1. *Representation*

Who can speak for the ecclesiastical community? In the texts compiled for Gratian's *Decretum* and in numerous papal decretals, there are as many monarchic as democratic elements. The canonists could simply pick and choose in this mass of material, which is what they did. In fact, they developed simultaneously two very different theories of representation.

One theory said that the "head" of the corporation could take all decisions—without vote or delegation—like a father for the family or a lord for his tenants. Thus, a bishop was authorized to assume the decision-making role for his diocese and an abbot for his abbey. According to the other theory, representation consisted of a mandate given by the corporation to one of its members.

Roman civil law supplied the models here. The *Digest* referred to "procurators" representing individuals in a legal suit. It also said that a community, taken as an abstract legal person, could be represented in court by a "syndic." Such procedures had been restored by civilists in the Middle Ages: the procurator, syndic, or advocate of a physical or abstract legal person could represent such a person in court, sign contracts, and agree to sales and purchases in his name.

Similar procedures were used in diocesan and general councils, and also in the general chapters of a monastic order. The rank and file began to send regularly elected "procurators" to these assemblies. The same procedures became customary in England, when towns and villages began to be represented at county courts.

However, initially, these representatives were sent to the assembly only to "listen and report," no more. They had no power to commit their principals, which made the assembly somewhat inefficient.

Some progress was made when someone had the idea to borrow from private law the method of representation with "full power" (*plena potestas*). Developed in the law courts in the twelfth century, this method was applied in ecclesiastical institutions at the beginning of the thirteenth century; subsequently, it became widespread; the delegates of parishes, dioceses, and monasteries could make decisions for their principals, who in turn were legally bound by these decisions. Thus came into being the intellectual mechanisms that made possible the development of "representative assemblies."

We should add that the first theory of representation never disappeared entirely. Because the canonists, after hesitating between the monarchic and democratic elements in the corpus of canon law, finally set out to conciliate the differences between the two, they read the praise for the "mixed constitution" in the ancient texts (in Aristotle and Cicero) and posited that a similar balance should exist in the church.

Johannes Teutonicus, for example, queries: "Is a prelate always obligated to seek a mandate from his church in all matters?" And he answers, "No, just as a tutor must not if he is properly appointed." Hostiensis thought likewise. For him, the bishop needed the chapter's approval only in important matters; he could do without his subordinates' consent in ordinary business.

Conversely, in the event of a prelatic vacancy, jurisdictional rights reverted to the chapter: the "headless corporation" had authority to act on a wide range of issues, notably in granting prebends.[65]

2. *Election*

In cases where the "head" alone was not entitled to make a decision, how could the "body" have a voice?

a. The Acknowledgment of Each Individual Vote by the Church

The canonists introduced an important idea: in a corporation every voice counted, and not a single one could be neglected *a priori*. The Rule of Saint Benedict,[66] it seems, was a distant source for this idea. The Rule provided for various elective procedures: the election of an abbot, the convening of monks for advice on important matters, and so on. It also had a "revolutionary"—specifically Christian—aspect, which broke with Roman voting practices. The least of the monks could be the innocent creature to whom God chooses to reveal his providential will. For this reason, everyone in the monastery must be consulted. The expression of the *sanior pars* (see below) is the usual rule, of course, but it is not always enough (see Rule, chapters 3, 64, 65).

The canonists reinforced this idea, invoking a rule of private law found in the Justinian code: *Quod omnes tangit ab omnibus approbari debet* ("What concerns all must be discussed and approved by all").

The original rule concerned primarily the issue of tutelage. When several tutors were responsible, a decision was valid only if everyone gave their consent. The canonists applied this rule to corporations: decisions concerning a corporation had to have been made by all its members. This did not mean that decisions had to be made unanimously, only that as a matter of principle no one was excluded from the procedure. This was the same as saying that the corporation was an *association of individuals* where each person had a worthwhile opinion; it was not an *organic body* where only the "head" thought and decided.

b. Major et Sanior Pars

Majority rule existed already in the *Digest:* "That which the major part of the city does is considered as if it had in fact been done by all." But what exactly is meant by "majority"? Is it an arithmetical or qualitative majority? And if it is arithmetical, is it a simple majority (half of the votes plus one) or two-thirds, or what?[67]

Before modern ideas of simple arithmetical majority triumphed, the canonists developed an innovative theory known as *major et sanior pars* ("the greater and sounder part"), which said that the idea of the majority was to be understood in qualitative terms as well as in arithmetical terms.

Huguccio, for example, identifies three elements: *number, zeal,* and *authority*. He posits that for a good decision at least two of these three elements have to concur. For Hostiensis, when the bishop states an opinion as prelate and not as an ordinary member of the chapter, his voice weighs as much as all the members of the corporation combined. Therefore, he is said to have the majority if he obtains just one more vote added to his own, unless fundamental issues of the church are at stake, in which case an arithmetical majority is necessary.

---

[65] See K. Pennington,"Law, Legislative Athority, and Theories of Government, 1150–1300," in Burns, *Cambridge History*, 445.

[66] See *The Holy Rule of Saint Benedict*, trans. Boniface Verheyen, OSB; available at www.ccel.org/ccel/benedict/rule2/files/rule2.html. Saint Benedict's text dates from ca. 535.

[67] See Quillet, "Community, Counsel, and Representation," 557.

At the beginning of the thirteenth century, Johannes Teutonicus advanced a more democratic principle: "Number always prevails over zeal and authority, unless it only slightly exceeds them; then I would combine either zeal or authority with number…and dignity should not be considered unless the electors were evenly divided."[68] Finally, Johannes Teutonicus approved a simple majority rule: "If the canons litigate among themselves, where the *major pars* lies, they may call themselves the chapter."[69] In the late Middle Ages, this generally agreed-upon opinion was adopted throughout the church and was also transposed to the secular state.

A simple majority principle was set down at the Fourth Lateran Council in 1215. In the middle of the thirteenth century it was applied by several religious orders, for example, the Templars and the Dominicans. Boniface VIII confirmed it. Later, secular assemblies adopted the same canonist model: for the election of the king of the Romans, such as in 1338, the election was conducted *concorditer vel a majori parte,* "unanimously or with a majority" (the principle was confirmed in the Golden Bull of 1356). In England, in the fifteenth century, the House of Commons sometimes elected its speaker by a majority of two or three votes. Although in the assemblies of the Three Estates—France, Brabant, and Holland—decisions had to be made unanimously by all three estates, the decision of each particular assembly was made by a simple arithmetical majority. The same was true of the German *Landtage* in the fifteenth century.

c. The Limits of the Election Principle: Jurisdiction and Ordination

There was a serious theological obstacle to the church's complete acceptance of these democratic principles. The apostles had not been elected by a corporation; they were chosen directly by Jesus Christ. In turn, did they not have to choose their own successors, and their successors *ad infinitum?* A God-given power cannot be instituted by a "bottom-up" election. The ritual of anointment, whether the anointment of biblical kings by the prophets or that of bishops by their predecessors, is a "top down" process, and it seems that it is always the case when the transmission of a sacramental character is at stake. And yet, the designation of bishops by election was a practice as old as the church itself.

The solution the canonists came up with was to make a distinction for the bishop between the effects of election and the effects of ordination (also called consecration). They posited that election gave the bishop his *jurisdictional powers* and ordination his *sacramental powers.*[70] In other words, while all power in the divinely instituted monarchy embodied by the church comes from God, it comes mediated through the electoral body of the clergy.

Initially formulated to handle the problems of small ecclesiastical communities (bishoprics and abbeys), corporate theory was applied by the canonists throughout the entire church: we will see this when we discuss the importance of Conciliar theory below.

3. *Application of Corporate Theory to Independent Cities and Kingdoms: The Reservations of the Nominalists*

Corporate theory was also applied, this time by the Romanists, to independent, small city-states and large, secular monarchies. It contributed to the abstract idea of the state, a public moral

[68] A remnant of this rule survives in our modern assemblies (in both public and private law) where, according to the statutes, the president generally casts the "deciding vote" in the event of a tie.

[69] Texts cited by Pennington, "Law, Legislative Authority," 451, 452. It is clear that non-unanimity in a community was not thought to be the normal situation: the rule was unanimity, and it was only in the event of disagreement that voices were counted. Pluralism was still regarded as a source of error and weakness, not an enrichment of the debate. All of this seems to be a step behind the Greek *agora*.

[70] See ibid., 449–50.

person, abstract and independent, not only from ordinary people but from the person of its leaders as well.

While the "Glossators" confused the corporation with its members,[71] the "Commentators"[72] made a distinction between the members of a political community, on the one hand, and the abstract corporative body that they formed, on the other. This abstraction, which only the intellect can grasp, is immortal and permanent, though its physical members are born and die. It is also distinct from its government. Thus, states are "legal persons." This abstract person can have one voice, one will, and one intelligence. Like ecclesiastical corporations, it needs only to give itself representatives.

It is important to signal the reservations of Nominalists the likes of Duns Scotus and William of Ockham, that is, thinkers who contested—from a general philosophical point of view—the reality of abstractions, since they believed only in the reality of concrete, individual objects, including individual human beings. With remarkable foresight the Nominalists anticipated the dangers concealed in the establishment of the state as an abstract person over its constituent members, on the grounds that the idea of "community" (and still more the idea that the community should be represented by some of its members or by a single person) contained the seeds that could lead to the crushing of the individual.

For Ockham, a political community is a relation between the human beings who comprise it; it is not a reality in itself, only a "concept", that is, a simple word: "A relation is only...a concept of the mind."[73] The unity of a concept should not prejudice the real unity of elements whose relation it conceives. "Something is said to be one [a unity] improperly and loosely, as when a kingdom is said to be one, or a people, or the world is said to be one."[74]

In modern terms, we would say that pluralism is irreducible. The idea of the "realm" is a dangerous fiction. Consequently, the idea of "representation" is also problematic: if the represented thing is a fiction, how can the representative not be as well? The entire process is illegitimate because all parties are irreducibly individual and unique.

Still, Ockham admits the legitimacy of emperors, popes, general councils, and other representatives of political communities, but at least he would like their legitimacy to be based on the "consent" of all interested individuals.

C. Conciliarism

Conciliarism is the idea that papal power must be controlled and limited by the church's General Council.[75] The Conciliar movement is rightly held to prefigure democratic ideals. The reason is that, while the debate between the advocates and adversaries of Conciliarism was fundamentally theological and in principal concerned only the church, its conclusions were easily transferable from the ecclesiastical to the secular realm; in this sense, they were "constitutional" questions.

The Great Schism (1378–1417) presented the opportunity for an expression of conciliar ideas. After the death of the Avignon pope, Gregory XI, who had returned to Rome in 1377, the election of Urban VI (April 1378) was rejected on the grounds that it was obtained under popular pressure; it is true that the people of Rome had insisted on an Italian pope. In September 1378,

---

[71] Accursius: "the corporation is nothing other than the men who are there." Quoted by Canning, "Law, Sovereignty," 471.

[72] In a gloss on Innocent IV's formulation that the corporation is a *persona ficta.*

[73] William of Ockham, *Quodlibet* VI, q. 15, quoted by Quillet 537n2.

[74] Ockham, quoted by Quillet, "Community, Counsel, and Representation," 537.

[75] This section is drawn from Chelini, *Histoire religieuse,* 524–57; Antony Black, "The Conciliar Movement," in Burns, *Cambridge History,* 573–87.

another pope, Clement VII, was elected by the cardinals, the majority of whom were French. Rejected in Rome, the new pope returned to Avignon. This was the start of the Schism. The two popes had two lines of successors for nearly 40 years; neither of the two parties was prepared to capitulate, and both received support of comparable weight from nation-states in full rise (the Avignon popes were supported by France and its allies—Scotland, Castille, and the rest of Spain—while the Roman popes were backed by England, Flanders, Poland, Hungary, the German territories of the Empire, and the Scandinavian kingdoms; Italy was divided between the two camps depending on diplomatic interests). As time went by, it became increasingly difficult to resolve the conflict: bishops, abbots, and other high dignitaries in each camp feared for their positions if the other side won; the kings of France and England were both pleased to have a "personal" pope at their beck and call.

Then, in 1409, the cardinals took a revolutionary initiative (from the standpoint of canon law) and assembled a Council in Pisa; it only succeeded in electing a third pope, Alexander V, who was succeeded by John XXIII in 1410. The latter was caught up in problems with the king of Naples, who appealed to the Holy Roman Emperor Sigismund. The emperor, in turn, demanded that the pope convene a new assembly, the Council of Constance (1414–18). By the decree *Hæc sancta* (1415), the council declared itself superior to the pope. Then it accepted the resignation of Pope Jean XXIII, unseated the two schismatic popes, and declared itself the depositary of the sovereignty of the church. It agreed upon a new program of reforms, and before concluding its deliberations it decided that the conclave should hold a papal election. This resulted in the election of Odo Colonna under the name of Martin V (November 11, 1417).

The moderates,[76] proponents of a constructive working relationship with the pope, prevented the council from slipping into revolutionary excess as some demanded. Yet, the moderates managed to uphold the principles expressed in the *Hæc sancta* decree, and they also voted a second decree, *Frequens* (1417), stipulating that a church council should be held periodically, and independently of the will of the pope.[77]

In application of this decree, an ecumenical council was to be held in Pavia in 1423, but because of the plague it was transferred to Siena, where it was finally dissolved. The quarrel simmering between the pope and the council erupted again at the next council in Basel (1430).

Martin V died in 1431 and was succeeded by Eugene IV, a less skillful man, who thought he could simply dissolve the council and eliminate it. But there were more and more doctors with extremist Conciliar views among its members. With the backing of Emperor Sigismund, they obtained the continuance of the council. Eugene IV was obliged to recognize the legitimacy of an assembly convened against his will, though he successfully isolated the extremists by relocating the council to Ferrara, then Florence, under the pretext of meeting with the Eastern Orthodox Church.[78] The extremists retreated to Basel, deposed the pope, and elected an antipope, Count Amadeus VIII of Savoy, under the name of Felix V; this new schism lasted until 1449. In fact, the Council of Basel heaped discredit on itself and ruined any chance of carrying out a serious church reform. At the same time, the meeting with the Greeks in Ferrara and Florence resulted in a reconciliation between East and West (the papal bull *Lætentur Cœli,* 1439), thanks to the efforts of Emperor John Palaeologus and the theologian Bessarion. The prestige of the papacy grew and, subsequently, the pope avoided convening the council and was able to restore the pontifical monarchy.

---

[76] Among these moderates were the celebrated canonist Francesco Zabarella and the chancellor of the University of Paris, Jean Gerson.

[77] The principle of a regular calendar meeting of a representative assembly, independent of the will of the monarch, became a central demand of constitutional advocates in modern times.

[78] The Greeks sought reconciliation with the western church because of the rising Turkish threat.

Before the Schism, and despite the claims of the *Dictatus papæ*, a conflict simmered between the doctrinal authority of the councils and the jurisdictional authority of the papacy. The dispute began in reaction to the growing centralization of the papacy during its period in Avignon. At this time, Marsilius of Padua made certain statements that could be called pre-Conciliar.

1. Every community needs protection from the usurpation of power by one of its parts; because any part is limited by definition, it can err "by ignorance or deceit, cupidity or ambition, or any other vicious passion" (*Defensor pacis* 2.20.6). The best protection against this danger is for the community as a whole to make decisions.

2. This is what the early church did, according to the Acts of the Apostles: since they considered themselves equals, the apostles adopted a method of "collective discussion" (*Defensor pacis* 2.16.5). Thus, "the assembly of the faithful, or the general council, represents the assembly of the apostles, the elders, and all other believers of this time" (2.19.2). That is to say, the general council was the successor of the deliberative assembly of the early church.

3. The corporation of citizens (*universitas civium*) coincides with the corporation (body) of the faithful (*universitas fidelium*); the leader of the former, the emperor, is responsible for convening the general council. Church history itself provides evidence of this: since the time of Constantine, general councils had been convened by the emperor, and their canons were implemented by the decrees of the emperors. Therefore, Louis IV of Bavaria, Constantine *redivivus*, is the one person with the authority to convene the general council (it should be remembered that Marsilius backed Philip the Fair's proposal to convene a council for the purpose of passing judgment on the pope).

1. *Conciliarism at the Time of the Great Schism*

Both at the time of the Great Schism and when ecumenical councils convened regularly in application of the *Frequens* decree, the Conciliar theorists developed and radicalized their ideas. Among the writers of Conciliar propaganda were Dietrich of Niem (Nieheim), Petrus de Allaco (Pierre d'Ailly), Jean Gerson, Francisco Zarbarella, Niccolò di Tudeschi, Andreas Escobar, John of Ragusa, Juan de Segovia, and Nicholas of Cusa.

In the wealth of doctrinal output, several ideas stand out:

a. the church, as a whole, is higher in authority than the pope because it is a "mystical corporation," of which the faithful are members; Christ—not the pope—is the head;

b. the council is said to represent the whole church because it represents all parishes, all religious orders, and all orders of knowledge (theology, canon law, etc.). This is why doctors, and not just abbots and bishops, can be members;

c. if there is a serious presumption that the pope is harmful to the church as a whole (for reasons of heresy, scandal, or poor administration), he must be able to be blamed and replaced.

Like the canonists, who proposed a "mixed constitution" for episcopal churches and religious orders, some moderate Conciliarists (d'Ailly, Gerson) made the same recommendation for the church itself (i.e., the government of the church would be exercised by the papacy, cardinals, and general council), but the idea was not adopted at the Councils of Constance and Basel. The dominant view in Basel was that the council, with its own executive organs, should exercise the power (*jurisdictio*) formerly in the sole hands of the pope.

Juan de Segovia, who represented the majority opinion, drew on the canonical doctrine of corporations and on the constitutional ideas put forward in defense of Italian republics to generalize the principle of the sovereignty of the council. The head of the community was sovereign in relation to each of its individual members, but its members as a whole, convened in general assembly, constituted a higher authority than the one head. The leader's authority prevailed only as long as his judgment was presumed to "conform to the will of all over whom he presides for the benefit of the republic and themselves. But if it happens that this whole community assembles together, and its assertions and wishes contradict those of the president, since truth is preferred to fiction, the community will deservedly prevail. For the truth is that this community is many persons, and the fiction is that this president, who is really one person, is said to be many by representation."[79] Segovia spoke of the *intentio omnium* ("will of all"), which can be likened to the modern expression of universal will for the common good. Jurisdictional authority existed only by *delegation* of this *intentio omnium:* "supreme power . . . exists first in the community itself [the church]; then in the rulers and magistrates, or consulate and senate [the council] . . . and subsequently in the executive or *podesta, dictator* or governor." The sovereignty of the community cannot be alienated. Segovia argued that the community "never abdicates its power . . . [which] belongs to it irretrievably."[80]

Finally, Segovia pursued the idea that necessarily each council delegate had an "equal voice" in relation to the others by virtue of the "mutual love" that prevailed among all participants regardless of differences of dignity and function. Superiors and subordinates were equal when they participated in council discussions. This stance presented a radical challenge to the very concept of *sanior pars*.

2. *The Conciliarism of Nicholas of Cusa*

The ideas of Nicholas of Cusa deserve very close attention. Nicholas of Cusa or Kues (1401–64), born in Kues near Trier, was German. He studied law and medicine in Padua, then became the bishop of Brixen, a cardinal, and the governor of Rome. In addition to *De concordantia catholica* (1433), in which he develops his Conciliar ideas, he wrote a work titled *De pace fidei* (On the peace of faith) about the time the Turks laid siege to Constantinople (1453); in it he attempts to show that Christians, Muslims, and Buddhists worship the same God. His best-known work is *De docta ignorantia* (Of learned ignorance) (1440), which shows the limits of reason: knowledge of God can only be attained by analogy. He also criticized Aristotle's cosmology and anticipated Copernicus.

Nicholas of Cusa developed the idea that government of any kind is lawful only if it is based on the "consent" of the governed; this stipulation is fundamental for the governed to be considered as "free men."

In the early church (Conciliarists make constant reference to this church), the "consent of the faithful" was a sign of doctrinal truth. Canon law admitted that bishops were elected by clerics "with the consent" of the laity.

Nicholas of Cusa combined the canonist notion of consent and the notion of cosmic "harmonious concord," borrowed from Neoplatonism, to establish just political authority, in the church and in the Empire. "The force of law subsists in the subjective concordance of those whom it obliges."[81] A prescription of power or a custom, if it goes against this feeling of concord or "oneness of spirit" (*unanimitas*) of the community, has no more worth than if it goes against divine law or natural justice. The collective opinion of the council has more authority than the pope as an individual. "It is beautiful to contemplate how in the people all powers, spiritual and temporal, are latent in potency"; that is, power inheres ultimately in the people. Consequently, all power

[79] Antony Black, "The Conciliar Movement," in Burns, *Cambridge History*, 581.
[80] Ibid., 582.
[81] Ibid., 583.

must be elected to be lawful. "So that in concord one body may be composed out of subjects and president, reason, natural law and divine law all require mutual consent, which we rightly understand to consist in election by all and consent by the one chosen, as in the spiritual marriage between Christ and the Church."

Therefore, the council was to be elected by priests directly or indirectly, and in turn it would elect the pope. And this principle would apply to all forms of government, including secular forms, because "all men by nature are free." Rulers obtained their authority to rule by the consent of men. "Thus all sovereignty... exists solely by concord and subjective consent. For, if men by nature are equally strong and equally free, the true and ordained power of one, by nature no stronger than the rest, can only be constituted by the election and consent of the others."[82]

The principle of the "universal council" was put into practice across the Empire through regularly held Diets—one or two a year—with the guarantee of free speech:[83] the resolutions of the Diets were "binding" for the laws of the Empire.

D. Humanism and Republicanism in Italian Cities during the Fifteenth Century

Feudalism had not developed very widely in Italy, and even less in very urbanized areas; before long, the commune movement led to the creation of autonomous city republics (Pisa in 1085; Milan in 1097; Arezzo in 1098; Lucca, Bologna, and Sienna ca. 1125).[84] Neither the Empire nor the papacy was able to stifle the movement. These republics subsequently saw a regime of consuls, followed by a regime of "podestas." But such regimes turned out to be weak because of the extreme political fragmentation of the region and the absence of a dominant power able to settle conflicts between cities, and because the city republics, in terms of domestic policy, were split. Various factions, with conflicting interests, represented the social classes; their quarrels were aggravated by systematic connections with one or the other of the great powers (the papacy or the Empire), as members of the Guelph or Ghibelline parties. The Guelphs, it is recalled, grouped together the notables and powerful merchants, the so-called *popolo grasso* (bourgeoisie), at ease in the representative structures of the city, which they controlled comfortably. The Ghibellines were the more popular party, headed by strong men, the so-called "captains of the people." Soon authoritarian forms of government sprang up wherever a strong man managed to eliminate his rivals and impose order, becoming a permanent podesta and even founding a dynasty (the Malatesta in Rimini after 1280, the Della Scala in Padua, the Visconti in Milan, at the end of the thirteenth century). When a tyranny of the "captain of the people" succeeded in establishing itself, the absence of feudalism proved a liability, since the potentate did not face the counterweight of councils and parliaments that existed in the feudal territories.

That said, the "brilliant flame of liberty"[85] continued to flicker in two Italian cities, Venice and Florence. Since Venice was in an outlying region, oriented toward its Adriatic commercial empire (Byzantium and the East), it was able to preserve its independence and republican regime. Florence, on the contrary, was vulnerable and exposed to ambitious Milan, which manifested threatening expansionist tendencies after 1350.

---

[82] Ibid., 584–85.

[83] According to the Conciliarists, the Holy Spirit would work through the council only if "freedom of speech" were guaranteed; the Conciliarists had rediscovered a long-forgotten principle, the *isegoria* of the Greek city (equality in freedom of speech), to which they gave new theological meaning.

[84] This section is drawn from Skinner, *Foundations of Modern Political Thought,* and Hans Baron, *The Crisis of Early Italian Renaissance* (Princeton, NJ: Princeton University Press, 1966).

[85] Skinner, *Foundations,* 23.

The conflict between the two cities was diplomatic at first: Milan sought an alliance with the French; it was finally concluded in favor of Florence in 1396. Earlier, in 1392, the conflict between Milan and Florence morphed into open war. One by one, Milan defeated the allies of Florence—Padua, Ferrara, Mantua, Bologna. Before very long Florence faced the powerful Lombard duchy alone (Emperor Wenceslas made Milan a duchy in 1395).

An ideological element played an important role in Florentine resistance to Milan. Thanks to the efforts of the humanists, certain texts by Cicero and Tacitus on the Roman Republic had been restored to honor. After reading Cicero's passages in praise of the moral superiority of the active life over the contemplative life (see above, pp. 300–02), various intellectuals took up active involvement in politics and persuaded the Florentines that their city was the sole heir of the Roman Republic and its civic virtues; and, they added, it was their calling to restore these virtues not just to Florence but to Italy as a whole.

Leonardo Bruni,[86] a leading humanist and intellectual of the time, stands out in particular. His *Panegyric to the City of Florence* argues that Florence is blessed with the best of what the Italian soil produces, since it is heir to both the Etruscan civilization and the Roman Republic. Furthermore, its constitution is a model of equilibrium and a rampart against tyranny. Just as the idea of Empire is defended at present by foreigners, the same idea was brought to ancient Rome by generals who had campaigned in the Orient. Empire is not an idea native to Italy.

Among the Florentine intellectuals of the age was Gregorio Dati, the author of *A History of the long and important Italian War in our day between the Tyrant of Lombardy and the magnificent Commune of Florence*. In his work, he argues (with words that evoke Herodotus's praise of the superiority of the Greek city-state over Persian monarchy)[87] that the fact that Florentines enjoy political freedom today proves that they elevate reason to the highest level in public affairs. It is precisely reason, Dati goes on to say, that gives them their superiority in diplomacy and war.

> The Florentines never believed that they could be vanquished or subjugated. Their minds were so contrary to an idea of the sort that they were fully incapable of imagining it. At all times, they invented the appropriate remedy.... They constantly placed their hope in the certainty that the Commune could not die, whereas the Duke [of Milan], a mere mortal, would take the Empire to his tomb.... And it can be said that the Florentines alone hold in their hands the freedom of all Italy, which no other power can corrupt.[88]

There were other Florentines, however, who saw the advantages of strong government. One was Coluccio Salutati, who in his early youth had been a staunch supporter of Republican ideas. The debate on this issue never ceased, not even in Florence.

These ideas frequently revolved around examples from ancient Rome. Who had helped Italy most? Caesar, who gave it greatness? Or Brutus, the republican, who assassinated a tyrant? In his *Divine Comedy*, Dante, a defender of the Empire, placed Brutus in hell. But was it not the Roman Empire that put an end to the civil wars of the Republic? Later, another Florentine praised the virtues of strong government out of concern for Italian national unity: his name was Machiavelli.

---

86 Leonardo Bruni wrote *Panegyric to the City of Florence* (after 1402), *History of the Florentine People, Eulogy to Nanni degli Strozzi* (1428) modeled on Pericles' funeral oration recorded by Thucydides, *Life of Dante, Life of Petrarch*, and *Dialogues I and II*.

87 See above, pp. 60–61.

88 Quoted by Louis Bodin, in Touchard, *Histoire des idées politiques*, 1:216.

Chapter 7

Medieval Millenarianism

The prophetic eschatology of the Bible is responsible for the fact that, in a West wholly and irreversibly converted to Christianity, time was seen as an anxious expectation of a different and better future (see above, pp. 445–46). While this expectation, filtered and moderated by ancient rationalism and law, determined the Papal Revolution and the social transformations following in its wake, it was also the source of a very different tradition: revolutionary millenarianism.

First, we will sketch briefly the *evolution of millenarian ideas* from biblical times until the dawn of the Middle Ages (section I).[1] Then, we will give a short *historical overview* of the social movements associated with millenarianism between the eleventh and sixteenth centuries (therefore, we will overstep slightly the conventional time frame of the Middle Ages) (section II). Finally, we will present the *ideologies* that sustained these movements (section III).

I. The Evolution of Millenarianism at the End of Antiquity

A. From the Revelation of Saint John the Divine to Saint Augustine

Millenarian belief—the literal interpretation of the Revelation of Saint John the Divine—which once found favor among many church fathers who did not dissociate it from Christian doctrine,

[1] Our guides for this topic are Norman Cohn, *The Pursuit of the Millennium: Revolutionary Millenarians and Mystical Anarchists of the Middle Ages*, rev. and expanded ed. (New York: Oxford University Press, 1970); Jean Delumeau, *History of Paradise: The Garden of Eden in Myth and Tradition* (New York: Continuum, 1995); Henri de Lubac, *La postérité spirituelle de Joachim de Flore* [The spiritual posterity of Joachim of Flora], 2 vols. (Paris: Lethielleux-Culture et Vérité, 1978). On the biblical sources of millenarianism, see above, pp. 441–45.

came under harsh criticism from Origen (ca. 185–254) (see p. 443). One of Origen's followers, Dionysius of Alexandria, went so far as to recommend the exclusion of the Revelation of Saint John the Divine from the Bible (the only divine source of millenarian ideas).[2]

The integration of the church into the Empire brought about an indirect solution to the problem by marginalizing in practice the social circles in which millenarianism had an appeal. The uncontrolled movements, which were inflamed by a restless hope for a profound and imminent transformation of the world, caused fear; efforts were made to deprive them of theological arguments that could be used to justify their cause. The definitive doctrinal condemnation of millenarianism is the work of Augustine.

In book 20, chapters 7–17, of his *City of God* (near the end of his work, where the author sets out his ideas on the doctrine of the last things, the Last Judgment, hell, and paradise), Augustine proposes a symbolic interpretation of the book of Revelation. When John the Divine writes that he saw "an angel coming down from heaven, having the key of the abyss, and a chain in his hand" to lay hold on Satan "and [bind] him for a thousand years," "and he cast him into the abyss" and "shut him up, and set a seal upon him," this is not in reference to future realities, Augustine says, but describes what had occurred since the coming of Christ. With his preaching, death, and Resurrection, Jesus triumphed over Satan and prevented him from doing evil (Mark 3:27; Luke 11:22), thereby delivering humankind. In establishing the church, Jesus had already established the kingdom of God on earth, and because Satan can no longer triumph over the predestined, the souls of the elect already have access to salvation. The "seal" that binds Satan means that the wicked are not known here below: they are inextricably interspersed among the elect. The book of Revelation speaks of "this kingdom militant (*de hoc regno militiæ*), in which conflict with the enemy is still maintained, and war carried on with warring lusts, or government laid upon them as they yield, until we come to that most peaceful kingdom (*illud pacatissimum regnum*) in which we shall reign without an enemy" (20.9.2). The separation of the wheat from the chaff in the City of God and the earthly City will occur only at the Last Judgment. As for the 1,000 years, it is simply a reference to a long and indefinite time: the time that the church will last on earth. After this time will come the *Parousia,* the resurrection of the dead, and the Last Judgment: they will come suddenly, and the current world will change directly into the everlasting kingdom of God.

Thus, Augustine excludes the notion of an intermediary time, that is, a future time on the same plane as history, in which evil has disappeared. Such a time is not to be hoped for, nor prepared for. Evil is and will always be present in *all* history. A new perspective of personal and supernatural redemption, reflecting what we noted earlier about the paradoxical eschatology of the Gospel (see above, pp. 434–36), replaces the old messianic vision of the world's transformation for all humankind.

Augustine's interpretation enabled the preservation of the Revelation—attributed to John the Beloved in his time—as part of the Bible while, at the same time, it mitigated the social restlessness that a literal interpretation aroused. Subsequently, Augustine's interpretation was accepted and adopted by the official church.

Millennial belief was condemned by the Council of Ephesus in 431. At the end of the fifth century, a decree by Pope Gelasius made obligatory the new allegorical interpretation of chapter 20 of Revelation. Thomas Aquinas repeated this condemnation in his controversy with Joachimism (see above, pp. 562–64); modern Catholicism accepted his doctrine on this point.

Be that as it may, the prophetic idea behind the millenarianism of Revelations never really disappeared. It could not, of course, if the interpretation we suggested above (pp. 412–30 and 434–36) as the *moral* source of messianism and millenarianism is accepted: as long as Christian

[2] See Delumeau, *History of Paradise,* chap. 1; G. Bardy, *La cité de Dieu de Saint Augustin* [Saint Augustine's *City of God*] (Paris: Desclée de Brouwer, 1960), no. 37, and special notes 26 and 27.

morality is preached and accepted in the hearts of all human beings, a sentiment and doctrines of changing times would return again and again in different incarnations. Consequently, millenarianism would remain buried in the depths of the Christian conscience and would, periodically, break to the surface.

B. Christian Sibyllines

Earlier, the Jews, for apologetical purposes, circulated Greek texts in hexameters in the style of the old Sibylline prophecies[3] (we noted, in part 2, an echo of pagan Sibylline prophecies in Virgil). Likewise, the Christians, who under the Roman imperial persecutions appropriated the Jewish apocalyptic heritage, adopted its forms of expression and added "Christian Sibyllines" to the established tradition. The oldest of these Sibyllines was the *Tiburtina,* dating from the fourth century.[4]

The Tiburtina was written in the context of Constantine's tumultuous succession. His two sons, Constantius and Constans, were embroiled in a bitter conflict; the victor, Constantius, converted to Arianism. Orthodox believers, in desperation at the situation, imagined that a savior king would come to put things right. His name would be Constans; he would be physically magnificent: tall, fine features, radiant. His reign would last 112 years, or perhaps 120; it would be prosperous. He would decimate the pagans and lay to waste their towns; in the end the Jews themselves would convert. Then the armies of Gog and Magog would rise up, but the emperor would trample them. Then he would make his way to Jerusalem where, on Golgotha, he would solemnly relinquish the imperial crown and give up the kingship to God. This would be the end of the Roman Empire and the beginning of the millennium. This final transition, however, would occur only after many trials: the Antichrist would also settle in Jerusalem and the archangel Michael would descend from heaven with his armies to destroy him once and for all. Thus, the Tiburtina created the theme of the emperor of the Last Days—the emperor as messiah—destined to run through all of Western history even into contemporary times.

This theme is developed in another Sibylline text from the end of the seventh century, titled the Revelations of Pseudo-Methodius. They too were prompted by a desperate situation: Muslims had overwhelmed Christian Syria. A powerful emperor, thought to be long dead, returns and routs the seed of Ishmael. Then, the same sequence of events occurs as in the Tiburtina: the emperor reigns in Jerusalem, lays down his crown on Golgotha, and the Antichrist appears, but he is defeated by the armies of heaven, anticipating the reign of Christ and the Last Judgment.

The Tiburtina was modified in a tenth century tract by the monk Adso; it enjoyed wide circulation and had many variants: the main difference was that the emperor of the Last Days was no longer Greek but a "king of the Franks." Other variations were created and circulated widely throughout the Middle Ages until the invention of the printing press.

Thus, with these texts adding to the tradition of commentaries on the book of Revelation, a powerful theme was forged that would traverse the Middle Ages and survive into modern times: a *savior king* will appear in the *Last Days;* a final *eschatological struggle* will erupt against the *forces of evil;* it will be resolved by *supernatural intervention.* Pagans, Jews, and Muslims will either be *converted* or *massacred;* the age will witness the brief triumph of the *Antichrist;*[5] then, a tiny number of *righteous ones, the Elect,* will witness the *final victory of Christ* and *1,000 years of bliss* will commence. At the end of this time, all humankind will be judged in a *Last Judgment.*

---

[3] See Cohn, *Pursuit of the Millennium,* 29–36.

[4] See Jeanne Baroin and Josiane Haffen, *La prophétie de la sibylle tiburtine* [The prophecy of the Tiburtine Sibyl] (Paris: Les Belles Lettres, 1987).

[5] See above, p. 442n102, for scriptural references to the Antichrist.

II. Medieval Millenarian Movements

Belief in the imminence of these events was deeply etched in the minds of ordinary people and functioned like a myth. In fact, the Middle Ages saw a series of *revolutionary millenarian agitations*. Here is a brief overview of some, drawn from Norman Cohn's comprehensive study of the topic.

A. Early Millenarian Agitation

Around 590 Gregory of Tours spoke of a miracle-working, faith-healing "Christ," who assembled an army of followers and attacked the official church; he was subsequently captured and killed in the town of Le Puy. Another similar figure, *Aldebert*, ran amuck in the mid-eighth century; after his condemnation by Saint Boniface, secular authorities put an end to his agitating.

There was a steep rise in agitation with millenarian overtones at the end of the eleventh century and in the early twelfth; it continued well into the sixteenth century. It engulfed most of Europe, but its active center was primarily in two regions of northern Europe: the region between the Somme and Rhine rivers (Flanders, Belgium, The Netherlands, Rhenish Germany) in the twelfth and thirteenth centuries; and the regions of Germany and Bohemia[6] between the fourteenth and sixteenth centuries. The phenomenon is clearly linked to the rapid economic growth and urban expansion of these regions, which created destabilized masses, isolated from their conservative rural milieu and available for social agitation.

B. Millenarian Agitation in the Context of the Crusades

The Crusades were motivated by a number of factors, but among them eschatological concerns played a leading role. Pope Urban II, preaching the First Crusade in Clermont in 1095, proposed to hasten the coming of messianic times with the reconquest of the Holy Land. Christianity must triumph in Jerusalem so that the Antichrist can rise up against Christians and Christ can return to destroy the Antichrist and inaugurate an everlasting reign.

Because the Crusader knights under the command of Godfrey of Bouillon and other princes believed in these things, they set out for the Holy Land and established Frankish realms there (the kingdom of Jerusalem, the counties of Edessa and Tripoli, the principality of Antioch). Soon these entities were being defended by the soldier-monk orders of the Hospitallers and the Knights Templar.

The same eschatological arguments inspired popular preachers like Peter the Hermit. These individuals played a prominent role in preaching about the Crusades and in mobilizing masses of fighting men from a populace destabilized by grinding poverty.

The *pauperes* ("paupers") did not share the same aim as the knights; their intention was not just to deliver Jerusalem, or make a pilgrimage there, it was also to settle permanently. What they were searching for in "Jerusalem" was a wondrous, earthly city where they would enjoy prosperity and justice. Before long they realized that their motivations differed from those of the nobles and came to see their own as superior. They believed themselves to be the true Elect of God.

Most of these poor died before reaching the Holy Land. Some arrived and formed the hordes of bloodcurdling fighters known as the *Tafurs* (their leader was called "King Tafur"). Armed only with scythes, practicing cannibalism, they were feared by Christians and Saracens alike. Their

[6] After the consolidation of a centralized, authoritarian France under the leadership of Charles V and his successors, the agitation drifted toward Germany, which was politically fragile after the Empire disintegrated into myriads of principalities and, at the same time, was experiencing strong economic development.

millenarian fanaticism drove them to unspeakable atrocities—genuine wars of extermination—against the Jews during their journey through France and Germany (in Rouen and the towns of the Rhine valley: Spire, Worms, Mainz, and Cologne, as well as in Metz, Trier, Regensburg, Prague, and so on) and all along the way to Jerusalem. In a sense, they were taking literally the biblical prophecies about the extermination or forcible conversion of the infidels in the Last Days. At virtually every step of the way, the fanatical masses overcame the resistance put up against them by the lords, bishops, and "official" Crusaders.

The same scenario played out again in the Second Crusade. Then, for over a century (between 1200 and 1320, more or less), the Crusades of the Poor People occurred alongside the official Crusades, following one after the other. A Children's Crusade took place in 1212, led by a "boy" who believed himself to be the Elect of God. The first Shepherd's Crusade took place in 1250 after Saint Louis's failed expedition.[7] It was led by an old apostate monk named Jacob, also known as the "Master of Hungary." This Crusade devastated France from north to south.

C. Agitation around the Emperor of the Last Days

Certain charismatic leaders of millenarian movements claimed to be the emperor of the Last Days mentionned in the old prophecies. Just as there was a *translatio imperii* ("transfer of rule") between the Greeks and the Franks, the emperor of the Last Days, thought to be an oriental emperor in the Tiburtina, became in the popular imagination a Western royal figure—either a king of France or a Germanic emperor.

Charlemagne was the first (with hindsight) to play the role of the emperor of the Last Days. It was claimed that he was not dead, but merely sleeping; that he would perform the feats ascribed to Constantius in the Tiburtina. Then, the role was transferred to the German emperor, Henry IV (Heinrich IV), an adversary of Gregory VII (the prophecy of Benzo, bishop of Alba). Later still, the role was assigned to different historical figures; some were leaders of the Crusades, both the "official" Crusades and the crusades preached by the millenarians: Godfrey of Bouillon, Duke of Lower Lorraine; Raymond IV of Saint-Gilles, Count of Toulouse; the King Tafur; Count Emmerich of Leiningen, instigator of massacres against the Jews during the First Crusade; Louis VII, King of France (Second Crusade), Baldwin IX, Count of Flanders;[8] and the "Master of Hungary."

Other prophecies concerned the king of France, who it was hoped would unite Christendom, together with a messianic pope, the *pastor angelicus*. These hopes surfaced again in the sixteenth century with a nationalist twist around the historic figure of Joan of Arc.

The most astonishing millenarian expression of an actual king being assimilated with the Emperor of the Last Days is the myth of the Emperor Frederick.[9] Initially, the phenomenon was similar to what we have described. When the German emperor, Frederick I Barbarossa, died during the Third Crusade to the Holy Land in 1190, prophecies began to circulate that he was not

---

[7] Saint Louis led two crusades: the seventh (1248–54), where at Al Mansurah he lost and was taken prisoner, and the eighth (1270), where he died at Tunis.

[8] In 1204 Baldwin was proclaimed emperor of Constantinople (the Crusaders had chased the Byzantines from the city), but he died the following year. Jeanne, his daughter, succeeded him in Flanders; at the same time, Philippe Augustus, the king of France, held the county under tight control. Then, in 1224, the local and largely anti-French populace enthusiastically welcomed a mysterious figure claiming to be the resurrected or reawakened Emperor Baldwin (he claimed to have lived hidden as a hermit in the forest for some 20 years). Recognized by a segment of the local nobility, the figure was crowned Emperor of Constantinople and Thessaloniki, Count of Flanders and Hainault, in front of delirious crowds. After seven months of deceit, he was unmasked and executed (he was, in fact, a serf and had been a minstrel in the First Crusade with Baldwin). None of this stopped popular imagination from hoping that Baldwin lived on or in believing in his prompt return (Cohn, *Pursuit of the Millennium*, 90–93).

[9] Ibid., chap. 6.

dead, that he would return as the eschatological savior and liberate the Holy Sepulchre, inaugurating the millennium. In no time, the phenomenon took on a whole new dimension.

Some 30 years later, these prophecies were transferred from Barbarossa to his grandson, Frederick II. Primarily because Frederick II was a harsh critic of the church and the papacy, he was seen as an instrument of absolute punishment against a corrupt clergy and a special protector of the poor. Combined in Frederick II were the two figures of the emperor as the messiah (the emperor of the Last Days) and the *novus dux* (the master of a new spiritual brotherhood, according to Joachimite prophecy, see below, pp. 627–29), who it was believed would rule the world at the time of the Third Era.

When Frederick II died in 1250, those who had placed their hopes in him did not accept that he was dead. They claimed that he had gone into hiding, that he was both alive and not alive (*vivit et non vivit*), that he was dwelling under the volcano Etna. In the course of the following years and decades, at least four or five instances of "Frederick's" resurrection or reappearance were recorded. One in particular, in 1284, involved a megalomaniac figure, who was embraced as a king in the town of Neuss, near Cologne; he held court there and planned to convene the imperial Diet. He was finally seized and handed over to the (true) emperor, Rudolph, who had him burned at the stake as a heretic. In his struggle with the authorities, this figure received the support of the poor, like Baldwin before him. The poor believed that he had miraculously escaped the flames after his execution and that he was alive somewhere, awaiting the moment for his triumphal return. It was said that he reappeared periodically in the disguise of a pilgrim.

The hope in an imminent return of a messiah of the poor fascinated the simple German populace well into the sixteenth century. In each new emperor—Sigismund, Frederick III, Maximilian, Charles V—the poor saw a reincarnation, albeit imperfect, of Frederick II. What differentiated the Frederick myth from similar myths was its vivacity, since it survived from the thirteenth until the middle of the sixteenth century in Germany.

Fascinating and highly characteristic of the collective frame of mind at the time is that the hope of the people never fully tumbled despite these repeated letdowns: each time a "king," in whom the poor and downtrodden had placed their hope, was vanquished, the very same king was transformed into a forerunner of the next king, and hope was revived again.

D. The Flagellants

Another form of social agitation in medieval society expressed millenarianism indirectly: the flagellant movement.[10]

As early as the eleventh century a new form of penitence appeared: self-flagellation. A grim, self-inflicted punishment, it was meant as an appeasement of God's anger and an expiation of one's sins—and perhaps those of others. Self-flagellation grew in popularity and became a group and public display before long. Enthralled spectators held flagellants for holy men. For over 200 years the movement spread throughout Germany and southern Europe; it became institutionalized when brotherhoods formed (the heads of some brotherhoods referred to a "heavenly letter" setting their mission, just as Peter the Hermit and the Master of Hungary had done earlier); fixed rites were established. The movement swelled suddenly in times of war or epidemic, such as during the Black Death of 1348.

The movement escaped church control entirely in Germany and Holland, turning violent, revolutionary, anticlerical, and brazenly millenarian. The flagellants believed that they were the "select few"; they alone would accomplish the journey to the end-time. Their blood was equal

[10] Ibid., chap. 7.

in worth to the blood of Christ. Flagellations were to last 33 days or 33 years to bring about the advent of the millennium. Flagellants played a central role in the massacres of Jews: pogroms were frequently held after flagellation ceremonies. In 1360, a flagellant messiah named Konrad Schmid appeared; he elaborated a genuine doctrine. The flagellant heresy lasted until the beginning of the fifteenth century, and as late as 1415 hundreds of flagellants were being burned at the stake every year.

E. The Free Spirit Heresy

The Free Spirit heresy was not, in itself, a particularly violent or revolutionary movement, but its ideas directly influenced numerous agitations in the Middle Ages. It lasted for some five centuries, from the beginning of the thirteenth until the seventeenth century.

The mendicant Beghards and Beguines traveled from town to town crying, "bread for the love of God." They preached, often successfully, to the people, who believed that their mendicant asceticism gave them thaumaturgical powers. The Beghards had great influence over single women and widows, many of whom formed the communities of the "Beguines"; they were primarily orthodox believers, but because of their contacts with the Beghards, suspicions of heresy existed. After 1320, these movements abandoned their mendicant character and went underground, though they remained known and feared by church authorities. Among them were the Little Brothers and Sisters of the Free Spirit, Beghards and Swestrones of Bread for God's Sake, *Homines Intelligentiae* ("men of intelligence"),[11] and the Society of the Poor (known to their opponents derisively as the Turlupins).

Their doctrine appears to have been inspired by Amaury of Bène (d. 1206); it was a pantheistic doctrine with inspirations from Neoplatonism and the commentaries of John Scottus Eriugena.[12] At the beginning of the thirteenth century, the followers of Amaury, clerics at the University of Paris, were condemned to the stake (the works of John Scottus Eriugena were condemned by a council in 1225). The movement was widespread in Germany and in the north of France.

F. The English Peasants' Revolt

There were three major peasant uprisings in the fourteenth century: the peasant revolt in Flanders (1323–28), the Jacquerie in France (1358), and the peasants' uprising in England (1381). This last rebellion—which involved urban as well as peasant populations—was millenarian in nature. Its leader was John Ball. The influence of John Wycliffe is evident as well. Other millenarian movements and social agitation sprang up at universities; John Bromyard, the chancellor of Cambridge University, was one of the leaders.

G. Taborism

Taborism was a millenarian movement of a very different sort. It appeared at the beginning of the fourteenth century in Bohemia, in the wake of the Hussite revolution. John Hus was rector of the University of Prague, an ordained priest and a popular preacher. He denounced the corruption and worldliness of the clergy and formulated a direct attack on the papacy against the sale of indulgences. Like Marsilius of Padua and William of Ockham, his contemporaries, he claimed

---

[11] *Intelligentiae* refers to the mystical faculty of the soul.

[12] A ninth century philosopher and theologian, perhaps a Scottish or Irish intellectual who arrived at the court of Charles the Bald, where he translated the works of Pseudo-Dionysius into Latin (it will be recalled that these works were of Neoplatonic inspiration).

that the papacy was just a human institution, that an unworthy pope could be unseated. Hus was excommunicated in 1412, condemned by the Council of Constance in 1414, and burned at the stake on July 6, 1415.

His death provoked an enormous reaction in Bohemia. The Hussite movement radicalized. The local church became increasingly national and adopted Hussite reforms. When King Wenceslas took the defense of the Roman church, the common people of the New Town of Prague (craftspeople, weavers, blacksmiths, and the like) broke into open revolt (1419). Catholics were driven from the town, the emperor's Catholic advisors were defenestrated, and the monasteries were expropriated. Then, under pressure from the lowest strata of the population,[13] the movement radicalized even more. Before long the urban masses and peasants, destabilized by the efforts of the nobles to increase seigneurial taxes, joined in open revolt.

Dissenting priests began to organize religious communities outside the normal system of parishes. These communities soon became permanent colonies patterned on the life of the early church. The hill on which the largest of these colonies had settled was renamed Mount Tabor.[14] The so-called Taborites gained a powerful foothold in five Bohemian towns. Before long they came under threat from the central power; this radicalized their revolt further. Under Martin Huska's leadership, various preachers announced the imminence of the millennium: the events would begin in February 1420; towns and villages would burn like Sodom; all those who did not gather "on the mountain" with the Saints would perish. Any association with the authorities would amount to dealing with the Antichrist.

In March 1420 war broke out with Sigismund, king of Bohemia and emperor of Germany. A Catholic army made up of German and Hungarian soldiers invaded Bohemia. The Taborites backed the national resistance effort led by Jan Žižka. Taborite communities enjoyed a brief respite, then Žižka decided to close them down because of their internal evolution.

In fact, after declaring the coming of the millennium, and imposing a regime of communal property and brotherhood, the Taborites simply ceased all work and productive activity. Then, something happened which is common in most (if not all) communist societies: they began to practice banditry outside the community (justified by the abolition of private property); and what was worse, the Taborite leaders began to exploit the members of the community proper by creating charges and levies that were harsher than the feudal servitudes they had abolished and that had won them the favors and support of the peasants in the first place. In the end, the community was obliged to restore institutions like those of the old feudal society (craft guilds, military hierarchy, etc.).

One minority radicalized even more and established a sect known as the Bohemian Adamites; its members adhered to a combination of Taborism and the heresy of the Free Spirit. After taking refuge on an island in the River Nežárka, the last Adamite colony was attacked and massacred by a detachment of Jan Žižka's army in 1421. But the Taborites had succeeded in developing a following throughout Germany and as far away as France and Spain.

[13] For years Prague's impoverished inhabitants had grown in number due to a steady influx from rural exodus.

[14] According to a third or fourth century tradition, Mount Tabor was the "high mountain" and site of the transfiguration of Jesus (Matt. 17:1–8; Mark 9:2–8; Luke 9:28–36). It was on this "mountain" that Christ delivered his great eschatological sermon and announced his Second Coming (Mark 13:24–27).

H. The German Peasants' Wars

Peasants' wars raged in southern and western Germany, and in Thuringia, in 1524 and 1525;[15] Marxists saw in these wars the first appearance in history of the proletariat.[16] The peasants' aims were primarily political, and not particularly radical or millenarian. However, in Thuringia, under the leadership of Thomas Müntzer, their intentions did take a millenarian turn.

Müntzer (1488–1525) was a former Augustinian monk who had studied the Holy Scriptures, medieval mysticism, and humanism. He came under the influence of Taborite ideas, those of the flagellants and of the Brethren of the Free Spirit; soon he was persuaded to side with millenarianism and Anabaptism. He was an itinerant preacher and met with great success among the ordinary people in every town he passed through (Zwickau, Wittenberg, Allstedt, and so on), and from which he was systematically expelled by the local authorities and by moderate segments of the population. Finally, in Mülhausen, he put together a resolute band of followers, including workers at the copper mines, and took command of a rebel army, promising them a miraculous victory over the army of the princes (a rainbow, the symbol of the movement, appeared in the sky when Müntzer announced their pending victory). But his "rabble army" was thoroughly crushed in May 1525.

I. The "New Jerusalem" in Münster

One peculiar millenarian experience demands our attention. The Anabaptists founded a "New Jerusalem"[17] in Münster in 1534–35. This political experience presents all the fully developed features of the later totalitarian "terrors" (the Jacobin Terror, Bolshevism, Nazism); arguably, the Anabaptist terrors equalled them in horror, if not in scope.

The Anabaptist movement took hold across Germany, Switzerland, and Holland, where it was harshly repressed (the Peasants' War had stung the authorities); the brutality of reaction bolstered Anabaptists in their conviction that they were truly God's Elect of the end-times, the same who would undergo messianic suffering for the salvation of all humankind. One of their leaders, Hans Hut, a former follower of Thomas Müntzer, prophesied the Second Coming of Christ for Pentecost 1528. It was expected that at this time Christ would hand over the sword of justice to the Saints and the millennium would begin under the banner of communal property and free love.

In 1528, at Esslingen on the Neckar, the Anabaptists attempted—or intended, at any rate—to establish the kingdom of God on earth, by force of arms. Their most memorable attempt, however, was the founding of a New Jerusalem in the bishopric of Münster (Rhein-Westphalia).

The Anabaptists seized power in Münster in February 1534; for some time the government of the bishopric had been weak due to the rebellion of the craft guilds and the devastating impact of the Lutheran reform on the church. Among the leaders were Bernt Rothmann, a blacksmith's son; Bernt Knipperdollinck, a draper; and, above all, two "apostles" by the names of Jan Matthys, a baker from Haarlem, and Jan Bockelson, also known as John of Leyden (in short, foreigners from Holland, a country where the number of impoverished, unsettled workers was enormous).

---

15 Between Bohemian Taborism and the Peasants' War in Germany, other movements of social agitation sprang to life under messianic leaders who were keen to inaugurate the Third Era by fire and blood; these movements targeted members of the clergy who were "happy to cover up their tonsure" (Cohn, *Pursuit of the Millennium*, 217). Examples include the brothers Janko and Livin of Winsberg (between 1450 and 1460), Hans Bohm (1476), the "Holy Boy of Nicklashausen," and Joss Fritz, who led the "Bundschuh" uprisings in Spire from 1502 to 1517 ("Bundschuh" refers to the footwear of the peasants and calls to mind the French *sans-culotte*).

16 See Friedrich Engels, *The Peasant War in Germany* (1850), in *The Collected Works of Karl Max and Friedrich Engels*, vol. 10 (New York: International Publishers, 1978).

17 Cohn tells the story remarkably (*Pursuit of the Millennium*, 261–80).

Matthys and Bockelson were held by the saints to be the prophets Enoch and Elijah, whose coming, according to the Scriptures, would be the imminent sign of the end-times.

The rebels rallied Anabaptist sympathizers from towns near and far, who were invited to occupy houses left abandoned by the fleeing bourgeoisie. Matthys and Bockelson created a theocracy with the broader intention of founding a New Jerusalem, purified of all stain. Unwelcome inhabitants—women, children, old people—were banished pitilessly: it was mid-winter; only the "Children of God" were authorized to stay for the purpose of establishing a community based on pure love.

As the town came under attack from the bishop's army, the young "ideal society" organized. A decree suppressed the use of money and all members of the community were required to hand over their coins to the leaders. Opponents of the measure ran the risk of immediate execution. Henceforth, craftspeople were to be paid in goods, and no longer in coin; the community leadership would decide autocratically all work assignments and resource allocations. Meals were to be taken communally in the refectory. Housing was requisitioned and lodging reassigned.

The movement was now entirely in the hands of half-literates, proud of their ignorance (God had chosen uneducated men and women for the salvation of the world). They openly displayed an anti-intellectual streak; books were collected and burned on bonfires. In fact, except for the Bible, all books were forbidden. The intention was clear: to make a clean break with the past and create a new human being: every theological tradition, every interpretation of the Scriptures that was not provided by the Anabaptists themselves was abolished.

Matthys died in March 1534. Bockelson replaced him and heightened the tyranny. Claiming a special revelation from God, he changed the constitution. All temporal and spiritual powers, all public and private affairs were to be held in his personal hands, with the support of a council of 12 elders under his control. Capital punishment was meted out for ordinary crimes, as well as for lies, slander, greed, and quarrels: it was a regime of fierce despotism. All craftspeople became public employees. Sexual conduct was regulated. Sexual relations with non-Anabaptists were held to be criminal. Bockelson imposed forced marriages and, bizarrely, polygamy (though not polyandry—several women were executed for having two partners). He kept a personal harem of 15 young women. Protests and resistance were punished by death (Bockelson participated in these executions personally). Although strict Puritanism had been the initial aim, in reality the town of Münster became a place of sexual promiscuity.

Then, after another "divine" revelation, Bockelson proclaimed himself king: king of Münster, then king of the world and messiah of the Last Days.

He had a court, court officers, and a corps of gentlemen-at-arms, all richly dressed and armed. He appeared in public with a crown and scepter and wore precious jewelry to enhance his appearance. One of his wives became queen. He changed the calendar, he chose the name of every newborn child. He even struck a coin in his effigy (though money no longer played a role, in principle). At the same time that he took the wealth of the community for himself and his court, he deprived the population of its last possessions, requisitioning lodging, clothes, and food. Even as the siege on the town intensified and famine raged, the king, his court, and his guard continued to seize all available supplies.

Bockelson's emissaries managed to ignite Anabaptist rebellions in Germany, Holland, and Switzerland; but all were harshly repressed. Finally, in June 1535, the town of Münster was retaken and the majority of Anabaptists were massacred. The entire experiment had lasted little more than 18 months.

The memory of the Anabaptist rebellion in Münster remained etched in the European conscience and fed official repression of all new expressions of millenarian agitation throughout the sixteenth, seventeenth, and eighteenth centuries.

III. Millenarian Myths and Ideologies

What did the participants in these movements have in mind as they engaged in social agitation and physical violence? We find a broad range of representations running from the irrational, spontaneous myth to the highly developed intellectual doctrine.

A. Jews, Clerics, Nobles, and the Rich

Whether during the Crusades or in the thrall of expectation of an emperor, or simply at the end of a flagellation ritual, the ensuing massacres targeted what René Girard might call well-identified "categories of victims": *the Jews (or Muslims), the clerics, the nobles,* and *the rich.*

Already in the *Song of Roland* at the end of the tenth century, the extermination of infidels—Jews and Muslims—was seen to be normal: "The Emperor has taken Saragossa. A thousand Franks are sent to search thoroughly the town, the mosques and synagogues. With iron hammers and axes they smash the images and all the idols; henceforth there will be no place there for spells or sorceries. The King believes in god, he desires to serve him. His bishops bless the water and the heathen are brought to the baptistery. If any one of them resists Charlemagne, the King has him hanged or burnt to death or slain with the sword."[18]

The conviction was held (by the "moderate" Saint Bernard of Clairvaux just as much as by anyone else) that the Saracens, their successors the Turks, and the Jews (all seen as related peoples) made up the armies of the Antichrist assembled for the last battle. One tradition claimed that the Antichrist would be a Jew from the tribe of Dan. Jews were increasingly portrayed as demons and represented in the iconography as horned devils. Unsurprisingly, they were held responsible for the Black Death of 1348: "these devils must have introduced into the water-supply a poison concocted of spiders, frogs, lizards, or other fantastical animals of the underworld."[19]

Massacres were perpetrated against regular and secular clergy as well. As far as the millenarian preachers were concerned, clerics had benefited excessively from recent economic developments, thereby excluding themselves from the army of the righteous who were called to participate in Christ's triumphant victory. The clergy came to be seen as a demonic brotherhood, the beast of the Apocalypse, wholly dedicated to a *vita animalis,* the life of the flesh, cut off from the life of the spirit. Centuries before Luther, the pope was identified with the Antichrist. Rome was the modern Babylon. A hatred of an enriched, corrupt clergy was also found among heretics like the Cathars, expressed more moderately; it could also be found within the church itself: the birth of the mendicant orders (Dominicans and Franciscans) can be explained as a reaction to the accumulation of wealth by the clergy and an attempt to return to the purity of the early church. The millenarians also attacked the nobles who were suspected of putting their political aspirations before the genuine eschatological aims of the Crusades.

Thus, it was common to combine the figures of the Jew, the cleric, and the noble into a single diabolical figure: the rich person (*dives*), systematically denounced as an egoist, a person without morals, a lecher. There is remarkable continuity between these medieval passions and the modern denunciations of the Jew by the Nazis and "capitalism" and the "bourgeoisie" by revolutionary socialists.

---

[18] Ibid., 57.

[19] Ibid., 69. See also René Girard, *The Scapegoat* (Baltimore: John Hopkins University Press, 1986), chap. 1.

B. Joachim of Flora

Joachim of Flora was born ca. 1135 in Calabria. He made a pilgrimage to the Holy Land, after which he became a Cistercian monk. But he soon left the order, probably because he aspired to a more perfect monastic life. He founded a new monastery, Saint John of Fiore, which soon became an order in its own right. When Joachim died in 1202, the order had 12 establishments. He is the author of a *Liber concordiae Novi ac Veteris Testamenti* (Harmony of the Old and New Testaments), an *Expositio in Apocalipsim* (Exposition of the Book of Revelation), a *Psalterium decem cordarum* (Psaltery of ten strings), and a treatise on the four Gospels. He also wrote *Preface,* an introduction to his works and his spiritual testament. Among other writings attributed to him is *The Figurae.* Though some of his followers broke with the church, Joachim of Flora insisted on his orthodoxy. He was protected by three popes and held to be a holy man in his lifetime. He was officially beatified.

Joachim's principal idea is that human life in this world passes through three states, corresponding to three ages and the three persons of the Trinity:

- *The age of the Father,* under the sign of natural law and Mosaic law. This is the age "before grace," a time of laity and marriage, lasting from the Creation until the coming of Christ.
- *The age of the Son,* under the doctrinal authority of "the Eternal Gospel," "the time of grace." This age is under the rule of the *ordo clericorum,* the order of secular clergy, who live between the flesh and the spirit; it will last from the Incarnation until a rapidly approaching date (around the year 1300).
- Finally, *the age of the Spirit,* lasting until the end of time. A "time of expectation of the end," "of more grace," "of the spiritual intelligence of the Scriptures," it is under the authority of the *ordo monachorum,* the order of the monks, devoted to the "freedom of contemplation"; they are dedicated to deciphering the totality of the divine message, while the church remains "under the veil of the letter." The "age of the Spirit" will bring "the hour of spiritual understanding and the manifest vision of God."

Reflecting a certain "ternarist" systematicism, which perhaps influenced Auguste Comte, Louis de Bonald, or Hegel when conceiving their own philosophical systems, Joachim wrote in his *Concordia:*

> The first state was the state of science, the second, the state of wisdom, and the third will be the state of plenitude of intelligence. The first, the state of servitude of slaves; the second, the state of filial dependence; the third, the state of freedom. The first state proceeded under the whip; the second, under the sign of action; the third, under the sign of contemplation. Fear characterized the first state; faith, the second; charity will mark the third. The first state was the age of slaves; the second the age of free men; the third will be the age of friends. The first state was the age of old men; the second, the time of young men; the third will be the time of children.[20] The first was under the stars of heaven; the second, at dawn; the third will be the time of broad daylight. The first was winter; the second, spring; the third will be the time of summer. The first brought nettles; the second brought roses; the third will bring lilies. The first produced grass; the second produced ears of grain; and the third will provide wheat. The first is comparable to water; the second to wine; the third to oil.[21]

[20] The maturation of the world takes place in reverse order to the maturation of the individual: it is an apparent regression. But, the *parvuli* (the children of God) will prevail over the powerful and the prosperous.

[21] Joachim of Flora, quoted in Delumeau, *History of Paradise,* 48.

Thus, in a clean break with Augustine's theology of history, Joachim of Flora imagines a divine doctrine in three phases, each revealing divine mysteries with increasing clarity. An understanding of the correspondences between the Old and New Testaments—the aim of Joachim's *Concordance*—enables the Christian to anticipate, to an extent at any rate, the age of the Spirit. Each age has a beginning (*initiatio*), an apogee (*fructificatio*), and an end (*consumatio*); the end of each phase overlaps with the start of the next. Just as the first age lasted 42 generations (according to the genealogy of Christ in Matt. 1:1–17), the second will also last 42 generations and will begin (if each generation lasts 30 years) around 1260. The transition period will begin as early as 1200.

This will not be a peaceful age. Joachim attempts to conciliate the Trinitarian model of the three ages and the classical theory of the cosmic "week."[22] He posits that the end of the second age will overlap with the sixth millennium of history, and the third with the seventh millennium, that is, the millennium proper. The book of Revelation announces that the passage from one millennium to the next will be a time of great conflict and crisis, characterized by the forcible conversion of the Jews, but above all by the advent of a king, the Antichrist, who will lead the forces of evil, and against whom it will be necessary to wrestle until the final victory.

Then the "eternal Gospel" will surpass the "Gospel according to the letter" as foretold in the book of Revelation (14:6).[23] There will be no further need for an interpretative effort of the Scriptures, which until now has been the particular province of the clergy. Contemplation of the naked truth will enable all "to dance for joy." There will be no need for a pope. John will succeed Peter as Solomon succeeded David.

> Oh pain! Today we are witness to the collapse of clerical life in flesh and blood, the breakdown of these men whose custom it was to shine their light on the people. Nothing in them appears spiritual any longer, nothing is directed towards the heavens as before. Almost everything has become lewd, carnal, flesh and blood, a weakening of the spirit. Where are the disputes today? Where the scandals? Where the fracas? Where the greed? Where the enmity, if not in the Church of the priests? Did they not have a duty to provide the people assembled at their feet with the simplicity of their example. In a word, we behold the crashing of the stars of heaven to earth in great number,[24] a fall provoked either by heretical deprivation, or a worse fall, the sin of the flesh, which is for the most part.[25]

So, the *institution itself must be superseded* (an old messianic theme, see above, pp. 419–21). Henceforth, monks, not the secular clergy, will govern the world.

This is a return of sorts to the theory of the *ordines* in the Early Middle Ages; more generally, it is a reaction to the Papal Revolution. Since the aim of the revolution was to christianize the world, it accepted a compromise with it. The church grew rich, and it started to confuse worldly and spiritual concerns. If monks take over the leadership of the church, they will be able to return it to its original vocation. Such an order, devoted entirely to contemplation, will come under a *novus dux*, a new supreme master; 12 patriarchs will stand up for the task of converting the Jews.

But the church rejected this doctrine. In a sense, Joachim's glorification of the age of the Spirit led somehow to a weakening of Christ's person and mission, which in the Joachimite perspective was no longer the end but a mere phase in the process of salvation, situated between John the Baptist and Elijah; in this perspective, Christ's return only precedes the coming of the Third

---

22 See above, pp. 444–45.

23 "Then I saw another angel flying in midheaven, with an eternal gospel to proclaim to those who dwell on earth, to every nation and tribe and tongue and people."

24 An allusion to Revelation 8:12.

25 Quoted in Delumeau, *History of Paradise*, 50–51.

Age. Although Joachim made no personal appeal for a holy war, his doctrine, in fact, provided arguments for those rejecting the new political order established by the papacy and Christian kingdoms. Joachimite thought reconnected with the prophetic eschatology of the Bible and, in so doing, represented a "reaction to a scouring of Augustine from eschatology."[26]

C. Franciscan "Spirituals"

Joachim's doctrine attracted no more than a small following during his lifetime and in the half-century after his death (first half of the thirteenth century). But its later success came from the fact that some Franciscans—one of the two major and recently established mendicant orders—adopted it as its quasi-official doctrine.

Created in 1210 by Saint Francis of Assisi—the *Poverello*—the Order of Friars Minor (or Franciscans, as they were also known) pursued an ideal of poverty and detachment from the world. Paradoxically, the order was so successful that it rapidly acquired enormous wealth and great power. Some of the Franciscans rejected this train of events; this is why they were called the "Spirituals." The thirteenth and fourteenth centuries became a theater of conflict between the Spirituals, on the one hand, and the leaders of the order and the papacy, on the other.

The Spirituals published Joachimite writings that until then had remained in the shadows; they added their own commentaries and contributed apocryphal supplements. The new prophecies embodied the belief that the spiritual brotherhood, imagined by Joachim as the ruling authority to come in the Third Era, was incarnated in the Franciscan order. The Franciscan Spirituals grew into a powerful force, in particular in Italy and Germany. In Germany they played a decisive role in shaping the myth of Emperor Frederick.

In 1356, at the time of the Battle of Poitiers (the second defeat of the Kingdom of France in its wars with the Kingdom of England), Jean de Roquetaillade, a French Franciscan, published a treatise titled *Vade mecum in tribulatione* (Guide for enduring tribulations). His text expresses various egalitarian social ideas close to core millenarian premises. Thus, we see how millenarianism evolved into a revolutionary social theory. Jean de Roquetaillade says that the great and worthy persons of this world failed their calling: the kingdom is humbled. A period of disorder will ensue. Antichrists will appear in the East and the West. But the people will rise up. It will chasten the clergy. A greater reformer, *reparator orbis,* will ascend to Peter's throne and the king of France will become emperor of the West. Together they will chase the Muslims and Tartars from Europe, suppress all heresy, and convert the infidels.

D. The Myth of the Emperor of the Last Days

The myth of Emperor Frederick was nourished by texts such as the political pamphlet *Gamaleon* (published in 1409 or 1429),[27] a fifteenth century pamphlet titled the *Reform of Sigismund* (published in 1439),[28] and the strange and disturbing book known as the *Book of One Hundred Chapters,* considered the first grand manifesto of German nationalism. This anonymous work dates from the early sixteenth century (its author is simply called the "Revolutionary from the Upper Rhineland"). It picks up the strands of the earlier apocalyptic tradition and pushes them to the limit.

---

[26] Henry Mottu, quoted in ibid., 46.

[27] The text glorifies Frederick the German emperor as the one who will liberate his country from pontifical domination, Italy, and Latinization, and who will go on to rule the world.

[28] It was a defense of an egalitarian social system and a harsh criticism of "capitalist" forms of the economy.

In a special revelation from heaven transmitted by the archangel Gabriel, the author learns that the world will be renewed by a brotherhood of pious laymen, wearing a yellow cross as their distinctive sign. Their leader will be the Emperor Frederick, the "Emperor of the Black Forest." He will be more than the emperor of the Last Days; he will be the messiah of the Apocalypse; he will establish a vast empire and reign 1,000 years.

But first, it will be necessary to eliminate all sinners. This will be the work of a new chivalrous order, the Brotherhood of the Yellow Cross. It will destroy Babylon and bend the world to the emperor's law. The massacre of all sinners will be viewed as a most holy act: "Soon we will drink blood instead of wine." Among the victims will be the emperor Maximilian and with him all the rich who thirst after *Avaritia* and *Luxuria,* including the clergy, who will have to be massacred at the rate of 2,300 priests a day for four and a half years ("Redouble your efforts. Kill them all from the pope to the novice!"), not to forget the usurers and traders. During the millennium all forms of capitalism and private property will be abolished. Property and goods will be held in common under the discretionary leadership of the emperor, who will control everything and punish the slightest deviation. "Pious Christians," that is, ordinary people, will be the stalwarts of the task.

In the main, these people will be *German*—this is where the author's social concerns take a radical, nationalist twist. For the revolutionary of the Upper Rhineland, the new millenarian society will simply restore the *early Germanic society* that Rome and the papacy had destroyed. The first men, from Adam down to Japhet (Abraham's son thought to be the ancestor of all Europeans), and their descendants until the tower of Babel, were all Germans: Germans, and not Jews, were the chosen people; German, and not Hebrew, was the first language. Once upon a time, a vast empire extended throughout Europe. It was a brotherly society without private property or commerce, living under a code of law known as the "Statutes of Trier," a law older and greater than the Decalogue of Moses.

This former Germanic empire was destroyed by Rome, which imposed the ideas of private property (*mine* and *yours*) inscribed in the codes of Roman and canon law.[29] Latin peoples were not natives of Europe; they were from Asia Minor and came to Europe as slaves. It is, therefore, necessary to restore the earlier German empire on the pillars of the statutes of Trier and vanquish the neighboring Latin peoples; this will be the work of Emperor Frederick. It will also be necessary to restore the early Christian religion, freed of its Jewish influences; the new capital will be Mainz, not Rome, and the new head will be the Emperor Frederick, not the pope. Frederick will be revered like a god. Spearheading this action will be a purely German, plebeian aristocracy.[30]

E. The Ideology of the Free Spirit

The heresy of the Free Spirit is known through polemical writings against the sect and through court records and diverse witness statements; we also know it through three works by former members: a fourteenth century work titled *Schwester Katrei* (Sister Catherine), a list of articles of faith discovered in a hermit's hut, and the *Mirror of Simple Souls* by Marguerite Porete, burned at the stake for heresy in 1310.

The doctrine of the Free Spirit changed very little over the five centuries of its existence. Its inspiration came from Neoplatonism, but it expunged the Christianizing elements in it developed by Pseudo-Dionysius and John Scottus Eriugena. Pantheism was restored to its full value. "God is all that is. God is in every stone and in every limb of the human body as surely as in the

[29] Roman law was introduced to Germany later and in more forced fashion than in the Latin countries.

[30] Cohn, *Pursuit of the Millennium,* stresses the astonishing proximity of this thinking with the German nationalists of the nineteenth and twentieth centuries and Nazism. See also Leon Poliakov, *The Aryan Myth* (New York: Plume Books, 1977), 118 and following.

Eucharistic bread." At the end of time, no emanation of God will remain, nothing will exist in separateness. Everything will return to God. Even the persons of the Trinity will be submerged in the undifferentiated Oneness.

Amaury of Bene wrote, "all things are one because whatever is, is God." One of his followers claimed when he was sentenced to die that he could not be "consumed by fire nor tormented by torture, for in so far as he was, he was God." Others claimed that they were "Christ and the Holy Spirit," superseding the idea of a single Incarnation. God the Father incarnated himself in Abraham and the other patriarchs; Christ the Son incarnated himself in Jesus of Nazareth. Now the time of the Third Age of history is come when the Holy Spirit will incarnate itself: the Amauricians claimed to be the first in whom the Holy Spirit would incarnate. Thus, they laid claim to being the original "spirituals." The Incarnation would spread and each would claim, with the words of Christ, "I am the Holy Spirit, and before Abraham was, I am." The Amauricians shared some of the earlier millenarian ideas as well; for example, they believed in the myth of the last emperor (for them, Philip Augustus was the last emperor; Amaury had been a close associate of Philip's son, the future Louis VIII). They also believed that the pope was the Antichrist.

The one true sin was to fail to recognize one's own divine origin. Most people committed this sin; only the elite of spirituals escaped it. The "perfects" ranked themselves above the saints, the angels, the Virgin, and even Christ. Some claimed to surpass even God. Devotees believed themselves completely transformed and claimed miraculous, thaumaturgical powers.

Above all, and this is what interests us in the context of political agitation, the Amauricians achieved a sort of *total amoralism*. Amoralism (i.e., antinomianism or anomism) was the dominant feature of the Free Spirit tradition, irrespective of its subsequent expression in other sects. Around 1230, Willem Cornelis claimed that voluntary poverty would wash away all sins. So, the poor were free to fornicate without sin. Other texts assert:

"He who recognizes that God does all things in him, he shall not sin. For he must not attribute to himself, but to God, all that he does."

"A man who has a conscience is himself Devil and hell and purgatory, tormenting himself. He who is free in spirit escapes from all these things."

"Nothing is sin except what is thought of as sin."

"One can be so united with God that whatever one may do one cannot sin."

"I belong to the Liberty of Nature, and all that my nature desires I satisfy.... I am a natural man."

"The free man is quite right to do whatever gives him pleasure."[31]

So followers could live in luxury like the noble *dives,* the cleric or the Jew, the very same people they had rebuked earlier as diabolical. In fact, the sect rejected all normal forms of social relations.

> When a man has truly reached the great and high knowledge he is no longer bound to observe any law or any command, for he has become one with God. God created all things to serve such a person, and all that God ever created is the property of such a man.... He shall take from all creatures as much as his nature desires and craves, and shall have no scruples of conscience about it, for all created things are his property.... A man who all heaven serves, all people and creatures are indeed obliged to serve and to obey; and if any disobeys, it alone is guilty.[32]

---

[31] Texts of various origins are cited in Cohn, *Pursuit of the Millennium,* 168.

[32] Ibid., 169.

By using all created things, these believers, who had "become God," drove "all things up to their first Origin." Women, like cattle, were created for the use of human beings. The sexual act itself had a transcendental, quasi-mystical value; it was regarded as a veritable sacrament, a "Christerie." It was said of adultery, "till acted that so-called sin, thou art not delivered from the power of sin."

The brethren of the Free Spirit had total contempt for private property. In 1317 the bishop of Strasbourg said about them, "They believe that all things are common, whence they conclude that theft is lawful for them." Johann Hartmann said, "The truly free man is king and lord of all creatures. All things belong to him, and he has the right to use whatever pleases him. If any one tries to prevent him, the free man may kill him and take his goods." Something given to an adept is "transmitted to Eternity"; if something is returned to its owner, it constitutes a regression "from the eternal to the temporal."[33]

F. From Taborite Eschatology to Anabaptism: The Ideology of Egalitarian Millenarianism

Toward the end of the Middle Ages, the ideologies of revolutionary prophets began to evolve significantly even within the millenarian framework itself. The emphasis changed from the Savior King to the egalitarianism hoped for in the New Jerusalem. In Norman Cohn's telling, this change resulted from a merging of Judeo-Christian messianic and apocalyptic themes with Greco-Roman myths from the Golden Age, giving rise to genuine *anarcho-communism:* anarchy because visionaries extolled the elimination of all institutions: clergy, state, social orders; and communism because the movement vowed to eliminate all private property and to achieve a community of goods.

1. *Egalitarian Nature*

At the same time that the Roman-canonic tradition was working to achieve a synthesis of legal and political ideas between Greco-Roman civism and Judeo-Christian morality, the opponents of the medieval feudal order were spontaneously, uncritically, and unconsciously working toward a retrospective fusion of Greco-Roman and biblical myths of an ideal age without private property, division of labor, wealth, or poverty. The Golden Age of the Greeks and Romans were combined and confounded with the earthly paradise of the Bible and the millennium it was intended to bring about. The result was a new, absolutely *unique* mythology, which would suffuse a discourse of discontent throughout the subsequent history of the West, from the utopias of the classical period to modern theories of revolution.

In parts 1 and 2 above, devoted to Greece and Rome, we quoted a number of authors (Hesiod, Aratus, Empedocles, Virgil, and so on) who described a Golden Age of a bygone time or—with the eternal return of the Great Year—of a time yet to come. Other texts proclaim the communistic practices of this earlier humankind: Ovid said that, in the Golden Age of Saturn, "the land... was once common to all, as the light of the sun... and the air" (*Metamorphosis* 1.135); Gnaeus Pompeius Trogus (a contemporary of Virgil) claimed that the "Aborigines" (the first inhabitants of Italy) held everything in common; Lucius (second century AD), contrasting the bliss of the Golden Age with the sadness of his present, said that human unhappiness was

[33] Ibid., 172. The amoralism and anti-institutionalism of the heresy of the Free Spirit evokes the ancient Cynics, and more recently various Marxist, Freudo-Marxist, and Leftist movements. There appears to be an intellectual link between an approach designed to bring about a radical social revolution and an effort on one's own behalf to become free of all moral constraint. Social institutions and moral norms are, apparently, understood indistinctly as arbitrary and irrational cultural realities of a fundamentally oppressive nature.

exacerbated by the spectacle of wealth inflicted by the rich on the poor (Letter 1); Diodorus Siculus recorded the myth of the Islands of the Blessed, whose inhabitants owned no property (in fact, the sun shone equally for all, an old Stoic theme from Cleanthes's *Hymn to Zeus*); and, finally, Epiphanes wrote of the "sect of the Carpocrats," who were against private property and a sense of *mine* and *yours*.

As early as the third century, patristic exegesis made the connection between the Stoic idea of the original equality of humankind and the biblical description of earthly paradise (Cyprian of Carthage, Ambrose of Milan, e.g.).

One text, which advocates the community of property as the norm, deserves attention because it is found in Gratian's *Decretum* and accordingly belongs to the official legal doctrine of the church. By this token, it was quoted by theologians, religious thinkers, and social critics throughout the history of Christianity. It is, nevertheless, an apocryphal text, falsely attributed to Pope Clement I, which found its way into the *Corpus iuris canonici* by an unusual set of circumstances, according to Cohn.

There are many apocryphal texts for Pope Clement I, a first century pope and thus a direct disciple of Peter. Around 265 AD the following speech was attributed to him (further amended a century later):

> For the use of all things that are in this world ought to have been common to all men, but through injustice one man says this is his, and another says that is his, and so division is created amongst mortals. In short, a very wise Greek, knowing these things to be so, says that all things should be in common among friends. And unquestionably, amongst "all things" spouses are included. He also says, just as the air cannot be divided up, nor the splendor of the sun, so the other things which are given in this world to be held in common by all ought not to be divided up, but really ought to be held in common.[34]

When, much later (ca. 850 AD), Pseudo-Isodore wrote the false decretals (see above, pp. 483–84), he included five epistles of Pope Clement, all apocryphal, three forged. The fifth, however, was not wholly invented, as it was based on the above-quoted text; it also added a commentary with an allusion to the alleged communism of the early Christian community according to chapter 4 of the Acts of the Apostles (see above, pp. 440–41).

Because Gratian believed in the authenticity of Clement's epistles, he included them in his *Decretum* (except for the one relating to free love), which is how it became a legal norm for the church until the sixteenth century, at which time the apocryphal nature of the false decretals was finally admitted. Theologians and canonists came to realize that the doctrine was essentially Stoic and not biblical.

2. *Bromyard and Ball*

From this period on, even in official circles, the Last Judgment was understood as essentially the *revenge of the poor*. In his description of the Last Judgment, included in his "guide for preachers," John Bromyard, the chancellor of the University of Cambridge, painted the following picture. Rich and poor debate before Christ, who sits in judgment; the poor exclaim, "[The lords] were served three or four courses out of our [the poor's] goods, which they took from us [while] we hungered and thirsted and were afflicted with cold and nakedness. And those robbers yonder gave not our own goods to us when we were in want, neither did they feed or clothe us out of them.... Their satiety was our famine; their merriment was our wretchedness.... Their

[34] Ibid., 184.

feasts, delectations, pomps, vanities, excesses and superfluities were our fastings, penalties, wants, calamities and spoliation."[35] Bromyard concludes, "Without a doubt, the just Judge will do justice to those clamouring thus!"[36]

It was only natural that such ideas were espoused by the agitators in a context of violent social troubles. About the time of the English Peasant War in 1381, the preacher John Ball says:

> And if we are all descended from one father and one mother, Adam and Eve, how can the lords say or prove that they are more lords than we are—save that they make us dig and till the ground so that they can squander what we produce? They are clad in velvet and satin, set off with squirrel fur, while we are dressed in poor cloth. They have wines and spices and fine bread, and we have only rye and spoilt flour and straw, and only water to drink. They have beautiful residences and manors, while we have the trouble and the work, always in the fields under rain and snow. But it is from us and our labour that everything comes with which they maintain their pomp.... Good folk, things cannot go well in England nor ever shall until all things are in common and there is neither villain nor noble, but all of us are of one condition.[37]

In another sermon, Ball quotes the parable of the wheat and the tares (Matt. 13:24–30, 36–43):

> He who sows the good seed is the Son of man; the field is the world, and the good seed means the sons of the kingdom; the weeds are the sons of the evil one, and the enemy who sowed them is the devil; the harvest is the close of the age, and the reapers are angels. Just as the weeds are gathered and burned with fire, so will it be at the close of the age. The Son of man will send his angels, and they will gather out of his kingdom all causes of sin and all evildoers, and throw them into the furnace of fire; there men will weep and gnash their teeth. Then the righteous will shine like the sun in the kingdom of their Father. He who has ears, let him hear.

Ball adds that this prophecy will soon be fulfilled. The poor, the righteous of the Gospel, must take up arms.

3. *The Taborites*

For the Taborites the millennium will be *anarcho-communistic*. All rents, taxes, and dues will be abolished; there will be no human authority in any form. The church will disappear; the sacrament will no longer be necessary. Illness and death will be unknown. Women will conceive without carnal knowledge and give birth without pain. In short, the millennium will restore the original Czech community described 300 years earlier by Cosmos of Prague, Bohemia's first historian:

> Like the radiance of the sun, or the wetness of the water, so the ploughed fields and the pastures, yea even the very marriages, were all in common.... For after the fashion of animals they entered on matings for a single night.... Nor did anyone know how to say "Mine,"

[35] Ibid., 192.

[36] Here we can see that theology—pastoral theology, at any rate—lacked the appropriate intellectual and analytical tools to understand the causes of economic development in the Middle Ages. It gave authority to the idea of a "zero-sum" economy involving equal or unequal sharing of scarce goods of natural origin only. Thus, this theology provided the basic arguments for simplistic and destructive political policies (against these ideas, it is possible to appreciate the depth of Aquinas's own thinking; he pursued passionately whatever bits and pieces of economic thought he could glean from classical authors and drew profit from the ideas and experience of the bankers and merchants of his time).

[37] Cohn, *Pursuit of the Millennium*, 189.

> but, as in the monastic life, they called whatever they had "Ours," with tongue and heart and in their deeds. There were no bolts to their shacks, they did not shut their doors against the needy, because there existed neither thief nor robber nor poor man.... But alas! They exchange prosperity for its opposite, and communal for private property...because the passion for possessing burns in them more fiercely than the fires of Etna.[38]

Thus, the myth takes on nationalist hues (like those of the Revolutionary of the Upper Rhineland somewhat later).

As for the Adamites, they saw themselves as the saints of the Last Days. They indulged in sexual promiscuity, lived almost continuously naked, dancing around the fire, singing hymns, claiming to live in the same state of innocence as Adam and Eve before the Fall.

4. *Thomas Müntzer*

Müntzer's mysticism is close to that of the followers of the Free Spirit: the person whose soul has been stripped naked by suffering "becomes God," and such a person can attain eschatological ends using any means; he or she will never be gripped by doubt. Through his contacts with Niklas Storch, another preacher who had spent time in Bohemia, Müntzer came under the influence of Taborite millenarianism. However, an important psychological parameter intervened as well. Müntzer was especially attracted to violence. He spoke complacently of the massacres recorded in the Bible, massacres and genocides perpetrated by prophets and kings in person.

For example, Elijah's massacre of the priests of Baal (1 Kings 18:40: Elijah ordered the people to seize the prophets of Baal by the hundreds and to butcher them all); or the massacre of the sons of Ahab by Jehu (2 Kings 10:1–11: the 70 sons of King Ahab were slaughtered and decapitated, then for good measure another 42 princes were murdered (verses 12–13), followed by a few hundred more priests of Baal later (verses 18–27). The Elect of Müntzer's time were expected to walk in the footsteps of these biblical assassins.

Müntzer's pamphlets grew increasingly violent, the more so when he realized that the reformed princes would not provide support and that he had become the target of Luther's criticism. Then he called his followers to a *holy war:*

> I tell you, if you will not suffer for God's sake, then you must be the Devil's martyrs. So take care! Don't be so disheartened, supine, don't fawn upon the perverse visionaries, the godless scoundrels! Start and fight the Lord's fight! It's high time. Keep all your brethren to it, so that they don't mock the divine testimony, otherwise they must all be destroyed. All Germany, France, and Italy on the alert....
>
> If there are but three of you who, trusting in God, seek only his name and honour, you will not fear a hundred thousand.
>
> Now go at them, and at them, and at them! It is time. The scoundrels are as dispirited as dogs.... It is very, very necessary, beyond measure necessary.... Take no notice of the lamentations of the godless! They will beg you in such a friendly way, and whine and cry like children. Don't be moved to pity.... Stir up people in villages and towns....
>
> At them, at them, while the fire is hot! Don't let your sword get cold! Don't let it go lame! Hammer cling, clang on Nimrod's anvil![39] Throw their tower to the ground! So long as they

---

[38] Ibid., 204.

[39] Nimrod (Gen. 10:8–10; 1 Chron. 1:10), "the first on earth to be a mighty man," was the king of Babel, later identified as the diabolical city of Babylon. In the mythology of the egalitarian millenarians, Nimrod, as the first builder of cities, was the quintessential archenemy because he destroyed humanity's primitive state of nature by introducing private property and class distinctions in society.

> are alive you will never shake off the fear of men. One can't speak to you about God so long as they are reigning over you. At them!, at them, while you have daylight! God goes ahead of you, so follow, follow![40]

5. *The Anabaptists*

The 40 or so sects that formed Anabaptism shared several ideas in common. They aspired to establish brotherly love on earth without institutions: no vast church, no state. The necessary condition for this is that people become "Saints"; this requires a second baptism (the root of the word "Anabaptism"). Again, the doctrine is exacerbated anarcho-communism. Private property appeared after the Fall.

> Shortly after that, Nimrod began to rule and then whoever could manage it got the better of the other. And they started dividing the world up and squabbling about property. Then *Mine and Yours* began. In the end people became so wild, they were just like wild beasts. Each wanted to be finer and better than the other, in fact wanted to be his master. Yet God had made all things common, as today still we can enjoy air, fire, rain and sun in common, and whatever else some thieving, tyrannical man cannot get hold of and keep for himself.[41]

These same ideas are of course found in the New Jerusalem in Münster. In October 1534, Rothmann produced a propaganda pamphlet in which he wrote:

> Amongst us God—to whom be eternal praise and thanks—has restored community, as it was in the beginning and as befits the Saints of God. We hope too that amongst us community is as vigorous and glorious, and is by God's grace observed with as pure a heart, as at any time before. For not only have we put all our belongings into a common pool under the care of deacons, and live from it according to our needs: we praise God through Christ with one heart and mind and are eager to help one another with every kind of service. And accordingly, everything which has served the purposes of selfseeking and private property, such as buying and selling, working for money, taking interest and practicing usury—even at the expense of unbelievers—or eating and drinking the sweat of the poor (that is, making one's own people and fellow-creatures work so that one can grow fat) and indeed everything which offends against love—all such things are abolished amongst us by the power of love and community. And knowing that God now desires to abolish such abominations, we would die rather than turn to them. We know that such sacrifices are pleasing to the Lord. And indeed no Christian or Saint can satisfy God if he does not live in such community or at least desire with all his heart to live in it.[42]

Bockelson, the king of Münster and the world, addressed the populace in the following terms:

> In like manner was David, a humble shepherd, anointed by the prophet, at God's command, as King of Israel. God often acts in this way; and whoever resists the will of God calls down God's wrath upon himself. Now I am given power over all nations of the earth, and the right to use the sword to the confusion of the wicked and in defence of the righteous. So let none in this town stain himself with crime or resist the will of God, or else he shall without delay be put to death with the sword.[43]

---

[40] Cohn, *Pursuit of the Millennium*, 237–38. The violence of tone in these exhortations is unmistakable. Luther's speech was not much different at this time. This style was cultivated in Germany until Marx and beyond.

[41] Ibid., 248.

[42] Ibid., 256.

[43] Ibid., 262.

And because there were murmurs in the crowd at these words, Bockelson continued: "Shame on you that murmur against the ordinance of the Heavenly Father! Though you were all to join together to oppose me, I shall still reign, despite you, not only over this town but over the whole world, for the Father will have it so; and my kingdom which begins now shall endure and know no downfall!"[44]

At the end of 1534, Rothmann produced two more pamphlets: *Restitution* and *Announcement of Vengeance*. He divided history into three ages: (1) the age of sin, beginning at Creation and culminating in the Flood; (2) the age of persecution and the cross, lasting until Rothman's present; and, in Rothmann's time, (3) the age of vengeance and the triumph of the saints. God enthroned a new David, John of Leyden. From now on, all Old Testament messianic prophecies would be fulfilled in Münster where universal love prevailed. But this new kingdom of God must reach throughout the world, and for this it must conquer the whole world and remove the wicked from its bosom.

It should be noted that many revolutionary themes, which appear in modern times in various expressions of Socialism, Marxism, Fascism, and Nazism, are already present in the writings of the millenarians, who seemingly influenced later theories unbeknownst to these modern authors. The very idea that there are great scansions of history—for example, the Marxist phases: primitive communism, feudalism, capitalism, and finally socialism when history ceases altogether—stands out clearly in the millenarian logic of time. As for the theme of violent revolution, justified because it will be the last and will inaugurate a final reign of justice and brotherhood, it too is an apocalyptic theme.

Of course, these analogies are by no means coincidental. At the dawn of the modern era, the West succeeded in fusing Greco-Roman and biblical traditions. However, the synthesis was imperfect and each family of ideas had its own conception of the synthesis. Some, in the line of the Papal Revolution, pursued the ideal of a regular improvement of the world: its driving force was the inner conversion of hearts, personal effort, and individual responsibility, supported by the tools of reason, science, and law. Others denied individual responsibility and designated a scapegoat for the evil in the world following in the footsteps of prerational and sacrificial thinking; they lived in the hope of an immediate coming of the millennium, even at the expense of a universal bloodbath.

It seems that the rest of the history of political ideas up to the modern era and contemporary times is, somehow, structured by this antagonism. The first family of ideas evolved into what is known as the "liberal democratic tradition." The second evolved into its radical adversaries: the "right" and the "left," unconscious millenarians themselves, who place their hope in new transcendent realities—the laws of history, the laws of race, and the destiny of nations—rather than in God like the Christians of the Middle Ages.

[44] Ibid., 262.

Selected Works Cited

Abelard, Peter. *Ethical Writings, Ethics.* Trans. Paul Vincent Spade. Cambridge, MA: Hackett, 1995.

Ambrose. *De officiis ministorum* [On the duties of the clergy]. Translated by H. de Romestin, E. de Romestin, and H. T. F. Duckworth. In *Nicene and Post-Nicene Fathers,* 2nd ser., vol. 10, edited by Philip Schaff and Henry Wace. Buffalo: Christian Literature Publishing, 1896.

Amidon, Philip R., S.J., trans. *The Church History of Rufinus of Aquileia, Books 10 and 11.* New York: Oxford University Press, 1997.

Aquinas, Thomas. *La loi nouvelle.* Translated by J. Tonneau. Paris: Éditions du Cerf, 1981.

———. *Somme théologique.* Vol. 3, *Prima pars.* Ed. Jean-Marie Aubert. Paris: Édition du Cerf, 1993.

———. *Summa theologica: La justice.* Edited by C. Spicq. Paris: Desclée et Cie, 1947.

———. *The Summa Theologica of St. Thomas Aquinas.* 2nd and rev. ed. 1920. Trans. Fathers of the English Dominican Province.

———. *The Summa Theologica of St. Thomas Aquinas.* Online ed., 2008 by Kevin Knight with corrections. Available at www.newadvent.org/summa.

———. *Summa theologica curia fratrum eiusdem Ordinis.* 5 vols. Salamanca: Bibliotecca de autores cristianos, 1964.

Arendt, Hannah. *The Origins of Totalitarianism.* 1948. Reprint, New York: Schocken Books, 2004.

Aristotle. *Athenian Constitution.* Translated by Frederic G. Kenyon. London: G. Bell, 1914.

———. *Nicomachean Ethics.* Translated by H. Rackham. Cambridge, MA: Harvard University Press, 1926.

———. *Nicomachean Ethics.* Translated by W. D. Ross. Oxford: Oxford University Press, 1925.

———. *The Politics of Aristotle.* Translated by Ernest Barker. Oxford: Clarendon Press, 1948.

———. *The Politics of Aristotle.* Translated by Benjamin Jowett. Oxford: Oxford University Press, 1905.

Arquillière, H.-X. *L'augustinisme politique: Essai sur la formation des théories politiques du Moyen Age* [Political Augustinism: Essay on the development of political theories in the Middle Ages]. 1933. Reprint, Paris: Vrin, 1972.

Augustine, Saint. *Against Julian.* Translated by Matthew A. Schumacher. New York: Fathers of the Church, 1957.

———. *La Cité de Dieu.* 5 vols. General introduction and notes by G. Bardy. Trans. G. Combès. Paris: Desclée de Brouwer, 1959–60.

———. *The City of God against the Pagans.* 7 vols. Trans. William M. Greene. Cambridge, MA: Harvard University Press, 1963.

Aurell, Martin. *La noblesse en Occident (Ve–XVe siècles)* [Nobility in the West]. Paris: Armand Colin, 1996.

Baczko, Bronislaw, ed. *Une éducation pour la démocratie: Textes et projets de l'époque révolutionnaire* [An education for democracy: Texts and proposals from the revolutionary era]. Paris: Garnier, 1982.

Balandier, Georges. *Anthropologie politique.* Paris: Presses Universitaires de France, 1967; Quadrige collection, 1991.

Balard, Michel, Jean-Philippe Genet, and Michel Rouche. *Le Moyen Age en Occident* [The Middles Ages in the West]. Paris: Hachette, 1990.

Barbey, Jean. "Le modèle du roi" [The example of the king]. In *Le miracle capétien* [The Capetian miracle], ed. Stéphane Rials. Paris: Librairie académique Perrin, 1987.

Bardy, G. *La cité de Dieu de Saint Augustin* [Saint Augustine's *City of God*]. Paris: Desclée de Brouwer, 1960.

Barker, Ernst. *From Alexander to Constantine: Passages and Documents Illustrating the History of Social and Political Ideas, 336 BC–AD 337.* Oxford: Clarendon Press, 1956.

Baroin, Jeanne, and Josiane Haffen. *La prophétie de la sibylle tiburtine* [The prophecy of the Tiburtine Sibyl]. Paris: Les Belles Lettres, 1987.

Baron, Hans. *The Crisis of Early Italian Renaissance.* Princeton, NJ: Princeton University Press, 1966.

Barthélémy, Dominique. *Nouvelle histoire de la France médiévale* [A new history of medieval France]. Vol. 3, *L'ordre seigneurial, XI–XII siècles.* Paris: Éditions du Seuil:, 1990.

Baslez, Marie-Françoise. *Histoire politique du monde grec antique* [A political history of the classical Greek world]. Paris: Nathan Université, 1994.

Beaune, Colette. "Les Capétiens et la naissance d'une histoire nationale" [The Capets and the birth of a national history]. In *Le miracle capétien* [The Capetian miracle], ed. Stéphane Rials. Paris: Librairie académique Perrin, 1987.

Benedict, Saint. *The Holy Rule of Saint Benedict.* Trans. Boniface Verheyen, OSB. Available at www.ccel.org/ccel/benedict/rule2/files/rule2.html.

Berman, Harold J. *Law and Revolution: The Formation of the Western Legal Tradition.* Cambridge: Cambridge University Press, 1983.

Bible. Revised Standard Version. New York: Thomas Nelson and Sons, 1959.

———. *Traduction oecuménique de la Bible.* Paris: Éditions du Cerf—Les Bergers et les Mages, 1976.

Black, Antony. "The Conciliar Movement." In *The Cambridge History of Medieval Political Thought,* ed. James Henderson Burns, 573–87. Cambridge: Cambridge University Press, 1988.

Bloch, Marc. *Feudal Society.* Translated by L. A. Manyan. Chicago: University of Chicago Press, 1961. Originally published in French as *La société féodale.*

———. *The Royal Touch: Sacred Monarchy and Scrofula in England and France.* London: Routledge & Kegan Paul, 1973. Originally published as *Les rois thaumaturges,* 1924.

Booker, Courtney M. *Past Convictions: The Penance of Louis the Pious and the Decline of the Carolingians.* Philadelphia: University of Pennsylvania Press, 2009.

Bottéro, Jean. *Mésopotamie* [Mesopotamia]. Paris: Gallimard, 1987. Translated by Zainab Bahrani and Marc Van De Mieroop as *Mesopotamia: Writing, Reasoning, and the Gods.* Chicago: University of Chicago Press, 1995.

Boulet-Dautel, Marguerite. "Le roi et l'empereur" [The king and the emperor]. In *Le miracle capétien* [The Capetian miracle], ed. Stéphane Rials. Paris: Librairie académique Perrin, 1987.
Boutruche, Robert. *Seigneurie et féodalité* [Seigneuralism and feudalism]. Paris: Aubier, Éditions Montaigne, 1968.
Branham, R. Bracht, and Marie-Odile Goulet-Cazé, eds. *The Cynics: The Cynic Movement in Antiquity and Its Legacy.* Berkeley and Los Angeles: University of California Press, 1997.
Bréhier, Emile. *Chrysippe et l'ancien stoïcisme* [Chrysippus and ancient Stoicism]. Amsterdam: Gordon & Breach, 1971.
———. *Les Stoïciens* [The Stoics]. Paris: Gallimard, 1962.
Bressolles, Monseignor. *Saint Agobard, évêque de Lyon, 769–840* [Saint Agobard, bishop of Lyon]. Vol. 1. Paris: Vrin, 1949.
Brun Jean. *Les Stoïciens: Textes choisis* [The Stoics: Selected texts]. Paris: Presses Universitaires de France, 1973.
Burns, James Henderson, ed. *The Cambridge History of Medieval Political Thought.* Cambridge: Cambridge University Press, 1988.
Caenegem, R. van. "Government, Law and Society." In *The Cambridge History of Medieval Political Thought,* ed. James Henderson Burns. Cambridge: Cambridge University Press, 1988.
Caesar. *De bello civili.* In *The Gallic War,* trans. H. J. Edwards. Cambridge, MA: Harvard University Press, 1917.
Canning, J. P. "Law, Legislative Authority and Theories of Government." In *The Cambridge History of Medieval Political Thought,* ed. James Henderson Burns, 424–76. Cambridge: Cambridge University Press, 1988.
———. "Law, Sovereignty, and Corporation Theory, 1300–1450." In *The Cambridge History of Medieval Political Thought,* ed. James Henderson Burns. Cambridge: Cambridge University Press, 1988.
———. "Politics, Institutions and Ideas," In *The Cambridge History of Medieval Political Thought,* ed. James Henderson Burns, 341–65. Cambridge: Cambridge University Press, 1988.
Caquot, André, and Marc Philonenko. *La Bible, Ecrits intertestamentaires* [Intertestamental writings]. Paris: Gallimard, 1987.
Carcopino, Jerome. *Virgile et le mystère de la IVe Eglogue* [Virgil and the mystery of the Fourth Eclogue]. Paris: L'Artisan du livre, 1930.
Chamoux, François. *Marc-Antoine.* Paris: Arthaud Éditions, 1986.
Chelini, Jean. *Histoire religieuse de l'Occident médiéval* [A religious history of the medieval West]. Paris: Armand Colin, 1997.
Chenu, Marie-Dominique. *Introduction à l'étude de saint Thomas d'Aquin* [An introduction to the study of St. Thomas Aquinas]. Paris: Vrin, 1974.
Chrysostom, Saint John. *Homily IV on Isaiah.* In *Old Testament Homilies: Homilies on Isaiah and Jeremiah,* vol. 2, trans. Robert Charles Hill. Brookline, MA: Holy Cross Orthodox Press, 2003.
Chuvin, Pierre. *A Chronicle of the Last Pagans.* Cambridge, MA: Harvard University Press, 1990.
Cicero, *De Republica.* Vol. 16. Translated by Clinton Walker Keyes. Cambridge, MA: Harvard University Press, 1928.
———. *On Duties* (*De officiis*). Vol. 21. Translated by Walter Miller. Cambridge, MA: Harvard University Press, 1913.
———. *De finibus bonorum et malorum* [On the ends of good and bad things]. Translated by H. Rackham. Cambridge, MA: Harvard University Press, 1914.

———. *De natura deorum* [On the nature of the gods]. Translated by H. Rackham. Cambridge, MA: Harvard University Press, 1933.

———. *The Republic* and *The Laws*. Translated by Niall Rudd. Oxford: Oxford University Press, 1998.

Cohen, A. *Everyman's Talmud*. New York: E. P. Dutton, 1975.

Cohn, Norman. *The Pursuit of the Millennium: Revolutionary Millenarians and Mystical Anarchists of the Middle Ages*. Rev. and expanded ed. New York: Oxford University Press, 1970.

Commynes, Philippe de. *The Reign of Louis XI*. Trans. with an introduction by Michael Jones. New York: Penguin, 1972.

Coppens, Yves. *Le singe, l'Afrique et l'homme* [The ape, Africa, and man]. Paris: Hachette-Pluriel, 1985.

Dante Alighieri. *The Divine Comedy: Inferno, Purgatorio, Paradiso*. Trans. Robin Kirkpatrick. London: Penguin Classics, 2012.

———. *Monarchy*. Ed. Prue Shaw. Cambridge: Cambridge University Press, 1996.

Daumas, François. *La civilisation de l'Egypte pharanoique* [The civilization of ancient Egypt]. Paris: Arthaud Éditions, 1987.

Davies, Brian, and G. R. Evans, eds. *On the Incarnation of the Word* in *"Anselm of Canterbury: The Major Works."* Oxford: Oxford University Press, 1998.

Davis, R. H. C. *A History of Medieval Europe: From Constantine to Saint Louis*. 3rd ed. New York: Pearson, 2005.

Delumeau, Jean. *History of Paradise: The Garden of Eden in Myth and Tradition*. New York: Continuum, 1995.

———. *Mille ans de bonheur* [A thousand years of bliss]. Paris: Fayard, 1995.

Demosthenes. *Demosthenes*. Vols. 1–7. Translated by J. H. Vince, A. T. Murray, and N. W. and N. J. De Witt. Cambridge, MA: Harvard University Press, 1930.

Diès, Auguste, ed. "Introduction." In Plato, *Republique*. Paris: Les Belles Lettres, 1932.

Diogenes Laertius. *The Lives and Opinions of Eminent Philosophers*. 2 vols. Translated by R. D. Hicks. 1925. Reprint, Cambridge, MA: Harvard University Press, 2006.

———. *The Lives and Opinions of Eminent Philosophers*. Translated by C. D. Yonge. London: Henry G. Bohn, 1853.

Dollinger, Philippe. *La Hanse, XIIe–XVIIe siècles* [The Hanseatic League from the twelfth to the seventeenth centuries]. Paris: Aubier, 1988.

Dumont, Jean-Paul, ed. *Les écoles présocratiques* [The pre-Socratic schools]. Paris: Gallimard, 1991.

Dunbabin, Jean. "Government." In *The Cambridge History of Medieval Political Thought*, ed. James Henderson Burns, 477–519. Cambridge: Cambridge University Press, 1988.

Durand, Matthieu de. *Précis d'histoire grecque* [An overview of Greek history]. Paris: Éditions du Cerf, 1991.

Engels, Friedrich. *The Peasant War in Germany*. 1850. In *The Collected Works of Karl Max and Friedrich Engels*, vol. 10. New York: International Publishers, 1978.

Epicurus. *Letters, Principal Doctrines, and Vatican Sayings*. Translated by Russell Geer. New York: Pearson, 1964.

Finley, Moses. *Early Greece: The Bronze and Archaic Ages*. New York: Norton, 1970.

Freeman, Kathleen. *Ancilla to Pre-Socratic Philosophers*. Cambridge, MA: Harvard University Press, 1948.

Ganshof, F.-L. *Feudalism*. New York: Harper & Row, 1964. Originally published in French as *Qu'est-ce que la féodalité?*, 1944.

Gaudemet, Jean. *Eglise et cité: Histoire du droit canonique* [Church and state: A history of canon law]. Paris: Éditions du Cerf, Montchrestien, 1994.
———. *Les institutions de l'antiquité* [The institutions of antiquity]. 3rd. ed. Paris: Montchrestien, 1991.
Gernet, Louis. *Droit et institutions en Grèce antique* [Law and institutions in ancient Greece]. Paris: Flammarion, 1982.
Gewirth, Alain. *Marsilius of Padua: Defensor Pacis.* New York: Columbia University Press, 2001.
Girard, René. *The Scapegoat.* Baltimore: Johns Hopkins University Press, 1986.
———. *Violence and the Sacred.* Baltimore: Johns Hopkins University Press, 1979.
Goldschmidt, Victor. *Le système Stoïcien et l'idée de temps* [Stoicism and the concept of time]. Paris: Vrin, 1969.
Gregory the Great, Saint. *Morals on the Book of Job.*, Vol. 3. Trans. John Henry Parker and F. and J. Rivington. Oxford: Oxford University Press, 1844.
———. *Selected Epistles of Gregory the Great,* in *Library of Nicene and Post Nicene Fathers.* 2nd ser. Vol. 12. Trans. J. Barmby. Buffalo: Christian Literature Publishing, 1895.
Grelot, Pierre. *L'espérance juive à l'heure de Jésus* [Jewish messianic expectations at the time of Jesus]. Paris: Desclée de Brouwer, 1994.
Grimal, Pierre. *Cicéron.* Paris: Fayard, 1986.
———. *Tacite.* Paris: Fayard, 1990.
Gross, Benjamin. *Messianisme et eschatologie* [Messianism and eschatology]. In *Encyclopédie de la mystique juive* [Encyclopedia of Jewish mysticism], ed. Armand Abécassis and Georges Nataf. Paris: Editions Berg International, 1977. Republished in one volume as *Messianisme et histoire juive, Encyclopédie juive.* Paris: Editions Berg International, 1994.
Gross, Berl. *Before Democracy: A Study in the History of Error and Justification.* Melbourne: Globe Press, 1992.
Guenée, Bernard. *L'Occident aux XIVe et XVe siècles: Les etats* [The West in the fourteenth and fifteenth centuries: The state]. Paris: Presses Universitaires France, 1993.
Guizot, François. *A Popular History of France, from the Earliest Times.* Vol. 1. Translated by Robert Black. Boston: Dana Estes and Charles Lauriat, n.d.
Haggenmacher, Peter. *Grotius et la doctrine de la guerre juste* [Grotius and the doctrine of the just war]. Paris: Presses Universitaires de France, 1983.
Halphen, Louis. *Charlemagne et l'Empire Carolingien* [Charlemagne and the Carolingian Empire]. 1947. Reprint, Paris: Albin Michel, 1968.
Hayek, Friedrich August. *The Road to Serfdom.* 1944. Reprint, Chicago: University of Chicago Press, 2007.
Henderson, Ernest F. *Select Historical Documents of the Middle Ages.* London: George Bell and Sons, 1910.
Herodotus. *The Histories.* Translated by George Rawlinson. New York: Alfred A. Knopf, 1997.
Hesiod. *The Works and Days, Theogony,* and *The Shield of Herakles.* Translated by Richard Lattimore. Ann Arbor: University of Michigan Press, 1959.
Hicks, R. D., trans. *The Lives and Opinions of Eminent Philosophers.* 2 vols. 1925. Reprint, Cambridge, MA: Harvard University Press, 2006.
Homer. *The Iliad.* Translated by A. T. Murray. Loeb Classical Library. Cambridge, MA: Harvard University Press, 1985.
Hugo, Victor. *Les voix intérieures* (Inner voices). Paris, 1837.
Humbert, Michel. *Institutions politiques et sociales de l'antiquité* [Social and political institutions in antiquity]. 4th ed. Paris: Précis Dalloz, 1991.

Husson, Geneviève, and Dominique Valbelle. *L'etat et les institutions en Egypte des premiers pharaons aux empereurs romains* [The Egyptian state and institutions from the early pharoahs until the Roman emperors]. Paris: Armand Colin, 1992.

Imbert, Jean. *Les hôpitaux en droit canonique* [Hospitals in canon law]. Paris: Vrin, 1947.

Isocrates. *Isocrates with an English Translation.* 3 vols. Translated by George Norlin. Cambridge, MA: Harvard University Press, 1980.

Jaeger, Werner. *Paideia: The Ideals of Greek Culture.* New York: Oxford University Press, 1945.

Jambet, Christian. "Le côté sombre de la loi, communication au Colloque Crimes et Vertus" [The dark side of the law, a conference communication at the Colloquium on Crimes and Virtues]. *Corbières matin, Cahier philosophique,* Aug. 11, 1997.

Joinville, Jean de. *Memoirs of Saint Louis.* Trans. Ethel Wedgwood. New York: E. P. Dutton, 1906.

Kantorowicz, Ernst. *Frederick the Second.* New York: Ungar, 1957.

Kramer, Samuel Noah. *History Begins at Sumer: Thirty-Nine Firsts in Recorded History.* Philadelphia: University of Pennsylvania Press, 1981.

Küng, Hans. *Judaism between Yesterday and Tomorrow.* New York: Crossroad, 1992.

Laburthe-Tolra, Philippe, and Jean-Pierre Warnier. *Ethnologie, Antropologie.* Paris: Presses Universitaires de France, 1993.

Ladurie, Emmanuel Le Roy, ed. *Les monarchies* [Monarchies]. Paris: Presses Universitaires de France, 1989.

Lebecq, Stéphane. *Les origines franques, V–IX siècles* [Frankish origins, fifth to ninth centuries]. Paris: Éditions du Seuil, 1990.

Le Glay, Marcel, Jean-Louis Voisin, and Yann Le Bohec. *Histoire romaine* [History of Rome]. Paris: Presses Universitaires de France, 1991.

Le Goff, Jacques. *Intellectuals in the Middle Ages.* London: Wiley-Blackwell, 1993. Translated as *Les intellectuels au Moyen Age.* Paris: Éditions du Seuil, 1985.

Lemaire, André. *Histoire du people hébreu* [History of the Hebrew people]. Paris: Presses Universitaires de France, 1981.

Lepointe, Gabriel. *Droit romain et ancien droit français (Droit des biens)* [Roman law and ancient French law (property law)]. Paris: Précis Dalloz, 1958.

Lévêque, Pierre. *L'aventure grecque* [The Greek adventure]. 1964. Rev. ed., Paris: Le Livre de Poche-Références, 1997.

Levinas, Emmanuel. *Difficult Freedom: Essays on Judaism.* Translated by Seán Hand. Baltimore: John Hopkins University Press, 1990.

———. *Otherwise than Being, or Beyond Essence.* Translated by Alphonso Lingis. Dordrecht: Kluwer Academic, 1981.

———. *Totality and Infinity.* Translated by Alphonso Lingis. Dordrecht: Kluwer Academic, 1961.

Lichardus, Jan, and Marion Lichardus-Itten. *La proto-histoire de l'Europe* [Proto-history of Europe]. Paris: Presses Universitaires de France, 1985.

Livy. *History of Rome.* Translated by B. O. Foster. Cambridge, MA: Harvard University Press, 1919.

Lombard-Jourdan, Anne. *Fleurs de lis et oriflamme: Signes célestes du royaume de France* [Fleur-de-lis and Oriflamme: Heavenly signs of the kingdom of France]. Paris: Presses du CNRS, 1991.

Lubac, Henri de. *La postérité spirituelle de Joachim de Flore* [The spiritual posterity of Joachim of Flora]. 2 vols. Paris: Lethielleux-Culture et Vérité, 1978.

Lucretius. *On the Nature of Things [De natura].* Translated by W. H. D. Rouse. Rev. Martin F. Smith. 1924. Reprint, Cambridge, MA: Harvard University Press, 1975.

Maddox, Graham. *Religion and the Rise of Democracy.* London: Routledge, 1996.

Margueron, Jean-Claude. *Les Mésopotamiens* [The Mesopotamians], 2 vols. Paris: Armand Colin, 1991.

Marrou, Henri-Irénée. *Histoire de l'éducation dans l'antiquité.* Paris: Éditions du Seuil, 1948. Translated as *A History of Education in Antiquity.* Madison: University of Wisconsin Press, 1982.

Martin, Jean-Pierre. *Les provinces romaines d'Europe centrale et occidentale* [The Roman provinces of central and western Europe]. Paris: Éditions SEDES, 1990.

Mayeur, J.-M., Ch. and L. Pietri, A. Vauchez, M. Venard, eds. *Histoire du christianisme* [A history of Christianity]. Vol. 5, *Apogée de la papauté et expansion de la chrétienté* [Apogee of the papacy and the spread of Christianity] (1054–1274). Paris: Desclée Fayard, 1990.

Mommsen, Theodore. *Droit public romain* [Roman public law]. Paris: De Boccard Édition Diffusion, 1984.

Moreau, Joseph. *Aristote et son école* [Aristotle and his school]. Paris: Presses Universitaires de France, 1962.

Mossé, Claude. *La Grèce archaique d'Homère à Eschyle* [Archaic Greece from Homer to Aeschylus]. Paris: Éditions du Seuil, 1984.

Moulin, Léo. *La vie des étudiants au Moyen Age* [Student life in the Middle Ages]. Paris: Albin Michel, 1991.

Nahm, Milton C. *Selections from Early Greek Philosophy.* New York: F. C. Crofts, 1947.

Neher, André. *L'essence du prophétisme* [Quality of prophecy]. 1955. Republished as *Prophètes et Prophéties* [Prophets and prophecies]. Paris: Payot, 1995.

Nelson, Janet. "Kingship and Empire." In *The Cambridge History of Medieval Political Thought,* ed. James Henderson Burns. Cambridge: Cambridge University Press, 1988.

Nemo, Capucine. *Louis le Pieux et les Juifs: Etude de trois diplômes de protection* [Louis the Pious and the Jews: A study of diplomas of protection]. Graduate thesis, University of Paris X-Nanterre, 1997.

———. *Rome et ses citoyens juifs* [Rome and its Jewish citizens]. Paris: Éditions Honoré Champion, 2010.

Nemo, Philippe. *Histoire des idées politiques aux temps modernes et contemporains* [A history of political ideas in modern and contemporary times]. Paris: Presses Universitaires de France, 2002.

Nicolet, Claude, et al. *Rome et la conquête du monde méditerranéen* [Rome and the conquest of the Mediterranean world]. 2 vols. Paris: Presses Universitaires de France, 1993–94.

Nizan, Paul. *Les matérialistes de l'antiquité* [Ancient Greek materialists]. 1938. Reprint, Paris: Maspero, 1968.

Olivier-Martin, François. *Histoire du droit français des origins à la Révolution* [A history of French law from the origins until the revolution]. Paris: Éditions du CNRS, 1988.

Orléans, Jonas d'. *Le métier du roi* [On the institution of kingship]. Ed. Alain Dubreucq. Paris: Éditions du Cerf, 1995.

Orrieux, Claude, and Pauline Schmitt Pantel. *Histoire grecque* [Greek history]. Paris: Presses Universitaires de France, 1995.

Pacaut, Marcel. *Les ordres monastiques et religieux au Moyen Age* [Monastic and religious orders in the Middle Ages]. Paris: Nathan Université, 1993.

Pennington, K. "Law, Legislative Authority, and Theories of Government, 1150–1300." In *The Cambridge History of Medieval Political Thought,* ed. James Henderson Burns. Cambridge: Cambridge University Press, 1988.

Pernoud, Régine. *Histoire de la bourgeoisie en France* [A history of the bourgeoisie in France]. Vol. 1, *Des origins aux temps modernes* [From its origins until modern times]. Paris: Éditions du Seuil, 1960.

Petit-Dutaillis, Charles. *La monarchie féodale en France et en Angleterre* [Feudal monarchy in France and England]. 1933. Reprint, Paris: Albin Michel, 1971.

Pindar. *Pythian II.* Translated by Diane Arnson Svarlien. Perseus Digital Library. Available at www.perseus.tufts.edu

Pinoteau, Hervé. "Armes de France et symboles capétiens" [Arms of France and Capetian emblems]. In *Le miracle capétien* [The Capetian miracle], ed. Stéphane Rials. Paris: Librairie académique Perrin, 1987.

Pizan, Christine de. *Le livre des faits et bonnes mœurs du roi Charles V* [The book of the deeds and good manners of the wise King Charles V]. Trans. and presented from Latin by Eric Hicks and Therese Moreau. Paris: Stock, 1997.

Plato. *Apology.* Translated by Harold North Fowler. In *Plato in Twelve Volumes,* vol. 1. Cambridge, MA: Harvard University Press, 1914.

———. *Gorgias* and *Symposium.* Translated by W. R. M. Lamb. In *Plato in Twelve Volumes,* vol. 3. Cambridge, MA: Harvard University Press, 1925.

———. *The Laws.* Translated by Benjamin Jowett. 1871. Available at www.gutenberg.org.

———. *The Laws.* Translated by R. G. Bury. In *Plato in Twelve Volumes,* vols. 10 and 11. 1926. Reprint, Cambridge, MA: Harvard University Press, 2001.

———. *Letters.* Translated by R. G. Bury. In *Plato in Twelve Volumes,* vol. 7. Cambridge, MA: Harvard University Press, 1966.

———. *Protagoras.* Translated by W. R. M. Lamb. In *Plato in Twelve Volumes,* vol. 2. Cambridge, MA: Harvard University Press, 1924.

———. *The Republic.* Translated by Paul Shorey. In *Plato in Twelve Volumes,* vols. 5 and 6. Cambridge, MA: Harvard University Press, 1969.

———. *The Statesman.* Translated by Harold N. Fowler. In *Plato in Twelve Volumes,* vol. 8. Cambridge, MA: Harvard University Press, 1925.

Plutarch. *Lives.* Translated by Bernadette Perrin. Cambridge, MA: Harvard University Press, 1921.

———. *Moralia: On the Fortune or the Virtue of Alexander.* Vol. 4. Loeb Classical Library. Cambridge, MA: Harvard University Press, 1936.

Poliakov, Leon. *The Aryan Myth.* New York: Plume Books, 1977.

Polybius. *Histoire* [The histories]. Translated, introduced, and annotated by Denis Roussel. Paris: Gallimard, 1970.

———. *The Histories.* Translated by W. R. Paton. Cambridge, MA: Harvard University Press, 1922.

Popper, Karl. *The Open Society and Its Enemies.* Princeton, NJ: Princeton University Press, 1950.

Poursin, Jean-Marie. *La population mondiale* [World population]. Paris: Éditions du Seuil, 1976.

Quillet, Jeannine. "Community, Counsel, and Representation." In *The Cambridge History of Medieval Political Thought,* ed. James Henderson Burns. Cambridge: Cambridge University Press, 1988.

———. *Marsile de Padoue, Le défenseur de la paix* [Marsilius of Padua, defender of peace]. Paris: Vrin, 1968.

Rat, Maurice. Introduction to *Virgile, L'Eneide.* Paris: Garnier-Flammarion, 1965.

Renouard, Yves. *Les hommes d'affaires italiens du Moyen Age* [Italian businessmen in the Middle Ages]. Paris: Armand Colin, 1972.

Rials, Stéphane, ed. *Le miracle capétien* [The Capetian miracle]. Paris: Librairie académique Perrin, 1987.

Robin, Léon. *Platon.* 1935. Reprint, Paris: Presses Universitaires de France, 1968.

Robinson, J. H. *Readings in European History.* Boston: Ginn, 1905.

Roussel, Denis, trans. and annot. Introduction to Polybius, *Histoire.* Paris: Gallimard, 1970.

Le sacre des rois [The consecration of the kings]. Collective work. Paris: Les Belles Lettres, 1985.

Sallust. *War with Catiline. War with Jugurtha. Selections from the Histories.* Translated by J. C. Rolfe. Cambridge, MA: Harvard University Press, 1921.

Schuhl, Pierre-Maxime. Preface to Bréhier, *Les Stoïciens* [The Stoics]. Paris: Gallimard, 1962.

"Seigneurs et seigneuries au Moyen Age" [Seigneurs and seigneuralism in the Middle Ages]. Proceedings of the 117th National Congress of Scholarly Societies. Paris: Éditions du CTHS, 1995.

Seneca. *Entretiens: Lettres à Lucilius.* Edited by Paul Veyne. Paris: Robert Laffont, 1993.

———. *Works.* 10 vols. Cambridge, MA: Harvard University Press, 1928–72.

Shorey, Paul, trans. *Plato in Twelve Volumes.* Vols. 5 and 6, *The Republic.* Cambridge, MA: Harvard University Press, 1969.

Sinclair, T. A. *History of Greek Political Thought.* London: Routledge & Kegan Paul, 1952.

Sirinelli, Jean. "Rome et les débuts du christianisme" [Rome and the beginnings of Christianity]. In *Histoire des idées politiques* [History of political ideas], vol. 1, ed. Jean Touchard. Paris: Presses Universitaires de France, 1959.

Skinner, Quentin. *The Foundations of Modern Political Thought.* Vol. 1, *The Renaissance.* Cambridge: Cambridge University Press, 1978.

Spicq, C., ed. *Summa theologica: La justice.* Paris: Desclée et Cie, 1947.

Sprague, Rosamond Kent, ed. *The Older Sophists: A Complete Translation by Several Hands of the Fragments in "Die Fragmente Der Vorsokraticker," Edited by Diels-Kranz with a New Edition of Antiphon and of Euthydemus.* Columbia: University of South Carolina Press, 1972.

Stein, P. G. "Roman Law." In *The Cambridge History of Medieval Political Thought,* ed. James Henderson Burns. Cambridge: Cambridge University Press, 1988.

Suger, Abbot of Saint Denis. *The Deeds of Louis the Fat.* Trans. with introduction and notes by Richard Cusimano and John Moorhead. Washington, DC: Catholic University of America Press, 1992.

———. *Life of King Louis VI the Fat.* Trans. Jean Dunbabin. Available at www.fordham.edu/halsall/basis/suger-louisthefat.html.

Tacitus. *Histories.* 2 vols. Translated by Clifford H. Moore and John Jackson. Cambridge, MA: Harvard University Press, 1925, 1931.

———. *Tacite, Oeuvres completes* [Tacitus, Works]. Translation, presentation, and commentary by Pierre Grimal. Paris: Gallimard, 1990.

———. *Works.* 6 vols. Cambridge, MA: Harvard University Press, 1914–32.

Tertullian. *The Address of Q. Sept. Tertullian to Scapula Tertullus, Proconsul of Africa.* Translated by Sir David Dalrymple. Edinburgh: Murray & Cochrane, 1790.

———. [Q. Septimi Florentis Tertulliani]. *Apologeticus: The Text of Oehler.* Annotated, with an introduction by J. E. B. Taylor. Translated by A. Souter. Cambridge: Cambridge University Press, 1917.

Thomas, Yann. Preface to Theodore Mommsen, *Droit public romain* [Roman public law]. Paris: De Boccard Édition Diffusion, 1984.

Thucydides. *History of the Peloponnesian War.* Vol. 1. Translated by C. F. Smith. Cambridge, MA: Harvard University Press, 1920.

Touchard, Jean. *Histoire des idées politiques* [A history of political ideas]. Vol. 1. Paris: Presses Universitaires de France, 1959.

Traduction oecuménique de la Bible [Ecumenical translation of the Bible]. Paris: Éditions du Cerf-Les Bergers et les Mages, 1976.

Usener, Hermann. *Epicurea.* Available at www.Epicurus.com.

Vernant, Jean-Pierre. *The Origins of Greek Thought.* New York: Cornell University Press, 1982.

Villiers, Robert. *Rome et le droit privé* [Rome and private law]. Paris: Albin Michel, 1977.

Virgil. *Eclogues, Georgics, Aeneid: Books 1–6.* Trans. H. Rushton Fairclough. Revised by G. P. Goold. Cambridge, MA: Harvard University Press, 1916.

von der Mühl, P. *Epicuri epistolae tres et ratae sententiae.* Leipzig: Teubner, 1922.

Watt, J. A. "Spiritual and Temporal Powers." In *The Cambridge History of Medieval Political Thought,* ed. James Henderson Burns. Cambridge: Cambridge University Press, 1988.

William of Ockham. *A Short Discourse on Tyrannical Government.* Ed. Arthur Stephen McGrade. Trans. John Kilcullen. Cambridge: Cambridge University Press, 1992.

Xenophon. *Cyropaedia.* 2 vols. Translated by Walter Miller. Cambridge, MA: Harvard University Press, 1914.

———. *Hellenica.* Vol. 2 (books 5–7). Translated by Carleton L. Brownson. Loeb Classical Library. Cambridge, MA: Harvard University Press, 1921.

———. *Memorabilia* and *Oeconomicus.* Translated by E. C. Marchant. Cambridge, MA: Harvard University Press, 1923.

———. *Scripta Minora.* Translated by E. C. Marchant and G. W. Bowersock. Cambridge, MA: Harvard University Press, 1925. Contains the following texts: *Agesilaus, Hiero, Constitution of the Lacedaemonians, Ways and Means, Cavalry Commander, Art of Horsemanship, On Hunting, Constitution of the Athenians.*

Index

Index